PRINCIPLES
OF
ADMINISTRATIVE
LAW

JONES & de VILLARS

Fourth Edition
2004

PRINCIPLES
OF
ADMINISTRATIVE
LAW

Fourth Edition

by

David Phillip Jones, Q.C.

B.A.(Hons.) (McGill), B.C.L., M.A. (Oxon.)

and

Anne S. de Villars, Q.C.

B.Sc. (Southampton), LL.B. (Alberta)

both of
de Villars Jones
Barristers and Solicitors
Edmonton

2004

THOMSON
™
CARSWELL

Library and Archives Canada Cataloguing in Publication

Jones, David Phillip, 1949–
    Principles of administrative law / by David Phillip Jones and Anne S. de Villars. – 4th ed.

Includes bibliographical references and index.
ISBN 0-459-24130-3 (bound).--ISBN 0-459-24137-0 (pbk.)

1. Administrative law – Canada. 2. Administrative law – Alberta.
3. Judicial review of administrative acts – Canada. 4. Judicial review of administrative acts – Alberta. I. De Villars, Anne S., 1946– II. Title.

KE5015.J66 2004   342.71'06   C2004-903964-4
KF5402.J66 2004

Composition: Computer Composition of Canada Inc.

THOMSON

CARSWELL

One Corporate Plaza   **Customer Service:**
2075 Kennedy Road   Toronto   1-416-609-3800
Scarborough, Ontario M1T 3V4   Elsewhere in Canada/U.S.   1-800-387-5164
                                                  Fax   1-800-298-5094
                    World Wide Web: http://www.carswell.com
                              E-mail: orders@carswell.com

To our families

PREFACE TO THE FOURTH EDITION

It seems impossible that five years have passed since the third edition, and that it is time to update this work once again.

Since the last edition, the Supreme Court of Canada has continued to refine its standards-of-review analysis, making it clear that this analysis applies to appeals as well as to applications for judicial review, clarifying that there is a spectrum of deference which results in only three possible standards – correctness, reasonableness *simpliciter*, and patent unreasonableness – and affirming that there now is no one-to-one relationship between any ground of review and any particular standard. Just before this edition went to press, Justice LeBel issued a significant *cri de coeur* in *Toronto (City) v. C.U.P.E., Local 79* about the complexity of the standards of review analysis, and the difficulty in distinguishing between the various standards (particularly the two reasonableness ones); and wondered whether one could get by with just correctness and reasonableness. It seems inevitable that further developments will occur as the courts take account of Justice LeBel's concerns.

In addition to the cases involving applications of procedural fairness, there have been new developments in the ability of administrative agencies to decide questions of constitutional law (including the *Charter*); the deflation of hopes that there might be a quasi-constitutional requirement for structural independence for administrative agencies; and further extension of the prohibition against collateral attacks by developing the concept of abuse of process.

We are grateful to the following for their generous and helpful contributions: Dale Gibson and Katharine Hurlburt (Chapter 2), Glenn Tait (Chapters 3, 6 and 13), Dwayne Chomyn (Chapter 7), David C. Elliott (Chapter 4), Professor Philip Bryden (Chapter 10), The Hon. Frans Slatter (Chapter 15), and Professor John Law (Chapter 16). Dawn Knowles and Richard Bruyer, research lawyers in our office, provided superb research and editing assistance. Our secretaries, Cheryl Robison, and the staff at Carswell provided wonderful technical expertise. As with the previous two editions, the net royalties from this edition will be donated to the Faculty of Law at the University of Alberta.

As we have noted in the prefaces to all of the previous editions, this is a book about *principles*. It is not a digest, and we have not attempted to deal with every case, much less cover the detailed law in all 14 Canadian jurisdictions. The "pragmatic and functional approach" which pervades virtually every part of contemporary Canadian administrative law can only do justice if the persons who must use it have a thorough understanding of the principles involved. This text will have performed its function if it helps students, counsel and judges organize their conceptual thinking about administrative law.

David Phillip Jones, Q.C.
Anne de Villars, Q.C.
New Year's Day 2004
Edmonton

PREFACE TO THE THIRD EDITION

Five years have now elapsed since the publication of the second edition of this work. In addition to the normal voluminous flow of Administrative Law decisions from the courts (which we have attempted to chronicle in the *Administrative Law Reports*, with the help of a number of dedicated readers), the Supreme Court of Canada has articulated the concept of a spectrum of "standards of review" and indicated that the appropriate standard must be addressed in every application for judicial review. There have also been significant developments in restricting collateral attacks on administrative decisions, institutional bias, various aspects of procedural fairness, the interplay between Administrative Law and Constitutional Law (particularly the *Charter*), and the availability of private law remedies against the Crown. We have tried to state the law as of December 1998.

We are grateful to the following for their generous and helpful contributions: Dale Gibson and Ritu Khullar (Chapter 2), Glenn D. Tait (Chapters 3, 6, 13 and 14), David C. Elliott (Chapter 4), Dwayne W. Chomyn (Chapter 7), Kathy Cherniawsky and Karen Munro (Chapter 9), Graham Steele (Chapter 10), Mary Henderson (Chapter 15), John Law (Chapter 16), and Frans Slatter (Chapter 17). Kathy Cherniawsky and Dawn Knowles provided superb research support; and our secretaries, Cheryl Holowaty, and the staff at Carswell provided technical expertise. As with the previous edition, the net royalties for this edition will be donated to the Faculty of Law at the University of Alberta.

As noted in the prefaces to the first and second editions, this is a book about *principles*. We have not attempted to deal with every case, much less to cover all 13 (soon 14) Canadian jurisdictions. If this text helps a student, counsel or judge organize their conceptual thinking about Administrative Law, it will have performed its function.

Appropriately, today is the 350th anniversary of the death of Charles Stuart, King, whose struggles with Parliament continue to echo through much of Administrative Law even now.

David Phillip Jones, Q.C.
Anne de Villars, Q.C.
30 January 1999
Edmonton

PREFACE TO THE SECOND EDITION

Almost nine years have elapsed since the publication of the first edition of this work. Over this period, there have been considerable changes – both in Administrative Law and in our lives. Although we have tried to keep up with developments in the area as they happened, the extremely busy demands of private practice and parenthood finally convinced us that the only way the second edition would see the light of day this century would be to "condominiumize" the book by asking other members of the Bar to help update various chapters: Dwayne Chomyn (Chapter 7), Dean Timothy Christian, Q.C. (Chapter 2), David C. Elliott (Chapter 4), Professor John Law (Chapter 15), Andrew C.L. Sims, Q.C. (parts of Chapter 9), Frans Slatter (Chapter 16), Grant Sprague (Chapter 14), Glenn Tait (Chapters 3, 6 and 12) and Karen Munro. We have been overwhelmed and delighted with the alacrity with which they have accepted this invitation! And we are also pleased that all of the contributors have agreed that the net royalties for this edition will be donated to the Faculty of Law at the University of Alberta.

We have tried to ensure that this change in authorship does not detract from the conceptual nature of this textbook on principles. We have used the organizing metaphor of Administrative Law as a river: the second edition should note if its course has changed, if there are new tributaries, if the delta splits up in some new way, or if there is pollution in the stream; but it is not necessary (or practical) to note all of the ever-rolling stream of new cases flowing along the previously well-identified riverbed. We have resisted the perfectionist's temptation to re-write the first edition completely, and tried to remember that writing a textbook (like politics) is the art of the possible.

We wish to reiterate the goals which we had when we set out to write this work. They are set out in the Preface to the First Edition, and we invite the reader to read that now. Some reviewers complained that the first edition did not mention a particular case – or all of the cases – decided in one or more of the 13 Canadian jurisdictions. After nine years of contemplating this criticism, we are still firmly of the view that our original conception of the work is right: namely, to provide a conceptual tool for students, practitioners and judges. There are other works available to assist those who need a casebook or a detailed digest of all of the Canadian cases ever decided on a particular point.

We also acknowledge the contribution by the following summer students and research assistants who have helped keep track of developments over various parts of the nine-year period since publication of the first edition: Patty Burchmore, Grant Cameron, Aaron Engen, Susan Fox, Peggy Kobly, Julie Lloyd, and Mary Peck.

The Bar and Bench have referred us to many interesting cases, comments, references and problems. We have tried to address these issues in this edition, and we gratefully solicit further contribututions of this sort.

Finally, we wish to thank those involved in the technical production of the text: our secretaries, Michael Storozuk from the Law Library at the University of Alberta who prepared the Index, and the staff at Carswell.

Generally, we have tried to state the law as of December 1993.

David Phillip Jones, Q.C.
Anne deV illars, Q.C.
New Year's Day 1994
Edmonton

PREFACE TO THE FIRST EDITION

The purpose of this book is to state the principles of Administrative Law. Our goal is to provide a conceptual analysis which will be useful to lawyer and lay man alike as a tool for approaching problems which arise in this ever-expanding field.

The use of the word "principles" is deliberate. First, in our experience, very few senior members of the Bar and Bench appear to realize that Administrative Law is a coherent system of principles. This may well result from the fact that Administrative Law is a relatively new addition to the curriculum of Canadian Law faculties. In addition, this unfamiliarity may reflect the slow and sometimes erratic evolution of the constitutional philosophy underlying the phenomenon of judicial review of administrative action, and the relationship between the legislature, the executive and the judiciary in a parliamentary democracy.

Secondly, we contrast "principles" with the "rules" which in most areas of law give definite answers to the legal problems arising from particular fact patterns. In Administrative Law, as in other areas of public law, there frequently is no single correct answer to a problem. Rather, competing principles of public policy are involved, and must be weighed against each other to reach a solution to the particular case.

Thirdly, the contexts in which an Administrative Law case can arise are so varied that it is almost impossible to develop a statement of the law without a great deal of generality. Indeed, one of the most difficult aspects of the practice of Administrative Law arises from the necessity of applying general principles to fact patterns which are complicated, frequently unique, and which involve adversaries who each may reasonably claim to have the law on his side. It is difficult, therefore, to glean precedential dicta from such cases without referring to general principles.

Fourthly, Parliament and the legislatures often appear to forget the principles of Administrative Law in enacting increasingly complex schemes of legislation. Without challenging the legislator's sovereign right to abolish, alter, amend, or displace any art of Administrative Law, it nevertheless would be exceedingly helpful if the intent to do so were clearly articulated in the statutes; and this can only be done if legislators clearly understand and continuously measure their enactments against the principles of Administrative Law.

Fifthly, any democratic state requires informed citizens. The Rule of Law not only implies a judiciary capable of declaring what the law is, and granting a remedy for infractions thereof; it also implies that citizens generally understand the principles underlying their relationship with governmental officials, and how to assert their rights. It is not reasonable to expect every citizen to be an administrative lawyer, but it is possible for them to understand when their rights and interests have been affected in a manner which Administrative Law would remedy.

CONTENTS

PART II
GROUNDS FOR JUDICIAL REVIEW

Chapter 5 **Introduction to the Grounds for Judicial Review** 133

PART III
STANDARDS OF REVIEW

PART IV
REMEDIES

A Note Regarding Case Citations

As part of Carswell's commitment to provide you with convenient and current legal information, case references added to this service also include WestlaweCARSWELL citations.

Carswell is pleased to provide WestlaweCARSWELL to law faculty and students attending a Canadian law school. Contact your Law Library Director to obtain a complimentary password.

The following is an example of the WestlaweCARSWELL citation format used on WestlaweCARSWELL and in this service:

2004 CarswellOnt 1234

- **"2004"** is the year of the decision
- **"CarswellOnt"** indicates that this is a decision from the courts of Ontario that has been added to WestlaweCARSWELL. Similarly, **"CarswellBC"** indicates a decision from the courts of British Columbia that has been added to WestlaweCARSWELL, and so on. Cases originating in Federal Courts have **"CarswellNat"** citations, while a decision from the Supreme Court of Canada will have a cite based on the jurisdiction in which it originated. Thousands of judicial decisions from every jurisdiction across Canada are available on WestlaweCARSWELL.
- **"1234"** indicates that this was the 1,234th decision from that jurisdiction that has been added to WestlaweCARSWELL in 2004.

The addition of WestlaweCARSWELL cites will provide a convenient point of reference for those who use WestlaweCARSWELL. Please note, however, that case citations previously added to this service may not necessarily contain WestlaweCARSWELL cites.

WestlaweCARSWELL is a leading, Internet-based legal research service which combines the Internet's simplicity with state-of-the-art searching capabilities. If you would like to learn more about WestlaweCARSWELL or are interested in seeing this valuable product, we invite you to call Customer Relations at 416-298-5140 (Toronto) or 1-800-387-5164 (North America) or visit our website at http://www.carswell.com/.

TABLE OF CASES

I

GENERAL PRINCIPLES

1

Introduction: What is Administrative Law?

1. What is Administrative Law?

Administrative law deals with the legal limitations on the actions of governmental officials, and on the remedies which are available to anyone affected by a transgression of these limits. The subject invariably involves the question of the lawful authority of an official to do a particular act which, in the absence of such authority, might well be illegal (or *ultra vires*) and give rise to an actionable wrong.[1] In our legal system, the mere fact that the government *is the government* does not give it any particular rights or powers. On the contrary, all governmental actions must be specially authorized by either legislation or the Royal Prerogative.[2] This need for governmental officials to be able to point

---

1 Is there a right without a remedy? Much of substantive administrative law derives from the availability of the prerogative remedies, and it is not surprising that some authorities first consider the nature and ambit of the remedies in administrative law, and only then look at the grounds for obtaining those remedies.

2 On the ambit of the Royal Prerogative, and the ability to override it by legislation, see O. Hood Phillips and Paul Jackson, *O. Hood Phillips' Constitutional and Administrative Law*, 7th ed. (London: Sweet & Maxwell, 1978), c. 14.

3

to the lawful authority permitting their actions makes administrative law a close cousin to constitutional law.

2. The Relationship of Administrative Law to Constitutional Law

In its broadest sense, constitutional law comprises all of the fundamental rules for determining who and which institutions have the right to make laws for the government of our society; it is "a law for the making of laws".[3] Administrative law, on the other hand, deals with the actions of administrators to whom powers have been granted by laws which have been validly enacted under the constitution. Logically, therefore, a finding that a particular law is unconstitutional will deprive the administrator (or "statutory delegate") of the legal basis upon which to justify its actions, which may give rise to a legal remedy in the hands of a person adversely affected thereby. Accordingly, any possible constitutional defect in legislation will be relevant to administrative law for the purpose of determining the legal validity of the governmental action complained of. Chapter 2 deals with "Constitutional Aspects of Administrative Law in Canada", and considers both the pure form of the doctrine of Parliamentary Sovereignty which exists in the United Kingdom, and the modifications which must be made to that doctrine in light of the federal nature of Canada, section 96 of the *Constitution Act*, 1867[4] and the *Canadian Charter of Rights and Freedoms*.[5]

3. Statutory Delegation of Governmental Powers

Once the constitutional validity of the legislation in question has been established, it is then necessary to determine the existence and exact scope of powers which that legislation delegates to the administration. The doctrine of Parliamentary Sovereignty gives the legislative branch authority to delegate powers, and the vast bulk of the business of government in fact takes place by virtue of delegated authority instead of being contained in laws passed by either the Federal Parliament or one of the provincial legislatures. The need to delegate authority can be justified in terms of the following factors, among others:

(a) The sheer magnitude of the business of government means that not everything can be dealt with by Parliament or a legislature.

(b) Much of governmental activity is technical in nature, and only broad principles should be contained in legislation.

(c) Delegating power to an administrator allows greater flexibility in applying broad statutory provisions to changing circumstances.

---

3 A phrase coined by the late Professor F.R. Scott from McGill.
4 30 & 31 Vict., c. 3; reproduced with amendments in R.S.C. 1970, App. II.
5 Part I of Sched. B to the *Canada Act*, 1982 (U.K.) (31 Eliz. 2, c. 11).

(d) It may not be possible to devise a general role to deal with all cases, which may be more conveniently determined in the discretion of a delegate.

(e) The need for rapid governmental action may require faster administrative response than can be accommodated by the necessity of legislative amendment.

(f) Innovation and experimentation in solving social problems may not be possible if legislation is required.

(g) Someone actually has to apply legislation, and that person has to have authority to do so.

(h) Emergencies may require broad delegation of powers with respect to a wide range of matters which would normally be dealt with by legislation.

It is not surprising, therefore, to discover that virtually all of the laws passed by the Federal Parliament or the provincial legislatures[6] delegate certain powers and duties, whether to the cabinet, a particular minister, a particular civil servant, a judge, a board, or someone else.[7] Although there are political conventions as to what types of powers should be delegated, there is no legal rule for determining what types of powers should be exercised by the legislative branch itself.[8] To some extent, these conventions are reflected in the rules of statutory construction, which assist in determining the exact meaning of legislation. The doctrine of Parliamentary Sovereignty, however, means that there is no legal – as opposed to political – limit on the ability of the legislative branch to use clear words to delegate virtually any power[9] to someone else. An important part of administrative law, therefore, deals with the controls which the Federal Parliament or the provincial legislatures themselves devise to supervise the exercise of their powers which they have delegated to administrators, which is examined in Chapters 3 and 4.

4. Delegation, Jurisdiction, and the Doctrine of Ultra Vires

Judicial review is probably the most important means of controlling illegal governmental actions. To the extent that such actions may constitute wrongs otherwise known to law, the delegate will have to demonstrate some statutory

---

6 Because of the federal nature of Canada, it is necessary to refer to both the Federal Parliament and the provincial legislatures when speaking of the primary level of legislators in Canada. This is not the case in a unitary state such as the United Kingdom, and English textbooks speak of the Sovereignty of Parliament to refer to one legislative body. It is important to remember this distinction when referring to English textbooks on administrative law.

7 Or to private individuals, for that matter.

8 In other words, legislation which delegates powers will generally be valid, provided its intent to do so is clear.

9 Whether legislative, judicial, executive or administrative in nature.

provision authorizing it to take the impugned action. The delegate must be able to demonstrate that its actions fall squarely within the power granted to it by the Federal Parliament or the provincial legislatures. If they do not, its actions are *ultra vires*, that is, beyond the delegate's jurisdiction. Most of administrative law involves the close scrutiny of the jurisdiction or authority of a particular governmental official to do a particular action which affects the rights or interests of another person, and this inevitably involves the application of rules of statutory construction[10] to determine precisely what the legislative branch meant to enact.

"Jurisdiction" is a difficult term of art in administrative law, and has a number of different meanings. It is frequently very difficult to determine whether the legislation does grant a particular delegate the "jurisdiction" to do the impugned act, or to do it in some particular way. Lack of jurisdiction makes the act *ultra vires*, and may make available a legal remedy. Chapter 5 examines both the concept of jurisdiction and the concomitant doctrine of *ultra vires*.

5. Grounds for Judicial Review

The superior courts have the inherent power to review the legality of administrative actions. On the one hand, this power is the natural consequence of the courts' role to interpret the meaning of statutes, including determining the ambit of statutes which delegate powers to administrators. In other words, the courts decide which administrative actions are *ultra vires*. On the other hand, the superior courts have historically used the prerogative remedies[11] such as *certiorari*, *mandamus*, prohibition, *quo warranto* and *habeas corpus* to exercise supervisory jurisdiction over inferior courts and other tribunals. As a result, there is considerable judicial review of administrative action in Canada.

"Judicial review" is not the same as an appeal. In general, the superior courts do not have the right to substitute their appraisal of the merits for any lawful action taken by an administrator. On the contrary, one of the consequences of the doctrine of Parliamentary Sovereignty is the right of the legislative branch to delegate powers to administrators without any right of appeal, whether to another administrator or to a court. Of course, legislation frequently does provide one or more levels of appeal, but there is no obligation for it to do so.

Judicial review, therefore, is generally limited to the power of the superior courts to determine whether the administrator has acted strictly within the

---

10 See J.A. Corry, "Administrative Law and the Interpretation of Statutes" (1935) 1 U.T.L.J. 286.

11 The remedies are called "prerogative" because they were historically available at the instance of the Crown. Hence, all such applications were made in the name of the Crown, on the instance of the applicant. Therefore, the proper style of the cause is *R. v. Commissioner of Police of the Metropolis*, [1968] 2 Q.B. 118 (Eng. C.A.). This nomenclature has for some reason fallen into disuse in Alberta, and the current usage would (incorrectly?) style the same case as *R. v. Commissioner of Police of the Metropolis*.

powers which have been statutorily[12] delegated to it. Judicial review concentrates almost completely on jurisdictional questions, and on the application of the *ultra vires* doctrine to the particular fact pattern surrounding the impugned administrative action.

For example, if legislation gives a municipality the power to expropriate private property for the purpose of redeveloping an area for the provision of houses, an attempt to expropriate for the purpose of developing a governmental or commercial centre will be void. The superior court can declare the expropriation scheme to be *ultra vires*, and no transfer of property will have occurred as the result of the city's filing the Notice of Intention to Expropriate against the title to the property in the Land Titles Office.[13]

Similarly, the revocation of a restaurant's liquor licence was struck down by the courts in *Roncarelli v. Duplessis*[14] because the Premier of Quebec had ordered the liquor licensing board to revoke the licence in light of Mr. Roncarelli's posting bond for bailing Jehovah's Witnesses out of jail. There were two jurisdictional errors in the administrative action taken in this case. First, the legislature had not delegated power to revoke liquor licences to the premier of the province, but rather to the board. As a result, only the board could exercise that discretionary power, and it had not done so, but had rather simply ratified or implemented the order of the premier, without considering the matter itself. Secondly, the courts held that the legislation did not allow the statutory delegate, the board, to exercise its discretion to revoke licences by referring to the licensee's unrelated activities of posting bond for arrested members of a religious group. That was an irrelevant consideration or an improper motive for the exercise of the power granted to the delegate by the provincial legislature. Accordingly, the delegate's purported action was *ultra vires*, and Mr. Roncarelli was in law entitled to keep his licence (and to damages).[15]

Judicial review of administrative action can occur for the following jurisdictional defects:

(a) substantive *ultra vires*, such as building a highway when the legislature has authorized building a park;[16]

(b) exercising a discretion for an improper purpose,[17] with malice,[18] in bad faith,[19] or by reference to irrelevant considerations,[20] as exempli-

---

12 Judicial review may also be available against certain actions taken pursuant to the Royal Prerogative (e.g., *R. v. Criminal Injuries Comp. Bd.; Ex parte Lain*, [1967] 1 Q.B. 864), and to correct breaches of the principles of natural justice committed by certain non-statutory domestic tribunals.

13 See *Ritchie v. Edmonton (City)* (1980), 108 D.L.R. (3d) 694 (Alta. Q.B.).

14 [1959] S.C.R. 121 (S.C.C.).

15 Indeed, the action was for damages, not for a prerogative remedy or a declaration that the licence was still in effect.

16 See *Ritchie v. Edmonton (City)* (the "Alberta Hotel" case), *supra* note 13.

17 *Ibid.*

18 See *Roncarelli v. Duplessis, supra* note 14.

19 See *Campeau Corp. v. Calgary (City)* (1978), 7 Alta. L.R. (2d) 294 (Alta. C.A.).

20 See *Padfield v. Min. of Agriculture, Fisheries and Food*, [1968] 2 W.L.R. 924 (H.L.), and *Ritchie v. Edmonton (City), supra* note 13.

fied in the *Alberta Hotel* case[21] and in *Roncarelli v. Duplessis* referred
to above;

(c) not considering relevant matters;[22]

(d) making serious procedural errors;[23]

(e) making an error of law,[24] in certain circumstances.

The inherent right of the courts to review the legality of administrative
action almost completely depends on the application of the *ultra vires* doctrine
to examine the jurisdiction of the statutory delegate whose action has been
impugned. It must be noted, however, that the courts' right to review certain
errors of law (ground (e) above, technically called "errors of law on the face
of the record") is not necessarily jurisdictional in nature, and has been explained
by Lord Denning in *R. v. Northumberland Compensation Appeal Tribunal*[25]
as an important historical anomaly.

Similarly, it has sometimes been suggested that the courts' right to review
administrative proceedings for serious procedural errors (technically called
breaches of the "principles of natural justice" or the "duty to be fair") is not
jurisdictional in nature. With respect, we submit that this view of the courts'
supervisory power is historically wrong, wrong in principle and dangerous in
the face of a privative clause purporting to deprive the courts of their inherent
power to review the merits of administrative action. The better view, we submit,
is that the legislation in question incorporates the common law relating to fair
procedures, and any serious deviation from fair procedure takes the statutory
delegate outside the ambit of the powers granted to it, even if he otherwise had
the power to take the particular action in question. In other words, procedural
error goes to jurisdiction, and entitles the superior courts to review the legality
of the delegate's actions.

The concept of jurisdiction is discussed in Chapter 5, and the jurisdictional
nature of a procedural error is discussed in Chapters 6, 8, 9 and 10.

6. Historical Development of Judicial Review of Administrative Action

Dicey observed many years ago that Britain, unlike France, had no "administrative law" because the ordinary courts – and not specialized administrative ones – determined the validity of governmental actions.[26] Even when

---

21 *Ritchie v. Edmonton (City), ibid.*
22 Which may be only the reverse of considering irrelevant matters.
23 *Québec (Commission des relations ouvrières) v. Alliance des professeurs catholiques de Montréal*, [1953] 2 S.C.R. 140 (S.C.C.); *Ridge v. Baldwin* (1963), [1964] A.C. 40 (U.K. H.L.); *Cooper v. Wandsworth Board of Works* (1863), 14 C.B.N.S. 180, 143 E.R. 414 (Eng. C.P.).
24 See the *Shaw* case, *infra* note 30.
25 *Infra* note 30.
26 A.V. Dicey, *Introduction to the Study of the Law of the Constitution*, 10th ed. by E.C.S. Wade (London: Macmillan Papermac, 1961).

made, this statement was deceptive, because English common law for centuries has provided for judicial review of the lawfulness of governmental actions, which surely puts the administration under the Rule of Law (which Dicey recognized). On the other hand, in recent years the administrative structure in common law countries has frequently included appeals from one administration to another, thereby making our system resemble the continental one much more closely than in Dicey's time. Further, at least one common law jurisdiction, Australia, has now established a specialized Administrative Law Court[27] to exercise the traditional judicial remedies for reviewing the legality of governmental actions. Still, the three central features of our system of administrative law would be recognized by Dicey, and remain (a) the Rule of Law (that is, the requirement for all governmental action to be expressly permitted by validly enacted laws); (b) the denial of any special status to the government merely because it *is* the government; and (c) the right of the ordinary courts to determine such questions of legality.

Where do the ordinary courts get their authority to review the lawfulness of governmental action? Nothing in the written constitutions of either the United Kingdom or Canada specifically gives the courts this important power. On the contrary, the superior courts have from time immemorial simply asserted their "inherent" jurisdiction to supervise the legality of actions taken by other officials, tribunals or delegates, which supervision was facilitated procedurally by the development of the prerogative remedies.

Historically, much of the administration of government in England was conferred on the local justices of the peace. When these officials were exercising judicial powers they were subject to the prerogative remedies (such as *certiorari*, *mandamus* and *habeas corpus*) issued by the superior courts. Perhaps illogically, the same prerogative remedies were used by the superior courts to control and review the administrative (as opposed to judicial) activities which Parliament delegated to these same justices of the peace. Later, the British Parliament created independent bodies (such as the Sewer Commissioners[28]) to exercise many of the administrative functions previously granted to the justices of the peace, as well as a vast array of new administrative powers. Again, the superior courts simply assumed that the prerogative remedies would be available to review actions taken by these non-judicial administrators, some of whom indeed exercised precisely the same functions which had previously been performed by the justices of the peace. In time, however, the theoretical error of this convenient historical development was recognized, and the superior courts restricted the availability of judicial review (in particular *certiorari*[29]) to those administrative functions which could be characterized as being "quasi-judicial" instead of "merely administrative" in nature. Although this distinction has become much less important in modern times, it will be nec-

---

27 See the discussion on the Australian Administrative Appeals Tribunal in Aronson and Franklin, *Review of Administrative Action* (Sydney: The Law Book Company, 1987): similarly, in Quebec, the *Tribunal Administratif du Québec* has been implemented. See chapter 14 for further discussion.

28 See for example, *Arthur v. Yorkshire Sewer Commr.* (1724), 8 Mod. 331, 88 E.R. 237.

29 See the discussion of the development of the duty to be fair in Chapter 8.

essary to examine the different types of functions which can be delegated in order to understand the development of modern administrative law.

7. Remedies and Standing

Most of administrative law involves applications for one of the prerogative remedies, a declaration, an injunction, damages or a statutory appeal to a court or to another administrative body. Considerable attention used to be given to choosing the right remedy and to making certain that the applicant had the proper standing to apply for it. However, a number of jurisdictions in the Commonwealth have modernized the procedures for seeking judicial review.

The prerogative remedies consist of *certiorari*, prohibition, *mandamus*, *habeas corpus* and *quo warranto*. *Certiorari* is an order from the superior court compelling an inferior tribunal or other statutory delegate to render up all of the record of its proceedings to permit the superior court to determine the lawfulness thereof. If the superior court's review indicates a jurisdictional error (or, in some circumstances, some other error of law on the face of the record)[30], it will quash the proceedings of the inferior body and remit the matter back to the statutory delegate to be determined according to law. An order of prohibition is similar to *certiorari*, except that it occurs prior to the final conclusion of the proceedings by the inferior body, and prohibits it from proceeding in a manner which would take it outside its jurisdiction (or would cause it to commit some other error of law on the face of the record).

Mandamus is a command by the superior court compelling an inferior body to fulfill a statutory duty delegated to it. Thus, an order of *mandamus* can be used to compel an immigration officer to permit a Canadian citizen to enter Canada, because the citizen has that right and the officer has a corresponding duty to permit him or her to do so. While *mandamus* can be used to compel a delegate to comply with a statutory duty to exercise its discretion, it generally cannot be used to make the delegate exercise its discretion in a particular way (unless, in the circumstances, there is only one way the discretion can lawfully be exercised: see the *Vic Restaurant* case[31]).

Habeas corpus is the most glorious prerogative remedy, with high constitutional importance going back to the *Magna Carta*.[32] It compels the respondent to bring the person of the application before the superior court in order to permit the court to determine the lawfulness of the respondent's detention of the applicant.

Quo warranto requires the respondent to demonstrate by what authority it exercises the powers of a particular statutory office. In practice, applications

---

30 *R. v. Northumberland Compensation Appeal Tribunal* (1951), [1952] 1 K.B. 338 (Eng. C.A.); see the discussion in Chapter 11.

31 *Vic Restaurant Inc. v. Montreal (City)* (1958), [1959] S.C.R. 58 (S.C.C.).

32 25 Edw. 1, c. 36. See R.J. Sharpe, *The Law of Habeas Corpus*, 2nd ed. (Oxford: Clarendon Press, 1989).

for *quo warranto* are rare, because alternative statutory procedures have been enacted, for example, those dealing with contested elections.[33]

A declaration[34] can be used to determine the lawfulness of an administrator's actions, or the validity of the parent legislation. In Alberta, a statement of claim can list a declaration as all or part of the relief sought in an action, and in certain other circumstances, a declaratory order can be obtained by the more summary notice of motion proceedings under Rule 410 or as part of the relief sought in the "application for judicial review". While declaratory relief may be useful in many circumstances involving illegal administrative action, it does not itself directly coerce the respondent, but merely declares rights; neither does it quash a decision or "speaking order" of an inferior tribunal.[35] Accordingly, a declaration may not always be an effective remedy in administrative law.

Because governmental officials in Canada have no general immunity from legal liability for their actions, a claim for damages may succeed whenever an illegal administrative action causes harm of a kind otherwise known to the private law of property, tort or contract. Difficult questions frequently arise as to the precise type of action to take to claim redress successfully, and it may be hard to determine who is the correct party to sue.[36] Nevertheless, it is important to remember that damages were awarded in two great administrative law cases: *Roncarelli v. Duplessis*,[37] and *Cooper v. Wandsworth Board of Works*.[38]

In addition to these methods of obtaining what might be called "inherent judicial review", the courts are sometimes expressly granted either review or appellate powers by the legislation setting up the administrative machinery in question. For example, the *Municipal Government Act* in Alberta[39] delegates the power to approve developments of land to municipal subdivision or Development Appeal Boards. Section 688 of the Act specifically gives the Court of Appeal the right to hear an appeal on any question of law or jurisdiction, providing leave to appeal has been granted by a single judge of that court. Indeed, the court is given power to draw inferences from the facts before the board, and has power to confirm, vary, reverse or vacate the board's decision.[40] Such statutory rights of review or appeal are quite common, and it is important to read the legislation in question to determine their precise ambit.

A number of Commonwealth jurisdictions have implemented reforms to the method by which courts control the legality of administrative action. For

---

33 See for example, the *Local Authorities Election Act*, R.S.A. 2000, c. L-21. Note that *quo warranto* is still sometimes used for this purpose in Quebec.

34 See L. Sarna, *The Law of Declaratory Judgments*, 2d ed. (Toronto: Carswell, 1988).

35 See for example, *Pyx Granite Co. v. Ministry of Housing & Local Government* (1959), [1960] A.C. 260 (U.K. H.L.).

36 Not all governmental bodies have legal status, and therefore may not be amenable to legal process, which may have to be taken against the individuals involved personally.

37 [1959] S.C.R. 121 (S.C.C.).

38 (1863), 143 E.R. 414 (Eng. C.P.).

39 R.S.A. 2000, c. M-26.

40 See s. 688 and s. 689.

example, in 1971 the *Ontario Judicial Review Procedure Act*[41] created a remedy called an "application for judicial review" which can be used whenever a prerogative remedy or a declaration would have been available. This reform has been widely copied in other jurisdictions (including Alberta), whether by statute[42] or by amendments to the rules of court (as originally in England[43]). Some reforms have also altered the court before which such applications may be made; for example, in Ontario they are dealt with by a three member Divisional Court,[44] and in New Zealand there is now an Administrative Division of the High Court.[45] The *Federal Courts Act*[46] in Canada has transferred virtually all applications for judicial review against federal boards, tribunals or commissions from the superior courts of the provinces to the Federal Court (except *habeas corpus*[47]). Important amendments were made in 1992 to the jurisdiction of the Trial and Appellate Divisions of the Federal Court.

Finally, some reforms have increased the grounds for judicial review of administrative action beyond those recognized by the common law. For example, sections 18.1 and 28 of the *Federal Courts Act* specifically permit the

---

41   R.S.O. 1990, c. J.1 (originally enacted in 1971).

42   In British Columbia, see the *Judicial Review Procedure Act*, R.S.B.C. 1996, c. 241. As well, the new *Administrative Procedures Act* received Royal Assent on May 20, 2004. For further background on B.C.'s substantial administrative law reforms, readers are directed to the British Columbia Administrative Justice Project and, in particular, its position paper on "Model Statutory Powers for Administrative Tribunals" issued in August 2003 by the Administrative Justice Office of the Ministry of the Attorney General (B.C.).

In the Commonwealth of Australia, see *Administrative Decisions (Judicial Review) Act*, 1977 (No. 59 of 1977), which was the outcome of the *Report of the Committee of Review on Prerogative Writ Procedures* (Parliamentary Paper No. 56, 1973, the "Elliott Committee Report") and the *Report of the Commonwealth Administrative Review Committee* (Parliamentary Paper No. 144, August 1971, the "Kerr Committee Report").

In the Australian State of Victoria, see *Administrative Law Act*, 1978, No. 9234, 1978 (preceded by the *Victoria Statute Law Revision Committee's Report on Appeals from Administrative Decisions*, 1968).

In New Zealand, see *Judicature Amendment Act*, 1972, no. 130 of 1972, as amended by No. 32 of 1977, ss. 10-15 (based on recommendations in the Fourth Report of the Public and Administrative Law Reform Committee entitled *Administrative Tribunals: Constitution, Procedure and Appeals*, January 1971, on a draft statute contained in the Fifth Report, January 1972 and on the Eighth Report, September 1975). See also J.F. Northey, "An Administrative Law Division of the New Zealand Supreme Court – A Proposal for Law Reform" (1969) 7 Alta. L. Rev. 62, and J.F. Northey, "The Administrative Division of the New Zealand Supreme Court – A Postscript" (1977) 17 Alta. L. Rev. 186.

43   Order 53 of the *Rules of the Supreme Court* as substituted in 1977 by the Rules of the Supreme Court (Amendment No. 3) 1977, s. 1. 1977 No. 1955 and enacted subsequently in statutory from in *Supreme Court Act*, 1981 (U.K.)., c. 54, s. 31. For current rules see *The Supreme Court Practice, 1999* (London: Sweet and Maxwell, 1998). Similar procedural reforms have been implemented in Alberta; see Chapter 14.

44   *Supra* note 41.

45   *Supra* note 42.

46   R.S.C. 1985, c. F -7; originally R.S.C. 1970, c. 10 (2nd Supp.). See Appendix 5.

47   *Habeas corpus* remains available only in the provincial superior courts, even against federal boards, tribunals or commissions. This can work hardship when other remedies, such as *certiorari*, are required to make *habeas corpus* effective because only the Federal Court can issue those other remedies against a federal body, thereby requiring one to go to two separate courts.

Federal Court or the Federal Court of Appeal (as the case may be) to quash any decision or order which a federal administrative body has made "on an erroneous finding of fact that it has made in a perverse or capricious manner or without regard to the material before it", as well as for any error of law whether or not it appears on the face of the record.[48]

Finally, one should note the existence and importance of non-judicial remedies against administrative action, even if it lies within the delegate's jurisdiction. First, the administration itself is sensitive to well-founded criticism, and may correct errors or unfair action. Secondly, statutory delegates receive their authority from legislation and are therefore responsible to the legislative body which enacted that legislation. Members of Parliament or of provincial legislative assemblies may be useful in drawing attention to unfair administrative action, particularly in light of the constitutional collective responsibility of cabinet members to the legislature for all actions taken by the various government departments. Finally, most provinces (but not the Federal Government) have created ombudsmen for the purpose of reviewing the propriety and fairness of governmental actions, even when clearly within the jurisdiction provided for by statute. Although the ombudsman's only real sanction is to report to the legislative assembly, with all of the attendant publicity which that would generate, in practice this office performs a very useful service and should not be overlooked in seeking to correct administrative errors or unfairness.[49] All of these non-judicial means of reviewing and perhaps changing administrative action are important, but lie outside the scope of this text.

8. Privative Clauses

Judicial review of illegal administrative action can be very significantly restricted under our system of government. In the first place, there is no explicit constitutional requirement in Canada that courts exist, and no explicit constitutional guarantee of their jurisdiction.[50] Although the Canadian courts have consistently held that neither federal nor provincial legislation can prevent judicial determination of the constitutional validity of legislation itself,[51] the doctrine of the Sovereignty of Parliament means that the legislative branch

---

48 For a detailed discussion, see the 1994 and subsequent annual editions of Sgayias, Kinnear, Rennie & Saunders, *Federal Court Practice* (Toronto: Carswell).

49 In Alberta, the Office of the Ombudsman is governed by the *Ombudsman Act*, R.S.A. 2000, c. 0-8. The ombudsman's annual reports are useful reading, and further information can be obtained from the International Ombudsman Institute. Although the ombudsman institution has spread widely throughout Canada, it has still not been adopted at the federal level.

50 See David Phillip Jones, "A Constitutionally Guaranteed Role for the Courts" (1979) 57 Can. Bar Rev. 669.

51 See B. Strayer, *The Canadian Constitution and the Courts: The Function and Scope of Judicial Review,* 3d ed. (Toronto: Butterworths, 1987); *Judicial Review,* 4th ed. (Toronto: University of Toronto Press, 1969), especially Chapter 4; *Amax Potash Ltd. v. Saskatchewan,* [1977] 2 S.C.R. 576 (S.C.C.); *Canada (Attorney General) v. Law Society (British Columbia),* [1982] 5 W.W.R. 289 (S.C.C.) at 306-08 (the *Jabour* case).

could oust the courts' ability to review actions taken by statutory delegates. Such legislative provisions are often called "privative clauses" because they deprive the courts of their inherent authority to review actions taken by statutory delegates.

The effect of privative clauses can be obtained in several different ways. As discussed above, the most obvious way is for the legislation to state expressly that the administrator's action shall not be reviewed in any court. The legislation could either specifically prevent the court from issuing any of the remedies available for judicial review, or could specifically abolish the grounds for judicial review, or both. Alternatively, the legislation could extend the jurisdiction of the delegate so far that the ambit for judicial review is reduced to virtually nothing. This results from the exact but inverse relationship between the ambit of the delegate's jurisdiction and the scope of the *ultra vires* doctrine. In particular, the possibility of judicial review becomes minimal if the legislation delegates powers in very subjective terms, such as the British courts held in *Liversidge v. Anderson*[52] where the Secretary of State was given power to intern anyone whom he suspected of being an enemy alien. Short of an out-and-out malicious formation of the suspicion,[53] it would be virtually impossible for the courts to say that the delegate had transgressed the ambit of the discretionary power granted to it by the legislation.

Astonishingly, privative clauses do not always achieve their objective. In particular, the courts historically held that a jurisdictional error by the delegate would mean that it had not made a lawful decision, so that there is nothing to be protected from judicial review by the privative clause.[54] Indeed, this view has frequently been applied to strike down breaches of natural justice (which could only be done if such breaches are jurisdictional in nature and therefore incapable of being preserved by a privative clause).[55]

The Supreme Court of Canada has recognized the tension created by the desirability for judicial review of administrative action and the sovereign

---

52 [1941] 3 All E.R. 338 (U.K. H.L.). The actual wording of delegation of power was in much more objective terms than the decision of their Lordships would lead one to believe, *viz.* [at 341]:

> If the Secretary of State has *reasonable cause* to believe any person to be of hostile origin or association...and that by reason thereof it is necessary to exercise control over him, he may make an order against that person directing that he be detained. [Emphasis added.]

> For an interesting postscript on the controversy caused by this case, and particularly by Lord Atkin's famous dissent, see Heuston, *"Liversidge v. Anderson* in Retrospect" (1970) 86 L.Q. Rev. 33.

53 Which would generally be very difficult to prove, particularly in a proceeding for a prerogative remedy where discovery is not available. Compare the situation in *Roncarelli v. Duplessis*, [1959] S.C.R. 121 (S.C.C.), which was an action for damages in delict (tort), where the premier's malice came out in cross-examination.

54 See for example, *Metropolitan Life Insurance Co. v. I.U.O.E., Local 796*, [1970] S.C.R. 425 (S.C.C.); *Anisminic Ltd. v. Foreign Compensation Commission* (1968), [1969] 2 A.C. 147 (U.K. H.L.).

55 *Québec (Commission des relations ouvrières) v. Alliance des professeurs catholiques de Montréal*, [1953] 2 S.C.R. 140 (S.C.C.); *Toronto Newspaper Guild v. Globe Printing Co.*, [1953] 2 S.C.R. 18 (S.C.C.).

ability of the legislative branch to enact privative clauses.[56] In the end, the "perfect" privative clause would prevent all judicial review, even on jurisdictional grounds.[57] Taken to the extreme, this suggests that the legislative branch could abolish the superior courts outright, notwithstanding the inclusion of section 96 in the *Constitution Act, 1867*. The solution to this problem may well put limits on the permissible content of privative clauses, thereby effectively constitutionalizing the courts' right to review the legality of administrative actions on jurisdictional grounds.[58]

In addition, the Supreme Court of Canada has focused its consideration of privative clauses as one element in the "pragmatic and functional approach" for determining the intention of the legislature about the appropriate standard of review to be used by the courts when hearing either an application for judicial review or an appeal from a decision by a statutory delegate. Accordingly, privative clauses are discussed in Chapter 12 dealing with Standards of Review.

9. Summary

Administrative law deals with the legal remedies available to a person affected by administrative action. In our system the government has no special rights or powers, but derives all of its authority either from statute or from the rights or powers of the Royal Prerogative. Much of administrative law involves determining the precise ambit of the powers which the Federal Parliament or provincial legislatures have granted to a particular statutory delegate. This frequently involves the principles of statutory interpretation. Similarly, the remedies generally available from the normal superior courts to correct administrative action which is *ultra vires* are subject to the doctrine of Parliamentary Sovereignty, and can be modified or abolished by validly enacted legislation. In the end, statutory construction is exceedingly important to determine precisely what the sovereign legislator has done.

In summary, virtually all of administrative law flows from two great principles: first, the Sovereignty of Parliament, and second, the right of the ordinary courts to determine the meaning of legislation and the corresponding lawfulness of governmental action. A consideration of these two great principles is necessary to appreciate the constitutional content of administrative law, and to understand the judges' reasoning processes in trying to determine whether a particular governmental action is legal or illegal.

---

56 *Crevier v. Quebec (Attorney General)*, [1981] 2 S.C.R. 220 (S.C.C.).
57 See for example, the now repealed *British Columbia Labour Code*, R.S.C. 1979, c. 212, s. 33, which provided as follows:
    The board has and shall exercise exclusive jurisdiction to determine the extent of its jurisdiction under this Act, a collective agreement or the regulations, to determine a fact or question of law necessary to establish its jurisdiction and to determine whether or in what manner it shall exercise its jurisdiction.
58 See the article referred to in note 50 *supra*.

10. Selected Bibliography

The standard texts and journals to which the reader might make reference are as follows:

Administrative Agency Practice.

Anisman, P. & Reid, R.F., *Administrative Laws: Issues and Practice* (Toronto: Carswell, 1995).

Aronson, N. & Franklin, N., *Review of Administrative Action* (Sydney: Law Book Co., 1987).

Blake, S., *Administrative Law in Canada*, 3d ed. (Toronto: Butterworths, 2001).

Brown D.J.M. & Evans J.M., *Judicial Review of Administrative Action in Canada*, looseleaf (Toronto: Canvasback, 2003).

Canadian Journal on Administrative Law and Practice.

Clarke, H.W., *Constitutional & Administrative Law* (London: Sweet & Maxwell, 1971).

Craig, P.P., *Administrative Law*, 5th ed. (London: Sweet & Maxwell, 2003).

Davis, K.C., *Administrative Law Treatise*, 3d ed. (Boston: Little, Brown, 1994).

de Smith, S.A., *Constitutional & Administrative Law*, 7th ed. by Brazier, R., ed. (London: Penguin, 1974).

de Smith, S.A., *Judicial Review of Administrative Action*, 5th ed. by Lord Woolf & Jowell J. (London: Sweet & Maxwell, 1995) and cumulative supplements (and previous editions).

Dussault, R. & Borgeat, L., *Administrative Law – A Treatise*, 2d ed. (Toronto: Carswell, 1986).

Emery, C., *Administrative Law: Legal Challenges to Official Action* (London: Sweet & Maxwell, 1999)

Evans, J.M. *et al.*, *Administrative Law Cases, Text & Materials*, 5th ed. (Toronto: Emond Montgomery, 2003).

Foulkes, D., *Administrative Law*, 5th ed. (London: Butterworths, 1982).

Galligan, D.J., *Discretionary Powers: A Legal Study of Official Discretion* (Oxford: Clarendon Press, 1986).

Garner, J.F., *Administrative Law*, 7th ed. by Jones B.L. (London: Butterworths, 1989).

Jennings, J., *The Law and the Constitution*, 5th ed. (London: University of London Press, 1959).

JUSTICE, *Administrative Justice – Some Necessary Reforms*, Report of the Committee of the Justice – All Souls Review of Administrative Law in the United Kingdom (1988).

Law Society of Upper Canada – Special Lectures series.

Macaulay, *Practice and Procedure Before Administrative Tribunals*, looseleaf (Toronto: Carswell, 1988).

Macaulay & Sprague, *Hearings Before Administrative Tribunals* (1995).

Moskoff, F.R., *Administrative Tribunals: A Practice Handbook for Legal Counsel* (1989).

Mullan, D.J., *Administrative Law,* 3d ed.(Toronto: Carswell, 1996), with cumulative supplements.

Oulette, *Les tribunaux administratifs* (1997).

Phillips, O. Hood, *Phillips' Constitutional & Administrative Law*, 7th ed. by Phillips & Jackson, eds. (London: Sweet & Maxwell, 1987).

Reid R.F. & David H., *Administrative Law and Practice*, 2d ed. (Toronto: Butterworths, 1978).

Supreme Court Law Review, annual updates on Administrative Law (Butterworths).

Wade & Bradley, *Constitutional and Administrative Law*, 11th ed. by Bradley, Ewing & Bates, eds. (1993)

Wade, W. & Forsyth C., *Administrative Law*, 8th ed., (Oxford: Clarendon Press, 2000) (and previous editions).

On the historical origins of judicial review:

dc Smith, S.A., *Judicial Review of Administrative Action*, 4th ed. by Evans, J.M. (London: Stevens, 1980), App. I, "The Prerogative Writs: Historical Origins".

Jenks, "The Prerogative Writs in English Law" (1923) 32 Yale L.J. 523.

Rubinstein, "On the Origins of Judicial Review" (1964) 1 U.B.C.L. Rev. 1.

Some review articles of a general nature are:

Angus, W., "The Individual and the Bureaucracy: Judicial Review – Do We Need It?" (1974) 20 McGill L.J. 177.

Arthurs, "Rethinking Administrative Law: A Slightly Dicey Business" (1979) 17 Osg. H.L.J. 1.

Couture, "Introduction to Canadian Federal Administrative Law" (1972) 22 U.T.L.J. 47.

Hendry, "Some Problems in Canadian Administrative Law" (1967) 2 Ottawa L. Rev. 71.

Hogg, "The Supreme Court of Canada and Administrative Law 1949-1971" (1973) 11 Osgoode Hall L.J. 187.

Jones, D.P., "Recent Developments in Administrative Law" presented to the Canadian Bar Association National Labour Administrative Law CLE Conference: Pushing the Boundaries: Standing, Privacy and Practical Issues, Ottawa, Ontario, November 21 and 22, 2003).

Lyon, "Reforming Administrative Law" (1988-89) 2 C.J.A.L.P. 315.

Macdonald, "Reflections on the Report of the Quebec Working Group on Administrative Tribunals (Ouellette Commission Report)" (1987-88) 1 C.J.A.L.P. 337.

McAllister, "Administrative Law" (1963) 6 Can. Bar J. 439.

Millward, "Judicial Review of Administrative Authorities in Canada" (1961) 39 Can. Bar Rev. 351.

Molot, "Annual Surveys of Canadian Law: Part 2 Administrative Law" Ottawa
    L. Rev. 435; (1975) 7 Ottawa L. Rev. 515.
Morden, "Recent Developments in Administrative Law" (1967) L.S.U.C. Spe-
    cial Lectures 275.
Rutherford, "Legislative Review of Delegated Legislation" (1969) 47 Can.
    Bar Rev. 352.
Scott, "Administrative Law 1923-1943" (1948) 26 Can. Bar Rev. 268.
Smillie, "Jurisdictional Review of Abuse of Discretionary Power" (1969) 47
    Can. Bar Rev. 623.
Wade, "Anglo-American Administrative Law: Some Reflections" (1965) 81
    L.Q. Rev. 357.
Weiler, P., "The Slippery Slope of Judicial Intervention" (1971) 9 Osgoode
    Hall L.J. 187.
Willis, "Administrative Law in Canada" (1939) 53 Harvard L. Rev. 251.
Willis, "Administrative Law in Canada" (1961) 39 Can. Bar Rev. 251.
Willis, "Civil Rights – A Fresh Viewpoint", (1965) 13 Chitty's L.J. 224.
Willis, "Three Approaches to Administrative Law", (1935) 1 U.T.L.J. 53.

Government studies:

Alberta Institute of Law Research and Reform, Report No. 40, *Judicial Review
    of Administrative Action: Application for Judicial Review* (1984).
Alberta Law Reform Institute, Final Report No. 79, *Powers and Procedures
    for Administrative Tribunals in Alberta* (1999).
B.C. Administrative Justice Office, Ministry of Attorney General, Position
    Paper on "Model Statutory Powers Provisions for Administrative Tribu-
    nals", Victoria, August 2003, and previous background papers.
English Law Commission, Working Paper No. 40, *Remedies in Administrative
    Law* (1971).
Law Reform Commission of Canada, *Towards a Modern Federal Administra-
    tive Law* (Ottawa, 1987).
Ontario Royal Commission: *Inquiry into Civil Rights, Report No. 1* (3 vols.
    1968), especially vol. 1 and parts of vol. 3 (the "McRuer Commission").
Report of the Committee on Administrative Tribunals and Enquiries (England,
    1957) (the "Franks' Committee Report").
Report of the Committee on Minister's Powers (England, 1932) (the Don-
    oughmore Committee").
Report of the Committee on the Organization of the Government of Ontario
    (1959) (the "Gordon Report").
*Report of the Special Committee on Boards and Tribunals to the Legislative
    Assembly of Alberta* (1966) (the "Clement Committee").
Royal Commission on Government Organization (5 vols., 1963) (the "Glassco
    Commission").
Scottish Law Commission, Memorandum No. 14, *Remedies in Administrative
    Law* (1970).
Third Report of Special Committee on Statutory Instruments, (1969) (the
    "MacGuigan Committee").

2

Constitutional Aspects of Canadian Administrative Law[1]

---

1 This chapter has been updated by Dale Gibson, Consulting Barrister, Edmonton, and Katharine L. Hurlburt, Barrister and Solicitor, also of Edmonton. It incorporates contributions made in the third edition by Dale Gibson and by Ritu Khullar of Chivers, Kanee and Carpenter, Edmonton; and in the second edition by Timothy J. Christian, Q.C., of Edmonton.

19

1. Introduction: The Relevance of British Law

Constitutional law is the law that all other laws must obey. Section 52(1) of the *Constitution Act, 1982* decrees that:

> The Constitution of Canada is the supreme law of Canada, and any law that is inconsistent with the provisions of the Constitution is, to the extent of the inconsistency, of no force or effect.

This means that the provisions of every other field of law must, to be valid, comply with the "supreme" requirements of constitutional law. In the case of administrative law, which deals, like constitutional law, with governmental conduct, the need to keep the constitutional backdrop constantly in mind is especially important. Administrative actions taken under constitutionally invalid laws are themselves illegal.

The preamble to the *Constitution Act, 1867* proclaims that Canada is to have a Constitution "similar in principle to that of the United Kingdom". It is not surprising, therefore, that much of our constitutional and administrative law derives from British sources. There are important differences, however, because of our federal system of government, certain specific provisions of the *Constitution Act, 1867,* and the *Canadian Charter of Rights and Freedoms.*[2]

The cornerstone of British constitutional law, and therefore of British administrative law, is the doctrine of Parliamentary Sovereignty (sometimes referred to as Parliamentary or Legislative Supremacy). That doctrine, if applied in unrestricted form, permits the legislative arm of government to enact whatever laws it chooses, entirely free from interference by the courts, so long

---

2   The latter is technically cited as Pt. I of Sched. B to the *Canada Act, 1982,* (U.K.) (31 Eliz. 2, c. 11); also reproduced in the *Constitution Act,* S.C. 1982, Pt. I. It will be referred to hereafter as the "*Charter*". The *Constitution Act, 1867* was known as the *British North America Act* until re-named by the *Constitution Act, 1982.*

as the laws are enacted in accordance with prescribed legislative procedures. It is therefore useful to begin our discussion of constitutional law with an examination of the operation of this doctrine in the United Kingdom at the time Canada came into being. The discussion will then point out that a modern state such as the United States can function without such a doctrine, and examine the extent to which Legislative Sovereignty has been modified in Canada.

2. The Sovereignty of Parliament in Britain

The hallmark of British constitutional law in 1867, when Canada received its constitution, was the Sovereignty of Parliament, a principle which entailed a number of consequences for the British legal system , as well as for the many other legal systems, Canada's included, that adopted elements of the British model. The following summary attempts to describe what might be called "classic" Parliamentary Sovereignty: the British model at the moment of Canada's creation. Since constitutions do not stand still, even in the United Kingdom, it probably does not describe the current British situation entirely accurately.[3] This discussion concerns only the British ideas from which Canadian constitutional and administrative law evolved.

(a) British Parliament Omnipotent

First, the British Parliament was considered omnipotent. There was no limitation, therefore, on the content or subject matter of an Act of the British Parliament. This differed sharply from the situation in the United States, where a written Constitution in general and the *Bill of Rights*[4] in particular prevents either Congress or the State Legislatures enacting certain laws. It also differed from the situation in Canada, where, ever since 1867, a written Constitution has placed judicially-reviewable constraints on both the Parliament of Canada and Provincial Legislatures. The entrenchment of the *Charter* in our Constitution in 1982 magnified the difference by placing extensive new fetters on the authority of Parliament and the Legislatures and their respective administrations.

(b) British Parliament Unfettered for the Future

Secondly, constitutional theory in the United Kingdom stipulated that the Sovereignty of Parliament necessarily implied that Parliament could not bind

---

3 A softening of classic Parliamentary Sovereignty has been noted by many modern observers. See for example: S.A. de Smith and R. Brazier, *Constitutional and Administrative Law*, 7th ed., 1994, c.4. An important factor in that process has been the impact of European Community law. See for example H.W.R. Wade, "Sovereignty – Revolution or Evolution?" (1996) 112 L.Q.R. 569; T.R.S. Allan, "Parliamentary Sovereignty: Law, Politics and Revolution" (1997) 113 L.Q.R. 443. See generally: J. Goldsworth, *The Sovereignty of Parliament – History and Philosophy* (2001) Oxford U. Press.

4 *I.e.*, the first ten amendments to the *Constitution of the United States of America*.

itself to act in a particular way in the future. If such undertakings as to the future were enforceable, that theory postulated, a future Parliament would not be sovereign. According to that view, commitments by one Parliament as to how it will act in the future would have no legal force, and a subsequent contradictory Act would be legally valid, even if morally wrong.[5]

(c) Courts Bound by Acts of Parliament

Thirdly, the courts were bound to apply Acts of Parliament.[6] Statutes superceded inconsistent common law principles and prior judicial rulings. This aspect of Parliamentary Sovereignty is still fully operational. The courts must abide by legislation regardless of their dislike, disapproval or disagreement with the provisions enacted by Parliament. Indeed, Parliament can pass an Act reversing any decision of any court.[7] Yet clear words are required in an Act of Parliament to override certain maxims of common law or certain methods of statutory construction applied by the courts.[8] This power of the courts to interpret the language of Parliament is the fountain of administrative law in the United Kingdom, where the only real question usually comes to: "Has Parliament authorized this delegate to do this action in this manner?"

(d) Administrative Powers Derive from Statute or the Royal Prerogative

Fourthly, aside from a few prerogative powers of the Crown, which will be discussed below, all the powers exercised by the executive derived from Parliament, and this remains the case today. Acts of Parliament frequently grant power to particular persons to do particular things: to make rules or

---

5   O. Hood Phillips & P. Jackson, *O. Hood Phillips' Constitutional and Administrative Law*, 7th ed. (London: Sweet & Maxwell, 1987), especially c. 3. There is another view: C. Dike, "The Case Against Parliamentary Sovereignty" [1976] P.L. 283; G. Winterton, "The British Grundnorm: Parliamentary Sovereignty Re-Examined" (1976) 92 L.Q.R. 591; G. Winterton, "Parliamentary Supremacy and the Judiciary" (1981) 97 L.Q.R. 265. See also note 3 above. The theoretical basis for the view that even sovereign legislatures may tie their own hands with respect to future legislation is provided by the "manner and form" principle, according to which legislatures, being bound by the "rule of law" to obey existing laws despite their power to amend those laws, must observe any procedural requirements they themselves may have imposed as to how those amendments are to be made. Thus, if a legislature enacted a statute containing a provision that it could only be amended by a two-thirds majority of the legislature, it would be bound by that "manner and form" for future changes. See: P.W. Hogg, *Constitutional Law of Canada*, 3d ed. (Toronto: Carswell, 1992) (Looseleaf) at 12.3(b). Although Hogg and other writers stress the procedural nature of the principle, there would seem to be no reason in logic not to apply it even to situations where a legislature created an *absolute* bar to future enactments.

6   O. Hood Phillips, *ibid.* at 50-54.

7   See *Burmah Oil Co. (Burma Trading) v. Lord Advocate* (1964), [1965] A.C. 75 (U.K. H.L.), which was reversed by a subsequent statute. See also the *K.V.P.* statute of Ontario referred to in note 13 below.

8   J. Willis, "Statutory Interpretation in a Nutshell" (1938) 16 Can. Bar Rev. 1; and see the bibliography on this topic in G. Gall, *The Canadian Legal System*, 4th ed. (Toronto: Carswell, 1995).

regulations, to decide individual cases, to perform various duties. Parliament grants powers to various delegates to perform assorted functions, as well as imposing duties on those or other persons.[9] The source of the delegates' powers (or of their obligation to perform duties) is Parliament. Parliament may delegate powers to or impose duties on anyone – whether or not that person is a Member of Parliament, an advisor to the Crown (such as a Minister), the Cabinet, a person permanently employed as a civil servant, an administrative agency, or a private citizen. Whoever is the delegate, the source of his or her power or duty is Parliament. In particular, members of the executive (whether the Cabinet, the "Government", civil servants or others) do not possess any inherent power due to their position or office.

The only exception to this rule is the limited ambit of the Royal Prerogative,[10] which historically permits the Crown in certain circumstances to perform certain acts (such as declaring war, prohibiting entry of aliens into the realm, dismissing the government or dissolving Parliament) independently of Parliament and without its consent. Parliament, being as sovereign over the executive as it is over the courts, may abolish any of the prerogative powers of the Crown. The courts also have the authority to define and restrict prerogative powers.[11] Failing such statutory or judicial restriction, though, the prerogative powers represent an exception to the rule that in the United Kingdom the ultimate lawful authority for all actions taken by the executive derives from Parliament, and not from the executive itself.

(e) No Constitutional Separation of Powers

Finally, the doctrine of the Sovereignty of Parliament necessarily implied in 1867, and still does, that there is no constitutional separation of powers in the United Kingdom.[12] It is wrong to assume that every Act of Parliament is necessarily "legislative" in nature. True "legislation" changes the law in a general way that applies to all similar future situations. In constitutional systems marked by separation of powers, legislative bodies are restricted to enacting such general "legislation". The British Parliament, however, has the power to enact, if it chooses, statutes that deal with the resolution of particular disputes, or the management of particular situations, which matters are essen-

---

9   For the distinction between powers and duties, see W.N. Hohfeld, *Fundamental Legal Conceptions* (New Haven: Yale University Press, 1919).

10 See Hood Phillips, *supra* note 5, Chapter 14 for a discussion of the Royal Prerogative. See also G. Winterton, "The Prerogative in Novel Situations" (1983) 99 L.Q. Rev. 407; C. Walker, "Review of the Prerogative: The Remaining Issues" [1987] P.L. 62; P. Lordon, *Crown Law* (Toronto: Butterworths, 1991) Chapter 3.

11 See for example: *Burmah Oil Co. (Burma Trading) v. Lord Advocate*, *supra* note 7; *Burmah Oil Co. v. Bank of England*, [1979] 3 All E.R. 700 (U.K. H.L.). In Canada, the courts' common law powers to review the Royal Prerogative are supplemented by the *Charter*: see D. Gibson, "Monitoring Arbitrary Government Authority: *Charter* Scrutiny of Legislative, Executive and Judicial Privilege" (1998) 61 Sask. L.R. 297.

12 Although *in fact* the legislative, executive and judicial powers are largely allocated to separate entities, there is no *legal* requirement for these institutional arrangements.

tially judicial or administrative in nature.[13] As will be seen later,[14] closer examination reveals great difficulty in clearly separating these three functions. For now, it is adequate to note that in Britain Parliament may pass any Act, whether its provisions are in substance "legislative", "judicial" or "executive" in nature.[15]

3. The United States: A Contrasting Model

In the United States, the written Constitution distributes governmental powers to three separate branches: legislative, executive and judicial, and prohibits any overlapping between these branches.[16] Thus the President and Cabinet members in the United States do not sit in Congress[17] and may not be judges. The United States Constitution also differs fundamentally from the British Constitution in that it divides governmental powers federally between national and state orders of government, and prohibits both Congress and the State Legislatures violating the various rights entrenched in the constitutionally entrenched *Bill of Rights*.[18] The courts are final arbiters of the legislative constraints imposed by the separation of powers, the federal/state division of powers, and the *Bill of Rights*. The U.S. situation resembles the British (and Canadian), however, in that U.S. courts also apply certain maxims of common law and certain principles of statutory construction in determining whether various actions taken under a particular Act of Congress or of a state Legislature fall within the terms of that Act.[19]

4. The Canadian Model

The original Constitution of Canada was the *British North America Act, 1867*.[20] Although it has been amended considerably over the years, and its

---

13 An example is the 1965 statute in which the British Parliament overturned the judicial decision in the *Burmah Oil* case: *supra* note 7. A Canadian *e.g.* is a 1950 Ontario statute, *An Act Respecting the KVP Company Limited*, S.O. 1950, c. 33, s. 1: ". . . [E]very injunction heretofore granted against the KVP Company Limited . . . restraining the Company from polluting the waters of the Spanish River, is dissolved."

14 See Chapter 3.

15 Similarly, there is no constitutional prohibition in the United Kingdom against one person's being a member of two or more of the legislative, judicial or executive branches of government. The Queen is both the head of the executive branch of government and one of the three components of Parliament, whose Royal Assent is required to complete the enactment of statutes. The House of Lords, which is another component of Parliament, and a legislative body, is also Britain's highest court. Members of the Cabinet (part of the executive) are normally members of one of the Houses of Parliament, and the Lord Chancellor not only sits in Parliament and is a member of Cabinet, but is also the chief judicial officer of the realm.

16 See Arts. I, II and III of the *Constitution of the United States of America*.

17 Although the Vice-President has the right to preside over the Senate.

18 As the first ten amendments thereto.

19 See, *e.g., Cleary v. Cardullo's, Inc.*, 198 N.E.2d 281 (Mass. S.C. 1964).

20 30 & 31 Vict., c. 3; reproduced with amendments in R.S.C. 1970, App. II.

name was changed in 1982 to the *Constitution Act, 1867*, it remains our basic constitutional document to this day. Its Preamble provides that Canada's Constitution is "similar in principle to that of the United Kingdom." This makes the British model of government relevant to constitutional and administrative law in Canada. It should not be supposed, however, that the Canadian model is identical, or even closely similar, to the British model. In fact, Canada's constitutional situation is somewhere between the British and United States positions.

The principle of separation of powers does not apply in Canada.[21] In that respect Canadian constitutional and administrative law resembles British law. On the other hand, the British principle of Legislative Sovereignty does not apply with full force in Canada. Some aspects of the principle, such as the paramountcy of statute over common law and executive edict, do apply to Canada.[22] However, our written constitution has always imposed judicially-enforced constitutional restrictions on both the Provincial Legislatures and the Parliament of Canada. While most of those restrictions related, before 1982, to the division of governmental powers between the federal and provincial orders of government, the advent of the *Charter*[23] that year imposed a whole new set of constitutionally-entrenched rights, many of which are highly applicable to the administrative arm of government. The section of this chapter devoted to the *Charter* and administrative law will explore the principles which may be discerned from *Charter* decisions since 1982, and will demonstrate that the *Charter* has made the American model of government considerably more relevant to Canadian administrative law than previously. This is because constitutional limitations on the power of our governments[24] to enact particular laws necessarily imply judicial review of whether such a prohibition has been breached in a specific case.

These differences between the Canadian and British systems of government place more arrows in the citizen's quiver for challenging questionable

---

21 See: P.W. Hogg, *supra* note 5 at 7.3(a). Note, however, that in *Babcock v. Canada (Attorney General)* (2002), 214 D.L.R. (4th) 193 at 212-13 (S.C.C.), where a challenge to legislation was based in part on a claim that it offended an unwritten constitutional principle of separation of powers, the Supreme Court of Canada, while rejecting the claim, did not deny that such a principle exists.

22 In the *Babcock* case, *ibid.*, the Supreme Court of Canada held that certain unwritten principles "must be balanced against the principle of Parliamentary sovereignty," thus adding the sovereignty concept to a number of other unwritten principles, including the Rule of Law, which in Canada must mutually accommodate each other.

23 *Supra* note 2. In the interests of completeness it should be mentioned that even before 1982 there were a few explicit constitutional constraints on Legislative Sovereignty that did not relate to the division of law-making powers. For example, s. 15 of the *Constitution Act, 1867* makes the Queen the Commander-in-Chief of Canada's military; s. 16 gives the Queen the power to decide where Canada's Seat of Government should be; s. 18 limits Parliamentary privilege; and ss. 56, 57 and 90 impose the (now theoretical) possibility of executive disallowance or reservation on both federal and provincial legislation.

24 Including municipal governments, which derive their authority from provincial legislation, and to which the *Charter* applies: *Godbout c. Longueuil (Ville)* (1997), 152 D.L.R. (4th) 577 (S.C.C.).

governmental actions than exist under British administrative law. Let us examine those differences and their consequences in greater detail.

(a) Structural Considerations

(i) Federalism and the Division of Legislative Powers

Unlike the United Kingdom, Canada is a federal state. The federal nature of Canada means that the sovereign right to legislate is split between two orders of government: federal and provincial.[25] If the Parliament of Canada or a Provincial Legislature purports to enact legislation on a subject matter which is not within its responsibilities under the Constitution, that legislation is unconstitutional: illegal and void.[26] This does not mean that provincial legislation must never refer to a matter within federal jurisdiction, or *vice versa*. When courts characterize legislation for constitutional purposes they do so on the basis of its overall essential nature – its so-called "pith and substance" – and disregard its lesser "incidental" characteristics.[27]The courts have the duty to determine whether particular legislation is unconstitutional, and they cannot be deprived of this power by procedural devices.[28]

It logically follows that neither the Federal Parliament nor a Provincial Legislature may attempt to enact legislation which purports to delegate powers which are not assigned to it under the Constitution. Thus, the validity of delegated legislation or of any other form of delegated powers depends upon the constitutional validity of the parent Act. Accordingly, the division of legislative competence under our federal system provides a fundamental departure from the British model of complete Parliamentary Sovereignty; and provides a limitation on the ability of either the Federal Parliament or a Provincial Legislature to delegate particular powers to the administration. Canadian administrative law is therefore broader than its British counterpart, and

---

25 The *Constitution Act, 1867* does not recognize municipal governments as sovereign partners in the federal system; but rather as mere creatures of Provincial Legislatures. Section 92(8) gives jurisdiction over "municipal institutions in the province" to Provincial Legislatures, which in turn bestow local government powers on municipalities. Laws enacted by municipal institutions pursuant to such delegations of authority are constrained by both the parameters of the delegated authority itself and the requirement that they must not conflict with federal or provincial legislation: *114957 Canada Ltée (Spray-Tech, Société d'arrosage) v. Hudson (Ville)*, [2001] 2 S.C.R. 241 (S.C.C.).

26 Section 52(1) of the *Constitution Act, 1982* states: "The Constitution of Canada is the supreme law of Canada, and any law that is inconsistent with the provisions of the Constitution is, to the extent of the inconsistency, of no force or effect." When the courts have determined that the legislation is unconstitutional, it will normally be held to have been always unconstitutional. Occasionally, however, the courts will grant temporary validity to unconstitutional legislation in order to give the government an opportunity to comply with constitutional requirements: *Reference re Language Rights Under s. 23 of Manitoba Act, 1870 & s. 133 of Constitution Act, 1867*, [1985] 1 S.C.R. 721 (S.C.C.).

27 *Paul v. British Columbia (Forest Appeals Commission)*, 2003 SCC 55 (S.C.C.). In this case it was held to be permissible for a provincial statute to confer upon a provincial administrative tribunal the power to determine a claim to Aboriginal rights with respect to forest products because it was incidental to general provincial jurisdiction over its natural resources.

28 *Amax Potash Ltd. v. Saskatchewan* (1976), [1977] 2 S.C.R. 576 (S.C.C.).

overlaps to this extent into constitutional law. This feature of Canadian government is generally discussed fully in books on constitutional law,[29] and will not be considered in any greater detail here.

(ii) The Ability to Delegate

Subject to constitutional constraints, both the Federal Parliament and the Provincial Legislatures are supreme or "sovereign" within their respective spheres of legislative competence.[30] Their powers are not considered to have been delegated to them, but to belong to them in their own right by reason of their sovereign constitutional status. This means, among other things, that the maxim *delegatus non potest delegare*, which restricts the authority of a person to whom powers have been delegated to further delegate those powers to someone else, does not apply to either the Federal Parliament or Provincial Legislatures. For example, in *Valin v. Langlois*,[31] the Supreme Court of Canada upheld the ability of the Federal Parliament to delegate the power to determine controverted federal elections to provincial superior courts, and clearly validated Parliament's ability to delegate its powers generally. Similarly, in *Hodge v. R.*,[32] the Privy Council upheld the right of a Provincial Legislature to delegate matters lying within its sphere of legislative competence. Accordingly, both the Parliament of Canada and the Provincial Legislatures have the same power to delegate as is possessed by the British Parliament, subject only to the constitutional restrictions imposed by the federal nature of Canada and by the *Charter*.

The delegation of powers is increasingly necessary in the modern state, where governments control so vast a segment of human activity. It would be virtually impossible for the Federal Parliament or a Provincial Legislature to spell out in each Act all of the detailed rules applicable to every situation, particularly if these rules are technical or likely to change rapidly. Similarly, it may not be possible to deal with every situation in terms of rules, and it may be desirable to delegate to a particular person the power to exercise his or her discretion to determine a matter, perhaps within the broad outlines of policy set down by statute.

(iii) Delegation, but not Abdication

Although the Federal Parliament and the Provincial Legislatures may delegate their powers, it has been said that they may not abdicate their legislative functions. While the abdication principle is a more important feature of administrative law in the United States, where it flows naturally from the notion

---

29 See P.W. Hogg, *supra* note 5.

30 Although one speaks about Parliamentary or Legislative "sovereignty", that word has other connotations generally reserved for members of the international community. In the context relevant to this Chapter the terms "sovereignty" and "supremacy" are often used interchangeably.

31 (1879), 3 S.C.R. 1 (S.C.C.), leave to appeal refused (1879), 1 Cart. B.N.A. 158 (Canada P.C.).

32 (1883), (1883-84) LR 9 App. Cas. 117 (Ontario P.C.).

of Separation of Powers, than in Canada, it has occasionally been recognized here as well.[33] This limitation on excessive delegation is thought by some to be inherent in the doctrine of Legislative Sovereignty: because sovereignty could not exist without a sovereign, and because "divided sovereignty" would be a contradiction in terms, the sovereign may not abolish itself; and may not bestow part of its sovereignty on another sovereign.[34]

However, it is extremely difficult to draw the line between proper delegation and improper abdication of legislative powers, and the courts lean heavily in favour of the former. Instances of delegation being held by the courts to constitute impermissible abdication are extremely rare. Nevertheless, the general lack of success in applying the abdication principle to strike down legislation does not detract from the importance of having some idea of which matters must be dealt with by the legislators themselves and not be delegated to others. Indeed, there is considerable current concern about the volume and breadth of delegated powers which have been authorized by all legislative bodies. If Parliament and the Legislatures are not to become mere formalities, delegating all their real powers to the executive (generally the leaders of the political party which controls a majority in the legislative body), some attempt must be made to determine the proper limits of delegation. The existence of such limits has been recognized in the cases. Even though it has seldom been applied in practice, the abdication doctrine provides a potentially important limitation on power granted to the administration.

It is important to bear in mind while examining the cases on abdication that abdication involves more than extensive delegation of power. As the Privy Council said in *Hodge v. R.*:[35]

> It was argued at the Bar that a legislature committing important regulations to agents or delegates effaces itself. That is not so. It retains its powers intact, and can, whenever it pleases, destroy the agency it has created and set up another, or take the matter directly into his own hands. How far it shall seek the aid of subordinate agencies, and how long it shall continue them, are matters for each legislature, and not for Courts of Law, to decide.

It is quite common for both the Federal Parliament and the Provincial Legislatures to grant very broad discretionary powers to their delegates. In Canada, the delegation of law-making powers usually goes either to the Governor in Council or to the Lieutenant Governor in Council, although it sometimes goes to a particular Minister, which is the general practice in the United Kingdom, or to some other administrative authority. Short of a permanent or near-permanent divestment of the legislative body's power to make laws and

---

33   See: J. Willis, "Administrative Law and the British North America Act" (1939) 53 Harv. L.R. 251 at 254.

34   Note, however, that the "manner and form" theory, discussed in note 5 above, explains how a sovereign legislature bound by the Rule of Law can create legal conditions or impediments to the exercise of its own sovereignty.

35   *Supra* note 32 at 132.

to supervise the exercise of delegated functions, very broad delegations are lawful.

(A) Cases dealing with provincial delegation

The prohibition against abdication has arisen in a few cases involving provincial legislation. In *Reference re Initiative & Referendum Act (Manitoba)*,[36] the Privy Council indicated that the courts might strike down an Act if the powers delegated therein were so broad as to constitute an abdication of a Provincial Legislature's powers. In that case, the legislation[37] provided a method by which the electors of the province could directly either institute or repeal legislation themselves, without further involving the provincial legislature. Although the Privy Council disposed of the case on the basis that the legislation unconstitutionally interfered with the office of the Lieutenant Governor, Viscount Haldane specifically recognized the existence of the doctrine against abdication when he noted that the ability of a Provincial Legislature to delegate power does not mean "that it can create and endow with its own capacity a new legislative power [or institution] not created by the [*B.N.A.* or *Constitution Act*] to which it owes its own existence".[38]

Similarly, in *Crédit foncier franco-canadien v. Ross*,[39] Chief Justice Harvey of the Appellate Division of the Supreme Court of Alberta indicated that it might be an unconstitutional abdication for the Provincial Legislature to delegate to the Lieutenant Governor in Council the ability to determine which particular debts were governed by the *Reduction and Settlement of Debts Act*.[40] Again, while the legislation was in fact struck down because it interfered with the functions of the Lieutenant Governor, and also because it trenched on federal legislative powers with respect to bankruptcy and interest, Chief Justice Harvey did note[41] that the Legislature could not constitutionally abdicate its legislative power to anyone else.[42] The Ontario Court of Appeal applied the

---

36   (1919), 48 D.L.R. 18 (Manitoba P.C.).

37   S.M. 1916, c. 59.

38   *Supra* note 36 at 25.

39   [1937] 3 D.L.R. 365 (Alta. C.A.). Hogg, *supra* note 5 at 14.1(c) and 14.2(a) suggests that this decision has been "effectively overruled" by *Shannon v. British Columbia (Lower Mainland Dairy Products Board)*, [1938] A.C. 708 (British Columbia P.C.), and *Reference re s. 16 of the Criminal Law Amendment Act, 1968-69 (Canada)*, [1970] S.C.R. 777 (S.C.C.).

40   S.A. 1936 (2nd Sess.) c. 2.

41   *Supra* note 39 at 368.

42   His Lordship went so far as to suggest that: "If there could be legislation by Orders in Council or in some other way than by Act of the Legislature there would be no power reserved in the Governor-General to disallow it" (*ibid.* at 369). Sections 90 and 56 of the *Constitution Act, 1867*, read together, give the Governor General in Council the power to disallow (annul) a provincial statute within two years of being notified of its passage. Although this anomalous power remains in the Constitution as a relic of a time when Canada's Federal and Provincial governments lacked complete autonomy, and was still occasionally employed at the time when the *Crédit Foncier* case was decided, it is unlikely that it will ever by used again. In any event, it is respectfully submitted that it does not follow logically from the fact that delegated legislation may not be disallowable that it involves an abdication of the Legislature's power to make laws.

abdication principle in *Outdoor Neon Displays Ltd. v. Toronto (City)*,[43] when striking down a statute which the Court interpreted as giving the provincial Municipal Board the power to validate a particular city bylaw, and future amendments to the bylaw. Although the Supreme Court of Canada affirmed the Court of Appeal decision, it did so on other grounds, and noted that it was not affirming the constitutional point.[44] The existence of the principle was also acknowledged by Ritchie J., of the Supreme Court of Canada, in *M.G.E.A. v. Manitoba*:[45]

> If the section could be read as giving legislative force to all agreements entered into under the authority of an order in Council . . . then this would appear to me to constitute a delegation of legislative power amounting to an abdication by the legislature of its ultimate authority to pass laws. . . .

(B) Cases dealing with federal delegation

This principle logically ought to apply to the Federal Parliament as well as to the Provincial Legislatures. Although it appears that no federal legislation has ever been struck down for this precise reason, the principle underlying the *Constitutional Validity of Bill No. 136 (Nova Scotia), Re*,[46] in which delegation of legislative powers from Parliament to a Provincial Legislature, and *vice versa*, was held to be constitutionally invalid, is closely related to the abdication principle. Moreover, the principle prohibiting abdication to administrative bodies has been considered in four important cases in the federal context. While the latter decisions suggest that the abdication principle may have a very narrow range of application, some of them may be explained by the wartime circumstances in which they arose.

In *Grey, Re*,[47] one of the issues involved the ability of the Parliament of Canada to delegate to the Cabinet the power to amend other Acts of Parliament. This, surely, is a very broad power to legislate. As Fitzpatrick C.J.C. said:[48]

> The practice of authorizing administrative bodies to make regulations to carry out the object of an Act, instead of setting out all the details in the Act itself, is well-known and its legality is unquestioned. But it is said that the power to make such regulations could not constitutionally be granted to such an extent as to enable the express provisions of a statute to be amended or repealed; that under the constitution parliament alone is to make laws, the Governor-in-Council to execute them, and the court to interpret them; that it follows that

---

43   (1959), 16 D.L.R. (2d) 624 (Ont. C.A.), affirmed [1960] S.C.R. 307 (S.C.C.).
44   [1960] S.C.R. 307 at 314 (S.C.C.).
45   (1977), [1978] 1 S.C.R. 1123 at 1143 (S.C.C.).
46   (1950), [1951] S.C.R. 31 (S.C.C.). Delegation to an *administrative* agency of the other order of government was held to be valid in *Prince Edward Island (Potato Marketing Board) v. H.B. Willis Inc.*, [1952] 2 S.C.R. 392 (S.C.C.).
47   (1918), 42 D.L.R. 1 (S.C.C.).
48   *Ibid.* at 2-3, 5.

no one of these fundamental branches of government can constitutionally either delegate or accept the functions of any other branch.

In view of *Rex v. Halliday*, [1917] A.C. 260, I do not think this broad proposition can be maintained. Parliament cannot, indeed, abdicate its functions, but within reasonable limits at any rate it can delegate its powers to the executive government. Such powers must necessarily be subject to determination at any time by parliament, and needless to say the acts of the executive, under its delegated authority, must fall within the ambit of the legislative pronouncement by which its authority is measured. . . .

There are obvious objections of a political character to the practice of executive legislation in this country because of local conditions. But these objections should have been urged when the regulations were submitted to parliament for its approval, or better still when the *War Measures Act* was being discussed. Parliament was the delegating authority, and it was for that body to put any limitations on the power conferred upon the executive.

In *Reference re Regulations (Chemical) under War Measures Act (Canada)*,[49] the question again arose whether Parliament could lawfully delegate such vast powers to the Governor in Council. Although the Supreme Court of Canada upheld the validity of the particular delegation in question, Duff C.J.C. clearly stated that "not . . . every matter within the jurisdiction of the Parliament of Canada, even in ordinary times, could be validly committed by Parliament to the Executive for legislative action in the case of an emergency".[50] His Lordship went on to say that ". . . the *War Measures Act* does not, of course, attempt to transform the Executive Government into a Legislature, in the sense in which the Parliament of Canada and the Legislatures of the Provinces are Legislatures".[51]

Both of these are wartime cases, and the necessities of emergencies such as war may require the courts to uphold broader delegation of legislative powers to the executive than might otherwise be the case: in effect to temporarily roll back the frontier of illegal abdication. Nevertheless, it is useful to note the limitations which the courts have indicated separate lawful delegation from the unlawful abdication of legislative power, even in wartime: (1) the delegation must be reasonably limited; (2) the legislative branch must always be able to terminate the delegate's authority and thereby resume its own legislative power; and (3) the doctrine of *ultra vires* must apply to permit the courts to determine the lawfulness of the delegate's actions. In summary, the ability of Parliament or the Legislature to supervise or review the delegate's actions may tip the scales in favour of validating the delegation.

---

49   [1943] 1 D.L.R. 248 (S.C.C.).
50   *Ibid.* at 253.
51   *Ibid.* at 256.

In a peacetime context, the Appeal Side of the Court of Queen's Bench of Quebec held in *R. v. Picard*[52] that the Federal Parliament had not abdicated its powers by providing that:[53]

> ... each collective agreement to which this Act applies shall be deemed to be amended by the incorporation therein of the conclusions [set forth in the Picard Commission's] report, with respect to each of the following matters concerning which [an] inquiry is to be made by [the Commission].

Note that here the Federal Parliament was not merely incorporating into legislation the recommendations of a report which had already been made. On the contrary, Parliament constituted a commission of inquiry, gave it *carte blanche ex ante* to regulate the longshoremen's strike, and purported to incorporate into the legislation a report which had not yet been written. Also note, however, that the delegation was not of a *permanent* nature. The lack of permanence appeared to influence the Court's decision.[54]

A similar problem arose tangentially in *Reference re s. 16 of the Criminal Law Amendment Act, 1968-69 (Canada)*.[55] Section 16 of that Act required drivers whom the police suspected of being impaired to breathe into a breathalyser. It also required the police officer to provide the suspected driver with a sample of the driver's own breath, for independent analysis if desired. However, no satisfactory and economical container had been developed to hold the driver's own sample. Section 120 of the Act provided that:[56]

> 120 This Act or any of the *provisions* of this Act shall come into force on a day or days to be fixed by proclamation.

The Governor General proclaimed that part of section 16 which required a driver to blow into the breathalyser; he did not, however, proclaim the accompanying requirement for the police officer to provide such a driver with a sample for the driver's own analysis. The question before the Court was whether Parliament had, in fact, granted the Governor in Council power to proclaim part of a section. To a large extent, the answer depended upon the proper meaning to be attached to the word "provisions" used in section 120. If "provisions" meant any section, subsection, or paragraph, then the Governor General's proclamation was valid; otherwise, it was *ultra vires*.[57] The majority of the Supreme Court of Canada upheld the validity of this delegation to the executive, and dealt with the problem as a strict matter of statutory construction, even though the whole import of section 16 as enacted was changed by the

---

52 (1967), 65 D.L.R. (2d) 658 (Que. Q.B.).

53 *Ibid.* at 661, quoting the *St. Lawrence Ports Working Conditions Act*, S.C. 1966-67, c. 49.

54 *Ibid.*, see remarks of Hyde J.A. at 661-63.

55 (1970), 10 D.L.R. (3d) 699 (S.C.C.).

56 S.C. 1968-69, c. 38, emphasis added.

57 One might ask how the Governor General's proclamation power here differs from the Lieutenant Governor in Council's power in the *Crédit Foncier* case, *supra* note 39. It is probably because of their similarity that Hogg suggests the *Breathalyzer Reference* "effectively overruled" *Crédit foncier*. See *supra* note 39.

action of Parliament's delegate. Indeed, Laskin J. specifically stated[58] that there was no "constitutional" issue in question in this case, obviously using the word "constitutional" to refer only to the division of legislative powers contained under sections 91 and 92 of the *Constitution Act, 1867,* and not in the broader sense to refer to other rules and conventions similar in principle to the Constitution of the United Kingdom. With respect, it would appear that this ruling is a product of the particular facts, and that it would be dangerous to assume that it stands for the proposition that there are no limits on the ability of the Federal Parliament to delegate (or abdicate) its powers.

Indeed, it is important to note that Martland J. dissented[59] because he construed "provision" in such a way that the Governor in Council could not proclaim only part of the relevant section. Although the technical *ratio decidendi* of this case focuses upon the proper interpretation to be given to the word "provision", and therefore deals only with the question whether the delegate's actions were *ultra vires* the proclamation power contained in section 120, it does seem clear that at least Martland J. recognized the broader concern that there must be some limits to the ability of Parliament to delegate powers to the executive to make autonomous laws, apart altogether from the question of whether the delegate's actions are *intra vires* the power purportedly delegated to it. In particular, if Parliament had expressly said that the executive could proclaim any provision of the *Criminal Law Amendment Act,* even if the proclamation changed the meaning of the entire Act as passed by Parliament, Martland J. seemed to indicate that that might have been unconstitutional.

The same division in judicial philosophy was apparent in the Supreme Court of Canada's decision in the *Reference re Amendment to the Constitution of Canada.*[60] That case involved the ability of the Parliament of Canada to pass a resolution asking the British Parliament to amend the *British North America Act, 1867* without the consent of Provincial Legislatures. The majority of the Court (Laskin C.J.C., Dickson, Beetz, Estey, McIntyre, Chouinard and Lamer JJ.) held that such a resolution breached constitutional conventions, but was not illegal. The minority, (Martland and Ritchie JJ.) however, held that it would be illegal for the Federal Parliament to take action which would have the effect of unilaterally altering its position with respect to the Provincial Legislatures.

Although few examples can be found in the cases of the abdication prohibition being applied to strike down illegal delegation and actions taken pursuant thereto, this ground for questioning the validity of legislation has been clearly acknowledged by courts at all levels over the years, and should not be forgotten by the administrative lawyer.

It must be acknowledged that the author of Canada's preeminent constitutional law treatise, Professor P.W. Hogg, seems skeptical about the concept. While noting that the four opinions comprising the Supreme Court of Canada's decision in *Grey, Re* "each contained indications that the power of delegation was not absolute, and that an 'abdication,' 'abandonment' or 'surrender' of

---

58 *Supra* note 55 at 717.
59 *Ibid.* at 708.
60 *Reference re Amendment to the Constitution of Canada,* [1981] 1 S.C.R. 753 (S.C.C.).

Parliament's powers would be invalid," he states that given the extremely extensive scope of the *War Measures Act* delegation involved in that case "it is not easy to imagine the kind of delegation that would be unconstitutional"; and he points out that none of the Supreme Court Justices in *Gray* indicated "what principle of constitutional law dictated the suggested limitation."[61]

It may be that the principle (or principles) which Professor Hogg seeks can be found among the "unwritten constitutional principles" to which Chapter 15.9(8) of his own book refers, admittedly also somewhat critically. Two such principles upon which the Supreme Court of Canada relied in the 1998 *Reference re Secession of Quebec*[62] – constitutionalism and democracy – would support the suggestions in *Gray* that an excessive hand-off of legislative powers to the executive would constitute unlawful abdication. Tolerating in time of war and other extraordinary situations such gross delegations of law-making powers as occurred in *Gray* can also find support in an "unwritten constitutional principle": the notion of constitutional necessity which the Supreme Court of Canada acknowledged in the *Reference re Language Rights Under s. 23 of Manitoba Act, 1870 & s. 133 of Constitution Act, 1867.*[63]

In short, the principle that Canada's sovereign legislative bodies, Federal and Provincial, may not abdicate their law-making responsibilities has been recognized by both the Privy Council and the Supreme Court of Canada, and is supported by fundamental constitutional doctrine. Although it has rarely been applied, it is available to be invoked against governments that attempt to circumvent the basic democratic precept that primary law-making must in normal circumstances take place through open debate in our principal elected legislative bodies: the Parliament of Canada and the Provincial Legislatures.[64]

(iv) Offices of Queen, Governor General and Lieutenant Governor Constitutionally Protected

When Canada's Constitution was first enacted in 1867 it contained a provision, s. 92(1), that permitted Provincial Legislatures to make laws in relation to "the amendment from time to time . . . of the constitution of the province", but exempted from that power "the office of Lieutenant Governor". The purpose of that restriction was presumably to ensure that any experiments the provinces might conduct with governmental structures within their own borders would not alter the fundamental model of British-style Parliamentary democracy, of which the Crown is a uniquely crucial component.

In the original Constitution, this restriction had no counterpart for the offices of either the Governor General or the Queen. This was simply because that document did not bestow any explicit amending powers on the Federal or

---

61 Hogg, *supra* note 5 at 14.1(d).
62 [1998] 2 S.C.R. 217 (S.C.C.). See: Dale Gibson, "'Constitutional Vibes' Reflections on the *Secession Reference* and the Unwritten Constitution" (1999) 11 N.J.C.L. 49.
63 [1985] 1 S.C.R. 721 (S.C.C.). See Dale Gibson, "The Rule of Non-Law: Implications of the Manitoba Language Reference" *Transactions of Royal Society of Canada*, 1986; Dale Gibson, "The Real Laws of the Constitution" (1990) 28 Alta. L.R. 589.
64 These concluding remarks – the text associated with notes 60 to 62 – express the views of Dale Gibson, and not necessarily of the authors.

Imperial Parliaments. Since any amendment to Federal or Imperial constitutional powers would require amendment by the Imperial Parliament itself, which could always be counted on to be conscious of the needs of Parliamentary democracy, no need was perceived for express provisoes concerning the Federal and Imperial Crowns. When the Constitution of Canada was patriated in 1982, however, and a new all-Canadian amending formula was created, constitutional protection for the Crown was extended to all orders of government. Section 92(1) was repealed, and replaced by s. 41(a) of the *Constitution Act, 1982*, which stipulates that one of several matters which cannot be amended without unanimous federal and provincial consent is "the office of the Queen, the Governor General and the Lieutenant Governor of a province".

This restriction presents another possible obstacle to the delegation of legislative powers. Its predecessor, section 92(1), was used to prevent certain types of delegation by Provincial Legislatures.

Indeed, it was the *ratio decidendi* of the Privy Council's judgment in *Reference re Initiative & Referendum Act (Manitoba)*,[65] referred to above:

> The references their Lordships have already made to the character of the office of the Lieutenant-Governor, and to his position as directly representing thc Sovereign in the Province, renders natural the exclusion of his office from the power conferred on the Provincial Legislature to amend the constitution of the Province. The analogy of the British constitution is that on which the entire scheme is founded, and that analogy points to the impropriety, in the absence of clear and unmistakable language, of construing s. 92 as permitting the abrogation of any power which the Crown possesses through a person who directly represents it. For when the Lieutenant-Governor gives to or withholds his assent from a Bill passed by the Legislature of the Province, it is in contemplation of law the Sovereign that so gives or withholds assent. . . . It follows that if the *Initiative and Referendum Act* has purported to alter the position of the Lieutenant-Governor in these respects, this Act was insofar *ultra vires*.
>
> Their Lordships are of opinion that the language of the Act cannot be construed otherwise than as intended seriously to affect the position of the Lieutenant-Governor as an integral part of the Legislature, and to detract from rights which are important in the legal theory of that position. For if the Act is valid it compels him to submit a proposed law to a body of voters totally distinct from the Legislature of which he is the constitutional head, and renders him powerless to prevent its becoming an actual law if approved by a majority of these voters. . . . S[ection] 11 of the *Initiative and Referendum Act* is not less difficult to reconcile with the rights of the Lieutenant-Governor. It provides that when a proposal for repeal of some law has been approved by the majority of the electors voting, that law is automatically to be deemed repealed at the end of 30 days after the Clerk of the Executive Council

---

65   (1919), 48 D.L.R. 18 at 23-25 (Manitoba P.C.).

shall have published in the "Manitoba Gazette" a statement of the result of the vote. Thus the Lieutenant-Governor appears to be wholly excluded from the new legislative authority.

These considerations are sufficient to establish the *ultra vires* character of the Act.

A similar conclusion was reached, in questionably similar circumstances, in *Crédit foncier franco-canadien v. Ross*.[66] Section 12 of the *Alberta Debt Reduction Act* gave the Lieutenant Governor in Council the power to declare that the Act did not apply to certain kinds of debts. Harvey C.J.A. held this to be an unconstitutional provincial interference with the office of the Lieutenant Governor:

> No doubt the Lieutenant-Governor is an integral part of the Legislature but his function is not to initiate or to enact legislation but merely to authorize the introduction to the Legislative Assembly of certain classes of legislation and to assent to or withhold assent from legislation proposed by the Legislative Assembly. What is intended by s. 12 is to confer a quite different function from any of those recognized by the Constitution. . . . This case is different [from the *Initiative and Referendum* case] only in that it adds to rather than subtracts from the Lieutenant-Governor's functions. That difference is in my opinion of no importance. In Lefroy's *Canada's Federal System*, p. 387, is a note giving the opinion of Sir John Thompson, Minister of Justice, in pursuance of which an Act of the Quebec Legislature declaring the Lieutenant-Governor a corporation sole was disallowed. His opinion was that "It is immaterial whether a Legislature by an Act seeks to add to or take from the rights, powers or authorities which by virtue of his office a Lieutenant-Governor exercises, in either case it is legislation respecting his office."

Notice, however, the manner in which the impugned Alberta Act affected the powers in question: the Lieutenant Governor and Council were delegated the power (under the Act, to which the Lieutenant Governor gave Royal Assent) to determine the debts to which the Act applied. This additional delegated power differed completely from the situation in the Manitoba Act, which purported to permit laws to be made without the Lieutenant Governor's assent. It is submitted that Harvey C.J.A. incorrectly overlooked this difference. The delegation would apparently have been valid, moreover, if the Legislature had granted the power to someone other than the Lieutenant Governor, say to a particular named Minister.

Such a limitation on the ability of Legislatures to delegate is untenable today, particularly in light of the general practice in Canada to delegate powers to the Lieutenant Governor in Council provincially and to the Governor in Council federally. There appears to be no other case where the courts have found such delegations to the Crown to be unconstitutional, and this practice

---

66   [1937] 3 D.L.R. 365 at 368 (Alta. C.A.). As was noted previously, *supra* note 57, Professor P.W. Hogg considers this decision to be a dead letter.

seems too strongly entrenched now to be challenged. Indeed, in *Shannon v. British Columbia (Lower Mainland Dairy Products Board)*,[67] Lord Atkin said:

> The third objection is that it is not within the power of the Provincial Legislature to delegate so-called legislative powers to the Lieutenant-Governor in Council, or to give him powers of further delegation. This objection appears to their Lordships subversive of the rights which the Provincial Legislature enjoys while dealing with matters falling within the classes of subjects in relation to which the constitution has granted legislative powers. Within its appointed sphere the Provincial Legislature is as supreme as any other Parliament; and it is unnecessary to try to enumerate the innumerable occasions on which the Legislatures, Provincial, Dominion and Imperial, have entrusted various persons and bodies with similar powers to those contained in this Act.

Accordingly, short of an attempt by Parliament or a Provincial Legislature to abolish or restrict the traditional rights of the Lieutenant Governor, it is unlikely that the courts will interfere on constitutional grounds with delegations made to representatives of the Crown.[68]

(v) No Inter-delegation

Parliament may not delegate its legislative powers to the Legislature of a Province, and the reverse is also prohibited. In *Constitutional Validity of Bill No. 136 (Nova Scotia), Re*,[69] it was held that such a delegation was invalid because it would permit a readjustment of the respective spheres of legislative authority, contrary to the essentially federal nature of Canada.

Nothing, however, prohibits the Federal Parliament from delegating powers to a person named by a Provincial Legislature. That person then becomes the delegate of the Federal Parliament when he or she is exercising the powers granted by Parliament, and remains the Legislature's delegate when exercising the powers granted by the Legislature. The legality of this delegation was established in *Prince Edward Island (Potato Marketing Board) v. H.B. Willis Inc.*,[70] and provides a very useful method for dealing with a problem which transcends federal and provincial legislative competence. Such a device will also permit a Provincial Legislature to delegate powers to a person nominated by the Federal Parliament.[71]

---

67 [1938] A.C. 708 at 722 (British Columbia P.C.).
68 For more on this subject, see J. Saywell, *The Office of the Lieutenant-Governor: a Study in Canadian Government and Politics* (Toronto: University of Toronto Press, 1957), especially c. 8.
69 (1950), [1951] S.C.R. 31 (S.C.C.).
70 [1952] 2 S.C.R. 392 (S.C.C.).
71 See G.V. La Forest, "Delegation of Legislative Power in Canada" (1975) 21 McGill L.J. 131.

(vi) The Section 96 Problem

Section 96 of the *Constitution Act, 1867*, requires the federal Governor General to appoint all "superior, district and county court judges".[72] This effectively limits the ability of either a Provincial Legislature or the Federal Parliament to delegate to other persons powers or functions which properly belong to a superior court.[73] Thus, for example, while a Provincial Legislature can constitutionally establish an administrative board or body which exercises the powers or functions of a superior court, it cannot appoint the members of such an administrative body. Note that the effect of section 96 applies to federal as well as provincial boards: if their jurisdiction broadly conforms to that of superior courts, only the Governor General (not even Parliament itself) may appoint the persons who exercise these powers. In fact, however, almost all federal appointees are coincidentally named by the Governor General, and it is therefore unlikely, as a matter of practice, that section 96 will be often invoked against a federal board or official.[74]

If a person exercising the powers of a superior court has not been correctly appointed under section 96, his or her actions are complete nullities. Section 96 therefore sometimes provides a fertile means for attacking the validity of actions taken by administrative agencies.

What constitutes a "superior, district or county court" for the purposes of section 96? Clearly, the phrase includes the courts having those names which were in existence at Confederation in 1867. However, merely declining to call a body to which powers are delegated a superior, district or county court does not necessarily avoid offending section 96. There is no doubt that section 96 reserves certain "core" powers to section 96 courts, such as the superior courts'

---

72 See the discussion paper by Hon. Mark MacGuigan entitled *The Constitution of Canada: A Suggested Amendment Relating to Provincial Administrative Tribunals*, August 1983, which proposed a constitutional amendment to change s. 96 by adding s. 96B:

> 96B(1) Notwithstanding section 96, the Legislature of each Province may confer on any tribunal, board, commission or authority, other than a court, established pursuant to the laws of the Province, concurrent or exclusive jurisdiction in respect of any matter within the legislative authority of the Province.
>
> (2) Any decision of a tribunal, board, commission or authority on which any jurisdiction of a superior court is conferred under subsection (1) is subject to review by a superior court of the Province for want or excess of jurisdiction.

This amendment was not enacted.

73 Because county courts and district courts have now been abolished in most, if not all, parts of Canada, the following commentary will use the term "superior courts" to refer to s. 96 courts. When enquiring into the historical jurisdiction of s. 96 courts, however, the functions of county and district courts should not be overlooked.

The jurisdictional implications of s. 96 are extensively examined by Hogg, *supra* note 5, c. 7.3. Professor Hogg is critical of the jurisprudence, which he refers to at one point as a "swamp of uncertainty" (c. 7.3(e)). It may be worth observing, however, that s. 96 has been the subject of relatively little litigation since the mid-1990s, perhaps a result of the trend to de-regulation.

74 But see *Babcock v. Canada (Attorney General)* (2002), 214 D.L.R. (4th) 193 (S.C.C.), discussed below.

extensive powers of contempt of court.[75] The question always is, are the particular impugned functions *peculiar* to such a court?

The Supreme Court of Canada has developed a three-step test to assist in determining whether certain judicial functions fall within the exclusive jurisdiction of section 96 courts, or can be conferred on inferior tribunals.[76] The first question asked by that test is whether the power conferred by the legislation "broadly conforms" to a power or jurisdiction exclusively exercised by a Superior, District or County Court at that time of Confederation? Second, if so, is it a judicial power? The third question – to be asked if the previous questions are both answered positively – is whether the power is subsidiary, ancillary, or necessarily incidental to a predominately administrative function or novel form of jurisdiction. As explained by McLachlin J., "the first two steps may be seen as identifying potential violations of section 96; the last step is setting up the circumstances in which the transfer of section 96 power to an inferior tribunal is 'transformed' and hence constitutionalized by the administrative context in which it is exercised".

Each of these aspects will be discussed in turn, but before doing so it should be noted that the enquiry must consider more than just the remedy involved in the impugned legislation. In some of the early jurisprudence under section 96, the courts concentrated on the nature of the *remedies* in question in characterizing the law for purposes of this inquiry. More recent decisions have indicated that in characterizing legislation it is also important to focus on the nature of the dispute or the *subject matter* at issue. Some decisions have seemed to suggest, in fact, that this should be done to the exclusion of the remedy or means of adjudication to obtain the remedy.[77] As in all constitutional litigation, much of the subsequent analysis will turn on how the law is initially characterized.

(A) The historical inquiry

The first of the three analytical steps to be applied is the historical inquiry, which asks whether the subject matter at issue is one which "broadly conforms" to the exclusive jurisdiction section 96 courts exercised at Confederation. If it is not, the function in question may be assigned to a person or body not appointed by the Governor General. In *Babcock v. Canada (Attorney General)*,[78] for example, a federal statute empowered the Clerk of the Privy Council

---

75 *MacMillan Bloedel Ltd. v. Simpson*, [1995] 4 S.C.R. 725, 130 D.L.R. (4th) 385 (S.C.C.).

76 *Reference re Act to Amend Chapter 401 of the Revised Statutes, 1989, the Residential Tenancies Act, S.N.S. 1992, c. 31*, [1996] 1 S.C.R. 186, 131 D.L.R. (4th) 609 at 640 (S.C.C.); *Reference re Residential Tenancies Act (Ontario)*, [1981] 1 S.C.R. 714 (S.C.C.).

77 *Reference re Act to Amend Chapter 401 of the Revised Statutes, 1989, the Residential Tenancies Act, S.N.S. 1992, c. 31, ibid.* at 625 and 640; *Sobeys Stores Ltd. v. Yeomans*, [1989] 1 S.C.R. 238, 57 D.L.R. (4th) 1 at 12 (S.C.C.); *Reference re Young Offenders Act (Canada)*, [1991] 1 S.C.R. 252, 77 D.L.R. (4th) 492 at 502 (S.C.C.). See also *Reference re Residential Tenancies Act (Ontario), ibid.*

78 (2002), 214 D.L.R. (4th) 193 (S.C.C.). See also: *Air Canada c. Canada (Commissaire de la concurrence)* (2003), 222 D.L.R. (4th) 385 (Que. C.A.), leave to appeal to S.C.C. allowed (August 14, 2003), Doc. 29660 (S.C.C.).

to certify information as a Cabinet confidence and thereby prevent its disclosure in the courts. The Supreme Court of Canada held that this did not make the Clerk a s. 96 judge because in 1867 no court had the power to compel the disclosure of Cabinet confidences.

It is important to bear in mind that it is only where the jurisdiction being challenged conforms *broadly* to the 1867 jurisdiction of a s. 96 court that the challenge will succeed. It will be remembered that when courts classify legislation for the purpose of determining its constitutionality they do so on the basis of its "pith and substance" – its essential character – and disregard its merely "incidental" features.[79] There is nothing to prevent certain *limited* functions or characteristics of a s. 96 judge being conferred on an inferior tribunal or other authority unless the conferral is so extensive as to convert that tribunal or authority, in effect, into a superior court. In *Nova Scotia (Labour Relations Board) v. Future Inns Canada Inc.*,[80] for instance, it was held that legislation which granted Commissioners of Inquiry "the same privileges and immunities as a judge of the Supreme Court" did not "grant powers that are 'broadly conformable or analogous to jurisdiction or powers exercised and exercisable by courts which are within s. 96'".

It should also be noted that the s. 96 question is not affected by whether the matters being adjudicated are governed by federal or provincial legislative jurisdiction. Some matters that are now within federal competence were historically determined by inferior courts, and some matters that are now provincial were dealt with historically by superior, district or county courts.[81]

The *Reference re Act to Amend Chapter 401 of the Revised Statutes, 1989, the Residential Tenancies Act, S.N.S. 1992, c. 31*[82] decision held that in answering this inquiry the courts will look to the jurisdiction of section 96 courts at Confederation in all *four* confederating provinces, in the hope of finding a general practice. In the event of a tie, the jurisdiction of the courts in England may be examined.[83] What is frozen in time is the exclusive jurisdiction or core-jurisdiction of section 96 courts only. The jurisdiction of *inferior* tribunals is not frozen at the time of Confederation, though it must not encroach upon the frozen exclusive domain of the higher courts.[84]

There are four possible results to this historical inquiry. The first would be that the jurisdiction of the issue "broadly conforms" to the type of jurisdic-

---

79   See text accompanying note 27.
80   (1999), 178 D.L.R. (4th) 202 at 226 (N.S. C.A.). The ruling relies for authority on what are acknowledged to be *obiter dicta* from the Supreme Court of Canada's decision in *Rivard c. Morier* (1985), 23 D.L.R. (4th) 1 at 736-37 (S.C.C.), a case in which s. 96 was neither argued not considered, but in which a similar bestowal of immunity was held to fall within provincial jurisdiction over "property and civil rights." It is consistent with s. 96 jurisprudence for the reason outlined in the text.
81   See: *Paul v. British Columbia (Forest Appeals Commission)*, 2003 SCC 55 (S.C.C.).
82   *Supra* note 76.
83   Note Professor Hogg's trenchant criticism of this approach, however: *supra* note 5, c. 7.3(e).
84   *Reference re Adoption Act (Ontario)*, [1938] S.C.R. 398, [1938] 3 D.L.R. 497 at 512 (S.C.C.); *Saskatchewan (Labour Relations Board) v. John East Iron Works Ltd.* (1948), [1949] A.C. 134 [1948] 4 D.L.R. 673 at 685 (Saskatchewan P.C.); *Ontario (Attorney General) v. Canada (Attorney General)*, [1982] 1 S.C.R. 62 (S.C.C.).

tion exercised exclusively by section 96 courts at the time of Confederation. If that were the case, it would be necessary to move on to the second and third elements of the test outlined above. A second alternative would be that the jurisdiction at issue does not conform to the jurisdiction of section 96 courts at the time of Confederation, but conforms instead to the functions of inferior tribunals at that time. In that case, there would be no question of infringing section 96, and the inquiry would be at an end. The third possibility would be that *both* the inferior courts and section 96 courts exercised jurisdiction in the area in 1867 – concurrent jurisdiction. The fourth alternative would be that *neither* court exercised jurisdiction in the area in 1867 – novel jurisdiction. It is worth reviewing the third and fourth possibilities, since they have given the courts pause. It will be seen, however, that those situations both produce the same result as the second: no constitutional impediment to inferior court jurisdiction.

The two leading cases with respect to what happens when there is concurrent jurisdiction are both decisions of the Supreme Court of Canada: *Sobeys Stores Ltd. v. Yeomans*,[85] and *Reference re Act to Amend Chapter 401 of the Revised Statutes, 1989, the Residential Tenancies Act, S.N.S. 1992, c. 31*. They establish that no section 96 problem exists in concurrent situations, so long as the historical jurisdiction of the inferior courts in the shared areas was substantial.

The sole fact that *some* jurisdiction may have been shared historically is not in itself sufficient to say that modern legislation conferring jurisdiction on an inferior tribunal would be valid. There must have been more than some small aspect of the jurisdiction that was shared. To establish concurrent jurisdiction it must be shown that there was a *practical* involvement of inferior tribunals that was "broadly co-extensive with the work of superior courts": *Sobeys Stores Ltd. v. Yeomans*. [86] The task assigned to the courts is to search for "a general shared involvement in a jurisdiction": *Sobeys Stores Ltd. v. Yeomans*.[87] One way of doing this is to consider the following aspects of inferior court jurisdiction:

- What was the geographic reach of the inferior courts?

- What were the pecuniary limitations if any?

- What were the range of disputes that it could determine?

Justice McLachlin in *Reference re Act to Amend Chapter 401 of the Revised Statutes, 1989, the Residential Tenancies Act, S.N.S. 1992, c. 31*[88] added two other criteria to this test:

- What was the percentage of the population which would have used inferior courts?

---

85 *Supra* note 77.
86 [1989] 1 S.C.R. 238 at 260 (S.C.C.).
87 *Ibid.* [emphasis in original].
88 (1996), 131 D.L.R. (4th) 609 at 641 (S.C.C.).

- What was the frequency with which disputes amenable to the process arose?

Justice McLachlin admonished that it is necessary to look to the actual powers exercised by superior courts at the time of Confederation.[89]

In *Sobeys Stores Ltd. v. Yeomans*, a majority of the Court held that the jurisdiction of a tribunal to adjudicate dismissal issues in employment law, and specifically the meaning of "just cause", was the type of jurisdiction that was concurrent or shared at Confederation. In *Reference re Act to Amend Chapter 401 of the Revised Statutes, 1989, the Residential Tenancies Act, S.N.S. 1992, c. 31*,[90] the majority of the Court upheld the jurisdiction of the Director and the Residential Tenancies Board on the basis that at Confederation both superior and inferior courts had a shared involvement in deciding residential tenancy disputes.

Interestingly, in both cases the dissenting justices would have upheld the jurisdiction on the basis of a "novel jurisdiction", which will be considered next.

It is well-established that novel jurisdiction, of a type that did not exist in 1867, can be conferred on inferior tribunals.[91] In *Reference Re Residential Tenancies Act*,[92] Chief Justice Lamer, writing for himself and Justices Sopinka and Cory (in dissent), stated a test for determining when novel jurisdiction exists:

    i.   Is the legislation an attempt to respond to a new societal interest and approach regarding the subject-matter of the legislation?

    ii. Is the legislation based on principles of law that make it distinct from similar legislation?[93]

    iii. Is there an identifiable social policy that is different from the policy goals of analogous legislation?

In that case Chief Justice Lamer and his fellow dissenters found that the landlord and tenant scheme in Nova Scotia was a novel jurisdiction. They were of the view that the jurisdiction was not meant to be a replica of the landlord and tenant law, but rather that it established a complete and comprehensive code independent of landlord and tenant law. While the majority of the Court

---

89 *Ibid.* at 642.
90 [1996] 1 S.C.R. 186, 131 D.L.R (4th) 609 (S.C.C.).
91 See: *Saskatchewan (Labour Relations Board) v. John East Iron Works Ltd.* (1948), [1949] A.C. 134, [1948] 4 D.L.R. 673 (Saskatchewan P.C.); and *Reference re Adoption Act (Ontario)*, [1938] S.C.R. 398, [1938] 3 D.L.R. 497 (S.C.C.), as explained by Justice Estey in *Ontario (Attorney General) v. Canada (Attorney General)*, [1982] 1 S.C.R. 62, 131 D.L.R. (3d) 257 at 283 (S.C.C.). In *Saskatchewan (Workers' Compensation Board) v. Wiebe* (1999), 174 D.L.R. (4th) 391 (Sask. C.A.), the Saskatchewan Court of Appeal upheld a trial decision (1998), 163 D.L.R. (4th) 336 (Sask. Q.B.) that found Boards of Inquiry under the *Saskatchewan Human Rights Code* not to be s. 96 courts, in part because anti-discrimination laws did not exist in 1867.
92 *Supra* note 90 at 627-28.
93 Here Lamer C.J.C. suggests that it may be useful to consider whether it is a distinct branch of law and whether there is a complete code to govern the area: *ibid.* at 632.

did not agree with that conclusion, there is no reason to doubt that the general principles expressed by the Chief Justice were accepted by the entire Court.

Those principles were drawn, in fact, from a previous decision in which a majority of the Supreme Court of Canada had accepted novelty as a basis for inferior court jurisdiction: *Reference re Young Offenders Act (Canada).*[94] The issue in that case was whether youth courts, which were inferior tribunals, could be given exclusive jurisdiction over young offenders. The Court characterized the law in question as relating to young persons charged with criminal offences. The historical inquiry showed that young persons charged with criminal offences had not been treated as a group in a significantly distinct way by any judicial body at Confederation. While there was some evidence of distinctions being made between adults and youths in criminal courts in 1867, it was clear that there had been no comprehensive scheme to deal especially with young persons in the criminal justice system at that time.

The Court therefore found that special legislation in relation to young offenders was the result of a new "interest and approach of society to the criminality and illegal conduct of its younger members."[95] It was part of a new scheme designed to respond to what was "a novel concern of society".[96] The Supreme Court of Canada was not saying that youths had never committed crime before, or had never been prosecuted and punished for it before, but rather that society was now approaching the problem of youth crime in a newly comprehensive and concerted way. Society had made a decision to try rehabilitating young offenders, as opposed to punishing them like adult criminal offenders. Since Confederation, the issue of "youth crime" *per se* had become a "novel concern of society".

Chief Justice Lamer, writing the majority decision in *Reference re Young Offenders Act (Canada)*, indicated that one question which must be asked is: if the subject matter of youth crime had existed in 1867, which level of court would have had jurisdiction over it? He concluded that since inferior courts then had jurisdiction over offences which had less stigma and carried lighter sentences, they would also have been given jurisdiction over young offenders.

It is worth noting the scathing critique that Justice McLachlin made of the "novel jurisdiction" approach in *Reference re Act to Amend Chapter 401 of the Revised Statutes, 1989, the Residential Tenancies Act, S.N.S. 1992, c. 31*[97] where she wrote the majority decision. (Justice McLachlin and Justice Wilson had dissented from the reasoning of the majority decision in *Reference re Young Offenders Act (Canada)*, not from the result.) In *Reference re Act to Amend Chapter 401 of the Revised Statutes, 1989, the Residential Tenancies Act, S.N.S. 1992, c. 31*,[98] Justice McLachlin upheld the Residential Tenancies scheme, as did Chief Justice Lamer, but she did so on the basis that there was a concurrent jurisdiction at the time of Confederation. In turning to the issue of novel jurisdiction, she stated that something is not novel just because it is

---

94 [1991] 1 S.C.R. 252, 77 D.L.R. (4th) 492 (S.C.C.).
95 *Ibid.* at 504.
96 *Ibid.* at 506.
97 [1996] 1 S.C.R. 186, 131 D.L.R. (4th) 609 (S.C.C.).
98 *Ibid.*

"simply a re-organization for administrative reasons of a jurisdiction which has been exercised by superior and inferior tribunals in Canada since before Confederation."[99] She emphasized that all legislation has social policy goals, but that in order for it to be novel, to create a new jurisdiction, it was necessary to have a "unifying concept or goal, and a sufficiently novel philosophy to belie any analogy with the powers previously exercised by superior courts."[100] She noted that almost any dispute regulated by section 96 courts of Confederation could be argued to have become modernized or urbanized and therefore changed, and that a lot of the policy issues being considered by some justices under the "novel jurisdiction" rubric were really issues to be addressed under stage three of the *Residential Tenancies* test.

(B) Judicial function

If after the historical inquiry one concludes that the jurisdiction at issue is one that broadly conforms to a jurisdiction exercised exclusively by section 96 courts at the time of Confederation, one proceeds to the second question, which is whether the jurisdiction is to be exercised in a judicial manner. The court will examine the functions of a tribunal with the functions of a section 96 court. The more a tribunal addresses broader social policy concerns in its decision-making, rather than considering the legal issues between parties, the less likely will it be considered to be exercising a judicial function.[101]

(C) Institutional setting

The third step in the *Residential Tenancies* analysis is based on a long-established principle of Canadian constitutional law that the constitutionality of legislation is to be determined by its substantial essence ("pith and substance"), rather than by its minor or "incidental" characteristics. Thus, a legislative scheme that establishes a fundamentally novel approach to some social problem will escape section 96 challenge even though some aspect of it, considered independently, may not be novel. Similarly, a scheme that is fundamentally administrative, rather than judicial, in nature, will not violate section 96 even if some of its incidental processes are judicial. When applying this principle at the third stage of the *Residential Tenancies* test, the courts must examine the particular feature or features of the scheme that have been attacked in the context of the *overall* institutional setting established.

A good illustration of the "institutional setting" factor is *MacMillan Bloedel Ltd. v. Simpson*,[102] which involved a provision of the *Young Offenders Act* in which Parliament attempted to give youth courts exclusive jurisdiction to try youths for contempt of court, including contempt of superior courts. The Supreme Court of Canada concluded that, apart from the exclusivity feature, the grant of jurisdiction to youth courts was permissible on the basis of the

---

99   *Ibid.* at 647.
100 *Ibid.* at 651.
101 *Reference re Residential Tenancies Act (Ontario)*, [1981] 1 S.C.R. 714 (S.C.C.); and *Sobeys Stores Ltd. v. Yeoman*, [1989] 1 S.C.R. 238, 57 D.L.R. (4th) 1 (S.C.C.).
102 [1995] 4 S.C.R. 725, 130 D.L.R. (4th) 385 (S.C.C.).

three-part *Residential Tenancies* test. First, on the historical test, the contempt of court power of superior courts was clearly within section 96 jurisdiction. Second, the jurisdiction of the youth court was unquestionably to be exercised judicially. However, third, in the context of the institutional setting of transferring of power to youth courts because of the novel policy objective of treating youths differently, it was held to be permissible to give the inferior tribunal, the youth court, the incidental jurisdiction to deal with contempt of superior courts by youths.

The real question in that case was whether such a grant of inferior court jurisdiction could be *exclusive*, with the result that superior court jurisdiction would be completely removed. The majority of the Court "read down" the legislation, interpreting its literally broad language narrowly, so as to permit only *concurrent* inferior court jurisdiction. The four dissenting judges thought that a grant of exclusive jurisdiction could be upheld under the third part of the *Residential Tenancies* test, the institutional setting. Further, the dissenters felt that the jurisdiction of the superior court had not been ousted, as it retained a supervisory function through judicial appeals. The majority view was based on comments by Gonthier J. in *Chrysler Canada Ltd. v. Canada (Competition Tribunal)*.[103]

(D) Deference and privative clauses

Section 96 has particular importance in administrative law for two reasons. First, it may hamper an attempt by the legislative branch to delegate certain judicial powers to an administrative tribunal, thereby retaining the historically important distinction between "judicial" and "administrative" matters which has been eroded in another context by the "duty to be fair".[104] Secondly, because one of the hallmarks of a superior court is its inherent power to determine the jurisdiction of statutory (or "inferior") tribunals, any attempt by the legislative branch to grant such a supervisory power (as opposed to an administrative appeal) to an administrative agency may well convert it into a superior court to which section 96 applies. Indeed, this latter proposition can be used to argue that a statutory provision (or "privative clause") which purports to oust the ordinary courts' inherent power to review decisions of administrative tribunals effectively gives that tribunal power to determine its own jurisdiction, and thus makes that tribunal a superior court whose members must be appointed in accordance with section 96. This argument can be used either to strike down the privative clause or to strike down every action taken by the administrative tribunal because its members have not been appointed correctly. In theory, the latter view appears to be better, because there is no doubt that the legislative branch could lawfully (i) enact a stringent privative clause provided (ii) the

---

103 [1992] 2 S.C.R. 394, 92 D.L.R. (4th) 609 at 615 (S.C.C.). See also: *Court of Unified Criminal Jurisdiction, Re*, [1983] 1 S.C.R. 704, 148 D.L.R. (3d) 25 (S.C.C.); *R. v. Trimarchi* (1987), 62 C.R. (3d) 204, 49 D.L.R. (4th) 382 (Ont. C.A.), leave to appeal to the S.C.C. refused [1988] 1 S.C.R. xiv (S.C.C.); and *Saskatchewan (Workers' Compensation Board) v. Saskatchewan (Board)* (1999), 174 D.L.R. (4th) 391 at 403 (Sask. C.A.), affirming (1998), 163 D.L.R. (4th) 336 at 342 (Sask. Q.B.).

104 See Chapter 8.

members of the administrative tribunal are appointed by the federal Governor General under section 96. Thus, the privative clause would appear to be valid; only the appointment of the delegates could be questioned.

The Supreme Court of Canada considered this argument about the constitutional importance of section 96 for determining the validity of privative clauses in *Crevier v. Quebec (Attorney General).*[105] Sections 194 and 195 of the *Professional Code of Quebec*[106] purported to preclude the availability of any of the remedies normally available from the superior court for the purpose of questioning the validity of any action taken by a wide range of officials and tribunals to whom various powers had been granted under the Code. Apart altogether from the question whether any of the provincially appointed officials and tribunals were themselves exercising the power of superior courts contrary to section 96 of the *Constitution Act*, Laskin C.J.C. held that the mere attempt to deprive the superior courts of their traditional supervisory function over the jurisdiction of these inferior delegates itself contravened the spirit of section 96.[107] In other words, the Supreme Court of Canada recognized that our Constitution protects some of the administrative law jurisdiction of the superior courts against privative clauses, and to that extent limits the legislative sovereignty of both Parliament and the Legislatures. As Laskin C.J.C. said:[108]

> It is true that this is the first time that this Court has declared unequivocally that a provincially constituted statutory tribunal cannot constitutionally be immunized from review of decisions on questions of jurisdiction. In my opinion, this limitation, arising by virtue of s. 96, stands on the same footing as the well-accepted limitation on the power of provincial statutory tribunals to make unreviewable determinations of constitutionality. There may be differences of opinion as to what are questions of jurisdiction but, in my lexicon, they rise above and are different from errors of law, whether involving statutory construction or evidentiary matters or other matters. It is now unquestioned that privative clauses may, when properly framed, effectively oust judicial review on question of law and, indeed, on other issues not touching jurisdiction. However, given that s. 96 is in the *British North America Act* and that it would make a mockery of it to treat it in non-functional formal terms as a mere appointing power, I can think of nothing that is more the hallmark of a superior court than the vesting of power in a provincial statutory tribunal to determine the limits of its jurisdiction without appeal or other review.

Distinguishing matters which go to jurisdiction from those which lie within it[109] may be exceedingly difficult, and will be considered in more detail in a

---

105 [1981] 2 S.C.R. 220 (S.C.C.).
106 R.S.Q. 1977, c. C-26.
107 *Supra* note 105 at 230.
108 *Ibid.* at 236.
109 Note the following sources quoted by Laskin C.J.C., *ibid.* at 237:
    There has been academic concern with the permitted scope of privative clauses referable to determinations of provincial adjudicative agencies. Opinion has varied from a position

later chapter.[110] Nevertheless, it is clear that the Supreme Court of Canada has recognized the importance of section 96 in administrative law, as a constraint on the unfettered ability of the legislative branch to enact broad privative clauses ousting judicial review of administrative actions.

5. The Canadian Charter of Rights and Freedoms and Administrative Law

(a) Introduction to the *Charter*

This part of the chapter examines the impact which the *Charter* has had on administrative law since it was enacted in 1982. Although there have been a myriad of court decisions, this section will not attempt to review them all, since it is intended to be a doctrinal overview of the principles developed by the Supreme Court of Canada to deal with some of the most difficult *Charter* problems which arise in administrative law.[111]

Prior to 1982, administrative law was largely a collection of common law rules which the courts developed to supervise the exercise of delegated authority by the bodies or persons upon whom such powers have been conferred. These rules were developed over a long period of time, and on an *ad hoc* basis. Before the *Charter*, there was no constitutional grant to the courts of the power of judicial review of administrative action.[112] The explicit exercise of such authority was simply assumed to be an inherent part of the judge's job of interpreting and enforcing legislation. The judge-made rules ensured that sub-

---

that even errors of law cannot validly be immunized from review (see J.N. Lyon, "Comment" (1971), 49 Can. Bar Rev. 365), to a position that at least jurisdictional review is constitutionally guaranteed (see W.R. Lederman, "The Independence of the Judiciary", (1956) 34 Can. Bar Rev. 1139, at p. 1174) to a position that jurisdictional determinations may, constitutionally, also be denied judicial review. See P.W. Hogg, "Is Judicial Review of Administrative Action Guaranteed by the British North America Act?" (1976), 54 Can. Bar Rev. 716, and see also Dussault, *Le contrôle judiciare de l'administration au Québec* (1969), especially at pp. 110-13.

See also D.J. Mullan, "The Uncertain Constitutional Position of Canada's Administrative Tribunals" (1982) 14 Ottawa L. Rev. 239, as well as *Québec (Procureur général) v. Farrah*, [1978] 2 S.C.R. 638 (S.C.C.) and *Tomko v. Nova Scotia (Labour Relations Board)* (1975), [1977] 1 S.C.R. 112 (S.C.C.).

110   See Chapter 12.

111   For more detailed discussions, see P.W. Hogg, *Constitutional Law of Canada*, *supra* note 5, especially c. 44 and 45; D. Gibson, *Law of the Charter: General Principles* (Toronto: Carswell, 1986); D.C. McDonald, *Legal Rights in the Canadian Charter of Rights and Freedoms*, 2d ed. (Toronto: Carswell, 1989); R.J. Sharpe, ed., *Charter Litigation* (Toronto: Butterworths, 1987); N.R. Finkelstein and B. Rogers, *Administrative Tribunals and the Charter* (Toronto: Carswell, 1990); G.A. Beaudoin and E. Mendes, eds., *The Canadian Charter of Rights and Freedoms*, 4th ed. (Toronto: Carswell, forthcoming); J.B. Laskin *et al.*, eds., *Canadian Charter of Rights Annotated*, (Canada Law Book).

112   There was (and continues to be) the *Canadian Bill of Rights, 1960*, of course, but its status, as an ordinary statute of the Parliament of Canada, is quasi-constitutional at best, but both it and its provincial counterparts can be significant in some instances. The "quasi-constitutional" status of such instruments derives from the "manner and form" principle, explained *supra* note 5 and in note 205, below.

ordinate agencies acted within jurisdiction, that they did not make errors of law, and that they followed a fair procedure when affecting rights. Behind these judge-made rules, however, was the fundamental notion that the elected legislative branch was supreme and could make or unmake any laws (subject, of course, to the structural constraints arising chiefly out of the federal nature of Canada, described above). For example, by specifically spelling out the statutory procedure to be used, the common law right to a fair hearing could be denied by the legislature. The courts had no power to consider the validity of federal or provincial laws passed by legislators within their jurisdiction.[113] Administrative law was concerned with formal validity and procedural propriety, not with the substantive justness of legislation.

The *Charter* has changed much of this. The courts have now been granted constitutional authority to review legislation and to declare it of no force or effect if it fails in either procedure or substance to measure up to the fundamental rights contained in the *Charter*.[114] The courts can also insist that fair procedures be used by administrative agencies wherever someone is deprived of the right to life, liberty or security of the person or other constitutionally guaranteed rights. Since 1982, therefore, there is a constitutional right to fair procedure which does not depend on the implied intention of the legislator.

These are the main changes which the *Charter* has brought to administrative law. The following sections of this chapter review the principal cases in which these basic principles have been elaborated and qualified; the application of the *Charter* to boards and agencies in the public sector; the power of tribunals to interpret and apply the *Charter*; the impact of section 7 on the administrative process (including the meaning which the courts have given to the principles of procedural and substantive fundamental justice); and, finally the effect of section 8 on the power of administrative tribunals to conduct searches and seize documents.

(b) To Whom Does the *Charter* Apply

The application of the *Charter* is prescribed in section 32(1) as follows:

> 32.(1) This Charter applies
>
> > (a) to the Parliament and government of Canada in respect of all matters within the authority of Parliament including all matters relating to the Yukon Territory and Northwest Territories; and

---

113   Subject to limitations provided for within the *Constitution Act, 1867* such as s. 93, or for that matter the "implied Bill of Rights". The latter notion is based on the theory that because the Constitution creates Parliamentary institutions, it impliedly guarantees the democratic freedoms that are essential to the survival of Parliamentary democracy. See: *Reference re Alberta Legislation*, [1938] S.C.R. 100 at 132-35 (S.C.C.), affirmed [1938] 3 W.W.R. 337 (Alberta P.C.), *per* Duff C.J.C; D. Gibson, "Constitutional Amendment and the Implied Bill of Rights" (1967) 12 McGill L. J. 497.

114   Sections 52(1) and 24(1) of the Constitution Act, 1982.

> (b) to the legislature and government of each province in respect of all matters within the authority of the legislature of each province.

Although section 32 refers, in the non-federal context, to only "the legislature and government of each province", the Legislatures and Governments of the Territories are also included by reason of section 30, which states:

> 30.   A reference in this Charter to a province or to the legislative assembly or legislature of a province shall be deemed to include a reference to the Yukon Territory and the Northwest Territories, or to the appropriate legislative authority thereof, as the case may be.

It should also be borne in mind that section 52(1) subjects all "laws", including subordinate legislation,[115] to *Charter* scrutiny.

The Supreme Court of Canada has dealt with section 32 in a number of circumstances and a set of principles has emerged. First, the Court has held that the *Charter* applies even to the exercise of prerogative powers by the executive.[116] Cabinet decisions fall under section 32(1) of the *Charter*, and are therefore reviewable in the courts for compatibility with the Constitution.

Second, the Court has said that the *Charter* applies to the common law, which must be interpreted and applied in a manner which is consistent with *Charter* values:[117]

> Historically, the common law evolved as a result of the courts making those incremental changes which were necessary in order to make the law comply with current societal values. The *Charter* represents a restatement of the fundamental values which guide and shape our democratic society and our legal system. It follows that it is appropriate for the courts to make such incremental revisions to the common

---

115   *Malartic Hygrade Gold Mines Ltd. v. Quebec* (1982), 142 D.L.R. (3d) 512 (Que. S.C.); *Baker v. Tanner* (1991), 77 D.L.R. (4th) 379 (N.S. C.A.).

116   *Operation Dismantle Inc. v. R.*, [1985] 1 S.C.R. 441 (S.C.C.) *per* Dickson C.J.C. at 455. See also Chapter 8, for a discussion of the issue of the applicability of the *Charter* to Cabinet decisions.

117   *Dolphin Delivery Ltd. v. R.W.D.S.U., Local 580* (1986), [1987] 1 W.W.R. 577, [1986] 2 S.C.R. 573 (S.C.C.). Significantly, McIntyre J. held that the action of the court in granting an order could not itself constitute such governmental action. If court orders were characterized as governmental actions virtually all private litigation would be subject to the *Charter*. McIntyre J. pointed out that this was not to say that the courts should ignore the values contained in the *Charter*. Indeed, he was of the view that the courts ought to ". . . apply and develop the principles of the common law in a manner consistent with the fundamental values enshrined in the Constitution." (*Ibid.* at 599.) The *Charter* may thus be considered an authoritative pronouncement of the rules of public policy which the courts may rely on in refusing to grant common law relief. For example, even though the *Charter* would not apply directly to a discriminatory contract between two private parties, the courts could refuse to enforce a discriminatory covenant on the ground that it was contrary to public policy as declared in the Constitution. See also *Pepsi-Cola Canada Beverages (West) Ltd. v. R.W.D.S.U., Local 558*, [2002] 1 S.C.R. 156 at 167-68 (S.C.C.).

law as may be necessary to have it comply with the values enunciated in the *Charter*.

Third, the *Charter* applies to all aspects of government, including the legislative, executive and administrative branches, as well as municipalities and municipal by-laws.[118]

In some cases, however, it is not immediately obvious whether a particular decision maker is part of "government" for the purposes of section 32. The analysis used by the Supreme Court of Canada to answer this question has undergone considerable development, beginning with a series of cases decided in 1990.

The first case was *McKinney v. University of Guelph*.[119] In *McKinney*, La Forest J. concluded that universities are not subject to *Charter* scrutiny. He came to this view after examining the statutory context in which universities operate. The deciding factor was that each of the universities had its own governing body, and in no case did the government appoint a majority of the members of that governing body. La Forest J. stated[120]:

> The government thus has no legal power to control the universities even if it wished to do so. Though the universities, like other private organizations, are subject to government regulations and to a large measure depend on government funds, they manage their own affairs and allocate these funds, as well as those from tuition, endowment funds and other sources.

> Though the legislature may determine much of the environment in which universities operate, the reality is that they function as autonomous bodies within that environment.

In *Harrison v. University of British Columbia*,[121] La Forest J. applied his decision in *McKinney*, despite some factual differences which he described as "relatively minor".[122] Under the applicable B.C. legislation, the Lieutenant Governor in Council appointed a majority of the members of the Board of Governors, and the Minister could require the university to submit various reports. La Forest J. stated that while these factors[123]

> suggested a higher degree of governmental control than was present in *McKinney*, I do not think they suggest the quality of control that would justify application of the *Charter*.

---

118   *Ramsden v. Peterborough (City)*, [1993] 2 S.C.R. 1084 (S.C.C.), where the Court struck down a by-law which prohibited placing posters on any public property. It was held that the by-law was overly broad and that its impact on freedom of expression was disproportionate to its objectives. See also: *Godbout c. Longueuil (Ville)*, [1997] 3 S.C.R. 844 (S.C.C.).

119   [1990] 3 S.C.R. 229 (S.C.C.).

120   *Ibid.* at 273-74.

121   [1990] 3 S.C.R. 451 (S.C.C.).

122   *Ibid.* at 463.

123   *Ibid.* at 463.

La Forest J. went on to adopt the words which the Court of Appeal had used below:[124]

> . . . the fact that the university is fiscally accountable does not establish government control or influence upon the core functions of the university, and, in particular, upon the policy and contracts in issue in this case.

Similarly, in *Stoffman v. Vancouver General Hospital*,[125] La Forest J. determined that a hospital was not a governmental actor and that its mandatory retirement policy was therefore not reviewable under the *Charter*. La Forest J. distinguished between "ultimate or extraordinary control and routine or regular control" over the affairs of an enterprise. Under the relevant statute, while the ultimate fate of the hospital was in the hands of the Government of British Columbia, responsibility for the daily or routine aspects of the hospital's operation rested with the hospital's Board of Trustees.

By contrast, the Court determined in *Douglas/Kwantlen Faculty Assn. v. Douglas College*[126] that a college (which was statutorily an agent of the Crown) was far less independent than the universities in *McKinney* and *Harrison*, and was "simply part of the apparatus of government both in form and in fact":[127]

> In carrying out its functions, . . . the college is performing acts of government, and I see no reason why this should not include its actions in dealing with persons it employs in performing these functions. Its status is wholly different from the universities in the companion cases of *McKinney v. University of Guelph*, and *Harrison v. University of B.C.*, which though extensively regulated and funded by government, are essentially autonomous bodies. Accordingly, the actions of the college in the negotiation and administration of the collective agreement between the college and the association are those of the government for the purposes of s. 32 of the *Charter*. The *Charter*, therefore, applies to these activities.

As a result, La Forest J. held that the collective agreement was "law", and therefore had to comply with the *Charter*.

A similar result was reached in *Lavigne v. O.P.S.E.U.*,[128] where the majority of the Court characterized the "Council of Regents" of the community college as an "emanation of government".[129] The Court was of the view that the government, through the Minister, had the power of "routine or regular control" over all of the activities of the Council of Regents, including collective bargaining with college employees (who were also Crown employees). Given these facts, the Council of Regents of the college was a governmental actor,

---

124   *Ibid.* at 464.
125   [1990] 3 S.C.R. 483 (S.C.C.).
126   [1990] 3 S.C.R. 570 (S.C.C.).
127   *Ibid.* at 584-85, *per* La Forest J.
128   [1991] 2 S.C.R. 211 (S.C.C.), reconsideration refused (1991), 4 O.R. (3d) xii (S.C.C.).
129   *Ibid.* at 311.

and the collective agreement between the Council and the Union was "law" to which the *Charter* applied.

La Forest J. went on to speak about the pervasive role of government in modern Canadian society and the need for *Charter* supervision of such government activities:[130]

> It was also argued that the *Charter* does not apply to the government when it engages in activities that are, in the words of the CLC and OFL, "private, commercial, contractual or non-public [in] nature". In my view, this argument must be rejected. In today's world it is unrealistic to think of the relationship between those who govern and those who are governed solely in terms of the traditional law maker and law subject model. We no longer expect government to be simply a law maker in the traditional sense; we expect government to stimulate and preserve the community's economic and social welfare. In such circumstances, government activities which are in form "commercial" or "private" transactions are in reality expressions of Canada's overall international competitiveness. In this context, one has to ask: why should our concern that government conform to the principles set out in the *Charter* not extend to these aspects of its contemporary mandate? To say that the *Charter* is only concerned with government as law maker is to interpret our Constitution in light of an understanding of government that was long outdated even before the *Charter* was enacted. . . .

> It must be borne in mind that the *Charter* is not intended to serve a simply negative role by preventing the government from acting in certain ways. It has a positive role as well, which might be described as the creation of as a society-wide respect for the principles of fairness and tolerance on which the *Charter* is based.

Eldridge v. British Columbia (Attorney General)[131] represents a significant development in the Court's analysis of the application of the Charter. The appellants, each of whom was born deaf, alleged that the failure to provide funding for sign language interpreters during the delivery of medical services to them violated their rights under section 15(1) of the *Charter*. Funding decisions were made by the Medical Services Commission in respect of medically required services delivered by doctors and other health care practitioners. Funding decisions were made by hospitals with respect to services delivered by the hospitals. Speaking for a unanimous Court, La Forest J. had no hesitation in concluding that the Medical Services Commission was subject to the *Charter* in this respect, because:[132]

> . . . the Commission implements a government policy, namely, to ensure that all residents receive medically required services without

---

130   *Ibid.*, per La Forest J. at 315*ff.*
131   [1997] 3 S.C.R. 624 (S.C.C.).
132   *Ibid.* at 666

charge. In lieu of setting out a comprehensive list of insured services in legislation, the government has delegated to the Commission the power to determine what constitutes a "medically required" service. There is no doubt, therefore, that in exercising this discretion the Commission acts in governmental capacity and thus is subject to the *Charter*.

The more controversial issue was whether the *Charter* applied to the hospitals. La Forest J. stated:[133]

> Stoffman made it clear that, as presently constituted, hospitals in British Columbia are non-governmental entities whose private activities are not subject to the *Charter*. It remains to be seen, however, whether hospitals effectively implement governmental policy in providing medical services under the *Hospital Insurance Act*.

La Forest J. analyzed the provisions of the *Hospital Insurance Act* and concluded:[134]

> The structure of the *Hospital Insurance Act* reveals, therefore, that in providing medically necessary services, hospitals carry out a specific governmental objective. The Act is not, as the respondents contend, simply a mechanism to prevent hospitals from charging for their services. Rather, it provides for the delivery of a comprehensive social program. Hospitals are merely the vehicles the legislature has chosen to deliver this program.

and:[135]

> The provision of these services is not simply a matter of internal hospital management; it is an expression of government policy. Thus, while hospitals may be autonomous in their day-to-day operations, they act as agents for the government in providing the specific medical services set out in the Act. The Legislature, upon defining its objective as guaranteeing access to a range of medical services, cannot evade its obligations under s. 15(1) of the *Charter* to provide those services without discrimination by appointing hospitals to carry out that objective. In so far as they do so, hospitals must conform with the *Charter*.

Thus, in *Eldridge,* the Court moved beyond the simple "autonomy" test enunciated in *McKinney* and its companion cases to ask whether an administrative body carries out governmental objectives or implements governmental policy. If so, then it will be part of "government" for *Charter* purposes. This means that a government cannot avoid application of the *Charter* simply by "privatizing" or "contracting out" responsibilities which have traditionally been performed by the public sector.

---

133   *Ibid.* at 662
134   *Ibid.* at 664-65.
135   *Ibid.* at 665.

The Court confirmed the *"Eldridge* approach" in the recent decision of *Blencoe v. British Columbia (Human Rights Commission)*[136]. In *Blencoe*, the respondent, a minister of the Government of British Columbia, was the subject of sexual harassment complaints which were filed with the British Columbia Human Rights Commission. The Commission carried out a lengthy investigation, then scheduled hearings before the British Columbia Human Rights Tribunal. The hearing dates were more than 30 months after the initial complaints were filed. A threshold issue in the case was whether the *Charter* applied to the actions of the Commission. The following factors were argued in support of a conclusion that the Commission was not subject to the *Charter*: (i) the Commission was required to be independent of the government; (ii) no statutory provisions were being challenged; and (iii) the Commission was performing a judicial function.

The Court had no hesitation in rejecting all three arguments. Bastarache J. stated:[137]

> The mere fact that a body is independent of government is not determinative of the *Charter's* application, nor is the fact that a statutory provision is not impugned.

> Bodies exercising statutory authority are bound by the Charter even though they may be independent of government.

Bastarache J. also made short work of the argument that the Commission was immune from the *Charter* because it exercises judicial functions. Relying on the Court's decision in *Slaight Commuinications Inc. v. Davidson*[138], Bastarache J. stated:[139]

> The facts in *Slaight* and the case at bar share at least one salient feature: the labour arbitrator (in *Slaight*) and the Commission (in the case at bar) each exercise governmental powers conferred upon them by a legislative body. The ultimate source of authority in each of these cases is government. All of the Commission's powers are derived from the statute. The Commission is carrying out the legislative scheme of the *Human Rights Code*. It is putting into place a government program or a specific statutory scheme established by the government to implement government policy [citations omitted]. The Commission must act within the limits of its enabling statute. There is clearly a "governmental quality" to the functions of a human rights commission which is created by government to promote equality in society generally.

> Thus, notwithstanding that the Commission may have adjudicatory characteristics, it is a statutory creature and its actions fall under

---

136 [2000] 2 S.C.R. 307 (S.C.C.), corrected [2001] 2 S.C.R. iv (S.C.C.). The Court split 5:4. The minority held that the issues fell to be determined on the basis of administrative law principles and, therefore, did not express an opinion on the *Charter* issues.

137 *Ibid.* at 332

138 [1989] 1 S.C.R. 1038 (S.C.C.)

139 *Supra* note 136 at 335-36.

the authority of the *Human Rights Code*. It is the administration of a government program that calls for *Charter* scrutiny. Once a complaint is brought before the Commission, the subsequent administrative proceedings must comply with the *Charter*. These entities are subject to *Charter* scrutiny in the performance of their functions just as government would be in like circumstances. To hold otherwise would allow the legislative branch to circumvent the *Charter* by establishing statutory bodies that are immune to *Charter* scrutiny.

In summary, any analysis of applicability of the *Charter* will necessarily be fact specific requiring a careful examination of the statutory framework, the nature of the actor, and the types of activities the actor engages in. The key question is whether the actor derives its authority to perform a particular function from statute. If the answer to that question is "yes", then performance of the function will very likely have sufficient "governmental quality" to attract application of the *Charter*.

(c) Jurisdiction over *Charter* Issues

(i) Introduction

Charter challenges before administrative tribunals frequently take the form of a challenge to the constitutional validity of the tribunal's enabling legislation. This raises the issue of whether the tribunal has jurisdiction to determine such challenges. Since a remedy must be fashioned once a breach of the *Charter* has been found, a related issue arises as to whether the tribunal has jurisdiction to grant *Charter* remedies.

There are two types of constitutional remedies that can be sought by parties. First, section 52 of the *Constitution Act, 1982* provides that the Constitution of Canada[140] is the supreme law of the land and any law that is inconsistent with the provisions of the Constitution is, to the extent of the inconsistency, of no force or effect. The leading case on remedies under section 52 is *Schachter v. Canada*.[141] *Schachter* says that once it has been decided that an enactment, or a portion of an enactment, violates the *Charter*, the choice of remedies are: (i) a declaration that the enactment is of no force and effect; (ii) severance of the offending portions; (iii) reading in words to make the enactment constitutional; and (iv) reading down, which means interpreting the enactment so that it is constitutional.

Second, under section 24 of the *Charter*, a party may seek a remedy for breach of a specific *Charter* right:

> 24(1) Anyone whose rights or freedoms, as guaranteed by this *Charter*, have been infringed or denied may apply to a court of competent jurisdiction to obtain such remedy as the court considers appropriate and just in the circumstances.

---

140 The entire *Constitution*, not just the *Charter*: see s. 52(2).
141 [1992] 2 S.C.R. 679 (S.C.C.).

This section grants very broad remedial powers to those administrative tribunals that are found to be courts of competent jurisdiction.

Thus, section 52 of the *Constitution Act, 1982* is the source of remedial power where a law is unconstitutional, whereas section 24 of the *Charter* is the source of remedial power for an action which was taken under a constitutional law, but which nonetheless violated an individual's *Charter* rights.

(ii) Section 52

Three cases, *Cuddy Chicks Ltd. v. Ontario (Labour Relations Board)*, *Tétreault-Gadoury*, and *Douglas College*, address the ability of an administrative tribunal to make findings about the constitutional validity of legislation.

In *Cuddy Chicks Ltd. v. Ontario (Labour Relations Board)*, La Forest J. put the matter succinctly:[142]

> An administrative tribunal which has been given the power to interpret law holds a concomitant power to determine whether that law is constitutionally valid.

In *Cuddy Chicks*, the Ontario Labour Relations Board was called on to decide whether the denial of trade union rights to agricultural workers was constitutionally valid. The question arose in the course of a certification application brought by a union on behalf of the agricultural workers. The Board had to answer the constitutional question before it could decide if it had jurisdiction to consider the certification application.

In determining that the Labour Relations Board had jurisdiction to deal with the constitutional question, La Forest J. noted that section 52(1) does not expressly confer such power on administrative tribunals. However, section 106(1) of the *Labour Relations Act* provided that the Board had exclusive jurisdiction "to determine all questions of fact or law that arise in any matter before it". La Forest J. held that this power to determine questions of law extended to questions such as whether a law violates the *Charter*. In coming to this conclusion he specifically did *not* rely on section 24 of the *Charter*. To do so would require an analysis of whether the administrative tribunal at issue was a court of competent jurisdiction:[143]

> In the present case, the relevant inquiry is not whether the tribunal is a "court" but whether the legislature intended to confer on the tribunal the power to interpret and apply the *Charter*.

The Court held that the Board did not have a general jurisdiction to deal with constitutional questions but did have power to decide constitutional matters which arose in its regulatory context. The nature of its jurisdiction was

---

142   [1991] 2 S.C.R. 5 at 14 (S.C.C.). See comments by J.L.H. Sprague, (1992-93) 6 C.J.A.L.P. 1; and J.M. Evans, (1990) 39 Admin. L.R. 87.

143   *Ibid.* at 14-15. In her concurring judgement, Wilson J. wrote that the absence of legislative authority to deal with the *Charter* may not be determinative and that there may be other sources of authority, including s. 24(1), upon which the jurisdiction of administrative tribunals to deal with *Charter* issues may be founded. *Ibid.* at 20.

limited. It could not make formal declarations of invalidity but could only treat an impeached provision as invalid in the matter before the Board. Such decisions of boards are not binding legal precedents. Furthermore, administrative tribunals have no right to be wrong about constitutional matters and they cannot expect judicial deference to their constitutional determinations.[144]

The Supreme Court has considered whether a tribunal which is not empowered with an exclusive jurisdiction privative clause is entitled to answer constitutional questions. In *Tétreault-Gadoury v. Canada (Employment & Immigration Commission)*,[145] the Supreme Court dealt with the power of a Board of Referees to interpret the *Charter*. The Board of Referees did not have the exclusive jurisdiction to decide questions of fact or law (unlike the Board in *Cuddy Chicks*). This power to decide question of fact or law was bestowed on the Umpire, to whom an appeal lay from a decision of the Board of Referees. Therefore, the Court concluded that only the Umpire could decide constitutional questions.

The Court has also dealt with the jurisdiction of labour arbitrators to decide *Charter* issues. In *Douglas/Kwantlen Faculty Assn. v. Douglas College*,[146] after deciding that the community college was a governmental actor and that the collective agreement was "law" subject to the *Charter*, La Forest J. went on to find that the arbitrator charged with determining questions of law and interpreting the collective agreement was bound to apply the *Charter*. He observed that[147] "there cannot be a Constitution for arbitrators and another for the courts". In this case, the arbitrator was acting pursuant to section 98 of the *Labour Code* which granted express authority to "provide a *final and conclusive* settlement of a dispute arising under a collective agreement". Under the section, arbitrators had a full range of remedies at their disposal. La Forest J. was of the view that the section empowered and required arbitrators to interpret collective agreements consistently with any statutes affecting the employment relationship, including the *Charter*:[148]

> The question here is whether an arbitrator in deciding a grievance under a collective agreement may apply the *Charter* and grant the relief sought for its breach. I have no doubt that he can.

This approach was confirmed in *Cooper v. Canada (Human Rights Commission)*.[149] The Court concluded that neither the Canadian Human Rights Commission nor any tribunal appointed by the Commission has the jurisdiction to interpret the *Charter* because neither has been given either the express or *implied* power by statute to determine questions of law. Justice McLachlin (L'Heureux-Dubé J. concurring) wrote a vigorous dissent arguing that the

---

144 See Chapter 12, for a discussion of the circumstances in which courts may show deference to decisions by statutory delegates.
145 [1991] 2 S.C.R. 22 (S.C.C.). See the comment by J.H.L. Sprague, *supra* note 142.
146 [1990] 3 S.C.R. 570 (S.C.C.). See also *Slaight Communications Inc. v. Davidson*, [1989] 1 S.C.R. 1038 (S.C.C.).
147 *Ibid.* at 597.
148 *Ibid.* at 596.
149 [1996] 3 S.C.R. 854, 140 D.L.R. (4th) 193 (S.C.C.).

power to determine questions of law could be *implied* from the enabling statute.[150] In so doing, she emphasized the important role of the *Charter* in Canadian society:[151]

> In my view, every tribunal charged with the duty of deciding issues of law has the concomitant power to do so. The fact that the question of law concerns the effect of the *Charter* does not change the matter. The *Charter* is not some holy grail which only judicial initiates of the superior court may touch. The *Charter* belongs to the people. All law and law-makers that touch the people must conform to it. Tribunals and commissions charged with deciding legal issues are no exception. Many more citizens have their rights determined by these tribunals than by the courts. If the *Charter* is to be meaningful to ordinary people, then it must find its expression in the decision of these tribunals.

She concluded that, in the absence of words in the enabling statute confining a tribunal's jurisdiction to determining questions of fact, a tribunal's ability to determine any question of law must include the ability to consider the *Charter*.

In stark contrast are the separate reasons of Lamer C.J. (concurring with the majority in the result).[152] He stated that the earlier case law was wrong and should be reconsidered by the Court. He argued that the power in section 52 should be reserved exclusively for the courts.[153]

Notwithstanding the divergence of approaches in *Cooper*, it appeared that the principles set out *Cuddy Chicks*, etc. remained the law in Canada. However, any doubt in that regard has been removed by Court in its very recent decision in *Martin v. Nova Scotia (Worker's Compensation Board)*.[154] One of the issues in that case was whether the Nova Scotia's Workers' Compensation Appeals Tribunal had jurisdiction to consider the constitutional validity of certain provisions in Nova Scotia's *Workers' Compensation Act*. Speaking for the Court, Gonthier J. stated:[155]

> ... Administrative tribunals which have jurisdiction – whether explicit or implied – to decide questions of law arising under a legislative provision are presumed to have concomitant jurisdiction to decide the constitutional validity of that provision. This presumption may only be rebutted by showing that the legislature clearly intended to exclude *Charter* issues from the tribunal's authority over questions of law. To the extent that the majority reasons in *Cooper v. Canada (Human*

---

150   *Ibid.* at 221-35.

151   *Ibid.* at 222.

152   *Ibid.* at 197-208.

153   Lamer C.J. focussed his discussion on declarations of invalidity. He did not expressly consider whether administrative tribunals should be debarred from access to any of the other remedies available under section 52.

154   2003 SCC 54, [2003] S.C.J. No. 54, 4 Admin. L.R. (4th) 1 (S.C.C.). See also the companion decision of *Paul v. British Columbia (Forest Appeals Commission)*, 2003 SCC 55 (S.C.C.) (dealing with Aboriginal rights – which is a constitutional issue but not a *Charter* issue).

155   *Ibid.* at para. 3

Rights Commission), [1996] 3 S.C.R. 854, are inconsistent with this approach, I am of the view that they should no longer be relied upon.

Gonthier J. stated[156] that the most important policy reason underlying the Court's approach on this issue is that the Constitution is the supreme law of the land; in principle, any unconstitutional legislative provision is invalid from the moment it is enacted, whether or not there has been a judicial ruling to that effect. The practical corollary to this principle is that any Canadian should be entitled to assert his or her constitutional rights and freedoms in the most accessible forum available. Further, any *Charter* decision by an administrative tribunal is subject to judicial review on a correctness standard. Gonthier J. did, however, place an important limitation on the scope of an administrative tribunal's jurisdiction with respect to *Charter* issues:[157]

> ... the constitutional remedies available to administrative tribunals are limited and do not include general declarations of invalidity. A determination by a tribunal that a provision of its enabling statute is invalid pursuant to the *Charter* is not binding on future decision makers, within or outside the tribunal's administrative scheme. Only by obtaining a formal declaration of invalidity by a court can a litigant establish the general invalidity of a legislative provision for all future cases. Therefore, allowing administrative tribunals to decide *Charter* issues does not undermine the role of the courts as final arbiters of constitutionality in Canada.

In summary, unless the legislature clearly intended the contrary, an administrative tribunal that has jurisdiction to decide questions of law also has jurisdiction to interpret and apply the *Charter*. Any *Charter* decision is, however, binding only on the parties to the particular proceeding in which the issue was raised and, in any event, is subject to review by the courts on a standard of correctness.

(iii) Section 24

R. v. Mills[158] is the leading case interpreting section 24 of the *Charter*. *Mills* says that to be a court of competent jurisdiction, and therefore to be able to grant remedies under section 24, a tribunal must have jurisdiction over: (i) the parties, (ii) the subject matter, and (iii) the remedy sought. This has come to be known as the *Mills* test.

In *Weber v. Ontario Hydro*,[159] the plaintiff's claim for damages against his employer as a result of alleged *Charter* breaches was not permitted to proceed because he was governed by a collective agreement which governed all employment-related issues between them. In this case, the key issue was whether an arbitrator appointed under the collective agreement would have jurisdiction to award damages as a result of a violation of a *Charter* right; that

---

156   *Ibid.* at paras. 27-30
157   *Ibid.* at para. 31.
158   [1986] 1 S.C.R. 863 (S.C.C.).
159   [1995] 2 S.C.R. 929, 30 Admin. L.R. (2d) 1 (S.C.C.).

is, was the arbitrator of competent jurisdiction? In this case the arbitration board met the criteria of *Mills*: it had jurisdiction over the parties, the subject matter and the remedy sought. The *Charter* issues (alleging violation of sections 7 and 8 of the *Charter* as a result of the employer's surveillance of the plaintiff while he was off work on a work-related injury) were a component of the labour dispute, and therefore the arbitrator had jurisdiction over the parties and the subject matter. Further, the arbitrator had the power to award damages and a declaration, which the Court found included damages for a *Charter* breach.

The dissenting reasons of Iacobucci J. (LaForest and Sopinka JJ. concurring) agreed that arbitrators must apply the law, including the *Charter*, but held that does not give them the power to grant a remedy for a *Charter* breach. Arbitrators cannot do so because they are not courts of competent jurisdiction as required by section 24. Iacobucci J. argued that *Mills*, a criminal case on preliminary inquiries, was not helpful in the context of determining whether an administrative tribunal is a court of competent jurisdiction.

A majority of the Court apparently applied the *Mills* test in *Mooring v. Canada (National Parole Board)*,[160] but concluded that the Parole Board was not a court of competent jurisdiction so as to be able to grant the *Charter* remedy of excluding evidence.

In *Ontario v. 974649 Ontario Inc.*,[161] the Court confirmed that the *Mills* test is the appropriate analysis to determine whether an administrative tribunal has jurisdiction to grant remedies under section 24. In particular, the Court set out a "functional and structural" analysis to be used in answering the third part of the *Mills* test, that is, whether the court or tribunal enjoys the power to grant the remedy sought. The Court stated:[162]

> Whether a court or tribunal enjoys the "power to grant the remedy sought" is, first and foremost, a matter of discerning the intention of Parliament or the Legislature. The governing question in every case is whether the legislator endowed the court or tribunal with the power to pronounce on *Charter* rights and to grant the remedy sought for the breach of these rights.[163]
>
> A legislative grant of remedial power under s. 24 may be either express or implied. It is express, for example, where the court or tribunal's constituting legislation explicitly authorizes the order sought as a remedy for *Charter* violations. Since the majority of existing courts and tribunals originated before the advent of the *Char-*

---

160 [1996] 1 S.C.R. 75 (S.C.C.), McLachlin and Major JJ. dissenting.

161 [2001] 3 S.C.R. 575 (S.C.C.). The issue in this case was whether a justice of the peace acting as a trial justice under Ontario's *Provincial Offences Act* had jurisdiction under s. 24(1) of the *Charter* to direct the Crown to pay costs for failure to disclose relevant information to the accused. One could argue for a restricted application of this case. However, the Court's use of the phrase "court or tribunal" throughout the judgment indicates that the principles enunciated in the case are intended to apply to administrative tribunals as well as provincial offences courts.

162 *Ibid.* at 589 per McLachlin C.J.

163 *Ibid.* at 590.

ter, however, express conferral of authority is likely to prove rare. The more common scenario, and the one presented by the case at bar, arises where the court or tribunal's enabling legislation is silent on the issue of its remedial jurisdiction under the *Charter*. In such cases, the grant of "power to grant the remedy sought" under s. 24, if it exists, must be implied.

The Court held that the appropriate approach to determining if an implied grant of power exists is a "functional and structural" approach. The question is, "whether the court or tribunal in question is suited to grant the remedy sought under s. 24 in light of its function and structure".[164] The courts will look to the language of the enabling legislation, interpreted in light of the advent of the *Charter*, and the history and accepted practice of the institution. Thus, factors such as the expertise of the tribunal, whether its proceedings are judicial or quasi-judicial, the tribunal's workload and the time constraints under which it operates are all relevant to the analysis of function and structure. The Court stated:[165]

> The question, in essence, is whether the legislature or Parliament has furnished the court or tribunal with the tools necessary to fashion the remedy sought under s. 24 in a just, fair and consistent manner without impeding its ability to perform its intended function.

Where the answer to that question is "yes", the administrative tribunal will meet the third branch of the *Mills* test. If the tribunal also has jurisdiction over the parties and the subject matter, then it will have the power to grant remedies under section 24.

(iv) Conclusion

In deciding what power an administrative tribunal has to interpret or apply the *Charter*, it is clear that the courts will carefully examine the statutory mandate of the tribunal to determine the degree of power granted to the tribunal by the legislator. The presumption is that a grant of power to decide questions of law includes the power to interpret or apply the *Charter*. Absent clear evidence rebutting that presumption, the courts will defer to the decision of the legislator, and find that the administrative tribunal has jurisdiction with respect to *Charter* issues. Any such decision, however, is binding only upon the parties to the particular administrative proceeding in which the issues were raised. It is also clear that, even where a tribunal has the authority to answer a constitutional question or to apply a *Charter* remedy, there will be no judicial deference to the decision of the tribunal. In such cases, the superior courts have a responsibility to ensure that the Constitution is correctly interpreted and applied, and the decisions of inferior tribunals must be right in law, and not merely one reasonable possible response.[166]

---

164   *Ibid.* at 597.
165   *Ibid.* at 598.
166   See the discussion of the "patently unreasonable" test in Chapters 11 and 12.

(d) The Impact of Section 7 on Administrative Law

(i) Introduction

Section 7 of the *Charter* provides:[167]

Everyone has the right to life, liberty and security of the person and the right not to be deprived thereof, except in accordance with the principles of fundamental justice.

"Everyone" may appear to include artificial persons such as corporations, but it is now clear that section 7 confers rights only on human beings, since corporations are not capable of enjoying life, liberty and security of the person.[168] However a corporation may rely on section 7 of the *Charter* to challenge the constitutionality of a law that is being used to prosecute that corporation in a criminal proceeding.[169] This principle has now been extended to include a corporation in a civil proceeding where the corporation is being subject to a statutory regulatory proceeding.[170] This extension to corporations as a "shield" reflects the concern that no one, including a corporation, should be subject to regulatory or criminal proceedings on the basis of an unconstitutional law.

It is also clear that "everyone" includes any human being physically present in Canada including illegal immigrants.[171]

A two-step analysis is called for in determining whether section 7 is applicable to a particular factual context. First, there must be a finding that there has been a deprivation of the right to "life, liberty and security of the person." Second, there must be a finding that such deprivation is contrary to the principles of fundamental justice.[172] It should also be noted that many decisions *assume*, without deciding, that section 7 applies to the first part of the test, then dispose of the case on the basis that there has been no violation of the principles of fundamental justice.[173] Thus, the impact of section 7 on administrative law rests primarily with the meaning given to the phrase "principles of fundamental justice."[174]

---

167 See D.J. Mullan, "The Reach of Section 7 of the Charter" (1987) 24 Admin. L.R. 203; J.M. Evans, "The Principles of Fundamental Justice" (1991) 29 Osgoode Hall L.J. 51.

168 *Irwin Toy Ltd. c. Québec (Procureur général)*, [1989] 1 S.C.R. 927 at 1004 (S.C.C.).

169 *R. v. Wholesale Travel Group Inc.*, [1991] 3 S.C.R. 154 (S.C.C.); see also *R. v. Big M Drug Mart Ltd.*, [1985] 1 S.C.R. 295 (S.C.C.) making the same point with respect to a corporation's ability to raise an argument that a law violates section 2(a) of the *Charter* – the right to freedom of conscience and religion.

170 *Canadian Egg Marketing Agency v. Richardson* (1998), 166 D.L.R. (4th) 1 (S.C.C.).

171 *Singh v. Canada (Minister of Employment & Immigration)*, [1985] 1 S.C.R. 177 (S.C.C.).

172 *R. v. Beare*, [1988] 2 S.C.R. 387 at 401 (S.C.C.).

173 See for instance, *Pearlman v. Law Society (Manitoba)*, [1991] 2 S.C.R. 869 (S.C.C.); *Béliveau c. Barreau (Québec)* (1992), 101 D.L.R. (4th) 324 (Que. C.A.), leave to appeal to S.C.C. refused (1993), 55 Q.A.C. 76 (S.C.C.); *Pierce v. Law Society (British Columbia)* (1993), 15 Admin. L.R. (2d) 235 (B.C. S.C.); *Khosla v. Alberta* (1993), 143 A.R. 295 (Alta. Q.B.).

174 See P.W. Hogg, *Constitutional Law of Canada, supra* note 5 at 44-17 to 44-22, where he critiques the Supreme Court of Canada's jurisprudence in this area.

(ii) Life, Liberty and Security of the Person

The first step of the test is problematic in the administrative law context: to what extent do administrative proceedings deprive a person of their life, liberty, or security of the person?

There appears to be no doubt that section 7 of the *Charter* can be engaged with respect to specific powers or steps exercised by an administrative tribunal. For instance, the liberty interest of section 7 is engaged at the point of compelling witnesses to testify in an administrative hearing, as the remedy for failing to testify is contempt of court and potential penal sanction.[175] Further, exercise of administrative audit or investigative powers may trigger the section 7 rights of the person under investigation. For example, in *R. v. Jarvis*,[176] the Supreme Court of Canada held that a taxpayer's section 7 liberty interest was engaged by the introduction at his trial for tax evasion of information which he was compelled to produce under the *Income Tax Act*, due to the possibility of imprisonment if the taxpayer was convicted. In that case, the specific liberty interest that was protected was the taxpayer's right against self-incrimination.

Clearly, the first part of the test is met where there are potential penal consequences for failing to comply with a procedural demand made by an administrative tribunal. In *Blencoe v. British Columbia (Human Rights Commission)*,[177] the Supreme Court of Canada had occasion to consider whether section 7 was engaged in the context of administrative proceedings in which there were no potential penal consequences to the individual who was the subject of the proceedings. Several sexual harassment complaints were made against Blencoe, both while he was serving as a minister in the Government of British Columbia and after he was removed from Cabinet and dismissed from the NDP caucus. Once the complaints were filed with the British Columbia Human Rights Commission, the Commission investigated the complaints, but there were lengthy delays. Over 30 months elapsed between the time the complaints were filed with the Commission and the dates set by the Commission for hearings before the British Columbia Human Rights Tribunal. Blencoe suffered considerable damage to his reputation as a result of the massive media attention given to the complaints. The issue was whether state-caused delay in human rights proceedings violated the respondent's rights under section 7 of the *Charter*. The Court concluded that there had been no violation of the respondent's right to liberty or to security of the person, and as a result, it was unnecessary to consider the principles of fundamental justice.

In *Blencoe*, the Court provided guidance as to the scope of the rights guaranteed by section 7. While acknowledging that the liberty interest protects more than the right to be free from physical restraint, and must be interpreted broadly, the liberty interest does not protect all aspects of personal autonomy. Bastarache J. stated:[178]

---

175 *British Columbia (Securities Commission) v. Branch*, (1995), 123 D.L.R. (4th) 462, [1995] 2 S.C.R. 3 (S.C.C.).

176 2002 SCC 73, 219 D.L.R. (4th) 233 (S.C.C.).

177 [2000] 2 S.C.R. 307 (S.C.C.), corrected [2001] 2 S.C.R. iv (S.C.C.).

178 *Ibid.* at 343

Although an individual has the right to make fundamental personal choices free from state interference, such personal autonomy is not synonymous with unconstrained freedom. In the circumstances of this case, the state has not prevented the respondent from making any "fundamental personal choices". The interests sought to be protected in this case do not in my opinion fall within the "liberty" interest protected by s. 7.

Similarly, while security of the person protects both the psychological and physical integrity of the individual:[179]

Not all state interference with an individual's psychological integrity will engage s. 7. Where the psychological integrity of a person is at issue, security of the person is restricted to "serious state-imposed psychological stress". . . . The words "serious state-imposed psychological stress delineate two requirements that must be met in order for security of the person to be triggered. First, the psychological harm must be state imposed, meaning that the harm must result from the actions of the state. Second, the psychological prejudice must be serious. Not all forms of psychological prejudice caused by government will lead to automatic s. 7 violations.

In the wake of *Blencoe*, it is clear that an individual's rights to liberty and to security of the person are engaged where an administrative tribunal can compel the person to testify or produce documents, since there may be penal consequences to a failure to comply with the tribunal's demand.[180] However, absent potential penal consequences, only the most serious intrusions into an individual's autonomy will trigger the application of section 7 in administrative processes.[181] Further, even if the applicant has been deprived of his or her right to liberty or to security of the person, the Court will not find that there has been a violation of section 7 if the deprivation has occurred in accordance with the principles of fundamental justice.

(iii) Principles of Fundamental Justice

At an early stage in its consideration of the *Charter*, the Supreme Court determined that the principles of fundamental justice are not simply procedural in nature. In *Reference re s. 94(2) of the Motor Vehicle Act (British Columbia)*,[182] Lamer J. said the principles of fundamental justice are to be found in the ". . . basic tenets of our legal system".[183] McIntyre J. concurred, but added fundamental justice ". . . involves more than natural justice (which is largely

---

179 *Ibid.* at 344
180 See for example, *R. v. Beare*, [1988] 2 S.C.R. 387 (S.C.C.); *Thomson Newspapers Ltd. v. Canada (Director of Investigation & Research)*, [1990] 1 S.C.R. 425 (S.C.C.).
181 For a more detailed discussion, see D.J. Mullan and D. Harrington, "The Charter and Administrative Decision-Making: The Dampening Effects of *Blencoe*" (2002) 27 Queen's L.J. 879-912.
182 (1985), [1986] 1 W.W.R. 481, [1985] 2 S.C.R. 486 (S.C.C.).
183 *Ibid.* at 496.

procedural) and includes as well a substantive element".[184] The substance, as well as the procedure, set out in a statute must not violate the principles of fundamental justice. Consistent with the Court's approach, therefore, it is useful to distinguish between the principles of *procedural* fundamental justice and *substantive* fundamental justice. The sources of both, however, are in the basic tenets and principles of the legal system. The cases illustrate aspects of what is a basic tenet and principle of the legal system. However, there remains much scope for debate about the content of these principles, particularly in the context of substantive principles, because of the novelty of the phrase "principles of fundamental justice" in our jurisprudence as compared to "natural justice" (procedural rights) or "due process" (which may include some substantive rights).[185]

(A) The principles of procedural fundamental justice

In several cases, the courts have considered the principles of procedural fundamental justice. In what has become a classic judgement, Wilson J. held in *Singh v. Canada (Minister of Employment & Immigration)* that the principles of fundamental justice include, at a minimum, the notion of procedural fairness including a fair tribunal; acting in good faith; and an opportunity to state one's case before the tribunal.[186] Wilson J. went on to find that the principles of procedural fundamental justice required that an oral hearing be afforded to an appellant for refugee status where the issue was one of credibility.[187]

Some principles may be stated about the tenets of procedural fundamental justice which have been elaborated in subsequent cases. First, there has been a complete incorporation of the common law rules of natural justice and the duty of fairness into the principles of fundamental justice as a matter of constitutional law. In *Pearlman v. Law Society (Manitoba)*, Iacobucci J. said:[188]

> . . . the principles of fundamental justice reflect the fundamental tenets on which our legal system is based. Those tenets include, but are not limited to, the rules of natural justice and the duty to act fairly that have been developed over the years in the administrative law context . . . It seems to me then that when deciding whether a law contravenes s. 7, one must examine the impugned legislation to ascertain whether it, viewed in a purposive manner, meets the fundamental precepts reflected in our system of justice.
>
> More specifically, it is well accepted that included in these fundamental principles is the concept of a procedurally fair hearing before an *impartial decision-maker* . . . Thus, in the administrative law con-

---

184   *Ibid.* at 486.
185   P.W. Hogg is highly critical of the S.C.C.'s approach to interpreting principles of fundamental justice: *Constitutional Law of Canada, supra* note 5 at c. 44.10.
186   [1985] 1 S.C.R. 177 at 212-13 (S.C.C.). See comment by S.K. McCallum, (1985) 12 Admin. L.R. 142.
187   *Ibid.* at 214.
188   [1991] 2 S.C.R. 869 at 882-83 (S.C.C.); emphasis added.

text, principles of fundamental justice include natural justice rules which in turn require that the members of the tribunal be impartial and disinterested: see de Smith's *Judicial Review of Administrative Action* (4th ed. 1980) at p. 248. Impartiality of the decision-making body is a critical feature of natural justice which is captured by the Latin maxim, nemo judex in causa sua debet esse – no one should be the judge in his own cause. There are many different factual settings which could place the impartiality of a decision making body in question. Among such contexts are situations where the decision-makers have or are perceived to have a pecuniary interest, either direct or indirect, in the outcome of the hearing before them. Another such context is where the relationship of the decision-maker to one of the parties or counsel is sufficiently close to give rise to a reasonable apprehension of bias.

Iacobucci J. went on to examine the rules of natural justice developed by the courts in the administrative law context and concluded that the fact that the professional discipline tribunal of the Law Society of Manitoba was empowered to award costs would not give rise to a reasonable apprehension of bias in a reasonable, well-informed person.

Second, the principles of procedural fundamental justice are not immutable, but change according to the context in which they are applied.[189]

Third, given that the principles of procedural fundamental justice are flexible and vary according to the context in which it is sought to apply them, it is important to try and identify the sorts of factors the courts are to consider in deciding what level of procedural protection is appropriate. As La Forest J. noted in *R. v. Lyons*:[190]

Section 7 of the Charter entitles the [accused] to a fair hearing; it does not entitle him to the most favourable procedures that could possibly be imagined.

In *R. v. Jones*, La Forest J. noted that:[191]

Some pragmatism is involved in balancing between fairness and efficiency. The provinces must be given room to make choices regarding the type of administrative structure that will suit their needs unless the use of such structure is in itself so manifestly unfair, having regard to the decisions it is called upon to make, as to violate the principles of fundamental justice.

---

189   *R. v. L. (T.P.)*, [1987] 2 S.C.R. 309 (S.C.C.) per La Forest J. at 361; *Idziak v. Canada (Minister of Justice)*, [1992] 3 S.C.R. 631 (S.C.C.), reconsideration refused (1992), 9 Admin. L.R. (2d) 1n (S.C.C.) per Cory J.
190   *Ibid.* at 361.
191   [1986] 2 S.C.R. 284 at 304 (S.C.C.).

In order to determine what the applicable principles of fundamental justice were in *Kindler v. Canada (Minister of Justice)*,[192] McLachlin J. looked to "the basic tenets of our judicial system and the system under scrutiny – this case our extradition system".[193] After reviewing the system of extradition McLachlin J. held that:[194]

> The test for whether an extradition law or action offends s. 7 of the *Charter* on account of the penalty which may be imposed in the requesting state, is whether the imposition of the penalty by the foreign state "sufficiently shocks" the Canadian conscience. . . .

She concluded, after reviewing the history of capital punishment in Canada, and current public opinion polls, Canadians would not be shocked by the execution of a fugitive in California or Pennsylvania.[195] Thus the law did not offend the principles of fundamental justice insofar as it did not require the Minister of Justice to obtain assurances that the death penalty would not be applied against the applicant fugitive before extradition occurred. Furthermore, the fugitive was not entitled to an oral hearing before the Minister in advance of the Minister's final decision to extradite him. The oral hearing afforded at the judicial stage of the extradition proceeding was sufficient to satisfy the principles of fundamental justice.

Along with the need to shock the conscience of Canadians before a law or practice violates the principles of fundamental justice, the court must also consider and balance the competing interests of the state and the individual.[196] In *Idziak v. Canada (Minister of Justice)*,[197] after a formal extradition hearing, the Minister of Justice decided to issue a warrant to surrender the accused to the U.S. authorities. The Minister took into account a memorandum which had been prepared by his officials, but refused to provide the accused with a copy of the memorandum. Cory J., in balancing the competing interests of the state and the individual, determined the principles of procedural fundamental justice were not breached by the Minister's refusal. The memorandum did not contain anything the fugitive did not already know[198] and it was not like evidence to be used in an adversarial proceeding. Instead, it was a briefing note to the Minister from a staff member who did not have any interest in the outcome.

Cory J. was of the view that the decision-making process was political in its nature and that the Minister had to weigh the representations of the fugitive against Canada's international treaty obligations. In analyzing the matter, Cory J. characterized the function being performed by the Minister, and found that

---

192 [1991] 2 S.C.R. 779 (S.C.C.).
193 *Ibid.* at 848.
194 *Ibid.* at 849.
195 *Ibid.* at 852.
196 *Idziak v. Canada (Minister of Justice)*, [1992] 3 S.C.R. 631 at 657 (S.C.C.).
197 *Ibid.*
198 But how would the accused know this?

the Minister's review of the extradition file was "at the extreme legislative end of the continuum of administrative decision-making":[199]

> The extradition hearing is clearly judicial in its nature while the actions of the Minister of Justice in considering whether to issue a warrant of surrender are primarily political in nature. This is certainly not a case of a single official's acting as both judge and prosecutor in the same case. At the judicial phase the fugitive possesses the full panoply of procedural protection available in a court of law. At the ministerial phase, there is no longer a *lis* in existence. the fugitive has by then been judicially committed for extradition. The act simply grants to the Minister a discretion as to whether to execute the judicially approved extradition by issuing a warrant of surrender.

In a highly significant passage, Cory J. invoked the "characterization of functions" approach to determine the degree of freedom from bias which was necessary in such a case:[200]

> The determination of bias in a specific case will depend upon the characterization of the decision-maker's function. Administrative decision-making covers a broad spectrum. At the adjudicative end of the spectrum, the appropriate test is: could a reasonably informed bystander reasonably perceive bias on the part of the adjudicator? At the opposite end of the continuum, that is to say the legislative end of the spectrum, the test is: has the decision-maker pre-judged the matter to such an extent that any representations to the contrary would be futile
> . . .
>
> The basis for the distinction is that, in an adjudicative proceeding, the parties' confidence in the result will depend upon the decision-makers' adhering to a standard of judicial impartiality. On the other hand, an administrative body created to determine policy issues may need the expert knowledge of members who are representative of interested parties. The legislative goal in creating such administrate bodies would be frustrated if courts held their members to the strict reasonable apprehension of bias standard.

A similar approach was taken by Iacobucci J. in *Dehghani v. Canada (Minister of Employment & Immigration)*,[201] where an applicant for refugee status was not entitled to counsel at a port of entry interview:

> While the right to counsel under s. 7 may apply in other cases besides those which are encompassed by s. 10(b), for example in cases involving the right to counsel at a hearing, it is clear from my earlier

---

199   *Supra* note 196 at 659-60.
200   *Ibid.* at 660-61.
201   [1993] 1 S.C.R. 1053 (S.C.C.).

comments that the secondary examination of the appellant at the port of entry is not analogous to a hearing. Certainly, factual situations which are closer or analogous to criminal proceedings will merit greater vigilance by the courts. However, in an immigration examination for routine information-gathering purposes, the right to counsel does not extend beyond those circumstances of arrest or detention described in s. 10(b).

Here, unlike in *Singh*[202] there was no serious issue of credibility to be determined. The Appellant was represented during the "credible basis" part of the refugee inquiry. The concern that the refugee be given the opportunity to state his case and know the case he had to meet was met by the requirement of a subsequent oral hearing:

> The purpose of the port of entry interview was, as I have already observed, to aid in the processing of the appellant's application for entry and to determine the appropriate procedures which should be invoked in order to deal with his application for Convention refugee status. The principles of fundamental justice do not include a right to counsel in these circumstances of routine information gathering.

Accordingly, it appears that the level of procedural protection provided by the principles of fundamental justice will vary depending on where the decision-maker is located on the continuum of different types of administrative decision-making. At the judicial or quasi-judicial end (such as criminal proceedings), a high degree of procedural fairness will be required, while a far lower standard will be imposed by the courts at the legislative or policy-making end. The use of the "characterization of functions" approach by the court is reminiscent of the technique employed in judicial review applications in Canada before the advent of the duty of fairness.[203] The old cases may well be resurrected in arguments about what sort of function is being performed by tribunals attacked under section 7 of the *Charter*.

In summary, the determination of what the principles of procedural fundamental justice require in a given case begins with the full range of safeguards which would be provided by the rules of natural justice or the duty of fairness.[204] These include the rights to notice, and a hearing, and unbiased decision-making and all the other related, procedural rights. One must then ask whether any particular procedural right should be afforded in the specific case. Several limiting factors should be examined. First, the purpose of the impugned legislation should be considered and a balance should be struck between the demands of fairness and efficiency. The competing interests of the state and the individual must be balanced. Second, in extradition matters at least (and perhaps more generally), the court may ask whether denying the remedy would

---

202 [1985] 1 S.C.R. 177 (S.C.C.).
203 See Chapter 8.
204 See Chapters 9 and 10.

"shock" the conscience of Canadians or violate the standards of the international community. Third, the nature of the decision-making function will be analyzed. Depending upon where the function resides on the continuum of administrative decision-making, a higher or lower degree of procedural fairness will be required. The closer the decision-maker is to the legislative (or policy) end of the spectrum, the lower the standard of procedural fundamental justice which is required. A higher degree of fairness is required as the decision-maker moves along the spectrum toward judicial or quasi-judicial deliberations.[205]

It will be interesting to see how the jurisprudence continues to develop with respect to the principles of fundamental justice in the context of administrative law. For example, it has long been established that there is no denial of fair procedure or natural justice where an apparent bias on the part of an administrative tribunal is authorized by the tribunal's enabling legislation, either expressly or by implication. However, the Supreme Court of Canada has yet to consider whether this defence of "statutory justification" is available in situations where an individual has been deprived of liberty or security of the person.

(B)   The principles of substantive fundamental justice and the doctrine of vagueness

The "doctrine of vagueness" is a principle of substantive fundamental justice under section 7 and is inherent in the phrase "prescribed by law" in section 1.[206] Two rationales are advanced to support the doctrine. First, a citizen

---

205   It is important not to forget the procedural guarantees set out in the *Canadian Bill of Rights*. While only a statute and only applicable to federal laws, it offers some broader procedural guarantees than s. 7 of the *Charter*:

   1. It is hereby recognized and declared that in Canada there have existed and shall continue to exist without discrimination by reason of race, national origin, colour, religion or sex, the following human rights and fundamental freedoms, namely,

      (a) the right of the individual to life, liberty, security of the person and enjoyment of property, and the right not to be deprived thereof except by due process of law;

   2. . . . no law of Canada shall be construed or applied so as to . . .

      (e) deprive a person of the right to a fair hearing in accordance with the principles of fundamental justice for the determination of his rights and obligations. . . .

Section 1(a) explicitly protects property, which was expressly excluded from the *Charter*, and s. 2(e) explicitly protects a person whose rights and obligations are being adjudicated. The *Bill of Rights* is still valid and has been relied upon by some members of the Supreme Court of Canada post-*Charter*. See for instance *Singh v. Canada (Minister of Employment & Immigration)*, [1985] 1 S.C.R. 177 (S.C.C.) *per* McIntyre J. and *MacBain v. Canada (Human Rights Commission)*, [1985] 1 F.C. 856 (Fed. C.A.).

   In addition, some provinces have their own *Bill of Rights*, which may be usefully applied in the administrative law context. The "quasi-constitutional" status that such instruments are sometimes said to have is rooted in the "manner and form" theory explained in note 5, *supra*.

206   In *Irwin Toy Ltd. c. Québec (Procureur général)*, [1989] 1 S.C.R. 927 (S.C.C.), Dickson C.J.C. considered whether provisions which were allegedly "confusing and contradictory" provided sufficient guidance to be immune from a vagueness attack. Dickson C.J.C. held at 983:

   Absolute precision in the law exists rarely, if at all. The question is whether the legislature

is entitled to fair notice about the law, and secondly, there must be a limit on the discretion by agents of the state to enforce the law.

The concept of fair notice to the citizen stems from the notion that it is not fair to penalize a person who does not know that what he or she is about to do is prohibited. Laws must be sufficiently precise to enable citizens to decide whether any proposed action will violate the law or not. There must be an "understanding that certain conduct is the subject of legal restrictions" so that citizens may know how to conduct themselves according to the law.[207] This principle strikes at legislation or rules which are so vague that a reasonable citizen cannot know whether or not a planned course of action is lawful.

The second rationale supporting the doctrine of vagueness is that there must be a limit upon the discretion of officials enforcing legislation. Laws

---

has provided an intelligible standard according to which the judiciary must do its work. The task of interpreting how that standard applies in particular instances might always be characterized as having a discretionary element, because the standard can never specify all the instances in which it applies. On the other hand, where there is no intelligible standard and where the legislature has given a plenary discretion to whatever seems best in a wide set of circumstances, there is no "limit prescribed by law".

Ultimately, it was held that the provisions of the *Consumer Protection Act* were satisfactory since they could be given a "sensible interpretation" and did not confer a power to ban any advertisements the court wished.

In *R. v. Zundel*, [1992] 2 S.C.R. 731 (S.C.C.), the majority of the Supreme Court of Canada struck down s. 181 of the *Criminal Code*, R.S.C. 1985, c. C-46, because it was so vague and broad that it could not be said to be a limitation "prescribed by law" pursuant to s. 1. The section of the Code prohibited "knowingly publish[ing] any false news or tale whereby injury or mischief is or is likely to be occasioned to any public interest". McLachlin J. concluded at 774 that:

> The broad, undefined term, "mischief to a public interest", ... is capable of almost indefinite extension.

She was concerned that the "undefined and virtually unlimited reach" of the phrase could:

> ... permit the state to restrict constitutional rights in circumstances and ways that may not be justifiable. The vague and broad wording of s. 181 leaves open that possibility (at 769-70).

In *Osborne v. Canada (Treasury Board)*, [1991] 2 S.C.R. 69 (S.C.C.) Sopinka J. discussed the impact of the vagueness doctrine on the phrase "prescribed by law" in s. 1. He said at 94:

> Vagueness can have constitutional significance in at least two ways in a s. 1 analysis. A law may be so uncertain as to be incapable of being interpreted so as to constitute any restraint on governmental power. The uncertainty may arise either from the generality of the discretion conferred on the donee of the power or from the use of language that is so obscure as to be incapable of interpretation with any degree of precision using the ordinary tools. In these circumstances there is no "limit prescribed by law" and no s. 1 analysis is necessary as the threshold requirement for its application is not met. The second way in which vagueness can play a constitutional role is in the analysis of s. 1. A law which passes the threshold test may, nevertheless, by reason of its imprecision, not qualify as a reasonable limit. Generality and imprecision of language may fail to confine the invasion of a *Charter* right within reasonable limits. In this sense vagueness is an aspect of overbreadth.

Ultimately, Sopinka J. held that the impugned words of the *Public Service Employment Act*, R.S.C. 1985, c. P-33, were not so vague or general that they failed to set out an intelligible standard.

207   *Canada v. Pharmaceutical Society (Nova Scotia)*, [1992] 2 S.C.R. 606 (S.C.C.), per Gonthier J. at 635.

must not be so vague that an official has unlimited discretion to define the prohibited conduct and to secure a conviction against anyone by simply laying a charge. In *Canada v. Nova Scotia Pharmaceutical Society (Nova Scotia)*,[208] Gonthier J. illustrated this proposition by referring to the vagrancy ordinance struck down by the United States Supreme Court in *Papachristou*.[209] The United States Supreme Court said the vagrancy ordinance:

> was so general and so lacked precision in its content that a conviction would ensue every time the law enforcer decided to charge someone with the offence of vagrancy. The words of the ordinance had no substance to them, and they indicated no particular legislative purpose. They left the accused completely in the dark, with no possible way of defending himself before the court.

The reason for striking down laws which do not give fair notice or which give unlimited discretion to officials is that laws which convey such a power are "unintelligible" because they do not give sufficient "guidance for legal debate". Gonthier J. expressed this rationale in the following words:[210]

> A vague provision does not provide an adequate basis for legal debate, that is for reaching a conclusion as to its meaning by reasoned analysis applying legal criteria. It does not sufficiently delineate any areas of risk, and thus can provide neither fair notice to the citizen nor a limitation of enforcement discretion. Such a provision is not intelligible, to use the terminology of previous decisions of this court, and therefore it fails to give sufficient indications that could fuel a legal debate. It offers no grasp to the judiciary. This is an exacting standard, going beyond semantics.

In *Pharmaceutical Society (Nova Scotia)*, however, the Court went on to hold that section 32(1)(c) of the *Combines Investigation Act*[211] was not unconstitutionally vague. The Act prohibits conspiracies to "prevent . . . or lessen, unduly, competition". The Court held these words were intelligible and could be interpreted. Parliament had "sufficiently delineated the area of risk and the terms of debate to meet the constitutional standard,"[212] which Gonthier J. summed in the following proposition:[213]

> . . . a law will be found unconstitutionally vague if it so lacks in precision as not to give sufficient guidance for legal debate. This statement of the doctrine best conforms to the dictates of the rule of

---

208   *Ibid.* at 636.
209   *Papachristou v. Jacksonville (City)*, 405 U.S. 156 (U.S. Fla., 1972).
210   *Supra* note 207 at 639-40.
211   R.S.C. 1970, c. C-23 [now s. 45(1)(c) of the *Competition Act*, R.S.C. 1985, c. C-34].
212   *Supra* note 207 at 657.
213   *Ibid.* at 643.

law in the modern State, and it reflects the prevailing argumentative, adversarial framework for the administration of justice.

However, even though statutory words may be difficult to interpret, or to apply in specific situations, this does not mean they fail to set out an intelligible standard. Difficulty of interpretation cannot be equated with the absence of any intelligible standard, and the doctrine of vagueness cannot be successfully invoked in such cases.[214] A court must consider the words in their interpretive context, by examining among other things, the purpose, subject-matter and nature of the impugned provision, societal values, related legislative provisions and prior judicial interpretations. Only after such an analysis can a court determine if the provisions provide sufficient guidance for legal debate.[215]

In the recent case of *Suresh v. Canada (Minister of Citizenship & Immigration)*,[216] the Court once again applied the test of "sufficient guidance for legal debate". In *Suresh*, the Court held that the terms "danger to the security of Canada" and "terrorism" in the federal *Immigration Act* are not unconstitutionally vague. The Court had no difficulty in arriving at definitions of these terms, and stated:[217]

> We are satisfied that the term "danger to the security of Canada", defined as here suggested, gives those who might come within the ambit of the provision fair notice of the consequences of their conduct, while adequately limiting law enforcement discretion. We hold, therefore, that the term is not unconstitutionally vague.

> In our view, it may safely be concluded, following the International Convention for the Suppression of the Financing of Terrorism, that "terrorism" in s. 19 of the Act includes any "act intended to cause death or serious bodily injury to a civilian, or to any other person not taking an active part in the hostilities in a situation of armed conflict, when the purpose of such act, by its nature or context, is to intimidate a population, or to compel a government or an international organization to do or to abstain from doing any act". . . . Parliament is not prevented from adopting more detailed or different definitions of terrorism. The issue here is whether the term as used in the Immigration Act is sufficiently certain to be workable, fair and constitutional. We believe that it is.[218]

Related to the doctrine of vagueness is overbreadth. A law prohibiting any person convicted of certain offences, including sexual offences, from loitering near school grounds, playgrounds, public parks or bathing areas was overbroad because it applied without prior notice to the accused, applied to too many

---

214 *Osborne v. Canada (Treasury Board)*, [1991] 2 S.C.R. 69 (S.C.C.), per Sopinka J. at 97.
215 *R. v. Canadian Pacific Ltd.*, [1995] 2 S.C.R. 1031 (S.C.C.).
216 [2002] 1 S.C.R. 3 (S.C.C.)
217 *Ibid.* at 52.
218 *Ibid.* at 55-56.

places and too many people, for an indefinite period with no possibility of review.[219]

Thus, the courts have determined that laws must contain an intelligible standard by which citizens can plan their conduct and against which the discretionary decisions of officials may be measured. Provisions which are difficult to interpret are not necessarily unconstitutionally vague. What is needed for an attack to succeed is such a lack of judicial, and legislative, guidance that there is no basis upon which legal debate can proceed.

(e) Section 8 and Administrative Law

Section 8 of the *Charter* provides that:

8. Everyone has the right to be secure against unreasonable search or seizure.

Many administrative tribunals are armed with powers allowing the forced production of documents or evidence, or allowing the entry of premises to conduct inspections[220] or searches. Section 8[221] of the *Charter* is engaged in such cases and the Supreme Court of Canada has set down some important guidelines which must be considered.

In *Canada (Director of Investigation & Research, Combines Investigation Branch) v. Southam Inc.*[222] the Supreme Court of Canada adopted the American approach and held the purpose of section 8 is the protection of the citizen's reasonable expectation of privacy.[223] Dickson J. (as he then was) stated that in the application of section 8, an assessment must be made as to whether in a particular situation the public's interest in being left alone by government must

---

219   *R. v. Heywood*, [1994] 3 S.C.R. 761 (S.C.C.) in a 5:4 split. See also *R. v. Canadian Pacific Ltd.*, *supra* note 215.

220   Inspections of documents or premises, which is narrower than an open-ended search, are considered "searches" for the purpose of s. 8: *Comité paritaire de l'industrie de la chemise c. Sélection Milton*, 115 D.L.R. (4th) 702, [1994] 2 S.C.R. 406 (S.C.C.).

221   See J.A. Fontana, *The Law of Search and Seizure in Canada*, 3d ed. (Toronto: Butterworths, 2002); S.C. Hutchison and J.C. Morton, *Search and Seizure Law in Canada*, (Toronto: Carswell, 1991); N. Finkelstein and M. Finkelstein, *Constitutional Rights in the Investigative Process*, (Toronto: Butterworths, 1991).

222   [1984] 2 S.C.R. 145 (S.C.C.).

223   By adopting the test of "reasonable expectation of privacy" from *Katz v. United States*, the court has based search and seizure in a broad privacy doctrine. In *Katz*, Mr. Justice Stewart stated:

The Fourth Amendment protects people, not places.

The Government's activities in electronically listening to and recording the petitioner's words violated the privacy upon which he justifiably relied while using the telephone booth and thus constituted a "search and seizure" within the meaning of the Fourth Amendment. The fact that the electronic device employed to achieve that end did not happen to penetrate the booth can have no constitutional significance.

See: K. Murray, "The 'Reasonable Expectation of Privacy Test' and the Scope of Protection Against Unreasonable Search and Seizure Under Section 8 of the *Charter of Rights and Freedoms*" (1987) Ottawa L.R. 25; and M. Rosenberg, "Unreasonable Search and Seizure: *Hunter v. Southam Inc.*" (1985) 19 U.B.C.L.R. 271.

give way to the government's interest in intruding on the individual's privacy in order to advance its goals, notably those of law enforcement.[224] The protection extended to the business premises of the corporate defendant. Accordingly, the Court held that an authorization to undertake a wide-sweeping, warrantless search of the *Edmonton Journal's* offices was unconstitutional. The Director of Combines, who issued the authorization, was not neutral and impartial. For this reason alone, the provision enabling the authorization was defective. Moreover, the Act was defective because it did not set out the criteria to be considered by an arbiter in deciding whether or not to authorize a search and seizure. Dickson J. held there must be objective criteria for granting prior authorization to conduct a search and seizure. This was necessary to ensure that the proper considerations were in mind when the arbiter decided the interests of the state prevailed over the privacy interests of the individual. It would be too low a standard to authorize a search and seizure merely because relevant evidence *may* be found. In such a case, the mere chance of discovering evidence would justify an intrusion. A higher standard was needed, which would be satisfied ". . . at the point where credibly based probability replaces suspicion".[225] The minimum acceptable standard was a statement on oath by the investigators that they believed an offence had been committed and that there was evidence at the place to be searched.

Dickson J. adopted the following procedural safeguards identified by Prowse J.A. in the Court of Appeal of Alberta as being necessary to satisfy the *Charter:*

(a) The power to authorize a search and seizure will be given to an impartial and independent person, who will be bound to act judicially in discharging that function.

(b) The arbiter will be required to satisfy himself that the person seeking the authority has reasonable grounds to suspect that an offence has been committed.

(c) The arbiter will be required to satisfy himself that the person seeking the authorization has reasonable grounds to believe that something which will afford evidence of the offence will be recovered.

(d) There will have to be evidence on oath before the arbiter.

The criteria set out in *Southam* are the high-water mark. In the administrative law context, most of the *Charter* cases involving section 8 have considered whether the formal process set out in *Southam* needs to be followed, or whether something less will do. The Supreme Court has decided that there is a sliding scale of privacy, and the amount of privacy to which one is entitled relates to the privacy one can reasonably expect in the particular circumstances.

---

224   *Supra* note 222 at 159-60.
225   *Ibid.* at 167.

Over and over again the court has emphasized that it is necessary to examine the full context of the claim.[226]

In *Thomson Newspapers Ltd. v. Canada (Director of Investigation & Research)*,[227] the Supreme Court considered a challenge to the power of the Director of Combines to order officers of a corporation to appear before the Restrictive Trade Practices Commission to be examined under oath and to produce documents. Such powers are common in many systems of administrative regulation. The Court held that corporations do not have the same reasonable expectation of privacy about their business records as individuals do about their personal papers and possessions.[228] Further, although a higher expectation of privacy is present when the state seeks information (even from a business) during the investigation of a criminal offence, those ordered to produce business documents during regulatory proceedings can only claim a limited expectation of privacy. The standard for deciding what is a reasonable search and seizure in the context of enforcing the criminal law is different from that in the administrative or regulatory context:[229]

> The application of a less strenuous and more flexible standard of reasonableness in the case of administrative or regulatory searches and seizures is fully consistent with a purposive approach to the elaboration of s. 8.

In *R. v. McKinlay Transport Ltd.*,[230] Wilson J. further observed:

> Since individuals have different expectations of privacy in different contexts with regard to different kinds of information and documents, it follows that the standard review of what is "reasonable" in a given context must be flexible if it is to be realistic and meaningful.

In this regard, the courts have noted the significance of the difference between a search and a demand for production, where the former authorizes state officials to conduct a broad based search of private premises while the latter merely compels production of certain business records.[231] Further, the

---

226 See for instance, *R. v. Wholesale Travel Group Inc.* (1991), 84 D.L.R. (4th) 161 at 211-12 (S.C.C.); *Comité paritaire de l'industrie de la chemise c. Sélection Milton*, 115 D.L.R. (4th) 702 at 732-34, [1994] 2 S.C.R. 406 (S.C.C.); *British Columbia (Securities Commission) v. Branch* (1995), 123 D.L.R. (4th) 462 (S.C.C.) at 483-85; *R. v. M. (M.R.)*, [1998] 3 S.C.R. 393 (S.C.C.).

227 [1990] 1 S.C.R. 425 (S.C.C.). Note that the agency itself had issued the notice, not an independent court that had established there were reasonable and probable grounds that a violation of the law had occurred.

228 See also *British Columbia (Securities Commission) v. Branch* (1995), 123 D.L.R. (4th) 462 at 488 (S.C.C.).

229 *Supra* note 227 at 506.

230 [1990] 1 S.C.R. 627 (S.C.C.), issued on the same day as *Thomson* at 645.

231 *Thomson Newspapers Ltd. v. Canada (Director of Investigation & Research)*, *supra* note 227; *R. v. McKinlay Transport Ltd.*, *ibid.*; *British Columbia (Securities Commission) v. Branch* (1995), 123 D.L.R. (4th) 462 (S.C.C.).

courts have recognized the difference between inspection of documents at a business premises and a search of business premises. The former is much narrower, and reasonable in the circumstances of inspectors enforcing or implementing the regulatory framework in a specific industry.[232] Finally, it is clear that in determining context, a court will consider a number of factors including: the realities of modern industrial society, the nature of the regulatory activity, the purpose of the regulation, the scope of the activity, and a balancing of the collective goals being achieved by the regulation with the right to privacy. Such an approach led to the conclusion that there was a low expectation of privacy in the securities trading industry[233] and in the field of labour and employment relations.[234]

Application of the contextual analysis gave an interesting result in the recent case of *R. v. Jarvis*.[235] Revenue Canada (as it then was) had received a tip that Mr. Jarvis had failed to report significant income on his tax returns. Revenue Canada decided to carry out an audit pursuant to its powers under the *Income Tax Act*. The taxpayer answered the auditor's questions and provided various records. The auditor concluded that the taxpayer had grossly omitted revenue in the relevant returns. She referred her file to the Special Investigations Section of Revenue Canada, but did not advise the taxpayer that she had done so. She held another meeting with the taxpayer during which the taxpayer provided further information. On the basis of all of the information contained in the auditor's file, the investigator obtained a search warrant. Some time later, the investigator obtained information about the taxpayer's affairs from various banks by issuing requirement letters under the *Income Tax Act*. At the taxpayer's trial for tax evasion, issues were raised as to the validity of the search warrant (and, therefore, admissibility of the information obtained under the search warrant) and admissibility of the banking information. The Court made a distinction between Revenue Canada's audit and investigation functions, holding that once the investigation function had been triggered, the taxpayer was entitled to full *Charter* protection as in any other criminal investigation. In the result, the search warrant was valid because the information upon which it was based had been properly obtained during the audit process. The banking information was inadmissible because the requirement letter procedure was only available to Revenue Canada during the audit process, and the requirement letters were issued after the matter had become an investigation.

R. v. Jarvis shows that it is possible for different levels of *Charter* protection to apply to different functions even when those functions are carried out by one agency acting under one statute. The question to be answered by the courts in each case is whether the search or seizure is unreasonable in light of the reasonable expectation of privacy of the person subjected to a search or compelled to produce evidence. It is clear the expectation of privacy varies

232   *Comité paritaire de l'industrie de la chemise c. Sélection Milton*, 115 D.L.R. (4th) 702, [1994] 2 S.C.R. 406 (S.C.C.).

233   *British Columbia (Securities Commission) v. Branch, supra* note 231.

234   *Sélection Milton, supra* note 232.

235   2002 SCC 73 (S.C.C.).

with the circumstances, depending upon the activities of the individual and, perhaps most importantly, the purpose and scope of the legislative scheme which purports to authorize the search, seizure, inspection, or requirement for production.

(f) Conclusion

The role of the courts in supervising governmental actions has changed considerably since the introduction of the *Charter* in 1982. The courts are no longer confined to merely interpreting and enforcing the positive law, which was the theoretical foundation of pre-*Charter* administrative law. The *Charter* has subjected the administrative process to intense judicial scrutiny. That judicial scrutiny has not produced a series of hard and fast rules. Instead, the Supreme Court of Canada has repeatedly said that a *Charter* analysis is contextual in nature, with the result that the impact of the *Charter* will vary from tribunal to tribunal – and may, indeed, vary from task to task carried out by a particular tribunal.

3

Statutory Delegation of Governmental Powers[1]

1. Institutions of Government

On an institutional level, it would be almost inconceivable to expect Parliament by itself to deal with all aspects of the laws it makes without the assistance of other governmental agencies. It is not surprising, therefore, to discover that legislation regularly delegates powers to the executive[2] and judicial[3] branches of government. One must, therefore, take account of the existence of these other two governmental institutions, even if the scope and

---

1 This chapter has been updated by Glenn Tait, of McLennan Ross, Barristers and Solicitors, Yellowknife.
2 For example, see the *School Act*, R.S.A. 2000, c. S-3, s. 39.
3 For example, see the Alberta *Rules of Court*, validated by the *Judicature Act*, R.S.A. 2000, c. J-2, s. 63.

very existence of their functions theoretically derive from Parliament,[4] which is pre-eminent in our constitutional system.

(a) The Judicial Branch

Let us first consider the position of the judicial institution in the British system of government which we have inherited in Canada. Because there is no entrenched constitutional separation of powers in the United Kingdom similar to the situation in the United States,[5] virtually all of the functions exercised by the British judiciary depend either upon authority statutorily delegated from the legislative branch, or upon common law tradition which can be specifically overridden by statute.[6] As a matter of practice, it is of course true that British constitutional convention has maintained a strongly independent judiciary, but there is no constitutional impediment to prevent the legislative branch from abolishing the courts entirely. Nor do the British courts have any inherent jurisdiction which could not be abolished by clear legislation. Therefore, the *de facto* independence of the judiciary in Britain is really a political matter, not a legal or constitutional necessity.[7]

The position of the judicial branch in Canada is similar, although complicated somewhat by both the *Canadian Charter of Rights and Freedoms*[8] and certain other provisions of the *Constitution Act, 1867*.[9] In theory, either the Federal Parliament or a provincial legislature could abolish the courts or abridge all or any part of their jurisdiction. Unlike the position under the Constitution of the United States, there is no constitutional guarantee in Canada that there will be independent courts with an irreducible minimum jurisdiction.[10] Thus, in Canada, at least certain "judicial functions" can be created by

---

4   The Crown itself, of course, predates Parliament, and the Royal Prerogative is an independent source of lawful power. On the other hand, legislation enacted by the Queen in Parliament can abridge all or any part of the Royal Prerogative, so that the better view seems to be that the Royal Prerogative continues to exist on the sufferance of Parliament. Further, the Queen herself does not constitute the entirety of the executive branch of government, most of which derives its powers from statutes. Even if the statutes delegate powers to the Queen (or the Queen in Council), the Queen is like any other statutory delegate in the exercise of those powers, who is subject to the doctrine of *ultra vires*, and the legality of which is capable of judicial review in the courts. In other words, one must identify the source of the Crown's powers, and not be content merely to identify the fact that it is the Crown which is exercising the power in question.

5   See arts. I, II and III of the *Constitution of the United States of America*.

6   Some judicial functions may derive from the Royal Prerogative, which can of course also be overridden by statute.

7   See David Phillip Jones, "A Constitutionally Guaranteed Role for the Courts" (1979) 57 Can. Bar Rev. 669.

8   Part 1 of Schedule B to the *Canada Act* (1982) (U.K.) (31 Eliz. 2, c. 11); also cited as the *Constitution Act*, S.C. 1982, Pt. I.

9   30 & 31 Vict., c. 3; reproduced with amendments in R.S.C. 1970, App. II, as further amended and renamed by the *Canada Act, ibid.*

10   It is true that s. 96 of the *Constitution Act, 1867* requires all functions of a superior, district or county court to be exercised by a judge named by the federal Governor in Council. On the other hand, there is no requirement for legislation to create judicial functions at all. It is conceivable – though obviously inconvenient – that all disputes between citizens could be

legislation but delegated to someone other than a judge sitting in a courtroom.[11] Against this theoretical position, however, it is important to note the existence in Canada of a political convention acknowledging the desirability of the existence of courts which in fact are independent,[12] and to whom a very wide range of judicial[13] and administrative[14] functions are delegated.

(b) The Executive or Administrative Branch

Similarly, no one can deny the *de facto* existence of a separate executive branch of government to which the legislative branch has delegated the power to administer its laws. The exact ambit of the executive may be difficult to identify with precision. It certainly includes the Crown, the Governor in Council (which in practice generally means the cabinet), and individual ministers[15] to whom particular powers have been delegated by legislation.[16] All of the foregoing statutory delegates sit in Parliament and are directly answerable to the legislative branch for the exercise of the powers which have been granted to them (and may of course be answerable in judicial proceedings to determine the lawfulness of their actions).[17] The doctrine of ministerial responsibility applies in these circumstances, even if some assistant or civil servant has in fact exercised the power in the name of the minister, the cabinet, or the

---

settled by legislation. In such a case, s. 96 would clearly be inapplicable. See Jones, *supra* note 7.

11 As noted by the Privy Council in *Saskatchewan (Labour Relations Board) v. John East Iron Works Ltd.*, [1948] 4 D.L.R. 673 (Saskatchewan P.C.). See also *Douglas/Kwantlen Faculty Assn. v. Douglas College* (1990), 77 D.L.R. (4th) 94 (S.C.C.) and the twin decisions of *Cuddy Chicks Ltd. v. Ontario (Labour Relations Board)* (1991), 81 D.L.R. (4th) 121, 50 Admin. L.R. 44 (S.C.C.) and *Tétreault-Gadoury v. Canada (Employment & Immigration Commission)* (1991), 81 D.L.R. (4th) 358 (S.C.C.), discussing the application of the *Canadian Charter of Rights and Freedoms* by administrative tribunals.

12 *Maîtres chez eux/Masters in their Own House* (the Deschênes Report) (Edmonton: Canadian Institute for the Administration of Justice, 1981).

13 That is, the vast bulk of judges' functions.

14 For example, the discretion to permit wire-tapping; taxing a lawyer's fee accounts; decrees absolute of divorce; approving the dissolution of corporations.

15 For example, the Minister of National Revenue under the *Income Tax Act*, R.S.C. 1985 (5th Supp.), c. 1.

16 Or their predecessors, as actions taken under such a delegation do not automatically come to an end when a particular delegate ceases to hold office; *Samson Indian Band No. 137 v. Canada (Minister of Indian Affairs & Northern Development)* (1988), 33 Admin. L.R. 141 (Fed. T.D.).

17 All statutory delegates are subject to judicial review for a breach of the *ultra vires* doctrine. Sometimes, however, the fact that a statutory delegate sits in the legislature and is subject to the doctrine of ministerial responsibility may cause the courts to give a rather broader construction to the ambit of discretionary powers delegated to that person. See *Liversidge v. Anderson* (1941), [1942] A.C. 206 (U.K. H.L.). Similarly, prior to the recent development of the duty to be fair, the applicability of the doctrine of ministerial responsibility sometimes inclined the courts to characterize a particular delegated function as merely administrative instead of being quasi-judicial (and therefore escaping the application of the principles of natural justice). See *Franklin v. Minister of Town & Country Planning* (1947), [1948] A.C. 87 (U.K. H.L.).

Governor in Council.[18] On the other hand, the executive branch also includes independent boards and tribunals which are not part of the organized departmental structure of the civil service,[19] but to whom the legislative branch has nevertheless delegated powers. Examples from Alberta include the Alberta Energy and Utilities Board, the Municipal Government Board, and the Surface Rights Board. Federal examples include the Canadian Transportation Commission, the National Energy Board, and the Canadian Radio-Television and Telecommunications Commission. All of these might be called "regulatory or administrative agencies", "tribunals", or "boards". Crown corporations such as Canadian National Railway or Alberta Science, Research and Technology Authority provide an example of governmental activities which are removed even further from political or civil service control by the government. These arrangements provide varying distances between the political executive which controls the departmentalized government and the independent boards, and relieves the former of direct political responsibility and accountability for the actions of the latter. Unfortunately, there is no legal or constitutional rule for determining which executive or administrative functions should be externalized to independent agencies. From time to time, the political government of the day reconsiders how independent particular agencies should be. Thus, legislation may provide for appeals to the cabinet from decisions of an independent administrative agency,[20] permit the cabinet to give policy directives to one of the agencies[21] or require ministerial approval prior to the conducting of certain activities by the agency.[22] Or, new legislation may be enacted to reorganize the administrative structure to move a particular function into one of the departments of state, or out to a totally or semi-independent agency.[23] It

---

18 See for example, the delegation provision in the *Public Service Act*, R.S.A. 2000, c. P-42, s. 9.

19 These independent boards or tribunals may report to Parliament directly (e.g., the Ombudsman and the Auditor-General in Alberta) and have their budgets set by the House itself. Alternatively, there may be a reporting relationship through a particular minister (e.g., the National Research Council reports to Parliament through the Minister responsible for the Council, who also has responsibility for the staff of the Council). There is no single paradigm.

20 Such as the Canadian Radio-Television and Telecommunications Commission. See for example *Inuit Tapirisat of Canada v. Canada (Attorney General)* on this point: (1980), 115 D.L.R. (3d) 1 (S.C.C.).

21 For example, the *Canadian Wheat Board Act*, R.S.C. 1985, c. C-24, s. 18(1) provides:
    The Governor in Council may, by order, direct the Board with respect to the manner in which any of its operations, powers and duties under this Act shall be conducted, exercised or performed.
    Similarly, the *Environmental Protection and Enhancement Act*, R.S.A. 2000, c. E-12, s. 100(1) (a) which provides that following receipt of a decision of the Environmental Appeal Board:
    . . . the Minister may, by order . . . confirm, reverse or vary the decision appealed and make any decision that the person whose decision was appealed could make.

22 For example, *Safety Codes Act*, R.S.A., 2000, c. s-1, s. 18(h) and (i) provides that the Safety Codes Council may only undertake certain tasks – such as the review, formulation and promulgation of safety codes – with the consent of the Minister.

23 For example, the transfer of employer's liability from tort law determined by the courts to an administrative matter dealt with by the Worker's Compensation Board. Conversely, note the privatization of the post office.

must also be remembered that the political executive (that is, the cabinet, and perhaps in practice the Prime Minister or Premier) almost invariably leads the party which has a majority in the legislative branch, and therefore is generally in a position to cause legislation to be enacted to alter the institutional arrangements for performing executive functions. Thus, in practice, it may be the executive which controls the legislative branch, although our constitutional philosophy states the reverse.

In summary, there are three great institutions of modern government: the legislative, the judicial and the executive. In the Anglo-Canadian tradition, the latter two institutions ultimately are subordinate to the legislature, although this is probably no longer strictly true in Canada under our written constitution and the *Charter of Rights and Freedoms*.[24] It is important, however, to remember that the existence of three separate institutions of government does not mean that each institution exercises only one particular type of function.

2. Institutions Versus Functions of Government

Altogether apart from the governmental institution involved, it is possible to identify three principal functions of government: (a) the legislative, which involves making general rules and regulations (such as the *Criminal Code*)[25] applicable to a wide range of people and fact patterns; (b) the executive, which involves the application and enforcement of the legislation to particular people in particular circumstances (such as an immigration officer's determination whether a particular person is a Canadian citizen entitled to enter Canada as of right)[26]; and (c) the judicial, which involves the independent determination by a judge whether a person has contravened the law. As noted earlier, however, the Canadian and British systems of government do not rigorously allocate the exercise of each of these three functions to the corresponding governmental institutions, as is done constitutionally in the United States. Thus, members of the departmentalized civil service form part of the executive branch of government but may be delegated powers that are not really executive in nature, such as powers (a) to make subordinate legislation; (b) to determine disputes in a judicial or quasi-judicial manner; or (c) to do some merely administrative act (such as issuing drivers' licences or admitting returning Canadian citizens to the country). Conversely, all Acts of Parliament are by their very nature "legislation", even if they are functionally judicial or administrative in nature and not general at all. Thus, a Bill of Attainder is legislation which declares a person to be guilty of a criminal offence and may forfeit his or her property – both of which would generally be considered to be judicial functions. Similarly,

---

24   Because section 52 of the *Constitution Act* makes the constitution the supreme law that overrides ordinary laws which conflict with it, and the *Charter* imposes certain limitations on the ability of either the Federal Parliament or provincial legislatures to enact certain types of laws, and gives the right to judicial redress for breaches of these limitations, thereby implying some irreducible role for the judicial branch of government.

25   R.S.C. 1985, c. C-46.

26   *Immigration and Refugee Protection Act* , S.C. 2001, c. 27, s. 19; *Citizenship Act*, R.S.C. 1985, c. C-29, s. 3.

divorces granted prior to the 1968 *Divorce Act*[27] were incorporated into Acts of Parliament, although they affected only two parties – very much the way that private Acts exempt particular persons from the operation of the general law.[28] All of these functions could have been delegated to judges or members of the executive, and the mere fact that Parliament itself exercises these functions through the vehicle of parent legislation does not really make them "legislative" in nature. Similarly, municipal by-laws which re-zone particular land have been held to be quasi-judicial in nature, even though they are delegated legislation in form.[29] These examples demonstrate the impossibility of characterizing a function as "legislative", "judicial" or merely "administrative" in nature simply by identifying the person or branch of government to whom the power has been delegated by the legislation in question, although some broad correlation may exist between institutions and functions of government.

---

27   R.S.C. 1970, c. D-8, now the *Divorce Act*, R.S.C. 1985 (3 Supp.), c. 3.

28   Although the Federal Parliament or a provincial legislature may enact legislation exempting a particular person from the general law, neither the Crown nor any other member of the executive has power to dispense from the general law of the land.

29   *Wiswell v. Winnipeg (Metropolitan)* (1964), 48 W.W.R. 193 (Man. C.A.), reversed on other grounds [1965] S.C.R. 512 (S.C.C.). As Freedman J.A. of the Manitoba Court of Appeal said at 194-95:

> Counsel's argument here is double-pronged. First, he contends that the Metropolitan council, when it was enacting bylaw No. 177, was engaged in a legislative function and not in a quasi-judicial act. If that were indeed the case, then it would have had the right to proceed without notice. But to say that the enactment of bylaw No. 177 was simply a legislative act is to ignore the realities and substance of the case. For this was not a bylaw of wide or general application, passed by the Metropolitan council because of a conviction that an entire area had undergone a change in character and hence was in need of reclassification for zoning purposes. Rather this was a specific decision made upon a specific application concerned with a specific parcel of land. . . . In proceeding to enact bylaw No. 177 Metro was essentially dealing with a dispute between Dr. Ginsberg, who wanted the zoning requirements to be altered for his benefit, and those other residents of the district who wanted the zoning restrictions to continue as they were. That Metro resolved the dispute by the device of an amending bylaw did indeed give to its proceedings an appearance of a legislative character. But in truth the process in which it was engaged was quasi-judicial in nature; and I feel I must so treat it.

Then counsel argues as well that the governing statute does not call for notice. Hence, he says, notice was not required. I am unable to accept this contention. A long line of authorities, both old and recent, establish that in judicial or quasi-judicial proceedings notice is required unless the statute expressly dispenses with it. The mere silence of the statute is not enough to do away with notice. In such cases, as has been said, the justice of the common law will supply the omission of the legislature. Some of the authorities dealing with this subject are referred to by Kirby, J. in the recent case of *Camac Exploration Ltd. v. Alberta (Oil & Gas Conservation Board)* (1964), 47 W.W.R. 81 (Alta. T.D.).

Compare the decision of the Alberta Court of Appeal in *Campeau Corp. v. Calgary (City)* (1978), 7 Alta. L.R. (2d) 294 (Alta. C.A.), and subsequent decision (1980), 12 Alta. L.R. (2d) 379 (Alta. C.A.), and the decision in *Harvie v. Calgary (City) Regional Planning Commission* (1978), 8 Alta. L.R. (2d) 166 (Alta. C.A.), reversing (1978), 5 Alta. L.R. (2d) 301 (Alta. C.A.).

3. Reasons for Characterizing Delegated Powers: "Legislative", "Judicial" or "Administrative"

The characterization of the function is important for determining the ambit of the power granted to the delegate,[30] the procedure which the delegate must follow in exercising that power and the remedies which may be available to challenge the legality of the delegate's action in court. Thus, the general rule is that both delegated legislative and judicial powers must be exercised by the very person to whom they have been granted, whereas merely administrative powers can be sub-delegated quite freely to others. For a long time, the principles of natural justice[31] were thought to be applicable only to the exercise of a judicial (or quasi-judicial) power, and not to the enactment of delegated legislation or to the exercise of a merely administrative action. Similarly, the availability of prerogative remedies of *certiorari* and prohibition was long restricted to correct procedural errors involved in the exercise of judicial (or quasi-judicial) powers, but not legislative or merely administrative ones.[32] So the functional characterization of delegated powers has been extremely important in administrative law.

In recent years, the necessity to characterize the nature of delegated functions has become considerably less important. In particular, the development of the general duty to be fair – whether comprised within the principles of natural justice, or in addition to them – has removed the distinction between judicial (or quasi-judicial) functions and merely administrative ones for the purpose of applying rules of fair procedure, as well as for determining the availability of *certiorari* and prohibition. This is a welcome advance, and is considered in detail in later chapters. Nevertheless, important distinctions still exist, particularly if the delegated power is characterized as being legislative in nature, because the principles of natural justice still do not apply to the exercise of such functions. Thus, considerable attention must be given throughout the study of administrative law to the courts' historical attempts to characterize the type of delegated powers impugned in litigation before them as being (a) legislative; (b) judicial (or quasi-judicial); or (c) executive (or merely administrative).[33]

4. Discretionary Powers

In addition to identifying the governmental institution involved and characterizing the type of function being exercised, it is also necessary to note the

---

30 It is submitted that, in applying the doctrine of *ultra vires*, the courts are likely to give a broader content to delegated legislative or administrative powers than they are to delegated judicial or quasi-judicial powers – always bearing in mind that there may be no doubt as to the ambit of the delegated power, however it is characterized.

31 See Chapter 8.

32 See David Phillip Jones, "Administrative Fairness in Alberta" (1980) 18 Alta. L.R. 351.

33 See S.A. de Smith *et al.*, *Judicial Review of Administrative Action*, 5th ed. (London: Sweet & Maxwell, 1995) at 1001-20.

distinction between (a) delegated powers which are really duties; and (b) those which are discretionary in nature.[34] It is obvious why legislation frequently imposes duties on delegates to enforce rules which are contained in the legislation itself, for example, the duty on a policeman to enforce the provisions of the *Criminal Code*. Frequently, however, it is not possible for Parliament to lay down a rule of general application in the legislation itself. On the contrary, it may be necessary for Parliament to provide the vehicle through which particular decisions are to be made by its delegates, rather than making those decisions itself. Such delegation of discretionary power may be necessary for a variety of reasons, including:

(a) the difficulty of providing a rule which is applicable to all cases;

(b) the difficulty of identifying all of the factors to be applied to a particular case;

(c) the difficulty of weighing those factors;

(d) the need to provide an easy vehicle for changing the considerations to be applied to the problem over time;

(e) the complexity of the issue; and

(f) the desire not to confer vested rights on a particular party (which might be called the "short leash" principle).

The delegate may be authorized to exercise its discretion in each particular case or to enact subordinate legislation governing all such cases (which itself can be changed more easily than the parent legislation). There is no general rule to determine when Parliament should enact a general rule governing all cases, or should delegate discretionary powers, or for determining whether the delegate should be required to exercise its discretion to enact a rule contained in subordinate legislation, or should be permitted to deal with each case individually.[35]

The rest of this section considers: (a) duties compared with discretionary powers; (b) the ambit of discretion; (c) pre-conditions to the exercise of discretion; and (d) the concept of a quasi-judicial power.

(a) Duties Compared with Discretionary Powers

Many delegated powers do not involve the exercise of discretion at all, but are really duties imposed upon the statutory delegate. Thus, an immigration officer has the duty to admit Canadian citizens into Canada; there is no discre-

---

34 See J.H. Grey, "Discretion in Administrative Law" (1979) 17 Osgoode Hall L.J. 107.

35 It is clear, however, that a delegate who has been authorized to make subordinate legislation cannot validly create a discretionary scheme for dealing with the matter in question; that is, converting a subordinate legislative power into a sub-delegated discretionary power is *ultra vires* because the parent legislation contemplated a system of rules being put in place, not a system of discretionary powers: see *Brant Dairy Co. v. Ontario (Milk Commission)* (1972), [1973] S.C.R. 131 (S.C.C.).

tion to refuse entry to any citizen.[36] It is, of course, true that the officer must make certain preliminary determinations, for example, whether the person is indeed a citizen. The officer may be right or wrong on that determination, but any error can be corrected by a court, because there is only one correct answer to this question. In other words, the immigration officer has no discretion to decide – as a matter of law – who is a citizen, or whether that citizen can be excluded from Canada; on the contrary, the officer has a duty to admit citizens into the country.

On the other hand, a law enacted by the legislative branch may grant the executive officer (or "delegate") the power to do or not do something as the delegate, in its discretion, thinks appropriate. For example, the Alberta Energy and Utilities Board has the power to set the price of natural gas supplied to consumers in Alberta; it has discretion as to the actual price to be charged. The price cannot be determined merely by reading the legislation itself, although it is the legislation which creates and delegates the discretion to the board to make such determinations from time to time.

(b) The Ambit of Discretion

It is extremely important to identify the ambit of the discretion[37] which legislation has delegated to the particular executive office in question. Very few discretions are completely unfettered. On the contrary, most legislation lays down at least general guidelines within which the delegate must exercise its discretion. Thus, section 38 of the *Public Service Employee Relations Act*[38] of Alberta delegates the power to a three-member arbitration board to settle the collective agreement between the provincial government as employer and a union, bearing in mind such factors as:

(a) the continuity and stability of public and private sector employment;

(b) the terms and conditions of employment in similar occupations outside the employer's employment including any geographic, industrial or other variations that the board considers relevant;

(c) the need to maintain appropriate relationships in the terms and conditions of employment as between different classification levels within an occupation and as between occupations in the employer's employment;

(d) the need to establish terms and conditions of employment that are fair and reasonable in relation to the qualifications required, the work performed, the responsibility assumed and the nature of the services rendered;

(e) the general economic conditions in Alberta;

(f) any other factor that to it appears to be relevant to the matter in dispute.

---

36 *Supra* note 26.
37 See J.H. Grey, *supra* note 34 at 110 and 114-28.
38 R.S.A. 2000, c. P-43.

The enumeration of these factors delimits the ambit of the discretion delegated by the legislature to the arbitration board. Thus, an arbitration board has no lawful power to go outside the area delegated to it, and any attempt to do so will be *ultra vires*.[39] Nevertheless, within the area delegated to it, an arbitration board is entitled to exercise its own discretion. Again, the discretionary nature of the power delegated to the arbitration board makes it impossible to determine from the legislation itself the precise terms of each collective agreement. The legislation merely creates the vehicle within which the statutory delegate will make its decision, within a certain area of discretion.

It is also important that where the legislature has delegated discretionary powers to a tribunal, that the tribunal actually exercise that discretion. It is not open for a tribunal to make its decision solely on the basis of policy, without consideration of the merits of a particular case.[40]

(c) Pre-Conditions to the Exercise of Discretion

It is important to note that some legislative provisions only delegate discretionary powers to the executive provided certain circumstances exist. For example, in *Bell v. Ontario (Human Rights Commission)*,[41] the commission could only exercise its powers if there was an allegation of discrimination with respect to the renting of a "self-contained domestic establishment". In the *Bell* case, the accommodation had shared bathroom and kitchen facilities. The Supreme Court of Canada decided that this meant that the property was not "self-contained", and therefore the commission had no jurisdiction to determine whether there had been unlawful racial discrimination involved by the owner's refusal to rent it to a particular applicant. In other words, the commis-

---

39   Although the discretionary nature of a statutory power may make the courts slow to interfere with the way in which the statutory delegate exercises its discretion, no discretion (indeed, no statutory power) is unlimited, and those limits demarcate the beginning of the doctrine of *ultra vires*. See *Ottawa-Carleton Dialysis Services v. Ontario (Minister of Health)* (1996), 41 Admin. L.R. (2d) 211 (Ont. Div. Ct.), additional reasons at (1996), 1996 CarswellOnt 4300 (Ont. Div. Ct.), leave to appeal allowed (1996), 1996 CarswellOnt 4691 (Ont. C.A.) and *Strait Crossing Development Inc. v. Canada (Attorney General)* (1995), 33 Admin. L.R. (2d) 9 (Ont. Gen. Div. [Commercial List]) for two cases with contrasting results.

40   In *Braden-Burry Expediting Services Ltd. v. Northwest Territories (Workers' Compensation Board)* (1999), 19 Admin. L.R. (3d) 208 (N.W.T. C.A.) a tribunal decision was set aside. The tribunal ruled that it was obliged to follow a policy which the court found should only have been a guide for the tribunal. See also *Braden-Burry Expediting Services Ltd. v. Northwest Territories (Workers' Compensation Board)* (2002), 50 Admin. L.R. (3d) 175 (N.W.T. S.C.) and Chapters 6 and 7, for a discussion on fettering of discretion.

41   [1971] S.C.R. 756 (S.C.C.). See also Peter Hogg, "The Jurisdictional Fact Doctrine in the Supreme Court of Canada: *Bell v. Ontario Human Rights Commission*" (1971) 9 Osgoode Hall L.J. 203; *R. v. Nat Bell Liquors Ltd.*, [1922] 2 A.C. 128 (Canada P.C.); *Parkhill Bedding & Furniture Ltd. v. I.M.A.U., Local 714* (1961), 26 D.L.R. (2d) 589 (Man. C.A.); *Lodum Holdings Ltd. v. B.C.W., Local 468* (1968), 3 D.L.R. (3d) 41 (B.C. S.C.); *Eastern Irrigation District v. Alberta (Industrial Relations Board)* (1970), 17 D.L.R. (3d) 192 (Alta. C.A.); H.W.R. Wade, "Anglo-American Administrative Law; More Reflections" (1966) 82 L.Q.R. 226; D.M. Gordon, "Jurisdictional Fact: An Answer" (1966) 82 L.Q.R. 515; D.M. Gordon, "The Relation of Facts to Jurisdiction" (1929) 45 L.Q.R. 459; and *Canada (Attorney General) v. P.S.A.C.* (1991), 80 D.L.R. (4th) 520, 48 Admin. L.R. 161 (S.C.C.) (the *Econosult* case).

sion's discretionary jurisdiction could only be exercised if certain facts or pre-conditions existed, but not otherwise.

Similarly, in *Anisminic Ltd. v. Foreign Compensation Commission*,[42] the legislation granted the commission jurisdiction to determine, in its discretion, how much compensation to pay British nationals or their successors-in-title for assets nationalized by the Egyptian government during the Suez affair. The commission refused even to entertain Anisminic's claim on the basis that it was not a successor-in-title to a person whose property had been nationalized. The House of Lords ruled that Anisminic was indeed a successor-in-title and that it had a right to file a claim which the commission must consider, although the commission could then exercise its discretion to determine how much (if anything) to pay Anisminic.

Both of these examples illustrate the conditional delegation of discretion-ary powers to the executive. This phenomenon is sometimes referred to as the "jurisdictional fact", "collateral fact", or "preliminary fact" doctrine. All of these phrases indicate that a certain state of affairs must exist before the delegate can exercise the power (generally discretionary in nature)[43] which the legisla-tive branch has delegated to it. Further, the courts – and not the statutory delegate – are entitled to determine whether the relevant pre-conditions do in fact exist which would permit the delegate to exercise the discretion in question.

(d) The Concept of a "Quasi-Judicial" Power

The phrase "quasi-judicial" refers to discretionary powers which are es-sentially judicial in nature, but which are exercised by officials other than judges in their courtrooms. Historically, quasi-judicial powers have been sub-ject to procedures which more or less resemble the formal ones used in liti-gation. As one moves further away from the judicial paradigm,[44] it becomes difficult to determine when the discretionary power can more properly be described as "merely administrative" or "ministerial". Nevertheless, the dis-tinction was formerly very important, because the procedural principles of natural justice were thought not to apply to the exercise of "merely adminis-trative" discretionary powers. In recent years, however, the development of the "duty to be fair" when exercising merely administrative powers has largely obliterated the importance of the distinction between them and quasi-judicial powers. Nevertheless, it is difficult to understand current administrative law without some familiarity with the old concept of a quasi-judicial power, its great (but not limitless) elasticity, and the procedural consequences of char-acterizing a particular discretionary power as being "quasi-judicial" in nature.

The concept of a quasi-judicial power takes its point of reference from the type of function exercised by a judge in litigation between two parties. The

---

42 (1968), [1969] 2 A.C. 147 (U.K. H.L.).

43 Sometimes a non-discretionary power or duty is involved, once the pre-conditions have been met.

44 For a discussion of various tests for determining whether a function is judicial, see S.A. de Smith *et al.*, *Judicial Review of Administrative Action*, 5th ed. (London: Sweet & Maxwell, 1995) at 1008-20.

formal procedures which have been developed over the centuries by the courts epitomize "natural justice" in its strongest form: there are pleadings; each side brings forward formal evidence; each side makes submissions of law and can answer the other's submissions; and the judge renders a decision in light of the law and the facts which have been proven before him or her in open court. These procedures are the hallmark of the judicial function. Many of these procedures have been made applicable to quasi-judicial functions exercised by officials who are not judges, although the exact content of the procedural requirements may differ with the type of quasi-judicial power involved.

It is important to remember that not all of a court's functions fit the model referred to above. On the one hand, many court functions are purely administrative in nature, and may not even involve the exercise of discretion, for example, the issuance of a writ or other proceedings. Other judicial proceedings do involve a formal hearing, but give the judge no discretion.[45] In yet other cases, the judge has a great deal of discretion under the applicable law.[46] In general, the procedural requirements of natural justice apply, in their strongest form, to all functions exercised by judges, whether or not discretionary in nature.

Over the years, the superior courts have been asked to review the procedures used by other officials in the exercise of powers delegated to them by legislation. The more closely those powers resembled ones exercised by judges in their courtrooms, the more likely it was that the superior courts would require some form of curial procedure to be used by the officials in the exercise of their powers; hence, the development of the phrase "quasi-judicial" powers. On the one hand, the content of the procedural requirements for exercising such non-curial powers differed enormously with the type and content of the power involved. The less the non-curial power resembled something done by a court, the less stringent was the requirement that court-like procedures be used to exercise that power. On the other hand, the concept of a quasi-judicial power is not infinitely elastic, and at some point it becomes impossible to characterize a particular non-curial power as being quasi-judicial instead of merely administrative – no matter how important it is, or how much it affects people, or how much discretion is involved. Although it was previously thought that no procedural safeguards were required for the exercise of merely administrative powers, administrative law has now developed the "duty to be fair"[47] in the method used to exercise even a merely administrative power. Accordingly, the distinction between quasi-judicial and merely administrative powers has become much less important. Nevertheless, it is probably accurate to state that the further one moves from the judicial model of decision-making, the

---

45   For example, the mandatory 25-year minimum sentence for first-degree murder: *Criminal Code*, R.S.C. 1985, c. C-46, s. 745.

46   For example, in deciding what is the appropriate sentence for certain offences; whether to exercise the court's discretion under the *Law of Property Act*, R.S.A. 2000, c. L-7, to relieve against a penalty or forfeiture with respect to land (particularly in the foreclosure context), or to exercise its discretion to refuse one of the prerogative remedies.

47   See Chapter 8, for a description of the development of the duty to be fair, and the varying content of natural justice in different circumstances.

less are the procedural requirements involved in adopting a "fair" procedure for the exercise of a statutory power delegated to someone who is not a judge.

Before leaving the topic of quasi-judicial functions, it is important to note two points: first, that section 96 of the *Constitution Act* prohibits the delegation of any judicial powers exercised by a superior, district or county court to anyone not appointed by the federal Governor in Council, and this constitutional limitation is still important today;[48] secondly, that there is no talisman to guide Parliament in determining whether it should (a) itself enact parent legislation containing all of the rules to govern a particular situation; (b) delegate discretion to an official to deal with each case, within broader or narrower policy guidelines contained in the Act; (c) provide specifically for some sort of procedure to be followed by such a delegate, or provide for an appeal to another official or to the courts; or (d) delegate the power to someone else to make rules and regulations which govern every case.[49] Although these choices are largely political matters, they are important both to good government and to the legal rights which arise as a result of the institutional framework within which the legislative branch chooses to delegate power.

5. Delegated Legislation

One of the most important methods of delegating power is the ability to enact subordinate legislation. Although discretion is obviously involved in determining the content of subordinate legislation, the courts have generally held that the procedural requirements of natural justice do not apply to the exercise of such legislative powers. Because subordinate legislation is as valid as if contained in the parent legislation itself, most legislatures have created systems for registering and publishing the subordinate legislation which has been enacted under their authority. Again, because delegation of power is involved, the ambit of that power can always be questioned and the doctrine of *ultra vires* permits judicial review to determine whether the delegate in fact has exercised the specific legislative power which has been granted to it. In addition, the Federal Parliament and some provincial legislatures have instituted standing "scrutiny" committees to review both the content and legality of the subordinate legislation which their servants have enacted with their authority. The great volume and importance of subordinate legislation makes this topic extremely important in administrative law, and it is discussed in detail in the next chapter.

---

48 See the discussion on this point in Chapter 2.
49 But see the caveat discussed in *supra* note 35, on the ability of a delegate to convert a legislative power into a discretionary one.

4

Subordinate
Legislation[1]

---

1 This chapter has been updated by David C. Elliott, Barrister and Solicitor, Edmonton.

1. Introduction

The previous chapter considered various types of statutory powers that can be delegated: duties, discretionary powers, judicial powers, and the power to enact subordinate legislation. This chapter considers subordinate legislation, including what it is, the reasons for it, how it is created, the effect it has, the systems some jurisdictions have created to make it accessible, who scrutinizes the legislation, and the kinds of court challenge that can be made against it.

2. What is Subordinate Legislation?

The Parliament of Canada and provincial legislatures each have sovereign authority within the Constitution of Canada to make law.[2] Either Parliament or a provincial legislature may, subject to limitations, delegate certain of their law-making powers.[3] When the delegate itself makes law, the result is subordinate legislation.[4] The legislation is "subordinate" in the sense that the right to make the subordinate law comes from a higher source – that source being legislation made by a sovereign parliament or legislature. The name "subordinate legislation" is a reminder that the subordinate law is constrained by what the parent Act says it can say.[5] In the event of conflict, subordinate legislation will, in most cases, give way to its parent legislation and other Acts.

---

2 *Hodge v. R.* (1883), (1883-84) LR 9 App. Cas. 117 at 132 (Ontario P.C.).
3 There is no constitutional principle preventing Parliament or legislatures from delegating the power to amend Acts to its delegates. See *Waddell v. British Columbia (Governor in Council)* (1983), 8 Admin. L.R. 266 (B.C. S.C.) (in particular at 289-91). This is not to say that Parliament should delegate the power to amend Acts as a matter of constitutional principle. For a discussion of this point see the annotation to the case at 268.
4 One Counsel to the Speaker of the House of Commons in the United Kingdom defined delegated legislation as "every exercise of a power to legislate conferred by or under an Act of Parliament or which is given the force of law by virtue of an Act of Parliament": *Statute Law Review*, Summer 1986, 115, fn 5.
5 *Royal Trust Corp. of Canada v. Law Society (Alberta)* (1985), 16 Admin. L.R. 317 (Alta. C.A.).

It goes without saying that subordinate legislation purportedly made without statutory authority is ineffective.[6]

The ability of Parliament and legislatures to delegate legislative power is constitutionally more restricted than in the United Kingdom.[7] Canada's federal system means that one level of the legislative branch (for example, the Federal Parliament) cannot delegate its law-making powers to the other level (for example, a provincial legislature). Similarly, the legislative branch cannot delegate such broad powers that it effectively effaces itself, nor can a provincial legislature delegate its legislative powers in such a way as to affect the Office of the Lieutenant Governor, or to breach section 96 of the *Constitution Act*.[8] Otherwise, however, there are no legal or constitutional limits on the ability of the legislative branch in Canada to delegate legislative powers, although again, political conventions do provide some common sense guide to what types of matters should be dealt with in parent legislation rather than in subordinate legislation.

3. Subdelegation

If legislation authorizes a delegate to make regulations, then the delegate must make them. The delegate cannot sub-delegate the law-making power without statutory authority to do so.[9]

4. Reasons for Subordinate Legislation

There are a variety of reasons for subordinate legislation, including:

(a) The sheer magnitude of the business of government means that not everything can be dealt with in parent legislation.

(b) The technical nature of much governmental activity requires that only

---

6 *Prospect Investments Ltd. v. New Brunswick (Liquor Licensing Board)* (1991), 48 Admin. L.R. 105 (N.B. Q.B.); *"Zamora" (The)*, [1916] 2 A.C. 77 (England P.C.); *Reference re Regulations (Chemical) under War Measures Act (Canada)*, [1943] S.C.R. 1 (S.C.C.) at 13; *Giant Grosmont Petroleums Ltd. v. Gulf Canada Resources Ltd.*, [2001] 10 W.W.R. 99 (Alta. C.A.), leave to appeal refused [2002] 1 S.C.R. vii (S.C.C.) at para. 17.

7 See Chapter 2.

8 30 & 31 Vict., c.3; reproduced with amendments in R.S.C. 1970, App. II, as further amended by the *Canada Act*, 1982 (U.K.) (31 Eliz. 2, c.11); also cited as the *Constitution Act*, 1982 (Can.).

9 *Canada (Attorney General) v. Brent*, [1956] S.C.R. 318 (S.C.C.); *Delight v. British Columbia (Egg Marketing Board)* (1991), 4 Admin. L.R. (2d) 31 (B.C. C.A.), leave to appeal refused (1992), 4 Admin. L.R. (2d) 31n (S.C.C.); *Dene Nation v. R.* (1984), 6 Admin. L.R. 268 (Fed. T.D.); *Normand v. Royal College of Dental Surgeons (Ontario)* (1985), 10 Admin. L.R. 196 (Ont. Div. Ct.); *Air Canada c. Dorval (Cité)* (1985), 13 Admin. L.R. 42 (S.C.C.), but contrast the delegation of administrative functions in *Forget c. Québec (Procureur général)* (1988), 32 Admin. L.R. 211 (S.C.C.). See also Keyes, *Executive Legislation* (Markam: Butterworths, 1992) at 252.

broad principles or a basic legislative framework can be contained in some Acts.

(c) The power to delegate to an administrator allows greater flexibility in applying statutory provisions to changing circumstances.

(d) The need for rapid governmental action may require faster administrative response than can be achieved by amending parent legislation.

(e) Innovation and experimentation in solving social problems may not be possible if parent legislation must be amended.

(f) Emerging situations or emergencies may require broad delegation of legislative powers with respect to a wide range of matters that would normally be dealt with in parent legislation.[10]

Regrettably, there is another reason for subordinate legislation – political expediency. This arises because the government of the day has not thought through how it will implement a legislative proposal (so it gives itself broad regulatory powers to do so in the future). Alternatively, when a government wishes to work out the implementation details of a legislative scheme with those most affected by the legislation, it may grant itself broad regulation-making powers.[11] Nor is it unknown for regulations to contain a particularly unpalatable provision which, if included in the parent Act, would have created a storm of protest in Parliament or a legislature. Although in many senses subordinate legislation is laudable and necessary in modern society, it can also have a dark side.[12]

5. The Growth of Subordinate Legislation

Subordinate legislation is by no means a new concept. One writer has traced the use of delegated powers to make law back to 1337[13] and a considerable amount of Government business was carried out by administrative regulations in the fifteenth and sixteenth[14] century in England. The modern

---

10 War is one example of an emergency. Alberta faced a volatile situation in the seventies in connection with energy development. The Legislature was of the opinion that the situation called for an extra-ordinary legislative response. See the former *Northeast Alberta Regional Commission Act*, R.S.A. 1980, c. N-8, rep. S.A. 1994, c. 23, s. 34, which permitted the Lieutenant Governor in Council to suspend, vary, or make inapplicable, by regulation, 12 Acts (including the *Municipal Government Act*, the *Planning Act*, and the *School Act* of the day).

11 See *Electric Utilities Act*, R.S.A. 2000, c. E-5.1, s. 94.

12 It is with respect to this dark side that Scrutiny Committees, where they exist, play such a vital role – bringing important matters to the attention of Parliament and legislatures – and to public attention. See discussion below.

13 The Hon. Justice V.C.R.A.C. Crabbe in *Statute Law Review*, Spring 1986, 4 at 5.

14 The *Statute of Wales* (1542) allowed Henry VIII to
    alter the laws of Wales and make ordinances for Wales, such alterations and new laws and ordinances to be published under the great seal and to be of as good strength, virtue and effect as if made by the authority of Parliament.

form of subordinate legislation – in the sense of an agent of the government making law as a result of powers conferred by Parliament – came into general use in the 19th century in the United Kingdom. A good example is the preamble to an 1832 Act to prevent the spread of cholera, which said:[15]

> Whereas it has pleased Almighty God to visit the United Kingdom with the disease called cholera . . . and whereas with a view to prevent as far as may be possible by the Divine Blessing the spreading of the said disease, it may be necessary that rules and regulations may from time to time be established within cities, towns or districts affected with or which may be threatened by the said disease, but it may be impossible to establish such rules and regulations by the authority of Parliament with sufficient promptitude to meet the exigency of any such case as may occur.

The technique of using subordinate legislation continued to grow through-out the 19th century in the United Kingdom. Writing at the turn of this century, Sir Courtney Ilbert said:[16]

> The increasing complexity of modern administration and the increas-ing difficulty of passing complicated measures through the ordeal of parliamentary discussion have led to an increase in the practice of delegating legislative power to executive authorities.

The benefits as well as the constitutional dilemma of delegated legislation were well summarized by the House of Commons (U.K.) Select Committee on Procedure:[17]

> The Executive is thereby freed from the necessity of introducing legislative proposals subject to the full parliamentary process; and Parliament is likewise freed from the obligation to subject such pro-posals to detailed scrutiny.

Canada and its provinces took to the concept of delegating legislative powers quickly.[18] The increasing volume of subordinate legislation, and its

---

15 Extracted from Miers and Page, *Legislation* (London: Sweet and Maxwell, 1990) at 106.

16 *Legislative Forms and Methods*, (1901) at 37.

17 First Report, H.C. 588-81 (1977-78) para. 3.3 (referred to in *Statute Law Review*, Summer 1986 at 114).

18 Holland and McGowan, *Delegated Legislation in Canada* (Toronto: Carswell, 1989) at 7 which records regulation making-powers being granted for the prevention of fires in the fifth statute enacted by the Parliament of Upper Canada in 1792. In Alberta, delegated powers were granted in the fourth Act to be passed by the Legislature (the *Public Service Act*, S.A. 1906, c. 4, s. 29).

increasingly varied forms, continue to challenge elected officials, administrators, the public-at-large, and professional advisors.[19]

6. Who Can Make Subordinate Legislation?

Parliament or a legislature may authorize virtually anyone, through its Acts, to make subordinate legislation.[20] Commonly, the Governor General in Council, Lieutenant Governor in Council, and Ministers are authorized to make regulations. But legislative powers are not infrequently delegated to Crown agencies.[21] Legislative powers are also often delegated to non-government agencies – professional bodies, like Provincial Law Societies and the Colleges of Physicians and Surgeons, to make regulations or bylaws governing their members. With the privatization of formerly government run institutions, even some law making powers are being delegated.[22]

7. Other Forms of Subordinate Legislation

Bylaws enacted by municipal councils are a form of subordinate legislation, because municipalities derive their powers from provincial legislation.[23] Not all bylaws are legislative in nature, and certain procedural requirements must be observed if they are properly characterized as being quasi-judicial.[24]

---

19 In 1977, the Joint Standing Committee of Parliament on Regulations estimated that there were more than 14,000 federal regulations then in force (more recent statistics are not readily available). In Alberta, it has been estimated that, in 2003, there were approximately 1,000 regulations in force. In 1990, the Parliament of Canada passed 54 statutes – in the same year 860 regulations were published in the Canada Gazette (Keys, *Executive Legislation, supra* note 9).

   In Alberta, in 2002, 42 public and private Acts were passed and 309 regulations were published in the Alberta Gazette.

   This is not just a Canadian phenomenon. In the United Kingdom during the 1980s, Parliament passed an average of 63 statutes a year and the average number of statutory instruments (just one form of delegated legislation) was approximately 2,000 a year. Miers and Page, *Legislation, supra* note 15 at 12, fn39. For other statistical information in the United Kingdom see "Making the Law", The Report of The Hansard Society Commission on The Legislative Process (1992).

   For a comment on the importance of subordinate legislation in Canada, see the Joint Committee's comments reproduced in the text accompanying note 131, in this chapter.

20 Subject to constitutional limitations mentioned earlier.

21 For example, broad regulation-making power is given to the Canadian Radio-television and Telecommunications Commission by the *Broadcasting Act*, S.C. 1991, c. 11. In Alberta, the Alberta Securities Commission has broad rule-making power, R.S.A. 2000, c. S-4, s. 224. Sometimes agencies are given regulation-making power subject to Governor in Council, Lieutenant Governor in Council, or Ministerial approval of the regulation. See for example regulations regarding security in connection with energy related matters, *Alberta Energy and Utilities Board Act*, R.S.A. 2000, c. A-17, s. 30(3).

22 See for example *Horse Racing Alberta Act*, R.S.A. 2000, c. H-11.3, s. 22, where regulation-making powers for horse racing, formerly exercised by the Lieutenant Governor in Council, are given to the Board of Directors of Horse Racing Alberta.

23 In Alberta, the *Municipal Government Act*, R.S.A. 2000, c. M-26.

24 See Chapter 3.

In Alberta, law-making powers have been delegated to Metis settlement councils.[25] Law-making powers have also been delegated to First Nations in British Columbia,[26] Quebec, and elsewhere. Self-government models, including the explicit delegation or recognition of law-making powers of First Nations, in one form or another, are likely to continue.[27]

Although in a category of their own, Federal legislation establishing the Yukon Territory, Northwest Territories and Nunavut delegates to Territorial jurisdictions law-making powers that are similar to Provincial legislative powers – although the Provincial jurisdiction is sovereign and the Territorial jurisdiction delegated.[28]

8. What Form Does Subordinate Legislation Take?

Unfortunately, subordinate legislation does not have one name, and even if it is given a particular name in one Act, the same kind of law may be given another name in another Act. Subordinate legislation is a hodgepodge of ordinances, regulations, rules, codes, bylaws, and sometimes even directives and policies. Names given to particular forms of subordinate legislation cannot be relied on for any purpose.

For the most part, this chapter is concerned with a particular form of subordinate legislation – the kind that falls within the meaning of "regulation".[29]

9. Examples of the Power to Enact Subordinate Legislation

Most significant Acts contain a regulation-making power, but the ambit within which the delegate may make regulations varies greatly from Act to Act. Sometimes the delegate is only empowered to make a regulation on a single topic – for example, the ability of the Lieutenant Governor in Council to designate the dates within which daylight savings time is to be observed each year in British Columbia[30]; or the establishment of a classification appeal board to settle disputes about the classification of civil service jobs under the *Public Service Act* (Alberta).[31]

---

25 *Metis Settlements Act*, R.S.A. 2000, c. M-14, Schedule 1.
26 *Sechelt Indian Band Self-Government Act*, S.C. 1986, c. 27.
27 We leave aside the inherent right of self-government claimed by First Nations and what it means in terms of law-making powers, but note its recognition in political statements and legislation throughout Canada.
28 For a discussion of the constitutional status of the Territories, see B.L. Willis, "*Bradash v. Warren*: Further Judicial Observations on the Constitutional Status of the Northern Territories" (1990-91) 4 C.J.A.L.P. at 175.
29 For the definition of "regulations", see later in this chapter.
30 *Interpretation Act*, R.S.B.C. 1996, c. 238, ss. 25(7), 26(a).
31 R.S.A. 2000, c. P-42, s. 12(1)(a).

On the other hand, some Acts delegate broad regulation-making power, like section 27 of the *Transportation of Dangerous Goods Act 1992* (Canada),[32] which among other things says,

27.(1) The Governor in Council may make regulations generally for carrying out the purposes and provisions of this Act, including regulations

    (a) prescribing products, substances and organisms to be included in the classes listed in the schedule . . .

    (g) prescribing circumstances in which any activity or thing is under the sole direction or control of the Minister of National Defence;

    (h) prescribing circumstances in which dangerous goods must not be handled, offered for transport or transported;

    (i) prescribing dangerous goods that must not be handled, offered for transport or transported in any circumstances;

    (j) prescribing safety marks, safety requirements and safety standards of general or particular application;

    (k) prescribing quantities or concentrations of dangerous goods in relation to which emergency response assistance plans must be approved under section 7. . . .

At the extreme, Parliament or a legislature may delegate such broad regulation-making power[33] that it is impossible to determine to what or to whom the Act applies, or how the administrative system in question operates, without reference to regulations dealing with substantive matters.

The Environmental Protection and Enhancement Act (Alberta)[34] provides a good example. Section 60 says that no person shall knowingly commence or continue any activity designated by the regulations as requiring an approval or registration, unless that person holds the appropriate approval or registration. An "activity" means an activity or part of an activity listed in the Schedule to the Act – but without looking at the regulations a person will not know whether an approval is required for a particular activity or not. For major legislation, this kind of approach is becoming more the rule than the exception.

A trend can now be seen which allows delegated legislation not only to deal with detail but with substance. Acts are occasionally seen that authorize regulations to be made that in effect amend not only the parent[35] Act but regulations made under other Acts as well.[36]

But even the broadest of Canadian delegated legislative powers pales in comparison to the *European Communities Act 1972* (UK) which empowers

---

32 S.C. 1992, c. 34.

33 For examples of some of the more common forms of Federal regulation-making power, see the second edition of E.A. Driedger, *Construction of Statutes* (Toronto: Butterworths, 1983) at 327.

34 R.S.A. 2000, c. E-12.

35 *Electric Utilities Act*, R.S.A. 2000, c. E-5.1, s. 142(2)(f) and (g).

36 See for example *Municipal Government Act*, R.S.A. 2000, c. M-26, ss. 585, 586(c).

the UK Government to legislate by statutory instrument to implement any European Community obligation of the United Kingdom. The closest Canadian equivalent might occur if Canada's obligations under the *North American Free Trade Agreement* could be implemented by Federal and Provincial regulations.

10. Subordinate Legislation is as Effective as Parent Legislation

Do not be misled by the name "subordinate" or "delegated" legislation into supposing that it is inferior, less important, or less effective than parent legislation. On the one hand, the doctrine of *ultra vires* applies to require the delegate to enact subordinate legislation within the constraints prescribed by the parent Act.[37] On the other hand, if this requirement is met, or if the regulation is both within the general purposes of the Act and within the general terms of the regulation-making authority[38] the subordinate legislation is as valid and effective as if it had been enacted by Parliament or a legislature itself.[39]

---

37 For example, see:
> (1) *Keough v. Memorial University of Newfoundland* (1980), 26 Nfld. & P.E.I.R. 386 (Nfld. T.D.), where the university was held not to have the power to make bylaws restricting parking;
> (2) *Herman Brothers Ltd. v. Regina (City)* (1977), [1978] 1 W.W.R. 97 (Sask. C.A.), where bylaws charging for services delivered outside the city were held to be invalid;
> (3) *British Columbia (Attorney General) v. Knapp*, [1971] 5 W.W.R. 727 (B.C. S.C.), where the city's power to regulate use of streets was held not to encompass the right to prohibit distribution of written material;
> (4) *Affleck v. Nelson (City)* (1957), 23 W.W.R. 386 (B.C. S.C.), where there was no power to declare a street a monument;
> (5) *Canadian Freightways Ltd. v. Calgary (City)* (1967), 58 W.W.R 601 (Alta. S.C.), where the power to license businesses was held not to give the right to license vehicles used by the business;
> (6) *Pacific Pilotage Authority v. Alaska Trainship Corp.*, [1981] 1 S.C.R. 261 (S.C.C.), where a requirement for compulsory pilots for U.S. ships was struck down.

For an example of an *ultra vires* exercise of delegated power which might or might not be legislative in nature, see the Fifteenth Report of the Joint Standing Committee on Regulations and Other Statutory Instruments to the First Session of the 32nd Parliament, 1980-81-82-83, dated 5 May 1983, relating to the exercise by the Minister of Indian and Northern Affairs of his power under the former s.12(1)(a)(iv) of the *Indian Act*, R.S.C. 1985, c. I-5, to exempt certain persons from various provisions of the Act, thereby effectively amending the Act.

38 See *Giant Grosmont Petroleums Ltd. v. Gulf Canada Resources Ltd.*, [2001] 10 W.W.R. 99 (Alta. C.A.), leave to appeal refused [2002] 1 S.C.R. vii (S.C.C.) where it was held that regulation-making powers can be inferred if the regulation is within the purposes of the statute and within the "sphere" of statutory authority authorizing the regulation [para. 39], adopting *British Columbia (Mill Board) v. Grisnich*, [1995] 2 S.C.R. 895 (S.C.C.) at para 19-20.

39 At one time it was the practice in the United Kingdom (and in some early Canadian Acts) to say that delegated legislation had the same force as if contained in an Act. This is not necessary and does not protect the subordinate legislation from an *ultra vires* challenge. See Bennion, *Statutory Interpretation:a Code*, 3d ed. (London, Toronto: Butterworths, 1997).

The validity of subordinate legislation was explicitly recognized by the Supreme Court of Canada in *McKay v. R.*[40] when Mr. Justice Cartwright said:

> ... if an enactment, whether of Parliament or of a legislature or of a subordinate body to which legislative power is delegated, is capable of receiving a meaning according to which its operation is restricted to matters within the power of the enacting body it shall be interpreted accordingly.

The constitutional relationship between parent and subordinate legislation bothered Harvey C.J.A. in *Crédit foncier franco-canadien v. Ross*:[41]

> It is important also to note that s. 92 [*Constitution Act*, 1867] author-izes and therefore makes valid only legislation by a Provincial Leg-islature and it is no doubt because of that fact that the power of disallowance given to the Governor-General in Council has reference only to Acts of Provincial Legislatures [as opposed to subordinate legislation]. If there could be legislation by Orders in Council or in some other way than by Act of the Legislature there would be no power reserved in the Governor-General to disallow it.[42]

The full force of this logic would be to prevent any use of subordinate legislation by provincial legislatures. This view is simply not sustainable in light of the recognition by the Privy Council in *Hodge v. R.*[43], and other authorities, of the right of provincial legislatures to delegate all or some of their powers, even if legislative in nature. But it does point out the concern that some legislative enactments should be regarded as so important that they should be debated openly in Parliament before enactment, that they should not be contained in subordinate legislation, and that Parliament and legislatures should supervise how their delegates exercise delegated law-making powers.

Not surprisingly, the principles of statutory interpretation apply equally to regulations[44] although for some forms of subordinate legislation (like munic-ipal bylaws) the courts have developed some distinct interpretive approaches.

---

40   [1965] S.C.R. 798 at 803 (S.C.C.). For additional comment on the presumption of validity of subordinate legislation, see P.A. Côté, *The Interpretation of Legislation in Canada*, 3d ed. (Toronto: Carswell, 2000) at 369-72; and *Waddell v. British Columbia (Governor in Council)* (1983), 8 Admin. L.R. 266 (B.C. S.C.).

41   [1937] 3 D.L.R. 365 at 369 (Alta. C.A.).

42   [1937] 3 D.L.R. 365 at 369 (Alta. C.A.).

43   (1883), (1883-84) LR 9 App. Cas. 117 (Ontario P.C.).

44   Côté, *The Interpretation of Legislation in Canada*, *supra* note 40 at 24-26. For observations on the principles to be applied see *Giant Grosmont Petroleums Ltd. v. Gulf Canada Resources Ltd.*, [2001] 10 W.W.R. 99 (Alta. C.A.), leave to appeal refused [2002] 1 S.C.R. vii (S.C.C.) at paras. 18-21.

11. The Preparation of Regulations

What process should a delegate follow in developing subordinate legislation? On first thought the delegate is in precisely the same position as any
other delegate who exercises discretionary powers to which the duty to be fair
applies. After all, the content of subordinate legislation is a matter of discretion.

However, in the absence of a specific statutory requirement for pre-publication of proposed regulations, judicial review is not available to challenge
the procedure used in developing legislation, whether parent or subordinate in
nature.[45] Indeed, in the sequel to the *Campeau* case,[46] the Alberta Court of
Appeal specifically excluded the availability of judicial review because a
legislative function was involved in the enactment of a municipal by-law. The
same point was made by D.C. McDonald J. in *Alberta v. Beaver (County No.
9)*,[47] involving the unsuccessful attempt to quash first reading of a municipal
by-law, and by Megarry J. in *Bates v. Lord Hailsham of St. Marylebone*,[48]
which involved the proclamation of a new tariff of solicitors' fees.

The circumstances in which Parliament or a provincial legislature chooses
to delegate legislative powers are many and varied. While it is not easy to
establish model procedures for consulting parties who might be affected by
subordinate legislation, it is clear that Parliament and legislatures should carefully consider whether consultation should take place, and in what form, when
considering the parent legislation itself.[49]

Some parent legislation requires regulations to be tabled in the House of
Commons or a provincial Legislative Assembly. In some cases, a legislative
body must specifically affirm the regulations in order to bring them into force.[50]
In other cases, the regulations automatically come into force after a certain
delay unless vetoed by a negative resolution of the House of Commons or a
Legislative Assembly.[51] Each of these systems provides a limited measure of

---

45   But see notes 60 and 168, below.

46   *Campeau Corp. v. Calgary (City)* (1980), 112 D.L.R. (3d) 737 (Alta. C.A.).

47   (1982), 20 Alta. L.R. (2d) 78 (Alta. Q.B.), reversed [1984] 4 W.W.R. 371 (Alta. C.A.).

48   [1972] 1 W.L.R. 1373 (Eng. Ch. Div.).

49   See Pt. E of the Fourth Report of the Scrutiny Committee, entitled "Drafting of Enabling
Powers and of Subordinate Laws" at 357*ff*, where the Scrutiny Committee recommends that
all enabling clauses in parent legislation should be referred to it prior to enactment.

50   The Scrutiny Committee states that it could only find two examples of federal statutes
requiring positive affirmation by Parliament to bring subordinate legislation into force: s. 18
of the *Government Organization Act*, R.S.C. 1970, c. 14 (2nd Supp.); and s. 4(2) of the
Unemployment Insurance Act, 1971, S.C. 1970-71-72, c. 48. See the Fourth Report at 340.

51   The federal Scrutiny Committee could only find twenty-one instances in all federal legislation
in force at the end of the 1976-77 Session where Parliament was afforded the opportunity to
disallow a statutory instrument or to prevent its coming into or continuing in force by refusing
to affirm it: see the Fourth Report at 337, 368-70. Other jurisdictions, such as the United
Kingdom and Australia, have general rules permitting motions to disallow subordinate
legislation to be brought to the floor of Parliament quite easily: see App. III to the fourth
Report at 382-84. Indeed, in 1975-76, the British House of Commons debated 92 motions
for disallowance of subordinate legislation (Fourth Report at 342). The Scrutiny Committee
was subsequently given power to require Parliament to positively affirm a regulation referred
to it by the Committee: see the discussion in the text following note 126, below.

pre-publication and control, and an opportunity for interested persons to make comments on the content and form of the proposed regulations.[52]

The quality of regulations will usually be improved as a result of publicity and comment by those likely to be affected by them. The public policy rationale underlying both the *audi alteram partem* rule and the duty to be fair appears to apply to subordinate legislation as well as to judicial, quasi-judicial or other discretionary powers that are subject to judicial review on procedural grounds. The desirability of prior consultation with affected persons is only occasionally recognized by Parliament and legislatures. Federally, some draft rules and regulations must be published and circulated before their final implementation: for example, in the *Tax Court of Canada Act*;[53] the *Broadcasting Act*;[54] and the *Canada Post Corporation Act*.[55] A system of prior consultation has long been the standard practice of the United States federal government under their *Administrative Procedures Act*,[56] and was strengthened by the *Negotiated Rulemaking Act 1991*.

Since 1983, the Federal Government has significantly improved the public consultation process by which it develops regulations. Based on Federal Government policies there is now a reasonably consistent process for publishing draft regulations, providing a Regulatory Impact Analysis Statement based on the draft, and limiting how quickly regulations are enacted after the draft is published. Although the process is not mandatory, it is followed and seems to be firmly entrenched.[57]

Note that the *Interpretation Act (Canada)*, R.S.C. 1985, c. I-21, s. 39 specifies the procedure to be used for affirmative or negative resolutions and the effect of those resolutions.

In a comparatively rare provision, Alberta regulations are permitted to be made by the Lieutenant-Governor in Council "for any matter that the Minister considers is not provided for or insufficiently provided for" in the *Municipal Government Act*, R.S.A. 2000, c. M-26, s. 603. The regulations last for a maximum of 2 years, giving the Government an opportunity to introduce appropriate legislation to deal with the matter.

52   The Scrutiny Committee called the procedure for determining the substance of subordinate legislation "truly the secret garden of the Crown" (Fourth Report at 343). It noted the increased requirement of pre-publication of draft subordinate legislation, and also the study by the Economic Council of Canada as to the need to know the impact of proposed subordinate legislation of a "social nature". It also noted how the U.S. system operates, and that the U.K. had abandoned its pre-publication scheme with the enactment of its *Statutory Instruments Act*, 1946 (9 & 10 Geo. 6, c. 36), in favour of a more comprehensive *ex post facto* scrutiny.

53   R.S.C. 1985, c. T-2, s. 22.

54   S.C. 1991, c. 11, s. 8.

55   R.S.C. 1985, c. C-10, s. 20.

56   The U.S. *Federal Administrative Procedure Act*, 5 U.S.C.A., ss. 551-556. See W. Gellhorn and C. Byse, *Administrative Law*, 8th ed. (Mineola: The Foundation Press, 1987). See also K.C. Davis, *Administrative Law*, (St. Paul: West Publishing Co., 1973), Chapters 11 and 12. And see also the discussion of the operation of the U.S. Act in App. V of the Fourth Report of the (Canadian) Federal Joint Standing Committee of the Senate and House of Commons on Regulations and Other Statutory Instruments (the "Scrutiny Committee") (17th July 1980), and contained in Hansard at 328*ff* as App. B to the proceedings of that day (referred to as the "Fourth Report"). Note that both the Fourth Report and the Second Report were published under separate cover. Page references here are to the versions published in Hansard.

57   See notes 60 and 168, below. See also *Submission to the Subcommittee on Bill C-25, the Regulations Act for the Standing Committee on Justice and Legal Affairs of the House of*

Quebec has a general pre-publication notice of regulations-in-process.[58] Although other Provinces have consultation policies of one sort or another they tend to be ineffective because they depend entirely on political and bureaucratic will to enforce the policy. The next decade will likely see a considerable amount of legislative activity to require consultation of one sort or another, particularly for regulations.[59]

12. The Filing and Publication of Regulations

Unlike parent legislation, which is enacted after three readings in a public forum, subordinate legislation is usually enacted relatively privately.[60] Consequently, it is important to have a scheme so that the public can determine the existence and content of subordinate legislation. All jurisdictions[61] in Canada require at least some of their subordinate legislation to be filed or registered in central registries, and to be published in an official gazette, before coming into force. Different jurisdictions, however, adopt somewhat different definitions of which "regulations" are subject to registration or filing, and publication, and provide for exceptions to both requirements.

In most provinces,[62] the method for making regulations accessible is based on a *Uniform Regulations Act*, recommended in 1943 by the Conference of Commissioners on the Uniformity of Legislation in Canada.[63] Although a number of provinces, including Alberta, have modified the original uniform

---

Commons Concerning Bill C-25, the Regulations Act (First Reading), March 22, 1996, presented by Philip Anisman on November 19, 1996, reproduced at (1997) 6 R.A.L. 73.

58 For a description of the Canadian, Quebec and Victoria (Australia) processes for consultation in rule-making, see Craven, "Consultation in Rule-Making – Some Lessons from Australia" (1990-91) 4 C.J.A.L.P. 221. And see also Holland and McGowan, *Delegated Legislation in Canada, supra* note 18 at 14-16.

59 For an argument that the *Charter of Rights and Freedoms* seeks and reinforces the need for participation in certain regulatory processes and decisions, see M. Jackman, "Rights and Participation: The Use of the *Charter* to Supervise the Regulatory Process" (1990-91) 4 C.J.A.L.P. 23. For the contrary view, see Keyes, *Executive Legislation, supra* note 9 at 97-98. For U.S. activity in the field see the *Act of Congress – Negotiated Rulemaking Act,* 1991, and for other Canadian comment see H.N. Janisch, "Tribunals and the Law" (1988-89) 2 C.J.A.L.P. 263 at 278 and Holland and McGowan, *Delegated Legislation in Canada, supra* note 18 at 142.

For Australian Commonwealth proposals see: Administrative Review Council: Rule Making by Commonwealth Agencies (1992), Report No. 35. For an example of a compulsory waiting period for regulatory review, see *Safety Codes Act* (Alberta), R.S.A. 2000, C. s-1, S. 65(3).

60 Municipal bylaws are an exception. They require three readings in public and sometimes are subject to public notice and hearing process requirements.

61 For a description, see Holland and McGowan, *Delegated Legislation in Canada, supra* note 18, Chapter 3.

62 For the differences among the provinces, see Holland and McGowan, *Delegated Legislation in Canada, supra* note 18 at 20-32.

63 Now called the Uniform Law Conference of Canada. The *Uniform Regulations Act* recommended in 1943, and the 1982 changes, are reproduced in Holland and McGowan, *Delegated Legislation in Canada, supra* note 18 at 297.

Act, based on recommendations made by the Uniform Law Conference in 1982, the basic elements of the 1943 proposal remain largely unchanged.

The applicable Alberta and federal legislation is now examined, in particular: (a) the definition of the "regulations" to which each system applies; (b) the filing or registration of regulations in a central public registry; and (c) the publication of regulations.

(a) What is a "Regulation"?

(i) The Alberta Definition of "Regulation"

In Alberta, there is a rather tortuous trail to find what a "regulation" is. The *Regulations Act*[64] defines "regulation" as follows:

> "regulation" means a regulation as defined in the *Interpretation Act* that is of a legislative nature;

The *Interpretation Act*[65] defines "regulation" as

> (c) "regulation" means a regulation, order, rule, form, tariff of costs or fees, proclamation, by-law or resolution enacted
>
> > (i) in the execution of a power conferred by or under the authority of an Act, or
> >
> > (ii) by or under the authority of the Lieutenant Governor in Council,
>
> but does not include an order of a court made in the course of an action or an order made by a public officer or administrative tribunal in a dispute between 2 or more persons;

But this is not the end of the trail because the *Regulations Act* (having adopted the *Interpretation Act* definition of regulation) then exempts certain things from being regulations under the *Regulations Act*, including bylaws, proclamations and documents adopted or incorporated by reference in a regulation.[66] In addition, other Alberta legislation from time to time excludes the *Regulations Act* from applying to regulations.[67] The end result is that the following are regulations in Alberta:

> regulations, orders, rules, forms, tariffs of costs or fees, bylaws and resolutions that are
>
> • of a legislative nature, and
>
> • enacted under or by an Act, or by the Lieutenant Governor in Council.

---

64 R.S.A. 2000, c. R-14, s. 1(1)(f).
65 R.S.A. 2000, c. I-8, s. 1(1)(c).
66 R.S.A. 2000, c. R-14, s. 1(2).
67 See note 69, below.

The following are not regulations under the *Regulations Act*:

- court orders

- orders made by a public officer or administrative tribunal in a dispute between 2 or more persons

- regulations, rules, orders, bylaws and resolutions made by local authorities,[68] and public or private corporations

- policies of the Metis Settlements General Council incorporated under the *Metis Settlements Act*

- proclamations

- documents adopted or incorporated by reference in a regulation (this might include, for example, various building and health and safety codes that theoretically are readily accessible through other means).

Even though some forms of subordinate legislation fall within the "regulation" definition, the *Regulations Act* does not apply to them if

- the regulations are exempted from the application of the *Regulations Act* by the Lieutenant Governor in Council under section 8(1)(g) of the Act, or

- another Act says that the *Regulations Act* does not apply to them.[69]

The power of the Lieutenant Governor in Council to exempt regulations from the application of the *Regulations Act* provides a means to validate regulations that would otherwise be ineffective as a result of a failure to file them.

The requirement that a regulation must be "of a legislative nature" was considered by the Ontario Court of Appeal in *Rose v. R.*[70] where the Court said:

> We are all of the opinion that the Order in question in this appeal is an act of a legislative and not of an administrative character. We have come to that conclusion upon a consideration of the terms of the Order in Council and of the legislation pursuant to which it was enacted. . . .
>
> The action of the Lieutenant-Governor in Council, as set out in the Order in Council referred to, in our opinion, clearly is of a legislative nature as I have said. We think that to an extent generally applicable to the public or large segments thereof it alters rights and

---

68   "Local authorities" includes municipalities, health regions, school boards, and various other local jurisdictions (R.S.A. 2000, c. R-14, s. 1(1)(b)).

69   For example, the *Engineering, Geological and Geophysical Professions Act*, R.S.A. 2000, c. E-11, s. 20(4), and the *Securities Act* R.S.A. 2000, c. S-4, s. 224(5).

70   (1960), 22 D.L.R. (2d) 633 at 634-36 (Ont. C.A.).

responsibilities and even the nature and extent of those responsibilities. Upon that ground alone we think sufficient has been said to indicate the legislative nature of the action taken by the Lieutenant-Governor in Council as set out in the Order in Council referred to. . . . In coming to a conclusion as to the nature of the act performed, not only must one look at the substance rather than the form but indeed in the inquiry upon which one must embark, all the surrounding circumstances must be looked at and by that I include the nature of the body enacting the Order in question, the subject-matter of the Order, the rights and responsibilities, if any, altered or changed by that Order. Significant in our opinion among these indicia to be considered in a determination of the legal question, is the fact that the Order here under review is an Order made formally by the Lieutenant-Governor in Council upon the recommendation of one of the Ministers of the Crown. That is to say it is an Order made by the executive of the Government and an Order that the executive could not have made unless the power to make it had been delegated to it by the Legislature. While this is not decisive it is, as I have said, one of the factors not without importance in the determination of the question.

It is important to keep in mind the distinction between delegated powers which are legislative in function and those which are merely legislative in form. Not all Orders in Council, for example, constitute subordinate legislation.[71] Conversely, not all subordinate legislation is enacted by an Order in Council (even if the power is granted to the Governor in Council)[72] – and as

---

71 See App. I to the federal Scrutiny Committee's Fourth Report, entitled "Subordinate Law, Orders in Council, 'Ministerial Orders', Regulations, Statutory Instruments and Official Documents" at 376-81.

72 The Scrutiny Committee noted at 337 of its Fourth Report:

> In Canada most regulations, and hence subordinate laws, are made by Order in Council of the Governor in Council. It is, therefore, commonly said that the regulations are made by the Cabinet. Your Committee thinks it important to place on public record that this is not strictly so. Since the Governor General does not preside at his Council, his assent to an Order in Council follows upon its earlier approval by Cabinet members. Very few draft regulations are actually considered by the Cabinet as a deliberative body. Some of these are first considered by Cabinet Subcommittees. By far the greatest number of regulations is recommended for His Excellency's approval by the Special Committee of Council which consists of ten Ministers with a quorum of four. The extent to which draft regulations are scrutinized as to policy, legality and propriety by the Special Committee will depend upon its membership. The decision as to whether a regulation should be considered by a Cabinet Committee or direct by the Cabinet rests fundamentally with the sponsoring Minister according to his view of the regulation's importance and implications. Occasionally, the Cabinet itself may decide that particular regulations when drafted should come before it. Your Committee records this information merely to disabuse the Houses and the public, if that be necessary, of the notion that all the Cabinet members turn their collective attention to each of the thousand and more regulations made each year. The way in which regulations by Order in Council are in fact made gives but little support to the view that there are safeguards in vesting subordinate law making powers in the Governor in Council rather than in individual Ministers. Furthermore, it

mentioned earlier, sometimes the power is granted to someone else entirely, such as the Benchers of the Law Society.[73]

It is for the registrar of regulations to decide,[74] in the first instance, whether any document, presented for filing is a regulation within the meaning of the *Regulations Act*. The registrar must refuse to file a regulation if a "Regulation Impact Report" has not been submitted and approved by the Chair of the Regulatory Reform Task Force, unless the requirement is waived.[75]

(ii) The Federal Definition of "Regulation"

The *Statutory Instruments Act* (Canada) has a more complicated scheme for determining which instruments must be registered and published as regulations. The federal definition of "regulation" reads as follows:[76]

2(1) . . . "regulation" means a statutory instrument

(a) made in the exercise of a legislative power conferred by or under an Act of Parliament, or

(b) for the contravention of which a penalty, fine or imprisonment is prescribed by or under an Act of Parliament,

and includes a rule, order or regulation governing the practice or procedure in any proceedings before a judicial or quasi-judicial body established by or under an Act of Parliament, and any instrument described as a regulation in any other Act of Parliament;

With one exception,[77] a regulation must be a "statutory instrument", which in turn is defined in the following way:[78]

"statutory instrument"

(a) means any rule, order, regulation, ordinance, direction, form, tariff of costs or fees, letters patent, commission, warrant, proclamation, by-law, resolution or other instrument issued, made or established

(i) in the execution of a power conferred by or under an Act of Parliament, by or under which that instrument is ex-

---

does nothing to satisfy the need for scrutiny of subordinate laws both as proposed and as made, by the public and particularly by Parliament.

73 *Legal Profession Act*, R.S.A. 2000, c. L-8, ss. 7, 8. Sometimes the delegate can only enact subordinate legislation if it is approved by the Lieutenant Governor in Council, e.g., the *Architects Act*, R.S.A. 2000, c. A-44, s. 9(2), or after consultation with another body, e.g., the *Engineering, Geological and Geophysical Professions Act*, R.S.A. 2000, c. E-11, s. 19(2).

74 *Regulations Act*, R.S.A. 2000, c. R-14, s. 5(1). There is also a reversal of decision process in s. 5(5).

75 Alberta Regulation A.R. 288/99, as amended, s. 3.

76 R.S.C. 1985, c. S-22 s. 2(1).

77 *Ibid*. s. 2(2).

78 *Ibid*. s. 2(1), definition of statutory instrument.

pressly authorized to be issued, made or established otherwise than by the conferring on any person or body of powers or functions in relation to a matter to which that instrument relates, or

(ii) by or under the authority of the Governor in Council, otherwise than in the execution of a power conferred by or under an Act of Parliament,

but

(b) does not include

(i) any instrument referred to in paragraph (a) and issued, made or established by a corporation incorporated by or under an Act of Parliament unless

(A) the instrument is a regulation and the corporation by which it is made is one that is ultimately accountable, through a Minister, to Parliament for the conduct of its affairs, or

(B) the instrument is one for the contravention of which a penalty, fine or imprisonment is prescribed by or under an Act of Parliament,

(ii) any instrument referred to in paragraph (a) and issued, made or established by a judicial or quasi-judicial body, unless the instrument is a rule, order or regulation governing the practice or procedure in proceedings before a judicial or quasi-judicial body established by or under an Act of Parliament,

(iii) any instrument referred to in paragraph (a) and in respect of which, or in respect of the production or other disclosure of which, any privilege exists by law or whose contents are limited to advice or information intended only for use or assistance in the making of a decision or the determination of policy, or in the ascertainment of any matter necessarily incidental thereto, or

(iv) an ordinance of the Northwest Territories, a law made by the Legislature of Yukon or the Legislature for Nunavut, a rule made by the Legislative Assembly of Yukon under section 16 of the *Yukon Act* or by the Legislative Assembly of Nunavut under section 21 of the *Nunavut Act* or any instrument issued, made or established under any such ordinance, law or rule.

The complicated federal scheme of identifying subordinate legislation governed by the registration and publishing system has been criticised.[79] However, the Federal Act goes considerably further in providing a vehicle for parliamentary scrutiny of delegated legislation than its typical Provincial equivalents.

(b) Filing or Registration of Regulations

The Alberta Act requires every regulation to be filed in duplicate with the registrar of regulations and specifies that, unless a later day is provided,[80]

a regulation comes into force on the day it is filed with the registrar[81] and in no case does the regulation come into force before the day of filing

Regulations that are not filed under the *Regulations Act* have no effect unless they are exempted from filing by the Act or another Act.[82] Registration requirements for regulations under the *Statutory Instruments Act* (Canada)[83] are similar to Alberta's filing requirements, but with three important additions. First, the federal scheme requires a pre-implementation examination of each federal regulation[84] by the Clerk of the Privy Council in consultation with the Deputy Minister of Justice to ensure that

3.(2) . . .

   (a) it is authorized by the statute pursuant to which it is to be made;

   (b) it does not constitute an unusual or unexpected use of the authority pursuant to which it is to be made;

   (c) it does not trespass unduly on existing rights and freedoms and is not, in any case, inconsistent with the purposes and provisions of the *Canadian Charter of Rights and Freedoms* and the *Canadian Bill of Rights*; and

   (d) the form and draftsmanship of the proposed regulation are in accordance with established standards.

---

79 The Fourth Report of the Scrutiny Committee strongly criticizes the federal definition of a "statutory instrument" and the distinction between it and a "regulation", and recommends a new definition along the lines originally proposed by the MacGuigan Committee: see paras. 56-65.

80 R.S.A. 2000, c. R-14, s. 2.

81 The registrar of regulations appointed by the Lieutenant Governor in Council under s. 7, *ibid.*

82 *Ibid.* s. 2(3). It is not uncommon to find Acts saying that the *Regulations Act* does not apply to a particular instrument.

83 R.S.C. 1985, c. S-22.

84 *Ibid.* s. 3, but note the exception provided for by s. 3(4).

The Deputy Minister of Justice is required to draw the attention of the regulation-making authority to any problem arising under these headings. There is nothing in the Act requiring the regulation-making authority to take account of criticism, although in practice the draft regulations probably would be amended before being made. In any event, no regulation is invalid only because it was not examined before implementation by the Deputy Minister of Justice, although the Governor in Council has the power to revoke such a regulation in whole or in part.[85]

Second, all federal regulations are required to be registered within seven days of their having been made[86] unless an exemption has been granted. In Alberta, there is no time limit for filing, although lack of filing will usually prevent the regulation from coming into effect.[87]

Third, unlike the Alberta Act, the federal scheme specifically provides a method for permitting regulations to come into force before their date of registration. This may occur if one of the following conditions is met:[88]

> 9(1) . . .
>
> (a) [the regulation] expressly states that it comes into force on a day earlier than that day and it is registered within seven days after it is made, or
>
> (b) [the regulation] is of a class that . . . is exempted [from filing][89]

In any of these cases, the regulation-making authority is required to advise the Clerk of the Privy Council in writing of the reasons why it was not practical to wait to bring the regulation into force on the date of registration.[90]

(c) Effect of Failure to File or Register Regulations

What is the legal effect of failing to register or file a regulation in accordance with the applicable legislation? In Alberta, an unfiled regulation has no effect whatever and will not be recognized by a court.[91] As Dêchene J. said in *C.S.A. of A. v. Farran (No. 2):*[92]

---

85 *Ibid.* s. 8.

86 *Ibid.* s. 5.

87 Section 2(2) of the *Regulations Act* (Alberta), provides that no regulation comes into force before being filed. However, s. 8(1)(g) of the Alberta Act provides a method for avoiding the filing requirement in certain circumstances.

88 R.S.C. 1985, c. S-22, s. 9(1).

89 In which case it comes into effect on the day it was made, or on such later date as is specified in the regulation.

90 R.S.C. 1985, c. S-22, s. 9(2).

91 See note 87.

92 (1977), 2 A.R. 500 at 504 (Alta. T.D.), affirmed [1979] 3 W.W.R. 385 (Alta. C.A.). The *Regulations Act*, R.S.A. 2000, c. R-14, s. 2(3) provides that unless otherwise provided to the contrary in another Act, a regulation not filed as provided in the *Regulations Act* has no effect.

It has not been filed and promulgated as a Regulation under the *Regulations Act* [R.S.A. 1970, c. 318], the filing of which is a prerequisite to its effectiveness under section 3 of the *Regulations Act*. It is, in my view, merely an internal document for the guidance of members of the Public Service. Indeed, the evidence before me indicates that it can be altered or disregarded, at least in part, on verbal or written instructions from the Commissioner.

A different result, however, was reached by the Federal Court of Appeal in *Melville (City) v. Canada (Attorney General)*,[93] which held the corresponding obligation under the federal Act to be merely directory and not mandatory, so that failure to register did not invalidate the Order in Council in question. It may be possible to distinguish these two cases in light of the much weaker filing requirement contained in the federal Act, which permits *ex post facto* filing as well as retroactive regulations, unlike the peremptory terms of the Alberta Act, which specifically states that no regulation has any effect until filed. The statement by the Alberta court certainly reinforces the policy of the Alberta legislation.

As noted earlier, the Alberta Act contains a provision[94] which permits the Lieutenant Governor in Council to enact regulations exempting any regulations from the provisions of the Act. The exempting regulation must itself be filed and otherwise comply with the *Regulations Act*,[95] and then relieves the regulation to which it applies from the consequences of non-filing. The ability to pass exempting regulations reinforces the view that the Alberta courts have correctly construed the mandatory nature of the filing requirement when no exemption has been enacted.

Obviously, the date of filing a regulation will usually precede the date of its publication, and may also precede the date upon which it is brought to the actual notice of a person affected by it. To this extent, therefore, it may be true that a person cannot be affected retroactively by a regulation if it cannot take effect before filing.[96] On the other hand, it is possible for a regulation to affect matters or to change the law with respect to a point in time before the date of filing. Although such a regulation will only become effective on the date of

---

93   (1982), 141 D.L.R. (3d) 191 (Fed. C.A.), reversing (1981), 129 D.L.R. (3d) 488 (Fed. T.D.).

94   R.S.A. 2000, c. R-14, s. 8(1)(g).

95   Alberta Regulation A.R. 288/99, s. 17, as amended, lists the regulations exempted from the provisions of the *Regulations Act*. In addition, other regulations have been exempted from publication (although they must be filed with the registrar of regulations). See the Index of Regulations to The Alberta Gazette.

96   Unless exempted from filing pursuant to s. 8 of the Act. Also, it is fairly common for an effective date to be different from the date of filing:

   (1) A regulation may specify an effective date in the future after filing (s. 2(2) of the *Regulations Act*).

   (2) Under the *Interpretation Act*, R.S.A. 2000, c. I-8, s. 7, regulations can be made and filed under an unproclaimed Act, but will only come into force on proclamation of the Act.

   (3) If the regulation specifies no date for effectiveness, it becomes effective on filing (s. 2(2) of the *Regulations Act* (Alberta)).

filing, it can, from that moment, validly alter the preceding law retrospec-tively.[97] Accordingly, the Alberta Act does not exclude the possibility of retrospective regulations that may well have a retroactive effect.[98]

The better view is that subordinate legislation not falling under the defi-nition of "regulation" – or to which the *Regulations Act* does not apply – becomes effective when it is issued, not when it becomes public or known.[99] However, the cases discussed below show that the courts do not always take this view, especially when some clear injustice is done through ignorance of the law.

(d) Publication of Regulations and Exemption From Publication

In principle, the maxim that "ignorance of the law is no excuse" should apply as much to subordinate legislation as to an Act of Parliament itself. As noted in *R. v. Ross*,[100] there are important differences between the manner of enacting parent legislation and the way in which most subordinate legislation is enacted:

> Briefly, amongst other things, before a public Act can receive the Royal assent and become law it must first, in the form of a bill, be presented to and deliberated upon and conveyed or passed, through its different stages at different times and on different days, by the action of the members of the Legislative Assembly in concourse duly assembled in the proper place designated for that purpose, at which the public, including representatives of the press, are generally per-mitted to be present. Therefore the proceedings necessary to enact and bring into force an Act or law binding upon the public give to it a certain measure of publicity, and it is not difficult to understand why it is a general rule of law that one cannot successfully plead ignorance of such an Act or law.

> But, on the other hand, an order made by a Minister, such as the one under discussion, is on a different footing than is an Act of the Leg-islature. The making of such an order is at the discretion of the Minister himself, as appears by the provisions of s. 119 of the *Forest Act* [R.S.B.C. 1936, c. 102], and is drawn up and signed in his private

---

97   For example, a regulation made and filed on 4 January 1994 may alter the rate of capital cost allowance available under the *Alberta Corporate Income Tax Act* for the 1983 taxation year. Under s. 2 of the *Regulations Act*, the regulation only comes into effect on 4 January 1994 – nevertheless, the consequence of that regulation is to change the law as it stood at some previous point in time, namely, 1983.

98   For the subtle and sometimes confusing distinction between retroactive and retrospective law, see *Sullivan and Driedger on The Construction of Statutes*, 4th ed. (Toronto: Butter-worths, 2002) at 547.

99   *Howe Sound School District No 48 v. Howe Sound Teachers' Assn.* (1985), 14 Admin. L.R. 263 (B.C. S.C.) See also the common law position discussed by A.I.L. Campbell in "The Publication of Delegated Legislation" (1982) Public Law 569. See also note 103, below.

100   (1944), [1945] 3 D.L.R. 574 at 576-77 (B.C. Co. Ct.) per Harrison Co. Ct. J.

office or some other private place, as I assume was the case with the order in question.

There does not appear to be any provisions in the *Forest Act*, or any other Act, that I can find, requiring promulgation of such an order, nor any provisions excluding such a requirement.

I think it hardly compatible with justice that a person may be convicted and penalized, and perhaps lose his personal liberty by being committed to jail in default of payment of any fine imposed, for the violation of an order of which he had no knowledge or notice at any material time.

I think this view of the matter, without the necessity of further enlargement, is fairly in accord with the decisions rendered, respectively, in *Johnson v. Sargant & Sons*, [1918] 1 K.B. 101, and *Brightman & Co. v. Tate*, [1919] 1 K.B. 463, 35 T.L.R. 209.

A similar result was reached by Tallis J. in the Supreme Court of the Northwest Territories in *Catholique v. R.*,[101] which was purportedly decided on common law principles because (at the time) no Territorial law dealt with the effect of publication. Indeed, His Lordship referred to the decision by Martin J.A. in *R. v. Molis*,[102] who expressly left open the question of whether ignorance of a regulation which has in fact been duly published might nevertheless in some circumstances still be a defence.[103]

Under the Alberta scheme, the registrar of regulations must publish the filed regulation in the Alberta Gazette within one month of receiving it, although this time limit can be extended. The Lieutenant-Governor in Council can dispense with publication of a regulation in two circumstances. The first is when the regulation has been available in printed form to all those likely to be interested in it. The second, when the regulation is of such a length as to render publication unnecessary or undesirable.[104] If the Lieutenant Governor in Council dispenses with publication, the unpublished regulation is, in effect, deemed to have been published.

The importance of filing and publishing regulations, in addition to making them accessible in a government publication, is to make them enforceable. Section 3(5) of the *Regulations Act* says

---

101 (1979), [1980] 1 W.W.R. 166 (N.W.T. S.C.). See also *Johnson v. Sargaunt & Sons*, [1918] 1 K.B. 101 (Eng. K.B.); *Jones v. Robson*, [1901] 1 Q.B. 673 (Eng. Q.B.); *Simmons Motor Units Ltd. v. Minister of Labour & National Service*, [1946] 2 All E.R. 201; *Simmonds v. Newell*, [1953] 1 W.L.R. 836; *R. v. Sheer Metalcraft*, [1954] 1 Q.B. 586 (Eng. Q.B.); *R. v. Villeneuve* (1967), 2 C.R.N.S. 301 (N.S. Co. Ct.); *Blackpool Corp. v. Locker* (1947), [1948] 1 K.B. 349 (Eng. C.A.).

102 (March 9, 1979), (Ont. C.A.) (unreported), affirmed [1980] 2 S.C.R. 356 (S.C.C.).

103 The generally held view in the United Kingdom is that, at common law, delegated legislation is valid even though it is not published. See for example, W. Wade and C. Forsyth, *Administrative Law*, 7th ed. (Oxford: Clarendon Press, 1994) at 892-93.

104 *Regulations Act*, R.S.A. 2000, c. R-14, ss. 3(2)-(4).

Unless expressly provided to the contrary in another Act, and subject to subsection (3),[105] a regulation that is not published is not valid as against a person who has not had actual notice of it.[106]

The registrar is required[107] to report to the Lieutenant Governor in Council[108] at least monthly concerning anything determined not to be a regulation, and the Lieutenant Governor in Council may approve the report or order that the document "be deemed to be a regulation", in which case it is considered to have been subject to the Act since it was passed.

The Lieutenant Governor in Council can pass a regulation[109] to exempt any other regulation from publication. A regulation exempted from publication by this method is not deemed by the Act to have been published, and it is an open question[110] as to whether actual notice of this type of exempted regulation must be given to the person to be affected by it. It is likely that actual or constructive notice will be necessary in most circumstances before the regulation will be enforceable.

The federal *Statutory Instruments Act*[111] requires all regulations to be published in the Canada Gazette within twenty-three days of registration of the regulation.[112] Although a regulation is not invalidated by lack of publication,[113] no one can be convicted of an offence consisting of a contravention of the regulation which occurred while the regulation was unpublished, unless both of the following conditions apply:

11.(2) ...

    (a) the regulation was exempted from [publication by a general regulation enacted by the Governor in Council,][114] or specifically on its face provides that it shall apply . . . before it is published in the Canada Gazette,[115]

---

105 Section 3(3) provides for dispensing with publication in which case the regulation is valid against all persons as if it had been published.

106 *Workers' Compensation Act*, R.S.A. 2000, c. W-15, s. 155, exempts orders, rulings, decisions or directions from publication in *The Alberta Gazette*.

107 Under the *Regulations Act*, R.S.A. 2000, c. R-14, s. 5(2).

108 This would be a rare occurrence. No report is made to the Legislature.

109 Under the *Regulations Act*, R.S.A. 2000, c. R-14, s. 8(1)(g), which regulation would itself have to comply with the Act. See *supra* note 95 for reference to regulations exempted from publication.

110 No cases appear to have been reported on this point.

111 For a brief history of the Federal requirements for publication see Holland and McGowan, *Delegated Legislation in Canada*, supra note 18 at 37-38.

112 R.S.C. 1985, c. S-22, s. 11.

113 *Ibid.* s. 11(2).

114 Pursuant to s. 20(c) of the *Statutory Instruments Act (Canada)*, R.S.C. 1985, c. S-22. The exempting regulation would itself have to be published.

115 Thereby permitting the regulation-making authority to decide whether to exempt it from publication. Compare this with the provision in s. 3 of the Alberta *Regulations Act* which grants a similar power to the Lieutenant Governor in Council (who may not be the regulation-making authority).

and

(b) it is proved that at the date of the alleged contravention reasonable steps had been taken to bring the purport of the regulation to the notice of those persons likely to be affected by it.

Regulations that are published in an official Gazette must be admitted in evidence in court proceedings and judicial notice must be taken of them.[116]

Finally, consider the effect of non-publication on the validity of a regulation required to be published. Although no one can be convicted of an offence created by an unpublished regulation,[117] not all regulations create offences, and people may therefore be affected in quite substantial ways by unpublished regulations. The Saskatchewan courts have reached this conclusion by upholding the validity of an unpublished Order in Council declaring California to be a reciprocal jurisdiction under the Saskatchewan *Reciprocal Enforcement of Maintenance Orders Act, 1968*.[118] This approach follows the English decision in *R. v. Sheer Metalcraft*,[119] (dealing with the *English Statutory Instruments Act*, 1946, which implies that unpublished regulations are nevertheless in existence and therefore have some legal effect).[120]

13. Subordinate Legislation that is not a Regulation

The preceding discussion of Alberta and federal legislative control over regulations centres on subordinate legislation that are "regulations". What is and what is not a "regulation" is largely based on decades old thinking, modified in 1982, by the Uniform Law Conference of Canada.

The concepts on which the first generation of *Regulation Acts* were premised are now somewhat dated. Not infrequently the *Regulations Act* is stated not to apply to significant regulations.[121] A new approach to the definition of "regulation" and to those rules that are not "regulations" is needed. Professor Janisch captured the point neatly in relation to the rules of internal administrative tribunals – what he says also holds true for internal government rules. Professor Janisch said:[122]

---

116 See for example *Alberta Evidence Act* R.S.A. 2000, c. A-18, ss. 28-32.

117 Unless one of the exceptions to publication applies.

118 S.S. 1968, c. 59 [now S.S. 1997, c. E-9.21]; see *Santa Clara (County) v. Hudson*, [1978] 6 W.W.R. 124 (Sask. Dist. Ct.).

119 [1954] 1 Q.B. 586 (Eng. Q.B.).

120 9 & 10 Geo. 6, c. 36. See s. 3(2) of the *English Act*, which specifically provides a defence for infringements of an unpublished statutory instrument. Because one can only infringe a prohibition which has existence, the wording of the *English Act* implies that the regulation is valid, and creates an offence, although a defence is available. If no offence is created, there is no need for a defence, but is it correct to assume that the unpublished regulation must therefore be in existence and valid? Such reasoning certainly flies in the face of the policy of the Act requiring publication.

121 For example, rule-making authority under the *Securities Act*, R.S.A. 2000, c. S-4, s. 224 which creates its own publication and notification regime.

122 H.N. Janisch, "Administrative Tribunals and the Law" (1988-89) 2 C.J.A.L.P. 263 at 279.

Quasi-law does not, in and of itself, affect legal rights – that only happens when the administrative tribunal in exercising its discretion gives effect to a pre-existing policy in an individual decision. In other words, as Ganz has pointed out, it may have no legal force, but significant legal effect. Or to put it another way, while internally binding on government officials, it does not create externally enforceable legal rights.

The area of subordinate legislation – or quasi legislation – is ripe for further research and commentary.

14. Parliamentary Scrutiny of Subordinate Legislation

An important aspect of the *Statutory Instruments Act* (Canada) is the provision[123] for the systematic review and scrutiny of virtually every federal statutory instrument. This provides a mechanism for Parliament, through a committee, to examine and supervise the exercise of those legislative powers which Parliament has delegated. Although the permanent existence of a joint committee of both Houses is not provided for by the federal Act,[124] in practice a Standing Joint Committee for the Scrutiny of Regulations of the House of Commons and Senate has been established during each session of Parliament since the Act was passed in 1977.[125]

(a) Standing Joint Committee for the Scrutiny of Regulations

The Joint Committee is comprised of members of both the House of Commons and the Senate. The particular Joint Committee established by each Parliament must adopt its own terms of reference for its review[126] of subordinate legislation. The current terms of reference are:[127]

Whether any Regulation or other Statutory Instrument within its terms of reference, in the judgment of the Committee:

1. is not authorized by the terms of the enabling legislation or has not complied with any condition set forth in the legislation;

---

123 R.S.C. 1985, c. S-22, s. 19.
124 Section 19 says that most statutory instruments "stand permanently referred" to any committee of the House of Commons, the Senate, or a joint committee established to consider them. The Act does not itself establish the Scrutiny Committee, nor does it require one to be established. The Fourth Report recommends that the Scrutiny Committee be put on a permanent statutory basis: see Recommendation No. 3.
125 For an overview of Parliamentary scrutiny in several Commonwealth jurisdictions see Keyes, *Executive Legislation, supra* note 9, Chapter 6.
126 A regulation may be within the power of government to enact but at the same time violate the criteria set out, thus requiring some action by the Committee.
127 Reproduced from the November 21, 2002 Report of the Joint Committee to both Houses of Parliament (the First Report to the 37th Parliament, Second Session) at 1:15-16.

2. is not in conformity with the *Canadian Charter of Rights and Freedoms* or the *Canadian Bill of Rights*;

3. purports to have retroactive effect without express authority having been provided for in the enabling legislation;

4. imposes a charge on the public revenues or requires payment to be made to the Crown or to any other authority, or prescribes the amount of any such charge or payment, without express authority having been provided for in the enabling legislation;

5. imposes a fine, imprisonment or other penalty without express authority having been provided for in the enabling legislation;

6. tends directly or indirectly to exclude the jurisdiction of the courts without express authority having been provided for in the enabling legislation;

7. has not complied with the *Statutory Instruments Act* with respect to transmission, registration or publication;

8. appears for any reason to infringe the rule of law;

9. trespasses unduly on rights and liberties;

10. makes the rights and liberties of the person unduly dependent on administrative discretion or is not consistent with the rules of natural justice;

11. makes some unusual or unexpected use of the powers conferred by the enabling legislation;

12. amounts to the exercise of a substantive legislative power properly the subject of direct parliamentary enactment;

13. is defective in its drafting or for any other reason requires elucidation as to its form or purport.

The Joint Committee has observed[128] that it has objected to a far higher proportion of the regulations it has scrutinized than have its counterparts in the United Kingdom, Australia and Ontario. In addition to looking beyond questions of *ultra vires* to the substance of delegated legislation, the Joint Committee has insisted that each statutory instrument identify the specific legislative provision relied on for the enactment of the subordinate legislation.[129] The entire record of the proceedings of the joint committees is an excellent source for studying problems of subordinate legislation. One wonders why the provinces have generally not adopted a scrutiny committee, particularly in light of

---

128 At 336 of the Fourth Report to the 1st Session of the 32nd Parliament.
129 As recommended in the Second Report of the Committee to the 2nd Session of the 30th Parliament (1976-77), paras. 56-69.

the fact that all who exercise delegated powers derive this authority from the sovereignty of Parliament.[130] As one of the joint committees said:[131]

> The maintenance of parliamentary supremacy and of parliamentary democracy is imperative. The inability of Parliament to consider or to make all the laws necessary in the modern state should not lead to a decrease in accountability to Parliament for law-making. Delegated law-making is far too wide-spread a practice to be without democratic participation, procedural safeguards and parliamentary accountability. Yet, our present practices are based on the premises that delegated legislation is abnormal, and that it is confined to matters of detail. There can be no doubt that delegated legislation is now the ordinary and indispensable way of making the bulk of the non-common law of the land. It is beyond question that subordinate legislation is not confined to detail and more often than not embodies and effects policy. The making and control of subordinate law must therefore be regularized and brought into harmony with our constitutional order.

The overall thrust of the 74 reports made by the Joint Committee to both Houses from 1977 to 2003 is to reiterate the need to reinforce Parliamentary control over both the content and the process making delegated legislation – matters which go far beyond merely requiring registration and publication as conditions precedent to the enforcement of subordinate legislation. Joint Committee recommendations include:[132]

1. Greater care in the use of legislative phrases which delegate powers, by instituting a procedure for referring all Bills containing such provisions to the Joint Committee after second reading but prior to enactment.[133]

2. Greater care in drafting subordinate legislation, in particular to prevent undue discretionary action by administrators which is incapable of judicial review.[134]

3. Developing a system for parliamentary scrutiny of the content of delegated legislation before it is enacted, perhaps by reference to the appropriate standing committees of the two Houses.[135]

---

130 It appears that Ontario is the only province to do so.

131 Second Report for the 2nd Session of the 30th Parliament (also published separately from Hansard). See App. VI to the Fourth Report to the 1st Session of the 32nd Parliament for a list of the government's non-action on the recommendations contained in the Second Report to the 2nd Session of the 30th Parliament.

132 Fourth Report to the 1st Session of the 32nd Parliament, Summary of Recommendations at 366*ff.*

133 *Ibid.* at 332, 357.

134 *Ibid.* at 360-62.

135 *Ibid.* at 334.

4. Providing for a standard method for Parliament to disallow subordinate legislation, along the lines adopted in Australia.[136]

5. Recognize that the scrutiny of delegated legislation provided for in the Act and in the *Canadian Bill of Rights* is really an internal administrative procedure, and not an independent parliamentary review of the draft subordinate laws.

6. Encourage the publication of draft versions of delegated legislation, along the lines of the system in use under the U.S. Federal *Administrative Procedures Act*.[137]

7. The definition of "regulations" should be expanded to include departmental directives, circulars and guidelines which direct public servants how to exercise discretions which have been delegated to them.[138]

8. A method should be devised to make certain that all regulations in fact are remitted to the Joint Committee for scrutiny.

9. The Joint Committee should be entitled to obtain copies of the legal opinions rendered by members of the Department of Justice advising as to the legality of proposed regulations.[139]

10. The complicated definitions of "regulation" and "statutory instrument" be replaced by a simpler, more comprehensive definition of "regulations", as recommended by the MacGuigan Committee in 1969.[140]

11. The Joint Committee should be put on a permanent, statutory basis, and its criteria for scrutinizing delegated legislation should be contained in that new *Subordinate Legislation Act*.

In 2003, the *Statutory Instruments Act* was specifically amended to provide a statutory disallowance procedure for all statutory instruments or delegated legislation subject to review and scrutiny by the Joint Committee.[141] Prior to this amendment, the Joint Committee could recommend the revocation of an objectionable regulation but the procedure was limited in scope and required the cooperation of the responsible Minister. The amendment makes the disallowance procedure more effective by giving it a statutory footing, making it applicable to virtually all subordinate legislation, and allowing a majority in Parliament to act with or without the concurrence of the responsible Minister.

The federal Joint Committee does excellent work on two separate fronts: one, on reviewing the legality and appropriateness of the content of one stream

---

136 *Ibid.* at 335, 338.
137 *Ibid.* at 338*ff.*
138 *Ibid.* at 356.
139 *Ibid.* at 363-64.
140 *Ibid.* paras. 57, 61.
141 See section 19.1 which was given Royal Assent on 19 June 2003 (formerly Bill C-205).

of the vast flow of subordinate laws enacted each year; the other, on finding methods to improve the Federal Parliament's conscious control over the circumstances in which it delegates powers to the executive, and over the executive's use of that delegated power.[142] Both goals represent a re-assertion of the supremacy of Parliament. It is regrettable that the Alberta Legislative Assembly has to date failed to act on the need for a provincial scrutiny committee,[143] even for the first purpose of scrutinizing the actual use of powers which the legislature has delegated to the provincial executive.[144]

15. Municipal Bylaws: a Particular Type of Subordinate Legislation

Municipal bylaws are an important species of subordinate legislation, affecting people more directly than many other types of regulation. The procedures required for the enactment, filing, publication, and validity of municipal bylaws differ from those contained in the provincial Regulations Acts.

Municipal bylaws are subordinate legislation because municipalities are the creatures of provincial legislation. This has two principal consequences. First, it means that municipal bylaws can only be valid if they fall within an area constitutionally allocated to the provinces under section 92 of the *Constitution Act*. Many bylaws have been struck down for trenching on areas of

---

142 The reader may also usefully refer to the following appendices to the Fourth Report: App. III, which describes the scrutiny systems used in the United Kingdom and in the Commonwealth of Australia for parliamentary control of delegated legislation; App. IV, which refers to the administrative requirement adopted by the federal Treasury Board for passing any "health, safety or fairness" regulation; App. V, which refers to the experience in the United States under the federal *Administrative Procedures Act*; App. VI, which lists the government's disposition of the recommendations made in the committee's Second Report (for the 1976-77 Session).

143 The Select Special Committee on Parliamentary Reform appointed in 1992 (but dissolved with the call for the Alberta Provincial election in May 1993, without reporting) might have considered this reform.

144 In November 1974, a Select Committee of the Legislative Assembly on Regulations in the Province of Alberta (the "Zander Committee") tabled its report in the legislature. It made 41 recommendations, including: (a) the establishment of a provincial scrutiny committee; (b) pre-publication of draft regulations, if possible accompanying the introduction of bills into the legislature; (c) the adoption of the guidelines set out in the McRuer Report (Ont.) for drafting regulations and the proper role and content thereof; (d) that regulation-making powers in legislation should be as specific as possible; (e) that regulations should be void if not published within 30 days of filing; (f) that all regulations should be published by the Queen's Printer; (g) that the indexing system for regulations should be improved; (h) that the regulations should be regularly revised and consolidated, like the statutes.

The response from the Alberta Government came in the form of a Ministerial Statement of Policy made in the Legislative Assembly on May 1, 1978. The Zander Committee Report is an extremely useful source, particularly on the history of the control of regulations in Alberta, Canada, the United Kingdom, and various other Commonwealth jurisdictions.

Note also the Report of the Special Committee on Boards and Tribunals to the Legislative Assembly of Alberta, 1965 (the "Clement Committee"), which also relates to the exercise and control of delegated statutory powers, although not just those of a legislative nature.

federal legislative authority.[145] Second, the doctrine of *ultra vires* applies to restrict bylaws to areas which the provincial legislatures have validly delegated to municipalities.[146] These legal constraints affect the validity of municipal legislation, even though municipalities are typically granted sweeping powers to make laws for the peace, order and good government of the municipality, its health, safety, morality and welfare.[147]

All municipal actions take place pursuant to either a by-law or a resolution, both of which are legislative in form. Nevertheless, the courts have long held that bylaws that are quasi-judicial in nature (for example, those dealing with re-zoning, subdividing or granting permission to develop an individual's land[148]) are subject to the procedural requirements of natural justice, even though these discretionary decisions are cast in legislative form.[149]

The *Regulations Act* (Alberta) specifically excludes municipal bylaws from the definition of "regulation", with the result that the filing and publication system of that Act does not apply to municipal bylaws. However, the *Municipal Government Act*[150] requires public hearings before many types of bylaws are enacted, and bylaws must be made generally available to the public.[151] These statutory provisions generally exceed and supplant any common law require-ment on the municipality to follow the principles of natural justice or fairness in enacting particular types of bylaws. In principle, the effect of a failure to comply with these statutory procedures should render the by-law void.[152] Ad-ditionally, the common law has long required notice and hearings prior to the enactment of certain types of bylaws – apart altogether from any statutorily imposed procedures.

---

145   For example, attempts to regulate prostitution have been held to infringe on the federal power to enact criminal law.

146   See the cases listed in *supra* note 37.

147   For a different formulation see ss. 7-9 of the *Municipal Government Act*, R.S.A. 2000, c. M-26 and the *School Act*, R.S.A. 2000, c. S-3, ss. 2-3.

148   *Wiswell v. Winnipeg (Metropolitan)* (1964), 45 D.L.R. (2d) 348 (Man. C.A.), reversed on other grounds [1965] S.C.R. 512 (S.C.C.); *Camac Exploration Ltd. v. Alberta (Oil & Gas Conservation Board)* (1964), 47 W.W.R. 81 (Alta. T.D.).

149   Indeed, the Legislature has considerably broadened the notice and hearing requirements for the enactment of land use bylaws that do not affect only one person's land and which therefore might not have been subject, at common law, to the principles of natural justice. See the *Municipal Government Act*, R.S.A. 2000, c. M-26, s. 692.

150   See *supra* note 147.

151   Although there is no general province-wide registry of municipal bylaws, and it may frequently be difficult to determine the exact extent of bylaws in force in a particular municipality. This problem was considered by the Zander Committee Report to the Alberta Legislature in 1974, which recommended "a centralized agency for the recording, reviewing and distribution of all municipal bylaws and resolutions in the Province of Alberta", much like the Ontario Municipal Board. This recommendation has not been implemented.

152   See *Harvie v. Calgary (City) Regional Planning Commission* (1978), 8 Alta. L.R. (2d) 166 (Alta. C.A.), reversing (1978), 5 Alta. L.R. (2d) 301 (Alta. T.D.). A question may arise whether such statutory procedures are mandatory or merely directory, in which case a failure to comply with them might not render the decision void. In such a case, however, what authority would the court have to strike down the bylaw, even if flagrant injustice had been done by not notifying a particular person affected by the bylaw?

Although all municipal bylaws and resolutions are legislative in form, the courts have long recognized the quasi-judicial nature of bylaws affecting the rights or property of particular individuals. Accordingly, a municipality can only pass such bylaws if it complies with the principles of natural justice or procedural fairness.[153] The exact content of these common law procedural requirements may be difficult to determine in particular circumstances,[154] as may be the border line between bylaws which are quasi-judicial in nature and those which are truly legislative.[155] In any event, the better view is that a breach of these common law procedural requirements renders the by-law void, not merely voidable.[156]

16. Challenging Subordinate Legislation

At the end of the day, most administrative law problems boil down to answering this question: Did the appropriate legislative body grant this particular power to this particular person to be exercised in this particular way?[157]

Too often it is accepted that a regulation, officially published in a government publication, (like the Canada or Alberta Gazette) must therefore be valid. Although regulations are presumed to be valid,[158] there are a variety of grounds on which subordinate legislation may be challenged. The following is a brief summary of the more important grounds.[159]

(a) Ultra Vires

The doctrine of *ultra vires* applies to the power of a delegate to enact subordinate legislation.[160] In other words, the delegate can only enact rules or

---

153 See for example *Wiswell v. Winnipeg (Metropolitan)* (1964), 48 W.W.R. 193 (Man. C.A.), reversed on other grounds [1965] S.C.R. 512 (S.C.C.); *Camac Exploration Ltd. v. Alberta (Oil & Gas Conservation Board)* (1964), 43 D.L.R. (2d) 755 (Alta. T.D.); *Campeau Corp. v. Calgary (City)* (1979), 7 Alta. L.R. (2d) 294 (Alta. C.A.), reversing (1977), 8 A.R. 77 (Alta. T.D.). In *Campeau Corp. v. Calgary (City)* (1980), 12 Alta. L.R. (2d) 379 (Alta. C.A.), the Court of Appeal declined to interfere with council's actions, which it specifically held to be legislative and not quasi-judicial in nature.

154 See Chapter 8.

155 See for example *Campeau (No. 1)* and *(No. 2)* on this point, *supra* note 153.

156 See H.W.R. Wade, "Unlawful Administrative Act: Void or Voidable?", Pt. I at (1967) 83 L.Q. Rev. 499; Pt. II at (1968) 84 L.Q. Rev. 95; Wade's *Administrative Law*, 7th ed. (Oxford: Clarendon Press, 1994) at 339-44 and 516-18. See also D.P. Jones, "Discretionary Refusal of Judicial Review in Administrative Law" (1981) 19 Alta. L. Rev. 483.

157 See D.P. Jones, "The Parliamentary Side of Administrative Law: The Standing Joint Committee of the Scrutiny of Regulations" (1996) 6 R.A.L. 25.

158 See Côté, *The Interpretation of Legislation in Canada, supra* note 40 at 309-10.

159 For a more detailed review, see Keyes, *Executive Legislation, supra* note 9 starting at 157, and Holland and McGowan, *Delegated Legislation in Canada, supra* note 18, Chapter 10 and following.

160 *McEldowney v. Forde*, [1969] 2 All E.R. 1039 (U.K. H.L.). The McRuer Report discusses various ways in which subordinate legislation may be *ultra vires* the parent enactment at 343-55 and at 380*ff.* The common law presumed that subordinate legislation could only validly do the following with specific authority in the parent act: amend another Act (or

regulations within the scope of the authority granted to the delegate by the parent legislation. The courts are entitled to review whether there is statutory authority for the enactment of any impugned subordinate legislation, just as the courts in general can review whether any other type of delegated action is *ultra vires*. It is unusual for legislation to contain a privative clause preventing judicial review of the vires of regulations.[161]

It is sometimes difficult to determine the specific statutory provision under which a particular regulation has been made. It is often not enough to learn that the regulation has been enacted pursuant to some Act without having the specific section in the Act identified. At the federal level, the Joint Standing Committee on Regulations and Other Statutory Instruments[162] has insisted that each regulation identify the specific statutory provision which is being relied upon by the delegate for authority to enact the regulation. This provides an opportunity for the delegate to consider carefully the specific statutory terms governing those regulations before enacting them, as well as a similar opportunity for the committee when reviewing them, or for an individual who might be affected by them.[163]

Legislation sometimes contains both specific regulation-making powers and an omnibus clause purporting to authorize the delegate to enact regulations for any matter considered "necessary or advisable to carry out effectively the intent and purpose of this Act".[164] The effectiveness of broad grants of powers varies.[165]

(b) Parent Act is Repealed

The fact that an Act under which regulations are made has been repealed does not necessarily mean that regulations made under the repealed Act are also repealed. The relevant *Interpretation Act* may save them if other powers to make regulations are substituted for the repealed Act – assuming those substituted provisions would authorize the existing regulations.[166]

---

regulations passed thereunder); amend the parent Act; impose penalties; sub-delegate; impose taxes or fees; operate retroactively; reverse the onus of proof; or exclude the jurisdiction of the courts.

161 As opposed to a privative clause preventing judicial review of a discretionary action by a delegate. For example, a decision of the Alberta Energy and Utilities Board setting natural gas prices.

162 See section 14 of this chapter, for a discussion of the Scrutiny Committee. In Alberta the registrar may refuse to register a regulation which does not show the provision of the Act authorizing the regulation (A.R. 288/99 s. 5).

163 It is equally difficult to find all of the regulations on a particular topic, since they are not usually indexed by subject matter. See Recommendation 22 of the Report of the Select Committee of the Legislative Assembly on Regulations in the Province of Alberta (the "Zander Committee") November 1974, and discussion at 84-90. See also D.S.M. Huberman, "Searching for Delegated Legislation or How to Find Your 'Red Tape'" (1966) 2 U.B.C.L. Rev. 467. Alberta has been one of the leaders in providing a statute law index. (See Index to the Statutes of Alberta prepared by the Canadian Law Information Council.)

164 For example, *Private Investigators and Security Guards Act*, R.S.A. 2000, c. P-23, s. 24(j).

165 See Keyes, "Expressio Unis: The Expression that Proves the Rule" (1989) Statute Law Review 1.

166 See for example s. 36(1)(e) *Interpretation Act* (Alberta), R.S.A. 2000, c. I-8.

(c) Parent Act is Ultra Vires

A parent Act that is *ultra vires* necessarily means that any subordinate legislation founded on that Act will also be *ultra vires*.

(d) Conditions Precedent

Some Acts require certain conditions to be met before subordinate legislation can be enacted: consultation, a report, an approval, a set of conditions to be met. Failure to meet the required conditions may render the subordinate legislation void.

(e) Composition or Procedure of the Delegate

When subordinate legislation can be made by a board or agency, the composition of that entity must comply with its Act and the manner in which it enacts subordinate legislation must also comply with its internal procedural rules on quorum, process, and voting. It is unlikely that any challenge on this ground could be mounted against the Governor in Council, Lieutenant-Governor in Council, or a Minister.

(f) Conflict with Other Acts

In principle, subordinate legislation in conflict with its parent Act or other legislation will be invalid unless its parent Act specifically provides for this.

(g) Implied Restrictions

(i) Good Faith

Canadian courts have, from time to time, intervened to satisfy themselves that subordinate legislation is enacted in good faith for the purpose for which the power was given. Challenges that subordinate legislation was enacted in bad faith are rarely successfully argued in Canada.[167]

(ii) Reasonableness

Although at one time municipal bylaws could be attacked on the basis of their unreasonableness, most jurisdictions have enacted legislation saying that

---

167   *Reference re Regulations (Chemical) under War Measures Act (Canada)*, [1943] S.C.R. 1 (S.C.C.); *Canada (Canadian Wheat Board) v. Manitoba Pool Elevators*, [1952] A.C. 427 at 444 (Manitoba P.C.). When the delegate performs a policy function (for example by setting utility rates after public hearings) in establishing regulations, the court may intervene if there was "a pre-judgement of the matter to such an extent that any representation to the contrary would be futile . . .". *Newfoundland Telephone Co. v. Newfoundland (Board of Commissioners of Public Utilities)* (1992), 134 N.R. 241 (S.C.C.).

For the basis of the rule see Holland and McGowan, *supra* note 18 at 215.

it is not open to question as to whether a by-law is reasonable.[168] Most subordinate legislation is not open to challenge on the basis of its supposed unreasonableness.[169]

(iii) The Legitimate Expectations Doctrine

The legitimate expectations doctrine has been applied by some courts to the enactment of subordinate legislation. Persons adversely affected by subordinate legislation typically claim an expectation that they would be consulted before enactment of the law. However, to date, appeal courts have rejected the argument on the basis that legislative functions do not attract procedural fairness. Despite the current state of the law, the doctrine may well yet gain some degree of acceptance in its application to the enactment of subordinate legislation.[170]

17. Summary

This chapter has focused attention on those delegated powers of a legislative nature. Although the doctrine of *ultra vires* applies to subordinate legislation, as it does to all delegated powers, if the delegate exercises its legislative powers correctly, the subordinate legislation is as valid as if it were contained in the parent Act. To keep the increasing volume of subordinate legislation relatively accessible, most jurisdictions have created systems for filing and publishing a large part of it. These systems are neither perfect nor complete. Particular regulations can be exempted from filing, publication, or both. But other forms of subordinate legislation need attention.

There are certain movements towards improving consultation before regulations are enacted and asserting Parliamentary or legislative control over regulations. We can anticipate that these trends will continue as the legislative branch, and the public at large, seek input into and some form of control over subordinate legislation. Subordinate legislation is a vital and important legal phenomenon affecting vast portions of the life of every citizen – it deserves more attention and study. No study of administrative law would be complete without examining it.

---

168   See for example *Municipal Government Act* (Alberta), R.S.A. 2000, c. M-26, s. 539, which reads: "No bylaw or resolution may be challenged on the ground that it is unreasonable." Note that although "reasonableness" is not open to challenge, the bylaw must be made "in good faith". For an analysis of the law on the basis of an assertion that delegated power must be exercised reasonably, see Holland and McGowan, *supra* note 18, Chapter 12.

169   See Keyes, *Executive Legislation, supra* note 9 at 229, for a helpful discussion.

170   For the development of the legitimate expectations doctrine, see Paula A. MacPherson, *The Legitimate Expectation Doctrine and Its Application to Administrative Policy* (1995-96) 9 C.J.A.L.P. 141.

18. Selected Bibliography

Most of the standard works referred to in the previous chapter have sections dealing with problems associated with delegation of powers. In addition, the reader might refer to:

Anisman, P., "Submission on Bill C-25, the *Regulations Act*" (1997) 6 R.A.L. 73.

Côté, *The Interpretation of Legislation in Canada*, 3d ed., (Toronto: Carswell, 2000).

Driedger, "The Enactment and Publication of Canadian Administrative Regulations" (1967) 19 *Administrative Law Review* 129.

Fairweather, G., "The Attitude of the Supreme Court of Canada toward Interdelegation: *Coughlin v. Ontario Highway Transport Board*" (1970) 5 U.B.C. L. Rev. 43.

Friedmann, "Statute Law and Its Interpretation in the Modern State" (1948) 26 Can. Bar Rev. 1277.

Gantz, *Quasi-Legislation: Recent Developments in Secondary Legislation* (1987).

Hayhurst and Wallington, "The Parliamentary Scrutiny of Delegated Legislation" [1988] P.L. 547.

Hewitt, *The Control of Delegated Legislation* (1953).

Holland and McGowan, *Delegated Legislation in Canada* (1989).

Janisch, H.N., "What is Law?" (1977) 55 Can. Bar Rev. 576.

Joint Standing Committee on Regulations and Other Statutory Instruments (Canada), Fourth Report for the 1st Session of the 32nd Parliament (Statutory Instruments No. 10).

Joint Standing Committee on Regulations and Other Statutory Instruments (Canada), Second Report for the Second Session of the 30th Parliament (Statutory Instruments No. 1), 1976-77.

Jones, D.P., "The Parliamentary Side of Administrative Laws" (1996) 6 R.A.L. 25.

Kerwell, *Parliamentary Supervision of Delegated Legislation, the United Kingdom, Australia, New Zealand and Canada* (1960).

Keyes, *Executive Legislation: Delegated Law Making by the Executive Branch* (1992).

Keyes, J.M., "Power Tools: The Form and Function of Legal Instruments for Government Action" (1996-97) 10 C.J.A.L.P. 133.

Lanham, D.J., "Delegated Legislation and the Alter Ego Principle" (1984) 100 L. Q. Rev. 587.

Lanham, "Delegated Legislation and Publication".

Leonard, *The New Wigmore: A Treatise on Evidence* (1996).

MacPherson, Paula A., "The Legitimate Expectation Doctrine and Its Application to Administrative Policy" (1995-96) 9 C.J.A.L.P. 141.

McCormick on Evidence, 4th ed. (1992), Strong, ed. at 757 *et seq.*

McIntosh, "Controls on Federal Legislation" (1970) 35 Sask. Bar Rev. 63.

Mullan, "Recent Developments in Nova Scotian Administrative Law" (1978) 4 Dalhousie L. J. 467 at 555.

Muylle, "Improving the Effectiveness of Parliamentary Legislative Procedures", Statute Law Review, Vol. 24, No 3, 2003, 169.

Powe, "The Georgia Straight and Freedom of Expression in Canada" (1970) 48 Can. Bar Rev. 410.

Report of the McRuer Royal Commission (Ontario), especially Vol. 1.

Report of the Second Commonwealth Conference on Delegated Legislation, Vol. 1 (Report), Vol. 2 (Documents), Vol. 3 (Transcript of Proceedings), Ottawa, April 1983.

Report of the Select Committee of the Alberta Legislature on Regulations (the "Zander Committee"), November 1974.

Report of the Special Committee on Boards and Tribunals to the Legislative Assembly of Alberta (the "Clement Committee"), 1965.

Rutherford, "Legislative Review of Delegated Legislation" (1969) 47 Can. Bar Rev. 352.

Third Report of the Special Committee of the House of Commons on Statutory Instruments (the "MacGuigan Committee"), 1968-69.

Twining and Miers, "How to do things with rules", 4th ed., (1994).

Wade & Forsyth, *Administrative Law*, 7th ed. (Oxford: Clarendon Press, 1994).

Weiler, T.J., "The Consultation Requirement in Regulatory Reform: Taking a Look at the Proposed *Regulatory Efficiency Act*" (1994-95) 8 C.J.A.L.P. 101.

Wigmore on Evidence, 3d ed. (1940), vol. 9 at 551 *et seq.*

Williams, "The Making of Statutory Instruments" (1970) 8 Alta. L. Rev. 324.

Willis, "Delegatus Non Potest Delegare" (1943) 21 Can. Bar Rev. 257.

Willis, "Statutory Interpretation in a Nutshell" (1938) 16 Can. Bar Rev. 1.

19. Reports of the Federal Scrutiny Committee

The Standing Joint Committee on the Scrutiny of Regulations has issued 74 Reports to both Houses of Parliament in a series starting in January 1977 and up to the fall of 2003.

II

GROUNDS FOR JUDICIAL REVIEW

5

Introduction to the Grounds for Judicial Review

1. General

Part II of this book deals with the *grounds* upon which superior courts may review the legality of a delegate's actions. It does not deal with either (a) the *standard* (or intensity) of review, which is discussed in Part III; or (b) the *remedies* or vehicles available for obtaining judicial review; these are discussed in Part IV.

Because most of administrative law deals with the right of the superior courts to review the legality of actions allegedly taken by delegates pursuant to statutory authority, a great deal of attention must be focused on the precise limits of the statutory power being exercised. Although the doctrine of Parliamentary Sovereignty generally means that specific legislation can be enacted to delegate virtually any power, the corollary is that any action taken outside of the area (or "jurisdiction") specifically delegated by statute will be *ultra vires*. In the end, the superior courts have the inherent right to construe the statutory language to determine whether the impugned administrative action is in fact authorized or instead is *ultra vires*.

This part examines possible jurisdictional defects from two aspects. First, Chapter 6 examines defects which prevent a delegate from acquiring jurisdiction "in the narrow sense". Secondly, it examines other errors which may subsequently cause the delegate to lose or exceed its jurisdiction. Chapter 7 considers the abuse of discretion; Chapters 8 and 9 deal with breaches of the *audi alteram partem* rule and the duty to be fair; and Chapter 10 examines the rule against bias *(nemo judex in sua causa debet esse)*.

Although all of the grounds for judicial review identified in the preceding paragraph are jurisdictional in nature, the superior courts have also historically asserted the anomalous power to issue *certiorari* to correct many *intra* jurisdictional errors of law on the face of the record. This is discussed in Chapter 11.

The examination will begin with a consideration of the various meanings which have been given to "jurisdiction".

2. The "Narrow" and "Wide" Meanings of "Jurisdiction"

"Jurisdiction" is one of the most elusive concepts in administrative law. In its broadest sense, "jurisdiction" means the authority to do every aspect of an *intra vires* action. In a narrower sense, however, "jurisdiction" means the power to commence or embark on a particular type of activity. A defect in jurisdiction "in the narrow sense" is thus distinguished from other errors – such as a breach of natural justice, considering irrelevant evidence, acting for an improper purpose, or reaching an unreasonable result – which take place *after* the delegate has lawfully started its activity, but which cause it to leave or exceed its jurisdiction. Lord Reid's analysis of these difficulties in defining "jurisdiction" in *Anisminic Ltd. v. Foreign Compensation Commission* is particularly useful:[1]

> It has sometimes been said that it is only where a tribunal acts without jurisdiction that its decision is a nullity. But in such cases the word "jurisdiction" has been used in a very wide sense, and I have come to the conclusion that it is better not to use the term except in the narrow and original sense of the tribunal being entitled to enter on the inquiry in question. But there are many cases where, although the tribunal had jurisdiction to enter on the inquiry, it has done or failed to do something in the course of the inquiry which is of such a nature that its decision is a nullity. It may have given its decision in bad faith. It may have made a decision which it has no power to make. It may have failed in the course of the inquiry to comply with the requirements of natural justice. It may in perfect good faith have misconstrued the provisions giving it power to act so that it failed to deal with the question remitted

---

1   (1968), [1969] 2 A.C. 147 at 171 (U.K. H.L.).

to it and decided some question which was not remitted to it. It may have refused to take into account something which it was required to take into account. Or it may have based its decision on some matter which, under the provisions setting it up, it had no right to take into account. I do not intend this list to be exhaustive. But if it decides a question remitted to it for decision without committing any of these errors it is as much entitled to decide the question wrongly as it is to decide it rightly. I understand that some confusion has been caused by my having said in *Reg. v. Governor of Brixton Prison, Ex parte Armah* [1968] A.C. 192, 234 that if a tribunal has jurisdiction to go right it has jurisdiction to go wrong. So it has, if one uses "jurisdiction" in the narrow original sense. If it is entitled to enter on the inquiry and does not do any of those things which I have mentioned in the course of the proceedings, then its decision is equally valid whether it is right or wrong subject only to the power of the court in certain circumstances to correct an error of law. I think that, if these views are correct, the only case cited which was plainly wrongly decided is *Davies v. Price* [1958] 1 W.L.R. 434. But in a number of other cases some of the grounds of judgment are questionable.

It is important to remember that virtually all grounds for judicial review of administrative action depend upon an attack on some aspect of the delegate's jurisdiction (in the wider sense) to do the particular activity in question.[2] Consequently, it is equally important to remember that any behaviour which causes the delegate to *exceed* its jurisdiction is just as fatal as any error which means that it never had jurisdiction "in the narrow sense" even to commence the exercise of its jurisdiction.

3. Judicial Review, Jurisdiction and Privative Clauses

The jurisdictional nature of most of judicial review is particularly important when the statute authorizing the delegate's action contains a privative clause.[3] Although such clauses purport to insulate the delegate's action from judicial review, the courts have consistently held that privative clauses cannot protect decisions taken outside the delegate's jurisdiction. The court can and must declare such decisions to be *ultra vires* and void. The exact ambit of the delegate's jurisdiction is an objective matter to be determined by the court's construction of the statute in question, and the delegate's jurisdiction is not invariably extended by the mere presence of a privative clause in the legislation. The existence of a privative clause may be one of the indicators that the

---

2 The exception is the court's anomalous power to correct an intra-jurisdictional error of law on the face of the record, which is discussed in Chapter 11.

3 For a discussion of the different types of privative clauses, their legal effect, and the "functional and pragmatic" approach for determining which errors of law go to jurisdiction, see Chapter 12.

legislature intended a particular matter to lie within the definitive authority of the statutory delegate.[4]

By contrast, a privative clause will prevent judicial review where the delegate has made an error of law *within* its jurisdiction[5] – which is the one ground for judicial review which is not jurisdictional in nature. If the error of law lies within jurisdiction, a privative clause has the effect of ousting the superior court's anomalous common law jurisdiction to correct the error, because the delegate's decision or action is not *ultra vires* – that is, it legally exists, and therefore there is something which can be protected by the privative clause.

No infallible test has been developed, however, for distinguishing errors of law which deprive a delegate of its jurisdiction from those which lie within it, although the Supreme Court of Canada has indicated that a "functional and pragmatic" approach should be used.[6]

4. Problems in Determining the Ambit of Jurisdiction

(a) Implied Statutory Intent

A precise delimitation of the ambit of the delegate's jurisdiction is frequently a very difficult matter of statutory interpretation. The object is to determine the intention of the legislature in creating the particular power in its entire context.[7] In most cases, the particular objection to the delegate's behaviour is not specifically dealt with by the authorizing statute; if it were, no argument could arise. For example, questions frequently arise as to specific aspects of the procedure to be adopted by the delegate in reaching its decision or prior to its taking action. In the absence of a comprehensive and specific statutory code of procedure,[8] the courts must determine whether the principles of natural justice or the duty to be fair apply to the governmental activity in question, and if so what their precise content is in all of the circumstances of

---

4   In addition, the presence or absence of a privative clause is one of the four factors considered in determining the standard (or intensity) of review: see Chapter 12.

5   See Chapter 11.

6   *Ibid.* The Supreme Court of Canada's decisions are *Bibeault*, (*Syndicate nationale des employés de la commision. scolaire régionale de l'Outaouais v. U.E.S., local 928* [1988] 2 S.C.R. 1048 (S.C.C.)); and *Econosult*, (*Canada (Attorney General) v. P.S.A.C.*) (1991), 80 D.L.R. (4th) 520 (S.C.C.)). For the subsequent development to use the pragmatic and functional approach in order to determine the standard of review, see *Pushpanathan v. Canada (Minister of Employment & Immigration)*, [1998] 1 S.C.R. 982 (S.C.C.), reasons amended [1998] 1 S.C.R. 1222 (S.C.C.), discussed in Chapter 12.

7   *Pushpanathan, ibid.*, which also deals with the related subject of determining the legislature's intention about the standard (or degree of intensity) which the courts are to apply in reviewing the statutory delegate's decision: see Chapter 12.

8   The *Administrative Procedures Act*, R.S.A. 2000, c. A-3 (reproduced in Appendix 1) is a partial code of procedure, but only applies to a very few provincial tribunals. No corresponding federal code exists to govern the procedure of federal tribunals, although one has been discussed. In Ontario, the *Statutory Powers Procedures Act* R.S.O. 1990, c. S.22 (reproduced in Appendix 2) codifies many aspects of procedural fairness for many bodies. On procedural fairness, see Chapter 8.

the case. In the end, the resolution of most jurisdictional questions involves application of the generally accepted rules of statutory construction,[9] which are, nevertheless, difficult to apply to particular statutes. Accordingly, it is extremely important to read the statute under which the delegate purports to act!

(b) Preliminary or Collateral Matters

Sometimes, the legislature only grants powers to a statutory delegate if–but only if–certain conditions precedent have been met. Lord Morris referred to this in its decision in *Anisminic*.[10]

> In all cases similar to the present one it becomes necessary therefore, to ascertain what was the question submitted for the determination of a tribunal. What were its terms of reference? What was its remit? What were the questions left to it or sent to it for its decision? What were the limits of its duties and powers? *Were there any conditions precedent which had to be satisfied before its functions began? If there were, was it or was it not left to the tribunal itself to decide whether or not the conditions precedent were satisfied? If Parliament has enacted that provided a certain situation exists then a tribunal may have certain powers, it is clear that the tribunal will not have those powers unless the situation exists.* The decided cases illustrate the infinite variety of the situations which may exist and the variations of statutory wording which have called for consideration. Most of the cases depend, therefore, upon an examination of their own particular facts and of particular sets of words. It is, however, abundantly clear that questions of law as well as of fact can be remitted for the determination of a tribunal.

An example of a preliminary or collateral issue arose in *Bell v. Ontario (Human Rights Commission).*[11] In that case, the Ontario Human Rights Commission only had jurisdiction with respect to a complaint about discrimination in rental housing if – but only if – the housing unit in question was a self-contained domestic establishment. As it was not, the condition precedent for the acquisition of jurisdiction was not met, and the courts prohibited the board of inquiry from dealing with the complaint.

In 1979, in *C.U.P.E., Local 963 v. New Brunswick Liquor Corp.,*[12] the Supreme Court of Canada strongly cautioned against lightly concluding that a matter was preliminary or collateral, indicating that in any case of doubt the matter should be treated as falling within the statutory delegate's jurisdiction.

---

9 For a discussion of the rules of statutory interpretation, see R. Sullivan, *Sullivan and Driedger on The Construction of Statutes*, 4th ed. (Toronto: Butterworths, 2002).

10 (1968), [1969] 2 A.C. 147 at 182 (U.K. H.L.), emphasis added.

11 [1971] S.C.R. 756 (S.C.C.).

12 [1979] 2 S.C.R. 227, 97 D.L.R. (3d) 417 (S.C.C.).

In some circumstances, therefore, the discretionary nature of the delegate's power may have the effect of widening its jurisdiction – and thereby reducing the ambit for judicial review on the ground of jurisdictional error.[13]

(c) Granting Delegated Powers in Broad or Subjective Terms

Sometimes, it is not possible to determine objectively the limits of the delegated power because the legislation is written in very broad or subjective terms–either (as Lord Morris noted) with respect to the fulfilment of conditions precedent to the acquisition of jurisdiction, or with respect to what can be done in the exercise of that jurisdiction. As long as the delegate acts *bona fide*, the courts will generally be very reluctant to second-guess its opinion, with the result that it is impossible to assert that the delegate's action is *ultra vires*.

For example, the *Royal Commission into the Donald Marshall, Jr. Prosecution* was granted jurisdiction to inquiry into the prosecution of Marshall, but also to:

> . . . inquire into . . . such other related matters which the Commissioners consider relevant to the Inquiry . . .

The very use of the word "consider" implies a subjective determination, and that subjective determination is to be made by the Commissioners and not by the courts. This subjective grant of power makes it very difficult to obtain judicial review on the basis that the delegate has acted outside of the ambit of its power. Thus, when the Commissioners decided to inquire into the general nature of Cabinet discussions on the *Marshall* case, but not into the views of individual Ministers, the Supreme Court of Canada[14] would not interfere:

> Here, the commission's opinion of "relevance" defines the issues themselves, *i.e.*, the mandate. The order in council gave this discretion only to the commission. If the commission did not "consider" the "other related matters" to be "relevant to the Inquiry", that, it seems to me, settles the question. There is nothing in the order in council that otherwise authorizes an inquiry into that matter. What the appellant seeks to do is to expand the commission's ruling beyond what the commission considers relevant. That he cannot do. Nor can a court on judicial review. The order in council gave to the commission, and to the commission only, power to define these other related matters which the *commissioners* consider relevant.

---

13 *Liversidge v. Anderson* (1941), [1942] A.C. 206 (U.K. H.L.), is probably the most striking example of this. There a majority of the House of Lords construed a delegation of internment powers in subjective terms, not objective ones, thereby making judicial review virtually impossible.

14 *Nova Scotia (Attorney General) v. Nova Scotia (Royal Commission into the Donald Marshall Jr. Prosecution)*, [1989] 2 S.C.R. 788, 50 C.C.C. (3d) 486, 62 D.L.R. (4th) 354, 41 Admin. L.R. 121 at 126 (S.C.C.); compare *Canada (Attorney General) v. Purcell* (1995), [1996] 1 F.C. 644, 40 Admin. L.R. (2d) 40 (Fed. C.A.).

A similar problem was presented in the famous case of *Liversidge v. Anderson*,[15] where the Secretary of State was authorized to order the detention of any person whom he had "reasonable cause to believe to be of hostile origin or association ... and that by reason thereof it is necessary to exercise control over him ...". The majority of the House of Lords held that they could not review the *bona fide* exercise of this delegated power because it was couched in terms of the Secretary of State's subjective belief as to Liversidge's hostile origins, as well as his subjective determination of the necessity to detain Liversidge. Lord Atkin dissented strongly from this subjective construction of the enabling legislation, preferring to construe the grant of power in much more objective terms which would permit the courts to determine the reasonability of the evidence upon which the Secretary of State made the decision to intern Liversidge.

The statute books are full of examples of delegated powers granted in subjective terms. For example, under section 28 of the *Energy Resources Conservation Act*,[16] the board is entitled to make quite wide subjective determinations about who qualifies as a "local intervenor" entitled to have his costs paid for participating in the board's proceedings. The statute reads as follows:

> 31(1) In this section, "local intervenor" means a person or group or association of persons who, *in the opinion of the Board*,
>
> (a) has an interest in, or
>
> (b) is in actual occupation of or is entitled to occupy
>
> land that is or may be directly and adversely affected by a decision of the Board. . . .

This legislative reference to the board's opinion greatly broadens the scope within which it can legally exercise its power, and correspondingly reduces the ambit of judicial review.

Another example of the subjective grant of power was contained in section 49(1) of the *Public Utilities Board Act* (and many other similar provisions for other delegates), which authorizes the board to issue subpoenas to compel testimony before it:[17]

> 49(1) The Board may, *when in its opinion* the attendance of any witness before the Board is desirable, cause to be served on the witness a notice requiring his attendance before the Board. . . .

---

15 (1941), [1942] A.C. 206 (U.K. H.L.); and see Heuston, "*Liversidge v. Anderson* in Retrospect" (1970) 86 L.Q. Rev. 33 for an interesting postscript on the controversy caused by this case. Compare the recent decision of the Supreme Court of Canada in *C.U.P.E. v. Ontario (Minister of Labour)*, [2003] 1 S.C.R. 539 (S.C.C.), where the Ontario legislation granted the Minister of Labour very wide subjective powers to appoint virtually anyone to chair an interest arbitration board.

16 R.S.A. 2000, c. E-10, emphasis added.

17 R.S.A. 2000, c. P-45, emphasis added.

This type of wording makes it very difficult to obtain a court order striking down the validity of the notice to attend, simply because it will generally be impossible to attack the board's opinion that the witness's testimony is desirable.

An example of this phenomenon in a rule-making context is found in section 138 of the *Employment Standards Code*.[18] Section 138 sets out the regulation-making authority of the Lieutenant Governor in Council and subsections 138(2) and (3) then state:

> (2) A regulation may be of particular or general application and applicable at particular times or in particular circumstances, may be subject to conditions and may delegate to or impose on the Director functions, powers or duties.

> (3) A regulation under subsection (1)(a) or (b) and any action or decision taken under or in accordance with the regulations under subsection (1)(a) or (b) apply *despite anything in the Act to the contrary*, except that no regulation overrides section 2.

Such a wide rule-making power effectively excludes the operation of the rule of *ultra vires*.

While there is no constitutional or other prohibition against the delegation of subjective or broadly worded powers, it is probably true to say that the courts strain against construing delegated powers in subjective or wide terms if the language can also be construed otherwise. Construing enabling legislation in objective terms has the result of extending the applicability of the *ultra vires* doctrine and therefore the ambit of judicial review of the legality of the delegate's actions. Conversely, a conscious and clearly-worded decision by the legislature to use a subjective or open-ended grant of power has the effect of widening the delegate's jurisdiction and therefore narrowing the ambit of judicial review of the legality of its actions.

(d) Incorporating the Delegate's Actions Into Legislation

Another way of effectively restricting judicial review is to incorporate the delegate's actions into legislation. Because the doctrine of Parliamentary Sovereignty prevents the courts from reviewing the contents of legislation itself (except for constitutional validity), administrative action which is incorporated into parent legislation is thereby also entitled to the protection of Parliamentary Sovereignty. As a result, no question can arise as to whether the delegate is acting within or outside the ambit of power granted to it by the legislature. In effect, the legislators adopt the delegate's actions as their own. Such legislative validation of a delegate's actions can occur at any point in time. Thus, the legislature may retroactively confirm or validate administrative action which has already occurred, or it may incorporate future actions by the delegate.[19] In

---

18 R.S.A. 2000, c. E-9.
19 For example, the Alberta Legislature has confirmed the *Alberta Rules of Court: Judicature Act*, R.S.A. 2000, c. J-2, s. 63.

any event, this legislative structure makes it very difficult to apply the *ultra vires* principle to strike down the validity of the governmental action in question.

A striking example can be given of the effectiveness of incorporation legislation as a means of preventing judicial review of the legality of administrative action. In *Chartered Institute of Patent Agents v. Lockwood*,[20] the Board of Trade was given power to make general rules regulating the registration of patents and trade marks, and these general rules were to have "the same effect as if they were contained in this Act, and shall be judicially noticed". The rules were also required to be laid before both Houses of Parliament where they could be annulled by positive resolution of either house within forty days; otherwise they came into effect. One of the rules made it illegal to act as a patent agent without being registered, and Mr. Lockwood was prosecuted for breaching this regulation. When the question arose about the validity of this rule, the House of Lords initially considered whether the rule was valid without regard to the statutory provision purporting to incorporate all of the rules into the parent legislation. They went on, however, to hold that the incorporation clause necessarily prevented judicial scrutiny of the validity of the regulations. As Lord Herschell L.C. said:[21]

> [The rules] are to be "of the same effect as if they were contained in this Act." My Lords, I have asked in vain for any explanation of the meaning of those words or any suggestion as to the effect to be given to them if, notwithstanding that provision, the rules are open to review and consideration by the Courts. The effect of an enactment is that it binds all subjects who are affected by it. They are bound to conform themselves to the provisions of the law so made. The effect of a statutory rule if validly made is precisely the same that every person must conform himself to its provisions, and, if in each case a penalty be imposed, any person who does not comply with the provisions whether of the enactment or the rule becomes equally subject to the penalty. But there is this difference between a rule and an enactment, that whereas apart from some such provision as we are considering, you may canvass a rule and determine whether or not it was within the power of those who made it, you cannot canvass in that way the provisions of an Act of Parliament. Therefore, there is that difference between the rule and the statute. There is no difference if the rule is one within the statutory authority, but that very substantial difference, if it is open to consideration whether it be so or not.
>
> I own I feel very great difficulty in giving to this provision that they "shall be of the same effect as if they were contained in this Act," any other meaning than this, that you shall for all purposes of construction or obligation or otherwise treat them exactly as if they were in the Act. No doubt there might be some conflict between a rule and

---

20   [1894] A.C. 347 (U.K. H.L.).
21   *Ibid.* at 359-60.

a provision of the Act. Well, there is a conflict sometimes between two sections to be found in the same Act. You have to try and reconcile them as best you may. If you cannot, you have to determine which is the leading provision and which the subordinate provision, and which must give way to the other. That would be so with regard to the enactment and with regard to rules which are to be treated as if within the enactment. In that case probably the enactment itself would be treated as the governing consideration and the rule as subordinate to it. Those are points which I need not dwell upon on the present occasion.

And Lord Russell reached the same conclusion:[22]

I think that if the rules are to be read as part of the Act (as I think they ought to be) it is not, in this case, competent to judicial tribunals to reject them. Such effect must be given to them by judicial construction as can properly be given to them taking them in conjunction with the general provisions of the Act or Acts of Parliament in connection with which they have been formulated.

These quotations demonstrate some judicial disquiet about how far an incorporation clause can go to prevent judicial review of the legality of a delegate's actions. Two quite distinct approaches to this problem arose in subsequent cases. In *R. v. Minister of Health*,[23] the House of Lords held that it had power to determine whether the delegate's actions were inconsistent with the Act, and therefore were not capable of being incorporated into it pursuant to a statutory provision that "the order of the Minister when made shall have effect as if enacted in this Act". This approach was adopted by the British Columbia Court of Appeal in *British Columbia (Minister of Finance) v. Woodward Estate*,[24] when it held that a decision which breached the principles of natural justice was void and therefore was incapable of being protected by legislation which purported to validate it retroactively. The Supreme Court of Canada, however, held that the proper construction of the legislation in question indicated that the legislature clearly intended to ratify and validate the previous decision of the Minister, notwithstanding the fact that it might otherwise have been invalid.

The proper approach, therefore, is to construe the parent legislation to determine how broadly it intends to protect or incorporate the delegate's actions. If one concludes that the legislation does incorporate the delegate's

---

22 *Ibid.* at 367. See also R. Ward, "Biting on the Bullet: The Constitutional Limits of Judicial Review" (1986) 49 Modern L. Rev. 645 on the effect of administrative action being approved by resolution of the House of Commons.

23 [1931] A.C. 494 (U.K. H.L.).

24 [1971] 3 W.W.R. 645 (B.C. C.A.), affirmed (1972), [1973] S.C.R. 120 (S.C.C.).

impugned actions, they are protected by the doctrine of Parliamentary Sovereignty from judicial review because by definition they cannot be *ultra vires*.[25]

5. Is an Ultra Vires Action Void or Voidable?

The question sometimes arises whether an *ultra vires* act is void or merely voidable.[26] The answer is important in order to determine whether the delegate's action has any legal effect prior to the declaration by the court that it is *ultra vires*. In principle, all *ultra vires* administrative actions are void, not voidable, and there are not degrees of invalidity. This is clearly true where the delegate is not even purporting to deal with the matter which the legislation grants to it: such substantive errors of jurisdiction "in the narrow sense" identified by Lord Reid are clearly void, and are not even arguably voidable. Similarly, Lord Reid indicated that subsequent errors which cause a delegate to exceed or lose its jurisdiction *(e.g.,* abuse of discretion, breaches of natural justice, certain errors of law) make its actions a nullity. Although people may have acted on the assumption that the delegate did have authority to do the impugned action, the effect of the court's granting of judicial review must be to declare that that was an erroneous state of affairs, that the delegate never had jurisdiction to do the particular action in the manner complained of. Contrary to the *dicta* by the Supreme Court of Canada in *Harelkin v. University of Regina*[27] to the effect that a breach of natural justice merely renders the delegate's action voidable, theoretical considerations require one to conclude that all of the types of excess of jurisdiction discussed in Chapters 7, 8, 9 and 10 render the decision or action void. This theoretical conclusion is of practical importance if there is a privative clause, because then the courts can only

---

25   The same types of problems arise with respect to statutory provisions which deem certain certificates or actions to be "conclusive for all purposes": see Vol. 1 of the McRuer Report at 273-74.

26   For a complete discussion of this point, see H.W.R. Wade, "Unlawful Administrative Action: Void or Voidable?", Part I at (1967) 83 L.Q. Rev. 499, Part II at (1968) 84 L.Q. Rev. 95; Wade's *Administrative Law*, 7th ed. (Oxford: Clarendon Press, 1994) especially at 339-44 and 516-18; G.L. Peiris, "Natural Justice and Degrees of Invalidity of Administrative Action" [1983] P.L. 634, and D.P. Jones, "Discretionary Refusal of Judicial Review in Administrative Law" (1981) 19 Alta. L. Rev. 483. The issue also arises in the context of collateral attacks on decisions by statutory delegates: see *R. v. Consolidated Maybrun Mines Ltd.*, [1998] 1 S.C.R. 706, 158 D.L.R. (4th) 193 (S.C.C.), affirming (1996), 5 Admin. L.R. (3d) 288, 133 D.L.R. (4th) 513 (Ont. C.A.); *R. v. Al Klippert Ltd.*, [1998] 1 S.C.R. 737, 158 D.L.R. (4th) 219, 216 A.R. 1 (S.C.C.), reversing (1996), 141 D.L.R. (4th) 80, 187 A.R. 241, 5 Admin. L.R. (3d) 274 (Alta. C.A.), reversing (1993), 146 A.R. 211 (Alta. Q.B.); *Danyluk v. Ainsworth Technologies Inc.*, [2001] 2 S.C.R. 460 (S.C.C.); as well as cases involving abuse of process: *Toronto (City) v. C.U.P.E., Local 79*, 2003 SCC 63 (S.C.C.) and *Toronto (City) v. C.U.P.E., Local 79*, 2003 SCC 64 (S.C.C.).

27   [1979] 2 S.C.R. 561 (S.C.C.). In the *A.U.P.E., Local 63 v. Alberta (Public Service Employees' Relations Board)*, [1982] 1 S.C.R. 923 (S.C.C.), discussed in Chapter 10, Chief Justice Laskin attempted to correct the dicta for *Harelkin v. University of Regina*, [1979] 2 S.C.R. 561 (S.C.C.) by saying: "Jurisdictional errors, *including want of natural justice . . .*". This position must be correct in theory.

review errors of *jurisdiction* (whether "narrow" or "wide"), *which can only occur if the action is void, not voidable.*

6. The Discretion to Refuse a Remedy Where Grounds for Judicial Review Exist

It has been noted that the courts have discretion to refuse at least some of the remedies for illegal administrative action even if grounds for judicial review have been established. Although the proper ambit for the exercise of this judicial discretion is dealt with in the context of the discussion about remedies in Part IV, it is important to remember that the existence of this discretion does not restrict the grounds for judicial review of illegal administrative action. Those cases in which the courts exercise their discretion to refuse a remedy even though grounds for judicial review undoubtedly exist should be identified and distinguished from those cases which refuse judicial review because no grounds for relief have been disclosed.

7. Summary

With the exception of the anomalous use of *certiorari* to correct certain intra-jurisdictional errors of law on the face of the record (discussed in Chapter 11), all grounds for judicial review depend upon a defect in the delegate's jurisdiction to do the particular act in question. This defect may occur in its acquisition of jurisdiction. Alternatively, an abuse of discretion, breach of natural justice or other error may cause the delegate to lose jurisdiction. All of these constitute grounds for judicial review. However, because the courts have the discretion to refuse certain remedies, a remedy may not be granted in every case where there are grounds to review an illegal administrative action.

The following chapters examine in some detail the separate grounds for judicial review of illegal administrative action.

8. Selected Bibliography

Akehurst, M.B., "Void or Voidable? – Natural Justice and Unnatural Meanings" (1968) 31 M.L.R. 138.

Arthurs, H.W., "Protection Against Judicial Review", in Canadian Institute for the Administration of Justice, *Judicial Review of Administrative Rulings* (Montreal: les Editions Yvon Blais Inc., 1983) at 149.

David, H., "Some Consequences of Procedural Error", in Canadian Institute for the Administration of Justice, *Judicial Review of Administrative Rulings* (Montreal: Les Editions Yvon Blais Inc., 1983) at 335.

Macdonald, R.A., "Absence of Jurisdiction: A Perspective", Canadian Institute for the Administration of Justice, *Judicial Review of Administrative Rulings* (Montreal: les Editions Yvon Blais Inc., 1983) at 179.

Oliver, D., "Void and Voidable in Administrative Law: A Problem of Legal Recognition" (1981) 34 Current Legal Problems 43.

Peiris, G.L., "Natural Justice and Degrees of Invalidity of Administrative Action" [1983] P.L. 634.

Rubinstein, A., *Jurisdiction and Illegality: A Study in Public Law* (Oxford: Clarendon Press, 1965).

Wade, H.W.R., "Unlawful Administrative Action: Void or Voidable?", Part I at (1967) 83 L.Q. Rev. 499.

Wade, H.W.R., "Unlawful Administrative Action: Void or Voidable?", Part II at (1968) 84 L.Q. Rev. 95.

6

Defects in Acquiring Jurisdiction

1. Introduction

Adopting Lord Reid's narrow meaning of jurisdiction,[1] one must first focus on the acquisition of the delegate's jurisdiction to do the particular act in question. This requires an examination of the statute to determine: (a) precisely what sort of thing the delegate is authorized to do, outside of which its actions are clearly *ultra vires*; (b) that the delegate has been validly constituted, by identifying who is the delegate, whether it can sub-delegate its responsibilities and powers, and has in fact been validly appointed; (c) whether the delegate has complied with all statutory requirements, such as advertising or giving notices to particular people; and (d) whether any other preliminary or collateral matters have been complied with in order to bring the delegate into the jurisdiction granted to it by statute. Errors on any one of these matters may prevent the delegate from acquiring jurisdiction in Lord Reid's narrow sense of the word, will render the delegate's actions *ultra vires*, and will provide grounds for judicial review.

---

1 In *Anisminic Ltd. v. Foreign Compensation Commission* (1968), [1969] 2 A.C. 147 at 171 (U.K. H.L.), quoted in Chapter 5.

147

2. Substantive Ultra Vires

It is obvious that a delegate can only acquire jurisdiction to do the type of activity authorized by the statute, and any other activity will be *ultra vires*. Thus, a delegate authorized to build a park has no jurisdiction to build a highway instead, and any attempt to do so will be *ultra vires* and therefore susceptible to judicial review. Likewise, an attempt by a professional governing body to conduct an investigation outside of the parameters set out in the governing statute causes that body to act without jurisdiction.[2]

3. Constitution of the Delegate

Jurisdiction can only be acquired by the person contemplated by the statute to do the particular activity in question. Accordingly, questions can always be raised as to whether the delegate has been properly constituted, which really breaks down into two separate questions: (a) in what circumstances can the delegate sub-delegate all or any of its powers and responsibilities to another person; and (b) what formalities, if any, must be observed in appointing a particular delegate?

(a) Sub-delegation

The maxim *delegatus non potest delegare*[3] states the general rule that a delegate may not sub-delegate statutory powers. The policy underlying the general rule reflects the Sovereignty of Parliament, which after all chose the specific delegate to whom it granted the statutory power in question.

Parliament may, of course, specifically authorize the sub-delegation of powers, and this has the effect of ousting the applicability of the maxim *delegatus non potest delegare* altogether. Thus the *Public Service Act*[4] sets out the duties of the deputy minister. That Act specifically delegates to the deputy minister the ability to perform the duties of the minister under the Act.[5] The deputy minister can, in turn, sub-delegate any of those powers to other officials within the department. Because the legislation specifically permits these instances of sub-delegation, no question of *ultra vires* can arise if it occurs.[6]

---

2   *Stephen v. College of Physicians & Surgeons (Saskatchewan)*, [1989] 6 W.W.R. 1 (Sask. C.A.) and *Goertz v. College of Physicians & Surgeons (Saskatchewan)*, [1989] 6 W.W.R. 11 (Sask. C.A.).

3   A delegate cannot delegate to another.

4   R.S.A. 2000, c. P-42.

5   *Ibid.* ss. 8, 9.

6   On the other hand, if sub-delegation has been validly done, only the sub-delegate can exercise the power; the delegate has given away its power and can no longer lawfully exercise it, unless the legislation specifically so provides, see e.g. *Securities Act*, R.S.A. 2000, c. S-4, s. 22(6) where after providing specific powers of delegation, provides:

>   Notwithstanding that the Commission has given an authorization [to another to perform a duty of the Commission] under this section, the Commission may do the act or thing in respect of which the authorization was given.

For other examples of specific statutory authority to sub-delegate powers, see: ss. 220 and 221

A more difficult question of statutory interpretation arises when Parliament does not use express language, but may nevertheless arguably be said to have intended to permit sub-delegation. Professor John Willis described the court's task in such a case as follows:[7]

> [If] the language of the statute does not, *ex hypothesi*, help it [a court], it is driven therefore to the scope and object of the statute. Is there anything in the nature of the authority to which the discretion is entrusted, in the situation in which the discretion is to be exercised, in the object which its exercise is to achieve to suggest that the legislature did not intend to confine the authority to the personal exercise of its discretion? This question is answered in practice by comparing the *prima facie* rule with the known practices or the apprehended needs of the authority in doing its work; the court inquires whether the policy-scheme of the statute is such as could not easily be realized unless the policy which requires that a discretion be exercised by the authority named thereto be displaced; it weighs the presumed desire of the legislature for the judgment of the authority it has named against the presumed desire of the legislature that the process of government shall go on in its accustomed and most effective manner and where there is a conflict between the two policies it determines which, under all the circumstances, is the more important.

The courts adopted this approach in *Reference re Regulations (Chemicals) under War Measures Act (Canada)*[8] to permit sub-delegation of the power to make regulations by the Governor in Council to the Controller of Chemicals, and a similar result occurred in *Fort Frances Pulp & Paper Co. v. Manitoba Free Press Co.*[9] On the other hand, this approach does not necessarily result in validating the impugned sub-delegation. For example, in *Canada (Attorney General) v. Brent*,[10] the Ontario Court of Appeal struck down regulations made by the Governor in Council which had the effect of sub-delegating to special inquiry officers the power to exercise their discretion to determine which immigrants should be granted landed immigrant status in Canada. As Aylesworth J.A. said:[11]

> In short, those limited powers of [subordinate] legislation, wide though the limits of the subject-matter be, which Parliament has delegated to His Excellency in Council have not been exercised by the

---

of the *Income Tax Act*, R.S.C. 1985 (5th Supp.), c.1; *Universities Act*, R.S.A. 2000, c. U-3, s. 37(c).

7   *"Delegatus Non Potest Delegare"* (1943) 21 Can. Bar Rev. 257 at 260-61.

8   [1943] S.C.R. 1 (S.C.C.).

9   [1923] 3 D.L.R. 629 (Ontario P.C.), affirming (1922), [1923] 3 D.L.R. 199 (Ont. C.A.) especially at 200, *per* Riddell J.

10 [1955] 3 D.L.R. 587 (Ont. C.A.), affirmed [1956] S.C.R. 318 (S.C.C.). See also *Brant Dairy Co. v. Ontario (Milk Commission)* (1972), [1973] S.C.R. 131 (S.C.C.) and *Canadian Institute of Public Real Estate Cos. v. Toronto (City)*, [1979] 2 S.C.R. 2 (S.C.C.).

11 *Ibid.* at 593.

delegate at all, but, on the contrary, by him have been re-delegated bodily, for exercise not merely by some one other individual but, respectively and independently of each other, by every Special Inquiry Officer who sees fit to invoke them and according to "the opinion" of each such sub-delegate.

I can find nothing in the Act expressly (or by inference, if that is permissible) manifesting any intention to permit or authorize any such procedure. On the other hand, it is reasonable to suppose that what Parliament had in contemplation was the enactment of such Regulations relevant to the named subject-matters, or some of them, as in His Excellency in Council's own opinion were advisable and as, therefore, would be of general application to persons seeking entry into Canada regardless of the particular port of entry involved. Surely, what was intended was legislation enacted by His Excellency in Council according to his wisdom and broad experience, prescribing standards for the general guidance of Immigration Officers and Special Inquiry Officers operating at or near the borders of the country, not a wide divergency of rules and opinions ever changing according to the individual notions of such officers. The Regulation is invalid and the order of deportation based upon it is invalid likewise, *delegatus non potest delegare . . .*

Other good examples of cases where the courts have applied the maxim include: *Behari Lal, Re*,[12] where it was held that the power conferred on the Governor in Council by section 30 of the *Immigration Act*[13] to prohibit the landing of immigrants of a specified class could not be delegated to the Minister of the Interior, because the exercise of power depended upon the Governor's opinion about the necessity and expediency of such a prohibition, and *Geraghty v. Porter*,[14] which required express words in the legislation before sub-delegation could be permitted.

Two particular circumstances, however, appear to incline the courts to conclude that Parliament must have intended sub-delegation to occur, even in the absence of express words permitting it. The first arises where the legislation delegates a power to a person who clearly will not be able to exercise it himself or herself personally, such as to a minister of the Crown who could not possibly personally exercise all of the statutory powers delegated to him or her.[15] Our constitutional practice generally permits ministers to delegate most of their

---

12   (1908), 13 B.C.R. 415 (B.C. S.C.).

13   R.S.C. 1906, c. 93.

14   [1917] N.Z.L.R. 554.

15   See Willis, *supra* note 7 at 260. See also *Peralta v. Ontario* (1988), 56 D.L.R. (4th) 575 (S.C.C.), affirming (1985), 16 D.L.R. (4th) 259 (Ont. C.A.). But compare this reasoning with that in *Behari Lal, Re, supra* note 12. Query: was the power to prohibit a particular immigrant so rarely used that Parliament must have intended the Governor in Council to do so itself? See also *Reference re Regulations (Chemical) under War Measures Act (Canada), supra* note 8.

powers to the civil servants in their department,[16] who exercise the powers in the minister's name.[17] This practice is specifically recognized in section 21 of the *Interpretation Act* (Alberta):[18]

(1) Words in an enactment directing or empowering a Minister of the Crown to do something, or otherwise applying to the Minister by the Minister's name of office, include

    (a) a Minister acting for another Minister or a Minister designated to act in the office, and

    (b) the deputy of the Minister or a person appointed as acting deputy,

but nothing in this subsection authorizes a deputy or acting deputy to exercise any authority conferred on a Minister to enact a regulation as defined in the *Regulations Act*.

(2) Words in an enactment directing or empowering a person to do something, or otherwise applying to the person by the person's name of office, include

    (a) a person acting for that person or appointed to act in the office, and

    (b) that person's deputy or a person appointed as that person's acting deputy

(3) This section applies whether or not the office of a Minister or other person is vacant.

Politically, the minister remains responsible for all actions taken in his or her name. Thus, the better view may be that civil servants merely act as agents helping the minister himself or herself to exercise his or her powers, instead of acting as sub-delegates in the place and stead of the minister. Certainly, the minister is politically responsible for all actions taken in his or her name, whether or not the minister even knew about them. And it is quite clear that the proper construction of some legislation may require the minister personally to exercise the particular statutory power in question, for example, deciding to prosecute for tax evasion under the *Income Tax Act*.[19] So provisions similar to

---

16 But see *Québec (Procureur General) v. Carrières Ste.-Thérèse Ltée*, [1985] 1 S.C.R. 831 (S.C.C.) where the legislation specifically provided that "the Minister may himself exercise directly the powers . . .". In the face of such a statutory direction, the Supreme Court found there could not be any sub-delegation of these powers.

17 This practice has been spelled out in statutes creating departments. For example, the *Government Organization Act*, R.S.A. 2000, c. G-10, s. 9 provides:

    (1) A Minister may in writing delegate any power, duty or function conferred on him by this Act or any other Act or Regulation to any person.

    (2) Subsection (1) does not apply to any power or duty of a Minister to make regulations as defined in the *Regulations Act*. Equivalent federal statutes do not contain such powers.

18 R.S.A. 2000, c. I-8.

19 *Granby Construction & Equipment Ltd. v. Milley* (1974), 47 D.L.R. (3d) 427 (B.C. S.C.), reversed (1974), 50 D.L.R. (3d) 115 (B.C. C.A.).

those in the *Interpretation Act* really do not permit sub-delegation in all circumstances,[20] but rather only add one more factor to be considered by the courts in construing legislation to try to eke out the implied intent of Parliament on this point.

Secondly, the courts appear to be more prepared to accept that Parliament intended to permit sub-delegation of merely administrative functions, but not legislative or judicial ones. This approach necessarily involves characterizing the function whose sub-delegation is in doubt – a futile process which has been made obsolete in other aspects of administrative law.[21] To some extent, however, this distinction makes good sense, because many merely administrative matters do not require the exercise of discretion or personal judgment, and it really does not matter which particular person in fact does the action in question. On the other hand, to the extent that the phrase "merely administrative" has been used in administrative law to encompass some discretionary functions which cannot be characterized as judicial or quasi-judicial, the policy underlying the rule against sub-delegation applies to require that particular administrator to exercise the discretion personally. In short, it is submitted that the real question is whether discretion must be exercised by the delegate. If so, there should be a strong presumption against sub-delegation, whatever the appellation of the function involved.

It may not always be easy to determine when sub-delegation has occurred. For example, the decisions in *Canada (Attorney General) v. Brent, Brant Dairy Co. v. Ontario (Milk Commission)* and *Canadian Institute of Public Real Estate Cos. v. Toronto (City)*[22] demonstrate an improper attempt to sub-delegate the power to enact subordinate legislation by converting it into a discretionary power to be exercised by sub-delegates. A similar situation arose in *R. v. Horback*,[23] where a municipal by-law purported to delegate judicial or discretionary power to the Superintendent of Motor Vehicles to determine which automobiles were unsafe, without setting out in the by-law the standards for what constituted safety. In *Saskatchewan (Labour Relations Borad) v. Speers*,[24] the Saskatchewan Court of Appeal found there to be an illegal sub-delegation when the board had its administrator determine how many of the employees wished to be represented by the respondent union instead of undertaking this task itself. Although the line between sub-delegation and using an agent or servant may be difficult to determine, stepping over it will generally be fatal to the validity of the administrator's action.

---

20 For example, see *Brent, supra* note 10.
21 See Chapter 8, for a discussion of the previous need to characterize functions as "judicial" or "quasi-judicial" (as opposed to "administrative" or "executive") in order to make the rules of natural justice applicable, or to make *certiorari* available to correct a breach of those rules. This need to characterize has been supplanted by the development of the "duty to be fair". Note the comments of Minuk Prov. J. in *R. v. Perimeter Airlines (Inland) Ltd.*, [1986] 6 W.W.R. 110 at 125 (Man. Prov. Ct.): "The cases I have been referred to indicate that there is sometimes a fine line to be drawn between powers that are legislative or administrative."
22 *Supra* note 10.
23 (1967), 64 D.L.R. (2d) 17 (B.C. S.C.).
24 (1947), [1948] 1 D.L.R. 340 (Sask. C.A.).

Altogether apart from determining whether sub-delegation is permitted in a particular context, it may frequently be difficult for the citizen to verify whether the governmental official with whom the citizen is dealing has in fact been sub-delegated the powers being exercised. On the one hand, some statutes specifically require some formal method by which the delegate must indicate that it is sub-delegating its statutory powers. Thus, sections 220 and 221 of the *Income Tax Act*[25] specifically permits the Minister of National Revenue to delegate certain of his or her powers to other departmental officials, which must be done by regulation.[26] Accordingly, one can look at the regulation to determine whether a particular departmental officer has been sub-delegated the particular power[27] being used. To some extent, such formality will only help the citizen after the fact, because a search-and-seizure raid by police and officials from the tax department is not likely to be delayed while the citizen roots around to find the regulation delegating the minister's authority to the person who in fact authorized the expedition. On the other hand, most federal and provincial statutes do not provide a formal method for recording sub-delegation of powers, nor is there often a written record of informal sub-delegation. For example, section 25 of the *Public Service Act*[28] of Alberta permits the department head to discipline or dismiss a member of the public service in certain circumstances, and section 8 authorizes the deputy head to exercise all of the powers of the department head. Section 9 in effect permits either of these to delegate any of their powers to any other designated officer of the department. It may be valid for the deputy to instruct such an officer verbally to discipline a particular public servant, even though the latter has no way at the time to determine that a sub-delegation has occurred.

To the extent that the sub-delegate's activity would otherwise constitute an actionable wrong known to law, the sub-delegate – and not the citizen – will have to bear the burden of proving the validity of the sub-delegation in order to raise a valid defence to the citizen's lawsuit. However, in other circumstances (such as getting a permit)[29] the burden of attacking the sub-delegation will lie on the citizen, and this burden will be compounded by the lack of any formal system of recording or registering sub-delegation of particular powers.

Sub-delegation may also effectively result where the delegate fetters its discretion by adopting a policy or contractually undertaking to exercise it only one way. Although "fettering discretion" is recognized as a separate ground for judicial review,[30] the practical result is the same as illegal sub-delegation

---

25 R.S.C. 1985 (5th Supp.), c.1.

26 For example, Regulation 900 under the *Income Tax Act*.

27 Generally discretionary in nature.

28 R.S.A. 2000, c. P-42, which provides as follows:

    8(2) For the purposes of this Act, a deputy head has the powers and may perform the duties of the deputy head's department head.

    9   A department head may, subject to the regulations, delegate any of the powers and duties granted to the department head by this Act to designated officials of the department head's department.

29 See *Vic Restaurant Inc. v. Montreal (City)* (1958), 17 D.L.R. (2d) 81 (S.C.C.).

30 See the discussion in Chapter 7, section 6.

because the discretion is not in fact exercised by the very delegate whom the legislation has designated. Thus, in *Vic Restaurant Inc. v. Montreal (City)*,[31] the Supreme Court of Canada struck down the city's practice of always accepting the advice of the police to refuse a restaurant licence to anyone whom the police had identified as undesirable. Adopting such a policy not only fettered the discretion specifically granted by statute to the city council, it effectively amounted to an illegal sub-delegation to the police, thereby making the administrative action *ultra vires*.

One must also consider the effect of a valid sub-delegation on the ability of the delegate personally to exercise the statutory power. Although the delegate may generally at any time rescind the sub-delegation, the better view appears to be that the delegate cannot exercise the statutory powers so long as the sub-delegation subsists.[32] What one has given away, one cannot continue to exercise! To this extent, therefore, delegation and sub-delegation operate differently from the law of agency, and the two concepts must be distinguished.

One must also distinguish between sub-delegation and agency when considering the applicability of the principles of natural justice or the duty to be fair. These procedural rules require the very person who is making a decision to give a fair hearing to anyone affected thereby. In sub-delegation situations, the sub-delegate clearly is making the decision and will be the one required to adopt a fair procedure. On the other hand, if the statutory delegate uses agents to help it exercise its power, the delegate itself – and not merely its agents – must comply with natural justice.[33] The coupling of natural justice considerations to the question of sub-delegation, therefore, may expand the ambit of judicial review of administrative actions.

In summary, the difficulties surrounding sub-delegation may affect the jurisdiction of the person purporting to exercise a statutory power. To the extent that there is a defect in that person's acquisition of jurisdiction, there is a ground for judicial review.

(b) Appointment of Members of the Delegate Body

Sometimes defects in the appointment of the members of a statutory body will render its actions void. Examples of fatal defects have included: failing to appoint persons with proper professional qualifications; appointing members for the wrong term of office;[34] not complying with a mandatory step in the appointment process;[35] adding unauthorized additional members to a tribunal;[36] and the lack of a quorum.[37]

---

31 *Supra* note 29.
32 But see the comments in *supra* note 6.
33 See *Arlidge v. Islington Corp.*, [1909] 2 K.B. 127 for a discussion of this problem.
34 *Hollenberg v. Optometric Assn. (British Columbia)* (1967), 61 D.L.R. (2d) 295 (B.C. C.A.).
35 *Wetaskiwin (Municipal District No. 74) v. Kaiser*, [1947] 4 D.L.R. 461 (Alta. T.D.), where the minister had the right to nominate one member for appointment by the council of one

4. Compliance with Statutory Requirements

Sometimes legislation prescribes specific matters that the delegate must attend to in the exercise of its powers. For example, the delegate may be required by statute to give notice to certain persons of its intended actions;[38] to give a hearing prior to acting;[39] to obtain someone else's approval;[40] to keep a written record of its proceedings;[41] or to do certain things within a prescribed period of time.[42] Questions often arise as to the legal consequence of the

---

member of the Agricultural Services Board, which was struck down because the council did not make the appointment, but let the minister do it directly.

36 *R. v. College of Physicians & Surgeons (British Columbia)*, [1942] 3 W.W.R. 510 (B.C. S.C.), where the executive committee added a county court judge as one of its members.

37 At common law, a quorum probably exists where half of the members are present: *Herring v. Mexia, Texas*, 290 S.W. 792 at 794 (Tex. C. Civ. A., 1927). This rule has been enacted in s. 17 of the *Interpretation Act* (Alberta), R.S.A. 2000, c. I-8. Sometimes legislation specifically deviates from this rule: see e.g. *Securities Act*, R.S.A. 2000, c. S-4, s. 23(2) and *Labour Relations Code*, R.S.A. 2000, c. L-1, s. 9(6). Also see *Strathcona (Municipality) v. Maclab Enterprises Ltd.* (1970), 75 W.W.R. 629 at 642-43 (Alta. T.D.), reversed [1971] 3 W.W.R. 461 (Alta. C.A.), leave to appeal refused [1971] S.C.R. xii (S.C.C.), where s. 7 of the *Planning Act*, S.A. 1963, c. 43, specifically permitted the board to fix its own quorum. See *R. v. Hatskin*, [1936] 3 D.L.R. 437 (Man. C.A.), for a case requiring all members to sit on an appeal under the *Minimum Wage Act*, 1924 (Man.), c. 128; or whether a member of a board can vote if he or she was not present at its proceedings: *Inter-City Freightlines Ltd. v. Swan River-The Pas Transfer Ltd.* (1971), [1972] 2 W.W.R. 317 (Man. C.A.); and McFadyen J.'s decision in *Hoyda v. Edmonton,* T.D. No. 7903-13252 (unreported), subsequently altered by an amendment to the *Municipal Government Act*.

38 See for example the *Labour Relations Code*, R.S.A. 2000, c. L-1, s. 16(6) and *Expropriation Act*, R.S.A. 2000, c. E-13, s. 24(2). Such a provision was held to be mandatory in *R. v. Ontario (Fuel Board)* (1959), 18 D.L.R. (2d) 73 (Ont. H.C.), where the applicant had never in fact received a notice sent by double registered mail, even though the board was given power to direct the manner of service of such notice. This provision, therefore, required the board to give actual notice to persons affected by its proceedings, and failure to do so resulted in the invalidity of its proceedings.

39 See for example the *Expropriation Act*, R.S.A. 2000, c. E-13, s. 15. Such a provision was held to be mandatory in *R. v. Alberta (Highway Traffic Board)*, [1947] 2 D.L.R. 373 (Alta. T.D.), where a *mandamus* was issued to require a hearing at which competitors could be heard prior to the issuance of an initial certificate of operation under s. 19 of the *Public Service Vehicles Act*, R.S.A. 1942, c. 276. Note that the specific statutory hearing provided for here was a pre-condition to the board's power to issue the certificate, and not necessarily implied by the common law requirement to follow the principles of natural justice.

40 See for example the *Safety Codes Act*, R.S.A. 2000, c. S-1, ss. 18(h) and (i). Such a provision was held to be mandatory in *Ross (Township) v. Cobden & Eganville (District High School Board)* (1967), 63 D.L.R. (2d) 390 (Ont. H.C.), where the minister's approval had not been obtained prior to the enactment of the by-law, as required under the Act. See also *Moshos v. Canada (Minister of Manpower & Immigration)*, [1969] S.C.R. 886 (S.C.C.).

41 See for example the *Expropriation Act*, R.S.A. 2000, c. E-13, s. 28(3). Such a provision was held to be mandatory in *Fitzpatrick v. Calgary (City)* (1964), 47 D.L.R. (2d) 365 at 369 (Alta. C.A.).

42 See for example the *Expropriation Act*, R.S.A. 2000, c. E-13, s. 8(4). The statutory requirement that arbitrators issue their decisions within a certain time was held to be merely directory in *Metropolitan Toronto (Municipality) Commissioners of Police v. Police Assn. (Metropolitan Toronto) (Unit B)* (1973), 37 D.L.R. (3d) 487 (Ont. Div. Ct.); *Assoc. catholique des institutrices rurales c. St-Pascal (Commission scolaire)*, [1948] R.L. 97 (Que. C.A.); *Lincoln*

delegate's failure to comply with such matters. On the one hand, if the statutory requirement is mandatory, failure to comply therewith will render the delegate's action void.[43] On the other hand, breach of a merely directory statutory provision does not affect the validity of the delegate's action.

Distinguishing between mandatory and directory statutory provisions can be an exceedingly tricky task. The *Interpretation Act* (Alberta) now provides[44] that "shall" and "must" have an imperative meaning, and "may" is to be construed as being permissive and empowering, without specifically stating any longer that these meanings shall not apply if the context of a particular statute requires some other construction. Accordingly, the true construction of a particular statute may still be subject to considerable debate. As noted by Maxwell on *The Interpretation of Statutes*,[45] the courts have sometimes taken the view that procedural requirements for public duties should generally be read as being directory, not mandatory:

> A strong line of distinction may be drawn between cases where the prescriptions of the Act affect the performance of a duty and where they relate to a privilege or power. Where powers, rights or immunities are granted with a direction that certain regulations, formalities or conditions shall be complied with, it seems neither unjust nor inconvenient to exact a rigorous observance of them as essential to the acquisition of the right or authority conferred, and it is therefore probable that such was the intention of the legislature. But when a public duty is imposed and the statute requires that it shall be performed in a certain manner, or within a certain time, or under other specified conditions, such prescriptions may well be regarded as intended to be directory only in cases when injustice or inconvenience to others who have no control over those exercising the duty would result if such requirements were essential and imperative.

On reflection, it may not be any easier to identify a public duty than to distinguish a mandatory statutory requirement from a merely directory one. It is clear that the courts in the end must make these distinctions in exercising their (public?) duty to construe the particular statute in question, having regard to the policy of the Act, all of its provisions, the reason for including the specific statutory requirement in question, whether any statutory consequence

---

(County) Roman Catholic Separate School Board v. Buchler, [1972] 1 O.R. 854 (Ont. C.A.). By contrast, time periods under the *Expropriation Act, ibid.* have been held to be mandatory.

43   Although the superior court may in an appropriate case exercise its discretion to refuse one of the prerogative remedies to a person attacking the delegate's action.

44   R.S.A. 2000, c. I-8, s. 28(2). See *Baron v. R.*, [1993] 1 S.C.R. 416 at 441 (S.C.C.) *per* Sopinka J. on the presumption that "shall" is intended to be mandatory.

45   10th ed. (1953) at 376-77, *quoted by* Edmund Davies J. in *Cullimore v. Lyme Regis (Borough)* (1961), [1962] 1 Q.B. 718 at 726-27 (Eng. Q.B.). See also: *Montreal Street Railway v. Normandin*, [1917] A.C. 170 at 174 (Quebec P.C.); *Metropolitan Toronto (Municipality) Commissioners of Police v. Police Assn. (Metropolitan Toronto) (Unit B), supra* note 43; *Anderson v. Stewart* (1921), 62 D.L.R. 98 at 109-10 (N.B. C.A.); *Liverpool Borough Bank v. Turner* (1860), 2 De G.F. & J. 502, 45 E.R. 715 (Eng. Ch. Div.).

is provided for failure to comply, and what the practical effect of non-compliance is on the complainant or any other person.

5. Preliminary or Collateral Matters

Sometimes, legislation only delegates powers to an administrator in conditional terms: if a certain state of affairs exists, then, but only then, does the administrator have authority to act or make a decision. It is important, therefore, to determine whether the delegate's jurisdiction depends upon any preliminary or collateral matter. If so, a defect or error in such a preliminary or collateral matter will prevent the delegate from having jurisdiction.

Let us examine a few examples of preliminary or collateral errors of jurisdiction. In *Anisminic Ltd. v. Foreign Compensation Commission*,[46] the commission was delegated authority to determine what compensation to pay British nationals or their successors-in-title for property confiscated by the Egyptian government during the Suez affair. The commission decided that Anisminic Ltd. was not a British successor-in-title to a British owner of expropriated property and declined to consider Anisminic's claim for recompense. The House of Lords, however, held that Anisminic was indeed in law a successor-in-title, with the result that the commission was bound to consider its claim. In other words, the status of being a successor-in-title was a precondition to the commission's jurisdiction to consider claims for compensation. Further, by making an erroneous determination of Anisminic's status as a successor-in-title, the commission could not deprive the company of its right to be considered for compensation. In short, the jurisdiction of the commission did not include the right to determine conclusively whether an applicant was a successor-in-title, but was consequent upon the right determination of that preliminary matter.

Similarly, in *Bell v. Ontario (Human Rights Commission)*,[47] the statutory delegate had certain powers if there was illegal racial discrimination with respect to renting a "self-contained domestic establishment". The Supreme Court of Canada upheld the issuance of an order of prohibition to stop the commission from exercising its powers with respect to a residential unit which was not self-contained. Again, the fact of being self-contained was preliminary to the jurisdiction of the statutory delegate. As Martland J. said:[48]

> The Act does not purport to place that issue [of whether there is a self-contained domestic establishment] within the exclusive jurisdiction of the board, and a wrong decision on it would not enable the board to proceed further.

---

46   (1968), [1969] A.C. 147 (U.K. H.L.).
47   [1971] S.C.R. 756 (S.C.C.).
48   *Ibid.* at 775. Query: if the Act had purported to place the determination of whether there was a self-contained domestic establishment within the exclusive jurisdiction of the commission, would this have breached s. 96 of the *Constitution Act*, 1867? See discussion in Chapter 2.

Accordingly, there was only one right answer to this question – and it was for the courts to determine that right answer.

As a final example, the decision in *Parkhill Bedding & Furniture Ltd. v. I.M.A.W., Local 714,5*[49] illustrates a collateral error of law which deprived the statutory delegate of jurisdiction.

The legislation provided that a collective agreement continued to apply to "any new employer to whom passes the ownership of the business of an employer who has entered into the agreement. . . ." The issue arose whether Parkhill was bound by the agreement when it purchased assets from the receiver of another company which had been party to the agreement. Section 59(1)(c) of the Manitoba *Labour Relations Act* provided as follows:[50]

> 59(1) Where in any proceeding before the board or otherwise in the course of the administration of this Act a question arises under this Act as to whether . . .
>
> > (c) in any case, a collective agreement has been entered into, and the terms thereof, and the persons who are parties to or are bound by the collective agreement or on whose behalf the collective agreement was entered into . . .
>
> the board shall decide the question and its decision shall be final and conclusive for all the purposes of this Act.

As Freedman J.A. said:[51]

> [T]he issue which the Board had to consider was whether the collective agreement was binding on Parkhill, and the Board came to the conclusion that it was. It must be remembered that neither Bastin, J., nor this Court can sit in appeal on the Board's decision. The Board has a right to be wrong, provided it acts within its jurisdiction. Did it so act in this case? That is the only question properly arising on this *certiorari* application.
>
> In my view the Board's order was made without jurisdiction. It is obvious that before the Board could make a final decision under s. 59(1)(c) it had to address itself to the question raised in s. 18(1)(c), namely, whether Parkhill was a new employer to whom the ownership of the business of Trysson had passed. Was this latter question, in the circumstances of this case, one that could properly be classified as preliminary or collateral, in the sense in which those terms are used in *certiorari* matters? Or was it part of the main issue which the Board had to decide? If it was the latter, then clearly the Board had exclusive jurisdiction to deal with it, and its decision would not be subject to review. If, on the other hand, it was the former, a different situation

---

49 (1961), 26 D.L.R. (2d) 589 (Man. C.A.).
50 R.S.M. 1954, c. 132, quoted *ibid.* at 592.
51 *Ibid.* at 593-94.

would arise. For the Board cannot give itself jurisdiction by a wrong decision on such a preliminary or collateral point upon which the limit to its jurisdiction depends (*Bunbury v. Fuller* (1853), 9 Exch. 111 at p. 140, 156 E.R. 47). An error by the Board on such a point is reviewable by the Court on *certiorari*.

I am aware that I am now entering upon fighting ground. Classification of a matter as preliminary or collateral is not always easy. Nor has an expanding jurisprudence on this branch of the law altogether removed its difficulties. For cases may be found on both sides of the question. Although the matter has been dealt with by the Supreme Court of Canada it has not come before it in circumstances which in my view are comparable to those of the present case. To the extent, however, that any general principles may be extracted from the decisions, the cases have been most helpful to me in the present controversy.

His Lordship noted[52] that the courts had intervened whenever "the point for determination involved an examination of legal principles and considerations that went beyond the simple confines of the statute under which the Board operated." Thus, in the present case:[53]

[b]efore the Board could determine whether the collective agreement was binding on Parkhill it had first of all to consider whether Parkhill was a "new employer" to whom had passed the business of Trysson. That question involved something more than the provisions of the *Labour Relations Act*, including specifically s. 59(1)(c) and s. 18(1)(c) thereof. It involved a consideration of the law pertaining to bankruptcy, to the effect of an assignment in bankruptcy upon the contracts of workmen, to the powers of a Trustee in Bankruptcy to sell, with the consent of inspectors, assets belonging to the bankrupt estate and to the title which a purchaser of assets from such Trustee acquires – including, in the latter question, whether such title is to be deemed encumbered by obligations under a collective agreement which had been entered into by the assignor in bankruptcy. These are matters entering into the determination of the question whether Parkhill was a "new employer" within the meaning of the Act. How can it be said that consideration of those matters is within the exclusive jurisdiction of the Board? Rather they are matters touching upon the status of Parkhill – a preliminary or collateral matter which the Board had first to deal with before it could proceed to adjudicate on whether the collective agreement was binding. On such a question the Board could be right or wrong. But since this was a preliminary or collateral matter the Board's decision thereon would be subject to review. If the Board were wrong and by its error assumed a jurisdiction it did not possess,

---

52   *Ibid.* at 596.
53   *Ibid.* at 597-98.

certiorari would lie, and the Court could correct the error, as in *Re Workmen's Compensation Act* and C.P.R. and as in the Lunenburg case. If the Board were right, a *certiorari* application could still be brought – because the matter involved was preliminary or collateral – but in that case the Court, once it agreed that the Board's jurisdiction had been established, could not interfere with whatever adjudication was made therein.

I do not wish to be taken as having attempted to lay down a definition of the phrase "a preliminary or collateral question", least of all an exhaustive definition. I am merely saying that the cases in Group B appear to possess a common factor that is also present in the case before us – namely, that before it can determine whether the Act applies at all, the Board must first consider legal principles that are outside the scope of the Act. Other forms of preliminary or collateral questions have arisen and doubtless will arise, but that is a field which I need not enter at this time.

Being of the view, then, that when the Board began to examine the status of Parkhill it entered upon a question that was truly preliminary or collateral to its jurisdiction, I must now ask whether the Board on that question arrived at the right or wrong decision. With respect, I believe its decision was wrong.

Accordingly, because a jurisdictional point was involved, the privative clause had no effect.

It is not always easy to determine from the legislation whether a particular matter is preliminary or collateral to a delegate's jurisdiction on the one hand, or lies within it on the other hand. As de Smith commented in the early 1980's:[54]

No satisfactory test has ever been formulated for distinguishing findings which go to jurisdiction from findings which go to the merits; and in some cases the courts, impressed by logical difficulties, have appeared to ignore the distinction altogether.

The Supreme Court of Canada, however, has clearly indicated that the court will not be hasty to characterize a particular matter as being jurisdictional in nature if there is any doubt. As Dickson J. said in the *C.U.P.E.* case:[55]

The question of what is and is not jurisdictional is often very difficult to determine. The Courts, in my view, should not be alert to brand as jurisdictional, and therefore subject to broader curial review, that which may be doubtfully so.

---

54 *Judicial Review of Administrative Action*, 4th ed. (London: Stevens & Sons Ltd., 1980) at 114.

55 *C.U.P.E., Local 963 v. New Brunswick Liquor Corp.* (1979), 97 D.L.R. (3d) 417 at 422 (S.C.C.).

Dickson J.'s reference to "broader curial review" is now perhaps not as accurate as it was in 1979. At that time the reference was to compare review of jurisdictional matters with the much more limited ambit of judicial review of intra-jurisdictional errors of law, to which the "patently unreasonable" test had been applied. Now, however, there are a spectrum of standards of review, once it has been determined that the delegate was operating solely within its jurisdiction.[56] In principle, however, the words of Dickson J. are still true today. No matter which standard of judicial review is going to be employed, that standard should not be applied once it has been determined that a jurisdictional matter is in question.[57]

The Supreme Court of Canada has had occasion to revisit this question, as part of a broader analysis of what constitutes jurisdictional errors.[58] In *Syndicat national des employés de la commission scolaire régionale de l'Outaouais v. U.E.S., local 298,6*[59] Beetz J. notes:

> The idea of the preliminary or collateral question is based on the principle that the jurisdiction conferred on administrative tribunals and other bodies created by statute is limited, and that such a tribunal cannot by a misinterpretation of an enactment assume a power not given to it by the legislator. The theoretical basis of this idea is therefore unimpeachable – which may explain why it has never been squarely repudiated: any grant of jurisdiction will necessarily include limits to the jurisdiction granted, and any grant of a power remains subject to conditions. The principle itself presents no difficulty, but its application is another matter.
>
> The theory of the preliminary or collateral question does not appear to recognize that the legislator may intend to give an administrative tribunal, expressly or by implication, the power to determine whether certain conditions of law or fact placed on the exercise of its power do exist. It is not always true that each of these conditions limits the tribunal's authority; but except where the legislator is explicit, how can one distinguish a condition which the legislator intended to leave to the exclusive determination of the administrative tribunal from a condition which limits its authority and as to which it may not err? One can make the distinction only by means of a more or less formalistic categorization. Such a categorization often runs the risk of being arbitrary and which may in particular unduly extend the superintending and reforming power of the superior courts by transforming it into a disguised right of appeal.
>
> The concept of the preliminary or collateral question diverts the courts from the real problem of judicial review: it substitutes the question "Is this a preliminary or collateral question to the exercise of

---

56 Or at least there is a spectrum of the amount of deference to be given to a statutory delegate. See the discussion of this issue in Chapter 12.

57 See the discussion on this point in Chapter 12.

58 See Chapter 11.

59 [1988] 2 S.C.R. 1048 (S.C.C.).

the tribunal's power" for the only question which should be asked, "Did the legislator intend the question to be within the jurisdiction conferred on the tribunal?"[60]

Then Beetz J. articulated his method for determining whether an alleged error is jurisdictional or not:[61]

> The formalistic analysis of the preliminary or collateral question theory is giving way to a pragmatic and functional analysis, hitherto associated with the concept of the patently unreasonable error. At first sight it may appear that the functional analysis applied to cases of patently unreasonable error is not suitable for cases in which an error is alleged in respect of a legislative provision limiting a tribunal's jurisdiction. The difference between these two types of error is clear: only a patently unreasonable error results in an excess of jurisdiction when the question at issue is within the tribunal's jurisdiction, whereas in the case of a legislative provision limiting the tribunal's jurisdiction, a simple error will result in a loss of jurisdiction. It is nevertheless true that the first step in the analysis necessary in the concept of a "patently unreasonable" error involves determining the jurisdiction of the administrative tribunal. At this stage, the Court examines not only the wording of the enactment conferring jurisdiction on the administrative tribunal, but the purpose of the statute creating the tribunal, the reason for its existence, the area of expertise of its members and the nature of the problem before the tribunal. At this initial stage a pragmatic or functional analysis is just as suited to a case in which an error is alleged in the interpretation of a provision limiting the administrative tribunal's jurisdiction: in a case where a patently unreasonable error is alleged on a question within the jurisdiction of the tribunal, as in a case where simple error is alleged regarding a provision limiting that jurisdiction, the first step involves determining the tribunal's jurisdiction.

This same "pragmatic and functional" approach was used again by the Supreme Court in *Canada (Attorney General) v. P.S.A.C.*,[62] (the *Econosult* case) where the majority of the Supreme Court ruled that the federal Public Service Staff Relations Board did not have jurisdiction to determine who was an "employee" of the federal Crown, given the definition of "employee" contained in the Act - notwithstanding the fact that the Board's functional approach might well have been reasonable and made labour relations sense. In other words, the objective reasonability of a delegate's decision does not

---

60   *Ibid.* at 1086-87.
61   *Ibid.* at 1088-89.
62   [1991] 1 S.C.R. 614 (S.C.C.).

ipso facto give it jurisdiction to make the decision if the courts decide that the legislature did not grant that jurisdiction to the delegate.[63]

In *Econosult*, all of the judges of the Supreme Court used the "pragmatic and functional" approach to determine whether Parliament intended to confer jurisdiction on the Public Service Staff Relations Board to determine who was an "employee" for the purposes of its Act.

Sopinka J., writing for the majority of the Court, held that Parliament did not intend to leave this matter to the Board's discretion, because: (1) Parliament had defined "employee" in section 2 of the Act, thereby indicating clearly its intention to limit the Board's jurisdiction to those who fell within that definition; (2) any other interpretation would recognize the creation of a category of de facto public servants, contrary to the purposes of the whole matrix of federal legislation on this subject; (3) this indicated that Parliament did not intend for the Board to rely on its general labour law expertise to extend its precise definition of "employee"; and (4) no previous decision of the Court contradicted the conclusion resulting from this pragmatic and functional approach.

Cory J. dissented, because he reached the opposite result after doing his pragmatic analysis. Nevertheless, all seven members of the Court agreed that characterization of a matter as jurisdictional or not was to be done on a "pragmatic and functional" basis. Only if this approach determined that Parliament had confided the matter to the delegate would the "patently unreasonable" test then be applied to determine whether the delegate had exceeded its jurisdiction. Finally, this standard was adopted again by the Supreme Court in a subsequent case involving these same parties.[64]

How can one demonstrate a preliminary or collateral jurisdictional defect? In some cases, it may be possible to demonstrate the defect from the face of the record of the proceedings. But, unlike the case involving intra-jurisdictional errors of law, a person alleging a jurisdictional error is not restricted to the record, but can lead any relevant evidence (usually in the form of affidavits) to cast light on the defect.[65]

In summary, therefore, preliminary and collateral matters operate to restrict the jurisdiction of statutory delegates. By definition, a statutory delegate has no discretion to make an error on a preliminary or collateral question upon which its jurisdiction depends. Although in practice it may be difficult to

---

63   Mr. Justice Cory neatly summarizes the evolution of the law in England, the United States and Canada in his dissent in *Econosult*. Note that although Cory J. dissented about whether the decision of the Public Service Staff Relations Board in that case was patently unreasonable, all of the judges accepted his statement about the law or standard to be applied in determining whether there was a jurisdictional error susceptible to judicial review.

64   *Canada (Attorney General) v. P.S.A.C.* (1993), 93 C.L.L.C. 14.022 at 125, 11 Admin. L.R. (2d) 59 (S.C.C.).

65   This was recognized by Lord Denning M.R. in *R. v. Northumberland Compensation Appeal Tribunal* (1951), [1952] 1 K.B. 338 (Eng. C.A.). It also arose in *Anisminic Ltd. v. Foreign Compensation Commission* (1968), [1969] 2 A.C. 147 (U.K. H.L.), where the commission's erroneous determination that Anisminic was not a successor-in-title was not disclosed on the face of the record but only in a subsequent affidavit explaining the basis of the commission's decision. Martland J. also refers to the admissibility of affidavits to show jurisdictional errors in the *Bell* case, [1971] S.C.R. 756 (S.C.C.).

determine whether preliminary or collateral matters are involved, the consequence of such a characterization is to bring that jurisdictional matter within the ambit of judicial review. A determination of what is and is not preliminary or collateral is but a part of a broader examination, that being whether or not the alleged error by the statutory delegate is or is not one of jurisdiction.

6. Summary

This chapter has examined the following types of defects which prevent a statutory delegate from acquiring jurisdiction:

(a) substantive *ultra vires*;

(b) improper constitution of the delegate;

(c) lack of compliance with mandatory procedural requirements; and

(d) errors on a matter preliminary or collateral to the delegate's jurisdiction.

All of these errors prevent the delegate from acquiring jurisdiction "in the narrow sense" of the word used by Lord Reid. Each of these errors results in a nullity, makes the delegate's actions *ultra vires*, and provides grounds for judicial review.

The next four chapters examine errors which the delegate can commit after having acquired jurisdiction "in the narrow sense", but which take it outside its jurisdiction and therefore also provide grounds for judicial review. Chapter 11 deals with the sole exception to the rule that all judicial review is jurisdictional in nature: the anomalous use of *certiorari* to correct errors of law within jurisdiction.

7. Selected Bibliography

Gordon, D.M., "Conditional and Contingent Jurisdiction of Tribunals" (1960) 1 U.B.C.L. Rev. 185.

Gordon, D.M., "Jurisdictional Fact: An Answer" (1966) 82 L.Q. Rev. 515.

Gordon, D.M., "The Observance of Law as a Condition of Jurisdiction" (1931) 47 L.Q. Rev. 386, 557.

Gordon, D.M., "The Relation of Facts to Jurisdiction" (1929) 45 L.Q. Rev. 459.

Hogg, P.W., "The Jurisdictional Fact Doctrine in the Supreme Court of Canada: *Bell v. Ontario*, Human Rights Commissions" (1971) 9 Osgoode Hall L.J. 203.

Keyes, J.M., "From *Delegatus* to the Duty to Make Law" (1987) 33 McGill L.J. 49.

Jaffe, L., "Judicial Review: Constitutional and Jurisdictional Fact" (1957) 70 Harv. L. Rev. 953.

Jaffe, L., "Judicial Review: Question of Fact", (1956) 69 Harv. L. Rev. 1020.

McRuer, "Objective Conditions Precedent to the Existence of the Power of Decision", Report of the Royal Commission, at 71*ff* and 250*ff*.

7

Losing Jurisdiction Through an Abuse of Discretion[1]

---

1 This chapter has been updated by Dwayne W. Chomyn of Neuman Thompson, Barristers and Solicitors, Edmonton.

1. Introduction

The doctrine of Parliamentary Sovereignty permits legislation to delegate very broad discretionary powers,[2] which Professor Julius Grey has described as follows:[3]

> Discretion may best be defined as the power to make a decision that cannot be determined to be right or wrong in any objective way. A university that interviews prospective students has the power to admit some applicants and reject some; an executive may choose a secretary out of a field of applicants; the sovereign may pardon some convicts and not others. While one could disagree with any of these decisions, there is no body or person entitled, as a general rule, to correct them and declare them wrong. Lord Diplock put it well in a recent case when he said:
>
> > The very concept of administrative discretion involves a right to choose between more than one possible course of action upon which there is room for reasonable people to hold differing opinions as to which is to be preferred.[4]
>
> It would not be incorrect to say that discretion involves the creation of rights and privileges, as opposed to the determination of who holds those rights and privileges.

Nevertheless, unlimited discretion cannot exist. The courts have continuously asserted their right to review a delegate's exercise of discretion for a wide range of abuses. It is possible to identify at least five generic types of abuses, which can be described as follows. The first category occurs when a delegate exercises its discretion with an improper intention in mind, which subsumes acting for an unauthorized purpose, in bad faith, or on irrelevant considerations. The second type of abuse arises when the delegate acts on inadequate material, including where there is no evidence or without considering relevant matters. Thirdly, the courts sometimes hold that an abuse of discretion has been committed where there is an improper result, including unreasonable, discriminatory or retroactive administrative actions. A fourth type of abuse arises when the delegate exercises its discretion on an erroneous view of the law. Finally, it is an abuse for a delegate to refuse to exercise its discretion by adopting a policy which fetters its ability to consider individual cases with an open mind.

---

2 See Chapter 2, for a discussion of constitutional limitations on the ability to delegate discretionary powers.

3 In "Discretion in Administrative Law" (1979) 17 Osgoode Hall L.J. 107.

4 *Secretary of State for Education & Science v. Thameside Metropolitan Borough Council* (1976), [1977] A.C. 1014 at 1064 (Eng. C.A.), affirmed (1976), [1977] A.C. 1014 at 1036 (U.K. H.L.).

An abuse of discretion is an error which is jurisdictional in nature, even though the statutory delegate is properly constituted, has complied with all mandatory requirements, is dealing with the subject matter granted to it by the legislation, and undoubtedly has the right to exercise the discretionary power in question. Again to quote from Lord Reid's decision in *Anisminic*:[5]

> [T]here are many cases where, although the tribunal had jurisdiction to enter on the inquiry, it has done or failed to do something in the course of the inquiry which is of such a nature that its decision is a nullity. It may have given its decision in bad faith. It may have made a decision which it had no power to make. It may have failed in the course of the inquiry to comply with the requirements of natural justice. It may in perfect good faith have misconstrued the provisions giving it power to act so that it failed to deal with the question remitted to it and decided some question which was not remitted to it. It may have refused to take into account something which it was required to take into account. Or it may have based its decision on some matter which, under the provisions setting it up, it had no right to take into account. I do not intend this list to be exhaustive.

Thus, these errors make the delegate's action a nullity. Because it is nonsensical to say that anyone has jurisdiction to commit a nullity, these errors must deprive the delegate of its jurisdiction to exercise its discretion in that particular manner.[6] And this brings into play the doctrine of *ultra vires*, which provides the theoretical basis upon which the courts are entitled to review[7] the manner in which the delegate has exercised the discretion which the sovereign legislature has conferred upon it.

It is also important to note that Lord Reid specifically states that his list of abuses of discretion and other errors is not meant to be exhaustive. The underlying theme connecting all of these errors is that they make the delegate's action so outrageous, unreasonable or unacceptable that the courts decide that the legislative branch could never have intended to grant the statutory delegate the power to act in such a manner. But this implied statement of legislative intent must necessarily yield whenever the legislative branch has used sufficiently specific words to indicate that the statutory delegate does in fact have the power to proceed in the manner complained of, for example, by specifically

---

5   (1968), [1969] 2 A.C. 147 at 171 (U.K H.L.). See also *Service Employees International Union, Local #33 v. Nipawin District Staff Nurses Association et al.* (1973), 41 D.L.R. (3d) 6 at 11-12 (S.C.C.).

6   *Syndicat des employés de production du Québec & de l'Acadie v. Canada (Labour Relations Board)* (1984), 14 D.L.R. (4th) 457 (S.C.C.); *I.A.F.F., Local 2130 v. St. Albert (City)* (1990), 109 A.R. 161 at 168 (Alta. C.A.).

7   Even in the face of a privative clause purporting to oust the court's supervisory jurisdiction. See the discussion on this point in Chapters 11 and 12.

ousting the applicability of the procedural requirements of natural justice,[8] or permitting a delegate to exercise its discretion in a discriminatory or retroactive manner. As Lord Reid suggests, it is possible that the courts will in the future find some other type of action by the statutory delegate so contrary to the presumed intention of the legislative branch that it takes the delegate outside of its jurisdiction, and therefore is susceptible to judicial review.

The labels used by the courts to describe various types of abuse of discretion may be unduly precise and may sometimes overlap. Thus, it may be difficult to determine whether a particular discretionary action is void because the delegate acted in bad faith, or for an improper purpose, or on irrelevant considerations – all of which phrases could be used to describe Mr. Duplessis's motivation in ordering the cancellation of Mr. Roncarelli's liquor permit because he posted bail for Jehovah's Witnesses charged with various offenses.[9] As Lord Greene M.R. said in *Associated Provincial Picture Houses Ltd. v. Wednesbury Corp.*:[10]

> Lawyers familiar with the phraseology commonly used in relation to the exercise of statutory discretions often use the word "unreasonable" in a rather comprehensive sense. It is frequently used as a general description of the things that must not be done. For instance, a person entrusted with a discretion must direct himself properly in law. He must call his own attention to the matters which he is bound to consider. He must exclude from his consideration matters which are irrelevant to the matter that he has to consider. If he does not obey those rules, he may truly be said, and often is said, to be acting "unreasonably". Similarly, you may have something so absurd that no sensible person could ever dream that it lay within the powers of the authority. Warrington, L.J., I think it was, gave the example of the red-haired teacher, dismissed because she had red hair. That is unreasonable in one sense. In another sense it is taking into consideration extraneous matters. It is so unreasonable that it might almost be described as being done in bad faith. In fact, all these things largely fall under one head.

And Lord MacNaughten put it similarly in *Westminster v. London & Northwestern Railway*:[11]

> There can be no question as to the law applicable to the case. It is well settled that a public body invested with statutory powers such as those

---

8   The principles of natural justice are not directly related to the proper exercise of discretion, and apply even to the exercise of non-discretionary powers. These principles are dealt with in Chapters 8, 9 and 10. Nevertheless, judicial review for a breach of natural justice occurs for precisely the same reason as judicial review for an abuse of discretion: the legislation is presumed not to permit that particular type of administrative action. This presumption, of course, must yield in the face of a specific statutory provision to the contrary, in all cases.

9   *Roncarelli v. Duplessis*, [1959] S.C.R. 121 (S.C.C.).

10   [1947] 2 All E.R. 680 at 682-83 (Eng. C.A.).

11   [1905] A.C. 426 at 430 (U.K. H.L.).

conferred upon the corporation must take care not to exceed or abuse its powers. It must keep within the limits of the authority committed to it. It must act in good faith. And it must act reasonably. The last proposition is involved in the second, if not in the first. But in the present case I think it will be convenient to take it separately.

Whatever the label used, the result is the same: judicial review of the delegate's jurisdiction to exercise its discretion in the manner complained of.

Finally, many of the cases referred to in this chapter deal with the content of delegated legislation, and not with the exercise of other forms of discretionary administrative actions. Nevertheless, it is submitted that, notwithstanding the odd pronouncement which might be misconstrued to the contrary,[12] the same principles of administrative law apply to determine the legality of all forms of delegated powers. First, one must of course acknowledge that the power to enact delegated legislation is discretionary in nature; after all, discretion is involved in determining the content of those legislative rules. Accordingly, the rules governing the exercise of this type of discretion should be applicable to other types as well. Secondly, one can indeed find examples where discretionary administrative decisions have in fact been struck down on these grounds, even though no legislative function is involved. Thus, all of these types of discretionary powers are dealt with together in this chapter.

Let us now consider the nature of these categories of abuse which the courts have held take a statutory delegate outside of its jurisdiction "in the narrow sense" used by Lord Reid.

2. The Abuse of an Improper Intention: Unauthorized or Ulterior Purpose, Bad Faith, Irrelevant Considerations

The courts have frequently held that it is *ultra vires* for a statutory delegate to use a power for some unauthorized or ulterior purpose, in bad faith, or acting on irrelevant considerations.

A clear example would be an attempt by a delegate who has been given power to expropriate land for creating a park to expropriate for the purpose of making a highway instead. Although the delegate undoubtedly has the power to expropriate land, it can only lawfully do so for the purpose for which that power was granted to it by the legislation; any other purpose is unauthorized, and therefore *ultra vires*. Of course, it will frequently be a nice question of statutory interpretation as to whether the particular purpose for which the

---

12 For instance, see *MacMillan Bloedel Ltd. v. British Columbia (Minister of Forests)* (1984), 4 Admin. L.R. 1 at 14-15 (B.C. C.A.), leave to appeal refused (1984), 4 Admin. L.R. 1n (S.C.C.) where the Minister made a policy decision after reviewing outdated factual material. The court said that the Minister was exercising a power "analogous to regulation-making" and since such a power is "more legislative than it is administrative" it "does not lend itself easily to judicial intervention" lest the court dictate "policy to policy makers." *Shawn v. Robertson* (1964), 46 D.L.R. (2d) 363 at 367 (Ont. H.C.), however, clearly indicates that all forms of delegated activities may be attacked.

statutory power is being exercised has been authorized or not by the legislation. Similarly, it may be difficult in some cases to establish precisely what the purpose is for which the statutory delegate is exercising the power in question.[13] However, this difficulty is somewhat alleviated by the fact that because a jurisdictional question is involved, extrinsic evidence is admissible concerning the purpose of the statutory delegate.[14]

"Bad faith", "unauthorized purpose", and "irrelevant considerations" are sometimes used interchangeably by the courts to describe the same defect. Thus, the use of a statutory power for an ulterior purpose may well constitute bad faith, and may also have resulted from irrelevant considerations. The *Roncarelli*[15] and *Padfield*[16] cases are examples of this type of interchangeability of terms. On the other hand, only one of these phrases may be applicable to describe the particular error committed by the statutory delegate. In particular, the courts may be reluctant to find the existence of bad faith, even where the delegate has acted for an improper purpose or on irrelevant considerations. Bearing in mind this terminological difficulty, it is useful to consider examples of each one of these categories.

(a) Unauthorized or Ulterior Purpose

Examples where the courts have struck down a delegate's actions on the ground that they were being taken for an unauthorized purpose include: the payment by a municipal council of higher wages than necessary in order to be a model employer even though the council was entitled to pay "such wages as [council] may think fit";[17] the enactment of a by-law[18] prohibiting pharmacists from advertising their professional services or fees, even though the association was entitled to enact by-laws concerning discipline of members, as well as any

---

13   An interesting question arises if there was more than one motive for an administrative action, if at least one was improper. Generally the courts will determine whether the action or decision is influenced by the improper consideration. Some English courts have sought to determine the "true purpose" or "dominant purpose" behind the action, discarding all others. It has been suggested that this test may be useful in instances concerning multimember bodies, such as municipal councils, school boards and the like. See H.W.R. Wade's description of the cases in *Administrative Law*, 7th ed. (Oxford: Clarendon Press, 1994), at 438-39. See also *Sawatzky v. Universities Academic Pension Plan Board* (1992), 9 Admin. L.R. (2d) 109 at 116*ff* (Alta. Q.B.); *Actus Management Ltd. v. Calgary (City)*, [1975] 6 W.W.R. 739 (Alta. C.A.); *Dallinga v. Calgary (City)* (1975), [1976] 1 W.W.R. 319 (Alta. C.A.).

14   As occurred in the *Anisminic* case, *supra* note 5, which dealt with a preliminary error of law. Indeed, the improper purpose in *Roncarelli v. Duplessis*, *supra* note 9, only came to light during examinations for discovery in a damage action, and probably never would have been disclosed on any record of the proceedings revoking the liquor licence. For the use of extrinsic evidence generally see *Securicor Investigations & Security v. Ontario (Labour Relations Board)* (1985), 18 D.L.R. (4th) 151 (Ont. Div. Ct.).

15   *Supra* note 9.

16   *Padfield v. Minister of Agriculture, Fisheries & Food*, [1968] A.C. 997 (U.K. H.L.), discussed below.

17   *Roberts v. Hopwood*, [1925] A.C. 578 (U.K. H.L.).

18   Approved by the Lieutenant Governor in Council pursuant to the statute.

other matter requisite for carrying out the objects of its Act;[19] the refusal of a
licence to carry on the business of a salvage yard on the ground that a pro-
spective zoning by-law would prohibit the use of that particular land for that
purpose;[20] or that the use of land for a restaurant would create traffic problems;[21]
the refusal to grant an extraprovincial trucking license in order to protect the
regulatory regime until a new regime was implemented;[22] the transfer of an
R.C.M.P. corporal as a reprisal for having submitted an unsubstantiated complaint against his superior officers;[23] the refusal to grant a billing number to a
physician wishing to practice in a city in order to encourage settlement in a
rural locality;[24] the exercise of a statutory provision to "refuse in any particular
case to grant the request of an applicant for a [business] licence . . . but the
granting or renewal of a licence shall not be unreasonably refused" where
members of the municipal council were apparently concerned about the morality of a sex shop. In the last case, Dickson J. stated that the specific statutory
power delegated to the municipal council to refuse a licence in "any particular
case"could not be construed to extend to refusing licences for any particular
type of business, such as "adult boutiques" which were not *ex hypothesi*
illegal.[25]

The courts' approach to this problem is well illustrated by the decision in
Tegon Developments Ltd. v. Edmonton (City).[26] The case involved a resolution
by city council prohibiting any development or demolition which might conflict with the historical character of the Old Strathcona area of Edmonton.
Although the *Planning Act*[27] specifically provided that a municipal council
might make resolutions respecting "(a) the use of land in specific areas, or (b)
any special aspects of specific kinds of development and the manner of their
control", Moir J.A. held that the resolution in question purported to use this
statutory power for an unauthorized purpose:[28]

> In my opinion council has the right to pass a resolution dealing with
> the "use" of land or "any . . . aspects of specific kinds of development".

19 *Bass v. Pharmaceutical Assn. (British Columbia)* (1965), 51 D.L.R. (2d) 552 (B.C. S.C.),
    affirmed (1965), 55 D.L.R. (2d) 476 (B.C. C.A.).
20 *Wilcox v. Pickering (Township)* (1961), 29 D.L.R. (2d) 428 (Ont. H.C.).
21 *Henry's Drive-In v. Hamilton (City) Commissioners of Police*, [1960] O.W.N. 468 (Ont.
    H.C.); and see also *Brampton Jersey Enterprises Ltd. v. Ontario (Milk Control Board)* (1955),
    1 D.L.R. (2d) 130 (Ont. C.A.).
22 *Lindsay v. Manitoba (Motor Transport Board)* (1989), 62 D.L.R. (4th) 615 at 629 (Man.
    C.A.), leave to appeal refused (1990), 65 Man. R. (2d) 160 (note) (S.C.C.).
23 *Desjardins v. Royal Canadian Mounted Police Commissioner* (1986), 18 Admin. L.R. 314
    (Fed. T.D.).
24 *Mia v. British Columbia (Medical Services Commission)* (1985), 15 Admin. L.R. 265 (B.C.
    S.C.).
25 *Prince George (City) v. Payne* (1977), [1978] 1 S.C.R. 458 (S.C.C.).
26 (1977), 5 Alta. L.R. (2d) 63 (Alta. C.A.), affirmed without written reasons (1978), 7 Alta.
    L.R. (2d) 292 (S.C.C.).
27 R.S.A. 1970, c. 276, s. 106(1) [now contained in the *Municipal Government Act*, R.S.A.
    2000, c. M-26].
28 *Tegon Developments Ltd. v. Edmonton (City)* (1977), 5 Alta. L.R. (2d) 63 at 68-69 (Alta.
    C.A.), affirmed (1978), [1979] 1 S.C.R. 98 (S.C.C.).

This resolution is not for that purpose but it is for the stated and express purpose of preserving the historical structures pending designation of certain sites in the area under the provisions of *The Alberta Heritage Act*, 1973 (Alta.), c. 5.

That statute empowers the Lieutenant-Governor in Council to designate any heritage site where preservation is in the public interest (s. 18). This is a procedure to safeguard the interest of the owner and of the public and it allows the owner to be heard. There is no power delegated to any municipal council to designate any area of building under that statute.

Further, the avowed purpose of the resolution is to enable the city to obtain contributions from Heritage Canada and the Devonian Foundation. It is said that the obtaining of such grants is "conditional, in part, on the adoption of the Resolution". Thus, in the guise of planning, the city has passed a resolution to freeze development in the area until the Lieutenant-Governor in Council acts and to enable the city to obtain grants from Heritage Canada and the Devonian Foundation.

The Old Strathcona Resolution is not concerned with the "use" of land as such but with preserving the existing structures. Neither can it be said that they set out "special aspects of specific kinds of development". The resolution in its latter aspect deals with all development and not with "specific kinds of development". The legislature of the province empowered the municipal council of the city of Edmonton to pass resolutions dealing with the use of land and in respect of "special aspects of specific kinds of development". However, the council, in purporting to act under that power, expressed other purposes, namely, to impose a freeze on land so that the powers given to the Lieutenant-Governor in Council by the *Alberta Heritage Act* could be exercised by the Lieutenant-Governor in Council. They also expressed the hope that funds would be forthcoming from Heritage Canada and from the Devonian Foundation. The freeze continues in effect as council has re-enacted the resolution for 1976 and again in 1977.

The power given to the council of the city of Edmonton must be exercised for the purpose for which it is given. It is not a valid exercise of the power to use it to preserve historical sites and to induce others to advance money to preserve historical sites. This division recently reviewed the authorities in respect of the right of the executive council of the province of Alberta to exercise a power given to it by the legislature of the province for a purpose not coming within the statute: *Heppner v. Min. of Environment of Alta.* (1977), 4 Alta. L.R. (2d) 139 (C.A.). The court has the right and the duty to ascertain if the power given was used for a proper purpose. Here the material before the council of the city of Edmonton, as produced in the affidavit filed on behalf of the city, clearly establishes the purpose. It was not a planning purpose.

It is a trite law that municipal governments are the creatures of statute. They can only do what they are authorized to do by statute. If there is no legislative authority for their actions, then those actions are beyond the competence of the municipal council. Here the resolution setting up the rules does not deal with the use of land but constitutes a freeze on the present development of the land and makes rules to preserve the existing development rather than dealing with the use of land as such. In my opinion the Old Strathcona Resolution is beyond the legislative competence of the council of the city of Edmonton.

In *Shell Canada Products Ltd. v. Vancouver (City)*[29] the municipality passed a resolution that it would not do business with Shell Canada "until Royal Dutch/Shell completely withdraws from South Africa." The purpose of the resolution was to express moral outrage against apartheid and join an international boycott against Shell. By a narrow majority, the Supreme Court of Canada struck down the bylaw holding that the boycott was not a municipal purpose consistent with the objects of the enabling statute and the *Vancouver Charter.*

Similarly, in *Columbia Estate Co. v. Burnaby (District)*,[30] the British Columbia Supreme Court struck down the re-zoning of private land to parking lot use when it was demonstrated that the true purpose of the re-zoning was to ensure that the land would be readily available for use in conjunction with a publicly operated transit system.

Another form of this error occurs when a delegate inadvertently fails to deal with the matter remitted and, instead, deals with some other matter. By doing so, the delegate exercises its power for an unauthorized purpose committing a jurisdictional error which renders the action or decision a nullity.[31] For instance, in *Ontario (Ministry of Community & Social Services) v. O.P.S.E.U.*,[32] a grievance arbitration board was called upon to adjudicate the dismissal of an employee alleged to have engaged in inappropriate sexual activity with a resident and to have violated internal policies and procedures rendering the employee vulnerable to such an accusation. The board found that the allegations concerning sexual activity had not been proven but that the employee had breached the ministry's policies. It also found that although the

---

29   [1994] 1 S.C.R. 231, 20 Admin. L.R. (2d) 202 (S.C.C.). But see the dissenting comments of McLachlin, J. at 225 (Admin. L.R.) where she states that the application of the doctrine of improper purposes to municipal authorities "remains problematic". Note that this case also deals extensively with standard of review of municipal decisions.

30   (1974), 49 D.L.R. (3d) 123 (B.C. S.C.).

31   *Anisminic Ltd. v. Foreign Compensation Commission* (1968), [1969] 2 A.C. 147 (U.K. H.L.); *S.E.I.U., Local 333 v. Nipawin District Staff Nurses Assn.* (1973), 41 D.L.R. (3d) 6 (S.C.C.); *I.A.F.F. Local 2130 v. St. Albert (City)* (1990), 109 A.R. 161 at 168 (Alta. C.A.); see the *obiter* comments of Laskin C.J.C. in *U.A.W., Local 720 v. Volvo Canada Ltd.* (1979), 99 D.L.R. (3d) 193 at 203-04 (S.C.C.) where the "wrong question" test of jurisdiction is discussed.

32   (1992), 97 D.L.R. (4th) 173, 10 Admin. L.R. (2d) 59 (Ont. C.A.).

policy said that such an infraction would result in a suspension, the employer did not act unreasonably in dismissing the employee.

The court found that the board was obliged to decide if there was just cause to dismiss the employee. If there was just cause for dismissal the board was then obliged to determine if the penalty was excessive and substitute a lesser form of discipline. Instead, the court found that the board had failed to answer the questions remitted, instead asking whether the employer had acted reasonably. By approaching the matter this way, the board failed to deal with the issues before it and the employee lost the opportunity to be reinstated to his employment, a right conferred by the statute.

In all of these cases, the statutory delegate undoubtedly had the power in certain circumstances to take the impugned actions. The question in each case, however, was whether the purpose for which the action was taken was authorized by the legislation in question. In other words, a power granted by legislation for one purpose cannot be used by a delegate for another purpose.

(b) Bad Faith

The phrase "bad faith" is frequently used to describe an abuse of a discretionary power. Such an abuse may be dishonest, malicious, fraudulent or *mala fides*. As Rand J. said in *Roncarelli v. Duplessis*:[33]

> In public regulation of this sort there is no such thing as absolute and untrammelled "discretion", that is that action can be taken on any ground or for any reason that can be suggested to the mind of the administrator; no legislative Act can, without express language, be taken to contemplate an unlimited arbitrary power exercisable for any purpose, however capricious or irrelevant, regardless of the nature or purpose of the statute. Fraud and corruption in the Commission may not be mentioned in such statutes but they are always implied as exceptions. "Discretion" necessarily implies good faith in discharging public duty; *there is always a perspective within which a statute is intended to operate*; and any clear departure from its lines or objects is just as objectionable as fraud or corruption. Could an applicant be refused a permit because he had been born in another province, or because of the colour of his hair? The ordinary language of the legislature cannot be so distorted.

It may well be that it is impossible for a tribunal to act in bad faith without doing so for an improper purpose, or without taking into account extraneous considerations. As Pennell J. said in *Smith v. Vanier (Minicipality)*, where there was an allegation of bad faith:[34]

---

33   [1959] S.C.R. 121 at 140 (S.C.C.), emphasis added. See also the decision in *Gershman v. Manitoba (Vegetable Producers' Marketing Board)* (1975), [1976] 2 W.W.R. 432 (Man. Q.B.), affirmed [1976] 4 W.W.R. 406 (Man. C.A.).

34   (1972), 30 D.L.R. (3d) 386 at 390-91 (Ont. H.C.). A similar result was reached in *Burns v. Haldimand (Township)* (1965), 52 D.L.R. (2d) 101 (Ont. C.A.), where bad faith was found

In the house of good faith there are many mansions. Good faith or want of it is not an external fact but rather a state of mind that can be judged by verbal or physical acts. To my mind good faith is a composite thing referable to all the relevant circumstances. Included in the circumstances is the manner in which the discretion was exercised.

In that case, the respondent had refused a building permit for renovations to construct a mini-cinema. On an application for *mandamus*, the respondent set forth only three defects in the application's compliance with the relevant by-law. When the applicant had remedied these three deficiencies, the respondent again refused to issue the licence. Although Pennell J. held that the members of the municipal council believed that refusing the licence would be for the public benefit, and noted that the council was not bound to give any reason for refusing the licence, His Lordship issued a second order of *mandamus* compelling the issuance of the licence because:[35]

> Good faith in law is not to be measured always by a man's own standard of right, but that which the law has prescribed as the standard for the observance of all men in their dealings with each other. The good faith must be determined by what has been done. Would not a reasonable man be entitled to assume from the posture of the Municipal Council on return of the first motion [for *mandamus*] that approval would be forthcoming if he remedied the deficiencies? In the present case the applicant ordered his affairs accordingly. Then, after completing the deficiencies with the financial consequences which that entailed he finds that the Council refused to issue the licence.
>
> Under such circumstances I believe a Court is entitled to look beyond the resolution to refuse the licence. I am of opinion that there was a want of good faith in law and accordingly an order of *mandamus* may issue.

On the other hand, although the courts have given a very broad definition to what constitutes "bad faith" in administrative law and particularly in municipal law, it nevertheless may be unwise to plead bad faith unless actual *mala fides* or malice can be demonstrated conclusively. In private law, the courts have tended to place a heavy onus on a person pleading bad faith,[36] and it is unnecessarily dangerous to count on the courts to remember that the term has

---

to exist when a city council purported to expropriate the applicant's lands for park purposes (which they undoubtedly had the power to do) when their real motive was to settle a law suit which the applicant had commenced against the municipality. It is submitted that this is the real *ratio decidendi* of the decision of the Alberta Court of Appeal in *Campeau Corp. v. Calgary (City)* (1978), 7 Alta. L.R. (2d) 294 (Alta. C.A.). See also *Multi-Malls Inc. v. Ontario (Minister of Transport & Communications)* (1976), 14 O.R. (2d) 49 at 60ff (Ont. C.A.).

35 *Smith v. Vanier (Municipality)*, *ibid*. at 392. See also *McIntyre Ranching Co. v. Cardston (Minicipality)* (1983), 28 Alta. L.R. (2d) 206 (Alta. C.A.).

36 See *Holt Renfrew & Co. v. Henry Singer Ltd.* (1982), 135 D.L.R. (3d) 391 (Alta. C.A.), leave to appeal refused [1982] 2 S.C.R. xi (S.C.C.), affirming (1980), 118 D.L.R. (3d) 645 (Alta. Q.B.).

taken on a much less odious meaning in public law. Because "unauthorized or ulterior purpose" or "irrelevant considerations" probably apply as well to virtually every abuse of discretion which could qualify as "bad faith", the latter phrase should be avoided whenever possible.

Not surprisingly, practical illustrations of bad faith are quite rare but examples where courts have struck down a delegate's actions on the grounds that they were taken in bad faith include: the "systemic targeting" of gay and lesbian literature by customs and immigration officials;[37] the failure to give notice of an expropriation resolution despite being aware that the land owner objected;[38] the transfer of an R.C.M.P. corporal as a reprisal for submitting an unsubstantiated complaint against superior officers;[39] the decision to provide the minimum allowable remuneration to a school principal with 39 years of service because he had been ill.[40]

(c) Irrelevant Considerations

A third category of improper intention arises when a delegate bases its decision on irrelevant considerations.

In *Associated Provincial Picture Houses Ltd. v. Wednesbury Corp.*,[41] the English Court of Appeal upheld the decision of a municipal corporation to prohibit children under the age of fifteen years from being admitted to a cinema on a Sunday, pursuant to a statutory provision which permitted cinemas to stay open on Sunday "subject to such conditions as the [council] think fit to impose. . . ". In determining whether this was a proper exercise of the municipality's discretion, Lord Greene M.R. said:[42]

> When an executive discretion is entrusted by Parliament to a local authority, what purports to be an exercise of that discretion can only be challenged in the courts in a very limited class of case. It must always be remembered that the court is not a court of appeal. The law recognizes certain principles on which the discretion must be exercised, but within the four corners of those principles the discretion is an absolute one and cannot be questioned in any court of law.
>
> What, then, are those principles? They are perfectly well understood. The exercise of such a discretion must be a real exercise of the discretion. If, in the statute conferring the discretion, there is to be found, expressly or by implication, matters to which the authority exercising the discretion ought to have regard, then, in exercising the

---

37 *Little Sisters Book & Art Emporium v. Canada (Minister of Justice)* (2000), 193 D.L.R. (4th) 193 (S.C.C.).

38 *McIntyre Ranching Co. v. Cardston (Minicipality)*, *supra* note 35.

39 *Desjardins v. Royal Canadian Mounted Police Commissioner* (1986), 18 Admin. L.R. 314 (Fed. T.D.).

40 *Fédération québecoise des Directeurs d'école v. Long-Sault (Commission scolaire)* (1983), 5 D.L.R. (4th) 444 (Que. S.C.).

41 (1947), [1948] 1 K.B. 223, [1947] 2 All E.R. 680 (Eng. C.A.).

42 *Ibid.* at 682-83, 685 [All E.R.]. This quotation is reported in a somewhat different form in K.B. (see at 228-30, 233-34).

discretion, they must have regard to those matters. Conversely, if the nature of the subject-matter and the general interpretation of the Act make it clear that certain matters would not be germane to the matter in question, they must disregard those matters. Expressions have been used in cases where the powers of local authorities came to be considered relating to the sort of thing that may give rise to interference by the court. Bad faith, dishonesty – those, of course, stand by themselves – unreasonableness, attention given to extraneous circumstances, disregard of public policy, and things like that have all been referred to as being matters which are relevant for consideration. In the present case we have heard a great deal about the meaning of the word "unreasonable". It is true the discretion must be exercised reasonably. What does that mean? Lawyers familiar with the phraseology commonly used in relation to the exercise of statutory discretions often use the word "unreasonable" in a rather comprehensive sense. It is frequently used as a general description of the things that must not be done. For instance, a person entrusted with a discretion must direct himself properly in law. He must call his own attention to the matters which he is bound to consider. He must exclude from his consideration matters which are irrelevant to the matter that he has to consider. If he does not obey those rules, he may truly be said, and often is said, to be acting "unreasonably". Similarly, you may have something so absurd that no sensible person could ever dream that it lay within the powers of the authority. Warrington, L.J., I think it was, gave the example of the red-haired teacher, dismissed because she had red hair. That is unreasonable in one sense. In another sense it is taking into consideration extraneous matters. It is so unreasonable that it might almost be described as being done in bad faith. In fact, all these things largely fall under one head. . . .

In the result, in my opinion, the appeal must be dismissed. I do not wish to repeat what I have said, but it might be useful to summarise once again the principle, which seems to me to be that the court is entitled to investigate the action of the local authority with a view to seeing whether it has taken into account matters which it ought not to take into account, or, conversely, has refused to take into account or neglected to take into account matters which it ought to take into account. Once that question is answered in favour of the local authority, it may still be possible to say that the local authority, nevertheless, have come to a conclusion so unreasonable that no reasonable authority could ever have come to it. In such a case, again, I think the court can interfere. The power of the court to interfere in each case is not that of an appellate authority to override a decision of the local authority, but is that of a judicial authority which is concerned, and concerned only, to see whether the local authority have contravened the law by acting in excess of the powers which Parliament has confided in it.

Similarly, in *R. v. Smith & Rhuland Ltd.*,[43] the Supreme Court of Canada held that it was not a relevant consideration for a Labour Relations Board to exercise its discretion to reject an application for certification of a union as a bargaining unit on the basis that the secretary-treasurer of the union was a communist. Rand J. said that he was unable to agree that[44]

> the Board has been empowered to act upon the view that official association with an individual holding political views considered to be dangerous by the Board proscribes a labour organization. Regardless of the strength and character of the influence of such a person, there must be some evidence that, with the acquiescence of the members, it has been directed to ends destructive of the legitimate purposes of the union, before that association can justify the exclusion of employees from the rights and privileges of a statute designed primarily for their benefit.

In light of the presumption that legislation is presumed not to infringe upon fundamental liberties, such as the freedom of speech and association, without specifically saying so, His Lordship held that the communist leanings of the secretary-treasurer of the union were an irrelevant consideration upon which the statutory delegate could exercise the discretionary powers which the legislature had undoubtedly granted to it. Cartwright and Taschereau JJ. each dissented, asserting that such political views were relevant to the exercise of the board's discretion. Unfortunately, none of the judges indicated a test for determining what matters are or are not relevant. Perhaps such a test could never be devised, and one must rest content with the ability to canvass the matter before the courts.

In another example, the Alberta Court of Appeal in *Campeau Corp. v. Calgary (City)*[45] held that the city's exercise of its power to enact a by-law zoning particular land as agricultural reserve could not be exercised for the improper purpose of creating a park without complying with the strict requirements of the *Planning Act*[46] requiring the city to purchase land designated as a park. Again, the *ratio* of the case rests on the exercise of a power which the legislative branch has undoubtedly granted to the statutory delegate, but for an unauthorized or improper purpose, or on irrelevant considerations. Similarly, in *Dallinga v. Calgary (City)*,[47] the court held that a development appeal board should not have considered evidence about the applicant's business methods in running an auto-wrecking yard when it exercised its statutory powers to determine whether to grant a development permit. And in *Doctors Hospital v. Ontario (Minister of Health)*,[48] an order of the provincial Cabinet exercising a statutory power to revoke the hospital's approval under the *Public Hospitals*

---

43   [1953] 2 S.C.R. 95 (S.C.C.).
44   *Ibid.* at 100.
45   (1978), 7 Alta. L.R. (2d) 294 (Alta. C.A.).
46   Now *Municipal Government Act*, R.S.A. 2000, c. M-26.
47   (1975), 62 D.L.R. (3d) 433 (Alta. C.A.).
48   (1976), 68 D.L.R. (3d) 220 (Ont. Div. Ct.).

Act[49] as part of an economy drive was struck down on the basis that budgetary considerations were irrelevant to the public health purposes for which the legislation had delegated that power to the Cabinet.

(d) Improper Intention Applies to all Types of Delegated Discretionary Powers

It is important to note that this ground for judicial review is available regardless of the characterization of the function exercised by the statutory delegate. In particular, it is not necessary to characterize the delegate's function as being judicial or quasi-judicial in nature; even a purely administrative or ministerial action must not be based on an irrelevant consideration, made in bad faith, or done for an improper or unauthorized purpose.[50] This point was made by Lord Denning M.R. in *Padfield v. Minister of Agriculture, Fisheries and Food*:[51]

> It is said that the decision of the Minister is administrative and not judicial. But that does not mean that he can do as he likes, regardless of right or wrong. Nor docs it mean that the courts are powerless to correct him. Good administration requires that complaints should be investigated and that grievances should be remedied. When Parliament has set up machinery for that very purpose, it is not for the Minister to brush it on one side. He should not refuse to have a complaint investigated without good reason.
>
> But it is said that the Minister is not bound to give any reason at all. And that, if he gives no reason, his refusal can not be questioned. So why does it matter if he gives bad reasons? I do not agree. . . . If the Minister is to deny the complainant a hearing – and a remedy – he should at least have good reasons for his refusal: and, if asked, he should give them. If he does not do so, the court may infer that he has no good reason. If it appears to the court that the Minister has been, or must have been, influenced by extraneous considerations which ought not to have influenced him – or, conversely, has failed, or must have failed, to take into account considerations which ought to have

---

49 R.S.O. 1970, c. 378 (now R.S.O. 1990, c. P.40).

50 See *Shawn v. Robertson*, [1964] 2 O.R. 696 (Ont. H.C.); *R. v. Brixton Prison Gov.; Ex parte Soblen*, [1963] 2 Q.B. 248 (C.A.); *Calgary Power Ltd. v. Copithorne* (1958), 16 D.L.R. (2d) 241 at 251 (S.C.C.), *per* Martland J.; *Desjardins v. Royal Canadian Mounted Police Commissioner*, *supra* note 39 where the court was urged not to "second guess" purely administrative decisions involving staffing. The court wrote at 322:
>   The notion of abuse of discretion is arguably the central and most controversial part of judicial review of administrative action. It is generally admitted, however, that the repository of the administrative discretion must act, in such a manner as not to abuse of his discretionary powers; in other words, he must not transgress the exercise of that discretion for ulterior motives, or act in bad faith.

51 [1968] 2 W.L.R. 924 at 928-29 (H.L.). Lord Reid noted that the words "if the Minister in any case so directs" are sufficient to show that he has some discretion, but they give no guide as to its nature or extent. That must be inferred from a construction of the Act read as a whole, which is the court's task.

influenced him – the court has power to interfere. It can issue a *mandamus* to compel him to consider the complaint properly.

This reasoning applies equally to all types of delegated discretionary powers: they must be exercised by the delegate for a proper purpose, in good faith, and on relevant considerations only.

As a practical matter though, in many cases courts have shown restraint when reviewing exercises of broad discretionary powers in situations which are heavily influenced by matters of public policy. For example, in *Thorne's Hardware Ltd. v. R.*,[52] Dickson, J. wrote:

> Decisions made by the Governor in Council in matters of public convenience and general policy are final and not reviewable in legal proceedings. Although, as I have indicated, *the possibility of striking down an Order in Council on jurisdictional or other compelling grounds remains open, it would take an egregious case to warrant such action. This is not such a case.*

The court noted that the action taken may have been moved by any number of political, economic, social or partisan considerations all of which were extensions of economic policy and politics and not of jurisdiction or jurisprudence.[53] This is not to suggest that such decisions are completely beyond review,[54] but that the exercise of discretion in some circumstances leaves little room for judicial intervention.[55]

3. The Abuse of Acting on Inadequate Material: No Evidence; Ignoring Relevant Considerations

The courts have tended to strike down purely arbitrary exercises of discretion. Thus, judicial review will occur where the delegate has acted upon no evidence whatever,[56] or has ignored relevant considerations.[57]

---

52 (1983), 143 D.L.R. (3d) 577 at 581 (S.C.C.). For an example of a case where an order-in-council was struck down on jurisdictional grounds, see *Alberta Teachers' Assn. v. Alberta* (2002), 40 Admin. L.R. (3d) 309 (Alta. Q.B.).

53 *Ibid.* at 580-84.

54 See for instance, *Roncarelli v. Duplessis*, [1959] S.C.R. 121 (S.C.C.).

55 *MacMillan Bloedel Ltd. v. British Columbia (Minister of Forests)* (1984), 4 Admin. L.R. 1 (B.C. C.A.), leave to appeal refused (1984), 4 Admin. L.R. 1n (S.C.C.); *Monsanto Canada Inc. v. Canada (Minister of Agriculture)* (1988), 34 Admin. L.R. 297 (Fed. C.A.), leave to appeal refused (1989), 100 N.R. 158 (note) (S.C.C.); *National Anti-Poverty Organization v. Canada (Attorney General)* (1989), 36 Admin. L.R. 197 at 215 (Fed. C.A.), leave to appeal refused (1989), 105 N.R. 160 (note) (S.C.C.).

56 See D.W. Elliott, "No Evidence – A Ground for Judicial Review in Canada?" (1972-73) 37 Sask. L.R. 48.

57 *R. v. Alberta (Labour Relations Board)* (1983), 27 Alta. L.R. (2d) 338 at 343 (Alta. Q.B.). See also *S.E.I.U., Local 333 v. Nipawin District Staff Nurses Assn.* (1973), 41 D.L.R. (3d) 6 (S.C.C.) and the cases cited therein.

Courts have narrowly constrained their review of jurisdiction on this basis. Unless satisfied that the delegate acted despite a "complete absence of evidence on an essential point"[58] or failed to "take into account highly relevant considerations",[59] courts have been unwilling to intervene. Even the complete failure to mention an argument or a point may not be fatal,[60] though the complete failure to even state an issue in an otherwise carefully constructed set of reasons is one fact the court can consider in reaching a decision.[61]

On the other hand, the courts are reluctant to attack the weight to be given to evidence or considerations which are clearly relevant. As Robins J. said in *Innisfil (Township) v. Barrie (City)*:[62]

> Once it is recognized that the Board is entitled to accept the policy statement, it follows, in my view, that it is for the Board to determine the weight to be given to it. It is not for the Court to enter the arena in such proceedings and judge the effect to be given material before the body charged with the decision. If a matter may properly be considered it is, I think, "scarcely possible for a court ever to say that too much weight was given to it or that it ought not to have been allowed to outweigh other considerations", to adopt the words of Windeyer, J. in *R. v. Anderson, Ex p. Ipec-Air Pty. Ltd.* (1965), 113 C.L.R. 177 at 205.

One of the challenges frequently facing the court is to determine which factors are relevant to the exercise of discretion. Clearly, if the legislation explicitly directs the statutory delegate to consider a factor, the statutory delegate must do so. But it often happens that there are relevant factors which are not explicitly set out in the legislation. In *C.U.P.E. v. Ontario (Minister of Labour)*,[63] the Supreme Court of Canada held that the Minister should have taken into account the need for recognized labour law experience when appointing retired judges to chair interest arbitration boards, although that factor was not explicitly set out in the legislation.

---

58 *Securicor Investigations & Security v. Ontario (Labour Relations Board)* (1985), 18 D.L.R. (4th) 151 at 154 (Ont. Div. Ct.); *R. v. Skogman* (1984), 9 Admin. L.R. 153 (S.C.C.); *H.F.I.A., Local 110 v. Construction & General Workers' Union, Local 92* (1986), 70 A.R. 228 at 235 (Alta. C.A.); *Lindsay v. Manitoba (Motor Transport Board)* (1989), 62 D.L.R. (4th) 615 (Man. C.A.), leave to appeal refused (1990), 5 Man. R. (2d) 160 (note) (S.C.C.) where the delegate's decision was based on assumptions, not facts.

59 *Oakwood Developments Ltd. v. St. François Xavier (Rural Municipality)* (1985), 18 Admin. L.R. 59 at 69 (S.C.C.).

60 *S.E.I.U., Local 333 v. Nipawin District Staff Nurses Assn.*, *supra* note 57 at 13; *I.W.A., Local 1-207 v. Zeidler Forest Industries Ltd.* (1989), 94 A.R. 293 at 296 (Alta. C.A.); *Stuart Olson Construction Ltd. v. Loyal Electric Ltd.* (1985), 61 A.R. 141 at 145 (Alta. Q.B.) where it was "assumed that the board considered or had in mind all legal principles open to it . . .".

61 *R. v. Alberta (Labour Relations Board)*, *supra* note 57.

62 (1977), 17 O.R. (2d) 277 at 287 (Ont. Div. Ct.). See also *R. v. Nat Bell Liquors Ltd.*, [1922] 2 A.C. 128 (Canada P.C.). For an example of a case where the court effectively re-weighed the evidence, see *Baker v. Canada (Minister of Citizenship & Immigration)*, [1999] 2 S.C.R. 817, 174 D.L.R. (4th) 193, 14 Admin. L.R. (3d) 173 (S.C.C.).

63 2003 SCC 29, 226 D.L.R. (4th) 193 (S.C.C.).

4. The Abuse of Improper Result: Unreasonable, Discriminatory, Retroactive or Uncertain Administrative Actions

Sometimes the court will look to the effect of the exercise of a discretion to determine whether an abuse has occurred. Thus, there is a presumption that discretionary powers should not be exercised unreasonably, discriminatorily, retroactively, or in an uncertain manner. As with all jurisdictional defects, extrinsic evidence is admissible to demonstrate whether one of these states of affairs exists.

(a) Unreasonableness

"Unreasonableness" has a very broad meaning in administrative law, as Lord Greene M.R. noted in *Associated Provincial Picture Houses Ltd. v. Wednesbury Corp.*:[64]

> Lawyers familiar with the phraseology commonly used in relation to the exercise of statutory discretions often use the word "unreasonable" in a rather comprehensive sense. It is frequently used as a general description of the things that must not be done. For instance, a person entrusted with a discretion must direct himself properly in law. He must call his own attention to the matters which he is bound to consider. He must exclude from his consideration matters which are irrelevant to the matter that he has to consider. If he does not obey those rules, he may truly be said, and often is said, to be acting "unreasonably". Similarly, you may have something so absurd that no sensible person could ever dream that it lay within the powers of the authority. Warrington, L.J., I think it was, gave the example of the red-haired teacher, dismissed because she had red hair. That is unreasonable in one sense. In another sense, it is taking into consideration extraneous matters. It is so unreasonable that it might almost be described as being done in bad faith. In fact, all these things largely fall under one head.

It is important to note – again! – that reasonableness is an *implied limitation* on the ability of a statutory delegate to exercise the discretion which undoubtedly has been granted to it by legislation. Because it is probably impossible to give a fool-proof litmus test to determine what particular results would constitute unreasonable exercises of statutory discretion, a few examples may be illuminating. In *Roberts v. Hopwood*,[65] the House of Lords held that it was an

---

64 (1947), [1948] 1 K.B. 223 at 229, [1947] 2 All E.R. 680 at 682-83 (Eng. C.A.). See also *Maple Lodge Farms Ltd. v. Canada*, [1982] 2 S.C.R. 2 (S.C.C.).

65 [1925] A.C. 578 (U.K. H.L.). See H.W.R. Wade's account of the subsequent history of the case in Wade & Forsyth, *Administrative Law*, 7th ed. (Oxford: Clarendon Press, 1994) at 420-23.

unreasonable and therefore *ultra vires* exercise of a municipal council's statutory discretion to pay its workers substantially more at a time of falling cost of living, even though the council wished to be "model employers". Coke reports a case where the court struck down charges levied by the commissioners of sewers against one owner of land adjacent to the river bank which they had repaired, instead of levying it against all of the owners who benefitted.[66] In *Claudio's Restaurant Group Inc. v. Calgary (City),*[67] the Municipality passed a bylaw prohibiting businesses from amplifying sound in a certain specified section of Calgary. The bylaw was struck down for being both discriminatory and unreasonable. The Court noted that if the purpose of the bylaw was to control noise, it was unreasonable to single out businesses in the bylaw because the sound would emanate to disturb people regardless of whether the source was "a business source, a residential source, a religious source or any other source".[68]

It may well be that unreasonableness can in some circumstances be treated as a synonym for the exercise of a discretion for an improper purpose, in bad faith, or on irrelevant considerations.[69] Nevertheless, it is possible that a delegate can act in good faith, closing its mind to irrelevancies and considering all relevant factors, but still come up with a result which the court might characterize as being unreasonable. In such circumstances, the court will probably be slow to strike down the decision which the legislation has clearly granted to the delegate and not to the courts.[70]

While it is clear that a delegate must not act unreasonably, it is equally clear that the courts apply a restrictive test refusing to substitute its view for that of the delegate except in the clearest of cases.[71] *Beltz v. Law Society (British Columbia)*[72] illustrates the point:

> The petitioner refers to Wade, *Administrative Law*, 5th ed., at 53, on the principle of reasonableness. As long ago as 1598, Coke said:
>
>> . . . notwithstanding the words of the commission give authority to the commissioners to do according to their discretions, yet their proceedings ought to be limited and bound with the rule of reason and law. For discretion is a science or understanding to discern between falsity and truth, between wrong and right, between shadows and substance, between equity and colourable

---

66 *Rooke's Case* (1598), 5 Co. Rep. 99b.
67 (1993), 10 Alta. L.R. (3d) 297 (Alta. Q.B.), additional reasons at (1993), 15 Alta. L.R. (3d) 141 (Alta. Q.B.).
68 *Ibid.* at 308
69 For example, *University Hospitals Board v. A.U.P.E., Local 54* (1989), 93 A.R. 141 (Alta. Q.B.).
70 Whether in first instance, or in appeal *de novo*.
71 See *Nottinghamshire County Council v. Secretary of State for the Environment,* [1985] 1 All E.R. 199 (U.K. H.L.) where it was said that the courts would not intervene on the grounds of unreasonableness unless the Minister had misconstrued the statute or had deceived the Commons.
72 (1986), [1987] 1 W.W.R. 427 (B.C. S.C.).

> glosses and pretences, and not to do according to their wills and private affections . . .

That view was expressed in 1905 in *Westminster Corp. v. L. & N. W. Railway Co.,* [1905] A.C. 426 at 430, in these words:

> It is well settled that a public body invested with statutory powers such as those conferred upon the corporation must take care not to exceed or abuse its powers. It must keep within the limits of the authority committed to it. It must act in good faith. And it must act reasonably. The last proposition is involved in the second, if not in the first.

However, when Wade turns at 362 to the standard of reasonableness, it becomes evident that it is a restrictive one indeed. It is often expressed by saying that the decision is unlawful if it is one to which no reasonable authority could have come, or so unreasonable that it might almost be described as being done in bad faith. As Wade puts it, the doctrine that powers must be exercised reasonably has to be reconciled with the no-less important doctrine that the court must not usurp the discretion of the authority which Parliament appointed to make the decision.

Even disregarding the doubt expressed in Driedger, *Construction of Statutes,* 2nd ed. (1983), at 317, as to whether the doctrine of unreasonableness applies to regulations other than the by-laws of municipal corporations, and there is certainly authority that it does not, the area within which the court may interfere on this ground is extremely narrow: see *MacDonald et al. v. Lambton County Board of Education* (1982), 37 O.R. (2d) 221 at 228 (Ont. H.C.). In *Re MacMillan Bloedel Ltd. and Appeal Board under the Forestry Act et al.* (1984), 8 D.L.R. (4th) 33 at 45, 51 B.C.L.R. 105, [1984] 3 W.W.R. 270 at 283 (B.C.C.A.), Macfarlane J.A. said in commenting upon the standard of reasonableness as it applied to the discretion of the Minister:

> It is clear that Lord Greene was not using "reasonable" in the sense of "appropriate or fitting". Rather the question was whether the local authority had acted in a manner so manifestly unreasonable or upon criteria so remote from that which was authorized by the Act as to exceed the authority conferred by the statute.

The Law Society submits that only where the integrity of the decision-making process is called into issue does the question of reasonableness arise. It is not what the court considers reasonable that should prevail. The court may well have different views to that of the authority. On policy matters, honest and sincere people often hold different views, but the court is not the arbiter of the correctness of one view over another: see *Associated Provincial Picture Houses Ltd. v. Wednesbury Corp.* [1984] 1 K.B. 223 at 230 (C. of A.).

Legislation, of course, can put this matter beyond dispute, as demonstrated by section 539 of the Alberta *Municipal Government Act*:[73] "No bylaw or resolution may be challenged on the ground that it is unreasonable."

This provision only insulates a by-law or resolution from attack on the ground of unreasonableness; it does not prevent attacking a discretionary action taken by a municipal officer pursuant to a by-law (or any other legislation) on the grounds of unreasonableness.

Unreasonableness has been dealt with here as a separate heading from the earlier one dealing with improper intentions[74] because unreasonableness – at least in one sense[75] – does not really go to the state of mind of the statutory delegate in the exercise of its discretion, but rather to the objective effect of the exercise of its discretion.

(b) Discrimination

There is also a presumption that a statutory delegate must not exercise its discretion in a discriminatory manner. Chief Justice McKeigan stated the test for what constitutes discrimination in *Lacewood Development Co. v. Halifax (City)*[76] as follows:

Wrongful discrimination involves two elements, both of which must be present before a by-law should be condemned on this ground:

(1) The by-law must discriminate in fact. To use the words of Middleton, J. in the "classic definition", by-laws discriminate if they "give permission to one and refuse it to another".

(0) The factual discrimination must be carried out with the improper motive of favouring or hurting one individual and without regard to the public interest.

Some more recent cases suggest that the second part of the *Lacewood* test—an improper motive—is no longer required to establish discrimination.[77]

---

73 R.S.A. 2000, c. M-26.
74 Including improper or ulterior purpose, bad faith, and irrelevant considerations.
75 Not the sense used by Lord Greene M.R. in the quotation from the *Associated Picture Houses* case, *supra* note 64.
76 (1975), 58 D.L.R. (3d) 383 at 395-96, 12 N.S.R. (2d) 692 (N.S. C.A.); *see also Carpenter Fishing Corp. v. Canada* (1996), [1997] 1 F.C. 874 (Fed. T.D.), reversed (1997), 155 D.L.R. (4th) 572 (Fed. C.A.), leave to appeal refused [1998] 2 S.C.R. vi (S.C.C.), reconsideration refused (November 19, 1998), Doc. 26484 (S.C.C.), leave to appeal refused (1999), 249 N.R. 200 (note) (S.C.C.).
77 See for example *Fountainhead Fun Centres Ltd. c. Montréal (Ville)*, [1985] 1 S.C.R. 368 (S.C.C.); *Shell Canada Products Ltd. v. Vancouver (City)* (1994), 20 Admin. L.R. (2d) 202 (S.C.C.); *R. v. Sharma*, [1993] 1 S.C.R. 650 (S.C.C.). See also discussion in D.J. Mullan, *Administrative Law*, 3d ed. (Toronto: Carswell, 1996) at 430.

These cases focus more on whether there has in fact been discrimination and on whether the enabling legislation authorizes it (either expressly or impliedly), or whether the discrimination was necessarily incidental to the exercise of the delegate's powers.

Most of the cases on discrimination deal with the exercise of the delegated discretionary power to enact legislation. For example in *Calgary (City) v. S. S. Kresge Co.*,[78] the court struck down a by-law requiring certain stores to close but permitting other stores to stay open on Sundays. In *Shell Canada Products Ltd. v. Vancouver (City)*,[79] a municipal bylaw boycotting Shell Products was struck down on the alternative footing that the bylaw was discriminatory (in a municipal law sense). The Court held that a municipality can only distinguish between classes of citizens if the enabling statute expressly or impliedly authorizes it. Nevertheless, the presumption against discrimination should in theory also apply to all forms of discretionary powers, and not just legislative ones.[80] Again, legislation may specifically permit discrimination with respect to certain matters.[81]

---

78   (1965), 51 W.W.R. 747 (Alta. S.C.). See also: *Sanbay Developments Ltd. v. London (City)* (1974), [1975] 1 S.C.R. 485 (S.C.C.), dealing with discriminatory spot zoning; *Rodenbush v. North Cowichan (District)* (1977), 76 D.L.R. (3d) 731 (B.C. S.C.); *Neilson Engineering Ltd. v. Toronto (City)* (1967), [1968] 1 O.R. 271 (Ont. H.C.).

79   [1994] 1 S.C.R. 231, 20 Admin. L.R. (2d) 202 (S.C.C.). See also: *Fountainhead Fun Centres Ltd. c. Montréal (Ville)*, [1985] 1 S.C.R. 368 (S.C.C.); *R. v. Sharma*, [1993] 1 S.C.R. 650, 10 Admin. L.R. (2d) 196 (S.C.C.); *R. v. Greenbaum*, [1993] 1 S.C.R. 674, 10 Admin. L.R. (2d) 161 (S.C.C.).

80   See *Desjardins v Royal Canadian Mounted Police Commissioner* (1986), 18 Admin. L.R. 314 (Fed. T.D.); *Fédération québecoise des Directeurs d'école v. Long-Sault (Commission scolaire)* (1983), 5 D.L.R. (4th) 444 (Que. S.C.); *Levesque c. Genest* (1985), 21 Admin. L.R. 219 (Que. S.C.); *Noel & Louis Holdings Ltd. v. R.* (1983), 1 Admin. L.R. 290 (Fed. T.D.); *Bingo Enterprises Ltd. v. Manitoba (Lotteries & Gaming Licensing Board)* (1983), 2 Admin. L.R. 286 (Man. C.A.).

81   See for example, s. 8 of the *Municipal Government Act*, R.S.A. 2000, c. M-26:

    8   Without restricting section 7, a council may in a bylaw passed under this Division may:
        (a) regulate or prohibit;
        (b) deal with any development, activity, industry, business or thing in different ways, divide each of them into classes and deal with each class in different ways;
        (c) provide for a system of licences, permits or approvals, including any or all of the following:
            (i) establishing fees for licences, permits and approvals including fees for licences, permits and approvals that may be in the nature of a reasonable tax for the activity authorized or for the purpose of raising revenue;
            (ii) establishing fees for licences, permits and approvals that are higher for persons or businesses who do not reside or maintain a place of business in the municipality;
            (iii) prohibiting any development, activity, industry, business or thing until a licence, permit or approval has been granted;
            (iv) providing that terms and conditions may be imposed on any licence, permit or approval, the nature of the terms and conditions and who may impose them;
            (v) setting out the conditions that must be met before a licence, permit or approval is granted or renewed, the nature of the conditions and who

But a delegate can not discriminate against an identifiable group when exercising a discretion. For instance, in *Little Sisters Book & Art Emporium v. Canada (Minister of Justice)*,[82] customs officers refused to allow large volumes of literature to enter Canada because of its gay and lesbian content. The effect was to equate homosexuality with obscenity and treat readers as sexual outcasts. The Court found this to be an improper exercise of discretion and issued declaratory relief giving specific guidance to Customs in respect of future action.

(c) Retroactivity

There is also a presumption that a delegated discretionary power shall not be exercised retroactively, unless the legislation expressly authorizes retroactivity. Most of the cases in this area deal with the discretion to enact delegated legislation, and not to other forms of discretionary action, but in theory the presumption against retroactivity should also apply to all other forms of discretionary powers.

For example, in *Canuck Holdings Western Ltd. v. Fort Nelson (Improvement District)*,[83] the court held that a by-law levying a hook-up charge with respect to service from a district's utilities could not be applied retroactively to require the plaintiffs to pay when they had completed the construction of their building and hooked it up to the utilities prior to the passage of the by-law. This reasoning is consistent with the principles set out in both the Alberta *Regulations Act* and the federal *Statutory Instruments Act*, which provide quite strict limitations on the ability to make delegated legislation retroactive.[84]

A problem does sometimes arise, however, in determining whether a decision has a retroactive effect. In the first place, a complaint about retroactivity can only arise where rights have already vested so as to be affected by the impugned retroactive decision.[85] Secondly, not every change in a rule is truly retroactive. For example, the implementation of a rule prohibiting an articling student from writing the bar admission examination more than three times is not necessarily retroactive if applied to students who have not yet written the examination three times (but, for example, only once and failed). In all likelihood, the student does not have a vested right to sit the examination

---

may impose them;
   (vi) providing for the duration of licences, permits, approvals and their suspension or cancellation for failure to comply with a term or condition or the bylaw or for any other reasons specified in the bylaw;
 (c.1) establish and specify the fees, rates, fares, tariffs or charges that may be charged for the hire of taxis or limousines;
   (d) provide for an appeal, the body that is to decide the appeal and related matters.

82 (2000), 193 D.L.R. (4th) 193 (S.C.C.).
83 (1963), 42 D.L.R. (2d) 313 (B.C. S.C.).
84 See the discussion on this point in Chapter 4.
85 See *Wilkin v. White* (1979), 11 M.P.L.R. 275 (B.C. S.C.), where the rules relating to subdivision were changed after an application had been made but no right had vested; *Hunter v. Surrey (District)* (1979), 108 D.L.R. (3d) 557 (B.C. S.C.), where the applicants were charged higher development cost charges under a new by-law passed after an application for subdivision had been made.

an unlimited number of times, and therefore his or her rights have not been affected by the imposition of a three-time rule. By contrast, if the three-time rule is subsequently amended to a two-time rule, it is conceivable that the application of that rule to anyone registered in the bar course who had not yet written three examinations might be a retroactive amendment to his or her right to write the examinations three times.

(d) Uncertainty

Administrative actions whose results are uncertain have also been held to be void on review by the superior courts. Again, most examples of this ground for judicial review relate to the content of delegated legislation. In *McEldowney v. Forde*,[86] a regulation was attacked for being uncertain. The legislation granted the government of Northern Ireland wide powers to preserve peace and maintain order, and a regulation was passed making it a criminal offence to belong to a "republican club" or "any like organization however described". Serious doubt was expressed by the courts about whether these phrases were so vague as to be incapable of enforcement. Of course, mere ambiguity is not sufficient to constitute uncertainty. On the contrary, the court's task is to resolve the ambiguity, to choose the one correct meaning – which in most cases would not itself be uncertain. Accordingly, the ambit within which uncertainty will be a useful ground for reviewing delegated legislation is likely to be narrow.

In principle, uncertainty should also be a ground for attacking the exercise of other discretionary administrative powers which are not legislative in nature; however, it is difficult to find a good example of this.

5. The Abuse of Misconstruing the Law

Certain errors of law will cause a delegate to lose its jurisdiction, unless the governing legislation specifically grants the delegate discretion to determine the meaning or content of the legal concept at issue.[87] Unfortunately, no satisfactory test has ever been devised to distinguish between those errors which constitute jurisdictional defects and those which are intra-jurisdictional in nature, although the Supreme Court of Canada has indicated that this characterization should be done on a "functional and pragmatic" basis.[88]

---

86 (1969), [1971] A.C. 632 (U.K. H.L.). See also *Transport Ministry v. Alexander*, [1978] 1 N.Z.L.R. 306 (New Zealand C.A.); *Hotel & Catering Indust. Training Bd. v. Automobile Pty. Ltd.*, [1969] 1 W.L.R. 697 (H.L.); *Red Hot Video Ltd. v. Vancouver (City)* (1985), 18 C.C.C. (3d) 153 (B.C. C.A.) where the words "graphic sexual material, sex act, pharmaceutical or educational products" was viewed as having "such wide and differing meanings that there are no reasonable standards for determining whether the books, films or other material fall within or without the purview of the bylaw."

87 For an example of a case involving this point, see *Barrie Public Utilities v. Canadian Cable Television Assn.*, 2003 SCC 28, 225 D.L.R. (4th) 206 (S.C.C.).

88 See the decisions in *Sydicat des employés de production du Québec & de l'Acadie v. Canada (Labour Relations Board)*, [1984] 2 S.C.R. 412 (S.C.C.); *Syndicat national des employés de la commission scolaire régionale de l'Outaouais v. U.E.S., local 298*, [1988] 2 S.C.R. 1048 (S.C.C.); *W.W. Lester (1978) Ltd. v. U.A., Local 740*, [1990] 3 S.C.R. 644 (S.C.C.); and

Nevertheless, the distinction between jurisdictional and intra-jurisdictional errors is important for at least six reasons. First, a privative clause cannot effectively prevent judicial review where the jurisdiction of the delegate is in question, but will be effective to prevent the superior courts from using *certiorari* to correct mere errors of law on the face of the record. Secondly, affidavits and other evidence are admissible, if necessary, to prove the existence of a jurisdictional error, but they cannot be considered by the court if a non-jurisdictional error of law is involved. Thirdly, the court's anomalous power to correct intra-jurisdictional errors is limited to errors of law only, and does not apply to errors of fact, whereas factual matters may give rise to a jurisdictional error, particularly in the context of the preliminary or collateral fact doctrine. Fourthly, this anomalous use of *certiorari* can only correct errors of law which appear on the face of the record, however that is defined, whereas jurisdictional errors do not have to be so disclosed. Fifthly, it may not be possible to correct intra-jurisdictional errors by any remedy other than this anomalous use of *certiorari*, although other remedies may frequently be available to review jurisdictional errors. Finally, the nature of the error may significantly impact the appropriate standard of review.

In theory, a distinction should be made between two kinds of jurisdictional errors of law. On the one hand, certain preliminary or collateral questions of law sometimes have to be determined correctly in order to bring the delegate within the jurisdiction granted to it by statute.[89] Errors on these preliminary matters constitute defects in the delegate's acquisition of jurisdiction, and are discussed more fully in Chapter 6. On the other hand, the delegate may undoubtedly have acquired jurisdiction to do the matter remitted to it by statute, but may subsequently make an error of law which causes it to lose jurisdiction. This type of error is discussed here and in Chapter 11.

Further, a theoretical distinction must be made between (1) errors of law which cause a delegate to lose jurisdiction and (2) intra-jurisdictional errors. Because of the jurisdictional nature of the former category, extrinsic evidence is admissible on any application for any remedy to correct such an error. By contrast, only an anomalous use of *certiorari* is available to quash an intra-jurisdictional error of law, and then only if the error is disclosed on the face of the record of the proceedings of the statutory delegate.[90]

The distinction between jurisdictional and intra-jurisdictional errors of law is brought into sharp relief if the legislation contains a privative clause which purports to prevent judicial review of a delegate's action. The courts have long held that such clauses only apply to administrative actions which are *intra vires*. Accordingly, a privative clause will not protect a jurisdictional error of

---

Canada (Attorney General) v. P.S.A.C., [1991] 1 S.C.R. 614 (S.C.C.). See also the discussion in Chapter 11.

89 See *Anisminic Ltd. v. Foreign Compensation Commission* (1968), [1969] 2 A.C. 147 (U.K. H.L.); *Canada (Attorney General) v. Canada (Public Service Staff Relations Board)* (1977), [1978] 2 S.C.R. 15 (S.C.C.); *Parkhill Bedding & Furniture Ltd. v. I.M.A.W., Local 714* (1961), 34 W.W.R. 13 (Man. C.A.); and *Associated Medical Services v. Ontario (Labour Relations Board)*, [1964] S.C.R. 497 (S.C.C.). See also the discussion in Chapter 11.

90 See Chapter 11.

law. The courts have used the phrase "patently unreasonable" to determine when an error of law is so serious that it should be characterized as being jurisdictional in nature.[91] This is discussed more fully in Chapters 11 and 12.

6. The Abuse of Fettering Discretion

Because administrative law generally requires a statutory power to be exercised by the very person upon whom it has been conferred,[92] there must necessarily be some limit on the extent to which the exercise of a discretionary power can be fettered by the adoption of an inflexible policy, by contract, or by other means. After all, the existence of discretion implies the absence of a rule dictating the result in each case; the essence of discretion is that it can be exercised differently in different cases. Each case must be looked at individually, on its own merits.[93] Anything, therefore, which requires a delegate to exercise its discretion in a particular way may illegally limit the ambit of its power. A delegate who thus fetters its discretion commits a jurisdictional error which is capable of judicial review.

On the other hand, it would be incorrect to assert that a delegate cannot adopt a general policy. Any administrator[94] faced with a large volume of discretionary decisions is practically bound to adopt rough rules of thumb. This practice is legally acceptable, provided each case is individually considered on its merits. As Bankes L.J. said in *R. v. Port of London Authority*:[95]

> There are on the one hand cases where a tribunal in the honest exercise of its discretion has adopted a policy, and, without refusing to hear an applicant, intimates to him what its policy is, and that after hearing him it will in accordance with its policy decide against him, unless there is something exceptional in his case. . . . [I]f the policy has been adopted for reasons which the tribunal may legitimately entertain, no objection could be taken to such a course. On the other hand there are cases where a tribunal has passed a rule, or come to a determination, not to hear any application of a particular character by whomsoever

---

91 See for example, *C.U.P.E., Local 963 v. New Brunswick Liquor Corp.*, [1979] 2 S.C.R. 227, 97 D.L.R. (3d) 417 (S.C.C.).

92 See Chapter 6, for a discussion of circumstances in which a delegate may validly sub-delegate certain statutory powers.

93 See W. Wade & C. Forsyth, *Administrative Law*, 7th ed. (Oxford: Clarendon Press, 1994) at 360: "It is a fundamental rule for the exercise of discretionary power that discretion must be brought to bear on every case: each one must be considered on its own merits and decided as the public interest requires at the time."

94 Or sometimes many administrators, all faced with exercising the same statutory discretion, for example, immigration officers deciding whether to grant landed immigrant status, tax inspectors, or prosecutors deciding whether to proceed by way of indictment or summary conviction. There is a natural tendency for the civil service to attempt to codify the way such discretions are to be exercised, to attempt to achieve consistency. Hence the various "guidelines", "interpretation bulletins" and other similar non-statutory material.

95 (1918), [1919] 1 K.B. 176 at 184 (Eng. C.A.). See also Lord Reid's comments in *British Oxygen Co. v. Board of Trade* (1970), [1971] A.C. 610 at 625 (U.K. H.L.).

made. There is a wide distinction to be drawn between these two classes.

Similarly, a delegate does not necessarily commit an error by referring to the policy adopted by another governmental agency when deciding to exercise its own discretion,[96] but may err if the delegate erroneously believes that it is bound by a decision of a different delegate and thereby fails to make an independent decision.[97] It is true that the principles of natural justice and fairness may in both cases require the delegate to disclose the existence of such policies so that a person affected thereby can intelligently make representations as to why the delegate should exercise its discretion differently in the particular case. Nevertheless, the legal issue boils down to whether the delegate in fact has exercised its discretion or fettered it.

(a) Inflexible Policy Fetters on the Exercise of Discretion

The adoption of an inflexible policy almost certainly means that the delegate has not exercised the discretionary power granted to it.[98] Accordingly, an order for *mandamus* in principle will issue to compel the delegate to decide the particular case on its own merits. This situation arose in *Lloyd v. British Columbia (Superintendent of Motor Vehicles)*,[99] where the Court of Appeal of British Columbia struck down the superintendent's invariable policy of suspending the licence of every driver convicted of driving while impaired. Bull J.A. dealt with the legal issues as follows:[100]

> With respect, I do not agree, but I prefer to base my conclusion on a somewhat different approach. As the proceedings are for *certiorari*, we are concerned with jurisdiction. Did the respondent Superintendent exceed or reject or decline the jurisdiction provided him by the statute, or put in another way, did he determine the question which he was required to determine? To my mind, the question of the justi-

---

96 *Innisfil (Township) v. Vespra (Township)*, [1981] 2 S.C.R. 145 (S.C.C.), varied [1982] 1 S.C.R. 1107 (S.C.C.); *R. v. Anderson* (1965), 113 C.L.R. 177 (Australia H.C.).

97 *Koopman v. Ostergaard* (1995), 34 Admin. L.R. (2d) 144 (B.C. S.C. [In Chambers])

98 On the contrary, the adoption of an inflexible policy constitutes converting a discretionary power into a rule applicable to all cases, rather similar to enacting delegated legislation with no discretionary element. This is the reverse of the problem in *Canada (Attorney General) v. Brent*, [1955] 3 D.L.R. 587 (Ont. C.A.), affirmed [1956] S.C.R. 318 (S.C.C.), and *Brant Dairy Co. v. Ontario (Milk Commission)* (1972), [1973] S.C.R. 131 (S.C.C.), discussed in Chapter 6, where the delegate purported to create a discretionary power by enacting delegated legislation. Both errors are fatal because they depart from the form of power delegated by the legislation to the administrator, who has no authority to make such changes.

99 (1971), 20 D.L.R. (3d) 181 (B.C. C.A.). See also *Jackson v. Beaudry* (1969), 70 W.W.R. 572 (Sask. Q.B.); and *Wimpey Western Ltd. v. Alberta (Department of the Environment)* (1983), 28 Alta. L.R. (2d) 193 (Alta. C.A.), affirming (1982), 21 Alta. L.R. (2d) 125 (Alta. Q.B.); *R. v. Bowman*, [1898] 1 Q.B. 663 at 667 (Div. Ct.); *R. v. London County Council*, [1918] 1 K.B. 68 (Eng. K.B.); *Alden v. Gaglardi* (1970), [1971] 2 W.W.R. 148 (B.C. C.A.), affirmed (1972), [1973] S.C.R. 199 (S.C.C.); *Alkali Lake Indian Band v. Westcoast Transmission Co.*, [1984] 4 W.W.R. 263 (B.C. C.A.).

100 (1971), 20 D.L.R. (3d) 181 at 188-89 (B.C. C.A.), emphasis added.

fication for a blanket policy decision as to unfitness is irrelevant in these proceedings. Once the Superintendent is carrying out his duties within his jurisdiction as required of him, it matters not how wrong or right he may be in the decisions he makes or the discretion he exercises. But where, as in *Board of Education v. Rice*, [1911] A.C. 179 [H.L.], and in *Toronto Newspaper Guild v. Globe Printing Co.*, [1953] 2 S.C.R. 18, 106 C.C.C. 225, [1953] 3 D.L.R. 561, the inferior tribunal, board or official has declined to enter upon, or has not entered upon, an inquiry upon which he was bound to enter, or where, as in numerous decisions of the Supreme Court of Canada and of this Court, having entered upon such inquiry the tribunal, board or official has exceeded the authority or jurisdictional boundary which the statute gave, a superior Court will interfere by the issue of one of the appropriate prerogative writs.

In my view it is crystal clear that the respondent Superintendent did not enter into any inquiry at all as to whether or not the appellant was or was not, by virtue of any reason, unfit to drive a motor vehicle. *He formed no opinion of the appellant's fitness at any time, and never at any time put his mind to that question. A pre-existing policy decision formed at some unknown earlier time would unquestionably, have bearing upon the formation of his opinion, had he put his mind to the appellant's fitness or otherwise, but that policy decision is not what the section required the Superintendent to make or to apply. He was required to form an opinion of fitness or unfitness as at the time of the formation of the opinion. Put simply, there never was any inquiry or consideration given to the situation of the person aggrieved by the official charged by the Legislature with judicial or quasi-judicial duties.* I fail to see on what valid grounds it can be said that the respondent Superintendent judicially formed an opinion of the appellant's unfitness to drive at the time of the opinion and which unfitness had been satisfactorily proved to him, when he did nothing more than give directions at some unknown earlier date to his staff to send out suspension notices to all persons who had been convicted of a violation of s. 222 of the Criminal Code and to place his stamped name thereon.

On the other hand, it is sometimes possible for a delegate to adopt a general policy without thereby fettering the exercise of its discretion in a particular case. At the minimum, it appears that the delegate must consider fairly those cases which run counter to the policy.[101] Fair consideration might require

---

101   *Maple Lodge Farms Ltd. v. Canada*, [1982] 2 S.C.R. 2, 137 D.L.R. (3d) 558 (S.C.C.); *R. v. Port of London Authority, supra* note 94; *R. v. Sylvester* (1862), 31 L.J. M.C. 93, 95; *H.E.U., Local 180 v. Peace Arch District Hospital* (1989), 57 D.L.R. (4th) 386 (B.C. C.A.); *Partridge v. Manitoba Securities Commission* (1989), 63 D.L.R. (4th) 564 (Man. Q.B.); *Hale v. White Rock (City) Board of Variance* (1985), 16 Admin. L.R. 313 (B.C. S.C.); *Brown v. Alberta* (1991), 2 Admin. L.R. (2d) 116 (Alta. Q.B.). In two colourful cases it was determined that the delegate failed to exercise its discretion. In *Veysey v. Canada (Commissioner of Correctional Service)* (1990), 43 Admin. L.R. 316 (Fed. C.A.), the court

disclosure of the existence of the policy to the person seeking to be exempted[102] therefrom. Provided that the policy is relevant to the purpose for which the discretion was granted,[103] the courts have upheld the validity of using a flexible policy in determining how to exercise the discretion. In such a case, the delegate has not relentlessly refused or declined to exercise its discretion on account of the policy, but rather has exercised its discretion in the very case before it.[104]

It has been suggested that the administrator's natural desire for consistency may sometimes amount to an illegal fettering of discretion,[105] as may adopting a policy of only acting on the recommendation of a third party.[106] This not only fetters discretion but also constitutes illegal sub-delegation.[107]

---

found that the denial of visiting privileges to a penitentiary inmate's homosexual partner on the basis that policy excluded homosexual partners constituted a failure to exercise a discretion. In the case of *Bourque c. Nouveau-Brunswick (Ministre des Resources naturelles & de l'Énergie)* (1992), 8 Admin. L.R. (2d) 50 (N.B. Q.B.), the applicant found two dead protected birds on his property. He applied to the minister to keep the birds which he proposed to have stuffed and displayed in his house. The permit was denied on the basis of a long standing policy to grant such permits only to universities, museums and other groups and organizations using such animals and birds for educational and scientific purposes. The application was granted insofar as the single minded pursuit of policy had the effect of fettering the discretion of the delegate.

102 *Innisfil (Township) v. Vespra (Township), supra* note 95; *Dale Corp. v. Nova Scotia (Rent Review Commission)* (1983), 2 Admin. L.R. 260 (N.S. C.A.).

103 *Ibid.* See also the *Wimpey Western* case, *supra* note 98, especially at 198-204 (C.A.), and 134-38 (Q.B.).

104 An interesting application of this rule is found in *Nastrani v. Canada (Minister of Citizenship & Immigration)* (1998), 148 F.T.R. 117 (Fed. T.D.), where an immigration officer fettered her own discretion by saying that she would never exercise her discretion in favour of an applicant on welfare. By adopting this blanket approach, the immigration officer failed to consider the applicant's individual circumstances.

105 See *Lewis v. British Columbia (Superintendent of Motor Vehicles)* (1979), 108 D.L.R. (3d) 525 at 528 (B.C. S.C.) where Taylor J. wrote:
     Those performing the Superintendent's duties quite understandably desire to avoid consideration of the merits of individual cases, and the controversy which arises when applicants are turned down on the basis of judgement. They prefer the strict application of rules to which reference can be made. Had the Legislature desired that the licenses be granted or refused on the basis of compliance with particular standards it would have authorized such standards to be established by regulation. Instead, it has determined that the decision should be based on "fitness" and "ability" and make the Superintendent and his delegates judges of these qualities in individual applicants.

106 See D.J. Mullan, "Natural Justice and Fairness – Substantive as well as Procedural Standards for the Review of Administrative Decision-Making?" (1982) 27 McGill L.J. 250; D.J. Mullan, "Recent Developments in Nova Scotian Administrative Law" (1978) 4 Dalhousie L.J. 467 at 538; H.W. MacLauchlan, "Some Problems with Judicial Review of Administrative Inconsistency" (1984), 8 Dalhousie L.J. 435. See also *Merchandise Transport Ltd. v. British Transport Commission*, [1962] 2 Q.B. 173 at 193 (Eng. Q.B.); *Capital Cities Communications Inc. v. Canada (Radio-Television & Telecommunications Commission)* (1977), 81 D.L.R. (3d) 609 at 629 (S.C.C.); *Hopedale Developments Ltd. v. Oakville (Town)* (1964), [1965] O.R. 259 (Ont. C.A.); *Alkali Lake Indian Band v. Westcoast Transmission Co.* (1984), 8 D.L.R. (4th) 610 (B.C. C.A.).

107 See *Vic Restaurant Inc. v. Montreal (City)* (1958), 17 D.L.R. (2d) 81 (S.C.C.), discussed in Chapter 6.

(b) Contractual Fetters on the Exercise of Discretion

A statutory delegate cannot validly contract to exercise its discretion in a particular way. As Lord Birkenhead said,[108] there is

> a well-established principle of law, that if a person or public body is entrusted by the legislature with certain powers and duties expressly or impliedly for public purposes, those persons or bodies cannot divest themselves of these powers and duties. They cannot enter into a contract or take any action incompatible with the exercise of their power or the discharge of their duties.

Thus, any contract which compels a municipality to re-zone land in a particular way is illegal, whether reliance is placed upon it by the municipality, the land-owner, or any third party.[109] Of course, a statute may specifically permit such contractual agreements on how a discretionary power is to be exercised.[110]

(c) Reference to Other Governmental Policies

A statutory delegate sometimes exercises its discretion by reference to a policy articulated by some other governmental body. On the one hand, such an external policy must clearly be relevant to the statutory question in issue.[111] If it is irrelevant or improper, the exercise of the delegated power is invalid for this reason.[112] On the other hand, even if the external policy is relevant, the rule against fettering requires the delegate to exercise its own discretion in deciding whether and how to accept the policy. In particular, the delegate

---

108 *Birkdale District Electric Supply Co. v. Southport (Corp.)*, [1926] A.C. 355 at 364 (U.K. H.L.). See also *Temiskaming Telephone Co. v. Cobalt (Town)* (1919), 59 S.C.R. 62 (S.C.C.), where Anglin J. said at 79: "A municipal corporation cannot validly contract not to use discretionary powers committed to it for the public good".

109 See *Pacific National Investments Ltd. v. Victoria (City)* (2003), 223 D.L.R. (4th) 617 (B.C. C.A.), leave to appeal allowed (2003), 2003 CarswellBC 2799 (S.C.C.), where the Court undertakes a thorough examination of the legal and policy principles relating the exercise of discretion by a municipality. See also *Vancouver (City) v. Vancouver (Registrar Land Registration District)*, [1955] 2 D.L.R. 709 (B.C. C.A.), where illegality was asserted against the city when the registrar refused to register an agreement which gave it an interest in land which it undertook to re-zone and *Osborne v. Amalgamated Society of Railway Servants* (1908), [1909] 1 Ch. 163 (Eng. C.A.), affirmed [1910] A.C. 87 (U.K. H.L.), where this principle was applied to strike down an agreement as to how trustees were to vote; *Egerton v. Earl of Brownlow* (1853), 4 H.L.C. 1 (U.K. H.L.) at 160-61.

110 Under s. 10 of the (now repealed) *Northern Canada Power Commission Act*, R.S.C. 1985, c. N-24 [Repealed R.S.C. 1985, c. 7 (4th Supp.), s. 1.], the commission was given broad discretion to determine the rates to be charged for power supplied by it. However, under s. 11, the commission could also enter into long-term contracts for the supply of power, and any such contract lawfully derogates from the commission's ongoing discretionary rate-setting power.

111 As it was held to be in both *Innisfil (Township) v. Vespra (Township)*, [1981] 2 S.C.R. 145 (S.C.C.), varied [1982] 1 S.C.R. 1107 (S.C.C.), and the *Wimpey Western* case (1983), 28 Alta. L.R. (2d) 193 (Alta. C.A.), affirming (1982), 21 Alta. L.R. (2d) 125.

112 See the discussion of this abuse in section 2 of this chapter, above.

cannot simply treat the external policy as a given, and may be required to permit cross-examination and refutation of that policy.[113] The expectation that a delegate will exercise its discretion in a manner so as to accommodate other governmental policies raises difficult legal issues about the relationship between apparently independent administrative bodies and more centralized government agencies,[114] which are only occasionally dealt with specifically by the legislature.[115]

In theory, all fetters on the ability of a delegate to exercise its discretion are an abuse, and result in a loss of jurisdiction[116] which can be reviewed by the courts, even in the face of a privative clause.

7. The Standard of Review of Discretionary Decisions

The standard of review that a court will use in reviewing the exercise of discretionary powers is discussed in Chapter 12.[117]

8. Summary

This chapter has considered the legal limitations on the ability of a statutory delegate to exercise discretionary powers. Although the essence of a discretionary power is that it can and should be exercised differently in different cases, this does not mean that discretionary administrative actions can never be challenged successfully in court. In the first place, the courts can review whether the legislation in fact grants the delegate authority to exercise the impugned discretion at all.[118] Even if the court upholds the ambit of the discretionary power upon which the delegate relies, judicial review nevertheless

---

113 This was the issue in the *Innisfil* case, *supra* note 111.

114 See *Parliament and Administrative Agencies*, prepared by F.F. Slatter as a Study Paper for the Law Reform Commission of Canada (1982); and *Public Participation in the Administrative Process*, prepared by David Fox as a Study Paper for the Law Reform Commission of Canada (1979).

115 See for example, s. 27 of the *Broadcasting Act*, S.C. 1991, c. 11, which permits the cabinet to give broad directions to the Canadian Radio-Television and Telecommunications Commission respecting the Free Trade Agreement, and the former s. 54 of the *Public Service Employee Relations Act*, R.S.A. 1980, c. P-33, as amended by the *Labour Statutes Amendment Act*, 1983 (Alta.), c. 34, s. 5(7), which required a board of arbitration to consider the Provincial Treasurer's written statements of fiscal policy.

116 The error is jurisdictional in nature because the policy fetter prevents the delegate from exercising its discretion at all. In the *Innisfil* case, *supra* note 111 however, some of the judges in the lower Ontario courts treated this type of error as one within jurisdiction. With respect, this approach is theoretically incorrect, as Estey J. recognized in the Supreme Court of Canada.

117 The applicable standard of review of a decision of a municipal corporation is discussed in *Shell Canada Products Ltd. v. Vancouver (City)*, [1994] 1 S.C.R. 231, 20 Admin. L.R. (2d) 202 (S.C.C.).

118 For example, see *Petrashuyk v. Law Society (Alberta)* (1983), 29 Alta. L.R. (2d) 251 (Alta. Q.B.), reversed (1984), 35 Alta. L.R. (2d) 259 (Alta. C.A.), reinstated (1988), 33 Admin. L.R. 145 (S.C.C.) 663; and *Liversidge v. Anderson* (1941), [1942] A.C. 206 (U.K. H.L.).

lies to ensure that there has been no abuse of that power in a particular case. Although the courts have frequently elided them together, this chapter has for convenience grouped possible abuses into the following categories:

(a) improper intention in exercising a discretionary power for an unauthorized or ulterior purpose, in bad faith, or for irrelevant considerations;

(b) acting on inadequate material where there is no evidence or by ignoring relevant considerations;

(c) exercising discretionary power so as to obtain an improper result, which may be unreasonable, discriminatory, retroactive or uncertain in operation;

(d) exercising discretionary power under a misapprehension of the law; and

(e) fettering the exercising of discretion by adopting a policy or entering into a contract.

In theory, all these abuses cause the delegate to lose jurisdiction,[119] and therefore are susceptible to judicial review even in the face of privative clauses.[120]

9. Selected Bibliography

Adkins, R.J.M. and Penner, H.D., "Absence of Evidence as Grounds for Appeal" (1990) 6 Admin. L. J. 28.

Brun, H., "La Mort de la discretion administrative" (1974) 52 Can. Bar Rev. 426.

Davis, K.C., *Discretionary Justice: A Preliminary Inquiry* (Baton Rouge: Louisiana State Press, 1969).

de Villars, A., "Administrative Action on the Side of Eagles: Proving Discrimination, Improper Purpose and Bad Faith: A "Mission Impossible" on the Gulf Islands" (1996) 5 R.A.L. 193.

Finkle, P. and Cameron, D., "Equal Protection in Enforcement Towards More Structured Discretion" (1989) 12 Dalhousie L. J. 34

Galligan, D.J., "The Nature and Function of Policies Within Discretionary Power" [1976] P. L. 332.

Grey, J.H., "Discretion in Administrative Law" (1979) 17 Osgoode Hall L. J. 107.

Grey, J.H. and Casgrain, L., "Jurisdiction, Fairness and Reasonableness" (1986/87) 10 Dalhousie L.J. 89.

Law Reform Commission of Canada, *A Catalogue of Discretionary Powers in the Revised Statutes of Canada 1970*, prepared by P. Anisman, 1975.

---

119 *Ibid.*
120 See Chapter 15.

MacLauchlan, H.W., "Some Problems with Judicial Review of Administrative Consistency" (1984) 8 Dalhousie L.J. 435.

Molot, H., "The Self-Created Rule of Policy and Other Ways of Exercising Administrative Discretion" (1972) 18 McGill L.J. 310.

Mullan, D.J., "Natural Justice and Fairness – Substantive as well as Procedural Standards for Review of Administrative Decision-Making" (1982) McGill L.J. 250.

Mullan, D.J., "Recent Developments in Nova Scotian Administrative Law" (1978) 4 Dalhousie L.J. 467 at 538*ff.*

Rogerson, P., "On the Fettering of Public Powers" [1971] P. L. 288.

Smillie, J.A., "Review of Abuse of Discretionary Power" (1969) 47 Can. Bar Rev. 623.

Wade, W.   & Forsyth C., *Administrative Law*, 7th ed. (Oxford: Clarendon Press, 1994), and 8th ed. (Oxford: Clarendon Press, 2000).

Wilson, H.J., "Discretion in the Analysis of Administrative Process

8

Natural Justice and the Duty to be Fair: Historical Development and General Principles

1. Introduction

This chapter describes the principles of natural justice and the later doctrine of procedural fairness as they apply to the work of administrative tribunals and other statutory delegates.[1]

We start with an historical review of the law as it related to the principles of natural justice in England and Canada. In particular, we note that the first part of the 20th century saw a gradual erosion of the vigour of the principles of natural justice, in Canada culminating with the decision in *Calgary Power Ltd. v. Copithorne.*[2] We catalogue the restoration of the principles of natural justice which began in England with *Ridge v. Baldwin,*[3] and which developed such momentum that it led to a tremendous extension of the principles into a new doctrine of procedural fairness.

We then trace the full flowering of the duty to be fair in Canada beginning in 1979 and through to today. This "duty to be fair" has now been extended to cover both quasi-judicial and executive decisions, thus eliminating the need to first characterize the nature of the delegate's function before determining whether the procedure used in exercising it must be "fair" and thereby amenable to *certiorari* or another remedy.[4]

The precise content of procedural fairness in any given circumstance may be very difficult to determine without litigation. This is considered in detail in Chapters 9 and 10. Chapter 12 deals with the standard of review – that is, the intensity of the scrutiny – that a court must bring to bear once it has determined that a decision is reviewable.

But first, a word about terminology: a discussion of the principles of natural justice and procedural fairness, and their history, necessarily entails the characterization of a delegate's function. Traditionally, the categories of legislative, judicial or quasi-judicial, and administrative (or ministerial, or executive) have been used. In this chapter, the term "executive" is used to describe the govern-

---

1 This chapter draws substantially on two articles written by Professor D.P. Jones: "Administrative Fairness in Alberta" (1980) 18 Alta. L. Rev. 351; and "Natural Justice and Fairness in the Administrative Process, published as a chapter in *Judicial Review of Administrative Rulings* arising out of the 1982 Annual Conference of the Canadian Institute for the Administration of Justice, also published in (1983) 43 Revue du Barreau 441.

2 (1958), [1959] S.C.R. 24 (S.C.C.).

3 (1963), [1964] A.C. 40 (U.K. H.L.).

4 The need to characterize a delegate's function may still be required where the decision may be characterized as a legislative function. The duty to be fair may not apply to all legislative functions: see section 5, below.

mental function of applying and enforcing legislation to particular people in particular circumstances. The term "administrative" will often be found in the cases used synonymously with "executive", but it has so many other meanings that we have tried to avoid it wherever possible.[5]

2. Historical Development

(a) Origins of the Phrase: "Judicial or Quasi-judicial"

"Natural justice" connotes the requirement that administrative tribunals, when reaching a decision, must do so with procedural fairness. If they err, the superior courts will step in to quash the decision by *certiorari* or prevent the error being made by prohibition. Such an error is jurisdictional in nature and renders the decision void.[6]

The prerogative writs of *certiorari* and prohibition were originally used by the superior courts to control the decisions of inferior courts. That is, the writs were originally used in a purely judicial context. Historically, not only the administration of justice but also other governmental functions were delegated by Parliament to local justices of the peace. They were originally legal officers who ran courts within a limited jurisdiction. But the justices of the peace also became administrators of local government in the sense that they were given duties in connection with the administration of the Poor Laws, the upkeep of roads and bridges, and the licensing of ale houses, for example. The two functions – judicial and executive – were not separated. As a result, administrative decisions were arrived at by a process similar to a trial of the issue.

With the growth of local government and statutory tribunals in the 19th century, many of the administrative duties of the justices of the peace were transferred to these new creations. Curiously, these transferred governmental tasks retained the characterization as "judicial" because they had previously been performed by judicial officers and not because their substance was necessarily judicial. This lead to much confusion later. Loosely, this meant that the new decision-makers were also required to proceed fairly (that is, they had to observe the principles of natural justice); and, secondly, of course, they were required to stay within their limited respective areas of jurisdiction. The new label "quasi-judicial" appeared in an effort to distinguish between the judicial decision-making of the judges on the one hand, and on the other hand the decision-making of members of administrative tribunals who were not judicial

---

5 See de Smith, Woolf & Jowell, "Classification of Functions" in *Judicial Review of Administrative Actions*, 5th ed. (London: Sweet & Maxwell, 1995) at 1001-19.

6 See H.W.R. Wade, "Unlawful Administrative Action: Void or Voidable?", Part I at (1967) 83 L.Q. Rev. 499; Part II at (1968) 84 L.Q. Rev. 95; W. Wade & C. Forsyth, *Administrative Law*, 7th ed. (Oxford: Clarendon Press, 1994) at 339-44; M.B. Akehurst, (1968) 31 M.L.R. 2, 138; J.F. Northey, [1977] N.Z.L.J. 284; D. Oliver, [1981] C.L.P.; G.L. Peiris, "Natural Justice and Degrees of Invalidity of Administrative Action" [1983] P.L. 634; *Harelkin v. University of Regina*, [1979] 2 S.C.R. 561 (S.C.C.), and comment by D.P. Jones "Discretionary Refusal of Judicial Review in Administrative Law" (1981) 19 Alta. L. Rev. 483.

officers, but who were nevertheless required to adopt at least some of the procedures reminiscent of those used in a courtroom.

Although the label "judicial" originally applied to all administrative acts, the courts subsequently narrowed the meaning. As a result, the characterization of powers as either "legislative", "judicial" or "executive" became a necessary prerequisite to judicial review because the principles of natural justice did not apply unless the power was characterized first as judicial or quasi-judicial in nature. As a corollary, prohibition and *certiorari* came to be available only against judicial or quasi-judicial functions. This restriction omitted the wide range of decision-making in the legislative and executive areas which could then proceed unimpaired by considerations of natural justice.

Natural justice was comprised of two main sub-rules: *audi alteram partem*[7] – that a person must know the case being made against him or her and be given an opportunity to answer it (which is discussed in Chapter 9); and *nemo judex in sua causa debet esse*[8] – the rule against bias (which is discussed in Chapter 10). For many years in Canada, these two great principles were held not to apply to a vast number of decisions said to be legislative or executive in nature. As a result, procedural error in those cases was generally not subject to judicial review.

In the last twenty-five years in Canada, the concept of the "duty to be fair" has developed to the point where it is now completely accepted and the need to characterize between quasi-judicial and executive has disappeared.[9] The result has been to re-assert the power of the courts to review governmental decisions which cannot be characterized as judicial or quasi-judicial in nature, and to eliminate some of the need for extreme care in choosing the correct remedy before seeking judicial review. It is possible to view the "duty to be fair" as being either an extension of the principles of natural justice, or as another way of stating those principles;[10] probably nothing hangs now on this distinction. A review of the history of the judicial versus executive function is still useful nonetheless.

(b) Early English Cases Applying Natural Justice: *Cooper* and *Rice*

The late 19th and early 20th centuries saw a huge increase in the number of statutory bodies and regulatory agencies created at all levels of government. The courts expected them to be no less governed by the principles of natural justice than the justices of the peace had been before them, since the powers they exercised in the administration of government were the same. This view was plainly stated by Earle C.J. in *Cooper v. Wandsworth Board of Works*:[11]

---

7   "Hear the other side."
8   "No man can be a judge in his own cause."
9   The English courts began their move in 1963 with *Ridge v. Baldwin, supra* note 3, which was adopted in Canada in *Nicholson v. Haldimand-Norfolk (Regional Municipality) Commssioners of Police* (1978), [1979] 1 S.C.R. 311 (S.C.C.).
10   For a discussion of this point, see D.P. Jones, "Administrative Fairness in Alberta" (1980) 18 Alta. L. Rev. 351.
11   (1863), 143 E.R. 414 at 418 (Eng. C.P.).

It has been said that the principle [to give notice to and allow the party affected to be heard] . . . is limited to a judicial proceeding, and that a district board ordering a house to be pulled down cannot be said to be doing a judicial act. I do not quite agree with that; . . . I think the appeal clause would evidently indicate that many exercises of the power of a district board would be in the nature of judicial proceedings. . . .

And *per* Willes J.:[12]

I am of the same opinion. I apprehend that a tribunal which is by law invested with power to affect the property of one of Her Majesty's subjects, is bound to give such subject an opportunity of being heard before it proceeds: and that that rule is of universal application, and founded upon the plainest principles of justice. Now, is the board in the present case such a tribunal? I apprehend it clearly is. . . .

The case stands for the proposition that the right to be heard is a fundamental principle of justice and of universal application even where the power in question is purely executive, even where it is not exercised by a judicial officer, and even where there is no requirement for a hearing in the enabling legislation. This view was subsequently applied in many decisions. In doing so, the courts characterized as judicial or quasi-judicial many powers which might more properly be considered executive. Why the courts felt the characterization was necessary is not clear. It could have been merely an unthinking linkage between the old functions of the justices of the peace as judicial officers and the new tribunals, or a justification of the court's desire to maintain jurisdiction over government officials. Unfortunately, as a result, emphasis came to be placed on the characterization dichotomy rather than on a universal application of the principles of natural justice whenever persons were adversely affected by any form of governmental decision. The results achieved may have been correct in some cases, but the process of reasoning involved led the development of the law astray.

Still, in 1911, the courts had not yet started to confuse themselves. In *Education Board v. Rice*,[13] Loreburn L.C. in the House of Lords said:

Comparatively recent statutes have extended, if they have not originated, the practice of imposing upon departments or officers of State the duty of deciding or determining questions of various kinds. In the present instance, as in many others, what comes for determination is sometimes a matter to be settled by discretion, involving no law. It will, I suppose, usually be of an administrative kind; but sometimes it will involve matter of law as well as matter of fact, or even depend upon matter of law alone. In such cases the Board of Education will

---

12 *Ibid.* at 418.
13 [1911] A.C. 179 at 182 (U.K. H.L.).

have to ascertain the law and also to ascertain the facts. I need not add that in doing either they must act in good faith and fairly listen to both sides, for that is a duty lying upon everyone who decides anything. But I do not think they are bound to treat such a question as though it were a trial. They have no power to administer an oath, and need not examine witnesses. They can obtain information in any way they think best, always giving a fair opportunity to those who are parties in the controversy for correcting or contradicting anything prejudicial to their view.

The declaration that to hear both sides "is a duty lying upon everyone who decides anything" could, if taken to its logical but ridiculous extreme, have gone too far. Certainly, there are thousands of decisions made every day which affect persons and which could not be made without prior notice and the opportunity to be heard having been given. But similarly, there are thousands of decisions made every day that affect persons where to give notice and have a hearing would grind the business of government to a halt. The problem was to set the boundaries of the duty. However, in attempting to do so over the next 50 years, the courts so severely narrowed the scope of natural justice that it appeared they had wrought its demise.

The erosion of the principles of natural justice took place in England mainly between the two World Wars and can be seen primarily in the plethora of cases arising out of the large number of slum clearance schemes which were instituted; and, secondarily, in the area of town and country planning. In the minds of the courts, the greater public advantage perceived as inherent in these schemes far outweighed the danger to individual rights which followed from the almost wholesale denial of the right to be heard.

By the time the Supreme Court of Canada caught up with the trend in England in the *Copithorne*[14] case, the English courts had already seen the error of their ways. It took the Supreme Court of Canada nearly 20 more years to restore natural justice to its rightful place in the scheme of administrative law in the *Nicholson* case.[15]

(c) The First Erosion of Natural Justice: Concentrating on the Identity of the Decision-Maker

The beginning of the erosion of the principle that there is a right to be heard whenever a person is affected by a tribunal's decision, be it executive or quasi-judicial in nature, occurred in *Local Government Board v. Arlidge*.[16] The House of Lords, reluctant to interfere with the sovereign power of Parliament, determined that the nature of the tribunal making the decision should (in modern times) determine the procedure to be followed. On the one hand, courts of law traditionally followed a procedure characterized as judicial. On

---

14 (1958), [1959] S.C.R. 24 (S.C.C.).

15 *Nicholson v. Haldimand-Norfolk (Regional Municipality) Commissioners of Police* (1978), [1979] 1 S.C.R. 311 (S.C.C.).

16 [1915] A.C. 120 (U.K. H.L.).

the other hand, administrative tribunals, having been given power over other governmental matters by Parliament, must (in the absence of any express intention to the contrary) have been intended by Parliament to follow procedures which were their own and which were necessary to obtain efficiency. This was the beginning of an emphasis on the identity of the decision-maker, instead of on the substance of the decision being made.

Secondly, the court expressly recognized the right of Parliament to delegate governmental powers to members of the executive, with no right of appeal to the courts. In the end Parliament was responsible for the exercise of these powers which it had delegated and for the procedures adopted by the non-judicial persons to whom they had been granted. Thus, the courts yielded their traditional supervisory power over the procedure adopted by such delegates to the doctrine of complete Parliamentary Responsibility – the ultimate in judicial deference!

Thirdly, the court was concerned about administrative efficiency, delay and expense. A full-blown court procedure, or something akin to it, offended against all of these worthwhile aims. Again, therefore, Parliament could not have intended this procedure to be followed. This was how individual rights were eroded in the face of administrative efficiency. The courts lost sight of the fact that government should serve the needs of the governed, and not the other way around.

In summary, the House of Lords fell into the error of regarding the identity of the decision-maker as determinative of what procedure should be applied, rather than looking at the nature of the decision itself and its effect on a subject. The error lay in the assumption that it was because administrative officials had previously been justices of the peace that they had to follow the principles of natural justice. In truth it was because the questions being determined by them were of such a nature as to require procedural fairness. When these powers were transferred from the inferior courts, only the identity of the decision-makers, and not the nature of the questions, changed. This first and fundamental misunderstanding by the courts was continued, fossilized, and compounded in subsequent cases.

(d) The Second Erosion of Natural Justice: The "Super-added Duty to Act Judicially"

The second misunderstanding had its origin in *R v. Electricity Commissioners*,[17] where the issue was whether the proceedings of the electricity commissioners were of an executive rather than judicial character. On the one hand, Banks L.J. cited authorities showing that the court would issue prohibition or *certiorari* to a body exercising judicial functions, even though the body could not be described as a court in the ordinary sense. On the other hand, while Atkin L.J. agreed that the operation of prohibition and *certiorari* had extended to control the proceedings of bodies which were not courts of justice, he went on to say that:[18]

---

17   (1923), [1924] 1 K.B. 171 (Eng. C.A.).
18   *Ibid.* at 205, emphasis added.

Wherever any body of persons having legal authority to determine questions affecting the rights of subjects, *and having the duty to act judicially*, act in excess of their legal authority they are subject to the controlling jurisdiction of the King's Bench Division exercised in these writs. (emphasis added)

Unfortunately, these words of Lord Atkin took on a life and meaning far beyond anything intended by him and were to cause the law in this area to stray far from its proper course.

In 1927 the King's Bench Division adopted these words in *R. v. Legislative Committee of the Church Assembly*,[19] where the issue was whether writs of prohibition and *certiorari* would lie against the church assembly or its legislative committee to prohibit them from proceeding further with the *Prayer Book Measure, 1927*. As a preliminary question, the court considered what kinds of bodies were involved, and whether either was[20]

[a] body of persons having legal authority to determine questions affecting the rights of subjects, *and having the duty to act judicially. . . .* (Emphasis added.)

This was a direct quote from Atkin L.J.'s judgment in the *Electricity Commissioners*. Lord Hewart L.C.J. emphasized that this was a double test, the two parts being joined by "and" not "or". He interpreted this to mean that:[21]

In order that a body may satisfy the required test it is not enough that it should have legal authority to determine questions affecting the rights of subjects; *there must be superadded to that characteristic the further characteristic that the body has the duty to act judicially. The duty to act judicially is an ingredient which, if the test is to be satisfied, must be present.* As these writs in the earlier days were issued only to bodies which without any harshness of construction could be called, and naturally would be called Courts, *so also today these writs do not issue except to bodies which act or are under the duty to act in a judicial capacity.* (Emphasis added.)

Note that he also made the *Arlidge* mistake of looking at the decision-maker, not the nature of the decision; and he compounded his error by adopting Atkin L.J.'s careless reference to the "superadded duty" test. He then went on to hold that the church assembly and the legislative committee did not have the duty to act judicially. Rather, he characterized their function as legislative and held that therefore *certiorari* was not available.[22]

---

19 (1927), [1928] 1 K.B. 411 (Eng. K.B.).
20 *Ibid.* at 415, emphasis added.
21 *Ibid.*, emphasis added.
22 Compare the decision of the Alberta Court of Appeal in *Campeau Corp. v. Calgary (City)* (1978), 7 Alta. L.R. (2d) 294 (Alta. C.A.) and the decision of the Supreme Court of Canada

The decision of the Privy Council in *Nakkuda Ali v. M.F. De S. Jayaratne*,[23] graphically illustrates the degree to which the principles of natural justice had been eroded. The question was whether the Controller of Textiles in Ceylon was required to hold a hearing before revoking Nakkuda Ali's textile licence. The Privy Council held that the double test of (a) affecting rights, and (b) the existence of a superadded duty to act judicially had to be met before the principles of natural justice applied. Although the words of the statute[24] imposed a condition that there must in fact exist such reasonable grounds known to the controller before he could validly exercise the power of cancellation (which undoubtedly affected the rights of the subject), the court held that this requirement did not of itself mean that the controller was under any superadded duty to act judicially. After all, the controller could have reasonable grounds for his belief without ever confronting the licence holder, and it could not be said that he could only arrive at this conclusion by a process analogous to the judicial process. As a result, the Privy Council held that *certiorari* was unavailable. In so deciding, the Privy Council relied on Atkin L.J.'s test in *Electricity Commissioners*, as interpreted by Hewart L.C.J. in *Church Assembly*.

(e) The Development of the Law in Canada

The Supreme Court of Canada was also wrestling with this knotty problem. However, at least until the *Copithorne* case,[25] Canadian courts did not veer as far off the path as the English courts had done.

(i) The Alliance Case

In *Québec (Commission des relations ouvrières) v. Alliance des professeurs catholiques de Montréal*,[26] the question was whether the Labour Relations Board had exceeded its jurisdiction in acting without notice to the union in cancelling the union's certificate of representation for calling an illegal strike.

The *Quebec Labour Relations Act* permitted the dissolution of a union but "après lui avoir donné l'occasion d'être entendue et de faire toute la preuve tendant à se disculper".[27]

The Supreme Court rejected the view that silence by the legislature with respect to the requirement to give notice to a party affected by any decision must be taken to mean that the legislature intended no notice to be given. Rather, it reasoned that since the legislature may be presumed to know the general law, which requires such notice, it would be necessary for it in explicit terms to absolve the board from the necessity of giving notice.

---

in *Inuit Tapirisat of Canada v. Canada (Attorney General)*, [1980] 2 S.C.R. 735 (S.C.C.), both discussed below.

23 (1950), [1951] A.C. 66 (Ceylon P.C.).

24 "Where the Controller has reasonable grounds to believe. . . ."

25 (1958), [1959] S.C.R. 24 (S.C.C.).

26 [1953] 2 S.C.R. 140 (S.C.C.).

27 R.S.Q. 1941, c. 162A, article 50. An unofficial translation: ". . . after having given it the opportunity to be heard and to prove anything tending to exculpate it."

Throughout the judgments, there is no mention of the *Electricity Commissioners*[28] case, the superadded duty test, or of *Nakkuda Ali*.[29] Indeed the court was following the principles enunciated early in the century to provide litigants with a fair procedure in the course of administrative decision-making.

(ii) Saltfleet v. Knapman

The Supreme Court continued its adherence to these principles in *Saltfleet (Municipality) Board of Health v. Knapman*,[30] where it was argued that the board's function was executive in deciding whether certain conditions precedent, which had to be met before the board could acquire jurisdiction, had been met. The court held that[31]

> in deciding whether or not such condition exists a duty to act judicially rests upon the board. It would, I think, require the plainest words to enable us to impute to the Legislature the intention to confer upon the local board the power to forcibly eject the occupants of a building for certain specified causes without giving such occupants an opportunity to know which of such causes was alleged to exist or to make answer to the allegation and I find no such words in the statute or the schedule.

Although the characterization of the function occupied the court's time, the double test was not used – so far, so good!

(iii) Calgary Power v. Copithorne

Something went seriously wrong when the case of *Calgary Power Ltd. v. Copithorne*[32] came before the Supreme Court of Canada. By now the Supreme Court of Canada knew what was happening in England.[33] The question before the court was the characterization of the Minister's powers under the *Alberta Water Resources Act*[34] to order the expropriation of land for a transmission line right-of-way. If quasi-judicial, the Minister was bound to give notice and hear the respondent; if purely executive, then there was no provision in the Act requiring the Minister to give notice or to hold a hearing.

On the one side, it was argued that these powers must be characterized as quasi-judicial because they extinguished or modified private rights or interests in favour of another person. However, Martland J. held that this effect was not sufficient to label the power as quasi-judicial; there must be additionally imposed a duty to act judicially. In support of this proposition he cited the *Church*

---

28   (1923), [1924] 1 K.B. 171 (Eng. C.A.).
29   *Supra* note 23.
30   [1956] S.C.R. 877 (S.C.C.).
31   *Ibid.* at 879.
32   *Supra* note 25.
33   Martland J. had been to Oxford.
34   R.S.A. 1942, c. 65.

Assembly[35] case, *Nakkuda Ali*,[36] and (through the latter), the *Electricity Commissioners*[37] and *Robinson v. Minister of Town & Country Planning*.[38]

The legislation in *Copithorne* contained no requirement about the giving of notice, nor the holding of an inquiry in relation to the expropriation itself, although there were requirements regarding the arbitration proceedings which would determine fair compensation. The Act gave the minister sole power to decide whether the lands were necessary for the authorized undertaking and there was no appeal provision from his decision.

Martland J. therefore concluded that the minister's decision was taken as a minister of the Crown and was therefore a policy decision for which he was answerable only to the legislature, and was made necessarily in consideration of the public interest.[39] Martland J. adopted the trial judge's extraordinary view that there was no contest here between Calgary Power and Mr. Copithorne to be decided by the minister, nor was there any specific issue between them which the minister was called upon to settle. Therefore, His Lordship held that none of the hallmarks of a quasi-judicial proceeding was present, nor was there a *lis inter partes*. He found a vast difference between a minister so acting and the position of some inferior administrative board called upon to decide a dispute between parties in particular circumstances which would be quasi-judicial. He gave no reasons or rationale for saying there was a vast difference.

Thus the Supreme Court held that the power of the minister was executive, not quasi-judicial. The minister's decision was to be made in accordance with the statutory requirements, and was to be guided by the minister's own views as to policy. Since the court characterized the minister's function as executive, there was no requirement to apply the principles of natural justice, *certiorari* was not available, and Mr. Copithorne lost his land without benefit of an opportunity to state his case.

Thus, Canadian jurisprudence was provided with a standard to be followed that was to colour the next 20 years.[40] Ironically, shortly afterwards, the English courts began a reversal of the process which had been strangling natural justice.

3. The Duty to be Fair

(a) *Ridge v. Baldwin*

In England, the principles of natural justice were restored to their rightful place in administrative decision-making beginning in the 1960's with a line of cases in which the old authorities once more held sway. The damage done to Canadian jurisprudence took more time to repair.

---

35   (1927), [1928] 1 K.B. 411 (Eng. K.B.).

36   (1950), [1951] A.C. 66 (Ceylon P.C.).

37   (1923), [1924] 1 K.B. 171 (Eng. C.A.).

38   [1947] K.B. 702 (Eng. C.A.).

39   Compare this to the reasoning adopted by the House of Lords in the *Arlidge* case.

40   The error propounded in *Copithorne* is still sometimes cited in Canadian courts; see *Johannesson v. Alberta (Workers' Compensation Board Appeals Commission)* (1995), 34 Admin. L.R. (2d) 64 (Alta. Q.B.), discussed later, *infra* note 139.

The restoration in England began with *Ridge v. Baldwin*,[41] when the House of Lords considered the case of Chief Constable Ridge of Brighton, who was dismissed by the Watch Committee without notice or a hearing. Lord Reid found it necessary to state that "the authorities on the applicability of the principles of natural justice are in some confusion . . .".[42] He went on:[43]

> In modern times opinions have sometimes been expressed to the effect that natural justice is so vague as to be practically meaningless. But I would regard these as being tainted by the perennial fallacy that because something cannot be cut and dried or nicely weighed or measured therefore it does not exist . . . It appears to me that one reason why the authorities on natural justice have been found difficult to reconcile is that insufficient attention has been paid to the great difference between various kinds of cases in which it has been sought to apply the principle. What a minister ought to do in considering objections to a scheme may be very different from what a watch committee ought to do in considering whether to dismiss a chief constable.

Lord Reid divided the various cases on dismissal into three classes: (a) dismissal of a servant by a master; (b) dismissal from offices held at pleasure; and (c) dismissal from an office where there must be something against a person to warrant dismissal. The present case, he held, fell into category (c). Lord Reid then referred to an unbroken line of authorities which required the chief constable to be told of the case against him and be given an opportunity to be heard.

To the contrary, the statutory board relied on a number of more recent cases which had dealt with decisions by ministers, officials and various other bodies which had adversely affected property rights or privileges of persons, and which found no fault with the lack of a proper hearing afforded to such persons. Lord Reid grouped these cases into three categories:

(a) There were many cases where attempts were made to apply the principles of natural justice to wider duties imposed by modern legislation on ministers and other organs of government. The principles were given limited application in these situations. For example, there were cases where the functions of a minister or department dealt more with questions of public interest and the merits of alternative schemes of action than with the effect on individuals, then the minister might attach more importance to public policy than to the fate of individuals. Further there were cases, such as *Arlidge*, where the minister could not do everything himself and an individual could not complain if the ordinarily accepted methods of doing public business did not give him

---

41   [1963] 2 All E.R. 66 (U.K. H.L.).
42   *Ibid.* at 71; a masterpiece of understatement!
43   *Ibid.*

as much procedural protection as he would be given by the principles of natural justice. However, Lord Reid pointed out that it would be incorrect to extrapolate this restriction on the applicability of natural justice to every circumstance in which a minister was involved.

(b) There were cases involving wartime legislation where the principles had been held to have limited applicability. But, this rationale for restricting natural justice cannot be taken to apply to peacetime legislation.

(c) There were cases showing a misunderstanding of Atkin L.J.'s judgment in the *Electricity Commissioners* as glossed upon by Lord Hewart in the *Church Assembly* case. Lord Reid quoted the latter and said:[44]

> I have quoted the whole of this passage because it is typical of what has been said in several subsequent cases. If Lord Hewart C.J. meant that it is never enough that a body simply has a duty to determine what the rights of an individual should be, but that there must always be something more to impose on it a duty to act judicially before it can be found to observe the principles of natural justice, then that appears to me impossible to reconcile with the earlier authorities. I could not reconcile it with what [various judges had said in various cases]. And, as I shall try to show, it cannot be what Lord Atkin meant.

Lord Reid referred to the cases considered by Atkin L.J. and found nothing in them that "superadded" to the duty itself. Rather, Atkin L.J. inferred the judicial character of the duty evolved from the nature of the duty itself. Indeed, the electricity scheme considered many matters, not just the treatment of an individual, yet still Lord Atkin inferred a judicial character to the powers involved in that legislation. Surely he would have inferred such a judicial character where the power involved related solely to the treatment of one individual.

The troublesome decision in *Nakkuda Ali* was summarily dismissed by Lord Reid as follows:[45]

> This House is not bound by decisions of the Privy Council and for my part nothing short of a decision of this House directly in point would induce me to accept the position that, although an enactment expressly requires an official to have reasonable grounds for his decision, our law is so defective that a subject cannot bring up such a decision for review however seriously he may be affected and however obvious it may be that the official acted in breach of his statutory obligation.

---

44 *Ibid.* at 77-78.
45 *Ibid.* at 79.

Lord Reid continued:[46]

> No case older than 1911 was cited in *Nakkuda Ali v. M.F. de S. Jayaratne* on this question, and this question was only one of several difficult questions which were argued and decided. So I am forced to the conclusion that this part of the judgment in *Nakkuda's* case was given under a serious misapprehension of the effect of the older authorities and therefore cannot be regarded as authoritative.[47]

As a result, Lord Reid held that the power of dismissal in the Act of 1882 could *not* – either in 1882 or now – be exercised until the Watch Committee had informed the constable of the grounds on which it proposed to proceed and given him a proper opportunity to submit his defence. Lord Reid also stated that decisions given without regard to the principles of natural justice are void, a conclusion reached time and time again in the authorities.[48]

Lord Hodson also squarely rebuffed the view that there had to be some superadded characteristic in the process over and above the fact that the decision affected rights. He first noted that the cases clearly showed that the absence of a *lis* or dispute between opposing parties was not a decisive feature in determining whether the principles of natural justice applied, although the presence of one certainly necessitated their application. He went on:[49]

> Secondly, the answer in a given case is not provided by the statement that the giver of the decision is acting in an executive or administrative capacity, as if that was the antithesis of a judicial capacity. The cases seem to me to show that persons acting in a capacity which is not on the face of it judicial, but rather executive or administrative, have been held by the courts to be subject to the principles of natural justice.

In effect, therefore, the House of Lords in *Ridge v. Baldwin* restored the reasoning in *Cooper* as the benchmark for the applicability of natural justice, and swept away the damaging confusion of 40 years. Although the scope of government in that time had expanded to cover many areas previously not

---

46 *Ibid.* at 80.
47 It is strange that *Cooper*, decided in 1863 was not cited in *Nakkuda Ali*, nor in *Rice* or *Arlidge*. One explanation might be that *Cooper* is found in *Halsbury's* 1st edition (1913) under "Statutes-Interpretation-Common Law Rules" and similarly in *Halsbury's* 2nd edition (1941) under the same heading. There is no heading for Administrative Law in either edition. Perhaps nobody found the reference to *Cooper*.
48 See H.W.R. Wade, "Unlawful Administrative Action: Void or Voidable?", Part I at (1967) 83 L.Q. Rev. 499; Part II at (1968) 84 L.Q. Rev. 95; W. Wade & C. Forsyth, *Administrative Law* 7th ed. (Oxford: Clarendon Press, 1994) at 339-44; M.B. Akehurst, (1968) 31 M.L.R. 2, 138; J.F. Northey, [1977] N.Z.L.J. 284; D. Oliver, [1981] C.L.P.; G.L. Peiris, "Natural Justice and Degrees of Invalidity of Administrative Action", [1983] P.L. 634; *Harelkin v. University of Regina*, [1979] 2 S.C.R. 561 (S.C.C.), and comment by D.P. Jones, "Discretionary Refusal of Judicial Review in Administrative Law" (1981) 19 Alta. L. Rev. 483.
49 *Supra* note 41 at 113.

regulated, the House of Lords found no justification for moving away from the old principles. In Lord Reid's words:[50]

> We do not have a developed system of administrative law – perhaps because until fairly recently we did not need it. So it is not surprising that in dealing with new types of cases the courts have had to grope for solutions, and have found that old powers, rules and procedure are largely inapplicable to cases which they were never designed or intended to deal with. But I see nothing in that to justify our thinking that our old methods are any less applicable today than ever they were to the older types of cases. And, if there are any *dicta* in modern authorities which point in that direction, then in my judgment they should not be followed.

(b) *Re H.K.*

By 1967, Lord Denning in *R. v. Gambling Board for Great Britain*[51] could state:

> At one time it was said the principles [of due process review] only apply to judicial proceedings and not to administrative proceedings. That heresy was scotched in *Ridge v. Baldwin.*

And Lord Parker C.J. in the same case held that there is a duty on an immigration officer to act fairly even though his function was not judicial or quasi-judicial in nature:[52]

> That is not, as I see it, a question of acting or being required to act judicially, but of being required to act fairly. Good administration and an honest or *bona fide* decision must, as it seems to me, require not merely impartiality, nor merely bringing one's mind to bear on the problem, but acting fairly; and to the limited extent that the circumstances of any particular case allow, and within the legislative framework under which the administrator is working, only to that limited extent do the so-called rules of natural justice apply, which in a case such as this is merely a duty to act fairly.

Wade summarizes the new approach to the judicial control of administrative action on procedural grounds as follows:[53]

> The courts now have two strings to their bow. An administrative act may be held to be subject to the requirements of natural justice either

---

50 *Ibid.* at 76.
51 [1970] 2 Q.B. 417 at 430 (Eng. C.A.).
52 [1967] 2 Q.B. 617 at 630 (Eng. Q.B.).
53 W. Wade & C. Forsyth, *Administrative Law*, 7th ed. (Oxford: Clarendon Press, 1994) at 515. For an excellent summary of the English cases on the "duty to be fair" see D.J. Mullan, "Fairness: The New Natural Justice" (1975) 25 U.T.L.J. 281.

because it affects rights or interests and therefore involves a duty to act judicially, in accordance with the classic authorities and *Ridge v. Baldwin*; or it may simply be held that, "in our modern approach", it automatically involves a duty to act fairly and in accordance with natural justice, without any of the analysis which has been made into such an unnecessary obstacle.

(c) Advantages of the New Approach

The new duty to be fair freed the law from the old tautological strait jacket which provided that if there was a quasi-judicial function, then the principles of natural justice applied, and *certiorari* was available to superintend any breach of those procedural requirements. Conversely, that tautology provided that if the function was not quasi-judicial in nature but rather merely executive, then the principles of natural justice did not apply, nor was *certiorari* available. Under this tautology, the question of fairness could only arise to determine the content of natural justice assuming that a quasi-judicial function was involved.

Unfortunately, the distinction was never clear between a quasi-judicial function on the one hand and a merely executive one on the other. However, because the availability of *certiorari* depended upon this characterization, a great deal of litigation occurred. Each case had to be determined by itself, and provided virtually no precedent for subsequent litigation. Although there is considerable elasticity in what constitutes a quasi-judicial function (and the courts variously stretched or narrowed the concept), at some point it is simply not possible to characterize something as quasi-judicial, no matter how unfair the procedure used, or how desirable it would be for *certiorari* to issue in the circumstances.

The concept of the "duty to be fair" is much more robust. In the first place, it avoids premising the availability of judicial review on the existence of a quasi-judicial function, which is not a clear concept in any event. Secondly, the "duty to be fair" openly articulates the question at least subconsciously asked by the courts in determining whether judicial review should issue for procedural reasons. And, finally, it provides an accurate rubric for administrators of all descriptions to bear in mind when exercising their various functions.

Of course there will still be continuous litigation over the question of whether a particular administrator's procedure was in fact fair. But this question has not generated any more litigation (and possibly less) than that previously arising out of the meaning of "quasi-judicial". Rather, the focus of argument has shifted to the real question at issue: was this decision arrived at fairly? And the judicial answers to this question, in each case, provide considerably better guidance about acceptable procedures in particular circumstances. No longer does a court's finding that no quasi-judicial function is involved effectively grant the administrator *carte blanche* to adopt any procedure, no matter how unfair.

It is not possible to dismiss the development of the duty to be fair as a mere fleshing-out of the content of natural justice.[54] On the contrary, it signif-

---

54 As has been suggested, while the essence of natural justice may be fairness, the duty to be

icantly extends the ambit of judicial review beyond the existence of quasi-judicial functions (to which it previously was argued that only natural justice applied). And the recent jurisprudence clearly holds that *certiorari* – which historically only issued to quash a quasi-judicial function – is available to remedy any breach of the duty to be fair, even if no quasi-judicial function is involved.[55] Accordingly, the old trilogy uniting the existence of a quasi-judicial function, the applicability of the rules of natural justice, and the availability of *certiorari* has now been shattered. It seems certain, therefore, that the reasoning of the Supreme Court of Canada in *Copithorne* is no longer good law.

4. The Development of the Duty to be Fair in Canada

(a) The *Nicholson* Case

The *Nicholson* case arose in Ontario under the *Judicial Review Procedure Act*,[56] and concerned the termination of a probationary police constable. Although section 27 of Regulation 680 of the *Police Act*[57] generally provided that

> [n]o chief of police, constable or other police officer is subject to any penalty under this Part except after a hearing and final disposition of a charge on appeal as provided by this Part . . .

there was a specific exception preserving the authority of a police board:

> (b) to dispense with the services of any [probationary] constable within eighteen months of his becoming a constable.

Nicholson was not told why he was dismissed, nor was he given notice or any opportunity to make representations before his services were terminated. He applied for judicial review. This was granted by Hughes J. at first instance,[58] who relied heavily on the reasoning of the House of Lords in *Ridge v. Baldwin*[59] to classify the legal position of a police constable as an "office". Therefore, notwithstanding the existence of section 27(b), His Lordship held that, while the board's[60]

---

fair applies even where natural justice may not. In particular, the requirement of fairness is not limited to quasi-judicial functions (however they may be defined).

55 Laycraft J.'s decision in *McCarthy* (discussed below), unanimously upheld by the Court of Appeal, is clear authority for this proposition. So is the reasoning of Dickson J. in *Martineau (No. 2)*, although Pigeon J.'s majority judgment in that case is less clear on this point.

56 S.O. 1971, c. 48 (now R.S.O. 1990, c. J.1).

57 R.S.O. 1970, c. 351 (now *Police Services Act*, R.S.O. 1990, c. P. 15).

58 (1975), 61 D.L.R. (3d) 36 (Ont. Div. Ct.), reversed (1976), 12 O.R. (2d) 337 (Ont. C.A.), reversed (1978), [1979] 1 S.C.R. 311 (S.C.C.).

59 (1963), [1964] A.C. 40 (U.K. H.L.).

60 *Supra* note 58 at 45.

deliberations may be untrammelled by Regulations made under the *Police Act*, . . . this court should not allow them to proceed as if the principles of natural justice did not exist.

The Court of Appeal, however, reversed the decision, answering the following question in the affirmative:[61]

> Can the services of a police constable be dispensed with within 18 months of his becoming a constable, without observance by the authority discharging him of the requirements of natural justice, including a hearing?

In effect, the Ontario Court of Appeal focused on the statutory provisions dealing with appeals for permanent constables, noted the absence of similar provisions for probationary members who were employed "at pleasure", applied the maxim *expressio unius est exclusio alterius*,[62] and washed their hands of any general judicial responsibility for enforcing the observance of fair procedures by administrative bodies. In a five-to-four decision,[63] however, the Supreme Court of Canada reversed the Ontario Court of Appeal, and reinstated the result reached by Hughes J. – thereby quashing the termination of Nicholson's employment (which by then had exceeded the 18-month probation period!).

Two principal issues underlie the majority decision of the Supreme Court, written by Laskin C.J.C.:

(a) Was the status of a probationary constable sufficient to attract the principles of natural justice to termination proceedings?

(b) Is there a general duty to be fair even if the principles of natural justice do not apply?

The first question raises the issue of whether a probationary constable occupies an "office" which cannot be terminated without cause (to which the principles of natural justice apply, following *Ridge v. Baldwin*) or whether he is a mere

---

61 (1976), 69 D.L.R. (3d) 13 at 14 (Ont. C.A.), reversed (1978), [1979] 1 S.C.R. 311 (S.C.C.).
62 *Ibid.* at 17-22: "to state one thing is to exclude others". See also the application of this maxim by the majority of the Supreme Court of Canada in *Law Society of Upper Canada v. French* (1974), [1975] 2 S.C.R. 767 (S.C.C.), affirmed (1974), 49 D.L.R. (3d) 1 (note) (S.C.C.). It is submitted that this application of the *expressio unius* rule is wrong in principle. Natural justice is presumed to apply to decisions, unless specifically ousted by Parliament. Specifying certain procedural steps in some circumstances only reinforces the applicability or fleshes out the content of natural justice in those cases; it does not indicate Parliament's intention specifically to exclude natural justice in other circumstances. In short, the onus is on the decision-maker to show Parliament's clear intent to exempt him from complying with natural justice or procedural fairness.
63 (1978), [1979] 1 S.C.R. 311, 88 D.L.R. (3d) 671 (S.C.C.), Laskin C.J.C.'s judgment was concurred in by Ritchie, Spence, Dickson and Estey JJ.; Martland J.'s dissent was concurred in by Pigeon, Beetz and Pratte JJ.

employee who can be dismissed at pleasure. Indeed, this precise issue divided Hughes J. and the Court of Appeal. Laskin C.J.C., however, held[64] that the lower courts' references to the common law position of policemen were inapt in light of the existence of the *Police Act*, which made no reference whatever to the concept of employment "at pleasure". It was therefore not necessary to rely upon the *Constitutional Reference* case[65] (as Hughes J. had done) to fit Nicholson's employment into the third category adopted by Lord Reid in *Ridge v. Baldwin*, instead of into the second.[66] Nor was it necessary to re-examine whether the law should continue to recognize employment at pleasure, even in light of the decision by the House of Lords in *Malloch v. Aberdeen Corporation*.[67] Rather, Laskin C.J.C. held that the *Police Act* forms a complete code, "a turning away from the old common law rule even in cases where the full [probationary] period of time has not fully run".[68] Accordingly, his Lordship was[69]

> of the opinion that although the appellant clearly cannot claim the procedural protections afforded to a constable with more than 18 months' service, he cannot be denied any protection. He should be treated "fairly" not arbitrarily.

It is important to note that this reasoning does not necessarily apply to an employee who truly is engaged at pleasure, although that precise issue did arise in the *McCarthy* case.[70] Indeed, this difference in the characterization of Nicholson's employment provides the basis for the dissenting judgment in the Supreme Court. Martland J. simply held that Nicholson was dismissable at pleasure, that that was the very purpose of the 18-month probationary period, and that, unlike *Malloch's* case, there were no procedures governing this type of case in the *Police Act*. According, Martland J. was of the opinion that there was no breach of any legal duty to the appellant in the exercise of this purely executive function.

This led to the second issue facing the court: was there a general duty to be fair even if the principles of natural justice did not apply? Martland J. did not even refer to the "duty to be fair", and it is clear that His Lordship did not recognize it as a concept different from natural justice. Because only an executive (and not quasi-judicial) function was involved in terminating a probationary constable, the rules of natural justice simply did not apply in this case. *Cedit questio.*

On the other hand, Laskin C.J.C. equally clearly recognized a distinction between the "duty to be fair" and the principles of natural justice. He specifi-

---

64   *Ibid.* at 677 [D.L.R.].

65   *Reference re Constitutional Questions Act (Ontario)*, [1957] O.R. 28 (Ont. C.A.).

66   *Supra* note 58. Lord Reid's three categories in *Ridge v. Baldwin* were: (a) pure master-servant relationships; (b) offices held at pleasure; and (c) offices terminable only for cause.

67   [1971] 2 All E.R. 1278 (U.K. H.L.).

68   *Supra* note 63 at 680 [D.L.R.].

69   *Ibid.*

70   Discussed in section (d), below.

cally adopted Megarry J.'s dictum in *Bates v. Lord Hailsham of St. Marylebone*:[71]

> that in the sphere of the so-called quasi-judicial the rules of natural justice run, and that in the administrative or executive field there is a general duty of fairness.

The chief justice also referred to de Smith's explanation[72] of the relationship between fairness and natural justice, and to the[73]

> realization that the *classification of statutory functions as judicial, quasi-judicial or administrative is often very difficult*, to say the least; and to endow some with procedural protection while denying others any at all would work injustice when the results of statutory decisions raise the same serious consequences for those adversely affected, regardless of the classification of the function in question . . .

Finally, the chief justice cited several English decisions[74] on the duty to be fair to support his view that this concept is now part of the common law. Because of the unfairness of the method adopted by the board in deciding to terminate Nicholson, its decision was quashed.

It is important to note that Laskin C.J.C. adopted the concept of the duty to be fair as a remedy for procedural unfairness where no quasi-judicial function was involved. He thus tacitly recognized the continuing need to characterize functions as quasi-judicial or merely executive, however difficult that characterization may be. While this approach was consistent with the English cases and it undoubtedly permitted judicial review of purely executive functions, it perpetuated the need to distinguish between quasi-judicial and merely executive functions, and it did not decide whether *certiorari* was available as a remedy for a breach of the duty to be fair where no quasi-judicial function was involved.[75] Although the seminal importance of *Nicholson* cannot be underestimated, these problems were precisely the issues which arose in *McCarthy*[76] and *Martineau*.[77]

---

71 [1972] 1 W.L.R. 1373 at 1378 (Eng. Ch. Div.).
72 S.A. de Smith, *Judicial Review of Administrative Action*, 3d ed. (Oxford: Clarendon Press, 1973) at 208-209.
73 *Supra* note 63 at 681 [D.L.R.], emphasis added.
74 *Pearlberg v. Varty (Inspector of Taxes)*, [1972] 1 W.L.R. 534 (U.K. H.L.); *Furnell v. Whangarei High Schools Board*, [1973] A.C. 660 (New Zealand P.C.); *Russell v. Duke of Norfolk* (1948), [1949] 1 All E.R. 109 at 118 (Eng. C.A.); *Selvarajan v. Race Relations Board* (1975), [1976] 1 All E.R. 12 (Eng. C.A.).
75 In *McCarthy v. Calgary Roman Catholic Separate School District No. 1*, [1979] 4 W.W.R. 725 (Alta. T.D.), affirmed (1979), 145 D.L.R. (3d) 765 (Alta. C.A.), it was argued by the school board that *Nicholson* should be confined to proceedings under the *Ontario Judicial Review Procedure Act*, S.O. 1971, c. 48 (now R.S.O. 1990, c. J.1), and should not be applied to *certiorari* in Alberta. Laycraft J. rejected this narrow interpretation of *Nicholson*, and Dickson J. in *Martineau (No. 2)* confirmed that the broader view is correct.
76 [1979] 4 W.W.R. 725 (Alta. T.D.), affirmed (1979), 145 D.L.R. (3d) 765 (Alta. C.A.).
77 *Martineau v. Matsqui Institution (No. 2)* (1979), [1980] 1 S.C.R. 602 (S.C.C.).

(b) The *Campeau* Case

The duty to be fair was also an important element in the decisions of the Appellate Division of the Supreme Court of Alberta in *Campeau Corp. v. Calgary (City)*,[78] and *Harvie v. Calgary (City) Regional Planning Commission*.[79]

Campeau involved an application to the city council to have the land use classification of certain lands changed from "agricultural-future residential" to "direct control" for a multiple-family development, pursuant to section 106(2) of the former *Planning Act*.[80] The lands in question, however, were ideally suited for a park. After lengthy proceedings, city council decided not to approve the requested amendment to the land use classification guidelines, even though it also declined to purchase the land for use as a park. The landowner applied to the Trial Division for an order either (a) approving the reclassification, or (b) directing council to re-hear the matter without taking into account the land's possible use as a park. Milvain C.J.T.D. rejected this application, after having noted that even an affirmative resolution by council to reclassify the land would have required further approval by the provincial planning board:[81]

> Such being the case I am satisfied the decision was no more than an administrative act, done in the performance of a divided concept as to what was a public duty. The decision is not subject to judicial review and the application before me is dismissed.

The Appellate Division unanimously reversed this decision. Lieberman J.A., writing the opinion for the court – one month before *Nicholson* was decided by the Supreme Court of Canada – noted the "difficulties and uncertainties inherent" in characterizing functions as quasi-judicial or merely administrative. He went on to note (indeed, predict!) that[82]

> there is a discernible trend in the decisions of the Supreme Court of Canada to examine the conduct of a tribunal's proceedings or even the exercise of ministerial discretion where a person's rights are affected in order to determine whether they were conducted and exercised fairly and in good faith. If not, the court will, wherever possible, intervene and right the injustice suffered by the aggrieved party by the use of one of the prerogative writs.

His Lordship then referred at length to the Supreme Court of Canada's decisions in *Roper c. Royal Victoria Hospital*,[83] *Hardayal v. Canada (Minister*

---

78 (1977), 8 A.R. 77 (Alta. T.D.), reversed (1978), 7 Alta. L.R. (2d) 294 (Alta. C.A.); see also *Campeau (No. 2)* (1980), 12 Alta. L.R. (2d) 379 (Alta. C.A.).

79 (1978), 8 Alta. L.R. (2d) 166 (Alta. C.A.).

80 R.S.A. 1970, c. 276 (now part of the *Municipal Government Act,* R.S.A. 2000, c. M-26).

81 (1978), 8 A.R. 77 at 86 (Alta. Q.B.).

82 (1978), 7 Alta. L.R. (2d) 294 at 302 (Alta. C.A.).

83 (1974), [1975] 2 S.C.R. 62 (S.C.C.).

of Manpower & Immigration),[84] and *St. John v. Fraser*,[85] as well as to the recent English cases on the duty to be fair in purely administrative proceedings.[86]

Notwithstanding this disquisition on the duty to be fair, Lieberman J.A. nevertheless held[87] that it was unnecessary to characterize the council's function in handling the application for reclassification of the land. The principal basis of His Lordship's judgment does not concern the duty to be fair at all, but rather the use of a statutory power for an improper purpose – namely, to acquire a park without paying full market value for it. Yet a breach of the principles of natural justice (or of the duty to be fair) has traditionally been treated as a separate ground for judicial review from actions made for an improper purpose, or based on irrelevant evidence, or on the lack of relevant evidence, or those which are simply *ultra vires* the governing legislation. Of course, in some circumstances, the procedures used by administrators acting in bad faith or for an improper purpose or on irrelevant evidence may also contravene the principles of natural justice (or the duty to adopt fair procedures). But, with respect, this coincidence of grounds for judicial review is precisely that: a coincidence. Accordingly, it is submitted that the real *ratio decidendi* of the *Campeau* decision concerns improper purpose, which is a substantive matter, and not procedural unfairness. Nevertheless, Lieberman J.A.'s *obiter dicta* on the duty to be fair accurately presaged the subsequent development of the law.[88]

(c) The *Harvie* Case

Although decided after *Nicholson* had been reported, and despite numerous references to the duty to be fair, the *ratio decidendi* of the unanimous judgment of the Appellate Division in *Harvie v. Calgary (City) Regional Planning Commission*[89] clearly characterizes the subdivision process in Alberta as quasi-judicial. Accordingly, the court held that Glenbow Ranches Ltd. had the right to notice and to appear before the planning commission on an application by a neighbouring landowner to subdivide the latter's land. The duty to be fair, in this case, did not stand in contradistinction to the principles of natural justice, but rather was relevant to concluding that there was a quasi-judicial function involved. The judgment, therefore, demonstrates the elastic nature of the concept of a quasi-judicial function.

To reach this conclusion, it was necessary for the court to overcome the judgment in a strikingly similar English case, *Gregory v. London Borough of Camden*,[90] to the effect that a neighbouring landowner had no "rights" affected when subdivision on development approval was granted to the applicant. This

---

84 (1977), [1978] 1 S.C.R. 470 (S.C.C.), reversing [1976] 2 F.C. 746 (Fed. C.A.).
85 [1935] S.C.R. 441 (S.C.C.).
86 *Supra* note 74.
87 *Supra* note 82.
88 Particularly in *Nicholson*, decided on 3rd October 1978 – just about a month after Lieberman J.A.'s judgment in *Campeau*, rendered 9th September 1978.
89 (1978), 8 Alta. L.R. (2d) 166 (Alta. C.A.).
90 [1966] 2 All E.R. 196 (Eng. Q.B.).

precedent, and the perception that subdivision was merely a "mechanical process",[91] had led Quigley J. to refuse judicial review over a purely executive function. Clement J.A., writing for the unanimous court[92] on appeal, came to a different conclusion. First, he noted that it is not possible to compartmentalize judicial and executive functions, and that the "quasi-judicial" label is apt to describe a composite function which involves both judicial and executive duties.[93] Secondly, His Lordship rejected the argument that a quasi-judicial function was not involved because none of Glenbow's rights were involved.[94] He quoted the following passage from the judgment of Martland J. in *Calgary Power Ltd. v. Copithorne*:[95]

> With respect to the first point, the respondent submitted that a function is of a judicial or quasi-judicial character when the exercise of it effects the extinguishment or modification of private rights or interests in favour of another person, unless a contrary intent clearly appears from the statute. This proposition, it appears to me, goes too far in seeking to define functions of a judicial or quasi-judicial character. In determining whether or not a body or an individual is exercising judicial or quasi-judicial duties, it is necessary to examine the defined scope of its functions and then to determine whether or not there is imposed a duty to act judicially . . .

Now Martland J.'s judgment in *Calgary Power*[96] has generally been interpreted to mean that there are two necessary requirements for the existence of a quasi-judicial function: first, that rights are affected; and, secondly, that there is a superadded duty to act judicially. Indeed, Martland J. in *Calgary Power* goes on to quote Hewart L.C.J.'s famous dictum to this effect from *R. v. Legislative Committee of the Church Assembly*:[97]

> In order that a body may satisfy the required test it is not enough that it should have legal authority to determine questions affecting the rights of subjects; there must be superadded to that characteristic the further characteristic that the body has the duty to act judicially.

Clement J.A., however, referred to *Nicholson*, and rejected this traditional test. To paraphrase, he said that the traditional proposition that rights must be

---

91 (1978), 5 Alta. L.R. (2d) 301 at 303 (Alta. T.D.).
92 Composed of Clement, Moir and Haddad JJ.A. – the latter two of whom formed the court with Lieberman J.A. in *Campeau*.
93 *Supra* note 89 at 180.
94 *Ibid.* at 180-85.
95 *Ibid.* at 180.
96 (1958), [1959] S.C.R. 24 at 30-34 (S.C.C.).
97 (1927), [1928] 1 K.B. 411 at 415 (Eng. K.B.).

affected went too far in seeking to define a judicial or quasi-judicial function.[98] He accepted de Smith's view[99] that

> the term "rights" is to be understood in a very broad sense, and is not to be confined to the jurisprudential concept of rights to which correlative legal duties are annexed. It comprises an extensive range of legally recognised interests, the categories of which have never been closed.

Although Glenbow Ranches did not have any cause of action against either the developer or the commission, nevertheless Clement J.A. held that its interests were so affected by the proposed subdivision that judicial review should issue in the circumstances.[100]

> Administrative law in the statutory sense reflects the concepts of legislatures to meet the difficulties in society arising out of increasing population densities, changing relationships between subjects and government, and other societal stresses. The new concepts are expressed in a legislative framework in which various rights, interests, duties and powers are created, for varied purposes and objectives, many unknown to the common law and some of far-reaching effect on traditional concepts. All of these must be given their proper effect. Jurisdiction over their administration is entrusted to newly-created tribunals or, in some cases, to existing tribunals. It is, in my view, necessary to the maintenance of the supervisory jurisdiction of the courts in the general public interest that these new rights and interests be viewed and weighed in the light of the legislative concept that created them, not in the shadow of narrower considerations expressed in times past under different societal conditions. When a new right or interest has been created by statute it must be examined, not in isolation, but in the context of the whole. I am of the opinion that the nature and extent of the right or interest is a vitally important facet of the complex judicial process necessary to determine whether, in a particular case, there is a duty on a tribunal to conform wholly or to some degree to the principles of natural justice in coming to a decision affecting the person asserting the interest.

This passage justifies the extension of the concept of a quasi-judicial function to a process which only affects "interests" and not technical "rights". Unfortunately, it still maintained the distinction between quasi-judicial and merely executive powers, and thus the need to characterize functions. At some point, it simply is not possible to stretch the elastic concept of quasi-judicial

---

98 *Supra* note 89 at 183.

99 S.A. de Smith, *Judicial Review of Administrative Action*, 3d ed. (Oxford: Clarendon Press, 1971) at 344.

100 *Harvie v. Calgary (City) Regional Planning Commission* (1978), 8 Alta. L.R. (2d) 166 at 184-85 (Alta. C.A.).

to cover a purely executive function that clearly cries out for judicial review. Thus, with respect, it was unfortunate that Clement J.A. did not follow *Nicholson* (from which he quoted extensively)[101] to its logical conclusion, nor did he in the end give effect to his bold statement of the expanding ambit of judicial review:[102]

> In late years there has been an emerging recognition that the supervisory jurisdiction of the court must keep pace with the increasing variety and scope of what are classified as administrative functions of tribunals, when a decision in the exercise of such functions has an appreciable effect on a right or interest of a subject which is, in the view of the court, of sufficient importance to warrant recognition.

The duty to be fair, therefore, in *Harvie* was relevant because its breach constituted a breach of the principles of natural justice, which applied because a quasi-judicial function was involved.

(d) The *McCarthy* Case

A bolder approach to the duty to be fair was taken by the Court of Appeal in unanimously upholding Laycraft J.'s judgment in *McCarthy v. Calgary Roman Catholic Separate School District No. 1*.[103] Mr. McCarthy was the superintendent of the Calgary separate school system, and was dismissed by the board without notice and without reasons. He sought (*inter alia*) *certiorari* to quash his purported dismissal, and the board countered by asking for a preliminary determination whether *certiorari* could even apply in these circumstances, which it said involved only a master-servant relationship. Milvain C.J.T.D. rejected[104] the board's application for a preliminary determination, but this was reversed by the Court of Appeal.[105]

Laycraft J.'s judgment, therefore, deals with the availability of *certiorari* in these circumstances.

Laycraft J. held[106] that McCarthy occupied a statutory office under the *School Act*,[107] and that the reasoning adopted by the majority of the Supreme Court of Canada in *Nicholson* applied squarely to this case. Nevertheless, the board argued that *Nicholson* was decided under the *Ontario Judicial Review Procedure Act*,[108] and was not authority in Alberta for extending the availability of *certiorari* to supervise the exercise of a purely administrative function. Laycraft J. rejected this argument, even though he specifically held that[109]

---

101 *Ibid.* at 185-87.
102 *Ibid.* at 185.
103 [1979] 4 W.W.R. 725 (Alta. T.D.), affirmed (1979), 145 D.L.R. (3d) 765 (Alta. C.A.).
104 On 20th November 1978, *ibid.* at 727.
105 *Ibid.* at 728-29.
106 *Ibid.* at 731-34.
107 R.S.A. 1970, c. 329 (now R.S.A. 2000, c. S-3).
108 S.O. 1971, c. 48 (now R.S.O. 1990, c. J.1).
109 *Supra* note 103 at 735.

[t]he function of the board in this case must be characterized as administrative and not as judicial or quasi-judicial in the sense that those terms have been distinguished from each other in Canadian cases.

This characterization clearly posed the problem so neatly avoided by Lieberman J.A. in *Campeau* and Clement J.A. in *Harvie*, who both managed to eke a quasi-judicial function out of the statutory powers involved in those cases. By holding that only an executive function was involved in *McCarthy*, Laycraft J. had to consider both (a) whether the duty to be fair had been breached, and also (b) whether *certiorari* was even available as a remedy for such a breach. His Lordship held that *Nicholson* not only recognized the right of the citizen to fairness in administrative procedure, but also necessarily recognized that *certiorari* was available to enforce that right:[110]

> to hold otherwise is to say that, though administrative acts in Alberta are subject to control by the courts, the only means of control is by the declaratory action. In some cases that result may follow as, for example, where the record produced on the motion under the *Crown Practice Rules* is inadequate or where the court in the exercise of its discretion decides that the case is not appropriate for a prerogative writ. In many cases, however, it would be highly undesirable that there be no power to quash an administrative decision made contrary to statutory power. When the Supreme Court of Canada recognized the right of the citizen to fair treatment in the exercise of such powers, it must also be taken to have recognized the traditional remedy by which the right might be enforced.

Accordingly, *certiorari* is available to correct a breach of the duty to be fair, even where only an executive function is involved. It is no longer necessary to stretch the concept of a quasi-judicial function to fit the particular facts in which it is alleged that a breach of procedural fairness has occurred. Nor is it necessary to find some other remedy (such as a declaration) for procedural unfairness in a purely executive matter. In other words, the tautology that *certiorari* is available only to correct breaches of the principles of natural justice, which are only relevant to quasi-judicial functions, has been broken.

Laycraft J.'s judgment was unanimously upheld by the Court of Appeal,[111] and now represents the law of Alberta – particularly in light of the subsequent decision of the Supreme Court of Canada in *Martineau (No. 2)*.

(e) *Martineau (No. 2)*

Precisely the same question which confronted Laycraft J. and the Alberta Court of Appeal in *McCarthy* was faced by the Supreme Court of Canada in *Martineau v. Matsqui Institution (No. 2)*:[112] Is *certiorari* available to remedy

---

110 *Ibid.* at 737.
111 October 1979 (unreported).
112 (1979), [1980] 1 S.C.R. 602 (S.C.C.).

a breach of the duty to be fair when a purely executive function is involved? Although the Supreme Court was unanimous in granting *certiorari*, it divided six-to-three[113] in the reasons for this outcome. The reasoning adopted by the court is, therefore, relevant to the Alberta cases on the duty to be fair, even though Martineau arose under the peculiar provisions of the *Federal Court Act*.[114]

Mr. Martineau was sentenced to 15 days in solitary confinement for a "flagrant or serious" disciplinary offence. His application for judicial review under section 28 of the *Federal Court Act* was rejected by the Supreme Court of Canada in *Martineau (No. 1)*[115] because the "directives" governing the procedure for dealing with disciplinary offences were executive rather than "law", and therefore could not be quasi-judicial in nature. Martineau, therefore, proceeded with his second action, under section 18 of the *Federal Court Act*, for an order of *certiorari* to quash the disciplinary board's decision. Mahoney J. at first instance, treating the matter as an application for a preliminary determination of a question of law, held that[116]

> a public body, such as the respondent, authorized by law to impose a punishment, that was more than a mere denial of privileges, had a duty to act fairly in arriving at its decision to impose the punishment. Any other conclusion would be repugnant. The circumstances disclosed in this application would appear to be appropriate to the remedy sought. I am not, of course, deciding whether the remedy should be granted but merely whether it could be granted by the Federal Court of Canada, Trial Division. In my view it could.

The Federal Court of Appeal reversed this[117] on the basis that a conviction for a disciplinary offence was a purely executive function with respect to which *certiorari* was not available. The consequence of this view, of course, is that Parliament must be taken to have transferred all supervising jurisdiction over quasi-judicial federal bodies to the Federal Court of Appeal under section 28 of the Act, so that the reference in section 18 to *certiorari* in the Trial Division is hollow, leaving no effective judicial review over purely executive functions.

Pigeon J., writing for the majority of the Supreme Court, refused to accept this view of the law. Rather, he understood *Nicholson* to stand for the "common law principle"[118]

---

113   Martland, Ritchie, Beetz, Estey and Pratte JJ., concurred with Pigeon J.; Laskin C.J.C. and McIntyre J. concurred with Dickson J.'s reasons.

114   R.S.C. 1970, c. 10 (2nd Supp.). See David J. Mullan, *The Federal Court Act: Administrative Law Jurisdiction* (Ottawa: Law Reform Commission of Canada, 1977). See also *Proposals to amend the Federal Court Act*, by the Hon. Mark MacGuigan, Minister of Justice, 29th August 1983.

115   [1976] 2 F.C. 198 (Fed. C.A.), affirmed (1977), [1978] 1 S.C.R. 118 (S.C.C.).

116   (1977), [1978] 1 F.C. 312 at 318-19 (Fed. T.D.), reversed [1978] 2 F.C. 637 (Fed. C.A.), reversed (1979), [1980] 1 S.C.R. 602 (S.C.C.).

117   [1978] 2 F.C. 637 (Fed. C.A.), reversed (1979), [1980] 1 S.C.R. 602 (S.C.C.).

118   *Supra* note 112 at 634, quoting from Megarry J.'s judgment in *Bates v. Lord Hailsham of St. Marylebone*, [1972] 3 All E.R. 1019 at 1024 (Eng. Ch. Div.) (emphasis is Pigeon J.'s);

> that in the sphere of the so-called quasi-judicial the rules of natural justice run, and that in the administrative or executive field there is a general duty of fairness. . . .

and the further principle that a breach of the duty could be enforced by judicial review. Policy may require that full-blown judicial procedures not be applicable to disciplinary proceedings,[119] (which would have prevented their characterization as quasi-judicial for the purpose of judicial review under section 28 of the 1970 version of the *Federal Court Act* which was subsequently amended in 1992 to eliminate this distinction). Although[120]

> [i]t is specially important that the remedy be granted only in cases of serious injustice and that proper care be taken to prevent such [disciplinary] proceedings from being used to delay deserved punishment so long that it is made ineffective, if not altogether avoided[.]

Pigeon J. upheld[121] Mahoney J.'s ruling that *certiorari* is available under section 18 of the *Federal Court Act* to supervise a breach of the duty to be fair in purely executive proceedings.

While the remaining three members of the court concurred in the outcome reached by Pigeon J., the reasons written on their behalf by Dickson J. were considerably lengthier, and addressed three specific issues: first, sorting out the respective supervisory jurisdictions of the Trial and Appellate Divisions of the Federal Court under sections 18 and 28 of the 1970 version of the Act (subsequently amended, effective in 1992); secondly, the duty to act fairly; and, finally, the ambit of *certiorari* in Canada.

On the first issue, Dickson J. agreed with Pigeon J., both in the present case and his *dicta* in *Howarth v. Canada (National Parole Board)*,[122] in rejecting the Federal Court of Appeal's interpretation that section 28 of the 1970 version of the Act completely supplanted the jurisdiction of the Trial Division to grant *certiorari*. While a breach of the duty to be fair alone is not sufficient to bring an administrative body within the definition of "quasi-judicial" (required to give the Federal Court of Appeal jurisdiction under the former version of section 28),[123] the converse is not true either. Therefore, while the lack of a quasi-judicial function may well have deprived the Court of Appeal of juris-

---

and referring specifically to *Nicholson* as the acceptance in Canada of the duty to be fair as a "common law principle".

119 *Supra* note 112 at 636-37.

120 *Ibid.* at 637.

121 *Ibid.* Note that curiously Pigeon J. referred to the proceedings under s. 28 of the *Federal Court Act* as being "in the nature of a right of appeal". Is this to be contrasted to judicial review?

122 (1974), [1976] 1 S.C.R. 453 (S.C.C.).

123 *Supra* note 112 at 613. Note, however, that a breach of the duty to act fairly may predispose the court to characterize an impugned function as being quasi-judicial, as occurred in both *Campeau (No. 1)* and *Harvie* cases discussed above. Section 28 was amended in 1990 (effective in 1992) to eliminate the reference to "judicial or quasi-judicial": see Appendix 5.

diction, it did not mean that the Trial Division could remedy a breach of the duty to be fair.[124] The duty to be fair is procedural in nature, and means more than merely good faith.[125]

Dickson J. then turned his attention to the availability of *certiorari* to remedy a breach of the duty to be fair procedurally. He referred to Atkin L.J.'s famous quotation in *R. v. Electricity Commissioners*:[126]

> Wherever any body of persons having legal authority to determine questions affecting the rights of subjects, and having the duty to act judicially, act in excess of their legal authority they are subject to the controlling jurisdiction of the King's Bench Division exercised in these writs.

Dickson J. noted the danger of construing this quotation too restrictively. In particular:[127]

> There has been an unfortunate tendency to treat "rights" in the narrow sense of rights to which correlative legal duties attach. In this sense, "rights" are frequently contrasted with "privileges", in the mistaken belief that only the former can ground judicial review of the decision-maker's actions.

His Lordship thus rejected such a narrow concentration on "rights", and focused instead on the public policy underlying judicial review:[128]

> When concerned with individual cases and aggrieved persons, there is the tendency to forget that one is dealing with public law remedies, which, when granted by the courts, not only set aright individual in justice, but also ensure that public bodies exercising powers affecting citizens heed the jurisdiction granted to them. *Certiorari* stems from the assumption by the courts of supervisory powers over certain tribunals in order to assure the proper functioning of the machinery of government. To give a narrow or technical interpretation to "rights" in an individual sense is to misconceive the broader purpose of judicial review of administrative action. *One should, I suggest, begin with the premise that any public body exercising power over subjects may be amenable to judicial supervision, the individual interest involved being but one factor to be considered in resolving the broad policy question of the nature of review appropriate for the particular administrative body.* [emphasis added]

---

124 See also *Hardayal v. Canada (Minister of Manpower & Immigration)* (1977), [1978] 1 S.C.R. 470 at 479 (S.C.C.); *Roper c. Royal Victoria Hospital* (1974), [1975] 2 S.C.R. 62 at 67 (S.C.C.).

125 *Supra* note 112 at 614.

126 (1923), [1924] 1 K.B. 171 (Eng. C.A.), quoted *supra* note 112 at 617.

127 *Supra* note 112 at 618.

128 *Ibid.* at 619, emphasis added.

If judicial review will issue even where "rights" are not technically affected, must there nevertheless be a duty to act judicially before *certiorari* is available? Again, Dickson J. rejected such a restriction on the availability of *certiorari* – relying principally upon Lord Reid's judgment in *Ridge v. Baldwin*, and on the now long line of English cases on the duty to be fair.[129] These authorities indicated to His Lordship that[130]

> the application of a duty of fairness with procedural content does not depend upon proof of a judicial or quasi-judicial function. Even though the function is analytically administrative, courts may intervene in a suitable case.
>
> In my opinion, *certiorari* avails as a remedy wherever a public body has power to decide any matter affecting the rights, interests, property, privileges, or liberties of any person.

What, then, is the relationship of the principles of natural justice to the duty to be fair? As the reader will recall, Laskin C.J.C. in the *Nicholson* case and Laycraft J. in the *McCarthy* case both treated the duty to be fair as quite distinct from the existence of a quasi-judicial power on the one hand, or natural justice on the other. Both Lieberman J.A. in *Campeau* and Clement J.A. in *Harvie*, by contrast, used the concept of fairness to establish that a quasi-judicial function was involved, and that the principles of natural justice had been breached. Dickson J. in *Martineau (No. 2)* deals with this contradiction expressly:[131]

> Conceptually, there is much to be said against such a differentiation between traditional natural justice and procedural fairness, but if one is forced to cast judicial review in traditional classification terms as is the case under the *Federal Court Act*, there can be no doubt that procedural fairness extends well beyond the realm of the judicial and quasi-judicial, as commonly understood.

Thus:[132]

> In general, courts ought not to seek to distinguish between the two concepts, for the drawing of a distinction between a duty to act fairly, and a duty to act in accordance with the rules of natural justice, yields an unwieldy conceptual framework. The *Federal Court Act*, however, compels classification for review of federal decision-makers.

---

129 In particular, *R. v. Hillingdon (London Borough Council)*, [1974] Q.B. 720 (Eng. Q.B.); *R. v. Barnsley Borough Council*, [1976] 3 All E.R. 452 (Eng. C.A.); *K. (H.), Re*, [1967] 2 Q.B. 617 (Eng. Q.B.); *R. v. Liverpool Corp.*, [1972] 2 Q.B. 299 (Eng. C.A.); *Furnell v. Whangarei High Schools Board*, [1973] A.C. 660 (New Zealand P.C.).

130 *Supra* note 112 at 622-23, emphasis added.

131 *Ibid.* at 623.

132 *Ibid.* at 629.

Finally, Dickson J. had to determine whether the duty to be fair applied in disciplinary cases. He noted that there were a number of precedents for the courts refusing to review disciplinary procedures.[133] Nevertheless, Dickson J. held that, while these may be counsels of caution, the rule of law must run within penitentiary walls:[134]

> It seems clear that although the courts will not readily interfere in the exercise of disciplinary powers, whether in the armed services, the police force or the penitentiary, there is no rule of law which necessarily exempts the exercise of such disciplinary powers from review by certiorari.

Accordingly, Dickson, J., on behalf of the minority of the court, concurred with Pigeon J.'s conclusion that, in principle, *certiorari* was available to review the disciplinary proceedings complained of by Mr. Martineau.

(f) Conclusion

In cases subsequent to these five, the Supreme Court has reinforced the extent of the duty to be fair. In *Cardinal v. Kent Institution*,[135] Le Dain J. noted:[136]

> There can be no doubt ... that the Director was under a duty of procedural fairness in exercising the authority conferred by s. 40 of the Regulations with respect to administrative dissociation or segregation. This Court has affirmed that there is, as a general common law principle, a duty of procedural fairness lying on every public authority making an administrative decision which is not of a legislative nature and which affects the rights, privileges or interests of an individual.

More recently, in *Baker v. Canada (Minister of Citizenship & Immigration)*,[137] L'Heureux-Dubé J. stated that the "fact that a decision is administrative and affects "the rights, privileges or interests of an individual" is sufficient to trigger the application of the duty of fairness."[138]

Thus, these cases significantly extend the ambit of judicial review in Canada. The duty to be fair is now undoubtedly part of our law and a breach

---

133 In particular, *R. v. Army Council*, [1917] 2 K.B. 504 (Eng. K.B.); *Dawkins v. Lord Rokeby* (1873), L.R. 8 Q.B. 255 (Eng. Q.B.); *Armstrong v. Whitehead*, [1973] 2 O.R. 495 (Ont. C.A.); *Fraser v. Mudge*, [1975] 3 All E.R. 78 (Eng. C.A.); *R. v. Hull Prison Board of Visitors*, [1979] Q.B. 425 (Eng. C.A.), reversing (1977), [1978] 2 W.L.R. 598 (Eng. Q.B.); *Daemar v. Hall*, [1978] 2 N.Z.L.R. 594 (New Zealand S.C.); *R. v. White* (1955), [1956] S.C.R. 154 (S.C.C.); *R. v. Beaver Creek Correctional Camp* (1968), [1969] 1 O.R. 373 (Ont. C.A.); *Wolff v. McDonnell*, 418 U.S. 539 (U.S. S.C., 1975).
134 (1979), [1980] 1 S.C.R. 602 at 628 (S.C.C.).
135 (1985), 16 Admin. L.R. 233 (S.C.C.).
136 *Ibid.* at 242.
137 (1999), 14 Admin. L.R. (3d) 173 (S.C.C.).
138 *Ibid.* at 191, citing from *Cardinal v. Kent Institution, supra* note 135.

of the duty to be fair can be corrected by *certiorari*, even if no judicial or quasi-judicial function is involved.[139]

Instead of characterizing functions as judicial or executive, the courts must now concentrate squarely on the real question which has always been before them: Was the procedure used in this case fair in all the circumstances?

The factors which determine whether the procedure was fair include (but are not limited to):

(i)   the nature of the decision and the process followed in making it;

(ii) the nature of the statutory scheme;

(iii) the importance of the decision to the individual affected (or, in other words, the effect of the decision on the individual's rights);

(iv) the legitimate expectations of the person challenging the decision; and

(v)   the choices of procedure made by the tribunal itself.[140]

While different judges may answer the question of whether a certain procedure was fair differently, and it will be difficult therefore to advise either clients or administrators of the answer, this approach is totally consistent with the policy underlying the historical judicial power to review procedures for breaches of natural justice – to ensure that justice is not only done, but manifestly and undoubtedly perceived to be done. The courts' recognition of the duty to be fair has been welcomed by everyone concerned with administrative law.

The concept of a quasi-judicial function is likely to remain important for determining whether that function may be delegated without breaching the rule that *delegatus non potest delegare*.[141] Similarly, administrators' immunity

---

139   Despite the entrenchment of the rule that a duty of fair procedure lies on all administrative delegates whether exercising a quasi-judicial or executive function, echoes of the past characterization necessity may still be found. See *Johannesson v. Alberta (Workers' Compensation Board Appeals Commission)* (1995), 34 Admin. L.R. (2d) 64 (Alta. Q.B.), which (incorrectly) ruled that Canadian law currently requires courts to distinguish between quasi-judicial and executive decisions and to apply Lord Atkin's two pronged test in order to determine whether judicial review is available. As we have stated, this characterisation exercise is no longer necessary. Unfortunately, the *Johannesson* case was referred to in a later case: *Friends of the Old Man River Society v. Assn. Professional Engineers, Geologists & Geophysicists (Alberta)* (1997), 2 Admin. L.R. (3d) 206 (Alta. Q.B.), reversed (2001), 93 Alta. L.R. (3d) 27 (Alta. C.A.), leave to appeal refused (2001), 299 A.R. 185 (note) (S.C.C.) as a proper statement of the law. See also *Saskatchewan Construction Labour Relations Council Inc. v. Saskatchewan (Minister of Labour)* (1993), 15 Admin. L.R. (2d) 143 (Sask. Q.B.).

140   *Baker v. Canada (Minister of Citizenship & Immigration)*, *supra* note 137 at 192*ff*; see also *Knight v. Indian Head School Division No. 19* (1990), 43 Admin. L.R. 157 (S.C.C.). For a more detailed discussion of these factors, see Chapter 9.

141   See for example, *Vic Restaurant Inc. v. Montreal (City)* (1958), [1959] S.C.R. 58 (S.C.C.); *Canada (Attorney General) v. Brent*, [1956] S.C.R. 318 (S.C.C.); and *Brant Dairy Co. v. Ontario (Milk Commiision)* (1972), [1973] S.C.R. 131 (S.C.C.).

from suit is likely to continue to refer to the qualified immunity of a judicial or quasi-judicial officer.[142]

Finally, the duty to be fair does not affect legislative functions at all, as is more fully described below.[143] Those cases which say that the exercise of a legislative function for an improper purpose is *ultra vires* do not relate to the procedure used. Hence, *Campeau* is not really on point. Indeed, for some reason the principles of natural justice have never applied to the exercise of a legislative power, and this principle has not been affected at all by the development of the duty to be fair. The distinction between a legislative function on the one hand, and a judicial, quasi-judicial or executive one on the other hand, will continue to be important.

5. The Applicability of the Duty to be Fair to Legislative Functions and to Decisions of the Cabinet

The duty to be fair regulates the procedure adopted by statutory delegates in the exercise of their powers. It generally applies to the exercise of discretionary powers.[144] One does not normally think of it in the context of an exercise of a duty where peremptory consequences follow the existence of a given state of facts, although *Cooper v. Wandsworth Board of Works*[145] involved precisely this circumstance (as does much of the courts' normal workload). Does the duty to be fair apply to a delegate exercising the power to make delegated legislation?[146] And does the duty to be fair apply to the cabinet,[147] exercising any kind of power which the Federal Parliament or a provincial legislature has delegated to it, or exercising the Royal Prerogative?

---

142   See de Smith, *supra* note 72 at 97-98, 106-07, 295-96.

143   See the decision of the Alberta Court of Appeal in *Campeau (No. 2)* (1980), 12 Alta. L.R. (2d) 379 (Alta. C.A.). *Sed quaere* the duty to be fair should not apply to the exercise of legislative powers – particularly delegated legislative powers.

144   A discretionary power is one granted by the legislative branch to a delegate to exercise his discretion to do (or not do) certain things or to choose among a number of alternatives. Not all delegated powers are discretionary; for example, some are duties. Similarly, some powers involve the promulgation of delegated legislation of general applicability, instead of decisions in individual cases. Finally, not all discretionary powers can be classified as "quasi-judicial" under the old classification of functions; some are "merely administrative".

145   (1863), 14 C.B.N.S. 180 (Eng. C.P.).

146   Difficulties arise in determining what constitutes "legislation" and "delegated legislation". For example, not all Orders in Council are legislative in nature, nor are all Acts of Parliament of general application. Similarly, land-use by-laws passed by municipalities are legislative in form but sufficiently quasi-judicial in nature that judicial review has frequently issued to strike down such by-laws enacted contrary to the principles of natural justice: see *Campeau Corp. v. Calgary (City)* (1978), 7 Alta. L.R. (2d) 294 (Alta. C.A.), and *Campeau Corp. v. Calgary (City)* (1980), 12 Alta. L.R. (2d) 379 (Alta. C.A.). As a result, the importance of "legislative" functions may give rise to as many characterization problems as the dichotomy between quasi-judicial and administrative functions.

147   Or the Governor in Council, or the Executive Council, or any other group or committee closely related to what we know as the Cabinet.

(a) Legislative Powers and the Duty to be Fair

Under the positivistic philosophy of our system of law, it is for Parliament to make the laws and for the courts to enforce them; and, assuming the constitutional requirements regarding the division of powers are met,[148] the courts will not generally inquire into procedure followed by Parliament in enacting laws, no matter how directly anyone's rights are affected. The only question is whether the Act in fact appears upon the Parliamentary roll.[149]

Thus, the duty of fairness does not generally apply to the exercise of legislative powers.[150] The Supreme Court of Canada has recently commented on the issue as follows:

> . . . legislative decision-making is not subject to any known duty of fairness. Legislatures are subject to constitutional requirements for valid law-making, but within their constitutional boundaries, they can do as they see fit. The wisdom and value of legislative decisions are subject only to review by the electorate. The judgment in *Reference Re Canada Assistance Plan* . . . was conclusive on this point in stating that: "the rules governing procedural fairness do not apply to a body exercising purely legislative functions."[151]

A more difficult problem arises when the power to legislate has been delegated to a subordinate. At first glance, the delegate is in precisely the same position as any other delegate who exercises discretionary powers to which the duty to be fair applies. After all, the content of the delegated legislation is a matter of discretion. Almost always, its quality will be improved as a result of publicity and comment by those likely to be affected by it. The public policy rationale underlying both the *audi alteram partem* rule and the duty to be fair appears to apply to delegated legislation as well as to judicial, quasi-judicial

---

148   And the requirements under the *Charter of Rights and Freedoms* of course: see Chapter 2. Thus, blind judicial obedience to legal positivism has never been total under our federal system, for the question could always be raised about whether a particular statute lay within the legislative competence of the legislative branch which purported to enact it. While the *Charter of Rights and Freedoms* has increased the ambit of judicial review of parent (and subsidiary) legislation even more, neither of these grounds has direct bearing on procedure or the duty to be fair.

149   Or has been printed by the Queen's Printer, and therefore is presumed to be an Act: *Alberta Evidence Act*, R.S.A. 2000, c. A-18, ss. 28, 32. Of course there is also the procedural requirement that proposed legislation receive three readings in the Senate and House of Commons and that it receive Royal Assent: see *Authorson (Litigation Guardian of) v. Canada (Attorney General)* (2003), 227 D.L.R. (4th) 385 (S.C.C.).

150   Unless there is a statutory provision to the contrary. See D.J.M. Brown and J.M. Evans, *Judicial Review of Administrative Action in Canada*, looseleaf, vol. 2 (Toronto: Canvasback, 2003) at 7-22ff.

151   *Wells v. Newfoundland*, [1999] 3 S.C.R. 199 (S.C.C.) at para. 59; see also *Apotex Inc. v. Canada (Attorney General)*, [2000] 4 F.C. 264 (Fed. C.A.), leave to appeal refused (2001), 268 N.R. 193 (note) (S.C.C.) and see *Authorson (Litigation Guardian of) v. Canada (Attorney General)* (2003), 227 D.L.R. (4th) 385 (S.C.C.), where the Supreme Court of Canada held that the *Canadian Bill of Rights* did not impose upon Parliament the duty to provide a hearing before the enactment of legislation.

or other discretionary powers which are subject to judicial review on procedural grounds. Indeed, this appears to have been recognized by the legislative branch in a number of cases where draft rules and regulations must be published and circulated prior to their final implementation: for example, under the *Canada Post Corporation Act*.[152] Further, this appears to be the standard practice of the United States Federal Government.[153]

Nevertheless, the law in Canada appears to be clear that judicial review is not generally available against the procedure used in implementing delegated legislation. Indeed, in the sequel to the *Campeau* case,[154] the Alberta Court of Appeal specifically excluded the availability of judicial review because a legislative function was involved. The same point was made by McDonald J. in *Alberta v. Beaver (County No. 9)*,[155] involving the unsuccessful attempt to quash the first reading of a municipal by-law; and by Megarry J., in *Bates v. Lord Hailsham of St. Marylebone*[156] which involved the proclamation of a new tariff of solicitors' fees.

Still, the concept of procedural fairness is important in the legislative context, and – as with all delegated powers – the legislative branch could pay considerably more attention to specifying the process by which its delegates are to determine the content of the legislation which they enact in the name of Parliament or the legislatures, as well as reviewing *ex post facto* the way the delegated legislative power in fact has been used.[157]

(b) The Cabinet and the Duty to be Fair

In principle, the duty to be fair applies to the exercise of all delegated discretionary powers,[158] including those exercised by the Cabinet.[159] The pre-

---

152 R.S.C. 1985, c. C-10, s. 20. See also the *Tax Court of Canada Act*, R.S.C. 1985, c. T-2, s. 22 regarding rules of that court; and the *Broadcasting Act*, S.C. 1991, c. 11, s. 8.

153 The *U.S. Federal Administrative Procedures Act*, 5 U.S.C.A., ss. 551-556. See W. Gellhorn *et al.*, *Administrative Law: Cases and Comments*, 8th ed. (Mineola, N.Y.: Foundation Press, 1987), c. 4 and Appendix A. See also K.C. Davis, *Administrative Law*, 6th ed. (St. Paul, Minn.: West Publishing Co., 1977), c. 11 and 12.

154 *Campeau (No. 2)*, *supra* note 143.

155 [1982] 4 W.W.R. 344 (Alta. Q.B.), reversed on another point at [1984] 4 W.W.R. 371 (Alta. C.A.).

156 [1972] 3 All E.R. 1019 (Eng. Ch. Div.).

157 As is done by the Joint Committee of the Senate and House of Commons on the Scrutiny of Regulations, whose proceedings are well worth reading. See the discussion in Chapter 4, about the Joint Committee. Virtually none of the provincial legislatures have such standing committees to review how their powers have in fact been used by their delegates.

158 As well as to certain non-discretionary powers.

159 See *Gray Line of Victoria Ltd. v. Chabot* (1980), [1981] 2 W.W.R. 635 (B.C. S.C.), supp. reasons (dealing with s. 96 of the *Constitution Act, 1867*, [1981] 5 W.W.R. 385 (B.C. S.C.); *South-West Oxford (Township) v. Ontario (Attorney General)* (1983), 8 Admin. L.R. 30 (Ont. H.C.); see also *C.U.P.E. v. Ontario (Minister of Labour)*, 2003 SCC 29 (S.C.C.), for a discussion of whether the doctrine of legitimate expectations applied to a Cabinet Minister's decision.

See also H.N. Janisch, "Case Comment: Cabinet Appeals" (1989) 32 Admin. L.R. 60; R. Macaulay, "Petitions to Cabinet; Power to Give Directions; Government Policy" (1988-89) 2 C.J.A.L.P. 206; M. Rankin, "The Cabinets and the Courts: Political Tribunals and

rogative remedies are traditionally not available against the Crown because they are the Crown's remedies, and the Crown can hardly grant a remedy against Herself. This rationale for restricting judicial review, however, is of an extremely personal and narrow nature, and cannot apply to any circumstance where Parliament has delegated powers to the cabinet or to a particular minister.[160] Such delegations are subject to all of the normal rules of administrative law, including the doctrine of *ultra vires* and the principles of natural justice (or the duty to be fair). The Cabinet – or executive committee[161] – is not immune from judicial review, and the fact that some – but by no means all – of its powers are exercised on behalf of the Crown does not entitle it to Her Majesty's extensive personal immunity from judicial action.

A good example of judicial review of a Cabinet decision can be found in *Gray Line of Victoria Ltd. v. Chabot.*[162] An appeal was made to Cabinet from a licensing body, the Motor Carrier Commission, for licences to operate sightseeing services. The Lieutenant Governor-in-Council (or a committee of it) allowed the appeal and granted the licences. A group of objectors applied for judicial review of the Cabinet's decision on two grounds. The first attack dealt with the fact that new evidence had been led on the appeal, contrary to the published rules governing such appeals. McEachern C.J.S.C. clearly asserted[163] the power of the courts to review the procedure used by the Cabinet in exercising the appellate function delegated to it by the legislature. On the facts, however, the Chief Justice held[164] that there was no unfairness involved in the procedure used because all the parties adduced new evidence, and all were represented by counsel who could answer the points made by other parties.

On the second point, also dealing with natural justice, McEachern C.J.S.C. struck down the Orders-in-Council implementing the Cabinet's decision on the appeal. These Orders-in-Council referred to the entire executive council, but in fact the appeal had been heard by only some members of it. His Lordship stated that[165]

Judicial Tribunals" (1989-90) 3 C.J.L.A.P. 302; M. Rankin, "The Cabinet and the Agencies: Toward Accountability in British Columbia" (1985) 19 U.B.C.L. Rev. 1; A.J. Roman, "Government Control of Tribunals: Appeals, Directives and Non-Statutory Mechanisms" (1985) 10 Queen's L.J. 476; D. Lemieux, "Cabinet and Tribunals: A Québec Perspective" (1990) 40 Admin. L.R. 118; Report of the Canadian Bar Association Task Force on *The Independence of Federal Administrative Tribunals and Agencies in Canada* (1990).

160   For some unknown reason, the Canadian practice favours delegation to the Cabinet, and, unlike the British practice, not to a particular minister. In principle, the distinction should make no difference to the amenability of the delegate to judicial review. See P.W. Hogg, "Judicial Review of Action by the Crown Representative" (1969) 43 A.L.J. 215; *Re Toohey (Aboriginal Land Commr.); Ex parte Nor. Land Council* (1981), 58 A.L.J.R. 164 (Australia H.C.); and *F.A.I. Insurances Ltd. v. Winneke* (1982), 56 A.L.J.R. 388 (Australia H.C.).

161   Not to be confused with Parliament or the legislatures. The distinction is important because only the latter bodies are "sovereign" whereas the executive government has no autonomous power apart from statutory delegation to it or the narrow remnants of the Royal Prerogative.

162   *Supra* note 159.

163   *Ibid.* at 641-42.

164   *Ibid.* at 642.

165   *Ibid.* at 646.

[t]he matter may be summarized by saying that in the discharge of its appellate jurisdiction natural justice and fairness requires [sic] the real decision to be made only by a majority of the members of the Executive Council who hear the parties if there is a hearing. Where there is no hearing, the real decision may only be made by a majority of those members of the Executive Council who consider the submissions of the parties and who give the parties the required opportunity to respond to adverse submissions, etc.

Of course if the powers exercised by Cabinet can be characterized as legislative, the duty of fairness will not apply. Moreover, what is classified as legislative in nature may extend beyond the legislative process itself to include matters of broad public convenience and general policy as opposed to private matters between parties. An example of this is found in the *Inuit Tapirisat*[166] case where the Supreme Court of Canada characterized the Cabinet's powers to issue an order in council dismissing an appeal from a CRTC decision on rates as "legislative action in its purest form".[167] Estey J. thought giving notice to everyone potentially affected by such rate-making power would be impractical for the Cabinet, and this too was relevant in minimizing the content of the procedural fairness required in the Cabinet's decision.

---

166   *Inuit Tapirisat of Canada v. Canada (Attorney General)* (1981), 115 D.L.R. (3d) 1 (S.C.C.); see also *National Anti-Poverty Organization v. Canada (Attorney General)* (1989), 36 Admin. L.R. 197 (Fed. C.A.), leave to appeal refused (1989), 105 N.R. 160 (note) (S.C.C.), reversing (1988), 32 Admin. L.R. 1 (Fed. T.D.). For a more detailed discussion on these cases see the third edition of this work at 218-28. See also H.N. Janisch, "Case Comment: Cabinet Appeals" (1988) 32 L.R. 60.

167   *Ibid.* at 15, and see also at 19, where Estey J. considered the *Bates* case and concluded that
    [i]t is clear that the orders in question in *Bates* and the case at bar were legislative in nature and I adopt the reasoning of Megarry J. to the effect that no hearing is required in such cases. I realize, however, that the dividing line between legislative and administrative functions is not always easy to draw: see *Essex County Council v. Minister of Housing*, (1967) 66 L.G.R. 23.
    The answer is not to be found in continuing the search for words that will clearly and invariably differentiate between judicial and administrative on the one hand, or administrative and legislative on the other. It may be said that the use of the fairness principle as in *Nicholson, supra,* will obviate the need for the distinction in instances where the tribunal or agency is discharging a function with reference to something akin to a lis or where the agency may be described as an "investigating body" as in the *Selvarajan* case, *supra.* Where, however, the executive branch has been assigned a function performable in the past by the Legislature itself and where the *res* or subject-matter is not an individual concern or a right unique to the petitioner or appellant, different considerations may be thought to arise. The fact that the function has been assigned as here to a tier of agencies (the CRTC in the first instance and the Governor-in-Council in the second) does not, in my view, alter the political science pathology of the case. In such a circumstance the Court must fall back upon the basic jurisdictional supervisory role and in so doing construe the statute to determine whether the Governor-in-Council has performed its functions within the boundary of the parliamentary grant and in accordance with the terms of the parliamentary mandate.

A more difficult issue is whether the duty to be fair applies to the Cabinet when exercising its powers pursuant to a Royal Prerogative.[168] Although this issue was raised in *Operation Dismantle*,[169] it was not clearly resolved.[170] While the majority of the Federal Court of Appeal held that section 7 of the *Charter* permits the courts to review the procedure used by the government in the exercise of a Royal Prerogative, the court did not rule on the applicability of the rules of natural justice. Likewise, the Supreme Court of Canada focussed on the application of the *Charter*, but did not consider the content of procedural fairness at all.

Other cases have held that the exercise of the Crown prerogative is beyond the scope of judicial review.[171] More recent decisions, however, seem to hold that, at least in principle, the duty to be fair does extend to the exercise of prerogative powers.[172] These cases suggest that the prevailing consideration in determining whether the duty of fairness extends to the exercise of a prerogative power is the subject matter involved, not the source of the power: that is, regardless of whether the decision stems from a prerogative power, does the decision affect the rights of an individual? If yes, the decision is subject to judicial review and the duty of fairness.[173]

---

168   As opposed to its statutory powers. Query the actual extent of the Royal Prerogative today, in light of the voluminous statutory provisions dealing with the military, external affairs and the like, which therefore no longer can globally be correctly described as falling under the Royal Prerogative. See C. Walker, "Review of the Prerogative: The Remaining Issues" [1987] P.L. 62; and *Council of Civil Service Unions v. Minister for the Civil Service*, [1984] 3 W.L.R. 1174 (H.L.).

169   *Operation Dismantle Inc. v. R.*, [1983] 1 F.C. 429 (Fed. T.D.), reversed [1983] 1 F.C. 745 (Fed. C.A.), affirmed S.C.C., Dickson C.J., Ritchie, Estey, McIntyre, Chouinard, Lamer, Wilson JJ., [1985] 1 S.C.R. 441 (S.C.C.). See also the discussion of this case in Chapter 2.

170   The majority of the Court of Appeal seems to assume that judicial review is not available at common law against the exercise of a prerogative power although it does not decide the matter one way or another. Marceau J. does hold that judicial review of the Royal Prerogative was almost unheard of (*ibid.* at 779-82). For a more detailed discussion of *Operation Dismantle* and the issue of the applicability of the duty to be fair to decisions involving the Royal Prerogative, see the Third Edition of this work at 224-28.

171   See for example *Multi-Malls Inc. v. Ontario (Minister of Transportation & Communications)* (1976), 14 O.R. (2d) 49 (Ont. C.A.). See also *Copello v. Canada (Minister of Foreign Affairs)* (2001), [2002] 3 F.C. 24 (Fed. T.D.), affirmed 2003 FCA 295 (Fed. C.A.).

172   See *Volker Stevin N.W.T. ('92) Ltd. v. Northwest Territories (Commissioner)* (1994), 113 D.L.R. (4th) 639 (N.W.T. C.A.).

173   See *Volker Stevin, ibid.*; *Black v. Canada (Prime Minister)* (2001), 199 D.L.R. (4th) 228 (Ont. C.A.); but see also *Copello v. Canada (Minister of Foreign Affairs)* (2001), [2002] 3 F.C. 24 (Fed. T.D.), affirmed 2003 FCA 295 (Fed. C.A.), and cases cited therein which suggest that the applicability of the duty of fairness to the exercise of prerogative powers may still be limited given the discretionary and non-justiciable nature of many of these decisions.

6. Theoretically Incorrect Attempts to Make the Duty to be Fair Apply to the Merits of a Decision

The phrase "duty to be fair" may give rise to misunderstanding because it does not clearly refer to procedural instead of substantive fairness. Its derivation, however, from the principles of natural justice[174] necessarily links it to questions of fair *procedure*. The obligation for a statutory delegate to adopt a fair procedure goes to the very terms of the power granted to it, and a breach of the duty to adopt a fair procedure renders the decision void and therefore capable of judicial review.[175] In the absence of a specific appellate power created by statute, the courts themselves have no jurisdiction to review the *substantive* fairness or any other aspect of the merits of a delegate's actions.[176] In other words, the distinction between judicial review and an appeal (of whatever breadth)[177] clearly endures notwithstanding the development of the duty to be fair.

Of course, certain substantive (as opposed to procedural) errors may sometimes also nullify a decision taken by a statutory delegate. For example, the legislature is generally presumed to have implicitly limited all delegated discretionary powers within the realm of reasonableness.[178] Accordingly, an unreasonable exercise of delegated power[179] will be *ultra vires*, and therefore capable of judicial review (though not of an appeal unless one is specifically created). Similarly, all statutory delegates are assumed to be under an obligation to act in good faith, and for no ulterior purpose,[180] not to act upon irrelevant considerations,[181] and not to ignore relevant ones.[182] All of these are implied substantive limitations which go to the ambit of the power granted by the legislative branch to its delegate. Any breach of these substantive limitations will render the delegate's action *ultra vires*, and give rise to judicial review (but not necessarily to an appeal).

---

174 See section 2, above.

175 See section 8, below.

176 See D.P. Jones, "Discretionary Refusal of Judicial Review in Administrative Law" (1981) 19 Alta. L. Rev. 483, especially at 485-87.

177 The word "appeal" does not connote any particular meaning, and in a particular context may mean an appeal *de novo*, an appeal on questions of law or jurisdiction, or (less frequently) a review of the record of the initial decision. See Chapter 14.

178 See W. Wade & C. Forsyth, *Administrative Law*, 7th ed. (Oxford: Clarendon Press, 1994) at 387*ff* for a discussion of the availability of judicial review on the ground of unreasonableness.

179 *Sed quaere* whether the same rule should apply to unreasonable parent legislation.

180 See *Roncarelli v. Duplessis*, [1959] S.C.R. 121 (S.C.C.); *Campeau Corp. v. Calgary (City) (No. 1)* (1978), 7 Alta. L.R. (2d) 294 (Alta. C.A.); *Padfield v. Minister of Agriculture, Fisheries & Food*, [1968] A.C. 997 (U.K. H.L.).

181 See *Padfield, ibid.*; *Dallinga v. Calgary (City)* (1975), [1976] 1 W.W.R 319 (Alta. C.A.); *R. v. Smith & Rhuland Ltd.*, [1953] 2 S.C.R. 95 (S.C.C.).

182 Which may only really be the reverse of acting on irrelevant evidence, "unreasonableness" or lack of evidence as grounds for judicial review. See *Sawatzky v. University Academic Pension Plan Board* (1992), 9 Admin. L.R. (2d) 109 (Alta. Q.B.) for a discussion about what happens if some but not all of the considerations are irrelevant.

To some extent, it may be possible to characterize all of these substantive limitations on the delegate's jurisdiction as a duty to be fair, although none of them deals with procedural matters. It is confusing to include these implied jurisdictional limitations on a delegate's powers under the rubric of the "duty to be fair", because there is a tendency to widen the use of that phrase even further to refer to the merits of the case before the delegate. For example, Professor David Mullan noted four cases where the courts may have over-stepped their review powers to interfere with a delegate's discretion solely because they found it "unfair" on the merits.[183] Judicial review is not an appeal on the merits and it is dangerous constitutionally for the courts to arrogate to themselves appellate powers which the legislative branch has not given to them.[184]

It may be difficult to distinguish the substance or merits of a delegate's decision from procedural limitations which administrative law has implied to circumscribe the ambit of power assumed to have been granted by the legis-lature.[185] Conversely, the temptation on the courts to interfere with the merits of an administrative decision may indicate that the legislative branch should take considerably more care in defining the relevant factors to be considered by its delegates when exercising the discretion granted to them, when deter-mining the procedures to be followed, and when determining the need for an appeal (including determining to whom the appeal should lie, and the nature of it).

7. Relationship Between the Duty to be Fair and the "Principles of Fundamental Justice" Contained in Section 7 of the Charter

"Substantive fairness" may also be constitutionally guaranteed by section 7 of the *Charter*[186] which provides as follows:[187]

> Everyone has the right to life, liberty and security of the person and the right not to be deprived thereof *except in accordance with the principles of fundamental justice.*

---

183 D.J. Mullan, "Natural Justice and Fairness – Substantive as Well as Procedural Standards for the Review of Administrative Decision-Making?" (1982) 27 McGill L.J. 250. The four cases are: (a) *R. v. Barnsley Borough Council*, [1976] 1 W.L.R. 1052 (Eng. C.A.); (b) *H.T.V. Ltd. v. Price Commission*, [1976] I.C.R. 170 (U.K. H.L.); (c) *Daganayais v. Min. of Immigration*, [1980] 2 N.Z.L.R. 130 (C.A.); (d) *Minister for Immigration & Ethnic Affairs v. Pochi* (1980), 31 A.L.R. 666 (Australia Fed. Ct.). Note also that the question of substantive fairness arose in the *Operation Dismantle, supra* note 169.

184 See D.P. Jones "A Constitutionally Guaranteed Role for the Courts" (1979) 57 Can. Bar Rev. 669.

185 See D.J. Mullan, *supra* note 183.

186 See Chapter 2.

187 Contained in the *Constitution Act, 1982*, which is Schedule B to the *Canada Act, 1982* passed by the Parliament of the United Kingdom, and proclaimed in Ottawa on April 17, 1982, emphasis added.

This phrase was borrowed from the earlier *Canadian Bill of Rights*,[188] and undoubtedly was intended to elevate the procedural aspects of natural justice to constitutional status in any matters dealing with life, liberty and the security of the person. Indeed, one of the Federal Government's legal advisors so testified to the Joint Parliamentary Committee during its hearings on the constitutional package.[189] However, the reference in section 7 to the "principles of fundamental justice" is not limited to procedural matters.[190] It also creates a substantive limitation on the content of parent legislation that can be enacted, as well as providing a method of scrutinizing the merits of a delegate's decision.

While section 7 impacts both procedural and substantial rights, as discussed in Chapter 2, there remains much scope for debate about the actual content of procedural versus substantive fundamental justice.

The concept of procedural fundamental justice includes, at a minimum, the procedural requirements required by the rules of natural justice and the duty of fairness. The level of procedural protection will then vary further according to the circumstances of the particular case and the type of tribunal or decision-maker being dealt with.[191]

The doctrine of substantive fundamental justice operates, first to require that laws be sufficiently clear to enable citizens to understand whether a contemplated action will contravene the law or not and, secondly, by limiting the amount of discretion a decision-maker has.[192] In other words, laws cannot be so vague that a reasonable citizen would not know whether a proposed action is legal or not, or so vague that it creates unlimited discretion.

Finally, on a different point, it is important to note that section 7 of the *Charter* at its very narrowest interpretation not only specifically imports procedural fairness into any decision affecting life, liberty and the security of the person, it also eliminates the sovereignty of the legislative branch with respect

---

188 R.S.C. 1970, App. III. Section 2(e) of the *Canadian Bill of Rights* stated that no law of Canada shall be construed or applied so as to "deprive a person of the right to a fair hearing in accordance with the principles of fundamental justice for the determination of his rights and obligations". This reference to the "principles of fundamental justice" is clearly procedural. See Fauteux C.J.'s comments on this point in *R. v. Duke*, [1972] S.C.R. 917 at 923 (S.C.C.). Note further that s. 7 of the *Charter* in fact corresponds to s. 1(a) – and not to s. 2(e) – of the *Canadian Bill of Rights*. Section 1 recognizes and continues the existence of certain human rights and fundamental freedoms, including "the right of the individual to life, liberty, security of the person and enjoyment of property, and the right not to be deprived thereof except by due process of law" (emphasis added). This reference to "due process" is (apart from the American concept of substantive due process) procedural in nature. Nevertheless, the substitution of "principles of fundamental justice" for "due process" in s. 7 of the *Charter* opens up the question of substantive justice now being protected.

189 See the testimony of Dr. Strayer, *Minutes of Proceedings and Evidence of the Special Joint Committee of the Senate and House of Commons on the Constitution of Canada*, Issue No. 46 at 32-33.

190 See discussion in Chapter 2, and *Reference re s. 94(2) of the Motor Vehicle Act (British Columbia)* (1985), [1986] 1 W.W.R. 481 (S.C.C.). See also J.H. Grey's comment "Can Fairness be Effective?" (1982) 27 McGill L.J. 360, for a good consideration of the extent to which requirements of procedural fairness ensure substantive justice on the merits.

191 See discussion in Chapter 2.

192 See discussion in Chapter 2.

to ousting the principles of natural justice, at least so far as any question of life, liberty and the security of the person is involved, and any attempt to do so will be unconstitutional.

8. Effect of a Breach of the Duty to be Fair

Notwithstanding heretical *dicta* to the contrary,[193] a breach of natural justice (or of the duty to be fair) renders the decision void, not voidable, and is therefore not protected by most privative clauses. The following explanation demonstrates the theoretical and practical importance of this statement.

Virtually all administrative law depends upon two maxims: (a) Parliament is sovereign; and (b) a delegate to whom Parliament has granted powers must act strictly within its jurisdiction, and the courts will determine whether the delegate's actions are *ultra vires*.

A delegate's jurisdiction may depend upon certain preliminary or collateral matters. Thus, in *Anisminic Ltd. v. Foreign Compensation Commission*,[194] the commission was bound to consider a claim for compensation filed by a party, or the party's successor-in-title, whose property was sequestrated by the Egyptian Government after Suez. Entertaining a claim from someone who did not meet those conditions would clearly have been *ultra vires* the power or jurisdiction granted to the commission by Parliament. Conversely, refusing even to receive a claim from a person who did meet those conditions would also have been *ultra vires*. Similarly, in *Bell v. Ontario (Human Rights Commission)*,[195] the commission could only hear complaints of discrimination relating to the rental of self-contained residential premises. The question whether particular premises were self-contained was obviously a jurisdictional one. Again, if Parliament gives a delegate power to make a park, it is *ultra vires* for the delegate to try to use that power to build a highway. All of these are examples of what may be called substantive *ultra vires*.

Even if the delegate is acting substantively within the subject matter granted to it by Parliament (that is, has correctly decided any preliminary or collateral point, or is in fact exercising the power granted to it), the actions may nevertheless be *ultra vires* if the delegate commits any of the following errors:

    (a) breaches the principles of natural justice or the duty to be procedurally fair;[196]

---

193 See *Harelkin v. University of Regina*, [1979] 2 S.C.R. 561 (S.C.C.), *per* Beetz J.; the *dicta* of Kerans J. in *Bridgeland Riverside Community Assn. v. Calgary (City)* (1982), 19 Alta. L.R. (2d) 361 (Alta. C.A.); and *United Food & Commercial Workers, Local 401 v. Canada Safeway Ltd.* (1989), 65 Alta. L.R. (2d) 420 (Alta. C.A.), leave to appeal refused (1989), 101 A.R. 80 (note) (S.C.C.).

194 (1968), [1969] 2 A.C. 147 (U.K. H.L.).

195 [1971] S.C.R. 756 (S.C.C.).

196 See for example, *Québec (Commission des relations ouvrières) v. Alliance des professeurs catholiques de Montréal*, [1953] 2 S.C.R. 140 (S.C.C.); *Ridge v. Baldwin* (1963), [1964]

(b) considers irrelevant evidence;[197]

(c) ignores relevant evidence;[198]

(d) acts for an improper purpose or out of malice.[199]

In each of these cases, the delegate has jurisdiction to commence action to deal with the matter, but steps outside the jurisdiction given by committing one of the errors listed above. The delegate's decision is clearly subject to judicial review. With one exception,[200] the only theoretical basis upon which the superior courts are entitled to review the legality of a delegate's action is based upon their inherent power to keep inferior tribunals within their respective jurisdictions. The concept of jurisdiction thus underlies these four grounds for judicial review every bit as much as it underlies review of other substantive *ultra vires* actions by a delegate of the legislature. The unstated premise, of course, is that Parliament never intended its delegate to act contrary to natural justice, or to consider irrelevant evidence, or to ignore relevant evidence, or to act maliciously or in bad faith, or unreasonably. Of course Parliament's sovereignty means that it could theoretically permit its delegates to act in any of these ways, and the courts would have to give effect to such specific legislative commandment. But the legislature rarely does this and the courts continue to construe legislation and other powers[201] on the assumption that these four requirements must be complied with in order for the delegate's action to be valid. In short, these requirements go to the substantive jurisdiction of the delegate, and must do so to authorize the courts to interfere with any such defective administrative action.

It is true that, for example, a breach of the principles of natural justice appears to be merely a procedural error, committed after the delegate has validly commenced the exercise of the power which Parliament has granted. But it would be incorrect to assume that such a procedural error is somehow less important or less substantive than a clear attempt by the delegate to do something completely unrelated to the power granted by Parliament (for example, to build a highway instead of a park). For more than a century the assumption has been that Parliament intends the procedural requirements of

---

A.C. 40 (U.K. H.L.); *Cooper v. Wandsworth Board of Works*, (1863), 14 C.B.N.S. 180 (Eng. C.P.).

197 *R. v. Smith & Rhuland Ltd.*, [1953] 2 S.C.R. 95 (S.C.C.); *Padfield v. Minister of Agriculture, Fisheries & Food*, [1968] A.C. 997 (U.K. H.L.); *Dallinga v. Calgary (City)* (1975), [1976] 1 W.W.R. 319 (Alta. C.A.).

198 See the discussion on this point in Chapter 7.

199 *Roncarelli v. Duplessis*, [1959] S.C.R. 121 (S.C.C.); *Campeau Corp. v. Calgary (City)* (1978), 7 Alta. L.R. (2d) 294 (Alta. C.A.), compare the *Padfield* case, *supra* note 197.

200 Error of law on the face of the record, even though the error does not go to the delegate's jurisdiction. For an excellent historical explanation of its anomaly, see *R. v. Northumberland Compensation Appeal Tribunal* (1951), [1952] 1 K.B. 338 (Eng. C.A.), compare Lord Reid's judgment in *Anisminic*, *supra* note 194. See Chapter 11.

201 Including delegated legislation such as rules and regulations, as well as delegated discretionary powers and duties.

natural justice to be observed by certain delegates, as part and parcel of the power granted to them; any default renders the decision void.[202] Nor is it possible to say that such a decision is voidable. If it were, what would entitle the courts to intervene to correct it? For the decision would – on the voidable assumption – lie within the jurisdiction of the delegate and would not be *ultra vires*. Of course such an error undoubtedly constitutes an error of law[203] which could be corrected by the court under its anomalous power to grant *certiorari* to correct even errors of law not going to jurisdiction. But this power to correct errors of law clearly is not available if there is a privative clause depriving the courts of their inherent power to review decisions of such a delegate made within jurisdiction nor, possibly, even where there is none.[204] Yet the courts have consistently held that privative clauses do not protect "decisions" which are made outside of the delegate's jurisdiction, because such decisions are void (not voidable), and therefore are not "decisions".[205] Nor is it difficult to find such cases involving breaches of natural justice, improper consideration of the evidence, or malice. None of these cases could have avoided the clear words of a privative clause if the decisions involved were merely voidable instead of being void, because then there would have been a "decision" protected by the privative clause. It must be concluded, therefore, that the rule that a breach of natural justice renders the decision void is of high constitutional importance, and must not be permitted to be eroded by loose *dicta* in cases where there is no privative clause.[206]

9. Summary on the Duty to be Fair

In conclusion, it can be seen that judicial review has long been available to control the procedure used to exercise many governmental powers. The ambit of this ground for judicial review has been expanding in Canada in the last few decades, in particular beyond the old category of "judicial and quasi-judicial" functions. The effect of a breach of procedural fairness is to render the delegate's actions void (that is, the error is jurisdictional in nature), and such a decision should not be insulated from judicial review by either a priv-

---

202 Otherwise the decision in *Cooper v. Wandsworth Board of Works* (1863), 14 C.B.N.S. 180 (Eng. C.P.), would have been opposite, for the demolition order there would have been valid and therefore a complete defence to the action in trespass (which is not a discretionary remedy). See H.W.R. Wade, "Unlawful Administration Action: Void or Voidable?" Part I at (1967) 83 L.Q. Rev. 499; Part II (1968) 84 L.Q. Rev. 95; W. Wade & C. Forsyth, *Administrative Law*, 7th ed. (Oxford: Clarendon Press, 1994), c. 10; and G.L. Peiris, "Natural Justice and Degrees of Invalidity", [1983] P.L. 634. Compare *Durayappah v. Fernando*, [1967] 2 A.C. 337 (Ceylon P.C.).

203 Because a breach of the principles of natural justice, or of the duty to be fair, obviously is an error of procedure.

204 See Chapter 11.

205 See for example, *Anisminic, supra* note 194; *Bell, supra* note 195; *Toronto Newspaper Guild v. Globe Printing Co.*, [1953] 2 S.C.R. 18 (S.C.C.). Compare *Pringle v. Fraser*, [1972] S.C.R. 821 (S.C.C.).

206 *Harelkin v. University of Regina*, [1979] 2 S.C.R. 561 (S.C.C.); and *Bridgeland Riverside Community Assn. v. Calgary (City)* (1982), 19 Alta. L.R. (2d) 361 (Alta. C.A.).

ative clause or the recently developed judicial deference towards intra-jurisdictional errors of law which are not "patently unreasonable".[207] Many questions still remain concerning the content of the duty to be fair. This will be
discussed in the following two chapters.

10. Selected Bibliography

Akehurst, C.M., "Statements of Reasons for Judicial and Administrative De-
    cisions" (1970) 33 M.L.R. 154.

Brown, D.J.M. and J.M. Evans, *Judicial Review of Administrative Action In
    Canada*, looseleaf (Toronto: Canvasback, 2003).

Flick, G.A., "Administrative Adjudications and the Duty to Give Reasons – A
    Search for Criteria" [1978] P.L. 16.

Fox, David, Public Participation in the Administrative Process, Study Paper
    for the Law Reform Commission of Canada, 1979.

Grey, J., "Can Fairness be Effective?" (1982) 27 McGill L.J. 360.

Hogg, P.W., "Judicial Review of Action by the Crown Representative" (1969)
    43 Australian L.J. 215.

Jones, D.P., "Administrative Fairness in Alberta" (1980) 18 Alta. L.R. 351.

Jones, D.P., "Discretionary Refusal of Judicial Review in Administrative Law"
    (1981) 19 Alta. L. Rev. 483.

Jones, D.P., "Natural Justice and Fairness in the Administrative Process" in
    Judicial Review of Administrative Rulings, arising out of the 1982 Annual
    Conference of the Canadian Institute for the Administration of Justice.

Leadbeater, A., Council on Administration, Study Paper for the Law Reform
    Commission of Canada, 1980.

Lynk, M., "Denny's Revenge: Judicial Formalism and the Application of
    Procedural Fairness to Internal Union Hearings" (1997) 23 Queen's L.J.
    115.

Morris, M.J., "Administrative Decision-Makers and the Duty to Give Reasons:
    An Emerging Debate" (1998) 11 C.J.A.L.P. 155.

Mullan, D.J., "Fairness: The New Natural Justice" (1975) 25 University of
    Toronto L.J. 281.

Mullan, D.J., "Natural Justice and Fairness – Substantive as Well as Procedural
    Standards for the Review of Administrative Decision-Making?" (1982)
    27 McGill L.J. 250.

Peiris, G.L., "Natural Justice and Degrees of Invalidity of Administrative
    Action" [1983] P.L. 634.

Reid, R.F., & David, H., *Administrative Law and Practice*, 2d ed. (Toronto:
    Butterworths, 1978) especially c. 2 and c. 3.

Report of the Committee on Administrative Tribunals and Inquiries, (the
    "Franks Committee Report"), England, 1957, Cmnd. 219.

Report of the Committee on Minister's Powers (the "Donoughmore Report"),
    England, 1932, Cmd. 4060.

---

207   For a discussion of "patently reasonable", see Chapters 11 and 12.

Report of the Special Committee on Boards and Tribunals to the Legislative Assembly of Alberta (the "Clement Report"), 1966.

Wade W. & Forsyth C., *Administrative Law*, 7th ed. (Oxford: Clarendon Press, 1994) and 8th ed. (Oxford: Clarendon Press, 2000).

9

The Duty to be Fair: Audi Alteram Partem

1. Introduction

As discussed in Chapter 8, following *Nicholson*, the old distinction be-tween quasi-judicial and administrative decisions has been rendered unimpor-tant and of little use "*. . . since both the duty to act fairly and the duty to act judicially have their roots in the same general principles of natural justice.*"[1] We now refer to the "duty to be fair" or "procedural fairness" as overarching terms which incorporate all of the rules of natural justice and which apply to all quasi-judicial and administrative decisions.

Thus, the duty to be fair has evolved so that it now applies to every public authority making an administrative decision which affects the rights, privileges or interests of an individual[2] (but not an administrative decision that is legis-lative in nature).[3] In Canada today, this includes a myriad of authorities ranging from the single delegate issuing dog licenses to major boards wielding great power over Canadian people and business.[4] This chapter and the next will

---

1   *Knight v. Indian Head School Division No. 19*, [1990] 1 S.C.R. 653 (S.C.C.); *Nicholson v. Haldimand-Norfolk (Regional Municipality) Commissioners of Police* (1978), [1979] 1 S.C.R. 311 (S.C.C.). For a discussion of the historical development of these principles see Chapter 8, and the Third Edition of this work, Chapters 8 and 9.
2   *Cardinal v. Kent Institution* (1985), 16 Admin. L.R. 233 (S.C.C.).
3   See *Authorson (Litigation Guardian of) v. Canada (Attorney General)*, 2003 SCC 39 (S.C.C.) and discussion in Chapter 8.
4   This was recently recognized by the Supreme Court of Canada in *C.U.P.E. v. Ontario (Minister of Labour)* (2003), 50 Admin. L.R. (3d) 1 (S.C.C.), where Justice Binnie stated at para. 149: "Given the immense range of discretionary decision makers and administrative bodies, the test [for determining the standard of review] is necessarily flexible, and proceeds

consider the *content* of the duty to be fair and its two fundamental principles: *audi alteram partem* (the right to hear the other side – discussed in this chapter) and *nemo judex in sua causa debet esse* (the rule against bias – discussed in the next chapter).

The principle *audi alteram partem* is an imperative which translated means "hear the other side!" More generally, it refers to the requirement in administrative law that a person must know the case being made against him or her and be given an opportunity to answer it before the person or agency that will make the decision. Beyond that, however, the content of the principle is often difficult to determine in particular circumstances, and what fairness requires has altered over time and continues to evolve.[5]

Overall, the scope and extent of the rule depends on the subject matter.[6] Since fairness depends on the specific context of the case, it is impossible to lay down hard and fast requirements about what does and does not constitute a fair hearing. In some cases, the enabling statute will provide a code of conduct for the hearing.[7] However, in many other cases, the statute is silent and the tribunal, and court if called upon, must determine what procedure is fair in the circumstances.

As noted by Madame Justice L'Heureux-Dube in *Baker v. Canada (Minister of Citizenship & Immigration)*[8] (with four other judges concurring) ". . . the duty of fairness is flexible and variable, and depends on an appreciation of the context of the particular statute and the rights affected . . .".[9] She observed that:[10]

> The existence of a duty of fairness does not determine what requirements will be applicable in a given set of circumstances. As I wrote in *Knight v. Indian Head School Division No. 19*, [1990] 1 S.C.R. 653, at p. 682, "the concept of procedural fairness is eminently variable and its content is to be decided in the specific context of each case". All of the circumstances must be considered in order to determine the content of the duty of procedural fairness: *Knight*, at pp. 682-83; *Cardinal, supra*, at p. 654; *Old St. Boniface Residents Assn. Inc. v. Winnipeg (City)*, [1990] 3 S.C.R. 1170, *per* Sopinka J.

---

by principled analysis rather than categories, seeking the polar star of legislative intent." Similarly, Justice Bastarache noted at para. 13: "[The pragmatic and functional approach] recognizes that the diversity of the contemporary administrative state includes different types of decision makers."

5 See R.F. Reid and H. David, *Administrative Law and Practice*, 2d ed. (Toronto: Butterworths, 1978) at 49-104.

6 Although the content of the rule has also varied with then current notions of the importance of individual rights as against the greater public good and vice versa and with the prevailing fashion of more or less judicial activism.

7 See for example the *Regulated Health Professions Act*, S.O. 1991, c. 18, sch. 2 and the *Police Act*, R.S.A. 2000, c. P-17, s. 20.

8 (1999), 14 Admin. L.R. (3d) 173 (S.C.C.).

9 *Ibid.* at 192.

10 *Ibid.* at 191-92.

She then went on, however, to enunciate certain factors relevant to determining the content of fairness:[11]

> Although the duty of fairness is flexible and variable, and depends on an appreciation of the context of the particular statute and the rights affected, it is helpful to review the criteria that should be used in determining what procedural rights the duty of fairness requires in a given set of circumstances. I emphasize that underlying all these factors is the notion that the purpose of participatory rights contained within the duty of procedural fairness is to ensure that administrative decisions are made using a fair and open procedure, appropriate to the decision being made and its statutory, institutional, and social context, with an opportunity for those affected by the decision to put forward their views and evidence fully and have them considered by the decision-maker.

The factors identified by L'Heureux-Dube J. include:

1. The nature of the decision being made and the process followed in making it. The closer the administrative process is to judicial decision-making, the more likely it is that procedural protections closer to the trial model will be required.

2. The nature of the statutory scheme and the terms of the statute pursuant to which the body operates. The role of the decision in the statutory scheme helps determine the content of the duty of fairness. Greater procedural protections are required when there is no appeal procedure or the decision determines the issue and further requests cannot be submitted.

3. The importance of the decision to the individual or individuals affected. The more important or the greater impact the decision has, the more stringent are the procedural protections. This is a significant factor. The court commented:

> The more important the decision is to the lives of those affected and the greater its impact on that person or those persons, the more stringent the procedural protections that will be mandated. This was expressed, for example, by Dickson J. (as he then was) in *Kane v. University of British Columbia* [1980] 1 S.C.R. 1105 (S.C.C.) at p. 1113:
>
> > A high standard of justice is required when the right to continue in one's profession or employment is at stake. . . . A disciplinary suspension can have grave and permanent consequences upon a professional career.[12]

---

11   *Ibid.* at 192-94.
12   *Ibid.*

4. The legitimate expectations of the person challenging the decision. The doctrine of legitimate expectations is part of the doctrine of procedural fairness. If a claimant has a legitimate expectation that a certain procedure will be followed, the duty of fairness requires this procedure to be followed. If a claimant has a legitimate expectation that a certain result will be reached, fairness may require more extensive procedural rights than might otherwise be accorded. The doctrine of legitimate expectations does not create substantive rights outside the procedural domain. The "circumstances" affecting procedural fairness take into account the promises or regular practices of administrative decision-makers. It will be generally unfair of the decision-makers to act contrary to their representations as to procedure or to go back on substantive promises without giving the person affected significant procedural rights.

5. The choices of procedure made by the agency itself, particularly if procedure is a matter of discretion or if the agency possesses expertise in determining appropriate procedures. Important weight must be given to the choice of procedures made by the agency and its institutional restraints.[13]

This list of factors is not exhaustive. Generally, however, it is imperative that individuals who are affected by administrative decisions be given the opportunity to present their case in some fashion. They are entitled to have decisions affecting their rights, interests, or privileges made using a fair, impartial, and open process which is appropriate to the statutory, institutional, and social context of the decision being made. With those factors enunciated in *Baker* in mind, a court must determine whether the procedure that was used in reaching any given decision was, in fact, fair, impartial, and open. This involves a detailed review of the circumstances of each case and a determination of whether the factors were applied properly.

Although it is clear that what constitutes a fair procedure depends on the context and the circumstances of each case, and although the concept is eminently variable, this chapter will attempt to flesh out the elements which go to make up a fair procedure. The chapter is divided into three main parts: the first part deals with the procedural steps taken by an administrative tribunal which lead up to a hearing, including a discussion of how the form of the hearing is determined; the second part discusses the elements of fair procedure during the course of an oral hearing; and the third part considers how a tribunal should handle any procedural post-hearing matters in a fair way.

2. Pre-Hearing Procedures

In many administrative structures, there are several stages in the decision-making process. For example, very often prior to the hearing itself, there is a

---

13 *Ibid.* at 192-94.

pre-hearing investigation which can range from merely an information gathering exercise to a full blown investigation. In addition to an investigation before the hearing, there are other pre-hearing procedures including the giving of notice and the requirement of disclosure. All of these procedural steps raise issues concerning the duty of fairness, such as the nature of the notice required and the necessary extent of disclosure, including a consideration of whether the delegate's file is available to the person affected. Of course there is also an issue concerning what kind of hearing is required, a formal hearing with all of the trappings of a court, or an informal process held by paper submission alone. Finally, the evolving doctrine of legitimate expectations must be considered. These issues, and how the duty of fairness relates to them, will each be discussed in turn.

(a) Investigation Stage

Whether the duty of fairness applies to the investigative stage is a question that has changed over time. This change has evolved from the historical emphasis on the characterization of function and focus on the greater public good (all of which came at the expense of individual rights)[14] to a consideration of how any particular decision affects individual rights and the need to allow administrative tribunals to carry out their functions efficiently and effectively.[15]

Traditionally, it was thought that the duty of fairness did not apply to the investigative stage. This view was expressed by the Supreme Court of Canada in *Guay v. Lafleur:* [16]

> . . . the maxim *"audi alteram partem"* does not apply to an administrative officer whose function is simply to collect information and make a report and who has no power either to impose a liability or to give a decision affecting the rights of parties.

Other courts followed suit. For example, the Alberta Court of Appeal in *Youngberg v. A.T.A.* stated:[17]

> The function of [the investigator] was to investigate, report and recommend. He was to gather the facts. He had no power to hear and determine at all. . . . The actions of [the investigator] were purely fact finding, reporting and recommending. Accordingly, his actions are not controllable by prerogative writ.

---

14 See note 87, below.
15 *Strauts v. College of Physicians & Surgeons (British Columbia)* (1997), 47 Admin. L.R. (2d) 79 (B.C. C.A.), where the function of the college to protect and serve the public necessitated that it not be trammelled by considerations of individual rights at the investigative stage.
16 (1964), [1965] S.C.R. 12 at 18 (S.C.C.).
17 (1977), [1978] 1 W.W.R. 538 at 548 (Alta. C.A.).

Other cases held the duty to be fair did not apply at the investigation stage as long as the investigation was conducted in accordance with the requirements of the relevant statute.[18]

However, there is now a discernible body of law which suggests that the old case law is no longer good law and that there is now a duty of fairness at the investigation stage of the administrative process. In *Stephen v. College of Physicians & Surgeons (Saskatchewan)*,[19] the Saskatchewan Court of Appeal noted:

> The college took the position that council was performing a mere investigative function which could not affect the rights of a party since there would be a future opportunity for a hearing before any disciplinary sanctions could be imposed. Thus it was not subject to judicial review. It relied on *Samuels, supra*, and *Jow v. College of Physicians and Surgeons* (1979), 91 D.L.R. (3d) 245, both judgments of the Queen's Bench where the Court refused to interfere with proceedings before a preliminary inquiry committee, because it had no power to make any final determination of the rights of the parties. Thus, it was not performing any judicial or quasi-judicial function and not amenable to supervision by the courts. It also relied on cases such as *Guay v. Lafleur*, [1965] S.C.R. 12 and *St. John v. Fraser*, [1935] S.C.R. 4 41. However, there has been a substantial movement in recent years toward extension of judicial review to investigatory bodies and the above cases may no longer be good law. Estey J., in *Irvine v. Canada (Restrictive Trade Practices Commission)*, [1987] 1 S.C.R. 181, undertook an extensive review of this evolution of the law. However, we need not examine this issue further than to say that these cases miss the point in issue here.

In the 1989 case of *S.E.P.Q.A. v. Canada (Human Rights Commission)*,[20] the Supreme Court of Canada specifically adopted the statement of Lord Denning in *Selvarajan v. Race Relations Board*:[21]

> In all these cases it has been held that the investigating body is under a duty to act fairly; but that which fairness requires depends on the nature of the investigation and the consequences which it may have on the persons affected by it. The fundamental rule is that, if a person may be subjected to pains or penalties, or be exposed to prosecution or proceedings, or deprived of remedies or redress, or in some such way adversely affected by the investigation and report, then he should be told the case made against him and be afforded a fair opportunity of answering it.

---

18 See J. T. Casey, *The Regulation of Professions in Canada* (Toronto: Carswell, 1994) (Looseleaf) at 7-6.1 (2002 - Rel. 1), fn. 23.

19 [1989] 6 W.W.R. 1 at 9 (Sask. C.A.).

20 [1989] 2 S.C.R. 879 (S.C.C.) at para. 27.

21 (1975), [1976] 1 All E.R. 12 at 19 (Eng. C.A.).

In recent years, however, Canadian courts have taken different approaches to this question. For example, a review board that annually reviewed the circumstances of individuals held on Lieutenant Governor's warrants at mental institutions, although without decision-making authority, was held to have the duty to proceed fairly;[22] there was held to be a limited duty of fairness at the investigation stage of a complaint against a certified general accountant where the investigator was exercising a degree of decision-making power when deciding whether or not to send the complaint on to an inquiry;[23] sending a copy of the investigation report to a human rights complainant and giving her an opportunity to respond was held to be sufficient to comply with the duty of fairness;[24] and procedural fairness was held not to entitle a doctor under investigation into chelation therapy to be shown copies of the complaint letters against him.[25]

The Supreme Court of Canada has considered whether a duty of fairness exists at the pre-hearing stage in a few cases. Following its obiter comments in *S.E.P.Q.A.*[26] (since the investigation process in *S.E.P.Q.A.* was not actually in dispute), in 1990 the court considered the case of *Knight v. Indian Head School Division No. 19.*[27] In a decision foreshadowing its subsequent decision in *Baker*, the court identified some of the factors upon which the existence of a general duty of fairness depends:

- the nature of the decision to be made by the administrative body;

- the relationship between the administrative body and the individual;

- the effect of the decision on the individual's rights; and

- how final the decision at the investigation stage is–a decision of a preliminary nature does not generally trigger the duty to act fairly; a decision of a more final nature may do so.

The Supreme Court considered the fourth factor in *Ruffo c. Québec (Conseil de la magistrature).*[28] The Court held that a judge accused of misconduct, who was refused an opportunity to express her views during an assessment to determine whether a formal inquiry should be held, had not been denied procedural fairness in this process. The assessment process by the disciplinary committee was only preliminary since it could only recommend that the government institute removal proceedings.

Generally speaking, the less final the tribunal's decision that affects the rights of an individual, the weaker the content of the duty of fairness in the pre-hearing stage; the content of the duty as always varying with the context.

---

22   *Abel v. Ontario (Advisory Review Board)* (1980), 119 D.L.R. (3d) 101 (Ont. C.A.).
23   *Tanaka v. Certified General Accountants' Assn. (Northwest Territories)*, [1996] N.W.T.R. 301 (N.W.T. S.C.).
24   *Williams v. First Air* (1998), 161 F.T.R. 34 (Fed. T.D.).
25   *Strauts, supra* note 15.
26   *Supra* note 20.
27   [1990] 1 S.C.R. 653 (S.C.C.).
28   [1995] 4 S.C.R. 267 (S.C.C.).

Further, the requirement to act fairly may depend on the requirements of the enabling statute. Many statutes are silent but some provide a process for the tribunal to follow in the pre-hearing stage. Failure to follow that process will invalidate the proceeding, thereby requiring the statutory delegate to start again. For example, in *Broda v. Law Society (Alberta)*,[29] Mr. Justice McDonald J. held that:

> During the course of the argument of this application I held, and I remain of the view, that the Deputy Secretary's memorandum dated September 18, 1991, did not qualify as a "report respecting the review" as required by s. 51(3)(b) [of the *Legal Profession Act*.] If my view the scheme of the Act creates a number of procedural steps which must be complied with before a member is exposed to the jeopardy of a hearing into his or her conduct by a Hearing Committee, bearing in mind that pursuant to s. 75(1) of the Act the general rule is that such hearings may be attended by the public. The potential glare of attendant publicity may work serious harm to the member. So the Act requires that, before that serious stage can be reached, there must be a review and report by the Secretary (or Deputy Secretary) to the Conduct Committee, and a review by the Conduct Committee (which may direct an investigation before completing its review) ending in a decision by that Committee either to dismiss the matter or that the conduct be dealt with by a Hearing Committee.
>
> The requirements of s. 57 may not be treated lightly. The review required by s. 51(1) must be a genuine and not a perfunctory review. The Legislature's direction that there be a review, and that if the matter is not dismissed he refer the matter "together with his report respecting the review", cannot be treated as mere surplusage. *Compliance with those requirements must have real meaning.* The purpose of requiring a "report" is to give the Conduct Committee the benefit of the Secretary's considered, experienced and rational views as to what the facts are and why it may be argued that the member's conduct constitutes conduct deserving of sanction. Merely delivering the Society's file on the member does not constitute a "report". . . .

Other examples of fairness in the investigation stage include *Tanaka*,[30] where the court imposed at least the minimum duty on the investigator to notify the individual involved of the investigation and to ask for a response and *Lindo v. Royal Bank*,[31] where the Federal Court Trial Division held that the duty of fairness required a copy of the report to be given to the parties and that they be given a reasonable opportunity to respond in writing in an investigation conducted for the Human Rights Commission.

---

29   (1993), 7 Alta. L.R. (3d) 305 at 311-12 (Alta. Q.B.).
30   *Tanaka v. Certified General Accountants' Assn. (Northwest Territories)* (1996), 38 Admin. L.R. (2d) 99 (N.W.T. S.C.).
31   (2000), [2000] F.C.J. No. 1101, 2000 CarswellNat 1483 (Fed. T.D.).

As administrative structures and processes differ so widely over the myriad of statutory tribunals, it is impossible to say in general what the content of the duty of fairness will be in the investigation stage and each case must be considered on its own facts. But it can be said that the existence of a duty of fairness at the investigation stage of the administrative process has been re-cognised and the courts will continue to flesh it out. Its content will vary with the context but it is likely to be of a more limited nature than is required at the hearing stage.

(b) Notice of the Hearing

Obviously, it is impossible to give a fair hearing to a person who has no notice of the action which a statutory delegate proposes to take. Conversely, it is not always possible to effect actual notice on every person who might potentially be affected by government action.[32] Accordingly, the question often arises whether individuals have been given proper notice, so that they can participate effectively in administrative procedures affecting them.[33]

Many statutes contain express provisions about how notice is to be given, to whom, and what it shall contain.[34] Sometimes, however, the statute may

---

32 In *Conception Bay South (Town) v. Newfoundland (Public Utilities Board)* (1991), 6 Admin. L.R. (2d) 287 (Nfld. T.D.), amended (1991), 6 Admin. L.R. (2d) 287 at 303 (Nfld. T.D.), the Newfoundland Supreme Court noted that, like other aspects of natural justice and the duty to be fair, the requirement of notice was dependent on the facts of the case. The court concluded that serving notice to all residents who might be potentially affected by a rate surcharge to be determined at a P.U.B. hearing would be unreasonable; however notice to each affected municipality would not. The decision itself was based on the inadequacy of the notice published in the media, which referred to the P.U.B. hearings but did not make specific reference to the surcharge until the last day of the hearings.

33 *T.W.U. v. Canada (Radio-Television & Telecommunications Commission)* (1995), 31 Admin. L.R. (2d) 230 (S.C.C.).

34 For example, Alberta's *Municipal Government Act*, R.S.A. 2000, c. 26 is quite specific in requiring a municipal council to give notice of its intention to pass certain types of land use by-laws:

    s. 606(2) Notice of the bylaw, resolution, meeting, public hearing or other thing must be

        (a) published at least once a week for 2 consecutive weeks in at least one newspaper or other publication circulating in the area to which the proposed bylaw, resolution or other thing relates, or in which the meeting or hearing is to be held, or

        (b) mailed or delivered to every residence in the area to which the proposed bylaw, resolution or other thing relates, or in which the meeting or hearing is to be held.

    s. 606(6) A notice must contain

        (a) a statement of the general purpose of the proposed bylaw, resolution, meeting, public hearing or other thing,

        (b) the address where a copy of the proposed bylaw, resolution or other thing, and any document relating to it or to the meeting or public hearing may be inspected,

        (c) in the case of a bylaw or resolution, an outline of the procedure to be followed by anyone wishing to file a petition in respect of it, and

        (d) in the case of a meeting or public hearing, the date, place and time where it will be held.

relieve the delegate from the obligation to give actual notice of proceedings, permitting a much more general form of publication.[35]

In the absence of a specific statutory prescription, the general rule of procedural fairness is that an administrator must give adequate notice to permit affected persons to know how they might be affected and to prepare themselves adequately to make representations.[36] Where the statute is silent as to the length of required notice, what is reasonable notice is contextual in nature.[37]

No notice is obviously inadequate notice.[38] Adequate notice has been held to require that the notice give an accurate description of the true nature and scope of the review[39] and it must be timely.[40] However, the exact content of this requirement may be difficult to determine without litigation since what is adequate or reasonable notice depends on the context of the case.[41] For example, where a tribunal could make a decision to terminate a person's employment, procedural fairness absolutely requires that the person is entitled to receive notice of the hearing before any decision is made.[42] Also, where the

---

35   For example, s. 51(3) of Alberta's *Public Utilities Board Act*, R.S.A. 2000, c. P-45 provides:
     s. 51(3) If, in a case within the jurisdiction of the Board, it is made to appear to the satisfaction of the Board that service of the notice cannot conveniently be made in the manner provided in subsection (2), the Board may order and allow service to be made by publication in The Alberta Gazette or by publication in a local newspaper, and that publication in each case is deemed to be equivalent to service in the manner provided in subsection (2).

36   See the discussion and cases referred to on this point in Reid and David, *supra* note 5 at 63-70. See also *Finch v. Assn. of Professional Engineers & Geoscientists (British Columbia)* (1994), 24 Admin. L.R. (2d) 227 (B.C. C.A.).

37   *C. (K.) v. College of Physical Therapists (Alberta)* (1999), 72 Alta. L.R. (3d) 77 (Alta. C.A.).

38   In *Sitler v. Alberta (Workers Compensation Board)*, 2003 ABQB 277 (Alta. Q.B.), Justice Sanderman found that a decision of the Appeals Commission established under the *Workers' Compensation Act* granting an estate status as an interested party without having given the original applicant the opportunity to argue against the position to be "inexcusable" and which "defies belief". Further, being "disturbed" by the adversarial tone of the Commission's brief before him, which he felt went beyond the function and role that the Commission should have taken in the proceedings, Sanderman J. also awarded solicitor/client costs against the Appeal Commission.

39   *Québec (Régie de L'assurance-maladie) v. Chamberland* (1986), 24 Admin. L.R. 304 (Que. C.A.) where the notice misled the appellant as to the seriousness of the charges and the appellant was thus unable to provide a full and adequate defence. See also *Rochon v. Spirit River School Division No. 47* (1994), 24 Admin. L.R. (2d) 115 (Alta. C.A.), where the Superintendent of the board was terminated midway through a meeting after an in camera discussion amongst board members and their counsel. The Superintendent received an agenda prior to the meeting; however, it made no mention that his employment would be considered. He had no formal notice, but on route to the meeting a third party informed him that he was to be terminated that evening.

40   *Forestell v. University of New Brunswick* (1988), 37 Admin. L.R. 290 (Visitor of the University of N.B.), where notice was received shortly before the proceeding was to begin. This defect can be cured by an adjournment sufficient to enable proper preparation.

41   *Dugas c. Commission d'aménagement de la péninsule acadienne* (1999), 6 M.P.L.R. (3d) 299 (N.B. C.A.); *Halfway River First Nation v. British Columbia (Ministry of Forests)* (1999), 178 D.L.R. (4th) 666 (B.C. C.A.); *Saskatchewan Broiler Hatching Egg Producers' Marketing Board v. Dubois* (1999), [2000] 5 W.W.R. 269 (Sask. Q.B.); *C. (K.) v. College of Physical Therapists (Alberta)* (1999), 72 Alta. L.R. (3d) 77 (Alta. C.A.).

42   *Lasch v. Miramichi Planning District Commission* (2000), 225 N.B.R. (2d) 66 (N.B. C.A.).

hearing is split into two parts, such as a hearing on liability separated from a hearing on penalty, reasonable notice must be given again prior to the hearing on penalty. General submissions on penalty at the liability phase of the hearing are insufficient.[43]

The effect of inadequate or no notice is to render the delegate's action void;[44] it is more than an administrative irregularity.[45] The fact that the applicant participated in the proceedings and was able to mount a defence, notwithstanding the absence of adequate notice, does not necessarily amount to a waiver of rights to adequate notice;[46] nor does a delay in bringing an application for judicial review.[47] The requirements of notice apply to all aspects of the proceedings, including the selection of date and location.[48] On the other hand, parties may in some circumstances have an obligation to take reasonable steps to inform themselves about proceedings,[49] and certainly cannot use a formal defect in giving notice to attack the validity of proceedings which they in fact knew about.[50]

Once adequate notice is provided, then the hearing may proceed as scheduled with or without the notified party in attendance.[51] As in most areas of procedural fairness, the test is whether the alleged lack of notice is so unfair that the proceedings in question should be set aside by the courts.

(c) Knowing the Case to be Met – Disclosure

The courts have consistently held that a fair hearing can only be had if the parties affected by the tribunal's decision know the case to be made against

---

43 *Watson v. British Columbia (Securities Commission)*, 1999 BCCA 625 (B.C. C.A.).

44 *Wiswell v. Winnipeg (Metropolitan)*, [1965] S.C.R. 512 (S.C.C.). A breach of natural justice does not mean that the decisionmaker never acquired jurisdiction to deal with the matter in issue, rather it means that the decisionmaker improperly exercised its decision making power. Thus to describe the decision as void is not to say that the body never possessed jurisdiction to deal with the matter. On the other hand, to describe the decision as voidable, as done in some cases (see for example *Morlacci v. British Columbia (Minister of Energy, Mines & Petroleum Resources)* (1997), 2 Admin. L.R. (3d) 242 (B.C. C.A.)) is problematic, as the decision would never have been valid and a court order would not be required to invalidate such a decision.

45 *Supermarchés Jean Labrecque Inc. v. Québec (Tribunal du travail)* (1987), 28 Admin. L.R. 239 (S.C.C.); *Pitt Polder Preservation Society v. Pitt Meadows (District)* (2000), 189 D.L.R. (4th) 219 (B.C. C.A.).

46 *Forestell v. University of New Brunswick* (1987), 84 N.B.R. (2d) 181 (N.B. Q.B.).

47 *Foothills (Municipal District No. 31) v. Alberta (Assessment Appeal Board)* (1986), 43 Alta. L.R. (2d) 282 (Alta. Q.B.).

48 *Supermarchés Jean Labrecque Inc. v. Québec (Tribunal du travail)* (1987), 28 Admin. L.R. 239 (S.C.C.).

49 *Tomko v. Nova Scotia (Labour Relations Board)* (1974), 9 N.S.R. (2d) 277 (N.S. C.A.), affirmed (1975), [1977] 1 S.C.R. 112 (S.C.C.); *Hretchka v. Chromex Investments Ltd.* (1971), [1972] S.C.R. 119 (S.C.C.).

50 Particularly if they waive the right to object to the defect: *Camac Exploration Ltd. v. Alberta (Oil & Gas Conservation Board)* (1964), 47 W.W.R. 81 (Alta. T.D.).

51 *Fischer v. Canadian Kennel Club* (1995), 31 Alta. L.R. (3d) 271 (Alta. Q.B.). Further, once notice has been provided, the decisionmaker need not serve notice of subsequent adjournments. See *Stuart v. Assiniboine Park-Fort Garry Community Committee of Winnipeg (City)* (1992), 4 Admin. L.R. (2d) 3 (Man. C.A.) dealing with an application for zoning variance.

them. Only in this circumstance can they rebut evidence prejudicial to their case and bring evidence to prove their position. But knowing the case that must be met is not enough, of course; the opportunity to present the other side of the matter must also be allowed.

The issue of whether and how much of the tribunal's file is available to the party affected is a source of difficulty for many tribunals. There is often a tendency to refuse to disclose the file to the parties involved. However, fairness generally requires that all information relied upon by the tribunal when making its decision be disclosed to the individual. Failure to do so deprives the tribunal of jurisdiction and renders the decision void.[52] The information to be disclosed includes reports prepared by the tribunal's staff[53] or any other report which the tribunal has relied on in making its decision. The contents of the file should be provided to the party in adequate time before the hearing so that the party can prepare its case.[54] This principle of procedural fairness has been approved by the courts.[55]

Nevertheless, as an element of procedural fairness, the extent of disclosure is context specific, having regard to the factors enunciated in *Baker*.[56] The process of determining whether the procedure used in reaching a decision was fair is not capable of a rigid, mechanical application.

Two recent immigration cases decided by the Supreme Court of Canada, *Suresh v. Canada (Minister of Citizenship & Immigration)*,[57] and *Ahani v. Canada (Minister of Citizenship & Immigration)*,[58] both in the context of section 7 of the *Charter*, illustrate how the same court can apply the same factors but reach different conclusions concerning the extent of disclosure required in the particular circumstances of the case. Both cases considered, generally, whether the procedures for deportation set out in the former *Immigration Act* were constitutionally valid in light of the procedural fairness component of "fundamental justice" contained in section 7 of the *Charter*. Further, both cases considered the extent of disclosure of the Minister's file that ought to be afforded to the claimants.

---

52 *Volkswagen Northern Ltd. v. Alberta (Industrial Relations Board)* (1964), 49 W.W.R. 574 (Alta. T.D.); *Anadarko Petroleum of Canada Ltd. v. Syd Johns Farms Ltd.*, [1975] 6 W.W.R. 350 (B.C. S.C.).

53 *Budge v. Alberta (Workers' Compensation Board)* (1985), 42 Alta. L.R. (2d) 26 (Alta. C.A.), where the court also found that it would be unsafe to allow the board to retroactively claim that it had not relied on the report when making its decision. See also *Tottrup v. Alberta* (1977), 79 D.L.R. (3d) 533 (Alta. T.D.), affirmed (1979), 17 A.R. 563 (Alta. C.A.), leave to appeal refused (1979), 19 A.R. 188n (S.C.C.); *Madison Development Corp. v. Alberta (Rent Regulation Appeal Board)* (1977), 7 A.R. 360 (Alta. T.D.).

54 The file might also reveal any irrelevant considerations or other matters such as bias.

55 *1185740 Ontario Ltd. v. Minister of National Revenue* (1999), 247 N.R. 287 (Fed. C.A.) – a party has the right to receive prior production of whatever documents will be placed before the tribunal; *Pitt Polder Preservation Society v. Pitt Meadows (District)* (2000), 189 D.L.R. (4th) 219 (B.C. C.A.) – where a public hearing is required, prior disclosure of all reports considered by the tribunal must be disclosed in order to make the hearing meaningful.

56 (1999), 14 Admin. L.R. (3d) 173 (S.C.C.).

57 2002 SCC 1, 37 Admin. L.R. (3d) 159 (S.C.C.).

58 2002 SCC 2 (S.C.C.).

Although the Supreme Court of Canada noted, in *Suresh*, that section 7 of the *Charter* has both procedural and substantive aspects, the procedural component requires compliance with the common law principles of procedural fairness.[59] After considering the factors articulated in *Baker*[60] and weighing these factors in the circumstances,[61] the Court held that the procedural protections required by section 7 of the *Charter* did not require the Minister to conduct a full oral hearing or a complete judicial process. Fairness did, however, require more than the total absence of procedural safeguards then contained in the former section 53(1)(b) of the *Immigration Act*[62] and certainly more than what Suresh received, particularly since he was facing deportation and potential torture. In particular, the Court required the Minister to reveal to Suresh all of the information she had on her file, including information from her staff and written assurances from a foreign government that the person would not be tortured.[63]

The Court emphasized, however, that these procedural safeguards would not necessarily arise in every case – and certainly not in the absence of the person affected establishing a threshold showing a risk of torture.[64]

Driving home the point that "context is everything" in procedural fairness cases,[65] the Supreme Court declined to grant relief[66] in its concurrent decision

---

59   Citing Wilson J. in *Singh v. Canada (Minister of Employment & Immigration)*, [1985] 1 S.C.R. 177 (S.C.C.).

60   For a discussion of these factors, see "Introduction", above.

61   With respect to the fifth factor, the Court made the following comments (at para. 120):
     The final factor we consider is the choice of procedures made by the agency. In this case, *the Minister is free under the terms of the statute to choose whatever procedures she wishes* in making a s. 53(1)(b) decision. As noted above, *the Minister must be allowed considerable discretion in evaluating future risk and security concerns*. This factor *also suggests a degree of deference to the Minister's choice of procedures since Parliament has signaled the difficulty of the decision by leaving to the Minister the choice of how best to make it*. At the same time, *this need for deference must be reconciled with the elevated level of procedural protections mandated by the serious situation of refugees* like Suresh, who if deported may face torture and violations of human rights in which Canada can neither constitutionally, nor under its international treaty obligations, be complicit. [Emphasis added.]

62   R.S.C. 1985, c. I-2 (since repealed). Now see *Immigration and Refugee Protection Act*, S.C. 2001, c. 27.

63   *Suresh, supra* note 57 at para. 122.

64   *Ibid.* at para. 127.

65   For other examples of the application of section 7 of the *Charter* to the requirement for disclosure in an administrative law context, see generally the Third Edition of this work at 263-69 and specifically: *Latham v. Canada (Solicitor General)* (1984), 9 D.L.R. (4th) 393, 5 Admin. L.R. 70 (Fed. T.D.); *Rice v. Canada (National Parole Board)* (1985), 16 Admin. L.R. 157 (Fed. T.D.); *Ross v. Kent Institution* (1987), 25 Admin. L.R. 67 (B.C. C.A.), leave to appeal refused (1987), 59 C.R. (3d) xxxiv (S.C.C.); *Chiarelli v. Canada (Minister of Employment & Immigration)* (1990), 42 Admin. L.R. 189, 67 D.L.R. (4th) 697 (Fed. C.A.), reversed [1992] 1 S.C.R. 711, 90 D.L.R. (4th) 289, 2 Admin. L.R. (2d) 125 (S.C.C.); *Singh v. Canada (Minister of Employment & Immigration)*, 12 Admin. L.R. 137, [1985] 1 S.C.R. 177, 17 D.L.R. (4th) 422 (S.C.C.); *Moumdjian v. Canada (Security Intelligence Review Committee)* (1999), [1999] F.C.J. No. 1160, 1999 CarswellNat 1420 (Fed. C.A.).

66   For an example in a non-*Charter* context, see *Romashenko v. Real Estate Council (British Columbia)*, 2000 BCCA 400 (B.C. C.A.) where the court refused to grant relief for lack of

in *Ahani*. In that case (unlike in *Suresh*), the appellant had not established a *prima facie* case that he faced torture upon deportation. Accordingly, the Court held that the additional procedural protections articulated in *Suresh* were not constitutionally required – it was sufficient for Ahani to be given notice of the Minister's intention to issue a danger opinion under section 53(1)(b) of the former *Immigration Act* and to allow him to provide submissions in that regard, even though he was not provided with a copy of the memorandum which had been provided to the Minister, nor given an opportunity to challenge the material in it. The Court stated its conclusion as follows[67]:

> We are satisfied that Ahani was fully informed of the Minister's case against him and given a full opportunity to respond. Insofar as the procedures followed may not have precisely complied with those we suggest in *Suresh*, we are satisfied that this did not prejudice him. We conclude that the process accorded to Ahani was consistent with the principles of fundamental justice. . . .

Thus, as evidenced by the decision in *Ahani*, the context of a case may limit the requirement of full disclosure. Another example can be found in the *Gaming Board* case,[68] where the intention of the Act under which the tribunal was operating required that the sources of the board's information not be disclosed. To do otherwise would prejudice the operation of the Act. Instead the board was to give sufficient indications of the objections to enable the person affected to answer them.

In other cases, service to and protection of the public has taken precedence over the requirement of fairness to the person affected. In *Strauts v. College of Physicians & Surgeons (British Columbia)*,[69] the British Columbia Court of Appeal affirmed the college's order requiring a doctor under investigation into chelation therapy to provide his records to the college. The doctor had refused on the grounds that procedural fairness required that he be given copies of any letters of complaint filed against him. As this was part of the investigative stage of the proceedings, the court found that the public factor and duties of the college to protect the public interest outweighed what the duty of fairness might otherwise require regarding full disclosure to the doctor. The court made it clear, however, that public interest considerations would not play any part in the adjudicative stage of any proceedings against the doctor.[70]

A further example of the limits on disclosure can be found in *Lazarov v. Canada (Secretary of State)*.[71] The Federal Court of Appeal set aside the Secretary of State's decision to refuse a certificate of citizenship to Lazarov

---

disclosure unless the aggrieved party showed prejudice and held that the tribunal need only disclose information that had not otherwise been disclosed in some other form.

67   *Ahani, supra* note 58 at para. 26.
68   *R. v. Gaming Board for Great Britain*, [1970] 2 All E.R. 528 (Eng. C.A.).
69   (1997), 47 Admin. L.R. (2d) 79 (B.C. C.A.).
70   *Ibid.* at 81-82.
71   (1973), 39 D.L.R. (3d) 738 (Fed. C.A.).

on the grounds that Lazarov had not been advised of pertinent facts alleged against him, so that he had no opportunity to reply to them.

The Canadian *Citizenship Act*[72] sets out several requirements which an applicant has to satisfy before the Citizenship Court can make a finding that the applicant is a fit and proper person to be granted Canadian citizenship. However, the Act also gives the Minister the discretion to decide whether or not to grant the citizenship. The Minister refused Lazarov on the basis of "... confidential information recently provided by the Royal Canadian Mounted Police".[73] Lazarov had been given no opportunity to be heard with respect to this information, the contents of which he also did not know.

Lazarov argued that the *audi alteram partem* rule applied to entitle him to know this information and make a reply to it. The Minister argued that his function was purely administrative, and that since Lazarov had no right to the certificate, no existing right was being affected or interfered with by the Minister's decision; therefore the *audi alteram partem* rule did not apply.

On the question of rights, Thurlow J. found for the court that there was no critical distinction between situations where existing rights were affected and situations which create rights. Rather, the question to be determined was whether the function of the Minister, although plainly administrative in nature, nevertheless required him to exercise his power on a quasi-judicial basis. His Lordship relied on Lord Upjohn's decision in *Durayappah v. Fernando*[74] to formulate a test. The factors he considered were the nature of the interest or right involved and its importance to the individual; the circumstances that entitled the decision-maker claiming the right to exercise control to intervene; and the nature of sanctions available to the tribunal.

In this case, Thurlow J. found that the importance of citizenship meant that Lazarov should have been given at least an opportunity to dispute the existence of the grounds on which he was refused, despite the discretionary nature of the Minister's decision. On the second point he noted, that although the Act gave the Minister very broad discretionary powers, that discretion did not extend to the procedure he adopted. If the Minister were to consider other facts apart from those appearing on the application, the applicant was to be given an opportunity to be heard with respect to them, prior to the exercise of the Minister's admittedly unfettered discretion. Thirdly, the sanction that could be imposed here was not a case of deprivation but rather more of a delay of the rights and advantages which citizenship confers. Nevertheless, His Lordship held that this did not excuse the lack of a fair hearing:[75]

> It is not a case of depriving a person of his property, and it is true that the applicant can apply again after two years, but the status of citizenship carries with it rights and advantages and to refuse the application of a person to whom it would otherwise be granted on the basis of matters of which he is not apprised and which he is given no oppor-

---

72 R.S.C. 1985, c. C-29.
73 *Lazarov, supra* note 71 at 740.
74 [1967] 2 A.C. 337 at 349 (Ceylon P.C.).
75 *Lazarov, supra* note 71 at 749-50.

tunity to dispute is shocking to one's sense of justice, even though he may lawfully apply again after a comparatively short time. It suggests that the applicant is not being fairly dealt with and that fairness demands that he at least be afforded an opportunity to state his position on them. . . .

In my opinion, therefore, the rule *audi alteram partem* applies whenever the Minister proposes to exercise his discretion to refuse an application on the basis of facts pertaining to the particular applicant or his application and where he has not already had an opportunity in one way or another of stating his position with respect to any matters which in the absence of refutation or explanation would lead to the rejection of his application. This is not to say that a confidential report or its contents need be disclosed to him but the pertinent allegations which if undenied or unresolved would lead to rejection of his application must, as I see it, be made known to him to an extent sufficient to enable him to respond to them and he must have a fair opportunity to dispute or explain them.

The exclusion of parties from the hearing will also result in their not knowing the case to be met and having no opportunity to reply, thereby breaching the *audi alteram partem* rule.

This problem arose in *Saltfleet (Municipality) Board of Health v. Knapman*,[76] where the Supreme Court of Canada considered the proper procedure to be followed by a local board of health in the exercise of its power to force occupants to vacate unfit premises. The board delivered the required notices to vacate but then, when it met to discuss the matter, refused to hear the submissions of the owner and several of the occupants who had attended the meeting in order to ascertain the nature of the complaints and to make submissions in answer to them. The board denied them any hearing at all. The board maintained that its action was administrative in nature and not quasi-judicial, so that no hearing was required.

The court found that, under the provisions of the enabling legislation, the board was required, as a condition precedent to the exercise of its authority, to be satisfied that the buildings were unfit or a nuisance or dangerous to health in some way. Once so satisfied, the board could proceed to issue its order to vacate. In so deciding whether or not a condition of unfitness existed, the court held that the board was required to act judicially and that only very plain words in the statute could oust this requirement. There were none and therefore the board was required to give the occupants an opportunity to know the case against them and to give an answer to the allegations. Since this had not been done, *certiorari* was issued to quash the eviction notices.

In cases dealing with prison and parole matters, a balance must be struck between protecting the confidentiality of sources and providing enough information about alleged offenses to allow applicants to respond intelligently in

---

76 [1956] S.C.R. 877 (S.C.C.).

their defence. In *Demaria v. Canada (Regional Classification Board)*,[77] Hugessen J. commented:

> In the final analysis, the test must be not whether there exist good grounds for withholding information, but rather whether enough information has been revealed to allow the person concerned to answer the case against him.[78]

In *Demaria*, the applicant was transferred from a medium security institution to a maximum security institution for disciplinary reasons. The substance of the allegations giving rise to the transfer were withheld from him, and neither he nor his lawyer were able to obtain particulars. The reason given was that "all preventive security information acquired by the Correctional Service of Canada was confidential and could not be released to an inmate's legal representative."[79] The court said that such a blanket claim was too broad, and that a burden lay on the authorities to demonstrate that they have withheld only such information as is necessary to protect confidentiality and informants.

Hugessen J. also discussed the relationship of notice, the right to a hearing and the right to know the case to be met:

> The purpose of requiring that notice be given to a person against whose interests it is proposed to act is to allow him to respond to it intelligently. If the matter is contested, such response will normally consist of either or both a denial of what is alleged and an allegation of other facts to complete the picture. Where, as here, it is not intended to hold a hearing or otherwise give the person concerned a right to confront the evidence against him directly, it is particularly important that the notice contain as much detail as possible, else the right to answer becomes illusory . . . In the absence of anything more than the bald allegation that there were grounds to believe that he had brought in cyanide, the appellant was reduced to a simple denial, by itself almost always less convincing than a positive affirmation, and futile speculation as to what the case against him really was.[80]

These cases all illustrate the change in the courts' focus to whether a delegate has acted fairly in the circumstances, rather than on the characterisation of the delegate's function and the requirement to act quasi-judicially.[81]

---

77 (1986), 21 Admin. L.R. 227 (Fed. C.A.).

78 *Ibid.* at 231.

79 *Ibid.* at 230.

80 *Ibid.* at 230-31.

81 For example in *A Solicitor v. Law Society (British Columbia)* (1995), 33 Admin. L.R. (2d) 314 (B.C. S.C.) the court stressed the importance of knowing adverse and favourable evidence to enable full answer and defence, particularly as the member was called as the first witness at her professional disciplinary hearing.

The stage of the proceedings,[82] the nature of the rights involved and the consequences to the individuals in question are now relevant to whether the tribunal acted fairly, and provided adequate disclosure.[83]

(d) Form of Hearing

The previous section discussed the requirement that parties have a right to know and answer any case to be made against them. However, the manner or form in which parties know the case being made against them and how they answer it varies from case to case and, like all aspects of procedural fairness, is context specific.

At one extreme, there is the full judicial procedure model where the administrative tribunal is formal, closely resembling a court. Apart from the manner of appointment of the adjudicator, it is hard to tell the two fora apart. Procedures before both involve oral hearings, swearing in of witnesses, cross-examination of witnesses, argument, and reply.[84] At the other extreme, there

---

82 Generally the level of disclosure is lower at the pre-hearing or investigative stages; see for example *Findlay v. College of Dental Surgeons (British Columbia)* (1997), 2 Admin. L.R. (3d) 1 (B.C. S.C.); *Howe v. Institute of Chartered Accountants (Ontario)* (1994), 27 Admin. L.R. (2d) 118 (Ont. C.A.), leave to appeal denied (1995), 85 O.A.C. 320 (note) (S.C.C.); and K.M. Munro, *"Howe* Troublesome – Do natural justice or fairness require full disclosure? When?"* (1995) 4 R.A.L. 97. Absent specific statutory authority a tribunal cannot order parties to produce documents per se prior to a hearing: *Canadian Pacific Air Lines Ltd. v. C.A.L.P.A.* (1993), 17 Admin. L.R. (2d) 141 (S.C.C.).

83 The adequacy of disclosure has been a contentious issue, particularly after the Supreme Court of Canada decision of *R v. Stinchcombe*, [1991] 3 S.C.R. 326 (S.C.C.), which dealt with the Crown's obligation to disclose information in criminal cases. There is mixed law on the applicability of the principles enunciated in *Stinchcombe* to the administrative context. The case has been applied in some, but not all administrative settings although the increasingly common application by courts of the *Stinchcombe* disclosure requirements suggest that the person affected would indeed have the right to see the report. See for example *Markandey v. Board of Ophthalmic Dispensers (Ontario)* (1994), [1994] O.J. No. 484, 1994 CarswellOnt 2601 (Ont. Gen. Div.); *Thompson v. Chiropractors' Assn. (Saskatchewan)* (1996), 36 Admin. L.R. (2d) 273 (Sask. Q.B.); the dissent in *Howe v. Institute of Chartered Accountants (Ontario)* (1994), 27 Admin L.R. (2d) 118 (Ont. C.A.), leave to appeal to S.C.C. refused (1995), 85 O.A.C. 320 (note) (S.C.C.); *Christian v. Northwestern General Hospital* (1993), 115 D.L.R. (4th) 279 (Ont. Div. Ct.), motion for leave to appeal to the Ontario Court of Appeal dismissed; *Dhanjal v. Air Canada* (1996), [1996] C.H.R.D. No. 4, 1996 CarswellNat 2962 (Can. Human Rights Trib.), affirmed (1997), 139 F.T.R. 37 (Fed. T.D.); and *I M P Group Ltd. v. Dillman* (1995), 143 N.S.R. (2d) 169 (N.S. C.A.); but see *Waterman v. National Life Assurance Co. of Canada* (1992), 18 C.H.R.R. D/173 (Ont. Bd. of Inquiry) (investigating officer's notes not ordered to be disclosed); *Nrecaj v. Canada (Minister of Employment & Immigration)* (1993), 14 Admin. L.R. (2d) 161 (Fed. T.D.); *Williams v. Canada (Regional Transfer Board, Prairie Region)* (1993), 15 Admin. L.R. (2d) 83 (Fed. C.A.). *Stinchcombe* is more likely to apply if the administrative setting closely resembles a criminal trial. For a discussion of these cases see J. Casey, "Disclosure in Administrative Proceedings – Does *Stinchcombe* Apply?" (1997) 6 R.A.L. 121. See also R.F. Reid & J. Mulcahy, "Pre-hearing discovery – Does *Stinchcombe* apply to administrative tribunals?" (1994) 3 R.A.L. 97 where the authors conclude that *Stinchcombe* does not add to the preexisting duty of disclosure.

84 For example, s. 47 (1) of *Police Act*, R.S.A. 2000, c. P-17 which deals with hearings into complaints as to the actions of a police officer. Most disciplinary proceedings of professionals contain similar statutory provisions, for example the *Architects Act*, R.S.A. 2000, c. A-44, and the *Legal Professions Act*, R.S.A. 2000, c. L-8 to name but two.

is a purely administrative model where the tribunal is very informal with no oral hearing (everything is done by paper), no opportunity for the parties to meet face to face, nor to put questions, no opportunity for parties to argue against each others' submissions, nor even often to know the identity of the decision-maker.[85] And there is every variation of procedure between these extremes. But whatever the procedure adopted by the decision-maker, it must be fair and impartial to those involved and be appropriate to the circumstances.[86]

As stated above, what is fair in the circumstances of an individual case has varied over time. Generally speaking, there is a greater degree of participation allowed to those affected by an administrative decision in the early 21st century than was the case 100 years ago. This reflects the changing public perspective of the greater importance of individual rights (as exemplified by the *Charter*) above the rights of society as a whole.

In the early 20th century, many areas of activity came to be regulated specifically by statutes. Many of these statutes, but not all, also contained explicit procedural provisions concerning notice and the right to a hearing. The courts then had to face the question of how far these provisions had gone in replacing the common law. Did the *absence* of procedural provisions in the statute mean that the tribunal was absolute governor of its own procedure and could ignore the right to notice and a hearing, or did the common law still operate? If the common law did still operate, to what extent did it supplement the incomplete statutory code of procedure?

The culmination of the long development of this area of the law[87] is exemplified in the decision of the Supreme Court of Canada in *Baker*,[88] which makes it clear that every person affected by an administrative decision has a right to a hearing. What *form* of hearing ". . . depends on an appreciation of the context of the particular statute and the rights affected . . .".[89] All of the circumstances must be considered in the specific context of the case in order to determine what kind of a hearing will be sufficient. What the court must keep in mind is how to ensure a fair and open procedure.[90]

---

85 For example, s. 77 (4) of the *Health Information Act*, R.S.A. 2000, c. H-5 gives Alberta's Information and Privacy Commissioner the discretion to order oral submissions only in inquiries under that Act.

86 The right to a hearing cannot be ousted by agreement by the parties where the statutory or regulatory context mandates a hearing: *Rosen v. Saskatoon District Health Board*, [2001] 10 W.W.R. 19 (Sask. C.A.).

87 For a review of the development of this aspect in England, see generally Third Edition of this work at 238-49 and, specifically: *Cooper v. Wandsworth Board of Works* (1863), 143 E.R. 414 (Eng. C.P.); *Local Government Board v. Arlidge*, [1915] A.C. 120 (U.K. H.L.) *(the "Arlidge Case")*; *Errington v. Minister of Health* (1934), [1935] 1 K.B. 249, [1934] All E.R. Rep. 154 (Eng. C.A.); *Franklin v. Minister of Town & Country Planning* (1947), [1948] A.C. 87, [1947] 2 All E.R. 289 (U.K. H.L.); *R. v. Gaming Board for Great Britain*, [1970] 2 All E.R. 528 (Eng. C.A.). For a review of the development of this aspect from the Canadian perspective, see Chapter 8.

88 (1999), 14 Admin. L.R. (3d) 173 (S.C.C.).

89 *Ibid.* at 192.

90 *Ibid.*

I emphasize that underlying all these factors is the notion that the purpose of participatory rights contained within the duty of procedural fairness is to ensure that administrative decisions are made using a fair and open procedure, appropriate to the decision being made and its statutory, institutional, and social context, with an opportunity for those affected by the decision to put forward their views and evidence fully and have them considered by the decision-maker.

Thus, although parties are entitled to a hearing, the duty to be fair does not necessarily mean an *oral* hearing is required[91] (or the other procedures that generally accompany the right to a hearing).[92] In fact, if it did, the process of government would grind to a halt because thousands of decisions are made every day without oral hearings. First resort must be had to the enabling statute giving the tribunal its jurisdiction. If the statute provides a code of procedure, then by *ipso facto* that defines the content of fair procedure.[93] Generally speaking, however, statutes do not contain a complete and detailed code of procedure. Some are silent and many more give only partial guidance. Within those parameters, a tribunal can set its own procedures. It could, for example, decide that a fair hearing can be extended without the decision-maker ever seeing the applicant in person. Provided the factors articulated in *Baker* for determining the scope of fairness are followed,[94] then it is likely that the procedure used by a tribunal will pass judicial muster.

Evans *et al.*, in the Third Edition of *Administrative Law: Cases, Text, and Materials* comment on the distinction:

> The phrase "oral hearing", like many of the terms in administrative law, can have different meanings, or no clear meaning at all. When "hearing" and "oral hearing" are contrasted, "hearing" refers to natural justice generally or the entire range of procedural elements, and the most useful meaning of "oral hearing" is a proceeding that includes a minimum of a face-to-face meeting with the other parties and the agency (or some official who will "hear" and report) and an opportunity to make representations orally.[95]

---

91 An exchange of written materials may suffice, *Mobil Oil Canada Ltd. v. Canada-Newfoundland (Offshore Petroleum Board)* (1994), 21 Admin. L.R. (2d) 248 (S.C.C.) at 269. See also *Murphy v. Dowhaniuk* (1986), 22 Admin. L.R. 81 (B.C. C.A.).

92 For example, the right to notice of a hearing is integral to the right to a hearing, whether oral or not. The requirement of a hearing may also entail the right to cross-examine witnesses, the right to counsel, the right to reasons, and the right to know the case to be met and to be heard by the party making the decision.

93 *Friends of the Old Man River Society v. Assn. of Professional Engineers, Geologists & Geophysicists (Alberta)* (2001), 199 D.L.R. (4th) 85 (Alta. C.A.), leave to appeal to the S.C.C. refused (2001), [2001] S.C.C.A. No. 366, 2001 CarswellAlta 1519 (S.C.C.) is an example of both the type of hearing and the type of notice being dependent upon the enabling statute.

94 For a review of the factors, see "Introduction", above.

95 (Toronto: Emond Montgomery, 1989) at 151-52. See also J.M. Evans, *et al.*, *Administrative Law*, 4th ed. (Toronto: Emond Montgomery, 1995) at 263, where the phrase "oral hearing"

If there is no statutory requirement for an oral hearing, the general presumption is that the tribunal may establish its own procedure.[96] However, in keeping with the movement towards a more functional and pragmatic analysis of what constitutes procedural fairness, the right to an oral hearing has been held to depend on the circumstances. In *Pett v. Greyhound Racing Assn. Ltd.*, Lord Denning stated that "[i]n matters affecting reputation or livelihood or serious import . . . fairness demands an oral hearing".[97] However in *Murphy v. Dowhaniuk*,[98] the British Columbia Court of Appeal noted that an oral hearing is not always necessary if an alternative means of placing evidence before the tribunal is sufficient.

Three Supreme Court of Canada decisions on the requirement of an oral hearing, all in the context of immigration cases, must be considered: *Singh v. Canada (Minister of Employment & Immigration)*,[99] *Suresh v. Canada (Minister of Citizenship & Immigration)*,[100] and *Chieu v. Canada (Minister of Citizenship & Immigration)*[101] where the court examined the issue in light of both the *Canadian Bill of Rights*[102] (in *Singh*) and the *Charter* (in all three).

(i) Constitutional and Quasi-Constitutional Rights to Oral Hearings

In *Singh v. Canada (Minister of Employment & Immigration)*,[103] there were two judgments, concurring in result, but differing in approach. Mr. Justice Beetz addressed the question of whether an oral hearing was required under the terms of the *Canadian Bill of Rights*; while Madame Justice Wilson examined the issue from the perspective of section 7 of the *Charter*. Both concluded that the circumstances of this case required an oral hearing.

---

is used in the sense of "a face to face encounter with the actual decision maker (or someone formally and legally deputed by that decision maker to hear and receive evidence) and, where relevant, the other party or parties."

96   But where a statute does contemplate an oral hearing, the failure to provide one amounts to a breach of procedural fairness: *Sarg Oils Ltd. v. Alberta (Environmental Appeal Board)* (1996), 36 Admin. L.R. (2d) 134 (Alta. Q.B.). See also *Robertson v. Edmonton (City)* (1990), 44 Admin. L.R. 27 (Alta. Q.B.), where the relevant statute, the *Planning Act*, contemplated some sort of oral hearing, but did not specify the exact procedure. The city council instituted a five minute time limit on presentations. This was acceptable, without more, as an appropriate exercise of its ability to use its own procedure. However, a breach of procedural fairness occurred in this case because the applicants had been told that there would be no time limitation.

97   (1968), [1968] 2 W.L.R. 1471, [1969] 1 Q.B. 125 (Eng. C.A.) at 1476. In *Willette v. Royal Canadian Mounted Police Commissioner* (1984), 10 Admin. L.R. 149 (Fed. C.A.), the Federal Court of Appeal ruled that an oral hearing was warranted in professional disciplinary matters. See also *Khan v. University of Ottawa* (1997), 2 Admin. L.R. (3d) 298 (Ont. C.A.). A majority of the Court of Appeal ruled that a law student appealing a grade deserved an oral hearing given the circumstances of the case and the consequences of an adverse finding with respect to her credibility.

98   (1986), 22 Admin. L.R. 81 (B.C. C.A.).

99   (1985), 12 Admin. L.R. 137 (S.C.C.).

100   (2002), 37 Admin. L.R. (3d) 159 (S.C.C.).

101   (2002), 37 Admin. L.R. (3d) 252 (S.C.C.).

102   R.S.C. 1970, App. III.

103   *Singh, supra* note 99.

The case dealt with the former *Immigration Act*[104] provisions relating to convention refugee status. Under the Act, a person claiming to be a refugee could apply to the Minister for a refugee designation. The Refugee Status Advisory Committee advised the Minister and, if the application was rejected, the applicant could seek a redetermination by the Immigration Appeal Board. The board was required to allow the matter to go to a hearing, if, on the basis of material submitted, ". . . there was reasonable grounds to believe that a claim would, upon a hearing of the application, be established."

There were seven appellants whose cases were consolidated because the main issues to be addressed were essentially the same. The Minister, acting on the advice of the Refugee Status Advisory Committee, determined that none of the appellants was a refugee. They appealed to the Immigration Appeal Board. The board denied the application to proceed to a hearing, based on section 71(1), that there were no ". . . reasonable grounds to believe that a claim could, upon the hearing of the application, be established. . .". Each appellant then sought judicial review by the Federal Court of Appeal, which was denied. The result of rejecting their appeals was either a deportation order (where the appellants were seeking admission into Canada at a port of entry) or a removal order (where the appellants were under investigation as to whether they should be removed after having been admitted to Canada).

Mr. Justice Beetz examined the scheme of the *Immigration Act* to determine whether section 71(1) infringed section 2(e) of the *Canadian Bill of Rights*.[105]

First, he concluded that the ". . . process of determining and redetermining appellants' refugee claims involves the determination of rights and obligations for which the appellants have, under s.2(e) . . . the right to a fair hearing in accordance with the principles of fundamental justice."[106] Secondly, the question was whether the appellants had received a ". . . fair hearing in accordance with principles of fundamental justice." Beetz J. noted that the appellants' claims to refugee status ". . . have been finally denied without their having been afforded a full oral hearing at a single stage of the proceedings before any of the bodies or officials empowered to adjudicate upon their claim on the merits."[107]

He emphasized, however, that the principles of fundamental justice will not always require an oral hearing, quoting the *Inuit Tapirisat* case for support:

---

104 R.S.C. 1985, c. I-2 (since repealed). Now see the *Immigration and Refugee Protection Act*, S.C. 2001, c. 27.

105 2. Every law of Canada shall, unless it is expressly declared by an Act of the Parliament of Canada that it shall operate notwithstanding the Canadian Bill of Rights, be so construed and applied as not to abrogate, abridge or infringe or to authorize the abrogation, the abridgement or infringement of any of the rights or freedoms herein recognized and declared, and in particular, no law of Canada shall be construed or applied so as to . . .

   (e) deprive a person of the right to a fair hearing in accordance with the principles of fundamental justice for the determination of his rights and obligations.

106 *Singh, supra* note 99 at 155.

107 *Ibid.*

the requirements of natural justice must depend on the circumstances of the case, the nature of the inquiry, the rules under which the Tribunal is acting, the subject-matter that is being dealt with, and so forth.[108]

Beetz J. accepted the appellants' submissions that where life or liberty may depend on findings of fact and credibility, the opportunity to make written submissions or to reply in writing to allegations, is not sufficient. He quoted portions of Pigeon J.'s dissenting judgment in *Ernewein v. Canada (Minister of Employment & Immigration)*[109] to illustrate that the principles of procedural fairness, even apart from the requirements of fundamental justice in the *Bill of Rights*, are that justice must appear to be done, and that these rights are not to be excluded by inference. He concluded that in all the circumstances of the case, the appellants were denied their fundamental right to a hearing. For Beetz J., the nature of the legal rights involved and the severity of the consequences to the individual concerned determined the content of fundamental justice.[110]

In her judgment, Madame Justice Wilson held that the procedures in the *Immigration Act* were incompatible with section 7 of the *Charter* and not justifiable under section 1. She noted that the Act imposes limitations on the hearing that are incompatible with principles of procedural fairness and therefore concluded that in order for the appellants to succeed they had to establish that Parliament's decision to exclude procedural fairness infringed the *Charter*.

She examined the nature of the right to an oral hearing, and its relationship to fairness, procedural fairness and fundamental justice. An oral hearing is not required in all circumstances.

If "the right to life, liberty and security of the person" is properly construed as relating only to matters such as death, physical liberty and physical punishment, it would seem on the surface at least, that these are matters of such fundamental importance that procedural fairness would invariably require an oral hearing. I am prepared, nevertheless, to accept for present purposes that written submissions may be an adequate substitute for an oral hearing in appropriate circumstances.

I should note, however, that even if hearings based on written submissions are consistent with principles of fundamental justice for some purposes, they will not be satisfactory for all purposes. In particular, I am of the view that where a serious issue of credibility is involved, fundamental justice requires that credibility be determined on the basis of an oral hearing . . .

---

108 [1980] 2 S.C.R. 735 at 747 (S.C.C.).

109 (1979), [1980] 1 S.C.R. 639 at 657 (S.C.C.).

110 *Singh, supra* note 99 at 157. He drew an interesting distinction in his discussion of the consequences. Threats to life and liberty are relevant, not to whether the *Bill of Rights* applies, "but with respect to the *type of hearing which is warranted in the circumstances*." [Emphasis added.]

As I have suggested, the absence of an oral hearing need not be inconsistent with fundamental justice in every case. My greatest concern about the procedural scheme envisaged by ss. 45 to 58 and 70 and 71 of the *Immigration Act* is not, therefore, with the absence of an oral hearing in and of itself, but with the inadequacy of the opportunity the scheme provides for a refugee claimant to state his case and know the case he has to meet.[111]

In this case, the issue focussed on legislation which specifically authorized the use of procedures that were not consonant with principles of fundamental justice, thus necessitating resort to the *Charter*. However, the judgments, although dealing with constitutional issues, also have much to say that may be equally applicable about the requirement of oral hearings in administrative law generally.

Although their arguments focus on the nature of "fundamental justice" under the *Bill of Rights* and the *Charter*, principles of procedural fairness in administrative law are elements of fundamental justice[112] and both judgments were directed to the procedural elements. Further, the interpretation of "fundamental justice" in the *Canadian Bill of Rights*, on which Beetz J. based his decision, has been quite narrow itself.

Wilson J. referred to a test of procedural fairness laid out in *R. v. Duke*[113] that held that fundamental justice includes, at least, that the tribunal ". . . must act fairly, in good faith, without bias and in a judicial temper, and must give to him the opportunity adequately to state his case."[114] Both Beetz J. and Wilson J. pointed to the importance of oral testimony when issues of credibility are involved. Clearly, the factors cited by the court in both judgments are important in assessing, in the administrative context, whether a tribunal will breach the duty to be fair if it refuses to hold an oral hearing.[115]

In another immigration case, *Suresh v. Canada (Minister of Citizenship & Immigration)*,[116] the court reiterated that what is required will depend on the circumstances. After a discussion of the factors from *Baker* and having weighed

---

111 *Ibid.* at 190.
112 For example, substantive issues of law are encompassed in principles of fundamental justice, but not in procedural fairness or fairness.
113 [1972] S.C.R. 917 (S.C.C.).
114 *Ibid.* at 923.
115 For example see *Idziak v. Canada (Minister of Justice)*, [1992] 3 S.C.R. 631, 9 Admin. L.R. (2d) 1 (S.C.C.), reconsideration refused (1992), 9 Admin. L.R. (2d) 1n (S.C.C.). Idziak was denied an oral hearing, because the decision to be made by the Minister was essentially one relating to whether there were any extenuating circumstances mitigating against his extradition. The extradition proceedings themselves were all conducted according to fair procedures. His application to the Minister had included all the relevant information; there was no case raised against him on the issue in question, therefore no need to cross-examine anyone. The information provided by him was all the information the Minister had before him when he made the decision.
116 2002 SCC 1, 37 Admin. L.R. (3d) 159 (S.C.C.).

these factors together in all of the circumstances,[117] the Court held that the procedural protections required by section 7 of the *Charter* did not extend to requiring the Minister to conduct a full oral hearing or a complete judicial process, but did require more than the total absence of procedural safeguards in section 53(1)(b) of the former *Immigration Act* and certainly more than what Suresh received. The "more" had to do with Suresh knowing all the information and material on which the Minister was relying to make her decision – ie. the requirement of disclosure[118] – and his having a full opportunity to respond to the case presented to the Minister. The Court held, however, that this could be adequately accomplished simply through written submissions.

In a third immigration case, *Chieu v. Canada (Minister of Citizenship & Immigration)*,[119] the issue focussed on whether the proper interpretation of section 70(1)(b) of the former *Immigration Act* permitted the Immigration Appeal Division (I.A.D.), when deciding whether to issue a removal order from Canada, to consider potential foreign hardship in the country to which a permanent resident would likely be removed. Pursuant to Section 52 of the Act, which controls the country of removal, either the individual being removed or the Minister, which is the usual case, selects the country of removal. Hence, the Minister argued that the potential foreign hardship in the country of removal was a consideration for the Minister to make, not the I.A.D.

A different form of hearing was contemplated for each section; a section 70 (1)(b) decision envisioned a full hearing while a section 52 decision not necessarily so. The Supreme Court held that Parliament intended the I.A.D. to have a broad discretion to allow permanent residents facing removal to remain in Canada if it would be equitable to do so. As a result, the court should not narrow this discretion contrary to the plain intention of Parliament and leave consideration of this factor only to the Minister or the courts on judicial review. This was not the intention of Parliament.[120]

> Parliament has equipped the I.A.D. with all of the tools necessary to ensure that the requirements of natural justice are met when removing individuals from Canada, including providing for an oral hearing, the calling and cross-examination of witnesses, the tendering of evidence,

---

117   With respect to the fifth factor, the court made the following comments (at para. 120):
    The final factor we consider is the choice of procedures made by the agency. In this case, *the Minister is free under the terms of the statute to choose whatever procedures she wishes* in making a s. 53(1)(b) decision. As noted above, *the Minister must be allowed considerable discretion in evaluating future risk and security concerns.* This factor *also suggests a degree of deference to the Minister's choice of procedures since Parliament has signaled the difficulty of the decision by leaving to the Minister the choice of how best to make it.* At the same time, *this need for deference must be reconciled with the elevated level of procedural protections mandated by the serious situation of refugees* like Suresh, who if deported may face torture and violations of human rights in which Canada can neither constitutionally, nor under its international treaty obligations, be complicit. [Emphasis added.]

118   For a review of this case from a disclosure perspective see "Knowing the Case to be Met – Disclosure", above.

119   2002 SCC 3, 37 Admin. L.R. (3d) 252 (S.C.C.).

120   *Ibid.* at paras. 69-71.

the giving of reasons (when requested), and a right to seek judicial review of the I.A.D.'s decision (during which time the statutory stay of the removal order is in place). That these procedures are designed to meet the requirements of natural justice can be inferred from Wilson J.'s statement in *Singh, supra*, at p. 199, that a hearing before the I.A.B., the I.A.D.'s predecessor, is "a quasi-judicial one to which full natural justice would apply". These procedures help ensure that any relevant *Charter* rights will be respected. Parliament did not give the Minister similar tools for making ss. 52 or 114(2) decisions, where no oral hearing is required, no witnesses can be called, and a statutory stay is not provided either pending the decision or if judicial review is sought.

As Cory J. stated, in dissent, in *Pushpanathan, supra*, at para. 157, when an individual faces removal from Canada:

> . . . it would be unthinkable if there were not a fair hearing before an impartial arbiter to determine whether there are "substantial grounds for believing" that the individual to be deported would face a risk of torture, arbitrary execution, disappearance or other such serious violation of human rights. In light of the grave consequences of deportation in such a case, there must be an opportunity for a hearing before the individual is deported, and the hearing must comply with all of the principles of natural justice. As well, the individual in question ought to be entitled to have the decision reviewed to ensure that it did indeed comply with those principles.

The protections provided in relation to a s. 70(1)(b) appeal to the I.A.D. satisfy these requirements. *While the Minister's decisions under ss. 52 and 114(2) may well accord with the requirements of natural justice in most cases, I am concerned that this will not always be the case. Baker, supra*, is one example of an instance where the Minister's decision was procedurally deficient. It fell to this Court to clarify that the principles of natural justice guarantee certain rights to individuals who make a s. 114(2) application, including a right to make written submissions to the Minister's delegate who actually makes the decision, a right to receive brief reasons for the decision, and a right to an unbiased decision maker. However, it is clear that the procedural protections required may vary with the context of the case: *Singh, supra*, at p. 213, per Wilson J.; *R. v. Lyons*, [1987] 2 S.C.R. 309, at p. 361, per La Forest J.; *Syndicat des employés de production du Québec et de l'Acadie v. Canada (Canadian Human Rights Commission)*, [1989] 2 S.C.R. 879, at pp. 895-96, per Sopinka J.; *Knight v. Indian Head School Division No. 19*, [1990] 1 S.C.R. 653, at p. 682, per L'Heureux-Dubé J.; *Pearlman v. Manitoba Law Society Judicial*

Committee, [1991] 2 S.C.R. 869, at p. 882; and *Dehghani, supra*, at p. 1076.

> *When faced with the problem of a statute which can be read in two ways, one that accords with the principles of natural justice and one that does not, this Court has consistently adopted the interpretation that favours a fuller assurance that the requirements of natural justice will be met*: Alliance des Professeurs Catholiques de Montréal v. Quebec Labour Relations Board, [1953] 2 S.C.R. 140, at p. 166, per Fauteux J.; *Nicholson v. Haldimand-Norfolk Regional Board of Commissioners of Police*, [1979] 1 S.C.R. 311, at p. 328, per Laskin C.J.; and *Singh, supra*, at p. 200, per Wilson J. Therefore, for the purposes of this appeal, a reading of the Act which allows permanent residents to have foreign hardship considered by the I.A.D., where a likely country of removal has been established, is preferable. [Emphasis added.]

(ii) Common law and Statutory Requirements for Oral Hearings

The cases consistently hold that there is no common law right to an oral hearing *per se*. In *Pacific Rim Credit Union v. British Columbia (Attorney General)*,[121] the court noted that the right to an oral hearing ". . . depends in large part on the terms of the statute and regulations which govern the procedures before a particular tribunal."[122]

In *McInroy v. R.*,[123] the Federal Court held that while the duty to act fairly applies to purely administrative actions, that duty does not necessarily include the requirement of an oral hearing. Interestingly, the case involved issues of credibility. A prison inmate was transferred to another institution on the basis of allegations that he was involved in certain disciplinary offenses. He denied the allegations in written submissions, but further requested an oral hearing which was denied. The court found that it was sufficient that he had notice of the proceedings and an opportunity to respond to the allegations in writing. The court found there was no duty at either common law or in the statute to hold a full hearing. This seems to be contrary to the position taken by the Supreme Court in *Singh*, but the two most important factors cited by Beetz J. were the nature of the legal rights at issue and the severity of the consequences to the individuals concerned. While not expressly examined in the Federal Court's decision, the fact that McInroy's rights were not substantially adversely affected may have been an element in the court's reasoning.

In *Murphy v. Dowhaniuk*,[124] the court accepted the Workers Compensation Board's conclusion that an oral hearing is unnecessary if the alternative means of placing evidence before it is sufficient. Dowhaniuk injured Murphy while at work. Murphy's counsel sought an oral hearing so that, in particular, he

---

121 (1988), 32 Admin. L.R. 49 (B.C. S.C.).
122 *Ibid.* at 58.
123 (1985), 13 Admin. L.R. 8 (Fed. T.D.).
124 *Murphy, supra* note 98.

could cross-examine witnesses to determine whether horseplay was involved in the accident.[125] The board denied him this opportunity and found that, although horseplay was involved, it was not a sufficient deviation from the course of Murphy's employment to take the situation out of the Act. The board reached this conclusion based on affidavit evidence only. The court upheld the board's decision because the board had reached the conclusion that Murphy's counsel wished to establish by cross-examination (that is, that horseplay had been involved). Written submissions were sufficient.

It might be argued that had counsel had the opportunity to cross-examine on the affidavit evidence, he might have been able to demonstrate a different degree of horseplay, thus taking the issue out of the Act and leading to a different conclusion. The facts were in dispute and Murphy's rights were adversely affected with serious consequences for him. This seems to satisfy the criteria established in *Singh* and should have secured Murphy an oral hearing.

In *Toronto Independent Dance Enterprise v. Canada Council*,[126] the Federal Court identified several factors to consider when determining whether an oral hearing is required. The dance enterprise had been receiving Canada Council grants for several years. After several warnings about the operation of the group, additional annual grant applications were rejected, without an oral hearing. In deciding that an oral hearing was not necessary, Rouleau J. raised the distinction between rights and benefits,[127] concluding that only a 'benefit' was involved here and when a benefit is involved, the decision to grant an oral hearing is purely discretionary. Secondly, he implied that the standard is lower because the Council was not staffed by public officials. Thirdly, he emphasized that the Council had the authority to establish its own procedures and that the courts should not be quick to interfere. Finally, he noted that it would be impossible to grant a hearing to all applicants. Thus, for the sake of efficiency, some should not be entitled to this aspect of *audi alteram partem*.

An oral hearing has been required for a rehearing, despite there being no new facts or legal arguments and where the same tribunal was sitting on review as had heard the original application;[128] the requirement has been extended to the sanctioning stage of an administrative process;[129] an oral hearing was held after a decision was insufficient;[130] and, when there was conflicting evidence

---

125 The issue was whether Murphy's injury "arose out of and in the course of his employment." If so, Murphy was restricted to a claim under the *Workers Compensation Act,* R.S.B.C. 1979, c. 437.

126 (1989), 38 Admin. L.R. 231 (Fed. T.D.).

127 Although note that in *Singh, supra* note 99, per Wilson J. at 187, this distinction was found to be irrelevant for *Charter* purposes.

128 *Assn. des consommateurs industriels de gaz c. Québec (Régie du gaz naturel)* (1988), 42 Admin. L.R. 291 (Que. S.C.).

129 *Fog Cutter Inc. v. New Brunswick (Liquor Licensing Board)* (1989), 38 Admin. L.R. 123 (N.B. Q.B.).

130 *Barrett v. Northern Lights School Division No. 133*, [1988] 3 W.W.R. 500 (Sask. C.A.).

regarding a central issue.[131] Oral hearings themselves must be conducted in accordance with principles of procedural fairness.[132]

The Supreme Court discussed the right to an oral hearing in *Baker v. Canada (Minister of Citizenship & Immigration).*[133] This case involved an applicant who had entered Canada illegally but who had supported herself for 11 years before being diagnosed as paranoid schizophrenic and obtaining welfare. She had four children, all born in Canada. She was ordered deported but she applied for an exemption from the requirement to apply for permanent residence from outside of Canada based on humanitarian and compassionate grounds. With counsel's help, she filed her application with supporting documentation which indicated she was making progress towards recovery but might relapse if forced to return to Jamaica where there was no treatment. She was the sole caregiver for two of her children and co-depended on her other two children. An immigration officer denied her request on the ground that there were insufficient humanitarian and compassionate grounds to warrant processing her application for permanent residence. No reasons were given. However, there were notes provided by the investigating immigration officer to the immigration officer who made the decision.[134] Ms. Baker applied for judicial review.

On the subject of the right to an oral hearing, Madam Justice L'Heureux Dube commented on what the duty of fairness required in these circumstances and held that, in this case, the circumstances did not warrant an oral hearing. In balancing these factors, the court held that the circumstances required:[135]

> . . . a full and fair consideration of the issues, and the claimant and others whose important interests are affected by the decision in a fundamental way must have a meaningful opportunity to present the various types of evidence relevant to their case and have it fully and fairly considered.

> *However, it also cannot be said that an oral hearing is always necessary to ensure a fair hearing and consideration of the issues involved. The flexible nature of the duty of fairness recognizes that meaningful participation can occur in different ways in different situations.* The Federal Court has held that procedural fairness does not require an oral hearing in these circumstances: see, for example, *Said, supra*, at p. 30.

---

131   *Cadillac Investments Ltd. v. Northwest Territories (Labour Standards Board)* (1993), 24 Admin. L.R. (2d) 81 (N.W.T. S.C.), but the court acknowledged that generally the type of hearing is a matter within the discretion of the board.

132   *Kane v. University of British Columbia*, [1980] 3 W.W.R. 125 (S.C.C.).

133   (1999), 14 Admin. L.R. (3d) 173 (S.C.C.).

134   The Supreme Court would later hold these notes as sufficient to constitute the reasons for the decision and sufficient to make a finding of bias on the part of the immigration officer.

135   *Baker, supra* note 133 at paras. 32-34.

I agree that an oral hearing is not a general requirement for H & C decisions. An interview is not essential for the information relevant to an H & C application to be put before an immigration officer, so that the humanitarian and compassionate considerations presented may be considered in their entirety and in a fair manner. In this case, the appellant had the opportunity to put forward, in written form through her lawyer, information about her situation, her children and their emotional dependence on her, and documentation in support of her application from a social worker at the Children's Aid Society and from her psychiatrist. These documents were before the decision-makers, and they contained the information relevant to making this decision. *Taking all the factors relevant to determining the content of the duty of fairness into account, the lack of an oral hearing or notice of such a hearing did not, in my opinion, constitute a violation of the requirements of procedural fairness to which Ms. Baker was entitled in the circumstances, particularly given the fact that several of the factors point toward a more relaxed standard.* The opportunity, which was accorded, for the appellant or her children to produce full and complete written documentation in relation to all aspects of her application satisfied the requirements of the participatory rights required by the duty of fairness in this case. [Emphasis added]

In *Baker*, the Supreme Court has confirmed that procedural fairness cannot only be satisfied through the means of an oral hearing because the flexible nature of the duty of fairness recognizes that meaningful participation can occur in different ways in different situations. Whether to grant an oral hearing is a matter of discretion. The form of hearing may be of a summary type procedure. A full blown traditional type of "judicial" hearing is not required absent statutory requirement.[136] The presence of conflicting evidence does not necessarily dictate that an oral hearing be necessary. In some cases, written submissions will suffice.[137]

(iii) Right of Reply

The right of reply is a right that almost invariably exists in an oral hearing, and may, in the appropriate circumstances exist where written representations are made.[138]

It is common ground that at oral hearings it is the invariable practice to allow reply by the party bearing the onus. It is not easy to see why this practice should vary where the representations are made in writing. . .(Here) fairness required that the party bearing the onus of proof

---

136 *LeClair v. Manitoba (Director, Residential Care)*, [1999] 9 W.W.R. 583 (Man. C.A.).
137 *Cougar Aviation Ltd. v. Canada (Minister of Public Works & Government Services)* (2000), [2000] F.C.J. No. 1946, 2000 CarswellNat 2925 (Fed. C.A.).
138 See for example *Madsen v. Canada (Attorney General)* (1996), 39 Admin. L.R. (2d) 248 (Fed. T.D.).

should have the right of reply, and that the failure to provide such an opportunity constituted a reviewable error.[139]

(e) Legitimate Expectations

Another issue which arises at the pre-hearing stage is the doctrine of legitimate expectations. The doctrine of legitimate expectations is part of the doctrine of fairness but it does not create substantive rights, only procedural protections. It is based on the principle that ". . . the 'circumstances' affecting procedural fairness take into account the promises or regular practices of administrative decision-makers, and that it will generally be unfair for them to act in contravention of representations as to procedure, or to backtrack on substantive promises without according significant procedural rights."[140]

In *Baker*, legitimate expectations were listed as the fourth factor affecting the content of the duty of fairness.[141]

> Fourth, the legitimate expectations of the person challenging the de-
> cision may also determine what procedures the duty of fairness re-
> quires in given circumstances. Our Court has held that, in Canada,
> this doctrine is part of the doctrine of fairness or natural justice, and
> that it does not create substantive rights: *Old St. Boniface, supra*, at
> p. 1204; *Reference re Canada Assistance Plan (B.C.)*, [1991] 2 S.C.R.
> 525, at p. 557. As applied in Canada, if a legitimate expectation is
> found to exist, this will affect the content of the duty of fairness owed
> to the individual or individuals affected by the decision. If the claimant
> has a legitimate expectation that a certain procedure will be followed,
> this procedure will be required by the duty of fairness: *Qi v. Canada
> (Minister of Citizenship and Immigration)* (1995), 33 Imm. L.R. (2d)
> 57 (F.C.T.D.); *Mercier-Néron v. Canada (Minister of National Health
> and Welfare)* (1995), 98 F.T.R. 36; *Bendahmane v. Canada (Minister
> of Employment and Immigration)*, [1989] 3 F.C. 16 (C.A.). Similarly,
> if a claimant has a legitimate expectation that a certain result will be
> reached in his or her case, fairness may require more extensive pro-
> cedural rights than would otherwise be accorded: D. J. Mullan, *Ad-
> ministrative Law* (3rd ed. 1996), at pp. 214-15; D. Shapiro, "Legiti-
> mate Expectation and its Application to Canadian Immigration Law"
> (1992), 8 *J.L. & Social Pol'y* 282, at p. 297; *Canada (Attorney Gen-
> eral) v. Human Rights Tribunal Panel (Canada)* (1994), 76 F.T.R. 1.
> Nevertheless, the doctrine of legitimate expectations cannot lead to
> substantive rights outside the procedural domain. This doctrine, as
> applied in Canada, is based on the principle that the "circumstances"
> affecting procedural fairness take into account the promises or regular

---

139   *Goyal v. Canada (Minister of Employment & Immigration)* (1992), 4 Admin. L.R. (2d) 159
     at 160-61 (Fed. C.A.). See also *Puxley v. Canada (Treasury Board - Transport Canada)*
     (1994), 24 Admin. L.R. (2d) 43 (Fed. T.D.).
140   *Baker, supra* note 133 at para. 26.
141   *Ibid.* at para. 26.

practices of administrative decision-makers, and that it will generally be unfair for them to act in contravention of representations as to procedure, or to backtrack on substantive promises without according significant procedural rights.

In *Centre hospitalier Mont-Sinaï c. Québec (Ministre de la Santé & des Services sociaux)*,[142] Mr. Justice Binnie considered whether the respondent hospital had a reasonable expectation that a permit recognized the de facto change in the character of the hospital's operations.

Over several years, with the full knowledge of government officials and with public funding, Mount Sinai Hospital changed the character of its operations, but not its permit. The hospital wished to obtain a permit which accurately reflected its mix of services. A series of Ministers were aware, cooperative and encouraging. They promised on several occasions to renew the permit to reflect the reality of the situation after the move.[143] After the move was complete, a formal application for an accurate permit was made. The formal request was refused based upon financial reasons (which all judges found to be groundless). However, the government continued to fund the new facility and allowed it to operate without the permit.

The hospital applied for *mandamus* to force the Minister to exercise his discretion to issue a permit reflecting reality.[144] The hospital argued it was entitled to the permit for several reasons:

- it had an acquired right to the permit and the factual situation should be regularized;

- procedural fairness entitled it to a permit;

- legitimate expectations entitled it to a permit;

- the Minister was estopped from refusing to issue the permit; and,

- the ongoing refusal constituted an abuse of discretion.

Most of these arguments would lead only to procedural relief – a new hearing. But the hospital sought substantive relief – a permit. The Minister

---

142   2001 SCC 41, 200 D.L.R. (4th) 193 (S.C.C.).

143   Justice Binnie for the minority sums up the interactions as follows at para. 8:
This case is not the simple scenario of an application for a permit followed by a refusal "in the public interest." From 1984 onwards the respondents worked closely with Ministry regulators. A web of understandings and incremental agreements came into existence with the concurrence indeed encouragement of successive Ministers. What perhaps began with an abstract notion of "the public interest" became, through private initiative and ministerial response, a specific embodiment of the public interest in terms of bricks and mortar, facilities and locations. Not only did successive Ministers subscribe to this embodiment of the public interest, they encouraged the respondents to act on it. If this were a private law situation there would likely be a breach of contract. This is not, of course, a private law situation.

144   The relevant law provided that the Minister was required to issue modified permits under s. 138 of the *Act respecting health services and social services*, R.S.Q., c. S-5 , if he formed the opinion, as a matter of policy, that the public interest was served by the modified permit.

argued that none of the grounds advanced entitled the hospital to substantive relief (the permit). In particular, it contended that estoppel could not be used against the Minister.

The Court rejected the hospital's arguments concerning legitimate expectations[145] on the basis that the doctrine can be used to compel only procedural – not substantive – relief. In doing so, the Supreme Court of Canada affirmed certain long-standing authorities including the principles about legitimate expectations established in *Old St. Boniface*.[146] Justice Binnie reiterated that the doctrine of legitimate expectations looks to the conduct of the delegate in the exercise of statutory power including established practices, conduct or representations that can be characterized as clear, unambiguous and unqualified.[147]

The Supreme Court of Canada held in two subsequent cases that the requirements for the application of the concept of legitimate expectation as a part of the principles of natural justice and procedural fairness had not been made out.

(i) *Moreau-Bérubé v. New Brunswick*

Although both of the lower courts[148] in *Moreau-Bérubé v. New Brunswick* had held that the principles of natural justice had been breached when the Judicial Council had not put the provincial court judge on notice that it was considering a penalty more severe than the one recommended by the investigative panel, the Supreme Court – surprisingly, in our view – held that the requirements of procedural fairness had been complied with.[149]

After acknowledging that the requirements of procedural fairness applied to the proceedings in question, Madam Justice Arbour noted that no assessment of the appropriate standard of judicial review was required, beyond "fairness" in the particular situation.[150] She then rejected the argument that the judge had

---

145 The majority did, however, rule that the past actions of the government and the successive Ministers amounted to an actual exercise of the Minister's discretionary authority and, therefore, the majority ordered the Minister to issue the modified permit as he had failed to act in accordance with a prior exercise of discretion so the criteria for the issuance of an order of mandamus were met. See Bastarache J.'s decision at paras. 99-100.

146 *Old St. Boniface Residents Assn. Inc. v. Winnipeg (City)* (1990), [1991] 2 W.W.R. 145 (S.C.C.) where Sopinka J. stated at 177:

> The principle developed in these cases is simply an extension of the rules of natural justice and procedural fairness. It affords a party affected by the decision of a public official an opportunity to make representations in circumstances in which there otherwise would be no such opportunity. The court supplies the omission where, based on the conduct of the public official, a party has been led to believe that his or her rights would not be affected without consultation.

147 *Centre hospitalier Mont-Sinaï, supra* note 142 at para. 29.

148 (1999), [1999] N.B.J. 320, 218 N.B.R. (2d) 256, 558 A.P.R. 256, 1999 CarswellNB 622 (N.B. Q.B.), affirmed [2000] N.B.J. 368, 2000 NBCA 12, 233 N.B.R. (2d) 205, 601 A.P.R. 205, 194 D.L.R. (4th) 664, 2000 CarswellNB 429 (N.B. C.A.), leave to appeal allowed (2001), 273 N.R. 200 (note) (S.C.C.), reversed [2002] 1 S.C.R. 249 (S.C.C.).

149 2002 SCC 11, 36 Admin. L.R. (3d) 1 (S.C.C.).

150 *Ibid.* at para. 74.

a reasonable expectation[151] that the Judicial Council would not impose a more serious penalty than the recommended reprimand, at least without putting her on specific notice that it was contemplating such a course of action:[152]

> The respondent argues that she had a reasonable expectation that the Council would not impose a penalty more serious than a reprimand for three main reasons:
>
> 1. The inquiry panel had recommended a reprimand, and had found that the respondent was able to continue performing her duties as a Provincial Court judge.
>
> 2. The Council, though it had the discretion to suspend her pending the inquiry's outcome, had allowed the respondent to discharge her judicial function for more than a year following her impugned comments. This, the respondent argues, created an expectation that the Council would proceed on the basis that she was able to continue performing her duties as a judge.
>
> 3. Dismissal had never been expressly contemplated or argued by any person at any level of the inquiry prior to the delivery of that sanction.
>
> Under section 6.11(3), the respondent had the "right to make representations to [the Council] either in person or through counsel and either orally or in writing, *respecting the [panel's report]* prior to the taking of action by the Judicial Council" (emphasis added). She essentially argues that when the panel recommended something less than removal from the bench, they indirectly took away her ability to argue against that sanction, and that her representations to the Council would have been affected had she known that a recommendation for removal from the bench was being considered.
>
> I am not persuaded by any of these arguments. *The doctrine of reasonable expectations* does not create substantive rights, and does not fetter the discretion of a statutory decision-maker. Rather, it *operates as a component of procedural fairness, and finds application when a party affected by an administrative decision can establish a legitimate expectation that a certain procedure would be followed*: Reference re Canada Assistance Plan (B.C.), [1991] 2 S.C.R. 525, at p. 557; Baker, supra, at para. 26. *The doctrine can give rise to a right to make representations, a right to be consulted or perhaps, if circumstances*

---

151   In their dissent in *Mackin v. New Brunswick (Minister of Justice)*, [2002] 1 S.C.R. 405 (S.C.C.), LeBel and Binnie JJ. rejected the application of the legitimate expectation doctrine as not being applicable either to substantive rights or legislative bodies, in the context of changes to the method of remunerating supernumerary provincial court judges (paras. 162-163).

152   *Moreau-Bérubé, supra* note 149 at paras. 76-83.

require, more extensive procedural rights. But it does not otherwise fetter the discretion of a statutory decision-maker in order to mandate any particular result: see D. Shapiro, *Legitimate Expectation and its Application to Canadian Immigration Law* (1992), 8 J.L. & Social Pol'y 282, at p. 297.

In the circumstances of this case, I cannot accept that the Council violated Judge Moreau-Bérubé's right to be heard by not expressly informing her that they might impose a sanction clearly open to them under the Act. The doctrine of legitimate expectations can find no application when the claimant is essentially asserting the right to a second chance to avail him- or herself of procedural rights that were always available and provided for by statute. . . . Regardless of the fact that the panel made a recommendation that it was not mandated to make, the Council had a clear and plain discretion to choose between three options. *I do not believe that the respondent, a judge, who had legal advice throughout, could have misapprehended the issues that were alive before the Judicial Council. She never asserted making such an error until it was raised by Angers J. on judicial review.*

The fact that a recommendation for dismissal was not discussed prior to being issued is also not relevant. The Council has no obligation to remind the respondent to read s. 6.11(4) carefully. While the Council might have opted, as a part of their procedure, to remind Judge Moreau-Bérubé that the Council would not be bound by any recommendations made by the inquiry panel, they chose not to, and that was within their discretion. . . .

In coming to the conclusions they did, the Court of Appeal and Angers J. relied in particular on *Michaud, supra.* I agree with Drapeau J.A. that *Michaud* is distinguishable. In that case, the recommended sanction was a product of a joint submission and the affected person made no representations. By contrast, *Judge Moreau-Bérubé's counsel made arguments before the tribunal to the effect that no reprimand should be administered, contrary to the recommendation of the inquiry panel. This demonstrates that the respondent was well aware that the Council was not bound by the recommendations of the inquiry panel and that it would come to its own independent decision about the sanction that was appropriate in light of the misconduct. She herself was urging the Council to disregard the recommendation of the inquiry panel.*

I agree with the comments of Drapeau J.A. who noted that [TRANSLATION] "it is undeniable that at each step where she had the right, Judge Moreau-Bérubé was fully heard" (para. 150). Acknowledging that the nature of these disciplinary proceedings imposes on the Coun-

cil a stringent duty to act fairly, I can find no breach of the rules of natural justice in the context of this case. [Emphasis added.]

With the greatest of respect, this passage seems to mix up two questions: (1) did the Judicial Council have the statutory power to impose removal from office, and (2) were the procedures which it used in exercising its powers "fair"? An affirmative answer to the first question does not necessarily entail an affirmative answer to the second question. Nor does the fact that a decision-maker has been given authority to choose its procedure necessarily determine whether the procedure actually chosen is "fair".

While there may be no obligation on a decision-maker to remind a party to read the applicable legislation carefully, and while there is no doubt that the decision-maker in this case had the power to impose the sanction it did, surely the central question has to be: "In all the circumstances, was the procedure which was used unfair to this particular person?" Ultimately, that is a question for the court – ultimately, indeed, for the highest court. Of course the Supreme Court's decision that the procedure in this case was not unfair is final; but it is troubling that two lower courts reached the opposite conclusion on this very point. This indicates that "fairness" – like other determinations of whether the appropriate standard of review has been breached – is clearly in the eye of the beholder.

(ii) The Retired Judges Case

The Supreme Court of Canada also held that the requirements for the application of the legitimate expectation doctrine had not been met in *C.U.P.E. v. Ontario (Minister of Labour).*[153] In rejecting the Ontario Court of Appeal's ruling that the unions had a legitimate expectation that the Minister would appoint arbitrators from the recognized list of labour arbitrators, Mr. Justice Binnie provided the following analysis:[154]

> The doctrine of legitimate expectation is "an extension of the rules of natural justice and procedural fairness": *Reference re Canada Assistance Plan (B.C.),* [1991] 2 S.C.R. 525, at p. 557. It looks to the conduct of a Minister or other public authority in the exercise of a discretionary power including established practices, conduct or representations that can be characterized as clear, unambiguous and unqualified, that has induced in the complainants (here the unions) a reasonable expectation that they will retain a benefit or be consulted before a contrary decision is taken. To be "legitimate", such expectations must not conflict with a statutory duty. See: *Old St. Boniface Residents Assn. Inc. v. Winnipeg (City),* [1990] 3 S.C.R. 1170; *Baker, supra; Mount Sinai, supra,* at para. 29; *Brown and Evans, supra,* at para. 7-2431. Where the conditions for its application are satisfied,

---

153 2003 SCC 29, 50 Admin. L.R. (3d) 1 (S.C.C.) (the *"Retired Judges Case"*).
154 *Ibid.* at paras. 131-133 and 146.

the Court may grant appropriate procedural remedies to respond to the "legitimate" expectation.

The Court of Appeal concluded, at para. 105, that "the Minister interfered with the legitimate expectations of the appellants and other affected unions, contrary to the principles and requirements of fairness and natural justice" and ordered the Minister to restrict his appointments to the s. 49(10) roster.

In my view, with respect, the conditions precedent to the application of the doctrine are not established in this case. . . .

In my view, the evidence does not establish a firm "practice" in the past of appointing from a HLDAA list, or from the s. 49(10) list, or proceeding by way of "mutual agreement". A general promise "to continue under the existing system" where the reference to the system itself is ambiguous, and in any event was stated by the Minister to be subject to reform, cannot bind the Minister's exercise of his or her s. 6(5) discretion as urged by the unions under the doctrine of legitimate expectation. [Emphasis added.]

Taken together, these two cases might well indicate that it will be quite hard to find cases where the legitimate expectation doctrine will be able to be successfully used.

However, by contrast, the decision of the British Columbia Court of Appeal in *British Columbia (Securities Commission) v. Pacific International Securities Inc.*[155] is an example of a case where the court found that a legitimate expectation did exist. Identifying legitimate expectation as to the procedure to be followed as one of the five factors from *Baker* to be used to determine the content of the duty of fairness in a particular context, Mr. Justice Smith held as follows:[156]

The legitimate expectations of participants in the hearing are another contextual consideration that informs the nature and degree of procedural fairness required. Here, the Commission has created legitimate expectations as to the level of particularization. Although it is not subjected to any statutory or regulatory requirement to provide particulars, it has prepared and published policy documents, including policies relating to Commission hearings. They proclaim a policy of full disclosure and provide, *inter alia*, that ". . . the Executive Director will disclose to each respondent particulars of the allegations in sufficient detail to give the respondent a fair opportunity to know and meet the case against the respondent" (Policy Doc. No. 15-601, s. 2.5(b)). Thus, the appellants are legitimately entitled to expect to receive particulars that meet this standard.

---

155 [2002] 8 W.W.R. 116 (B.C. C.A.).
156 *Ibid.* at para. 14.

However, although the appellants had a legitimate expectation to receive particulars of the alleged offence, the Court of Appeal ruled that the Commission had in fact complied with that obligation.

(f) Summary of Duty of Fairness in Pre-Hearing Procedures

It is now generally accepted that the duty of fairness applies to the pre-hearing stages of the administrative process where decisions are made that affect individuals. But the duty of fairness is flexible and variable, and its content depends on the context of the particular statute and the circumstances of the case, including the rights affected. Just because the duty exists, its existence does not determine what requirements will be applicable in a given set of circumstances.

In *Baker*, the Supreme Court provided a list of factors which courts must consider when determining the content of the duty of fairness, but the list is not exhaustive.

3. Oral Hearing Processes

This part of the chapter will examine what elements of fair procedure apply in the context of oral hearings.[157] Where a tribunal has granted a party an oral hearing, the content of the required duty of fairness varies, as always, with the context and the circumstances of each case. The trappings and formalities of the traditional court room setting often do not lend themselves well to the administrative context. In many cases, one of the advantages of the administrative tribunal's process is its informality. The rules of judicial procedure do not apply to administrative tribunals where each tribunal, subject to its enabling statute, is master of its own procedures.

(a) Cross-examination of Witnesses

When an oral hearing is held, rather than a hearing based solely on written submissions and documents, the right to call witnesses and to cross-examine them is generally part of the procedure protected by the duty of fairness.

The right to cross-examination, like the right to an oral hearing, depends on a variety of circumstances. Clearly it may be required by statute, but where the statute is silent, and the tribunal is the governor of its own procedure, the common law is reluctant to impose courtroom procedures and technical rules of evidence. The tribunal is master of its own procedure and a right to cross-examine witnesses does not necessarily follow from a right to be represented by counsel.[158] The very nature of cross-examination is adversarial, and this

---

157   As discussed in the previous section, it is important to emphasize that the rules of procedural fairness do not require that a hearing be oral. See for example *Stuart v. Haughley Parochial Church Council*, [1935] Ch. 452, affirmed [1936] Ch. 32 (lay electoral commission). See also discussion under "Pre-Hearing Procedures – Form of Hearing", above.

158   *Del Zotto v. Minister of National Revenue*, [2000] 4 F.C. 321 (Fed. C.A.), leave to appeal refused (2001), 268 N.R. 196 (note) (S.C.C.).

may be incompatible with the nature of the tribunal.[159] Neither the right to call witnesses, nor the right to cross-examine witnesses is unlimited. A tribunal can reasonably limit both.[160] However, cross-examination may be a necessary element of procedural fairness where important issues of credibility are raised, or where there is no other effective means of refuting the allegations or arguments of the other side.[161]

(i) Innisfil (Township) v. Vespra (Township)

The Supreme Court of Canada has also examined the issue of when a tribunal will be required to allow cross-examination in order to fulfil the requirements of procedural fairness. In *Innisfil (Township) v. Vespra (Township)*,[162] Estey J. provided the historical backdrop for the differences in requirements between courts of law and administrative tribunals, and in particular the requirement for the opportunity to cross-examine:[163]

> It is within the context of a statutory process that it must be noted that cross-examination is a vital element of the adversarial system applied and followed in our legal system, including, in many instances, before administrative tribunals since the earliest times. Indeed the adversarial system, founded on cross-examination and the right to meet the case being made against the litigant, civil or criminal, is the procedural substructure upon which the common law itself has been built. That is not to say that because our court system is founded upon these institutions and procedures that administrative tribunals must apply the same techniques. Indeed, there are many tribunals in the modern community which do not follow the traditional adversarial road. On the other hand, where the rights of the citizens are involved and the statute affords him the right to a full hearing, including a hearing of his demonstration of his rights, one would expect to find the clearest statutory curtailment of the citizen's right to meet the case made against him by cross-examination. . . .

---

159   See *Wolfe v. Robinson* (1961), [1962] O.R. 132 (Ont. C.A.), where the Ontario Court of Appeal held that there was no right to cross-examine witnesses at a coroner's inquest because there is no accused; see also *Syncrude Canada Ltd. v. Michetti* (1993), 7 Alta. L.R. (3d) 382 (Alta. Q.B.) where Perras J. noted that the Workers' Compensation Board Appeals Commission operated on an inquiry model, and had no procedure or practice for cross-examination. Given that, and the applicant's ability to respond both orally and in written submissions, there was no breach of procedural fairness. This was reversed on appeal (1994), 28 Admin. L.R. (2d) 155 (Alta. C.A.), additional reasons at (1995), 165 A.R. 89 (Alta. C.A.). According to the appellant court, as the expert sought to be cross-examined was also an advisor to the decision maker, the boards' refusal to allow either cross-examination or the use of written interrogations, as well as other deficiencies, took the board out of jurisdiction.

160   *Kirchmeir v. Boulanger*, 2000 ABCA 324 (Alta. C.A.).

161   See *Puxley v. Canada (Treasury Board - Transport Canada)* (1994), 24 Admin. L.R. (2d) 43 (Fed. T.D.).

162   [1981] 2 S.C.R. 145 (S.C.C.), varied [1982] 1 S.C.R. 1107 (S.C.C.).

163   *Ibid.* at 166-68.

The procedural format adopted by the administrative tribunal must adhere to the provisions of the parent statute of the Board. The process of interpreting and applying statutory policy will be the dominant influence in the workings of such an administrative tribunal. Where the Board proceeds in the discharge of its mandate to determine the rights of the contending parties before it on the traditional basis wherein the onus falls upon the contender to introduce the facts and submissions upon which he will rely, the Board's technique will take on something of the appearance of a traditional court. Where, on the other hand, the Board, by its legislative mandate or the nature of the subject matter assigned to its administration, is more concerned with community interests at large, and with technical policy aspects of a specialized subject, one cannot expect the tribunal to function in the manner of the traditional court. This is particularly so where the Board membership is drawn partly or entirely from persons experienced or trained in the sector of activity consigned to the administrative supervision of the Board. Again where the Board in its statutory role takes on the complexion of a department of the executive branch of government concerned with the execution of a policy laid down in broad concept by the Legislature, and where the Board has the delegated authority to issue regulations or has a broad discretionary power to license persons or activities, the trappings and habits of the traditional courts have long ago been discarded.

In this case the Court found that the appellant had a right to cross-examine a ministry official who had introduced a letter stating government policy. It further held that he could not be deprived of that right only because an appellate court thought that it would not advance his case. Nor was the right to cross-examination being used to challenge the executive level of government and engage the tribunal in political action. "It is merely an exercise by a party properly before the Board on an annexation application of a right accorded to that party by the Legislature."[164]

(ii) County of Strathcona v. MacLab Enterprises

In *Strathcona (Municipality) v. Maclab Enterprises Ltd.*,[165] the Alberta Court of Appeal refused to quash a decision by the Provincial Planning Board. The board had admitted into evidence a report by an expert who was unavailable for cross-examination. The court noted that the board had allowed the parties an opportunity to answer any of the points raised by the expert's report, and that they had done so by filing reports by two other experts. Given the board's statutory right to determine its own procedure and rules of practice, this and the fact that the respondents were able to respond with their own experts' reports meant that they had received a fair opportunity to correct or contradict the evidence of the other expert:

---

164 *Ibid.* at 174.
165 [1971] 3 W.W.R. 461 (Alta. C.A.), leave to appeal refused [1971] S.C.R. xii (S.C.C.).

It does not follow that the refusal of or the placing of limitations upon
the right of cross-examination will always require that the court quash
an order made in proceedings in which these restrictions are enforced.
If he is afforded an equally effective method of answering the case
against him, in other words is given "a fair opportunity to correct or
controvert any relevant statement brought forward to his prejudice . . .
the requirements of natural justice will be met.[166]

(iii) Murray v. Council of Municipal District of Rockyview

In *Murray v. Rockyview (Municipal District No. 44)*,[167] the Alberta Court
of Appeal used the same reasoning to determine that the Development Appeal
Board had not met the requirements of procedural fairness in its refusal to
allow cross-examination. The issue arose over development approval of a park.
Three members of the board chose to go on a fact-finding mission and visited
several parks similar to the one proposed. The court found that the refusal to
allow cross-examination, by itself, was not contrary to procedural fairness.
However, when combined with the new evidence gathered by the board members, which the parties were unable to contradict or correct in any other manner,
the limitation of cross-examination was unfair and contrary to the principles
of procedural fairness. A new appeal was ordered to be heard by members of
the board who had not visited the other sites.

In summary, the courts will examine a refusal to allow cross-examination
upon the basis of whether the procedure is fair, whether the tribunal exercises
its discretion in good faith and whether the tribunal listens to both sides.[168] The
relevant circumstances will include whether there is a *lis inter partes*, whether
someone's rights are affected and whether there is conflicting evidence.[169] For
example, in a disciplinary hearing, where someone's reputation and livelihood
is at stake, or where issues of credibility arise, the right to cross-examine will
usually be present.[170] However, if there are no issues of credibility and there

---

166   *Ibid.* at 464.
167   (1980), 12 Alta. L.R. (2d) 342 (Alta. C.A.), leave to appeal refused (1980), 14 Alta. L.R.
      (2d) 86 (Alta. C.A.).
168   *Lipkovits v. C.R.T.C.* (1982), [1983] 2 F.C. 321 (Fed. C.A.), leave to appeal refused (1983),
      72 C.P.R. (2d) 288 (S.C.C.).
169   *Jackson v. Region 2 Hospital Corp.* (1994), 24 Admin. L.R. (2d) 220 (N.B. Q.B.).
170   *Carlin v. Registered Psychiatric Nurses' Assn. (Alberta)* (1996), 39 Admin. L.R. (2d) 177
      (Alta. Q.B.); *Willette v. Royal Canadian Mounted Police Commissioner* (1984), 10 Admin.
      L.R. 149 (Fed. C.A.); *B. v. W.* (1985), 16 Admin. L.R. 99 (Ont. H.C.); *Armstrong v. Royal
      Canadian Mounted Police Commissioner* (1994), 24 Admin. L.R. (2d) 1 (Fed. T.D.),
      affirmed (1998), 156 D.L.R. (4th) 670 (Fed. C.A.) where the court held that the absence of
      a statutory right of cross-examination did not violate the principles of procedural fairness;
      but see *Kuntz v. College of Physicians & Surgeons (British Columbia)* (1987), 24 Admin.
      L.R. 187 (B.C. S.C.) where, although the court recognized that the petitioner's right to
      continue his profession was at stake, and thus there was a high standard of justice required,
      the court found that there was no right to cross-examine. The court found that the petitioner
      would be able to correct or controvert any facts through means other than cross-examination.
      The Court of Appeal affirmed this decision noting that the matter was only at a preliminary
      stage and that the judge did not preclude the possibility that such a right could exist at a
      later stage in the proceedings: (1988), 31 Admin. L.R. 179 (B.C. C.A.).

are other means to determine the facts and ensure full and fair disclosure, cross-examination will not necessarily be required.[171] Similarly, where proceedings are at a preliminary or investigatory stage, there is no right to cross-examination.[172] Tribunals must treat evidence, such as depositions which cannot be cross-examined on, with caution, and keep in mind the fact that there has not been cross-examination on the evidence when determining its weight.[173]

(b) Evidentiary Considerations

The fact that the strict traditional rules of evidence do not apply to administrative tribunals does not mean that tribunals have complete discretion to determine what evidence they will hear.[174] Firstly, the tribunal must not abuse its discretion by basing its decision on insufficient or no evidence, nor on irrelevant considerations.[175] As in other areas of the *audi alteram partem* rule, the tribunal must exercise its discretion to hear evidence in a manner consistent with procedural fairness. In *R. v. Deputy Industrial Injuries Commissioner,*[176] Diplock L.J. listed certain rules for the tribunal. He first confirmed that, in the absence of any statutory requirement, a hearing need not be held. In that case, a delegate *must* consider all written material submitted to him, including the written decision of the lower tribunal which is being appealed. He *may* also consider material from other sources which constitutes "evidence". Such "evidence" is:

> . . . not restricted to evidence which could be admissible in a court of law. For historical reasons, based on the fear that juries who might be illiterate would be incapable of differentiating between the probative values of different methods of proof, the practice of the common law courts has been to admit only what the judges then regarded as the best evidence of any disputed fact, and thereby to exclude much material which, as a matter of common sense, would assist a fact-finding tribunal to reach a correct conclusion: *cf. Myers v,. Director of Public Prosecutions*, [1964] 3 W.L.R. 145.

> These technical rules of evidence, however form no part of the rules of procedural fairness. The requirement that a person exercising quasi-judicial functions must base his decision on evidence means no more than it must be based upon material which tends logically to

---

171 See *B. v. W., ibid.*

172 *Onischak v. British Columbia (Council of Human Rights)* (1989), 38 Admin. L.R. 258 (B.C. S.C.); *Irvine v. Canada (Restrictive Trade Practices Commission)* (1987), 24 Admin. L.R. 91 (S.C.C.).

173 *Four Star Management Ltd. v. British Columbia (Securities Commission)* (1990), 43 Admin. L.R. 274 (B.C. C.A.), leave to appeal refused [1991] 1 S.C.R. xv (S.C.C.).

174 For further discussion on evidence and administrative tribunals see J.L.H. Sprague, "Evidence before Administrative Agencies: Let's All Forget the "Rules" and Just Concentrate on What We're Doing" (1994-1995) 8 C.J.A.L.P. 263.

175 See Chapter 7.

176 (1964), [1965] 1 Q.B. 456 at 488, 490 (Eng. C.A.).

show the existence or non-existence of facts relevant to the issue to be determined, or to show the likelihood or unlikelihood of the occurrence of some future event the occurrence of which would be relevant. It means that he must not spin a coin or consult an astrologer, but he may take into account any material which, as a matter of reason, has some probative value in the sense mentioned above. If it is capable of having any probative value, the weight to be attached to it is a matter for the person to whom Parliament has entrusted the responsibility of deciding the issue. The supervisory jurisdiction of the High Court does not entitle it to usurp this responsibility and to substitute its own view for his.

Many boards and tribunals are explicitly exempted from the traditional judicial rules of admissibility by their empowering statute.[177] This exemption does not mean, however, that tribunals are free to accept or reject evidence as they please.[178] In general, the courts have found that tribunals are ". . . entitled to act on any material which is logically probative, even though it is not evidence in a court of law."[179]

The law of evidence dealing with such issues as hearsay, requirements for disclosure, and taking views, while not technically determinative, will often still be relevant. These rules were developed within the context of ensuring relevance and reliability,[180] and relevance and reliability are vital to the determination of whether the admission of certain evidence in an administrative proceeding would jeopardize the fairness of the proceeding.[181] Factors such as expediency, the (sometimes) limited legal expertise of tribunal members, and the perception that administrative tribunals are intended to be less formal mitigates against strict observance of the technical rules. The overriding factor is whether the hearing is fair given all the circumstances.

(i) Judicial Notice

Members of administrative tribunals are very often distinguishable from judges in the amount of specialised knowledge they bring with them to the

---

177 For example, the *Labour Relations Code*, R.S.A. 2000, c. L- 1, s. 14(5) provides that:
   The Board
    (a) may accept any oral or written evidence that it, in its discretion, considers proper, whether admissible in a court of law or not, and
    (b) is not bound by the law of evidence applicable to judicial proceedings.

178 Boards are bound by the duty to be fair and must act on reliable and persuasive information: *Mooring v. Canada (National Parole Board)* (1996), 38 Admin. L.R. (2d) 149 (S.C.C.). The court ruled that the Parole Board did not possess the authority to exclude evidence obtained in violation of the *Charter*.

179 *T.A. Miller Ltd. v. Minister of Housing & Local Government*, [1968] 1 W.L.R. 992 (Eng. C.A.), per Lord Denning at 995.

180 Note the prevailing movement towards a more flexible approach to evidence law, emphasizing reliability, relevance and necessity exemplified in cases such as *R. v. Khan*, 59 C.C.C. (3d) 92, [1990] 2 S.C.R. 531 (S.C.C.); *R. v. Smith* (1992), 75 C.C.C. (3d) 257 (S.C.C.).

181 See also M.R. Gorsky, "Effective Advocacy and the Continuing Significance of the Rules of Evidence before Administrative Tribunals" (1989) 2 C.J.A.L.P. 47.

task at hand. Judges rarely have more than a general knowledge of the subject matter they are dealing with. However, many tribunals are composed of members appointed specifically because they have personal knowledge in a particular area. Yet judicial notice has traditionally been restricted.[182] Courts have been able to take judicial notice of facts which are (a) so notorious as not to be the subject of dispute among reasonable persons, or (b) capable of immediate and accurate demonstration by resorting to readily accessible sources of indisputable accuracy.[183]

To restrict their ability to take judicial notice of only notoriously known or verifiable facts would defeat one of the rationales for the appointment of specialized tribunals. The courts have recognized that this difference between themselves and tribunals implies that the more restrictive rules do not apply to administrative bodies. The requirement is that the procedure be fair.[184] This generally involves a certain degree of disclosure concerning the tribunal member's background. The difficult issue is what knowledge must be disclosed.

Clearly, where an adjudicator has sought information from identifiable sources, these sources must be disclosed so that the individual may raise evidence to answer it. A more difficult problem arises in trying to determine what portion of a tribunal member's background of personal knowledge must be disclosed. This knowledge will include information acquired through education, experience and participation in the tribunal itself.[185] In his article, "The Problem of "Official Notice": Reliance by Administrative Tribunals on the Personal Knowledge of their Members", J.A. Smillie[186] formulates the problem this way:

> The courts have appreciated that the requirement of disclosure cannot normally be extended to the subjective reasoning and mental processes of an adjudicator, and some have attempted to draw a distinction for the purposes of disclosure between a tribunal's use of *facts*

---

182 *Anadarko Petroleum of Canada Ltd. v. Syd Johns Farms Ltd.*, [1975] 6 W.W.R. 350 (B.C. S.C.); *Johnston v. Canada (Minister of Veteran Affairs)* (1990), 108 N.R. 306 (Fed. C.A.). However, in *Countertop Microwave Ovens, Re* (1984), 8 Admin. L.R. 173 (Fed. C.A.), the court held that failure to disclose a report was not fatal to the decision because the report contained only general or public information.

183 J. Sopinka, S.N. Lederman & A.W. Bryant, *The Law of Evidence in Canada* (Toronto: Butterworths, 1992) at 976. In *Gargoyles Lounge Inc. v. New Brunswick (Minister of Finance)* (1996), 48 Admin. L.R. (2d) 157 (N.B. C.A.), the court noted that an adjudicator should not impose a sentence based in part upon the unproven personal belief that the violation was not an isolated event.

184 *Huerto v. College of Physicians & Surgeons (Saskatchewan)* (1996), 34 Admin. L.R. (2d) 159 (Sask. C.A.) the court ruled that a disciplinary tribunal acted unfairly in relying upon the personal knowledge of its members to determine the proper standard of care. The committee effectively denied the member before them of the ability to test or cross examine on this key issue. See also I.F. Ivankovich, "Case Comment: Heurto v. College of Physicians & Surgeons (Saskatchewan)" (1995) 29 Admin. L.R. (2d) 121.

185 However, an adjudicator cannot use his or her own specialized training or expertise as a substitute for evidence: *Dennis v. British Columbia (Superintendent of Motor Vehicles)*, 2000 BCCA 653 (B.C. C.A.).

186 [1975] *Public Law* 64 at 69.

within its knowledge to *supplement*, or as a *substitute for*, evidence properly and openly presented to it, and its use of its accumulated background of special knowledge, understanding and experience to *evaluate and assess* the evidence properly presented. By this view, the principles of natural justice require factual information within the knowledge of a tribunal to be disclosed to the parties for comment and rebuttal if the tribunal intends to place reliance upon it in reaching its decision, but a tribunal is entitled to use, without any obligation of disclosure, its accumulated background of experience, skill, and specialized knowledge in analysing and evaluating the evidence properly presented to it, assessing the weight to be placed upon specific items of evidence, and drawing conclusions of "ultimate" fact from the "basic" or "primary" facts proved in evidence.

In *Singh v. Canada (Minister of Employment & Immigration)*,[187] the Federal Court of Appeal allowed a decision by the Immigration Appeal Board to stand, although the board's decision was based on information it considered to be common knowledge. The board made reference to the political situation in India at the time that Singh, an applicant for convention refugee status, alleged he had been abused. This information was used to discredit Singh's testimony given under oath during the hearing. No evidence of the political situation was presented during the hearing, and the applicant was unaware of the board's reliance upon the information until the reasons for the decision were released.

Heald J., writing for himself and Pratte J., concluded that the board could take judicial notice of information it had acquired during the day to day workings of the board. Heald J. quoted *Maslej v. Canada (Minister of Manpower & Immigration)*:[188]

> . . . no tribunal can approach a problem with its collective mind blank and devoid of any of the knowledge of a general nature which had been acquired in common with other members of the general public, through the respective life-times of its members, including perhaps most importantly that acquired from time to time in carrying out their statutory duties.

Thurlow C.J., writing in dissent, argued that the board could not take judicial notice of such 'facts', unless there was evidence to establish them. He further added that if he was wrong on that point, the applicant was entitled to be informed that these facts would be taken into account and to be given an opportunity to refute them.

The analysis by Smillie proves to be of little assistance here. The distinction between facts which are used as evidence, and facts which are used to evaluate and assess evidence is not as clear cut when applied to *Singh*. It could be argued

---

187   (1984), 6 Admin. L.R. 38 (Fed. C.A.).
188   (1976), [1977] 1 F.C. 194 at 198 (Fed. C.A.), quoted in *Singh, ibid.* at 49.

that the board used the information acquired through day to day operations to assess the credibility and weight to be given to the evidence given by Singh. It could also be argued that it used its knowledge to supplement and substitute evidence properly presented before it. The better approach is that taken by Thurlow C.J. The test is one of fairness, and here the applicant's credibility was put into question and he was given no opportunity to refute or explain.[189]

(ii) Taking Views

Closely related to principles of judicial notice are rules relating to the tribunal gathering its own evidence and taking views. Some tribunals and administrative bodies are expressly granted the right to investigate.[190] However, the right to investigate must be expressly provided for in the tribunal's empowering legislation. If a tribunal conducts its own investigation, it violates the rules of procedural fairness, particularly where the information gathered is not disclosed to the parties or they are not provided with an opportunity to refute it.[191]

When members of a tribunal conduct a view,[192] it must be in accordance with generally accepted evidentiary rules. The tribunal cannot do so in the absence of, or without the knowledge of, the parties. For example in *Teneycke v. Matsqui Institution*,[193] the applicant was charged with a disciplinary offence for indecently exposing himself to an officer through the window of his cell. The chairman of the disciplinary court viewed the cell himself to determine whether the offence was possible, or if the window was too high, as alleged by the applicant. The court held that the procedure violated the rules of procedural fairness because it was done in the absence of the applicant or his representative. In *Lewis v. Surrey (District)*,[194] two tribunal members viewed the site which was the subject of a public hearing process. The view took place after the public hearing and was significant in that the members changed their vote. However, the court found that this did not invalidate the by-law. It noted

---

189   S. 68 of the former *Immigration Act*, for example, included provisions concerning judicial notice:

>   (4) The Refugee Division may, in any proceedings before it take notice of any facts that may be judicially noticed and, subject to subsection (5), of any other generally recognized facts and any information or opinion that is within its specialized knowledge.

>   (5) Before the Refugee Division takes notice of any facts, information or opinion, other than facts that may be judicially noticed, in any proceedings, the Division shall notify the Minister, if present at the proceedings, and the person who is the subject of the proceedings of its intention and afford them a reasonable opportunity to make representations with respect thereto.

190   See for example, *Securities Act*, R.S.A. 2000, c. S-4.

191   *Vance v. Hardit Corp.* (1985), 18 Admin. L.R. 111 (Ont. Div. Ct.); *Murray v. Rockyview (Municipal District No. 44)* (1980), 12 Alta. L.R. (2d) 342 (Alta. C.A.), leave to appeal refused (1980), 14 Alta. L.R. (2d) 86 (Alta. C.A.).

192   "The act or proceeding by which tribunal goes to an object which cannot be produced in court because it is immovable or inconvenient to remove, and there observes it." *Black's Law Dictionary* (6th ed.) (St. Paul: West Publishing Co., 1990).

193   (1990), 43 Admin. L.R. 294 (Fed. T.D.).

194   (1979), 99 D.L.R. (3d) 505 (B.C. S.C.).

that the legislature did not intend council members to remain totally incommunicado, and that it would be impractical to require a new public hearing each time this sort of event occurred. The difference between these two cases may lie in the degree of fairness required. In *Teneycke*, an individual's rights and liberties were involved, while in *Re Lewis* the public hearing process involved more diffuse and undifferentiated rights.

(iii) Hearsay

Not all tribunals are governed by the strict evidentiary rules of a court of law and in many instances hearsay is properly admitted and acted on.

For example, both the *Labour Relations Code*[195] and the *Public Service Employee Relations Act*[196] specifically provide that boards of arbitration constituted thereunder are not bound by the rules of evidence. In fact, arbitrators very frequently admit hearsay to the extent that it is relevant to the issue at hand, giving it whatever weight is appropriate in the circumstances. In light of the statutory provisions governing their powers, such a procedure is clearly permissible – and may well be appropriate in other contexts.

However, where a tribunal relies almost entirely on hearsay evidence to reach its decision, it will generally breach the duty of fairness.[197] This is because the person whose rights are being adjudicated is not given an opportunity to cross-examine the makers of the statements.[198] In particular, courts have suggested that where the maker of the statement is available to testify and be cross-examined, oral testimony is required.[199] The particular facts of the case will also be relevant. For example, in *McInnes v. Simon Fraser University*,[200] a university appeal committee considered three written reports when deciding whether or not to require a student to withdraw from a department. The report writers did not testify. The court found that reliance on the reports did not breach the duty of fairness because *inter alia* the hearing took place six or seven years after the event in the reports, and thus cross-examination would not be particularly helpful. Also there was no evidence of bad faith, and there was other evidence to support the committee's conclusion.

---

195   R.S.A. 2000, c. L-1.

196   R.S.A. 2000, c. P-43.

197   *Bond v. New Brunswick (Board of Management)* (1992), 8 Admin. L.R. (2d) 95 (N.B. Q.B.), reversed (1992), 8 Admin. L.R. (2d) 100 (N.B. C.A.), leave to appeal refused (1993), 10 Admin. L.R. (2d) 57 (note) (S.C.C.). The court held that reliance on hearsay despite direct contradictory testimony was a breach of procedural fairness in the circumstances.

198   *Girvin v. Consumers' Gas Co.* (1973), 40 D.L.R. (3d) 509 (Ont. Div. Ct.); *Ontario Jockey Club v. Restaurant, Cafeteria & Tavern Employees' Union, Local 254* (1977), 15 L.A.C. (2d) 273 (Ont. Arb. Bd.).

199   *B. (J.) v. Catholic Childrens' Aid Society of Metropolitan Toronto* (1987), 27 Admin. L.R. 295 (Ont. Div. Ct.). In *Rubia v. Assn. of Registered Nurses (Newfoundland)* (1996), 39 Admin. L.R. (2d) 143 (Nfld. T.D.), the court ruled that fairness was denied because a disciplinary committee lacked a subpeona power and consequently the applicant could not fully defend himself through *viva voce* evidence, but rather had to rely upon affidavits.

200   (1983), 3 D.L.R. (4th) 708 (B.C. C.A.).

In the case of *R. v. Khan*,[201] the Supreme Court of Canada revised the rules relating to the admissibility of hearsay evidence. In the subsequent professional misconduct hearing,[202] the Ontario Divisional Court found that the admission of hearsay evidence in the disciplinary hearing necessitated a new hearing. On appeal, the Ontario Court of Appeal[203] found that the principles of reliability and necessity outlined by the Supreme Court applied to administrative tribunals, as well as to criminal proceedings, and the evidence was ruled to be admissible.

(iv) Parol Evidence

It is generally true that extrinsic evidence of intention is inadmissible in a court proceeding on grounds of irrelevancy. However, such evidence may be necessary and therefore admissible to resolve ambiguities. It is a clear principle of administrative law that written instruments, if they are clear, must be construed according to the plain and unambiguous language of the instrument itself.[204] Evidence of relevant surrounding circumstances may be admitted when necessary to clarify the meaning of the document. Such evidence may also indirectly disclose the true intentions of the parties. However, a party cannot attempt to give a contract a meaning other than its apparent meaning by establishing that the parties intended to say something other than what they said.[205] When evidence is admitted under an assertion that there is an ambiguity in the written documents and no ambiguity is found to exist but is acted upon to give a construction to the agreement which departs from the meaning of the words used, there is an error on the face of the record.[206]

(v) Privileged Communications

Privileged communications, such as those between spouses, are protected by section 4(3) of the *Canada Evidence Act.*[207] In *Wylie v. British Columbia (Police Commission)*,[208] it was held to be a breach of procedural fairness to include privileged communications, gathered by a judicially approved wiretap, as evidence. The serious consequences of police discipline require that proceedings be conducted with scrupulous regard to the rights of the person charged. The effect of such a breach of procedural fairness is that the contaminated proceedings are void and not merely voidable.[209]

---

201 [1990] 2 S.C.R. 531 (S.C.C.).
202 *Khan v. College of Physicians & Surgeons (Ontario)* (1990), 76 D.L.R. (4th) 179, 48 Admin. L.R. 118 (Ont. Div. Ct.), reversed (1992), 57 O.A.C. 115 (Ont. C.A.).
203 (1992), 94 D.L.R. (4th) 193, 11 Admin. L.R. (2d) 147 (Ont. C.A.).
204 *Inland Cement Industries Ltd. v. C.L.C.W., Local 359*, [1981] 3 W.W.R. 65 (Alta. C.A.) at 71.
205 *Doyon v. Canada (Public Service Staff Relations Board)* (1977), [1978] 1 F.C. 31 (Fed. C.A.).
206 *Ibid.* at 75.
207 R.S.C. 1985, c. C-5; see also s. 189(6) of the *Criminal Code*, R.S.C. 1985, c. C-46 regarding private communications.
208 [1985] 5 W.W.R. 326 (B.C. C.A.).
209 *Ibid.* at 331.

Solicitor-client communications are also privileged information in administrative proceedings, unless the enabling legislation says otherwise. If the statute is silent, *bona fide* solicitor-client communications are inadmissible.[210]

(c) Open Court

The tradition of the common law has always required that judicial proceedings be conducted in public so that justice will manifestly be seen to be done. The exceptions to this rule occur where, for public policy reasons, it has been decided that the case should not be subjected to the full glare of publicity, for example, in adoption cases concerning infants or where matters of national security are at stake.

The openness of judicial proceedings does not have a general counterpart in the actions of statutory delegates. There is no rule that such proceedings must be held in public. Indeed, a huge number of merely administrative acts are carried out by public servants every day not in a public forum – nor would such a suggestion be made.[211]

But the question becomes more difficult where the nature of the administrative proceedings leans more towards a judicial model. Many statutes provide that deliberations of the various administrative tribunals set up under them be in public. Some, for example the former *Immigration Act*, provide that an immigration inquiry be held in camera.[212] In the absence of such statutory provisions, however, the courts have had to decide when the requirement of a public hearing shall operate and when it shall not. For example, in *Edmonton Journal (The) v. Canada (Attorney General)*,[213] the court found that a coroner's inquest was not a "court proceeding", noting that there was no *lis*, no accused, no charge and no penalty. In *Southam Inc. v. Canada (Minister of Employment & Immigration)*,[214] the court determined that a detention review hearing under the former *Immigration Act*[215] was quasi-judicial and that, therefore, the general rule of open court proceedings applied.

(i) Re Millward

In *Millward v. Canada (Public Service Commission)*,[216] the Federal Court had to determine whether proceedings before an appeal board established under

---

210 *Shell Canada Ltd. v. Canada (Director of Investigation & Research)*, [1975] F.C. 184 (Fed. C.A.).
211 *Omineca Enterprises Ltd. v. British Columbia (Minister of Forests)* (1992), 7 Admin. L.R. (2d) 95 (B.C. S.C.), affirmed (1993), 18 Admin. L.R. (2d) 210 (B.C. C.A.), leave to appeal refused (1994), 23 Admin. L.R. (2d) 319 (note) (S.C.C.).
212 S.C. 1976-77, c. 52 (am. by S.C. 1985, c. 26), s. 29(3). (Repealed and replaced with the *Immigration and Refugee Protection Act*, S.C. 2001, c. 27.)
213 (1983), 5 D.L.R. (4th) 240 (Alta. Q.B.), affirmed (1984), 37 Alta. L.R. (2d) 287 (Alta. C.A.), leave to appeal refused (1984), 56 N.R. 398n (S.C.C.).
214 [1987] 3 F.C. 329 (Fed. T.D.).
215 S.C. 1976-77, c. 52 (am. by S.C. 1985, c. 26) (Repealed and replaced by the *Immigration and Refugee Protection Act*, S.C. 2001, c. 27.)
216 (1974), 49 D.L.R. (3d) 295 (Fed. T.D.).

the *Public Service Employment Act*[217] had to be held in public or private, or whether there was discretion in the board to conduct the proceedings either in public or in private or partly in each. The purpose of the board was to inquire into the appeal of an unsuccessful candidate for a federal government job against the appointment of the successful candidate.

Cattanach J. stated the rule of open court as applied to Courts of Law and Justice and quoted Lord Haldane from *Scott v. Scott*:[218]

> If there is any exception to the broad principle which requires the administration of justice to take place in open Court, that exception must be based on the application of some other and overriding principle which defines the field of exception and does not leave its limits to the individual discretion of the judge.

Although no principles have emerged to justify the exception, two principles have been advanced: first, that the public will be excluded when it is necessary to secure that justice is done;[219] and secondly, that the court only hears cases *in camera* in exceptional classes established by judicial decisions and statutes. Cattanach J. then went on to list the rules of common law:[220]

(1) the fundamental rule is open Court;

(2) the Court may hear an application for trial *in camera* where justice cannot be administered otherwise;

(3) the Court may hear matters *in camera* in specific cases, such as when a statute so provides, wards, lunacy, secret processes and keeping order;

(4) the Court has no power at common law, beyond these exceptions, to hear cases *in camera* and has no arbitrary discretion, it does not have such power in divorce or nullity proceedings;[221]

(5) at one time the Courts have exercised this power to hear matters *in camera* on consent of the parties but this has been doubted in *Nagle-Gillman v. Christopher*[222] and . . . overruled in *Scott v. Scott, supra.*

In *Millward,* the Public Service Commission had published a "Guide to the Public Service Appeals System" which stated that every appeal hearing was open to the public. The court emphasized that this was merely a guide and

---

217 R.S.C. 1970, c. P-32.

218 [1913] A.C. 417 at 435*ff* (U.K. H.L.), quoted by Cattanach J. at 303.

219 Viscount Haldane in *Scott v. Scott, ibid.*; Lush J. in *Norman, Ex parte* (1916), 85 L.J.K.B. 203 (Eng. K.B.).

220 *Supra* note 216 at 304.

221 *McPherson v. McPherson* (1935), [1936] 1 D.L.R. 321 (Alberta P.C.) at 326-27.

222 *Nagle-Gillman v. Christopher* (1876), 4 Ch. D. 173.

not a statement of the law. Indeed it was dangerously misleading to the lay persons who would read it, since it purported to oust the discretion vested in the board.

Having disposed of the guide, the court then sought help in the statute as a whole and found none. As a result, the decision whether to hold the inquiry in public or private was held to be a matter solely in the board's discretion.

It may be relevant that the parties consent to one form or another,[223] although this may only govern if the tribunal is a creature of those parties.[224] It is also important to note that where a tribunal has the discretion to decide whether the hearing be public or not, the request by one party to hold the hearing *in camera*, does not oust that discretion.[225]

However, there is no requirement for non-judicial bodies to sit in public in the absence of statutory direction to the contrary.[226] Where the statute is silent, then the tribunal in question has the discretion to decide in that particular case, it generally being the governor of its own proceedings.

(ii) The McVey Case

The question of open court proceedings and public and media accessibility have also arisen in relation to section 2(b) of the *Charter*.[227] A case that received considerable press attention at the time in the United States and British Columbia concerned the extradition of an American citizen arrested in Canada, Charles McVey.[228]

The British Columbia Court of Appeal found that the offenses with which he was charged were not extraditable.[229] Following that judgment, an immigration officer filed a report against McVey, alleging violations of subsections 27(2)(e) and 27(2)(g) of the former *Immigration Act*[230] dealing with overstaying after entering as a visitor and entering under a false name. In the subsequent

---

223   If for no other reason than because they would be estopped from later asserting their right to privacy to prevent a public (or private) hearing. See also A. Walton, ed. *Russell on the Law of Arbitration*, 18th ed., (London: Stevens, 1970) at 220, referred to (dubiously) by Grange J. in *Toronto Star, infra* at 375; and the 20th ed., (London: Stevens, 1982) at 260.

224   *Toronto Star Ltd. v. Toronto Newspaper Guild* (1976), 73 D.L.R. (3d) 370 (Ont. Div. Ct.).

225   *Ibid.*

226   See for example *Tafler v. British Columbia (Commissioner of Conflict of Interest)* (1995), 31 Admin. L.R. (2d) 6 (B.C. S.C. [In Chambers]), affirmed (1998), 11 Admin. L.R. (3d) 228 (B.C. C.A.). See also (1995), 31 Admin. L.R. (2d) 1 (B.C. C.A. [In Chambers]). But see *Vancouver (City) v. British Columbia (Assessment Appeal Board)* (1996), 39 Admin. L.R. (2d) 129 (B.C. C.A.) where the Court of Appeal ruled that notwithstanding that the appeal process was not a judicial proceeding, the process was public and therefore, in absence of a specific statutory provision, the board did not have authority to receive evidence in camera.

227   2. Everyone has the following fundamental freedoms: . . .
     (b) freedom of thought, belief, opinion and expression, including freedom of the press and other media of communication

228   *United States v. McVey* (1988), [1989] 2 W.W.R. 673 (B.C. C.A.), reversed (1992), [1993] 1 W.W.R. 289 (S.C.C.).

229   The Supreme Court of Canada in *United States v. McVey* (1992), [1993] 1 W.W.R. 289 (S.C.C.), subsequently found that the offenses were, in fact, extraditable.

230   Since repealed, see now the *Immigration and Refugee Protection Act*, S.C. 2001, c. 27.

inquiry, the adjudicator held that the inquiry should be closed to the public on the authority of section 29 of the former *Immigration Act*.[231]

The decision to close the inquiry to the public was challenged in the Federal Court of Appeal by members of the news media wishing access to the proceedings.[232] The applicants argued, firstly, that section 29 was contrary to section 2(b) of the *Charter* and secondly, that the decision was not based on any evidence. Mahoney J., for the Court, held that it was not the appropriate time to rule on the constitutionality of the section since there was a similar motion awaiting reserved judgment in the trial division.[233] He held that the section placed an onus on a member of the public who wished the inquiry to be open to establish that conducting the inquiry in public would not impede it and that it would not have an adverse effect on the person or any member of the person's family. The mere assertion of the right to access was sufficient to satisfy this burden and shift the onus to the person seeking to exclude the public. McVey's submissions (that his terminally ill wife in the United States would be adversely affected by publicity surrounding the inquiry) were not sufficient grounds for the adjudicator to order the inquiry closed to the public. Mahoney J. therefore set aside the adjudicator's decision and ordered him to reconsider the matter.

On rehearing, the adjudicator again ordered that the inquiry be held *in camera* and he also ordered a publication ban. The basis of his decision this time was McVey's own health (his wife having passed away in the meantime). An application to the Federal Court of Appeal was again made to set aside the decision. MacGuigan J., for the Court, ordered the decision set aside and found that section 29(3) was contrary to section 2(b) of the *Charter* and was not justified under section 1.[234]

MacGuigan J. referred extensively to the decision of Martin J. in *Toronto Star Newspapers Ltd. v. Kenney*,[235] and in particular to his discussion of the legislative history of the section.

---

231 S. 29 then read:

> (1) An inquiry by an adjudicator shall be held in the presence of the person with respect to whom the inquiry is to be held wherever practicable.

> (2) At the request or with the permission of the person with respect to whom an inquiry is to be held, an adjudicator shall allow any person to attend an inquiry if such attendance is not likely to impede the inquiry.

> (3) Except as provided in subsection (2), an inquiry by an adjudicator shall be held in camera unless it is established to the satisfaction of the adjudicator, on application by a member of the public, that the conduct of the inquiry in public would not impede the inquiry and that the person with respect to whom the inquiry is to be held or any member of that person's family would not be adversely affected if the inquiry were to be conducted in public.

232 *Pacific Press Ltd. v. Canada (Minister of Employment & Immigration)*, [1990] 1 F.C. 419, 10 Imm. L.R. (2d) 42, 104 N.R. 228 (Fed. C.A.).

233 See *Toronto Star,* note 235, below.

234 [1991] 2 F.C. 327 (Fed. C.A.).

235 (1990), 33 F.T.R. 194 (Fed. T.D.). The original section made an *in camera* proceeding virtually mandatory and the government became concerned about its constitutionality after the decision in *Reference re s. 12 (1) of the Juvenile Delinquents Act (Canada)* (1983), 41 O.R. (2d) 113 (Ont. C.A.). That decision by the Supreme Court had held that public

However, MacGuigan J. rejected Martin J.'s approach to the matter and instead ruled on the constitutionality of the section.[236] He first noted the importance of media access to the courts, even before the *Charter*[237] and concluded that an immigration inquiry was analogous to judicial proceedings since it met the tests in *Coopers and Lybrand* and the general rule of open proceedings applied.[238]

On the question then of the constitutionality of section 29(3), the court found that the activity fell within the protection of section 2(b) and that the purpose of the legislation was clearly to restrict freedom of expression. Furthermore, section 29(3) could not be justified under section 1 of the *Charter*. While there was a pressing and substantial objective – the protection of refugees – the proportionality test was not met. MacGuigan J. found little rational connection between the provision and the objective, since the section applies

---

accessibility to the courts by the media was an element of s. 2(b), and that s. 12(1) of the *Juvenile Delinquents Act* requiring juvenile trials to be held *in camera* infringed that section. The government amended s. 29 by adding subsection 29(3). The government's intention as indicated by an excerpt from the discussions of the parliamentary committee studying the bill was to protect convention refugees. MacGuigan J. concluded (note 223, above, at 337):

It seems very clear from this account of the genesis of this legislative provision that its very purpose was to prevent access to immigration inquiries by the press and the public, except in limited circumstances, in order to enable Convention refugees to speak freely of their experiences, without danger of reprisals from those from whom they have fled.

236 In *Toronto Star*, Martin J. considered himself bound by the decision in the first *McVey* case, but suggested that he would have found the section to be unconstitutional but for Mahoney J.'s decision. Instead, he read the decision as standing for the proposition that the section was to be read as providing the adjudicator with real discretion "to determine on a case by case basis and on the particular circumstances of each case" whether the hearing should be *in camera*. MacGuigan J. argued that this "reading down" of the provision was essentially judicial re-drafting, which was inappropriate where the result of the impugned legislation was exactly what was intended by the legislation.

237 He quoted Dickson J. in *MacIntyre v. Nova Scotia (Attorney General)*, [1982] 1 S.C.R. 175 at 185-86 (S.C.C.): "curtailment of public accessibility can only be justified where there is present the need to protect social values of superordinate importance" and Cory J. in *Edmonton Journal v. Alberta (Attorney General)* (1989), [1989] 2 S.C.R. 1326, [1990] 1 W.W.R. 577 at 612 and 619 (S.C.C.):

There can be no doubt that the courts play an important role in any democratic society. They are the forum not only for the resolution of disputes between citizens, but for the resolution of disputes between the citizens and the state in all of its manifestations. The more complex society becomes, the more important becomes the function of the courts. As a result of their significance, the courts must be open to public scrutiny and to public criticism of their operation by the public. . . . In today's society it is the press reports of trials that make the courts truly open to the public.

238 To reach this conclusion, he referred to the decision of Rouleau J. in *Southam Inc. v. Canada (Minister of Employment & Immigration)*, [1987] 3 F.C. 329 (Fed. T.D.) where it was held that a detention review hearing was quasi-judicial on the basis of a four-fold test enumerated by Mr. Justice Dickson in *Minister of National Revenue v. Coopers & Lybrand* (1978), [1979] 1 S.C.R. 495 at 504 (S.C.C.). The test included:

1. whether a hearing is contemplated before a decision is reached;
2. whether the decision or order will directly affect the rights and obligations of persons;
3. whether the process is adversarial and;
4. is there an obligation to apply substantive rules to many individual cases, rather than implementing broad social and economic policy?

to inquiries of every kind, not just refugee inquiries. The section was over-inclusive.[239]

Nevertheless, MacGuigan J. chose to deem the section temporarily valid for one year, in order to give Parliament time to amend it.[240]

The rationale for an open court system was addressed by Wilson J. in *Edmonton Journal v. Alberta (Attorney General).*[241] She noted that the importance of an open court to the public at large rested on four factors: maintaining an effective evidentiary process, ensuring a judiciary and jury that behave fairly and sensitively to society and its values, promoting a shared sense that our courts operate with integrity and dispense justice and lastly, serving an educational function.[242]

(d) Right to Counsel

A party before an administrative tribunal does not have an absolute right to counsel pursuant to the principles of procedural fairness. Indeed there are situations where courts have upheld the denial of the right to counsel, such as where regulations exclude it;[243] where it is excluded in the rules of an association;[244] in prison disciplinary hearings which require a rapid hearing and decision;[245] or where no oral hearing is required at all by the governing legislation.[246] However, there are also many situations where courts have quashed decisions by administrative tribunals which were made in the absence of

---

239 "The interference in the case at bar cannot in my view be said to be 'of a minimal nature'. While less maximal than a total prohibition of access, it nevertheless wrongly reverses the onus of proof, makes no provision for anything between total access and total prohibition, and applies not only to the refugee class Parliament aimed to protect but to all inquiries for whatever purpose. The respondents did not even seek to defend the application of s. 29(3) to non-refugees except in the secondary sense that it protected refugees by helping to obscure who were and who were not refugee claimants."

240 Had the section been struck down, the effect would have been to require that all inquiries be conducted *in camera* except with the specific permission of the claimant. In the meantime, MacGuigan J. provided guidelines as to what the words "adversely affected" meant. His guidelines exclude embarrassment or humiliation, privacy interests, and stress and tension. The inquiry subjects may establish adverse effects by showing that their concerns are consistent with the policy objectives of s. 29(3) and with *Charter* principles, and they must also show some direct link between the publicity and personal danger.

241 *Edmonton Journal, supra* note 237.

242 In determining whether an administrative proceeding should be open or not, perhaps these factors are more relevant than the factors cited in *Minister of National Revenue v. Cooper & Lybrand* (1978), [1979] 1 S.C.R. 495 (S.C.C.). Those factors relate to narrow functional characteristics but there may be situations where the proceeding is not adversarial, but which, under the factors discussed by Wilson J., would appropriately be held in public. For example, in *Edmonton Journal v. Alberta (Attorney General)*, [1989] 2 S.C.R. 1326 (S.C.C.), the public may well have had a public interest in learning the details of how an inmate died in the Edmonton Detention Centre, whether or not the proceeding was adversarial or anyone's individual rights or obligations were being ascertained.

243 *Maynard v. Osmond*, [1976] 3 W.L.R. 711 (Eng. C.A.).

244 *Enderby Town Football Club v. Football Assn. Ltd.* (1970), [1971] Ch. 591 (Eng. C.A.).

245 *Fraser v. Mudge*, [1975] 1 W.L.R. 1132 (Eng. C.A.). However, see note 256, below, and accompanying discussion.

246 *R. v. Melbourne; Ex parte Whyte*, [1949] V.L.R. 257.

counsel for one party after a denial of the opportunity to be represented by counsel.

(i) The Guay v. Lafleur Case

The traditional approach – that representation by counsel is purely discretionary on the part of the statutory delegate or tribunal – was articulated by the Supreme Court of Canada in *Guay v. Lafleur*.[247] This case involved a purely administrative procedure, an investigation conducted by a delegate of the Minister. The delegate did not have authority to decide or adjudicate on any of the issues; the Minister made the final decision. The delegate did have recommendation-making power within an inquiry under the *Income Tax Act*[248] into the affairs of the respondent and others. The delegate, an inquiry officer, called a number of witnesses to be questioned under oath and allowed them to be represented by counsel. The respondent wished to be present and to be represented by counsel during the examination of those witnesses. Despite the quasi-judicial trappings of the inquiry, the court held that its nature remained administrative and that the *audi alteram partem* maxim did not apply in the same way as it would if the inquiry officer was making a final determination.

Hall J. dissented on the basis that the inquiry officer had authority to make recommendations, which involved some judgment of the facts. Hall J. noted that had the Minister himself held the inquiry instead of delegating this task, he would have had to act fairly and impartially, and would undoubtedly have had to have allowed the respondent the right to counsel. He noted that while the decision was issued in another name, it was in fact made by the inquiry officer, which he would have held would make the need for compliance with the principles of procedural fairness even more strong.

Given the evolution that has occurred in the development of the doctrine of fairness, one wonders whether *Guay v. Lafleur* would be decided the same way today.[249]

(ii) The Pett Case

The type of reasoning in the dissent in *Guay v. Lafleur* was, at about the same time, being applied by the English Court of Appeal. In *Pett v. Greyhound Racing Assn. Ltd.*,[250] the track stewards of a greyhound racing stadium held an inquiry into whether or not drugs had been administered to a dog trained by Pett. An unfavourable decision could have resulted in Pett losing his licence as a trainer and thus have damaged his reputation and livelihood. When he obtained his licence, he had agreed to abide by the rules of the National Greyhound Racing Club, which did not prescribe any procedure to be followed at an inquiry. In fact, the procedure used allowed Pett to be present, and to hear evidence and cross-examine witnesses. However, Pett also wished to be

---

247   (1964), [1965] S.C.R. 12 (S.C.C.).
248   R.S.C. 1952, c. 148, as amended by S.C. 1970-71-72, c. 63 and subsequent amendments.
249   See also the discussion of *Guay v. Lafleur* under "Investigation Stage", above.
250   (1968), [1969] 1 Q.B. 125 (Eng. C.A.).

represented by counsel. The Court quashed the track stewards' refusal of the request to be represented by counsel.

The Racing Club argued on appeal that the Court could not interfere with the absolute discretion of the track stewards to determine all procedural matters in such inquiries. Secondly, the Club alleged that legal representation would cause delay and complications which would frustrate the object of completing inquiries expeditiously and with complete fairness.

Lord Denning M.R. did not accept either of these submissions. He considered the serious consequences to Pett of being found guilty and held that Pett was entitled to appear himself and to appoint an agent to act for him. The Court held that the agent could be a lawyer, which the Court viewed as particularly appropriate given that a lawyer is trained in the arts of cross-examination and advocacy and an average layman is not. In Lord Denning's view, therefore, when a person's reputation or livelihood is at stake, he or she has a right to speak by his or her own mouth or by counsel. Lord Denning also dismissed the view of Maugham J. in *Maclean v. Workers' Union*[251] that there was no right of audience to counsel before a domestic tribunal. He noted that while a lack of representation might have been acceptable when applied to tribunals dealing with minor matters, it did not apply to those dealing with very serious matters. Procedural fairness therefore required the right to counsel.

(iii) The Irvine Case

Subsequent Canadian cases have followed the *Pett* line of reasoning, and suggest that *Guay v. Lafleur* is no longer good law. None of these cases, however, holds that there is an absolute right to counsel.

In *Irvine v. Canada (Restrictive Trade Practices Commission)*,[252] the Supreme Court of Canada again dealt with the issue of right to counsel and the role of counsel. Investigated persons under the Restrictive Trade Practice regime were allowed to be represented by counsel, but counsel was limited to an extremely restricted role which specifically did not include the right to cross-examine adverse witnesses. The Court held that the distinction between administrative or investigation proceedings (as in *Guay v. Lafleur*) and quasi-judicial proceedings was no longer determinative of whether the principles of procedural fairness apply. Accordingly, the basis for which the right to counsel was denied in *Guay v. Lafleur* is no longer an appropriate basis for such a finding.

The Court divided the history of a party's legal right to participation in administrative hearings into three phases: (1) "pre-fairness", when the nature of the tribunal proceeding was determinative, based on the distinction between administrative proceedings and quasi-judicial proceedings; (2) when the doctrine of fairness applied to administrative proceedings; and (3) post-*Charter*.[253]

---

251   [1929] 1 Ch. 602 (Eng. Ch. Div.).
252   24 Admin. L.R. 91, [1987] 1 S.C.R. 181 (S.C.C.).
253   Because of some procedural rulings prior to the hearing of the actual case and lack of notice to the respective Attorneys-General, the Court in *Irvine* did not deal with any constitutional issues, though some had been raised.

The Court in *Irvine* discussed at length the application of the principles of procedural fairness to administrative proceedings, and held that these principles did apply to administrative proceedings such as those of the Restrictive Trade Practice Commission investigations. However, the Court held that the principles of procedural fairness in these circumstances did not entitle all investigated persons to counsel. This is because the investigator had only a private investigative and recommendation-making power, and because the statute provided ample protections for persons being investigated. The Hearing Officer did not have authority to publish the results of his or her investigation, but provided a private statement of evidence to the Commission (i.e., the actual decision-maker) and affected persons; and when the Commission considered the statement of evidence, it must also consider any other evidence or material as it considered advisable and must also provide the full opportunity to all investigated persons to be heard in person or by counsel. Indeed, if the investigation went to a criminal prosecution, the Court held, no evidence could be used in the criminal proceedings unless the accused against whom the evidence was used had had an opportunity for cross-examination by counsel. The Supreme Court held that these circumstances were not so unfair that the Courts must intervene to "supply the legislative omission":[254]

> Courts must, in the exercise of this discretion, remain alert to the danger of unduly burdening and complicating the law enforcement investigative process. Where that process is in embryonic form engaged in the gathering of the raw material for further consideration, the inclination of the Courts is away from intervention. Where, on the other hand, the investigation is conducted by a body seized of powers to determine, in a final sense or in the sense that detrimental impact may be suffered by the individual, the Courts are more inclined to intervene. In the present case it was sufficient that the hearing officer allowed all the parties to be represented by counsel who could object to improper questioning and re-examine their clients to clarify the testimony given and to ensure that the full story was communicated by the witness counsel represented.

Accordingly, the Supreme Court of Canada in *Irvine* held that the determinative factor in right to counsel cases is not the type of proceedings or the nature of the tribunal, but the potential risk to the affected party and whether these risks were sufficiently significant to entitle the person to be represented by counsel. That is, the determination is based on the content of procedural fairness in the particular circumstances of the case, not whether procedural fairness applies to the tribunal proceedings.[255]

---

254   *Irvine, supra* note 252 at 140.

255   This position has been followed a number of times. See for example *Stephen v. College of Physicians & Surgeons (Saskatchewan)*, [1989] 6 W.W.R. 1 (Sask. C.A.), where the court held that procedural fairness applied to the investigation process within disciplinary proceedings; *Gaetz v. Palacios-Boix* (1993), 121 N.S.R. (2d) 324 (N.S. T.D.), where the principles of procedural fairness were applied to the tribunal's dealing with a complainant

(iv) The Right to Counsel in the Charter Context

After the *Charter* was enacted in Canada, parties before administrative tribunals began asserting that the right to counsel may be constitutionally required in some cases. However, although section 10(b) of the *Charter* grants a right to counsel, that right is only available upon "arrest or detention". Therefore, this section of the *Charter* does not give a right to counsel in an administrative law context. The other section of the *Charter* which was argued to provide a right to counsel in proceedings of an administrative tribunal is section 7. Applicants argued that section 7 of the *Charter* must be interpreted to entitle a person to counsel where "life, liberty or security of the person" is at stake.

This application of section 7 of the *Charter* was first argued in *Howard v. Stony Mountain Institution, Presiding Officer of Inmate Disciplinary Court.*[256] In *Howard*, the Federal Court of Appeal found (in two separate, but concurring judgments) that there was no absolute right to counsel in prison disciplinary hearings pursuant to the principles of procedural fairness. The Court also found that there is no absolute right to counsel pursuant to section 7 of the *Charter*, but that the *Charter* enhanced existing rights and in the appropriate circumstances, a prisoner in disciplinary proceedings is entitled to be represented by counsel.

Chief Justice Thurlow concluded that there was no absolute right to counsel, but that a presiding officer had discretion to permit counsel in the appropriate circumstances. The factors relevant to the exercise of the discretion included the seriousness of the charge, the likelihood that points of law might arise, the inmate's capacity to present his own case, procedural problems, the need for speed, and the need for fairness as between prisoners and as between prisoners and prison officers.[257] He concluded from this analysis that the right to counsel in this context arises from the ". . . requirement to afford the person an opportunity to adequately present his case."[258] In assessing whether section 7 of the *Charter* changed this position, he articulated a broad and purposive approach to the interpretation of the section and raised the question to a matter of right rather than a matter of discretion where the circumstances warrant it:[259]

> I am of the opinion that the enactment of section 7 has not created any absolute right to counsel in all such proceedings. It is undoubtedly of

---

in disciplinary proceedings; *Tanaka v. Certified General Accountants' Assn. (Northwest Territories)* (1996), 38 Admin. L.R. (2d) 99 (N.W.T. S.C.), where the court held that procedural fairness applied to the investigation stage of discipline proceedings; and *Assn. of Optometrists (British Columbia) v. British Columbia (Minister of Health)* (1998), 5 Admin. L.R. (3d) 216 (B.C. S.C. [In Chambers]), which held that fairness applies to administrative proceedings. All of these cases specifically note that *Guay v. Lafleur* is no longer a correct statement in the law of Canada.

256 (1985), 11 Admin. L.R. 63 (Fed. C.A.), appeal quashed for mootness [1987] 2 S.C.R. 687 (S.C.C.).

257 *R. v. Secretary of State for the Home Department* (1983), [1984] 1 All E.R. 799, [1984] 2 W.L.R. 613 (Eng. Q.B.).

258 *Howard, supra* note 256 at 84.

259 *Ibid.*

the greatest importance to a person whose life, liberty or security of the person are at stake to have the opportunity to present his case as fully and adequately as possible. The advantages of having the assistance of counsel for that purpose are not in doubt. But what is required is an opportunity to present the case adequately and I do not think it can be affirmed that in no case can such an opportunity be afforded without also as part of it affording the right to representation by counsel at the hearing. . . .

. . . whether or not the person has a right to representation by counsel will depend on the circumstances of the particular case, its nature, its gravity, its complexity, the capacity of the inmate himself to understand and present his defence. The list is not exhaustive. And from this, it seems to me, it follows that whether or not an inmate's request for representation by counsel can lawfully be refused is not properly referred to as a matter of discretion but is a matter of right where the circumstances are such that the opportunity to present the case adequately calls for representation by counsel.

MacGuigan J. addressed the issue of whether the common law duty of fairness required that an inmate be represented by counsel. On the basis of such cases as *Davidson v. Prison for Women*,[260] *Minott v. Stony Mountain Penitentiary*,[261] and *Blanchard v. Millhaven Institution*,[262] he concluded that the Canadian position, pre-*Charter*, was that there was no absolute right to counsel, only a discretion. He then analysed the principles of fundamental justice, as developed in both the *Charter* context and in the context of procedural fairness. He noted that the *Charter* does not merely confirm the *status quo*, but that it can enhance existing common law rights. He concluded that a right to counsel is not discretionary when circumstances require representation by counsel. His main point of departure from Thurlow C.J. was that wherever a person's rights to "life, liberty and security of the person" were implicated, the right to counsel was a presumption that would have to be rebutted:[263]

In sum, other than, perhaps, in fact situations of unique simplicity, I cannot imagine cases where a possible penalty of earned remission would not bring into play the necessity for counsel. Indeed, in my view the probability that counsel will be required for an adequate hearing on charges with such consequences is so strong as to amount effectively to a presumption in favour of counsel, a departure from which a presiding officer would have to justify. The right-enhancing effect of the *Charter* thus greatly increases the ambit of protection afforded.

---

260 (1981), 61 C.C.C. (2d) 520 (Fed. T.D.).
261 (1981), [1982] 1 F.C. 322 (Fed. T.D.).
262 (1982), [1983] 1 F.C. 309, 69 C.C.C. (2d) 171 (Fed. T.D.).
263 *Howard, supra* note 256 at 106-07.

The case clearly raises the issue of whether the principles of fundamental justice in section 7 of the *Charter* provide greater procedural protection than the doctrine of procedural fairness. While the Court here was determined to limit the *Charter's* scope and insisted that section 7 created no new rights but enhanced existing ones, it also clearly suggested that the right to counsel was a right that only arose under the *Charter* as a matter of right, not discretion, in the appropriate circumstances.[264]

The right to present one's case adequately is a question of fairness,[265] and where interests of life, liberty and security of the person are involved, the context is surely one where the requirements of fairness dictate the right to counsel. However, the same factors as those enumerated by Thurlow C.J. and MacGuigan J. for the operation of section 7 – the nature of the case including its gravity, complexity, and whether complex issues of law arise – are equally applicable in determining the extent of the duty of fairness outside of a section 7 context.[266]

In a series of cases following *Howard*,[267] the courts tended to restrict *Howard* to its facts, and took a very narrow approach to the right to counsel.[268] These cases hold that the right to counsel exists only where loss of earned

---

264 Yet, the requirements of procedural fairness, as developed in *Nicholson v. Haldimand Norfolk (Regional Municipality) Commissioners of Police* (1978), [1979] 1 S.C.R. 311 (S.C.C.), and *Martineau v. Matsqui Institution (No. 2)* (1979), [1980] 1 S.C.R. 602 (S.C.C.), and in such cases as *Irvine v. Canada (Restrictive Trade Practices Commission)*, *supra* note 252; *I.W.A. Local 2-69 v. Consolidated Bathurst Packaging Ltd. v. International Woodworker of America, Loc. 2-69* (1990), 42 Admin. L.R. 1; and *Newfoundland Telephone Co. v. Newfoundland (Board of Commissioners of Public Utilities)* (1992), 4 Admin. L.R. (2d) 121 (S.C.C.), suggest that a right to counsel might now be founded without the assistance of the *Charter*. Thurlow C.J. himself noted that the *Tarrant* decision appears "to amount in substance to a right to have counsel when the facts indicate the need for it, and to a discretion to allow it in other cases as well." The spectrum of obligations of procedural fairness are equally context dependent.

265 See the sections on the right to a hearing, the right to an oral hearing, the right to cross-examination, and the right to know the case to be met, above.

266 Both Chief Justice Thurlow and Justice MacGuigan emphasized the distinction between the common law discretion to disallow counsel and a right to counsel arising under the *Charter*. The distinction they draw relates to the scope of judicial review. Breaches of procedural fairness are cured by *certiorari*, a discretionary remedy. Breaches of the *Charter* result in a declaration that the impugned action is invalid. *Charter* remedies may be breached (s. 24) and legislation may override a common law right to counsel which the *Charter* may then invalidate.

267 Following the decision in *Howard*, changes to the *Penitentiary Service Regulations* were made. The regulations added a third category of offences, intermediary, to the existing two, minor and serious. Both intermediary and serious offences are adjudicated by disciplinary boards, but only serious offences may be punished by a loss of remission. The other possible punishments are the same for both intermediary and serious offences.

268 *Kelly v. Joyceville Institution* (1987), 25 Admin. L.R. 303 (Fed. T.D.); *Savard v. Edmonton Institution Disciplinary Bd.* (1986), 44 Alta. L.R. (2d) 353, 3 F.T.R. 1 (Fed. T.D.); *Walker v. Kingston Penitentiary* (1986), 52 C.R. (3d) 106, 3 F.T.R. 109 (Fed. T.D.). For a discussion of the principles applied to the penalty of dissociation and its effects on liberty and security of the person, see M. Jackson, "The Right to Counsel in Prison Disciplinary Hearings" (1986) 20 U.B.C. Law Rev. 221; *Engen v. Kingston Penitentiary* (1987), 12 F.T.R. 7, 60 C.R. (3d) 109 (Fed. T.D.).

remission is a possible penalty and where issues of law are at stake. The right
to counsel remains a matter of discretion in intermediary offenses, in situations
where punitive dissociation (solitary confinement) is the penalty, and where
the issues involve questions of fact.[269] This retrenchment means that the right
to counsel has not advanced very much further under the *Charter* than it had
under the doctrine of procedural fairness.[270]

Outside the prison context, a right to counsel has been said to be based on
such factors as the consequences of the hearing, the penalties involved, and
the nature of the proceedings.[271] A right to counsel includes the right to careful
and competent counsel;[272] and, where an applicant was denied an adjournment
in order to obtain and instruct new counsel, this amounted to a denial of the
applicant's right to counsel.[273] The right to counsel has not been held to include
a right to state-funded counsel in an Administrative Law context, though that
argument has been made.[274]

In conclusion, neither the principles of procedural fairness nor the *Charter*
entitle a person to representation by counsel in all proceedings by all administrative tribunals or statutory delegates. Both the common law principles of
procedural fairness and constitutionally-entrenched fundamental justice require a decision-maker to consider whether, in the circumstances of each
individual case, a party before the decision-maker is entitled to counsel. Decision-makers who deny representation by counsel in circumstances which the
court later rules are sufficiently serious or complex so as to require counsel, or
in which there is a sufficiently difficult question of law that the party cannot
adequately present his case without representation by counsel, will be reviewable on both procedural fairness grounds and on the basis of a breach of

---

269   The decision to transfer an inmate to another institution, or from open to closed or closer
custody has been found not to require a right to counsel: *Jacobson v. Regional Transfer
Board (Pacific)* (April 14, 1987), Doc. T-2307-86 (Fed. T.D.); *Norton v. Saskatchewan
(Director of Corrections)* (1986), 47 Sask. R. 265 (Sask. Q.B.). But see *Hay v. Canada
(National Parole Board)* (1985), 21 C.C.C. (3d) 408, 18 C.R.R. 313 (Fed. T.D.) where a
decision to put into effect on involuntary transfer, not based on the inmate's fault or
misconduct, was found to offend ss. 7 and 9 of the *Charter*.

270   Perhaps a return to the issue is warranted based on the principles developed in other aspects
of procedural fairness. Given the serious consequences of many disciplinary offenses,
fairness requires that access to counsel not be restricted on the basis of narrow and inflexible
classifications of offenses, but on the recognition that
    . . . justice and fairness cannot tolerate a procedure where a layman is expected to deal
    with legal concepts which are strange to him, and at the same time advise himself
    objectively:
       Joplin v. Vancouver (City) Commissioners of Police (1982), [1983] 2 W.W.R. 52
       (B.C. S.C.), affirmed (1985), 10 Admin. L.R. 204 (B.C. C.A.).

271   *Irvine v. Canada (Restrictive Trade Practices Commission), supra* note 252.

272   *Mathon v. Canada (Minister of Employment & Immigration)* (1988), 38 Admin. L.R. 193
(Fed. T.D.).

273   *De Sousa v. Canada (Minister of Employment & Immigration)* (1988), 32 Admin. L.R. 140
(Fed. C.A.).

274   See for example *Jones v. Canada (Royal Canadian Mounted Police Public Complaints
Commission)* (1998), 162 D.L.R. (4th) 750 (Fed. T.D.); *Groenewegen v. Northwest Terri-
tiories (Speaker of the Legislative Assembly)* (1998), [1998] N.W.T.J. No. 129 (N.W.T.
S.C.).

fundamental justice. Each case turns on its own unique circumstances, because there is neither an absolute right to counsel nor an absolute discretion to deny counsel.

(e) Availability of an Adjournment

The refusal by an administrative tribunal to grant an adjournment may amount to a denial of procedural fairness, if the refusal to grant the adjournment is unreasonable in the circumstances. If one party cannot be present or cannot present his or her case adequately because his or her request for an adjournment is denied, the hearing will not be fair and courts can step in to remedy the situation. However, there is no absolute right to an adjournment, and a tribunal undoubtedly has the jurisdiction to grant or to refuse an adjournment on proper grounds:[275]

> but in the exercise of that discretion the court will not permit a board to act capriciously, or in disregard of the rights of others, or be motivated by bias towards any interested party. Where such conduct appears and results in a denial of natural justice, the courts will not hesitate to intervene in order that justice may be done.

Granting an adjournment is a discretionary matter. Refusing an adjournment may amount to a breach of procedural fairness but not every refusal to grant an adjournment will amount to a denial of fairness.

In *R. v. Saskatchewan (Labour Relations Board)*, the Labour Relations Board of Saskatchewan had refused a request for a one-day adjournment by the employer who wished to bring an officer of the employer company as a witness to testify on the issue in dispute. Davis J. held that the dispute could only have been properly resolved by the Board once it had heard this testimony, that the request was genuine and entirely reasonable, and that none of the parties would have been prejudiced by an adjournment. Therefore, Davis J. held that the Board's refusal was unjustified and resulted in a denial of procedural fairness.

On appeal, however, a unanimous Court of Appeal held that in refusing the adjournment, the Board:[276]

> . . . exercised a discretion which it had, and, in my respectful view, did not do so wrongfully. The company, in my opinion, in waiting until the morning of 4th April before asking for an adjournment or asking for another date for the hearing, did not act reasonably. The need for an adjournment was not something that arose unexpectedly. The company had known for a considerable length of time of Piggott's commitment. In spite of this it never at any time, although there was ample opportunity to do so, advised the Board that the date of 4th

---

275 *R. v. Saskatchewan (Labour Relations Board)* (1972) [1973] 1 W.W.R. 331 at 336 (Sask. C.A.), reversed [1973] 6 W.W.R. 165 (Sask. C.A.).

276 *Ibid.* at 171.

April was not a satisfactory one for a hearing. Had it done so, the Board might have arranged for a date mutually agreeable to both parties. The Board was not given an opportunity to do so.

After a very careful consideration of all the evidence, and with every deference to the learned Chambers Judge, in my opinion, to hold that under the facts as disclosed under this application the Board wrongfully exercised its discretion in refusing to grant an adjournment, would be an improper interference with those discretionary powers vested in the Board.

Similarly, in *C.U.P.E., Local 30 v. WMI Waste Management of Canada Inc.*[277] the Court upheld the denial of an adjournment:[278]

Nor do we see any error in the conclusion that the denial of the adjournment was not a breach of natural justice. The notice provided was adequate as to the issues to be addressed, and as to its timeliness. With knowledge of the nature of the issue to be addressed and of the possibility that some parties may be filing briefs, the parties had adequate opportunity to seek legal counsel in advance, but chose not to do so. The appellants were not caught by surprise, and were not entitled to delay proceedings through their own failure to seek legal counsel in advance.

The decision whether to adjourn is a discretionary power of the tribunal. We cannot conclude that the failure to grant an adjournment in this case was so unfair that the decision should be set aside.

Accordingly, an administrative tribunal may correctly take into account the timing of the application for an adjournment. A party seeking an adjournment, particularly in circumstances where the tribunal has convened for only that hearing, may be denied the adjournment on the basis that the need for an adjournment was not brought to the attention of the tribunal in a timely fashion.

The right to an adjournment cannot be defeated by rigid policies and guidelines. In *Mackey v. Saskatchewan (Medical Care Insurance Commission)*,[279] the Court held that it was ". . . improper to have a rigid policy with respect to the length of hearings, particularly given the variety of issues that hearings before Commissions might involve." The Court held that the applicant deserved a full and fair hearing and that the applicant's right to procedural fairness overrode the policy of the Board. Similarly, in the case of *Assn. of Professional Engineers (Ontario) v. Smith*,[280] the Association had a policy of denying adjournments when one was requested on the basis that a party had

---

277   (1996), 34 Admin. L.R. (2d) 172 (Alta. C.A.).
278   *Ibid.* at paras. 9, 10.
279   (1988), 32 Admin. L.R. 279 (Sask. Q.B.).
280   (1989), 38 Admin. L.R. 212 (Ont. H.C.).

changed counsel. The applicant had changed counsel and his adjournment request was denied on the basis of this policy. The applicant's counsel applied for a court order to prohibit the committee from proceeding until he had time adequately to prepare for the hearing. The court granted this application and stated that rigid guidelines cannot be used to avoid the basic principles of procedural fairness. If a fair hearing depends upon counsel being informed and prepared, then sufficient time must be provided to allow for this.

A request for an adjournment may be properly refused where the tribunal believes that the request is a stalling tactic or is otherwise not genuine. In *Stolove v. College of Physicians & Surgeons (Ontario)*,[281] the applicant delayed the hearing process by continually changing counsel and requesting adjournments. Eventually, the tribunal dismissed his requests on the grounds that he had ample time to retain and instruct counsel. The applicant was denied a remedy on judicial review, and the Court held that the denial of an adjournment in these circumstances did not amount to a breach of procedural fairness. The Court held that the primary concern – whether the applicant has been prejudiced – must be balanced against the interest of the public in the speedy resolution of such matters. The adjournment requested in *Stolove* was largely for the convenience of counsel, and specifically was not related to the merits or preparation of the hearing. The Court held that the applicant had ample time and opportunity to retain and instruct counsel.

Requests for an adjournment must frequently be balanced against the value of continuing with the hearing in a timely fashion, particularly where the administrative tribunal has a public interest mandate. For example, in *Pomeroy v. Law Society (British Columbia)*,[282] the refusal to grant an adjournment was held not to have been made capriciously or arbitrarily, and was accordingly held not to be a denial of procedural fairness. This was despite the Law Society having amended one allegation against the applicant Pomeroy less than a week before the hearing. The amendment changed the allegation from an allegation of entering into an inappropriate loan with a client into an allegation of theft from the client. In refusing the adjournment in this case, the Chairman of the Discipline Committee of the Law Society took into account the difficulty of reconvening the decision-making panel, as well as the circumstances of the alleged victims and potential impact on the prosecution's evidence. The Court on judicial review held that these were legitimate factors to consider, and that in proceedings such as these, the tribunal is entitled to take into account the public interest in having a "reasonably expeditious resolution" of disciplinary proceedings.[283]

The same principles apply to a grant or refusal of an adjournment, despite whether the adjournment request occurs at the beginning of the hearing or during the hearing. Occasionally, an adjournment request will occur during

---

281   (1988), 30 O.A.C. 236 (Ont. Div. Ct.).

282   (1998), [1998] B.C.J. No. 347, 1998 CarswellBC 327 (B.C. S.C.).

283   *Ibid.* at para. 8. Public interest was also a factor in *R. (J.) v. College of Psychologists (British Columbia)* (1995), 33 Admin. L.R. (2d) 174 (B.C. S.C. [In Chambers]), where the court held that an applicant, having successfully obtained an adjournment, could not later bring an application based on improper delay by the College.

the course of a hearing, rather than at the beginning. Courts have held that, where circumstances warrant an adjournment, the time of the request does not change whether a denial may breach procedural fairness. For example, in *Bailey v. Registered Nurses' Assn. (Saskatchewan)*,[284] the prosecution in professional disciplinary proceedings failed to disclose relevant materials to defence counsel until mid-way through the oral hearing, and then the tribunal refused counsel's adjournment request to allow time to review those materials. On judicial review, the Court held that an adjournment was warranted in the circumstances and that the refusal of an adjournment ". . . may have affected the appellants' ability to make full answer and defence . . . [and] may have resulted in prejudice . . .".[285] The Court in *Bailey* also held that natural breaks in a hearing day, i.e. lunch breaks, were not to be confused with adjournments, and that breaks such as a lunch break ought not to be viewed by the tribunal as preparation time.

As was the case in *Bailey* where the applicants had not received disclosure of material documents until mid-way through the hearing of the allegations, requests for adjournments often accompany other allegations of a breach of procedural fairness. The combined effect of these may be taken into account by a reviewing Court. In *Atwal v. Canada (Minister of Citizenship & Immigration)*,[286] the Court first held that the Board's refusal to grant two adjournments constituted a denial of procedural fairness for the applicant refugee. In *Atwal*, the Board (on a second request) granted one adjournment of a particular refugee hearing. However, in the late afternoon of the hearing, counsel for the applicant sought a further adjournment of the proceedings to another day, on the basis of another commitment and also that there was no likelihood of completing the whole hearing even if the hearing continued into the evening. The Board refused this request without seeking any information about the competing commitment. After an acrimonious exchange, counsel for the applicant and the applicant left the hearing. The Board then decided to treat the proceedings as an abandoned refugee claim and issued a notice for an Abandonment Hearing. The Board sent the notice of the Abandonment Hearing to the applicant but not to counsel for the applicant, ostensibly because the counsel's leave-taking constituted a withdrawal as counsel. On the day of the Abandonment Hearing, an agent for counsel for the applicant appeared and sought an adjournment of the abandonment proceedings. The Board denied this request, and indeed denied numerous requests for a two-minute adjournment for the agent to speak with the applicant about the merits of the abandonment proceedings.

On judicial review, the Court held that, with respect to the denial of the adjournment during the first hearing, the Board was not entitled to force a hearing into the evening, unless that decision to continue later than usual had been given with reasonable notice, done by consent of all parties, or decided

---

284　(1998), 167 Sask. R. 232 (Sask. Q.B.). See also *Penton v. Métis Nation of Alberta Assn.*, 29 Alta. L.R. (3d) 223, [1995] 8 W.W.R. 39 (Alta. Q.B.).

285　*Ibid.* at 272.

286　(1998), [1998] F.C.J. No. 1693 (Fed. T.D.).

after hearing the reason counsel for the applicant had to leave and found those reasons wanting. The Court noted that, in the circumstances, it was unlikely that the Board hearing would have been completed by 6:00 p.m. and that in these circumstances the refusal of an adjournment was a breach of procedural fairness. This breach was compounded by the decision of the Board to later issue a Notice of the Abandonment Hearing to the applicant but not to counsel for the applicant, and then to refuse an adjournment of the Abandonment Hearing on the day set out in the Notice. The Court held [at para. 21] that:

> [t]he Board displayed a serious lack of judgment when it proceeded with the abandonment proceedings at a time when it was still angry with Mr. Rowe [counsel for the applicant]. This may explain why it gave fairly short Notice of the Abandonment Hearing to the Applicant and no notice to Mr. Rowe. These procedural choices seriously prejudiced the Applicant's ability to proceed on the merits on February 10, 1998, either with Mr. Rowe or with another counsel. The result was that, at the Abandonment Hearing, the Board would very likely be able to order that the Applicant's refugee claim had been abandoned. Essentially, the Board "set up" the Applicant to fail at the Abandonment Hearing.

It was clear in this case that the Applicant had not had an opportunity to present his case adequately to the Board, because of the repeated denials of adjournment requests. The lack of notice to counsel for the Applicant made worse the denial of procedural fairness due to the refused adjournments. However, reviewing courts are able to take into account the fact that two breaches of procedural fairness, operating together, may result in a more serious breach than either of them alone.

The governing principle must be that all interested parties have a right to a fair hearing. If, for good reason, one party cannot put its case squarely before the tribunal, then procedural fairness requires that the party be granted its requested adjournment.

(f) Stay of Proceedings

A stay of proceedings and an interlocutory injunction are remedies that have sufficiently common characteristics that they are governed by the same rules. The test for granting a stay of proceedings or interlocutory injunction is set out in *Metropolitan Stores (MTS) Ltd. v. Manitoba Food & Commercial Workers, Local 832*[287] In this case, an employer sought to set aside a provision of the Manitoba *Labour Relations Act,* which allowed the Labour Board to impose a collective agreement in certain circumstances. The employer alleged that the provisions were contrary to the *Charter,* and applied to the Court of

---

287   25 Admin. L.R. 20, [1987] 1 S.C.R. 110 (S.C.C.). This test was reiterated by the Supreme Court of Canada in an application for a stay pending appeal in a constitutional challenge to the validity of tobacco products legislation: *RJR-MacDonald Inc. v. Canada (Attorney General)*, [1994] 1 S.C.R. 311 (S.C.C.).

Queen's Bench for an order staying the proceedings of the Manitoba Labour Board until the validity of the legislation was determined.

The case was ultimately determined by the Supreme Court of Canada, where a unanimous Court outlined the test for whether to grant a stay of proceedings. The court will consider:

1. whether there is a serious question to be tried;
2. whether irreparable harm, that is harm not susceptible or difficult to be compensated in damages, will result; and
3. where the balance of convenience lies.

The Court in *Metropolitan Stores* noted that a judge determining a stay or interlocutory injunction application has only a "limited role" and ought not to attempt to determine the case. This is because at the interlocutory stage of the proceedings, the motions judge will usually not have heard evidence, will have little or no pleadings or submissions in writing, and not all parties will necessarily have been notified. The Court also held that the public interest mandate of an administrative tribunal was an important factor in determining the issue of balance of convenience.[288] In *Metropolitan Stores*, the Court held that the public interest was best served by ensuring administrative efficiency and certainty in public administration, and accordingly set aside the grant of a stay of proceedings by the lower court.

An illustration of these principles comes from *Everingham v. Ontario*[289] where patients at the Oak Ridge Division of the Mental Health Centre in Penetanguishene applied for a declaration that the Social Behaviour Management Program violated section 35 of the *Mental Health Act* and sections 2, 7 and 12 of the *Charter*. The Court, applying the *Metropolitan Stores Ltd.* test, determined there was a serious issue to be tried, but that there was no evidence adduced regarding harm and that even if there was harm, such harm could be recompensed by damages. As well, the Court held that the balance of convenience favoured not suspending the program because to do so would endanger the safety and security of other patients, staff and visitors.

Although the Supreme Court in *Metropolitan Stores* formulated these rules in the context of a question of constitutional validity,[290] lower courts have applied the same principles to stays pending other kinds of determinations. For example, in *Everingham*,[291] the stay was requested pending a determination of whether, *inter alia*, the complained of procedures violated the *Mental Health Act*. In *Northern Alberta Dairy Pool Ltd. v. Miscellaneous Teamsters, Local 987*,[292] the Canada Labour Relations Board held that the factors identified by the Supreme Court in *Metropolitan Stores*, including the public interest, were applicable to stay applications in labour relations matters.

---

288 *Ibid.*
289 (1991), 5 O.R. (3d) 149 (Ont. Gen. Div.).
290 The Supreme Court heard argument on a similar point in *Phillips v. Nova Scotia (Commissioner, Public Inquiries Act)*, [1995] 2 S.C.R. 97 (S.C.C.), but declined to deal with the issue because it had become moot.
291 *Everingham, supra* note 289.
292 (1991), 12 C.L.R.B.R. (2d) 28 (Alta. L.R.B.).

Frequently, a party to proceedings by an administrative tribunal will apply for a stay of proceedings pending the determination of another proceeding. This often occurs in professional discipline proceedings where there is either a civil action or criminal charges arising from the same set of facts. In such circumstances, the appropriate test to be applied by the administrative tribunal is that set out in *Metropolitan Stores*, taking into account the public interest mandate of the professional governing body and the need for speedy resolution of such matters. In *Howe v. Institute of Chartered Accountants (Ontario)*,[293] the applicant accountant applied to the Chairman of the Discipline Committee of the Institute of Chartered Accountants for a stay of the disciplinary proceedings pending the outcome of a civil trial arising from the same facts. Howe argued that he would suffer prejudice in the civil action because the plaintiffs would have access to evidence adduced during the disciplinary proceedings, that running both the civil action and the disciplinary defence would be too costly and an unreasonable burden, and that findings by the disciplinary tribunal could improperly influence the civil action. The Court in *Howe* held (at 125) that:

> . . . to permit the disciplinary hearing in the case at bar to be blocked indefinitely by the existence of civil actions which may not be prosecuted expeditiously and which may ultimately be settled, would be quite inconsistent . . . with a recognition of the public interest in the disciplinary proceedings.

An application for a stay of proceedings pending the result of a criminal trial arising out of the same facts is more likely to be successful. Here, the question of harm will be determined by reference to potential prejudice to the fair criminal trial of the accused.[294] The applicant for a stay of disciplinary proceedings pending a criminal trial will be required to demonstrate that he or she will suffer irreparable harm in the criminal proceedings; indeed that proceeding with the disciplinary proceedings will essentially defeat his or her right to silence in the criminal proceedings. Many statutes granting professional governing bodies the authority to discipline members include provisions protecting against the use of evidence tendered in the disciplinary proceedings in subsequent civil proceedings. Such provisions make it less likely that a person subject to both proceedings will suffer prejudice in subsequent proceedings, and also make it less likely that the applicant will satisfy the test for a stay of the disciplinary proceedings.

---

293   (1995), 31 Admin. L.R. (2d) 133 (Ont. C.A.), affirming (1994), 31 Admin. L.R. (2d) 119 (Ont. Div. Ct.), leave to appeal allowed (April 18, 1995), Doc. CA M14986 (Ont. C.A.). A separate issue in the same proceedings is reported at *Howe v. Institute of Chartered Accountants (Ontario)* (1994), 27 Admin. L.R. (2d) 118 (Ont. C.A.), leave to appeal refused (1995), 27 Admin. L.R. (2d) 118 (note) (S.C.C.).
294   See for example *Voutsis v. College of Physicians & Surgeons* (1987), 41 D.L.R. (4th) 378 (Sask. Q.B.).

The Supreme Court of Canada's decision in *Blencoe v. British Columbia (Human Rights Commission)*[295] is frequently cited for the proposition that delay justifies obtaining a stay in administrative law proceedings on the ground that it is an abuse of process. *Blencoe* dealt primarily with whether section 7 of the *Charter* was violated by state-caused delay in human rights proceedings. The majority refused to grant a stay in these circumstances, stating that the onus is heavy and should only be granted in the "clearest of cases" in administrative law cases. Mr. Justice Bastarache, on behalf of the majority, noted:[296]

> In order to find an abuse of process, the court must be satisfied that, "the damage to the public interest in the fairness of the administrative process should the proceeding go ahead would exceed the harm to the public interest in the enforcement of the legislation if the proceedings were halted" (Brown and Evans, supra, at p. 9-68). According to L'Heureux-Dubé J. in Power, supra, at p. 616, "abuse of process" has been characterized in the jurisprudence as a process tainted to such a degree that it amounts to one of the clearest of cases. In my opinion, this would apply equally to abuse of process in administrative pro-ceedings. For there to be abuse of process, the proceedings must, in the words of L'Heureux-Dubé J., be "unfair to the point that they are contrary to the interests of justice" (p. 616). "Cases of this nature will be extremely rare" (Power, supra, at p. 616). In the administrative context, there may be abuse of process where conduct is equally oppressive.

The Supreme Court's decision in *Blencoe* did not leave much room for the direct application of section 7 of the *Charter*[297] to the practices and pro-cedures adopted by administrative authorities in crafting a suitable remedy.[298]

---

295 [2000] 2 S.C.R. 307, 23 Admin. L.R. (3d) 175 (S.C.C.).
296 *Ibid.* at para. 120.
297 S. 7 of the *Charter* reads as follows:
   Everyone has the right to life, liberty and security of the person and the right not to be deprived thereof except in accordance with the principles of fundamental justice.
298 *Blencoe* has been cited in some lower court decisions to grant stays for delay under the common law. In *Crown Packaging Ltd. v. British Columbia (Human Rights Commission)*, 2000 BCSC 1809 (B.C. S.C.), reversed (2002), 98 B.C.L.R. (3d) 250 (B.C. C.A.), an employer successfully argued that a stay against referral of a complaint of workplace harassment was in order because the Human Rights Commission had delayed the process for over five years, causing actual and potential prejudice. Justice Taylor concluded that (at para. 134):
   . . . there has been an impairment of the process that led to the referral to the Tribunal that will impact upon the fairness, whether perceived or real of that hearing, and that the delay has prejudiced the petitioner on an evidentiary basis and amounts to an abuse of process. Because of these and the position taken by the Tribunal in relation to the Commission I am of the opinion that this Court could and should intervene. This case is one in which the relief sought should be granted notwithstanding the observations of many courts that a stay of proceedings is a remedy that should be reserved for the clearest of cases. In my view, because of the two bases which I have discussed, this is such a

Subsequently, there have been a number of lower level court decisions confirming that section 7 was not engaged in various administrative law contexts. For example, in *Starzynski v. Canada Safeway Ltd.*,[299] the Court of Queen's of Alberta denied section 7 protection to a union in a human rights matter. In *Anhgang v. Law Society (Manitoba)*,[300] the Court ruled that delay in an investigation by the Law Society did not engage the "right to life, liberty and security of the person" protected by section 7. While the unexplained 16-month delay was unreasonable, the applicants failed to establish any prejudice, so there was no violation of the administrative law principles of fundamental justice (including the right to a fair hearing) as described in *Blencoe*.

A subsequent Supreme Court of Canada case involving delay and section 7 of the *Charter* was *Winnipeg Child & Family Services (Central Area) v. W. (K.L.).*[301] This case involved an unsuccessful challenge to legislation authorizing the apprehension of children by child welfare authorities in non-emergency situations and without prior judicial authorization. Given earlier cases such as *Blencoe*, it is probably beyond doubt that section 7 would apply to this situation. The Court was split on whether the section 7 rights to life, liberty and security of the person required prior judicial authorization as a prerequisite to lawful apprehension in non-emergency cases.

The majority addressed whether the delay of the post-apprehension hearing violated the section 7 principles of fundamental justice. The majority noted that the scheme must minimize family disruption (and respect a child's need for continuity) as much as possible through fair and prompt post-apprehension hearings which allowed reasonable notice, disclosure of particulars and an opportunity for meaningful parental participation. The majority found that the legislation which allowed for a two-week delay between removal and the interim child protection hearing seemed "to lie at the outside limit of what is constitutionally acceptable".[302] However, the majority warned that limits must be somewhat flexible:[303]

> . . . it does not seem advisable in this case to state a precise constitutional standard for delays in the child protection context. There may be several means by which constitutionally-sufficient safeguards could be implemented. As this court recognized in *R. v. Jones*, [1986] 2 S.C.R. 284, at p. 304, the principles of fundamental justice do not require total uniformity among provinces and territories; they must be

---

case.
See also *Stearns v. Alberta Insurance Council*, 2001 ABQB 752 (Alta. Q.B.), additional reasons at 2001 ABQB 863 (Alta. Q.B.) for another example where the court has relied on the principles of natural justice to stay proceedings because of delay.
299   (2000), 86 Alta. L.R. (3d) 366 (Alta. Q.B.), affirmed (2003), 330 A.R. 340 (Alta. C.A.).
300   (2001), 2000 MBQB 157 (Man. Q.B.), affirmed 2001 MBCA 137 (Man. C.A.).
301   2000 SCC 48 (S.C.C.).
302   *Ibid.* at para. 125.
303   *Ibid.*

given some flexibility in designing administrative regimes in light of the particular needs of their respective communities.[304]

The majority ruled that additional delays should not generally be tolerated if the parents are ready for a hearing on the date the application is returnable. Having found the legislation to be in conformity with section 7 of the *Charter*, the majority of the Supreme Court denied the application to invalidate the law pursuant to section 52. Then the majority turned to the issue of individual remedies under section 24, and ultimately denied any personal *Charter* remedy for the delay.

The minority also addressed the issue of delay. According to the minority, the length of delay and its cause and effect should be assessed together, rather than in isolation. Further, the remedial action must be appropriate – it could take the form of a stay or of an expedited hearing and costs.

(g) Legislative Prescriptions for Administrative Procedures

Many authority-granting statutes contain provisions setting out specific procedures to be adopted by the delegate. However, more general attempts have also been made to provide an all-encompassing code of procedure for statutory delegates. For example, the Alberta *Administrative Procedures Act*[305] governs many aspects of the procedure used by the few bodies[306] to which it has been applied.[307] The same approach was adopted subsequently in the Ontario *Statutory Powers Procedure Act*,[308] which is not only more comprehensive in dealing with every aspect of procedure, but also applies to considerably more statutory delegates. Both of these models follow the lead of the American *Federal Administrative Procedures Act*.[309]

Just as *ad hoc* statutory provisions as to procedure do not totally supplant the common law rule of procedural fairness, it is probably true that these uniform procedures Acts provide minimum requirements for procedural fairness, leaving the courts with the power to impose the additional procedural requirements of the residual common law if the ends of fairness so require.

The English approach goes considerably further. On the one hand, it is true that the 1958, 1971 and 1992 versions of the *Tribunals and Inquiries Acts*[310] attempt to provide a comprehensive code of procedure for a large

---

304 The Act had been amended between the time of apprehension and the trial to shorten the delay.
305 R.S.A. 2000, c. A-3, reproduced in Appendix 1.
306 See note 439, below.
307 The Alberta Law Reform Institute has proposed the adoption of a comprehensive code of procedures which would apply to all administrative tribunals. This is a far more comprehensive code of procedural rules for administrative agencies than is found in the *Administrative Procedures Act*. See *Powers and Procedures for Administrative Tribunals in Alberta*, ALRI Final Report No. 79, December 1999. The code would cover all aspects of administrative process and would apply to all administrative tribunals. As of December 2003, these proposals had not been implemented by the Alberta Legislature.
308 R.S.O. 1990, c. S-22, reproduced in Appendix 2.
309 5 U.S.C.A.
310 1958 (6 & 7 Eliz. 2, c. 66); 1971, c. 62; 1992, c. 53.

number of statutory tribunals. On the other hand, the Acts also create a Council on Tribunals[311] which is charged with the task of reviewing and approving the procedures adopted by these tribunals. This allows for considerable attention to adapting general procedural guidelines to the requirements of individual and quite diverse statutory schemes. It also permits close scrutiny of the content of any delegated legislation enacted by the tribunal to govern its own procedures. There is a great deal to be said for the two-pronged English approach to ensuring the adoption of fair administrative procedures.[312]

More recently, the *Administrative Justice Project* in British Columbia has gone even further and proposed that the legislature articulate such matters including the standard of review which a court is to apply on judicial review or on appeal.[313] This would signal the legislature's intention about which items it intends to be left to the tribunal and which it intends to be reviewed by the courts.

(h) Role of Board Counsel During the Hearing

A tribunal cannot delegate any of its obligations to conduct the hearing or to make the final decision to its own counsel. Any extensive participation by counsel will amount to the denial of a fair hearing.[314] For example, in *Matthews v. Board of Directors of Physiotherapy (Ontario)*,[315] the Board's counsel adopted a very aggressive and interventionist approach to his role in the hearing. It was found that counsel appeared on crucial issues to assume ". . . the mantle of Chairman to the extent that he, rather than the tribunal, appeared to be deciding the matter in issue."[316] This resulted in an appearance of unfairness and consequently a loss of jurisdiction.[317]

---

311 See discussion on "Statutory requirements for reasons", below.
312 The Law Reform Commission of Canada considered the desirability of this approach in A. Leadbeater's Study Paper entitled *Council on Administration*, 1980. In Ontario, the Statutory Powers Procedure Review Committee performs this function.
313 The BC's *Administrative Tribunals Act* received Royal Assent on May 20, 2004. See Frank A.V. Falzon's Background Paper for the B.C. Administrative Justice Project entitled "Standard of Review on Judicial Review or Appeal" 2001 at 45*ff*. This excellent paper and other material from the Project can be found at www.gov.bc.ca/ajp/rpts/.
314 *Venczel v. Assn. of Architects (Ontario)* (1989), 45 Admin. L.R. 288 (Ont. Div. Ct.), additional reasons at (1990), 45 Admin. L.R. 288 at 289 (Ont. Div. Ct.).
315 (1990), 44 Admin. L.R. 147 (Ont. Div. Ct.).
316 *Ibid.* at 148.
317 See also *Venczel v. Assn. of Architects (Onatrio)* (1990), 45 Admin. L.R. 288 (Ont. Div. Ct.), additional reasons at (1990), 45 Admin. L.R. 288 at 289 (Ont. Div. Ct.) where the court stated (at 289):
　　In our view, it is intolerable that a man faced with a disciplinary hearing should have to face not only the discipline committee that has been provided for by the legislature, but in addition, the counsel hired by it who runs the hearing, makes the decisions for the committee, and makes those decisions without even consulting the committee. A person facing such a hearing would not know whether he has been tried by the committee appointed under the Act or by someone hired to assist it.
　　See also *Brett v. Ontario (Directors, Physiotherapy Board)* (1991), 77 D.L.R. (4th) 144 (Ont. Div. Ct.), affirmed (1993), 64 O.A.C. 152 (Ont. C.A.).

Similarly, in *Carlin v. Registered Psychiatric Nurses' Assn. (Alberta)*,[318] the Court held that counsel to the decision-making Discipline Committee of the Nurses' Association "... dominated the Hearing as to the issue of jurisdiction".[319] Binder J. held that it was quite proper for the Discipline Committee to rely on legal counsel for advice, particularly on legal issues such as jurisdiction, but that in this case, the role of counsel went beyond a consulting role and moved into a decision-making role.

Legal counsel to the tribunal also cannot be legal counsel for one of the parties appearing before the tribunal, nor can the counsel be too closely aligned with one of the parties appearing before the tribunal. For example, in *Hutterian Brethren Church of Starland v. Starland (Municipal District No. 47)*,[320] legal counsel acted for both the municipality (a party) and the Development Appeal Board (the decision-maker). While this situation was determined on the basis that legal counsel's dual role resulted in a biased panel, not on the basis of improper consultation, it is nonetheless an important aspect of the role of legal counsel, and the constraints on the role of legal counsel because of the requirements of procedural fairness. In *Starland*, counsel for the municipality retired with the Development Appeal Board, thus resulting in the ultimate decision of the Board being quashed.[321]

In *Omineca Enterprises Ltd. v. British Columbia (Minister of Forests)*,[322] the Supreme Court of British Columbia held that counsel retained by the Appeal Board properly exercised his duty to the Board. The court outlined the permissible extent of a solicitor's involvement:[323]

> [I]t is important for counsel to proceed in a spirit of disinterested inquiry and to avoid the appearance of partisanship on behalf of any interest. It is undesirable to be too dogmatic in attempting to define the proper functions of counsel to administrative tribunals in all circumstances. The overriding objective is always to ensure that the proceedings are fair and impartial.

In *Snider v. Assn. of Registered Nurses (Manitoba)*,[324] the Manitoba Court of Appeal held that the mere presence of the tribunal's lawyer during the deliberation stage does not, without more, establish a breach of procedural

---

318   [1996] 8 W.W.R. 584 (Alta. Q.B.).

319   *Ibid.* at 604.

320   (1993), 9 Alta. L.R. (3d) 1, 14 Admin. L.R. (2d) 186 (Alta. C.A.).

321   See the discussion of a similar allegation and finding in *Bailey v. Registered Nurses' Assn. (Saskatchewan)* (1998), 167 Sask. R. 232 (Sask. Q.B.), where counsel to the Association had discussed the disciplinary proceedings against Bailey with members of the Discipline Committee, and subsequently appeared for the prosecution before the Discipline Committee. See also a discussion of a similar overlapping of roles of legal counsel in *Regie*, note 369, below.

322   (1992), 7 Admin. L.R. (2d) 95 (B.C. S.C.), affirmed (1993), 18 Admin. L.R. (2d) 210 (B.C. C.A.), leave to appeal refused (1994), 23 Admin. L.R. (2d) 319 (note) (S.C.C.).

323   *Ibid.* at 99-100.

324   [2000] 4 W.W.R. 130 (Man. C.A.), leave to appeal refused (2000), 262 N.R. 396 (note) (S.C.C.).

fairness. However, the court found it "desirable" for counsel to advise and confer with the tribunal in the presence of the parties in order to avoid allegations of a breach of procedural fairness.

Accordingly, Board counsel must confine his or her role to that of consultant, and is precluded from taking too active a role during the hearing itself, in questioning witnesses or asking questions about the submissions made by the parties. If Board counsel strays into decision-making, the ultimate decision will be quashed by a reviewing Court on the basis of a breach of procedural fairness.

(i) Summary on Procedural Fairness During Oral Hearings

It is now well established that an administrative tribunal must proceed fairly when making its decision. Precisely what this means will be the subject of innumerable cases, all of which will have to seek that fine line between procedural fairness and procedural arbitrariness. It must be remembered that the proliferation of administrative decision-makers throughout the multitude of Canadian federal, provincial, and territorial statutes represents the intention of legislatures to have the process of governing made fast, efficient, and readily accessible to the general public. In achieving this objective, however, the courts will not allow the decision-makers to lose sight of those elements of fair procedure contained in the rules of procedural fairness. However, from the above discussion, it can be seen that the contents of the rules are flexible and must be tailored to each situation as it arises.

It cannot be said precisely what the content of the rules of procedural fairness require in every circumstance. Nevertheless, the courts are and will continue to be called upon to define the rules. While the occasional egregious excess will occur, most judicial review on the basis of procedural fairness involves careful case-by-case analysis of the alleged unfairness. Because the principles of procedural fairness vary in content from one case to another and from one administrative tribunal to another, reviewing courts must always examine the facts and context individually in order to determine whether a breach of procedural fairness occurred.

4. Post-Hearing Processes

Generally the duty to be fair arises during the oral hearing. However, the administrative tribunal's duty to determine issues before it in a fair and impartial manner does not end with the conclusion of the oral hearing. Issues which may arise post-hearing include: the extent of consultation which panel members can engage in with other members of the administrative agency (or its staff) after the hearing has ended; the role of counsel in helping to draft reasons; the duty of a decision-making panel to consult together in reaching a decision; and whether changes in the circumstances necessitate or allow a new hearing.

(a) Hearing Before the Person Making the Decision

Procedural fairness requires that "the person who decides must hear". Several considerations justify the rule. First, it is based on statutory intention and the maxim *delegatus non potest delegare*.[325] Second, it is based on the need for independence. Procedural fairness requires that decisions be made without inappropriate influences upon the decision-makers. Third, it reinforces the rule that parties must be given the chance to address the points raised against them. Accordingly, the rule is an aspect of the *audi alteram partem* rule. Allowing persons to participate as decision-makers when they have not participated in the hearing raises the obvious possibility that new matters will be introduced without an opportunity for a response.

In general, the person upon whom the statutory power to decide has been conferred must make the decision. No delegation of this power is allowed. However, the rule is relaxed in various circumstances where administrative efficiency and possibility demand it. For instance, many statutes require the Minister to make the decision. It would be physically impossible for one person to investigate, hear and decide all the matters which the statute calls upon that person to decide. The courts have therefore often allowed such powers to be exercised by officials in the Minister's department who are his or her subordinates. In most cases, this is a form of valid sub-delegation.[326]

By contrast there are some cases where a subordinate official conducts an investigation, hears submissions, examines witnesses and so on, and then reports everything fully to the person with the statutory power to decide. If that person makes a decision based on the full information, there is no breach of procedural fairness. Of course, the question is raised of whether the person affected by that report is entitled to see it.[327]

---

325 See Chapters 3 and 4 for a discussion of this maxim.

326 For example, under the *Income Tax Act*, specific provision is made to permit the delegation *by regulation* of certain of the Minister's powers to various departmental officials. Similarly, statutes creating government departments often expressly authorize Ministerial delegation. See, for example the former *Department of Education Act*, R.S.A. 1980, c. D-17, s. 5.1. The text did not refer to these forms of formally recognized delegation, but rather to less formal institutional delegation.

327 The increasingly common application by courts of the disclosure requirements in *R. v. Stinchcombe*, [1991] 3 S.C.R. 326 (S.C.C.) suggest that the person affected would indeed have the right to see the report. See for example *Markandey v. Board of Ophthalmic Dispensers (Ontario)* (1994), [1994] O.J. No. 484, 1994 CarswellOnt 2601 (Ont. Gen. Div); *Thompson v. Chiropractors' Assn. (Saskatchewan)* (1996), 36 Admin. L.R. (2d) 273 (Sask. Q.B.); the dissent in *Howe v. Institute of Chartered Accountants (Ontario)* (1994), 27 Admin L.R. (2d) 118 (Ont. C.A.), leave to appeal to S.C.C. refused (1995), 27 Admin. L.R. (2d) 118 (note) (S.C.C.); *Christian v. Northwestern General Hospital* (1993), 115 D.L.R. (4th) 279 (Ont. Div. Ct.), motion for leave to appeal to the Ontario Court of Appeal dismissed; *Dhanjal v. Air Canada* (1996), [1996] C.H.R.D. No. 4, 1996 CarswellNat 2962 (Can. Human Rights Trib.), affirmed (1997), 139 F.T.R. 37 (Fed. T.D.); and *I.M.P. Group Ltd. v. Dillman* (1995), 143 N.S.R. (2d) 169 (N.S. C.A.); but see *Waterman v. National Life Assurance Co. of Canada* (1992), 18 C.H.R.R. D/173 (Ont. Bd. of Inquiry) (investigating officer's notes not ordered to be disclosed); *Nrecaj v. Canada (Minister of Employment & Immigration)* (1993), 14 Admin. L.R. (2d) 161 (Fed. T.D.); *Williams v. Canada (Regional Transfer Board, Prairie Region)* (1993), 15 Admin. L.R. (2d) 83 (Fed. C.A.); see also

Another aspect of the rule that "persons who hear cases must decide them" usually means *only* those persons must decide and no others. However, some challenges arise when a panel member is absent for some of the proceedings, but participates in the end result. The result of such an absence is to vitiate the decision unless the legislation provides express authorization for such absences.[328] It is not uncommon for municipal government statutes and others governing quasi-political decision making bodies to make such statutory exceptions.[329]

Despite these particular circumstances, the general rule is that persons who make decisions must themselves conduct the hearing (whatever the content of that hearing may be) and must make the decision.[330] A breach of this aspect of procedural fairness in effect constitutes an illegal sub-delegation.

The bigger issue in the "persons who hear cases must decide them" rule occurs within standing boards. The bulk of administrative law decision-making occurs in the context of administrative tribunals or standing boards. Single or multi-person panels hear and decide individual cases but often do so within an institutional framework. Tribunals administer important statutory schemes. They employ support staff and often legal counsel who, along with members and chairs, participate in the tribunals' processes. Consistency in decision making is often an important institutional value. Tension exists between the institutional environment and its need to preserve consistency and predictability, and the dictates of the rule that the person who hears must decide.

Courts have accepted the reality of, and necessity for, collegial consultation amongst tribunal members, and to some extent their staff advisors. At the same time, they have articulated rules to limit such consultation in the interests of due process for litigants and independence for decision-makers. Two cases illustrate the permissible limits of collegial consultation and the consequences of unacceptable intervention in the post-hearing decision-making process.

(i) The Consolidated Bathurst Case

Consolidated Bathurst involved a challenge to a long standing practice of the Ontario Labour Relations Board of holding "full-board" meetings.[331] Dur-

---

Suresh v. Canada (Minister of Citizenship & Immigration), 2002 SCC 1 (S.C.C.) and discussion in section "Knowing the Case to be Met – Disclosure", above.

328 See for example the former *Planning Act*, R.S.A. 1980, c. P-9, s. 140(3), repealed S.A. 1995, c. 24, s.103.

329 *Doyle v. Canada (Restrictive Trade Practices Commission)* (1985), 21 D.L.R. (4th) 366 at 371 (Fed. C.A.), leave to appeal refused (1985), 7 C.P.R. (3d) 235n (S.C.C.).

330 See *Hoyda v. Edmonton*, No. 7903-13252 (Alta. Q.B.) (unreported), where some members of city council voted on a matter when they were not present for the hearing; and *Western Realty Projects Ltd. v. Edmonton (City)*, [1974] 5 W.W.R. 131 (Alta. Dist. Ct.), affirmed (1974), [1975] 1 W.W.R. 681 (Alta. C.A.). The reverse problem sometimes also arises, where not all of the people who heard the matter participate in the actual decision. See also *C.R.T.C. v. C.T.V. Television Network Ltd. v. Canada (Radio-Television & Telecommunications Commission)*, [1982] 1 S.C.R. 530 (S.C.C.), where some members left during the hearing.

331 *I.W.A. Local 2-69 v. Consolidated Bathurst Packaging Ltd.*, 42 Admin. L.R. 1, [1990] 1 S.C.R. 282 (S.C.C.). For comments, see D.J. Mullan, *"Consolidated-Bathurst and the*

ing such meetings, the Chairman, the Vice-Chairs, the members, and some senior staff, would consider the policy implications of particular decisions about to be rendered by three person panels of the Board. Panels facing decisions with policy implications could, but were not obliged to, ask for the full Board's input. Discussion proceeded on the basis that the facts, as found by the panel, would be taken as given. The full Board would then discuss, without minutes or recorded vote, the policy implications of the proposed decision. Later, the panel would meet on its own to arrive at its decision, informed, but not bound, by the advice of colleagues within the Board.

In *Consolidated Bathurst*, one of the parties learned that a full board discussion had taken place in a case they had lost. That party sought Board reconsideration on the basis that the full-board procedure was illegal. The Board declined reconsideration, but took the opportunity to set out the institutional and social policy reasons for engaging in voluntary full-board consultation. Paramount amongst these reasons stood the need to maintain consistency when administering major social legislation.

The Supreme Court upheld the full-board practice. In the Court's view it involved an acceptable balance between the need for independence, the right to be heard and the advantages of full-board consultation.

The Court accepted that:[332]

> ... the rules of natural justice must take into account the institutional constraints faced by an administrative tribunal. These tribunals are created to increase the efficiency of the administration of justice and are often called upon to handle heavy caseloads. It is unrealistic to expect an administrative tribunal such as the Board to abide strictly by the rules applicable to courts of law.

The full-board process involved a policy debate within an informed and expert collegial body. This encouraged consistency and predictability in decision-making. Consistency enabled members of the public to plan those of their activities regulated by the statute, and enabled the Board to achieve a high ratio of settlement of its cases.

The Court emphasized that:[333]

> [i]ndependence is an essential ingredient of the capacity to act fairly and judicially, and any procedure or practice which unduly reduces this capacity must surely be contrary to the rules of natural justice.

Dominion Stores Pension Fund cases: Different Approaches or Reconcilable Differences?" (1986-87) 21 Admin. L.R. 215; M. Falardeau-Ramsay, "Collegiality and Decision-Making in the Aftermath of the *Consolidated-Bathurst* Decision" (1987-88) 1 C.J.A.L.P. 207; and "Is it Show-and-Tell Time for the Tribunals?" (1992) 2 R.A.L. 38.

332 *Ibid.* at 25.

333 *Ibid.* at 24.

The institutionalized protections which saved the full-board procedure from being an undue threat to this independence were:

- the process was voluntary at the instance of the panel involved,

- meetings were without recorded attendance or vote;

- panels, throughout, remained free to make and responsible for making, the final decisions;

- panels decided the facts first which were then taken as given, and

- (while this is not clearly expressed, it is implicit), all this took place within the tribunal with no external influence or pressure.

The Court imposed a further constraint, in the interest of due process, by saying that the parties must be advised of any new evidence or grounds and be given the opportunity to respond.[334]

(ii) The Tremblay Case

The decision making quorum in *Tremblay* consisted of two people, a Commissioner and an Assessor. They heard an appeal, on a question of law, over a person's entitlement to "medical aid." There was no hearing. The parties agreed on the facts and filed written argument.

The Commission had a standard practice that all draft decisions should be sent to the Commission's legal counsel for review. Counsel being on vacation, the President of the Commission reviewed the draft. He disagreed, and sent the two decision-makers a memorandum to that effect. One of the two then asked for a "consensus table" meeting, which, not unlike the "full-board" meeting in *Consolidated Bathurst*, involved a plenary meeting of the Commission.

The discussion at this consensus table led one of the two adjudicators to change her mind. Under the statute, where the two adjudicators differed, the President decided the case. He did so, deciding on the basis of the position he had taken in his earlier memorandum.

During a Court challenge, the Commission explained the reasons for mandatory counsel review and the "consensus table" mechanism. Again, this emphasized the need for maintaining consistency within a large tribunal.

The Court overturned the tribunal decision.[335] Unlike in *Consolidated Bathurst*, the institutional setting within which the consultation process occurred involved constraints that interfered with the independence of the decision-makers. The mandatory nature of the solicitor's review, and the ability of the President, as well as the individual adjudicators, to request a preliminary discussion influenced the Court's view. It found a coercive atmosphere in the

---

334   *Ibid.*
335   *Québec (Commission des affaires sociales) c. Tremblay*, 3 Admin. L.R. (2d) 173, [1992] 1 S.C.R. 952 (S.C.C.).

plenary meetings, which involved recorded votes, minutes and other formalities.

The Court reinforced the "he who decides must hear rule" by saying:[336]

> ... the statute clearly provides that it is the decision-makers who must decide a matter. Accordingly, it is those decision-makers who must retain the right to initiate consultation; imposing it on them amounts to an act of compulsion towards them and a denial of the choice expressly made by the legislature.

The Commission apparently wishes by this machinery to make the expertise of the Commission as a whole available to its members and to inform them of existing precedents. This is a praiseworthy motive. If the quorum has the advantage of the experience and opinions of its colleagues it may be in a position to render a more thoughtful decision. However, it is the quorum, and *only the quorum*, which has the responsibility of rendering the decision. If it does not wish to consult, it must be truly free not to do so. This constraint, which is subjective for the decision-makers, may also cause litigants to have an impression of objective bias. Compulsory consultation creates at the very least an appearance of a lack of independence, if not actual constraint.

(iii) Evidence About Consultation and the Deliberative Process[337]

With *Consolidated Bathurst* and *Tremblay*, the Courts arrived at a balance between the personal, institutional and social interests involved in administrative decision-making. However, there is a side effect that requires serious assessment as the law continues to unfold. Judicial review of administrative law decision-making has customarily been restricted to a review of a more or less extended record.[338] Decision-making as a process, however, is almost entirely "off the record" in the customary sense of "the record". *Tremblay* opened the door on deliberative secrecy within administrative tribunals. The Court's comments focussed upon the institutionalized controls on the panel's decision-making freedom, like Rules and objective institutional arrangements. However, the Courts' closing remarks on the point have encouraged wider scrutiny:[339]

> ... it seems to me that by the very nature of the control exercised over their decisions administrative tribunals cannot rely on deliberative secrecy to the same extent as judicial tribunals. Of course, secrecy remains the rule, but it may none the less be lifted when the litigant

---

336 *Ibid.* at 217.
337 Much of the text in this section is revised from a paper by K.M. Munro, "Potential Problems with Multi-Member Standing Boards", published by the Legal Education Society of Alberta for a seminar on Dealing with Government Boards and Agencies, April 25-28, 1997.
338 See the discussion of the "Record" in Chapter 11.
339 *Tremblay, supra* note 335 at 210.

can present valid reasons for believing that the process followed did not comply with the rules of natural justice.

Since *Tremblay*, other cases have built on this opening to examine the full details of administrative tribunal decision-making. Deliberative secrecy is still the rule, unless there is an allegation of a breach of procedural fairness. If this is the case, courts may review the process of decision-making as well as the actual decision. Applicants seeking to examine board members with respect to the process followed, either by seeking a subpoena requiring decision-makers to attend examination for discovery or seeking disclosure of documents with respect to the consultative process, are increasingly successful. Thus, an administrative tribunal may well be required to justify in detail its general consultative process or policy; alternatively, a panel of a standing board may well be required to justify in detail the actual consultation which occurred in a particular decision. Courts are increasingly prepared to shine a bright light into the otherwise unobserved (though not necessarily dark) processes of a standing board. Decisions of panels of the board may be quashed for breaches of procedural fairness unless the board is able to justify its consultative procedure within the ambit of *Consolidated-Bathurst, Tremblay* and *Régie*.[340]

The process of adjudication is generally not required to be an open process: parties are not allowed to inquire about the actual thinking process or consideration about the issues in the decision by the decision-maker.[341] Deliberative secrecy is not absolute, but it is nonetheless heavily protected. Deliberative secrecy, or confidentiality about decision-making, makes it very difficult for parties to know (and therefore assess) whether the decision-making process was fair. Deliberative secrecy also makes it very difficult for a party to challenge the process, because the knowledge and evidence of any alleged breach is in the possession of the decision-makers.

For example, the reported decision in *Consolidated-Bathurst* does not make it clear how the parties learned of the full board meeting held to discuss the policy implications of the decision to be made by the panel of the Board.[342] However the appellant learned of the full board meeting, it sought a reconsideration of the issue on the basis that the full board meeting had vitiated the first decision. In its reconsideration decision, the panel of the Board provided all of the "evidence" of the consultative process, essentially as a defence to the submissions that the earlier decision had been vitiated. That is, the decision-making panel in *Consolidated-Bathurst* volunteered the information about the

---

340   *2747-3174 Québec Inc. c. Québec (Règie des permis d'alcool)*, [1996] 3 S.C.R. 919, 42 Admin. L.R. (2d) 1 (S.C.C.).

341   See the remarks by Mr. Justice Gonthier in *Tremblay, supra* note 335, for example. At 209, he distinguishes between review by the court of the "formal process" for consultation and "matters of substance or the decision-makers' thinking on such matters."

342   Mr. Justice Gonthier in *Consolidated-Bathurst, supra* note 331, says at 11-12: "Counsel for the appellant then learned that a full Board meeting had been called to discuss the policy implication of its decision when it was still in the draft stage. The parties were neither notified of nor invited to participate in this meeting."

process, and this process was later reviewed by the Court on the basis of the information in the reconsideration decision.

Later cases did not involve disclosure in such a voluntary and co-operative manner. Whether a decision-making body must provide evidence of its consultative process has been the subject of considerable litigation. In *Tremblay*, the Commission argued that it was protected by deliberative secrecy from being required to give evidence about the consultative process. Dugas J. ordered the Commission secretary to answer questions about the process for dealing with draft decisions, and one of the decision-makers gave *viva voce* evidence.[343] In deciding that Dugas J. did not err in requiring the Commission secretary to give evidence, the unanimous Supreme Court drew a distinction between evidence of the process of consultation and evidence about the actual making of the decision by the decision-maker:[344]

> The questions raised by the respondent did not touch on matters of substance or the decision-makers' thinking on such matters. These questions were directed instead at the formal process established by the commission to ensure consistency in its decisions. They were concerned first with the institutional setting in which the decision was made and how it functioned, and second with its actual or apparent influence on the intellectual freedom of the decision-makers. This distinction was noted by Dugas J. during the interrogatories themselves.

> In the case of administrative tribunals, the difficulty of distinguishing between facts relating to an aspect of the deliberations which can be entered in evidence and those which cannot is quite understandable. The institutionalization of the decisions of administrative tribunals creates a tension between on one hand the traditional concept of deliberative secrecy and on the other the fundamental right of a party to know that the decision was made in accordance with the rules of natural justice. The institutionalized consultation process involving deliberation is the subject of rules of procedure designed to regulate the "consensus tables" process. Paradoxically, it is the public nature of these rules which, while highly desirable, may open the door to an action in nullity or an evocation. It may be questioned whether justice is seen to be done.

The Court in *Tremblay* drew a distinction between an administrative tribunal and a judge: a judge has a right to refuse to answer how and why he or she arrived at a particular conclusion; this is fundamental to judicial independence. However, an administrative tribunal is subject to review by a court on the basis of procedural fairness, which specifically involves review of the

---

343   *Tremblay, supra* note 335 at 215-18. Indeed, the testimony of Mr. Pothier was decisive in the case and appears to have been given voluntarily.

344   *Ibid* at 209.

process of the decision-making. Some of judicial review involves examination of the internal decision-making process; this implies that administrative tribunals are not as protected as judges by deliberative secrecy:[345]

> Accordingly, it seems to me that by the very nature of the control exercised over their decisions administrative tribunals cannot rely on deliberative secrecy to the same extent as judicial tribunals. Of course, secrecy remains the rule, but it may nonetheless be lifted if the litigant can present valid reasons for believing that the process followed did not comply with the rules of natural justice.

The principles of procedural fairness, therefore, may require a decision-maker to give evidence about some aspects of the process of decision-making. Particularly, the principles of procedural fairness may require a tribunal to provide evidence to a reviewing court about the consultative processes followed in general or in a particular case.

The enabling statutes of some standing boards contain provisions protecting board members from giving testimony. In *Ellis-Don Ltd. v. Ontario (Labour Relations Board)*,[346] prior to the hearing of its application for judicial review, the company unsuccessfully sought an interlocutory order to stay the decision of the Ontario Labour Relations Board, and also requested that several members of the Board be summoned for examination before an official examiner and that certain documents be produced. Steel J. granted an order compelling the members to appear, but refused the stay and the production order.[347] On appeal, the Divisional Court reversed this decision and ruled that the members of the Board could not be compelled to appear before an official examiner, based upon the common law rule respecting the compellability of administrative tribunal members and on section 117 (formerly section 111) of the *Ontario Labour Relations Act*.[348] Leave to appeal this interlocutory order to the Court of Appeal and the Supreme Court of Canada was denied.

In the substantive application for judicial review, the Supreme Court did not break any new judicial ground on this issue. It affirmed that deliberative secrecy will be maintained, particularly where constituent legislation provides additional protection, at the cost of frustrating attempts to seek evidence for judicial review. However, the majority went further to frustrate those seeking to quash administrative decisions by actively protecting the privacy of deliberations by applying the presumption of regularity to official proceedings and determinations.

---

345   *Ibid.* at 210.
346   2003 SCC 39 (S.C.C.).
347   (1992), 95 D.L.R. (4th) 56 (Ont. Div. Ct.).
348   (1994), 16 O.R. (3d) 698 (Ont. Div. Ct.), leave to appeal refused (1994), 24 Admin. L.R. (2d) 122n (Ont. C.A.), leave to appeal refused [1995] 1 S.C.R. vii (S.C.C.). S. 117 provides: Except with the consent of the Board, no member of the Board, nor its registrar, nor any of its other officers, nor any of its clerks or servants shall be required to give testimony in any civil proceeding or in any proceeding before the Board or in any proceeding before any other tribunal respecting information obtained in discharge of their duties or while acting within the scope of their employment under this Act.

Speaking about the trade-offs between fairness and deliberative secrecy in the substantive judicial review, Justice LeBel for the majority commented on the evidentiary aspect of the case:[349] "[u]ndoubtedly, the principle of deliberative secrecy creates serious difficulties for parties who fear that they may have been the victims of inappropriate tampering with the decision of the adjudicators who actually heard them."

However, in his view it was a fair cost that the process becomes less open and that litigants face tough hurdles when trying to build the evidentiary foundation necessary for a successful challenge based on alleged breaches of natural justice. Deliberative secrecy played an important role in safeguarding the independence of administrative adjudicators. It enhanced administrative consistency by granting protection to a consultative process that involved interaction between the adjudicators who heard the case and members who did not. Without secrecy, there would be a chilling effect on consultation and independence, as well as a negative impact for consistency.

Speaking about the presumption of regularity, Justice LeBel further ruled that this presumption could not be reversed simply because of a change in the reasons for the decision, especially when the change is limited on its face to questions of law and policy. A contrary approach to the presumption would deprive administrative tribunals of the independence that deliberative secrecy assures, and would jeopardize the consistency brought about through full board consultations.

Justice Binnie, speaking for the minority, held a somewhat different view. He agreed that secrecy may be justified on policy grounds, but recognized that it creates problems. He was clearly troubled by the Board relying upon its own successful denial of access to relevant information to feed the presumption of regularity and thereby defeat the appellant's complaint about the process. His negative reaction to the Board's refusal to provide evidence could be music to the ears of litigants attempting to overturn administrative decisions.

According to Justice Binnie, section 117 prevented Ellis-Don from getting to the bottom of the Board's decision-making process, but did not preclude judicial review in this type of case:[350]

> The Court ought not to be blind to the difficulties of proof in determining whether the appellant has made out its case. Otherwise the limitation imposed by *Consolidated-Bathurst* becomes a pious sentiment rather than an enforceable rule of law.

He stressed that the Courts have a real expectation that the limits on full board discussions set out in *Consolidated-Bathurst* will be enforced. He conceded that the Board is responsible for maintaining its deliberative secrecy, but was concerned that inside information from a whistle-blower could not be ignored. He held that it is the nature of judicial review to relax some of the secrecy in the decision-making process in order to dispel concerns about unfairness in

---

349 *Ellis-Don, supra* note 346 at para. 52.
350 *Ibid.* at para. 101.

the process, and suggested that the price of the Board's preserving the secrecy could be vacating the decision:[351]

> . . . the Board cannot have it both ways. It cannot, with the assistance of the legislature, deny a person in the position of the appellant all legitimate access to relevant information, then rely on the absence of this same information as a conclusive answer to the appellant's complaint. We are not in the business of playing Catch 22. The record discloses a change of position by the panel on an issue of fact. This runs counter to *Consolidated-Bathurst* and has to be dealt with properly if confidence in the integrity of the Board's decision making is to be maintained.

By contrast, in *Payne v. Ontario (Human Rights Commission),*[352] the majority of the Ontario Court of Appeal[353] allowed a limited examination of the registrar under Rule 39.03 of the Ontario *Rules of Civil Procedure* with respect to what documents, facts, considerations or recommendations not already revealed by the record[354] filed in the judicial review proceedings were before the Commissioners, to inquire as to whether "strategic factors" formed a basis for the Commissioners' decisions, and to inquire whether there were any reasons for the determination not revealed in the reasons given to the complainant.

Writing for the majority, Sharpe J.A. stated the Ontario law on examinations in the course of an application for judicial review as follows:[355]

> As I explain below, these authorities hold that a party to an application for judicial review is entitled to adduce evidence by way of examination, provided the evidence sought to be adduced is relevant to an issue properly raised on the judicial review application and is not specifically excluded by statute or some applicable legal principle, and provided that the examination is not being used for an ulterior or improper purpose and does not constitute an abuse of process of the court.

His analysis started with the Ontario Court of Appeal's decision in *Canada Metal Co. v. Heap,*[356] which is authority for the proposition that no prior leave

---

351 *Ibid.* at para. 105. See also paras. 108, 109.

352 (2000), 25 Admin. L.R. (2d) 255, 192 D.L.R. (4th) 315 (Ont. C.A.).

353 Sharpe and O'Connor JJ.A.; Abella J.A. dissented.

354 As Sharpe J.A. noted at para.161: "A statutory body subject to judicial review cannot immunize itself or its process by arriving at decisions on considerations that are not revealed by the record it files with the court." On the other hand, there is a distinction between a motion requiring the decision-maker to file a better and more complete record (of documents which should properly be included in the record), and the right to examine members or staff of the decision-maker.

355 *Supra* note 352 at para. 162.

356 (1975), 7 O.R. (2d) 185 at 191-92 (Ont. C.A.).

or order is required prior to issuing a subpoena under Rule 39.03, and that no onus of proving justification arises against the party issuing it.

He then considered concerns about deliberative secrecy and whether a factual foundation was required as possible limitations to the right to examine witnesses in the context of an application for judicial review. Sharpe J.A. noted that Rule 39.03 cannot generally be used to breach deliberative secrecy, to avoid exposing tribunal members to unduly burdensome examinations, to achieve finality, and to protect the process of debate/discussion/compromise inherent in collegial decision-making: *Agnew v. Assn. of Architects (Ontario)*[357] and *Ellis-Don*.[358] Nevertheless, the deliberative secrecy limitation must be balanced with the right of the citizen to effective judicial review of adminis-trative (as opposed to judicial) decisions: *Tremblay*.[359] In the present case, the Commissioners' claim to the protection of deliberative secrecy was weakened by the fact that they conducted their discussions at the same time they enter-tained submissions and input from staff members, so it was not possible to identify a discrete, deliberative phase in the process.

Further, an applicant for judicial review who seeks to conduct an exami-nation that will touch upon the deliberative secrecy of the decision-maker must present some basis for a clearly articulated and objectively reasonable concern that a relevant legal right may have been infringed; examinations based on conjecture or mere speculation will not be allowed. This having been said, Sharpe J.A. disagreed that it was necessary in all cases to establish a "reasonable evidential foundation" (as the Commission had urged) or that there was a "heavy onus" requiring the party seeking the examination to provide "reason-able, reliable, relevant evidence" to meet a "high threshold" (as Abella J.A. stated in dissent). This would be contrary to *Canada Metal*, and would effec-tively make Rule 39.03 redundant:[360]

---

357   (1987), 64 O.R. (2d) 8 (Ont. Div. Ct.).

358   (1994), 24 Admin. L.R. (2d) 122, 68 O.A.C. 216, 110 D.L.R. (4th) 731 (Ont. Div. Ct.), leave to appeal refused (1994), 24 Admin. L.R. (2d) 122n (Ont. C.A.), leave to appeal refused [1995] 1 S.C.R. vii (S.C.C.), reversing (1992), 6 Admin. L.R. (2d) 318, 57 O.A.C. 306, 95 D.L.R. (4th) 56 (Ont. Div. Ct.) (Steele J.).

359   *Québec (Commission des affaires sociales) c. Tremblay*, [1992] 1 S.C.R. 952 (S.C.C.) (per Gonthier J.), at 965-66:

> Additionally, when there is no appeal from the decision of an administrative tribunal, as is the case with the Commission, that decision can only be reviewed in one way: as to legality by judicial review. It is of the very nature of judicial review to examine *inter alia* the decision maker's decision-making process. Some of the grounds on which a decision may be challenged even concern the internal aspect of that process: for example, was the decision made at the dictate of a third party? Is it the result of the blind application of a previously established directive or policy? All these events accompany the deliberations or are part of them.
>
> *Accordingly, it seems to me that by the very nature of the control exercised over their decisions[,] administrative tribunals cannot rely on deliberative secrecy to the same extent as judicial tribunals. Of course, secrecy remains the rule, but it may nonetheless be lifted when the litigant can present valid reasons for believing that the process followed did not comply with the rules of natural justice.* [Emphasis added.]

360   *Payne*, *supra* note 352 at paras. 170, 171.

Simply put, an applicant for judicial review should not have to prove his or her case before securing access to the very process designed by the *Rules of Civil Procedure* to adduce evidence. It is also my view that to pitch the test so high in a case such as the present one would be inimical to the inherent power of judicial review and the importance of having a full and accurate record of what transpired before the decision-maker. To fulfill their constitutionally protected mandate of ensuring that statutory procedures are followed in a manner that accords with the principles of natural justice, the superior courts must afford litigants adequate procedures to ensure that all relevant facts are presented. Accordingly, it is sufficient if the proposed examination is focussed on facts relevant to an issue properly raised by way of judicial review. I hardly need to add that facts relevant to an issue properly raised by way of judicial review is a very specific and narrowly circumscribed classification.

. . . In my view, requiring the applicant for judicial review to satisfy a "heavy onus" by providing "reasonable, reliable, relevant evidence" would effectively deny access to Rule 39.03 to anyone who was not already in a position to prove his or her case. I do not agree that such a standard would achieve an appropriate balance.

Finally, Sharpe J.A. commented that, unlike section 111 of the *Ontario Labour Relations Code* (considered in *Ellis Don*), section 30 of the *Ontario Human Rights Code*[361] does not provide a blanket prohibition against any testimony in any civil proceedings, but only against what occurred during the investigation stage (not during the subsequent decision stage). Examinations were therefore ordered.

There have been two subsequent Ontario cases of interest: *Ontario Federation of Anglers & Hunters v. Ontario (Ministry of Natural Resources)*,[362] where the Court of Appeal held that there was no reasonable evidentiary basis to permit the examinations of either the Premier or the responsible Minister with respect to the Cabinet's decision to cancel the spring bear hunt; and *Pritchard v. Ontario (Human Rights Commission)*,[363] where the Divisional Court ordered the production of all information pertaining to the complaint

---

361 30(1) No person who is a member of the Commission shall be required to give testimony in a civil suit or any proceedings as to information obtained in the course of an investigation under this Act.

(2) No person who is employed in the administration of this Act shall be required to give testimony in a civil suit or any proceeding other than a proceeding under this Act as to information obtained in the course of an investigation under this Act.

362 (2002), 211 D.L.R. (4th) 741 (Ont. C.A.), leave to appeal refused (2003), 313 N.R. 198 (note) (S.C.C.).

363 (2001), [2001] O.J. No. 2788, 148 O.A.C. 260, 2001 CarswellOnt 2423 (Ont. Div. Ct.), affirmed (2002), 2002 CarswellOnt 4626 (Ont. Div. Ct.), reversed (2003), 63 O.R. (3d) 97 (Ont. C.A.), leave to appeal allowed (2003), 2003 CarswellOnt 5833 (S.C.C.), affirmed (2004), 2004 CarswellMan 97 (S.C.C.).

which formed the basis for the judicial review application, including written, oral,[364] electronic or other information.

It is therefore fair to say that the potential for discovery in applications for judicial review is not nearly as wide-ranging as discovery in other civil litigation, although it is possible in order to give citizens an effective judicial review. As ever, it is contextual and it is difficult to know where the impenetrable border protecting deliberative secrecy might be. The Court of Appeal of Nova Scotia referred to discovery in judicial review applications as a ". . . restricted right of discovery of administrative decision-makers or decision-making tribunals".[365] The Court suggested that the form of discovery itself must be quite focussed, and also that "valid reasons" for concern must actually exist in order to obtain discovery:[366]

> A distinction exists between discovery, which is a somewhat unfocused fact gathering exercise, and the examination of witnesses in the course of a judicial review, when issues are more defined and questions must be relevant to them. In either case, discovery or testimony, a proper evidentiary foundation must be created, generally by affidavit evidence, to establish that valid reasons exist for concern that there has been a want of natural justice or procedural fairness, or that the discretionary authority has been otherwise exceeded.

The requirement for "valid reasons for concern" was stated alternatively as a requirement for a "reasonable *prima facie* case" by the Ontario General Division Court in *Bettes*.[367] Similarly, the Court of Queen's Bench of Alberta cited Gonthier J. in *Tremblay* in holding that deliberative secrecy ". . . may be lifted when the litigant can present valid reasons for believing that the process followed did not comply with the rules of natural justice".[368]

However, *Régie* and *Payne* suggest a less stringent requirement. Indeed, *Régie* could *perhaps* support an argument that there is no requirement for a reasonable *prima facie* case, for obtaining an order compelling evidence or disclosure of records by the decision-maker. The Court in *Régie* was not required to deal directly with the issue of whether decision-makers could be

---

364   It is not clear how one produces "oral" communication.

365   *Waverley (Village) v. Nova Scotia (Acting Minister of Municipal Affairs)* (1994), 26 Admin. L.R. (2d) 302 at 310 (N.S. C.A.), leave to appeal refused (1995), 34 C.P.C. (3d) 130 (note) (S.C.C.).

366   *Ibid.*

367   *Bettes v. Boeing Canada DeHavilland Division* (1992), 8 Admin. L.R. (2d) 232 (Ont. Gen. Div.), affirmed [1993] O.L.R.B. Rep. 275 (Ont. Div. Ct.).

368   *Apotex Inc. v. Alberta* (1996), 38 Alta. L.R. (3d) 153 (Alta. Q.B.) at 190. Here, Hutchinson J. held that the provisions in the Alberta *Rules of Court* allowing a litigant to compel the other party to attend examination for discovery extended to applications for judicial review. This decision was referred to favourably in *Athabasca Tribal Council v. Alberta (Minister of Environmental Protection)* (1998), [1998] A.J. No. 1157, 1998 CarswellAlta 978 (Alta. Q.B. [In Chambers]). However, see also *Canada (Attorney General) v. Canada (Commission of the Inquiry on the Blood System)* (1996), 37 Admin. L.R. (2d) 241 (Fed. T.D.), where Richard J. refused disclosure requested pursuant to the *Federal Court Rules* dealing with discovery, on the basis that the request was nothing more than a fishing expedition.

subpoenaed to give testimony or provide documents about the consultative process. However, Mr. Justice Gonthier made strong adverse comments about the Régie's decision *not* to provide evidence about its consultative process. He determined that the decision-makers were not sufficiently impartial and independent to comply with the principles of procedural fairness, notwithstanding that the evidence the Court was looking for may well have existed. The "missing evidence" was evidence about structures prohibiting overlapping of roles between the investigatory, prosecutorial and adjudicative stages of the Régie's authority. The Court impliedly drew an adverse inference from the lack of evidence, by virtue of the fact that the evidence which was in front of them did not make it clear that there was not an overlapping of roles:[369]

> Evidence as to the role of the lawyers and the allocation of tasks among them is incomplete, but the possibility that a jurist who has made submissions to the directors might then advise them in respect of the same matter is disturbing, especially since some of the directors have no legal training. . . .

> A lack of evidence makes it difficult to assess the Régie's operations. . . .

> The fact that the Régie, as an institution, participates in the process of investigation, summoning and adjudication is not in itself problematic. However, the possibility that a particular director could, following the investigation, decide to hold a hearing and could then participate in the decision-making process would cause an informed person to have a reasonable apprehension of bias in a substantial number of cases. It seems to me that, as with the Régie's jurists, a form of separation among the directors involved in the various stages of the process is necessary to counter that apprehension of bias.

The best reading of existing jurisprudence is that if an allegation of a breach of procedural fairness is made, decision-makers may be compelled to testify about their consultative processes, and standing boards may be compelled to disclose policy documents about that same process. Legislative prohibitions against decision-makers being required to testify may well be read down in order to allow the reviewing Court to ensure that the decision-makers have complied with the principles of procedural fairness. Even if the applicant does not specifically request a subpoena or disclosure, the reviewing Court may draw an adverse inference if the standing board fails to provide evidence that there is no interference with independence of the decision-making panels.

---

369 *2747-3174 Québec Inc. c. Québec (Régie des permis d'alcool)* (1996), 42 Admin. L.R. (2d) 1 (S.C.C.) at 124, 126-27. However, see also *I.B.E.W., Local 894 v. Ellis-Don Ltd.* (1998), 38 O.R. (3d) 737 (Ont. C.A.), leave to appeal allowed (1999), 236 N.R. 183 (note) (S.C.C.), affirmed [2001] 1 S.C.R. 221 (S.C.C.) where the Ontario Court of Appeal refused to draw an adverse inference.

The net result of these cases is to extend the body of information upon which judicial scrutiny can be based, and to provide more transparency into the decision-making process (though none of the cases have extended into the content of deliberations). An allegation of a breach of procedural fairness in post-hearing consultation may well result in an order for decision-makers to provide evidence about the deliberative process. Improper use of consultation—that is, consultation which in essence delegates the function of decision-making—will be reviewable on the basis of a breach of procedural fairness. During that review, the reviewing court will have access to better and more evidence in order to make the determination about whether the use of consultation has indeed been improper.

(b) Role of Counsel to the Decision-Maker

The role of counsel in administrative proceedings has also become an important issue facing the courts, particularly in cases where a tribunal has its own counsel or it consults with independent counsel.[370] Indeed, a common form of post-hearing consultation involves a tribunal's legal counsel. Provided board counsel plays no adversarial role in the hearing process, and neither usurps nor accepts an invitation to take over the decision-making role, such consultation is unobjectionable.[371]

Administrative boards may retain legal counsel for advice and assistance in the proceedings before them. A tribunal may also look to outside legal counsel for assistance in the preparation of its reasons. A board is comprised of experts in a particular field and as laymen may not be competent to resolve jurisdictional and fairness problems that arise with regard to the rights defined by a statutory scheme. Accordingly, legal counsel and advice is permissible as long as the role of counsel is confined, in fact and appearance, to be consistent with principles of procedural fairness. In addition, many of the same principles set out in *Consolidated Bathurst* and *Tremblay* apply with equal force to the consultative role of legal counsel to the decision-maker.

The role of legal counsel to the administrative tribunal generally becomes an issue in two areas: counsel behaviour during the hearing and the role of counsel in post-hearing consultation or in writing reasons for the decision. No matter what stage of the decision-making process, the decision-makers must not delegate the decision-making power of a board – or, conversely, legal counsel for the tribunal must not usurp the role of the decision-maker. Courts upon review have held that:[372]

It is true that the board in rendering its decision made reference to the advice of its legal counsel and his opinion, but it is equally clear that

---

370   See also "Role of Board Counsel During the Hearing", above.

371   For an extended discussion of the role of the solicitor in the post-hearing process, see M. Rankin and L. Greathead, "Advising the Board: The Scope of Counsel's Role in Advising Administrative Tribunals" (1993) 7 C.J.A.L.P. 29.

372   *Canadian Pacific Ltd. v. Carlyle (Town)*, [1987] 4 W.W.R. 232 (Sask. C.A.) at 252.

the board itself made the decision and did not delegate that decision-making power to its solicitor.

An example of acceptable consultation with counsel post-hearing is set out in *Bovbel*.[373] Here, the decision-maker was the Immigration and Refugee Board, which had denied the applicant Convention refugee status. The Board's policy was described by Pratte J.A., writing for a unanimous Court (at 171), as one which:

> . . . encourages the members of the board, the great majority of whom have no legal training, to submit their reasons for decision to the Legal Services Branch (which is composed of lawyers who do not participate in the hearings of the board) prior to putting their reasons in final form.

In *Bovbel*, the Court of Appeal approved the Board policy, and held (at 176):

> There is no doubt that the participation of "outsiders" in the decision-making process of an administrative tribunal may sometimes cause problems. The decisions of the tribunal must, indeed, be rendered by those on whom Parliament has conferred power to decide and their decisions must, unless the relevant legislation impliedly or expressly provides otherwise, meet the requirements of natural justice. However, when the practice followed by members of an administrative tribunal does not violate natural justice and does not infringe on their ability to decide according to their opinion even though it may influence that opinion, it cannot be criticized.

The Court cited *Consolidated Bathurst* and *Tremblay* for the above-stated principle. Accordingly, counsel to the administrative tribunal may well play a consulting role in the deliberation of the tribunal, but is constrained by the same constraints as colleague board members. Consultation may occur on matters of policy and legal interpretation, but cannot go beyond influence to coercion, and cannot deal with findings of fact.

An administrative tribunal frequently requires legal advice from its own counsel during a hearing, or wishes to have counsel retire with the panel in order to provide legal advice should the need arise during deliberations. In *Omineca Enterprises Ltd. v. British Columbia (Minister of Forests)*,[374] the Appeal Board hearing an appeal from a decision of the Chief Forester regarding time sale harvesting licenses retained legal counsel. Omineca Enterprises objected to the retaining of legal counsel at the outset of the hearing of the appeal. Counsel retired with the Appeal Board during deliberations on whether the

---

373 *Bovbel v. Canada (Minister of Employment & Immigration)* (1994), 18 Admin. L.R. (2d) 169 (Fed. C.A.), leave to appeal refused (1994), 23 Admin. L.R. (2d) 320 (note) (S.C.C.).

374 *Omineca Enterprises Ltd. v. British Columbia (Minister of Forests)* (1992), 7 Admin. L.R. (2d) 95, 71 B.C.L.R. (2d) 247 (B.C. S.C.), affirmed (1993), 18 Admin. L.R. (2d) 210 (B.C. C.A.), leave to appeal refused (1994), 23 Admin. L.R. (2d) 319 (note) (S.C.C.).

Appeal Board had authority to retain him, and whether to grant an adjournment so that Omineca could petition the Supreme Court for an order removing him as counsel. The Board returned and ruled that it would continue to retain legal counsel, but that it would allow the adjournment to allow Omineca to seek a remedy from the courts. Ultimately the case was heard by the Court of Appeal. The British Columbia Court of Appeal held that the Appeal Board did have authority to retain its own independent legal counsel,[375] and that the procedure involving that counsel retiring with the Board was not a breach of procedural fairness.[376]

However, in *Carlin*,[377] counsel to the tribunal retired with the tribunal and the Court reached an opposite conclusion about the fairness of the process. In *Carlin*, after deliberations were complete, the tribunal released written reasons which referred to case law which had neither been raised by the parties nor discussed by the parties in their submissions to the tribunal. Binder J. found as a fact that the case law must have been provided to the tribunal by its own counsel, and further found that the tribunal breached the principles of procedural fairness by referring to case law of which the parties were not aware and were not given an opportunity to address. In this case, the Court quashed the decision of the Discipline Committee.

As with the trend toward disclosure of evidence related to the consultation process, there is also a trend toward disclosure of legal advice provided to administrative tribunals. The traditional view has been that administrative tribunals are entitled to take legal advice and that advice will be privileged and need not be disclosed to the parties (provided there is no evidence to suggest that counsel actually made the decision for the statutory delegate).[378] Indeed, in the *Khan* case,[379] the Court of Appeal noted that not all advice given by counsel will necessarily be legal advice:[380]

---

375   The court also held that it was not objectionable that independent legal counsel would be paid by the Ministry of the Attorney General, notwithstanding that the Ministry was a party to the appeal.

376   In *Snider v. Assn. of Registered Nurses (Manitoba)*, [2000] 4 W.W.R. 130 (Man. C.A.), leave to appeal refused (2000), 262 N.R. 396 (note) (S.C.C.), the Manitoba Court of Appeal found that the mere presence of the tribunal's lawyer during the deliberation stage does not, without more, establish a breach of procedural fairness. Further, it is "desirable" for counsel to advise and confer with the tribunal in the presence of the parties in order to avoid allegations of a breach of procedural fairness.

377   *Carlin v. Registered Psychiatric Nurses' Assn. (Alberta)*, [1996] 8 W.W.R. 584 (Alta. Q.B.).

378   *Jackman v. Dental Board (Newfoundland)* (1990), 82 Nfld. & P.E.I.R. 91 (Nfld. T.D.); *R. v. East Kerrier JJ.*, [1952] 2 Q.B. 719 (Eng. C.A.); *R. v. Public Accountants Council (Ontario)*, [1960] O.R. 631, 25 D.L.R. (2d) 410 (Ont. C.A.); *Glassman v. College of Physicians & Surgeons (Ontario)*, [1966] 2 O.R. 81, 55 D.L.R. (2d) 674 (Ont. C.A.); *Bernstein v. College of Physicians & Surgeons (Ontario)* (1977), 15 O.R. (2d) 447, 76 D.L.R. (3d) 38 (Ont. Div. Ct.); *Sawyer v. Ontario (Racing Commission)* (1979), 24 O.R. (2d) 673, 99 D.L.R. (3d) 561 (Ont. C.A.); see also the decision of Feehan J. in *Sawatzky v. Universities Academic Pension Plan Board (No. 1)*, Action No. 9003-10621 (Alta. Q.B.) [unreported]; and by analogy with Gonthier J.'s analysis in *I.W.A. Local 2-69 v. Consolidated Bathurst Packaging Ltd.* (1990), 105 N.R. 161 at 192, 194. (S.C.C.)

379   *Khan v. College of Physicians & Surgeons (Ontario)* (1992), 11 Admin. L.R. (2d) 147, 94 D.L.R. (4th) 193 (Ont. C.A.).

380   *Ibid.* at 177 [Admin. L.R.].

Advice intended to improve the quality of the Committee's reasons by, for example, deleting erroneous references to the evidence or adding additional relevant references to the evidence, is not advice on a matter of law but is rather advice as to how the Committee should frame its reasons in support of its decision.

However, later cases suggest that disclosure of, for example, legal opinions provided to decision-makers by their counsel, is required by the principles of procedural fairness and that those legal opinions are not privileged. In *Melanson v New Brunswick (Workers' Compensation Board)*,[381] the Court of Appeal of New Brunswick held that legal opinions on the issue in question and provided by the Workers' Compensation Board by its own counsel are not privileged and must be disclosed to the parties. Ryan J.A. writing for the majority stated:[382]

Legal opinions given in relation to the interpretation of legislation which is germane to a claim before one of the Board's tribunals is not privileged. Such professional opinions are, in my view, for the benefit of employers, employees and dependants in the processing of claims by the Workers' Compensation Board, not simply something for the exclusive use of the Board. When the W.C.B. is in an adversarial position or has caused the legal opinion to be generated for matters unrelated to claims, a solicitor-client privilege relationship arises vis-a-vis other parties. However, when the legal opinions relate to the interpretation of W.C.B. legislation or the duty or obligation to pay claims, they must not be withheld from the employers, employees or their dependants. Privilege does not attach.

Similarly, the Court in *Carlin* held that, with the exception of special circumstances, legal advice provided to a tribunal by its own counsel must be provided openly and in the presence of all parties. Binder J. stated that:[383]

[in general, it is proper for counsel to] . . . attend at the hearing of a tribunal, to provide advice to the tribunal, when *requested* by the tribunal to do so, provided, except in very special circumstances, that such advice is given *openly and in the presence of all interested parties*.

Binder J. also cited with approval the "half-way house" position suggested by James T. Casey:[384]

---

381 (1994), 25 Admin. L.R. (2d) 219 (N.B. C.A.), leave to appeal refused (1994), 154 N.B.R. (2d) 320 (note) (S.C.C.).
382 *Ibid.* at 228-29.
383 *Carlin, supra* note 377 at 605.
384 *Ibid.* at 606, citing J.T. Casey, *Regulation of Professions in Canada* (Toronto: Carswell, 1994) at 8-38 to 8-39. See also J.T. Casey, "A Pot-Pourri of Recent Developments in Administrative Law" published by the Legal Education Society of Alberta, papers for a seminar on "Dealing with Government Boards and Agencies", April 25-28, 1997.

> . . . the solution lies in the adoption of a procedure which permits counsel to a discipline tribunal to be present during deliberations but which also ensures that the dictates of procedural fairness are met. A commitment that the "prosecutor" and counsel to the member facing charges will be given the opportunity to address any new legal issues or arguments which arise during deliberations and which were not previously canvassed by the parties in open hearing, should alleviate most of the concerns.

This suggested solution to the seemingly intractable problem of the role of counsel to the tribunal during deliberations is entirely consistent with the principles set out in *Consolidated Bathurst* and *Tremblay*, and provides the better view of what are the appropriate constraints on counsel to an administrative tribunal.

The role of counsel to the tribunal can also become important and controversial during preparation of written reasons for the decision. In *Khan v. College of Physicians & Surgeons (Ontario)*,[385] the Ontario Court of Appeal addressed the issue of counsel's participation in the writing and delivering of reasons for the decision. The reasons of the Board were delivered three months after the completion of the hearing. The original draft was written by the chairman of the committee, reviewed by the solicitor and then rewritten and approved by the committee without further involvement from the solicitor. The Court held that involvement of counsel did not interfere with the freedom of the decision-makers to decide according to their consciences and opinions, but that instead the aim of the drafting process was to produce a set of reasons which accurately and fully reflected the thought processes of the committee. To the extent that consultation with counsel promotes that aim, it is to be encouraged. The Court unanimously held, though, that the line between permissible assistance and interference must be drawn having regard to the effect of counsel's involvement in the drafting process on the fairness of the proceedings, and on the integrity of the overall discipline process:[386]

> It must also be recognized that the volume and complexity of modern decision making all but necessitates resort to "outside" sources during the drafting process. Contemporary reason writing is very much a consultive process during which the writer of the reasons resorts to many sources, including persons not charged with the responsibility of deciding the matter, in formulating his or her reasons. It is inevitable that the author of the reasons will be influenced by some of these sources. To hold that any "outside" influence vitiates the validity of the proceedings or the decision reached is to insist on a degree of isolation which is not only totally unrealistic but also destructive of effective reason writing.[387]

---

385   (1992), 11 Admin. L.R. (2d) 147 (Ont. C.A.).
386   *Ibid.* at 178-79.
387   *Ibid.* at 179.

The process must also, even if it does not interfere with the actual freedom of the decision-makers, not be designed so as to create an appearance of bias or lack of independence.[388]

> Where counsel is connected with one of the parties to the hearing an appearance of bias will result if that counsel participates in the drafting process . . . or where the decision-maker is compelled to consult with others, who are not charged with the responsibility of deciding the case, the appearance of independence may be lost.[389]

The reasons for a decision made by a tribunal must be the reasons of that tribunal. However, the Court of Appeal looked to the decision of the Supreme Court in *I.W.A. Local 2-69 v. Consolidated Bathurst Packaging Ltd.*[390] for the principle that outside sources of assistance are permissible within certain bounds:

> The ultimate aim of the drafting process is a set of reasons which accurately and fully reflects the thought processes of the Committee. To the extent that consultation with the counsel promotes that aim, it is to be encouraged. The debate must fix, not on the Committee's entitlement to assistance in the drafting of reasons, but on the acceptable limits of that assistance.[391]

The Court of Appeal noted that there was no single formula or procedure to determine the appropriate degree of assistance in the preparation of reasons. The Court suggested that many factors were involved in a determination of what is a permissible level of assistance by tribunal counsel: the nature of the proceedings, the issues raised, the composition of the tribunal, the terms of the enabling legislation, the available support structure, and the tribunal's workload. The Court then determined that the process in the case of Dr. Khan was fair because:
1. The first draft had been prepared by a committee member.
2. Counsel revised and clarified the first draft in consultation with the Chairman of the committee.
3. The committee then met to consider and revise the second draft, and counsel played no role in this review and revision.
4. The final draft was signed by each member of the committee.

In *Carlin* by contrast, counsel to the Discipline Committee took a more active role in the writing of the reasons of the Committee and the Court held that this role breached the principles of procedural fairness. Here, the Court drew an inference that counsel had "prepared" the reasons, which were then signed by the members of the Discipline Committee, because of the fact that

---

388 *Ibid.*
389 *Ibid.* at 180, citing *Sawyer v. Ontario (Racing Commission)* (1979), 24 O.R. (2d) 673 at 676, 99 D.L.R. (3d) 561 at 564-65 (Ont. C.A.).
390 [1990] 1 S.C.R. 282, 42 Admin. L.R. 1 (S.C.C.).
391 *Khan, supra* note 385 at 178.

the footer at the bottom of the page of the written reasons included the initials of legal counsel.[392] While the Court held that it is acceptable for legal counsel to "assist the hearing tribunal in preparing" reasons and even to assist in drafting reasons, the implication is that the complete writing cannot be done by legal counsel to the committee.[393]

Similarly, in *Wolfrom v. Assn. of Professional Engineers & Geoscientists (Manitoba)*[394], the majority of the Manitoba Court of Appeal upheld a trial judge's conclusion that reasons, prepared and revised by counsel for a disciplinary committee, did not satisfy the statutory requirement that the Committee ". . . make a written decision on the matter consisting of the reasons for its decision" imposed by section 49(1) of *The Engineering and Geoscientific Professions Act*.[395] The Court emphasized that the evidence clearly showed that the Committee's counsel prepared and revised the reasons and because the Committee chose not to adduce any evidence suggesting that the reasons were, in fact, its own, the presumption of regularity did not apply.

(c) Duty to Counsel Prior to Making a Final Decision

A decision by a multi-member panel must be made by all members of the panel, though the process for decision-making may vary from case to case. In *Calgary General Hospital v. U.N.A., Local 1*,[396] the tribunal was a tripartite board composed of a labour nominee, a management nominee and a chairman. The Board was unable to meet immediately after the hearing, and the members agreed to meet at a later date. The Chairman was unable to arrange a meeting where all members of the Board could meet together. He met with the management nominee and prepared a draft award. He later met with the labour nominee, discussed the draft award, and agreed to take the labour nominee's notes which he later reviewed. He then issued a decision as a majority award, concurred in by the management nominee. The decision contained only minor changes from the draft award. On judicial review of that decision, Mr. Justice Virtue held that procedural fairness required that there be consultation and deliberation, but not that all the members meet at the same time. Procedural fairness requires only that, at the least, each member must have an opportunity to hear and respond to the other members' positions.

The Alberta Court of Appeal[397] held that it was unnecessary to decide whether the rules of procedural fairness required face to face communication among the members. The Court found that because the members of the Board had agreed on a procedure (that they would meet), the Board was bound to abide by that agreement. The failure to do so went to jurisdiction and the award was quashed.

---

392   *Carlin, supra* note 377.
393   *Ibid.*
394   (2001), [2002] 2 W.W.R. 616 (Man. C.A.).
395   S. M. 1998, c. E120.
396   (1990), 16 L.A.C. (4th) 14 (Alta. Arb. Bd.).
397   *U.N.A., Local 1 v. Calgary General Hospital* (1990), 46 Admin. L.R. 245 (Alta. C.A.).

Accordingly, all members of a multi-member decision making panel must take part in the decision, and some form of communication is required in order to ensure input from all members of the decision-making panel.

(d) Changes in Circumstances: Rehearings and Re-openings

Sometimes a change in circumstances after a hearing may be a reason to require a rehearing or a new hearing. The issue which then arises is whether the tribunal can reopen the oral hearing to hear new evidence or submission, or whether the tribunal can change or amend its decision. To rehear or continue a hearing, the tribunal cannot be *functus officio*.[398] The doctrine of *functus officio*, though, only arises when the final decision of the tribunal is issued (either orally or in writing). In addition, a tribunal may correct obvious technical or clerical errors in a decision without breaching the doctrine of *functus officio*.

In *Salinas v. Canada (Minister of Employment & Immigration)*,[399] the presiding member of a Refugee Division panel attempted to reconvene an immigration hearing because of a change in the political situation in Panama, the homeland of the appellant. The Federal Court of Appeal held that until a decision was rendered, the panel was not *functus* and could therefore reconvene to hear new evidence.

An administrative tribunal may retain jurisdiction over a certain matter, and therefore, retain the possibility of hearing further evidence or considering more issues raised by the parties. An example of this occurs in the case of approval in principle of development permits by municipalities. In *Jones v. Delta*,[400] a developer applied to the municipality seeking to rezone agricultural land to be used for golf courses. Under section 956 of the provincial *Municipal Act*, developments of this type must be approved by law. The normal procedure in British Columbia is for a municipal council to give a proposed bylaw first and second readings, then send the matter to a public hearing, followed by two more readings for final approval. At the hearing in this case, there were strong objections posed by public and environmental groups. Notwithstanding these objections, the municipality gave the bylaw a third reading and approved the golf course in principle.

Over the next 15 months, the municipality negotiated with the developers to obtain concessions and changes in order to alleviate many of the concerns raised by those opposed at the public hearing. Some electors opposed to the golf course, appealed on the ground that the municipality should not have considered any new information from one side without giving the public a further opportunity to be heard. The British Columbia Court of Appeal held that a public hearing can only be meaningful where there is something new or

---

398 See the discussion about the applicability of *functus officio* to administrative agencies in *Chandler v. Assn. of Architects (Alberta)*, [1989] 6 W.W.R. 521 (S.C.C.) at 542, per Sopinka J.

399 (1992), 6 Admin. L.R. (2d) 154 (Fed. C.A.).

400 (1992), 92 D.L.R. (4th) 714 (B.C. C.A.), leave to appeal refused (1993), 14 M.P.L.R. (2d) 287 (note) (S.C.C.).

material to be disclosed. The basis of the *audi alteram partem* rule is the concept that the opposing side will have something new to say, not just repeat arguments already made. The Court held that to give effect to the concerns raised by the electors would mean that municipal councils could never address concerns raised at a public hearing without having another public hearing. Accordingly, the municipal council was not required by the principles of procedural fairness to reopen the hearing regarding the golf course, notwithstanding that it had only approved the golf course in principle and had retained jurisdiction to make a further decision about the development (the final approval).

Another circumstance in which a tribunal may receive a request to reopen a hearing might involve any situation where an applicant is denied the opportunity to place his entire case before the tribunal. If the failure to present evidence is due to the intervention of the board, as was the case in *I.A.M., Lodge 2309 v. Canada (Labour Relations Board)*,[401] the court will find a violation of the *audi alteram partem* rule. If failure to present evidence is the failure of the applicant, then the tribunal is under no obligation to allow a reopening. As stated in *Mansingh v. Canada (Minister of Manpower & Immigration) (No. 2)*,[402] the tribunal cannot be expected to monitor the evidence before it, making sure that all relevant evidence is provided. If the grounds advanced for re-opening a case are irrelevant, the tribunal is not obliged to grant such an application. Although it may be difficult to determine relevancy without hearing the whole of the case, the tribunal, as experts in the area, can certainly assess relevancy in a cursory manner in order to avoid frivolous reopenings.[403]

Further, the question sometimes arises whether a tribunal may correct procedural or substantive errors by holding a re-hearing.[404] Apart from correcting obvious slips and technical errors,[405] the tribunal has no general power to re-open a matter that has been decided, because the tribunal is then *functus officio*.[406]

---

401   (1988), 33 Admin. L.R. 227 (Fed. C.A.).

402   (1978), 24 N.R. 576 (Fed. C.A.).

403   *Sparrow v. Canada (Minister of Employment & Immigration)*, [1977] 2 F.C. 403 (Fed. T.D.), C.C.H. D.R.S. at 26-598.

404   For a comprehensive consideration of this topic, see R.F. Reid and H. David, *Administrative Law and Practice*, 2d ed. (Toronto: Butterworths, 1978) at 105-15. See also R.A. Macdonald, "Reopenings, Rehearings and Reconsideration in Administrative Law" (1979) 17 Osgoode Hall L.J. 207.

405   *Wilkes v. Interlake Tissue Mills Co.* (1969), [1970] S.C.R. 441 (S.C.C.); *British Columbia Forest Products Ltd., Re* (1961), 36 W.W.R. 145 (B.C. S.C.). Sometimes legislation specifically gives the power to correct errors: see *Heller v. British Columbia (Registrar, Vancouver Land Registration District)*, [1963] S.C.R. 229 (S.C.C.); and s. 80(2) of the *Public Service Employee Relations Act*, R.S.A. 1980, c. P-33, which provides that "a tribunal may in any proceeding, award or decision correct any clerical mistake, error or omission."

406   *Windsor Consruction (1962) Ltd. v. I.U.O.E., Local 115* (1968), 1 D.L.R. (3d) 683 (B.C. S.C.).

The concept of *functus officio* was discussed extensively in *Chandler v. Assn. of Architects (Alberta)*, where Sopinka J. held that the doctrine extended to administrative tribunals:[407]

> I do not understand Martland J. [in previous case] to go so far as to hold that *functus officio* has no application to administrative tribunals. Apart from the English practice, which is based on a reluctance to amend or reopen formal judgments, there is a sound policy reason for recognizing the finality of proceedings before administrative tribunals. As a general rule, once such a tribunal has reached a final decision in respect to the matter that is before it in accordance with its enabling statute, that decision cannot be revisited because the tribunal has changed its mind, made an error within jurisdiction or because there has been a change of circumstances. It can only do so if authorized by statute or if there has been a slip or error within the exceptions enunciated in *Paper Machinery Ltd. v. J.O. Ross Engr. Corp, supra* [which dealt with an error in expressing the manifest intention of the Court].

> To this extent, the principle of *functus officio* applies. It is based, however, on the policy ground which favours finality of proceedings rather than the rule which was developed with respect to formal judgments of a court whose decision was subject to a full appeal. For this reason I am of the opinion that its application must be more flexible and less formalistic in respect to the decisions of administrative tribunals which are subject to appeal only on a point of law. Justice may require the reopening of administrative proceedings in order to provide relief which would otherwise be available on appeal.

> Accordingly, the principle should not be strictly applied where there are indications in the enabling statute that a decision can be reopened in order to enable the tribunal to discharge the function committed to it by enabling legislation. . . .

However, a number of statutes[408] specifically permit re-hearings, reconsideration and variations of previous decisions.[409] In circumstances where the statute allows a rehearing of the same matter, the administrative tribunal would

---

407 [1989] 6 W.W.R. 521 (S.C.C.) at 541-42.

408 For example, the *Income Tax Act* permits the Minister to re-assess a taxpayer within three years after the date of the original assessment. Such a re-consideration will re-verify the taxpayer's right to object or appeal within 90 days.

409 One example is s. 64 of the *Public Utilities Board Act*, R.S.A. 2000, c. 45 which provides that:

> The Board may rehear an application before deciding it, and may review, rescind or vary any order or decision made by it.

A similar (though wider ranging) provision exists in the *Environmental Protection and Enhancement Act*, R.S.A. 2000, c. E-12, s. 101. See also *Nurani v. Alberta (Environmental Appeal Board)* (1997), 1 Admin. L.R. (3d) 248 (Alta. Q.B.).

not fall into error on the basis that it reconsidered an issue. For example, in *Johannesson v. Alberta (Workers' Compensation Board, Appeals Commission)*,[410] Veit J. held that a decision by the Appeals Commission about whether to reconsider an earlier decision was a separate decision subject to judicial review. While the issue before the Court was not the validity of the reconsideration decision, the fact that the Commission dealt with the reconsideration request was certainly not remarked upon unfavourably by the Court. The enabling legislation for the Workers' Compensation Board allows for reconsideration of the same issues already dealt with earlier by other decision-making panels of the Board.

A perhaps more interesting decision was reached by the Court of Queen's Bench of Alberta in *Nurani v. Alberta (Environmental Appeal Board)*.[411] Here, the applicant Nurani sought an order for prohibition against the Environmental Appeal Board, arguing that it had no jurisdiction to reconsider its earlier decision to permit him to operate a beverage container depot. The Board, in hearing appeals from permit applications for beverage container depots, had a recommendation-making power only, and the Minister of Environment had final decision-making authority. The statute in question specifically provided for reconsideration by the Board, but did not provide for reconsideration by the Minister. Nurani argued that the Board's statutory reconsideration power only extended until such times as the Minister made the final decision, because the Minister had no reconsideration power and therefore any recommendation after the Minister was *functus* and would be moot. The Court of Queen's Bench denied the application for prohibition on the basis that it was only the Board's reconsideration power which was at issue and noted that any further reconsideration by the Minister would have to be considered if and when it happened.

Generally, for an administrative tribunal to reconsider a decision or to rehear a matter, it must have statutory authority to do so. Even without statutory authority, the tribunal may correct minor technical errors without erring. However, in the absence of statutory authority, an administrative tribunal cannot reconsider a decision or rehear a matter. If there is statutory authority to reconsider a decision or rehear a matter, the extent of the reconsideration authority must be determined by interpretation of that provision. Note, however, that the doctrine of *functus officio* does not preclude a tribunal from re-opening the oral hearing in order to hear more evidence or submissions, or from seeking further written submissions from parties prior to making its decision. The doctrine of *functus* comes into play only when a final decision is rendered.

In principle, the same components of fairness apply to any such re-hearing as would apply to the board's initial proceedings, including adequate notice of the rehearing and the matters that will be considered, an open hearing, the right to cross-examine witnesses, the obligation to give reasons, and the like. Nevertheless, the precise nature of the proceedings must – as always in adminis-

---

410   (October 29, 1996), Doc. Edmonton 9403 19547, [1996] A.J. No. 917 (Alta. Q.B.).
411   (1997), 1 Admin. L.R. (3d) 248 (Alta. Q.B.).

trative law – be determined in the context of the specific statutory provisions involved.

(e) *Res Judicata*

Res judicata is the rule that establishes that the final judgment of a court on any particular issue may not be disputed by the parties or their successors in any subsequent legal proceeding.[412] This doctrine may be applied in the administrative setting to ensure that all matters dealing with a case are brought forward at first instance in order to allow a tribunal to adjudicate on them all at the same time. Failure to do so will violate the *res judicata* rule and any subsequent application may be dismissed.[413] Even where the doctrine of *res judicata* does apply, this type of repetition does not constitute a patently unreasonable error.[414]

The doctrine of *res judicata* does not apply simply because the same parties have litigated a similar issue in a different forum. In *Saggers v. Alberta (Human Rights Commission)*,[415] the applicant filed a grievance under his collective agreement about workplace discrimination, and also filed a complaint with the Human Rights Commission. The Arbitration Board heard the grievance prior to the Human Rights Commission dealing with its complaint. The Commission dismissed the complaint on the basis that it was *res judicata*. On judicial review the Court held that, in order for the doctrine of *res judicata* to apply, the legal and factual issues must be the same. The Court held that while there were similarities between the two complaints filed by Saggers, and the parties were the same, the legal and factual issues were not identical, and ordered a reconsideration of the complaint by the Human Rights Commission.

Similarly, the doctrine of *res judicata* does not apply to preclude a full hearing of a similar issue, when the evolving facts result in changed legal or factual issues. If there is an issue of whether *res judicata* might apply, the tribunal must hear arguments from both parties about whether the doctrine applies before deciding the question.[416]

(f) Waiver

Courts may deny judicial review to an applicant based on the principles of waiver or acquiescence. This is because the remedies available on judicial review are discretionary, and the court may refuse to grant them on the basis that the applicant waived his or her rights or acquiesced in the errors subsequently alleged. However, jurisdiction cannot be conferred on statutory au-

---

412 R.W.M. Dias, *Jurisprudence*, 5th ed. (London: Butterworths, 1985) at 126. See also *R. v. Manchuk*, [1938] O.R. 385 (Ont. C.A.), reversed [1938] S.C.R. 341 (S.C.C.).

413 See *Melcor Developments Ltd. v. Edmonton (City)* (1982), 20 Alta. L.R. (2d) 179 (Alta. Q.B.).

414 *Pacific Press Ltd. v. Vancouver-New Westminster Newspaper Guild, Local 115* (1988), 31 Admin. L.R. 227 (B.C. S.C.), affirmed on other grounds (1989), 34 B.C.L.R. (2d) 339 (B.C. C.A.).

415 (1997), 46 Admin. L.R. (2d) 290 (Alta. Q.B.), affirmed (2000), 90 Alta. L.R. (3d) 25 (Alta. C.A.), leave to appeal refused (2001), 274 N.R. 198 (note) (S.C.C.).

416 *A.T. Farms Ltd. v. Byrnes* (1995), 32 Admin. L.R. (2d) 284 (Sask. Q.B.).

thorities by consent or acquiescence, so an error in the acquisition of jurisdiction cannot be refused on the basis of waiver or acquiescence.[417] Courts have historically retained authority to review cases with constitutional considerations to prevent the acquisition of jurisdiction by a statutory delegate, despite the existence of waiver or estoppel. In the case of *Scivitarro v. British Columbia (Minister of Human Resources)*,[418] there was no common law or statutory authority for the Board to re-hear the matter remitted to it once an original order was made. It was found that non-compliance with statutory requirements prevented the Board from acquiring jurisdiction to deal with the matter. The Court held that it was not possible for the doctrines of waiver and estoppel to confer jurisdiction on a second board with the consent of the parties and thereby preclude judicial review.

In *E.C.W.U., Local 916 v. Atomic Energy of Canada Ltd.* (hereinafter *Atomic Energy*),[419] the Court held that a simple apprehension of bias did not go to the jurisdiction of the tribunal. Thus the procedures acquiesced to by the applicant were not reviewable and the applicant's allegation of bias was dismissed. They accordingly applied the doctrine of waiver to deny judicial review of the tribunal's proceedings.[420] Because most alleged errors in judicial review are issues of procedural fairness or exceeding jurisdiction rather than an error in jurisdiction, waiver will be a proper consideration for a court exercising its discretion to refuse a remedy for much illegal governmental action.

(g) Reasons for Decisions

(i) The Common Law Position

Traditionally, at common law, there was no obligation on a statutory tribunal to provide written reasons for a decision, and a failure to give reasons in and of itself was not regarded as a breach of procedural fairness.[421] This

---

417   *Rosenfeld v. College of Physicians & Surgeons (Ontario)* (1969), 11 D.L.R. (3d) 148 (Ont. H.C.).

418   [1982] 4 W.W.R. 632 (B.C. S.C.).

419   (1985), 17 Admin. L.R. 1 (Fed. C.A.), leave to appeal refused (1986), 22 Admin. L.R. xxviii (note) (S.C.C.). See also *Winn v. Alta. Guild of Ophthalmic Dispensers* (1986), 68 A.R. 251 (Alta. Q.B.).

420   See D.P. Jones, "A Note on the Relationship of Waiver and Estoppel to Jurisdictional Defects in Administrative Law" (1986) 25 Alta. L.R. 487.

421   See *Pure Spring Co. v. Minister of National Revenue* (1946), [1947] 1 D.L.R. 501 at 534 (Can. Ex. Ct.); *K.E. Roessler Construction Co. v. Thiessen*, [1976] 4 W.W.R. 529 (Man. Q.B.); *Gill Lumber Chipman, (1973) Ltd. v. C.J.A.* (1973), 42 D.L.R. (3d) 271 (N.B. C.A.); *Lazar v. Assn. of Professional Engineers (Manitoba)* (1971), 23 D.L.R. (3d) 614 (Man. Q.B.); *British Columbia (Minister of Highways) v. Toop* (1972), [1973] 4 W.W.R. 219 (B.C. S.C.); *Dobson v. Edmonton (City)* (1959), 27 W.W.R. 495 (Alta. T.D.); *Andreas v. Edmonton Hospital*, [1944] 3 W.W.R. 599 (Alta. C.A.); M. Akehurst, "Statements of Reasons for Judicial and Administrative Decisions" (1970) 33 M.L.R. 154; G.A. Flick, "Administrative Adjudications and the Duty to Give Reasons: A Search for Criteria" [1978] P.L. 16; R.A. Macdonald & D. Lametti, "Reasons for Decisions in Administrative Law" (1989-90) 3 C.J.A.L.P. 124; H.L. Kushner, "The Right to Reasons in Administrative Law" (1986) 24 Alta. L.R. 305; M.C. Lévesque-Crévier, "La Motivation en droit administratif" (1980) 40 Rev. du B. 535; G. Richardson, "The Duty to Give Reasons: Potential and

traditional approach[422] has now been all but ousted by the decision of the Supreme Court of Canada in *Baker v. Canada (Minister of Citizenship & Immigration)*[423] where L'Heureux Dube, for a unanimous court, stated:[424]

> In my opinion, it is now appropriate to recognize that, in certain circumstances, the duty of procedural fairness will require the provision of a written explanation for a decision. *The strong arguments demonstrating the advantages of written reasons suggest that, in cases such as this where the decision has important significance for the individual, when there is a statutory right of appeal, or in other circumstances, some form of reasons should be required. This requirement has been developing in the common law elsewhere.* The circumstances of the case at bar, in my opinion, constitute one of the situations where reasons are necessary. The profound importance of an H & C decision to those affected, as with those at issue in Orlowski, Cunningham, and Doody, militates in favour of a requirement that reasons be provided. It would be unfair for a person subject to a decision such as this one which is so critical to their future not to be told why the result was reached. [Emphasis added.]

The requirement to give reasons is still dependent on there existing "certain circumstances" which, in *Baker*, were the significance of the decision on the individual involved, the existence of a statutory right of appeal, and "other circumstances" in which some form of reasons should be required. The category is not closed. Courts can no longer rely on the traditional common law position but must now determine on a case by case basis when procedural fairness requires a tribunal to provide written reasons for its decision, even where there is no statutory requirement to do so.

There were three cases shortly before *Baker* which deserve mention. In one, the Federal Court of Appeal concluded that there was no common law right to reasons and in the other two, the Nova Scotia and the British Columbia Courts of Appeal came to the opposite conclusion with respect to whether a statutory delegate is required to give reasons for a decision. The cases are *Williams v. Canada (Minister of Citizenship & Immigration),*[425] on the one

---

Practice" [1986] P.L. 437; Report of the Committee of the Justice – All Souls Review of Administrative Law in the United Kingdom (1988) c. 3; S.R. Ellis, C. Tretheway & F. Rotter, "Tribunals – Reasons, and Reasons for Reasons" (1990-91) 4 C.J.A.L.P. 105.

422 For a historical review of the common law requirement to give reasons, see the Third Edition of this work at 333-38.

423 [1999] 2 S.C.R. 817, 174 D.L.R. (4th) 193 (S.C.C.). The case concerned the deportation of an illegal immigrant with four Canadian-born children and the refusal of an immigration officer to allow Ms. Baker to stay on humanitarian and compassionate grounds. The applicant succeeded on judicial review on the grounds of bias and an unreasonable exercise of discretion.

424 *Ibid.* at para. 43.

425 (1996), 4 Admin. L.R. (3d) 226 (Fed. T.D.), reversed (1997), 4 Admin. L.R. (3d) 200 (Fed. C.A.), leave to appeal refused (1997), 224 N.R. 320 (note) (S.C.C.).

hand, and *Future Inns Canada Inc. v. Nova Scotia (Labour Relations Board)*[426] and *British Columbia (Judicial Compensation Committee), Re*[427] on the other. The Supreme Court denied leave to appeal on both *Williams* and *Future Inns*.[428] It can now be said that *Future Inns* was the forerunner of the position now articulated in *Baker*. Not all statutory delegates will be required to give reasons but courts must consider each case on its individual facts even where the decision in question is purely discretionary.

The rationale for requiring a statutory delegate to provide reasons can be found in the *Future Inns* case. In *Future Inns*, the Labour Relations Board found the employer Future Inns guilty of unfair labour practices, apparently for firing five housekeeping employees because they were attempting to form a union. The Board did not provide reasons. There was no direct evidence that the employer was aware of the union activities; the employer manager testified to the contrary, specifically that she was unaware of the union activities until after the firings.

The Court could have followed the traditional approach, which did not require reasons, yet still have quashed the decision as being an exceptional case where the decision is inexplicable and, since it is not explained by reasons, it must be held to be patently unreasonable. However, the Court did not make such a finding but instead held that there is a common law requirement for a statutory delegate to provide reasons for its decision and quashed the decision of the Board on the basis that it had not complied with this requirement. The unanimous Court of Appeal held that:[429]

> The preparation of supporting reasons is the best self-assessment a decision-maker can make of his or her decision.
>
> The greater the protection from judicial review accorded to a Tribunal, the greater may be the need for reasons. . . .
>
> Counsel for the Board emphasizes that no case has been found where a court has held that failure to give reasons makes a tribunal's decision patently unreasonable. No case on point is needed. The principle is clear. Patent unreasonableness can assume many forms. I am prepared to reach the result here on the application of fundamental principles.
>
> As well, the cases I have reviewed support the conclusion that in such cases there is an implied duty to give reasons. Breach of this duty is a breach of the rules of natural justice. . . .

---

426   (1997), 4 Admin. L.R. (3d) 248 (N.S. C.A.), leave to appeal refused (1997), 224 N.R. 154 (note) (S.C.C.).

427   (1998), 160 D.L.R. (4th) 477 (B.C. C.A.), leave to appeal to the S.C.C. refused (1999), [1998] S.C.C.A. No. 401, 236 N.R. 185 (note) (S.C.C.).

428   (1997), [1997] S.C.C.A. No. 332, 224 N.R. 320 (note) (S.C.C.) and (1997), [1997] S.C.C.A. No. 265, 224 N.R. 154 (note) (S.C.C.). See also *Brochu v. Bank of Montreal* (1996), 45 Admin. L.R. (2d) 312 (Fed. T.D.), reversed (1999), 251 N.R. 207 (Fed. C.A.).

429   *Future Inns, supra* note 426 at 259, 263 and 268-69.

In the circumstances, the Board acted in a patently unreasonable man-ner in giving this decision without reasons. There was an implied duty on the Board here to furnish reasons. It was in breach of the rules of natural justice or fair play. . . . Counsel for the Union suggested that this Court remit the matter to the Board with an order that it furnish reasons for its decision. The Board has already made its decision. It was a decision reached in a patently unreasonable manner and contrary to the rules of natural justice. To ask it to make up reasons after the fact would be a futile exercise.

Similarly, the British Columbia Court of Appeal also held that a decision-maker is required to provide reasons for its decision, notwithstanding that there is no statutory requirement to provide reasons in the *Provincial Court Judges' Association* case. The issue was whether the Legislature of British Columbia had appropriately dealt with recommendations regarding the remuneration of Judges of the Provincial Court. The Province had established a Compensation Advisory Committee to provide non-binding recommendations about remu-. neration and benefits for Provincial Court Judges. The statute provided that the Legislature could depart from the recommendations of the Compensation Advisory Committee if the Legislature deemed them to be "unfair and unrea-sonable". The following resolution was moved in the Legislature by the Min-ister of Finance:

> Be it resolved that this House reject as unfair and unreasonable all of the recommendations made by the Judicial Compensation Committee established under section 7.1(9) of the *Provincial Court Act* and tabled in the Legislature on May 11, 1995, and that this House substitute the current salary, benefit and other remuneration arrangements for the period January 1, 1995 to December 31, 1997.

This resolution was passed unanimously by the Legislature of British Columbia, and the Provincial Court Judges' Association petitioned to the Supreme Court of British Columbia for a declaration that the resolution was void and of no effect and also declaring that the Judges are entitled to the remuneration, allowances and benefits recommended by the Judicial Compen-sation Committee. This case was ultimately decided by the Court of Appeal. While the unanimous Court stated that its comments ought not to be construed as supporting a "general duty to give reasons", it nonetheless held that the resolution was void on the basis of no reasons:[430]

> The reasons for this decision would be found either in the report of the executive responding to the contents of the commission's report, or in the recitals to the resolution of the legislature on the matter. An unjustified decision could potentially lead to a finding of unconstitu-

---

430 *British Columbia (Judicial Compensation Committee), Re, supra* note 427 at 491, citing Lamer C.J.

tionality. The need for public justification, to my mind, emerges from one of the purposes of s. 11(d)'s guarantee of judicial independence – to ensure public confidence in the justice system. A decision by the executive or the legislature, to change or freeze judges' salaries, and then to disagree with a recommendation not to act on that decision made by a constitutionally mandated body whose existence is premised on the need to preserve the independence of the judiciary, will only be legitimate and not be viewed as being indifferent or hostile to judicial independence, if it is supported by reasons.

The importance of reasons as the basis for the legitimate exercise of public power has been recognized by a number of commentators.

The Supreme Court has not gone so far as to say that all decisions by all statutory delegates require reasons, but there is now no doubt that, in certain circumstances, procedural fairness requires a written explanation for a decision. The question now becomes which circumstances will trigger the right to reasons.

Future Inns does not contain a detailed articulation of the factors to be taken into account in order to determine when a decision-maker will be subject to a common-law requirement to provide reasons. However, if courts are to find a common law requirement to provide reasons for a decision, they may well look to the basis articulated by Madam Justice Reed in *Williams* at the Trial Division, some of which the Supreme Court has now confirmed in *Baker*. These factors are whether:

- there are significant consequences for the individual,

- the decision-making process gives no assurance that the ultimate decision-maker considered the applicant's submissions directly,

- there is unclear reasoning leading to the finding, and

- there is inability of a reviewing court on judicial review to determine whether the decision-makers applied consistent and lawful criteria.

It is difficult to imagine where to draw the line based on Madam Justice Reed's reasons. The last factor she mentions is present in all judicial reviews, that is, that the decision is incapable of being judicially reviewed unless the delegate provides reasons. One of the other factors is arguably present in most judicial review proceedings, which is that there is an important issue at stake for the applicant.

The British Columbia Court of Appeal in *British Columbia (Judicial Compensation Committee), Re.* did not attempt to provide a list of factors but emphasised the need for reasons as providing a public justification for the legitimate exercise of public power.

In *Baker*, Madam Justice L'Heureux Dube emphasized the importance of the decision to the individual as a basis for the requirement of reasons as well as the advantage to a court on a statutory appeal to know the reasons for the decision. She called these "strong arguments" in favour of the requirement to give reasons. Madam Justice L'Heureux Dube specifically agreed that written reasons have significant benefits because they:[431]

- ensure fair and transparent decision-making,

- reduce arbitrary or capricious decisions,

- reinforce public confidence in the judgement and fairness of tribunals,

- afford parties the opportunity to assess the question of appeal,

- foster better decision-making by ensuring that issues and reasoning are well articulated and therefore more carefully thought out,

- the process of writing may guaranty a better decision,

- allow the parties to see that the applicable issues have been carefully considered,

- are invaluable if a decision is to be appealed, questioned, or considered on judicial review,

- those affected may be more likely to feel that they were treated fairly and appropriately.

She also dealt with concerns that have been expressed if written reasons become a requirement for all administrative tribunals – that it would be an inappropriate burden to impose on them and may lead to increased costs and delay, and that it might induce a lack of candour on the part of administrative officers – by noting:[432]

> In my view, however, these concerns can be accommodated by ensuring that any reasons requirement under the duty of fairness leaves sufficient flexibility to decision-makers by accepting various types of written explanations for the decision as sufficient.

In *Baker* itself, the Supreme Court exercised this flexibility and found as sufficient the immigration officer's notes which were taken, by inference, to be the reasons for the decision:[433]

> In my view, however, the reasons requirement was fulfilled in this case since the appellant was provided with the notes of Officer Lorenz. The notes were given to Ms. Baker when her counsel asked for reasons. Because of this, and because there is no other record of the reasons for making the decision, the notes of the subordinate reviewing officer

---

431 *Baker, supra* note 423.
432 *Ibid.* at para. 40
433 *Ibid.* at para. 44. The court also used the notes to find that the immigration officer had not approached the case with appropriate impartiality.

should be taken, by inference, to be the reasons for decision. Accepting documents such as these notes as sufficient reasons is part of the flexibility that is necessary, as emphasized by Macdonald and Lametti, supra, when courts evaluate the requirements of the duty of fairness with recognition of the day-to-day realities of administrative agencies and the many ways in which the values underlying the principles of procedural fairness can be assured. It upholds the principle that individuals are entitled to fair procedures and open decision-making, but recognizes that in the administrative context, this transparency may take place in various ways. I conclude that the notes of Officer Lorenz satisfy the requirement for reasons under the duty of procedural fairness in this case, and they will be taken to be the reasons for decision.

It is difficult to predict when a court will require that procedural fairness requires the provision of written reasons at common law for a tribunal's decision and when it will not, because, like all aspects of procedural fairness, the content of the rule is context specific. Fairness in administrative decision-making may well dictate that the persons affected by a decision should know why it has been reached.[434] This is all the more true where the right of appeal, or where the availability of judicial review, depends on the ability to demonstrate that the delegate's reasoning contained an error of law. Without reasons, it may be impossible to demonstrate to the reviewing court that an error of law occurred, and therefore impossible to correct a result arrived at on irrelevant evidence, in bad faith, or for an improper purpose.[435]

It is clear, however, that reasons will not be required for every administrative decision; and it is clear that different forms of reasons will suffice. It may be that courts, over time, will develop a list of factors which will indicate when written reasons are required and will articulate which administrative tribunals have a common law requirement to provide written reasons and which do not. It bears watching to see how this development will impact the operations of administrative decision-makers, particularly on those with a high volume of decision-making.

It should also be noted that there is one well-established exception to the traditional view that there is no common law requirement to provide reasons for a decision. This exception occurs when, if there are no written reasons to demonstrate the reasonableness of a decision, the decision (when viewed in the context) can only be viewed as unreasonable.

(ii) Statutory Requirements for Reasons

Of course, where the delegate is statutorily required to provided reasons, failure to do so will certainly violate procedural fairness and, moreover, will

---

434   There has also been some support for the requirement of reasons under s. 7 of the *Charter*. See *D & H Holdings Ltd. v. Vancouver (City)* (1985), 15 Admin. L.R. 209 (B.C. S.C.) and *Canada (Department of Employment & Immigration) c. Cushnie* (1988), 35 Admin. L.R. 38 (Que. C.A.).

435   For example, in *Roncarelli v. Duplessis*, [1959] S.C.R. 121 (S.C.C.) where the Premier (in discovery) gave his improper reason for cancelling Roncarelli's liquor licence.

amount to a jurisdictional error by the statutory delegate.[436] One example is section 7 of Alberta's *Administrative Procedures Act*,[437] which provides:

> When an authority exercises a statutory power so as to adversely affect the rights of a party, the authority shall furnish to each party a written statement of its decision setting out
>
> (a) the findings of fact on which it based its decision, and
>
> (b) the reasons for the decisions.

The Lieutenant Governor in Council is given power under the Act to prescribe the statutory authorities to whom the procedural requirements of the *Administrative Procedure Act* apply.[438] Unfortunately, to date only a few bodies have been brought under this regime.[439]

Similar general legislation exists in a number of other provinces requiring some or all of their statutory delegates to give reasons.[440] Unfortunately, no corresponding general requirement yet exists at the federal level in Canada.[441]

---

436 *Morin v. Alberta (Provincial Planning Board)*, [1974] 6 W.W.R. 291 (Alta. T.D.); *Hannley v. Edmonton (City)* (1978), 7 Alta. L.R. (2d) 394 (Alta. C.A.); *Dome Petroleum Ltd. v. Alberta (Public Utilities Board)* (1976), 2 A.R. 453 (Alta. C.A.), affirmed [1977] 2 S.C.R. 822 (S.C.C.).

437 R.S.A. 2000, c. A-3, reproduced in Appendix 1.

438 *Ibid.*, s. 2.

439 Alberta Regulation No. 135/80, as amended, designates as authorities to which the *Administrative Procedures Act* applies as:

> (a) the Alberta Agricultural Products Marketing Council (in some circumstances);
> (b) the Surface Rights Board;
> (c) the Alberta Motor Transport Board;
> (d) the Irrigation Council;
> (e) the Local Authorities Board;
> (f) the Energy Resources Conservation Board;
> (g) the Public Utilities Board (in some circumstances); and
> (h) the Assessment Review Board (in some circumstances).

The Assessment Review Board is only required to give reasons when one of the parties requests that the Board do so. This request must be made in a timely fashion or the Board no longer has the obligation: *Inter-Meridian Investing Ltd. v. Alberta (Assessment Appeal Board)* (1997), 4 Admin. L.R. (3d) 244 (Alta. C.A.). However, only final decisions must be in writing: *TransAlta Utilities Corp. v. Alberta (Energy & Utilities Board)* (1997), [1997] A.J. No. 1077, 1997 CarswellAlta 1021 (Alta. C.A. [In Chambers]).

The ALRI's Final Report No. 70, December 1999, *Powers and Procedures for Administrative Tribunals in Alberta* recommends that all tribunals be required to give reasons. As of December 2003, the Alberta government had not implemented this report.

440 For example, see s. 17 of the *Statutory Powers Procedure Act*, R.S.O. 1980, c. S. 22, which requires a tribunal to whom the Act applies to "give reasons in writing . . . if requested by a party."

441 See however, the *Report of the Law Reform Commission of Canada on a Council on Tribunals*. For the position in Australia, see s. 13 of the *Administrative Decisions (Judicial Review) Act, 1977* (affecting federal decisions and s. 8 of the *Administrative Law Act, 1978* (Victoria).

In addition, however, a number of individual Acts contain similar specific provisions requiring the persons to whom statutory powers have been delegated to give reasons for their decisions.[442] As in most of administrative law therefore, it is important to study the particular legislation involved to know what legal obligations are imposed on the administrator.

(iii)   The Effect of Giving "Wrong" Reasons

If a statutory delegate provides reasons for its decision (whether it is required to do so or does so voluntarily),[443] the possibility exists that the reasons will demonstrate some fatal error in the way in which the delegate purported to exercise the power delegated to it – thereby opening the door to judicial review. This is demonstrated extremely well in the *Padfield* case.[444]

The case involved provisions of the *Agricultural Marketing Act 1958*,[445] which regulated the marketing of milk under the Milk Marketing Board. The Board fixed different prices for milk in the eleven regions into which England and Wales were divided, the price differential among the regions reflecting differences in transportation costs. The south east region was unhappy with this and since they could not get a majority on the Board, which was made up representatives from the eleven regions, they asked the Minister to appoint a committee of investigation to look into their complaints. He refused to do so and gave certain reasons for his refusal. The House of Lords considered the lawfulness of these reasons.

Under the Act, a complaint would go to a committee of investigation ". . . if the Minister in any case so directs . . .".[446] The committee had to consider whether any act or omission of the Board was ". . . contrary to the interests of any persons affected by the scheme and is not in the public interest."[447]

The Minister refused to refer the matter to the committee, for the following stated reasons:

(a)   If the complaint were upheld, he would be expected to make a statutory order to remedy the situation.

(b)   The complaint would open up too wide an issue.

(c)   The decision was one for the Board, not the committee of investigation.

On a challenge to this approach, the Court first had to consider the nature of the authority given to the Minister. It was argued that the Minister was

---

442   For example, see s. 687(2) of the *Municipal Government Act*, R.S.A. 2000, c. M-26, which requires a Subdivision and Development Appeal Board to give reasons in writing.

443   See the discussion on this point in the *Padfield* case, note 444, below. See also *Sawatzky v. Universities Academic Pension Plan Board* (1992), 9 Admin. L.R. (2d) 109 at 116-20 (Alta. Q.B.); *Actus Management Ltd. v. Calgary (City)*, [1975] 6 W.W.R. 739 (Alta. C.A.); *Dallinga v. Calgary (City)* (1975), [1976] 1 W.W.R. 319 (Alta. C.A.).

444   *Padfield v. Minister of Agriculture, Fisheries and Food*, [1968] 2 W.L.R. 924 (H.L.).

445   6 & 7 Eliz. 2, c. 47.

446   *Ibid.*, s. 19(3)(b).

447   *Ibid.*, s. 19(6).

subject to *mandamus* since there was a duty imposed on him to refer serious complaints to the committee. The court considered the distinction between a power coupled with a duty and a complete discretion. All five law lords held that this was not a duty but a discretion in the Minister. The question was whether he had exercised his discretion lawfully with four of the five law lords[448] holding that the Minister had acted unlawfully. The difference of opinion among the judges lay in the nature and extent of the discretion conferred, whether it was unfettered and whether the reasons which the Minister had given constituted unlawful conduct.

In Lord Reid's view, refusing the complaint on the ground that it raised wide issues which he might have to remedy constituted a misdirection by the Minister, since the legislation clearly contemplated this very eventuality by providing for amendment and revocation of the scheme first through the means of the committee's investigation.

Secondly, the reason that the issue should be resolved through the Board was also insufficient. The Minister could not absolve himself from his responsibility. He had a duty to act where the Board had acted contrary to the public interest and a duty to investigate complaints.

Lord Reid was also of the view that if the Minister was suggesting that the result of the committee's investigation might lead to his later embarrassment, this would be a bad reason.

While the Minister was not bound to give reasons, his failure to do so did not mean that his decision could not be questioned by a court. The Court could act if it could be inferred from all the circumstances that the effect of the refusal was to frustrate the policy and objects of the Act. Merely because the Act conferred a power (as distinct from a duty) did not prevent the Court from going behind the words and determining that the circumstances warranted coupling the power with a duty. In this case, the Minister's discretion was not unlimited and it had been used in a manner that did not accord with the intention of the Act which conferred it. Lord Hodson said:[449]

> The reasons disclosed are not, in my opinion, good reasons for refusing to refer the complaint seeing that they leave out of account altogether the merits of the complaint itself.

Lord Pearce said:[450]

> Thus the independent committee of investigation was cornerstone in the structure of the Act. It was a deliberate safeguard against injustices that might arise from the operation of the scheme. . . .
>
> It is quite clear from the Act in question that the Minister is intended to have *some* duty in the matter. It is conceded that he must properly consider the complaint. He cannot throw it unread into the

---

448   Lord Morris of Borth-y-Gest dissented.
449   *Padfield, supra* note 444 at 958.
450   *Ibid.* at 960-61, 962.

waste paper basket. He cannot simply say (albeit honestly) "I think that in general the investigation of complaints has a disruptive effect on the scheme and leads to more trouble than (on balance) it is worth; I shall therefore never refer anything to the committee of investigation." To allow him to do so would be to give him power to set aside for his period as Minister the obvious intention of Parliament, namely that an independent committee set up for the purpose should investigate grievances and that their report should be available to Parliament. This was clearly never intended by the Act.

A general abdication of the Minister's power and duty in this fashion was not in accord with Parliament's intention. Similarly, Lord Upjohn outlined what might constitute unlawful behaviour by the Minister:

(a) an outright refusal to consider a relevant matter;

(b) misdirecting himself on a point of law;

(c) taking into account some wholly irrelevant or extraneous consideration; or

(d) wholly omitting to take into account a relevant consideration.

If the reasons disclosed that the Minister had committed one of these errors and thereby acted unlawfully, he had exceeded his jurisdiction. Even if his discretion was said to be unfettered, this did not unfetter the control which the judiciary had over the executive, namely that in exercising its powers, the latter had to act lawfully; this the Court determined by looking at the scope and purpose of the Act in conferring a discretion. The Minister, by failing to understand the scope and object of section 19, and of his functions and duties under it, so misdirected himself in law.

(iv) What Constitutes "Reasons"

As the Appeal Division of the Supreme Court of Alberta noted in *Dome Petroleum Ltd. v. Alberta (Public Utilities Board)*, the rationale for requiring an administrator to give reasons is:[451]

to enable persons whose rights are adversely affected by an administrative decision to know what the reasons for that decision were. The reasons must be proper, adequate and intelligible. They must also enable the person concerned to assess whether he has grounds of appeal.

This mirrors the approach adopted by the English courts in *Poyser v. Mills' Arbitration*.[452] The reasons were held to be inadequate because the arbitrator

---

451   (1976), 2 A.R. 453 at 472 (Alta. C.A.), affirmed [1977] 2 S.C.R. 822 (S.C.C.).
452   (1963), [1964] 2 Q.B. 467 (Eng. Q.B.).

had indicated in his report that certain items were bad and others were good, but he did not identify which was which. As Megaw J. stated:[453]

> I am bound to say this, and again I do not think it was disputed by [counsel for the landlord], that a reason which is as jejune as that reason is not satisfactory, but in my view it goes further than that. The whole purpose of section 12 of the *Tribunals and Inquiries Act,* 1958, was to enable persons whose property, or whose interests, were being affected by some administrative decision or some statutory arbitration to know, if the decision was against them, what the reasons for it were. Up to then, people's property and other interests might be gravely affected by a decision of some official. The decision might be perfectly right, but the person against whom it was made was left with the real grievance that he was not told why the decision had been made. The purpose of section 12 was to remedy that, and to remedy it in relation to arbitrations under this Act. Parliament provided that reasons shall be given, and in my view that must read as meaning that proper, adequate reasons must be given. The reasons that are set out must be reasons which will not only be intelligible, but which deal with the substantial points that have been raised. In my view, it is right to consider that statutory provision as being a provision as to the form which the arbitration award shall take. If those reasons do not fairly comply with that which Parliament intended, then that is an error on the face of the award. It is a material error of form. Here, having regard to paragraph 3, this award, including the reasons, does not comply with the proper form, and that is, in my view, an error of law on the face of the award. . . . I do not say that any minor or trivial error, or failure to give reasons in relation to every particular point that has been raised on the hearing, will be sufficient ground for invoking the jurisdiction of this court.

Merely parroting the matters which a delegate is required to consider does not constitute a "reason" for its action. For example, a development appeal board was given discretion under the former *Planning Act (Alberta)* to approve certain non-conforming developments if they did not adversely affect the amenities of the neighbourhood.[454] In *Hannley v. Edmonton (City),*[455] the Appellate Division of the Supreme Court of Alberta struck down a board's decision which merely repeated that the particular development ". . . would not adversely affect the amenities of the neighbourhood . . ." because that did not constitute a "reason" but rather stated a conclusion. A similar result was reached

---

453   *Ibid.* at 477-78. Even if the duty to give reasons is not mandatory, failure to do so may imply inadequate reasons, which Megaw J. suggested might constitute a reviewable intra-jurisdictional error of law.

454   R.S.A. 1980, c. P-9, s. 69(5), repealed S.A. 1995, c. 24, s. 103.

455   (1978), 7 Alta. L.R. (2d) 394 (Alta. C.A.).

in both *Morin v. Alberta (Provincial Planning Board)*[456] and *Dome Petroleum Ltd. v. Alberta (Public Utilities Board).*[457]

The fact that reasons are obscure will not of itself make them bad when an inference can be drawn from them to enable a court to deal with the matter.[458] Similarly, although the reasons must demonstrate (necessarily or by implication) that the delegate considered the matters required by statute,[459] the delegate does not need to enumerate each finding of fact.[460] However, if reasons are unintelligible and therefore incapable of proper judicial scrutiny they are inadequate.[461] It is not satisfactory that a board restates its policy guidelines to comply with requirements of providing reasons.[462] Although reasons may not be meaningful, the court may not intervene if there are other grounds to support the decision.[463] In *Baker*, the immigration officer's notes were sufficient reasons as:[464]

> . . . part of the flexibility that is necessary . . . when courts evaluate the requirements of the duty of fairness with recognition of the day-to-day realities of administrative agencies and the many ways in which the values underlying the principles of procedural fairness can be assured. It upholds the principle that individuals are entitled to fair procedures and open decision-making, but recognizes that in the administrative context, this transparency may take place in various ways.

One recent example of where the court was asked to consider whether reasons were adequate is *BP Canada Energy Co. v. Alberta (Energy & Utilities Board)*,[465] in which the applicant successfully sought leave to appeal a decision of the EUB on the basis of inadequate reasons. In *BP Canada Energy*, the board was required to give reasons under the *Administrative Procedures Act.*[466] The applicants argued that without adequate reasons explaining the discrepancy between the Board's findings and the interpretive evidence in front of it,

---

456   [1974] 6 W.W.R. 291 (Alta. T.D.).

457   (1976) 2 A.R. 453 (Alta. C.A.), affirmed [1977] 2 S.C.R. 822 (S.C.C.).

458   *Earl of Iveagh v. Minister of Housing & Local Government* (1963), [1964] 1 Q.B. 395 (Eng. C.A.).

459   *Morin v. Alberta (Provincial Planning Board)*, [1974] 6 W.W.R. 291 (Alta. T.D.).

460   *S.E.I.U., Local 333 v. Nipawin District Staff Nurses Assn.* (1973), [1975] 1 S.C.R. 382 (S.C.C.); *Woolaston v. Canada (Minister of Manpower & Immigration)* (1972), [1973] S.C.R. 102 (S.C.C.).

461   *R. v. Sheppard*, [2002] 1 S.C.R. 869 (S.C.C.).

462   *Consumers' Assn. of Canada (Alberta) v. Alberta (Public Utilities Board)* (1985), 10 Admin. L.R. 137 (Alta. C.A.).

463   *Chen v. Law Society (Manitoba)* (1999), 141 Man. R. (2d) 116 (Man. Q.B.), affirmed 2000 MBCA 26 (Man. C.A.), where the court found that a Complaints Resolution Committee had failed to give meaningful reasons when it suspended a lawyer pending a hearing. The lawyer was entitled to know the basis on which she had been suspended and needed to be able to assess whether to appeal. However, as there were grounds to support the suspension, the court refused to intervene on this ground.

464   *Baker, supra* note 423 at para. 44.

465   2003 ABCA 285 (Alta. C.A. [In Chambers]).

466   R.S.A. 2000, c. A-3.

a concern exists that the Board arrived at its conclusions as a result of interpretive and opinion evidence heard in the absence of the parties, either during or after the hearing. The applicants submitted that the case was all about interpretive evidence and, in such a case, it is necessary for the Board to say what interpretations it accepts and why. The applicants pointed out that the Board did not explain why its map differed from all maps submitted by the parties. Madam Justice Conrad, in determining whether to grant the applicant leave to appeal, concluded:[467]

> The test for me is to determine whether the adequacy of the reasons raises a serious arguable issue. Notwithstanding the length of the reasons, I am of the view that the Applicants have met the required threshold on this issue. The Applicants have demonstrated a serious arguable issue as to the Board's failure to provide an adequate explanation as to why it reached the conclusions it did. There is an issue as to whether the reasons make the requisite findings of fact or disclose all the evidence behind the Board's Decision in such a way as to make the parties understand the reasons and assess whether the Board erred in law or jurisdiction. In *Lor-Al Springs Ltd. v. Ponoka (County) Subdivision and Development Appeal Board* (2000), 271 A.R. 149, [2000] A.J. No. 1286, 2000 ABCA 299 at para. 15, Picard J.A. agreed with the statement that "the test for determining whether the reasons given by a delegate are adequate in law is whether they show why or how or on what evidence the delegate reached the conclusion." It is at least a serious arguable issue that the Board's Decision failed to meet this standard, and I therefore grant leave to appeal on this issue.

In summary, it appears that the test for determining whether the reasons given by a delegate are adequate in law is whether they show why or how or on what evidence the delegate reached its conclusion.[468] If so, then any common law or statutory requirement to give reasons will be satisfied (although the reasons given may disclose another fatal error); if not, that fact alone will constitute a fatal flaw in the exercise of the delegate's power.

(v) The Effect of Failing to Give Reasons

The failure to give reasons may invalidate the statutory delegate's actions in two possible ways. First, as the House of Lords noted in *Padfield*,[469] the failure of the decision-maker to give reasons for a decision may lead the court to conclude that the delegate had no proper reason for the decision, and must therefore have acted for some improper purpose. Accordingly, the delegate's decision must be held to be void. In effect, this reasoning assumes that silence or lack of a proper reason constitutes no lawful reason and an abuse of discre-

---

467 *BP Canada Energy, supra* note 465 at para. 22.
468 *Couillard v. Edmonton (City)* (1979), 10 Alta. L.R. (2d) 295 (Alta. C.A.).
469 [1968] 2 W.L.R. 924 (H.L.).

tion.[470] However, the court cannot be counted on always to impugn the integrity of a delegate who emulates the "inscrutable face of the Sphinx", to quote Lord Sumner's famous judgment in the *Nat Bell Liquors* case.[471]

Secondly, the failure to give reasons will more directly deprive the delegate of jurisdiction if the delegate is under a common law or statutory obligation to do so. Failure to do so renders the decision void.[472] In some cases, it may be both possible (and appropriate) for the delegate to articulate the reasons for the decision afterwards in proper form, without having to recommence the hearing *de novo*.[473]

5. Conclusion

The principles of procedural fairness have been applied by the courts for many years to determine whether delegates have adopted a fair procedure in the exercise of their statutory powers. Procedural fairness is presumed by the common law to be an implied limitation on the exercise of delegated power. The courts have adopted these rules from their own procedures, and have applied them to statutory delegates generally, whether or not quasi-judicial functions are involved. Because of the doctrine of the Sovereignty of Parliament, legislation may specifically prescribe the procedure to be adopted by a delegate, but very specific words are required to oust the common law's presumption in favour of fairness and the requirement to comply with the principles of procedural fairness.

What constitutes "fairness" may be difficult to determine in particular circumstances. The cases have identified many types of unfair procedures. But what is unfair in one context may be fair in another, and *vice versa*. Accordingly, it is dangerous to generalize about the nature of a fair hearing in the abstract. Nevertheless, the courts' insistence on a fair procedure is an extremely important vehicle for judicial review of administrative action, and for maintaining regularity and decency in the workings of our large and complicated modern government.

---

470   For other examples of this reasoning, see *Wrights' Canadian Ropes Ltd. v. Minister of National Revenue* (1946), [1947] A.C. 109 at 123 (Canada P.C.); *Norton Tool Co. v. Tewson* (1972), [1973] 1 W.L.R. 45 (N.I.R.C.); *Pepys v. London Tpt. Executive*, [1975] 1 W.L.R. 234 (C.A.). In *Poyser v. Mills' Arbitration* (1963), [1964] 2 Q.B. 467 (Eng. Q.B.), Megaw J. considered that lack of reasons could also constitute an intra-jurisdictional error of law reviewable in certain circumstances by *certiorari* (see Chapter 11) or on appeal.

471   [1922] 2 A.C. 128, 65 D.L.R. 1 at 25 (Canada P.C.).

472   *Morin v. Alberta (Provincial Planning Board)*, [1974] 6 W.W.R. 291 (Alta. T.D.); *Hannley v. Edmonton (City)* (1978), 7 Alta. L.R. (2d) 394 (Alta. C.A.); *Dome Petroleum Ltd. v. Alberta (Public Utilities Board)* (1976), 2 A.R. 453 (Alta. C.A.), affirmed [1977] 2 S.C.R. 822 (S.C.C.).

473   This procedure may be more apt under the English Act than under the Alberta one which *requires* the tribunal to give reasons in writing, not merely on request. This implies a condition precedent, the non-fulfilment of which could possibly not be cured by a subsequent issuance of reasons. For a discussion of the timing for asking for and giving reasons under the English Act, see W. Wade & C. Forsyth, *Administrative Law*, 7th ed. (Oxford: Clarendon Press, 1994) at 942.

6. Selected Bibliography

Akehurst, C.M., "Statements of Reasons for Judicial and Administrative Decisions" (1970) 33 M.L.R. 154.

Brown, D.J.M. and Evans, J.M. (The Hon.), *Judicial Review of Administrative Action in Canada,* looseleaf (Toronto, Canvasback, 2003), c. 7.

Berkenbosch, W. & Casey, J.T., *The Duty of Fairness in the Investigative Stage of Administrative Proceedings* (2002) 40 Admin. L.R. (3d) 50.

Casey, J.T., *Regulation of Professions in Canada,* looseleaf (Toronto: Carswell, 1994) at 8-38 to 8-39.

Casey J.T., "A Pot-Pourri of Recent Developments in Administrative Law" published by the Legal Education Society of Alberta, papers for a seminar on "Dealing with Government Boards and Agencies, April 25-28, 1997.

Casey, J.T., "Disclosure in Administrative Proceedings – Does *Stinchcombe* Apply?" (1997) 6 R.A.L. 121.

de Villars, A.S., "Staff in the Decision-Making Process", a paper presented at a symposium held in Ottawa, November 1994.

Flick, G.A., "Administrative Adjudications and the Duty to Give Reasons – A search for Criteria" [1978] P.L. 16.

Fox, D., Public Participation in the Administrative Process, Study Paper for Law Reform Commission of Canada (1979).

Grey, J., "Can Fairness be Effective?" (1982) 27 McGill L.J. 360.

Hogg, P.W., "Judicial Review of Action b the Crown Representative" (1969) 43 Australian L.J. 215.

Janisch, H.N., "Consistency, Rule Making and Consolidated Bathurst" (1991) 16 Queens Law Journal 95.

Jones, D.P., "Administrative Fairness in Alberta" (1980) 18 Alta. L.R. 351.

Jones, D.P., "Discretionary Refusal of Judicial Review in Administrative Law" (1981) 19 Alta. L. Rev. 483.

Jones, D.P., "Natural Justice and Fairness in the Administrative Process" in *Judicial Review of Administrative Rulings,* arising out of the 1982 Annual Conference of the Canadian Institute for the Administration of Justice.

Jones, D.P., "A Comment on Legitimate Expectations and the Duty to Give Reasons in Administrative Law" (1986) 25 Alta. L.Rev. 512.

Kushner, H.L., "The Right to Reasons in Administrative Law" (1986) 24 Alta. L. Rev. 305.

Leadbeater, A., Council on Administration, Study Paper for the Law Reform Commission of Canada, 1980.

Lévesque-Crévier, M.C., "La Motivation en droit administratif" (1980) 40 Rev. du Barreau 535.

MacPherson, P.A., "The Legitimate Expectations Doctrine and its Application to Administrative Policy" (1996) 9 C.J.A.L.P. 141.

Macdonald, R.A. and Lametti, D., "Reasons for Decisions in Administrative Law" (1989-90) 3 C.J.A.L.P. 124.

Morris, M., "Administrative decision-makers and the duty to give reasons: an emerging debate" (1997-1998) 11 C.J.A.L.P. 155.

Mullan, D.J., "Fairness: The New Natural Justice" (1975) 25 University of Toronto L.J. 281.

Mullan, D.J., "Natural Justice and Fairness – Substantive as Well as Procedural Standards for the Review of Administrative Decision-Making?" (1982) 27 McGill L.J. 250.

Munro, K.M., "Potential Problems with Multi-Member Standing Boards", published by the Legal Education Society of Alberta for a seminar on Dealing with Government Boards and Agencies, April 25-28, 1997.

Munro, K.M., "Howe troublesome: Do Natural Justice or Fairness Require Full Disclosure?" (1995) 4 R.A.L. 97.

Peiris, G.L., "Natural Justice and Degrees of Invalidity of Administrative Action" [1983] P.L. 634.

Reid, R.F., and David, H., *Administrative Law and Practice*, 2d ed. (Toronto: Butterworths, 1978) especially c. 2 and c. 3.

Report of the Committee on Administrative Tribunals and Inquiries (the "Franks Committee Report"), England, 1957, Cmnd. 219.

Report of the Committee of the JUSTICE – All Souls Review of Administrative Law in the United Kingdom (1988), especially c. 2 on "The Formulation of Principles – Good Administration", and c. 3 on "The Duty to Give Reasons".

Report of the Committee on Minister's Powers (the "Donoughmore Report"), England, 1932, Cmd. 4060.

Report of the Special Committee on Boards and Tribunals to the Legislative Assembly of Alberta (the "Clement Report"), 1966.

Richardson, G., "The Duty to Give Reasons: Potential and Practice" [1986] P.L. 437.

Steel, G., "Tribunal Counsel" (1997-1998) 11 C.J.A.L.P. 57.

Sprague, J.L.H., "Evidence before Administrative Agencies: Let's All Forget the 'Rules' and Just Concentrate on What We're Doing" (1994-1995) 8 C.J.A.L.P. 263.

Wright, D., "Rethinking the doctrine of legitimate expectations in Canadian Administrative Law" (1997) 350 Osgoode Hall L.J. 139.

10

The Duty to be Fair: the Rule Against Bias[1]

---

1 This chapter has been revised by Professor Philip Bryden, Dean at the Faculty of Law, University of New Brunswick.

1. Introduction to the Rule

The second principle of natural justice is sometimes referred to as "the rule against bias."[2] The rule, in its simplest form, is that decision-makers must base their decisions, and must be seen to be basing their decisions, on nothing but the relevant law and the evidence that is properly before them. The integrity of our system of administrative adjudication depends on the exclusion of extraneous factors such as the self-interest or the prejudices of decision-makers from the considerations that are brought to bear on decisions[3] and the rule is designed to preserve public confidence in the system's impartiality. Although the rule against bias has not received the same attention as *audi alteram partem*, the policy underlying both aspects of natural justice is identical: justice must not only be done, but must manifestly and undoubtedly be seen to be done.[4]

The conundrum posed by bias cases is that everyone approaches legal issues with certain predispositions. Many of our predispositions take the form of "common sense" – for example, how cause-and-effect works, how people interact, what makes a story plausible or not – and no-one will suggest that tribunal members are not entitled to apply these views to the case at hand. Other predispositions may include an opinion on the meaning of statutes or judicial precedents, or on the merits of a variety of political and economic theories. Cases would be interminable if literally *everything* had to be proved. So the question is not so much *whether* predispositions are impermissible, but rather *which* predispositions are impermissible, and under what circumstances.[5]

The questions that will be addressed in this chapter are:

– To whom does the rule against bias apply?
– What is the legal test for bias?
– How is that test applied in different settings?
– How do institutional arrangements give rise to legal concerns about bias and lack of independence?

---

2 The rule against bias is also sometimes referred to as the "nemo judex" rule, from the Latin phrase *nemo judex in sua causa debet esse* (a literal translation of which might be "no one shall be judge in their own cause"). Although the Latin phrase is somewhat narrower than the rule against bias, one should be aware of its use as a shorthand.

3 See J. McCormack, "The Price of Administrative Justice" (1998) 6 Can. Lab. & Emp. L.J. 1 at 16.

4 To paraphrase the words of Lord Chief Justice Hewart in *R. v. Justices of Sussex* (1923), [1924] 1 K.B. 256 at 259 (Eng. K.B.).

5 See *R. v. S. (R.D.)*, [1997] 3 S.C.R. 484 (S.C.C.) at paras. 103-108 (per Cory J.) and paras. 32-45 (per L'Heureux-Dubé and McLachlin JJ.).

- What is the legal effect of a finding that a situation gives rise to a reasonable apprehension of bias?
- Can failure to raise a concern about bias constitute a waiver of the right to raise that concern later on?

2. To Whom Does the Rule Against Bias Apply?

As with the first principle of natural justice, application of the rule against bias does not depend on a rigid categorization of functions. It applies to all statutory delegates and persons exercising public authority whose decisions are required to meet the standards of procedural fairness.

In *S.E.P.Q.A. v. Canada (Human Rights Commission)*,[6] Sopinka J. for the Supreme Court of Canada discussed and adopted the modern, flexible approach to the application of the rules of natural justice and fairness to all types of administrative bodies:

> Both the rules of natural justice and the duty of fairness are variable standards. Their content will depend on the circumstances of the case, the statutory provisions and the nature of the matter to be decided. The distinction between them therefore becomes blurred as one approaches the lower end of the scale of judicial or quasi-judicial tribunals and the high end of the scale with respect to administrative or executive tribunals. Accordingly, the content of the rules to be followed by a tribunal is now not determined by attempting to classify them as judicial, quasi-judicial, administrative or executive. Instead, the court decides the content of these rules by reference to all the circumstances under which the tribunal operates.[7]

Thus, the usual issue is not *whether* the rule against bias applies to a given public decision-maker, but rather *how* it applies, in the environment of that particular decision-maker. If a subordinate who makes a recommendation to the ultimate decision-maker plays an important role in the decision-making process, a finding of bias on the part of the subordinate can invalidate the decision even if there is no suggestion of bias on the part of the decision-maker himself or herself.[8]

3. The Test for Bias

In earlier times, there was considerable debate over the content of the test for bias. The principal debate was whether an applicant had to show only a reasonable apprehension of bias, a real suspicion of bias, or a real likelihood of bias, or indeed whether there was any real difference between them. In

---

6 [1989] 2 S.C.R. 879, 62 D.L.R. (4th) 385, 89 C.L.L.C. 17,022 (S.C.C.).

7 *Ibid.* at 895-96 [S.C.R.].

8 *Baker v. Canada (Minster of Citizenship & Immigration)*, [1999] 2 S.C.R. 817 (S.C.C.) at para. 45.

Canada, this debate was finally settled in *Committee for Justice & Liberty v. Canada (National Energy Board)*,[9] in which the Supreme Court of Canada adopted the "reasonable apprehension of bias" test. The *National Energy Board* case is now the leading Canadian case on bias. Indeed, this test is applied in determining whether judges as well as administrative decision-makers are subject to disqualification for bias.[10] The basic difference between the bias rules governing judges and the bias rules governing administrative decision-makers is the way in which the institutional context of administrative decision-making is employed to shape the application of the "reasonable apprehension of bias" test set out in the *National Energy Board* case.[11] The case itself is therefore worth examining in some detail.

(a) The Facts of the National Energy Board Case

The case arose from the formation in June 1972 of the Arctic Gas consortium to build a natural gas pipeline from the Arctic to southern markets. The Canada Development Corporation, wholly owned by the Government of Canada, became a shareholder in the new corporation, and contributed some $1.2 million to the pipeline project. Marshall Crowe was President of the Canada Development Corporation from the date of its entry into the project until October 1973, when he was appointed Chairman of the National Energy Board. During this period, he attended various meetings and took part in numerous decisions made by several of the committees of the consortium.

In 1975, Arctic Gas and a number of competitors made applications to the board for permission to construct pipelines to move natural gas from the Arctic to southern markets. In April 1975 the board, which at that time had eight

---

9   (1976), [1978] 1 S.C.R. 369 (S.C.C.). Although Canadian law concerning bias has its roots in English law, English courts currently adopt a two-part approach to determining whether a decision-maker ought to be disqualified. The first question is whether the decision-maker has a personal interest in the case that effectively makes him or her a party to the dispute, and in these situations the decision-maker is automatically disqualified. If this issue is resolved in favour of allowing the decision-maker to take part, the second question is whether the circumstances are such that there is a "real likelihood" or "real danger" that the decision-maker is biased. *R. v. Bow Street Metropolitan Stipendiary Magistrate ex. p. Pinochet Ugarte (No. 2)*, [2000] 1 A.C. 119 (H.L.). The differences between the "real danger" or "real likelihood" of bias test and the "reasonable apprehension of bias" test may be more apparent than real, and the outcomes of most cases will be the same using either test. See *Locabail (U.K.) Ltd. v. Bayfield Properties Ltd.*, [2000] 1 All E.R. 65 (Eng. C.A.); *Auckland Casino Ltd. v. Casino Control Authority*, [1995] 1 N.Z.L.R. 142 (New Zealand C.A.). In case there was any practical difference between the "real danger of bias" and "reasonable apprehension of bias" tests, the House of Lords in *Porter v. Magill*, [2002] A.C. 357 (H.L.) has decided to remove any reference in English law to a "real danger" of bias and has concentrated on whether there is a "real possibility" of bias. This change was designed to bring this aspect of English law into line with the law of the European Community and the law of most other Commonwealth jurisdictions, including Canada.

10   See for example *R. v. S. (R.D.)*, *supra* note 5.

11   See *2747-3174 Québec Inc. c. Québec (Régie des permis d'alcool)*, [1996] 3 S.C.R. 919 (S.C.C.) at paras. 112-115 (per L'Heureux-Dubé J., concurring with the majority on this point); *Newfoundland Telephone Co. v. Newfoundland (Board of Commissioners of Public Utilities)*, [1992] 1 S.C.R. 623, 4 Admin. L.R. (2d) 121 (S.C.C.).

members, assigned Crowe and two others to constitute the panel to hear these competing applications. The applications were subsequently directed to be heard together at public hearings commencing in October 1975.

In the meantime, counsel for Arctic Gas approached the board's counsel and raised the question whether Crowe should participate in the hearings. A third party, it was argued, might reasonably apprehend that Crowe was biased in favour of Arctic Gas. Crowe therefore prepared a statement which was sent to all of the applicants and intervenors shortly before the hearings, setting out his previous involvement with the Arctic Gas project. When this was read at the opening of the hearings, five of the intervenors objected to Crowe's participation. The National Energy Board therefore decided to state a case to the Federal Court of Appeal under section 28(4) of the *Federal Court Act* in the following terms: "Would the board err in rejecting the objections and in holding that Mr. Crowe was not disqualified from being a member of the panel on the grounds of reasonable apprehension or reasonable likelihood of bias?"

(b) The Judgments

After first considering its own jurisdiction to decide the question put to it, the five members of the Court of Appeal unanimously held that the board would not err in permitting Crowe to participate in the hearings. In giving reasons for the court's decision, Thurlow J. surveyed the wide range of factual circumstances in which bias may be alleged, and noted that there was no suggestion that Crowe was actually biased or had a pecuniary interest in the outcome of the hearings. He then considered the two submissions made by the intervenors: first, that a third party could reasonably apprehend that Crowe's previous involvement with Arctic Gas would incline him to favour its application; or, secondly, that Crowe was in favour of building a pipeline (which the intervenors opposed).

Thurlow J. only dealt with these submissions by recognizing that bias might theoretically be established in "predetermination cases, cases where there has been some expression of views indicating . . . prejudgment."[12] But he said that

> [e]ven in such cases it becomes necessary to consider whether there is reason to apprehend that the person whose duty it is to decide will not listen to the evidence and decide fairly on it.[13]

After noting that Crowe's previous participation in the Arctic Gas consortium "might give rise in a very sensitive or scrupulous conscience to the uneasy suspicion that he might be unconsciously biased,"[14] the judge rejected such a subjective test for bias. Rather, he said the rule against bias was cast in terms of:

> [W]hat would an informed person, viewing the matter realistically and practically–and having thought the matter through–conclude[?]

---

12 (1975), 65 D.L.R. (3d) 660 at 667 (Fed. C.A.), reversed (1976), [1978] 1 S.C.R. 369 (S.C.C.).
13 *Ibid.*, emphasis added.
14 *Ibid.*

> Would he think that it is more likely than not that Mr. Crowe, whether consciously or unconsciously, would not decide fairly?[15]

Applying this test, the Court of Appeal held that reasonable and right-minded people had no cause to apprehend bias in Crowe. Therefore, the decisions of the National Energy Board panel over which Crowe was scheduled to preside would be valid.

It is interesting to note that the Court of Appeal buttressed this conclusion by referring to the fact that Crowe's participation in the consortium was of a representative nature only. While he was President of the Canada Development Corporation, he had no financial interest either in it or in the consortium; he "was essentially a person acting in the interest of the Government of Canada." He therefore had nothing to gain or lose from any decision which might be reached by the board. Accordingly, Thurlow J. held that there was no

> reason for apprehension that he would be likely to be unable or un- willing to disabuse his mind of preconceptions he may have in the face of new material [coming before the Board] pointing to a different view of matters considered in the course of his participation in activ- ities of the study group, or that he would be unconsciously influenced by decisions which he had supported as a participant in the study group.[16]

Furthermore, the Court of Appeal noted that a two-year period had elapsed between Crowe's tenure as President of the Canada Development Corporation and the Arctic Gas application to the board, and it held that the issues now to be decided by the board were "widely different from those to which the study group devoted its attention." Thus

> there appear[ed] to be no valid reason for apprehension that Mr. Crowe . . . cannot approach these new issues with the equanimity and impar- tiality to be expected of one in his position.[17]

In summary, the *ratio decidendi* of the Court of Appeal's judgment appears to have centered on its appraisal of Crowe's actual ability to keep an open mind, and not on what a bystander would reasonably perceive. In other words, the Court of Appeal arguably stated one test but applied another.

The Supreme Court of Canada reversed the decision of the Court of Appeal by a five-to-three margin.[18] The analyses adopted by the majority and minority in the Supreme Court were diametrically opposed. On the one hand, Laskin C.J.C., writing for the majority, concentrated almost exclusively on the partic- ular facts. In a rather cantankerous judgment, the Chief Justice does not clearly state the legal test he is applying. The closest he comes is in the following paragraph:

---

15 *Ibid.*
16 *Ibid.*
17 *Ibid.* at 669.
18 (1976), [1978] 1 S.C.R. 369 (S.C.C.). Note that the Supreme Court did not award costs to the appellants.

This Court in fixing on the test of reasonable apprehension of bias, as in *Ghirardosi v. Minister of Highways for British Columbia* [[1966] S.C.R. 367], and again in *Blanchette v. C.I.S. Ltd.* [[1973] S.C.R. 833], (where Pigeon J. said at p. 842-43, that "a reasonable apprehension that the judge might not act in an entirely impartial manner is ground for disqualification") was merely restating what Rand J. said in *Szilard v. Szasz* [[1955] S.C.R. 3], at pp. 6-7 in speaking of the "probability or reasoned suspicion of biased appraisal and judgment, unintended though it be". This test is grounded in a firm concern that there be no lack of public confidence in the impartiality of adjudicative agencies, and I think that emphasis is lent to this concern in the present case by the fact that the National Energy Board is enjoined to have regard for the public interest.[19]

In contrast, the dissenting judgment from de Grandpré J. is much plainer in its endorsement of the Federal Court of Appeal's test:

The proper test to be applied in a matter of this type was correctly expressed by the Court of Appeal. As already seen by the quotation above, the apprehension of bias must be a reasonable one held by reasonable and right minded persons, applying themselves to the question and obtaining thereon the required information. In the words of the Court of Appeal, that test is "what would a informed person, viewing the matter realistically and practically–and having thought the matter through–conclude. Would he think that it is more likely than not that Mr. Crowe, whether consciously or unconsciously, would not decide fairly."

I can see no real difference between the expressions found in the decided cases, be they 'reasonable apprehension of bias', 'reasonable suspicion of bias, or 'real likelihood of bias'. The grounds for this apprehension must, however, be substantial and I entirely agree with the Federal Court of Appeal which refused to accept the suggestion that the test be related to the "very sensitive or scrupulous conscience".[20]

Ironically, it is this passage from the dissenting judgment that is now widely quoted for its statement of the correct test for bias. The majority judgment is largely ignored.

It is in the application of the "reasonable apprehension of bias" test that de Grandpré J.'s dissenting judgment departs markedly from the majority judgment. De Grandpré J. not only denied the quasi-judicial nature of the National Energy Board, and therefore even the applicability of the rule against bias to its proceedings, but also was particularly hostile to the possibility that personal attitudes or previous experiences might ever amount to a disqualifying bias. After pointing out that "the National Energy Board is a tribunal that must

---

19 *Ibid.* at 391.
20 *Ibid.* at 394-95.

be staffed with persons of experience and expertise," he quoted the following passage from *R. v. Picard*:[21]

> Professional persons are called upon to serve in judicial, quasi-judicial and administrative posts in many fields and if Governments were to exclude candidates on such ground, they would find themselves deprived of the services of most professionals with any experience in the matters in respect of which their services are sought. Accordingly, I agree with the Court below that this ground was properly rejected.

Justice de Grandpré emphasized that "mere prior knowledge of the particular case or preconceptions or even prejudgments cannot be held *per se* to disqualify a panel member."[22] His Lordship then accepted the distinction made in the American decision of *New Hampshire Milk Dealers' Association v. New Hampshire Milk Control Board* between a "predisposed view . . . about public or economic policies" (attitudinal bias) and "a prejudgment concerning issues of fact in a particular case" (bias in law):[23]

> It is a well established legal principle that a distinction must be made between a preconceived point of view about certain principles of law or a predisposed view about the public or economic policies which should be controlling and a prejudgment concerning issues of fact in a particular case. 2 Davis, *Administrative Law Treatise*, s. 12.01, p. 131. There is no doubt that the latter would constitute a cause for disqualification. However, "Bias in the sense of crystallized point of view about issues of law or policy is almost universally deemed no ground for disqualification." (. . .) If this were not the law, Justices Holmes and Brandeis would have been disqualified as would be others from sitting on cases involving issue of law or policy on which they had previously manifested strong diverging views from the holdings of a majority of the members of their respective courts.

Thus de Grandpré J. rejected the appellant's submission that Crowe should be disqualified because his background would naturally incline him to favour the building of a pipeine.

In the wake of *Canada (National Energy Board)*, the easiest part of the rule against bias has been stating the test. It is whether "an informed person, viewing the matter realistically and practically – and having thought the matter through," would have "a reasonable apprehension of bias."[24] This test has been endorsed over and over again in the cases. Of course, no-one claims that the

---

21   (1967), 65 D.L.R. (2d) 658 at 661 (Que. Q.B.).

22   *Supra* note 18 at 397, quoting MacKeigan C.J.N.S in *Tomko v. Nova Scotia (Labour Relations Board)* (1974), 9 N.S.R. (2d) 277 at 298 (N.S. C.A.), affirmed (1975), 69 D.L.R. (3d) 250 (S.C.C.). De Grandpré J. also referred to *Schabas v. University of Toronto* (1974), 6 O.R. (2d) 271 (Ont. Div. Ct.); *United States v. Morgan*, 313 U.S. 409, 1 Hals. (4th) 83 (U.S. S.C., 1940), para. 69; *R. v. Commonwealth Conciliation & Arbitration Commission* (1969), 122 C.L.R. 546 (Australia H.C.).

23   222 A.2d 194 at 198 (1967), quoted in *Canada (National Energy Board)*, *ibid.* at 399-400.

24   (1976), [1978] 1 S.C.R. 369 (S.C.C.).

Canada (National Energy Board) test is easy to apply–the courts have shown repeatedly that they differ on what the reasonable, well-informed person would decide–but at least there is a firm consensus on what the correct test for administrative bias is.

4. What Constitutes Bias In Law?

For analytical purposes it is helpful to begin by distinguishing five types of cases in which arguments concerning the presence of a reasonable apprehension of bias can arise. The first is when the decision-maker (for present purposes we include in this term an individual who may contribute to a decision, such as counsel for a tribunal) has a personal financial interest in the outcome of the matter being decided. The second is when the decision-maker's impartiality can be said to be impaired because of his or her personal relationship with one or more of the parties whose case is being decided or some other person who has a significant role in the case. The third type of situation is when the decision-maker has acquired knowledge of or has been involved in the matter in some capacity other than his or her current capacity as a decision-maker. The fourth situation is when the words or behaviour of the decision-maker form the basis of a challenge to his or her impartiality. Cases in the fourth category are sometimes described as "actual bias" cases, but for reasons that we will set out below, it is normally extremely unproductive to frame arguments or analysis in "actual bias" terms. Finally, the fifth type of case involves institutional arrangements that are said to give rise to a reasonable apprehension of bias. These institutional bias cases bring into play a sufficiently distinctive set of considerations that are best treated separately from the other four categories of cases, where the concern is with characteristics or behaviour of the decision-maker as an individual.

In this section, we will consider the test for, and some examples of, reasonable apprehension of bias based on the characteristics or behaviour of the decision-maker as an individual, something that is sometimes described as personal bias. In the following section we will look at institutional bias.

(a) Financial Interest in the Outcome of the Dispute

The courts have consistently held that the existence of a direct financial interest in the outcome of the matter in dispute almost always disqualifies a statutory delegate from acting. In other words, a pecuniary interest gives rise to a "reasonable apprehension of bias", no matter how open-minded in fact the delegate might be. This rule was applied by the House of Lords in the celebrated case of *Dimes v. Grand Junction Canal Co.*,[25] where the Lord Chancellor had affirmed the order of the Vice-Chancellor granting relief to a company in

---

25   (1852), 3 H.L.C. 759 (U.K. H.L.). See also *R. v. London Rent Assessment Panel Committee* (1968), [1969] 1 Q.B. 577 (Eng. C.A.), concerning a pecuniary interest by the chairman of the appeal board against local taxes; *Innisfail (Town) By-Law No. 724, Re* (1957), 23 W.W.R. 184 (Alta. T.D.).

which, unknown to the defendant, the Lord Chancellor had an interest as a shareholder. As Lord Campbell said: [26]

> No one can suppose that Lord Cottenham could be, in the remotest degree, influenced by the interest that he had in this concern; but, my Lords, it is of the last importance that the maxim that no man is to be a judge in his own cause should be held sacred. And that is not to be confined to a cause in which he is a party, but applies to a cause in which he has an interest. Since I have had the honour to be Chief Justice of the Court of Queen's Bench, we have again and again set aside proceedings in inferior tribunals because an individual who had an interest in a cause, took a part in the decision. And it will have a most salutary influence on these tribunals when it is known that this high Court of last resort, in a case in which the Lord Chancellor of England had an interest, considered that his decision was on that account a decree not according to law, and was set aside. This will only be a lesson to all inferior tribunals to take care not only that in their decrees they are not influenced by their personal interest, but to avoid the appearance of labouring under such an influence.

Sometimes legislation specifically reiterates the common law view that a direct financial interest gives rise to a reasonable apprehension of bias.[27]

Obviously, the mere existence of a financial interest in the outcome of the dispute may not in fact influence the decision-maker. Indeed, when the finan-

---

26   *Ibid.* at 793-94.
27   For example, s. 172 (1) of the Alberta *Municipal Government Act*, R.S.A. 2000, c. M-26, provides that:

> 172(1) When a councillor has a pecuniary interest in a matter before the council, a council committee or any other body to which the councillor is appointed as a representative of the council, the councillor must, if present,
>> (a) disclose the general nature of the pecuniary interest prior to any discussion of the matter,
>> (b) abstain from voting on any question relating to the matter,
>> (c) subject to subsection (3) abstain from any discussion of the matter, and
>> (d) subject to subsections (2) and (3), leave the room in which the meeting is being held until discussion and voting on the matter are concluded.

> "Pecuniary interest" is defined in s. 170:
> 170(1) Subject to subsection (3), a councillor has a pecuniary interest in a matter if
>> (a) the matter could monetarily affect the councillor or an employer of the councillor, or
>> (b) the councillor knows or should know that the matter could monetarily affect the councillor's family.

> (2) For the purposes of subsection (1), a person is monetarily affected by a matter if the matter monetarily affects
>> (a) the person directly,
>> (b) a corporation, other than a distributing corporation, in which the person is a shareholder, director or officer,
>> (c) a distributing corporation in which the person beneficially owns voting shares carrying at least 10% of the voting rights attached to the voting shares of the corporation or of which the person is a director or officer, or
>> (d) a partnership or firm of which the person is a member.

cial interest at stake is sufficiently small, it is probably unreasonable for anyone to apprehend that it would do so. Traditionally, however, the common law has been reluctant to take into account the size of the financial interest in determining that a decision-maker ought to be disqualified.[28] In more recent cases, the courts have tended to relax the strict application of this rule and apply a *de minimis* principle to avoid disqualification for trivial financial interests.[29] This exception is limited to situations in which "the potential effect of any decision on the [decision-maker's] personal interest is so small as to be incapable of affecting his or her decision one way or the other; but it is important, bearing in mind the rationale of the rule, that any doubt should be resolved in favour of disqualification."[30]

There are, in addition, four other situations in which a person who has a direct financial interest in the outcome of a decision is entitled to take part in the decision-making process notwithstanding the general prohibition discussed above: (1) where legislation specifically permits a decision-maker to have a pecuniary interest;[31] (2) where the financial impact of the decision on the

---

28 *Dimes v. Grand Junction Canal Co.*, *supra* note 25.

29 See *Ebner v. The Official Trustee in Bankruptcy* (2000), 176 A.L.R. 644 (Australia H.C.); *Locabail (U.K.) Ltd. v. Bayfield Properties Ltd.*, [2000] 1 All E.R. 65 (Eng. C.A.); *Auckland Casino Ltd. v. Casino Control Authority*, [1995] 1 N.Z.L.R. 142 (New Zealand C.A.).

30 *Locabail (U.K.) Ltd. v. Bayfield Properties Ltd.*, *ibid.* at para. 10.

31 For example, s. 170(3) of the *Municipal Government Act*, *supra* note 27, provides that a member of council does not have a pecuniary interest by reason only of any interest:

> (a) that the councillor, an employer of the councillor or a member of the councillor's family may have as an elector, taxpayer or utility customer of the municipality,
>
> (b) that the councillor or a member of the councillor's family may have by reason of being appointed by the council as a director of a company incorporated for the purpose of carrying on business for and on behalf of the municipality or by reason of being appointed as the representative of the council on another body,
>
> (c) that the councillor or member of the councillor's family may have with respect to any allowance, honorarium, remuneration or benefit to which the councillor or member of the councillor's family may be entitled by being appointed by the council to a position described in clause (b),
>
> (d) that the councillor may have with respect to any allowance, honorarium, remuneration or benefit to which the councillor may be entitled by being a councillor,
>
> (e) that the councillor or a member of the councillor's family may have by being employed by the Government of Canada, the Government of Alberta or a federal or provincial Crown corporation or agency, except with respect to a matter directly affecting the department, corporation or agency of which the councillor or family member is an employee,
>
> (f) that a member of the councillor's family may have by having an employer, other than the municipality, that is monetarily affected by a decision of the municipality,
>
> (g) that the councillor or a member of the councillor's family may have by being a member or director of a non-profit organization as defined in section 241(f) or a service club,
>
> (h) that the councillor or member of the councillor's family may have
>
>> (i) by being appointed as the volunteer chief or other volunteer officer of a fire or ambulance service or emergency measures organization or other

decision-maker is indistinguishable from the impact the decision is likely to have on most other members of the community;[32] (3) where the decision-maker is the only person who can make the decision;[33] and (4) possibly, where the parties have agreed to waive any objections to the decision-maker's interest.[34]

Direct financial interest raises relatively few problems. An interest that is more indirect is likely to create more controversy. In *Black & McDonald Ltd. v. Construction Labour Relations Assn. (British Columbia)*,[35] the potential for financial advantage resulted in a finding that there was a reasonable apprehension of bias. Black & McDonald was a corporate member of an employers' bargaining association. It negotiated an independent agreement with the plumbers' union, which it argued it was entitled to do on the basis of recent changes in the *Labour Code* which excluded routine maintenance work from the definition of "construction." The employers' organization unsuccessfully applied for an order from the Labour Relations Board that the work was, in fact, construction. On a reconsideration of that decision, the second panel included Mr. McAvoy, who was a representative of labour on the Board. At the time, however, he was also the business agent of the electrical workers' union, whose work consisted of approximately 85% new construction and 15% service and maintenance work. Both the refrigeration workers' union and the plumbers' union were involved primarily in maintenance work, and both objected to Mr. McAvoy's presence on the panel. The Board dismissed the

---

volunteer organization or service, or

    (ii) by reason of remuneration received as a volunteer member of any of those voluntary organizations or services,

  (i) of the councillor, an employer of the councillor or a member of the councillor's family that is held in common with the majority of electors of the municipality or, if the matter affects only part of the municipality, with the majority of electors in that part,

  (j) that is so remote or insignificant that it cannot reasonably be regarded as likely to influence the councillor, or

  (k) that a councillor may have by discussing or voting on a bylaw that applies to businesses or business activities when the councillor, an employer of the councillor or a member of the councillor's family has an interest in a business, unless the only business affected by the bylaw is the business of the councillor, employer of the councillor or the councillor's family.

  (4) Subsection (3)(g) and (h) do not apply to a councillor who is an employee of an organization, club or service referred to in those clauses.

32 See *R. v. Justices of Sunderland*, [1901] 2 K.B. 357 (Eng. C.A.), where the justices had the same pecuniary interest as any other ratepayer. The Canadian Judicial Council's publication *Ethical Principles for Judges* (Ottawa: Canadian Judicial Council, 1998) states at 42 that "Owning an insurance policy, having a bank account, using a credit card or owning shares in a corporation through a mutual fund would not, in normal circumstances give rise to conflict or the appearance of conflict unless the outcome of the proceedings before the judge could substantially affect such holdings."

33 *R. v. Campbell*, [1998] 1 S.C.R. 3 (S.C.C.); *Judges v. A.G. Sask* (1931), 53 T.L.R. 464 (P.C.); *Martel v. Minister of National Revenue*, [1970] Ex. C.R. 68 (Can. Ex. Ct.).

34 See the discussion of waiver in section 8 of this chapter.

35 (1985), 19 Admin. L.R. 43 (B.C. L.R.B.), set aside/quashed (1985), 19 Admin. L.R. 65 (B.C. S.C.), affirmed (1986), 19 Admin. L.R. 73 (B.C. C.A.), and comments by T.S. Kuttner, "Is the Doctrine of Bias Compatible with the Tri-Partite Labour Tribunal" (1986) 19 Admin. L.R. 81 and "Bias and the Labour Boards Redux" (1989) Admin. L.R. 216.

application to disqualify Mr. McAvoy because the electrical workers' union was not a party to the action, and therefore its interest was too indirect. However, the B.C. Supreme Court[36] held that the Board was in error, noting that it did not matter that the interest was indirect, or that the electrical workers' union was not a party to the proceedings before the Board. What was relevant in determining whether there was a reasonable apprehension of bias was whether the union's interests might be affected by the outcome. On appeal to the Court of Appeal,[37] Nemetz J.A. found the Board's decision to be patently unreasonable,[38] rejected counsel's argument that the principles of "free, independent and impartial minds" be watered down because the board was made up of representatives from labour and management and held that the members of the panel were required to be as impartial as judges.[39]

A similar problem arose in *U.F.C.W., Local 1252 v. Prince Edward Island (Labour Relations Board).*[40] Mr. MacDonald was a member of the Labour Relations Board, and the business agent for the C.A.W. Union. Previously, he had been a member of a rival union, the U.F.C.W. Several contentious cases between the two unions had either come or were about to come before panels of the board. Although Mr. MacDonald was not sitting on those particular panels, he had sat with some of the panel members on other matters. On application for judicial review it was alleged that there was a reasonable apprehension of bias. The judge noted that Mr. MacDonald's employment with C.A.W. was dependent upon its success in the province, thus raising the spectre of some form of pecuniary bias. On appeal,[41] the issue of pecuniary bias was again indirectly raised. In dismissing the appeal, Mitchell J.A. noted: "It may be understood that union employees will serve on labour relations boards from time to time, but surely it cannot be taken as accepted that these employees will continue to sit as active board members while their employer has a contentious application before the board."[42] However, it is difficult to identify this supposed pecuniary bias in light of the fact that Mr. MacDonald was not sitting on the impugned panel.

Pecuniary interest has, however, been found to be too indirect when it was only a contingent interest,[43] and where the tribunal members' jobs might be at stake as the result of pending legislation.[44]

---

36   (1985), 19 Admin. L.R. 65 (B.C. S.C.), affirmed (1986), 19 Admin. L.R. 73 (B.C. C.A.).

37   (1986), 19 Admin. L.R. 73, [1986] 4 W.W.R. 223 (B.C. C.A.).

38   Query: What is the relationship between the patently unreasonable doctrine and the reasonable apprehension of bias? See *Witte v. Northwest Territories (Workers' Compensation Board)* (1999), 19 Admin. L.R. (3d) 185 (N.W.T. C.A.), additional reasons at (2000), [2001] 1 W.W.R. 440 (N.W.T. C.A.), leave to appeal refused (2000), 261 N.R. 199 (note) (S.C.C.) and the discussion in Chapter 12 dealing with standards of review.

39   *Supra* note 37 at 79 [Admin. L.R.].

40   (1988), 31 Admin. L.R. 200 (P.E.I. T.D.).

41   (1988), 31 Admin. L.R. 196. (P.E.I. C.A.).

42   *Ibid.* at 198.

43   *Energy Probe v. Canada (Atomic Energy Control Board)* (1984), 11 Admin. L.R. 287 (Fed. C.A.), leave to appeal refused (1985), 15 D.L.R. (4th) 48n (S.C.C.); see Case Comments by D.J. Mullan (1984), 5 Admin. L.R. 191 and (1986), 16 Admin. L.R. 311.

44   *Sethi v. Canada (Minister of Employment & Immigration)* (1988), 31 Admin. L.R. 123 (Fed.

(b) Relationships with Persons Involved with the Dispute

Where a decision-maker has a sufficiently close personal relationship with someone who has a direct interest in the outcome of the decision, that relationship will give rise to a reasonable apprehension of bias and that person is disqualified from taking part in the decision. It is evident from the examples given below that the types of relationships that can give rise to a reasonable apprehension of bias are not confined to relationships with one of the parties to the proceeding but can include a relationship with a lawyer representing one of the parties or even, in some situations, a relationship with a key witness. The central issue in these cases is typically whether the relationship between the decision-maker and the person involved with the dispute is sufficiently close that a reasonable person would have concerns about the decision-maker's ability to judge that matter impartially.[45] In addition, the interest of the person with whom the decision-maker has a relationship in the outcome of the decision must be sufficiently significant that a reasonable person would conclude that the decision-maker's impartiality could be impaired.[46]

Although no exhaustive catalogue can be given, the courts have sometimes found the following situations to contravene the rule against bias: where the decision-maker is now or previously has been the solicitor or client of one of the parties in the proceedings;[47] where the decision-maker in an employment insurance proceeding is a notary who was regularly retained by the employer who is a party to the proceeding;[48] where the daughter of the decision-maker in a disciplinary proceeding is a witness in another proceeding against the individual who is the subject of the disciplinary proceedings;[49] where the decision-maker is the employer of a party to the proceedings;[50] and where the decision-maker in a securities proceeding is a director of a company that is in competition with the person who is the subject of the proceeding.[51]

C.A.), leave to appeal refused (1988), 36 Admin. L.R. xl (S.C.C.). But see *Canadian Pacific Ltd. v. Matsqui Indian Band*, [1995] 1 S.C.R. 3 (S.C.C.), and the discussion of structural independence in section 6 of this chapter.

45　*Cougar Aviation Ltd. v. Canada (Minister of Public Works & Government Services)* (2000), 26 Admin. L.R. (3d) 30 (Fed. C.A.); *Banyay v. Insurance Corp. of British Columbia* (1996), 17 B.C.L.R. (3d) 216 (B.C. C.A.); *Huchette c. Québec* (1992), 12 C.R. (4th) 393 (Que. C.A.); *President of the Republic of South Africa v. South African Rugby Football Union*, [1999] 4 S.A. 147 (South Africa Constitutional Ct.).

46　See for example *G.W.L. Properties Ltd. v. W.R. Grace & Co. of Canada* (1972), 74 B.C.L.R. (2d) 283 (B.C. C.A.) (*per* McEachern, C.J. in chambers); *Assn. of Optometrists (British Columbia) v. British Columbia (Minister of Health)* (1998), 5 Admin. L.R. (3d) 216 (B.C. S.C. [In Chambers]).

47　*Ghirardosi v. British Columbia (Minister of Highways)*, [1966] S.C.R. 367 (S.C.C.).

48　*Marsan v. Canada (Employment & Immigration Commission)* (1996), 39 C.C.L.I. (2d) 161 (Fed. C.A.).

49　*Spence v. Prince Albert Board of Police Commissioners* (1987), 25 Admin. L.R. 90 (Sask. C.A.), leave to appeal refused (1987), 80 N.R. 316 (note) (S.C.C.).

50　*U.F.C.W., Local 1252 v. Prince Edward Island (Labour Relations Board)* (1988), 31 Admin. L.R. 200 (P.E.I. T.D.), affirmed (1988), 31 Admin. L.R. 196 (P.E.I. C.A.).

51　*Bennett v. British Columbia (Superintendent of Brokers)* (1993), 17 Admin. L.R. (2d) 222 (B.C. C.A.).

It is often useful to draw a distinction between the current or ongoing relationships held by a decision-maker and associations or relationships that occurred in the past. Courts tend to be reluctant to accept the argument that a decision-maker's past professional associations or activities betoken a general sympathy with a party that forms a basis for disqualification.[52] In particular, the passage of time is thought to be relevant in determining whether a past business or professional relationship gives rise to a reasonable apprehension of bias.[53]

(c) Outside Knowledge of or Involvement with the Matter in Dispute

It sometimes happens that a decision-maker is not merely associated in some way with a person who is involved in the dispute but has outside knowledge of or involvement with the subject matter in dispute. In general, courts are inclined to accept arguments that this type of knowledge or involvement gives rise to a reasonable apprehension of bias that disqualifies the person who is in this situation from taking part in the decision-making process. The concern in these cases is not simply that the decision-maker will be predisposed to come to a particular conclusion, but that the decision-maker will be unable to avoid making use of information that was obtained outside the hearing, thus violating the rule that the decision must be based solely on the information available on the record of the proceeding. The classic example of disqualification in this type of situation is the *National Energy Board* case discussed in detail above. Other examples include cases where a decision-maker sits on appeal from his or her own decision;[54] where a person acts as both prosecutor and judge in disciplinary proceedings;[55] and a case where a judge had access to the full police report on an accused person which the judge had obtained in his capacity as counsel on a bail application for a co-accused prior to the judge's appointment to the bench.[56]

Typically these cases arise because of activity that took place earlier in the decision-maker's career, often prior to his or her appointment to a court,

---

52 *Arsenault-Cameron v. Prince Edward Island*, [1999] 3 S.C.R. 851 (S.C.C.) (*per* Bastarache J.); *President of the Republic of South Africa v. South African Rugby Football Union, supra* note 45.

53 *Zündel v. Citron* (2000), 25 Admin. L.R. (3d) 113 (Fed. C.A.), leave to appeal refused (2000), 266 N.R. 200 (note) (S.C.C.); *Marques v. Dylex Ltd.* (1977), 81 D.L.R. (3d) 554 (Ont. Div. Ct.).

54 *R. v. Alberta (Securities Commission)* (1962), 36 D.L.R. (2d) 199 (Alta. T.D.); *Glassman v. College of Physicians & Surgeons (Ontario)*, [1966] 2 O.R. 81 (Ont. C.A.). Note that there was no common law ban on a member of the Court of Appeal sitting on an appeal from his own decision at trial. See also section 5 below on "Institutional Bias". And compare *Dancyger v. Pharmaceutical Assn. (Alberta)* (1970), [1971] 1 W.W.R. 371 (Alta. C.A.); *Ringrose v. College of Physicians & Surgeons (Alberta)*, [1976] 4 W.W.R. 712 (S.C.C.).

55 *Maillet v. College of Dental Surgeons (Quebec)* (1919), 58 D.L.R. 210 (Que. C.A.); but compare *Re Solicitor* (1967), 60 W.W.R. 705 (Alta. C.A.).

56 *R. v. Catcheway*, [2000] 1 S.C.R. 838 (S.C.C.). See also *R. v. Laframboise* (1997), 200 A.R. 75 (Alta. C.A.); *R. v. Hayward* (1997), 31 O.T.C. 150 (Ont. Gen. Div.); and *R. v. Ewen* (1994), 98 Man. R. (2d) 1 (Man. Q.B.).

board or tribunal. It is equally objectionable, however, for the decision-maker to seek or obtain such outside information during the course of the proceedings or prior to issuing a decision. For example, a reasonable apprehension of bias has been found where one party's solicitor or officer has participated in the decision-maker's deliberations after the hearing[57] and where a decision-maker receives off-record advice from persons who had acted in a prosecutorial role in relation to the proceedings.[58]

While prior involvement in a case will usually result in disqualification, this is not invariably the case. For example, in *Roberts v. R.*[59] the Supreme Court of Canada addressed an application to vacate its earlier judgment on the merits of the appeal because Mr. Justice Binnie, the author of the decision on the merits, had played a limited role as counsel in the case prior to his appointment to the Court. When the appeal on the merits was heard in 2001, Mr. Justice Binnie no longer recalled the supervisory role he had played in the litigation when he was Assistant Deputy Minister of Justice some fifteen years earlier, in 1985-86. The Court (without the participation of Mr. Justice Binnie) concluded that this situation did not give rise to a "reasonable apprehension of bias" and therefore dismissed the application. The Court rejected the application of the English line of "automatic disqualification" cases, of which the *Pinochet* decision is the most prominent recent example, to situations in which the only "interest" the decision-maker had in the case was his or her prior involvement in the litigation as counsel. The Court also concluded that the passage of time was a relevant consideration in determining whether or not Mr. Justice Binnie's prior involvement with the case gave rise to a reasonable apprehension of bias. Mr. Justice Binnie's lack of recollection of the events was also relevant, although not dispositive, since the Court was concerned about the possibility that his earlier participation in the case may have affected his thinking unconsciously. The Court decided, however, that when the lapse of time was combined with the limited nature of Mr. Justice Binnie's supervisory role in the litigation while he was Assistant Deputy Minister of Justice, reasonable people would not conclude that this involvement had affected Mr. Justice Binnie's ability, even unconsciously, to remain impartial in rendering judgment in this case.

It is important to draw a distinction between situations where the decision-maker's outside knowledge of the matter flows from the administrative structure of the decision-making agency and situations where that knowledge results from activities unconnected to the structure of the agency. An example of the

---

57   See *Such v. Alberta (Minister of Forestry, Lands & Wildlife)* (1991), 6 Admin. L.R. 174 (Alta. C.A.); *R. v. Justices of Sussex* (1923), [1924] 1 K.B. 256 (Eng. K.B.); *Cooper v. Wilson*, [1937] 2 K.B. 309 (Eng. K.B.); *R. v. Hendon R.D.C.; Ex parte Chorley*, [1932] 2 K.B. 696.

58   See *Braemar Bakery Ltd. v. Manitoba (Liquor Control Commission)* (1999), 20 Admin. L.R. (3d) 27 (Man. C.A.), additional reasons at [2000] 4 W.W.R. 167 (Man. C.A.), where the tribunal invited prosecution witnesses to stay behind after the conclusion of the hearing; *Fooks v. Assn. of Architects (Alberta)* (1982), 21 Alta. L.R. (2d) 306 (Alta. Q.B.), where the registrar and solicitor of the association met privately with the discipline committee and the council of the association.

59   2003 SCC 45 (S.C.C.).

first type of situation occurs where an agency is statutorily authorized to perform both investigative and adjudicative functions and these duties are undertaken by the same individual in a particular case.[60] These types of cases deserve special consideration and we will discuss them below under the heading of institutional bias.[61]

(d) Inappropriate Comments or Behaviour

Comments or other behaviour on the part of a decision-maker that are inconsistent with that individual's being perceived by reasonable people as impartial will result in the disqualification of the decision-maker. This aspect of the rule against bias is sometimes thought of as the rule against actual bias, but this can be misleading. It is, of course, the case that where it can be demonstrated that a decision-maker is not, in point of fact, impartial, the decision-maker is biased.[62] It is not necessary, however, to prove actual bias, and it is possible for a court to find that a decision-maker's comments gave rise to a reasonable apprehension of bias in circumstances in which an argument that the decision-maker was actually biased would not succeed.[63] In addition, a court might be somewhat reluctant to make a finding that a decision-maker was actually biased since this could call into question not only the legitimacy of the person's decision in that particular case but the suitability of that person to exercise decision-making authority in other cases.[64] Since the types of comments or behaviour that would support a finding that a decision-maker was actually biased would inevitably support a finding of a reasonable apprehension of bias, it is not surprising that in most cases courts prefer to focus their observations on the issue of a reasonable apprehension of bias.

It is useful to begin by observing that not every expression by a decision-maker of a predisposition with regard to a particular issue will be regarded as giving rise to a reasonable apprehension of bias. As Mr. Justice Cory stated in *R. v. S. (R.D.)*: "not every favourable or unfavourable disposition attracts the label of bias or prejudice. For example, it cannot be said that those who condemn Hitler are biased or prejudiced. This unfavourable disposition is

---

60 See for example *Barry v. Alberta (Securities Commission)*, [1989] 1 S.C.R. 301 (S.C.C.); *W.D. Latimer Co. v. Bray* (1974), 6 O.R. (2d) 129, 52 D.L.R. (3d) 161 (Ont. C.A.).

61 See section 5 of this chapter.

62 See *Godbout v. Alberta (Driver Control Board)* (1998), 5 Admin. L.R. (3d) 40 (Alta. Q.B.) at para. 45.

63 See for example *R. v. S. (R.D.)*, [1997] 3 S.C.R. 484 (S.C.C.) at paras. 21-22 (per Major J. dissenting); *Sawridge Band v. R.*, [1997] 3 F.C. 580 (Fed. C.A.), leave to appeal refused (December 1, 1997), Doc. 26169, [1997] S.C.C.A. No. 430 (S.C.C.). In *Braemar Bakery Ltd. v. Manitoba (Liquor Control Commission)*, *supra* note 58 the Manitoba Court of Appeal observed that where an allegation is made concerning conduct that might give rise to a reasonable apprehension of bias, evidence that might negate the existence of actual bias is irrelevant. The court stated (at para. 17) that "The concepts [of actual bias and reasonable apprehension of bias] are quite different and cannot be used interchangeably. It is an error of law to deal with the concept of actual as opposed to apprehended bias just as it is an error to place any weight or consideration on the fact that the adjudicating body might have reached a decision that appears to be eminently reasonable."

64 Compare *Moreau-Bérubé v. Nouveau-Brunswick*, [2002] 1 S.C.R. 249 (S.C.C.).

objectively justifiable – in other words, it is not "wrongful or inappropriate" . . .".[65] In addition, courts are very reluctant to assume that simply because a decision-maker has made certain types of decisions in the past,[66] has been associated with a particular organization or political party,[67] or has expressed views as an advocate or as an academic,[68] this betokens the type of predisposition to make decisions in accordance with those views that would give rise to a reasonable apprehension of bias.[69]

The situations that are more likely to cause problems involve behaviour or comments that take place during the course of a hearing or during the deliberative process. There are, for example, cases where a tribunal member, or tribunal counsel, has so descended into the fray as to destroy any sense of impartiality.[70] In addition, comments made in providing reasons for decision may stray sufficiently outside the realm of proper considerations to be addressed by the decision-maker as to give rise to a reasonable apprehension of bias.[71] Some care must be taken, however, in determining when actions or comments that a party to the proceedings finds offensive can be said to give rise to a reasonable apprehension of bias. This issue was addressed by the

---

65 *R. v. S. (R.D.), supra* note 63 at para. 105, referring to the reasons of Scalia J. in *Liteky v. U.S.*, 114 S. Ct. (U.S.S.C., 1994) at 1155. See also *Zündel v. Citron, supra* note 53 at paras. 38-39.

66 *Ellis-Don Ltd. v Ontario (Labour Relations Board)* (1992), 98 D.L.R. (4th) 762 (Ont. Div. Ct.); *Locabail (U.K.) Ltd. v. Bayfield Properties Ltd.*, [2000] 1 All E.R. 65 (Eng. C.A.).

67 *Samson Indian Band & Nation v. Canada* (1998), 227 N.R. 386 (Fed. C.A.), affirming (1997), [1998] 3 F.C. 3 (Fed. T.D.); *Fogal v. Canada* (1999), [1999] F.C.J. No. 129, 1999 CarswellNat 164 (Fed. T.D.), affirmed (2000), [2000] F.C.J. No. 916, 2000 CarswellNat 1229 (Fed C.A.), leave to appeal refused (2001), 273 N.R. 400 (note) (S.C.C.); *President of the Republic of South Africa v. South African Rugby Football Union*, [1999] 4 S.A. 147 (South Africa Constitutional Ct.).

68 *Arsenault-Cameron v. Prince Edward Island, supra* note 52; *Large v. Stratford (City) Police Department* (1992), 92 D.L.R. (4th) 565 (Ont. Div. Ct.), affirmed (1993), 110 D.L.R. (4th) 435 (Ont. C.A.), leave to appeal allowed (1994), 112 D.L.R. (4th) vii (S.C.C.), reversed on other grounds [1995] 3 S.C.R. 733 (S.C.C.), reconsideration refused (January 25, 1996), Doc. 2400 (S.C.C.).

69 There are, however, cases where courts have found that a decision-maker's personal connection with the issues in disputes or the tone in which his or her academic or professional views have been expressed gives rise to a reasonable apprehension of bias. See *Gale v. Miracle Food Mart* (1993), 13 O.R. (3d) 824 (Ont. Div. Ct.); *Timmins v. Gormley,* a companion case to *Locabail (U.K.) Ltd. v. Bayfield Properties Ltd.*, *supra* note 66 at para. 85.

70 See *Sawridge Band v. R., supra* note 63; *Yusuf v .Canada (Minister of Employment & Immigration)* (1991), 7 Admin. L.R. (2d) 86 (Fed. C.A.); *Brett v. Ontario (Directors, Physiotherapy Board)* (1991), 77 D.L.R. (4th) 144 (Ont. Div. Ct.), affirmed (1993), 104 D.L.R. (4th) 421, 13 Admin. L.R. (2d) 217 (Ont. C.A.); *U.S.W.A., Local 4444 v. Stanley Steel Co.* (1974), 6 O.R. (2d) 385 (Ont. Div. Ct.); *Golomb v. College of Physicians & Surgeons (Ontario)* (1976), 12 O.R. (2d) 73 (Ont. Div. Ct.); but compare *Casullo v. College of Physicians & Surgeons (Ontario)* (1976), 67 D.L.R. (3d) 351 (S.C.C.), where the committee was annoyed by the evasiveness of the complainant; and *Hawkins v. Halifax (County) Residential Tenancies Board* (1974), 47 D.L.R. (3d) 117 (N.S. T.D.), where the tribunal compelled a person to appear before it. The *Sawridge* and *Brett* cases are particularly instructive because of the extensive quotation by the reviewing court of the comments that were considered offensive.

71 See for example *Baker v Canada (Minister of Citizenship & Immigration)*, [1999] 2 S.C.R. 817 (S.C.C.).

Supreme Court of Canada in *R. v. S. (R.D.),*[72] a case in which it was argued that certain comments made by a trial judge in acquitting a black youth accused of assaulting a police officer gave rise to a reasonable apprehension that she was biased against the police.[73] The Nova Scotia Supreme Court allowed the Crown's appeal on this basis and ordered a new trial[74] and the Nova Scotia Court of Appeal, by a 2-1 majority, upheld this decision.[75] The Supreme Court of Canada, by a 6-3 majority, reversed this decision and restored the trial's judge's acquittal of the accused. It is clear that we do not expect decision-makers to pretend to decide issues without regard to their own common sense and wisdom gained from their own personal experience. At the same time, it is generally important that decision-makers do not convey, through their behaviour or comments, an impression that their decisions are based on their own preconceptions or prejudices rather than on the applicable law and relevant evidence before them. While there is general agreement on the relevant legal test to be applied, the divergence of opinion among the judges who address this issue (and, indeed, the divergence of opinion among the members of the Supreme Court of Canada majority)[76] suggests that the precise point at which a decision-maker's comments cross the boundary into the realm of the unacceptable may be difficult to ascertain.

A final consideration that must be taken into account is the fact that there are many different kinds of administrative decision-makers, operating in very widely differing statutory and policy contexts. Because of this, an overly rigid application of the "reasonable apprehension of bias" test might actually defeat the purpose for which some tribunals have been set up. For example, some

---

72 [1997] 3 S.C.R. 484 (S.C.C.).

73 The following comments gave rise to the Crown appeal. In the course of giving her oral reasons for dismissing the charge, the judge stated. "The Crown says, well, why would the officer say that events occurred the way in which he has relayed them to the Court this morning. I am not saying that the Constable has misled the court, although police officers have been known to do that in the past. I am not saying that the officer overreacted, but certainly police officers do overreact, particularly when they are dealing with non-white groups. That to me indicates a state of mind right there that is questionable. I believe that probably the situation in this particular case is the case of a young police officer who overreacted. I do accept the evidence of [R.D.S.] that he was told to shut up or he would be under arrest. It seems to be in keeping with the prevalent attitude of the day." See *R. v. S. (R.D.)*, [1997] 3 S.C.R. 484 (S.C.C.) at paras. 4 (per Major J.), 53 (per L'Heureux-Dubé and McLachlin JJ.), and 74 (per Cory J.).

74 (1995), [1995] N.S.J. No. 184, 1995 CarswellNS 608 (N.S. S.C.), affirmed (1995), 145 N.S.R. (2d) 284, 102 C.C.C. (3d) 233 (N.S. C.A.), leave to appeal allowed (1996), 203 N.R. 392 (note) (S.C.C.), reversed [1997] 3 S.C.R. 484 (S.C.C.).

75 (1995), 145 N.S.R. (2d) 284, 102 C.C.C. (3d) 233 (N.S. C.A.), leave to appeal allowed (1996), 203 N.R. 392 (note) (S.C.C.), reversed [1997] 3 S.C.R. 484 (S.C.C.).

76 The majority in the result was composed of Cory, Iacobucci, L'Heureux-Dubé, McLachlin, LaForest and Gonthier JJ. Iacobucci J. agreed with the reasons for judgment of Cory J. and LaForest and Gonthier, JJ concurred with the reasons for judgment jointly authored by L'Heureux-Dubé and McLachlin JJ. Major J. wrote dissenting reasons with Lamer, C.J. and Sopinka J. concurring. These three judges expressed a preference for the reasoning of Cory J. over that of L'Heureux-Dubé and McLachlin JJ., however, (see para. 23) and the approach to the reasonable apprehension of bias employed by Cory J. should probably be considered to represent the majority view.

tribunals include politicians (like municipal councillors) who may very well have been elected because they supported or opposed a particular point of view. Some tribunals have members who are appointed precisely because of their identification with particular interests, such as labour, management, or consumers. The Supreme Court of Canada has concluded in recent years that the "reasonable apprehension of bias" test must be applied in a manner that is sensitive to the institutional context in which the decision is being made in order to deal with this kind of situation. Especially on tribunals with a strong policy or legislative function, members are permitted to hold firm views, provided they show themselves to be "amenable to persuasion." In other words, the members must not have formed an irreversible view before they hear any evidence.

This variation on the *National Energy Board* theme is well-illustrated by three Supreme Court of Canada decisions – two dealing with municipal councillors, and one dealing with a public utilities board member who was a self-proclaimed champion of consumer rights.

(i) Municipal Councillors: Old St. Boniface and Save Richmond Farmland

In *Old St. Boniface Residents Assn. Inc. v. Winnipeg (City)*,[77] a rezoning application came before a committee of the municipal council. One of the members sitting on the committee had previously spoken on behalf of the applicant developer at a finance committee meeting. At first instance, Schwartz J. concluded that, although there was no suggestion that the councillor had any personal interest in the outcome beyond what he thought to be his duty, he should not have participated in the decision process as both advocate and judge. The Court of Appeal disagreed, noting that the scheme of legislation contemplated that municipal councillors could be called upon to consider the same matter at various committee stages prior to the eventual vote by council, and that all that was required was that the councillor retain an open mind.

In writing for the majority of the Supreme Court of Canada, Sopinka J. noted that there had been recent changes in the law of the rules of natural justice and fairness. Where previously the content of these rules had been based on rigid classifications of a tribunal's function, the content of the rules is now based on such factors as the terms of the enabling statute, the nature of the particular function with which the tribunal is seized and the type of decision it is required to make.[78] He then examined the factors under which a committee of city council operates, and concluded that the Legislature's intent could not have been to apply the rule against prejudgment there with the same rigour and force as in the case of other tribunals "whose character and function more

---

77   (1990), [1990] 3 S.C.R. 1170, [1991] 2 W.W.R. 145 (S.C.C.).
78   See the quotation accompanying note 7, above.

closely resemble those of a court."[79] Justice Sopinka described the hurdle the applicant has to overcome as follows:[80]

> The party alleging a disqualifying bias must establish that there is a prejudgment of the matter, *in fact*, to the extent that any representations at variance with the view, which has been adopted, would be futile. *Statements by individual members of council, while they may very well give rise to an appearance of bias, will not satisfy the test unless the court concludes that they are the expression of a final opinion on the matter, which cannot be dislodged.*

It will be seen that this test is quite different from the usual "reasonable apprehension of bias." According to Sopinka J., the usual "reasonable apprehension of bias" test is applicable only where the councillor has – or appears to have – an interest, either pecuniary or by virtue of some sort of special relationship, in the outcome. In other cases, Sopinka J. asserted that the test for bias was one of fact, i.e. whether the councillor's mind is or was in fact so closed that further representations would be futile.

The Supreme Court's decision in *Save Richmond Farmland Society v. Richmond (Township)*[81] was released concurrently with the decision in *Old St. Boniface*, and involved essentially the same legal issues. Again, a member of a municipal council had been reported as stating that he was unlikely to change his mind on a zoning issue. At trial, Prowse J. held that the alderman had not closed his mind to all argument, noting (among other things) the alderman's attendance at public hearings. In the Court of Appeal,[82] Southin J.A. found that a reasonable person might conclude that the alderman had a closed mind, but that in relation to the particular statute in question and given the broad policy issues involved, a closed mind (not the result of corruption) would not disqualify him. The Supreme Court, in another majority decision written by Sopinka J., applied the test from *Old St. Boniface* and found that there was no disqualifying bias, specifically reiterating that the test is whether the councillor in fact had a closed mind, not whether a reasonable person would think he had.

La Forest J. concurred in the result, but differed on the point of whether a municipal councillor may have a closed mind. He approved the approach taken by Southin J.A. in the Court of Appeal to the effect that a closed mind (that was not corrupt) should not be grounds for finding bias in an elected official acting legislatively. La Forest J. noted the difficulty in gauging the "openness" of a person's mind, and suggested that requiring an "open mind" would lead to "posturing" and to politicians paying lip service to the possibility of changing their minds. Justice La Forest noted that if the result is to make the public

---

79 *Supra* note 77 at 169 [W.W.R.].
80 *Ibid.*, emphasis added at 172 [W.W.R.]. See S.K. McCallum, "Fairness and the Limits of Adjudication" (1992-93) 6 C.J.A.L.P. 57 for a discussion of the decisions in *Old St. Boniface, Save Richmond Farmland*, and *Newfoundland Telephone*.
81 (1990), [1990] 3 S.C.R. 1213, [1991] 2 W.W.R. 178, 46 Admin. L.R. 264 (S.C.C.).
82 (1989), 36 B.C.L.R. (2d) 49, 36 Admin. L.R. 155, 43 M.P.L.R. 88 (B.C. C.A.).

hearing process nothing more than a charade, then that is something the legislature must address.[83]

(ii) The Newfoundland Telephone Case

In *Newfoundland Telephone Co. v. Newfoundland (Board of Commissioners of Public Utilities)*,[84] a commissioner on the public utilities board was a self-styled champion of consumers' rights. (This predisposition was well-known when he was appointed, and may well have been the reason he was appointed.) He expressed his opinions publicly and vocally regarding an issue that was to come before the Board in a public hearing. The issue was the appellant's wage and benefits policy for its executives.[85] The Newfoundland Court of Appeal found that although there was a reasonable apprehension of bias, the Board's subsequent decision revealed that there had been no actual bias and the Board's ruling was therefore upheld.[86]

---

83 See also *Save St. Ann's Coalition v. Victoria (City)* (1991), 5 M.P.L.R. (2d) 331 (B.C. C.A.) and *Brentwood Lakes Golf Course Ltd. v. Central Saanich (District)* (1991), 6 M.P.L.R. (2d) 1 (B.C. S.C.). In both cases municipal councillors deposed that they had open minds, despite their previously stated positions. The onus of proving a closed mind, incapable of being persuaded, lies on the party challenging a decision. For a discussion on the "almost insurmountable evidentiary burden on those parties alleging disqualifying bias against municipal councillors," see J. Mascarin, "Tolerance for the Biased Municipal Councillor: The Amenable to Persuasion Test – Case Comment: *Old St. Boniface Residents Assn. Inc. v Winnipeg (City)* and *Save Richmond Farmland Society v. Richmond (Township)*" (1991) 2 M.P.L.R. (2d) 322; and M. R. O'Connor, "Bias and the Open-Minded Councillor" (1993) 11 M.P.L.R. (2d) 250.

84 [1992] 1 S.C.R. 623, 4 Admin. L.R. (2d) 121 (S.C.C.).

85 The commissioner made such statements as:"If they want to give Brait [the Chief Executive Officer of the appellant] and the boys extra fancy pensions, then the shareholders should pay it, not the rate payers," Mr. Wells said. ..."So I want the company hauled in here–all them fat cats with their big pensions–to justify (these expenses) under the public glare ... I think the rate payers have a right to be assured that we are not permitting this company to be too extravagant." ..."Who the hell do they think they are?" Mr. Wells asked. "The guys doing the real work, climbing the poles never got any 21 percent increase." ...The telephone company wants the report kept confidential, "but, who do they think they are," said Mr. Wells. "This document should be public."

86 In *Newfoundland Light & Power Co. v. Newfoundland (Public Utilities Commissioners Board)* (1987), 25 Admin. L.R. 180 (Nfld. C.A.), leave to appeal refused (1987), 82 N.R. 205n (S.C.C.) the Newfoundland Court of Appeal had addressed a similar application involving the same commissioner. In that case, the Court found (at 187-188) that "A close examination of the statements made by and attributed to Mr. Wells at the time of his appointment would leave little doubt in anybody's mind that he looked upon his position as that of a consumer advocate and that he perceived himself in a role closely allied to an intervenor in any application involving the utility company. For whatever reason, Mr. Wells' perception of his role seems to have changed dramatically by the time the application was made in the spring of 1986. A careful perusal of the newspaper clippings and transcripts of the television and radio programs at that time does not lead this Court to conclude that any decision of Mr. Wells would have been based on anything other than the evidence adduced at the hearings . . .". This comment is less clear than it might be since it is not evident whether or not the Court addressed its mind to the question of whether any of the commissioner's comments at the relevant time would give rise to a reasonable apprehension of bias. It may be possible to reconcile the result in this case with the Supreme Court of Canada's later decision in *Newfoundland Telephone* by noting that in this case the statements by the

On appeal, the Supreme Court of Canada overturned that decision. Cory J., writing for a unanimous Court, noted that the extent of the duty depends upon the nature and function of the particular tribunal. He referred to the Court's decisions in *Old St. Boniface*[87] and *Save Richmond Farmland Society*[88] which required a determination of the location of the delegate along "the spectrum of administrative bodies whose functions vary from being almost purely adjudicative to being political or policy-making in nature."[89] He concluded that, with respect to elected officials, the test of a reasonable apprehension of bias was whether the decision-maker had an open mind. However, a board exercising adjudicative functions would be expected to more closely comply with the standards applicable to the courts. A board exercising a policy function was more likely to have greater leeway similar to an elected body.

In *Newfoundland Telephone*, the Court found that the board was performing different functions at different times. At the point at which the Board was performing its investigative function, the Court said that

> wide licence must be given to board members to make public comment. As long as those statements do not indicate a mind so closed that any submission would be futile, they should not be subject to attack on the basis of bias.[90]

The Court held that because the comments made by the commissioner prior to the commencement of the hearing did not indicate that he had a closed mind, these comments would not be sufficient to cause his disqualification.[91]

But the Court found that once the Board had reached the hearing stage, greater discretion was called for in order to avoid the creation of a reasonable apprehension of bias. The nature of the commissioner's comments after the hearing process had begun was found to have created a reasonable apprehension of bias, and therefore the proceedings were found to be unfair and invalid.

5. Institutional Bias

(a) Introduction

Institutional bias cases concern situations in which a reasonable apprehension of bias is alleged to be generated by the structure or operation of a decision-making body, rather than by the words or actions of an individual decision-

---

commissioner that indicated a lack of impartiality appear to have been made well in advance of the hearing. His statements during and after the hearing do not appear to have been of a character that would give rise to a reasonable apprehension of bias. In other words, during the hearing of the *Newfoundland Light & Power* case, the commissioner behaved in a manner that showed that, notwithstanding his strong policy views, he was prepared to approach the case itself with an open mind.

87   [1990] 3 S.C.R. 1170 (S.C.C.).
88   [1990] 3 S.C.R. 1213 (S.C.C.).
89   *Supra* note 84 at 134 [Admin. L.R.].
90   *Ibid.* at 138 [Admin. L.R.].
91   *Ibid.* at 138 [Admin. L.R.].

maker. We have already seen that the institutional character of the decision-making body is significant to the determination of what types of conduct on the part of decision-makers will give rise to a reasonable apprehension of bias. The issue in institutional bias cases is: when will the way that the decision-making institution itself functions or is structured give rise to a reasonable apprehension of bias? The appearance of impartiality is important for public confidence in the system, and it is important for the public to have confidence not only in the impartiality of individual decision-makers but in the system itself.[92] The difficulty in institutional bias cases lies in reconciling a concept of impartiality that is based on a judicial model with a legislature's choice to adopt a decision-making structure that does not necessarily correspond to this model.

Many of the most significant recent developments in the law of bias are on this subject of institutional bias.[93] It is an outgrowth of the modern reality that many public decision-makers, like the Immigration and Refugee Board or a Workers' Compensation Board, are large bodies with multiple decision-makers and complex internal and external relationships. The Supreme Court of Canada has overcome its earlier reluctance to deal with the issue,[94] and has in recent years grappled with several cases in which it has been alleged that the very structure of a tribunal would pre-dispose its members to decide a certain way. In order to understand the case law in this area, however, it is essential to distinguish between arguments that attack a statutory scheme itself and arguments that merely attack the way the scheme is administered. The common law rules of natural justice and procedural fairness cannot be used to attack the validity of legislation,[95] although these doctrines can be employed successfully to challenge the validity of decision-making structures adopted

---

92   On this point, see in particular *Lippé c. Charest* (1990), [1991] 2 S.C.R. 114 (S.C.C.).

93   The leading cases include: *Bell Canada v. C.T.E.A.* (2003), [2003] S.C.J. No. 36, 2003 CarswellNat 2427 (S.C.C.); *C.U.P.E. v. Ontario (Minister of Labour)* (2003), 50 Admin. L.R. (3d) 1 (S.C.C.); *Ocean Port Hotel Ltd. v. British Columbia (General Manager, Liquor Control & Licensing Branch)*, [2001] 2 S.C.R. 781 (S.C.C.); and *2747-3174 Québec Inc. c. Québec (Régie des permis d'alcool)*, [1996] 3 S.C.R. 919 (S.C.C.). See also *Canadian Pacific Ltd. v. Matsqui Indian Band*, [1995] 1 S.C.R. 3 (S.C.C.), where Lamer C.J.C. and Cory J. (concurring in the result) consider both institutional bias and structural independence. It is difficult to draw any firm conclusions from *Matsqui*, however, because of the way the court divided. The other three judges in the majority did not deal with the issue of institutional bias. The four dissenting judges held the issue was premature, although Sopinka, writing for the dissenting judges, did express agreement with Chief Justice Lamer's reasoning with respect to institutional bias although not with respect to institutional independence (at 63). The existence of an institutional aspect of impartiality was first affirmed in *Lippé c. Charest*, *ibid.,* which dealt with part-time judges who continued to carry on the practice of law. Lamer C.J. held that "whether or not any particular judge harboured pre-conceived ideas or biases, if the system is structured in such a way as to create a reasonable apprehension of bias on an institutional level, the requirement of impartiality is not met" (1990), [1991] 2 S.C.R. 114 at 140 (S.C.C.). See also *Ruffo c. Québec (Conseil de la magistrature)*, [1995] 4 S.C.R. 267 (S.C.C.).

94   For example, in *King v. University of Saskatchewan*, [1969] S.C.R. 678 (S.C.C.), the Supreme Court of Canada rejected an attempt to invoke the concept of institutional bias.

95   *Ocean Port Hotel*, *supra* note 93.

through delegated legislation.[96] Using relevant constitutional or quasi-constitutional principles, however, it is possible to attack the validity of decision-making structures embedded in legislation.[97] The discussion of institutional bias in the recent cases therefore tends to concentrate on two issues. The first issue is the extent to which statutory schemes expressly or impliedly authorize the use of decision-making structures that are difficult to reconcile with ideas of institutional impartiality that are based on a judicial model. In these cases, the common law rules of natural justice and procedural fairness will not enable parties to attack institutional bias flowing from the structures themselves, though sometimes the common law has been useful in shaping the operation of these structures.[98] The second issue is the extent to which courts are prepared to use constitutional or quasi-constitutional principles to invalidate elements of statutory schemes that give rise to institutional impartiality concerns.[99]

Related to this topic is the case law on the subject of structural independence.[100] Institutional bias arguments attack elements of a decision-making structure that are said to create the concern that decision-makers will be predisposed to decide cases in particular ways. Structural independence arguments, on the other hand, attack the absence or insufficiency of structural guarantees that decision-makers are free to decide cases without regard to improper external influences. There is a family resemblance between institutional bias and structural independence cases in the sense that both branches of the law are designed to provide assurances to the parties to decisions, and the public, that decisions will be made impartially.[101] The difference between these two branches of the law lies mainly in the types of institutional assurances of impartiality that are sought in each case. The structural independence cases address the need for and extent of guarantees concerning the security of tenure, security of remuneration and administrative independence afforded to members of administrative tribunals.[102] It is convenient, therefore, to discuss these cases separately from the decisions concerning institutional bias.

---

96 See *Canadian Pacific Ltd. v. Matsqui Indian Band*, *supra* note 93.

97 See for example *Singh v. Canada (Minister of Employment & Immigration)*, [1985] 1 S.C.R. 177 (S.C.C.); *MacBain v. Canada (Human Rights Commission)*, [1985] 1 F.C. 856, 16 Admin. L.R. 109 (Fed. C.A.); compare *Québec (Régie des permis d'alcools)*, *supra* note 93.

98 See for example *C.U.P.E. v. Ontario (Minister of Labour) supra* note 93; *Ocean Port Hotel*, *supra* note 93; *Québec (Régie des permis d'alcools)*, *ibid.* (per 'Heureux-Dubé J. concurring).

99 See *Bell Canada*, *supra* note 93; *Québec (Régie des permis d'alcools)*, *ibid.* (per Gonthier J. writing for the majority); *Pearlman v. Law Society (Manitoba)*, [1991] 2 S.C.R. 869 (S.C.C.).

100 For a general discussion of this topic, see P. Bryden, "Structural Independence of Administrative Tribunals in the Wake of *Ocean Port*" (2003) 16 C.J.A.L.P. 125 and K. Wyman, "The Independence of Administrative Tribunals in an Era of Ever Expansive Judicial Independence" (2001) 14 C.J.A.L.P. 61.

101 See for example *Bell Canada*, *supra* note 93 at para. 17; *Québec (Régie des permis d'alcools)*, *supra* note 93 at paras. 41-43 (per Gonthier J.) and paras. 105-107 (per L'Heureux-Dubé J.).

102 See for example, *Bell Canada*, *ibid.*; *C.U.P.E. v. Ontario (Minister of Labour)*, *supra* note 93; *Ocean Port Hotel*, *supra* note 93; *Québec (Régie des permis d'alcools)*, *supra* note 93; *Katz v. Vancouver Stock Exchange*, [1996] 3 S.C.R. 405 (S.C.C.); *Canadian Pacific Ltd. v. Matsqui Indian Band*, *supra* note 93.

(b) The General Test for Institutional Bias

For cases of institutional bias, the Supreme Court has retained the *Canada (National Energy Board)* test, but has added a slight wrinkle:[103]

> As a result of *Lippé, supra,* and *Ruffo v. Conseil de la magistrature,* [1995] 4 S.C.R. 267, *inter alia,* the test for institutional impartiality is well established. It is clear that the governing factors are those put forward by de Grandpré J. in *Committee for Justice and Liberty v. National Energy Board,* [1978] 1 S.C.R. 369, at p. 394. The determination of institutional bias presupposes that a well-informed person, viewing the matter realistically and practically – and having thought the matter through – would have a reasonable apprehension of bias *in a substantial number of cases.* In this regard, all factors must be considered, but the guarantees provided for in the legislation to counter the prejudicial effects of certain institutional characteristics must be given special attention.

Thus we can see that the unique feature of the test for institutional bias is the requirement that the apprehension of bias exist in "a substantial number of cases." As demonstrated in the *Québec (Régie des permis d'alcools)* case itself, the facts of any particular case before the tribunal can be of limited significance with respect to a finding of institutional bias. What tends to be more important is whether the legislature has expressly or impliedly authorized a decision-making scheme that gives rise to this type of apprehension of bias and, if so, whether that legislative decision can be successfully challenged using the *Charter* or a quasi-constitutional statute such as the *Canadian Bill of Rights,* the *Alberta Bill of Rights* or the *Quebec Charter of Rights and Freedoms.*

(c) Some Examples of Institutional Bias

As with most cases of bias, the difficulty in institutional bias cases is not stating the test. After *Québec (Régie des permis d'alcools),* the test is well-settled. The difficulty comes in applying the test to a particular set of circumstances. Broadly speaking, institutional bias arguments have tended to be made in five types of situations: (i) where a tribunal member carries out more than one function in relation to a particular case; (ii) where tribunal staff are employed in ways that give rise to bias concerns; (iii) where a party to the proceeding has an institutional role in the proceeding that might be thought to bias the outcome; (iv) where the tribunal itself might be thought to have a financial interest in a particular outcome; and (v) where a tribunal engages in internal consultations concerning a case that is before it in a manner that is thought to be improper. These categories are not closed, and they are better understood as illustrations of a general principle rather than as a set of hard and fast rules.

---

103 *Québec (Régie des permis d'alcool), ibid.* at para. 44 (emphasis in original).

(i) Tribunal Members Exercising Overlapping Functions

Legislation very often establishes a hierarchy of administrative proceedings to deal with a particular matter. Thus, a committee which is entitled to exercise a particular power (for example, to discipline a member of a profession) may appoint a sub-committee solely to investigate and report on the facts to the parent committee, or to decide the matter tentatively subject to a final hearing or appeal before the parent committee. Is the rule against bias breached if the members of the sub-committee also participate in the deliberations of the parent committee? Similarly, is the rule against bias breached where there is an appeal to a person or a body which is reasonably apprehended to be unlikely to deviate from the previous decision taken elsewhere in the decision-making institution, even if no actual overlap of personnel occurs between the two different decisions?

Canadian courts have never invalidated legislation on the basis that the decision-making structure chosen by the legislature gives rise to a reasonable apprehension of bias because it locates a multiplicity of functions within a single institution. As Gonthier J. observed in the *Québec (Régie des permis d'alcool)* case, ". . . a plurality of functions in a single administrative agency is not necessarily problematic . . . Some boards will have a function that is investigative, prosecutorial and adjudicative. It is only boards with these three powers that can be expected to regulate adequately complex or monopolistic industries that supply essential services."[104] The issue for Canadian courts in these types of cases typically has been whether an individual tribunal member can play more than one role in respect of any given case without that conduct giving rise to a reasonable apprehension of bias.

Until relatively recently, the dominant view among Canadian courts had been that where a statute authorizes a board, commission or tribunal to perform a multiplicity of functions, this has the implicit effect of authorizing individual members of the decision-making body to exercise more than one of these functions in any given case. For example, in *Law Society of Upper Canada v. French*,[105] the respondent had been found guilty of professional misconduct by the discipline committee of the law society. Its report was sent to convocation for final decision, along with a recommendation that Mr. French be suspended for three months. All members of the discipline committee were benchers and therefore also members of convocation. Two of them asserted their right to participate in convocation's disposition of the discipline committee's report. The majority of the Supreme Court held that the legislature had impliedly intended to authorize the members of the discipline committee to participate in convocation's disposition of the committee's report.

Similarly, in *Barry v. Alberta (Securities Commission)*,[106] the Supreme Court of Canada held that the fact that the chairman of the Securities Commission's disciplinary panel received information from an internal investigation prior to sitting on the hearing panel did not give rise to a successful claim

---

104   *Québec (Régie des permis d'alcool)*, *supra* note 93 at para. 47.
105   (1974), [1975] 2 S.C.R. 767 (S.C.C.), affirmed (1974), 49 D.L.R. (3d) 1 (note) (S.C.C.).
106   [1989] 1 S.C.R. 301 (S.C.C.); commented on by S. McCallum, (1989) 35 Admin. L.R. 315.

of institutional bias since this type of activity was impliedly authorized by the Commission's enabling statute. Madam Justice L'Heureux-Dubé wrote that "the courts must be sensitive to the nature of body created by the legislator"[107] in order to determine whether there was legislative authority for the alleged breach. She concluded that the Act contemplates the participation of the chairman at several stages of the proceedings. She drew a distinction between the formal requirements of investigations ordered by the commission under section 28 of the Alberta *Securities Act* and the more routine and administrative types of investigations that are essential to the efficient operation of the commission:[108]

> Because of the formalities surrounding the s. 28 investigation, and because of the broad powers conferred, I am inclined to agree that the commission must have the implied authority to conduct a more informal internal review. It would be unreasonable to say that the security commission requires express statutory authority to review the documents it has on file, or to keep itself informed of the course of an R.C.M.P. investigation. To do so would be to make mandatory a resort to a s. 28 investigation for what are often simple administrative purposes.

The court also considered the functions of a securities commission in determining whether there was statutory authority for its actions. The protective role of a securities commission was held to give the commission a special character, and thus the chairman's dual role did not give rise to a reasonable apprehension of bias.[109]

There have been signs, however, that Canadian courts would be willing to take a closer look at the question of whether the fact that a legislature authorizes an institution to carry out more than one function should carry with it the implication that an individual adjudicator is impliedly authorized to carry out a multiplicity of functions in relation to the same case. Obviously, if the legislation specifically authorizes duplication at an individual level, the doctrine of Parliamentary supremacy means that, absent a constitutional or quasi-constitutional challenge to the legislation itself, the rule against bias must yield. On the other hand, legislation is seldom so specific, and it has been suggested that it would be better if the courts were more reluctant to imply an unnecessary restriction on the application or content of the rule against bias. The better approach appears to be the one advocated by Dickson J. in dissent in *Ringrose v. College of Physicians & Surgeons (Alberta)*[110] and employed by the Alberta Court of Appeal in *Duncan v. Law Society of Alberta Investigating Commit-*

---

107 *Brosseau, ibid.* at 310 [S.C.R.].
108 *Ibid.* at 312 [S.C.R.].
109 For another securities case that came to the same conclusion, see *W. D. Latimer Co. v. Bray* (1974), 6 O.R. (2d) 129, 52 D.L.R. (3d) 161 (Ont. C.A.).
110 (1976), [1977] 1 S.C.R. 814 (S.C.C.).

tee.[111] That is to determine first whether the facts of the particular case give rise to a reasonable apprehension of bias as a result of functional overlap at an individual level and second to determine whether the legislative scheme can be made to work without permitting this form of institutional bias.

It appeared to some commentators that the Supreme Court of Canada had embraced this approach in its 1996 decision in *2747-3174 Québec Inc. c. Québec (Régie des permis d'alcool).*[112] In that case, the neighbours of a bar complained to the Quebec Liquor Licensing Board (the Régie) about noise and drug-dealing at the bar, and asked that the bar's license be suspended. The Board concluded, after fourteen days of hearings, that the licenses should be suspended. The bar owners sought to quash the Board's decision for reasons having nothing to do with whether there was substance to the neighbours' complaints. They alleged that a number of the Régie's structural features raised a reasonable apprehension of bias or lack of independence. The Supreme Court of Canada accepted that there was a reasonable apprehension of bias, and quashed the license suspension (by implication, all other proceedings of the Board were invalid as well). The Court addressed concerns about institutional bias relating to the roles of the institution's directors and its staff and concerns about the independence of the directors. We will consider the issue of institutional bias relating to the role of the directors here and discuss the other aspects of the case below.

In a decision based on the requirement of impartiality found in s. 23 of the *Quebec Charter of Rights and Freedoms*, Mr. Justice Gonthier wrote:

> ... The fact that the Régie, as an institution, participates in the process of investigation, summoning and adjudication is not in itself problematic. However, the possibility that a particular director could, following the investigation, decide to hold a hearing and could then participate in the decision-making process would cause an informed person to have a reasonable apprehension of bias in a substantial number of cases. It seems to me that, as with the Régie's jurists, a form of separation among the directors involved in the various stages of the process is necessary to counter that apprehension of bias.[113]

It is useful to note that there was no evidence that a director played more than one role in relation to the case of the bar itself. The possibility that a director *might* play more than one role was held to be sufficient to invalidate the proceedings.

Despite the fact that Gonthier J., writing for the majority of the Court, based his decision on the *Quebec Charter*, he did not find it necessary to issue a declaration that any of the provisions of the Régie's enabling legislation were inconsistent with the *Charter*. This was because the deficiencies he identified

---

111 (1991), 79 Alta. L.R. (2d) 228 (Alta. C.A.), leave to appeal denied (1991), 7 Admin. L.R. (2d) 219n (S.C.C.). For an example of the use of the same methodology in a slightly different context, see *Calgary General Hospital v. U.N.A., Local 1* (1983), 29 Alta. L.R. (2d) 3 (Alta. C.A.), leave to appeal refused (1984), 52 N.R. 400 (S.C.C.).

112 [1996] 3 S.C.R. 919 (S.C.C.).

113 *Ibid.* at para. 60.

in the institution's structure were not imposed by the legislation or regulations but instead flowed from the way in which the Régie's directors chose to administer the statutory scheme.[114] It could be argued, therefore, that the same outcome could have been reached using the common law, and indeed Madam Justice L'Heureux-Dubé came to exactly that conclusion in her reasons for judgment concurring in the result.[115]

Nevertheless, the Supreme Court of Canada's more recent decision in *Ocean Port Hotel Ltd. v. British Columbia (General Manager, Liquor Control & Licensing Branch)*[116] has cast a shadow over this optimistic assessment of the significance of the *Québec (Régie des permis d'alcool)* decision. While the central issue in the *Ocean Port Hotel* case was the argument that the Liquor Appeal Board's decision should be set aside because of a lack of tribunal independence, the court also considered the question of functional overlap between investigation and decision-making at the initial stage of the proceedings. In addressing this issue, Chief Justice McLachlin wrote:[117]

> . . . The mere fact that senior inspectors functioned both as investigators and as decision makers does not automatically establish a reasonable apprehension of bias. The respondent relies on *Régie*, where the Court held that an apprehension of bias arose from the plurality of functions performed by the Régie's lawyers and directors. *Régie*, however, is clearly distinguishable from the case at bar. The apprehension of bias in Régie resulted from the possibility of a single officer participating at each stage of the process, from the investigation of a complaint through to the decision ultimately rendered. The central concern in *Régie*, succinctly stated by Gonthier J., was that "prosecuting counsel must in no circumstances be in a position to participate in the adjudication process" (para. 56; see also paras. 54 and 60).
>
> The respondent makes no similar allegations in the present case. Its concern hinges solely on the fact that the Branch's hearing officers were employed by the same authority as its prosecuting officers. However, as Gonthier J. cautioned in *Régie*, "a plurality of functions in a single administrative agency is not necessarily problematic" (para. 47). The overlapping of investigative, prosecutorial and adjudicative functions in a single agency is frequently necessary for a tribunal to effectively perform its intended role: *Newfoundland Telephone Co. v. Newfoundland (Board of Commissioners of Public Utilities)*, [1992] 1 S.C.R. 623. Without deciding the issue, I would note that such flexibility may be appropriate in a licensing scheme involving purely economic interests.
>
> Further, absent constitutional constraints, it is always open to the legislature to authorize an overlapping of functions that would otherwise contravene the rule against bias. . . .

---

114   *Ibid.* at para. 71.
115   *Ibid.* at paras. 75, 130 and 260.
116   [2001] 2 S.C.R. 781 (S.C.C.).
117   *Ibid.* at paras. 40-43.

Thus, even assuming the plurality of functions performed by senior inspectors would otherwise offend the rule against bias, it may well be that this structure was authorized by the Act at the relevant time.

The Court remanded the case to the British Columbia Court of Appeal, which agreed with this "provisional opinion".[118] Donald J.A., writing for a unanimous court, went on to observe:[119]

> ... I am persuaded that when compliance with the terms of a licence is in issue and regard is had to the entirety of the liquor licensing scheme, the full panoply of a quasi-judicial hearing, including a distinct separation between the presenter of the allegation and the decision-maker, is not required to conform to the principles of natural justice. At that point the general manager and his delegates are administering the licensing scheme. The Branch's decision to suspend is subject to an adjudication in the fullest sense by a de novo hearing before the Liquor Control Board whose members are independent of the general manager and thus the Branch.
>
> The potential for bias arising from the equal standing of the two senior inspectors who participated in the compliance hearing is inconsequential in this case. Both are delegates of the general manager. Under the Act the general manager could have performed both functions herself – marshalling the evidence and making a decision – and no complaint could be taken.

On the surface, the institutional bias aspect of the *Ocean Port* case is distinguishable from *Régie des permis d'alcool* on a number of grounds. First of all, even though there was a lack of institutional separation between investigative and decision-making functions within the Branch's administrative structure, the *Ocean Port* case itself did not involve a single official carrying out both investigative and decision-making functions.[120] Secondly, the institutional bias challenge in *Ocean Port* concerned decision-making at an administrative level which was subject to a *de novo* hearing before a quasi-judicial appeal body (the Liquor Appeal Board) and there was no suggestion of functional overlap between the Branch and the Board. On the other hand, the observations concerning statutory authorization made by McLachlin, C.J. and particularly by Donald J.A. suggest that Canadian courts may continue to be prepared, at least in some instances, to imply from general statutory language conferring multiple functions on an institution the right of an individual official

---

118   *Ocean Port Hotel Ltd. v. British Columbia (General Manager, Liquor Control & Licensing Branch)* (2002), 40 Admin. L.R. (3d) 103 (B.C. C.A.).

119   *Ibid.* at paras. 9-10.

120   As we noted above in our discussion of *Québec (Régie des permis d'alcool)*, there was no evidence that the same individuals *actually* performed both investigative and decision-making functions in that particular case. The mere possibility that this might happen gave rise to a reasonable apprehension of institutional bias. In *Ocean Port* there was evidence before the court that this had not taken place.

within that institution to perform both decision-making and investigative or other functions in respect of a single case.

(ii) Tribunal Staff With Overlapping Functions

It is not just tribunal members who may have overlapping functions. Tribunal staff may also serve multiple levels of a multi-tiered decision-making structure. As we noted above, this issue arose in the *Québec (Régie des permis d'alcool)* case,[121] and there the Supreme Court of Canada affirmed that over-lapping staff functions may also lead to a reasonable apprehension of institutional bias.

The Court's principal concern was that the Board's legal counsel *could have* participated (there was no finding that they did in fact participate) in various stages of the decision-making process, from investigation through to decision:

> . . . the issue of the role of the lawyers employed by legal services is at the heart of this appeal. In my view, an informed person having thought the matter through would in this regard have a reasonable apprehension of bias in a substantial number of cases. The Act and regulations do not define the duties of these jurists. The Régie's annual report, however, and the description of their jobs at the Régie, show that they are called upon to review files in order to advise the Régie on the action to be taken, prepare files, draft notices of summons, present arguments to the directors and draft opinions. The annual report and the silence of the Act and regulations leave open the pos-sibility of the same jurist performing these various functions in the same matter. The annual report mentions no measures taken to sepa-rate the lawyers involved at different stages of the process. Yet it seems to me that such measures, the precise limits of which I will deliberately refrain from outlining, are essential in the circumstances. Evidence as to the role of the lawyers and the allocation of tasks among them is incomplete, but the possibility that a jurist who has made submissions to the directors might then advise them in respect of the same matter is disturbing, especially since some of the directors have no legal training.[122]

The overlapping of staff functions will not always result in a finding of insti-tutional bias. "Although an overlapping of functions is not always a ground for concern," wrote Gonthier J. for the majority, "it must nevertheless not result in excessively close relations among employees involved in different stages of the process."[123]

In other cases, the institutional bias concern is that tribunal staff members are overstepping the scope of their authority and effectively deciding the case.

---

121 [1996] 3 S.C.R. 919 (S.C.C.).
122 *Ibid.* at 956-57 [S.C.R.].
123 *Ibid* at 954 [S.C.R.].

For example, in *Misra v. College of Physicians & Surgeons (Saskatchewan)*,[124] the appellant physician was facing disciplinary charges. On his way into the hearing, he overheard the registrar, who was not a member of the panel hearing his case, dictating the suspension order. The court rejected the argument that the registrar was merely fulfilling his administrative role efficiently.[125]

> Any person about to have his rights judged by a tribunal, who hears the chief administrative officer of that tribunal, dictating an order of the tribunal surely has a reasoned suspicion of biased appraisal and judgment, unintended though it be.

An apparently similar case with a different result is *Spring v. Law Society of Upper Canada*.[126] Mr. Spring was disbarred by convocation on the adoption of the discipline committee's reasons and recommendations. These reasons had been prepared in draft form by the clerk to the discipline committee. He prepared the draft findings of fact and reasons based on a five minute phone call with a member of the committee. He had not been present during the committees deliberations. The court found that there was no reasonable apprehension of bias because the member had reviewed the draft and made several changes. The decision-making process had not been delegated, and the reasons given were in fact the reasons of the discipline committee. In a strongly worded dissent, however, Trainor J. suggested that an informed and objective observer would not conclude that the reasons were those of the committee. He noted that the phone call was brief and that the final version was largely unchanged from the first draft. He also noted that, although the clerk was not on the prosecutorial team, he was an employee of the prosecutor. He suggested that the Law Society "should be a flagship of administrative tribunals" and that the committee members themselves should have at least drafted an outline of their reasons.[127]

Finally, there are cases where outside counsel retained to perform a prosecutorial function on behalf of a regulatory body may find themselves in a conflict of interest because of their firm's simultaneous representation of another client in separate proceedings in which the other client is adverse in interest to the person who is subject to the prosecution. This situation has been held to give rise to a reasonable apprehension of bias that invalidates the regulatory proceedings.[128] In the absence of evidence of personal animus on the part of the lawyer, however, such a finding does not bar that lawyer or his

---

124   (1988), 36 Admin. L.R. 298 (Sask. C.A.), leave to appeal allowed (1989), 79 Sask. R. 80n (S.C.C.), commented on by I. Ivankovich, (1990) 41 Admin. L.R. 111.

125   *Ibid.* at 322.

126   (1988), 30 Admin. L.R. 151 (Ont. Div. Ct.).

127   *Ibid.* at 164. As discussed in section (v) below, the mere fact that tribunal staff review the reasons for decision prepared by members and provide other advice and assistance to them does not, in and of itself, give rise to a reasonable apprehension of bias. See *Weerasinge v. Canada (Minister of Employment & Immigration)* (1993), [1994] 1 F.C. 330 (Fed. C.A.); *Bovbel v. Canada (Minister of Employment & Immigration)*, [1994] 2 F.C. 563 (Fed. C.A.), leave to appeal refused (1994), 23 Admin. L.R. (2d) 320 (note) (S.C.C.).

128   *Kaburda v. College of Dental Surgeons (British Columbia)* (1997), 30 B.C.L.R. (3d) 345 (B.C. C.A.).

or her firm from acting in a prosecutorial capacity in relation to the same individual in subsequent proceedings where there is no longer a conflict of interest between the individual and the firm's other clients.[129]

(iii) Institutional Role of Interested Parties

A third situation that can give rise to institutional bias concerns is when a party to the proceedings or someone who is thought to be aligned in interest to a party has an institutional role that may allow that person to influence the outcome of the proceedings. The classic example of this type of situation is found in *MacBain v. Canada (Human Rights Commission)*.[130] In this case, the Canadian Human Rights Commission had assigned an investigator to assess allegations of sexual harassment. The investigator had determined that the complaint was "substantiated." After this, the Commission decided to establish a tribunal to inquire into the matter. The Commission, as required by the *Canadian Human Rights Act* at the time, selected the members to sit on the tribunal, and then proceeded to act in an adversarial role by presenting the case against the defendant before the tribunal it had appointed. The Federal Court of Appeal held that the process, although authorized by statute, violated the *Canadian Bill of Rights*. In so doing, the Court based its decision on two factors: first, the use of the word "substantiated" in two sections of the Act, denoting that this involved a pre-judgement by the Commission, prior to its appointing the tribunal members; and secondly, the direct connection between the prosecutor of the complaint (the Commission itself) and the decision-maker (the tribunal, which was appointed by the Commission), giving rise to a suspicion of influence or dependency. The fact that the Commission appointed the Tribunal violated the principle that no one should judge his or her own cause, "since it cannot be said that there is any meaningful distinction between being your own judge and selecting the judge in your own cause."[131]

It is important to note, however, that specific legislative sanction will generally override the principles of natural justice such as the rule against bias. In *MacBain*, the Court found that the legislation that authorized the scheme infringed the *Canadian Bill of Rights*, and therefore the legislation was inoperative within the context of this particular case. In *C.U.P.E. v. Ontario (Minister of Labour)*,[132] trade unions opposed to the appointment of retired judges to hear interest arbitrations under the Ontario *Hospital Disputes Labour Arbitration Act* argued that the Minister of Labour was barred from doing so because he was a member of a government that had a financial interest in the outcome of the arbitrations. The Supreme Court of Canada rejected the Minister's argument that his interest was too attenuated or remote to give rise to a reasonable apprehension of bias on his part. Binnie J., writing for the majority,

---

129   *Kaburda v. College of Dental Surgeons (British Columbia)* (2002), 45 Admin. L.R. (3d) 213 (B.C. S.C.). For the Supreme Court of Canada's most recent discussion of when law firms find themselves in a conflict of interest, see *R. v. Neil*, 2002 SCC 70 (S.C.C.).

130   [1985] 1 F.C. 856, 16 Admin. L.R. 109 (Fed. C.A.).

131   *Ibid.* at 125 [Admin. L.R.] (per Heald J.).

132   (2003), 50 Admin. L.R. (3d) 1 (S.C.C.).

stated: "This approach, I think, is unrealistic. It underestimates the Minister's collective responsibility with his colleagues at a time of pitched confrontation with the unions over reductions in public sector staffing and financing. At the very least, there was an appearance that he had a significant interest in outcomes as well as process."[133] Nevertheless, the Supreme Court of Canada rejected the unions' institutional bias argument, even though the unions succeeded on other grounds. Binnie J. went on to observe:[134]

> The legal answer to this branch of the unions' argument, however, is that the legislature specifically conferred the power of appointment on the Minister. Absent a constitutional challenge, a statutory regime expressed in clear and unequivocal language on this specific point prevails over common law principles of natural justice, as recently affirmed by this Court in *Ocean Port Hotel, supra.*

The unions argued that in the past Ministers had delegated their appointment authority to a senior civil servant and the Act authorized this form of delegation. The Court held, however, the power to delegate the authority to make appointments was permissive not mandatory, and this did not detract from the general power conferred on the Minister to make appointments personally.[135] Accordingly, the Court concluded that "the Minister's perceived interest in the outcome of s. 6(5) arbitrations does not bar him from exercising a statutory power of appointment conferred on him in clear and unequivocal language."[136]

Institutional bias concerns will not arise every time a person interested in a dispute has a role that could influence the tribunal. In the *Bell Canada* case,[137] for example, Bell argued that the power of the Canadian Human Rights Commission, which was a party to pay equity hearings before the Canadian Human Rights Tribunal, to issue binding guidelines to the Tribunal gave rise to a reasonable apprehension of bias. The Supreme Court of Canada rejected this argument. The Court observed that the "guidelines" were in fact regulations that had the force of law and that it was not an interference with the Tribunal's impartiality for it to be bound by the law.[138] The Court then noted that "Bell's real objection may be that placing the guideline power and the prosecutorial function in a single agency allows the Commission to manipulate the outcome of a hearing in its favour."[139] The concern the Court raised in response to this line of argument was that Bell had not introduced any evidence of actual abuse of the Commission's authority to issue guidelines. In the absence of this type of evidence, the Court concluded that the mere existence of the possibility of

---

133 *Ibid.* at para. 116.
134 *Ibid.* at para. 117.
135 *Ibid.* at paras. 123-125.
136 *Ibid.* at para. 126. For a case where the court was prepared to impose a limit on a party's choice of a labour arbitrator who was thought to be too closely aligned in interest to the party notwithstanding the fact that there was no apparent statutory restriction on the choice of that individual, see *Calgary General Hospital v. U.N.A., Local 1* (1983), 29 Alta. L.R. (2d) 3 (Alta. C.A.), leave to appeal refused (1984), 52 N.R. 400 (S.C.C.).
137 (2003), [2003] S.C.J. No. 36, 2003 CarswellNat 2427 (S.C.C.).
138 *Ibid.* at paras. 34-38.
139 *Ibid.* at para. 44.

abuse was an insufficient basis for a reasonable observer to conclude that there was a real likelihood of bias.[140] This line of reasoning represents another example of the Supreme Court of Canada's shift away from the view found in *Régie des permis d'alcool* that in institutional bias cases it is sufficient to raise the mere possibility that a reasonable apprehension of bias could be demonstrated in a substantial number of cases. This does not mean that a party alleging institutional bias needs to show evidence of actual bias, but it does suggest that the courts are more reluctant to entertain institutional bias arguments that are excessively abstract than might have been the case even a few years ago.

(iv) Tribunal Interest in the Outcome

It is not uncommon for regulatory regimes to authorize a disciplinary tribunal to make an award of costs against a person who has found guilty of an infraction. Where the disciplinary tribunal is part of the regulatory body, it could be said to have an interest in finding people guilty since the costs award can be employed to defray the regulatory body's expenses. In *Pearlman v. Law Society (Manitoba)*[141] the Supreme Court of Canada rejected a constitutional challenge to a professional discipline regime that had these features. Assuming without deciding that s. 7 of the *Charter* was applicable in this situation, the court nevertheless concluded that this type of scheme did not give rise to a reasonable apprehension of bias and therefore was not inconsistent with s. 7's guarantee that deprivations of liberty and security of the person must take place in a manner that accords with the principles of fundamental justice. Iacobucci J., writing for a unanimous Court, accepted the propositions that the principles of fundamental justice in this context required a hearing before an impartial tribunal and that the test for impartiality was whether the proceedings gave rise to a reasonable apprehension of bias. The issue was whether the Law Society Discipline Committee's power to award costs in this situation would give rise to a reasonable apprehension of bias, and the answer he gave to that question was no.

Iacobucci J. identified three considerations that contradicted the argument that reasonable people would harbour a concern with respect to bias as a result of this scheme. The first was that the power to award costs did not result in a profit to the Law Society but merely allowed it to recover expenses incurred in investigating what proved to be misconduct on the part of a lawyer. Second, the costs award did not accrue to the benefit of the individual members of the Discipline Committee but to the Law Society as a whole. Finally, any financial benefit the costs award might provide to Committee members in their capacity as members of the Law Society in the form of reductions to their professional fees was so miniscule and indirect as to make it unreasonable to believe that such a benefit might predispose members of the Committee to find an accused lawyer guilty of misconduct.

---

140 *Ibid.* at paras. 45-50.
141 [1991] 2 S.C.R. 869 (S.C.C.).

(v) Internal Tribunal Consultations

A final problem area arises when a tribunal makes formal arrangements for consultation between the decision-maker and other tribunal members after the hearing but prior to making the actual decision in a particular case.[142] This problem frequently arises where an agency's workload is done by panels, and there is a need to achieve some degree of coherence and consistency on an agency-wide basis. A variation on this situation arises when the agency consults with its own staff, such as legal counsel or other experts.[143] The principles are well illustrated by three cases from the Supreme Court of Canada.

(A) Consolidated-Bathurst

The issue in *Consolidated Bathurst Packaging Ltd.*[144] was the degree of independence required for a small adjudicative panel of a much larger board.

During its deliberation concerning a labour dispute, a three-member panel of the Ontario Labour Relations Board took a draft of its decision to a meeting of the full Board to discuss the policy issues involved. The parties involved in the labour dispute were not given notice of this meeting and had no opportunity to appear before the entire Board. The applicant argued that there was a breach of natural justice because the parties did not have the opportunity to be heard by the actual tribunal making the decision. Although the question of bias was not expressly raised in the case, it was clearly an unstated element in the reasoning of the court.

The majority's decision stressed the fact that discussions about a case with someone who has not heard the evidence does not automatically prejudice the decision-maker's ability to make an independent determination. The Court concluded that this type of caucus procedure should not be used to compel or induce panel members to change their minds due to moral suasion or in the interests of adjudicative coherence. Nor should the meetings be used to interfere with the factual findings of the tribunal members who have actually heard the evidence. The Court examined how the full board meetings had in fact

---

142   No one really knows how much judges talk informally to each other about pending cases. See Gonthier J.'s comments about this practice in *I.W.A. Local 2-69 v. Consolidated Bathurst Packaging Ltd.* (1990), 105 N.R. 161 at 192 and 194 (S.C.C.), quoting Meredith C.J.C.P. in *Toronto & Hamilton Highway Commission v. Crabb* (1916), 37 O.L.R. 656 (Ont. C.A.) at 659:[B]ut it is only fair to add that if every judge's judgment were vitiated because he discussed the case with some other judge a good many judgments existing as valid and unimpeachable ought to fall; and that if such judgments might fall in an appellate court because of a defect which must have been detected if the subject had been so discussed.On the role of tribunal counsel after a hearing, including decision-writing, see Graham Steele, "Tribunal Counsel" (1997) 11 C.J.A.L.P. 57.

143   See cases cited *supra* at note 127.

144   *I.W.A. Local 2-69 v. Consolidated Bathurst Packaging Ltd.*, [1990] 1 S.C.R. 282, 42 Admin. L.R. 1 (S.C.C.). For comments, see D.J. Mullan, "*Consolidated-Bathurst* and the *Dominion Stores Pension Fund* cases: Different Approaches or Reconcilable Differences?" (1986-87) 21 Admin. L.R. 215; M. Falardeau-Ramsay, "Collegiality and Decision-Making in the Aftermath of the *Consolidated-Bathurst* Decision" (1987-88) 1 C.J.A.L.P. 207; B. Crane, "Case Comment on the *Consolidated Bathurst* Decision" (1987-88) 1 C.J.A.L.P. 215; and "Is it Show-and-Tell Time for the Tribunals?" (1992) 2 R.A.L. 38.

operated. It noted that the meetings were not imposed and were structured to promote discussion without forcing consensus, as indicated by the absence of voting, taking of minutes and attendance records. The overarching factor was not whether the tribunal members were influenced by others, but whether that influence was such that it restricted their freedom to decide independently. On the basis of the above factors, the Court determined that the consultation process with the full Board did not compromise natural justice principles.

In a strong dissent,[145] Sopinka J. argued that it was contradictory to state that the purpose of a full Board meeting was to achieve uniformity and coherence in the decision-making process, and at the same time to state that the panel members would not be influenced by the discussions. In Sopinka J.'s view, the independence of the individual panel which actually heard the matter was lost, thereby tainting the fairness of the hearing. In addition, he was of the view that the meeting interfered with the ability of the parties to have a full opportunity to present evidence and to make submissions.

(B) Tremblay

In *Québec (Commission des affaires socials) c. Tremblay,*[146] the Supreme Court applied the rules it had laid down in *Consolidated-Bathurst*. The case concerned an internal consultation process that had been established by the Commission to ensure consistent decision-making. Ms. Tremblay had applied to the Ministry to be reimbursed for the costs of dressings and bandages as "medical equipment" and was turned down. She appealed to the Commission. The appeal proceeded by way of admissions and written arguments. The panel consisted of two members who prepared and accepted a draft decision favourable to the appellant. Pursuant to the established practice, however, the decision was forwarded to the Commission's legal counsel for verification. Because the legal counsel was on vacation,[147] the decision was forwarded to the president of the Commission, who wrote a memo disagreeing with the decision. The issue was then directed to be submitted to the consultation process created by the Commission. After the meeting, where most of the members present disagreed with the draft decision, one of the original panel members changed her mind. Since there was then no majority agreement by the panel quorum, the decision was then referred back to the President to make the final determination, as required by the legislation.

These facts raise several issues, but the one that the Court found to be central was whether the "institutionalized" decision-making process was legal. Gonthier J. quoted *Consolidated Bathurst*:[148]

---

145   *Ibid.* at 13 [Admin. L.R.].

146   [1992] 1 S.C.R. 952, 3 Admin. L.R. (2d) 173 (S.C.C.).

147   Query whether consultation with legal counsel would have been permissible. Would it depend upon the extent to which the members of the panel felt compelled to accept counsel's advice? See M. Rankin and L. Greathead, "Advising the Board: The Scope of Counsel's Role in Advising Administrative Tribunals" (1993) 7 C.J.A.L.P. 29.

148   (1992), 3 Admin. L.R. (2d) 173 at 213 (S.C.C.) (emphasis in original), citing from *Consolidated Bathurst, supra* note 144 at 18 [Admin. L.R.].

*But this institutional purpose is subject to the clear understanding
that it is for the panel hearing the case to make the ultimate decision
and that discussion at the "Full Board" meeting is limited to the
policy implications of a draft decision . . .* The facts set out in the draft
decision are taken as given and do not become the subject of discussion. No vote is taken at these meetings nor is any other procedure
employed to identify a consensus . . . *No minutes are kept of such
meetings nor is actual attendance recorded.* [Emphasis added.]

He noted that a "plenary meeting designed to promote adjudicative coherence may thus prove acceptable and even desirable for a body like the
commission, provided this process does not involve any interference with the
freedom of decision-makers to decide according to their consciences and opinions."[149] Nevertheless, the Court in *Tremblay* found that there was a reasonable
apprehension of bias, unlike the situation in *Consolidated Bathurst*. The court
particularly noted the compulsory nature of the consultation, the systemic
pressure created by such factors as the taking of votes by a show of hands and
the fact that minutes were kept and attendance recorded.

(C) Ellis-Don

The difficulty of proving that a tribunal has not, in fact, respected the
restrictions on consultation set out in *Consolidated-Bathurst* is illustrated by
the Supreme Court of Canada's decision in *I.B.E.W., Local 894 v. Ellis-Don
Ltd.*[150] In that case, a panel of the Board prepared a draft set of reasons for
decision that were the subject of consultation at a meeting of the full Board.
As a result of this consultation, the outcome of the decision changed from the
outcome reached in the draft reasons. The draft reasons were then leaked to
Ellis-Don by a retired member of the Board. Ellis-Don sought judicial review
on the basis that the changes between the draft reasons and the final outcome
of the case demonstrated that the Board had failed to observe the limits on
consultation found in *Consolidated-Bathurst*, and in particular the limitation
on attempts to interfere with factual findings. Ellis-Don also sought to obtain
an order for examination of members of the Board concerning what had actually
happened at the full Board meeting. Its application was rejected by the Ontario
Divisional Court[151] on the basis of the testimonial immunity conferred on the
Board by s. 111 of the Ontario *Labour Relations Act*.

The Supreme Court of Canada, in a majority decision written by LeBel J.,
rejected Ellis-Don's argument that the Board had violated the rules of natural
justice. The Court held the mere fact that the outcome of the case changed as
a result of the full Board meeting did not carry with it the implication that
anything untoward had occurred at the meeting. In addition, the Court found
that the alteration of the Board's findings with respect to the union's abandon-

---

149 *Tremblay, ibid.* 214.
150 [2001] 1 S.C.R. 221 (S.C.C.).
151 *Ellis-Don Ltd. v. Ontario (Labour Relations Board)* (1994), 16 O.R. (3d) 698 (Ont. Div.
Ct.), leave to appeal refused 1994), 24 Admin. L.R. (2d) 122n (Ont. C.A.), leave to appeal
refused [1995] 1 S.C.R. vii (S.C.C.), reversing (1992), 95 D.L.R. (4th) 56 (Ont. Div. Ct.).

ment of its bargaining rights should be characterized as flowing from the interplay between policy and fact rather than as evidence of interference with the hearing panel's factual findings. Accordingly, Ellis-Don had not demonstrated that the Board had failed to observe the rules governing consultation laid down in *Consolidated Bathurst*, and its application to have the Board's decision quashed was dismissed.

Like *Consolidated-Bathurst* itself, this decision attracted a vigorous dissent, this time authored by Binnie J. He rejected the majority's description of the change in the Board's reasoning as the result of the interplay between policy considerations and fact. He concluded that the difference between the draft reasons and the final outcome of the case could only be explained as the product of the Board's interference with the panel's factual findings. In addition, Binnie J. objected to the Board's assertion of its testimonial immunity to prevent Ellis-Don's attempts to find out what had actually happened at the full Board meeting.[152] He acknowledged the legitimacy of the rationale for testimonial immunity as a general proposition. Nevertheless, he did not believe that it served the rationale underlying the immunity to allow the Board, in the face of evidence that there may have been an irregularity, to argue that Ellis-Don had failed to prove the existence of the irregularity and at the same time to assert its immunity and thereby prevent Ellis-Don from gathering the information that might have permitted it to make out its case.

6. Structural Independence

Over the past decade, the Supreme Court of Canada has engaged in the cautious development of a principle that certain types of administrative decision-makers must be protected from the threat of improper interference with the independent exercise of their adjudicative functions by guarantees of security of tenure, security of remuneration and administrative control over case management. The case law concerning the structural independence of administrative tribunals has two important elements in common with the law governing institutional bias. The first is that it is essential to distinguish between arguments grounded in constitutional or quasi-constitutional legal principles, which can be used to attack a statutory scheme itself, and arguments grounded in the common law, which are constrained by the statutory structure adopted by the legislature. As Chief Justice McLachlin observed in *Ocean Port Hotel Ltd. v. British Columbia (General Manager, Liquor Control & Licensing Branch)*:[153]

> . . . like all principles of natural justice, the degree of independence required of tribunal members may be ousted by express statutory

---

152   See R. Hawkins, "Behind Closed Doors II: The Operational Problem–Deliberative Secrecy, Statutory Immunity and Testimonial Privilege" (1996), 10 C.J.A.L.P. 39 and D. Mullan, "Policing the Consolidated-Bathurst Limits–Of Whistleblowers and Other Assorted Characters" (1993), 10 Admin. L.R. (2d) 241 at 242, cited with approval by Binnie J. at paras. 97 and 101 respectively.

153   [2001] 2 S.C.R. 781 (S.C.C.) at para. 22 (case references omitted).

language or necessary implication. . . . Ultimately, it is Parliament or the legislature that determines the nature of a tribunal's relationship to the executive. It is not open to a court to apply a common law rule in the face of clear statutory direction. Courts engaged in judicial review of administrative decisions must defer to the legislator's intention in assessing the degree of independence required of the tribunal in question.

The second point of commonality is that the structural independence principle is a vehicle for attacking institutional arrangements that might be thought to give rise to concerns about impartial decision-making in a substantial number of cases. Like the law governing bias at an individual level, the objective is to provide both parties to disputes and members of the public with appropriate assurances that the decisions of tribunals are not only made impartially but seen to be made impartially.

As indicated above, what makes tribunal independence cases distinct from institutional bias cases is that the structural independence principle is concerned with the need for and extent of guarantees concerning the security of tenure, security of remuneration and administrative independence afforded to members of administrative tribunals. The concern that animates the structural independence doctrine is that if there are no adequate guarantees of this type of independence, reasonable people might be concerned that decision-makers were vulnerable to interference by those who control their employment security, their remuneration or the management of their work. These are the same types of concerns that form the rationale for the guarantees of judicial independence found in ss. 96-100 of the *Constitution Act, 1867*, s. 11(d) of the *Canadian Charter of Rights and Freedoms* and the commitment found in the preamble to the *Constitution Act 1867* to a system of government "similar in principle to that of the United Kingdom".[154] Canadian courts have not been prepared to accept the argument that administrative tribunals that perform purely adjudicative functions are the equivalent of courts and are therefore entitled to the same level of protection of their independence as judges.[155] On the other hand, it is possible, at least in theory, to argue that a statutory scheme that fails to provide appropriate independence guarantees to administrative decision-makers fails to meet the constitutional requirements of s. 7 of the *Charter* or the quasi-constitutional guarantees of ss. 1(a) and 2(e) of the *Canadian Bill of Rights*, s. 1(a) of the *Alberta Bill of Rights* or s. 23 of the *Quebec*

---

154 See *R. v. Campbell*, [1997] 3 S.C.R. 3 (S.C.C.), additional reasons at [1998] 1 S.C.R. 3 (S.C.C.).

155 *Bell Canada v. C.T.E.A.* (2003), [2003] S.C.J. No. 36, 2003 CarswellNat 2427 (S.C.C.) at para. 29; *Ocean Port Hotel Ltd. v. British Columbia (General Manager, Liquor Control & Licensing Branch)*, [2001] 2 S.C.R. 781 (S.C.C.) at paras. 29-33; *Barreau de Montréal v. Québec (Procureur général)*, [2001] R.J.Q. 2058, 48 Admin. L.R. (3d) 82 (Que. C.A.) at paras. 108-112, leave to appeal denied (2002), 2002 CarswellQue 2078, 48 Admin. L.R. (3d) 82n (S.C.C.), reconsideration refused (2002), 2002 CarswellQue 2683 (S.C.C.). Compare *R. v. Wigglesworth*, [1987] 2 S.C.R. 541 (S.C.C.) and *R. v. Shubley*, [1990] 1 S.C.R. 3 (S.C.C.), restricting the applicability of the protections of s. 11(d) of the *Charter* to tribunals that adjudicate cases involving true penal consequences.

Charter of Human Rights and Freedoms. The decisions discussing the constitutional or quasi-constitutional concept of tribunal independence indicate that even if the principles governing judicial independence represent the model for tribunal independence guarantees, these guarantees must be applied flexibly in light of the functions and characteristics of the particular tribunal.[156]

The common law principle guaranteeing tribunal independence has the same general objective as the constitutional or quasi-constitutional principle, but it is subject to the restriction that such guarantees can be ousted by express statutory language or by necessary implication. Thus, in the *Ocean Port Hotel* case,[157] the Supreme Court of Canada held that the common law principle of tribunal independence could not be employed to invalidate a Liquor Appeal Board decision rendered by Board members whose appointments were effectively at the pleasure of the Lieutenant Governor in Council, since the Board's enabling legislation expressly contemplated the use of "at pleasure" appointments. Similarly, in *C.U.P.E. v. Ontario (Minister of Labour)*[158] the Supreme Court of Canada was unanimous in its conclusion that the common law principle of tribunal independence could not be used to invalidate the appointment of interest arbitrators in health care disputes on an *ad hoc* basis where this method of appointment was statutorily mandated. On the other hand, in *Canadian Pacific Ltd. v. Matsqui Indian Band*,[159] two members of the Supreme Court of Canada (Lamer, C.J. and Cory J.) concluded that property tax assessment appeals boards created by the bands pursuant to delegated legislative authority did not represent an adequate alternative to judicial review of the assessments because the members of the boards did not have sufficient security of tenure or security of remuneration to meet common law standards.[160]

Whether the requirement of structural independence is a constitutional or quasi-constitutional one, or one that flows from the common law, it is still

---

156   *Bell Canada, ibid.* at paras. 21-31; *2747-3174 Québec Inc. c. Québec (Régie des permis d'alcool),* [1996] 3 S.C.R. 919 (S.C.C.) at paras. 61-64.

157   *Supra* note 155.

158   (2003), 50 Admin. L.R. (3d) 1 (S.C.C.) at para. 190 (per Binnie J. writing for the majority) and paras. 43-44 (per Bastarache J. dissenting, but not on this point). The majority upheld the unions' challenge to the appointment of retired judges to carry out the interest arbitration role. It did so not on the basis that the retired judges lack institutional independence, however, but on the ground that the Minister of Labour's appointment of retired judges who lacked labour relations expertise was, in light of the requirements of the statutory scheme, patently unreasonable.

159   [1995] 1 S.C.R. 3 (S.C.C.).

160   Similarly, in *Sekela v. British Columbia (Police Complaint Commissioner)* (2001), 93 B.C.L.R. (3d) 208 (B.C. C.A.), the British Columbia Court of Appeal (in a majority decision) ruled that a decision of an adjudicator in a complaint under the B.C. *Police Act* should be quashed because the contract for the adjudicator's services entitled the Police Complaint Commissioner, who was a party to the proceedings, to view drafts of the adjudicator's reasons and to terminate the contract on 10 days notice. According to the reasons of Levine J.A. writing for the majority, these contractual provisions (which were not mandated by the *Police* Act) violated the structural independence requirement found in the common law and gave rise to a reasonable apprehension of bias. Interestingly, Southin J.A. dissented on the basis that there was no evidence of actual interference by the Commissioner in the adjudicator's performance of his duties in this case.

necessary to determine precisely what types of independence guarantees are necessary to convince reasonable people that the members of the tribunal are not vulnerable to improper influence. Although some commentators have suggested that it would be desirable to develop a distinctive concept of tribunal independence that is not modeled on judicial independence,[161] the case law to date has relied on a flexible adaptation of the principles of security of tenure, security of remuneration and administrative control employed to protect the independence of judges. It is not easy to determine precisely how flexible the courts will be in their adaptation of the principles of judicial independence to the tribunal setting. Several considerations do, however, appear consistently in the judicial discussions of structural independence for tribunals.

In general, the more closely the functions and powers of the tribunal are to those of specialized courts, the more appropriate it is to demand a high level of independence for the members of the tribunal. The nature of the interests affected by the tribunal's decisions also appears to be relevant. For example, in the *Bell Canada* case, the Supreme Court of Canada observed:

> The fact that the Tribunal functions in much the same way as a court suggests that it is appropriate for its members to have a high degree of independence from the executive branch. A high degree of independence is also appropriate given the interests that are affected by proceedings before the Tribunal – such as the dignity interests of the complainant, the interest of the public in eradicating discrimination, and the reputation of the party that is alleged to have engaged in discriminatory practices.[162]

Similarly, in *Barreau de Montréal v. Québec (Procureur général)*[163] the Quebec Court of Appeal concluded that the status of the Tribunal administratif de Québec as a purely adjudicative body and the fact that it has powers not enjoyed by all tribunals, such as the authority to make initial determinations concerning the constitutional validity of its own enabling legislation and the statutory regimes it administers, entitle it to a high degree of structural independence. In addition, some decisions suggest that the fact that the tribunal is in a position of potential conflict with the person who exercises control over his or her appointment or remuneration justifies a high degree of independence.[164]

On the other side of the ledger, several factors have been used by courts to indicate that guarantees of independence that might not be acceptable in the judicial arena are adequate for administrative tribunals. The most significant

---

161   See K. Wyman, "The Independence of Administrative Tribunals in an Era of Ever Expansive Judicial Independence", *supra* note 100; N. Des Rosiers, "Toward an Administrative Model of Independence and Accountability for Administrative Tribunals", in H. Dumont and G.A. Smith, eds. *Justice to Order – Adjustment to Changing Demands and Coordination Issues in the Justice System in Canada* (Montreal: Éditions Thémis, 1998) at 53.

162   *Supra* note 155 at para. 24.

163   *Supra* note 155 at paras. 128-133.

164   See *Canadian Pacific Ltd. v. Matsqui Indian Band, supra* note 159 at 56-57 [S.C.R.] (per Lamer, C.J.); *Barreau de Montréal, ibid.* at paras. 144-48. This consideration is not, however, always given significant weight by courts. See *Katz v. Vancouver Stock Exchange*, [1996] 3 S.C.R. 405 (S.C.C.).

of these considerations is the past practice of the tribunal itself or of other comparable bodies. For example, in *Canadian Pacific Ltd. v. Matsqui Indian Band*,[165] Sopinka J. expressed the view that it was premature to determine whether or not the tax assessment appeal boards were sufficiently independent from the Band councils that appointed their members since it was necessary to take into account the actual practices of the boards in making that determination. Similarly, in *C.U.P.E. v. Ontario (Minister of Labour)*[166] the Court found that the past practice of successful use of arbitrators appointed on an *ad hoc* basis in the labour relations context supported its conclusion that concerns with respect to structural independence did not justify judicial interference with the system of *ad hoc* appointments. In addition, courts seem to take a more flexible approach to self-regulating bodies or other institutions that do not easily with fit within the traditional model than they do toward classic adjudicative tribunals appointed by government.[167]

When all of these factors are taken into account, it is not easy to make categorical statements about what types of institutional arrangements will be found to offer adequate guarantees of security of tenure, security of remuneration or administrative control in any particular context. In the *Régie des permis d'alcool* case, Gonthier J. stated:[168] "In my view, the directors' conditions of employment meet the minimum requirements of independence. These do not require that all administrative adjudicators, like judges of courts of law, hold office for life. Fixed-term appointments, which are common, are acceptable. However, the removal of adjudicators must not simply be at the pleasure of the executive." In *Bell Canada* the Supreme Court of Canada found that the general system of fixed term appointments for members of the Canadian Human Rights Tribunal was satisfactory and that the power of the Tribunal's Chairperson to extend a member's appointment in ongoing inquiries did not compromise the independence of members of the Tribunal.[169] On the other hand, the courts have been prepared to accept the legitimacy of much more flexible *ad hoc* arrangements in other settings.[170]

7. The Legal Effect of a Reasonable Apprehension of Bias

As a general rule, where a party has established a reasonable apprehension of bias on the part of an individual decision-maker or with respect to the decision-making institution itself, any decision taken in respect of that person is invalid. Normally it will not matter that the other members of a multi-member

---

165   *Ibid.* at 67-70 [S.C.R.]. In addition, see *Alex Couture Inc. c. Canada (Procureur général)* (1991), 83 D.L.R. (4th) 577 (Que. C.A.), leave to appeal refused [1992] 2 S.C.R. v (S.C.C.).

166   *Supra* note 158 at paras. 191-193.

167   See *Katz v. Vancouver Stock Exchange, supra* note 164; *Mohammad v. Canada (Minister of Employment & Immigration)* (1988), [1989] 2 F.C. 363 (Fed. C.A.), leave to appeal denied (1989), 101 N.R. 157n (S.C.C.).

168   *Supra* note 156 at para. 67.

169   *Supra* note 155 at paras. 24 and 51-53.

170   See *C.U.P.E. v. Ontario (Minister of Labour), supra* note 158; *Katz v. Vancouver Stock Exchange, supra* note 164.

panel were impartial or that the decision on the merits was sound in other respects.[171] As Cory J. wrote in the *Newfoundland Telephone* case:[172]

> Everyone appearing before administrative boards is entitled to be treated fairly. It is an independent and unqualified right. As I have stated, it is impossible to have a fair hearing or to have procedural fairness if a reasonable apprehension of bias has been established. If there has been a denial of a right to a fair hearing it cannot be cured by the tribunal's subsequent decision. A decision of a tribunal which denied the parties a fair hearing cannot be simply voidable and rendered valid as a result of the subsequent decision of the tribunal. Procedural fairness is an essential aspect of any hearing before a tribunal. The damage created by apprehension of bias cannot be remedied. The hearing, and any subsequent order resulting from it, is void.

This statement, while sound as a general proposition, should not in our view be taken too literally. No court has ever gone so far as to hold that a decision tainted by bias is void for all time against the whole world. As H.W.R. Wade has pointed out forcefully,[173] the "void/voidable" distinction is almost incoherent when applied to administrative law. Wade argues persuasively that calling a decision "void" in administrative law means, at most, that it is subject to being set aside at the suit of an eligible person. If no eligible person challenges the decision, or if the time limit for challenging the decision has passed, the so-called "void" decision will stand.

In any event, an inflexible rule–to the effect that an order tainted by an apprehension of bias *must* be quashed in its entirety–may well be at odds with

---

171   In *Roberts v. R.*, 2003 SCC 45 (S.C.C.), the Supreme Court of Canada observed at para. 93 that:

> In the circumstances of the present case [where the nine judges who sat on these appeals shared the same view as to the disposition of the appeals and the reasons for judgment] even if it were found that the involvement of a single judge gave rise to a reasonable apprehension of bias, no reasonable person informed of the decision-making process of the Court, and viewing it realistically, could conclude that it was likely that the eight other judges were biased, or somehow tainted, by the apprehended bias affecting the ninth judge.

The significance of this observation is unclear. In the *Baker* case, [1999] 2 S.C.R. 817 (S.C.C.), the Court concluded at para. 45 that if a person plays an important part in a decision-making process, including merely making a recommendation, "and if a person with such a central role does not act impartially, the decision itself cannot be said to have been made in an impartial manner." The *Baker* approach is also consistent with authorities that hold that a decision is invalidated if any member of a panel making the decision has not heard all the evidence since that individual may have influenced the thinking of those panel members who did hear all the evidence. See *Mehr v. Law Society of Upper Canada*, [1955] S.C.R. 344 (S.C.C.). It may be that the Court's comment in the *Roberts* case is best explained as a reflection of the principle, discussed below, that courts retain a residual discretion in appropriate cases not to invalidate a decision in which there is a reasonable apprehension of bias.

172   (1992), 4 Admin. L.R. (2d) 121 at 140 (S.C.C.).

173   H.W.R. Wade, "Unlawful Administrative Action: Void or Voidable?", Part I at (1967) 83 L.Q.R. 499; Part II at (1968) 84 L.Q.R. 95.

practical justice for the applicant. In many cases, declaring a proceeding void means that the tribunal has to start afresh. That will often be precisely what the applicant wants, but not always. The prospect of re-calling all the witnesses, paying for counsel, and taking the time, energy and money to re-do the whole tribunal proceeding, may be more than the applicant can bear. Even if the applicant is awarded costs of the judicial review proceeding, it will almost certainly be only a partial indemnity for the costs incurred. In these cases, it seems odd for the court to insist that the tribunal start over again. Parties may be put in the unpalatable pickle of having to choose between continuing with a hearing tainted by bias, or seeking an unattractive judicial remedy. The reverse danger is that a party with deeper pockets than its adversaries may use the apocalyptic consequences of a judicial review proceeding as a bargaining chip.

A view more in keeping with what the courts actually do is that the court retains a discretion to fashion a remedy that suits the circumstances of the case. This discretion may be used to fashion a practical remedy for the applicant, but also to protect the integrity and efficiency of the justice system. The discretion is used not to excuse a tainted hearing, but rather to ensure fairness.

This theory of a residual discretion to fashion a practical remedy explains, for example, the courts' great willingness to find that a party has, by its conduct, waived its right of objection to bias.[174] The conventional view is at a loss to explain the doctrine of waiver – if a biased hearing is a nullity, how can a party's conduct lend it substance?

The courts have also shown that they are willing, where there is no practical way for the tribunal to hold a fresh hearing, to grant an order that amounts to a stay[175] or to provide a disposition on the merits.[176] Admittedly, this jurisdiction is exercised sparingly, generally limited to the following circumstances:

- It is impossible, because of the abolition or alteration of the tribunal, to remit the matter to a tribunal with jurisdiction over the same subject-matter.

---

174 See the discussion of waiver at section 8 of this chapter.

175 *Bailey v. Registered Nurses' Assn. (Saskatchewan)*, [1996] 7 W.W.R. 751, 137 D.L.R. (4th) 224 (Sask. Q.B.), reversed on other grounds (1996), 140 D.L.R. (4th) 547, 148 Sask. R. 156 (Sask. C.A.). In what has to be one of the strongest condemnations of tribunal conduct, the court quashed the tribunal's decision, awarded solicitor-client costs to the applicants, and ordered that the charges of professional misconduct against the applicants not be raised again. The decision was reversed on appeal, but on the grounds that the trial judge erred in not receiving certain evidence from the respondents.

176 *Després c. Assoc. des Arpenteurs-géomètres* (1992), 8 Admin. L.R. (2d) 136, 130 N.B.R. (2d) 210 (N.B. C.A.), reversing (1992), 124 N.B.R. (2d) 254 (N.B. Q.B.); *Leshner v. Ontario (Deputy Attorney General)* (1992), 8 Admin. L.R. (2d) 132, 96 D.L.R. (4th) 41, 10 O.R. (3d) 732 (Ont. Div. Ct.); *Chipman Wood Products (1973) Ltd. v. Thompson* (1996), 42 Admin. L.R. (2d) 259, 181 N.B.R. (2d) 386 (N.B. C.A.), citing rule 62.21(1) of the New Brunswick Rules of Court as authority for doing so; *Chanteur v. Ordre des audioprothésistes (Québec)*, [1996] R.J.Q. 539 (Que. C.A.). See also *R. v. Secretary of State for the Home Department*, [1991] 1 A.C. 696 (U.K. H.L.), per Lord Ackner at 757-58, on why this remedy is generally not appropriate.

- It is impossible, or at least highly unlikely, that the tribunal will be able to hold a fair hearing.
- The time and expense attendant on remitting the matter to the tribunal will cause irreparable harm to the applicant.
- The evidence available to the court is complete enough and clear enough for the court to find that there is only one lawful decision the tribunal can make.

The courts' reluctance to make a decision on the merits properly reflects the nature of judicial review, the efficient operation of the justice system, and the relative expertise of courts and tribunals.

The Supreme Court of Canada has recently endorsed this pragmatic approach to the consequences of administrative decisions that are made in violation of the principles of procedural fairness in *Danyluk v. Ainsworth Technologies Inc.*[177] In that case, the issue was whether an employee whose claim for unpaid wages under the Ontario *Employment Standards Act* was dismissed by an employment standards officer in a manner that was procedurally unfair was estopped from asserting a breach of contract claim for the same wages in court. The Court made the following observation in response to the argument that the officer's violation of the rules of natural justice made the decision incapable of grounding an estoppel argument:[178]

> In my view, with respect, the theory that a denial of natural justice deprives the ESA decision of its character as a "judicial" decision rests on a misconception. Flawed the decision may be, but "judicial" (as distinguished from administrative or legislative) it remains. Once it is determined that the decision maker was capable of receiving and exercising adjudicative authority and that the particular decision was one that was required to be made in a judicial manner, the decision does not cease to have that character ("judicial") because the decision maker erred in carrying out his or her functions. As early as *R. v. Nat Bell Liquors Ltd.*, [1922] 2 A.C. 128 (H.L.), it was held that a conviction entered by an Alberta magistrate could not be quashed for lack of jurisdiction on the grounds that the depositions showed that there was no evidence to support the conviction or that the magistrate misdirected himself in considering the evidence. The jurisdiction to try the charges was distinguished from alleged errors in "the observance of the law in the course of its exercise" (p. 156). If the conditions precedent to the exercise of a judicial jurisdiction are satisfied (as here), subsequent errors in its exercise, including violations of natural justice, render the decision voidable, not void: *Harelkin v. University of Regina*, [1979] 2 S.C.R. 561, at pp. 584-85. The decision remains a "judicial decision", although seriously flawed by the want of proper notice and the denial of the opportunity to be heard.

---

177   [2001] 2 S.C.R. 460, 34 Admin. L.R. (3d) 163 (S.C.C.).
178   *Ibid.* at para. 47.

This was not the end of the matter as far as the Court was concerned. The mere fact that the decision was capable of supporting an estoppel argument did not mean that the court seized of the breach of contract action should automatically give effect to that argument. It was necessary for the court to exercise discretion whether or not to do so, taking into account all the relevant considerations including the relevant statutory language, the purpose of the administrative scheme, whether or not an appeal was available from the administrative decision, what procedural safeguards were in place in the administrative scheme, the expertise of the administrative decision-maker, the circumstances of the particular case and the potential for unfairness.

8. Can the Rule Against Bias be Waived?

One of the controversial questions of bias law is whether the courts will *require* that bias be raised before the tribunal. Many courts have held that disqualification for bias is waived if it is not raised at the first practical opportunity.[179] According to this view, a remedy for bias is in the court's discretion, and the court will not assist a party that has not moved promptly to protect its rights.

Courts do tend, however, to treat waiver with some caution. Waiver will be inferred only where the party alleging bias has full knowledge or the means of knowledge of the problem, and an opportunity to object.[180] In a New Bruns-

---

179   Innumerable examples of "waiver" could be given. The following list is very much a partial one: *Canada (Human Rights Commission) v. Taylor*, [1990] 3 S.C.R. 892 (S.C.C.); *Canada (Anti-Dumping Tribunal), Re* (1975), [1976] 2 S.C.R. 739 (S.C.C.), where the Attorney General waited two years before bringing an application to quash a tribunal decision; *E.C.W.U., Local 916 v. Atomic Energy of Canada Ltd.* (1985), [1986] 1 F.C. 103 (Fed. C.A.), leave to appeal refused (1986), 72 N.R. 77 (note) (S.C.C.); *Huyck v. Musqueam Indian Band* (2000), 23 Admin. L.R. (3d) 28 (Fed. T.D.), additional reasons at (2000), 2000 CarswellNat 2632 (Fed. T.D.), affirmed 2001 FCA 150 (Fed. C.A.), leave to appeal refused (2002), 293 N.R. 191 (note) (S.C.C.); *Fischer v. Canadian Kennel Club* (1995), 31 Alta. L.R. (3d) 271, 170 A.R. 395 (Alta. Q.B.); *Zaroud v. Canada (Secretary of State)* (1995), 45 Admin. L.R. (2d) 318 (Fed. T.D.), where applicant's counsel had raised the issue of bias but did not specifically ask the member to withdraw; *Balka v. McDonald* (1994), 120 Nfld. & P.E.I.R. 7 (Nfld. T.D.), where the chair had disclosed a previous relationship with a party and offered to remove himself from the hearing if either party objected; *Mitchell v. Institute of Chartered Accountants (Manitoba)*, [1994] 3 W.W.R. 704, 22 Admin. L.R. (2d) 182 (Man. Q.B.), affirmed [1994] 10 W.W.R. 768 (Man. C.A.), where an objection was raised late in a hearing; *Callahan v. Newfoundland (Deputy Minister of Social Services)* (1993), 23 Admin. L.R. (2d) 32, 113 Nfld. & P.E.I.R. 1 (Nfld. T.D.); *Robinson v. Comité Garderie Plein Soleil* (1992), 8 Admin. L.R. (2d) 304 (N.W.T. S.C.); *West Region Tribal Council v. Canada (Adjudicator appointed pursuant to s. 242 of the Canada Labour Code)* (1992), 55 F.T.R. 28 (Fed. T.D.); *Woodard v. Prince Edward Island (Minister of Provincial Affairs)* (1996), 140 Nfld. & P.E.I.R. 282 (P.E.I. T.D.); *S.C.F.P., local 1378 c. Résidences Mgr. Chiasson Inc.* (1996), 172 N.B.R. (2d) 308 (N.B. C.A.); *Moharib v. Misericordia General Hospital* (1996), 107 Man. R. (2d) 283 (Man. C.A.).

180   See G.S. Lester, "Bias: How and When to Raise the Objection" (1997) 3 A.A.P. 49 at 50, citing *French v. Law Society of Upper Canada (No. 2)* (1973), 1 O.R. (2d) 514 at 534 (Ont. H.C.), reversed on other grounds (1975), 8 O.R. (2d) 193 (Ont. C.A.), leave to appeal to S.C.C. refused (1975), 8 O.R. (2d) 193n (S.C.C.); *Halfway River First Nation v. British*

wick case, the Court of Appeal held that a party's failure to attend a tribunal hearing meant that it could not object to the merits of the tribunal's decision, but non-attendance did not act as a waiver of a reasonable apprehension of bias.[181] Other courts have held that it is not necessary to make the allegation of bias to the tribunal.[182] According to this view, a biased proceeding is a nullity, and cannot be lent substance by the acts or omissions of a party. It has even been held that the tribunal has no jurisdiction to rule on an allegation of bias, or if it does, the ruling is only a piece of evidence for consideration of the reviewing court.[183] If that is the case, there is little point in going through the motions of putting a bias argument to the tribunal.

Which view is the better? In our opinion, the better view is that the court has a discretion depending on the circumstances of the particular case and tribunal. It should not be an inflexible rule that bias must be raised before the tribunal, and neither should it be an inflexible rule that bias need not be raised before the tribunal. The principal value at stake is the efficient administration of justice. Sometimes it will be more efficient for a bias allegation to be heard and decided by the tribunal, other times by the court. The following factors might be taken into account:

(a) The time and expense, and the effect on the parties, the tribunal, and the public interest, involved in continuing a proceeding that may later be quashed. Evaluation of this factor will depend, for example, on the nature of the proceeding and its anticipated length.

(b) The strength of the applicant's case. The stronger the case for a disqualifying bias, the more efficient it is for the court to decide the matter as quickly as possible.

(c) The completeness of the record. The court should consider whether the evidence will be more complete if the matter is heard and decided by the tribunal.

(d) Whether the allegation of bias is, by its nature, something that could be remedied by the tribunal. For example, an allegation of personal bias on the part of a potential panel member can generally be resolved internally. An allegation of institutional bias may require judicial intervention.

(e) Whether the tribunal is sophisticated enough to apply correctly the

---

   Columbia (Ministry of Forests) (1997), 39 B.C.L.R. (3d) 227 (B.C. S.C.), affirmed (1999), 178 D.L.R. (4th) 666 (B.C. C.A.); *Mitchell v. Institute of Chartered Accountants (Manitoba)*, [1994] 3 W.W.R. 704 (Man. Q.B.), affirmed [1994] 10 W.W.R. 768 (Man. C.A.).

181 *Chipman Wood Products (1973) Ltd. v. Thompson* (1996), 181 N.B.R. (2d) 386 (N.B. C.A.).

182 Some courts, though very much a minority, have concluded that the right to object to bias cannot be waived: e.g., *Devries v. Canada (National Parole Board)* (1993), 12 Admin. L.R. (2d) 309, 21 C.R. (4th) 36 (B.C. S.C.); or that the applicant's failure to object cannot be determinative of whether a remedy will be granted: *Milne v. Saskatchewan (Joint Chiropractic Professional Review Committee)* (1992), 90 D.L.R. (4th) 634 at 639 (Sask. C.A.).

183 *Beno v. Canada (Somalia Inquiry Commission)*, [1997] 1 F.C. 911, 47 Admin. L.R. (2d) 206 (Fed. T.D.), reversed on other grounds (1997), 146 D.L.R. (4th) 708, 47 Admin. L.R. (2d) 244 (Fed. C.A.), leave to appeal refused (1997), 224 N.R. 395 (note) (S.C.C.).

law on bias. Many smaller tribunals will have no legally-trained members and no access to legal advice.

(f) Whether the court believes there is any value in having the tribunal's own opinion on the allegations of bias.

(g) Whether the threshold test for discovery of the tribunal has been met. If it has, and discovery is ordered, the tribunal will be in the untenable position of having to adjudicate a dispute in which it has, in effect, become one of the parties.

The application of these factors will generally be enough to differentiate between cases where bias ought to have been raised before the tribunal, and cases where it may be raised for the first time on judicial review. There is no need to add an additional hurdle, namely whether the objection was raised in a timely way.

The doctrine of waiver is initially attractive. It is universally accepted that, in the interests of the efficient administration of justice, an appeal court should not normally hear issues that were not raised in the court below. By analogy, a bias allegation not made to the tribunal should not be allowed on judicial review. In our view, the analogy is not a good one. The doctrine of waiver has been applied too harshly and ought to be softened.

The fact that is often overlooked by courts is the practical difficulty that many parties face in making allegations of bias. "Bias" is a dreadfully loaded word. Tribunals frequently treat allegations of a reasonable apprehension of bias as an allegation of actual bias. It is hard for some tribunal members not to feel that their honour and integrity is at stake. Consequently, it is difficult for a party to risk alienating the tribunal. For all these reasons, it is often better to hope for the best in the tribunal's decision than to make allegations of bias. This choice is not really a choice to sit on one's rights, but rather a choice to make the allegation of bias in the forum best equipped to deal with it.

It is important to underline that the tactical use of an allegation of bias should never be acceptable. Our argument is that an allegation of bias made solely as a tactic will fail *because it has no merit*. It ought to be handled on that basis. If the allegation does have some merit – i.e. if there really is a reasonable apprehension of bias – it seems more than a little odd to uphold the tribunal's decision anyway, just because someone did not raise the issue as quickly as they might have.

9. Evidence of Bias

It is one thing to suspect bias, or to allege an apprehension of bias. It is quite another thing to prove it. If one thing is certain, it is that there must be an evidentiary foundation for the court to find there is a reasonable apprehension of bias.[184] But what evidence does, or might, the court have? And what does the applicant have to show before discovery of the tribunal is ordered?

---

184 *Finch v. Assn. of Professional Engineers & Geoscientists (British Columbia)* (1996), 38

(a) The Record and Affidavits

In a typical judicial review application, the only evidence before the court is the record of the tribunal's proceedings. The court is not interested in hearing new evidence. The limitations on the record follows from the theory of judicial review, which is that the reviewing court is checking to make sure that the tribunal did its job, not determining whether the tribunal reached the correct result. The contents of the record varies from jurisdiction to jurisdiction, but will typically consist at least of the tribunal's decision, the evidence and written submissions before the tribunal, and, if there is one, a transcript.

This theory, strictly applied, would prevent most bias cases from going forward. The reason is that most forms of bias are not, by their nature, on the record. Just about the only form that *is* on the record is inappropriate interference in the hearing itself and that is only if there is a transcript. It is therefore universally accepted that additional evidence may be brought forward to establish a breach of natural justice, including bias,[185] provided, of course, that the evidence is otherwise admissible.

Typically, the evidence dealing with a reasonable apprehension of bias is brought forward by affidavit.[186] The deponent of an affidavit is subject to cross-examination. This method of bringing forward evidence with respect to bias is convenient and generally speedy, but it will tend to produce unsatisfactory evidence. There are several reasons:

- Many tribunal proceedings are not truly adversarial. The affidavit evidence will therefore tend to be unconstrained by the salutary effect of having the other side file its own affidavits, or having the other side cross-examine on the affidavits.

- The tribunal has a limited role on judicial review.[187] The tribunal can hardly descend into the adversarial fray, and yet the member's evidence may be indispensable if the court is to have a realistic idea of what happened. Affidavits from tribunal members are admissible,[188] except that no evidence is admissible to show whether a tribunal member is in fact biased.[189] If there are disputes on the facts, or cross-examination on the member's affidavit, it will be difficult for the

---

Admin. L.R. (2d) 116, [1996] 5 W.W.R. 690 (B.C. C.A.), leave to appeal refused [1996] 10 W.W.R. lix (note) (S.C.C.).

185 The leading case is *R. v. Northumberland Compensation Appeal Tribunal* (1951), [1952] 1 All E.R. 122, [1952] 1 K.B. 338 (C.A.), *per* Denning L.J. at 131.

186 For example, *Stellarton (Town) v. Nova Scotia (Commissioner, Public Inquiries Act)* (1996), (sub nom. *Stellarton (Town) v. Richard, J.*) 150 N.S.R. (2d) 11 (N.S. S.C.).

187 The Federal Court of Appeal has even gone so far as to hold that the tribunal itself is not a proper party in judicial review proceedings: *Canada (Attorney General) v. Bernard*, [1994] 2 F.C. 447, 17 Admin. L.R. (2d) 2 (Fed. C.A.).

188 *S.C.F.P., local 1378 c. Résidences Mgr. Chiasson Inc.* (1996), 172 N.B.R. (2d) 308 (N.B. C.A.).

189 Such evidence is irrelevant to determining whether there is an *apprehension* of bias, and therefore is inadmissible.

tribunal then to dispense impartial justice in any further proceedings before the tribunal.

• Dueling affidavits are not, for the most part, a suitable means to resolve substantial disputes of fact.

All courts make provision for converting applications into actions, where there are substantial disputes of fact.[190] Others provide for discovery even on applications.[191]

(b) Voluntary and Compulsory Disclosure[192]

If something more is required than just the record and affidavits based on evidence already available, the tribunal may be asked for voluntary disclosure.[193]

Clearly, a tribunal will not always be willing to be forthcoming with evidence of what goes on behind the scenes. Can a tribunal be *forced* to give evidence? The answer is yes production of documents and oral discovery may be ordered in appropriate circumstances.[194] In the case that looked like it was going to set a precedent on the scope of discovery, the tribunal voluntarily turned over its files and discovery became unnecessary.[195]

When evaluating whether the circumstances are appropriate, there is a balance to be struck between deliberative secrecy (which is necessary to the free flow of ideas necessary for effective decision-making) and deliberative openness (which is necessary to meaningful judicial review).[196] The courts,

---

190   For example, Nova Scotia Civil Procedure Rule 37.10(e).

191   See, for example, *Apotex Inc. v. Alberta*, [1996] 7 W.W.R. 207, 182 A.R. 321 (Alta. Q.B.).

192   Portions of the following discussion are based on G. Steele, "Tribunal Counsel" (1997) 11 C.J.A.L.P. 57 at 91-94.

193   This appears to be what happened in *Khan v. College of Physicians & Surgeons (Ontario)* (1992), 9 O.R. (3d) 641, 11 Admin. L.R. (2d) 147, 97 D.L.R. (4th) 193 (Ont. C.A.), and *Jennifer's of Nova Scotia Inc. v. Clark* (1994), 136 N.S.R. (2d) 110 (N.S. C.A.).

194   *Québec (Commission des affaires sociales) c. Tremblay*, [1992] 1 S.C.R. 952, 90 D.L.R. (4th) 609 at 618-19, 3 Admin. L.R. (2d) 173 (S.C.C.). It is possible that the tribunal is protected by the Crown's traditional immunity from discovery, but many tribunals are not part of the Crown, and Crown immunity may in any event be inapplicable: see, for example, *Apotex Inc. v. Alberta*, [1996] 7 W.W.R. 207, 182 A.R. 321 (Alta. Q.B.).

195   *Glengarry Memorial Hospital v. Ontario (Pay Equity Hearings Tribunal)* (1993), 99 D.L.R. (4th) 682 (Ont. Div. Ct.), varied (1993), 99 D.L.R. (4th) 706 (Ont. Div. Ct.), leave to appeal to Ont. C.A. refused on natural justice issue. This case is discussed in detail in the Ellis/ Aterman and Hawkins articles, note 223 below, and R.E. Hawkins, "Behind Closed Doors I: The Substantive Problem—Full Boards, Consensus Tables and Caucus Cabals" (1996) 9 C.J.A.L.P. 267.

196   It appears that courts may also give some weight to a statutory provision stating that tribunal members are not compellable witnesses: *Ellis-Don Ltd. v. Ontario (Labour Relations Board)* (1992), 95 D.L.R. (4th) 56, 6 Admin. L.R. (2d) 318 (Ont. Div. Ct.), reversed (1994), 24 Admin. L.R. (2d) 122, 110 D.L.R. (4th) 731 (Ont. Div. Ct.), leave to appeal to S.C.C. denied (1994), 24 Admin. L.R. (2d) 122n (Ont. C.A.), leave to appeal refused (1995), 184 N.R. 320 (note) (S.C.C.). This non-compellability should be treated cautiously, however, and not used as a pretext to permit a tribunal to escape scrutiny for bias.

and academic commentators, have been equivocal about where the balance lies.[197]

Deliberative secrecy is premised on the assumption that the best decision-making comes out of a process in which judges are permitted to keep their private thoughts private. An incidental advantage of deliberative secrecy is that it tends to keep litigation focused on substantive issues. Every lawyer knows that procedure can be used for purposes other than speedy resolution on the merits. Deliberative secrecy prevents disputes from corkscrewing into routine inquiries about the resolution process. To put it bluntly, extensive inquiries into the decision-making process are disruptive.

The values served by deliberative openness are more straightforward: Justice must not only be done, but must be manifestly and undoubtedly be seen to be done.[198] It increases the confidence of the parties and the public in the decision-making process. It also produces better decisions.

By the very nature of judicial review, administrative tribunals cannot rely on deliberative secrecy to the same extent as courts. But what is the appropriate threshold that must be crossed? If the standard is set too low, then there is the very real danger that the tribunal will become the target of routine and disruptive attacks on its decision-making process. If the standard is set too high, real injustice could escape undetected.

A standard requiring clear evidence of bias seems too high,[199] while mere speculation or hearsay is too low.[200] Two intermediate standards are:

(a) A *prima facie* case. A *prima facie* case is one that is logically sufficient to establish, on a balance of probabilities, facts from which a reasonable apprehension of bias can reasonably be inferred.[201]

(b) A reasonable possibility. This standard is lower than a *prima facie* case, and would require the court to be satisfied of facts that justify

---

197 R. Ellis and P. Aterman, "Deliberative Secrecy and Adjudicative Independence: The *Glengarry* Precipice" (1993) 7 C.J.A.L.P. 171, are alarmed at the intrusion into deliberative secrecy. Still, they recognize that the courts will order discovery in some cases. Their "Protocol for Adjudicator Examinations" at 190-91, is interesting. Another view supporting more openness is R.E. Hawkins, "Behind Closed Doors II: The Operation Problem—Deliberative Secrecy, Statutory Immunity and Testimonial Privilege" (1996) 10 C.J.A.L.P. 39.

198 *Supra* note 3.

199 *Seliski v. Assn. of Naturopathic Physicians (British Columbia)* (1996), 36 Admin. L.R. (2d) 307 (B.C. S.C.).

200 Further inquiry was rejected in *Bettes v. Boeing Canada DeHavilland Division)* (1992), 10 O.R. (3d) 768, 8 Admin. L.R. (2d) 232 (Ont. Gen. Div.), affirmed [1993] O.L.R.B. Rep. 275 (Ont. Div. Ct.), leave to appeal to Ont. C.A. refused, where there was only hearsay evidence of improper influences; and in *Kuntz* and *Hammami*, note 182 above, where a majority of a five-judge bench concluded the allegations of bias were speculative. See also *Ross v. New Brunswick School District No. 15 Board of Education* (1990), 110 N.B.R. (2d) 107, 78 D.L.R. (4th) 392 (N.B. C.A.).

201 *Penton v. Métis Nation of Alberta Assn.* (1995), 29 Alta. L.R. (3d) 223, [1995] 8 W.W.R. 39, 171 A.R. 140 (Alta. Q.B.) comes close to formulating the test in these terms.

further inquiry.[202] The objective is to leave open promising lines of inquiry, while forestalling wild goose chases, red herrings and fishing expeditions.

In our view, the second option (reasonable possibility) is to be preferred, but it must be carefully handled. The difference between the two standards might best be illustrated by the *Glengarry Hospital* case.[203]

Briefly, a decision of the Ontario Pay Equity Tribunal contained a dissent. The dissenting member wrote that there had been, in his view, a breach of natural justice, but that his oath of office prevented him from saying what it was. The employer applied for discovery. On a standard of a *prima facie* case, the application may well have failed. The only evidence was the uncorroborated opinion of a single member of the panel (an opinion that, in the result, was rejected by the court). On a standard of a reasonable suspicion, however, the application would succeed, as indeed it did in the Ontario Divisional Court. Given the source of the suspicion, any reasonable person would want to inquire further.

10. Summary

The overriding principle of the rule against bias is to protect the administration of justice from disrepute. In order to function properly, a justice system has to be held in high esteem by the public. Few things will destroy public confidence in the administrative justice system more quickly than a sense that a decision-maker is biased. That is why the courts have moved decisively to quash tribunal decisions where there is a reasonable apprehension of bias.

The tests for bias are well-settled. For most situations, the "reasonable apprehension of bias" test, as stated in *Canada (National Energy Board)*, will be applied. For allegations of institutional bias, as in *Québec (Régie des permis d'alcools)*, this test is modified so that the reasonable observer has to have a apprehension of bias in a substantial number of cases. In addition, it is possible to argue that a tribunal's institutional arrangements give rise to a reasonable apprehension of bias because it lacks sufficient structural guarantees of independence. Finally, a much less restrictive test is applied to tribunals with a strong policy or legislative element, because it is appropriate and even necessary for members of such tribunals to have formed an opinion on contentious issues. The requirement, as stated in *Old St. Boniface*, is that the member be

---

202 Something akin to this test is expressed by the Nova Scotia Court of Appeal in *Waverley (Village) v. Nova Scotia (Acting Minister of Municipal Affairs)* (1994), 26 Admin. L.R. (2d) 302, 129 N.S.R. (2d) 298 at 303 (N.S. C.A.), leave to appeal refused (1995), 26 Admin. L.R. (2d) 302 (note), 140 N.S.R. (2d) 240 (note) (S.C.C.): "In either case, discovery or testimony, a proper evidentiary foundation must be created, generally by affidavit evidence, to establish that *valid reasons exist for concern* that there has been a want of natural justice or procedural fairness, or that the discretionary authority has been otherwise exceeded." (Emphasis added.)

203 *Supra* note 221.

"amenable to persuasion," or in other words, that the member not have an entirely closed mind.

The real difficulty in bias cases is establishing whether the test has been met. The courts have held repeatedly that each case must be evaluated on its own facts. The simplest case is where a tribunal member blurts something in the hearing room, and is recorded on tape. The offended party gets a copy of the transcript, and off to court they go. But this kind of straightforward bias case is relatively rare. On other occasions, a party has only an uneasy feeling that the deck is stacked against them, but is unable or unwilling to go about the difficult task of gathering evidence of some of the subtler forms of bias. Although the Supreme Court of Canada's cases on institutional bias and structural independence represent an astonishing new chapter in the law of bias, it may be that the cost and time involved in mounting a case of institutional bias or lack of structural independence will deter most litigants.[204]

11. Selected Bibliography

Arthurs, H.W., "The Three Faces of Justice – Bias in the Tripartite Tribunal" (1963) 28 Sask. Bar Rev. 147.

Bryden, P., "Structural Independence of Administrative Tribunals in the Wake of *Ocean Port*" (2003) 16 C.J.A.L.P. 125.

Canadian Bar Association, *Report of the Task Force on The Independence of Federal Administrative Tribunals and Agencies in Canada*, 1990.

Haigh, R. & Smith, J., "Independence after *Matsqui*?" (1998) 11 C.J.A.L.P. 101.

Hawkins, R.E., "Behind Closed Doors I: The Substantive Problem – Full Boards, Consensus Tables and Caucus Cabals" (1995-96) 9 C.J.A.L.P. 267.

Jones, D.P., "Comment on *P.P.G. Industries Canada* v. *The Attorney-General of Canada*" (1977) 55 Can. Bar Rev. 718.

Jones, D.P., "Institutional Bias: The Applicability of the Nemo Judex Rule to Two-Tier Decisions" (1977) 23 McGill L.J. 605.

Jones, D.P., "The *National Energy Board* Case and the Concept of Attitudinal Bias" (1977) 23 McGill L.J. 459.

Kligman, R., *Bias* (Markham, Ontario: Butterworths, 1998).

Kuttner, T.S., "Is the Doctrine of Bias Compatible with the Tri-Partite Labour Tribunal?" (1986) 19 Admin. L.R. 81.

Kuttner, T.S., "Bias and the Labour Boards Redux" (1978) 31 Admin. L.R. 216.

Lester, G.S., "Bias: How and When to Raise the Objection" (1997) 3 Admin. Agen. P. 49.

Mullan, D., "*Consolidated-Bathurst* and the *Dominion Stores Pension Fund* case: Different Approaches or Reconcilable Differences?" (1986-87) 21 Admin. L.R. 215.

---

204 See R. Haigh and J. Smith, "Independence After *Matsqui*?" (1998) 11 C.J.A.L.P. 125.

Report of the Committee on Ministers' Powers, (the "Donoughmore Committee") England (1932) at 76-79.

Sedgewick, R.M. Jr., "Disqualification on the Ground of Bias as Applied to Administrative Tribunals" (1945) 23 Can. Bar Rev. 453.

Shores, W. & Jardine, D., "Institutional Bias – A Sharpened Sword for Attacking the Administrative Structure of Tribunals" (1997) 6 R.A.L. 197.

Wyman, K., "The Independence of Administrative Tribunals in an Era of Ever Expansive Judicial Independence" (2001) 14 C.J.A.L.P. 61.

Yee, G., "Procedures in Dealing with Bias: the adjudicator's perspective" (1997) 3 Admin. Agen. P. 54.

11

Errors of Law on the Face of the Record

1. Introduction

The purpose of this chapter is to examine the anomalous[1] use of *certiorari* to correct certain intra-jurisdictional errors of law on the face of the record[2] of proceedings taken by a statutory delegate.

Although almost all grounds for judicial review concentrate on the jurisdiction of a statutory delegate, *certiorari* is also sometimes available to correct errors of law made by the delegate within its jurisdiction. This anomalous use of *certiorari* was referred to by Lord Sumner in *R. v. Nat Bell Liquors Ltd.*,[3] and resuscitated by Denning L.J. in *R. v. Northumberland Compensation Appeal Tribunal.*[4] In theory, this use of *certiorari* permits the court to make sure that all statutory delegates abide by the law of the land, which is conceived as being a unitary whole.[5]

An example of this ground of judicial review can be found in labour arbitration. The courts have often held that an arbitration board does not have any jurisdiction to err in its interpretation of an external statutory provision which arises in the course of the arbitration (although, as discussed below, careful attention must now be paid to identifying the appropriate standard of review, which if less stringent than correctness may have the practical result of the court's not in fact intervening). In *McLeod v. Egan*,[6] Laskin C.J.C. commented that:

---

1   "Anomalous" because this use of *certiorari* is the only example of judicial review which can be used to correct an error *within* jurisdiction. All other examples of judicial review require there to be some form of jurisdictional defect.

2   Note that the Federal Court has never required the alleged error to be disclosed on the face of the record. See s. 18 (pre-1992) and s. 18.1 (post-1991) (the latter reproduced in Appendix 5; see Appendix 5 of the Third Edition of this work for both pre- and post-1991 sections). For an excellent discussion of judicial review of decisions of federal boards, tribunals and commissions, see Sgayias, Kinnear, Rennie and Saunders, *Federal Court Practice 1998* (Scarborough: Carswell, 1998). Note also that s. 2(2) of the Ontario *Judicial Review Procedure Act*, R.S.O. 1990, c. J.1 (reproduced in Appendix 3) requires the error of law to be "on the face of the record" (although it extends the availability of the remedy to "*any* decision made in the exercise of any statutory power...", and not just those for which *certiorari* might have been available).

3   [1922] 2 A.C. 128 (Canada P.C.).

4   (1951), [1952] 1 K.B. 338 (Eng. C.A.), affirming (1950), [1951] 1 K.B. 711 (Eng. K.B.).

5   In other words, legal concepts do not have one meaning in the courts, and different meanings in administrative tribunals. See note 53.

6   (1974), [1975] 1 S.C.R. 517 (S.C.C.). See also: *Calgary (City) v. C.U.P.E., Calgary Civic Employees Local 37* (1992), 2 Alta. L.R. (3d) 389 (Alta. Q.B.), reversed (1994), 149 A.R. 313 (Alta. C.A.), where the court held that the arbitrator's interpretation of the external statutory provision had to be correct, not just not patently unreasonable; *Toronto Transit Commission v. A.T.U., Local 113* (1992), 6 Admin. L.R. (2d) 15 (Ont. Div. Ct.), where the arbitrator's decision was protected by the patently unreasonable doctrine and a privative clause; *O.S.S.T.F., District 53 v. Haldimand Board of Education* (1991), 6 Admin. L.R. (2d) 177 (Ont. Div. Ct.), where the privative clause did not protect the arbitrator's decision because the governing legislation provided that a collective agreement could not conflict with the provisions of certain human rights statutes; and *Ontario (Legal Aid Plan) v. O.P.S.E.U.* (1991), 5 Admin. L.R. (2d) 113 (Ont. C.A.) where the Ontario Court of Appeal quashed a common employer declaration by the Ontario Labour Relations Board because it had not properly construed and applied the regulation governing the operation of different aspects of the *Legal Aid Plan*.

Although the issue before the arbitrator arose by virtue of a grievance under a collective agreement, it became necessary for him to go outside the collective agreement and to construe and apply a statute which was not a projection of the collective bargaining relations of the parties but a general public enactment of the superior provincial legislature. On such a matter, there can be no policy of curial deference to the adjudication of an arbitrator, chosen by the parties or in accordance with their prescriptions, who interprets a document which is in language to which they have subscribed as a domestic charter to govern their relationship. . . .

That is not to say that an arbitrator, in the course of his duty, should refrain from construing a statute which is involved in the issues that have been brought before him. In my opinion, he must construe, but at the risk of having his construction set aside by a court as being wrong.

A second example of this ground of review can be found in the decision of the Supreme Court of Canada in *Canada (Attorney General) v. Mossop*,[7] where the Court corrected the interpretation of the Human Rights Tribunal about whether prohibition against discrimination on the basis of "family status" under the *Canadian Human Rights Act* applied to same-sex couples. La Forest J. noted that:[8]

[The superior expertise of an *ad hoc* human rights tribunal] does not extend to questions of law such as the one at issue in this case. These are ultimately matters within the province of the judiciary, and involve concepts of statutory interpretation and general legal reasoning which the courts must be supposed competent to perform. The courts cannot abdicate this duty to the tribunal. They must, therefore, review the tribunal's decisions on questions of this kind on the basis of correctness, not on a standard of reasonability.

In practice, the availability of judicial review to correct errors of law on the face of the record is subject to three complications. First, the availability of judicial review to correct errors of law may be restricted by the enactment of a privative clause.[9] Secondly, the appropriate standard of review may be less stringent than correctness, which may in practical terms prevent the court

---

7   [1993] 1 S.C.R. 554, 13 Admin. L.R. (2d) 1 (S.C.C.). For other examples in the human rights context where the courts have considered whether there was an error of law on the face of the record, see *Gould v. Yukon Order of Pioneers* (1996), 37 Admin. L.R. (2d) 1 (S.C.C.); *Attis v. New Brunswick District No. 15 Board of Education* (1996), 37 Admin. L.R. (2d) 131 (S.C.C.); *Berg v. University of British Columbia*, [1993] 2 S.C.R. 353 (S.C.C.), additional reasons at (June 30, 1993), Doc. 22638, 22640 (S.C.C.); *University of Alberta v. Alberta (Human Rights Commission)*, [1992] 2 S.C.R. 1103 (S.C.C.); and *Zurich Insurance Co. v. Ontario (Human Rights Commission)*, [1992] 2 S.C.R. 321 (S.C.C.). Note that some of these cases involve appeals from human rights adjudicators, rather than applications for judicial review.

8   *Ibid.* at 28 [Admin. L.R.]

9   For a more detailed analysis of privative clauses and other restrictions on judicial review, see Chapter 12.

from remedying what might otherwise be characterized as an error of law. Finally, the availability of review on this ground is always subject to the court's inherent discretion to refuse prerogative remedies. All three of these restrictions seriously complicate this area of administrative law in Canada, and will be considered in detail in the rest of this chapter and the next chapter.

In order to understand the availability of judicial review for an intra-jurisdictional error of law, one must consider:

(a)   the importance of the distinction between errors of law which are not jurisdictional in nature, and errors which deprive a statutory delegate of its jurisdiction;

(b)   the general limitations on *certiorari* as a remedy;

(c)   the extent of the "record";

(d)   the distinction between an error of "law" and other kinds of errors (such as errors of fact);

(e)   the effect of a privative clause to prevent review of errors of law; and

(f)   the standard(s) of review applicable to this ground.

2. The Importance of the Distinction Between Jurisdictional and Non-Jurisdictional Errors of Law

Although the courts' emphasis in the last few years on the standard of review[10] may have made it unfashionable to speak of "jurisdictional" and "non-jurisdictional" errors, it is nevertheless still important to take account of the vast jurisprudence relating to this distinction in order to understand the ambit of the availability of error of law on the face of the record as a ground for judicial review.

All jurisdictional errors necessarily involve an error of law, although not all errors of law prevent a statutory delegate from acquiring jurisdiction or cause the statutory delegate to lose jurisdiction. Unfortunately, no completely satisfactory test has ever been developed for distinguishing between jurisdictional and non-jurisdictional errors, although the Supreme Court of Canada originally developed the "pragmatic and functional" approach to determine the intention of the legislature about what the statutory delegate was to have authority to do or decide.[11]

However difficult it may be to make the distinction between jurisdictional and intra-jurisdictional errors, the distinction is still important for at least five

---

10   See Chapter 12.

11   See *Syndicat des employés de production du Québec & de l'Acadie v. Canada (Labour Relations Board)*, [1984] 2 S.C.R. 412 (S.C.C.); *Syndicat national des employés de la commission scolaire régionale de l'Outaouais v. U.E.S., local 298*, [1988] 2 S.C.R. 1048 (S.C.C.); *W.W. Lester (1978) Ltd. v. U.A., Local 740*, [1990] 3 S.C.R. 644, 48 Admin. L.R. 1 (S.C.C.); and *Canada (Attorney General) v. P.S.A.C.* (1991), 48 Admin. L.R. 161 (S.C.C.) (hereinafter *Econosult*).

reasons. First, for constitutional reasons, the existence of a privative clause will generally not prevent judicial review where the jurisdiction of the delegate is in question (although there may be questions about the applicable standard of review even in this category of case); but the presence of a privative clause will generally hallmark the legislature's intention for the courts to use a more deferential standard of review with respect to mere (i.e. non-jurisdictional) errors of law on the face of the record. Secondly, affidavits and other evidence are admissible if necessary to prove the existence of a jurisdictional error; but they cannot be considered by the court if a non-jurisdictional error of law is involved.[12] Thirdly, the court's anomalous power to correct intra-jurisdictional errors is limited to errors of law only, and does not apply to errors of fact (although note that factual matters may give rise to a jurisdictional error, particularly in the context of the preliminary or collateral fact doctrine). Fourthly, this anomalous use of *certiorari* can only correct errors of law which appear on the face of the record, however that is defined, whereas jurisdictional errors do not have to be so disclosed. Finally, other remedies besides this anomalous use of *certiorari*[13] may not be available to correct intra-jurisdictional errors, although other remedies may sometimes be available to review jurisdictional errors.[14]

3. Inherent Limitations on the Availability of Certiorari as a Remedy to Correct Non-Jurisdictional Errors of Law

Because errors of law on the face of the record can sometimes be corrected by *certiorari*, this ground for judicial review will generally only be available to the extent to which *certiorari* is available as a remedy.

(a) The Ambit of Certiorari Against Administrative Decisions

Formerly, it was thought that *certiorari* was only available against judicial or quasi-judicial bodies, and not against merely administrative ones. However, at least since the *Nicholson v. Haldimand-Norfolk (Regional Municipality) Comissioners of Police*[15] and *Martineau v. Matsqui Institution (No. 2)*[16] cases, the ambit of *certiorari* has been expanded to supervise the procedural fairness of merely administrative bodies. In principle, therefore, *certiorari* should be available to correct errors of law committed by merely administrative bodies,

---

12 See for example *I.B.E.W., Local 424 v. TNL Industrial Contractors Ltd.*, [1998] 10 W.W.R. 47 (Alta. Q.B.).

13 For example, by a declaration, which will not quash the delegate's decision. See *Punton v. Ministry of Pensions & National Insurance (No. 2)* (1963), [1964] 1 W.L.R. 226 (Eng. C.A.).

14 Although the courts' recent restrictive approach to collateral attacks may in at least some cases have the practical effect of restricting the availability of other remedies even for jurisdictional errors. See Chapter 14, for a discussion of collateral attacks.

15 (1978), [1979] 1 S.C.R. 311 (S.C.C.).

16 (1979), [1980] 1 S.C.R. 602 (S.C.C.).

and should not be restricted to those which are exercising judicial or quasi-judicial functions.[17]

(b) Is a Statutory Delegate Involved?

Certiorari is also generally only available against the exercise of a statutory power. Thus, in *Alberta (Minister of Education) v. C.S.A. of A.*,[18] the Alberta Court of Appeal held that *certiorari* was not available to supervise the exercise of judicial powers created by an agreement. The same difficulty has long plagued attempts to obtain *certiorari* against labour arbitration boards. On the one hand, some labour arbitration boards are established by statute, and *certiorari* will[19] be available to correct at least some errors of law made on the face of their records. On the other hand, other labour legislation merely provides the vehicle through which collective agreements are reached, including a statutory obligation to include an arbitration clause in such agreements. The courts have vacillated about the availability of *certiorari* to correct errors of law committed by such consensual arbitration boards. This point appears to have been settled affirmatively by the Supreme Court of Canada in *Roberval Express Ltd. v. Transport Drivers Warehousemen & General Workers' Union, Local 106.*[20] This decision in effect converts many labour arbitrations into statutory proceedings, thereby bringing them within the ambit of *certiorari*.[21]

---

17 S. 2(2) of the Ontario *Judicial Review Procedure Act* R.S.O. 1990, c. J-1 (reproduced in Appendix 3) specifically grants the court power to review "*any* decision made in the exercise of a statutory power of decision to the extent it is not limited or precluded by the Act conferring such power of decision" for error of law on the face of the record.

18 (1976), 70 D.L.R. (3d) 696 at 699 (Alta. C.A.). See also the reasoning of Clement J.A. in *Inland Cement Industries Ltd. v. C.L.G.W., Local 359*, [1981] 3 W.W.R. 65 (Alta. C.A.), to the effect that arbitration boards constituted under the *Labour Relations Act*, S.A. 1980, c. 72 [now *Labour Relations Code*, R.S.A. 2000, c. L-1], are indeed statutory, following the Ontario decision in *International Nickel Co. v. Rivando*, [1956] O.R. 379 (Ont. C.A.). In 1977, the words "or otherwise" were removed from the *Alberta Labour Act*, thereby putting the statutory nature of labour arbitration boards beyond question in this province. This realization would have pre-empted a considerable part of the subsequent judgment by Kerans J.A. in *Suncor Inc. v. McMurray Independent Oil Workers, Local 1* (1982), [1983] 1 W.W.R. 604 (Alta. C.A.), discussed *infra*. See also *R. v. Visitors to Lincoln's Inn, ex p. Persaud and Colder* (*The Times*, 26 January 1993) and *R. v. Birmingham City Council, ex p. Dredger* (*The Times*, 28 January 1993), both discussed by J. Mulcahy in "Scope of Judicial Review: Susceptible Bodies" (1993) 2 R.A.L. 110.

19 In the absence of an effective privative clause.

20 [1982] 2 S.C.R. 888 (S.C.C.), reversing its previous decision in *Howe Sound Co. v. International Union of Mine, Mill & Smelter Workers (Can.), Local 663*, [1962] S.C.R. 318 (S.C.C.), which held that there could be a statutory arbitrator only if the parties were compelled by statute to submit their disputes to that person, and did not have the option of settling those disputes by some other method. Such compulsion was the case in *U.S.W.A. v. Port Arthur Shipbuilding Co.* (1968), [1969] S.C.R. 85 (S.C.C.), and *International Nickel Co. v. Rivando*, [1956] O.R. 379 (Ont. C.A.).

21 In Alberta, s. 145(2) of the *Labour Relations Code*, R.S.A. 2000, c. L-1 and s. 63(2) of the *Public Service Employee Relations Act*, R.S.A. 2000, c. P-43 specifically allow for *certiorari* and *mandamus* against an arbitration or adjudication award under a collective agreement governed by either of those Acts. However, not all collective agreements are governed by these two Acts (for example, those under the *Colleges Act*, R.S.A. 2000, c. C-19 and *Technical*

Nevertheless, *certiorari* is still not available against non-statutory decisions. In the arbitration context, it is important to remember the existence of the separate common law remedy to quash and remit a consensual arbitrator's decision for misconduct, as well as the court's appellate and review jurisdiction under the Alberta *Arbitration Act*[22] (both of which are discussed below). In purely non-statutory contexts, private law remedies may have to be used instead of *certiorari*,[23] and those remedies may or may not be available to correct a mere intra-jurisdictional error of law. This result would seem to be perverse, particularly in those jurisdictions which have amalgamated the old administrative law remedies into a uniform application for judicial review.[24]

4. The Record

As errors of law must be apparent upon the face of the record, the extent of the record is a key consideration.

What, then, constitutes the record? Lord Denning said this in the *R. v. Northumberland Compensation Appeal Tribunal* case:[25]

> It has been said to consist of all those documents which are kept by the tribunal for a permanent memorial and testimony of their proceedings: see *Blackstone's Commentaries*, Vol. III, at p. 24. But it must be noted that, whenever there was any question as to what should, or should not be, included in the record of any tribunal, the Court of King's Bench used to determine it. It did it in this way: When the tribunal sent their record to the King's Bench in answer to the writ of *certiorari*, this return was examined, and if it was defective or incom-

---

Institutes Act, R.S.A. 1000, c. T-3, so there may be a question about the availability of administrative law remedies with respect to arbitration awards under those collective agreements.

22   R.S.A. 2000, c. A-43, ss. 44 & 45.

23   An exception may occur where the procedural rules for obtaining *certiorari* have been merged into a broader statutory application for judicial review. See, *e.g.*, the decision of Hunt J. in *Kaplan v. Canadian Institute of Actuaries* (1994), 28 Admin. L.R. (2d) 265 (Alta. Q.B.), affirmed (1997), 50 Admin. L.R. (2d) 72 (Alta. C.A.), additional reasons at (1998), 60 Alta. L.R. (3d) 251 (Alta. C.A.), leave to appeal to S.C.C. refused (1998), 227 N.R. 89 (note) (S.C.C.).

24   For example, in Alberta, Rule 753.14 (reproduced in Appendix 4) contemplates that a return may be filed – either voluntarily, or pursuant to a court order – where the application for judicial review asks for "relief other than an order to set aside a decision or act". In such a case, it seems likely that the court would consider any alleged error of law disclosed by the return, even though the form of relief sought was not in the nature of *certiorari*.

25   (1951), [1952] 1 K.B. 338 at 352 (Eng. C.A.). See also the decision in *Baldwin & Francis Ltd. v. Patent Appeal Tribunal*, [1959] 2 All E.R. 433 at 445 (U.K. H.L.); *Stedelbauer Chevrolet Oldsmobile Ltd. v. Alberta (Industrial Relations Board)* (1967), 59 W.W.R. 269 at 278 (Alta. C.A.), affirmed (1968), [1969] S.C.R. 137 (S.C.C.); *R. v. Preston Supplementary Benefits Appeal Tribunal*, [1975] 1 W.L.R. 624, 628 (Eng. C.A.); *R. v. Knightsbridge Crown Court*, [1982] Q.B. 304 (Eng. Q.B.). The most comprehensive Alberta case is *Alberta (Labour Relations Board) v. I.B.E.W., Local 1007* (1991), 5 Admin. L.R. (2d) 301, 83 Alta. L.R. (2d) 253 (Alta. Q.B.). For a consideration of the common law position, see Abel, "Materials for Consideration in *Certiorari*" (1963) 15 U. of T.L.J. 102.

plete it was quashed: see *Apsley's* case,[26] *Rex v. Levermore*,[27] and *Ashley's* case,[28] or, alternatively, the tribunal might be ordered to complete it: *Williams v. Bagot*[29] and *Rex v. Warnford*.[30] It appears that the Court of King's Bench always insisted that the record should contain, or recite, the document or information which initiated the proceedings and thus gave the tribunal its jurisdiction; and also the document which contained their adjudication. Thus in the old days the record sent up by the justices had, in the case of a conviction, to recite the information in its precise terms; and in the case of an order which had been decided by quarter sessions by way of appeal, the record had to set out the order appealed from: see *Anon*.[31] The record had also to set out the adjudication, but it was never necessary to set out the reasons (see *South Cadbury (Inhabitants) v. Braddon, Somerset (Inhabitants)*)[32] nor the evidence, save in the case of convictions. Following these cases, I think the record must contain at least the document which initiates the proceedings; the pleadings, if any; and the adjudication; but not the evidence, nor the reasons, unless the tribunal chooses to incorporate them. If the tribunal does state its reasons, and those reasons are wrong in law, *certiorari* lies to quash the decision.

A nice question arises whether the record includes the evidence presented to a statutory delegate during the course of its proceedings. On the one hand, the decision in *Farrell v. British Columbia (Workmen's Compensation Board)*,[33] specifically holds that the record consists only of the initiating document, the pleadings (if any), and the adjudication (including the reasons if incorporated therein), but not the evidence or the supporting documents referred to in the decision. In Alberta, the *Rules of Court*[34] effectively deem the following documents to be part of the record which the decision-maker is required to return to the Court of Queen's Bench in an application for *certiorari*: the judgment, order or decision (as the case may be) and reasons therefor, together with the process commencing the proceedings, the evidence and all exhibits filed (if any), and all things touching the matter, together with the notice of motion for *certiorari*. Accordingly, it appears that the definition of the record has been extended in Alberta to include all of the evidence.[35] To

---

26 (1648), Sty. 86.

27 (1700), 1 Salk. 146.

28 (1697), 2 Salk. 479.

29 (1824), 4 Dow. & Ry. K.B. 315.

30 (1825), 5 Dow. & Ry. K.B. 489.

31 (1697), 2 Salk. 479.

32 (1710), 2 Salk. 607.

33 (1960), 26 D.L.R. (2d) 185 (B.C. C.A.), affirmed (1961), [1962] S.C.R. 48 (S.C.C.).

34 Part 56.1 in civil matters (reproduced in Appendix 4); R. 831 in criminal matters.

35 In *Woodward Stores (Westmount) Ltd. v. Alberta (Assessment Appeal Board, Division No. 1)* (1976), 69 D.L.R. (3d) 450 (Alta. T.D.), McDonald J. queried whether such an extension to the record could be accomplished by Rule of Court, in light of the fact that such an extension might affect the substantive law which could not be changed by rule. This possible

this extent, therefore, it may be possible to use the extended record in Alberta to demonstrate errors of law which can be corrected by the anomalous use of *certiorari*. On the other hand, administrative bodies often do not make verbatim transcripts or tape recordings of their proceedings, and are generally under no duty to do so.[36] As a result, it may not be possible to show an error of law on the face of even the extended record: the delegate's decision may still be "the inscrutable face of the Sphinx",[37] immune from judicial review.

Secondly, a similar problem relates to whether notes taken by a statutory delegate form part of the record. These notes are not themselves evidence, but may be summaries of the evidence. In *Walker v. Keating*,[38] the Appeal Division of the Nova Scotia Supreme Court declined to include the hand-written notes of the chairman of a three-member tribunal as part of the record. By contrast, the Trial Division of that same court subsequently did order the notes of a sole arbitrator to be included in the record in *Construction Assn. Management Labour Bureau Ltd. v. I.B.E.W., Local 625*,[39] apparently because there could be no possibility of a difference in the notes taken by the various members of the tribunal. On the other hand, this last case holds that copies of decisions and other authorities submitted to the tribunal do not form part of its record, even though they are "other papers or documents in the proceeding"[40] and "touch the matter"[41] being questioned by *certiorari*. Oddly, the dissenting decision of a multi-member statutory body has been held not to constitute part of the

---

problem no longer exists because s. 63(2) of the *Judicature Act*, R.S.A. 2000, c. J-2, validates the *Rules of Court* notwithstanding that any provision therein may affect substantive rights.

36   *I.A.M., Local 1722 v. Northgate International Trucks* (June 11, 1987), Doc. 8703-10088 (Alta. Q.B.) *per* Veit J.; *Rhéaume v. Canada* (1992), 11 Admin. L.R. (2d) 124 (Fed. C.A.), leave to appeal to S.C.C. denied (1993), 11 Admin. L.R. (2d) 126n (S.C.C.); *Kandiah v. Canada (Minister of Employment & Immigration)* (1992), 6 Admin. L.R. (2d) 42, 141 N.R. 232 (Fed. C.A.). Compare the entitlement to a transcript of court proceedings: *Janitzki v. Canada (Health & Welfare)* (1991), 128 N.R. 394, 398 (Fed. C.A.), leave to appeal refused (1992), 138 N.R. 405 (note) (S.C.C.); *Tung v. Canada (Minister of Employment & Immigration)* (1991), 124 N.R. 388, 391 (Fed. C.A.). On the question of whether a party is entitled to make a verbatim record of the proceedings at its own expense, see: *Alberta (Labour Relations Board) v. I.B.E.W., Local 1007* (1991), 83 Alta. L.R. (2d) 253 (Alta. Q.B.); and *Eastern Provincial Airways Ltd. v. Canada (Labour Relations Board)* (1983), [1984] 1 F.C. 732 (Fed. C.A.). If proceedings are tape recorded, the practice in Alberta appears to be to include the untranscribed tape as part of the record returned to the court. See *Alberta (Labour Relations Board) v. I.B.E.W., Local 1007* (1991), 5 Admin. L.R. (2d) 301 (Alta. Q.B.); *A.U.P.E. v. R.* (1978), 11 A.R. 1 (Alta. T.D.); *Fort McMurray School District No. 2833 v. Fort McMurray Roman Catholic Separate School District No. 32* (1984), 53 A.R. 191 at 196, 9 D.L.R. (4th) 224 (Alta. Q.B.), affirmed (1985), 71 A.R. 251 (Alta. C.A.); *Blagdon v. Canada (Public Service Commission Appeal Board)* (1975), [1976] 1 F.C. 615 (Fed. C.A.). However, the court has held that no jurisdictional error arises where the tape is unintelligible: see *B.S.O.I.W., Local 725 v. Canron Inc.* (1983), 43 A.R. 299 (Alta. Q.B.).

37   *R. v. Nat Bell Liquors Ltd.* (1922), 65 D.L.R. 1 at 25 (Canada P.C.), *per* Lord Sumner.

38   (1973), 6 N.S.R. (2d) 1 (N.S. C.A.). See also *Yorke v. Northside-Victoria District School Board* (1992), 6 Admin. L.R. (2d) 183 (N.S. C.A.). The same result was reached in *Alberta (Labour Relations Board) v. I.B.E.W., Local 1007* (1991), 5 Admin L.R. (2d) 301 (Alta. Q.B.).

39   (1983), 34 C.P.C. 65 (N.S. T.D.).

40   Nova Scotia rule.

41   Alberta Rule 753.13 (reproduced in Appendix 4).

record.[42] In principle, correspondence between members of a statutory body, written after the hearing for the purpose of discussing the issues, should not form part of the record, because it does not affect the proceedings at the hearing. If such documents exist, the person making the return to the court cannot sign the certificate as drafted in Rule 753.13,[43] and should probably alter the certificate to reflect that certain listed documents in his possession are not properly returnable to the court as part of the record. At least such a procedure discloses the existence of such materials, and leaves it open to the judge to determine whether they are part of the record.

Thirdly, it is sometimes possible to extend the record by agreement. As Lord Denning noted in the *R. v. Northumberland Compensation Appeal Tribunal* case:[44]

> Notwithstanding the strictness of the rule that the error of law must appear on the face of the record, the parties could always by agreement overcome this difficulty. If they both desired a ruling of the Court of King's Bench on a point of law which had been decided by the tribunal, but which had not been entered on the record, the parties could agree that the question should be argued and determined as if it were expressed in the order. The first case I have found in which this was done was in 1792, *Rex v. Essex*,[45] but thereafter it was quite common. It became a regular practice for parties to supplement the record by affidavits disclosing the points of law that had been decided by the tribunal. This course was only taken if no one objected. It seems to have been adopted by litigants as a convenient alternative to asking the tribunal to make a speaking order. Thus, in the numerous cases on the validity of a sewer's rate, it was the regular course of proceeding for affidavits to be lodged stating the objections in law to the rate; and the case was decided on the objections stated in the affidavits: see, for instance, *Rex v. Tower Hamlets*.[46] Recent cases such as *Rex v. West Riding of Yorkshire Justices*[47] and *General Medical Council v. Spackman*[48] show that the practice continues today. The explanation of all these cases is, I think, that the affidavits are treated by consent as if they were part of the record and make it into a speaking order.

---

42   *Regina (City) v. A.T.U., Local 588* (1975), 61 D.L.R. (3d) 376 (Sask. Q.B.), affirmed (1976), 67 D.L.R. (3d) 533 (Sask. C.A.); *Manitoba Telephone System v. Greater Winnipeg Cablevision Ltd.* (1984), 5 D.L.R. (4th) 28 at 33 (Man. C.A.). However, counsel often puts the dissenting reasons before the court by affidavit. For a different view, see *Milan v. Cominco Ltd.* (November 28, 1972), Morrow J. (N.W.T. S.C.) (unreported).

43   Reproduced in Appendix 4.

44   (1951), [1952] 1 K.B. 338 at 353 (Eng. C.A.).

45   (1792), 4 Term Rep. 591.

46   (1829), 9 B. & C. 517.

47   [1910] 2 K.B. 192.

48   [1943] A.C. 627 (U.K. H.L.), affirming *R. v. General Medical Council*, [1942] 2 K.B. 261 (Eng. C.A.).

This quotation contemplates agreement in the context of the application for judicial review. Conceivably, the parties to an administrative proceeding might agree at the outset of those proceedings that certain material (such as the chairman's notes) will constitute the record, and therefore will become part of any return to the court on an application for *certiorari*.

If there is doubt about whether something should be included in the return, or whether the return is complete, the proper procedure is to apply to the court for a determination of this question prior to the hearing of the application for judicial review. Similarly, the court may in an appropriate case dispense with filing unnecessary parts of the return.[49] In other cases, it may be necessary to obtain a court order to seal the return to prevent other people accessing it inappropriately.

Finally, in proceedings which are governed by the *Federal Courts Act*, both divisions of the Court may grant relief if the federal board, commission or other tribunal "erred in law in making a decision or an order, *whether or not the error appears on the face of the record*".[50]

5. Errors of Law Versus Errors of Fact

As its name implies, the anomalous use of *certiorari* to quash errors of law on the face of the record requires there to be an error of law, and not some other type of mistake. Thus, *certiorari* will not issue to correct an error of fact.[51] Nevertheless, what constitutes an "error of law" is to be widely construed, and probably has a meaning similar to the phrase used for determining the right of appeal on a point of law.

(a) What is an Error of "Law"?

In his fourth edition, Wade[52] described the distinction as follows:

> There is only one clear and logical point at which the line [between errors of law and errors of fact] can be drawn, and it has been recognized in many judgments. This is that questions of fact are the primary facts of the particular case which have to be established before the law can be applied, the "facts which are observed by the witnesses and proved by testimony", to which should be added any facts of

---

49 For example, see Alberta Rule 753.14(2), which codifies the existing common law on this point (reproduced in Appendix 4).

50 S. 18.1(4)(c) (emphasis added), which applies to applications that go to the Trial Division. S. 28(2) extends this to applications which go directly to the Federal Court of Appeal: both sections are reproduced in Appendix 5.

51 See *R. v. Criminal Injuries Comp. Bd.; Ex parte Staten*, [1972] 1 W.L.R. 569 (Div. Ct.). This of course assumes that the error of fact is made within the delegate's jurisdiction, and is not a preliminary, collateral or other matter upon which the delegate's jurisdiction depends. Further, in *Blanchard* (discussed below), the Supreme Court of Canada (*per* Lamer J.) suggested that an unreasonable finding of fact could constitute a jurisdictional error.

52 *Administrative Law*, 4th ed. (Oxford: Clarendon Press, 1977) at 775. For a lengthier discussion, see pp. 946-50 of Wade's, 7th ed. (Oxford: Clarendon Press, 1994).

common knowledge of which the court will take notice without proof. Whether these facts, once established, satisfy some legal definition or requirement is a question of law, for the question then is how to interpret and apply the law to those established facts. If the question is whether some building is a "house" within the meaning of the Housing Acts, its location, condition, purpose of use and so forth are questions of fact. But once these facts are established, the question whether it counts as a house within the meaning of the Act is a question of law . . .

In principle, therefore, an appeal on a point of law should be available on every question of legal interpretation arising after the primary facts have been established. It ought to cover all legal "inferences from facts", as they are often called. It should cover all questions of causation. But the courts have laid down a narrower doctrine, designed to give greater latitude to tribunals where there is room for difference of opinion. The rule is that the application of a legal definition or principle to ascertained facts is erroneous in point of law only if the conclusion reached by the tribunal is unreasonable. If it is within the range of interpretations within which different persons might reasonably reach different conclusions, the court will hold that there is no error of law.

While this quotation from *Wade* focuses on what constitutes an error of law in the context of an appeal, similar considerations logically should apply to determine what constitutes an error of law in the context of an application for judicial review.[53] To the extent that the quotation refers to "unreasonableness" as a basis for determining whether there is an error of law, this probably belongs more appropriately in a discussion about the standard which the court will use in reviewing an alleged error. It does, however, raise the issue about the extent to which the courts should inexorably apply their views about what the law is, rather than allow the statutory delegate to determine that question or have a different view, or conclude that the legislature intended some other meaning to be given to the legal phrase in question.[54]

---

53   For some time, there was doubt about whether the Supreme Court's decisions in *Pezim v. British Columbia (Superintendent of Brokers)* (1994), 22 Admin. L.R. (2d) 1 (S.C.C.) and *Canada (Director of Investigation & Research) v. Southam Inc.* (1997), 50 Admin. L.R. (2d) 199 (S.C.C.) [hereafter *Southam*] applied only to appeals, or also to applications for judicial review. In *Pushpanathan v. Canada (Minister of Employment & Immigration)*, [1998] 1 S.C.R. 982 (S.C.C.), reasons modified [1998] 1 S.C.R. 1222 (S.C.C.), the Court made it clear that the same considerations apply to both vehicles. Accordingly, the same uniformity should apply to determining what constitutes an "error of law."

54   See Evans, *et al., Administrative Law Cases, Text, and Materials*, 4th ed. (Toronto: Edmond Montgomery Publications Ltd., 1995) at 760, and their reference to the decision in *National Labour Relations Board v. Hearst Publications*, 322 US 111 (U.S. Sup. Ct., 1944) and *Cormier v. Alberta (Human Rights Commission)* (1984), 14 D.L.R. (4th) 55 (Alta. Q.B.); see also Evans, *et al., Administrative Law Cases, Text and Materials*, 5th ed. by D.J. Mullan (Toronto: Edmond Montgomery Publications Ltd., 2003), c. 9.

As the Supreme Court of Canada noted in *Southam*[55] (which also involved a statutory appeal, rather than an application for judicial review), it may be very difficult to determine whether a particular alleged error is an error of law, an error of fact, or a mixed error of law and fact (and the correct characterization of the error will probably have significant consequences for the determining the appropriate standard of review):

> The parties vigorously dispute the nature of the problem before the Tribunal. The appellants say that the problem is one of fact. The respondent insists that the problem is one of law. In my view, the problem is one of mixed law and fact.
>
> Section 12(1) of the *Competition Tribunal Act* contemplates a tripartite classification of questions before the Tribunal into questions of law, questions of fact, and questions of mixed law and fact. Briefly stated, questions of law are questions about what the correct legal test is; questions of fact are questions about what actually took place between the parties; and questions of mixed law and fact are questions about whether the facts satisfy the legal tests. A simple example will illustrate these concepts. In the law of tort, the question what "negligence" means is a question of law. The question whether the defendant did this or that is a question of fact. And, once it has been decided that the applicable standard is one of negligence, the question whether the defendant satisfied the appropriate standard of care is a question of mixed law and fact. *I recognize, however, that the distinction between law on the one hand and mixed law and fact on the other is difficult. On occasion, what appears to be mixed law and fact turns out to be law, or vice versa.*
>
> For example, the majority of the British Columbia Court of Appeal in *Pezim, supra*, concluded that it was an error of law to regard newly acquired information on the value of assets as a "material change" in the affairs of a company. It was common ground in that case that the proper test was whether the information constituted a material change; the argument was about whether the acquisition of information of a certain kind qualified as such a change. To some extent, then, the question resembled one of mixed law and fact. But the question was one of law, in part because the words in question were present in a statutory provision and questions of statutory interpretation are generally questions of law, but also because the point in controversy was one that might potentially arise in many cases in the future: the argument was about kinds of information and not merely about the particular information that was at issue in that case. The rule on which the British Columbia Securities Commission seemed to rely – that newly acquired information about the value of assets can constitute a material change – was a matter of law, because it had the potential to apply widely to many cases.

---

55   (1997), 50 Admin. L.R. (2d) 199 at 212-15 (S.C.C.).

By contrast, the matrices of fact at issue in some cases are so particular, indeed so unique, that decisions about whether they satisfy legal tests do not have any great precedential value. If a court were to decide that driving at a certain speed on a certain road under certain conditions was negligent, its decision would not he any great value as a precedent. *In short, as the level of generality of the challenged proposition approaches utter particularity, the matter approaches pure application, and hence draws nigh to being an unqualified question of mixed law and fact.* See R.P. Kerans, *Standards of Review Employed by Appellate Courts* (1994), at pp. 103-108. *Of course, it is not easy to say precisely where the line should be drawn; though in most cases it should be sufficiently clear whether the dispute is over a general proposition that might qualify as a principle of law or over a very particular set of circumstances that is not apt to be of much interest to judges and lawyers in the future.*

Part of the confusion in this case arises from the fact that the parties are arguing about two different questions. On the surface, it appears that the parties agree about the law: both say that, in determining the dimensions of the relevant market, the Tribunal must consider indirect evidence about cross-elasticity of demand. No one quarrels with the Tribunal's understanding of the kinds of indirect evidence it should consider.

However, the respondent says that, having informed itself correctly on the law, the Tribunal proceeded nevertheless to ignore certain kinds of indirect evidence. Because the Tribunal must be judged according to what it does and not according to what it says, the import of the respondent's submission is that the Tribunal erred in law. After all, if a decision-maker says that the correct test requires him or her to consider A, B, C, and D, but in fact the decision-maker considers only A, B, and C, then the outcome is as if he or she had applied a law that required consideration of only A, B, and C. If the correct test requires him or her to consider D as well, then the decision-maker has in effect applied the wrong law, and so has made an error of law.

The appellants, for their part, maintain that the Tribunal considered all the relevant kinds of indirect evidence, including the kinds that the respondent says it ignored. Accordingly, the appellants argue that if the Tribunal erred, it can only have been in applying the correct legal test to the facts. Such an error, say the appellants, is an error of fact. . . .

Both positions, so far as they go, are correct. If the Tribunal did ignore items of evidence that the law requires it to consider, then the Tribunal erred in law. Similarly, if the Tribunal considered all the mandatory kinds of evidence but still reached the wrong conclusion, then its error was one of mixed law and fact. The question, then, becomes whether the Tribunal erred in the way that the respondent says it erred. . . . [Emphasis added.]

To the extent that the *Southam* decision makes the distinction between the three categories of errors for the purpose of determining the applicable standard of review, rather than as a ground of review, this is discussed more thoroughly later in this chapter and in the next chapter. For the moment, the important thing is to try to determine what constitutes an error of law which can, at least potentially, be corrected by *certiorari*.

(b) Other Circumstances in Which an Error of Fact May be Reviewed

It would be wrong, however, to assume that errors of fact made by an administrative tribunal can never be the subject of judicial review, although such review clearly would necessarily relate to jurisdiction. To the extent that a statutory delegate has discretion to determine the facts, it must exercise its discretion reasonably. If it does so, it is acting within its jurisdiction, and no judicial review can arise (because there is no jurisdictional error, and there is no error of law within jurisdiction). On the other hand, if the statutory delegate exercises its discretion to determine the facts in an unreasonable manner, it has not in law exercised its discretion, but rather has declined jurisdiction. The normal grounds for reviewing a jurisdictional error, therefore, should in principle be available in such a circumstance.

Further, in circumstances which are governed by the *Federal Courts Act*, sections 18 and 28 of that Act explicitly give both divisions of the Federal Court authority to review a decision by a federal board, commission or other tribunal if it "based its decision or order on an erroneous finding of fact that it made in a perverse or capricious manner or without regard for the material before it".[56]

(c) Is Lack of Evidence an Error of Law?

An issue sometimes arises about whether the court can review the decision of a statutory delegate on the basis that there was no, or insufficient, evidence before it to support its finding.

The courts appear to have adopted the view in *Nat Bell Liquors*[57] that the sufficiency of evidence is not a question of law, and therefore an erroneous appraisal of the evidence by a statutory delegate will not give rise to the anomalous use of *certiorari* to correct an error of law on the face of the record. (If, however, the proceedings are governed by the *Federal Courts Act*, sections 18.1(4)(d) and 28(2) give both the Federal Court and the Federal Court of Appeal authority to grant relief if a federal board, commission or other tribunal has "based its decision or order on an erroneous finding of fact that it made in a perverse or capricious manner or without regard for the material before it".)

---

56   Section 18.1(4)(d), which applies to applications which go to the Trial Division. S. 28(2) extends this ground to applications which go directly to the Federal Court of Appeal: See Appendix 5.

57   (1922), 65 D.L.R. 1 (Canada P.C.). See also D.W. Elliott's excellent article entitled "No Evidence – A Ground for Judicial Review in Canada?" (1972-73) 37 Sask. L.R. 48.

On the other hand, total lack of evidence appears to be a jurisdictional error capable of judicial review, even in the face of a privative clause. Similarly, it is submitted that an unreasonable appreciation of the facts may sometimes constitute a jurisdictional defect in the tribunal's proceedings. This point was clearly recognized by the Supreme Court of Canada in *Blanchard v. Control Data Canada Ltd.*, where Lamer J. provided the following analysis:[58]

> In looking for an error which might affect jurisdiction, the emphasis placed by this Court on the dichotomy of the reasonable or unreasonable nature of the error casts doubt on the appropriateness of making, on this basis, a distinction between error of law and error of fact. In addition to the difficulty of classification, the distinction collides with that given by the courts to unreasonable errors of fact. An unreasonable error of fact has been categorized as an error of law. The distinction would mean that this error of law is then protected by the privative clause unless it is unreasonable. What more is needed in order that an unreasonable finding of fact, in becoming an error of law, becomes an unreasonable error of law? An administrative tribunal has the necessary jurisdiction to make a mistake, and even a serious one, but not to be unreasonable. The unreasonable finding is no less fatal to jurisdiction because the finding is one of fact rather than law. An unreasonable finding is what justifies intervention by the courts.
>
> Not only is the distinction between error of law and of fact superfluous in light of an unreasonable finding or conclusion, but the reference to error itself is as well. Indeed, though all errors do not lead to unreasonable findings, every unreasonable finding results from an error (whether of law, fact, or a combination of the two), which is unreasonable.
>
> In conclusion, an unreasonable finding, whatever its origin, affects the jurisdiction of the tribunal. I hasten to add that the distinction between an error of law and one of fact is still entirely valid when the tribunal is not protected by a privative clause. Indeed, though all errors of law are then subjected to review, only unreasonable errors of fact are, but no others.

As noted above, sections 18.1(d) and 28(2) of the *Federal Courts Act* would achieve the same result, but without having to characterize the unreasonable finding of fact as being jurisdictional in nature, because any such decision would undoubtedly have been made "in a perverse or capricious manner or without regard to the material before it".

6. The Effect of a Privative Clause

Although privative clauses are now generally dealt with in the context of the four *Pushpanathan* factors involved in determining the appropriate stan-

---

58 [1984] 2 S.C.R. 476 at 494-95 (S.C.C.).

dard of review, the presence of a statutory[59] privative (or preclusive) clause traditionally prevented the anomalous use of *certiorari* to correct errors of law on the face of the record that lie within the delegate's jurisdiction. Of course privative clauses[60] cannot constitutionally be effective to oust judicial review of jurisdictional questions, on the rationale that a statutory delegate cannot lawfully make a decision outside its jurisdiction, so there is nothing to be protected by the privative clause. Precisely because intra-jurisdictional errors of law lie within the delegate's jurisdiction, however, there is a decision or action which can be protected by the privative clause. In order to succeed in obtaining judicial review when there is a privative clause, therefore, one must show that a jurisdictional error has been committed by the delegate. As noted earlier in this chapter, while no satisfactory test had ever been devised to differentiate intra-jurisdictional errors of law from those which go to jurisdiction, a vast number of cases can be used to illustrate attempts to characterize particular errors of law as "going to jurisdiction", and therefore escaping the protection of a privative clause.

(a) Preliminary or Collateral Matters

By definition, preliminary or collateral matters are jurisdictional in nature; they are not intra-jurisdictional. Although a privative clause will not protect errors about a preliminary or collateral matter, this chapter deals with intra-jurisdictional errors of law, so further discussion about review of preliminary or collateral errors is out of place here, but this issue will be addressed in the next chapter.

(b) A patently Unreasonable Interpretation of Law Converts an Intra-Jurisdictional Error into a Jurisdictional Error which is not Protected by a Privative Clause

A line of cases has developed the doctrine that all errors of law which are "patently unreasonable" are jurisdictional in nature, and therefore cannot be immunized from judicial review by a privative clause. The clearest statement

---

59 That is, in the same statute as creates the delegate's power to do the act in question. There may be some doubt as to the precise meaning of a privative clause, particularly where the Act specifically provides that *certiorari* or some other remedy is available in some short period of time (for example 30 days): *A.U.P.E., Local 63 v. Alberta (Public Service Employees' Relations Board)* (1982), 21 Alta. L.R. (2d) 104 (S.C.C.); *U.N.A., Local 11 v. Alberta (Board of Arbitration)*, [1983] 6 W.W.R. 1 (Alta. C.A.); and *Suncor Inc. v. McMurray Independent Oil Workers, Local 1* (1982), [1983] 1 W.W.R. 604 (Alta. C.A.). Does a "no *certiorari*" clause have the same effect as a "final and binding" clause? These are difficult questions of statutory construction. See S. Chumir, "The *Rammell* and *Farrell* Cases" (1963) 3 Alta. L. Rev. 124, for a discussion of different types of privative clauses, and R. Carter, "The Privative Clause in Canadian Administrative Law, 1944-1985: A Doctrinal Examination" (1986) 64 Can. Bar Rev. 241; and H.W. Arthurs, "Protection Against Judicial Review" (1983) Rev. du B. 277. See also *Pringle v. Fraser*, [1972] S.C.R. 821 (S.C.C.); *British Columbia (Minister of Finance) v. Woodward Estate* (1972), [1973] S.C.R. 120 (S.C.C.); and *Toronto Newspaper Guild v. Globe Printing Co.*, [1953] 2 S.C.R. 18 (S.C.C.).

60 The term is loosely defined. There is quite a range of stronger and weaker wording used in privative clauses (or "glosses"). See Chapter 12.

of this doctrine occurs in the Supreme Court of Canada's decision in *Blanchard v. Control Data Canada Ltd.*, where Beetz J. said:[61]

> According to the prior decisions of this Court, a patently unreasonable error by an administrative tribunal in interpreting a provision which it has to apply within the limits of its jurisdiction will in itself cause the tribunal to lose its jurisdiction.

and Lamer J. put it this way in the same case:[62]

> In principle, where there is a privative clause the superior courts should not be able to review errors of law made by the administrative tribunals. However, it is now settled that some errors of law can cause the arbitrator to lose his jurisdiction. The debate turns on the question of which errors of law result in the loss of jurisdiction. Contrary to the decision of Lord Denning in *Pearlman v. Keepers and Governors of Harrow School*, [1979] 1 All E.R. 365, where he said (at p. 372) that "no court or tribunal has any jurisdiction to make an error of law on which the decision of the case depends" (subsequently disapproved by the Privy Council in *South East Asia Fire Bricks Sdn. Bhd. v. Non-Metallic Mineral Products Manufacturing Employees Union*, [1980] 3 W.L.R. 318, and *Re Racal Communications Ltd.*, [1980] 2 All E.R. 634), this Court has tended since *Nipawin* . . . and *C.U.P.E.* . . . to avoid intervening when the decision of the administrative tribunal was reasonable, whether erroneous or not. In other words, only unreasonable errors of law can affect jurisdiction. The following extract from *C.U.P.E.* . . . has become the classic statement of the approach taken by this Court:

> > Put another way, was the Board's interpretation so patently unreasonable that its construction cannot be rationally supported by the relevant legislation and demands intervention by the court upon review?

> This is a very severe test and signals a strict approach to the question of judicial review. It is nevertheless the test which this Court has applied and continues to apply. . . .

While the *C.U.P.E.*[63] decision is frequently quoted as support for a standard of review involving curial deference, it also stands for the proposition that a patently unreasonable interpretation of the statutory provisions in question constitutes a jurisdictional error (which therefore would not be protected by a

---

61 [1984] 2 S.C.R. 476 at 479 (S.C.C.). See also *C.A.I.M.A.W., Local 14 v. Canadian Kenworth Co.*, [1989] 2 S.C.R. 983 at 1003-04, 40 Admin. L.R. 181, 62 D.L.R. (4th) 437 (S.C.C.).

62 *Ibid.* at 492-93.

63 (1979), 97 D.L.R. (3d) 417 (S.C.C.).

privative clause). Thus, "patently unreasonable" is one test[64] for determining which errors are so serious as to become jurisdictional in nature. The effect of a successful application of the "patently unreasonable" doctrine is to evade the operation of a privative clause; that is, the use of the "patently unreasonable" test is a sword for judicial review of administrative action–it creates a ground for review. Conversely, however, errors of law which are not "patently unreasonable", and which do not relate to a matter which is preliminary or collateral to the delegate's jurisdiction in the narrow sense,[65] are intra-jurisdictional in nature and will be immunized from judicial review whenever there is a privative clause. This is the result of the doctrine of Parliamentary Sovereignty, under which the legislative branch may specifically exclude judicial review (within certain limitations).[66]

7. Standards of Review, Curial Deference, and Intra-Jurisdictional Errors of Law

In principle, *certiorari* should always be available to correct any error of law on the face of the record which is not protected by a privative clause.[67] In fact, however, the courts have retreated somewhat from such a bold assertion of their jurisdiction, and have tended to restrict the anomalous use of *certiorari* to correct only certain errors of law.

In England, as Wade noted in his fourth edition,[68] the courts have sometimes held that there is no error of law if the legal conclusion is "within the range of interpretations within which different persons might reasonably reach

---

64 Presumably, other tests would apply in those circumstances where the court determines that the legislature intended a different standard of review to be applicable. For example, if "reasonableness *simpliciter"* is the appropriate standard (*Southam* (1997), 50 Admin. L.R. (2d) 199 (S.C.C.)) then an unreasonable decision will take the statutory delegate outside of its jurisdiction.

65 Preliminary and collateral matters are, by definition, jurisdictional in nature. As will be seen in the next chapter, this usually means that the appropriate standard of review for preliminary and collateral matters is correctness.

66 See the section in Chapter 12, dealing with "Constitutional limitations on privative clauses in Canada".

67 As Lamer J. noted in *Blanchard v. Control Data Canada Ltd.*, [1984] 2 S.C.R. 476 at 495 (S.C.C.):

> ... [A]n unreasonable finding, whatever its origin, affects the jurisdiction of the tribunal. *I hasten to add that the distinction between an error of law and one of fact is still entirely valid when the tribunal is not protected by a privative clause. Indeed, though all errors of law are then subjected to review*, only unreasonable errors of fact are, but no others. [Emphasis added.]

See also *Canadian Imperial Bank of Commerce v. Alberta (Assessment Appeal Board),* [1990] 6 W.W.R. 425 (Alta. Q.B.), reversed [1992] 4 W.W.R. 419 (Alta. C.A.); *Alberta (Minister of Social Services) v. Alberta (Widow's Pension Appeal Panel)* (1988), 64 Alta. L.R. (2d) 126 (Alta. Q.B.); *Barron v. Foothills (Municipal District No. 31)* (1984), 36 Alta. L.R. (2d) 27 (Alta. C.A.); *Shell Canada Ltd. v. Pincher Creek No. 9 (Municipal District)* (1975), 59 D.L.R. (3d) 262 (Alta. C.A.).

68 *Administrative Law*, 4th ed (Oxford: Clarendon Press, 1977) at 776. For a more detailed discussion, see *Administrative Law*, 7th ed. (Oxford: Clarendon Press, 1994) at 948.

different conclusions". With respect, this is inconsistent with the philosophy that there is only one correct construction of any legal phrase in a particular context, and it is the responsibility of the courts to determine that correct construction.[69]

In Canada, the courts over the last twenty-five years have been struggling with the concept of the applicable standard of review to be applied when scrutinizing various alleged defects in particular statutory contexts. Early on in this process, the courts applied the correctness standard to closely scrutinize defects in the acquisition of jurisdiction, such as preliminary or collateral errors, and used the "not patently unreasonable" test to refuse to issue *certiorari* to correct an intra-jurisdictional error of law even where no privative clause existed.[70] After the decisions in *Pezim*,[71] *Southam*[72], *Pushpanathan*[73], *Dr. Q*,[74] and *Ryan*,[75] it has become clear that there is a spectrum of deference which gives rise to three possible standards of review, and that there is no automatic connection between a particular ground of review and any particular standard of review.[76] In particular, it is clear that the correctness standard does not necessarily apply to all errors of law. Justice LeBel described this state of affairs in *Toronto (City) v. C.U.P.E., Local 79* as follows:[77]

> This Court has been very careful to note, however, that not all questions of law must be reviewed under a standard of correctness. As a prefatory matter, as the Court has observed, in many cases it will be

---

69 See the comments by Laskin C.J.C. in *McLeod v. Egan* (1974), [1975] 1 S.C.R. 517 (S.C.C.), to the effect that there is only one correct interpretation of statutory provisions which arbitration boards must construe in the course of their inquiries.

70 See for example *A.U.P.E., Local 63 v. Alberta (Public Service Employees' Relations Board)*, [1982] 1 S.C.R. 923, 21 Alta. L.R. (2d) 104 (S.C.C.), especially the dissent by Martland and Beetz JJ.; and the comment by Mullan in (1983) 5 S.C. Rev. 24. See also *Suncor Inc. v. McMurray Independent Oil Workers, Local 1* (1982), [1983] 1 W.W.R. 604 (Alta. C.A.); the dissent by Moir J.A. in *U.N.A. Local 11 v. Alberta (Board of Arbitration)*, [1983] 6 W.W.R. 1 (Alta. C.A.); and the Supreme Court's decision in *Shalansky v. Regina Pasqua Hospital* (1983), 145 D.L.R. (3d) 413 (S.C.C.), affirming (1982), 15 Sask. R. 253 (Sask. C.A.), affirming (1980), 10 Sask. R. 225 (Sask. Q.B.), dismissing an application for judicial review of an arbitration award. Compare the previous decisions in *Yellow Cab Ltd. v. Alberta (Industrial Relations Board)* (1979), 11 Alta. L.R. (2d) 97 at 103 (Alta. C.A.), reversed on other grounds [1980] 2 S.C.R. 761 (S.C.C.), where the Court of Appeal had ruled that the legislation permitted the issuance of *certiorari* to correct *any* error of law, not just patently unreasonable ones, following *Stedelbauer Chevrolet Oldsmobile Ltd. v. Alberta (Industrial Relations Board)* (1968), [1969] S.C.R. 137 (S.C.C.). These cases are discussed in some detail at 391-400 of the second edition of this work.

71 [1994] 2 S.C.R. 557 (S.C.C.).

72 [1997] 1 S.C.R. 748 (S.C.C.).

73 *Pushpanathan v. Canada (Minister of Employment & Immigration)*, [1998] 1 S.C.R. 982 (S.C.C.), reasons varied [1998] 1 S.C.R. 1222 (S.C.C.).

74 *Q v. College of Physicians & Surgeons (British Columbia)*, [2003] 1 S.C.R. 226 (S.C.C.).

75 *Ryan v. Law Society (New Brunswick)*, [2003] 1 S.C.R. 247 (S.C.C.).

76 Except for constitutional issues, which must always engage the correctness standard: *Paul v. British Columbia (Forest Appeals Commission)*, 2003 SCC 55 (S.C.C.) at para. 31; and *Martin v. Nova Scotia (Workers' Compensation Board)*, 2003 SCC 54 (S.C.C.) at para. 31.

77 2003 SCC 63 (S.C.C.) at paras. 71 through 74. Note that all of the judges agreed that correctness was the appropriate standard of review in this case.

difficult to draw a clear line between questions of fact, mixed fact and law, and law; in reality, such questions are often inextricably intertwined (see *Pushpanathan v. Canada (Minister of Citizenship and Immigration)*, [1998] 1 S.C.R. 982, at para. 37; *Canada (Director of Investigation and Research) v. Southam Inc.*, [1997] 1 S.C.R. 748, at para. 37). More to the point, as Bastarache J. stated in *Pushpanathan*, *supra*, "even pure questions of law may be granted a wide degree of deference where other factors of the pragmatic and functional analysis suggest that such deference is the legislative intention" (at para. 37). The critical factor in this respect is expertise.

As Bastarache J. noted in *Pushpanathan*, *supra*, at para. 34, once a "broad relative expertise has been established", this Court has been prepared to show "considerable deference even in cases of highly generalized statutory interpretation where the instrument being interpreted is the tribunal's constituent legislation": see, for example, *Pezim v. British Columbia (Superintendent of Brokers)*, [1994] 2 S.C.R. 557, and *National Corn Growers Assn. v. Canada (Import Tribunal)*, [1990] 2 S.C.R. 1324. This Court has also held that, while administrative adjudicators' interpretations of external statutes "are generally reviewable on a correctness standard", an exception to this general rule may occur, and deference may be appropriate, where "the external statute is intimately connected with the mandate of the tribunal and is encountered frequently as a result": see *Toronto (City) Board of Education*, *supra*, at para. 39; *Canadian Broadcasting Corp.*, *supra*, at para. 48. And, perhaps most importantly in light of the issues raised by this case, the Court has held that deference may be warranted where an administrative adjudicator has acquired expertise through its experience in the application of a general common or civil law rule in its specialized statutory context: see *Ivanhoe*, *supra*, at para. 26; L'Heureux-Dubéé J. (dissenting) in *Canada (Attorney General) v. Mossop*, [1993] 1 S.C.R. 554, at pp. 599-600, endorsed in *Pushpanathan*, *supra*, at para. 37.

In the field of labour relations, general common and civil law questions are often closely intertwined with the more specific questions of labour law. Resolving general legal questions may thus be an important component of the work of some administrative adjudicators in this field. To subject all such decisions to correctness review would be to expand the scope of judicial review considerably beyond what the legislature intended, fundamentally undermining the ability of labour adjudicators to develop a body of jurisprudence that is tailored to the specialized context in which they operate.

Where an administrative adjudicator must decide a general question of law in the course of exercising its statutory mandate, that determination will typically be entitled to deference (particularly if the adjudicator's decisions are protected by a privative clause), inasmuch as the general question of law is closely connected to the adjudicator's core area of expertise. This was essentially the holding of this Court in *Ivanhoe, supra*. In *Ivanhoe*, after noting the presence of a privative clause, Arbour J. held that, while the question at issue involved both civil and labour law, the labour commissioners and the Labour Court were entitled to deference because "they have developed special expertise in this regard which is adapted to the specific context of labour relations and which is not shared by the courts" (para. 26; see also *Pasiechnyk v. Saskatchewan (Workers' Compensation Board)*, [1997] 2 S.C.R. 890). This appeal does not represent a departure from this general principle.

The practical result of this approach, of course, will frequently prevent the courts from achieving consistency and coherence in differing decisions by administrative bodies. As Moir J.A. put it earlier in his dissent against the application of deference in the *U.N.A.* case:[78]

> The result of this decision is to leave the question to the individual arbitration boards who hear grievances under collective agreements. Whatever these boards decide will be protected unless their decisions are "patently unreasonable" or "clearly wrong". To my mind this is not a desirable result but it must follow from the decision in *Suncor* and probably *Shalansky*.

The use of any standard of review which is less stringent than correctness will in practice necessarily limit the prior availability of *certiorari* to correct intra-jurisdictional errors of law where no privative clause exists. Conversely, to the extent that correctness is found to be the applicable standard of review even in the face of a privative clause (which is perhaps an unlikely outcome of the pragmatic and functional analysis, but theoretically possible), or where the delegate's interpretation of law is found to be unreasonable[79] even in the face of a privative clause, it is possible that the availability of judicial review for errors of law on the face of the record might be somewhat more expansive

---

78 [1983] 6 W.W.R. 1 at 6 (Alta. C.A.). See *Domtar Inc. c. Quebec (Commission d'appel en matière de lesions professionelles)*, [1993] S.C.R. 756, 15 Admin. L.R. (2d) 1 (S.C.C.) recognizing that conflicting decisions between two administrative tribunals do not give an independent basis for judicial review; commented on by P. Mercer at (1993) 2 R.A.L. 237. See also *Foothills Provincial General Hospital v. U.N.A., Local 115* (1993), 10 Alta. L.R. (3d) 254 at 272-73 (Alta. Q.B.), additional reasons at (1994), 150 A.R. 81 (Alta. Q.B.); and *A.U.P.E. v. University Hospitals Board*, [1991] 2 S.C.R. 201 at 202 (S.C.C.), to the effect that the Court will not intervene where there is another reasonable interpretation, "even possibly a better one than that adopted by the Board", so long as the Board's was not patently unreasonable (or deal with a jurisdictional matter).

79 If the interpretation was patently unreasonable (as opposed to simply unreasonable), the previous jurisprudence would say that the decision was made outside of jurisdiction, so that it would not be protected by any privative clause. It is the development of the reasonableness *simpliciter* standard which gives rise to the possibility that the court would intervene, even though on traditional analysis the privative clause ought to protect a decision which is unreasonable but not patently unreasonable. See Justice LeBel's *cri de coeur* doubting the robustness of the distinctions between these two standards of review in *Toronto (City) v. C.U.P.E., Local 79*, 2003 SCC 63 (S.C.C.).

than the cases prior to the development of the standards-of-review might suggest.

8. The Discretion to Refuse the Remedy

Certiorari, like all of the prerogative remedies, is discretionary in nature. In the previous edition of this work, it was suggested that this rationale could be used to explain why the courts were reluctant to correct errors of law which were not patently unreasonable, but subsequent jurisprudence has not described this in terms of the discretionary refusal of a remedy, but rather as a jurisdictional limitation on the courts' power to do so as a consequence of the applicable standard of review. So the discretion to refuse a remedy must be considered as a separate and additional ground upon which the courts might decline to correct an intra-jurisdictional error of law on the face of the record.

Professor de Smith recognized[80] only three cases in which the courts exercised their discretion to refuse prerogative remedies:

(a) where there is an appeal which provides a more effective remedy;

(b) where the applicant's conduct has disentitled him or her to relief; and

(c) where it would be pointless to issue the remedy.[81]

It is important to remember that the discretion to refuse prerogative remedies is precisely that: discretionary. Thus, none of these considerations should bind the courts to refuse judicial review where other considerations require it – such as those referred to by Moir J.A. in the *U.N.A.* case.[82] Finally, it is important to remember that not all remedies for illegal administrative action are discretionary in nature.[83]

9. Summary on Intra-Jurisdictional Errors of Law on the Face of the Record as a Ground for Judicial Review

Anomalously, the common law recognizes that *certiorari* is available to correct an error of law which is otherwise within the jurisdiction of the statutory

---

80 J.M. Evans, *de Smith's Judicial Review of Administrative Action*, 4th ed. (London: Stevens & Sons, 1980) at 422-28. For an expanded discussion of the role of discretion in granting or refusing administrative law remedies, see c. 20 of the 5th ed. of *de Smith* by Woolf & Jowell (London: Sweet & Maxwell, 1995). See also D.P. Jones, "Discretionary Refusal of Judicial Review in Administrative Law" (1981) 19 Alta. L. Rev. 483.

81 For an example, see *Canadian Kellogg Co. v. Alberta (Industrial Relations Board)* (1975), [1976] 2 W.W.R. 67 (Alta. I.R.B.), where the error would not have affected the result. Alberta Rule 753.07 specifically provides that the court may validate the impugned decision and refuse relief where the sole ground is a defect in form or a technical irregularity, where no substantial wrong or miscarriage of justice has been made.

82 *Foothills Provincial General Hospital v. U.N.A., Local 115* (1993), 10 Alta. L.R. (3d) 254 (Alta. Q.B.), additional reasons at (1994), 150 A.R. 81 (Alta. Q.B.).

83 For example, the right to damages is not discretionary (although the amount thereof may be). See the discussion of the consequences of this point in D.P. Jones, *supra* note 80.

delegate. This use of *certiorari* is anomalous because all other grounds for judicial review require there to be some defect in jurisdiction.

At common law, the intra-jurisdictional error had to be apparent on the face of the record. However, this requirement has become less stringent because of the greatly expanded statutory definition of the record (or the return) in many jurisdictions. In addition, the Federal Court can correct all errors of law regardless of whether they appear on the record.

Because this ground for judicial review is limited to errors of *law*, it is important to note the distinction between errors of law, errors of fact, and mixed errors of law and fact. Errors of fact are not reviewable under this anomalous use of *certiorari*, but unreasonable findings of fact may constitute an error of jurisdiction (and the Federal Court has specific authority to correct decisions or orders which a federal board, commission or other tribunal based on an erroneous finding of fact that was made in a perverse or capricious manner or without regard for the material before it).

The development of the concept of standards of review may practically impact the availability of *certiorari* to correct an error of law to the extent that correctness is not the applicable standard of review.

Finally, even if there is an error of law, which meets the appropriate standard of review, the court always has discretion to refuse to issue *certiorari*.

10. Selected Bibliography

Abel, A., "Materials for Consideration in *Certiorari*: 1" (1963-64) 15 U. of T. L.J. 102.

Beatson, J., "The Scope of Judicial Review for Error of Law", 4 Oxford J. of Legal Studies 22.

Carter, R., "The Privative Clause in Canadian Administrative Law, 1944-1985: A Doctrinal Examination" (1986) 64 Can. Bar Rev. 241.

Lord Cooke, 1997 *Hamlyn Lectures, "Turning Points in the Common Law"*, Lecture 4 on *Anisminic*.

de Smith, S.A., "*Certiorari* and Speaking Orders" (1951) 14 Mod. L. Rev. 207.

Lord Diplock, "Administrative Law: Judicial Review Reviewed" [1974] Camb. L.J. 233.

Emery, C.T., and Smythe,B., "Error of Law in Administrative Law" (1984) 100 L.Q. Rev. 612.

Emery, C.T., "Appellate Jurisdiction to Correct Errors of Law" (1987) 103 L.Q. Rev. 264.

Flood, C., "The Correctness Standard and Labour Remedies" (1992) 2 R.A.L. 41.

Gordon, D.M., "Quashing on *Certiorari* for Error of Law" (1951) 67 L.Q. Rev. 452.

Gould, B., "*Anisminic* and Judicial Review" [1970] P.L. 358.

Grey, J. & Casgrain, L.M., "Jurisdiction, Fairness and Reasonableness" (1988) 4 Admin. L.J. 43.

Jones, T.H., "Mistake of Fact in Administrative Law" [1990] P.L. 507.

Law Reform Commission of British Columbia, *Report on Arbitration*, May 1982, especially c. IX, "Judicial Supervision of Awards", and c. X, "Judicial Supervision of Awards: Reform".

MacLauchlan, H.W., "Judicial Review of Administrative Interpretations of Law: How much formalism can we reasonably bear?" (1986) 36 U. of T.L.J. 343.

MacLauchlan, H.W., "Approaches to Interpretation in Administrative Law" (1987-88) 1 C.J.A.L.P. 293.

MacLauchlan, H.W., "Reconciling Curial Deference with a Functional Approach in Substantive and Procedural Judicial Review" (1993) 7 C.J.A.L.P. 1

McRuer Report, Vol. 1 at 302-15.

Morden, D., "Recent Developments in Administrative Law" [1967] Law Soc. of Upper Can. Special Lectures 275 at 295-98.

Norman, K., "The Privative Clause: Virile or Futile?" (1969) 34 Sask. L. Rev. 334.

Sawer, G., "Error of Law on the Face of the Administrative Record" (1954) 3 U.W. Aust. Ann. L. Rev. 24.

Yardley, D.C.M., "The Grounds for *Certiorari* and Prohibition" (1959) 37 Can. Bar Rev. 294 at 323-37.

III

STANDARDS OF REVIEW

The examination of these four factors [from Pushpanathan], and the "weighing up" of contextual elements to identify the appropriate standard of review, is not a mechanical exercise. Given the immense range of discretionary decision makers and administrative bodies, the test is necessarily flexible, and proceeds by principled analysis rather than categories, seeking the polar star of legislative intent.

— Justice Binnie in *C.U.P.E. v. Ontario (Minister of Labour)*, 2003 SCC 29 at paragraph 149

12

Standards of
Review

1. Introduction

Like Gaul, all of administrative law is conceptually divided into three parts: (1) the grounds for review; (2) the applicable standard of review; and (3) the available remedies.

By "standard of review", we mean the degree of intensity with which the courts[1] will examine the decision of a statutory delegate, whether on an appeal or on an application for judicial review. Will the court examine the decision to determine whether it is correct in the court's eyes? Reasonable? Not patently unreasonable? Or will the court use some other standard? To put it another way, to what extent will the court defer to the decision of the statutory delegate,

---

1 Conceivably, a statutory delegate which hears an appeal from another statutory delegate may also have to determine the appropriate standard of review. For an example, see *College of Hearing Aid Practitioners (Alberta) v. Zieniewicz*, 2003 ABCA 346 (Alta. C.A.).

even if the court itself might have done something different? What are the justifications for any level of "curial deference"?

Although the courts have long shown varying degrees of deference in reviewing decisions of statutory delegates, they have only relatively recently started to explicitly articulate the "standard of review" as a discrete step which must be performed in each administrative law case. The genesis of standard of review analysis is the 1979 decision by the Supreme Court of Canada in *C.U.P.E.*[2] which recognized the distinction between "preliminary and collateral matters" on which the acquisition of jurisdiction depend (and upon which the statutory delegate must be correct), and those matters within the statutory delegate's jurisdiction which the Legislature intended the statutory delegate's decision to be final (with which the courts should only interfere if they were "patently unreasonable"). For twenty years after *C.U.P.E.*, much of the jurisprudence was devoted to identifying other circumstances (usually involving other aspects of jurisdiction) where the courts would use a more stringent standard than "patently unreasonable" in reviewing the statutory delegate's decision. In the course of this jurisprudence, the Court adopted a "pragmatic and functional approach" for analyzing the constellation of factors for determining whether the legislators intended a particular matter to be a "jurisdictional given" or to be within the authority of the statutory delegate to decide definitively.[3] Initially, the analysis contemplated only two different standards of review ("correctness" or "patently unreasonable"), which operated rather like a toggle switch. However, in 1994 the Court in *Pezim*,[4] articulated the concept of a "spectrum of standards of review" applicable to different types of alleged defects by statutory delegates, and in 1997 in *Southam*[5] it actually applied an intermediate standard of review ("reasonableness *simpliciter*") rather than just using one of the endpoints ("correctness" and "patent unreasonableness") – thereby effectively trading a toggle switch for a dimmer switch.

In the benchmark decision for contemporary standard of review analysis, *Pushpanathan*[6] in 1998, the Court made it clear that (a) the analysis applies both to appeals and to applications for judicial review, (b) the applicable standard of review must be identified in every case, and (c) a functional and pragmatic approach is to be used to weigh the various factors which determine the applicable standard of review to be applied in the particular circumstances. The principal factors to be considered in determining the applicable standard of review in any particular case are (1) whether there is a privative clause or an appeal; (2) the comparative expertise of the court and the statutory delegate

---

2 *C.U.P.E., Local 963 v. New Brunswick Liquor Corp.*, [1979] 2 S.C.R. 227, 97 D.L.R. (3d) 417, 25 N.B.R. (2d) 237 (S.C.C.).

3 *Syndicat des employés de production du Québec & de l'Acadie v. Canada (Labour Relations Board)*, [1988] 2 S.C.R. 1048 (S.C.C.) ("*Bibeault*").

4 *Pezim v. British Columbia (Superintendent of Brokers)*, [1994] 2 S.C.R. 557, (1994), 22 Admin. L.R. (2d) 1 at 27-28 (S.C.C.). Although it referred to a spectrum of standards of review, the Supreme Court actually only referred to two possible standards of review – correctness and patent unreasonableness (which it selected).

5 *Canada (Director of Investigation & Research) v. Southam Inc.*, [1997] 1 S.C.R. 748, 50 Admin. L.R. (2d) 199 (S.C.C.) (hereafter "*Southam*").

6 [1998] 1.S.C.R. 982 (S.C.C.), reasons modified [1998] 1 S.C.R. 1222 (S.C.C.).

about the particular matter; (3) the purpose of the statutory delegate's enabling statute, and the particular provision in question; and (4) the nature of the particular problem – whether it is a question of law, fact, or mixed law and fact. In all cases, the central question in ascertaining the applicable standard of review is to determine the intention of the legislature – not only its intention in conferring the particular jurisdiction on the particular administrative tribunal in question, but also its intention about what the court is to do when it is reviewing the particular matter in question.[7] After *Pushpanathan*, it was assumed that there were other possible standards of review along the spectrum, such as "correctness with an appropriate measure of deference",[8] and "deference absent a nearly patently unreasonable error".[9] However, in 2003, somewhat surprisingly, the Court in *Dr. Q.*[10] and *Ryan*[11] restricted the number of standards to three – correctness, reasonableness *simpliciter*, and patent unreasonableness – and effectively transferred the spectrum concept to the amount of deference to be given to a particular statutory delegate, which in turn engages one of the three recognized standards of review.

The existence of different possible standards of review requires an understanding of the following issues:

(a) The constitutional rationale for judicial review which underpins the existence of different tests for different types of alleged defects – in other words, the court needs to be clear about *its* role in the particular circumstance at hand (which applies both to applications for judicial review and to statutory appeals).

(b) The historical development of judicial review over the last 25 years, ranging from the high-water mark of judicial review in *Anisminic*[12] through the low-water mark resulting from the development of the "patently unreasonable" test in *C.U.P.E.*[13] as a shield to protect virtually all administrative decisions from judicial review, to the realization that "correctness" must be applied to jurisdictional questions,

---

7 Legislative intent is the "polar star" of standard-of-review analysis: Binnie J. in *C.U.P.E. v. Ontario (Minister of Labour)*, 2003 SCC 29, 226 D.L.R. (4th) 193 (S.C.C.) at para. 149 (the "*Retired Judges Case*").

8 *Northwood Inc. v. British Columbia (Forest Practices Board)*, 2001 BCCA 141 (B.C. C.A.), leave to appeal refused (2001), [2001] S.C.C.A. No. 207, 2001 CarswellBC 2119 (S.C.C.) (*Northwood*); *Van Unen v. British Columbia (Workers' Compensation Board)*, 2001 BCCA 262 (B.C. C.A.), leave to appeal to SCC denied on 4 October 2001 without reasons (2001), [2001] S.C.C.A. No. 288, 2001 CarswellBC 2117 (S.C.C.) (*Van Unen*). See also *Skyline Roofing Ltd. v. Alberta (Workers' Compensation Board)* (2001), 34 Admin. L.R. (3d) 289 (Alta. Q.B.).

9 *Rickard Realty Advisors Inc. v. Calgary (City)*, 216 A.R. 271, 63 Alta. L.R. (3d) 248, 1998 ABCA 173 (Alta. C.A.) at para. 7.

10 *Q. v. College of Physicians & Surgeons (British Columbia)*, [2003] 1 S.C.R. 226, 48 Admin. L.R. (3d) 1 (S.C.C.).

11 *Ryan v. Law Society (New Brunswick)*, [2003] 1 S.C.R. 247, 48 Admin. L.R. (3d) 33 (S.C.C.).

12 *Anisminic Ltd. v. Foreign Compensation Commission* (1968), [1969] 2 A.C. 147 (U.K. H.L.).

13 *C.U.P.E. Local 963 v. New Brunswick Liquor Corp.*, [1979] 2 S.C.R. 227, 97 D.L.R. (3d) 417 (S.C.C.).

the development of the "pragmatic and functional approach" to distinguish between jurisdictional and intra-jurisdictional matters, the development of the spectrum of standards of review and the extension of the "pragmatic and functional approach" to determine the applicable standard of review, and the recent restriction on the number of possible standards of review.

(c) The concept of curial deference, and the factors which will locate a particular case at a particular point on the spectrum of deference, thereby in turn engaging one of the three recognized standards of review.

(d) The differences between the three recognized standards of review, and how they are applied.

(e) The role of an appellate court when hearing an appeal from a lower court's selection or application of the standard of review for a particular decision of a statutory delegate.

and

(f) Whether the same spectrum applies to other grounds for judicial review – such as natural justice and abuse of discretion.

The purpose of this chapter is to examine the historical, theoretical and practical dimensions of the "standard of review" in administrative law.

2. The Constitutional and Conceptual Basis for Different Standards of Review

Administrative law raises fundamental questions about the constitutional relationship between the legislature, the courts and statutory delegates – which in turn provide the clue to the constitutional and conceptual basis for different standards of judicial review. Do the courts have a general power to overturn *all* administrative decisions with which they do not agree? If not, why not? Even when the courts do have the power to review decisions of other statutory delegates, when (if ever) should they consciously defer to the delegate's decision? Why?

The traditional – or Diceyan[14] – view of judicial review explains this constitutional relationship of the courts to the legislature and the administration as follows:

• With certain constitutional limitations, the legislature can confer virtually any power on a statutory delegate, and not on the court. The

---

14 Named after the description of the British constitution by A.V. Dicey in *Introduction to the Study of the Law of Constitution*, 10th ed. by E.C.S. Wade (London: Macmillan Papermac, 1961). See H. Arthurs, "Rethinking Administrative Law: A Slightly Dicey Business" (1979) 17 Osg. Hall L.J. 1; and the dissenting judgment by Wilson J. in *W.W. Lester (1978) Ltd. v. U.A., Local 740*, [1990] 3 S.C.R. 644 (S.C.C.).

Canadian Constitution does not require all executive or administrative powers to be exercised by the courts.

- Apart from the constitutional authority of the courts to decide cases involving the allocation of legislative powers in the Canadian federation or limitation on those powers under the *Charter*, the superior court's own power to review decisions by statutory delegates derives either directly or indirectly from the legislature. The court possesses *direct* authority to review the decisions of other statutory delegates when legislation contains a specific right of appeal to the court.[15] The court possesses *indirect* or *inherent* authority to review decisions of other statutory delegates as a result of the constitutional presumption that all "inferior" tribunals have limited jurisdiction, and the superior courts themselves have jurisdiction to see that the inferior bodies stay within their limited jurisdictions.

- With certain constitutional limitations, the legislature can provide that the court must not interfere with the decision of the statutory delegate. The Constitution does not give the courts *carte blanche* to sit in appeal or review from the decisions of all statutory delegates with which it does not agree. The courts must obey the legislature's directions limiting the courts' own jurisdiction.[16]

- The legislature can confer a wide spectrum of powers on its delegates. At the one end, it can clearly indicate its intention to limit the statutory delegate's jurisdiction, so that the delegate's decision on this matter must be correct (in the court's eyes). At the other end, the legislature can clearly indicate that a particular matter lies completely within the jurisdiction of the statutory delegate, and shall not be interfered with by the courts for any reason whatever.

Unfortunately, the legislature frequently does not articulate its intentions about what powers it intends to grant to the statutory delegate, or the relationship it wants between the statutory delegate and the court's superintending power.[17] Further, the meaning of language is frequently imprecise, so controversies often arise about whether a particular statutory provision does or does

---

15 Sometimes legislation specifically grants a right to judicial review, rather than providing for an appeal. For example, see the Alberta *Labour Relations Code*, R.S.A. 2000, c. L-1, sections 19, 127, 145 and 204; or the *Freedom of Information and Protection of Privacy Act*, R.S.A. 2000, c. F-25, section 74. These are examples of *direct* or *explicit*, not *indirect* or *inherent*, authority for the courts to review the decisions of statutory delegates.

16 Unless the legislature attempts to prevent all forms of judicial review, which would be unconstitutional: *Crevier v. Quebec (Attorney General)*, [1981] 2 S.C.R. 220, 127 D.L.R. (3d) 1 (S.C.C.). Similar constitutional considerations might prevent a legislature from specifying a standard of review less than correctness for constitutional questions.

17 The B.C. Administrative Justice Project has recommended that legislation should specify the different standards of review which are to be applied by the courts. The legislation received Royal Assent on May 20, 2004. The B.C. language is set out in Appendix 6 below. For the full discussion, see "Model Statutory Powers Provisions for Administrative Tribunals", August 2003, which can be found at www.gov.bc.ca/ajp/rpts, at 88-104 and 132-42.

not limit a particular delegate's jurisdiction, or whether the legislature intended the court to be able to review the delegate's decision and if so, in what circumstances.

In each case, the court must determine what powers the legislature intended to give to the statutory delegate and to the court itself. The answer to those questions inexorably dictates what standard of review the court should apply in reviewing the administrative decision in question.

3. Historical Development of Different Standards

The courts have used various approaches for determining when to intervene in a statutory delegate's decision.

(a) The High-Water Mark for Judicial Review: Anisminic

The high water mark for intensive judicial review is epitomized by the 1968 decision of the House of Lords in *Anisminic*.[18] Because the legislation in question contained a strong privative clause, the court could only review the administrative agency's decision if a jurisdictional defect was involved. To achieve this end, the House of Lords effectively magnified the number of ways in which an administrative agency may fail to acquire jurisdiction, or lose jurisdiction:[19]

> It has sometimes been said that it is only where a tribunal acts without jurisdiction that its decision is a nullity. But in such cases the word "jurisdiction" has been used in a very wide sense, and I have come to the conclusion that it is better not to use the term except in the narrow and original sense of the tribunal being entitled to enter on the inquiry in question. But there are many cases where, although the tribunal had jurisdiction to enter on the inquiry, it has done or failed to do something in the course of the inquiry which is of such a nature that its decision is a nullity. It may have given its decision in bad faith. It may have made a decision which it had no power to make. It may have failed in the course of the inquiry to comply with the requirements of natural justice. It may in perfect good faith have misconstrued the provisions giving its power to act so that it failed to deal with the question remitted to it and decided some question which was not remitted to it. It may have refused to take into account something which it was required to take into account. Or it may have based its decision on some matter which, under the provisions setting it up, it had no right to take into account. I do not intend this list to be exhaustive. But if it decides a question remitted to it for decision without committing any of these errors it is as much entitled to decide that question wrongly as it is to

---

18 *Anisminic Ltd. v. Foreign Compensation Commission* (1968), [1969] 2 A.C. 147 (U.K. H.L.). See the interesting discussion of this case by Lord Cooke in *The Hamlyn Lectures* on "Turning Points in English Law" (London: Sweet and Maxwell, 1997) at 63*ff.*
19 *Ibid.* at 171.

decide it rightly. I understand that some confusion has been caused by my having said in *Reg. v. Governor of Brixton Prison, Ex parte Armah* [1968] A.C. 192, 234 that if a tribunal has jurisdiction to go right it has jurisdiction to go wrong. So it has, if one uses "jurisdiction" in the narrow original sense. If it is entitled to enter on the inquiry and does not do any of those things which I have mentioned in the course of the proceedings, then its decision is equally valid whether it is right or wrong subject only to the power of the court in certain circumstances to correct an error of law. I think that, if these views are correct, the only case cited which was plainly wrongly decided is *Davies v. Price* [1958] 1 W.L.R. 434. But in a number of other cases some of the grounds of judgment are questionable.

In effect, the *Anisminic* approach allows the courts to use a microscopic examination of the delegate's actions in order to find jurisdictional defects which the courts can correct.

The Supreme Court of Canada adopted the *Anisminic* approach in three notable cases:

- *Metropolitan Life Insurance Co. v. I.U.O.E., Local 796.*[20]

- *Bell v. Ontario (Human Rights Commission)*[21] (dealing with a preliminary or collateral question).

- *Blanco v. Rental Commission.*[22]

Cory J. has described these decisions in *Econosult* as follows:[23]

All of these decisions relied upon the principle set out in *Anisminic*. . . . They all took the position that a definition of jurisdictional error should include any question pertaining to the interpretation of a statute made by an administrative tribunal. In each case, this court substituted what was, in its opinion, the correct interpretation of the enabling provision of the tribunal's statute for that of the tribunal. These cases appear to expand, in a significant manner, a court's role upon an application for judicial review.

(b) The English Extension: All Errors of Law are Jurisdictional

The English courts have extended *Anisminic* to the point where it is now simply assumed in England that *all* errors of law can be reviewed and corrected by the courts: *Racal Communications, Re:*[24]

---

20 [1970] S.C.R. 425 (S.C.C.).

21 [1971] S.C.R. 756 (S.C.C.).

22 [1980] 2 S.C.R. 827 (S.C.C.).

23 *Canada (Attorney General) v. P.S.A.C.* (1991), 80 D.L.R. (4th) 520 (S.C.C.) (hereinafter *Econosult*) at 544-45.

24 [1980] 2 All E.R. 634 (U.K. H.L.) per Lord Diplock, at 638-39. See also *O'Reilly v. Mackman*, [1983] A.C. 120 (H.L.); *Millbanks v. Secretary of State for Home Dept.*, [1983] A.C. 120 (H.L.); and Lord Diplock, "Administrative Law: Judicial Review Reviewed" [1974] Camb.

[W]here Parliament confers on an administrative tribunal or authority, as distinct from a court of law, power to decide particular questions defined by the Act conferring the power, Parliament intends to confine that power to answering the question as it has been so defined, and if there has been any doubt as to what that question is this is a matter for the courts of law to resolve in fulfilment of their constitutional role as interpreters of the written law and expounders of the common law and rules of equity. So, if the administrative tribunal or authority have asked themselves the wrong question and answered that, they have done something that the act does not empower them to do and their decision is a nullity. . . . *The breakthrough made by Anisminic* [[1969] 2 A.C. 147] was that, as respects administrative tribunals and authorities, the old distinction between errors of law that went to jurisdiction and errors of law that did not was for practical purposes abolished. Any error of law that could be shown to have been made by them in the course of reaching their decision on matters of fact or of administrative policy would result in their having asked themselves the wrong question with the result that the decision they reached would be a nullity. [Emphasis added.]

Curiously, the English Parliament had abandoned the use of privative clauses[25] almost entirely after *Anisminic* and long before *Racal* and *O'Reilly*. As a result, it was not actually necessary for the House of Lords to treat all errors of law as going to jurisdiction in order for the courts to have the power to review, because in fact there were no privative clauses to prevent the historical and anomalous use of *certiorari* to correct intra-jurisdictional errors on the face of the record (as described in Chapter 11).

Indeed, it may be that the English approach will permit the courts to correct *any* error of law, whether or not it is apparent on the face of the record. As Lord Diplock said:[26]

Any error of law that could be shown to have been made by them in the course of reaching their decision on matters of fact or of administrative policy *would result in their having asked themselves the wrong question with the result that the decision they reached would be a nullity.* [Emphasis added.]

The implication is that there is only one right interpretation of the law, the interpretation of the courts, and there is little effective room for Parliament to delegate discretion to administrative agencies about the meaning or application of legal concepts. Accordingly, the standard for judicial review in England appears to be "correctness", at least as far as any question of law is concerned.

L.J. 233. But compare the decision of the Privy Council in *South East Asia Fire Bricks Sdn. Bhd. v. Non-Metallic Mineral Products Manufacturing Employees' Union* (1980), [1981] A.C. 363 (Malaysia P.C.), rendered ten days before *Re Racal*.

25 Privative clauses are discussed in more detail below.

26 *Supra* note 24 at 639.

One of the consequences of the absence of using privative clauses in England – and the English courts' assumption that any interpretation by an administrative agency of legal concepts which differs from the courts' interpretation will take the administrators outside their jurisdiction – is that English law does not contain our Canadian erudition on "patent unreasonableness", "curial deference", the "pragmatic and functional approach" to determining which matters are jurisdictional and which lie within the jurisdiction of the statutory delegate, or the concept of a spectrum of standards of review (or deference). As will be seen below, the law of Canada now differs from the law of England because our courts will not necessarily correct all errors of law.

(c) The Low-Water Mark for Judicial Review in Canada: C.U.P.E. and the "Not Patently Unreasonable" Test as a Shield from Judicial Review

The decision of the Supreme Court of Canada in *C.U.P.E., Local 963 v. New Brunswick Liquor Corp.*[27] marked a significant turning point in the Canadian courts' attitude towards statutory delegates, greatly minimizing the circumstances in which the courts would review administrative decisions. In effect, the courts applied the "not patently unreasonable test" to shield an enormous range of alleged administrative errors from judicial review.

C.U.P.E. involved a decision of the New Brunswick Public Service Labour Relations Board which interpreted a provision in its Act that an "employer shall not replace . . . striking employees or fill their positions with any other employee". The question was whether the Board had jurisdiction to interpret "other employee" to include management personnel, or whether the Court should impose its interpretation on the Board. Cory J. has described the Court's approach in *C.U.P.E.* as follows:[28]

> Dickson J. (as he then was), writing for the court, noted that the section in question was replete with ambiguity. He then set out with compelling force the rationale for *protecting decisions of administrative tribunals which were made within their jurisdiction.* He wrote at 424 [D.L.R.]:
>
>> The labour board is a specialized tribunal which administers a comprehensive statute regulating labour relations. In the administration of that regime, a board is called upon not only to find facts and decide questions of law, but also to exercise its understanding of the body of jurisprudence that has developed around the collective bargaining system, as understood in Canada, and its labour relations sense acquired from accumulated experience in the area.
>>
>> The usual reasons for judicial restraint upon review of labour board decisions are only reinforced in a case such as the one at

---

27 [1979] 2 S.C.R. 227, 97 D.L.R. (3d) 417 (S.C.C.).
28 In *Econosult, supra* note 23 at 545.

bar. Not only has the Legislature confided certain decisions to an administrative board, but to a separate and distinct Public Service Labour Relations Board. That Board is given broad powers – broader than those typically vested in a labour board – to supervise and administer the novel system of collective bargaining created by the *Public Service Labour Relations Act*. The Act calls for a delicate balance between the need to maintain public services, and the need to maintain collective bargaining. Considerable sensitivity and unique expertise on the part of Board members is all the more required if the twin purposes of the legislation are to be met.

He went on to stress that judicial restraint should be exercised in reviewing the P.S.L.R.B.'s interpretation of the words in issue, since an interpretation of the provision in question was a function that "would seem to lie logically at the heart of the specialized jurisdiction confided to the board" (p. 424). From this, it followed that "not only would the Board not be required to be 'correct' in its interpretation but one would think that *the Board was entitled to err and any such error would be protected from review by the privative clause*". He then defined the appropriate *standard for judicial review* in these words at 237 [S.C.R.]:

> Did the Board here so misinterpret the provisions of the Act as to embark on an inquiry or answer a question not remitted to it? Put another way, *was the Board's interpretation so patently unreasonable that its construction cannot be rationally supported by the relevant legislation and demands intervention by the court upon review*? [Underlined emphasis added; italicized emphasis added by Cory J.]

(i) Post-C.U.P.E. Euphoria

The euphoric (but ultimately incorrect) reaction by many administrative law observers[29] to *C.U.P.E.* was that the "patent unreasonableness" test should be applied in *all* circumstances – jurisdictional or not, with or without a privative clause – to protect *all* decisions of *all* statutory delegates from *all* forms of judicial review. As Cory J. described it:[30]

> The immediate effect of the *C.U.P.E.* decision has been charted by Wilson J. in her reasons in *National Corn Growers Assn.* . . . Legal writers hailed the decision as setting out a "restricted and unified theory of judicial review". The *C.U.P.E.* test of reasonableness was applied in situations where labour boards were protected by a privative clause[,] in cases of consensual arbitrators, statutory arbitrators and, as well, to labour relations board decisions not protected by a privative

---

29   Members of the "Central Canadian Anti-Judicial Review Establishment"!
30   *Supra* note 23 at 546.

clause [though perhaps by a privative "gloss"[31]]. Generally, these cases preclude judicial interference with interpretations made by a board as long as they are not patently unreasonable. . . .

The principle adopted in *C.U.P.E.* reached its zenith when it was applied in *Teamsters Union Local 938 v. Massicotte* (1982) 1134 D.L.R. (3d) 385, [1982] 1 S.C.R. 710. . . . In that case Laskin C.J., at p. 724, stated that: *"mere doubt as to correctness* of labour board interpretation of its statutory power *is no ground for finding jurisdictional error*, especially when the labour board is exercising powers confided to it in wide terms to resolve competing contentions".

C.U.P.E. and the decisions referred to above, make it clear that an administrative tribunal will, in ordinary circumstances, lose jurisdiction only if it acts in a patently unreasonable manner. [Emphasis added.]

The cases cited by Cory J. are:

- *U.A.W., Local 720 v. Volvo Canada Ltd.*[32]

- *Douglas Aircraft Co. of Canada v. McConnell.*[33]

- *A.U.P.E., Local 63 v. Alberta (Public Service Employees' Relations Board)*,[34] which assimilates the "privative gloss" of a final and binding clause to a "privative clause" ousting judicial review.

- *C.A.I.M.A.W., Local 14 v. Canadian Kenworth Co.*[35]

- *I.B.T., Local 938 v. Massicotte.*[36]

Thus, the immediate reaction to the *C.U.P.E.* case was the assertion that reasonableness was a complete shield against judicial review on *all* grounds. This minimalist standard for judicial review was subsequently eloquently restated in Wilson J.'s dissents in *National Corn Growers*[37] and *Lester*[38] – although the majority of the Supreme Court has clearly now recognized that this is not an accurate statement of either the law or the court's own constitutional role.

---

31 The concept of a "privative gloss" comes from *A.U.P.E., Local 63 v. Alberta (Public Service Employees' Relations Board)*, [1982] 1 S.C.R. 923 (S.C.C.), where the privative clause specifically permitted applications for judicial review within a certain window of time.

32 (1979), [1980] 1 S.C.R. 178 (S.C.C.).

33 (1979), [1980] 1 S.C.R. 245 (S.C.C.).

34 [1982] 1 S.C.R. 923 (S.C.C.).

35 [1989] 2 S.C.R. 983 at 1003-04 (S.C.C.).

36 [1982] 1 S.C.R. 710 (S.C.C.).

37 *National Corn Growers Assn. v. Canada (Canadian Import Tribunal)*, [1990] 2 S.C.R. 1324 (S.C.C.).

38 *W.W. Lester (1978) Ltd. v. U.A., Local 740*, [1990] 3 S.C.R. 644 (S.C.C.).

(d) The Subsequent Clarification: The "Correctness Test" Applied to Jurisdictional Matters

The subsequent cases make it clear that the post-*C.U.P.E.* euphoria was not justified, and that the patently unreasonable test could not be applied to all applications for judicial review. The unstated assumption in the generalized use of the "patently unreasonable" test was that one is talking about a delegate who had otherwise undoubtedly acquired jurisdiction, and who also would normally have undoubted jurisdiction to take the action in question. Thus, a more accurate and complete statement of the test would read as follows:

> *C.U.P.E.*, and the decisions referred to above, make it clear that an administrative tribunal will, in ordinary circumstances *lose jurisdiction [which it has undoubtedly already acquired, and would normally be able to exercise]* only if it acts in a patently unreasonable manner.

In a long line of cases, the Supreme Court subsequently clarified *C.U.P.E.* and restricted the application of the patently unreasonable test to a broad – but nevertheless limited – range of circumstances. As will be seen below, it is now clearly established that the "patently unreasonable" test has no application to matters that clearly involve jurisdictional givens, including constitutional questions.[39] In at least those circumstances, the correctness test must be applied.

(i) The "Correctness Test" Applied to Preliminary or Collateral Matters

As Dickson J. acknowledged in *C.U.P.E., Local 963* itself, the category of preliminary or collateral errors still conceptually exists (although the courts may not be astute to find that a particular alleged error fits into these categories), and other matters can also be clearly jurisdictional (although if there was any doubt, the courts may treat the matter as being one within the delegate's jurisdiction):[40]

> With respect, I do not think that the language of "preliminary or collateral matter" assists in the inquiry into the Board's jurisdiction. One can, I suppose, in most circumstances subdivide the matter before an administrative tribunal into a series of tasks or questions and, without too much difficulty, characterize one of those questions as a "preliminary or collateral matter". As Wade suggest in his *Administrative Law* (4th ed. 1977) at p. 245, questions of fact will naturally be regarded as "the primary and central questions for decision", whereas the "prescribed statutory ingredients will be more readily found to be collateral". This is precisely what has occurred in this

---

39   And perhaps also to questions involving the interpretation of "external" statutes (as opposed to the "constituent" statute of the tribunal). Depending upon how important the construction of the external statute is to the mandate of the statutory delegate, the courts may show some deference to its interpretation: *A.C.T.R.A. v. Canadian Broadcasting Corp.*, [1995] 1 S.C.R. 157, 27 Admin. L.R. (2d) 1 (S.C.C.); *C.U.P.E. v. Ontario (Minister of Labour)*, 2003 SCC 29 (S.C.C.) (the *Retired Judges Case*).

40   [1979] 2 S.C.R. 227 at 233 (S.C.C.).

case, the existence of the prohibition [against filling a striker's position with another "employee"] described in the statute becoming the "collateral matter", and the facts possibly constituting breach of the prohibition, however interpreted, the "primary matter for enquiry". Underlying this sort of language is, however, another and, in my opinion, a preferable approach to jurisdictional problems, namely, that jurisdiction is typically to be determined at the outset of the inquiry.

The question of what is and is not jurisdictional is often very difficult to determine. The courts, in my view, should not be alert to brand as jurisdictional, and therefore subject to broader curial review, that which may be doubtfully so. [Emphasis added.]

(ii) The "Correctness Test" Applied to Other Types of Jurisdictional Issues Too

The mere fact that a delegate's decision is reasonable does not protect it from judicial review on jurisdictional grounds; mere reasonableness neither clothes the delegate with jurisdiction if the legislature has not done so itself, nor insulates the delegate's decision from judicial review. This proposition was unequivocally re-established in two post-*C.U.P.E.* decisions written by Beetz J.: *Syndicat* and *Bibeault*.

(A) The Syndicat case

In *Syndicat des employés de production du Québec & de l'Acadie v. Canada (Labour Relations Board)*,[41] the question was whether the federal Labour Relations Board – which undoubtedly had general jurisdiction over the parties and the dispute – had jurisdiction to refer a particular matter to arbitration. Beetz J. unequivocally held that the patently unreasonable test had no application once it had been determined that a jurisdictional question was involved:[42]

> [A jurisdictional error] relates generally to a provision which confers jurisdiction, that is, one which describes, lists and limits the powers of an administrative tribunal, or which is [TRANSLATION] "intended to circumscribe the authority" of that tribunal, as Pigeon J. said in *Komo Construction Inc. v. Commission des relations de travail du Québec,* [1968] S.C.R. 172 at p. 175. A jurisdictional error results generally in an excess of jurisdiction or a refusal to exercise jurisdiction, whether at the start of the hearing, during it, in the findings or in the order disposing of the matter. Such an error, even if committed in the best possible good faith, will result nonetheless in the decision containing it being set aside. . . .

---

41   [1984] 2 S.C.R. 412 (S.C.C.).
42   *Ibid.* at 420-21.

Once the error was classified as jurisdictional, the reasonableness – or lack of patent unreasonableness – was irrelevant:[43]

> Unquestionably, as has already been noted, it is often difficult to determine what constitutes a question of jurisdiction, and administrative tribunals like the Board must generally be given the benefit of any doubt. Once the classification has been established, however, it does not matter whether an error as to such a question is doubtful, excusable or not unreasonable, or on the contrary is excessive, blatant or patently unreasonable. What makes this kind of error fatal, whether serious or slight, is its jurisdictional nature. . . .
>
> *Once a question is classified as one of jurisdiction, and has been the subject of a decision by an administrative tribunal, the superior court exercising the superintending and reforming power over that tribunal cannot, without itself refusing to exercise its own jurisdiction, refrain from ruling on the correctness of that decision, or rule on it by means of an approximate criterion.*
>
> *This is why the superior courts which exercise the power of judicial review do not and may not use the rule of the patently unreasonable error once they have classified an error as jurisdictional.* [Emphasis added.]

As Cory J. subsequently noted in *Econosult*,[44] this statement of the law was strongly criticized by many commentators, including Wilson J. in her dissent in *National Corn Growers Assn.* (discussed below). However, it is now clear that Beetz J. stated the law correctly in *Syndicat*, and that this was unequivocally accepted by Cory J. and the rest of the Supreme Court in *Econosult*.

(e) The "Functional and Pragmatic" Test for Identifying Jurisdictional Matters: Bibeault and Econosult

The difficulty, however, was to have some method of determining whether a particular matter is a jurisdictional given or not. While some matters may clearly be jurisdictional, and other questions may clearly not be jurisdictional, there may be a large grey area of uncertainty about whether the delegate has jurisdiction to decide other matters. What test was to be applied to determine whether the delegate has jurisdiction to deal with a particular matter or not?

(i) The Bibeault case

In *Syndicat national des employés de la commission scolaire régionale de l'Outaouais v. U.E.S., local 298*,[45] Beetz J. observed:[46]

---

43 *Ibid.* at 441-42.
44 *Canada (Attorney General) v. P.S.A.C.* (1991), 80 D.L.R. (4th) 520 (S.C.C.).
45 [1988] 2 S.C.R. 1048 (S.C.C.).
46 *Ibid.* at 1086-87.

The idea of the preliminary or collateral question is based on the principle that the jurisdiction conferred on administrative tribunals and other bodies created by statute is limited, and that such a tribunal cannot by a misinterpretation of an enactment assume a power not given to it by the legislator. The theoretical basis of this idea is therefore unimpeachable – which may explain why it has never been squarely repudiated: any grant of jurisdiction will necessarily include limits to the jurisdiction granted, and any grant of a power remains subject to conditions. The principle itself presents no difficulty, but its application is another matter.

The theory of the preliminary or collateral question does not appear to recognize that the legislator may intend to give an administrative tribunal, expressly or by implication, the power to determine whether certain conditions of law or fact placed on the exercise of its power do exist. It is not always true that each of these conditions limits the tribunal's authority; but *except where the legislator is explicit, how can one distinguish a condition which the legislator intended to leave to the exclusive determination of the administrative tribunal from a condition which limits its authority and as to which it may not err?* One can make the distinction only by means of a more or less formalistic categorization. Such a categorization often runs the risk of being arbitrary and which may in particular unduly extend the superintending and reforming power of the superior courts by transforming it into a disguised right of appeal.

The concept of the preliminary or collateral question diverts the courts from the real problem of judicial review: it substitutes the question "Is this a preliminary or collateral question to the exercise of the tribunal's power?" for the only question which should be asked, "Did the legislator intend the question to be within the jurisdiction conferred on the tribunal?" [Emphasis added.]

Then Beetz J. articulated his method for determining whether an alleged error is jurisdictional or not:[47]

The formalistic analysis of the preliminary or collateral question theory is giving way to a pragmatic and functional analysis, hitherto associated with the concept of the patently unreasonable error. At first sight it may appear that the functional analysis applied to cases of patently unreasonable error is not suitable for cases in which an error is alleged in respect of a legislative provision limiting a tribunal's jurisdiction. *The difference between these two types of error is clear: only a patently unreasonable error results in an excess of jurisdiction when the question at issue is within the tribunal's jurisdiction, whereas in the case of a legislative provision limiting the tribunal's jurisdiction, a simple error will result in a loss of jurisdiction. It is nevertheless*

_____

47 *Ibid.* at 1088.

*true that the first step in the analysis necessary in the concept of a
"patently unreasonable" error involves determining the jurisdiction
of the administrative tribunal. At this stage, the Court examines not
only the wording of the enactment conferring jurisdiction on the administrative tribunal, but the purpose of the statute creating the tribunal, the reason for its existence, the area of expertise of its members
and the nature of the problem before the tribunal.* At this initial stage
a pragmatic or functional analysis is just as suited to a case in which
an error is alleged in the interpretation of a provision limiting the
administrative tribunal's jurisdiction: in a case where a patently unreasonable error is alleged on a question within the jurisdiction of the
tribunal, as in a case where simple error is alleged regarding a provision limiting that jurisdiction, the first step involves determining the
tribunal's jurisdiction. [Emphasis added.]

(ii) The Econosult Case

In *Econosult*,[48] the majority of the Supreme Court ruled that the federal
Public Service Staff Relations Board did not have jurisdiction to determine
who was an "employee" of the federal Crown, given the definition of "employee" contained in the Act – notwithstanding the fact that the Board's functional approach might well have been reasonable and made labour relations
sense. In other words, the objective reasonability of a delegate's decision did
not *ipso facto* give it jurisdiction to make the decision if the courts decide that
the legislature did not grant that jurisdiction to the delegate. Mr. Justice Cory
neatly summarized the evolution of the law in England, the United States and
Canada in his dissent in *Econosult*.[49]

In *Econosult*, all of the judges of the Supreme Court used the "pragmatic
and functional" approach to determine whether Parliament intended to confer
jurisdiction on the Public Service Staff Relations Board to determine who was
an "employee" for the purposes of its Act. However, the members of the Court
reached different conclusions about the results of applying this approach.

Sopinka J., writing for the majority of the Court, held that Parliament did
not intend to leave this matter to the Board's discretion, because (1) Parliament
had defined "employee" in section 2 of the Act, thereby indicating clearly its
intention to limit the Board's jurisdiction to those who fell within that definition; (2) any other interpretation would recognize the creation of a category of
de facto public servants, contrary to the purposes of the whole matrix of federal
legislation on this subject; (3) this indicated that Parliament did not intend for
the Board to rely on its general labour law expertise to extend its precise

---

48   (1991), 80 D.L.R. (4th) 520 (S.C.C.).

49   Cory J. dissented about the actual disposition of the appeal, because he reached the opposite
result after doing his pragmatic and functional analysis. Although Cory J. dissented about
whether the decision of the Public Service Staff Relations Board in that case was patently
unreasonable, all of the judges accepted his statement about the law or standard to be applied
in determining whether there was a jurisdictional error susceptible to judicial review.

definition of "employee"; and (4) no previous decision of the Court contradicted the conclusion resulting from this pragmatic and functional approach.

All seven members of the Court agreed that characterization of a matter as jurisdictional or not was to be done on a "pragmatic and functional" basis.[50] If this approach determined that Parliament had confided the matter[51] to the delegate, then the "patently unreasonable" test should be applied to determine whether the delegate had exceeded its jurisdiction. If this approach determined that Parliament intended the matter to be a "jurisdictional given" as far as the statutory delegate was concerned, then the "correctness" test should be applied. Up to this point, there were only two standards – "correctness" and "not patently unreasonable" – which operated rather like an "on/off" switch, with nothing in between.

(iii) The Fact That There are "Jurisdictional Consequences" Does Not Necessarily Mean That the Correctness Standard Applies

In *Alberta v. Alberta (Labour Relations Board)*,[52] the Court of Appeal of Alberta made the distinction between a "jurisdictional given" (about which the Legislature did not intend the statutory delegate's decision to be determinative) and a matter which the Legislature clearly intended the statutory delegate to determine definitively even though its decision might have "jurisdictional consequences".

The issue involved a determination about whether four newly-created municipalities were "successor employers" and therefore governed by the existing collective agreement which the Crown had previously entered into with AUPE when the functions in question were carried on by Crown employees. If the Board determined that the municipalities were successors, then it had jurisdiction to go on and deal with the collective agreement regime resulting therefrom. On the other hand, if the Board determined that the municipalities were not successors, then it had no jurisdiction to go further. The

---

50   The court has continued to use the functional and pragmatic test: see for example, *I.L.W.U., Ship & Dock Foremen, Local 514 v. Prince Rupert Grain Ltd.* (1996), 40 Admin. L.R. (2d) 1 at 15-17 (S.C.C.), per Cory J.

51   How does one identify the "matter" in question? Is the "matter" to be defined broadly or narrowly?

See the decision of the Supreme Court of Canada in *A.C.T.R.A. v. Canadian Broadcasting Corp.*, [1995] 1 S.C.R. 157, 27 Admin. L.R. (2d) 1 (S.C.C.). McLachlin J. (dissenting) held that the functional test is question-specific and must be applied to each question which the Board considered, and the appropriate standard of review must then be applied to its answer to that specific question. She held that this requirement is not obviated by the fact that the question is part of the substance of the dispute, or is preliminary or jurisdictional. The majority used a broader approach to characterize the "matter" in question.

See the recent decisions in *C.U.P.E. v. Ontario (Minister of Labour)*, 2003 SCC 29, 226 D.L.R. (4th) 193 (S.C.C.) (the *Retired Judges Case*) at para. 97 (Binnie J.) and paras. 6-13 (Bastarache J.); and *Barrie Public Utilities v. Canadian Cable Television Assn.*, 2003 SCC 28, 225 D.L.R. (4th) 206 (S.C.C.) at paras. 59-66 and 125 (Bastarache J.).

52   (2002), 2001 ABCA 299, 40 Admin. L.R. (3d) 115 (Alta. C.A.), application for leave to appeal dismissed by S.C.C. at (2002), [2002] S.C.C.A. No. 100, 2002 CarswellAlta 1135 (S.C.C.), additional reasons at [2003] 8 W.W.R. 397 (Alta. C.A.).

relevant legislation specifically conferred the power to make this decision on the Board, made its decision final and binding, and provided several further layers of privative clauses. The chambers judge[53] quashed the Board's decision on the basis that this matter was a jurisdictional given, which the Board had answered incorrectly. By contrast, the Court of Appeal noted that the legislation specifically provided that this matter was to be determined by an expert Board, whose decision was final and binding and protected by several layers of privative clauses, all of which made the patently unreasonable standard of review applicable. As the Board's decision was not patently unreasonable, it should not have been quashed.

Accordingly, the fact that there may be jurisdictional consequences flowing from the decision of a statutory delegate does not necessarily mean that the legislators intended the matter to be a jurisdictional given, as opposed to intending the statutory delegate to make the definitive decision on that matter. As the Supreme Court of Canada subsequently made clear in the companion cases of *Q.*[54] and *Ryan*,[55] there is no necessary relationship between particular types of errors and particular standards of review – it all depends on applying a pragmatic and functional approach to how much deference the legislators intended.

(f) The "Patently Unreasonable" Test

The "patently unreasonable" test was initially used in the context of alleged errors in the statutory delegate's interpretation of its constituent legislation, principally where there was a privative clause preventing judicial review. Issues arose about what "patently" meant, what was the relationship between a patently unreasonable decision and jurisdiction, and whether the test applied in circumstances beyond the interpretation of the statutory delegate's constituent legislation.

(i) What Does "Patently" Mean?

Historically, one referred to a "patent" error – that is, one which appears on the face of the record – as contrasted with a latent error. With respect to errors of law, the reference to "patent" relates to the anomalous[56] use of *certiorari* to correct intra-jurisdictional errors of law on the face of the record – a doctrine which was resuscitated in 1952 by Denning L.J. (as he then was) in *R. v. Northumberland Compensation Appeal Tribunal*.[57] In the absence of

---

53 (1998), 30 Admin. L.R. (3d) 24 (Alta. Q.B.), additional reasons at (1998), 30 Admin. L.R. (3d) 62 (Alta. Q.B.), reversed (2002), 40 Admin. L.R. (3d) 115 (Alta. C.A.), leave to appeal refused (2002), 300 N.R. 200 (note) (S.C.C.), additional reasons at [2003] 8 W.W.R. 397 (Alta. C.A.).

54 *Q. v. College of Physicians & Surgeons (British Columbia)*, [2003] 1 S.C.R. 226, 48 Admin. L.R. (3d) 1 (S.C.C.).

55 *Ryan v. Law Society (New Brunswick)*, [2003] 1 S.C.R. 247, 48 Admin L.R. (3d) 33 (S.C.C.).

56 "Anomalous" because all of the other uses of *certiorari* relate to jurisdictional defects of one sort or another, whereas *Shaw's* case shows that *certiorari* can be used to correct an intra-jurisdictional error of law on the face of the record (in the absence of a privative clause).

57 (1951), [1952] 1 K.B. 338 (Eng. C.A.), affirming (1950), [1951] 1 K.B. 711 (Eng. K.B.).

a privative clause, the courts assumed the right to correct *all* errors of law which appeared on the face of the record[58] of an inferior tribunal – regardless of whether the error was jurisdictional or not, and regardless of whether the error involved the delegate's interpretation of its own ("constituent") statute or some other question of law.[59]

Secondly, "unreasonableness" – whether apparent on the face of the record or not – has always been recognized as a ground for judicial review, particularly in the context of discretionary decisions. Alleging unreasonableness is effectively a sword to eviscerate the statutory delegate's decision.

However, to the extent that "not patently unreasonable" was a justification for not granting judicial review – for showing deference to the statutory tribunal, particularly in the face of a privative clause – the concept was effectively used as a shield. In this sense, the term took on more of a qualitative rather than a locational meaning. Only if a decision was "patently unreasonable" – "clearly irrational" or "off-the-wall" – would judicial review be issued.[60] In this sense, "patently unreasonable" was a standard of review which determined how stringently the court would examine the statutory delegate's decision.

As will be seen below, exactly how one determines whether something is "patently unreasonable" may be a matter of some debate about which different judges may have different appreciations. In addition, it has become necessary to distinguish "patent unreasonableness" from "reasonableness *simpliciter*" when the Supreme Court of Canada recognized the existence of the latter standard of review in the *Southam* case.

---

58 What constitutes the "record" is rather complicated. The common law position is rather well explained in *Shaw*'s case. Sometimes legislation changes the common law. Thus, in *R. v. Nat Bell Liquors Ltd.*, [1922] 2 A.C. 128 (Canada P.C.), legislation cut down the record to the bare bones, making it virtually impossible to demonstrate an error of law on the face of the record (see Chapter 11). On the other hand, most jurisdictions have now increased the scope of the record – or, at least, of the return which must be made of the record under the court's rules of civil practice. See for example Rules 753.13 and 753.14 of the Alberta *Rules of Court*, reproduced in Appendix 4.

59 For an example of some other question of law, see *McLeod v. Egan* (1974), [1975] 1 S.C.R. 517 (S.C.C.).

60 As La Forest J. put it in *C.A.I.M.A.W., Local 14 v. Canadian Kenworth Co.*, [1989] 2 S.C.C. 983 at 1003-04 (S.C.C.):

> . . . [A] tribunal has the right to make errors, even serious ones, provided it does not act in a manner 'so patently unreasonable that its conclusion cannot be rationally supported by the relevant legislation and demands intervention by the court upon review'.

But compare the following comments by Wilson J. (dissenting) at 1022:

> I am not sure how helpful it is to substitute one adjectival phrase for another and define patent unreasonableness in terms of rational indefensibility. It seems to me that this simply injects one more opportunity for ambiguity into a test which is already fraught with ambiguity. There is, it seems to me, a good argument to be made that "rational indefensibility" is an even stricter test than "patent unreasonableness". Be that as it may, both tests pose problems for the courts which, as my colleague points out, are to be viewed as lacking the special expertise required for the resolution of labour disputes which specialized labour boards enjoy.

(ii) "Unreasonableness" Goes Beyond Questions of Law

The courts have not restricted the eviscerating use of the "unreasonableness" test to the delegate's interpretation of its own legislation (its "constituent statute" or "constating legislation"), but have extended it to all aspects of the delegate's decision-making process, including evidentiary questions and findings of fact.

As Lamer J. noted in *Blanchard v. Control Data Canada Ltd.*:[61]

> In looking for an error which might affect jurisdiction, the emphasis placed by this Court on the dichotomy of the reasonable or unreasonable nature of the error casts doubt on the appropriateness of making, on this basis, a distinction between error of law and error of fact. In addition to the difficulty of classification, the distinction collides with that given by the courts to unreasonable errors of fact. An unreasonable error of fact has been categorized as an error of law. The distinction would mean that this error of law is then protected by the privative clause unless it is unreasonable. What more is needed in order that an unreasonable finding of fact, in becoming an error of law, becomes an unreasonable error of law? An administrative tribunal has the necessary jurisdiction to make a mistake, and even a serious one, but not to be unreasonable. The unreasonable finding is no less fatal to jurisdiction because the finding is one of fact rather than law. An unreasonable finding is what justifies intervention by the courts.

> Not only is the distinction between error of law and of fact superfluous in light of an unreasonable finding or conclusion, but the reference to error itself is as well. Indeed, though all errors do not lead to unreasonable findings, every unreasonable finding results from an error (whether of law, fact or a combination of the two), which is unreasonable.

> In conclusion, an unreasonable finding, whatever its origin, affects the jurisdiction of the tribunal. I hasten to add that the distinction between an error of law and one of fact is still entirely valid when the tribunal is not protected by a privative clause. Indeed, though all errors of law are then subjected to review, only unreasonable errors of fact are, but no others.

As discussed in Chapter 7, unreasonableness may also be grounds for judicial review of the exercise of a discretionary power.

(iii) The Relationship Between a Patently Unreasonable Decision and Jurisdiction

The conceptual basis for permitting the court to intervene (even in the face of a privative clause) when a decision is patently unreasonable lies in the presumption that the Legislature never intended to grant the statutory delegate

---

61   [1984] 2 S.C.R. 476 at 494-95 (S.C.C.).

jurisdiction to do any such thing: *C.A.I.M.A.W., Local 14 v. Canadian Kenworth Co.*[62]

As a result of this jurisdictional aspect of a finding that a statutory delegate's action is patently unreasonable, the delegate has standing to defend the reasonableness of its decision – and therefore its jurisdiction – in judicial review proceedings.[63]

(g) The Development of the Concept of a Spectrum of Standards of Review, the Articulation of the Intermediate Standard of "Reasonableness Simpliciter", and Using the Functional and Pragmatic Approach to Determine the Applicable Standard of Review

Although credit for articulating the concept of different standards of review belongs to Roger Kerans J.A. of the Court of Appeal of Alberta,[64] three decisions of the Supreme Court of Canada developed the concept of a spectrum of standards of review applicable to both statutory appeals and applications for judicial review, articulated "reasonableness *simpliciter*" as an intermediate standard of review, and prescribed a functional and pragmatic approach to determine the applicable standard of review in a particular case:

- *Pezim v. British Columbia (Superintendent of Brokers).*[65]

- *Canada (Director of Investigation & Research) v. Southam Inc.*[66]

- *Pushpanathan v. Canada (Minister of Employment & Immigration).*[67]

(i) Pezim

Pezim is the first instance in which the Supreme Court of Canada referred to the concept of a spectrum of standards of review. It involved a statutory

---

62   [1989] 2 S.C.R. 983 at 1003-04 (S.C.C.).

63   *Ibid.* See comment by R.W. Macaulay, (1990-91) 4 C.J.A.L.P. 85; *B.C.G.E.U. v. British Columbia (Industrial Relations Council)* (1988), 32 Admin. L.R. 78 at 91 (B.C. C.A.) per Taggart J.A. For a critical comment about a board exercising this right to be heard, see *Ferguson Bus Lines Ltd. v. A.T.U., Local 1374*, 43 Admin. L.R. 18 at 38-40, [1990] 2 F.C. 586, 68 D.L.R. (4th) 699 (Fed. C.A.), leave to appeal refused at (1990), 74 D.L.R. (4th) viii (S.C.C.). The general rule, of course, is that a statutory delegate should be very circumspect in any submissions it makes in an application for judicial review or an appeal, whether a party or an intervener: *Northwestern Utilities Ltd. v. Edmonton (City)* (1978), 7 Alta. L.R. (2d) 370 (S.C.C.) at 387-389; *Alberta v. Alberta (Labour Relations Board)* (2001), 30 Admin. L.R. (3d) 24 (Alta. Q.B.) at 43-44, additional reasons at (1998), 30 Admin. L.R. (3d) 62 (Alta. Q.B.), reversed (2002), 40 Admin. L.R. (3d) 115 (Alta. C.A.), leave to appeal refused (2002), 300 N.R. 200 (note) (S.C.C.), additional reasons at [2003] 8 W.W.R. 397 (Alta. C.A.); *Bransen Construction Ltd. v. C.J.A., Local 1386* (2002), 39 Admin. L.R. (3d) 1 (N.B. C.A.).

64   See his judgment in *Alberta (Workers' Compensation Board, Appeals Commission) v. Penny* (1993), 12 Alta. L.R. (3d) 238 (Alta. C.A.), and his subsequent book on this topic: *Standards of Review Employed by Appellate Courts* (Edmonton: Juriliber, 1994).

65   [1994] 2 S.C.R. 557 (S.C.C.).

66   [1997] 1 S.C.R. 748 (S.C.C.).

67   [1998] 1 S.C.R. 982 (S.C.C.), amended [1998] 1 S.C.R. 1222 (S.C.C.).

appeal from a decision of the superintendent of brokers revoking the right to be an officer of a publicly traded corporation. Because there was a right of appeal, and therefore no privative clause, the issue arose about the standard of review the court should use when reviewing the superintendent's decision:[68]

> From the outset, it is important to set forth certain principles of judicial review. There exist various standards of review with respect to the myriad of administrative agencies that exist in our country. The central question in ascertaining the standard of review is to determine the legislative intent in conferring jurisdiction on the administrative tribunal. In answering this question, the courts have looked at various factors. Included in the analysis is an examination of the tribunal's role or function. Also crucial is whether or not the agency's decisions are protected by a privative clause. Finally, of fundamental importance, is whether or not the question goes to the jurisdiction of the tribunal involved.
>
> Having regard to the large number of factors relevant in determining the applicable standard of review, *the courts have developed a spectrum that ranges from the standard of reasonableness to that of correctness*. Courts have also enunciated a principle of deference that applies not just to the facts as found by the tribunal, but also to the legal questions before the tribunal in the light of its role and expertise. *At the reasonableness end of the spectrum*, where deference is at its highest, are those cases where a tribunal protected by a true privative clause is deciding a matter within its jurisdiction, and where there is no statutory right of appeal. . . .
>
> *At the correctness end of the spectrum*, where deference in terms of legal questions is at its lowest, are those cases where the issues concern the interpretation of a provision limiting the tribunal's jurisdiction (jurisdictional error) or where there is a statutory right of appeal which allows the reviewing court to substitute its opinion for that of the tribunal and where the tribunal has no greater expertise than the court on the issue in question, as for example in the area of human rights. . . . [Emphasis added.]

Notwithstanding the reference to a *spectrum* of standards of review,[69] at the end of the day the Court settled on the patent unreasonableness standard – one of the end points on the spectrum. Because the decision of the superintendent (who was specialized in this regulatory area) was not patently unreasonable, it was not set aside by the Court.

---

68 [1994] 2 S.C.R. 557, 22 Admin. L.R. (2d) 1 at 27-28 (S.C.C.).

69 As noted below, the subsequent decisions in *Q. v. College of Physicians & Surgeons (British Columbia)*, [2003] 1 S.C.R. 226 (S.C.C.) and *Ryan v. Law Society (New Brunswick)*, [2003] 1 S.C.R. 247 (S.C.C.) make it plain that there is not a spectrum of *standards of review*, but rather a spectrum of *deference* which in turn determines which of the three recognized standards of review is to be used in a particular case.

(ii) Southam

Subsequently, however, the Court in *Southam* – another appeal case – not only reiterated the concept of a spectrum of standards of review, but actually applied a new intermediate standard of review ("reasonableness *simpliciter*") which was found along the spectrum:[70]

F. The Standard

In my view, considering all of the factors I have canvassed, what is dictated is a standard more deferential than correctness but less deferential than "not patently unreasonable". Several considerations counsel deference: the fact that the dispute is over a question of mixed law and fact; the fact that the purpose of the *Competition Act* is broadly economic, and so is better served by the exercise of economic judgment; and the fact that the application of principles of competition law falls squarely within the area of the Tribunal's expertise. Other considerations counsel a more exacting form of review: the existence of an unfettered statutory right of appeal from decisions of the Tribunal and the presence of judges on the Tribunal. *Because there are indications both ways, the proper standard of review falls somewhere between the ends of the spectrum.* Because the expertise of the Tribunal, which is the most important consideration, suggests deference, a posture more deferential than exacting is warranted.

I wish to emphasize that the need to find a middle ground in cases like this one is almost a necessary consequence of our standard-of-review jurisprudence. Because appeal lies by statutory right from the Tribunal's decisions on questions of mixed law and fact, the reviewing court need not confine itself to the search for errors that are patently unreasonable. The standard of patent unreasonableness is principally a jurisdictional test [to determine whether the statutory delegate has exceeded or left its jurisdiction] and, as I have said, the statutory right of appeal puts the jurisdictional question to rest. See *New Brunswick Liquor Corp. v. C.U.P.E., Local 963* . . ., [1979] 2 S.C.R. 227, at p. 237. But on the other hand, appeal from a decision of an expert tribunal is not exactly like appeal from a decision of a trial court. Presumably if Parliament entrusts a certain matter to a tribunal and not (initially at least) to the courts, it is because the tribunal enjoys some advantage that judges do not. For that reason alone, review of the decision of a tribunal should often be on a standard more deferential than correctness. Accordingly, a third standard is needed.

I conclude that the third standard should be whether the decision of the Tribunal is unreasonable. This test is to be distinguished from the most deferential standard of review, which requires courts to consider whether a tribunal's decision is patently unreasonable. *An unreason-*

---

able decision is one that, in the main, is not supported by any reasons that can stand up to a somewhat probing examination. Accordingly, a court reviewing a conclusion on the reasonableness standard must look to see whether any reasons support it. The defect, if there is one, could presumably be in the evidentiary foundation itself or in the logical process by which conclusions are sought to be drawn from it. An example of the former kind of defect would be an assumption that has no basis in the evidence, or that was contrary to the overwhelming weight of the evidence. An example of the latter kind of defect would be a contradiction in the premises or an invalid inference. [Emphasis added.]

The distinction between "unreasonable *simpliciter*" and "patently unreasonable" is discussed in greater detail below.

(iii) Initial Doubt About Whether the Spectrum Applies Both to Appeals and to Applications for Judicial Review

Curiously, almost immediately after *Southam*, the Supreme Court issued two *judicial review* decisions (both from Quebec) which (a) did not refer to *Pezim* or *Southam* at all, (b) did not refer to the concept of a spectrum of possible standards of review, (c) did not refer to the standard of "reasonableness *simpliciter*", and (d) simply applied the "not patently unreasonable" test without any conceptual discussion at all: *Pointe-Claire (Ville) c. S.E.P.B., Local 5*[71] and *S.C.F.P., Local 301 c. Québec (Conseil des services essentiels).*[72] This raised a doubt about whether the law with respect to standards of review differed for appeals compared with applications for judicial review. Were there any circumstances in which the court – on an application for judicial review – should apply a more stringent standard than "not patently unreasonable", but less stringent than "correctness"? For example, if the legislation did not contain a privative clause? Or if the statutory delegate did not have any particular expertise about the matter? Would it depend on the nature and wording of the power being exercised?[73] Certainly the constellation of factors involved in the pragmatic and functional analysis developed in *Bibeault* to determine whether a matter is a jurisdictional given or lies within jurisdiction had been applied to

---

71   [1997] 1 S.C.R. 1015 (S.C.C.).

72   [1997] 1 S.C.R. 793 (S.C.C.).

73   For example, in *Miller v. Newfoundland (Workers' Compensation Commission)* (1997), 2 Admin. L.R. (3d) 178 (Nfld. T.D.) at 183-84, the reviewing judge applied the reasonableness standard, in light of the fact that the statute authorized the original decision-maker (the Chief Review Commissioner) to draw *reasonable* inferences from the facts:

But often, as in the present case, the alleged error is one of fact in the inferences drawn from the evidence or one of mixed law and fact. The standard of review would then normally be that of patent unreasonableness, because of the strong privative clause in the legislation. At worst, from the Commission's perspective, the standard of review for s. 60(1), as opposed to other provisions, would be the standard of reasonableness incorporated into s. 60(1) by the reference to "reasonable inferences". This "reasonableness" standard has recently been adopted as a third standard by the Supreme Court of Canada [in *Southam*].

both applications for judicial review and appeals – why wouldn't the concept of a spectrum of standards also apply?[74]

In *Pushpanathan*,[75] the Supreme Court of Canada made it clear that the spectrum *does* apply both to applications for judicial review and to appeals.

(iv) Pushpanathan

The issue in *Pushpanathan* arose as follows. The Federal Court Trial Division had dismissed the appellant's application for judicial review of a decision of the Convention Refugee Determination Division of the Immigration and Refugee Board, and certified the following "serious question of general importance" for consideration by the Federal Court of Appeal: *"Is it an error of law for the Refugee Division to interpret Art. 1F(c) of the Convention to exclude from refugee status an individual guilty of a serious* Narcotics Control Act *offence committed in Canada?"*.[76]

Although none of the lower decisions nor the written submissions addressed the standard of review, Bastarache J. identified this as the very first question to be answered (and must be answered in every case):[77]

> The certification of a "question of general importance" is the trigger by which an appeal [from the Trial Division] is justified. The object of the appeal is still the judgment itself, not merely the certified question. *One of the elements necessary for the disposition of an application for judicial review is the standard of review of the decision of the administrative tribunal whose decision is being reviewed, and that question is clearly in issue in this case.* Reluctant as this Court is to decide issues not fully argued before it, determining the standard of review is a prerequisite to the disposition of this case. [Emphasis added.]

Bastarache J. identified the two traditional standards of review, and then noted the development of the spectrum or range of standards in *Southam*:[78]

> The central inquiry in determining the standard of review exercisable by a court of law is the legislative intent of the statute creating the tribunal whose decision is being reviewed. More specifically, the reviewing court must ask: "[W]as the question which the provision raises one that was intended by the legislators to be left to the exclusive

74 For further discussion see D.P. Jones, "The Concept of a Spectrum of Standards of Review: Is There a Different Standard of Review for Appeals?" (1997) 6 R.A.L. 169.

75 [1998] 1 S.C.R. 982 (S.C.C.), reasons modified [1998] 1 S.C.R. 1222 (S.C.C.).

76 *Ibid.* at 1001. The Court has subsequently frequently reiterated the necessity of addressing the applicable standard of review in every case in *Moreau-Bérubé c. Nouveau-Brunswick*, [2002] 1 S.C.R. 249, 36 Admin. L.R. (3d) 1 (S.C.C.) at para. 36 (per Arbour J.); in *Chieu v. Canada (Minister of Citizenship & Immigration)*, [2002] 1 S.C.R. 84, 37 Admin. L.R. (3d) 252 (S.C.C.) at para. 20 (per Iacobucci J.); and in *Q. v. College of Physicians & Surgeons (British Columbia)*, [2003] 1 S.C.R. 226 (S.C.C.) at para. 40 (per Iacobucci J.).

77 *Ibid.* at 1004.

78 *Ibid.* at 1004-05.

jurisdiction of the Board?" (*Pasiechnyk v. Saskatchewan (Workers' Compensation Board)*, [1997] 2 S.C.R. 890, at para. 18, per Sopinka J.).

Since *U.E.S., Local 298 v. Bibeault*, [1988] 2 S.C.R. 1048, this Court has determined that the task of statutory interpretation requires a weighing of several different factors, none of which are alone dispositive, and each of which provides an indication falling on a spectrum of the proper level of deference to be shown the decision in question. This has been dubbed the "pragmatic and functional" approach. This more nuanced approach in determining legislative intent is also reflected in *the range of possible standards of review*. Traditionally, the "correctness" standard and the "patent unreasonableness" standard were the only two approaches available to a reviewing court. But in *Canada (Director of Investigation and Research) v. Southam Inc.*, [1997] 1 S.C.R. 748, a "reasonableness *simpliciter*" standard was applied as the most accurate reflection of the competence intended to be conferred on the tribunal by the legislator. Indeed, *the Court there described the range of standards available as a "spectrum" with a "more exacting end" and a "more deferential end"* (para. 30). [Emphasis added.]

(h) The Four Factors to be used in the Functional and Pragmatic Approach to Determine the Applicable Standard of Review

Bastarache J. then went on to identify four factors to be taken into account in the functional and pragmatic approach for determining the applicable standard of review, referring to many of the previous cases:[79]

- Whether there is a privative clause which would speak in favour of a more deferential standard (although absence of a privative clause does not necessarily invoke the correctness standard).

- Whether the statutory delegate has greater expertise on the matter in question.

- The purpose of the Act as a whole, and the provision at issue in particular.

- The "nature of the problem" – whether a question of law or fact.

Each of these factors will be considered more thoroughly below.

(i) *The Fleeting Thought There might be Many Standards along the Spectrum*

In the interval after *Pezim*, *Southam* and *Pushpanathan*, it was assumed that there were other possible standards of review along the spectrum, such as

---

79 *Ibid.* at 1006-12.

"correctness with an appropriate measure of deference",[80] and "deference absent a nearly patently unreasonable error".[81] In addition, "reasonableness *simpliciter*" was conceived of as being very contextual, occupying a broad band on the spectrum, with a variable content depending upon the circumstances. A great deal of time was taken up by counsel and the courts in trying to determine precisely at what point the particular standard of review lay on the spectrum in each particular case.

(k) *Dr. Q* and *Ryan*: The Transference of the Concept of a Spectrum from Standards to Deference, Three Standards of Review, and a Constant Meaning for "Reasonableness Simpliciter"

In 2003, in the companion cases of *Q*.[82] and *Ryan*,[83] the Court restricted the number of standards to three – correctness, reasonableness *simpliciter*, and patent unreasonableness; effectively transferred the concept of a spectrum to the amount of deference to be given to a particular statutory delegate, which in turn engages one of the three recognized standards of review; made it clear that there is a fixed meaning for "reasonableness *simpliciter*"; and reiterated that there is no necessary relationship between particular types of errors and particular standards of review – it all depends on applying a pragmatic and functional approach to determine how much deference the legislators intended the courts to apply in the particular case.

(i) *Only Three Standards*

With respect to limiting the number of standards of review, Justice Iacobucci made it clear in *Ryan* that there are only three standards of review:[84]

> [24] In the Court's jurisprudence, only three standards of review have been defined for judicial review of administrative action (*Chamberlain v. Surrey School District No. 36*, 2002 SCC 86, at para. 5, per McLachlin C.J.; *Baker v. Canada (Minister of Citizenship and Immigration)*, [1999] 2 S.C.R. 817, at para. 55; see also *Pezim v. British Columbia (Superintendent of Brokers)*, [1994] 2 S.C.R. 557, at pp. 589-90; *Canada (Director of Investigation and Research) v. Southam Inc.*, [1997] 1 S.C.R. 748, at para. 30;

---

80 *Northwood Inc. v. British Columbia (Forest Practices Board)*, 2001 BCCA 141 (B.C. C.A.), leave to appeal refused (2001), [2001] S.C.C.A. No. 207, 2001 CarswellBC 2119 (S.C.C.) (*Northwood*); *Van Unen v. British Columbia (Workers' Compensation Board)*, 2001 BCCA 262 (B.C. C.A.), leave to appeal to SCC denied on 4 October 2001 without reasons: (2001), [2001] S.C.C.A. No. 288, 2001 CarswellBC 2117 (S.C.C.) (*Van Unen*). See also *Skyline Roofing Ltd. v. Alberta (Workers' Compensation Board)* (2001), 34 Admin. L.R. 289 (Alta. Q.B.).

81 *Rickard Realty Advisors Inc. v. Calgary (City)*, 216 A.R. 271, 63 Alta L.R. (3d) 248, 1998 ABCA 173 (Alta. C.A.) at para. 7.

82 *Q. v. College of Physicians & Surgeons (British Columbia)*, [2003] 1 S.C.R. 226 (S.C.C.).

83 *Ryan v. Law Society (New Brunswick)*, [2003] 1 S.C.R. 247 (S.C.C.).

84 See also his article "Articulating a Rational Standard of Review Doctrine: A Tribute to John Willis" (2002) Queen's L.J. 809 at para. 31.

Pushpanathan, supra, at para. 27. The pragmatic and functional approach set out in *Bibeault, supra,* and more recently in *Pushpanathan, supra,* will determine, in each case, which of these three standards is appropriate. *I find it difficult, if not impracticable to conceive more than three standards of review. In any case, additional standards should not be developed unless there are questions of judicial review to which the three existing standards are obviously unsuited.*

[25] To elaborate on this point, in *Southam, supra,* the Court held that an unreasonable decision was one that did not stand up to a somewhat probing analysis. It is not clear that there is helpful language to describe a conceptually distinct fourth standard that would be less deferential than reasonableness *simpliciter* but more deferential than correctness. At this point, *the multiplication of standards past the three already identified would force reviewing courts and the parties that appear before them into complex and technical debates at the outset.* I am not convinced that the increase in complexity generated by adding a fourth standard would lead to greater precision in achieving the objectives of judicial review of administrative action.

[26] *A pragmatic and functional approach should not be unworkable or highly technical.* Therefore I emphasize that, as presently developed, there are only three standards. Thus a reviewing court must not interfere unless it can explain how the administrative action is incorrect, unreasonable, or patently unreasonable, depending on the appropriate standard. [Emphasis added.]

Accordingly, it should only be necessary to choose between these three standards of review in virtually all cases.

(ii) The Spectrum is a Spectrum of Deference, Not a Spectrum of Standards

The restriction of the number of standards of review does not mean that the concept of a spectrum has been abandoned, however. Rather, the Court has converted the spectrum of standards of review into a spectrum of deference. This is how Iacobucci J. put it in *Ryan*:

[45] *It is true that the Court has resorted to the metaphor of a spectrum in order to explain the relative ordering of the three recognized standards of review.* The idea is that the standards could be arranged from least deferential to most deferential with reasonableness as the intermediate standard of review. *The metaphor suggests standards arranged along a gradient of deference but it was never meant to suggest an infinite number of possible standards. That the metaphor relates to a spectrum of deference and not a spectrum of standards has become increasingly clear*

> *since the use of the term "spectrum" in Pezim, supra*, at p. 590
> (see *Baker, supra* at para. 55, per L'Heureux-Dubé J.; *Pushpan-*
> *athan, supra*, at para. 27, per Bastarache J.). As Major J. recently
> wrote: "[T]he various standards of review are properly viewed
> as points occurring on a spectrum of curial deference. They range
> from patent unreasonableness at the more deferential end of the
> spectrum, through reasonableness *simpliciter*, to correctness at
> the more exacting end of the spectrum" (*Mattel, supra*, at para.
> 24). [Emphasis added.]

Accordingly, the four factors from the pragmatic and functional approach
set out in *Pushpanathan* will be used to determine where a particular case lies
on the spectrum of deference, and that will in turn determine which of the three
recognized standards of review will be engaged.

(iii) The Fixed Meaning of Reasonableness Simpliciter

In *Ryan*, the Supreme Court also made it clear that the standard of "reasonableness *simpliciter*" does not have a variable content: it is a discrete point,
with constant content, which requires the court to determine whether "after a
somewhat probing examination, can the reasons given, when taken as a whole,
support the decision?"[85] While the answer to this question must bear careful
relation to the context of the decision, the question (or standard or test) remains
the same:[86]

> The suggestion that reasonableness is an "area" allowing for more or
> less deferential articulations would require that the court ask different
> questions of the decision depending on the circumstances and would
> be incompatible with the idea of a meaningful standard.

As discussed in greater detail below in the section dealing with the content of
the three standards of review, "reasonable" of course is not the same as either
"correct" or "patently unreasonable".

(iv) The Overall Functional and Pragmatic Approach – No Necessary Correlation Between a Particular Type of Error and a Particular Standard of Review

Finally, Chief Justice McLachlin made it clear in *Dr. Q* that there is no
necessary relationship between particular types of errors and particular standards of review – it all depends on applying a pragmatic and functional approach to determine how much deference the legislators intended in the particular case:

> [25] ... [I]t is no longer sufficient to slot a particular issue into a
> pigeon hole of judicial review and, on this basis, demand cor-

---

85   [2003] 1 S.C.R. 247 (S.C.C.) at para. 47.
86   *Ibid.* at para. 47.

rectness from the decision-maker. Nor is a reviewing court's interpretation of a privative clause or mechanism of review solely dispositive of a particular standard of review: *Canada (Deputy Minister of National Revenue) v. Mattel Canada Inc.*, [2001] 2 S.C.R. 100, 2001 SCC 36, at para. 27. The pragmatic and functional approach demands a more nuanced analysis based on consideration of a number of factors. This approach applies whenever a court reviews the decision of an administrative body. As Professor D.J. Mullan states in *Administrative Law* (2001), at p. 108, with the pragmatic and functional approach, "the Court has provided an overarching or unifying theory for review of the substantive decisions of all manner of statutory and prerogative decision makers". Review of the conclusions of an administrative decision-maker must begin by applying the pragmatic and functional approach.

Accordingly, much of the long, tortuous jurisprudence which has led us to this point probably cannot be cited directly as authority to determine the outcome of a case today, but the principles underlying the earlier cases should still be of some assistance in locating particular cases at particular points on the new spectrum of deference, thereby determining which of the three recognized standards of review should be applied (and with what result).

Notwithstanding the generality of Chief Justice McLachlin's statement, special consideration needs to be given to (a) whether a less stringent standard than correctness could ever apply to a constitutional issue;[87] (b) whether a less stringent standard than correctness could ever apply to a clearly "jurisdictional" matter or a "jurisdictional given" without running into the constitutional limitations from *Crévier*; (c) whether a more stringent standard than "not patently unreasonable" would ever be applied where the legislature has enacted a strong privative clause; (d) whether the same standard of review analysis applies to all grounds for judicial review – particularly, to breaches of the principles of natural justice and procedural fairness, and (e) how the standard of review analysis is to be applied to discretionary decisions. These issues are discussed more fully below.

(l) Justice LeBel's cri de coeur in *Toronto (City) v. C.U.P.E., Local 79*

The concurring *obiter* reasons issued by Justice LeBel (with Justice Deschamps) in *Toronto (City) v. C.U.P.E., Local 79*[88] is a startling and refreshing curial *cri de coeur* about the complexity of modern standards of review anal-

---

87   Two subsequent cases make it clear that constitutional issues will always attract the correctness standard: see *Paul v. British Columbia (Forest Appeals Commission)*, 2003 SCC 55 (S.C.C.) at para. 31 (per Bastarache J.); *Martin v. Nova Scotia (Workers' Compensation Board)*, 2003 SCC 54, 4 Admin. L.R. (4th) 1 (S.C.C.) at para. 31 (per Gonthier J.). Are there any circumstances in which the four *Pushpanathan* factors would conclude that a lesser standard of review would be applicable to a constitutional issue?

88   2003 SCC 63 (S.C.C.).

ysis. Although the parties had made no submissions about the need for a fundamental re-thinking of this area (because they would necessarily be trying to fit their clients' cases within the framework of the existing law),[89] Justice LeBel noted the growing criticism with the ways in which the standards of review currently available within the pragmatic and functional framework are conceived of and applied; and the need for the law governing the standards of review to be predictable, workable and coherent.

Justice LeBel particularly focused on (a) the interplay between correctness and patent unreasonableness, and (b) the distinction between patent unreasonableness and reasonableness. With respect to the former, he noted:[90]

> At times the Court's application of the standard of patent unreasonableness may leave it vulnerable to criticism that it may in fact be doing implicitly what it has rejected explicitly, intervening in decisions that are, in its view, incorrect, rather than limiting any intervention to those decisions that lack a rational foundation. In the process, what should be an indelible line between correctness, on the one hand, and patent unreasonableness, on the other hand, becomes blurred. It may very well be that review under any standard of reasonableness, given the nature of the intellectual process it involves, entails such a risk. Nevertheless, the existence of two standards of reasonableness appears to have magnified the underlying tension between the standards of reasonableness and correctness.

With respect to the latter, Justice LeBel noted that the patent unreasonableness standard was used in contradistinction to the correctness standard, and was developed prior to the birth of the pragmatic and functional approach and prior to (and not in conjunction with) the formulation of the concept of reasonableness *simpliciter*.[91] The current attempts to distinguish between the two reasonableness standards is problematic both conceptually and practically:[92]

> Because patent unreasonableness and reasonableness *simpliciter* are both rooted in this guiding principle [that there is not only one acceptable solution], it has been difficult to frame the standards as analytically, rather than merely semantically, distinct. The efforts to sustain a workable distinction between them have taken, in the main, two forms, which mirror . . . two definitional strands of patent unreasonableness. One of these forms distinguishes between patent unreasonableness and reasonableness *simpliciter* on the basis of the relative magnitude of the defect. The other looks to the "immediacy or obvi-

---

89   Because the matter had not been raised at the hearing, the majority of the Court was not prepared to deal with the issues raised by Justices LeBel and Deschamps. Note, however, that the absence of submissions did not prevent the Court from embarking on the standard of review analysis in *Pushpanathan*.

90   *Supra* note 88 at paras. 99 and 100.

91   *Ibid.* at para. 101.

92   *Ibid.* at para. 103.

ousness" of the defect, and thus the relative invasiveness of the review necessary to find it. Both approaches raise their own problems.

Justice LeBel queried whether the theoretical effort necessary to keep these two reasonableness standards conceptually distinct is productive,[93] or consistent with the legislature's intent or the rule of law:[94]

> On the assumption that we can distinguish effectively between an unreasonable and a patently unreasonable decision, there are situations where an unreasonable (*i.e.*, irrational) decision must be allowed to stand. This would be the case where the standard of review is patent unreasonableness and the decision under review is unreasonable, but not patently so. As I have noted, I doubt that such an outcome could be reconciled with the intent of the legislature which, in theory, the pragmatic and functional analysis aims to reflect as faithfully as possible. As a matter of statutory interpretation, courts should always be very hesitant to impute to the legislature any intent to let irrational administrative acts to stand, absent the most unequivocal statement of such intent. . . . As a matter of theory, the constitutional principle of the primacy of the rule of law, which is an ever-present background principle of interpretation in this context, reinforces the point: if a court concludes that the legislature intended that there be no recourse from an irrational decision, it seems highly likely that the court has misconstrued the intent of the legislature.

Finally, Justice LeBel concluded that the courts may need to rethink some of the fundamentals in the standards of review analysis:

> Administrative law has developed considerably over the last 25 years since *CUPE v. New Brunswick Liquor Board*. This evolution, which reflects a strong sense of deference to administrative decision makers and an acknowledgment of the importance of their role, has given rise to some problems or concerns. It remains to be seen, in an appropriate case, what should be the solution to these difficulties. Should courts move to a two standard system of judicial review, correctness and a revised unified standard of reasonableness? Should we attempt to more clearly define the nature and scope of each standard or rethink their relationship and application? This is perhaps some of the work which lies ahead for courts, building on the developments of recent years as well as on the legal tradition which created the framework of the present law of judicial review.

Obviously, this area of the law is still going to develop over the next few years.

---

93   *Ibid.* at para. 121. In para. 127, Justice LeBel suggests that the distinction between the two reasonableness standards is about as unproductive as differentiating between "illegible" and "patently illegible".

94   *Ibid.* at paras. 127 and 133.

4. Distinguishing among the Three Standards of Review

Because applying a different standard of review may well result in a different outcome, how do the three standards of review differ (bearing in mind Justice LeBel's recent *cri de coeur*[95] about the robustness of some of this analysis)?

(a) The Correctness Standard

Obviously, the correctness standard allows the court to determine whether it agrees with the decision of the statutory delegate; and, if not, to substitute its own view of the correct outcome.[96] Correctness is the most stringent standard that could be employed by the reviewing court.[97]

(b) The Reasonableness Standard

By contrast, the reasonableness *simpliciter* standard is less stringent than correctness, but more stringent than patent unreasonableness. The decision of the Supreme Court of Canada in *Law Society of New Brunswick v. Ryan*,[98] is the most recent attempt to give meaning to what constitutes an "unreasonable decision":

> [55] *A decision will be unreasonable only if there is no line of analysis within the given reasons that could reasonably lead the tribunal from the evidence before it to the conclusion at which it arrived.* If any of the reasons that are sufficient to support the conclusion are tenable in the sense that they can stand up to a somewhat

---

95 *Toronto (City) v. C.U.P.E., Local 79*, 2003 SCC 63 (S.C.C.).

96 Query: normally in a successful application for judicial review, the court does not actually dispose of the matter itself but rather remits it to the statutory delegate to make the decision in accordance with the directions of the court. Is there any purpose to this remittance where the standard of review is correctness, and the court has determined that the statutory delegate's decision is incorrect?

97 To the extent that the reviewing court agrees that the decision of the statutory delegate *is* correct, it might be thought that there is no need to go further to identify the applicable standard of review, because a decision which meets the correctness standard will necessarily meet the less stringent standards of reasonableness *simpliciter* and patent unreasonableness. This was the approach adopted by the late Justice Sopinka in *C.A.I.M.A.W., Local 14 v. Canadian Kenworth Co.*, [1989] 2 S.C.R. 983 at 1017-1018, 40 Admin. L.R. 181 at 214 (S.C.C.):

> I share La Forest J.'s opinion of the importance of curial deference in the review of specialist tribunals' decisions. But, in my view, curial deference does not enter the picture until the court finds itself in disagreement with the tribunal. Only then is it necessary to consider whether the error (so found) is within or outside the boundaries of reasonableness. . . . So long as the Court is satisfied with the correctness of the tribunals' decision, any reference to reasonableness is superfluous.

Today, however, it is probably necessary to go through the entire *Pushpanathan* analysis rather than adopting this type of shortcut. See Justice LeBel's discussion of this point in *Toronto (City) v. C.U.P.E., Local 79*, 2003 SCC 63 (S.C.C.) at paras. 85 to 95.

98 *Ryan v. Law Society (New Brunswick)*, [2003] 1 S.C.R. 247, 48 Admin. L.R. (3d) 33 (S.C.C.).

probing examination, then the decision will not be unreasonable and a reviewing court must not interfere (see *Southam, supra,* at para. 56). This means that a decision may satisfy the reasonableness standard if it is supported by a tenable explanation even if this explanation is not one that the reviewing court finds compelling (see *Southam, supra,* at para. 79).

[56] *This does not mean that every element of the reasoning given must independently pass a test for reasonableness. The question is rather whether the reasons, taken as a whole, are tenable as support for the decision.* At all times, a court applying a standard of reasonableness must assess the basic adequacy of a reasoned decision remembering that the issue under review does not compel one specific result. Moreover, *a reviewing court should not seize on one or more mistakes or elements of the decision which do not affect the decision as a whole.* [Emphasis added.]

Does this explanation of what "reasonableness" means restrict either the court or the parties to a mere examination of the statutory delegate's reasons without more? Clearly Justice Iacobucci contemplated that applying the reasonableness standard may involve "significant searching or testing", and explaining the defect in the reasons "may require a detailed exposition to show that there are no lines of reasoning supporting the decision which could reasonably lead that tribunal to reach the decision it did".[99] Note that earlier cases have also found the *outcome* – the decision itself – to be unreasonable, not just the underlying reasoning.[100]

(c) Distinguishing Between "Unreasonable" and "Incorrect"

Justice Iacobucci distinguished between the "reasonable" and "correct" standards of review in the following terms in *Ryan*:[101]

¶ 50 At the outset it is helpful to contrast judicial review according to the standard of reasonableness with the fundamentally different process of reviewing a decision for correctness. When undertaking a correctness review, the court may undertake its own reasoning process to arrive at the result it judges correct. In contrast, when deciding whether an administrative action was unreasonable, a court should not at any point ask itself what the correct decision would have been. Applying the standard of reasonableness gives effect to the legislative intention that a specialized body will have the primary responsibility of decid-

---

99 *Ibid.* at para. 53.
100 See the majority's decision in *National Corn Growers Assn. v. Canada (Canadian Import Tribunal)*, [1990] 2 S.C.R. 1324, 74 D.L.R. (4th) 449 (S.C.C.).
101 *Ryan v. Law Society (New Brunswick)*, [2003] 1 S.C.R. 247, 48 Admin. L.R. (3d) 33 (S.C.C.). See also Justice LeBel's concurring *obiter* reasons in *Toronto (City) v. C.U.P.E., Local 79*, 2003 SCC 63 (S.C.C.).

ing the issue according to its own process and for its own reasons. The standard of reasonableness does not imply that a decision maker is merely afforded a "margin of error" around what the court believes is the correct result.

¶ 51   There is a further reason that courts testing for unreasonableness must avoid asking the question of whether the decision is correct. Unlike a review for correctness, there will often be no single right answer to the questions that are under review against the standard of reasonableness. For example, when a decision must be taken according to a set of objectives that exist in tension with each other, there may be no particular trade-off that is superior to all others. Even if there could be, notionally, a single best answer, it is not the court's role to seek this out when deciding if the decision was unreasonable.

(d) Distinguishing Between Unreasonableness and Patent Unreasonableness

Justice Iacobucci described the distinction between "unreasonable" and "patently unreasonable" as follows:[102]

> [52]   The standard of reasonableness *simpliciter* is also very different from the more deferential standard of patent unreasonableness. In *Southam, supra*, at para. 57, the Court described the difference between an unreasonable decision and a patently unreasonable one as rooted "in the immediacy or obviousness of the defect". Another way to say this is that a patently unreasonable defect, once identified, can be explained simply and easily, leaving no real possibility of doubting that the decision is defective. A patently unreasonable decision has been described as "clearly

---

102   In *Canada (Director of Investigation & Research) v. Southam Inc.*, [1997] 1 S.C.R. 748 (S.C.C.), Justice Iacobucci described the difference between "unreasonable *simpliciter*" and "patently unreasonable" as follows (at para. 57):

> *The difference between "unreasonable" and "patently unreasonable" lies in the immediacy or obviousness of the defect. If the defect is apparent on the face of the tribunal's reasons, then the tribunal's decision is patently unreasonable. But if it takes some significant searching or testing to find the defect, then the decision is unreasonable but not patently unreasonable.* As Cory J. observed in *Canada (Attorney General) v. P.S.A.C.*, [1993] 1 S.C.R. 941, at p. 963, "[i]n the *Shorter Oxford English Dictionary* 'patently', an adverb is defined as 'openly, evidently, clearly'". This is not to say, of course, that judges reviewing a decision on the standard of patent unreasonableness may not examine the record. If the decision under review is sufficiently difficult, then perhaps a great deal of reading and thinking will be required before the judge will be able to grasp the dimensions of the problem. See *National Corn Growers Assn. v. Canada (Canadian Import Tribunal)*, [1990] 2 S.C.R. 1324, at p. 1370, per Gonthier J.; see also *Toronto (City) Board of Education v. O.S.S.T.F., District 15*, S.C.C., No. 24724, February 27, 1997, at para. 47, per Cory J. But once the lines of the problem have come into focus, if the decision is patently unreasonable, then the unreasonableness will be evident. [Emphasis added.]

irrational" or "evidently not in accordance with reason" (*Canada (Attorney General) v. Public Service Alliance of Canada*, [1993] 1 S.C.R. 941 at pp. 963-64, per Cory J.; *Centre communautaire juridique de l'Estrie v. Sherbrooke (City)*, [1996] 3 S.C.R. 84 at paras. 9-12, per Gonthier J.). A decision that is patently unreasonable is so flawed that no amount of curial deference can justify letting it stand.

Note that this description of a "patently unreasonable" decision does not require the error either to appear on the face of the record,[103] or be restricted to an interpretation of the statutory delegate's constituent statute.[104] In addition, the court can conduct a much more searching inquiry into the reasonableness of the statutory delegate's decision under the "reasonableness *simpliciter*" test than under the "not patently unreasonable" test. The court may have to consider a much wider range of evidence and argument about why a particular decision is "unreasonable" in all of the circumstances. The conceptual and practical difficulties of making these distinctions between the two reasonableness standards is reviewed extensively in Justice LeBel's *cri de coeur* in *Toronto (City) v. C.U.P.E., Local 79*.[105]

As discussed below, even where judges agree about the appropriate standard of review to be applied in a particular case, they may well disagree about whether that standard has been met.[106]

5. The First Factor in the Functional and Pragmatic Approach to Deference – the presence or absence of a privative clause or an appeal

The first factor which Justice Bastarache identified in *Pushpanathan* was the presence or absence of a privative clause (or, conversely, a right of appeal):[107]

---

103   Which is the source of the court's anomalous power to correct an error of law on the face of the record: *Shaw's case*; see Chapter 11, above.

104   See the sharp division on this point in *National Corn Growers Assn. v. Canada (Canadian Import Tribunal)*, [1990] 2 S.C.R. 1324, 74 D.L.R. (4th) 449 (S.C.C.), where the court did not restrict itself to questions about the reasonableness of the Tribunal's interpretation of its own statute (as Justice Wilson in dissent thought appropriate) but looked at the reasonableness of the Tribunal's decision in light of Canada's various trade obligations.

105   2003 SCC 63 (S.C.C.), starting at para. 96.

106   *Pushpanathan* is a good example of this. Although all judges agreed that correctness was the appropriate standard of review, the majority held that the immigration officer's interpretation of the legislation was incorrect, whereas the minority reached the opposite conclusion.

107   [1998] 1 S.C.R. 982, 160 D.L.R. (4th) 193 (S.C.C.) at 1006. Note that it would be very unusual for there to be both a privative clause and a right of appeal applicable to a particular issue simultaneously; they would generally be mutually exclusive.

The absence of a privative clause does not imply a high standard of scrutiny, where other factors bespeak a low standard. However, *the presence of a "full" privative clause is compelling evidence that the court ought to show deference to the tribunal's decision, unless other factors strongly indicate the contrary as regards the particular determination in question.* A full privative clause is "one that declares that decisions of the tribunal are final and conclusive from which no appeal lies and all forms of judicial review are excluded" (*Pasiechnyk, supra,* at para. 17, per Sopinka J.). Unless there is some contrary indication in the privative clause itself, actually using the words "final and conclusive" is sufficient, but other words might suffice if equally explicit (*United Brotherhood of Carpenters and Joiners of America, Local 579 v. Bradco Construction Ltd.,* [1993] 2 S.C.R. 316, at pp. 331 and 333). *At the other end of the spectrum is a clause in an Act permitting appeals, which is a factor suggesting a more searching standard of review.*

Some Acts will be silent or equivocal as to the intended standard of review. The Court found in *Bradco* that the submission of a dispute to a "final settlement" of an arbitrator was "somewhere between a full privative clause and a clause providing for full review by way of appeal" (pp. 331 and 333). Sopinka J. went on to examine other factors to determine that some degree of deference was owed to the arbitrator's ruling. In essence, a partial or equivocal privative clause is one which fits into the overall process of evaluation of factors to determine the legislator's intended level of deference, and does not have the preclusive effect of a full privative clause. [Emphasis added.]

(a) The Absence of a Privative Clause Does Not Automatically Engage the Correctness Standard

At the outset, it is important to note Justice Bastarache's statement that the absence of a privative clause does not thereby necessarily engage a high standard of review such as correctness. This is at variance with English law, where the courts have asserted the right to correct all errors of law on the face of the record (at least in the absence of a privative clause): *Shaw's Case.* In Canada, it may be more accurate to say that the courts have the *right* to correct all errors of law on the face of the record, but should not therefore necessarily employ the correctness standard to determine whether there is or is not an error. As Justice Bastarache said in *Pushpanathan*, ". . . even pure questions of law may be granted a wide degree of deference where other factors of the pragmatic and functional analysis suggest that such deference is the legislative intention."[108]

---

108   *Ibid.* at para. 37.

(b) The Presence of a Privative Clause Implies Deference

On the other hand, the presence of a privative clause is "compelling evidence" that the legislators intended the courts to show deference to the statutory delegate, at least with respect to those matters covered by the privative clause.

A "privative clause" is a statutory provision which purports to oust the inherent jurisdiction of the superior courts to review the legality of actions taken by statutory delegates. In theory, the doctrine of Parliamentary Sovereignty means that the courts must give effect to such legislative provisions. On the other hand, the courts were initially quite creative in finding ways to evade the effect of privative clauses, largely by holding that the legislature could not have intended to confer power on a statutory delegate to exceed the bounds of the jurisdiction which the legislature had conferred on it. If the statutory delegate exceeded its jurisdiction, then its decision was void, and there was therefore no lawful action which could be protected by the privative clause. Accordingly, the distinction between jurisdictional and intra-jurisdictional errors was extremely important in understanding the courts' approach to privative clauses. Although the concept of "jurisdiction" has largely been subsumed in the functional and pragmatic approach to determining the appropriate standard of review, each privative clause must be construed in light of its own wording and on the statutory context in which it is found. Some general types of privative clauses may be identified.

(i) Final and Binding Clauses

Many statutes contain provisions which state that the delegate's decision shall be "final", "binding", "conclusive", "not subject to appeal", "unappealable" or "not subject to be questioned". The courts have almost universally treated such provisions as meaning that no appeal lies from the delegate's decision, which merely reiterates the common law rule that no appeal lies without being specifically created by statute.[109] On this view, such clauses did not have the effect of depriving the superior courts of their inherent jurisdiction to review the legality of a delegate's actions. The courts' power in this regard undoubtedly extended to correcting any jurisdictional defects in the delegate's actions, and one prevailing view was that "final and binding" clauses did not affect the courts' right to correct intra-jurisdictional errors of law as well.[110]

However, that did not answer the question as to how intensive a level of review should be applied. Laskin C.J.C. in *A.U.P.E., Local 63 v. Alberta (Public Service Employees' Relations Board)* indicated that the privative "gloss" of a final and binding clause should restrict the courts to correcting only those intra-jurisdictional errors of law which are "patently unreasona-

---

109 See the discussion on this point in Chapter 14. This reasoning has been criticized as giving no meaning to the provision: *O.P.S.E.U. v. Forer* (1985), 52 O.R. (2d) 705 at 722, 15 Admin. L.R. 145 (Ont. C.A.). For a decision reiterating the more traditional view, see *Dayco (Canada) Ltd. v. C.A.W.*, [1993] 2 S.C.R. 230, 14 Admin. L.R. (2d) 1 (S.C.C.) (per La Forest J.).

110 See the discussion on this point in Chapter 11.

ble".[111] A similar conclusion was reached by Gonthier J. speaking for the majority in *National Corn Growers Assn. v. Canada (Canadian Import Tribunal)*.[112] The Court has subsequently held in *Dayco (Canada) Ltd. v. C.A.W.* that the presence and strength of a privative clause would not only affect the standard of review of intra-jurisdictional errors, but would also have an impact on the breadth of a tribunal's jurisdiction.[113] In the *Dayco* case, the Court found a "final and binding" clause to be a relatively weak privative provision, and that its wording did not indicate that the decision actually made by the delegate (a labour arbitrator) was intended to be within its exclusive jurisdiction, or that it was to be unreviewable by the court (even though it was said to be "final and binding"):

> Here the privative clause in s. 108 [a no *certiorari* clause] applies only to the Board, and there is no comparable provision with respect to the arbitrator. The union contends, however, that the phrase "final and binding . . . between the parties" in s. 44 constitutes a privative clause, a contention accepted by the Court of Appeal. However, the most that can be said for the phrase is that it has limited privative effect on the issues in this appeal. . . .

> Whatever the status of the clause in s. 44, the section should be contrasted with the strong and explicit privative clause in s. 108 protecting decisions of the Labour Relations Board. Clearly, if the legislature had intended to mandate the same judicial deference to an arbitrator as to the Board, it could simply have brought the arbitrator under the shelter of s. 108. That is not the case, and I am left with the conclusion that the legislation contemplates a more limited shield against judicial review for decisions of an arbitrator. . . .

In *Dayco*, the weak privative clause was taken as one signal to the Court that, in the application of the "pragmatic and functional test", the delegate was intended to have a limited jurisdiction, and that the error under review was of a jurisdictional nature.

In a subsequent unanimous decision, the Supreme Court explained the *Dayco* decision as turning on the "specific question in issue, which involved a general question of law".[114] The general question was whether a promise in a collective agreement can survive the expiry of the agreement, and on such a

---

111 [1982] 1 S.C.R. 923 at 927 (S.C.C.), emphasis added (hereafter "*Olds College*".) This decision is criticized in Chapter 11 dealing with the court's power to correct errors of law on the face of the record.

112 *National Corn Growers Assn. v. Canada (Canadian Import Tribunal)*, [1990] 2 S.C.R. 1324 at 1370 (S.C.C.).

113 [1993] 2 S.C.R. 230, 14 Admin. L.R. (2d) 1 (S.C.C.). See also *C.J.A., Local 579 v. Bradco Construction Ltd.*, [1993] 2 S.C.R. 316 at 333, 12 Admin. L.R. (2d) 165, 106 Nfld. & P.E.I.R. 140, 102 D.L.R. (4th) 402 (S.C.C.), commented on by D.J. Mullan, "*Bradco*: Refined Reiterations of the Rubric of Review" (1993) 12 Admin. L.R. (2d) 219. *Bradco* was decided 13 days after *Dayco* and discusses the same issues.

114 *Ross v. New Brunswick School District No. 15*, [1996] 1 S.C.R. 825 at 848 (S.C.C.).

question the arbitrator had to be correct even if the issue was within jurisdiction. As a general proposition, a "final and binding" clause is seen as having lesser privative effect, and the presence of such a clause will usually therefore engage a lesser standard of deference to the decision under review.[115] However, a "final and binding" clause might have full privative effect if the overall statutory context calls for that interpretation.[116]

(ii) Exclusive Jurisdiction Clauses

A great deal of legislation goes further than stating that the delegate's decisions are final and binding by going on to provide that the delegate has exclusive jurisdiction to determine those matters remitted to it. This literally implies that the courts have no jurisdiction to deal with any of those matters. Such a provision undoubtedly prevents an appeal to the courts on the merits. It also prevents judicial review for an intra-jurisdictional error of law. But it does not confer on the delegate the authority to determine which matters are within or outside of its jurisdiction: the courts assert the right to make such determinations,[117] notwithstanding such an "exclusive jurisdiction" clause. The courts use the same legal reasoning to reach this result as they apply to "no *certiorari*" clauses.

(iii) No-certiorari Clauses

Legislation also frequently contains a provision preventing the issuance of any prerogative remedy, declaration or other court order to call into question the validity of the delegate's actions.[118] The courts have traditionally treated a no-*certiorari* type of clause as effective to prevent judicial review of any intra-jurisdictional error of law, but not effective to prevent judicial review of any jurisdictional defect in the delegate's actions. The constitutional rationale for holding that these clauses do not oust the courts' right to scrutinize jurisdictional defects is the assumption that Parliament cannot ever have intended inferior delegates to act outside their jurisdiction; any such action is *ultra vires*

---

115 In *Dayco (Canada) Ltd. v. C.A.W.*, [1993] 2 S.C.R. 230, 14 Admin. L.R. (2) 1 (S.C.C.) Cory J. (dissenting) minimized the importance of the precise wording of the privative clause. The majority, however, disagreed, holding that the wording actually used is an important component of the pragmatic and functional search for the specialized jurisdiction which was given to the delegate by the legislature. The weak privative clause, coupled with the court's view of the narrow expertise of the delegate, tended to shrink the arbitrator's jurisdiction, causing the issue in question (whether the collective agreement had expired) to be characterized as a "judicial given", upon which the arbitrator had to be correct.

116 See *Pushpanathan v. Canada (Minister of Employment & Immigration)*, [1998] 1 S.C.R. 982 at 1006 (S.C.C.), amended [1998] 1 S.C.R. 1222 (S.C.C.).

117 See the clear reasoning to this effect by Beetz J. in the decision of the Supreme Court of Canada in *Syndicat des employés de production du Québec & de l'Acadie v. Canada (Labour Relations Board)*, [1984] 2 S.C.R. 412 (S.C.C.); and by Cory J. in *Canada (Attorney General) v. P.S.A.C.*, [1991] 1 S.C.R. 614, 80 D.L.R. (4th) 520 (S.C.C.) ("*Econosult*").

118 For example, s. 42 of the *Energy Resources Conservation Act*, R.S.A. 2000, c. E-10.

and void; and therefore there is in law nothing to be protected by the privative clause. As Lord Morris put it in the *Anisminic* case:[119]

> The control which is exercised by the High Court over inferior tribunals . . . is of a supervisory but not of an appellate nature. It enables the High Court to correct errors of law if they are revealed on the face of the record. The control cannot, however, be exercised if there is some provision (such as a "no *certiorari*" clause) which prohibits removal to the High Court. But it is well settled that even such a clause is of no avail if the inferior tribunal acts without jurisdiction or exceeds the limits of its jurisdiction.

To the extent that no-*certiorari* clauses are still prevalent in Canada, the supervisory power of the courts depends upon the ability to characterize any alleged error by the delegate as being jurisdictional in nature. On the one hand, both the English and the Canadian courts recognize that a jurisdictional defect can occur at the very beginning of a delegate's functions (either because it has no statutory authority whatever to do the act in question, or because some matter preliminary or collateral to its jurisdiction has not been fulfilled),[120] in the course thereof (either because it has breached the principles of natural justice and procedural fairness, or because it has in some manner abused its discretion)[121] or at the very moment it makes its determination.[122] In general, none of these jurisdictional errors will be protected from judicial review by a no-*certiorari* clause. On the other hand the presence or absence of a privative clause will effect the scope of the tribunal's jurisdiction, as is discussed in the next section.

There may be considerable difficulty in determining the precise ambit of the power which Parliament granted to the statutory delegate. As a result, it may not be easy to determine whether the delegate has made an error within or outside of the jurisdiction granted to it. The cases referred to in this and the previous chapter clearly demonstrate the difficulties which the Canadian courts have experienced in drawing the line between intra-jurisdictional errors which are protected by no-*certiorari* clauses and jurisdictional errors which are not immune from judicial review. The matter is made even more complicated because a patently unreasonable interpretation of an intra-jurisdictional question of law is a jurisdictional error.[123] Thus, some errors which were previously considered to be protected by a no-*certiorari* clause might now be subject to review by the superior courts.

---

119 *Anisminic Ltd. v. Foreign Compensation Commission* (1968), [1969] 2 A.C. 147, [1969] 1 All E.R. 208 at 222 (U.K. H.L.).

120 See Chapter 6.

121 See Chapters 7, 8, 9 and 10.

122 As occurred in *Syndicat des employés de production du Québec & de l'Acadie v. Canada (Labour Relations Board)*, [1984] 2 S.C.R. 412, 14 D.L.R. (4th) 457 (S.C.C.).

123 *C.A.I.M.A.W., Local 14 v. Canadian Kenworth Co.*, [1989] 2 S.C.R. 983 at 1003-04 (S.C.C.) (per La Forest J.); and *Syndicat des employés de production du Québec & de l'Acadie v. Canada (Labour Relations Board)*, [1984] 2 S.C.R. 412, 14 D.L.R. (4th) 457 (S.C.C.) (per Beetz J.).

A no-*certiorari* clause is considered to have stronger privative effect than a "final and binding" clause. In *Dayco*, the no-*certiorari* clause was described as being "strong and explicit", as compared to the "final and binding" clause which was said to be "limited". Accordingly in applying the "pragmatic and functional" test in determining the intended scope of the delegate's jurisdiction, the presence of a no-*certiorari* clause will signal to the court that the legislature intended a wider jurisdiction for the delegate. This will result in higher curial deference by the court.

(iv) "Full" or "True" Privative Clauses

Some privative clauses incorporate characteristics of all of the types of clauses discussed so far. A good example is section 22 of the Saskatchewan *Workers' Compensation Act*.[124] This clause provides that the Board has "exclusive jurisdiction" over certain matters, and that the Board's decisions are "final and conclusive" and may not be removed by *certiorari*. The Supreme Court of Canada has described this type of clause as being a "full" or "true" privative clause:[125]

> A "full" or "true" privative clause is one that declares that decisions of the tribunal are final and conclusive from which no appeal lies and all forms of judicial review are excluded. . . . Where the legislation employs words that purport to limit review but fall short of the traditional wording of a full privative clause, it is necessary to determine whether the words were intended to have full privative effect or a lesser standard of deference.

The presence of a full privative clause will signal a wide jurisdiction and a high degree of deference to the delegate, which when considered with the expertise of the tribunal and the nature of the question will determine the intensity of judicial review. But even a full privative clause does not prevent review of jurisdictional error.

(v) Elastic Jurisdiction Clauses

In theory and subject to the constitutional limitations discussed below, Parliament might delegate the power to an inferior tribunal to determine the limit of its own jurisdiction. If coupled with a no-*certiorari* clause, such an elastic delegation of jurisdiction appears to prevent all forms of judicial review. Precisely because the statutory delegate has the power to determine its own jurisdiction, none of its actions can ever be *ultra vires*.[126] Because of the strong form in which the doctrine of Parliamentary Sovereignty exists in England, the British courts would have to give effect to such legislation, and would not

---

124   S.S. 1979, c. W-17.1

125   *Pasiechnyk v. Saskatchewan (Workers' Compensation Board)*, [1997] 2 S.C.R. 890 at 905 (S.C.C.).

126   Subjective discretionary powers may functionally achieve the same result. See the discussion below about standard of review of discretionary powers.

be able to review the legality of such a delegate's actions for any reasons, including jurisdictional defects.

The only Canadian example of such a strong clause, to the authors' knowledge, was at one time contained in section 33 of the *Labour Code* of British Columbia:[127]

> 33. The board has and shall exercise exclusive jurisdiction to determine the extent of its jurisdiction under this Act, a collective agreement or the regulations, to determine a fact or question of law necessary to establish its jurisdiction and to determine whether or in what manner it shall exercise its jurisdiction.

This provision has now been replaced with a more conventional "final and conclusive" clause. However even its existence in this strong form did not prevent the courts from asserting a right to review the decisions of the Labour Board for jurisdictional error.[128]

(vi) Constitutional Limitations on Privative Clauses in Canada

As explained in greater detail in Chapter 2, there are certain constitutional limitations in Canada affecting the validity of privative clauses.[129] The most important is section 96 of the *Constitution Act, 1867*, which requires the judges of all superior, district and county courts to be appointed by the federal Governor in Council. This has the effect of limiting the range of persons to whom certain judicial powers can be granted. It also has the effect of preventing the legislative branch from granting unlimited or unreviewable jurisdiction to a statutory delegate, because one of the hallmarks of a superior court is its inherent power to determine the jurisdiction of statutory (or "inferior") tribunals. This proposition can be used to argue that a privative clause which purports to oust the ordinary superior court's inherent power to review a decision of an administrative tribunal effectively gives that tribunal power to determine its own jurisdiction, and thus makes that tribunal into a superior court whose members must be appointed in accordance with section 96. This argument allows the courts either to strike down the validity of such a privative clause, or to strike down every action taken by the administrative tribunal because its members have not been appointed correctly in accordance with section 96.

On the one hand, the latter view appears to be more correct in theory, because there is no doubt that the legislative branch could lawfully enact a stringent privative clause provided the members of the administrative tribunal

---

127 R.S.B.C. 1979, c. 212, s. 33; repealed and substituted, S.B.C. 1987, c. 24, s. 23.

128 See *C.A.I.M.A.W., Local 14 v. Canadian Kenworth Co.*, [1989] 2 S.C.R. 983 (S.C.C.); *Lorne W. Camozzi Co. v. I.U.O.E., Local 115* (1985), 68 B.C.L.R. 338, 17 Admin. L.R. 78, [1986] 3 W.W.R. 312, 24 D.L.R. (4th) 266 (B.C. C.A.); and *G & L Transfer Ltd. v. General Truck Drivers' & Helpers' Union, Local 31* (1981), 30 B.C.L.R. 258 (B.C. S.C.).

129 See D.P. Jones, "A Constitutionally Guaranteed Role for the Courts" (1979) 57 Can. Bar Rev. 669; P.W. Hogg, "Privative Clauses", Part 7.3(f) in *Constitutional Law of Canada*, 3d ed. (Toronto: Carswell, 1992) (Looseleaf).

are appointed by the federal Governor in Council under section 96. Thus, the privative clause would appear to be valid; only the appointment of the delegates could be questioned.

Nevertheless, the Supreme Court of Canada has used section 96 to strike down the validity of a privative clause. In *Crevier v. Quebec (Attorney General)*,[130] sections 194 and 195 of the *Professional Code of Quebec*[131] purported to preclude the availability of any of the remedies normally available from the Superior Court for the purpose of questioning the validity of any action taken by a wide range of officials and tribunals to whom various powers had been granted under the Code. Laskin C.J.C. held that the mere attempt to deprive the superior courts of their traditional supervisory function over the jurisdiction of these inferior delegates itself contravenes the spirit of section 96. In other words, the Supreme Court of Canada has recognized that our Constitution protects some of the administrative law jurisdiction of the superior courts against privative clauses, and to that extent thereby limits the legislative sovereignty of both Parliament and the legislatures. As Laskin C.J.C. said:[132]

> It is true that this is the first time that this Court has declared unequivocally that a provincially constituted statutory tribunal cannot constitutionally be immunized from review of decisions on questions of jurisdiction. In my opinion, this limitation, arising by virtue of s. 96, stands on the same footing as the well-accepted limitation on the power of provincial statutory tribunals to make unreviewable determinations of constitutionality. There may be differences of opinion as to what are questions of jurisdiction but, in my lexicon, they rise above and are different from errors of law, whether involving statutory construction or evidentiary matters or other matters. It is now unquestioned that privative clauses may, when properly framed, effectively oust judicial review on questions of law, and, indeed, on other issues not touching jurisdiction. However, given that s. 96 is in the *British North America Act* and that it would make a mockery of it to treat it in nonfunctional formal terms as a mere appointing power, I can think of nothing that is more the hallmark of a superior court than the vesting of power in a provincial statutory tribunal to determine the limits of its jurisdiction without appeal or other review.

While it may be exceedingly difficult to determine which matters go to jurisdiction, as opposed to those which lie within it, nevertheless it is clear that the *Crevier* decision elevates and reinforces the importance of section 96 as a weapon against the unfettered ability of the legislative branch to enact broad privative clauses ousting judicial review of administrative actions. It is also clear that this case now casts grave doubts on the validity of legislation which

---

130   [1981] 2 S.C.R. 220 (S.C.C.). The rule has been affirmed since, as for example in *U.N.A. v. Alberta (Attorney General)*, [1992] 1 S.C.R. 901 at 936 (S.C.C.) and *C.J.A., Local 579 v. Bradco Construction Ltd.*, [1993] 2 S.C.R. 316 (S.C.C.).

131   R.S.Q. 1977, c. C-26, s. 194-95 [re-en. 1982, c. 16, s. 2-3].

132   *Supra* note 130 at 236-37 [S.C.R.].

purports to give a statutory delegate jurisdiction to determine the limits of its own jurisdiction – legislation so clearly epitomized by the "elastic jurisdiction" clause formerly contained in section 33 of the *Labour Code of British Columbia*.[133]

An open question is whether the *Crevier* principle applies to federal tribunals. On the face of it section 96 would not apply to federally appointed tribunals. The *Crevier* decision could be taken to have silently reversed Laskin J.'s earlier decision for the Supreme Court of Canada in *Pringle v. Fraser*,[134] which upheld Parliament's right to enact legislation depriving the courts of their inherent jurisdiction to review a decision of the Immigration Appeal Board because the latter was given "sole and exclusive jurisdiction to hear and determine all questions of fact and law, including questions of jurisdiction". The issue is whether the Constitution provides some protection for judicial review generally. One commentator has pointed out that the Supreme Court's pronouncements on this issue have been worded generally, and have not been limited to provincial tribunals.[135] This may give some indication of the Court's attitude, but none of the cases raises the point directly. In *MacMillan Bloedel Ltd. v. Simpson*[136] the Supreme Court held that there is constitutional protection for the core or inherent jurisdiction of the superior courts, and that the contempt of court power was part of that core jurisdiction. While the Court cited *Crevier* as a precedent for its decision, it did not expressly deal with its applicability to federal tribunals.

(vii) Statutory Abolition of Privative Clauses

Some governments have had the courage to eschew their reliance on privative clauses. As early as 1932, the Donoughmore Committee on Ministers' Powers in England recommended the abandonment of such clauses.[137] In 1957, the Franks Committee recommended that no statute should purport to preclude judicial review,[138] and this recommendation was incorporated in the 1958, 1971 and 1992 versions of the *Tribunals and Inquiries Acts*:[139]

As respects England and Wales –

---

133 *Supra* note 127. On the validity of a time limitation clause on seeking *certiorari*, see D.P. Jones, "Case Comment on *Wainwright School Div. v. C.U.P.E.*" (1988) 55 Alta L.R. (2d) 323.

134 [1972] S.C.R. 821 (S.C.C.).

135 D.J. Mullan, "*Bradco*: Refined Reiterations of the Rubric of Review" (1993) 12 Admin. L.R. (2d) 219.

136 [1995] 4 S.C.R. 725 at 751 (S.C.C.).

137 Cnd. 4060 (1932), at 65.

138 Cmnd. 218 (1957) at para. 117. See the similar recommendations of the Law Reform Commission of Canada, *Report on Independent Administrative Agencies: A Framework for Decision-making (#26)* (1985) at 41-42.

139 6 & 7 Eliz. 2, c. 66; 1971 (Eng.) c. 62; 1992 (Eng.) c. 53. Reproduced here is s. 12 of the 1992 Act. See *R. v. Registrar of Companies, ex parte Central Bank of India*, [1986] 1 All E.R. 105 (C.A.).

(a) any provision in an Act passed before 1st August 1958 that any order or determination shall not be called into question in any court, or

(b) the provision in such an Act which by similar words excludes any of the powers of the High Court,

shall not have effect so as to prevent the removal of the proceedings into the High Court by order of *certiorari* or to prejudice the powers of the High Court to make orders of *mandamus*.

Only a very few privative clauses were excepted from this general provision, including (at the time) the one protecting decisions of the Foreign Compensation Commission which gave rise to the famous *Anisminic* decision,[140] as well as certain time-delayed ouster clauses.[141] In general, the British government has not relied on privative clauses for almost forty years, with no obvious impediment to the efficiency of their administrative machinery. As a result, English administrative law has not been troubled by the "patently unreasonable" doctrine or the need for a "pragmatic and functional approach" to determine jurisdiction.[142]

A similar renunciation of privative clauses was at one time enacted by the federal Parliament of Canada. Section 28 of the *Federal Court Act*[143] as originally enacted in 1970 provided for a statutory "application for judicial review" against most federal boards, commissions and other tribunals "notwithstanding the provisions of any other Act". This was held to nullify the effect of privative clauses in statutes enacted before the *Federal Courts Act* came into force, as well as in subsequent statutory re-enactments which the *Interpretation Act*[144] did not treat as being "new law".[145] Unfortunately, the "notwithstanding" clause disappeared in the 1990 amendments[146] to the Act that clarified the division of jurisdiction between the Trial Division and the Court of Appeal (with effect from 1 February 1992). The amended Act now merely says that the Court has jurisdiction to review the decisions of "any federal board". Whether this bare and general grant of jurisdiction will be held to be sufficient to override more specific privative clauses in particular statutes is unclear, but such an effect would appear unlikely. Accordingly, after 1992 privative clauses in federal

---

140   *Supra* note 119; this privative clause was repealed by s. 3(2) and (10) of the *Foreign Compensation Act* 1969.

141   For example, see *Smith v. East Elloe (Rural District)*, [1956] A.C. 736 (U.K. H.L.). Compare the similar legislative provision in the *Olds College* case (*A.U.P.E., Local 63 v. Alberta (Public Service Employees' Relations Board)*, [1982] 1 S.C.R. 923 (S.C.C.)).

142   See section 3(b), above.

143   R.S.C. 1970, c. 10 (2nd Supp.), reproduced in Appendix 5, below (now the *Federal Courts Act*).

144   R.S.C. 1985, c. I-21.

145   See *Howarth v. Canada (National Parole Board)* (1974), [1976] 1 S.C.R. 453 at 475 (S.C.C.); *Canada (Attorney General) v. Canada (Public Service Staff Relations Board)*, [1977] 2 F.C. 663 (Fed. C.A.).

146   *Federal Court, Crown Liability and Supreme Court Amendment Act*, S.C. 1990, c. 8. The current version of the *Federal Courts Act* is reproduced in part in Appendix 5, below.

statutes will probably be treated by the Federal Court in the same way as their provincial counterparts.

It appears that none of the Canadian provinces has enacted provisions to eviscerate the effectiveness of privative clauses, nor has the practice of enacting sweeping privative clauses fallen into disuse.[147] The approach of the Supreme Court of Canada[148] regarding privative clauses as an important signal by the legislature that considerable deference was intended to be shown to the tribunal can only serve to acknowledge the legitimacy of privative clauses and to encourage their continued use.

(viii) Summary on Privative Clauses

The courts' treatment of privative clauses illustrates the tension which exists in our constitutional system of government between the doctrine of Parliamentary Sovereignty and the presumed right of the courts to rule on the legality of governmental action.

In the past, the courts used the *ultra vires* doctrine quite effectively to prevent statutory delegates from exceeding their jurisdiction. As a result, the effect of most privative clauses was restricted by the courts to protecting *intra vires* decisions by delegates, and perhaps also intra-jurisdictional errors which are not patently unreasonable.

As the first of the four *Pushpanathan* factors, the presence of a privative clause connotes the intention of the legislature for the courts to show deference to the decision of the statutory delegate. The presence of a strongly worded privative clause probably engages the "not patently unreasonable" standard of review, although it is of course possible that the legislature could specify some other standard of review to be used. Without such an explicit legislative statement, it is probably unlikely that any of the other three *Pushpanathan* factors would increase the standard of review in the face of a privative clause to (say) reasonableness *simpliciter*. On the other hand, the absence of a privative clause does not necessarily engage the correctness standard – one must complete the analysis by weighing the absence of a privative clause with the other three *Pushpanathan* factors.

Legislators are perfectly entitled to use clear words to define which matters lie within the jurisdiction of its statutory delegates (to use old language) or which should be shown extreme deference (to use more modern language). The real question is why legislators would choose to oust the courts' historic role of determining questions of law. For more than thirty years, England has accepted the desirability of having the courts determine almost all questions of law arising in the course of administrative action – whether intra-jurisdictional or jurisdictional in nature[149] – with no obvious impediment to the effi-

---

147 In some provinces privative clauses do not affect the Ombudsman: *Ontario (Ombudsman) v. Ontario (Labour Relations Board)* (1985), 23 Admin. L.R. 63 (Ont. Div. Ct.), affirmed (1987), 23 Admin. L.R. 71 (Ont. C.A.), leave to appeal refused (May 5, 1987), Doc. 20329 (S.C.C.); *Ombudsman Act*, R.S.A. 2000, c. O-8, s. 12(3).

148 See *Dayco (Canada) Ltd. v. C.A.W.*, [1993] 2 S.C.R. 230 (S.C.C.).

149 See the discussion on the English position in Chapter 11.

ciency of government. Why do Canadian legislators so fear judicial review that they insist on inserting privative clauses in almost all important pieces of legislation?

(c) The Presence of an Appeal Provision Implies Less Deference

Conversely, the presence of an appeal provision suggests a more searching standard of review. However, this does not necessarily mean that the correctness standard applies. Depending upon the wording of the appeal provision, and the effect of the other three factors in the pragmatic and functional analysis, it might be appropriate for the appellate court to apply a less stringent standard than correctness.

(i) *Examples of Appeal Cases Where the Correctness Standard was Applied*

The following are examples of cases where the courts have applied the correctness standard in appeals from a statutory delegate:

- *Bell Canada v. Canada (Canadian Radio-Television & Telecommunications Commission).*[150]

- *Zurich Insurance Co. v. Ontario (Human Rights Commission).*[151]

- *University of Alberta v. Alberta (Human Rights Commission).*[152]

- *Canada (Attorney General) v. Mossop.*[153]

- *Berg v. University of British Columbia,*[154] where Chief Justice Lamer noted that the question of what constitutes a "service customarily available to the public" is a general question of law, for which there is no reason to show deference by this Court."

- *Gould v. Yukon Order of Pioneers*, where La Forest J. said:[155]

    I note that we are here once again involved in an issue of statutory interpretation and general legal reasoning. On that basis, I would have thought that a reviewing court, and ultimately this Court, has the duty under s. 26(3) of the Act, which provides for an

---

150 [1989] 1 S.C.R. 1722 at 1746-7 (S.C.C.). Although the Court considered whether curial deference should be applied to the decision of the CRTC, which it recognized as an expert body, it decided (at para. 34) that ". . . the decision impugned by the respondent is not a decision which falls within the appellant's area of special expertise and is therefore pursuant to s. 68(1) subject to review in accordance with the principles governing appeals" (*i.e.*, on a correctness standard).

151 [1992] 2 S.C.R. 321, 93 D.L.R. (4th) 346 (S.C.C.).

152 [1992] 2 S.C.R. 1103, 95 D.L.R. (4th) 439, 127 A.R. 241 (S.C.C.).

153 [1993] 1 S.C.R. 554, 13 Admin. L.R. (2d) 1, 100 D.L.R. (4th) 658 (S.C.C.).

154 [1993] 2 S.C.R. 353 (S.C.C.), additional reasons at (June 30, 1993), Doc. 22638, 22640 (S.C.C.).

155 [1996] 1 S.C.R. 571, 37 Admin. L.R. (2d) 1 at 26-27, 133 D.L.R. (4th) 449 (S.C.C.).

appeal on "questions of law" to consider the correctness of the Board's decision. . . .

On the basis of the foregoing, *it is quite clear that the question* of what constitutes "services to the public" for the purposes of s. 8(a) of the *Yukon Act is a general question of law, one which an appellate court must review on the basis of correctness.* [Emphasis added.]

- *Attis v. New Brunswick District No. 15 Board of Education.*[156]

- *Dell Holdings Ltd. v. Toronto Area Transit Operating Authority.*[157]

- *Barrie Public Utilities v. Canadian Cable Television Assn.*[158]

Where the appeal provision contemplates appeals on questions of law or jurisdiction, it is likely that the courts will apply a correctness test, concluding that the legislature intended the courts to substitute their view on the legal or jurisdictional issue. The correctness standard may also be applied where there is an appeal *de novo*, because presumably the legislators intended the appellate court to make its own determination about all aspects of the matter being appealed. However, the mere fact that there is an appeal does not necessarily engage the correctness standard if the other three *Pushpanathan* factors indicate that some deference to the original decision-maker was intended by the legislature.

In addition, where there is an appeal from one court to a higher court, the latter will apply the correctness standard to both the lower court's selection and application of the proper standard of review.[159]

---

156 37 Admin. L.R. (2d) 131, 171 N.B.R. (2d) 321, [1996] 1 S.C.R. 825, 133 D.L.R. (4th) 1 (S.C.C.). Technically, *Ross* was an application for judicial review, not an appeal. After *Q.*, the distinction probably does not matter.

157 (1997), 45 Admin. L.R. (2d) 1 (S.C.C.) at 22-23. Iacobucci J. dissented, but not about the standard to be applied.

158 2003 SCC 28 (S.C.C.) per Binnie J. for the majority. Bastarache J. dissenting would have selected the less stringent reasonableness standard.

159 *Alberta (Minister of Municipal Affairs) v. Alberta (Municipal Government Board)*, 2002 ABCA 199, 218 D.L.R. (4th) 61 (Alta. C.A.), leave to appeal refused (2003), 314 N.R. 208 (note) (S.C.C.), additional reasons at (2003), 41 M.P.L.R. (3d) 20 (Alta. C.A.). With respect to the second point, the majority of the Court of Appeal referred to the Supreme Court of Canada's decision in *Housen v. Nikolaisen*, 2002 SCC 33, 211 D.L.R. (4th) 577, 286 N.R. 1 (S.C.C.) at paras. 33 through 36. Hunt J.A. dissented on the basis that it was not necessary to answer the second question, and that there might be some circumstances in which an appellate court should show some deference to the way the lower court applied the appropriate standard of review.

The same issue arose in *C.U.P.E. v. Ontario (Minister of Labour)*, 2003 SCC 29, 226 D.L.R. (4th) 193 (S.C.C.) (the *"Retired Judges Case"*) in the context of identifying the test for determining whether there had been a breach of the requirement of impartiality, and the way the proper test is applied (per Justice Binnie at para. 200):

> The unions contend that this Court should defer to the Court of Appeal's findings of fact. Reliance is placed on the observation of Gonthier J. that "[t]he principle of non-intervention on questions of fact is also applicable to a second appellate

(ii) Examples of Appeal Cases Where the Reasonableness Standard was Applied

The following are examples of appeal cases where the courts have applied the less stringent reasonableness standard instead of correctness, after weighing the other three *Pushpanathan* factors:

- *Southam*,[160] which involved an appeal on a question of law, fact or mixed law and fact, where deference was shown to the statutory decision-maker (which consisted of economists as well as judges) because the issue was a question of mixed fact and law.

- *Dr. Q.*,[161] which involved an appeal "on the merits", where deference was shown to the statutory decision-maker (the physician's peers in a professional regulatory scheme) on a question of fact about credibility of the complainant and the accused physician.

- *Ryan*,[162] which involved an appeal "on a question of law or fact" where the Court of Appeal was empowered to make any order "as may be just", where deference was shown to the statutory decision-maker (the lawyer's peers in a professional regulatory scheme) about the appropriate penalty for sanctionable conduct.

- *Deputy Minister of National Revenue v. Mattel Canada Inc.*[163]

- *Committee for Equal Treatment of Asbestos Minority Shareholders v. Ontario (Securities Commission).*[164]

- *C.J.A., Local 579 v. Bradco Construction Ltd.*[165]

The decision not to apply the correctness standard in these cases, even though there was a specific statutory right of appeal, resulted from weighing

---

court such as this Court *vis-à-vis* a first appellate court" (*St-Jean v. Mercier*, [2002] 1 S.C.R. 491, 2002 SCC 15, at para. 37). *However, we are not thusly inhibited if the Court of Appeal applied the wrong test.* The correct viewpoint [for the determination of whether a decision-maker is impartial] is that of an informed observer who is detached from a personal interest in the controversy [not that of one of the parties].

With respect to the second point from *Telus*, for good examples of cases where the Supreme Court of Canada applied the same standard of review but reached a different result than the lower courts, see: *Ryan v. Law Society (New Brunswick)*, [2003] 1 S.C.R. 247 (S.C.C.) (different result from applying the reasonableness standard); and *Chieu v. Canada (Minister of Citizenship & Immigration)*, 2002 SCC 3, 37 Admin. L.R. (3d) 252 (S.C.C.) (different result from applying the correctness standard).

160 *Canada (Director of Investigation & Research) v. Southam Inc.*, [1997] S.C.R. 748, 50 Admin. L.R. (2d) 199, 144 D.L.R. (4th) 1 (S.C.C.).

161 *Q. v. College of Physicians & Surgeons (British Columbia)*, [2003] 1 S.C.R. 226 (S.C.C.).

162 *Ryan v. Law Society (New Brunswick)*, [2003] 1 S.C.R. 247 (S.C.C.).

163 [2001] 2 S.C.R. 100 (S.C.C.) at para. 27 (per Major J.).

164 [2001] 2 S.C.R. 132 (S.C.C.) at para. 49.

165 [1993] 2 S.C.R. 316 at 335 (S.C.C.).

the three other *Pushpanathan* factors. In some cases, the fact that the decision involved questions of fact or mixed fact and law inclined the court not to substitute its own view but to grant deference to the decision-maker's determination on these points. In other cases, the decision-maker's expertise was the critical factor. In yet other cases, the appeal was from the exercise of a discretion.[166]

(iii) Example of an Appeal Case Where the Patently Unreasonable Standard Was Applied

The following is an example of a case where the courts applied the patently unreasonable standard, even where there was a specific statutory right of appeal:

- *Pezim*[167] where there was an appeal from a specialized securities regulator on any question of law or jurisdiction.

Conceptually, it is arguable that *Pezim* would be decided differently today. How can the three other *Pushpanathan* factors possibly be given so much weight in a particular case that it would be treated as though the legislature had enacted the strongest form of privative clause instead of making specific provision for an appeal? Perhaps both of these cases can be explained by the fact that they were decided before the recognition of the reasonableness *simpliciter* standard in *Southam* as part of the complete development of the contextual, pragmatic and functional test.

What is clear is that the mere provision of a right of appeal is not sufficient to engage the correctness standard of review. If this is the result intended by the legislature, it will need to use very clear language to achieve this result.

---

166 See the discussion below on standards of review for discretionary decisions. The reluctance by the courts to substitute their view of how a statutory delegate should exercise its discretion is particularly marked in the case of appeals from the imposition of discipline by governing bodies of a profession. See *Q. v. College of Physicians & Surgeons (British Columbia)*, [2003] 1 S.C.R. 226 (S.C.C.); *Ryan v. Law Society (New Brunswick)*, [2003] 1 S.C.R. 247 (S.C.C.); *Lazar v. Assn. of Professional Engineers (Manitoba)*, [1971] 5 W.W.R. 614 (Man. Q.B.); *Marten v. Disciplinary Committee of the Royal College of Veterinary Surgeons*, [1965] 1 All E.R. 949 (Eng. Q.B.); *K. v. College of Physicians & Surgeons (Saskatchewan)* (1970), 72 W.W.R. 321 (Sask. Q.B.); *Rajasooria v. Disciplinary Committee*, [1955] 1 W.L.R. 405; *A Solicitor, Re*, [1912] 1 K.B. 302 at 312 (Eng. K.B.); *Weber v. Toronto (Metropolitan) Licencing Commission*, [1963] 2 O.R. 286 (Ont. H.C.), reversed [1964] 1 O.R. 621 (Ont. C.A.). See also *Canadian Western Natural Gas Co. v. Alberta (Public Utilities Board)* (1984), 33 Alta. L.R. (2d) 185 (Alta. C.A.), where the Court of Appeal refused to second-guess the discretion exercised by the board not to re-hear a matter.

167 *Pezim v. British Columbia (Superintendent of Brokers)*, [1994] 2 S.C.R. 557, 22 Admin. L.R. (2d) 1, 114 D.L.R. (4th) 385 (S.C.C.). Query: would the Court today select the reasonableness standard, rather than patently unreasonable? Would it have made any difference to the outcome?

(d) Specific Statutory Identification of the Standard of Review to be Applied

Because the entire *Pushpanathan* analysis is aimed at identifying the legislature's intention about the standard of review to be applied by the courts, it ought to be possible for the legislature to explicitly specify the applicable standard. This was suggested by the British Columbia Administrative Justice Project and legislation to accomplish this is currently being implemented in British Columbia.[168] It remains to be seen whether sufficiently specific language can be identified to make it clear without argument what standard is to be applied in practice to which issues. If this can be achieved, it would remove a great deal of the present doubt, argument and expense which is necessarily caused by having to address the present Byzantine jurisprudence about the applicable standard of review at the outset of every case involving judicial review or an appeal.

6. The Second Factor in the Functional and Pragmatic Approach to Deference – Expertise

In *Pushpanathan*, Mr. Justice Bastarache discussed the second (and most important) factor – expertise – in the following terms:

> Described by Iacobucci J. in *Southam*, *supra*, at para. 50, as "the most important of the factors that a court must consider in settling on a standard of review", this category includes several considerations. If a tribunal has been constituted with a particular expertise with respect to achieving the aims of an Act, whether because of the specialized knowledge of its decision-makers, special procedure, or non-judicial means of implementing the Act, then a greater degree of deference will be accorded. In *Southam*, the Court considered of strong importance the special make-up and knowledge of the *Competition Act* tribunal relative to a court of law in determining questions concerning competitiveness in general, and the definition of the relevant product market in particular.
>
> Nevertheless, expertise must be understood as a relative, not an absolute concept. As Sopinka J. explained in *Bradco*, *supra* at 335: "On the other side of the coin, a lack of *relative expertise* on the part of the tribunal vis-à-vis the particular issue before it as compared with

---

168 See Frank A.V. Falzon's proposal that legislation could specify the standard of review: Background Paper entitled "Standard of Review on Judicial Review or Appeal" at www.gov.bc.ca/ajp/rpts/. See also the policy paper issued by the B.C. Attorney General in August 2003 entitled "Model Statutory Powers Provisions for Administrative Tribunals" at 88-104 and 132-142. The proposed language is contained in the B.C. Administrative Tribunal Act (Bill 56), reproduced in Appendix 6. The B.C. Act received Royal Assent on May 20, 2004. One might question why the second statutory standard (in addition to correctness) is patently unreasonable, rather than unreasonable.

the reviewing court is a ground for a refusal of deference" (emphasis added). Making an evaluation of relative expertise has three dimensions: the court must characterize the expertise of the tribunal in question; it must consider its own expertise relative to that of the tribunal; and it must identify the nature of the specific issue before the administrative decision-maker relative to this expertise. Many cases have found that the legislature has intended to grant a wide margin for decision-making with respect to some issues, while others are properly subject to a correctness standard. Those cases are discussed in the fourth section below, the *"Nature of the Problem"*. The criteria of expertise and the nature of the problem are closely interrelated.

Once a broad relative expertise has been established, however, the Court is sometimes prepared to show considerable deference even in cases of highly generalized statutory interpretation where the instrument being interpreted is the tribunal's constituent legislation. In *Pezim v. British Columbia (Superintendent of Brokers)*, [1994] 2 S.C.R. 557, the B.C. Securities Commission's definition of the highly general question of what constituted a "material change" under the *Securities Act* was subjected to an unreasonableness standard. Iacobucci J. stated that "[c]ourts have also enunciated a principle of deference that applies not just to the facts as found by the tribunal, but also to the legal questions before the tribunal in the light of its role and expertise" (p. 590). This can include the interpretation of a statute which requires recourse to the treaty which it was intended to implement, as was the case in *National Corn Growers Assn. v. Canada (Import Tribunal)*, [1990] 2 S.C.R. 1324, where a patently unreasonable-ness test was applied to the interpretation of a treaty provision because the regulatory and economic nature of the determination counselled deference notwithstanding the generality of its application.

In short, a decision which involves in some degree the application of a highly specialized expertise will militate in favour of a high degree of deference, and towards a standard of review at the patent unreasonableness end of the spectrum.

(a) Different Types of Expertise

"Expertise" is a chameleon-like concept that has many possible manifestations. As the quotation above indicates, Justice Bastarache recognized the following forms of expertise in *Pushpanathan*: (a) the specialized knowledge of the statutory delegate, (b) the use of a special procedure, or (c) the non-judicial means of implementing an Act.[169]

---

169   By definition, whenever legislation confers powers on a statutory delegate who is not a judge, there is a "non-judicial means of implementing the Act". This covers virtually all of administrative law. But surely that fact alone does not in any meaningful sense force one to conclude that the statutory delegate is an "expert" or has "expertise".

Other cases have recognized other forms of expertise: (d) expertise arising from the specialization of function, such as the use of a judicial council for disciplining judges;[170] (e) expertise in the choice of sanctions;[171] (f) the expertise of lay persons about the general public's perception;[172] (g) expertise from experience in the repeated application of the statute, regulations, guidelines or policy in question;[173] (h) expertise as a result of the independent nature of the statutory delegate;[174] (i) the expertise of a Minister with respect to the matters in his or her portfolio;[175] (j) a Minister exercising a discretionary power;[176] (k) the expertise of a specialized administrative tribunal which possesses considerable expertise over the subject matter of its jurisdiction;[177] (l) the expertise of a statutory delegate charged with developing policy;[178] (m) the expertise of fact-finders with respect to findings of fact.[179]

---

170   *Moreau-Bérubé c. Nouveau-Brunswick*, 2002 SCC 11, 36 Admin L.R. (3d) 1 (S.C.C.).

171   *Ryan v. Law Society (New Brunswick)*, [2003] 1 S.C.R. 247 (S.C.C.) at para. 31.

172   *Ibid.*, at para. 32.

173   *Ibid.*, at para. 33. There is considerable difference of opinion in the courts about whether they should defer to a statutory delegate's experience in interpreting legislation – whether the statutory delegate's constitutive legislation, or other legislation which it is required to interpret in the course of its duties. See *Macdonell v. Quebec (Commission d'accès d'information)*, 2002 SCC 71, 219 D.L.R. (4th) 193 (S.C.C.) at para. 8; *C.U.P.E. v. Ontario (Minister of Labour)*, 2003 SCC 29, 226 D.L.R. (4th) 193 (S.C.C.) (the *Retired Judges Case*) at para. 17 (per Bastarache J. dissenting as to outcome, but not about the expertise of the Minister); *Barrie Public Utilities v. Canadian Cable Television Assn.*, 2003 SCC 28 (S.C.C.) per Bastarache J. (dissenting) at paras. 73-91; *National Corn Growers Assn. v. Canada (Canadian Import Tribunal)*, [1990] 2 S.C.R. 1324, 74 D.L.R. (4th) 449 (S.C.C.) (per Wilson J. dissenting). By contrast, the courts have not recognized human rights commissions to have expertise about what constitutes a breach of their legislation, even though they have repeated experience in applying their statutes: see the cases discussed in the section dealing with appeals where the correctness standard of review has been applied.

174   See *MacDonell c. Québec (Commission d'accès à l'information)*, 2002 SCC 71, 219 D.L.R. (4th) 193 (S.C.C.) at paras. 7-8; *Canada (Information Commissioner) v. Royal Canadian Mounted Police Commissioner*, 2003 SCC 8, 224 D.L.R. (4th) 1 (S.C.C.) at paras. 15-19; *3430901 Canada Inc. v. Canada (Minister of Industry)* (2001), [2002] 1 F.C. 421 (Fed. C.A.), leave to appeal refused (2002), 293 N.R. 400 (note) (S.C.C.) at para. 30.

175   *C.U.P.E. v. Ontario (Minister of Labour)*, 2003 SCC 29, 226 D.L.R. (4th) 193 (S.C.C.) (the *Retired Judges Case*) at paras. 150-152 (per Binnie J.) and at paras. 16-17 per Bastarache J. (dissenting as to outcome, but not on this point).

176   *Ibid.*, per Bastarache J. at para. 17. See also *Suresh v. Canada (Minister of Citizenship & Immigration)*, [2002] 1 S.C.R. 3 (S.C.C.) at para. 30; *Centre hospitalier Mont-Sinaï c. Québec (Ministre de la Santé & des Services sociaux)*, [2001] 2 S.C.R. 281 (S.C.C.) at para. 57; *Baker v. Canada (Minister of Citizenship & Immigration)*, [1999] 2 S.C.R. 817 (S.C.C.) at para. 59.

177   *British Columbia Telephone Co. v. Shaw Cable Systems (B.C.) Ltd.*, [1995] 2 S.C.R. 739 (S.C.C.) at paras. 30-31.

178   *Deputy Minister of National Revenue v. Mattel Canada Inc.*, [2001] 2 S.C.R. 100 (S.C.C.) at para. 16 (per Major J.).

179   *Q. v. College of Physicians & Surgeons (British Columbia)*, [2003] 1 S.C.R. 226 (S.C.C.) (findings of credibility). Although a statutory delegate may have expertise in fact-finding, the factual nature of an issue may also be relevant to the fourth *Pushpanathan* factor – namely, the "nature of the problem". Problems which involve findings of fact or mixed fact and law attract more deference, even if the statutory delegate is not an expert at fact-finding. By contrast, note that the Supreme Court of Canada has not deferred to facts found by human rights tribunals, at least in cases where the evidence was all in written form: *Gould*

(b) Relative Expertise

Even if a statutory delegate has some form of expertise, it will only command deference if it has greater relative expertise than the court on the matter at hand. In other words, expertise is a relative – not an absolute – concept. As Sopinka J. put it in *Bradco*:[180]

> On the other side of the coin, a lack of *relative expertise* on the part of the tribunal *vis-à-vis* the particular issue before it as compared with the reviewing court is a ground for a refusal of deference". [Emphasis added.]

Note that it is not sufficient for the statutory delegate to have some form of *general* expertise,[181] perhaps arising from the fact that it deals with a specialized subject or was set up as a separate regulatory agency. Rather, it is necessary to determine the *particular issue* that is before the court, and then determine whether the statutory delegate has greater relative expertise with respect to that issue. For example, in two cases[182] the Supreme Court of Canada has acknowledged the considerable expertise of the CRTC over the subject matter of its jurisdiction, but nevertheless held that the court had greater expertise with respect to the questions of law which were involved in those cases. The Supreme Court has used a similar analysis to justify employing the correctness standard of review in appeals from decisions of various human

---

v. Yukon Order of Pioneers, [1996] 1 S.C.R. 571, 37 Admin. L.R. (2d) 1 at 14-15 (S.C.C.) (per Iacobucci J.); *University of Alberta v. Alberta (Human Rights Commission)*, [1992] 2 S.C.R. 1103 at 1124-26 (S.C.C.) (per Dickson C.J.). See Hon. Robert F. Reid, Q.C.'s comment on *Dickason* at (1992) R.A.L. 2 at 4 indicating "[queasiness] about equating fact-finding by trial judges who have training and experience in the art to fact-finding by "administrative decision-makers" who in the human rights field could be moonlighting professors having neither, and who are moreover not even bound by the rules of evidence".

180 *C.J.A., Local 579 v. Bradco Construction Ltd.*, [1993] 2 S.C.R. 316 at 335 (S.C.C.), quoted by Bastarache J. in *Pushpanathan* at para. 33.

181 But see the dissent by Bastarache J. in *Barrie Public Utilities v. Canadian Cable Television Assn.*, 2003 SCC 28, 225 D.L.R. (4th) 206 (S.C.C.) at paras. 73-91.

182 *British Columbia Telephone Co. v. Shaw Cable Systems (B.C.) Ltd.*, [1995] 2 S.C.R. 739 (S.C.C.) at paras. 30-31 (per L'Heureux-Dubé J.); and *Barrie Public Utilities v. Canadian Cable Television Assn.*, 2003 SCC 28, 225 D.L.R. (4th) 206 (S.C.C.) at paras. 12-16 (per Gonthier J.). As Gonthier J. put it in *Barrie Public Utilities* (at para. 16):

> Deference to the decision maker is called for only when it is in some way more expert than the court and the question under consideration is one that falls within the scope of its greater expertise (*Dr. Q.*, at para. 28). In my view, this is not such a case. The proper interpretation of the phrase "the supporting structure of a transmission line" in s. 43(5) is not a question that engages the CRTC's special expertise in the regulation and supervision of Canadian broadcasting and telecommunications. This is not a question of telecommunications policy, or one which requires an understanding of technical language. Rather, it is a purely legal question and is therefore, in the words of La Forest J., "ultimately within the province of the judiciary" (*Ross v. New Brunswick School District No. 15*, [1996] 1 S.C.R. 825, at paras. 28). This Court's expertise in matters of pure statutory interpretation is superior to that of the CRTC. This factor suggests a less deferential approach.

rights commissions.[183] Similarly, the courts have held that various privacy commissioners do not have greater expertise about the meaning of certain concepts found in their respective statutes which limit or define their authority (such as what constitutes solicitor-client privilege).[184] On the other hand, it does not necessarily follow that the courts will always have greater expertise with respect to every question of law – it will depend upon whether the issue is a specialized legal concept instead of a general one, whether that legal question falls within the greater expertise of the statutory delegate, and whether the legislature clearly intended the statutory delegate to be able to make that determination definitively.[185] As Chief Justice McLachlin put it in *Dr. Q.*, merely identifying something as "a purely legal question" does not automatically engage any particular standard of review (or mean that the courts have a greater expertise than the statutory delegate with respect to that legal question).[186]

Further, note that the concept of relative expertise also requires the courts to determine or characterize what is the *particular issue* or *matter* that is before the court. Different judges may do this differently, with the possibility of different results.[187] To the extent that a party can convince the court that the matter in question involves a constitutional issue[188] or a jurisdictional limita-

---

183 See the cases referred to in Part 5(c) above dealing with the correctness standard of review in the context of statutory appeals.

184 *Dagg v. Canada (Minister of Finance)*, [1997] 2 S.C.R. 403 (S.C.C.); *MacDonell c. Quebec (Commission d'accès à l'information)*, 2002 SCC 71, 219 D.L.R. (4th) 193 (S.C.C.); *Canada (Information Commissioner) v. Royal Canadian Mounted Police Commissioner*, 2003 SCC 8, 224 D.L.R. (4th) 1 (S.C.C.); *Ontario (Attorney General) v. Ontario (Information & Privacy Commissioner)* (2001), 41 Admin. L.R. (3d) 117 (Ont. Div. Ct.), affirmed (2002), 48 Admin. L.R. (3d) 279 (Ont. C.A.), leave to appeal refused (2003), 2003 CarswellOnt 1841 (S.C.C.).

185 See the dissent by Bastarache J. in *Barrie Public Utilities v. Canadian Cable Television Assn.*, 2003 SCC 28, 225 D.L.R. (4th) 206 (S.C.C.) at paras. 83-91, and the authorities referred to therein.

186 *Q. v. College of Physicians & Surgeons (British Columbia)*, [2003] 1 S.C.R. 226 (S.C.C.) at para. 25.

187 *A.C.T.R.A. v. Canadian Broadcasting Corp.*, [1995] 1 S.C.R. 157, 27 Admin. L.R. (2d) 1 (S.C.C.); and the comment by D.P. Jones, Q.C. entitled "What's the 'matter'? What's the standard of review?" (1995) 4 R.A.L. 74.

188 See *Barrie Public Utilities v. Canadian Cable Television Assn.*, 2003 SCC 28, 225 D.L.R. (4th) 206 (S.C.C.) at para. 66 (per Binnie J.) and at para. 125 (per Bastarache J. dissenting about the characterization of the issue as constitutional). See also *Paul v. British Columbia (Forest Appeals Commission)*, 2003 SCC 55 (S.C.C.) at para. 31; *Martin v. Nova Scotia (Workers' Compensation Board)*, 2003 SCC 54, 4 Admin. L.R. (4th) 1 (S.C.C.) at para. 31; *Westcoast Energy Inc. v. Canada (National Energy Board)*, [1998] 1 S.C.R. 322 (S.C.C.) at para. 40 (per Major and Iacobucci JJ); *K Mart Canada Ltd. v. U.F.C.W., Local 1518*, [1999] 2 S.C.R. 1083 (S.C.C.); *Cooper v. Canada (Human Rights Commission)*, [1996] 3 S.C.R. 854 (S.C.C.); *Attis v. New Brunswick School District No. 15 Board of Education*, [1996] 1 S.C.R. 825 (S.C.C.); *Tétreault-Gadoury v. Canada (Employment & Immigration Commission)*, [1991] 2 S.C.R. 22 (S.C.C.); *Cuddy Chicks Ltd. v. Ontario (Labour Relations Board)*, [1991] 2 S.C.R. 5 (S.C.C.); *Douglas/Kwantlen Faculty Assn. v. Douglas College*, [1990] 3 S.C.R. 570 (S.C.C.); *Slaight Communications Inc. v. Davidson*, [1989] 1 S.C.R. 1038 (S.C.C.). Are there any circumstances in which a statutory delegate could have greater expertise with respect to this type of question?

tion,[189] it will be unlikely that the court will find that the statutory delegate has greater expertise with respect to that issue.

(c) How is Expertise Established?

Unfortunately, none of the recent cases addresses how one determines whether a particular statutory delegate has expertise with respect to the particular issue in question.

Is expertise discerned by simply reading the statute? Does it derive from the qualifications or experience of the particular members of the tribunal making the decision – or the tribunal as a whole?

Does the fact that a tribunal has a long history necessarily give it expertise? Does expertise depend upon how independent the tribunal is? Or how comprehensively and credibly it writes the reasons for its decisions? Would this expertise relate to all matters?

How would these facts be established? Is evidence admissible on these points? If so, when and how does one get this evidence on to the record – during the tribunal's proceedings, or somehow during the appeal or application for judicial review?

Can members of a tribunal be compelled to describe their training, skills and experience? Is the expertise of the particular individual decision-makers relevant? Would this differ if the statutory delegate is a standing body, as compared to an *ad hoc* decision-maker?

(d) Expertise is only Important as an Indicator of Legislative Intent

It is very easy to be so blinded by the gleam of "expertise" that one forgets that the whole purpose of the pragmatic and functional approach from *Pushpanathan* is to determine the intent of Parliament. Did Parliament intend the court to have the final say about the meaning of the particular statutory phrase, or did it intend the statutory delegate to have some discretion to determine that meaning?

By itself, unrooted from legislative intent, expertise (however it is defined) does not provide a justification for judicial deference. The accuracy of this statement can be demonstrated by the very possibility that the legislature could specifically provide that the courts are to employ the correctness standard when reviewing an expert tribunal's decision.[190] In these circumstances, the fact that the tribunal is expert would simply be irrelevant to the standard of review to be employed by the court. It is only when the legislature has not stated its intention clearly that one must resort to the four *Pushpanathan* factors –

---

189 For a good discussion about jurisdictional limitations, see Veit J.'s decision in *Alberta v. Alberta (Labour Relations Board)* (2001), 30 Admin. L.R. (3d) 24 (Alta. Q.B.), additional reasons at (1998), 30 Admin. L.R. (3d) 62 (Alta. Q.B.), reversed at (2002), 40 Admin. L.R. (3d) 115 (Alta. C.A.), leave to appeal dismissed by S.C.C. at (2002), [2002] S.C.C.A. No. 100, 2002 CarswellAlta 1135 (S.C.C.), additional reasons at (2003), 16 Alta. L.R. (4th) 24 (Alta. C.A.).

190 See the B.C. attempt to legislate the standard of review: *supra* note 168 and Appendix 6, below.

including expertise – in order to determine "the polar star of legislative intent".[191] The mere fact that a statutory delegate is expert does not necessarily or definitively determine what was the legislature's intent about the degree of scrutiny to be employed by the courts in reviewing the statutory delegate's decisions.

7. The Third Factor in the Functional and Pragmatic Approach to Deference – the Purpose of the Act as a Whole, and the Provision in Particular

In *Pushpanathan*, Justice Bastarache described the third factor – the purpose of the Act as a whole, and the purpose of the provision in question in particular – in the following terms:

> As Iacobucci J. noted in *Southam, supra*, at para. 50, purpose and expertise often overlap. The purpose of a statute is often indicated by the specialized nature of the legislative structure and dispute-settlement mechanism, and the need for expertise is often manifested as much by the requirements of the statute as by the specific qualifications of its members. Where the purposes of the statute and of the decision-maker are conceived not primarily in terms of establishing rights as between parties, or as entitlements, but rather as a delicate balancing between different constituencies, then the appropriateness of court supervision diminishes. Thus, in *National Corn Growers, supra*, at p. 1336, Wilson J. characterized the function of the board in question as one of "management", partially because of the specialized knowledge of the members of the board, but also because of the range of remedies available upon a determination, including the imposition of countervailing duties by the Minister (at p. 1346). In *Southam*, the Court found (at para. 48) that the "aims of the Act are more 'economic' than they are strictly 'legal'" because the broad goals of the Act "are matters that business women and men and economists are better able to understand than is a typical judge". This conclusion was reinforced by the creation in the statute of a tribunal with members having a special expertise in those domains. Also of significance are the range of administrative responses, the fact that an administrative commission plays a "protective role" *vis-à-vis* the investing public, and that it plays a role in policy development; *Pezim, supra*, at p. 596. That legal principles are vague, open-textured, or involve a "multi-factored balancing test" may also militate in favour of a lower standard of review (*Southam*, at para. 44). These considerations are all specific articulations of the broad principle of "polycentricity" well known to academic commentators who suggest that it provides the best rationale

---

191   To use Binnie J.'s phrase from *C.U.P.E. v. Ontario (Minister of Labour)*, 2003 SCC 29, 226 D.L.R. (4th) 193 (S.C.C.) (the *Retired Judges Case*) at para. 149.

for judicial deference to non-judicial agencies. A "polycentric issue is one which involves a large number of interlocking and interacting interests and considerations" (P. Cane, *An Introduction to Administrative Law* (3rd ed. 1996), at p. 35). While judicial procedure is premised on a bipolar opposition of parties, interests, and factual discovery, some problems require the consideration of numerous interests simultaneously, and the promulgation of solutions which concurrently balance benefits and costs for many different parties. Where an administrative structure more closely resembles this model, courts will exercise restraint. The polycentricity principle is a helpful way of understanding the variety of criteria developed under the rubric of the "statutory purpose".

8. The Fourth Factor in the Functional and Pragmatic Approach to Deference – The "Nature of the Problem": A Question of Law or Fact?

In *Pushpanathan*, Justice Bastarache discussed the fourth factor – the nature of the problem, whether it is a general question of law or a specific determination of fact – in the following terms:

> As mentioned above, even pure questions of law may be granted a wide degree of deference where other factors of the pragmatic and functional analysis suggest that such deference is the legislative intention, as this Court found to be the case in *Pasiechnyk, supra*. Where, however, other factors leave that intention ambiguous, courts should be less deferential of decisions which are pure determinations of law. The justification for this position relates to the question of relative expertise mentioned previously. There is no clear line to be drawn between questions of law and questions of fact, and, in any event, many determinations involve questions of mixed law and fact. An appropriate litmus test was set out in *Southam, supra*, at para. 37, by Iacobucci J., who stated:

> Of course, it is not easy to say precisely where the line should be drawn; though in most cases it should be sufficiently clear whether the dispute is over a general proposition that might qualify as a principle of law or over a very particular set of circumstances that is not apt to be of much interest to judges and lawyers in the future.

This principle was also articulated by L'Heureux-Dubé J. in *Canada (Attorney General) v. Mossop*, [1993] 1 S.C.R. 554, at pp. 599-600, who sought to clarify the limitations of distinctions based on this criterion:

> In general, deference is given on questions of fact because of the 'signal advantage' enjoyed by the primary finder of fact. Less defer-

ence is warranted on questions of law, in part because the finder of fact may not have developed any particular familiarity with issues of law. While there is merit in the distinction between fact and law, the distinction is not always so clear. Specialized boards are often called upon to make difficult findings of both fact and law. In some circumstances, the two are inextricably linked. Further, the 'correct' interpretation of a term may be dictated by the mandate of the board and by the coherent body of jurisprudence it has developed. In some cases, even where courts might not agree with a given interpretation, the integrity of certain administrative processes may demand that deference be shown to that interpretation of law.

Her dissent in that case was founded essentially on her disapproval of the views of the majority on the characterization of the human rights tribunal as enjoying no expertise relative to courts in the understanding and interpretation of human rights Acts. Nevertheless, the principles discussed in the above quotation correctly state the law. This was confirmed in *Pasiechnyk*, at paras. 36 to 42, where the broad expertise of the Workers' Compensation Board to determine all aspects of "eligibility" under that system was considered sufficiently broad to include the determination that the term "employer" included claims against the government for its alleged negligence in regulating the works of two companies which had led to workers' injuries. Claims against the government as regulator were thus barred by virtue of the determination in issue. To allow such a claim "would undermine the purposes of the scheme" which was to "solve . . . the problem of employers becoming insolvent as a result of high damage awards" (para. 42). Such a finding falls squarely within Iacobucci J.'s description of a question of law: a finding which will be of great, even determinative import for future decisions of lawyers and judges. The creation of a legislative "scheme" combined with the creation of a highly specialized administrative decision-maker, as well as the presence of a strong privative clause was sufficient to grant an expansive deference even over extremely general questions of law.

Keeping in mind that all the factors discussed here must be taken together to come to a view of the proper standard of review, the generality of the proposition decided will be a factor in favour of the imposition of a correctness standard. This factor necessarily intersects with the criteria described above, which may contradict such a presumption, as the majority of this Court found to be the case in *Pasiechnyk*, *supra*. In the usual case, however, the broader the propositions asserted, and the further the implications of such decisions stray from the core expertise of the tribunal, the less likelihood that deference will be shown. Without an implied or express legislative intent to the contrary as manifested in the criteria above, legislatures should be assumed to have left highly generalized propositions of law to courts.

9. Practical Issues in the Identification and Application of the Appropriate Standard of Review

The contextual, pragmatic and functional approach involved in applying the four *Pushpanathan* factors in order to find the appropriate standard of review raises a number of practical issues.

(a) The Standard of Review must be Addressed in Every Case

The Supreme Court of Canada has made it clear that the standard of review must be addressed at the outset of every application for judicial review and appeal.[192] This means quite a bit of work for counsel and the courts before the principal issue can even be addressed.

(b) Lack of Predictability

The courts have not given any guidance about how one is to weigh the four *Pushpanathan* factors together in order to arrive at the appropriate standard of review.

For example, given that Chief Justice McLachlin in *Q.*[193] did not conclude that the provision of an appeal "on the merits" was determinative of the Legislature's intent, precisely how did she weigh the four factors from the pragmatic and functional approach? Two factors (the existence of a broad right of appeal, and no greater expertise in the Committee compared to the court) suggested a low degree of deference, one factor was ambivalent (the purpose of the statute and the provision in particular), and the fourth factor (the nature of the problem – credibility) suggested deference. We know the various considerations identified by the court with respect to each of the four factors, and the outcome, but we don't know the weight applied to each of the factors. But precisely why did the fourth factor outweigh all the others?

As Justice Binnie puts it in the *Retired Judges Case*:[194]

> The examination of the four factors, and the "weighing up" of contextual elements to identify the appropriate standard of review, is not a mechanical exercise. Given the immense range of discretionary decision makers and administrative bodies, the test is necessarily flexible, and proceeds by principled analysis rather than categories, seeking the polar star of legislative intent.

---

192   *Pushpanathan v. Canada (Minister of Employment & Immigration)*, [1998] 1 S.C.R. 982 at 1004 (S.C.C.), amended at [1998] 1 S.C.R. 1222 (S.C.C.) (per Bastarache J.); *Suresh v. Canada (Minister of Citizenship & Immigration)*, [2002] 1 S.C.R. 3, 37 Admin. L.R. (3d) 159 (S.C.C.) (per Iacobucci J.); and *Q. v. College of Physicians & Surgeons (British Columbia)*, [2003] 1 S.C.R. 226 (S.C.C.) at para. 40 (per McLachlin C.J.).

193   *Q. v. College of Physicians & Surgeons (British Columbia)*, *ibid.*

194   *C.U.P.E. v. Ontario (Minister of Labour)*, 2003 SCC 29, 226 D.L.R. (4th) 193 (S.C.C.) at para. 149.

This lack of a method of weighing the various factors causes uncertainty, unpredictability, and the possibility of different judges reaching different results about which standard of review is to be applied.[195]

(c) Issues of Proof

There may often be practical issues about how to prove various matters which could be relevant to the selection of the appropriate standard of review in a particular case. Issues about how to establish expertise have been discussed above, in that section. In addition, it may be necessary to enter evidence in order to permit the court to be able to make an appraisal about whether a particular decision is either unreasonable or patently unreasonable (as the case may be). How is this evidence to get before the court? Can it be led in front of the statutory delegate? Can it be led in the subsequent judicial review or appeal proceedings?

(d) Distinction Between the Standard to be Applied by the Statutory Delegate at First Instance and the Appropriate Standard of Review to be Applied by the Courts

There may well be a difference between the standard which must be applied by the statutory delegate in doing its job ("clear and cogent evidence" in *Q.*) and the standard of review which must be applied by the reviewing court:[196]

> [19] The standard of clear and cogent evidence [which the Committee had to apply] does not permit the reviewing judge to enter into a re-evaluation of the evidence. . . . The requirement for "clear and cogent evidence" is a matter relating to the standard of proof employed at the Committee level, ensuring that the Committee is alive to the gravity of the consequences of their decision. It is a legal standard that the administrative decision-maker must apply to the evidence in order to determine the outcome of the case. It does not instruct a reviewing court on how to scrutinize the decision of the administrative decision-maker. This is solely a question of standard of review, to be resolved by applying the pragmatic and functional approach.

(e) A Higher Court will Apply the Correctness Standard to a Lower Court's Choice and Application of Standard of Review

Q. makes it clear that the choice of standard of review is to be done correctly by the chambers judge; no deference is to be shown by a higher court to the

---

195 This problem is demonstrated by the majority and the minority analyses in *Barrie Public Utilities v. Canadian Cable Television Assn.*, 2003 SCC 28, 225 D.L.R. (4th) 206 (S.C.C.).

196 [2003] 1 S.C.R. 226 (S.C.C.) at paras. 16-19. A similar point was made by Justice Iacobucci in *Suresh v. Canada (Minister of Citizenship & Immigration)*, [2002] 1 S.C.R. 3, 37 Admin. L.R. (3d) 159 (S.C.C.) at para. 40: ". . . [I]t is useful to underline the distinction between standard of review [to be employed by the reviewing court] and the evidence required to establish particular facts in issue [in front of the original decision-maker]."

standard selected by the lower court judge. In addition, a higher court can substitute its own view of (*i.e.*, correct) how the applicable standard is to be applied.[197] No deference is to be shown by the higher court to these determinations by the lower court. The practical effect may be to simply encourage litigants to appeal.

(f) Different Judges may Apply the same Standard Differently

Even where all of the judges agree on the selection of the appropriate standard, different judges may apply that standard differently to reach different results.

For example, in *Chieu v. Canada (Minister of Citizenship & Immigration)*, all of the courts agreed on the appropriateness of the correctness standard of review, but the Supreme Court of Canada's view of the correct legal interpretation differed from the lower courts' interpretation – thereby reaching a different outcome. In *Pushpanathan*,[198] all of the judges in the Supreme Court of Canada agreed that correctness was the applicable standard of review, but the majority differed from the minority about what was the correct interpretation of the legislation.

Similarly, although all the judges may agree that either the reasonableness *simpliciter* standard or the "patent unreasonableness" standard applies, they may reach different conclusions about whether the statutory delegate did or did not breach the standard in question – just like in olden times different Chancellors had different lengths of feet. See:

- *Macdonell v. Quebec (Commission d'accès à l'information)*, 2002 SCC 71, where the court split 5 to 4 in holding that the Commissioner's decision was reasonable.[199]

- *C.U.P.E. v. Ontario (Minister of Labour)* 2003 SCC 29 (S.C.C.), where the 6 members of the majority held that the Minister's appointment of retired judges was patently unreasonable, but the 3 members of the minority perceived that it was not.

- *Barrie Public Utilities v. Canadian Cable Television Assn.*, 2003 SCC 28 (S.C.C.), where the majority of the Supreme Court used the cor-

---

197 *Q. v. College of Physicians & Surgeons (British Columbia)*, [2003] 1 S.C.R. 226 (S.C.C.) at paras. 43-44. See also *Alberta (Minister of Municipal Affairs) v. Alberta (Municipal Government Board)*, 2002 ABCA 199, 218 D.L.R. (4th) 61 (Alta. C.A.), leave to appeal refused (2003), 314 N.R. 208 (note) (S.C.C.), additional reasons at 2003 ABCA 260 (Alta. C.A.) and *C.U.P.E. v. Ontario (Minister of Labour)*, 2003 SCC 29, 226 D.L.R. (4th) 193 (S.C.C.) (the *Retired Judges Case*) at para. 200 (per Binnie J. in the context of correcting wrong test used by the Ontario Court of Appeal for the determination of whether a decision-maker is impartial).

198 *Pushpanathan v. Canada (Minister of Employment & Immigration)*, [1998] 1 S.C.R. 982 (S.C.C.), amended at [1998] 1 S.C.R. 1222 (S.C.C.).

199 By contrast, the Quebec Superior Court had adopted the patently unreasonable test (and held that the Commissioner's decision *was* patently unreasonable!). The Court of Appeal adopted the reasonableness standard, and held that the Commissioner's decision was not unreasonable.

rectness standard of review and set aside the CRTC's decision, but Justice Bastarache would have applied the reasonableness standard (and would have held that the CRTC's decision was reasonable).[200]

• *Starson v. Swayze*, 2003 SCC 32 (S.C.C.), where the majority and minority differed about whether the decision of the Capacity and Consent Board was reasonable.

Does this possibility of different outcomes – even applying the same standard – simply encourage losing litigants to appeal?

When there is a three-member court, does the fact that one judge finds the decision *not* to be patently unreasonable by definition mean that it is not? Does this imply that a finding of patent unreasonableness should be required to be unanimous?

(g) Different Standards of Review may Apply to Different Issues

It is clear that different standards of review may apply to different issues. For example, the Supreme Court of Canada held that the correctness standard applied to the issue which arose under the *Immigration Act* in *Pushpanathan*,[201] but the reasonableness *simpliciter* standard applied to the issue which arose in *Baker*. Accordingly, it is generally not possible to state that a particular standard of review will apply to all questions which arise under a particular statute, or all decisions made by a particular statutory delegate.

Similarly, there may be different standards of review applicable to different issues involved in any particular decision by a statutory delegate. For example, there were three separate questions in *Suresh*,[202] and a separate standard-of-review analysis was required with respect to each issue. Care must be taken to deal with each issue separately, so that the standard applicable to one issue (perhaps a constitutional issue) is not simply assumed to apply to all of the other issues.[203]

---

200 There was no privative clause in the legislation, but there was a statutory right of appeal, so the patently unreasonable standard of review was virtually excluded.

201 *Pushpanathan v. Canada (Minister of Employment & Immigration)*, [1998] 1 S.C.R. 982 (S.C.C.), amended at [1998] 1 S.C.R. 1222 (S.C.C.); *Baker v. Canada (Minister of Citizenship & Immigration)*, [1999] 2 S.C.R. 817 (S.C.C.).

202 *Suresh v. Canada (Minister of Citizenship & Immigration)*, [2002] 1 S.C.R. 3, 37 Admin. L.R. (3d) 159 (S.C.C.) (per Iacobucci J.) See also *Pushpanathan, ibid.*, at para. 49 (per Bastarache J.); and *MacDonell c. Québec (Commission d'accès à l'information)*, 2002 SCC 71, 219 D.L.R. (4th) 193 (S.C.C.) at para. 58 (per Bastarache J.).

203 This point was made by Bastarache J. in his dissent in *Barrie Public Utilities v. Canadian Cable Television Assn.*, 2003 SCC 28, 225 D.L.R. (4th) 206 (S.C.C.) at para. 125:

By failing to separate out the constitutional issue from the ordinary judicial review process, Rothstein J.A. introduced constitutional concerns into the standard of review [of the second issue]. He held that the question could not have been intended to be left to the exclusive determination of the CRTC because it might extend the CRTC's power to entities not otherwise subject to its jurisdiction. This is a veiled constitutional concern. *The result was a determination of a correctness standard for an expert agency's inter-pretation of its enabling legislation.* Neither Rothstein J.A. nor Gonthier J. conducted a full constitutional analysis. Had they done so, they would have concluded that the CRTC's

On the other hand, it may sometimes be difficult to know whether a particular case presents just one issue or multiple issues. In the *Retired Judges Case*,[204] Binnie J. acknowledged that the Union's legal challenge contained many sub-parts, but concluded that it would be wrong to isolate the issues and subject each of them to possibly differing standards of review:

> ¶ 97 Although the net result of a s. 6(5) appointment is the naming of a particular individual as a chairperson, the appointment is inevitably the product of a number of issues or determinations, some of them having to do with procedural fairness (*e.g.*, do I first have to consult with the parties?), some of them legal (*e.g.*, to what extent is my choice constrained by HLDAA?), some of them factual (*e.g.*, what qualifications am I looking for?), and others of mixed fact and law (*e.g.*, is this individual "qualified" within the range of choice permitted to me by HLDAA?) *The Court's task on judicial review is not to isolate these issues and subject each of them to differing standards of review.* The unions' attack is properly aimed at the ultimate s. 6(5) appointments themselves. Nevertheless, as a practical matter (and practicality is a welcome virtue in this area of the law), it is convenient to group these issues in order to facilitate the judicial review of the s. 6(5) decision. [Emphasis added.]

Justice Bastarache agreed that there was only one issue in this case, which engaged only one standard of review (which was patent unreasonableness), but he issued a strong warning against the temptation to inappropriately identify sub-issues which might attract different standards of review:

> ¶ 6 Binnie J. and I agree ultimately on the appropriate standard of review. This agreement masks, however, some disagreement on the pragmatic and functional approach adopted by this Court.

> ¶ 7 As this Court recognized in *Pushpanathan v. Canada (Minister of Citizenship and Immigration)*, [1998] 1 S.C.R. 982, this approach focusses on "the particular, individual provision being invoked and interpreted by the tribunal" (para. 28). The result is that *some provisions within the same statute may require greater deference than others*, depending on the factors (para. 28). *It does not follow, however, that exercise of a discretionary power under a single provision, such as s. 6(5) in this appeal, should be viewed as "the product of a number of issues or determinations"* (Binnie

---

interpretation of s. 43(5) was not *ultra vires* Parliament. *In effect, Rothstein J.A.'s decision demonstrates to parties dissatisfied with an administrative decision that they need only frame a constitutional argument – it need not be a sound one – in order to have the decision reviewed by a court on a correctness basis.* The mere suggestion of unconstitutionality is enough. [Emphasis added.]

204 *C.U.P.E. v. Ontario (Minister of Labour)*, 2003 SCC 29, 226 D.L.R. (4th) 193 (S.C.C.).

J.'s reasons, at para. 97) *with the decision maker's statutory interpretation singled out for closer scrutiny. Binnie J.'s citations to this Court's decision in Canadian Broadcasting Corp. v. Canada (Labour Relations Board)*, [1995] 1 S.C.R. 157 ("*CBC*"), support the impression that a single administrative decision contains within it parts that are independently reviewable on a more or, more likely, less deferential standard. That appeal related to the standard of review for an agency's decision that required it to interpret a statute other than its enabling legislation. The passage from the plurality, to which Binnie J. refers, concludes that where the standard of review for a decision as a whole is patent unreasonableness, the correctness of the interpretation of an external statute may nevertheless affect the overall reasonableness of that decision. That authority is not apparently relevant to a case such as the present appeal, where the Minister exercises a power under a single statute, his enabling legislation. *Given the present context, reference to that authority can only suggest, wrongly, that even in these circumstances a patent unreasonableness standard must make room, within the broader decision, for review of statutory interpretation on a correctness basis.* The obvious exception, where a legal question will take a different standard from the global decision, is when an agency's decision engages constitutional issues. Constitutional questions will necessarily be reviewable on a correctness standard. Special cases like *CBC* will be dealt with on a case-by-case basis. *In this case, however, the main issue is that of deciding whether the Minister failed to consider proper factors when making appointments under s. 6(5). It is a single issue.*

¶ 8 *It is true that some enabling statutes distinguish between the agency's factual and legal determinations. Such statutes may contemplate an appeal from the agency's legal determinations while protecting, with a privative clause, findings of fact.* See *e.g. Telecommunications Act*, S.C. 1993, c. 38, s. 64(1). *Yet, where there is no basis for dividing a decision into component questions* – here the privative clause in s. 7 of the HLDAA expressly shields the entire appointment – *the single appropriate standard of review, and the deference it dictates, apply to all aspects of the decision.* There is no basis for the view that an expert decision maker due deference with regard to a discretionary appointment power is due less deference because the power is circumscribed by legislation, the suggestion being that there is a statutory interpretation aspect to his or her decision. The authorities that Binnie J. cites for the self-evident proposition that a discretion is never untrammelled and that "there is always a perspective within which a statute is intended to operate" (*Roncarelli v. Duplessis*, [1959] S.C.R. 121, at p. 140; *Padfield v. Minister of Agriculture, Fisheries and Food*, [1968] A.C. 997

(H.L.)) do not indicate that each administrative action necessarily involves a distinct and identifiable exercise of statutory interpretation. . . .

¶ 12 *The difficulty may stem from Binnie J.'s importing a practical sense of how decisions are actually made into the specialized judicial review context. Obviously, one could divide nearly every administrative decision into preliminary determinations. Even a purely legal question of statutory interpretation relies on the prior factual determination that the decision maker was reading the correct version of the Act and not some other document. In the course of selecting a chairperson for an arbitral board, the Minister made choices concerning for instance which officials to consult and determined how many options were open to him. But for judicial review to be workable, courts generally operate on the assumption that they can isolate a single decision to be reviewed. They then determine one standard of review for that decision. For present purposes, it is unworkable to view the Minister's naming of an individual as comprising multiple determinations.*

¶ 13 Admittedly, the pragmatic and functional approach may require different standards of review for different questions. This recognizes that the diversity of the contemporary administrative state includes different types of decision makers. Parliament and the provincial legislatures have not structured or qualified every agency to determine finally the same types of question. But *judicial review would become grossly unwieldy and complex if each decision was to be viewed as a multiplicity of preliminary determinations.* [Emphasis added.]

Obviously, in many cases there may be considerable disagreement about how many issues are involved – and therefore about how many times the standard-of-review analysis needs to be performed.[205]

(h) The Possibility that the Appropriate Standard may Change Over Time

The Supreme Court of Canada has also recognized that the appropriate standard of review for a particular statutory provision may change over time, given supervening events. In *Ivanhoe inc. c. Travailleurs & travailleuses unis de l'alimentation & du commerce, section 500*,[206] the court applied the patent unreasonableness standard to the Labour Court's interpretation of the very same statutory provision to which the Court had previously applied the cor-

---

205 See also Justice LeBel's analysis of the two standards of review applicable in *Toronto (City) v. C.U.P.E., Local 79*, 2003 SCC 63 (S.C.C.), starting at para. 67.

206 [2001] 2 S.C.R. 565 (S.C.C.).

rectness standard in *Bibeault.*[207] In the interval between the two decisions, the Quebec legislature had amended the legislation, and slightly strengthened the privative clause, and the Labour Court had acquired greater expertise, with the result that greater deference was now called for.

(i) Number of Standards

To be the devil's advocate (but not the devil!): *Why* do we need three standards? *Why* wouldn't correctness and reasonableness suffice?[208] *Why* do legislators continue to use privative clauses?

10. The Distinction Between the Standard of Review and the Content of the Duty of Procedural Fairness – Do the Three Standards of Review Apply to Breaches of Procedural Fairness?

While the courts have spent a lot of time and energy developing the spectrum of deference and the three standards of review, it is not at all clear that this analysis applies to every ground for judicial review. For example, the test – the standard of review used by the courts – for determining whether there has been a breach of natural justice or procedural fairness is whether a reasonable person, reasonably apprised of the facts, would reasonably apprehend that the procedure used was not fair. It is not easy to correlate "fairness" to "correctness", "reasonableness" or "patent unreasonableness", and there is no justification for deferring to a statutory delegate's use of an unfair procedure.

In *Moreau-Bérubé v. Nouveau-Brunswick,*[209] Justice Arbour recognized that no assessment of the appropriate standard of review is required in determining whether there has been a breach of procedural fairness:

> (3) Procedural Fairness
>
> ¶74 The third issue requires no assessment of the appropriate standard of judicial review. Evaluating whether procedural fairness, or the duty of fairness, has been adhered to by a tribunal requires an assessment of the procedures and safeguards required in a particular situation. (See generally, *Knight v. Indian Head School Division No. 19*, [1990] 1 S.C.R. 653, and *Baker, supra.*)

---

207 *Syndicat national des employés de la commission scolaire régionale de l'Outaouais v. U.E.S., local 298*, [1988] 2 S.C.R. 1048 (S.C.C.).

208 As tentatively suggested in Justice LeBel's *cri de coeur* in *Toronto (City) v. C.U.P.E., Local 79*, 2003 SCC 63 (S.C.C.) at para. 134. The Administrative Justice Project in B.C. has also suggested having only two standards – correctness and *patent* unreasonableness: see Appendix 6, below.

209 [2002] 1 S.C.R. 249 (S.C.C.).

Justice Binnie also recognized this distinction in the *Retired Judges Case*:[210]

(A) Some Preliminary Observations

¶ 96   Given the range and variety of the unions' objections, it might be useful to do a little organization at the outset.

¶ 97   Although the net result of a s. 6(5) appointment is the naming of a particular individual as a chairperson, the appointment is inevitably the product of a number of issues or determinations, some of them having to do with procedural fairness (*e.g.*, do I first have to consult with the parties?), some of them legal (*e.g.*, to what extent is my choice constrained by HLDAA?), some of them factual (*e.g.*, what qualifications am I looking for?), and others of mixed fact and law (*e.g.*, is this individual "qualified" within the range of choice permitted to me by HLDAA?) *The Court's task on judicial review is not to isolate these issues and subject each of them to differing standards of review.* The unions' attack is properly aimed at the ultimate s. 6(5) appointments themselves. Nevertheless, as a practical matter (and practicality is a welcome virtue in this area of the law), it is convenient to group these issues in order to facilitate the judicial review of the s. 6(5) decision.

¶ 98   The first order of business is to examine the legislative scheme of HLDAA in general and s. 6(5) in particular. As Beetz J. pointed out, "[t]o a large extent judicial review of administrative action is a specialized branch of statutory interpretation": *U.E.S., Local 298 v. Bibeault*, [1988] 2 S.C.R. 1048, at p. 1087 (emphasis deleted), quoting S. A. de Smith, H. Street and R. Brazier, *Constitutional and Administrative Law* (4th ed. 1981), at p. 558. The Court's mandate on judicial review is to keep the statutory decision maker within the boundaries the legislature intended.

¶ 99   In performing that mandate, of course, administrative law supplies certain inferences and presumptions. For example, as this Court recently affirmed in *Ocean Port Hotel Ltd. v. British Columbia (General Manager, Liquor Control and Licensing Branch)*, [2001] 2 S.C.R. 781, 2001 SCC 52, at para. 21, "courts generally infer that Parliament or the legislature intended the tribunal's process to comport with principles of natural justice". More broadly, it is presumed that the legislature intended the statutory decision maker to function within the established principles and constraints of administrative law.

¶100   *The second order of business is to isolate the Minister's acts or omissions relevant to procedural fairness, a broad category*

---

210   *C.U.P.E. v. Ontario (Minister of Labour)*, 2003 SCC 29, 226 D.L.R. (4th) 193 (S.C.C.) at para. 103.

which extends to, and to some extent overlaps, the traditional principles of natural justice: Nicholson v. Haldimand-Norfolk Regional Board of Commissioners of Police, [1979] 1 S.C.R. 311, per Laskin C.J., at p. 325. The unions, for example, question whether the Minister was right to refuse to consult with them before making the appointments. *These questions go to the procedural framework within which the Minister made the s. 6(5) appointments, but are distinct from the s. 6(5) appointments themselves.* It is for the courts, not the Minister, to provide the legal answer to procedural fairness questions. *It is only the ultimate exercise of the Minister's discretionary s. 6(5) power of appointment itself that is subject to the "pragmatic and functional" analysis, intended to assess the degree of deference intended by the legislature to be paid by the courts to the statutory decision maker, which is what we call the "standard of review".*

¶101   The third order of business, accordingly, is to determine the degree of judicial deference which, having regard to HLDAA and all the relevant circumstances, the Minister is entitled to receive in the exercise of his discretionary s. 6(5) power. In assessing the Minister's appointments, the court may need to take into consideration some of the determinations made by the Minister as input into the exercise of his discretion. For example, if, as I believe, the Minister is entitled to make any appointment that is not patently unreasonable, his interpretation of the scope of his power of appointment under s. 6(5) will affect the reasonableness of his ultimate appointment: *Canadian Broadcasting Corp. v. Canada (Labour Relations Board)*, [1995] 1 S.C.R. 157, at para. 49.

¶102   *The content of procedural fairness goes to the manner in which the Minister went about making his decision, whereas the standard of review is applied to the end product of his deliberations.*

¶103   *On occasion, a measure of confusion may arise in attempting to keep separate these different lines of enquiry. Inevitably some of the same "factors" that are looked at in determining the requirements of procedural fairness are also looked at in considering the "standard of review" of the discretionary decision itself.* Thus in *Baker, supra,* a case involving the judicial review of a Minister's rejection of an application for permanent residence in Canada on human and compassionate grounds, the Court looked at "all the circumstances" on both accounts, but overlapping factors included the nature of the decision being made (procedural fairness, para.23; standard of review, para. 61); the statutory scheme (procedural fairness, para. 24; standard of review, para. 60); and the expertise of the decision maker (procedural fairness, para. 27; standard of review, para. 59). Other factors, of course, did not overlap. In procedural fairness, for example, the Court was concerned with "the importance of the decision to the individual or individuals affected" (para. 25), whereas determining the standard of review included such factors as the existence of a privative clause (para. 58). *The point is that, while there are some common "factors", the object of the court's inquiry in each case is different.* [Emphasis added.]

Writing for the dissenting minority, Justice Bastarache also noted a distinction between the duty of procedural fairness and the standard of review:

¶ 5 I do not share Binnie J.'s appreciation of the potential confusion in determining, as separate exercises, the content of the duty of procedural fairness and the standard of review. Both exercises examine the context of an administrative decision. The same factor may be salient for both exercises. Nevertheless, the two inquiries proceed separately and serve different objectives. The content of the duty of procedural fairness seeks to ensure the appropriate relationship between the citizen and the administrative decision maker. In contrast, the standard of review speaks to the relationship between the administrative decision maker and the judiciary. In the former case, there is no need to determine a degree of deference.

As it happened, Justice Binnie did not find a breach of procedural fairness (the "second order of business") in this particular case. If he had, the appointment would have been set aside on that ground all by itself. What standard of review – what test – would the court have applied to determine whether a breach of procedural fairness had occurred? Surely, *fairness*. While the appraisal of what is "fair" is undoubtedly contextual, it does not engage the spectrum of deference (as Justice Bastarache noted). Nor does it engage the resulting three standards of review which are applied to other aspects of the decision including issues of statutory interpretation (the "first order of business"), the exercise of discretionary powers, or the substance of the actual decision (the "third order of business"). These standards of review simply do not apply to a breach of procedural fairness.

As noted earlier, Chief Justice McLachlin observed in *Q.* that there is no longer a one-to-one relationship between a particular *ground* for judicial review and the *standard* of review applicable to that ground in all contextual circumstances. However, it would not be accurate to say that the four *Pushpanathan* factors or the three standards of "correctness", "reasonableness" or "patent unreasonableness" are applicable to breaches of natural justice and procedural fairness.[211]

---

211 However, note the following statement by Justice Binnie in his dissent in *I.B.E.W., Local 894 v. Ellis-Don Ltd.*, [2001] 1 S.C.R. 221 (S.C.C.), para. 65:

(a) The Standard for Reviewing the Adequacy of Reasons

The same question arises about the standard for reviewing the adequacy of reasons. Assuming that the statutory delegate gives reasons – either in fulfilment of an obligation to do so, or voluntarily[212] – what standard does the court apply in reviewing the adequacy of those reasons?

The courts require there to be something more than a passage in a decision which is simply called "reasons". They also require the articulated reasons to be more than a mere restatement of criteria or statutory formulae which the delegate is supposed to consider in reaching its decision: *Hannley v. Edmonton (City)*,[213] *Morin v. Alberta (Provincial Planning Board)*,[214] and *Dome Petroleum Ltd. v. Alberta (Public Utilities Board)*.[215] Although the reasons do not need to set out all of the evidence, findings of fact or submissions,[216] they must demonstrate to the court that the delegate considered all the matters required by the statute.[217] The reasons also must not demonstrate that the delegate erred by considering irrelevant matters, asking the wrong question, or committed some other error which the court can correct.

In sum, the test for determining whether the reasons given by a delegate are adequate in law is whether they show why or how or on what evidence the

---

Compliance with the rules of natural justice is a legal issue. The standard of review is correctness as noted in D.J.M. Brown and J.M. Evans, *Judicial Review of Administrative Action in Canada,* loose-leaf (Toronto: Canvasback, 2003) vol. 2, at para. 14:2300, pp. 14-14 and 14-15:

> [W]hether the administrative decision-maker has breached the rules of natural justice or the duty of procedural fairness by failing to permit any, or adequate, participation by the person concerned will usually be assessed on the basis of "correctness". And the presence of a privative clause will be of no consequence in this regard.

See also *British Columbia (Securities Commission) v. Pacific International Securities Inc.,* 2002 BCCA 421, 215 D.L.R. (4th) 58 (B.C. C.A.), where Smith J.A. states as follows (at para. 5):

> The standard of review on questions of natural justice and procedural fairness is one of correctness, but correctness must be considered in the context of the proper approach to the review of the Commission's decision.

If by "correctness" one means that the court agrees or disagrees with the decision without any deference to the decision-maker, perhaps the analysis of *Brown and Evans* makes some sense. However, the true question the court seeks to ask with respect to alleged breaches of natural justice is: was the procedure fair or not? That is the standard – the test.

212   On the obligation to give reasons and the effect of a failure to do so, see Chapter 9.
213   (1978), 7 Alta. L.R. (2d) 394 (Alta. C.A.).
214   [1974] 6 W.W.R. 291 (Alta. T.D.).
215   (1977), 2 A.R. 453 at 472 (Alta. C.A.), affirmed [1977] 2 S.C.R. 822 (S.C.C.). See also *Consumers' Assn. of Canada (Alberta) v. Alberta (Public Utilities Board)* (1985), 10 Admin. L.R. 137 (Alta. C.A.).
216   *S.E.I.U., Local 333 v. Nipawin District Staff Nurses Assn.* (1973), [1975] 1 S.C.R. 382 (S.C.C.); *Woolaston v. Canada (Minister of Manpower & Immigration)* (1972), [1973] S.C.R. 102 (S.C.C.).
217   *Morin v. Alberta (Provincial Planning Board)*, [1974] 6 W.W.R. 291 (Alta. T.D.).

delegate reached the conclusion.[218] If so, then any statutory requirement to give reasons will be satisfied.

Of course, the reasons given may disclose another fatal error – such as being unreasonable! It seems likely that the reasonableness of the reasons will be measured against a standard similar to "reasonableness *simpliciter*" described in *Southam*. But the reasonableness of reasons is different from whether the delegate has complied with its obligation to give reasons in the first place.

11. The Application of the Standard of Review Analysis to Discretionary Decisions

Conceptually, the review of a discretionary decision involves at least two separate inquiries:

- First, did the statutory delegate act within the ambit of the discretion granted to it, by considering relevant factors and not considering irrelevant factors? Answering this question involves a determination of what is or is not a relevant factor. Sometimes, the legislation explicitly indicates at least some of the factors that it intends the decision-maker to take into account in exercising the discretion. However, questions may arise about whether other non-enumerated factors can be taken into account. Ultimately, the courts must determine who the legislature intended to make the determination about whether a particular factor is or is not relevant – the courts, or the statutory delegate? Using the pragmatic and functional approach and the four factors identified in *Pushpanathan*, this analysis will identify the standard of review to be applied in reviewing statutory delegate's determination of what factors are or are not relevant to the exercise of the discretion.

- Second, assuming the statutory delegate did act within the ambit of the discretion granted to it (however that is determined), was the way the statutory delegate exercised the discretion unreasonable (or patently unreasonable, depending upon the standard of review to be applied)?[219]

Although not always sharply delineating these two separate concepts, the Supreme Court of Canada has spent considerable effort in the last few years trying to articulate the proper approach to reviewing the exercise of discretionary powers.

Following on from its seminal decision in *Baker v. Canada (Minister of Citizenship & Immigration)*[220] which provided that the pragmatic and func-

---

218   *Couillard v. Edmonton (City)* (1979), 10 Alta. L.R. (2d) 295 (Alta. C.A.).

219   Presumably, the correctness standard of review would never be applied to this second question, precisely because the power being exercised is discretionary in nature, which means that there is more than one possible right outcome.

220   [1999] 2 S.C.R. 817, 14 Admin. L.R. (3d) 173 (S.C.C.) (per L'Heureux-Dubé J., especially at paras. 51-62).

tional approach from *Pushpanathan* is to be applied to determine the standard of review for reviewing the exercise of discretionary decisions, there have been four other recent important Supreme Court of Canada decisions involving the review of discretionary decisions: *Suresh*, *Chieu*, *Moreau-Bérubé*, and the *Retired Judges Case*.

(a) Suresh v. Canada (Minister of Citizenship & Immigration)

Suresh involved four issues: (1) constitutional review of the provisions of the *Immigration Act*; (2) the Minister's decision whether Suresh's presence in Canada constituted a danger to national security; (3) the factual question whether Suresh faced a substantial risk of torture upon return to Sri Lanka; and (4) whether the procedures used by the Minister under the Act were adequate to protect Suresh's constitutional rights. Issues 2 and 3 were discretionary decisions.

In determining the standard of review applicable to these two discretionary decisions, the Court reiterated the *Baker* analysis, but made it clear that the courts' role does not include the weighing of relevant factors when reviewing the exercise of a ministerial decision:

¶29 The first question is what standard should be adopted with respect to the Minister's decision that a refugee constitutes a danger to the security of Canada. We agree with Robertson J.A. that the reviewing court should adopt a deferential approach to this question and should set aside the Minister's discretionary decision if it is patently unreasonable in the sense that it was made arbitrarily or in bad faith, it cannot be supported on the evidence, or the Minister failed to consider the appropriate factors. *The court should not reweigh the factors or interfere merely because it would have come to a different conclusion.*

¶30 This conclusion is mandated by *Pushpanathan v. Canada (Minister of Citizenship and Immigration)*, [1998] 1 S.C.R. 982, which reviewed the principles for determining the standard of review according to the functional and pragmatic approach. In *Pushpanathan*, the Court emphasized that the ultimate question is always what the legislature intended. One looks to the language of the statute as well as a number of factors to determine that intention. *Here the language of the Act (the Minister must be "of the opinion" that the person constitutes a danger to the security of Canada) suggests a standard of deference. So, on the whole, do the factors to be considered: (1) the presence or absence of a clause negating the right of appeal; (2) the relative expertise of the decision-maker; (3) the purpose of the provision and the legislation generally; and (4) the nature of the question. (Pushpanathan, supra, at paras. 29-38).*

¶31 The first factor suggests that Parliament intended only a limited right of appeal. Although the Minister's s. 53(1)(b) opinion is not protected by a privative clause, it may only be appealed by leave of the Federal Court - Trial Division (s. 82.1(1)), and that leave decision may not itself be appealed (s. 82.2). The second factor, the relative expertise of the decision-maker, again favours deference. As stated in *Baker v. Canada (Minister of Citizenship and Immigration)*, [1999] 2 S.C.R. 817, "[t]he fact that the formal decision-maker is the Minister is a factor militating in favour of deference" (para. 59). The Minister, as noted by Lord Hoffmann in *Secretary of State for the Home Department v. Rehman*, [2001] 3 W.L.R. 877, at para. 62, "has access to special information and expertise in . . . matters [of national security]". The third factor - the purpose of the legislation - again favours deference. This purpose, as discussed in *Pushpanathan, supra*, at para. 73, is to permit a "humanitarian balance" of various interests — "the seriousness of the danger posed to Canadian society" on the one hand, and "the danger of persecution upon refoulement" on the other. Again, the Minister is in a superior position to a court in making this assessment. Finally, the nature of the case points to deference. The inquiry is highly fact-based and contextual. As in *Baker, supra*, at para. 61, the s. 53(1)(b) danger opinion "involves a considerable appreciation of the facts of that person's case, and is not one which involves the application or interpretation of definitive legal rules", suggesting it merits a wide degree of deference.

¶32 *These factors suggest that Parliament intended to grant the Minister a broad discretion in issuing a s. 53(1)(b) opinion, reviewable only where the Minister makes a patently unreasonable decision.* It is true that the question of whether a refugee constitutes a danger to the security of Canada relates to human rights and engages fundamental human interests. However, it is our view that a deferential standard of ministerial review will not prevent human rights issues from being fully addressed, provided proper procedural safeguards are in place and provided that any decision to deport meets the constitutional requirements of the *Charter*.

¶33 The House of Lords has taken the same view in *Rehman, supra*. Lord Hoffmann, following the events of September 11, 2001, added the following postscript to his speech (at para. 62):

I wrote this speech some three months before the recent events in New York and Washington. They are a reminder that in matters of national security, the cost of failure can be high. *This seems to me to underline the need for the judicial arm of government to respect the decisions of ministers of the Crown on the question of whether support for terrorist activities in a foreign country constitutes a threat to national security.* It is not only that the executive has access to special information and expertise in these matters. It is also that such decisions, with serious potential results for the community, require a legitimacy which can be conferred only by entrusting them to persons responsible to the community through the democratic process. If the people are to accept the consequences of such decisions, they must be made by persons whom the people have elected and whom they can remove. [Emphasis added.]

¶34   *It follows that the weighing of relevant factors is not the function of a court reviewing the exercise of ministerial discretion* (see, for instance, *Pezim v. British Columbia (Superintendent of Brokers)*, [1994] 2 S.C.R. 557, at p. 607, where Iacobucci J. explained that a reviewing court should not disturb a decision based on a "broad discretion" unless the tribunal has "made some error in principle in exercising its discretion or has exercised its discretion in a capricious or vexatious manner").

¶35   *The Court's recent decision in Baker, supra*, did not depart from this view. Rather, it confirmed that the pragmatic and functional approach should be applied to all types of administrative decisions in recognition of the fact that a uniform approach to the determination of the proper standard of review is preferable, and that there may be special situations where even traditionally discretionary decisions will best be reviewed according to a standard other than the deferential standard which was universally applied in the past to ministerial decisions (see *Dagg v. Canada (Minister of Finance)*, [1997] 2 S.C.R. 403).

¶36   *The Court specified in Baker, supra*, that a nuanced approach to determining the appropriate standard of review was necessary given the difficulty in rigidly classifying discretionary and non-discretionary decisions (paras. 54 and 55). The Court also made it clear in *Baker* that its approach "should not be seen as reducing the level of deference given to decisions of a highly discretionary nature" (para. 56) and, moreover, that any ministerial obligation to consider certain factors "gives the applicant no right to a particular outcome or to the application of a particular legal test" (para. 74). To the extent this Court reviewed the Minister's discretion in that case, its decision was based on the ministerial delegate's failure to comply with *self-imposed* ministerial guidelines, as reflected in the objectives of the Act, international treaty obligations and, most importantly, a set of published instructions to immigration officers.

¶37   *The passages in Baker* referring to the "weight" of particular factors (see paras. 68 and 73-75) *must be read in this context*. It is the Minister who was obliged to give proper weight to the relevant factors and none other. *Baker* does not authorize courts reviewing decisions on the discretionary end of the spectrum to engage in a new weighing process, but draws on an established line of cases concerning the failure of ministerial delegates to consider and weigh implied limitations and/or patently relevant factors: see *Anisminic Ltd. v. Foreign Compensation Commission*, [1969] 2 A.C. 147 (H.L.); *Sheehan v. Ontario (Criminal Injuries Compensation Board)* (1974), 52 D.L.R. (3d) 728 (Ont. C.A.); *Maple Lodge Farms Ltd. v. Canada*, [1982] 2 S.C.R. 2; *Dagg*, *supra*, at paras. 111-12, per La Forest J. (dissenting on other grounds).

¶38   This standard appropriately reflects the different obligations of Parliament, the Minister and the reviewing court. Parliament's task is to establish the criteria and procedures governing deportation, within the limits of the Constitution. The Minister's task is to make a decision that conforms to Parliament's criteria and procedures as well as the Constitution. *The court's task, if called upon to review the Minister's decision, is to determine whether the Minister has exercised her decision-making power within the constraints imposed by Parliament's legislation and the Constitution. If the Minister has considered the appropriate factors in conformity with these constraints, the court must uphold her decision. It cannot set it aside even if it would have weighed the factors differently and arrived at a different conclusion.*

¶39   This brings us to the question of the standard of review of the Minister's decision on whether the refugee faces a substantial risk of torture upon deportation. This question is characterized as constitutional by Robertson J.A., to the extent that the Minister's decision to deport to torture must ultimately conform to s. 7 of the *Charter*: see *Kindler v. Canada (Minister of Justice)*, [1991] 2 S.C.R. 779, per La Forest J.; and *United States v. Burns*, [2001] 1 S.C.R. 283, 2001 SCC 7, at para. 32. As mentioned earlier, whether there is a substantial risk of torture if Suresh is deported is a threshold question. The threshold question here is in large part a fact-driven inquiry. It requires consideration of the human rights record of the home state, the personal risk faced by the claimant, any assurances that the claimant will not be tortured and their worth and, in that respect, the ability of the home state to control its own security forces, and more. It may also involve a reassessment of the refugee's initial claim and a determination of whether a third country is willing to accept the refugee. Such issues are largely outside the realm of expertise of reviewing courts and possess a negligible legal dimension. We are accordingly of the view that the threshold finding of whether Suresh faces a substantial risk of torture, as an aspect of the larger s. 53(1)(b) opinion, attracts deference by the reviewing court to the Minister's decision. *The court may not reweigh the factors considered by the Minister, but may intervene if the decision is*

> *not supported by the evidence or fails to consider the appropriate factors.* It must be recognized that the nature of the evidence required may be limited by the nature of the inquiry. This is consistent with the reasoning of this Court in *Kindler, supra,* at pp. 836-37, where considerable deference was shown to ministerial decisions involving similar considerations in the context of a constitutional revision, that is in the context of a decision where the s. 7 interest was engaged. [Emphasis added.]

The reader might wonder whether this discussion about *Baker* provides a convincing explanation of why reasonableness *simpliciter* was the applicable standard of review in that case, or why the Court determined that the Minister's delegate's decision in that case was unreasonable. Or is the Court – without undercutting the rhetoric of *Baker* – actually indicating that the outcome in *Baker* is an anomaly, and that the most frequent result of applying the *Pushpanathan* analysis when reviewing the merits of most discretionary decisions will be the application of the patently unreasonable standard?

In what circumstances might the application of the *Pushpanathan* analysis result in the unreasonableness *simpliciter* standard applying to the review of the exercise of a discretionary decision? One possibility might be where there is an appeal to the court from the exercise of a statutory discretion. By definition, there would be no operative privative clause where there is such an appeal, and the court might well conclude that the intention of the legislature was for the court to exercise its own discretion in determining the matter. This would be reinforced more or less depending upon the presence, or absence, and nature of any expertise of the original decision-maker with respect to the discretionary matter being decided.

Of course, to the extent that unreasonableness *simpliciter* is determined to be the applicable standard, one must then appreciate the distinction between something which is "unreasonable" and something which is "patently unreasonable", which Iacobucci J. described in *Southam* as follows:[221]

> An unreasonable decision is one that, in the main, is not supported by any reasons that can stand up to a somewhat probing examination. Accordingly, a court reviewing a conclusion on the reasonableness standard must look to see whether any reasons support it. The defect, if there is one, could presumably be in the evidentiary foundation itself or in the logical process by which conclusions are sought to be drawn from it.

(b) Chieu v. Canada (Minister of Citizenship & Immigration)[222]

In *Chieu,* the sole issue was whether the words "having regard to all the circumstances of the case" in section 70(1)(b) of the *Immigration Act* allows

---

221 *Canada (Director of Investigation & Research) v. Southam Inc.,* [1997] 1 S.C.R. 748 (S.C.C.) at para. 56.
222 [2002] 1 S.C.R. 84, 37 Admin. L.R. (3d) 252 (S.C.C.).

the I.A.D. to consider potential foreign hardship when reviewing a removal order made against a permanent resident. The lower courts had answered this question in the negative, dismissing Chieu's application for judicial review of the adjudicator's decision ordering his removal from Canada. The Supreme Court answered this question affirmatively and allowed Chieu's appeal.

In reaching this decision, the Supreme Court first addressed the applicable standard of review – something which the lower courts had not done explicitly.[223]

An interesting aspect of Iacobucci J.'s going through the "pragmatic and functional" approach from *Pushpanathan* is the following comment on the effect of the requirement in the *Immigration Act* which makes an appeal to the Federal Court of Appeal conditional on the Trial Division's certifying that "a serious question of general importance is involved":

> ¶23 The resolution of a certified question will generally be of considerable precedential value. The legislative scheme recognizes this fact by providing that questions of general importance, *i.e.* those that will be applicable to numerous future cases, may be reviewed by the F.C.A. and, with leave, by this Court. The Act thus evinces a particular concern that questions of general importance be appropriately resolved. For this reason, Bastarache J. concluded in *Pushpanathan, supra*, that "s. 83(1) would be incoherent if the standard of review were anything other than correctness" (para. 43). However, in *Baker, supra*, a decision by the Minister under s. 114(2) of the Act was reviewed by L'Heureux-Dubé J. on the intermediate standard of reasonableness *simpliciter*, even though a question had been certified in that case. *In my opinion, the presence of s. 83(1) is not determinative of the standard of review on its own. As this Court stated in Southam, supra, at paras. 36-37, the precedential value of a case is only one factor relevant to the determination of the appropriate standard of review. While the review of an issue of "general importance" weighs in favour of a correctness standard, other factors relevant to the pragmatic and functional approach must still be considered.* Indeed, both Bastarache J. in *Pushpanathan* and L'Heureux-Dubé J. in *Baker* went on to examine a number of additional factors. [Emphasis added.]

Iacobucci J. then went on to consider the following factors, in the course of concluding that correctness was indeed the appropriate standard of review in this case:

> ¶24 *In this case, the relevant additional factors also favour the correctness standard.* The I.A.D. enjoys no relative expertise in the

---

223   Although, as the Supreme Court recognized, the lower courts must implicitly have used the correctness standard – even though the result of their application of that standard differed from the Supreme Court's application of the same standard.

matter of law which is the object of the judicial review. While in *Pushpanathan* the matter under review was a human rights issue, an area of law in which deference is usually not given, the issue here is one of jurisdiction, a similar area where little deference is shown. Administrative bodies generally must be correct in determining the scope of their delegated mandate, given that they are entirely the creatures of statute. *As Bastarache J. stated in Pushpanathan*, at para. 28, "it is still appropriate and helpful to speak of 'jurisdictional questions' which must be answered correctly by the tribunal in order to be acting *intra vires*". While the I.A.D. has considerable expertise in determining the weight to be given to the factors it considers when exercising the discretionary jurisdiction conferred by s. 70(1)(b) of the Act, the scope of this discretionary jurisdiction itself is a legal issue ultimately to be supervised by the courts. The legal nature of the issue is particularly evident in cases like the one before us, where the Minister is arguing that the I.A.D. has usurped her jurisdiction. The factor of expertise weighed in the opposite direction in *Baker*, because the Minister "has some expertise relative to courts in immigration matters, particularly with respect to when exemptions should be given from the requirements that normally apply" (para. 59). The issue under review in *Baker* did not involve a jurisdictional issue like the one presently before this Court, and therefore a more deferential standard of review was appropriate.

¶25 In addition, Parliament has not enacted a strong privative clause for decisions of the I.A.D. (s. 69.4(2)). As Bastarache J. stated in *Pushpanathan* (at para. 49), in relation to the similarly worded privative clause for the C.R.D.D. (s. 67(1)), "read in the light of s. 83(1), it appears quite clear that the privative clause, such as it is, is superseded with respect to questions of 'general importance'". In my opinion, this is also the case for the privative clause contained in s. 69.4(2).

¶26 Finally, appeals under s. 70(1)(b) do not engage the I.A.D. in a polycentric balancing of competing interests, but instead require the resolution of an issue in which an individual's rights are at stake. The I.A.D. is not involved in a managing or supervisory function, but is adjudicating the rights of individuals *vis-à-vis* the state. This factor also weighs in favour of a less deferential standard of review. For all of these reasons, I conclude that a correctness standard should be applied in reviewing the decision of the I.A.D. in this case. However, it may well be that a more deferential standard would apply to decisions of the I.A.D. in other contexts, particularly if the issue under review were to fall squarely within the specialized expertise of the board. [Emphasis added.]

(c) Moreau-Bérubé c. Nouveau-Brunswick[224]

The second of the three issues in *Moreau-Bérubé v. New Brunswick* was whether the ultimate decision of the Judicial Council to recommend the removal of the judge from office was justifiable. Arbour J. described this question as "one of mixed law and fact", which required the court to "pass judgment on the Council's ability to assess, weigh, and apply the evidence to a particular legal threshold while discharging its core function". Without much analysis with respect to the standard applicable to this particular issue,[225] she agreed with the standard imposed by Drapeau J.A. (who alone expressed a position on the applicable standard of review) that determinations of this sort should not be interfered with unless they are patently unreasonable.[226]

Applying this standard, she found nothing patently unreasonable in the Council's decision to draw its own conclusions with regard to whether the judge's comments created an apprehension of bias sufficient to justify a recommendation for her removal as a provincial court judge. Indeed, Arbour J. went on to state that she would have reached the same conclusion even if she had applied the reasonableness *simpliciter* standard of review to this issue.

(d) The Retired Judges Case[227]

The *Retired Judges Case* involved the courts' review of the way the Minister of Labour exercised his discretion to appoint the chair of various interest arbitration boards. While the majority of the Supreme Court of Canada held that the way the Minister exercised his discretion was patently unreasonable, the minority sharply criticized this result (even though they agreed on the same standard of review).

Writing for the majority, Justice Binnie held that the appointment of retired judges had the effect of frustrating "the very legislative scheme under which the power is conferred".[228] While the court was not entitled to re-weigh the factors considered by the Minister, it was entitled to review the factors which the Minister took into account or ignored. Although not every relevant factor excluded by the Minister from consideration would necessarily be fatal under the patent unreasonableness standard of review,[229] it was patently unreasonable

---

224 [2002] 1 S.C.R. 249, 36 Admin. L.R. (3d) 1 (S.C.C.).
225 There is considerable discussion about how the *Pushpanathan* analysis applies to the first issue.
226 (2000), 194 D.L.R. (4th) 664 (S.C.C.), leave to appeal allowed (2001), 273 N.R. 200 (note) (S.C.C.), reversed [2002] 1 S.C.R. 249 (S.C.C.) at para. 69. This differed from the reasonableness *simpliciter* standard of review applicable to the first issue, which involved the interpretation given by the Council to section 6.11(4) of the enabling statute, relating to the scope of its mandate. Arbour J. held that the lower courts should not have substituted their interpretation of that provision for the one adopted by the Council (para. 67).
227 *C.U.P.E. v. Ontario (Minister of Labour)*, 2003 SCC 29, 226 D.L.R. (4th) 193 (S.C.C.).
228 *Ibid.* at para. 174.
229 *Ibid.* at para. 176. Under what circumstances would the court permit a discretionary decision-maker to ignore a relevant factor? Only if (a) the appropriate standard of review is patent unreasonableness, and (b) the failure to take the factor into account is not immediate and obvious?

for the Minister to exclude altogether any consideration of the need for the appointed arbitrators to have labour relations expertise and general accepta-bility by the labour relations community.[230] The decision to appoint inexpert, inexperienced and not generally acceptable chairs is a defect which is both immediate and obvious[231] – the test for whether a decision is patently unrea-sonable.

Although the majority's result is tantalizing, in many ways the dissenting judgment (written by Justice Bastarache for himself, Chief Justice McLachlin and Justice Major) is more interesting from an analytical point of view. Justice Bastarache starts with the following discussion of how the courts should go about determining whether a particular factor is or is not relevant to the exercise of a discretion:

¶ 27 Binnie J. concludes that the appointments were patently unrea-sonable because the Minister's approach excluded relevant cri-teria (labour relations experience and broad acceptability) and substituted another criterion (prior judicial experience).

¶ 28 *This assessment requires that we determine the relevant criteria for exercise of the discretion, or at least whether the Minister relied upon irrelevant criteria or failed to consider a relevant and important criterion.* I agree with Binnie J. that a contextual approach to statutory interpretation of the enabling legislation is necessary for determining the relevant criteria. We disagree, however, as to what the essential criteria ultimately turn out to be. We [also] disagree as to which factor or factors must be given primary importance for an appointment to survive review as not "clearly irrational" or patently unreasonable.

¶ 29 *In the clearest of cases, the criteria constraining the exercise of a discretion will be spelled out in the legislation itself. In other cases, the relevant factors to consider will be specified in reg-ulations or guidelines.* For example, in *Baker, supra*, this Court quashed the immigration officer's decision. In making the de-cision, the officer had failed to consider a factor expressly in-cluded in the relevant guidelines issued by the Minister of Cit-izenship and Immigration. Other indications of the important considerations were found in the specific purposes of the rele-vant Act and in international instruments (*Baker, supra*, at para. 67). In that appeal, the appropriate standard of review was the less deferential standard of reasonableness *simpliciter*. In other words, *Baker* says nothing one way or the other as to whether the failure to weigh heavily the interests of the children – a factor explicitly stated in the relevant documents – would have vitiated the decision as patently unreasonable. *In yet an-*

---

230 *Ibid.* at para. 176.
231 *Ibid.* at para. 184.

other category of cases, the relevant factors may be unwritten, derived from the purpose and context of the statute. For example, in *Roncarelli, supra,* this Court reasonably inferred that denying or revoking a liquor permit for reasons irrelevant to the sale of liquor in a restaurant lay beyond the scope of the discretion conferred upon the Commission by the *Alcoholic Liquor Act. Note, however, that it was an irrelevant factor that was inferred in Roncarelli.* A statute cannot reasonably spell out and exclude in advance every irrelevant, bad faith or abusive consideration. It is much simpler for a legislator to spell out the relevant factors, and we often expect it to have done so. I would caution, then, against reviewing courts too easily concluding that implied factors are relevant and that failure, first to perceive them at all, and second to consider them, vitiates a decision. What, then, are the relevant factors in this case?

¶ 30   In this case, the statute does not say very much. It stipulates that appointees must be "qualified to act". It also states, significantly, that it is "in the opinion of the Minister" that such persons must be qualified to act. In other words, the statute expressly contemplates that the Minister's opinion is important. I have already noted these words in determining the appropriate degree of deference. There are no relevant regulations, guidelines, or other instruments. Are there other relevant factors? In other words, can the reviewing court infer other factors relevant to the Minister in appointing a chairperson under s. 6(5) from the legislative context? [Emphasis added.]

Justice Bastarache concluded that the Court should *not* infer that the Legislature intended the Minister to take into account, in exercising his entirely subjective power of appointment, a need for the chair to have labour relations expertise and broad acceptability in the labour relations community, for three reasons:

(1) This factor was not stipulated in the Act, the regulations or any guidelines.[232] The fact that various Ministers had referred to this factor, or that this factor may have appeared essential in other circumstances, did not constitute a basis for implying that it was a dominant fact, or treating it as though it had been specifically referred to in legislation, regulations or guidelines.

(2) The relevance of this factor was not obvious (unlike in *Roncarelli* where it was obvious that the discretion to renew a liquor licence must not be wielded to punish a person who posted bail for fellow members of a religious minority). Given that the standard of review was patent

---

232 *Ibid.* at para. 31.

unreasonableness, it required the relevance of this factor to be immediately identifiable or obvious:

¶ 32   I have already noted that a patently unreasonable decision is one marked by the immediacy or obviousness of the defect. *Where the alleged defect is failure to consider relevant factors, I think it important that those factors must themselves be immediately identifiable or obvious.* In accordance with their duty, counsel for the respondents have assiduously compiled a record that presents the need for labour relations expertise and broad acceptability in its best light. They have collected excerpts from various reports, the legislative history of the HLDAA, and statements by Ministers of Labour. The fact that these materials are neatly compiled in the respondents' record makes the significance of those criteria obvious, or at least much more obvious, than it has ever been. *I do not dispute that the respondents made a good case for the importance of reading those factors into the statute, but doing so was a difficult task. In my view, the general affirmations and aspirations Binnie J. refers to in para. 110 came nowhere near the evidentiary threshold for imposing a specific restriction on the wide discretion set out in s. 6(5).* Would the factors Binnie J. relies upon have been obvious to a new Minister of Labour called on to exercise his discretion under s. 6(5)? Could the Minister have been expected to compile a thorough history of the HLDAA before acting? I do not believe so. [Emphasis added.]

Note that Justice Bastarache at this stage is focusing on whether a particular *additional* factor, not specified in the statute, is to be inferred as being relevant to the exercise of the discretion in question. This issue is conceptually anterior to the later question about whether the Minister's actual exercise of the discretion was patently unreasonable. If one concludes that it is not patently unreasonable not to take into account this additional factor, then that would be the end of the matter; there would be no need to go on to make a determination about whether the actual exercise of the discretion is also patently unreasonable.

Could there be an argument that the correctness standard should have applied to the question about whether the additional factor was or was not relevant? Or is the application of the correctness standard excluded in this particular case – but perhaps not in other cases – because this particular statute grants the discretion in such subjective terms ("in the opinion of the Minister", without specifying factors to be taken into account)?

In passing, note Justice Bastarache's reference to "the evidentiary threshold for imposing a specific restriction on the wide discretion set out in s. 6(5)". What sort of evidence would this be? How would it be gathered? How would it be placed in front of the court? What evidence has been in front of other courts in other cases where they have decided to infer additional factors relevant to the exercise of a discretion (or held that particular factors were *not* relevant: *Roncarelli*)?

(3) The majority underestimated the very subjective nature of the discretion which the Legislature granted to the Minister:

> ¶ 35 The Minister in the present appeal developed an opinion as to who was qualified to act. He determined that judging experience was relevant. He valued professional experience as an impartial decision maker. He recognized that judges are typically generalists who quickly learn the necessary substance within the context of each case. The Minister clearly gave experience in the health field less weight than some would have preferred; this is because he was dealing with parties unable to agree on a mutually acceptable qualified person and thought experience as an impartial decision maker was more crucial. All we can presume is that, all things considered, he found independence and experience at judicially resolving disputes to be more important. *The HLDAA* called for the Minister to reach his own opinion, not to consider a specific determining factor. In my view, Binnie J. has effectively read out of the provision one of its most important elements, that it is in the Minister's opinion, not viewed objectively by some constant standard, that persons are to be qualified. This is not to say that the opinion of the Minister is totally unfettered, as I will explain later in these reasons. [Emphasis added.]

(Justice Bastarache subsequently explained[233] that the list of prohibited appointees contained in section 6(12)[234] was not an exhaustive listing of all possible disqualifying factors, or all possible factors that would render an appointment patently unreasonable. In addition, the Minister's discretion to appoint is not unfettered and must be exercised within the scope of the Act, so the Minister would not be authorized to decide to appoint only members of his own political caucus, hospital CEOs, or union business agents.)

Apart from the difficulty in determining whether labour relations expertise and broad acceptability was to be implied as a relevant factor, Justice Bastarache was also not prepared to accept that it was patently unreasonable for the Minister to weigh that factor less heavily than the other, also-unwritten factor of judicial experience.[235] The Minister's weighting was not patently unreasonable, because "it takes some significant searching or testing to find the defect". It is difficult to argue that the appointment of retired judges was "evidently not

---

233 *Ibid.* at paras. 38 to 40.
234 Those who had a pecuniary interest in the matters before the board, or who had acted as counsel for one of the parties within the previous six months.
235 *Supra* note 227 at paras. 36, 37.

in accordance with reason", or "clearly irrational", or "so flawed that no amount of curial deference" could justify letting them stand. All of these verbal formulations of the content of the standard of review point to the conclusion that the appointments were not patently unreasonable.

(e) Summary on the Review of the Exercise of Discretionary Powers

In summary, the recent cases indicate that the Court is still working out the consequences of its decision in *Baker* that the pragmatic, functional and contextual approach from *Pushpanathan* is to be applied to the review of the exercise of discretionary powers. This requires the courts to engage in the complex and evolving standards-of-review analysis in order to determine which of the three recognized standards of review is to be applied when reviewing a particular discretionary decision. In addition, it will be necessary to identify whether the issue in question involves delimiting the boundaries of the discretion (determining what factors are relevant or irrelevant), or involves a determination about the reasonableness or patent unreasonableness of the decision itself (assuming it is within those boundaries), or both. Different standards of review might be applicable to each of these questions depending upon the nature and structure of the particular discretionary power. Even with respect to the same issue, different judges might identify different standards of review; and, even where they identify the same standard of review, may reach different conclusions about whether that standard has been complied with or not.

12. Does the Standards of Review Analysis Apply to Consensual Tribunals?

Most of administrative law deals with *statutory* bodies, but many of the principles also apply to domestic or consensual tribunals which derive their jurisdiction from a contract between the parties, rather than from a statute. In principle, the standards-of-review analysis should apply to consensual tribunals, even though different remedies might be available.

The reader is referred to previous editions of this work for a consideration of the applicability of the standards of review analysis to consensual tribunals.[236]

13. Summary on Standards of Review

As can be seen from this chapter, the development of the standards of review analysis has been long and tortuous. However, it is now clear that the standard of review must be identified for each issue in each case. Because of the doctrine of Parliamentary sovereignty, if the legislature states its intention clearly and explicitly, whatever standard it specifies must be used by the court

---

236 See section 7 of Chapter 12 of the Third Edition, starting at 508.

when reviewing the actions of a statutory delegate.[237] However, because the legislature often does not clearly specify the standard of review to be used for the particular issue in question, it becomes necessary for the courts to use the four *Pushpanathan* factors to perform a pragmatic and functional analysis. In these circumstances, the point – the polar star – of that contextual analysis is to determine the intention of the legislature about how intensely the courts are to review what a statutory delegate has done. It remains to be seen whether the courts will take up Justice LeBel's recent *cri de coeur* in *Toronto (City) v. C.U.P.E., Local 79*[238] about whether the current standards of review analysis needs more work.

14. Selected Bibliography

B.C. Administrative Justice Office, Ministry of Attorney General, Position Paper on "Model Statutory Powers Provisions for Administrative Tribunals", Victoria, August 2003, and previous background papers which can be found at www.gov.bc.ca/ajp/rpts.

Blais, M.et al., *Standards of Review of Federal Administrative Tribunals* (Toronto: Butterworths, 2003).

Brown D.J.M. & Evans, J.M. (The Hon.), *Judicial Review of Administrative Action in Canada*, looseleaf (Toronto: Canvasback, 2003).

Craig. P.P., *Administrative Law*, 5th ed. (London: Sweet & Maxwell, 2003).

Hogg, P.W., *Constitutional Law of Canada*, 3d ed., looseleaf (Toronto: Carswell, 1992), Part 7.3(f)

Iacobucci, F. (The Hon.), "Articulating a Rational Standard of Review Doctrine: A Tribute to John Willis" (2002) Queen's L.J. 809.

Jones, D.P., "The Concept of a Spectrum of Standards of Review: Is There a Different Standard of Review for Appeals?" (1997) 6 R.A.L. 169.

Jones, D.P., "What's the 'matter'? What's the standard of review?" (1995) 4 R.A.L. 74.

Jones, D.P., "Notes on *Dr. Q.* and *Ryan*: Two More Decisions by the Supreme Court of Canada on the Standard of Review in Administrative Law" presented to the Canadian Institute for the Administration of Justice Western Roundtable, April 25, 2003, Edmonton, Alberta.

Jones, D.P., "Recent Developments in Administrative Law"presented to the Canadian Bar Association National Labour/Administrative Law CLE Conference: Pushing the Boundaries: Standing Privacy and Practical Issues, November 21 and 22, 2003, Ottawa, Ontario.

Kerans R.P. (The Hon.), *Standards of Review Employed by Appellate Courts* (Edmonton: Juriliber, 1994).

Mullan D.J., "*Bradco*: Refined Reiterations of the Rubric Of Review" (1993) 12 Admin. L.R. (2d) 219.

Mullan, D.J., *Administrative Law* (Toronto: Irwin Law, 2001).

---

237 Subject, however, to the restriction that the legislature almost certainly could not specify a different standard than correctness for constitutional questions.

238 2003 SCC 63 (S.C.C.).

Wade H.W.R. & Forsyth C.F., *Administrative Law*, 7th ed. (Oxford: Clarendon Press, 1994), and 8th ed. (Oxford: Clarendon Press, 2000).

IV
REMEDIES

13

Introduction To Remedies[1]

Because of the common law view that there is generally "no right without a remedy", it is not sufficient to be familiar just with the grounds for seeking judicial review of administrative action: a determination must be made as to whether there is a remedy available to correct the illegal administrative action in question.

There are three broad classes of remedies which might be available in a particular circumstance.

1. Appeals

First, the legislature may have provided a specific method of appealing the action or decision taken by its delegate in first instance. In general, the right of appeal does not derive from the common law, but must be expressly provided for by statute. As a result, the legislation in question will determine to whom the appeal lies, the procedure that must be followed and the scope of the appeal. The existence of an appeal – to whatever body – frequently inclines the superior courts to exercise their discretion to refuse one of the other possible remedies for illegal administrative action. Chapter 14 discusses appeals.

---

1 This chapter has been updated by Glenn Tait, of McLennan Ross, Barristers and Solicitors, Yellowknife.

2. Prerogative Remedies

Secondly, one of the "prerogative" remedies may be available from one of the superior courts to correct an administrative illegality. This family of remedies includes *certiorari* (which permits the court to determine whether a statutory delegate's decision has been made within its jurisdiction), prohibition (which prevents the delegate from making a decision which will take it outside its jurisdiction), *mandamus* (which compels a delegate to fulfil its statutory duties), *quo warranto* (which requires a person to justify the authority by which he or she occupies an office), and – probably most famous of them all–*habeas corpus* (which requires the production of a person into the face of the court to explain why the person is being detained). These remedies are called "prerogative" because the Crown is nominally the applicant. This is indicated by the style of the cause of action as follows: "*R. v. Delegate; Ex parte Affected Person*". The prerogative remedies are discretionary in nature, and can be refused by the courts in certain circumstances. These circumstances include cases where the applicant has slept on his or her rights or does not come to court with clean hands, where there is an equally effective appeal provided by statute, where the applicant does not have a sufficient interest or standing to challenge the administrative act in question, and perhaps where the delegate's interpretation of the law is not "patently unreasonable". The prerogative remedies are discussed in Chapter 15.

3. Private law Remedies

Thirdly, some remedies from private law may be available in the public law context. Thus, certain illegal administrative actions may give rise to an actionable wrong for which the ordinary private law provides an adequate remedy. For example, a delegate acting outside its jurisdiction may well commit a tort – as occurred in *Cooper v. Wandsworth Board of Works*[2] when a partially built house was torn down pursuant to statutory authority without complying with the principles of natural justice. In principle, administrators may be liable for any form of tort or breach of contract unless their actions are justified by specific statutory authority. Similarly, an injunction may be available in certain circumstances to prevent some types of anticipated illegal administrative actions. Further, a declaration or a declaratory order may be available to proclaim the illegality of certain forms of administrative action. Nevertheless, not all illegal administrative actions necessarily give rise to an actionable wrong known to the common law; and illegal administrative action does not *per se* constitute a tort. Therefore, the common law maxim that there is "no right without a remedy" is still very important in attempting to apply the ordinary civil law to some forms of illegal administrative action. On the other hand, some private law remedies, such as a damage action, are not discretionary in nature, and therefore may be available to obtain a remedy in

---

2   (1863), 14 C.B.N.S. 180 (Eng. C.P.).

circumstances when the courts would otherwise be inclined to exercise their discretion to refuse a prerogative remedy. Some of the applications of private law remedies to the public law context are discussed in Chapter 16.

4. Ontario Procedural Reforms

Over the years, there have been a number of reforms to the procedure for obtaining judicial review of illegal administrative actions. In particular, the 1971 Ontario *Judicial Review Procedure Act*[3] merged most of the prerogative and private law remedies into one "application for judicial review" – reminiscent of the abolition in the late 1800's of the forms of action in tort. Such a reform minimizes the importance of choosing the correct remedy to rectify a particular type of administrative wrong, and permits the court to determine whether there are any grounds for judicial review without regard to the confines of one of the nominate remedies. This type of procedural reform has been widely copied in varying forms throughout much of the common law world.

5. Alberta Procedural Reforms

To accomplish many of the same reform ideals, the Alberta *Rules of Court* were amended in 1987 to deal with remedies available in administrative law matters. The rules in Part 56.1 create a remedy called an "Application for Judicial Review" which encompasses the prerogative remedies of *mandamus*, prohibition, *certiorari*, *quo warranto* and *habeas corpus*, as well as private law remedies of declarations and injunctions.[4] The revised procedure makes judicial review simpler but does not reform or alter the grounds upon which judicial review may be granted. It is not necessary to specify the nature of the application or the remedy desired, although it is possible and probably desirable to do so. The Court has jurisdiction to award any of the remedies, whether specified or not, providing the grounds for establishing that remedy has been established.

6. Federal Procedural Reforms

In the early 1970s, the Federal Parliament took a different approach to reforming the procedure for obtaining judicial review of federal administrative action. The *Federal Court Act* (now the *Federal Courts Act*)[5] transferred review of the legality of federal administrative acts from the provincial superior courts to the Trial Division of the Federal Court (with the exception of *habeas corpus*, which remained with the provincial superior courts). The legislation then

---

3 Originally S.O. 1971, c. 48, now R.S.O. 1990, c. J.1, reproduced in Appendix 3.
4 Reproduced in Appendix 4.
5 Originally R.S.C. 1970, c. 10 (2nd Supp.); now R.S.C. 1985, c. F-7, as (*inter alia*) amended by S.C. 1990, c. 8 (in effect from 1 February 1992), and by S.C. 2002, c. 8, s. 14 (effective July 2, 2003).

creates a generalized "application for judicial review" instead of the old nominate prerogative remedies. The application for judicial review is available from the Federal Court of Appeal. Unfortunately, the application for judicial review was originally only available with respect to activities which were "judicial or quasi-judicial in nature" (which was not defined in the Act). This perpetuated an untenable characterization of the nature of delegated functions, and also created an important procedural dilemma about which division of the Federal Court had jurisdiction to hear a particular case involving an alleged illegality by a federal administrator. The *Federal Courts Act* was amended to cure these defects.

7. Substantive Reforms

Other reforms have included legislative expansions of the grounds for judicial review (see, for example, the grounds set out in section 27 of the *Federal Courts Act*), the creation of ombudsmen to deal with complaints about maladministration even where there is no illegality involved, the creation in some jurisdictions of a "council on tribunals"[6] to comment upon the types of powers which should be delegated to administrators and to supervise the rules and procedures which they adopt for exercising those delegated powers.

8. Privative Clauses

Sometimes legislation contains a "privative clause" which purports to prevent judicial review of administrative action. Various forms of privative clauses exist, ranging from simple time limits within which applications for judicial review must be brought to more comprehensive attempts to prevent any direct or collateral attempt to challenge the legality or the merits of a delegate's action in any court proceeding whatever. For many years, the courts have resisted giving literal effect to most of these clauses by asserting that an *ultra vires* administrative action is a nullity which does not exist in the eyes of the law, and which therefore cannot attract the protection of a privative clause. To a certain extent, this approach flies in the face of clear parliamentary intent to prevent judicial review of a particular administrator's actions, but the courts' persistence in asserting the principle of legality is now so engrained (and probably so desirable) that the only real questions today revolve around the types of errors that prevent a delegate from acquiring jurisdiction or that subsequently cause it to lose jurisdiction. Thus, the concept of "jurisdiction" is central to any discussion of the effectiveness of privative clauses. Chapter 12 examines different types of privative clauses, and how the courts have dealt with them in the context of standards of review.

---

6 Following the English model which was instituted by the *Tribunals and Inquiries Act, 1957*. See D.G.T. Williams, "The Council on Tribunals: The First Twenty-Five Years", [1984] P.L. 73; and (for a comparative appraisal of the situation in Alberta) G. Sprague, "Thirty Years After the Franks' Committee Report" (1989) 5 Admin. L.J. 66.

14

Appeals from Administrative Decisions

1. Introduction

Unlike judicial review of administrative action, the general rule is that no appeal exists unless specifically provided for by statute. Particular legislation does, of course, very frequently provide for appeals, either within the administrative hierarchy, to the courts, or both. The range of these appeals is very broad, going from a complete new hearing on the one hand to a mere review of the original delegate's jurisdiction and correctness in law on the other hand. In each case, the appellate body will need to determine the standard of review which it must apply when hearing the appeal. In general, judicial review of administrative action is not available where an equally effective appeal exists. It is useful, therefore, to consider some examples of statutory appeals from administrative decisions. It is also useful to consider other possible routes for redress, such as the Ombudsman and direct political intervention in the administrative process. All of these remedies are to be distinguished from those more familiar to administrative law: the prerogative remedies (discussed in Chapter 15) and private law remedies applied to administrative action (discussed in Chapter 16).

2. Examples of Circumstances Where There is No Appeal

There is no legal or constitutional requirement that an appeal should exist from any decision made by a statutory delegate.

It is possible to find numerous examples where legislation has made no provision for an appeal, whether to another step in the administrative hierarchy or to the courts. For example, under the *Municipal Government Act*,[1] the Municipal Government Board has the final power to determine the amount of municipal taxes, and no appeal lies from its decision.[2] Accordingly, there is no other person, court or body which has jurisdiction to consider the merits of a particular tax assessment on property (except, in theory, the legislature itself, which could enact legislation altering a particular assessment, even retroactively).[3] By contrast, an application for judicial review can be made to the courts to review the jurisdiction of the Board in any matter before it, although such judicial review would probably not deal directly with the merits of the case.

The principles of good public administration usually require that at least one level of appeal exist with respect to any delegate's decision. It may happen, therefore, that the administrators will themselves try to fashion an appeal mechanism even where none exists under the legislation. Unfortunately, the creation of such an appeal mechanism may be *ultra vires*, and therefore would not withstand judicial scrutiny if attacked. An example would be to have a small group (perhaps of one) make a tentative decision, which would become the final decision if no one objects, but which could be "appealed" to the full

---

1   R.S.A. 2000, c. M-26, s. 506.

2   Other examples where no appeal has been provided for include (a) decisions of the Information and Privacy Commissioner under the *Freedom of Information and Protection of Privacy Act*, R.S.A. 2000, c. F-25, s. 73, the *Health Information Act*, R.S.A. 2000, c. H-5, s. 81, or the *Personal Information Protection Act*, S.A. 2003, c. P-6.5, s. 53, although all three statutes specifically contemplate that applications for judicial review may be made to the Court of Queen's Bench; (b) decisions of the federal Immigration and Refugee Appeal Board, although applications for judicial review are available to the Federal Court; and (c) decisions of the Pension Review Board, although they are susceptible to an application for judicial review to the Federal Court of Appeal under s. 28 of the *Federal Courts Act*, R.S.C. 1985, c. F-7, as amended. Many other examples can be found where legislation does not provide any right of appeal.

3   See for example, the *Municipal Taxation Amendment Act*, S.A. 1981, c. 26, s. 2, which amended the definition of "improvement" in the former parent Act [*Municipal Taxation Act*, R.S.A. 1980, c. M-31] to include huge mobile diggers which the Board had held not to come within the definition and therefore not to be taxable (currently the *Municipal Government Act*, *supra* note 1, s. 284(1)(j)).

body if someone did object. Obviously, it would be better for the legislation to make explicit provision for an appeal.

A variant on an administrative appeal is to give the initial decision-maker the specific power of reconsideration. This may involve the matter going to the very same person who made the initial decision, or to a different panel of the same administrative agency.[4]

3. Appeals to Other Administrators

Of course, legislation very frequently does provide a right of appeal from one delegate to another. Thus, the Alberta *Workers' Compensation Act*[5] provides two levels of administrative appeals:

46(2) On receiving a request for review [of any person who has a direct interest in a claim for compensation under this Act] the Board shall cause all the information in the Board's possession in respect of the matter that is the subject of the review to be reviewed by the review body.

13.2

(1) A person who has a direct interest in and is dissatisfied with

(a) a decision under section 46 made by a review body appointed under section 45,

(b) a decision under section 120 made by a review body appointed under section 119, or

(c) a determination of the Board under section 21(3)

may, in accordance with this section, the regulations and the Appeals Commission's rules, appeal the decision or determination to the Appeals Commission.

Similarly, the *Municipal Government Act* provides for an appeal to the Development Appeal Board from a decision made by a development authority with respect to the proposed development of land;[6] the *Legal Profession Act* permits an appeal to the Benchers from a disposition by the Hearing Committee of a charge of misconduct against a member;[7] and the *Hospitals Act* permits an appeal to the Hospital Privileges Appeal Board by a doctor whose medical privileges have been cancelled or not renewed by the governing body of a

---

4 For example, the Alberta Labour Relations Board has the power to reconsider its decisions: *Labour Relations Code*, R.S.A. 2000, c. L-1, s. 12(4).

5 R.S.A. 2000, c. W-15. For another example, see ss. 118 to 120 of the *Child Welfare Act*, R.S.A. 2000, c. C-12.

6 R.S.A. 2000, c. M-26, ss. 683 to 688.

7 R.S.A. 2000, c. L-8, s. 75.

hospital;[8] and the *Environmental Protection and Enhancement Act*[9] provides for an appeal from a decision of the director to the Environmental Appeal Board, which (in most cases) makes a recommendation to the Minister who makes the final decision. The statute books are replete with other examples of administrative appeals from one statutory delegate to another.

There does not appear to be any particular logic in whether the appeal lies from one public servant to another, to a standing board or tribunal, or to a minister or the cabinet;[10] or from a minister to cabinet or to a standing board or tribunal.

Finally, one must remember that more than one level of appeal may be provided,[11] and that the existence of any right of appeal may affect the availability of the forms of judicial review discussed in this book.[12]

4. Specific Statutory Appeals to the Courts

The general rule that appeals must be specifically created by legislation also applies with respect to appeals to the courts of law. In many cases, legislation does provide for such appeals, although again there does not appear to be a discernible pattern about which level of court should hear such an appeal.

In some cases, legislation provides for an appeal to the Court of Queen's Bench. Thus, the *Human Rights, Citizenship and Multiculturalism Act* grants a right of appeal to that superior court from a decision of a panel constituted under that Act;[13] the *Marketing of Agricultural Products Act* grants a similar

---

8   R.S.A. 2000, c. H-12, s. 21.

9   R.S.A. 2000, c. E-12, Part 4.

10   For example, from the C.R.T.C. to the federal cabinet. Under s. 28 of the *Broadcasting Act*, S.C. 1991, c. 11:

> the Governor in Council may, within ninety days after the date of the decision, on petition in writing of any person received within forty-five days after that date or on the Governor in Council's own motion, by order, set aside the decision or refer the decision back to the [Canadian Radio and Telecommunications] Commission for reconsideration ... if the Governor in Council is satisfied that the decision derogates from the attainment of the broadcasting policy ... .

See H.N. Janisch, "Case Comment: Cabinet Appeals" (1989) 32 Admin. L.R. 60; R. Macaulay, "Petitions to Cabinet; Power to Give Directions; Government Policy" (1988-89) 2 C.J.A.L.P. 206; M. Rankin, "The Cabinets and the Courts: Political Tribunals and Judicial Tribunals" (1989-90) 3 C.J.A.L.P. 302; M. Rankin, "The Cabinet and the Agencies: Toward Accountability in British Columbia" (1985) 19 U.B.C.L. Rev. 1; A.J. Roman, "Government Control of Tribunals: Appeals, Directives and Non-Statutory Mechanisms" (1985) 10 Queen's L.J. 476; D. Lemieux, "Cabinet and Tribunals: A Quebec Perspective" (1990) 40 Admin. L.R. 118; Report of the Canadian Bar Association Task Force on *The Independence of Federal Administrative Tribunals and Agencies in Canada* (1990).

11   For example, to the Appeals Commission under the *Workers' Compensation Act*, R.S.A. 2000, c. W-15.

12   See the discussion on this point later in this chapter.

13   R.S.A. 2000, c. H-14, s. 37. For other examples of appeals from an administrative body to the courts, see: s. 70 of the *Engineering, Geological and Geophysical Professions Act*, R.S.A. 2000, c. E-11; and s. 71 of the *Chiropractic Profession Act*, R.S.A. 2000, c. C-13.

right of appeal to any party who considers a decision of an appeal tribunal under the Act to be "unfair or prejudicial to his interests";[14] and the *Surface Rights Act* provides for an appeal *de novo* with respect to a compensation order made by the Board for the use of land.[15] On the federal level, Parliament has provided a right of appeal to the Tax Court of Canada against a tax assessment and certain other determinations under the *Income Tax Act*.[16] In principle, any appellate decision rendered by one of these courts of first instance may itself be appealed further up the court hierarchy to the Court of Appeal[17] and (with leave) to the Supreme Court of Canada.[18]

In other cases, an appeal is provided directly to the Court of Appeal from the decision of a statutory delegate. For example, the Court of Appeal of Alberta has jurisdiction to hear an appeal from a decision of the Benchers that a member of the Law Society is guilty of conduct unbecoming.[19] Similarly, that court is empowered to hear an appeal on any point of law or jurisdiction arising from a decision of the Development Appeal Board,[20] the Alberta Energy and Utilities Board,[21] with leave of the Court of Appeal. In theory, a further statutory right of appeal lies from the Court of Appeal to the Supreme Court of Canada, generally with leave of the latter court.[22]

Sometimes an appeal is provided to a court which has been specially created for this purpose. Thus, the Tax Court of Canada was established to discharge the functions previously performed by the Tax Review Board in hearing appeals from income tax assessments.[23] That court has also been given jurisdiction to hear appeals against assessments in employment insurance matters,[24] which were previously dealt with by umpires appointed under the *Employment Insurance Act*.[25] Other examples of special appellate courts include the Competition Tribunal,[26] and the Employment Insurance Board of Referees.[27] Again, decisions of any of these specially created courts may sometimes be appealed further up the court hierarchy.[28] The question sometimes arises whether the members of these special courts must be appointed by the Gov-

---

14 R.S.A. 2000, c. M-4, s. 42.

15 *Surface Rights Act*, R.S.A. 2000, c. S-24, s. 26. Note that a further appeal lies with leave to the Court of Appeal, s. 26(8). Query whether this appeal is also *de novo*.

16 R.S.C. 1985, (5th Supp.) c. 1, s. 140(1). See also s. 17.6 of the *Tax Court of Canada Act*, R.S.C. 1985, c. T-2, which permits a further appeal to the Federal Court of Appeal in certain circumstances.

17 See s. 3(b)(iv) of the *Judicature Act*, R.S.A. 2000, c. J-2 and RR. 501 to 543 of the *Rules of Court* of Alberta.

18 *Supreme Court Act*, R.S.C. 1985, c. S-26.

19 *Legal Profession Act*, R.S.A. 2000, c. L-8, s. 80.

20 *Municipal Government Act*, R.S.A. 2000, c. M-26, s. 688.

21 *Alberta Energy and Utilities Board Act*, R.S.A. 2000, c. A-17, s. 26.

22 *Supreme Court Act*, R.S.C. 1985, c. S-26.

23 *Tax Court of Canada Act*, S.C. 1980-81-82-83, c. 158, now R.S.C. 1985, c.T-2.

24 *Ibid*. at s. 12.

25 S.C. 1996, c. 23.

26 *Competition Tribunal Act*, R.S.C. 1985, c. 19 (2nd. Supp.).

27 *Employment Insurance Act*, S.C. 1996, c. 23, s. 111.

28 For example, income tax appeals now go from the Tax Court of Canada directly to the Federal Court of Appeal.

ernor-in-Council under section 96 of the *Constitution Act, 1867*, especially if there is any attempt to make their decisions final without recourse to further steps in the court hierarchy.[29]

It can readily be seen that no uniform pattern has developed concerning the appropriate court to hear an appeal from a decision of a statutory delegate. Similarly, no uniform procedure is prescribed for taking such an appeal. On the one hand, an appeal to the Alberta Court of Queen's Bench under the *Human Rights, Citizenship and Multiculturalism Act*[30] must be taken by an originating notice, whereas no procedure is specified for an appeal to the same court under the *Marketing of Agricultural Products Act*.[31] On the other hand, an application for leave to appeal must first be granted on a point of law or jurisdiction by one of the judges of the Court of Appeal against a decision of a Development Appeal Board under the *Municipal Government Act*,[32] or against a decision of the Energy and Utilities Board,[33] and only if leave is granted can the appeal be proceeded with to the full Court of Appeal. A similar diversity exists with respect to the time limits within which an appeal must be taken to the court.[34] One must, therefore, study the appropriate legislation very carefully to make certain that the proper procedure is taken within the correct time to the specific court designated to hear the particular appeal.

5. Nature and Scope of Appeals

The exact ambit of an appeal from a statutory delegate may not be clearly stated in the legislation.

On the one hand, a number of statutes[35] provide for an appeal from the decision of a statutory tribunal to the courts restricted to questions of law or jurisdiction. Such appeals may be restricted to just determining from the record whether the first delegate erred in determining its jurisdiction or otherwise

---

29 See the discussion on this problem in Chapter 2.

30 R.S.A. 2000, c. H-14, s. 37, which also requires the appeal to be taken within 30 days of the date of receipt of the order of the panel.

31 R.S.A. 2000, c. M-4.

32 R.S.A. 2000, c. M-26, s. 688.

33 *Alberta Energy and Utilities Board Act*, R.S.A. 2000, c. A-17, s. 26.

34 Under s. 26 of the *Alberta Energy and Utilities Board Act*, R.S.A. 2000, c. A-17, leave to appeal "may be obtained ... within 30 days" or "within any further time as granted by the judge". By contrast, s. 688 of the *Municipal Government Act*, R.S.A. 2000, c. M-26, only requires that the application for leave to appeal be made within 30 days of the decision appealed from, not necessarily disposed of within that time. There is no time limit set out under s. 42 of the *Marketing of Agricultural Products Act*, R.S.A. 2000, c. M-4. The time limit under the *Human Rights, Citizenship and Multiculturalism Act*, for filing an appeal is 30 days from the date that the appellant receives a copy of the order of the panel: R.S.A. 2000, c. H-14, s. 37(2). By contrast, the time limit for an appeal by a lawyer who has been found to be guilty of conduct deserving of sanction is 30 days from the finding of guilt or order of punishment, apparently regardless of when it was communicated to him however, the Court may extend the time: s. 80 of the *Legal Profession Act*, R.S.A. 2000, c. L-8. See also *Frost v. Suffesick* (1998), 61 Alta. L.R. (3d) 261 (Alta. C.A. [In Chambers])

35 For example, s. 688 of the *Municipal Government Act*, R.S.A. 2000, c. M-26; s. 26 of the *Alberta Energy and Utilities Board Act*, R.S.A. 2000, c. A-17.

erred in law, which may not be broader than an application for judicial review which generally does not consider the merits of the delegate's decision but only the legality thereof.[36]

On the other hand, an appeal on the merits may take many forms. It may involve a complete hearing *de novo*, with there being no reference to the proceedings before the first delegate in the administrative appeal[37] (although courts may be reluctant to find, in the absence of some specific language, the right to a hearing *de novo).*[38] Alternatively, the appellate body may well be aware of the first delegate's decision,[39] and may treat that decision with some deference, particularly if the delegate has some expertise,[40] although the Court

---

36 There may be an issue about whether the material that would be in front of the court on an appeal is more or less extensive than what would be contained in the Return on an application for judicial review: see *BP Canada Energy Co. v. Alberta (Energy & Utilities Board)*, 2003 ABQB 875 (Alta. Q.B.), leave to appeal allowed 2004 ABCA 32 (Alta. C.A. [In Chambers]).

37 As occurred when an appeal was formerly taken from the Tax Court to the Trial Division of the Federal Court. (Since 1991, appeals from the Tax Court go directly to the Federal Court of Appeal, and are not appeals *de novo*: s. 17.6 of the *Tax Court of Canada Act*, R.S.C. 1985, c. T-2 and s. 27 of the *Federal Courts Act,* R.S.C. 1985, c. F-7).

38 See *Canadian Tire Corp. v. C.T.C. Dealer Holdings Ltd.* (1987), 23 Admin. L.R. 285 (Ont. Div. Ct.), leave to appeal refused (1987), 35 B.L.R. xx (Ont. C.A.) where the Court determined that an unrestricted right of appeal was "not a warrant for us to retry the case." See also *Abbotsford School District 34 v. Shewan* (1987), 47 D.L.R. (4th) 106 (B.C. C.A.) and *Riverside Terrace Realty Ltd. v. North Vancouver (District)* (1992), 6 Admin. L.R. (2d) 73 (B.C. S.C.). Even when the Court considers an appeal as a trial *de novo*, the decision of the statutory body may still be afforded substantial evidential value; *Lamb v. Canadian Reserve Oil & Gas Ltd.* (1976), [1977] 1 S.C.R. 517 (S.C.C.); *Imperial Oil v. Smulski* (1981), 18 Alta. L.R. (2d) 200 (Alta. C.A.) and *Champlin Canada Ltd. v. Calco Ranches Ltd.* (1986), 46 Alta. L.R. (2d) 182 (Alta. Q.B.).

39 See *Dudley v. Chiropractic Assn. (Alberta)* (1977), 2 Alta. L.R. (2d) 384 (Alta. Dist. Ct.), where there was an appeal on the merits, but the court had the previous decision before it, even though it permitted further evidence to be led on the appeal.

40 *Caswell v. Alexandra Petroleums Ltd.*, [1972] 3 W.W.R. 706 (Alta. C.A.), leave to appeal refused [1972] S.C.R. ix (S.C.C.); *Lamb v. Canadian Reserve Oil & Gas Ltd.* (1976), [1977] 1 S.C.R. 517 (S.C.C.); *Chieftain Development Co. v. Lachowich* (1981), [1982] 1 W.W.R. 37 (Alta. Q.B.); *Livingston v. Siebens Oil & Gas Ltd.*, [1978] 3 W.W.R. 484 (Alta. C.A.); *Morgan v. Vancouver (City)* (1988), 33 Admin. L.R. 160 (B.C. C.A.); *Imperial Oil, supra* note 38. In *Transalta Utilities Corp. v. Alberta (Public Utilities Board)* (1986), 43 Alta. L.R. (2d) 171 (Alta. C.A.), Kerans J.A. noted at 180 that "[t]he use of elastic adjectives is usually considered by a court as an implicit granting of a power to the tribunal to form its own "opinion" or make "policy" or to exercise a "discretion" – in fine, to make law." See also *Mobil-GC Canada Ltd. v. Mackey* (1987), 51 Alta. L.R. (2d) 283 (Alta. Q.B.). The Supreme Court of Canada has explicitly recognized this in *Bell Canada v. Canada (Canadian Radio-Television & Telecommunications Commission)*, [1989] 1 S.C.R. 1722 (S.C.C.), where Gonthier J. for the Court said at 1745-46:

> It is trite to say that the jurisdiction of a court on appeal is broader than the jurisdiction of a court on judicial review. In principle, a court is entitled, on appeal, to disagree with the reasoning of the lower tribunal.

> However, within the context of a statutory appeal from an administrative tribunal, additional consideration must be given to the principle of specialization of duties. Although an appeal tribunal has the right to disagree with the lower tribunal on issues which fall within the scope of the statutory appeal, curial deference should be given to the opinion

of Appeal has asserted its right to hear evidence and decide about the merits of an appeal from a specialized statutory body (particularly where the decision did not disclose on its face any reliance on expertise).[41]

Other types of difficulties arise in determining the scope of an appeal to a court. Because the right of appeal must be specifically provided for by statute, it is clearly possible for legislation to prescribe what issues can be appealed, who bears the burden of proof, whether new evidence can be led, what procedure is to be adopted by the court in hearing the appeal, what remedies the court can order, whether costs can be awarded, and similar problems. Sometimes legislation does deal with these matters specifically. Thus, the *Income Tax Act* provides that the Tax Court or the Federal Court of Appeal may "confirm, vary or vacate" any assessment at issue before it[42] and the former *Health Disciplines Act* of Ontario provided that:[43]

> Any party to proceedings before a discipline committee may appeal from its decision or order to the Divisional Court ... and the court may affirm or may rescind the decision of the committee appealed from and may exercise all powers of the committee and may direct the committee or the College to take any action which the committee or the College may take and as the court considers proper, and for such purposes the court may substitute its opinion for that of the committee, or the court may refer the matter back to the committee for rehearing, in whole or in part, in accordance with such directions as the court considers proper.

---

of the lower tribunal on issues which fall squarely within its area of expertise.

This approach was further refined in *Zurich Insurance Co. v. Ontario (Human Rights Commission)* (1992), 93 D.L.R. (4th) 346 (S.C.C.) where Sopinka J., writing for the majority, noted at 373:

> In spite of the ability to overturn decisions of the board on findings of fact, this court has indicated that some curial deference will apply even to cases without privative clauses to reflect the principle of the specialization of duties: see *Bell Canada v. Canada (C.R.T.C.)*. While curial deference may apply to findings of fact, which the board of inquiry may have been in a better position to determine, such deference will not apply to findings of law in which the board has no particular expertise.

See also *University of Alberta v. Alberta (Human Rights Commission)* (1992), 95 D.L.R. (4th) 439 (S.C.C.) where Cory J. stated, following a reference to *Bell Canada* (at 494):

> However the situation is different when there is neither specialized skill and knowledge exercised by an administrative decision-maker nor a statutory restriction imposed upon the court's review of these decisions.

See also the comments, *infra*.

41 *Whitehouse v. Sun Oil Co.*, [1982] 6 W.W.R. 289 (Alta. C.A.) at 295 (*per* Stevenson J.A. as he then was).

42 See s. 169 of the *Income Tax Act*, R.S.C. 1985 (5th Supp.) c. 1; combined with s. 17.6 of the *Tax Court of Canada Act*, R.S.C. 1985, c. T-2, and s. 27 of the *Federal Courts Act*, R.S.C. 1985, c. F-7.

43 R.S.O. 1990, c. H-4. For another example, see s. 167 of the *Securities Act*, R.S.B.C. 1997, c. 418.

By contrast, section 689 of the Alberta *Municipal Government Act* limits the powers of the Court of Appeal by providing that:[44]

> 689(1)   On the hearing of the appeal
>
> (a) no evidence other than the evidence that was submitted to the ... board ... may be admitted, but the Court may draw any inferences
>
> > (i) that are not inconsistent with the facts expressly found by the ... board ... and
> >
> > (ii) that are necessary for determining the question of law or the question of jurisdiction,
>
> and
>
> (b) the Court may confirm, vary, reverse or cancel the decision.

Under some legislation (such as the *Municipal Government Act*)[45], therefore, the court is bound by the findings of fact made by the administrative tribunal from whom the appeal lies, but other legislative provisions (such as the power of either the Tax Court or the Federal Court of Appeal under the *Income Tax Act*)[46] impose no such limitations. In many cases, however, the legislative provision granting the appeal is sufficiently vague that litigation is required to determine its precise nature and form in the circumstances: see *Dudley v. Chiropractic Assn. (Alberta)*[47] where Stevenson D.C.J. (as he then was) said that "[i]n principle an appeal 'on the merits' authorizes a retrial of the facts" so that "this court is not bound by the fact findings [of the statutory delegate] and is not precluded from hearing evidence to the extent that there are fact issues".

In the absence of a specific statutory statement as to the *form* of the appellate hearing (as opposed to its *scope*–that is, what can be appealed), there would appear to be no requirement on the appellate body to hear the appellant in person or through counsel, and it may be difficult to lead further evidence[48] or make additional submissions which were not before the original decision-maker from whom the administrative appeal has been taken. Of course, the rules of natural justice require the appeal to be "fair" in all of the circumstances, but it is impossible to lay down a code of what fairness requires in the absence of a specific statutory provision as to the procedure to be adopted on appeal.

---

44 R.S.A. 2000, c. M-26.

45 *Ibid.*

46 *Supra* note 42.

47 (1977), 2 Alta. L.R. (2d) 384 at 386, 388 (Alta. Dist. Ct.).

48 For example, the legislation at issue in the *Dudley* case, *ibid.*, specifically stated that the appeal was to be "on the merits". Note the comments of the Alberta Court of Appeal in *Imperial, supra* note 38.

The appellate body may sometimes even permit the original decision-maker to participate in the appellate proceedings. Indeed, legislation sometimes specifically permits such adversarial participation.[49]

Sometimes, legislation creates a board or tribunal to deal with a particular matter, and one or more members of that body is a judge.[50] The mere presence of a judge on the appellate body does not make it a court; one should not infer any restrictions on the ambit of the proceedings merely because a judge is involved as a *persona designata*; and the mere involvement of a judge does not necessarily make available appeal procedures which would otherwise apply to his or her decisions when acting as a judge.

6. Appellate Exercise of Discretion

Difficult issues arise when considering whether the appellate body has the right to exercise a statutory discretion differently from the way chosen by the original statutory delegate. Occasionally, the legislation in question may specifically prevent the appellate body from doing so, but this would appear to be rare.[51] In principle, the general rule should be the reverse: where an appeal is provided from the exercise of a statutory power which is discretionary in nature, the appellate body itself should be able to exercise the discretion granted by

---

49   See s. 688(6) of the *Municipal Government Act*, R.S.A. 2000, c. M-26 which entitles the Board to be represented by counsel at the appeal. The Supreme Court of Canada construed the predecessor to this provision extremely narrowly in *Northwestern Utilities Ltd. v. Edmonton (City)* (1978), [1979] 1 S.C.R. 684 (S.C.C.); *Canada (Labour Relations Board) v. Transair Ltd.* (1976), [1977] 1 S.C.R. 722 (S.C.C.); *Central Broadcasting Co. v. Canada (Labour Relations Board)* (1976), [1977] 2 S.C.R. 112 (S.C.C.). Compare the subsequent more generous role accorded to administrative bodies defending their actions in an appeal enunciated in *Sheckter v. Alberta (Planning Board)* (1979), 9 Alta. L.R. (2d) 45 (Alta. C.A.) and in *Calgary Reg. Planning Comm. v. Mun. Dist. of Foothills No. 31* (March 28, 1979) (unreported) and in *Rocky View (Municipal District No. 44) v. Alberta (Planning Board)* (1982), 40 A.R. 344 (Alta. C.A.). Curiously, the Supreme Court of Canada permitted the statutory delegate to participate fully in the judicial review proceedings in *Law Society of Upper Canada v. French* (1974), [1975] 2 S.C.R. 767 (S.C.C.), affirmed (1974), 49 D.L.R. (3d) 1 (note) (S.C.C.). See also *C.A.I.M.A.W., Local 14 v. Canadian Kenworth Co.* (1989), 62 D.L.R. (4th) 437 (S.C.C.) which applies the conclusion from *Northwestern Utilities* to a case of judicial review, rather than appeal. But see the comments of Mahoney J.A. in *Ferguson Bus Lines Ltd. v. A.T.U., Local 1374* (1990), 43 Admin. L.R. 18 at 38-40 (Fed. C.A.), leave to appeal refused (1990), 127 N.R. 240 (note) (S.C.C.) concerning the appearance by a statutory tribunal at an application for judicial review when the initial jurisdiction of the tribunal is not being questioned, although the reasonableness of its decision (and therefore its jurisdiction) was the issue.

50   See for example, the former s. 20(2) of the *Teaching Profession Act*, R.S.A. 1980, c. T-3, which made a judge of the Court of Queen's Bench chairman of the three-member Teaching Profession Appeal Board to hear appeals from teachers found to be guilty of unprofessional or unethical conduct. Similarly, judges used to be Referees determining whether teachers' contracts had been properly terminated. Both functions are now done by persons who are not judges.

51   See s. 18 of the 1983 draft *Planning Act* in B.C., which limited the powers of the appeal board to a number of legal questions, and s. 40 which specifically stated that the appeal board must not substitute its decision for that of the local government or officer.

statute on the delegate from whom the appeal lies. This is particularly clear where the only matter capable of being appealed is discretionary in nature, and the appeal is said to be "on the merits"–obviously the legislature intended the appellate body to exercise its own plenipotentiary discretion in a second hearing of the matter.[52] However, as discussed below, the courts have sometimes taken the view that they themselves should show curial restraint in exercising any appellate powers which they may have from the exercise of a discretionary power by adopting a less stringent standard of review. This concept of curial restraint can be criticized if the very matter with respect to which the appeal is provided is a discretionary power.

Nevertheless, the courts have often been very reluctant to substitute their own discretion for that of a statutory delegate, even where that very discretion is capable of being appealed to the court.[53] As Lord Greene said in *Wrights' Canadian Ropes Ltd. v. Minister of National Revenue*,[54] which dealt with an appeal from the Minister's discretionary decision to disallow a claim for expenses:

> [U]nless it be shown that the Minister has acted in contravention of some principle of law the Court, in their Lordships' opinion, cannot interfere: the section makes the Minister the sole judge of the fact of reasonableness or normalcy and the Court is not at liberty to substitute its own opinion for his ...

> The Court is, in their Lordships' opinion, always entitled to examine the facts which are shown by evidence to have been before the Minister when he made his determination. If those facts are in the opinion of the Court insufficient in law to support it the determination cannot stand. In such a case the determination can only have been an arbitrary one. If, on the other hand, there is in the facts shown to have been before the Minister sufficient material to support his determination *the Court is not at liberty to overrule it merely because it would itself on those facts have come to a different conclusion. As has already been said, the Minister is by the subsection made the sole judge of the fact of reasonableness and normalcy* but as in the case of any other judge of fact there must be material sufficient in law to support his decision.

This reluctance by the courts to substitute their view of how a statutory delegate should exercise its discretion is particularly marked in the case of appeals from the imposition of discipline by governing bodies of a profession.[55]

---

52 But see the recent decisions by the Supreme Court of Canada in *Q v. College of Physicians & Surgeons (British Columbia)*, [2003] 1 S.C.R. 226 (S.C.C.) and in *Ryan v. Law Society (New Brunswick)*, [2003] 1 S.C.R. 247 (S.C.C.), where the Court adopted a deferential *standard* of review (reasonableness) even though these cases both involved appeals on the merits.

53 See the cases cited in note 38.

54 (1946), [1947] 1 D.L.R. 721 at 730-31 (Canada P.C.), emphasis added.

55 See *Lazar v. Assn. of Professional Engineers (Manitoba)*, [1971] 5 W.W.R. 614 (Man. Q.B.);

7. Standard of Appellate Review

One of the most difficult issues is to determine the standard of review which courts will use when hearing a particular appeal. Since the recent decisions of the Supreme Court of Canada in Q.[56] and $Ryan$,[57] it is clear that the mere existence of a right of appeal "on the merits" does not determine the standard of review to be applied by the appellate body.[58] Rather, the appropriate standard of review by the appellate body must be determined by using the same pragmatic and functional approach and the four *Pushpanathan* factors which is used in the context of applications for judicial review. This analysis is considered in greater detail in Chapter 12 above.

8. Isolated Reforms to Permit Appeals to the Courts

Although the common law provides no automatic right of appeal to the courts from an administrative decision (so that such a right must be specifically provided for by statute), there have been a number of recommendations and attempts to reverse this rule so as to provide a generalized right of appeal to the courts on various legal matters involved in the exercise of statutory powers. For example, the Franks Committee in England recommended that there should be a general right of appeal on "fact, law and merits". This recommendation was implemented in a more restricted form by the *Tribunals and Inquiries Act, 1958*,[59] which provides for a right of appeal to the High Court on a point of law only from those specific tribunals enumerated in the schedule to the Act.

In 1965, the Special Committee on Boards and Tribunals appointed by the Legislative Assembly of Alberta was asked to consider whether there should be a greater provision for appeals to the courts from the decisions of such boards and tribunals. The committee made the following observations[60]:

> It has already been noted in this report that a widespread and nearly unanimous desire for a right of appeal to the Courts was ex-

---

Marten v. Disciplinary Committee. of the Royal College of Veterinary Surgeons, [1965] 1 All E.R. 949 (Eng. Q.B.); *K. v. College of Physicians & Surgeons (Saskatchewan)* (1970), 72 W.W.R. 321 (Sask. Q.B.); *Rajasooria v. Disciplinary Committee*, [1955] 1 W.L.R. 405; *A Solicitor, Re*, [1912] 1 K.B. 302 at 312 (Eng. K.B.); *Weber v. Toronto (Metropolitan) Licensing Commission*, [1963] 2 O.R. 286 (Ont. H.C.), reversed [1964] 1 O.R. 621 (Ont. C.A.). See also *Canadian Western Natural Gas Co. v. Alberta (Public Utilities Board)* (1984), 33 Alta. L.R. (2d) 185 (Alta. C.A.), where the Court of Appeal refused to second-guess the discretion exercised by the board not to re-hear a matter.

56 *Q. v. College of Physicians & Surgeons (British Columbia)*, [2003] 1 S.C.R. 226 (S.C.C.).

57 *Ryan v. Law Society (New Brunswick)*, [2003] 1 S.C.R. 247 (S.C.C.).

58 Whether the appellate body is a court or another administrative agency: *College of Hearing Aid Practitioners (Alberta) v. Zieniewicz*, 2003 ABCA 346 (Alta. C.A.).

59 6 & 7 Eliz. 2, c. 66; replaced without substantial variation by the *Tribunals and Inquiries Act, 1971* (c. 62).

60 *Report of the Special Committee on Boards and Tribunals to the Legislative Assembly of Alberta*, (1966) (the "Clement Committee") at 12-14.

pressed to the Committee in submissions which dealt with particular tribunals. ... It is said that if the recommendations of the Committee respecting minimum uniform standards of procedures are implemented, the occasions would be diminished on which an appeal would be required to obtain justice: this may be so. Nevertheless, there is embedded in the democratic principles of the administration of justice a right to appeal by a person who considers himself aggrieved, and the Committee is of the view that this principle should be more fully recognized in administrative law than it is at present. It would give citizens who are affected by the decisions of a tribunal a right comparable to the one they have traditionally had in respect of judgments of the Courts. And, as with the Courts, a right of appeal would impose a measure of discipline on the tribunal and a sense of responsibility in maintaining proper standards in its procedures. The growth and extent of a new system of administration of justice created by Legislatures in administrative law requires that all reasonable steps be taken to assure the society in which it operates that it is indeed doing justice. This is not to say that at the present stage of the development of administrative law in Alberta the Committee as a whole is prepared to recommend a full right of appeal to the Courts in all cases, or to recommend the establishment of an over-all appeal tribunal even if it were constitutionally possible to do so.

The Committee is unanimously and firmly of the view that in every case there should be a right of appeal to the Supreme Court of Alberta on a question of jurisdiction and a question of law. No legitimate reason can be put forward why a tribunal to whom the legislature has delegated certain defined authority should be permitted with impunity to transgress the bounds of the jurisdiction that it was intended it should exercise. Similarly, there should be no excuse for a tribunal misapplying law, or ignoring law, to which all citizens of the Province are subject, in favour of its own views as to what should be applicable to the persons that are affected by its decisions. No leave should be required for such an appeal, and simple and expeditious procedures should be provided. By this stroke there would be cut away the privative clauses still remaining in some statutes whereby the Legislature seeks to protect its tribunals from the disciplines of the Rule of Law; and in place of the old and difficult prerogative writs persons who felt themselves aggrieved by excesses of jurisdiction or misapplication of law would have a simple and easy access to the Courts to determine the point.

Appeals on facts, which might be described as appeals from the quality of decisions, are subject to several considerations. ...

By statute tribunals are not required to judge the acceptability of evidence by any established standards. If there are no accepted standards for determining facts, then an appeal on facts could be taken, not because a standard has been departed from in the exercise of the judicial function, but in the hope that the appeal tribunal of itself might come to a different result by applying different standards or taking a different approach. It is difficult to see how the ends of justice would be advanced by a contest to have the facts determined on some amorphous basis other than that adopted in the particular case by the tribunal of first instance. This would be so even if, as in Court procedures, the appeal is based on the trial proceedings: that is to say, the oral evidence is transcribed and it, together with whatever documentary evidence is involved, is put before the appeal tribunal. Further than that, if the members of the tribunal of first instance have been appointed because they possess expert knowledge which would promote administrative efficiency in attaining the objective of the legislature, then the appeal tribunal would require to be constituted with members having at least comparable expert knowledge, otherwise this purpose would be stultified. The alternative would be a re-hearing before the appeal tribunal so that expert evidence could be called to inform it on matters for which the tribunal of first instance itself provided the expert knowledge. Thus, considerations of expediency and efficiency that the Legislature had thought desirable in the general interests in establishing such a tribunal would be lost. In the area of administrative law the claims of the public are in reality foremost in the statutory enactments, and the degree to which individual interests must be sacrificed for the general good must be a matter of balance for the legislature to determine. ...

In the result, the Committee as a whole is of the view that at the present time there cannot be generalizations on the question of appeals on facts. A specific solution should be sought for each specific problem: the nature of the jurisdiction exercised by each tribunal requires examination, a balance must be struck between efficiency of administration and the interests of the individuals having regard to the purpose of the statute, and a conclusion then reached as to whether an appeal to the Courts is on balance warranted, or whether an effective appeal tribunal can be provided. In the *Securities Act*, the Legislature determined that a full appeal is appropriate, and it may be that on close consideration the Legislature might find others in which it would be appropriate also ...

Unfortunately, these recommendations have never been implemented in Alberta, even though the subsequent adoption of the *Administrative Procedures Act*[61] would have provided an appropriate vehicle for a generalized right of appeal (whether restricted to law and jurisdiction, or extending to merits as well), at least with respect to the ten tribunals which have been made subject to it. Frankly, it is unrealistic to expect that the members of the legislature will be able to give reasoned, detailed consideration to the need for an appeal – or its nature and extent – from each statutory power contained in each piece of

---

61   R.S.A. 2000, c. A-3.

legislation which they enact. To some extent, the Sovereignty of Parliament could be used to solve this problem if the provincial legislature were to create a Scrutiny Committee on Regulations, such as exists federally and in England. Such a committee could use its power to review systematically how administrators exercise their statutory powers to insist that rights of appeal be implemented whenever possible in administrative schemes created by delegated legislation. But this goal would be achieved even more effectively if the Scrutiny Committee were given the power, sought by the federal committee, to review the enabling legislation itself to make sure that the question of appeals has been carefully dealt with. Similarly, a Council on Tribunals (such as exists in England) might help concentrate proper attention on the existence and scope of appeals, in at least some contexts. In short, what is required is a commitment, a statement of policy, that Canadian society requires and values the right of appeal, so that the onus should be on our governments to justify why no appeal exists in particular circumstances.

9. Administrative Appeals Tribunals

This type of reform has been made at the federal level in Australia by the creation of the Administrative Appeals Tribunal,[62] which hears appeals from the merits of decisions made from a large number of designated statutory delegates.[63] Professor Mullan has described and criticized the idea and operation of this general administrative appeals tribunal.[64] In particular, some difficulties appear to arise from the wide variety of matters which can be appealed, so that the Appeals Tribunal is not guaranteed to have any particular expertise in the subject matter of each appeal.[65] Similarly, the Australian model appears to have succumbed to an overly judicial procedure which may just encumber the whole administrative process and compete unnecessarily with more conventional routes for judicial review and with the broader powers of the Om-

---

62 *Administrative Appeals Tribunal Act*, 1975. By contrast to the Australian system, Quebec recently enacted *An Act Respecting Administrative Justice*, L.Q. 1996, c. 54, which assimilated most administrative tribunals into a single body, the Administrative Tribunal of Quebec. The Tribunal is divided into four specialized divisions. Unlike the Administrative Appeals Tribunal, the Administrative Tribunal is the original decision maker.

63 *Ibid.* at s. 25 (permitting other statutes to confer appellate jurisdiction on the A.A.T.) and s. 26 (giving the A.A.T. appellate jurisdiction over the bodies listed in Sched. 1 to the Act). In 1998 the Administrative Appeals Tribunal indicated that the Tribunal had jurisdiction over 302 enactments. See (1998) 50 Admin. Rev. 30.

64 See D.J. Mullan, "Alternatives to Judicial Review of Administrative Action – The Commonwealth of Australia's Administrative Appeals Tribunal" in *Judicial Review of Administrative Rulings* (Montreal: Les Editions Yvon Blais, Inc., 1983), at 441-66, for The Canadian Institute for the Administration of Justice; also found at (1983) 43 *Revue du Barreau* 569. This article contains a large number of references to extremely good articles on the whole gamut of the reforms which have been made to Australian administrative law.

65 The Tribunal appears to be conscious of this problem. One of the recommendations in *Review of the Administrative Appeals Tribunal*, a report presented to the Attorney General in 1991, was that the Tribunal include in its membership experts in environmental law and science, to ensure that the Tribunal had expertise in such matters. See (1992) 30 Admin Review 18.

budsman to correct maladministration.[66] It may be, therefore, that considerable care should be given to the format and vehicle for implementing the desirable policy of full right of appeal from every administrative decision,[67] whether that appeal lies to the ordinary courts, to a specially created administrative court, or to an *ad hoc* administrative body.

A similar general administrative appeal structure has been implemented in Quebec by the creation of the *Tribunal Administratif du Québec*.[68] It is too early to tell how successful it will be, and whether it could usefully be copied in other Canadian jurisdictions.

10. The Ombudsman

Another possible route for preventing abuse of delegated powers is to invoke the help of the Ombudsman. Borrowed in 1962 by New Zealand[69] from the Scandinavian countries, the idea of the Ombudsman has spread throughout the British Commonwealth[70] and beyond. Alberta[71] was the first province in Canada to create an Ombudsman, and now they exist everywhere[72] except in Prince Edward Island, Newfoundland, the Territories, and federally.

Section 12 of the Alberta *Ombudsman Act* sets out the functions of the Ombudsman, which are almost the same in all jurisdictions:

---

66 Another recommendation from the 1991 *Review of the Administrative Appeals Tribunal*, *ibid* was the implementation of case management time limits, including a guideline of 12 months from receipt of application to final disposition of the case. These reviews are ongoing, for example in 1998 the Council considered the merits of expanding the role of the Federal Court to hear appeals from the A.A.T. on matters of fact in addition to questions of law as currently allowed under s. 44 of the *Administrative Appeals Tribunal Act*, 1975. The Council also considered the merits of creating a separate regime for taxation and patents appeal: see (1998) 50 Admin. Rev. 20-25 for a summary of the Council Report.

67 Thus, Mullan suggests not only the creation of a federal Ombudsman, but also the need to rationalize existing statutory appeal procedures, making them as uniform as possible, and grouping them under a single umbrella whenever common issues are involved (such as Quebec tried in its Tribunal on the Professions): *supra* note 64 at 465.

68 For further information on the *Tribunal Administratif du Québec*, see its website at *www.taq.gouv.qc.ca*. See also *Barreau de Montréal c. Québec (Procureur général)* (2001), 48 Admin. L.R. (3d) 82 (Que. C.A.), leave to appeal refused (2002), 302 N.R. 200 (note) (S.C.C.), reconsideration refused (2002), 2002 CarswellQue 2683 (S.C.C.). Also note that a bill has been introduced before the Québec Legislature to refine the role and structure of the Tribunal Administratif du Québec.

69 *Parliamentary Commissioner (Ombudsman) Act*, 1962 (N.Z.).

70 Note the work of the International Ombudsman Institute. See also c. 5 ("Ombudsmen") in the *Report of the Committee of the JUSTICE – All Souls Review of Administrative Law in the United Kingdom* (1988).

71 R.S.A. 2000, c. O-8.

72 New Brunswick: R.S.N.B. 1973, c. 0-5; Quebec: *Public Protector Act*, R.S.Q. 1977, c. P-32; Manitoba: C.C.S.M., c. O45; Nova Scotia: R.S.N.S. 1989, c. 327. Saskatchewan: R.S.S. 1978, c. 0-4; Ontario: R.S.O. 1990, c. O.6; British Columbia: R.S.B.C. 1996, c. 340; Newfoundland had an ombudsman, but now does not; *Parliamentary Commissioner (Ombudsman) Act*, R.S.N. 1970, c. 285.

12(1) It is the function and duty of the Ombudsman to investigate any decision or recommendation made, including any recommendation made to a Minister, or any act done or omitted, relating to a matter of administration and affecting any person or body of persons in his or its personal capacity, in or by any department or agency, or by any officer, employee or member thereof in the exercise of any power or function conferred on him by any enactment.

(2) The Ombudsman may make an investigation either on a complaint made to him by any person or of his own motion, and he may commence an investigation notwithstanding that the complaint may not on its face be against a decision, recommendation, act or omission as mentioned in subsection (1).

(3) The powers and duties conferred on the Ombudsman by this Act may be exercised and performed notwithstanding any provision in any Act to the effect

(a) that any decision, recommendation, act or omission mentioned in subsection (1) is final,

(b) that no appeal lies in respect thereof, or

(c) that no proceeding or decision of the person or organization whose decision, recommendation, act or omission it is shall be challenged, reviewed, quashed or called in question. ...

The Ombudsman does not have jurisdiction whenever there is a right of appeal, objection or review on the merits of a case to a court or statutory tribunal,[73] so his or her role is complementary to rights of appeal provided under legislation. The real powers of the Ombudsman lie in his or her right to investigate the propriety of governmental action, even if it is not *ultra vires* in administrative law terms. Section 21 of the Alberta Act demonstrates the width of these powers in a somewhat convoluted way:

21(1) This section applies when, after making an investigation under this Act, the Ombudsman is of the opinion that the decision, recommendation, act or omission that was the subject matter of the investigation

(a) appears to have been contrary to law,

(b) was unreasonable, unjust, oppressive or improperly discriminatory or was in accordance with a rule of law, a provision

---

73 See s. 13 of the Alberta *Ombudsman Act*. Note, however, that the Ombudsman will gain jurisdiction once an appeal has been exercised (unsatisfactorily?) or the right to appeal has lapsed, or been abandoned: see *Ontario (Ombudsman) v. Board of Radiological Technicians (Ontario)* (1990), 68 D.L.R. (4th) 311 (Ont. Div. Ct.). Further, note that s. 13 does not require a person to seek judicial review (as opposed to an appeal) before going to the Ombudsman.

of any Act or a practice that is or may be unreasonable, unjust, oppressive or improperly discriminatory,

(c) was based wholly or partly on a mistake of law or fact, or

(d) was wrong.

(2) This section also applies when the Ombudsman is of the opinion

(a) that in the making of the decision or recommendation, or in the doing or omission of the act, a discretionary power has been exercised

(i) for an improper purpose,

(ii) on irrelevant grounds, or

(iii on the taking into account of irrelevant considerations,

or

(b) that in the case of a decision made in the exercise of a discretionary power, reasons should have been given for the decision.

(3) If, when this section applies, the Ombudsman is of the opinion

(a) that the matter should be referred to the appropriate authority for further consideration,

(b) that the omission should be rectified,

(c) that the decision should be cancelled or varied,

(d) that any practice on which the decision, recommendation, act or omission was based should be altered,

(e) that any law on which the decision, recommendation, act or omission was based should be reconsidered,

(f) that reasons should have been given for the decision, or

(g) that the matter should be reheard or reconsidered by the appropriate authority, or

(h) that any other steps should be taken,

the Ombudsman shall report that opinion and the Ombudsman's reasons for it to the appropriate Minister and to the department or agency concerned ... and may make any recommendations the Ombudsman thinks fit and in that case the Ombudsman may request the department, agency or administrative head of the professional organization to notify the Ombudsman within a specified time of the steps, if any, that it proposes to take to give effect to the Ombudsman's recommendations.

(4) If within a reasonable time after the report is made under subsection (3) to the administrative head of a professional orga-

nization no action is taken which seems to the Ombudsman to be adequate and appropriate, the Ombudsman, in his discretion after considering the comments, if any, made by or on behalf of the department or agency affected, may send a copy of the report and recommendations to the Lieutenant Governor-in-Council and may thereafter make any report to the Legislature on the matter that he thinks fit.

(5) If, within a reasonable time after the report is made to the appropriate Minister and the department or agency under subsection (3) or to the administrative head of a professional organization under subsection (3) and to the appropriate Minister under subsection (4), no action is taken that seems to the Ombudsman to be adequate and appropriate, the Ombudsman, in the Ombudsman's discretion after considering the comments, if any, made by or on behalf of the department, agency or professional organization, may send a copy of the report and recommendations to the Lieutenant Governor in Council and may afterwards make any report to the Legislature on the matter that the Ombudsman thinks fit.

(6) The Ombudsman shall attach to every report sent or made under subsection (5) a copy of any comments made by or on behalf of the department, agency or professional organization concerned.

Thus, the Ombudsman is empowered to ask very searching questions about the way statutory delegates exercise their powers. Merely having the Ombudsman ask questions and make recommendations will very often cause a statutory delegate to revise a questionable action or policy: the effectiveness of the Ombudsman's function is not to be underestimated.[74] The Ombudsman does have the power to inquire into and investigate both adjudicative and administrative decisions made by statutory delegates.[75] On the other hand, in the final analysis the Ombudsman has no legal means for compelling a recal-

---

74 As demonstrated by a review of any of the annual reports filed by the various Ombudsmen. For litigation concerning the Ombudsman's powers under their respective Acts, see the decision of the Supreme Court of Canada in *British Columbia Development Corp. v. Friedmann* (1984), [1985] 1 W.W.R. 193 (S.C.C.); *Ombudsman Act, Re* (1970), 72 W.W.R. 176 (Alta. S.C.); *Ontario (Ombudsman) v. Ontario (Health Disciplines Board)* (1979), 26 O.R. (2d) 105 (Ont. C.A.); *Ontario (Ombudsman) v. R.* (1979), 26 O.R. (2d) 434 (Ont. H.C.), affirmed (1980), 30 O.R. (2d) 768 (Ont. C.A.); *Ombudsman Act (Saskatchewan), Re*, [1974] 5 W.W.R. 176 (Sask. Q.B.); *Nova Scotia (Ombudsman) v. Sydney Steel Corp.* (1976), 17 N.S.R. (2d) 361 (N.S. C.A.); *Friedmann v. British Columbia (Attorney General)* (1985), 20 D.L.R. (4th) 7 (B.C. S.C.); *Ontario (Ombudsman) v. Ontario (Ministry of Financial Institutions)* (1989), 66 D.L.R. (4th) 358 (Ont. Div. Ct.).

75 *Ontario (Ombudsman) v. Ontario (Labour Relations Board)* (1985), 21 D.L.R. (4th) 631 (Ont. Div. Ct.), affirmed (1987), 44 D.L.R. (4th) 312 (Ont. C.A.), leave to appeal refused (May 5, 1987), Doc. 20329 (S.C.C.); *Levey v. Friedman* (1985), 18 D.L.R. (4th) 641 (B.C. S.C.).

citrant administrator to correct maladministration or to avoid it in the future: his or her sole sanction is to make a public report to the legislature.[76] To this extent, therefore, the Ombudsman does not have the same legal power as the Australian Administrative Appeals Tribunal, or any other appellate mechanism, to implement the results of his or her investigation.

11. The Effect of an Appeal on the Availability of Judicial Review

The existence of an appeal may have the effect of causing the courts to exercise their discretion to refuse to grant judicial review of an administrator's decision by way of one of the prerogative remedies, a declaration or an injunction.[77] As McDermid J.A. stated in *Chad Investments Ltd. v. Longson Tammets & Denton Real Estate Ltd.*:[78]

> It is a wrongful exercise of judicial discretion, unless there are special circumstances, to grant an order of *certiorari* where the party aggrieved has been given an effective right of appeal which the party has not taken advantage of and which has expired. I think this is supported by the majority of the authorities.

> Here the Legislature has given the right of appeal upon a question of jurisdiction or law, but has provided that application for leave must be made within 30 days after the making of the decision, and that the Appellate Division shall hear the appeal as speedily as practicable. Under the Alberta *Rules of Court* an application for *certiorari* must be made within six months of the decision. To grant *certiorari* in a situation such as this would, in effect, circumvent the clear intention of the Legislature that time is a critical and important factor in planning matters.

> *A Court, therefore, should not exercise its discretion which would effect such a result unless there are special circumstances, and I do not find any such special circumstances in this case.*

---

76 See s. 20 of the Alberta Act.

77 There is a *right* to damages, however, and the court has no discretion to refuse damages if a case is made out, although it may have a discretion as to the amount. In England, there appears to be no requirement for an applicant to exhaust alternative remedies before applying for judicial review: see W.R. Wade, *Administrative Law*, 5th ed. (Oxford: Clarendon Press, 1982) at 593*ff.* and Viscount Simonds' *dicta* in *Pyx Granite Co. v. Minister of Housing & Local Government* (1959), [1960] A.C. 260 at 286 (U.K. H.L.). For more recent developments in England, see W. Wade and c. Forsyth, *Administrative Law*, 7th ed. (Oxford: Clarendon Press, 1994) at 721-29.

78 (1971), 20 D.L.R. (3d) 627 at 631-32 (Alta. C.A.), emphasis added. See also *Edith Lake Service Ltd. v. Edmonton (City)* (1981), 132 D.L.R. (3d) 612 (Alta C.A.), leave to appeal refused (1982), 42 N.R. 358 (note) (S.C.C.) which incorporates the comments of the Supreme Court of Canada in *Harelkin v. University of Regina* (1979), 96 D.L.R. (3d) 14 (S.C.C.), in determining whether "special circumstances exist" and *Bromley v. Assn. of Professional Engineers, Geologists & Geophysicists (Alberta)* (1989), 64 Alta. L.R. (2d) 306 (Alta. Q.B.)

Thus, the Appellate Division held that the trial judge had erred in granting *certiorari* to quash the issuance of a development permit after the 30-day appeal period had elapsed.[79]

The policy of refusing judicial review appears now to apply whether the appeal lies to the courts or to another administrative body. In *Harelkin v. University of Regina*,[80] the Supreme Court of Canada refused to issue a prerogative remedy to quash the decision that a student be required to withdraw from the University because the Supreme Court held that his right to appeal to a committee of the University Senate would constitute an "adequate alternative remedy" to judicial review. Until the *Harelkin* case, a credible argument could be made that appeals to another administrative body should not be treated with the same deference as appeals to the courts, so that a greater claim to judicial review would exist in the former case notwithstanding the existence of an appeal in the legislation in question. However, the decision of the majority of the Supreme Court in *Harelkin* clearly focuses on whether the appeal – to whatever body – is an adequate remedy in the circumstances.[81]

It may be difficult to second-guess the courts' view on whether a particular appeal is or is not an adequate alternative remedy to judicial review.[82] Beetz J. set out the following criteria in his decision for the majority in *Harelkin*:[83]

> In order to evaluate whether appellant's right of appeal to the senate committee constituted an adequate alternative remedy and even a better remedy than a recourse to the Courts by way of prerogative writs, several factors should have been taken into consideration among which[:] the procedure on the appeal, the composition of the senate committee, its powers and the manner in which they were probably to be exercised by a body which was not a professional court of appeal and was not bound to act exactly as one nor likely to do so. Other relevant factors include the burden of a previous finding, expeditiousness and costs.

---

79 But see *Hung Ly v. Toronto (City) Chief Building Official* (1988), 39 M.P.L.R. 103 (Ont. Dist. Ct.) where an initial application for a building permit was denied. No appeal was taken from the denial, but subsequently a second application was filed. That application was also denied, and the denial was appealed. The court found that this was not an abuse of process.

80 (1979), 96 D.L.R. (3d) 14 (S.C.C.).

81 See *Chad Investments Ltd. v. Longson Tammets & Denton Real Estate Ltd.*, *supra* note 78 at 632; *Madison Development Corp. v. St. Albert (Town)*, [1975] 6 W.W.R. 345 (Alta. S.C.); *Alberta (Minister of Education) v. C.S.A. of A.* (1976), 70 D.L.R. (3d) 696 (Alta. C.A.); *Spalding, Re* (1955), 16 W.W.R. 157 (B.C. C.A.); *R. v. Postmaster-Gen., Ex parte Carmichael*, [1928] 1 K.B. 291 at 299 (D.C.); *BP Canada Energy Co. v. Alberta (Energy & Utilities Board)*, 2003 ABQB 875 (Alta. Q.B.), leave to appeal allowed 2004 ABCA 32 (Alta. C.A. [In Chambers]); compare *Alberta Giftwares Ltd. v. Calgary (City)* (1979), 10 Alta. L.R. (2d) 221 (Alta. Q.B.).

82 See how the various courts dealt this question with *Harelkin*, *supra* note 80.

83 *Ibid.* at 51. A similar list was adopted by the Alberta Court of Appeal in *Edith Lake Service Ltd. v. Edmonton (City)* (1981), 20 Alta. L.R. (2d) 1 (Alta. C.A.), leave to appeal to S.C.C. refused at (1982), 42 N.R. 358 (note) (S.C.C.).

On the one hand, the courts have concluded that it would be unfair to prevent judicial review where the applicant was not a party to the proceedings in question, had not received notice of the decision, and therefore could not in practice take advantage of the statutory right of appeal;[84] or where the material which would be available to the appellate body would be less complete than that before the court in an application for *certiorari*;[85] where the appeal procedure did not provide for a hearing *de novo*;[86] where the issues raised in judicial review are broader than those which could be raised at an appeal;[87] and possibly in circumstances of bias or improperly obtained evidence which would eviscerate the appeal.[88] Similar questions were asked in determining whether an "appeal" under the *Child Welfare Act* was sufficient to oust the Court's *parens patriae* jurisdiction.[89] By contrast, the courts have held that the following factors do not prevent the appeal route from being effective, adequate and exclusive: difficulty in getting a lawyer within the appeal period;[90] being lulled into not appealing because legislative or administrative changes would be made to permit the application to be granted;[91] or the mere fact that the original administrator made an error of law.[92]

On the other hand, difficult conceptual problems arise if there is a jurisdictional defect in the administrative proceedings from which an appeal lies. In the first place, it may be extremely efficient and speedy to use judicial review to identify and determine the effect of a jurisdictional error, particularly if it involves a preliminary or collateral matter so that the delegate has no jurisdiction whatever. To force a party to exhaust his or her statutory appeals instead of applying for judicial review not only undercuts the *ultra vires* principle by breathing life into a void decision, it may well delay the clarifi-

---

84   See *Canadian Industries Ltd. v. Edmonton (Development Appeal Board)* (1969), 71 W.W.R. 635 (Alta. C.A.); *Harvie v. Alberta (Provincial Planning Board)* (1977), 5 A.R. 445 (Alta. T.D.).

85   *Solicitor, Re* (1967), 60 W.W.R. 705 (Alta. C.A.), leave to appeal refused (1967), 66 W.W.R. 427n (S.C.C.).

86   *Fooks v. Assn. of Architects (Alberta)* (1982), 21 Alta. L.R. (2d) 306 (Alta. Q.B.).

87   *Sterzik v. Beattie* (1985), 39 Alta. L.R. (2d) 375 (Alta. Q.B.), reversed (1985), 76 A.R. 112 (Alta. C.A.); *Eric D. McLaine Construction Ltd. v. Southport (Community)* (1990), 257 A.P.R. 158 (P.E.I. T.D.).

88   *Obiter* in *Rozander v. Alberta Energy Resources Conservation Board* (1978), 8 Alta. L.R. (2d) 203 (Alta. C.A.), leave to appeal to S.C.C. refused (1979), 14 A.R. 540 (note) (S.C.C.). See *Connor v. Law Society (British Columbia)*, [1980] 4 W.W.R. 638 (B.C. S.C.) for a case involving an allegation of bias, and where there was some doubt as to the existence of an appeal in any event.

89   *M. (B.) v. Alberta* (1985), 37 Alta. L.R. (2d) 52 (Alta. Q.B.).

90   Though note that this may cause the court to extend the appeal period if it can do so under the legislation. See also *Rozander v. Alberta Energy Resources Conservation Board, supra* note 88; *North American Montessori Academy Ltd. v. Edmonton (Development Appeal Board)* (1977), 7 A.R. 39 (Alta. C.A.).

91   The *Montessori* case, *ibid.*

92   *Saratoga Processing Co., Re* (1979), 10 Alta. L.R. (2d) 193 (Alta. Q.B.). Compare *Winter v. Newfoundland (Residential Tenancies Board)* (1980), 31 Nfld. & P.E.I.R. 148 (Nfld. T.D.), where the court held that the jurisdictional nature of the alleged error committed by the delegate constituted a special circumstance for permitting judicial review rather than forcing the citizen through the appellate process.

cation of an important point of law.[93] The same argument for expeditious judicial review can be made – with less force – when it is alleged that the statutory delegate has committed an error (like a breach of natural justice)[94] which causes it to lose the jurisdiction which it undoubtedly had. In such a circumstance, it may well be the case that a robust right of appeal would provide ample opportunity to correct any such error made by the original delegate.[95] At least, this reasoning was accepted by the majority of the Supreme Court of Canada in the *Harelkin* case to deny judicial review when there was a right of appeal from a decision made in breach of natural justice.[96] By contrast, the minority of the court dissented strongly on this point, as demonstrated by the following quotation from Dickson J.:[97]

> This point raises the general issue of the discretionary nature of *certiorari*. In this context the authorities ... draw a distinction between jurisdictional and non-jurisdictional error and between a right of appeal to an administrative or domestic tribunal and a right of appeal to the Courts. Generally speaking, the rule is that, if the error is jurisdictional, *certiorari* will issue *ex debito justitiae*, but if the error is error

---

93 Of course, it may be that the delegate will be able (and will agree) to state a case to the courts at the outset, instead of compelling the parties to complete a hearing before it (and perhaps other statutory appeals) before finally being able to get the matter before a court, if an appeal is provided to the court: see the *Committee for Justice & Liberty v. Canada (National Energy Board)* (1976), [1978] 1 S.C.R. 369 (S.C.C.), for an example of the use of this sensible procedure. For an example of the opposite approach, see the *Saratoga* case, *ibid.*

94 Beetz J. heretically suggests in *Harelkin, supra* note 80, that a breach of the principles of natural justice may not constitute a jurisdictional error. This reasoning is insupportable, and has been criticized by D.P. Jones, "Discretionary Refusal of Judicial Review in Administrative Law" (1981) 19 Alta. L. Rev. 483 at 485-87.

95 On the other hand, it also has the effect of expropriating the appellant's right to two proper hearings. Using a criminal law paradigm, a procedural irregularity at trial is grounds for appeal, which would result in the whole matter being remitted for a complete re-hearing to the trial court, from which a further appeal on the merits would lie to the court of appeal. In *Harelkin, ibid.*, the problem was that the appellate body not only would be unlikely to understand the procedural defects of the first proceedings, but would not then remit the matter back for re-hearing by the Council. Rather, the appeal body would simply dispatch the case on its own merits, thereby expropriating the student of his right to two complete hearings.

96 See also *North American Montessori Academy Ltd. v. Edmonton Development Appeal Board* (1977), 7 A.R. 39 (Alta. C.A.); *Dierks v. Altermatt*, [1918] 1 W.W.R. 719 (Alta. C.A.); *R. v. s. (G.)*, [1959] S.C.R. 638 (S.C.C.); *Cathcart v. Lowery* (1962), 37 W.W.R. 612 (Sask. C.A.), *Rozander v. Alberta Energy Resources Conservation Board* (1978), 8 Alta. L.R. (2d) 203, 93 D.L.R. (3d) 271, 13 A.R. 461 (Alta. C.A.), leave to appeal refused (1979), 14 A.R. 540 (note) (S.C.C.); *Saratoga Processing Co., Re* (1979), 10 Alta. L.R. (2d) 193 (Alta. Q.B.); and *Danyluk v. Ainsworth Technologies Inc.*, [2001] 2 S.C.R. 460 (S.C.C.).

97 (1979), 96 D.L.R. (3d) 14 at 27 (S.C.C.). This comment was explicitly adopted by the Saskatchewan Court of Appeal as the rationale for not refusing judicial review in an instance where the statutory body was found to have acted completely without jurisdiction: *Goertz v. College of Physicians & Surgeons (Saskatchewan)*, [1989] 6 W.W.R. 11 (Sask. C.A.). There the Court, after reciting the quotation from Dickson J., went on to note:

> While the majority [in *Harelkin*] refused to recognize the distinction between errors within and without jurisdiction, it is not apparent that it would have reached the same result had the tribunal there acted throughout without jurisdiction.

in law, then in the absence of a privative clause, *certiorari* may issue. The discretion is broad when the error is non-jurisdictional and there is an appeal to the Courts, but virtually disappears when the error is jurisdictional and the right of appeal, if any, is to an administrative or domestic tribunal sitting in a purely appellate role.

Professor de Smith expresses the point admirably ...:

> Nor will a person aggrieved by an invalid decision be required first to exhaust administrative or domestic appellate remedies as a condition precedent to impugning that decision in the courts.

The loosely-formulated American doctrine of exhaustion of remedies has simply no Canadian or English counterpart ...

Accordingly, the argument is about the width of the court's discretion to refuse judicial review of a jurisdictional error in a delegate's decision if an adequate alternative remedy is provided in the legislation. It is important to note again that the policy of refusing judicial review where there is an adequate right of appeal is not an inflexible rule of law but is the result of the court's discretion to refuse certain remedies. Further, the applicability of the policy does not depend upon the presence of a privative clause in the legislation to protect the decision from which the appeal is to be taken,[98] which would clearly indicate the legislature's intention to provide the appeal instead of judicial review. Nevertheless, the implied legislative intention to oust judicial review must underlie the existence of the court's discretion to refuse judicial review even where there is no privative clause to highlight the exclusivity of the appeal. Yet, this very assumption points to the fallacy inherent in the discretionary nature of the policy. For either the legislature intended the appeal to be exclusive, or it did not; either judicial review should be precluded in all cases where there is an appeal, or in none.

How can one appeal from a void decision? The courts have dealt with this intellectual conundrum by holding that a statutory right of appeal must be intended to permit an appeal from all determinations, whether valid or void. As Beetz J. said for the majority in *Harelkin*:[99]

> [E]ven if it can be said that the decision of the council committee was a nullity, I believe it was still appealable to the senate committee for the simple reason that the senate committee was given by statute the power to hear and decide upon appeals from the decisions of the council, whether or not such decisions were null.

and referred[100] to the earlier decision of the court in *Provincial Secretary of Prince Edward Island v. Egan*:

---

98   For example, see *Pringle v. Fraser*, [1972] S.C.R. 821 (S.C.C.).
99   *Supra* note 97 at 49.
100   *Ibid.* at 50 (quoting Sir Lyman Duff C.J.C.).

The fact that the County Judge has acted without jurisdiction does not, in my opinion, affect this right of appeal. Once the conclusion is reached that the section intends to give an appeal to the Supreme Court ... I can see no reason for limiting the scope of the appeal in such a way as to exclude questions of jurisdiction. As the Attorney-General observed in the course of his argument, lawyers are more familiar with the practice of dealing with questions of jurisdiction raised by proceedings by way of *certiorari* and prohibition. A tribunal exercising a limited statutory jurisdiction has no authority to give a binding decision upon its own jurisdiction and where it wrongfully assumes jurisdiction it follows, as a general rule, that, since what he has done is null, there is nothing to appeal from. But here we have a statute and this is only pertinent on the point of the meaning and effect of the statute.

It has always seemed to me that the proceeding by way of appeal would be the most convenient way of questioning the judgment of any judicial tribunal whose judgment is alleged to be wrong, whether in point of wrongful assumption of jurisdiction, or otherwise. There is no appeal, of course, except by statute and, I repeat, the question arising upon this point is entirely a question of the scope and effect of this statute.

This approach clears away a great deal of pointless abstruse learning about whether there can be an appeal from a void decision,[101] and permits one to focus on whether the appeal is or is not a more efficient way of correcting errors than judicial review.

12. Restrictions on Collateral Attacks Where Appeal Available

The Supreme Court of Canada has largely – but not entirely – restricted the ability to make a collateral attack on a previous administrative order. Previously, one could simply ignore an order or decision which was null and void (for whatever reason) and plead that nullity as a defence in any enforcement proceedings.

In *R. v. Consolidated Maybrun Mines Ltd.*,[102] the Ontario Ministry of the Environment issued an order requiring the respondent to clean up various aspects of its mine site. It ignored the order, and did not appeal the order to the Environmental Appeal Board. In due course, the Ministry charged the respon-

---

101 For an excellent discussion of this problem, see H.W.R. Wade, "Unlawful Administrative Action: Void or Voidable?" Part I at (1967) 83 L.Q.R. 499; Part II at (1968) 84 L.Q.R. 95; and G.L. Peiris, "Natural Justice and Degrees of Invalidity of Administrative Action" [1983] P.L. 634.

102 [1998] 1 S.C.R. 706 (S.C.C.), affirming (1996), 5 Admin. L.R. (3d) 288 (Ont. C.A.), leave to appeal allowed (1996), 110 C.C.C. (3d) vi (S.C.C.).

dent with failing to comply with the order. In these proceedings, the respondent pleaded the invalidity of the original order. The court of first instance ruled that it could look at the original order, concluded that only part of it was valid, and fined the respondent only with respect to that part. On appeal to the General Division of the Ontario Court, it held that the trial court had exceeded its jurisdiction and effectively encroached on the functions of the Environmental Appeal Board. The Ontario Court of Appeal and the Supreme Court of Canada upheld this ruling.

Madam Justice L'Heureux-Dubé, writing for the unanimous court, observed that the question of whether a penal court may determine the validity of an administrative order on a collateral basis depends on the statute under which the order was made – in other words, on the intention of the Legislature. She ruled that the best way to decide this question, taking into account both the integrity of the administrative process and the interests of litigants, is to focus the analysis on the legislature's intention as to the appropriate forum. It must be presumed that the legislature did not intend to deprive a person against whom an order is directed of an opportunity to assert his or her rights. One must look at (1) the wording of the statute from which the power to issue the order derives, the purpose of the legislation, the availability of an appeal, the nature of the collateral attack taking into account the appeal tribunal's expertise and *raison d'être*,[103] and the penalty on a conviction for failing to comply with the order. This is an important – but not exhaustive – catalogue of the factors for determining the legislature's intention. Using that catalogue in this case, Her Ladyship concluded that the legislature did not intend a person like the respondent to be able to make a collateral attack on the Ministry order, but rather contemplated that the affected party would take advantage of the appeal mechanisms provided by the Act. Permitting a collateral attack would encourage conduct contrary to the Act's objectives (what collateral attack wouldn't?), and the appeal mechanism under the Act was adequate and the Board could fully remedy any deficiency there might be in the original order.

Finally, it was important to Her Ladyship that the nature of the penal consequences were just a fine – with the implication that a more drastic penalty might incline the court more readily to permitting a collateral attack.

Like its decisions in *Pezim* and *Southam* dealing with standard of review, the Court has not set out a categorical rule, but rather (1) referred to a panoply of possible factors it might take into account, which will vary in different cases, making it very difficult for counsel to give advice to clients in advance of litigation, thereby increasing both uncertainty and the courts' workload; and (2) eked out its understanding of the intention of the Legislature – which, however, had not seen fit to include anything about this issue in the legislation itself. Query: Will legislative draftsmen now be tempted to put something into statutes specifically dealing with the ability to controvert an order collaterally?

---

103   Note the reference to both expertise and *raison d'être*, not just expertise. Is this a recognition that the claim to expertise has been coming under sustained attack, with considerable attention to characterizing the precise issue about which the delegate might (or might not) be said to have expertise?

Perhaps a privative clause applying to collateral attacks on penal orders? To what extent is the existence – and adequacy? – of an appeal mechanism an absolutely necessary underpinning for the Court's analysis?

Perplexingly, Her Ladyship also specifically stated that the nature of the collateral attack – whether alleging a lack of jurisdiction *ab initio* or a subsequent loss of jurisdiction – was irrelevant, because the question was to identify on whom the legislature intended to confer jurisdiction to hear and determine the question raised. Does this comment pose a problem under section 96 of the Constitution Act, along the lines raised in *Crévier*? How does it square with the realization in *Syndicat* that curial deference cannot apply to jurisdictional defects, even when "not patently unreasonable" was so in vogue?

Is this just a refinement of the rule (used, for example, in *Harelkin*) that judicial review is not available where there is an adequate right of appeal – with the refinement that now a person must actually take the appeal, rather than wait for enforcement action to occur? As the French saying goes, *Les absents ont toujours tort!*

A similar result was reached in *R. v. Al Klippert Ltd.*,[104] which involved a stop-use order issued by the development officer of the City of Calgary with respect to a gravel pit. The owner thought that the pit had been a valid nonconforming use going back to an era before it had been annexed to the City. Consequently, the owner ignored the order, and did not attempt to appeal to the Development Appeal Board or to the Court of Appeal on a point of law or jurisdiction. When charged with failing to comply with the order, the respondent submitted that the predecessor municipality had granted its predecessor valid authority to operate the gravel pit, so the stop-order could not be valid. The provincial court judge accepted this, and acquitted the respondent. The Court of Queen's Bench reversed this ruling, but the Court of Appeal restored the acquittal. Cross-referencing the *Consolidated Maybrun* decision (and noting that the appeal process was public and adversarial, and afforded the affected party the opportunity to present his or her point of view and assert his or her rights and be informed of the reasons for the Board's decision), the Supreme Court of Canada again held that the trial judge lacked jurisdiction to determine the merits of the order.

However, *Danyluk v. Ainsworth Technologies Inc.*,[105] is an example of a subsequent case where the Supreme Court of Canada applied the factors from *Consolidated Maybrun* to permit a lawsuit for wrongful dismissal to continue, even though an inspector under the Employment Standards legislation had already made a final and binding decision about the amount of pay to which the plaintiff was entitled.

On a related topic, in a pair of recent decisions, the Supreme Court of Canada has used the concept of abuse of process to prevent statutory delegates from hearing attempts to relitigate matters which have been previously decided

---

104 [1998] 1 S.C.R. 737 (S.C.C.), reversing (1996), 5 Admin. L.R. (3d) 274 (Alta. C.A.), leave to appeal allowed (1997), 214 N.R. 160 (note) (S.C.C.), reversing (1993), 146 A.R. 211 (Alta. Q.B.).

105 [2001] 2 S.C.R. 460 (S.C.C.).

by the courts: *Toronto (City) v. C.U.P.E., Local 79*,[106] and *Toronto (City) v. C.U.P.E., Local 79.*[107]

13. Conclusion

The discussion in this chapter indicates that our legislators have not developed a comprehensive philosophy concerning the desirability and establishment of appeals from administrative decisions. It is apparent that there is no rationale to whether an appeal lies to another statutory tribunal or whether it lies to a court (and, if so, to which level of court), whether the appeal is to be *de novo* (with or without the appellate body knowing the result of the lower decision) or limited to a question of law or jurisdiction, and what standard of review the legislature intended the court to apply when dealing with the appeal. This state of affairs is unsatisfactory. The legislative branch should give considerably more attention to whether there should be an appeal, to whom it is to lie, and upon what basis it is to be heard; and these decisions should be based on discernible policy considerations and should constitute a rational scheme.

The nature of modern society necessitates that legislators will delegate a wide range of governmental powers simply because the process of modern government cannot be handled in any other way. Thus, persons other than judicial officers are given the responsibility of making decisions which affect people's lives in significant ways. In most cases, the decisions made by these delegates affect people quite directly, and range from minutiae which hardly make a ripple on the consciousness of the citizenry to comprehensive legislation which directly affects their lives and livelihoods and which may be the subject of intensive public and media attention. Within this vast range, the legislators must decide whether there is to be an appeal to another level of decision-maker. Generally speaking, the more directly an administrative decision affects a person's life, the greater the moral claim to a right of appeal, and the more likely that one will in fact be provided by statute. As the Special Committee on Boards and Tribunals reported in 1965:[108]

> Nevertheless, there is embedded in the democratic principles of the administration of justice a right to appeal by a person who considers himself aggrieved, and this Committee is of the view that this principle should be more fully recognised in administrative law than it is at present. It would give citizens who are affected by the decisions of a tribunal a right comparable to the one they have traditionally had in respect of judgments of the Courts.

However, this democratic principle is difficult to apply to administrative agencies which have been created precisely to keep matters out of the courts.

---

106 2003 SCC 63 (S.C.C.).
107 2003 SCC 64 (S.C.C.).
108 *Supra* note 60 at 12.

On the one hand, any presumption that the delegate has specialized knowledge implies that an appeal should go to someone else who also possesses that specialized knowledge, and not to a generalist judge. On the other hand, judges are specialists in the area of errors of law and jurisdiction. Indeed, this has always been the role of the superior courts. No statutory delegate can be said to have greater competence in this area. Accordingly, there should be no requirement upon an applicant to appeal through the hierarchy of statutory appeals on a question of law or jurisdiction before gaining access to a court which is the proper forum for such questions. Rather, it should be possible to have such legal questions determined immediately by a court (whether using traditional judicial review or through a specific legislative right of appeal to the courts on such questions). Further, such legal determinations should be done preferably at the Queen's Bench level, which would be simple, expeditious, and efficient, and would also allow for a normal further appeal – perhaps only with leave – to the Court of Appeal.

There can be no reasoned argument against such judicial review of legal questions. There can be no support for any argument that a statutory tribunal should be allowed to transgress its jurisdictional bounds with impunity or should be able to determine the law wrongly, nor that another administrative tribunal is better able to judge such legal matters than a court of law.

Appeals on the merits of decisions should, however, lie to other statutory bodies and not to the courts. (In any given case, the legislature might determine that a court is the proper forum for an appeal, perhaps because of the prestige or perceived independence of judges; but it is suggested that this would be the exception and not the rule and that it would be done after proper consideration of the subject area in question and not, as it now appears, by default.) In principle, appeals on the merits would progress up the statutory appeal chain. Whether such appeals would be strictly *de novo* or on the merits should be determined in every case. Proper considerations might include whether the first decision-maker was only one person or a multiple-member board, his or her (or their) competence, the specialized nature of the decision being made, what procedure is to be used in reaching the decision, whether reasons are to be given, and how directly a person might be affected by the decision.

This then makes some sense of the problem of "appealing" a void decision. A decision that is void for error of law or lack of jurisdiction would not be appealed under this scheme but would be reviewed judicially instead. If there has been an error, the decision will be quashed and remitted to the tribunal to be made again properly, according to law. If there has not been an error of law, then the tribunal's decision will stand and the applicant may exercise his or her right of a statutory appeal on the merits. This would particularly make sense of the present absurdity of requiring that an applicant who alleges that a tribunal has made an error on a preliminary point of law exhaust the statutory route of appeals on the merits.

This is obviously an area for considerable further thought and rationalization by the legislature when it creates administrative schemes for implementing governmental objectives.

14. Selected Bibliography

Giles, J., "Should there be Judicial Review where there is an Adequate Right of Appeal?" (1983) 43 Revue du Barreau 497; also published as a chapter in Judicial Review of Administrative Rulings, (Montreal: Les Editions Yvon Blais, Inc., 1983).

Jones, D.P., "Discretionary Refusal of Judicial Review in Administrative Law" (1981) 19 Alta. L. Rev. 483.

JUSTICE – All Souls Review of Administrative Law in the United Kingdom, *Administrative Justice: Some Necessary Reforms* (1988), c. 5 on "Ombudsmen".

Katz, L., "Australian Federal Administrative Law Reform" (1980) 58 Can. Bar Rev. 341.

Lawrence, J.E., "Powers of the Governor in Council over Administrative Tribunals: Appeals and Directions" (1987-88) 1 C.J.A.L.P. 327.

Marshall M. & Reif L., "The Ombudsman: Maladministration and alternative dispute resolution" (1995) Alta. L.R. 215.

Rankin, M., "The Cabinets and the Courts: Political Tribunals and Judicial Tribunals" (1988-89) 2 C.J.A.L.P. 302.

Sprague, G., "Thirty years After the Franks' Committee Report – Alberta's Report Card" (1989) 5 Admin. L.J. 66.

Williams, D.G.T., "The Council on Tribunals: The First Twenty-Five Years" [1984] P.L. 73.

15

The Prerogative Remedies[1]

1. Introduction

Although a number of jurisdictions have created an "application for judicial review" as the standard procedure for challenging illegal governmental

---

1 This chapter has been updated by Justice Frans Slatter of the Court of Queen's Bench of Alberta.

actions,[2] the adoption of this uniform procedure does not really constitute a new substantive remedy. Although one speaks of "an application for judicial review in the nature of *certiorari*" (or "... in the nature of *mandamus*" or "... a declaration"), it is still necessary to examine the scope, availability and limitations of the various prerogative and private law remedies which have traditionally been available to obtain judicial review, even though there is now a uniform procedure for obtaining those remedies. This chapter examines the prerogative remedies; Chapter 16 looks at private law remedies which are used in administrative law.

The prerogative remedies have an ancient history,[3] and are the primary vehicles through which the superior courts review the legality of government actions. The five prerogative remedies in use today are *habeas corpus, certiorari*, prohibition, *mandamus* and *quo warranto*.[4] Each is used for a specific purpose. *Habeas corpus* requires a person to identify some lawful authority for detaining the applicant. *Certiorari* permits the court to review the legality of the decision of a delegate and to quash it if defective. Prohibition is used anticipatorily to prevent a delegate from committing certain kinds of errors. *Mandamus* compels a delegate to perform statutory duties imposed upon it. Finally, *quo warranto* is used to determine the right of the respondent to occupy a public office.

The "prerogative" nature of the remedies derives from the fact that they were issued by the Crown to control the actions of its servants taken in its

---

2   Ontario was the first Canadian jurisdiction to reform its procedure: See the *Judicial Review Procedure Act*, S.O. 1971, c. 48 [now R.S.O. 1990, c. J.1], reproduced in Appendix 3. Many other jurisdictions have more or less adopted the Ontario model: New Zealand, *Judicature Amendment Act, 1972*; N.S. by amending its Rules of Court in 1972; B.C., *Judicial Review Procedure Act*, S.B.C. 1976, c. 25 [now R.S.B.C. 1996, c. 241]; England, by an amendment in 1977 to Order 53 of the *Rules of the Supreme Court*, subsequently confirmed by statute in 1981 (c. 54); Alberta, by amendments to the Rules of Court in 1987, reproduced in Appendix 4 (authorized by S.A. 1987, c. 17). Section 28 of the 1970 version of the *Federal Court Act* created an "application for judicial review", but it was a more substantive reform; the 1990 amendments (effective in 1992) made the federal procedure accord more with the current provincial models. For a more detailed discussion of the reforms, see Chapter 15 of the first edition of this work.

   For a discussion of the procedure for obtaining judicial review in Quebec, see G. Steele, "Judicial Review in Quebec: A Primer on Evocation for Common Law Jurists" (1990-91) 4 C.J.A.L.P. 129.; D. Lemieux, "Supervisory Judicial Control of Federal and Provincial Public Authorities in Quebec" (1979) 17 Osgoode Hall L.J. 133, and *Société d'énergie de la Baie James c. Noël*, [2001] 2 S.C.R. 207 (S.C.C.) at para. 27.

3   See J.M. Evans, *de Smith's Judicial Review of Administrative Law*, 4th ed. (London: Stevens & Sons Ltd., 1980), App. 1, for a historical description of the various prerogative writs. See also the bibliography to this Chapter.

4   de Smith identifies three other writs which are probably now obsolete: (a) *de non procedendo rege inconsulto* to prevent the common law courts from dealing with matters in which the King had an interest; (b) *scire facias* for the purpose of rescinding royal grants, charters and franchises; and (c) *ne exeat regno* to prevent subjects leaving the Kingdom: *ibid.* at 585.

name.[5] In time, the Crown delegated these remedies to the superior courts. Royal writs[6] were used to compel the administrators to come before the courts to justify their actions. Traditionally, the proper nomenclature for a prerogative remedy was "*R. v. Delegate; Ex parte Applicant*". In the first stage of what was a two-step procedure, the applicant applied for the writ *ex parte*, based on an affidavit indicating the applicant's knowledge, information or belief about the invalidity of the delegate's decision.[7] The writ was issued if there was a *prima facie* case of illegality (although this was not required if the Crown itself was the applicant).[8] The delegate was required by the writ to come to court to justify its actions. The second stage of the procedure involved an application at which the court determined the issue of illegality. If illegality was demonstrated, the court would generally issue an order for the respective prerogative remedy. However, the court always retained the discretion to refuse to issue such an order even if the case was made out by the applicant.[9]

In Alberta, this two-step procedure was abolished many years ago.[10] It was replaced with a one-step procedure involving a notice of motion.[11] The rules still provide that no actual *writ* is issued; rather, an order in the nature of the prerogative relief sought is granted.

As indicated above, a further significant procedural reform was implemented in Alberta in 1987 when the "application for judicial review" was created as the uniform procedure for obtaining the traditional prerogative remedies as well as two private law remedies (injunctions and declarations)[12]

---

5 Because the writs issue in the name of the Crown, they are not available against the Crown: *R. v. British Columbia (Minister of Finance)*, [1935] S.C.R. 278 at 285 (S.C.C.); *R. v. Lords Commissioners of the Treasury* (1872), L.R. 7 Q.B. 387 (Eng. Q.B.); *Alberta Mortgage & Housing Corp. v. Hindmarsh* (1987), 77 A.R. 263 (Alta. C.A.); *O.P.S.E.U. v. Ontario (Attorney General)* (1995), 26 O.R. (3d) 740 (Ont. Div. Ct.). But see the discussion at note 68 *infra* and in Chapter 16 about who constitutes "the Crown".

6 We sometimes still refer to the "prerogative writs" when we really mean the corresponding modern orders issued by the court. See Alberta *Rules of Court*, Rules 738(2) and 753.04.

7 Because the writ was the first step in a two-step procedure, it was not a final order. Therefore, the affidavit did not have to be on the applicant's personal knowledge but could be on information and belief. Query: whether the conversion in Alberta to a one-step procedure which might result in a final order makes R. 305(1) applicable so that the affidavit must be based on the applicant's knowledge, not merely on information and belief. D.C. McDonald J. adopted this view in *Alberta v. Beaver (County No. 9)*, [1982] 4 W.W.R. 344 (Alta. Q.B.), reversed on another point [1984] 4 W.W.R. 371 (Alta. C.A.). See also *I.B.E.W., Local 424 v. TNL Industrial Contractors Ltd.* (1998), 61 Alta. L.R. (3d) 60 (Alta. Q.B.); *Moldeveanu v. Canada (Minister of Citizenship & Immigration* (1999), 235 N.R. 192 (Fed. C.A.).

8 Because the Crown had a right to the initial writ – as opposed to the final order – as of right. See D.P. Jones, "Comment on *P.P.G. Industries Canada Ltd. v. A.G. Canada*" (1977) 55 Can. Bar Rev. 718, for a discussion of this distinction.

9 See section 7 of this chapter, below.

10 Under the 1914 R. 824, borrowed in turn from Ontario's 1897 R. 1294. English Order 53 maintains the two-step procedure.

11 Not an *Originating* Notice. Hence, only two days' notice needed to be given instead of ten, and no fee was payable on filing the notice with the court.

12 These private law remedies are discussed in Chapter 16.

which are frequently used in administrative law.[13] The purpose for creating the new procedure for obtaining judicial review was two-fold. First, different rules governed the availability of different remedies, resulting in differences with respect to standing to commence proceedings, the time within which different remedies had to be sought and the grounds which had to be proved in order to obtain the different remedies. Although more than one remedy may have been available in certain circumstances, the remedies were not completely fungible and care had to be taken to choose the correct one. Secondly, an application for one or more prerogative remedies could not be joined with an action at private law.[14] Notwithstanding the implementation of this significant procedural change, the substantive law relating to the remedies has generally not changed. Therefore, it is still important to understand the scope, advantages and limitations of the different prerogative remedies.

Despite the procedural reforms implemented in Alberta and elsewhere, limitations continue to exist in obtaining judicial review to correct illegal governmental action. In the first place, it is necessary in our federal system to determine whether the federal courts or a provincial superior court has authority to issue a remedy to supervise the particular delegate's actions. Secondly, while the Crown always has the right to apply for a prerogative remedy, the standing of a private person to do so may be problematic. Thirdly, the courts have discretion to refuse to issue a prerogative remedy, even where the applicant has otherwise demonstrated entitlement thereto.

2. *Habeas Corpus*

Habeas corpus has probably the greatest constitutional importance of all of the prerogative remedies.[15] The writ is mentioned in the Magna Carta and has become synonymous with legal systems in which the state must justify the detention of citizens to the courts.

In administrative law, *habeas corpus* is used in cases dealing with detention of would-be immigrants,[16] prisoners,[17] children,[18] and mentally incapaci-

---

13 The procedural changes were proposed in 1984 in a Report by the Institute of Law Research and Reform (now the Alberta Law Reform Institute) entitled *Judicial Review of Administrative Action: Application for Judicial Review* (Report No. 40). These proposals were discussed in Chapter 15 of the First Edition of this work. The reforms which were actually implemented differ somewhat from the proposals.

14 *O.C.A.W., Local 9-14 v. Polymer Corp.*, [1966] 1 O.R. 774 (Ont. H.C.); and see also *McCarthy v. Calgary Roman Catholic Seperate School District No. 1*, [1979] 4 W.W.R. 725 at 730 (Alta. T.D.), affirmed (1979), 145 D.L.R. (3d) 765 (Alta. C.A.).

15 See J.M. Evans, *de Smith's Judicial Review of Administrative Law, supra* note 3, Appendix 2, for a detailed discussion of *habeas corpus*; as well as D.A.C. Harvey, *The Law of Habeas Corpus in Canada* (Toronto: Butterworths, 1974); R.J. Sharpe, *The Law of Habeas Corpus*, 2d ed. (Oxford: Clarendon Press, 1989); and M. Cohen (1938) 16 Can. Bar Rev. 92, and (1940) 18 Can. Bar Rev. 10 and 172. *Habeas Corpus* is now one of the protected legal rights set out in section 10 of the *Charter of Rights and Freedoms*.

16 *R. v. Pentonville Prison Governor* (1973), [1974] A.C. 18 (U.K. H.L.); *De Marigny v. Langlais*, [1948] S.C.C. 155 (S.C.C.). In immigration matters the provincial superior courts often defer to the federal courts where there is an equally effective remedy available: *Reza*

tated persons.[19] The issue of *habeas corpus* quashes the illegal detention of the applicant.

In reviewing such detentions, the courts review for errors of law or jurisdiction that make the decision to detain *ultra vires*: *habeas corpus*, like the other judicial review remedies, is not an appeal on the merits. In *Armah v. Ghana*,[20] the House of Lords confirmed that *habeas corpus* extends to include errors of law on the face of the record. The courts have generally treated the issue of the order as not being discretionary once a defect has been found in the legality of the detention of the applicant. However, the best view is likely that the courts still retain discretion to refuse *habeas corpus* in an appropriate case, although they may not be quick to exercise this discretion.[21]

Often it is necessary for an applicant to seek *habeas corpus* together with some other remedy, such as *certiorari-in-aid*, so that the basis for a detention can be reviewed and quashed.[22] Standing to apply for *habeas corpus* may be granted to the person detained, to someone acting on his or her authority if he or she cannot act,[23] or to someone acting without the authority of the person so detained.[24] The burden of proof is on the respondent, who will normally be

---

v. *Canada*, [1994] 2 S.C.R. 394 (S.C.C.); *Peiroo v. Canada (Minister of Employment & Immigration)* (1989), 69 O.R. (2d) 253, 38 Admin. L.R. 247 (Ont. C.A.), leave to appeal refused (1989), 104 N.R. 319 (note) (S.C.C.).

17 *Cardinal v. Kent Institution*, [1985] 2 S.C.R. 643 (S.C.C.); *R. v. Miller*, [1985] 2 S.C.R. 613 (S.C.C.); *Morin v. Canada (National Special Handling Unit Review Committee)*, [1985] 2 S.C.R. 662 (S.C.C.); *R. v. Mitchell* (1975), [1976] 2 S.C.R. 570 (S.C.C.); *Hicks v. R.* (1981), [1982] 1 W.W.R. 71 (Alta. C.A.).

18 *Stawiarski, Re* (1970), 13 D.L.R. (3d) 507 (N.B. C.A.); *D., Ex parte* (1970), [1971] 1 O.R. 311 (Ont. H.C.); *Berg v. Young* (1982), 22 Alta. L.R. (2d) 235, 140 D.L.R. (3d) 451 (Alta. Q.B.).

19 *Brooks, Re* (1961), 38 W.W.R. 51 (Alta. S.C.); *Perry v. Steele* (1959), 129 C.C.C. 206 (P.E.I. C.A.); *Re S-C (Mental Patient: habeas corpus)*, [1996] Q.B. 599 (C.A.).

20 [1968] A.C. 192 (U.K. H.L.).

21 It may be academic whether this is an exception to the general rule that all prerogative remedies are discretionary, or is merely a strong guideline as to how the courts will exercise their discretion. The Ontario Court of Appeal in *Peiroo v. Canada, supra* note 16, exercised its discretion not to grant the remedy and referred an immigration matter to the federal Court. See also *Armaly v. Canada (Correctional Service)* (2001), 299 A.R. 188 (Alta. C.A.), leave to appeal refused (2002), 301 N.R. 390 (note) (S.C.C.) and *Hickey v. Kent Institution* (2003), 176 B.C.A.C. 272 (B.C. C.A.) where the courts declined to grant *habeas corpus* as other appeal remedies were available.

22 Historically, an application for *habeas corpus* did not cause a record to be filed with the court; it was necessary to apply for *certiorari* for this purpose. Hence the development of the use of *certiorari-in-aid*. This remedy caused some difficulties immediately after the creation of the Federal Courts, in situations where a federal authority was the respondent. This was because *certiorari* is the only remedy available in the Federal Courts, whereas *habeas corpus* is generally only available in provincial superior courts. The law was eventually clarified to allow an application for *habeas corpus* with *certiorari-in-aid* to proceed in the provincial superior courts: *R. v. Miller, supra* note 17. Under R. 753.14, the Alberta Court may require a return of the record even in an application for judicial review that is not in the nature of *certiorari*.

23 For example, in cases of legal or mental incapacity by someone with a special interest such as the parent or guardian.

24 D.A.C. Harvey, *The Law of Habeas Corpus in Canada, supra* note 15 at 76, 93; R.J. Sharpe, *The Law of Habeas Corpus, supra* note 15.

the person who is actually detaining the applicant. Unlike the other prerogative remedies, *habeas corpus* lies against anyone, and not just someone purporting to act under statutory authority.

Section 18 of the *Federal Courts Act*[25] does not transfer *habeas corpus* applications from the provincial superior courts to the Federal Court with respect to detentions by a federal board, tribunal or commission. This has the advantage of making the remedy available from the local superior court instead of the itinerant Federal Court.[26] It may be the case that a separate and other remedy may be conjoined in the provincial superior court to ensure *habeas corpus* is a useful remedy.[27]

3. *Certiorari* and Prohibition

Certiorari and prohibition are discussed together because they are the reverse faces of each other.[28] *Certiorari* is used to bring decisions of lower tribunals before the superior court, where the decisions can be quashed if the tribunals have acted without jurisdiction, or where they have made an intra-jurisdictional error on the face of the record.[29] Prohibition is issued to prevent a tribunal from embarking upon or continuing upon a procedure for which it has no jurisdiction, or to prevent it from making an intra-jurisdictional error of law. Prohibition is forward-looking, designed to prevent something from being done, and is therefore invoked earlier in the proceedings than *certiorari*, which only comes into play once an erroneous decision has been made.

As Atkin L.J. said in *R. v. Electricity Commissioners*:[30]

> I can see no difference in principle between *certiorari* and prohibition, except that the latter may be invoked at an earlier stage. If the pro-ceedings establish that the body complained of is exceeding its juris-diction by entertaining matters which would result in its final decision being subject to being brought up and quashed on *certiorari*, I think that prohibition will lie to restrain it from so exceeding its jurisdiction.

The history of how these remedies were extended to control a wide range of *ultra vires* governmental actions that were not strictly "judicial" in nature has been described in detail in Chapter 8. The superior courts originally su-

---

25 *Federal Courts Act*, R.S.C. 1985, c. F-7, reproduced in Appendix 5. Note that the Federal Court does have exclusive jurisdiction to hear applications for *habeas corpus* for members of the Canadian Forces serving outside Canada: s. 18(2).

26 As noted, *supra* note 16, the provincial courts will often defer to the federal courts on matters of federal law, if an effective remedy is available.

27 See *Cardinal* and *Miller*, *supra* note 17; *Dumas c. Centre de détention Leclerc de Laval*, [1986] 2 S.C.R. 459, 22 Admin. L.R. 205 (S.C.C.).

28 For a discussion of the equivalent remedy in Quebec (which, like the rest of Canada, derives its administrative law from England), see *supra* note 2.

29 The concept of an intra-jurisdictional error of law is discussed in detail in Chapter 11; and section 2 discusses what constitutes the "record".

30 (1923), [1924] 1 K.B. 171 at 206 (Eng. C.A.).

pervised the lower courts when they were acting judicially in the traditional sense, and continued that supervisory role as the lower courts came to perform much wider and non-judicial functions in the administration of government. As the duties of the magistrates in the administration of local government were subsequently transferred to a multitude of local government authorities and other statutory delegates in the late 19th century, the traditional supervisory role of the superior courts nevertheless remained available. Where Parliament had made no other provision, the common law remedies of *certiorari* and prohibition continued to be used to ensure that the various statutory delegates acted within their respective jurisdictions. Thus, these prerogative remedies came to be used outside the traditional judicial context.

The courts were later led astray by the heresy that *certiorari* and prohibition would only be available if the nature of the impugned decision could be characterized as "judicial" or "quasi-judicial". Atkin L.J. said in the *Electricity Commissioners case*:[31]

> Wherever any body of persons having legal authority to determine questions affecting the rights of subjects *and having the duty to act judicially*, act in excess of their legal authority they are subject to the controlling jurisdiction of the King's Bench Division exercised in these writs.

Whether or not the decision-maker was "acting judicially" (or "quasi-judicially") came to be the rock upon which many litigants floundered. *Certiorari* and prohibition were held not to be applicable to actions that could be described as being merely "administrative" in nature. In retrospect, this approach entirely misread the *Electricity Commissioners* case, which undoubtedly involved an administrative act, that is one performed by statutory delegates who were not judges; and, on the other hand, ignored the long history of supervision by the courts of all kinds of governmental action which, although exercised by judicial officers, could not be said to be judicial in nature. The courts, however, have now long asserted their right to step in to supervise both "judicial" and "administrative" actions. Nevertheless, the course of administrative law was severely skewed for many years by the adoption of the "quasi-judicial" terminology. Although it has been suggested that the quasi-judicial restriction only applied to determine the applicability of the principles of natural justice to the exercise of a statutory power, in fact this terminology was also used to seriously restrict the ambit of *certiorari* and prohibition as vehicles for judicial review of the legality of governmental action on grounds which either did not include or went beyond breaches of natural justice.[32]

---

31 *Ibid.* at 205, emphasis added. The quasi-judicial terminology was clearly accepted by the Supreme Court of Canada in *Calgary Power Ltd. v. Copithorne* (1958), [1959] S.C.R. 24 (S.C.C.).

32 This is explained in Chapter 8. For a good example of the distinction between what constitutes grounds of judicial review (for example, a breach of natural justice) and the availability of *certiorari*, see D.C. McDonald J.'s judgment in *Alberta v. Beaver (County No. 9)*, [1982] 4 W.W.R. 344 (Alta. Q.B.), reversed on another point [1984] 4 W.W.R. 371 (Alta. C.A.).

The courts started to abandon this heresy after *Ridge v. Baldwin*[33] in England and *Nicholson*,[34] *Martineau (No. 2)*[35] and *Knight*[36] in Canada. It is now quite clear that both *certiorari* and prohibition are available to control purely administrative actions.

Before an order of *certiorari* will be issued, there must be a decision or determination of some kind made by a delegate. A mere recommendation, investigation or report not constituting a determination did not always attract the remedy.[37] But the development of the wider doctrine of fairness now means that some mere recommendations and investigations will be reviewed.[38] A preliminary decision by a delegate is not reviewable: only a final decision is reviewable.[39] The traditional position was that when a decision was quashed, the effect was as if it had not been made. Therefore, no one need follow it. To the extent that the quashed decision involved a jurisdictional error,[40] it was always void[41] *ab initio* and could have been ignored with impunity. But the

---

33   (1963), [1964] A.C. 40 (U.K. H.L.).

34   *Nicholson v. Haldimand-Norfolk (Regional Municipality) Commissioners of Police*, [1979] 1 S.C.R. 311 (S.C.C.).

35   *Martineau v. Matsqui Institution* (1979), [1980] 1 S.C.R. 602 (S.C.C.).

36   *Knight v. Indian Head School Division No. 19*, [1990] 1 S.C.R. 653 (S.C.C.).

37   See *Guay v. Lafleur* (1964), [1965] S.C.R. 12 (S.C.C.). Thus, a coroner's inquest is generally not subject to *certiorari*: *Wolfe v. Robinson* (1961), [1962] O.R. 132 (Ont. C.A.); *Young v. Manitoba* (1960), 33 W.W.R. 3 (Man. C.A.), but see *Evans v. Milton* (1979), 24 O.R. (2d) 181 at 219 (Ont. C.A.), leave to appeal refused (1979), 28 N.R. 86 (note) (S.C.C.) allowing review for bias.

38   In *Baker v. Canada (Minister of Citizenship & Immigration)*, [1999] 2 S.C.R. 817 (S.C.C.) at para. 45 it was held that a junior immigration officer who only made recommendations was under a duty to act fairly. In *British Columbia (Securities Commission) v. Branch*, [1995] 2 S.C.R. 3 (S.C.C.) at para. 76 the Court said that all investigators are under a duty to act fairly. In *Irvine v. Canada (Restrictive Trade Practices Commission)*, [1987] 1 S.C.R. 181 (S.C.C.) the Court discussed the traditional rule, and at para. 87 held that the closer the investigation was to the final decision, the higher the standard of fairness required. See also S.A. deSmith, Wolf & J. Jowell, *Judicial Review of Administrative Action*, 5th ed. (London: Sweet & Maxwell, 1995) at 491 *et seq.* where the authors suggest that the degree of proximity between the investigation and the decision and the exposure of the person investigated to harm are matters of paramount concern in determining when a recommendation will be reviewable.

39   *Zündel v. Canada (Human Rights Commission)*, [2000] 4 F.C. 255 (Fed. C.A.), leave to appeal refused (2000), 266 N.R. 392 (note) (S.C.C.); *Edmonton (City) v. Alberta (Human Rights & Citizenship Commission)* (2002), [2003] 3 W.W.R. 731 (Alta. Q.B.); *Howe v. Institute of Chartered Accountants (Ontario)* (1994), 19 O.R. (3d) 483 (Ont. C.A.), leave to appeal refused (1995), 21 O.R. (3d) xvi (S.C.C.). Review can proceed in exceptional cases: *Great Atlantic & Pacific Co. of Canada v. Ontario (Minister of Citizenship)* (1993), 62 O.A.C. 1 (Ont. Div. Ct.) (bias, proper parties and timeliness of the decision were in issue); *Canada (Attorney General) v. Leonarduzzi* (2001), 205 F.T.R. 238 (Fed. T.D.); *McIntosh v. College of Physicians & Surgeons (Ontario)* (1998), 116 O.A.C. 158 (Ont. Div. Ct.).

40   The law may differ with respect to an intra-jurisdictional error of law.

41   See H.W.R. Wade, "Unlawful Administrative Action: Void or Voidable?" Pt. I at (1967) 83 L.Q. Rev. 499; Pt. II at (1968) 84 L.Q. Rev. 104; W. Wade & C. Forsyth, *Administrative Law*, 8th ed. (Oxford: Clarendon Press, 2000) at 466 *ff* and 488 *ff*; M.B. Akehurst, (1968) 31 Mod. L. Rev. 2; J.F. Northey, [1977] N.Z.L.J. 284; G.L. Peiris, "Natural Justice and Degrees of Invalidity of Administrative Action" [1983] P.L. 634; *Harelkin v. University of Regina*, [1979] 2 S.C.R. 561 (S.C.C.), and comment by D.P. Jones, "Discretionary Refusal of Judicial Review in Administrative Law" (1981) 19 Alta. L. Rev. 483.

court has a discretion to refuse a remedy even if the decision is void,[42] and the Supreme Court of Canada has now limited the situations in which such decisions can be attacked collaterally,[43] so it is generally safer to get an order of *certiorari* to quash any challenged administrative action.

Certiorari and prohibition are now used exclusively to control the exercise of statutory authority[44] and are confined to the public law field. They play no part in private law and thus, for example, will lie neither to compel compliance with a private right[45] nor to review the award of a consensual authority arbitrator.[46] On the other hand, a person may sometimes seek one of the private law remedies discussed in Chapter 16 in the context of an illegal governmental action, instead of obtaining *certiorari* or prohibition.[47]

It is important to recognize the limitations on the availability of *certiorari* or prohibition even in the context of controlling illegal governmental action. First, although judicial and administrative decisions are fully within the sphere of *certiorari* and prohibition, legislative decisions are still not.[48] This limitation

---

42   See section 7 of this chapter.

43   *R. v. Consolidated Maybrun Mines Ltd.*, [1998] 1 S.C.R. 706 (S.C.C.); *R. v. Al Klippert Ltd.*, [1998] 1 S.C.R. 737 (S.C.C.).

44   Although they have been applied to prerogative powers: *R. v. Secretary of State for the Home Department, Ex parte Bentley*, [1994] Q.B. 349 (Div. Ct.); *Black v. Canada (Prime Minister)* (2001), 54 O.R. (3d) 215 (Ont. C.A.). See also L. Sossin, "The Rule of Law and the Justiciability of Prerogative Powers" (2002) 47 McGill L.J. 435. Compare *Operation Dismantle Inc. v. R.*, [1985] 1 S.C.R. 441 (S.C.C.) on *Charter* review of the prerogative.

45   *Skoreyko v. Belleville* (1991), 115 A.R. 61 (Alta. C.A.); *C.U.P.E., Local 3197 v. Edmonton (City)* (1998), 212 A.R. 71 (Alta. C.A.); *Associated Respiratory Services Inc. v. British Columbia (Purchasing Commission)* (1992), 70 B.C.L.R. (2d) 57 (B.C. S.C.), reversed (1994), 87 B.C.L.R. (2d) 70 (B.C. C.A.), additional reasons at (1994), 95 B.C.L.R. (2d) 357 (B.C. C.A.), leave to appeal refused (1995), 192 N.R. 78 (note) (S.C.C.). On the "public" reach of the *Charter*, compare *Godbout c. Longueuil (Ville)*, [1997] 3 S.C.R. 844 (S.C.C.).

46   *Howe Sound Co. v. International Union of Mine, Mill & Smelter Workers (Can.), Local 663*, [1962] S.C.R. 318 (S.C.C.); compare *U.S.W.A. v. Port Arthur Shipbuilding Co.* (1968), [1969] S.C.R. 85 (S.C.C.). The Supreme Court of Canada has greatly expanded the category of statutory arbitrations: see *Roberval Express Ltd. v. Transport Drivers Warehousemen & General Workers' Union, Local 106*, [1982] 2 S.C.R. 888 (S.C.C.), and *A.U.P.E. v. Alberta* (2002), 5 Alta. L.R. (4th) 238 (Alta. C.A.).

47   But a private law remedy will only lie against the government if it would lie against a private defendant for the same act; and, even then, the Crown has more extensive immunities and defences from suit. Accordingly, private law remedies cannot always be substituted for prerogative remedies: see Chapter 16.

48   *Campeau Corp. v. Calgary (City)* (1980), 12 Alta. L.R. (2d) 379 (Alta. C.A.); *Alberta v. Beaver (County No. 9)* (1982), 20 Alta. L.R. (2d) 78 (Alta. Q.B.), reversed (1984), 31 Alta. L.R. (2d) 174 (Alta. C.A.); compare *Bates v. Lord Hailsham of St. Marylebone*, [1972] 1 W.L.R. 1373 (Eng. Ch. Div.); *Inuit Tapirisat of Canada v. Canada (Attorney General)*, [1980] 2 S.C.R. 735 (S.C.C.); *TransCanada Pipelines Ltd. v. Beardmore (Township)* (2000), 186 D.L.R. (4th) 403 (Ont. C.A.), leave to appeal refused (2000), [2000] S.C.C.A. No. 264, 2000 CarswellOnt 4248 (S.C.C.). On the review of legislative acts on procedural grounds, see *Authorson (Litigation Guardian of) v. Canada (Attorney General)* (2003), 227 D.L.R. (4th) 385 (S.C.C.).

also seems to apply to delegated legislation.[49] Second, *certiorari* and prohibition lie only against public bodies whose authority is derived from statute.[50] Third, these remedies do not lie against the Crown,[51] although they do lie against the Crown and her ministers when exercising statutory functions.[52] Fourth, visitors to universities may perform the same function as *certiorari* and prohibition, thereby effectively preventing the application of these remedies to universities.[53] Fifth, *certiorari* and prohibition do not lie to enforce contractual or other private law rights, perhaps even where there is a "public law" back-drop to these rights.[54] Sixth, the anomalous use of *certiorari* to correct an intra-jurisdictional error of law on the face of the record is often subject to the "patently unreasonable" test.[55] Finally, legislation frequently attempts to oust the availability of *certiorari* or prohibition to review the legality of particular governmental action through privative clauses. The role of these "privative clauses" in determining the appropriate standard of review is discussed in Chapter 12.

Section 28 of the *Federal Courts Act*[56] transfers the judicial review authority with respect to certain listed federal boards to the Federal Court of

---

49 Both *Campeau* and the *Beaver* cases dealt with municipal by-laws, which are a form of delegated legislation. The power of the court to grant declaratory relief as an alternative to certiorari may overcome this limitation: *S.G.E.U. v. Saskatchewan*, [1997] 4 W.W.R. 41 (Sask. Q.B.), affirmed [1997] 6 W.W.R. 605 (Sask. C.A.).

50 Or from the Royal Prerogative? See *Ex parte Bentley*, *supra* note 44 and the cases at notes 45 and 46.

51 See *supra* note 5. See also *Local Government Board v. Arlidge*, [1915] A.C. 120 (U.K. H.L.), where *certiorari* was issued. But who precisely is the "Crown"? See *supra* note 44 and note 68, *infra*.

52 *R. v. British Columbia Provincial Police Commissioner*, [1940] 3 W.W.R. 39 (B.C. C.A.), affirmed [1941] S.C.R. 317 (S.C.C.); *R. v. British Columbia (Workers' Compensation Board)*, [1942] 2 W.W.R. 129 (B.C. C.A.); *R. v. Leong Ba Chai* (1953), [1954] S.C.R. 10 (S.C.C.); *M. v. Home Office*, [1993] 1 A.C. 377 (U.K. H.L.); *Manitoba v. Christie, MacKay & Co.* (1992), 83 Man. R. (2d) 197 (Man. C.A.).

53 See the decision of the Alberta Court of Appeal in *Vanek v. University of Alberta*, [1975] 5 W.W.R. 429 (Alta. C.A.), where *certiorari* was refused because s. 5 of the *Universities Act* made the Lieutenant Governor the visitor to the University. The Legislature subsequently abolished the office of visitors: S.A. 1976, c.88, s. 2.

For a more detailed discussion of the law in Canada, see the Third Edition of this book, and for the English position see *R. v. Hull University Visitor, ex parte Page*, [1993] A.C. 682.

54 See the cases at *supra* notes 45 and 46. The distinction between "private law" and "public law" has become very important in England after the reform of the remedies there. See *O'Reilly v. Mackman*, [1983] A.C. 120 (H.L.); *Cocks v. Thanet Dist. Council*, [1983] A.C. 286 (H.L.). See also C. Harlow, " 'Public' and 'Private' Law: Definition without Distinction" (1980) 43 Mod. L. Rev. 241; The Rt. Hon. Lord Justice Woolf, "Public Law – Private Law: Why the Divide? A Personal View" [1986] P.L. 220, and Wade & Forsyth, *supra* note 41 at 649-66.

55 See Chapter 11.

56 R.S.C. 1985, c. F-7, reproduced in Appendix 5. The list of tribunals to be reviewed by the Federal Court of Appeal was added in 1990, and replaced the earlier provisions which gave the Court of Appeal jurisdiction over certain federal decisions which were made on a "judicial or quasi-judicial basis". See section 9, below for a more detailed discussion of the operation of the *Federal Courts Act*; and see Sgayias et al, *Federal Court Practice* (Toronto: Thomson Carswell, published annually).

Appeal. Section 18 transfers the jurisdiction to issue *certiorari* and prohibition against any other "federal board, commission or other tribunal"[57] from the provincial superior courts exclusively to the Federal Court. In both cases, the procedure is an application for judicial review.

4. *Mandamus*

An order of *mandamus* compels the performance of a statutory duty owed to the applicant.[58] The remedy has never been confined to judicial or quasi-judicial functions but has always covered all forms of administrative action (or, more properly, inaction). Unlike *certiorari* and prohibition, which prevent statutory delegates from exercising a power unlawfully, *mandamus* is used where the statutory delegate refuses to exercise power it is compelled to use. In legal theory, an order of *mandamus* is a royal command to perform a public duty; failure to obey is contempt of court. Like *certiorari* and prohibition, *mandamus* is a discretionary remedy that may be refused by the court even though the applicant has otherwise made out its case.[59]

Certain conditions must be fulfilled before a court will issue an order of *mandamus*. The Federal Court of Appeal in *Apotex Inc. v. Merck & Co. and Merck Frosst Canada Inc.*[60] summarized those conditions as follows:

(1) There must be a public legal duty to act.[61]

---

57 Section 2 defines a "federal board, commission or other tribunal" to mean:

> . . . any body, person or persons having, exercising or purporting to exercise jurisdiction or powers conferred by or under an Act of Parliament or by or under an order made pursuant to a prerogative of the Crown, other than the Tax Court of Canada or any of its judges, any such body constituted or established by or under a law of a province or any such person or persons appointed under or in accordance with a law of a province or under section 96 of the *Constitution Act, 1867*.

For a discussion of this definition, see D.J. Mullan's study for the Law Reform Commission of Canada entitled *The Federal Court Act: A Study of the Court's Administrative Law Jurisdiction* (1977) at 17-22.

58 Normally, the applicant for *mandamus* will be a private citizen. It may sometimes happen, however, that one public body will seek to enforce a duty lying upon another public body, as occurred in *Canada (Anti-Dumping Tribunal), Re* (1975), 65 D.L.R. (3d) 354 (S.C.C.); and *Alberta v. Beaver (County No. 9)* (1982), 20 Alta. L.R. (2d) 78 (Alta. Q.B.), reversed (1984), 31 Alta. L.R. (2d) 174 (Alta. C.A.).

59 *Apotex Inc. v. Canada (Attorney General)* (1993), [1994] 1 F.C. 742, 18 Admin. L.R. (2d) 122 (Fed. C.A.), affirmed [1994] 3 S.C.R. 1100, 29 Admin. L.R. (2d) 1 (S.C.C.); *Mobil Oil Canada Ltd. v. Canada-Newfoundland (Offshore Petroleum Board)*, [1994] 1 S.C.R. 202, 21 Admin. L.R. (2d) 248 (S.C.C.). See also section 7 of this chapter, below.

60 *Ibid.* See also *Karavos v. Toronto (City)* (1947), [1948] 3 D.L.R. 294 (Ont. C.A.).

61 *Mandamus* only operates in the public law arena, and cannot be used to enforce private contractual rights. A mandatory injunction or an order of specific performance would be the appropriate private law remedies. Further, one must ensure the legislation in issue imposes a duty on and does not grant a mere power to the delegate. It must impose a duty and that duty must be a public duty as opposed to a private duty. On the difference between public and private duties see *Skoreyko v. Belleville* (1991), 115 A.R. 61 (Alta. C.A.) and *Dombrowski v Dalhousie University* (1974), 55 D.L.R. (3d) 268 (N.S. T.D.), affirmed (1976), 79 D.L.R.

(2) The duty must be owed to the applicant. In other words, the applicant must satisfy the *locus standi* requirements discussed in section 6 of this chapter.

(3) There must be a clear right to expect performance of the duty, specifically:

   (a) the applicant must satisfy all conditions precedent giving rise to the duty, and

   (b) the applicant must have made a demand that the duty be performed, and the decision-maker must have failed to comply with the demand either expressly, for example by an outright refusal, or impliedly by, for example, failing to respond to the demand within a reasonable time.[62]

(4) Where the duty owed is one that is discretionary in nature, the following conditions must be met:

   (a) the decision-maker must not exercise its discretion in a manner which might be characterised as "unfair", "oppressive" or which demonstrates "flagrant impropriety" or "bad faith";

   (b) the decision-maker must not exercise its discretion in a manner which might be characterised as "unqualified", "absolute', "permissive", or "unfettered";

   (c) the decision-maker must act upon relevant as opposed to irrelevant considerations;[63]

   (d) the decision-maker cannot be compelled to exercise its discretion in a particular manner.[64] In some cases, however, where there is

---

(3d) 355 (N.S. C.A.). Whether or not a statutory duty exists can only be determined from the legislative language. See *Vancouver Island Railway, An Act Respecting, Re*, [1994] 2 S.C.R. 41 (S.C.C.) and the discussion in Chapter 6, on the distinction between a mandatory and a merely directory statutory provision. See also *Nguyen v. Canada (Minister of Employment & Immigration)* (1993), 16 Admin. L.R. (2d) 1 (Fed. C.A.), leave to appeal refused (1994), 17 Admin. L.R. (2d) 67 (note) (S.C.C.), where the Federal Court held that an immigration policy constituted an implied statutory duty, the performance of which could be compelled by an order of *mandamus*.

62 *Hamilton Dairies Ltd. v. Dundas (Town)* (1927), 33 O.W.N. 113 at 114 (Ont. Div. Ct.); *Hughes v. Henderson* (1963), 46 W.W.R. 202 (Man. Q.B.) where the delegate refused to act despite a demand to act having been made, and *Chandler v. Assn. of Architects (Alberta)*, [1989] 2 S.C.R. 848 (S.C.C.) at para. 68 (L'Heureux-Dubé dissenting). Where a delegate's conduct or lack of action was, by implication, sufficient evidence of a refusal, see *R. v. Alberta (Highway Traffic Board)*, [1947] 2 D.L.R. 373 (Alta. T.D.); *Sarcee Gravel Products Inc. v. Alberta (Workers' Compensation Board)* (2002), 44 Admin. L.R. (3d) 1 (Alta. Q.B.); *Apotex Inc. v. Alberta* (2001), 302 A.R. 80 (Alta. Q.B.).

63 *Oakwood Development Ltd. v. St. François Xavier (Rural Municipality)*, [1985] 2 S.C.R. 164 (S.C.C.).

64 *R. v. Gloucester (Bishop)* (1831), 2 B. & Ad. 158 at 163; *Pecover v. Bowker* (1957), 20 W.W.R. 561 (Alta. T.D.); *Campeau Corp. v. Calgary (City)* (1978), 7 Alta. L.R. (2d) 294 (Alta. C.A.); *A.U.P.E. v. Alberta* (1991), 85 Alta. L.R. (2d) 266 (Alta. C.A.). In *Apotex Inc.*

only one legal way in which the delegate can exercise its discretion in the particular circumstances, the courts have been known to order this result.[65] At the other extreme, the delegate may have discretion whether to act at all, and no *mandamus* can lie in these circumstances precisely because there is no duty to act at all[66]; and

(e) the applicant must have a vested right to the performance of the duties;

(5) The applicant must have no other remedy available to it.

(6) The order sought must be of some practical value or effect.

(7) There must be no equitable bar to the court granting *mandamus.*

(8) The balance of convenience must favour the granting of *mandamus.*[67]

Mandamus does not lie against the Crown[68] or its agents. This reflects the general rule that none of the prerogative remedies is available against the Crown, because in theory the court cannot treat the monarch as both applicant and respondent in the same action at the same time, nor could it commit itself in contempt for disobedience.[69] On the other hand, the number of people

---

v. *Alberta* (2001), 302 A.R. 80 (Alta. Q.B.) the court held that while the decision-maker could not be told how to exercise its discretion, it had to make a decision one way or the other by a fixed date.

65 See for example, *Trinity Western University v. College of Teachers (British Columbia),* [2001] 1 S.C.R. 772 (S.C.C.); *Vic Restaurant Inc. v. Montreal (City)* (1958), [1959] S.C.R. 58 (S.C.C.); *R. v. Baker,* [1923] 1 W.W.R. 1430 at 1434 (Alta. C.A.); *Brampton Jersey Enterprises Ltd. v. Ontario (Milk Control Board)* (1955), [1956] O.R. 1 (Ont. C.A.); *R. v. British Columbia (Workmen's Compensation Board),* [1942] 2 W.W.R. 129 (B.C. C.A); *R. v. London Licensing Justices; Ex parte Stewart,* [1954] 1 W.L.R. 1325.

66 *Re Fletcher,* [1970] 2 All E.R. 527n (Eng. C.A.); *Poizer v. Ward,* [1947] 2 W.W.R. 193 (Man. C.A.); *R. v. British Columbia (Labour Relations Board),* [1949] 2 W.W.R. 873 (B.C. S.C.); *R. v. Marshland Smeeth & Fen District Commissioners,* [1920] 1 K.B. 155 at 165 (Eng. K.B.). In *Centre hospitalier Mont-Sinaï c. Québec (Ministre de la Santé & des Services sociaux),* [2001] 2 S.C.R. 281 (S.C.C.) it was held the Minister had previously exercised his discretion, and he was ordered to implement it.

67 In *Devinat v. Canada (Immigration & Refugee Board)* (1999), [2000] 2 F.C. 212 (Fed. C.A.), leave to appeal refused (2000), [2002] 2 S.C.R. vii (S.C.C.) the Court refused to order the translation of all prior decisions of the Commission based on the balance of convenience.

68 But "the Crown" must be distinguished from the Governor (alone or in Council), the Cabinet, a Minister, or any other public servant to whom the legislature has delegated a statutory duty. In the latter case, *mandamus* will lie: see *Newfoundland Assn. of Provincial Court Judges v. Newfoundland* (2000), 191 D.L.R. (4th) 225 (Nfld. C.A.); *R. v. British Columbia (Workmen's Compensation Board),* [1942] 2 W.W.R. 129 (B.C. C.A.); *R. v. Saskatchewan (Minister of Mineral Resources),* [1973] 2 W.W.R. 672 (S.C.C.); *Gajic v. British Columbia (Ministry of Finance & Corporate Relations)* (1996), 19 B.C.L.R. (3d) 169 (B.C. C.A.) and the excellent analysis of the rule in the Report by the Law Reform Commission of B.C. on Civil Rights, Pt. I: "Legal Position of the Crown" (1972) at 32-34.

69 *Massey Manufacturing Co., Re* (1886), 13 O.A.R. 446 (Ont. C.A.); *Canadian Broadcasting Corp. v. Ontario (Attorney General),* [1959] S.C.R. 188 at 204 (S.C.C.); *R. v. Powell* (1841), 1 Q.B. 352 at 361. See the powerful criticisms of these justifications for Crown immunity in the Report of the B.C. Law Reform Commission, *ibid.*

entitled to this immunity is quite restricted. In particular, it does not apply to the Queen, the Lieutenant-Governor, cabinet ministers or public servants when they are exercising a power conferred by statute, for then they are *personae designatae*.[70]

Again, it is important to remember that section 28 of the *Federal Courts Act* transfers the authority to grant *mandamus* in respect of certain listed federal delegates to the Federal Court of Appeal. Likewise section 18 transfers the judicial review authority against any other "federal board, commission or other tribunal" from the provincial superior courts to the Federal Court.

5. *Quo Warranto*

Quo warranto is used to challenge the right of a person to hold a public office, whether created by the Crown, by charter or by statute.[71] The Rules of Court govern the procedure. The courts will generally exercise their discretion to refuse the remedy to the extent that an equivalent alternative procedure is provided by statute,[72] which may explain why this remedy is not frequently sought.

6. *Locus Standi*

The law does not permit just any concerned citizen to challenge the decision of a public delegate. In order to possess standing to obtain one of the prerogative remedies, an applicant must be "aggrieved",[73] "affected"[74] or have

---

70   *Supra* note 68.

71   See *Sargent v. McPhee* (1967), 60 W.W.R. 604 (B.C. C.A.), challenging the appointment of a member of a public inquiry, compare *R. v. Trainor* (1967), 66 D.L.R. (2d) 605 (P.E.I. C.A.); *R. v. Gee* (1965), 51 W.W.R. 705 (Alta. Dist. Ct.) but compare *R. v. Clark*, [1943] O.R. 501 (Ont. C.A.), leave to appeal refused (1943), [1944] S.C.R. 69 (S.C.C.) and *R. v. Steinkopf* (1964), 49 W.W.R. 759 (Man. Q.B.), set aside/quashed (1964), 50 W.W.R. 643 (Man. C.A.), and the comment thereon by F. Muldoon, "*Quo Warranto* and the Legislator: Stubbs and Steinkopf Revisited" (1970) 4 Man. L.J. 178.

72   For example, under Pt. 5 of the *Local Authorities Election Act*, R.S.A. 2000, c. L-21 ("Controverted Elections"); see also *Jock v. R.*, [1991] 2 F.C. 355 (Fed. T.D.). See section 7(e), below.

73   *R. v. Justices of Surrey* (1870), L.R. 5 Q.B. 466 (Eng. Q.B.), per Blackburn J. at 473:

>   In other cases where the application is by the party grieved . . . we think that it ought to be treated . . . as *ex debito justitiae*; but where the applicant is not a party grieved (who substantially brings error to redress his private wrong), but comes forward as one of the general public having no particular interest in the matter, the Court has a discretion, and if it thinks that no good would be done to the public by quashing the order, it is not bound to grant it at the instance of such a person.

A person "aggrieved" has been viewed as one who suffers some "peculiar grievance of their own beyond some grievance suffered by them in common with the rest of the public": *Civil Service Assn. of Alberta v. Farran* (1976), 68 D.L.R. (3d) 338 at 341 (Alta. C.A.).

On standing generally, see T.A Cromwell, *Locus Standi, A Commentary on the Law of Standing in Canada* (Toronto: Carswell, 1986); D.J. Mullan, *Administrative Law,* (Toronto:

some other "sufficient interest".[75] In general, mere busy-bodies need not apply.[76] The decision as to when standing ought to be granted is always one in the court's discretion and as noted by T.A. Cromwell in *Locus Standi, A Commentary on the Law of Standing in Canada:*[77]

> The cases [on standing] are not decided upon verbal formulae or lists of protected interests, but on the basis of the Court's perception of the relationship between the applicant and the challenged decision, the nature of the statutory scheme out of which the decision issued, and the merits of the complaint. In addition to these factors, the courts are recognising that who is a person aggrieved is a matter of degree rather than a test, the application of which results in clear-cut answers.

The Attorney General, as protector of the public interest, always has standing.[78]

Irwin Law, 2001) at 445 *ff* and the *Report of the English Law Commission on Remedies in Administrative Law*, Cmnd. 6407, 1976; Chapter 8 of the *Report of the Committee of the JUSTICE – All Souls Review of Administrative Law in the United Kingdom* (1988); Sir Konrad Schiemann, *"Locus Standi"* [1990] P.L. 342.

74 In *Canadian Motion Picture Distributors Assn. v. Partners of Viewer's Choice Canada* (1996), 42 Admin. L.R. (2d) 280 (Fed. C.A.) the applicant film producers and distributors were denied standing to seek judicial review as they were not found to be directly affected by the decision in issue as the decision did not affect the applicants more than it did every other film producer and distributor. For a statutory interpretation of "directly affected" see *C.U.P.E., Local 30 v. WMI Waste Management of Canada Inc.* (1996), 34 Admin. L.R. (2d) 172 (Alta. C.A.), affirming (February 9, 1994), Doc. Edmonton 9603-21182 (Alta. Q.B.) where the common law definition of "directly affected" described as ". . . a personal and individual interest as distinct from the general interest which appertains to the whole community" was accepted. See also *Friends of the Athabasca Environmental Assn. v. Alberta (Public Health Advisory & Appeal Board)* (1994), 24 Admin. L.R. (2d) 156 (Alta. Q.B.), affirmed [1996] 4 W.W.R. 604 (Alta. C.A.).

Pursuant to s.18.1(1) of the *Federal Courts Act*, R.S.C. 1985, c. F-7, an application for judicial review may be made by ". . . anyone directly affected by the matter in respect of which relief is sought." In *Nova Scotia (Attorney General) v. Ultramar Canada Inc.* (1995), 35 Admin. L.R. (2d) 124 (Fed. T.D.), the Court held that the Province of Nova Scotia was directly affected within the meaning of the statute by the decision of a government delegate as there were genuine, important public interests in issue which the Province could adequately represent, such as the interest in competition in the local petroleum market and continued economic activity and employment in the Province. See also *Shiell v. Canada (Atomic Energy Control Board)* (1995), 33 Admin. L.R. (2d) 122 (Fed. T.D.).

75 English Order 53, Rule 3(7); *R. v. Manchester Corp.*, [1911] 1 K.B. 560. See also S.M. Thio, [1966] P.L. 133.

76 *Finlay v. Canada (Minister of Finance)*, [1986] 2 S.C.R. 607, 23 Admin. L.R. 197 at 220 (S.C.C.). See also *Gouriet v. Union of Post Office Workers* (1977), [1978] A.C. 435 (U.K. H.L.), dealing with an injunction; *Blackburn v. Attorney General*, [1971] 1 W.L.R. 1037 (Eng. C.A.); *McWhirter v. A.G.*, [1972] C.M.L.R. 882 (C.A.); *League for Life in Manitoba Inc. v. Morgentaler*, [1985] 4 W.W.R. 633 (Man. Q.B.).

77 *Supra* note 73 at 107.

78 *Federal Courts Act*, R.S.C. 1985, c. F-7, s. 18.1(1), and see cases at note 85, below.

The traditional rationales for limiting standing may be summarised as follows:[79]

(1) the doctrine of standing promotes the efficient use of judicial resources by ensuring the court hears only those persons truly aggrieved by the decision in issue;

(2) the doctrine of standing assists in the efficient presentation of issues before the court. This rationale is premised on the view that only those with a direct, personal interest in the matter before the court will present well prepared argument based on firm legal issues;

(3) the doctrine of standing ensures that rights are not determined by the court in the absence of those with the most at stake;

(4) the doctrine of standing helps to define the appropriate role of the court in the administrative law process, by vetting those matters that are reviewed by the court and ensuring only those which are legitimate questions for review are before it.

(a) Standing Under the Common Law

The courts have had considerable difficulty over the years in determining who qualifies under these terms, but there are some consistencies in the case law. A person "aggrieved" or "affected" by a decision generally includes one whose interest is affected more than those of the general public or community in issue.[80] In addition, if the applicant belongs to a class which is directly affected or aggrieved by a decision, that will generally be sufficient to be granted standing[81] and the applicant need not be the person in the class whom the decision primarily affects.[82] However, the ability of persons merely indi-

---

79 For a discussion of the traditional rationales, see T.A. Cromwell, *Locus Standi, A Commentary on the Law of Standing in Canada, supra* note 73 at 9, 10, 11; R. Tim Hay, "Exactly Who is 'Directly Affected'? – A Trilogy on Public Standing Before Administrative Tribunals" (1996) 5 R.A.L. 148; J.M. Ross, "Standing in *Charter* Declaratory Actions" (1995) 33 Osgoode Hall L.J. 151, and *Finlay v. Canada (Minister of Finance), supra* note 76.

80 *Supra* notes 73 and 74.

81 *Berg v. British Columbia (Attorney General)* (1991), 48 Admin. L.R. 82 (B.C. S.C.) where standing was granted to apply for *certiorari*.

82 See *Noddle v. Toronto (City)* (1982), 37 O.R. (2d) 421 (Ont. H.C.) and *Appleton v. Eastern Provincial Airways Ltd.* (1983), 6 Admin. L.R. 128 (Fed. C.A.) where standing to apply for *certiorari* was granted, but compare *Canadian Motion Picture Distributors Assn. v. Partners of Viewer's Choice Canada* (1996), 42 Admin. L.R. (2d) 280 (Fed. C.A.) where standing was denied because all film distributors were equally affected. Compare *Union of Northern Workers v. Northwest Territories (Minister of Mining Safety)* (1991), 49 Admin. L.R. 280 (N.W.T. S.C.) where a Union was found to be "aggrieved" and given standing in an action for *mandamus,* when a Minister failed to comply with his statutory duty to appoint persons to the Mine Occupation Health and Safety Board. The duty was owed to more than just the Union, but the Union was in the class or group affected.

rectly affected by a decision to apply for judicial review on the basis of a denial of natural justice to another person who has been primarily affected is limited.[83]

Although traditionally the whole world had the right to make an application for a prerogative writ, the courts would usually only issue one to a person so "aggrieved" or "affected" by the governmental action that he or she had a "sufficient interest" to have standing to require the delegate to come to court to explain the legality of its actions. The courts have vacillated between a wider and a narrower concept of standing with two clearly identifiable extremes. On the one hand, the courts will often grant standing to a private citizen in constitutional cases,[84] as well as to the Crown in all cases.[85] On the other hand, common law standing will not be granted to a person merely because they have concerns and have resolved to become involved in an issue.[86]

Under the wider view, standing was granted in the following cases: to a recycling depot objecting to the granting of a permit to a competitor;[87] to an adjoining landowner challenging a permit for an intensive livestock operation;[88] to a neighbour complaining about an illegal use of lands;[89] to a chief of police to enforce police regulations;[90] to a union seeking to enforce worker safety legislation;[91] and to members of a public interest group.[92]

---

83 Standing to apply for *certiorari* was denied in *Cunningham Drug Stores Ltd. v. British Columbia (Labour Relations Board)* (1972), [1973] S.C.R. 256 (S.C.C.) and *U.S.W.A. v. American Barrick Resources Corp.* (1991), 2 O.R. (3d) 266 (Ont. Div. Ct.). Compare *Sanders v. Chester (District) Municipal School Board* (1979), 102 D.L.R. (3d) 486 (N.S. T.D.) where parents of the students of a terminated teacher were granted standing.

84 *Thorson v. Canada (Attorney General) (No. 2)* (1974), [1975] 1 S.C.R. 138 (S.C.C.); *MacNeil v. Nova Scotia (Board of Censors)* (1975), [1976] 2 S.C.R. 265 (S.C.C.); *Borowski v. Canada (Minister of Justice)*, [1981] 2 S.C.R. 575 (S.C.C.); *Canadian Egg Marketing Agency v. Richardson*, [1998] 3 S.C.R. 157 (S.C.C.).

85 *Canada (Anti-Dumping Tribunal), Re* (1975), [1976] 2 S.C.R. 739 (S.C.C.); *Alberta v. Beaver (County No. 9)* (1984), 31 Alta. L.R. (2d) 174 (Alta. C.A.); Compare *Alberta v. Canadian Wheat Board* (1997), [1998] 2 F.C. 156 (Fed. T.D.), affirmed (1998), 13 Admin. L.R. (3d) 4 (Fed. C.A.) on the standing of the provincial Attorney General in federal matters.

86 See *supra* note 76. Being "interested" means having a legally recognized interest, as opposed to a philosophical or personal interest. Persons with the latter type of interest are sometimes granted public interest standing: see subsection 6(b), below.

87 *Northeast Bottle Depot Ltd. v. Alberta (Beverage Container Management Board)* (2000), 82 Alta. L.R. (3d) 346 (Alta. Q.B.).

88 *Bengston v. Alberta (Natural Resources Conservation Board)* (2003), 330 A.R. 81 (Alta. C.A.) (a statutory appeal).

89 *Woodman v. Capital (Regional District)* (1999), 6 M.P.L.R. (3d) 128 (B.C. S.C.), additional reasons at ((1999), 1999 CarswellBC 2735 (B.C. S.C.); compare *Harvie v. Calgary (City) Regional Planning Commission* (1978), 8 Alta. L.R. (2d) 166 (App. Div.). See also the Comment by E.A. Bastedo and A.W. MacKay, "Citizen Access to Nova Scotia Planning Appeals: From Interested to Aggrieved Persons" (1987) 23 Admin. L.R. 246.

90 *McCormack v. Lymer* (1992), 97 D.L.R. (4th) 740 (Ont. Gen. Div.), leave to appeal refused (1992), 97 D.L.R. (4th) 749 (Ont. Gen. Div.).

91 *Union of Northern Workers v. Northwest Territories (Minister of Mining Safety)* (1991), 49 Admin. L.R. 280 (N.W.T. S.C.).

92 See comments by D.J. Mullan on *Saanich Inlet Preservation Society v. Corwichan Valley (Regional District)* (1983), 2 Admin. L.R. 12 (B.C. C.A.); by A.J. Roman on *Sea Shepherd Conservation Society v. British Columbia* (1984), 11 Admin. L.R. 190 (B.C. S.C.); by A. Wayne Mackay on *Friends of Public Gardens v. Halifax (City)* (1985), 13 Admin. L.R. 272

The narrower view[93] denied standing in the following circumstances: to a bank seeking to challenge a Real Estate Council policy dealing with referrals of mortgage business;[94] to the owner of a cabin seeking to stop logging in a provincial park;[95] to parents challenging closure of a school not attended by their children;[96] to an employer trying to enforce the rights of employees[97] and to an environmentalist who lived several hundred miles from the project.[98]

The cases are not easily reconcilable, but the different tests for standing can to some extent be explained by noting which prerogative remedy was being sought,[99] as well as by noting the type of defect being attacked.[100] Since the 1986 decision in *Finlay*,[101] the courts have been more willing to grant standing.

(b) Public Interest Standing

Under certain circumstances, the courts have the discretion to grant standing to those who individually do not meet those specific requirements outlined above: those whom the court nonetheless regards as proper representatives of the larger public interest.[102] Courts may consider granting public interest stand-

---

(N.S. T.D.); by L.M. Fox on *Canadian Abortion Rights Action League Inc. v. Nova Scotia (Attorney General)* (1989), 39 Admin. L.R. 171 (N.S. T.D.), reversed (1990), 43 Admin. L.R. 134 (N.S. C.A.), leave to appeal refused (1990), 100 N.S.R. (2d) 90 (note) (S.C.C.); by L.M. Fox on *Energy Probe v. Canada (Attorney General)* (1989), 37 Admin. L.R. 1 (Ont. C.A.), leave to appeal refused (1989), 102 N.R. 399 (note) (S.C.C.), and by R. Binch, "The Mere Busybody: Autonomy, Equality and Standing" (2002) 40 Alta. Law Rev. 367.

93 For a discussion of the narrower view, see W. Wade and C. Forsyth, *Administrative Law*, 8th ed. (Oxford: Clarendon Press, 2000), c. 20, especially at 667-77.

94 *Toronto Dominion Bank v. Real Estate Council (Alberta)* (2002), 1 Alta. L.R. (4th) 154 (Alta. Q.B.).

95 *Denys v. Saskatchewan (Minister of the Environment & Public Safety)* (1993), 107 Sask. R. 295 (Sask. Q.B.).

96 *Potter v. Halifax Regional School Board* (2001), 196 N.S.R. (2d) 330 (N.S. S.C.), reversed other grounds (2002), 206 N.S.R. (2d) 18 (N.S. C.A.), leave to appeal refused (2003), 313 N.R. 193 (note) (S.C.C.).

97 *U.S.W.A. v. American Barrick Resources Corp.* (1991), 2 O.R. (3d) 266 (Ont. Div. Ct.).

98 *Shiell v. Canada (Atomic Energy Control Board)* (1995), 33 Admin. L.R. (2d) 122 (Fed. T.D.); *Shiell v. Amok Ltd.* (1987), 27 Admin. L.R. 1 (Sask. Q.B.).

99 Although there may previously have been different tests for standing for different remedies, a majority of the House of Lords has held that there is now only one rule: *Inland Revenue Commissioners v. National Federation of Self-Employed & Small Businesses Ltd.* (1981), [1982] A.C. 617 (U.K. H.L.), compare *Lord Nelson Hotel Ltd. v. Halifax (City)* (1972), 33 D.L.R. (3d) 98 (N.S. C.A.).

100 *Supra* note 73.

101 [1986] 2 S.C.R. 607 (S.C.C.). *Finlay* is a case on public interest standing, but it has also influenced the test for common law standing.

102 See the trilogy of Supreme Court of Canada cases, *Thorson v. Canada (Attorney General) (No. 2)* (1974), [1975] 1 S.C.R. 138 (S.C.C.); *MacNeil v. Nova Scotia (Board of Censors)* (1975), [1976] 2 S.C.R. 265 (S.C.C.) and *Borowski v. Canada (Minister of Justice)*, [1981] 2 S.C.R. 575 at 606 (S.C.C.). The Court in *Borowski* interpreted *Thorson* and *McNeil* as deciding that "to establish status as a plaintiff in a suit seeking a declaration that legislation is invalid, if there is a serious issue as to its invalidity, a person need only show that he is affected by it directly or that he has a genuine interest as a citizen in the validity of legislation and that there is no other reasonable and effective manner in which the issue may be brought before the court". See T.A. Cromwell, *Locus Standi: A Commentary on the Law of Standing*

ing if three criteria are satisfied: the applicant must be raising a serious issue as to the invalidity of the decisions complained of;[103] the applicant must demonstrate a genuine interest in the matter; and another reasonable and effective way to bring the issue before the court must not be available.[104] Further, the courts may exercise their discretion to grant standing in judicial review proceedings to mere strangers in limited circumstances.[105]

(c) Standing Under Statutory Provisions

The terms, "directly affected" and "aggrieved", used to assist the court in determining standing at common law, have also been incorporated into various statutes[106] and interpreted by the courts with varying results.

In *Friends of the Island Inc. v. Canada (Minister of Public Works)*,[107] the Federal Court rejected an interpretation of "directly affected" in section 18.1 (1) of the *Federal Courts Act*, which would narrow its meaning and restrict the judicial discretion regarding standing. The Court effectively held that the scope of public interest standing in the federal sphere is not narrower than the common law position. The Court held:[108]

> ... s. 18.1 (1) allows the Court discretion to grant standing when it is convinced that the particular circumstances of the case and the type of interest which the applicant holds, justify status being granted. (This assumes there is a justiciable issue and no other effective and practical means of getting the issue before the courts) ...

in *Canada, supra* note 73 at 68-100 for further discussion of these cases. See also *Finlay v. Canada (Minister of Finance)*, [1986] 2 S.C.R. 607 (S.C.C.) and *Canadian Council of Churches v. R.*, [1992] 1 S.C.R. 236, 2 Admin. L.R. (2d) 229 (S.C.C.). All of these cases support the view that the court has an overriding discretion to grant standing to a person who might not possess such standing individually. In *Remmers v. Lipinski* (2001), 95 Alta. L.R. (3d) 209 (Alta. C.A.), leave to appeal denied (2002), [2001] S.C.C.A. No. 502, 2002 CarswellAlta 784 (S.C.C.), ratepayers were given public interest standing to claim the private law remedy of damages on behalf of a municipality.

103 The applicant will have to present some evidentiary base in support of the "serious issue": *Corp. of the Canadian Civil Liberties Assn. v. Canada (Attorney General)* (1998), 40 O.R. (3d) 489 (Ont. C.A.), leave to appeal refused (1999), 237 N.R. 393 (note) (S.C.C.).

104 See *Canadian Council of Churches, supra* note 102 and *Sierra Club of Canada v. Canada (Minister of Finance)* (1998), [1999] 2 F.C. 211, 13 Admin. L.R. (3d) 280 (Fed. T.D.).

105 *Energy Probe v. Canada (Atomic Energy Control Board)* (1984), [1985] 1 F.C. 563 (Fed. C.A.), leave to appeal to S.C.C. refused (1985), 15 D.L.R. (4th) 48n (S.C.C.); *Reese v. Alberta* (1992), 87 D.L.R. (4th) 1 (Alta. Q.B.), additional reasons at (1992), 11 Admin. L.R. (2d) 265n (Alta. Q.B.); and *Florence v. Canada (Air Transport Committee)* (1988), 34 Admin. L.R. 36 (Fed. T.D.).

106 The most important provision is s.18.1 (1) of the *Federal Courts Act*, R.S.C. 1985, c. F-7, and see s. 5(b) of the *Judicial Review Act*, R.S.P.E.I. 1988, c. J-3, and s. 5(2) of the *Public Health Act*, R.S.A. 2000, c. P-37.

107 [1993] 2 F.C. 229, 102 D.L.R. (4th) 696 (Fed. T.D.), reversed (1995), 106 F.T.R. 320 (note) (Fed. C.A.), leave to appeal refused (1996), 206 N.R. 76 (note) (S.C.C.)

108 *Ibid.*at 737.

Read literally, this view does not follow the rationales traditionally used to justify limitations on the doctrine of standing.[109]

While the reasoning in *Friends of the Island* has been followed in other Federal Court decisions where section 18.1 (1) has been in issue,[110] the Alberta Courts have rejected this more relaxed view of judicial discretion in favour of a view implicitly based upon the traditional rationale.[111] In *C.U.P.E., Local 30 v. WMI Waste Management of Canada Inc.,*[112] five applicants sought to appeal a decision of the Edmonton Board of Health ("EBH") to the Alberta Public Health Advisory and Appeal Board ("PHAAB"). They were denied standing before the PHAAB. The applicants then applied to the Court of Queen's Bench for judicial review of the PHAAB's decision on standing. The PHAAB's constating statute permitted a person "directly affected" by a decision of the EBH, who considered himself "aggrieved" by that decision, the right to appeal to the PHAAB. Both the Court of Queen's Bench and the Court of Appeal found that the applicants were not "directly affected" within the meaning of the legislation.[113] Some effect had to be given to the word "directly", and it limited standing. The Court of Appeal held that the term "directly affected" did not carry with it a judicial discretion to grant public interest standing before an administrative tribunal (the position advocated by the applicants).

(d) Legal Personality and Standing of Decision-Makers

Difficulties sometimes arise in determining whether the applicant has sufficient legal personality to participate in legal proceedings, and the reverse problem sometimes arises in identifying the correct legal entity to be the respondent. A related issue involves the standing or role of the administrative agency to participate in the proceedings for judicial review before the various courts.

In general, the applicant for a prerogative remedy must be recognized as a person in law. Thus unincorporated associations have been held to lack status

---

109   See *supra* note 79.

110   See for example, *Sunshine Village Corp. v. Superintendent of Banff National Park* (1996), 44 Admin. L.R. (2d) 201 (Fed. C.A.), leave to appeal refused (February 20, 1997), Doc. 25583, [1996] S.C.C.A. No. 498 (S.C.C.); *Sierra Club of Canada v. Canada (Minister of Finance)*, *supra* note 104.

111   R. Tim Hay, "Exactly Who is 'Directly Affected'? – A Trilogy on Public Interest Standing Before Administrative Tribunals", supra note 79.

112   (1996), 34 Admin. L.R. (2d) 172 (Alta. C.A.), affirming (February 9, 1994), Doc. Edmonton 9603-21182 (Alta. Q.B.). The decision in *WMI Waste Management* was followed in two subsequent Alberta decisions, *Friends of the Athabasca Environment Assn. v. Alberta (Public Health Advisory & Appeal Board)* (1994), 24 Admin. L.R. (2d) 156 (Alta. Q.B.), affirmed (1996), 34 Admin. L.R. (2d) 167 (Alta. C.A.), and *Kostuch v. Alberta (Director, Air & Water Approvals Division, Environmental Protection)* (1996), 35 Admin. L.R. (2d) 160 (Alta. Q.B.).

113   The court, at both levels, applied *Endowed Schools Act, Re*, [1898] A.C. 477 (P.C.) where the Privy Council stated: ". . . that the term 'directly affected' points rather to a personal and individual interest as distinct from the general interest which appertains to the whole community among which the endowment works".

both in administrative proceedings,[114] and in applications for a prerogative remedy to verify the legality of such proceedings.[115] Nevertheless, there are a number of cases, principally dealing with labour unions, which go the other way.[116]

The courts have also had to consider the reverse question of the necessity for the respondent administrator to have legal personality.[117] In the public law context of the prerogative remedies, however, the legal personality of the respondent is irrelevant. After all, the prerogative remedies supervise the exercise of statutory power. If Parliament has seen fit to grant such powers to boards, tribunals or other entities that are not legally persons, that fact alone is sufficient to permit the courts to recognize their existence for the purpose of the prerogative remedies.[118]

Finally, the issue arises as to the standing of a statutory delegate to participate in proceedings for a prerogative remedy challenging the validity of its decision, or to appeal from an adverse ruling of a lower court on this point. In England it seems that all delegates have standing to participate fully at every level of judicial review of their decisions, even to the point of defending the merits of their actions.[119] In Canada, however, the Supreme Court has unmistakably restricted statutory delegates to the more neutral role of making representations about jurisdictional matters only in proceedings for judicial re-

---

114 *Ladies of the Sacred Heart of Jesus v. Armstrong's Point Assn.* (1961), 36 W.W.R. 364 (Man. C.A.).

115 *Sisters of Charity, Providence Hospital v. Saskatchewan (Labour Relations Board)*, [1950] 2 W.W.R. 1046 (Sask. K.B.), affirmed (1951), 2 W.W.R. (N.S.) 66 (Sask. C.A.); *Canada Morning News Co. v. Thompson*, [1930] S.C.R. 338 at 342 (S.C.C.); *Hoechst Marion Roussel Canada v. Canada (Attorney General)* (2001), [2002] 1 F.C. 76 (Fed. T.D.). Federal Court Rule 2 contemplates applications by unincorporated associations.

116 *R. v. Saskatchewan (Labour Relations Board)* (1966), 56 W.W.R. 133 (Sask. Q.B.); *Professional Institute of the Public Service of Canada v. Canada (Attorney General)* (2002), 62 O.R. (3d) 682 (Ont. C.A.); *Berry v. Pulley* (2002), 211 D.L.R. (4th) 651 (S.C.C.). Section 1 of the *Judicial Review Procedure Act*, R.S.O. 1990, c. J.1 gives status to unions (see Appendix 3. Compare *S.G.E.U. v. Saskatchewan* (1998), 172 Sask. R. 83 (Sask. C.A.).

117 *MacLean v. Ontario (Liquor Licence Board)* (1975), 9 O.R. (2d) 597 (Ont. Div. Ct.); *Westlake v. R.*, [1971] 3 O.R. 533 (Ont. H.C.), affirmed [1972] 2 O.R. 605 (Ont. C.A.), affirmed [1973] S.C.R. vii (S.C.C.); *Perehinec v. Northern Pipeline Agency* (1980), [1981] 2 W.W.R. 566 (Alta. C.A.), affirmed [1983] 2 S.C.R. 513 (S.C.C.); *Canada (National Harbours Board) v. Langelier* (1968), [1969] S.C.R. 60 (S.C.C.). Most of the cases do not involve a prerogative remedy, but rather a private law action where the legal personality of the respondent or defendant is critical.

118 See the *Nor. Pipeline* case, *ibid.*, and Federal Court Rule 2. Compare *Smith v. New Brunswick (Human Rights Commission)* (1997), 185 N.B.R. (2d) 301 (N.B. C.A.), leave to appeal refused (1997), 192 N.B.R. (2d) 198 (note) (S.C.C.) holding that the Commission is not a suable entity for purposes of declaratory relief, with the suggestion in *Smith v. New Brunswick (Human Rights Commission)* (1999), 217 N.B.R. (2d) 336 (N.B. C.A.), leave to appeal refused (2000), 259 N.R. 200 (note) (S.C.C.) that the decision of the Commission would have been reviewable by *certiorari* but for the lateness of the motion.

119 For example, *Education Board v. Rice*, [1911] A.C. 179 (U.K. H.L.). The authors understand the text to reflect the state of English law, although Wade & Forsyth, *supra* note 41, do not appear to deal with this point specifically.

view, almost like an *amicus curiae*.[120] The Canadian courts, however, have recognized the right of one administrative body to participate in hearings by another statutory delegate.[121] Legislation sometimes specifically grants this right.[122]

(e) Timing

In theory, the question of standing is a preliminary matter which should be determined at the outset of the application for a prerogative remedy, even under the modern procedure which has been telescoped into one step.[123] In *Finlay v. Canada (Minister of Finance)*, the Supreme Court concluded that whether the issue of standing is to be determined as a preliminary matter or reserved for consideration with the merits of the case "... depends on the nature of the issues raised and whether the court has sufficient material before it, in the way of allegations of fact, considerations of law, and argument, for a proper understanding at a preliminary stage, of the nature of the interest asserted".[124]

(f) Intervention

Sometimes one party will apply to intervene in a judicial review application brought by another.[125] Intervention differs from standing to commence

---

120   *Northwestern Utilities Ltd. v. Edmonton (City)* (1978), [1979] 1 S.C.R. 684 (S.C.C.); D.J. Mullan, "Recent Developments in N.S. Administrative Law" (1978) 4 Dalhousie L.J. 467 at 486-97; L.A. Jacobs and T.S. Kuttner, "Discovering What Tribunals Do: Tribunal Standing Before the Courts" (2002) 81 Can. Bar Rev. 616; *Bransen Construction Ltd. v. C.J.A., Local 1386* (2002), 39 Admin. L.R. (3d) 1 (N.B. C.A.). In *C.A.I.M.A.W., Local 14 v. Canadian Kenworth Co.*, [1989] 2 S.C.R. 983 at 1003-04 (S.C.C.), La Forest J. recognized that a patently unreasonable finding was a jurisdictional error, and therefore the delegate has standing to participate in the judicial review proceedings. See comment by R.W. Macaulay, (1990-91) 4 C.J.A.L.P. 85. For a critical comment about a board exercising this right to be heard, see *Ferguson Bus Lines Ltd. v. A.T.U., Local 1374* (1990), 43 Admin. L.R. 18 at 38-40 (Fed. C.A.), leave to appeal refused (1990), 127 N.R. 240 (note) (S.C.C.) per Mahoney J.

121   See for example, *Rocky View (Municipal District No. 44) v. Alberta (Planning Board)* (1982), 22 Alta. L.R. (2d) 87 (Alta. C.A.); *O'Hanlon v. Foothills (Municipal District No. 31)*, [1979] 6 W.W.R 709 (Alta. C.A.), affirmed (1979), [1980] 1 W.W.R. 304 (Alta. C.A.); *Sarcee Gravel Products Inc. v. Alberta (Workers' Compensation Board)* (2002), 44 Admin. L.R. (3d) 1 (Alta. Q.B.).

122   See R.F. Reid and H. David, *Administrative Law and Practice*, 2d ed. (Toronto, Butterworths, 1978), Chapter 10, "Appearances by Tribunals in Court"; *Canada Labour Code*, R.S.C. 1985, c. L-2, sec. 22(1.1); *Energy Resources Conservation Act*, R.S.A. 2000, c. E-10, s. 41(8) (right to be heard on appeal).

123   English Order 53, Rules 3(1) and (7) require a preliminary application for permission to seek judicial review, and require the applicant to show a "sufficient interest".

124   (1986), 23 Admin. L.R. 197 at 206-07 (S.C.C.); and see *Sierra Club of Canada v. Canada (Minister of Finance)* (1999), 13 Admin. L.R. (3d) 280 (Fed. T.D.) and the *Inland Revenue* case (1981), [1982] A.C. 617 (U.K. H.L.).

125   Intervention is provided for in some rules of court: see for example Ontario R. 13 and Federal Court R. 109. See s. 28 of the *Energy Resources Conservation Act*, R.S.A. 2000, c. E-10, and s. 95(3) of the *Environmental Protection and Enhancement Act*, R.S.A. 2000, c. E-12 for statutory recognition of interveners; see also A.J. Roman and M.R. Hemingway, "Standing to Intervene" (1988) 26 Admin. L.R. 49; and S.J. McWilliams, "Ontario *Inter-*

proceedings, because intervention assumes there is another party that qualifies for full standing. Thus the test for intervention is whether the proposed inter-venor will bring a helpful perspective to the case without causing undue repetition or complexity.[126] Sometimes, of course, the intervenor may also be an aggrieved party that could obtain standing on its own.[127]

7. Discretionary Nature of the Prerogative Remedies

The discretionary nature of the prerogative remedies (and of the remedy of "judicial review"[128]) in effect amounts to a restriction on a citizen's right to obtain redress for illegal governmental action. The court's discretion permits it to deny relief to an applicant even though the applicant has made out its case.[129]

In addition to the express provisions of the rules or statutes, the common law outlined several bases upon which the court may exercise its discretion to refuse a remedy. The courts have recognized the following broad categories in which they have sometimes exercised their discretion to refuse prerogative remedies: (a) where the applicant has waived its right to object to the defect in the statutory delegate's proceedings, or acquiesced in them; (b) where there is unreasonable delay in bringing the application to the court; (c) where the applicant's conduct disentitles it to the remedy; (d) where granting the remedy would be moot, academic or futile; and (e) where there is an equally effective alternative remedy.

(a) Waiver and Acquiescence

The parties cannot validly confer jurisdiction on an administrative body if that jurisdiction is lacking under its constituent legislation.[130] Where a tribunal

---

venor Funding Project: The Experience of the Ontario Energy Board" (1991-92) 5 C.J.A.L.P. 203; M.I. Jeffrey, "Ontario's Intervenor Funding Project Act" (1989-90) 3 C.J.A. L.P. 69; J. Keeping, "Interveners' Costs" (1989-90) 3 C.J.A.L.P. 81.

126   The cases are summarized in Halpern v. Toronto (City) (2000), 51 O.R. (3d) 742 (Ont. Div. Ct.), Halpern v. Canada (Attorney General) (January 19, 2001), Doc. 684/00, [2001] O.J. No. 879 (Ont. Div. Ct.), and Halpern v. Toronto (City) (2003), 169 O.A.C. 172 (Ont. C.A. [In Chambers]). See also Clark v. Canada (Attorney General) (1977), 17 O.R. (2d) 593 (Ont. H.C.); Benoit v. Canada (2001), 272 N.R. 169 (Fed. C.A.); R. v. Finta, [1993] 1 S.C.R. 1138 (S.C.C.).

127   See for example Assn. of Parents for Fairness in Education, Grand Falls District 50 Branch v. Société des Acadiens du Nouveau-Brunswick Inc., [1986] 1 S.C.R. 549 (S.C.C.), granting a non-party leave to appeal.

128   The common law discretion is expressly preserved in the Judicial Review Procedure Act, R.S.B.C. 1996, c. 241, s. 8; and the Judicial Review Procedure Act, R.S.O. 1990, c. J.1, s. 2(5).

129   For the implications of this discretion, see Rt. Hon. Sir Thomas Bingham, "Should Public Law Remedies be Discretionary?" [1991] P.L. 64. Even the Attorney General can be denied a remedy: Canada (Auditor General) v. Canada (Minister of Energy, Mines & Resources), [1989] 2 S.C.R. 49 (S.C.C.) at para. 53. Damages are not discretionary: see Chapter 16.

130   Because the delegate's action would still be ultra vires the legislative authority granted to it. But the parties may waive this defect, and this waiver may cause the courts to exercise their discretion to refuse a prerogative remedy.

commits a jurisdictional error, its decision is void. No amount of acquiescence by the parties can legally validate its non-decision. Nevertheless, because the prerogative remedies are discretionary, it does not follow that a person who acquiesced in the invalid proceedings will necessarily be granted a remedy: the applicant's conduct may disentitle it to relief. Such a discretionary with-holding of the remedy, however, will not thereby make the tribunal's proceed-ings valid.[131] It simply means that a particular applicant's conduct was such that the court decided to exercise its discretion to refuse a remedy.

Acquiescence or implied waiver may occur when no objection is made to the tribunal's jurisdiction although the defect was apparent. Where there is a breach of the rules of natural justice or procedural fairness, continued partici-pation in the proceedings may deprive the applicant of the right to a prerogative remedy. For example, the court may refuse relief where the applicant raises an allegation of bias after the proceedings have gone adversely, but the applicant knew of all the facts relating to bias before or at the time of the hearing;[132] where the applicant failed to object to procedures adopted by a tribunal;[133] or where the applicant failed to object to procedural rulings made by a tribunal during a hearing.[134]

(b) Unreasonable Delay

Where an applicant is guilty of unreasonable delay in bringing its appli-cation before a court, it may find the remedy barred.[135] This is especially true

131   See W. Wade and C. Forsyth, *supra*, note 41, c. 10; *Zündel v. Canada (Human Rights Commission)* (2000), 30 Admin. L.R. (3d) 77 (Fed. C.A.); *Immeubles Port Louis Ltée c. Lafontaine (Village)*, [1991] 1 S.C.R. 326 (S.C.C.).

132   *Canada (Human Rights Commission) v. Taylor*, [1990] 3 S.C.R. 892 (S.C.C.); *Huyck v. Musqueam Indian Band* (2000), 23 Admin. L.R. (3d) 28 (Fed. T.D.), additional reasons at (2000), 2000 CarswellNat 2632 (Fed. T.D.), affirmed (2001), 272 N.R. 188 (Fed. C.A.), leave to appeal refused (2002), 293 N.R. 191 (note) (S.C.C.); *C.A.L.P.A. v. Canadian Pacific Air Lines Ltd.* (1966), 57 D.L.R. (2d) 417 (B.C. C.A.); compare *Committee for Justice & Liberty v. Canada (National Energy Board)* (1976), [1978] 1 S.C.R. 369 (S.C.C.).

133   *Camac Exploration Ltd. v. Alberta (Oil & Gas Conservation Board)* (1964), 47 W.W.R. 81 (Alta. T.D.); *R. v. Canada (Labour Relations Board)* (1966), 58 D.L.R. (2d) 134 (Ont. C.A.); *Seaside Real Estate Ltd. v. Halifax-Dartmouth Real Estate Board* (1964), 44 D.L.R. (2d) 248 (N.S. C.A.); *Dunluce Steak House & Pizza Ltd. v. Alberta (Liquor Control Board)* (1992), 7 Admin. L.R. (2d) 31 (Alta. Q.B.); *Archer c. Université de Moncton* (1992), 9 Admin. L.R. (2d) 200 (N.B. Q.B.); *Radhakrishnan v. U.C.F.A.* (2002), 5 Alta. L.R. (4th) 1 (Alta. C.A.); *Immeubles Port Louis Ltée v. Lafontaine (Village)*, [1991] 1 S.C.R. 326 (S.C.C.); *Mohammadian v. Canada (Minister of Citizenship & Immigration)*, [2001] 4 F.C. 85 (Fed. C.A.), leave to appeal refused (2002), 292 N.R. 195 (note) (S.C.C.).

134   See for example *Yuz, Re* (1986), 24 Admin. L.R. 276 (Ont. C.A.), leave to appeal to S.C.C. refused (1987), 80 N.R. 317 (note) (S.C.C.). Compare *Hryciuk v. Ontario (Lieutenant Governor)* (1996), 31 O.R. (3d) 1 (Ont. C.A.), leave to appeal refused (1997), 223 N.R. 222 (note) (S.C.C.), reversing (1994), 18 O.R. (3d) 695 (Ont. Div. Ct.).

135   *Canada (Anti-Dumping Tribunal), Re* (1975), [1976] 2 S.C.R. 739 (S.C.C.); *Babiuk v. Calgary (City)* (1992), 12 M.P.L.R. (2d) 197 (Alta. Q.B.); *Carpenter v. Vancouver (City) Commissioners of Police* (1986), 34 D.L.R. (4th) 50 (B.C. C.A.), leave to appeal refused (1987), 79 N.R. 79 (note) (S.C.C.); *Harelkin v. University of Regina*, [1979] 2 S.C.R. 561 (S.C.C.); *Angus v. R.*, [1990] 3 F.C. 410 (Fed. C.A.). See also *Immeubles Port Louis Ltée*

where the delay would result in hardship or prejudice to the public interest or to third parties who have acted in good faith on the strength of the delegate's apparently valid decision.[136] Rule 743.06 of the Alberta Rules of Court provides that an application for judicial review to quash or overturn a decision shall be filed and served within six months after the order to which it relates, and further expressly provides that the court cannot enlarge or abridge this time limitation.[137] It does not necessarily follow, however, that an applicant can safely wait for six months without running the risk of the court finding there to have been an unreasonable delay.[138] What constitutes unreasonable delay is a question to be decided in each case. One primary consideration must be the need for effective and reliable administration, which must entail the notion of finality in decision-making.

Delay in bringing an application for prohibition may mean that the tribunal has reached its decision and there is nothing that the court can prohibit: an attempt would have to be made to quash the decision by *certiorari* instead.[139]

(c) Clean Hands and the General Conduct of the Applicant

Apart from the two examples already described (waiver and delay) where the applicant's conduct may lead to a refusal of the remedy, other forms of conduct may also be taken into consideration. For instance, the court may exercise its discretion to refuse a prerogative remedy if the applicant has dealt with the tribunal in bad faith, been deceitful, withheld evidence or engaged in fraudulent conduct.[140] Where the applicant's motives can be called into ques-

---

   c. Lafontaine (Village), [1991] 1 S.C.R. 326 (S.C.C.) and *Ostrowski v. Saskatchewan (Beef Stabilization Board)* (1993), 109 Sask. R. 40, 9 Admin. L.R. (2d) 227 (Sask. C.A.).

136   See for example the injustice which resulted in *Welbridge Holdings Ltd. v. Greater Winnipeg (Municipality)* (1970), [1971] S.C.R. 957 (S.C.C.). See also *R. v. Canada (Board of Broadcast Governors)* (1962), 33 D.L.R. (2d) 449 (Ont. C.A.); *J.G. Morgan Development Corp. v. Canada (Minister of Public Works)* (1992), 8 Admin. L.R. (2d) 247 (Fed. T.D.); *Chippewas of Sarnia Band v. Canada (Attorney General)* (2000), 51 O.R. (3d) 641 (Ont. C.A.), additional reasons at (2001), 14 C.P.C. (5th) 7 (Ont. C.A.), leave to appeal refused (2001), 158 O.A.C. 199 (note) (S.C.C.), reconsideration refused [2002] 3 C.N.L.R. iv (note) (S.C.C.). But see *Friends of the Oldman River Society v. Canada (Minister of Transport)*, [1992] 1 S.C.R. 3, 3 Admin. L.R. (2d) 1 (S.C.C.), where a substantial delay was viewed as reasonable in the circumstances.

137   Query: whether the six-month rule applies to an application by the Crown for *certiorari*. This raises the vexed question of whether or not the Crown is bound by the Rules Of Court. To the extent that this Rule is substantive, it has been ratified by statute: *Judicature Act*, R.S.A. 2000 c. J-2, s. 63. Compare *Ostrowski v. Saskatchewan, supra* note 135, declaring invalid the former Saskatchewan Rule 675(2).

138   *R. v. Justices of Stafford*, [1940] 2 K.B. 33 at 46-47 (Eng. C.A.); *Inter-Meridian Investing Ltd. v. Alberta (Assessment Appeal Board)* (1997), 55 Alta. L.R. (3d) 113 (Alta. C.A.).

139   With the current procedure in Alberta, the court may choose another appropriate remedy at the hearing: Rule 753.04.

140   *Cock v. British Columbia (Labour Relations Board)* (1960), 33 W.W.R. 429 (B.C. C.A.); *Burgin v. King (Township)*, [1973] 3 O.R. 174 (Ont. Div. Ct.); *Rodd v. Essex (County)* (1910), 44 S.C.R. 137 (S.C.C.); *Ex parte Fry*, [1954] 1 W.L.R. 730 (C.A.); *Glynn v. Keele University*, [1971] 1 W.L.R. 487 (Eng. Ch. Div.); *R. v. Tucker* (1992), 9 O.R. (3d) 291 (Ont. C.A.), leave to appeal refused (1993), 150 N.R. 393 (note) (S.C.C.); *Khalil v. Canada (Secretary of State)*, [1999] 4 F.C. 661 (Fed. C.A.).

tion, the application may fail.[141] Thus, a remedy may be refused where the motive behind the application is really to further the applicant's own pecuniary interests or for some other purely personal motive considered improper by the court.[142]

(d) Futility, Mootness and Non-Material Errors

Prerogative remedies will not be issued where it would be futile to do so. For instance, once a tribunal has made a decision, prohibition is no longer useful.[143] Similarly, *mandamus* is unnecessary where the tribunal has agreed to perform its statutory duty.[144] Remedies that are incapable of meaningful implementation will not be granted.[145] If subsequent events have made the issue moot, the remedy can be withheld.[146] Minor procedural irregularities which in fact, or in all likelihood, had no effect on the ultimate decision have also been ignored by the courts.[147] On the other hand, it is not the court's task to second-guess the result if the statutory delegate had performed its function correctly, so that the court generally will not exercise its discretion to refuse a

---

141   *Swim, Ex parte* (1921), 49 N.B.R. 207 (N.B. C.A.); *Concerned Citizens Committee (Borden & Carleton Siding) v. Prince Edward Island (Minister of Environmental Resources)* (1994), 24 Admin. L.R. (2d) 149 (P.E.I. T.D.).

142   *Homex Realty & Development Co. v. Wyoming (Village)*, [1980] 2 S.C.R. 1011 (S.C.C.); *Solex Developments Co. v. Taylor (District)* (1998), 60 B.C.L.R. (3d) 53 (B.C. C.A.), additional reasons at (1999), 1999 CarswellBC 463 (B.C. C.A.).

143   Although *certiorari* may be used to quash an improper decision that has been made.

144   *Tetzlaff v. Canada (Minister of the Environment)* (1991), 47 Admin. L.R. 290 (Fed. T.D.), varied other grounds (1991), [1992] 2 F.C. 215 (Fed. C.A.).

145   *Scholton v. Chemainus Health Care Centre* (1995), 29 M.P.L.R. (2d) 249 (B.C. S.C.); *Clubb v. Saanich (District)* (1996), 35 Admin. L.R. (2d) 309 (B.C. S.C.); *Canadian Pacific Forest Products Ltd. v. British Columbia (Minister of Forests)* (1993), 17 Admin. L.R. (2d) 261 (B.C. S.C.). But compare *Friends of the Oldman River Society v. Canada (Minister of Transport)*, *supra* note 136.

146   *Lavoie v. Canada (Minister of the Environment)* (2002), 43 Admin. L.R. (3d) 209 (Fed. C.A.); *Wiebe v. Alberta (Labour Relations Board)* (2001), 93 Alta. L.R. (3d) 47 (Alta. C.A.); *Society of the Friends of Strathcona Park v. British Columbia (Minister of the Environment, Lands & Parks)* (1999), 20 Admin. L.R. (3d) 125 (B.C. S.C.); *Narvey v. Canada (Adjudicator appointed under Immigration Act)* (2000), 265 N.R. 205 (Fed. C.A.), affirming (1997), 140 F.T.R. 1 (Fed. T.D.). The Court has a discretion to decide an issue even if the case is moot: *Borowski v. Canada (Attorney General)*, [1989] 1 S.C.R. 342 (S.C.C.).

147   *R. v. Canada (Board of Broadcast Governors)*, [1962] O.R. 657 (Ont. C.A.); *Duperron v. Fort McMurray School District No. 2833* (1990), 74 Alta. L.R. (2d) 420 (note) (Alta. C.A.); *Caddy Lake Cottagers Assn. v. Florence-Nora Access Road Inc.* (1998), 129 Man. R. (2d) 71, 12 Admin. L.R. (3d) 24 (Man. C.A.); *Bridgeland Riverside Community Assn. v. Calgary (City)* (1982), 19 Alta. L.R. (2d) 361 (Alta. C.A.) at 368; *Wayzhushk Onigum Nation v. Kakeway* (2001), 35 Admin. L.R. (3d) 1 (Fed. T.D.). Compare *Costello v. Calgary (City)*, [1983] 1 S.C.R. 14 (S.C.C.) where the statute called for 21 days' notice, and only 17 days' notice was given; the mandatory statutory language resulted in the quashing of the decision. See Alberta Rule 753.07; *Federal Courts Act*, R.S.C. 1985, c. F-7, s. 18.1(5); *Judicial Review Act*, R.S.P.E.I. 1988, c. J-3, s. 6; *Judicial Review Procedure Act*, R.S.O. 1990, c. J.1, s. 3 and *Judicial Review Procedure Act*, R.S.B.C. 1996, c. 241, s. 9 covering defects in form and technical irregularities.

prerogative remedy where a breach of natural justice has occurred.[148] But where the decision under review would have been the same despite the error, the remedy may be withheld.[149]

(e) Availability of Alternative Remedies

The courts have sometimes exercised their discretion[150] to refuse a prerogative remedy when an equally effective alternative remedy (such as an appeal) is, or was, available to the applicant.[151] The courts' approach on this aspect of discretion has diverged in recent years in England and in Canada. The English courts have tended to assert their right to issue prerogative remedies to correct illegality without requiring the applicant to exhaust its statutory or administrative rights of appeal.[152] By contrast, the decision of the majority of the Supreme Court of Canada in *Harelkin v. University of Regina*[153] is a clear indication to Canadian courts to give precedence to the alternative remedy prescribed by the legislators, even if *habeas corpus* is involved.[154] This approach has recently been reinforced by the Supreme Court of Canada in *R. v. Consolidated Maybrun Mines Ltd.*[155] and *R. v. Al Klippert Ltd.*[156] On the other hand, when the appeal would be of little value and the result must be clear, the court may grant

---

148   See Dickson J.'s dissenting judgment in *Harelkin v. University of Regina*, [1979] 2 S.C.R. 561 (S.C.C.); *Friends of the Oldman River Society, supra* note 136; *Cardinal v. Kent Institution*, [1985] 2 S.C.R. 643 (S.C.C.); *Newfoundland Telephone Co. v. Newfoundland (Board of Commissioners of Public Utilities)*, [1992] 1 S.C.R. 623 (S.C.C.).

149   See for example *Mobil Oil Canada Ltd. v. Canada-Newfoundland (Offshore Petroleum Board)*, [1994] 1 S.C.R. 202, 21 Admin. L.R. (2d) 248 (S.C.C.). See also P.D. Ruby, "Remedial Discretion: When Should the Court Right the Wrong?" (1997) 11 C.J.A.L.P. 259.

150   Judicial review of a federal tribunal is not available when an appeal exists, under s. 18.5 of the *Federal Courts Act*, R.S.C. 1985, c. F-7. Under the *Judicial Review Act*, R.S.P.E.I. 1988, c. J-3, s. 4(2) the applicant must elect between the appeal and judicial review. Section 2(1) of the *Judicial Review Procedure Act*, R.S.O. 1990, c. J.1 allows judicial review "despite any right of appeal".

151   *Harelkin v. University of Regina*, [1979] 2 S.C.R. 561 (S.C.C.); *Canadian Pacific Ltd. v. Matsqui Indian Band*, [1995] 1 S.C.R. 3 (S.C.C.); *Canada (Auditor General) v. Canada (Minister of Energy, Mines & Resources)*, [1989] 2 S.C.R. 49 (S.C.C.); *R. v. Dubois*, [1986] 1 S.C.R. 366 (S.C.C.), reconsideration refused (1986), 22 Admin. L.R. xxviii (S.C.C.). In *Harelkin* and the *Auditor General's* case the alternative remedy was found to be adequate, but in *Matsqui* and *Dubois* it was not. See the further discussion in Chapter 12.

152   See W. Wade & C. Forsyth, *supra* note 41, c. 20.

153   *Harelkin, supra* note 151.

154   See the cases at *supra* note 21.

155   [1998] 1 S.C.R. 706 (S.C.C.), affirming (1996), 5 Admin. L.R. (3d) 288 (Ont. C.A.), leave to appeal allowed (1996), 206 N.R. 319 (note) (S.C.C.).

156   [1998] 1 S.C.R. 737 (S.C.C.), reversing (1996), 5 Admin. L.R. (3d) 274 (Alta. C.A.), leave to appeal allowed (1997), 214 N.R. 160 (note) (S.C.C.), reversing (1993) 146 A.R. 211 (Alta. Q.B.) See also D.P. Jones, "Recent Restrictions on Collateral Attacks on Administrative Decisions" presented at B.C. C.L.E. Program on *Recent Developments in Administrative Law*, November 1998, Vancouver.

the relief and thereby avoid further proceedings and expense.[157] Prerogative relief may also be available once the appeal process has been exhausted.[158]

8. The Application for Judicial Review in Alberta

Since 1987, there has been a single process for the review of administrative action in Alberta:[159]

753.04

> (1) On an application for judicial review, the court may grant any relief that the applicant would be entitled to in proceedings for any one or more of the following remedies:
>
> > (a) an order in the nature of *mandamus*, prohibition, *certiorari, quo warranto* or *habeas corpus*;
> >
> > (b) a declaration or injunction.

Accordingly, all applications for judicial review are commenced by way of Originating Notice.[160] They use the same style of cause as would be used in other civil applications (*"Applicant" v. "Delegate"*), rather than the traditional style of clause which invoked the name of the Crown as nominal applicant on behalf of the party truly aggrieved (*R. v. "Delegate, ex parte Aggrieved"*).[161] The Rules require the application to be served on both the delegate and the Attorney General (whether or not the Attorney General is a party to the application),[162] as well as any other party interested in the applications.[163] Rule 753.10 allows the court to ensure that any party who may otherwise be effected

---

157   *Voermans v. Alberta (Surface Rights Board)* (1988), 58 Alta. L.R. (2d) 277 (Alta. Q.B.); *Imperial Oil Ltd. v. British Columbia (Regional Waste Manager)* (1998), 51 B.C.L.R. (3d) 93 (B.C. S.C. [In Chambers]); *Québec (Commission des accidents du travail) c. Valade*, [1982] 1 S.C.R. 1103 (S.C.C.).

158   *Khan v. University of Ottawa* (1997), 34 O.R. (3d) 535 (Ont. C.A.).

159   Alta. Reg. 457/87, authorized by S.A. 1987, c. 10; reproduced in Appendix 4. Part 56.1 of the *Alberta Rules of Court* supplants most of the old *Crown Practice Rules in Civil Matters* and governs the process for applications for judicial review. Note however that Part 56 (entitled *Crown Practice Rules*) has not be replaced *in toto*: certain old rules continue in force. For a more detailed consideration of the Rules, see D.P. Jones, "The Judicial Review Rules – Part 56.1" contained in *Papers presented at the Mid-Winter Meeting of the Alberta Branch of the Canadian Bar Association, 1992*.

160   Rules 753.02 and 753.03

161   Rule 753.08, which refers to Form G being used. Prior to the implementation of the reforms in 1987, the practice in Alberta was mixed about how to style an application for a prerogative remedy.

162   Rule 753.10(2) states that the Attorney General is entitled as of right to be heard on the application, which clearly applies even when the Attorney General is not a party.

163   Rule 753.09. Subsection (2) allows the Court to direct service of the Originating Notice on any other person (not a party). Rule 753.10(1) permits the Court to direct the addition or striking out of any person as a party to the proceedings for judicial review, and Rule 753.10(3) allows any affected person to apply to become a party.

by the proceedings be given notice.[164] Rule 753.12 and Rule 753.13 set out the procedure for obtaining the record from the decision-maker that is being reviewed.[165]

There is a mandatory six-month time limit for seeking judicial review in the nature of *certiorari*.[166] The wording of the rule indicates that the six-month time limit applies to the other judicial review remedies (such as declarations) that have the effect of quashing the delegate's decision.[167]

Part 56.1 of the Alberta Rules allows the application for judicial review to be used in a number of novel ways. The most important aspect of the procedure is the ability to combine applications for prerogative relief with an application for a private law injunction or declaration.[168] (It is not possible, however, to combine an application for prerogative relief with an action for damages.[169]) Further, the court has the power to grant any remedy to the applicant which would be appropriate in the circumstances, whether or not the formal pleadings specifically identified that remedy. Hence an applicant may apply for several types of relief and let the court determine which is the most appropriate.[170] The court also has discretion to convert the process of judicial review into a much more broadly based action involving discoveries and potentially *viva voce* evidence.[171]

Rule 753.14 gives the court the power to require the delegate to file a Return, even in circumstances where the relief sought does not involve an order to set aside the decision, if the record is necessary to establish the

---

164   This has been a concern especially if a remedy is granted and third parties will have their rights affected: *Can Am Simulation Ltd. v. Newfoundland (Minister of Works, Services & Transportation)* (1991), 92 Nfld. & P.E.I.R. 227 (Nfld. T.D.)

165   See *Yorke v. Northside-Victoria District School Board* (1992), 90 D.L.R. (4th) 643 (N.S. C.A.) where the British Columbia Court of Appeal discusses its equivalent of R. 753.12 and 753.13 of the Alberta *Rules of Court*.

166   Rule 753.11. The six-month time limit cannot be extended or waived: subsection 2. Note that this provision requires the application to be filed *and served* (presumably on everyone necessary, including the Attorney General) within the six-month time frame.

167   *Dwyer v. College of Physicians & Surgeons (Alberta)* (1989), 98 A.R. 81 (Alta. Q.B.). But a bylaw is not a "decision or act" so it is not covered by the Rule: *United Taxi Drivers' Fellowship of Southern Alberta v. Calgary (City)* (2002), 3 Alta. L.R. (4th) 211 (Alta. C.A.), leave to appeal allowed (2003), 311 N.R. 198 (note) (S.C.C.), reversed 2004 SCC 19 (S.C.C.).

168   Rule 753.04

169   *Graduate Students' Assn. of the University of Alberta v. University of Alberta* (1991), 80 Alta. L.R. (2d) 280 (Alta. C.A.). English Order 53, Rule 7 allows a claim for damages to be added.

170   For instance in converting an application for one kind of relief into another: *Chandler v. Assn. of Architects (Alberta)* (1988), 92 A.R. 161 (Alta. C.A.); *University of Alberta v. Alberta (Human Rights Commission)* (1988), 61 Alta. L.R. (2d) 330 (Alta. Q.B.). See also Rules 753.04(2) and 753.16.

171   Rule 753.16. Query whether discoveries are available on an application for judicial review itself: see *Broda v. Edmonton (City)* (1989), 102 A.R. 255 (Alta. Q.B.) at 260 per Trussler J., and the commentary on this rule in A. Fradsham, *Alberta Rules of Court Annotated* (Toronto: Carswell, published annually). Note that in England it is possible, but unusual, to call *viva voce* evidence: *R. v. Secretary for Transport, ex parte Sheriff and Sons Ltd.* (*The Times*, Dec. 18 1986): see the comment by A.W. Bradey, [1987] P.L. 141.

applicant's claim. Conversely, the court may dispense with the filing of all or part of the record in appropriate circumstances.

The court is also given a general power to stay any proceeding pending the determination of an application for judicial review, provided it would not be detrimental to the public interest or to public safety to do so.[172] Prior to 1987, it appears to have been the law that it was contemptuous for the delegate to proceed in the face of an application for judicial intervention,[173] although this was not universally held to be the case.[174]

Rule 753.07 authorizes the court to refuse relief if the sole established ground for complaint is a defect in form or a technical irregularity, provided no substantial wrong or miscarriage of justice has occurred.

An appeal lies to the Court of Appeal from an order granted by the Court of Queen's Bench on an application for judicial review.[175] The Appeal is a matter of right; no leave is required.

9. The *Federal Courts Act*[176]

As noted in the discussion above about each of the prerogative remedies, it is extremely important to make an application against a "federal board, commission or other tribunal" in the correct court, whether the superior court of a province on the one hand, or the Federal Court or Federal Court of Appeal on the other.[177]

The original version of the *Federal Courts Act* passed in 1970 had a long and confusing history in administrative law. The wording of the original version of the Act divided the responsibility for reviewing the conduct of federal delegates between the Trial Division and the Appellate Division depending on whether or not the delegate was obligated to act on a "judicial or quasi-judicial basis". The *Federal Courts Act* was amended in 1990 to eliminate this unsatisfactory distinction.[178] The judicial review for most federal delegates now rests with the Federal Court. However, the Federal Court of Appeal has jurisdiction to hear applications for judicial review concerning certain listed federal delegates, including the following important tribunals:[179] the Canadian Radiotelevision and Telecommunications Commission, the National Energy Board, the Canada Industrial Relations Board, the Public Service Staff Relations

---

172　Rule 753.15, discussed in *U.F.C.W., Local 401 v. Economic Development Edmonton*, 2002 ABQB 590 (Ata. Q.B.). Under English Order 53, Rule 3(10) a stay is automatic.

173　See observations of Kerans J.A. in *Law Society (Alberta) v. Black* (1983), 29 Alta. L.R. (2d) 326 at 329 (Alta. C.A.).

174　*U.A., Local 488 v. Fish International Canada Ltd.* (1985), 61 A.R. 9 (Alta. Q.B.).

175　Rule 753.17.

176　For an excellent and detailed discussion of the jurisprudence under the relevant provisions of the Act, see Sgayias *et al.*, *Federal Court Practice* (Toronto: Thomson Carswell, published annually).

177　See *Carruthers v. Lions Gate Hospital* (1983), 4 Admin. L.R. 51 (Fed. C.A.), leave to appeal refused (1984), 4 Admin. L.R. 51n (S.C.C.) for a consideration of what constitutes a "Federal Board, Commission or other tribunal".

178　S.C. 1990, c. 8, which was effective on February 1, 1992.

179　Section 28.

Board, the Canadian Transportation Agency, Umpires under the *Employment Insurance Act*, and the Competition Tribunal.

The procedure in both the Federal Court and the Federal Court of Appeal is an "application for judicial review". As in Alberta, the relief which may be obtained on an application for judicial review includes the relief which formerly would have been obtained by injunction, *certiorari*, prohibition, *mandamus*, *quo warranto* or by way of declaratory relief. It is not possible to join an application for *habeas corpus* (which the statute left in the provincial superior courts) against a federal body with an application for any other prerogative remedy, nor any private law remedy in an application for judicial review pursuant to either section 18 or 28.[180]

Unlike most provincial procedure reforms,[181] the *Federal Courts Act* specifically articulates the grounds[182] upon which the Federal Courts can review a decision of a federal board, commission or other tribunal – namely, that it:

(a)   acted without jurisdiction, acted beyond its jurisdiction or refused to exercise its jurisdiction;

(b)   failed to observe a principle of natural justice, procedural fairness or other procedure that it was required by law to observe;

(c)   erred in law in making a decision or an order, whether or not the error appears on the face of the record;

(d)   based its decision or order on an erroneous finding of fact that it made in a perverse or capricious manner or without regard for the material before it;

(e)   acted, or failed to act, by reason of fraud or perjured evidence; or

(f)   acted in any other way that was contrary to law.

Finally, it is important to remember that the jurisdiction of the Federal Courts is entirely statutory; they do not have the same inherent jurisdiction possessed by the provincial superior courts to correct all governmental illegalities.

10.   Conclusion

The prerogative remedies have a long history of being used to control illegal governmental action. The reforms in Alberta and under the *Federal Courts Act* provide a uniform procedure for obtaining relief from illegal governmental activity. It is vital to know the purpose, scope and limitations of the prerogative remedies when using the procedure to apply for judicial review of the legality of a delegate's decision.

---

180   *R. v. Mitchell* (1975), [1976] 2 S.C.R. 570 (S.C.C.).
181   Grounds for review are found in the *Judicial Review Act*, R.S.P.E.I. 1998, c. J-3, s. 4.
182   S. 18.1(4) and s. 28(2) of the *Federal Courts Act*, R.S.C. 1985, c. F-7.

11. Selected Bibliography

Procedural Reform

Alberta Institute of Law Research and Reform, Report No. 40, *Judicial Review of Administrative Action: Application for Judicial Review* (1984).

Alberta Law Reform Institute, Report No. 79, *Powers and Procedures for Administrative Tribunals in Alberta* (1999).

Beatson & Matthews, "Reform of Administrative Law Remedies: The First Step" (1978) 41 Mod. L. Rev. 437.

British Columbia Law Reform Commission, Report No. 18, A Procedure for *Judicial Review of the Actions of Statutory Agencies* (1974).

English Law Commission, *Remedies in Administrative Law, Working Paper No. 40*, 1971.

English Law Commission, *Report on Remedies in Administrative Law*, No. 73, Cmnd. 6407, 1976.

Jones, D.P., "The Judicial Review Rules – Part 56.1", in *Papers presented at the Mid-Winter Meetings of the Alberta Branch of the Canadian Bar Association, 1992.*

Law Reform Commission of Canada, Report No. 14, *Judicial Review and the Federal Court* (1980).

Mullan, D.J., *The Federal Court Act: A Study of the Court's Administrative Law Jurisdiction*, prepared for the Law Reform Commission of Canada, 1977.

Northey, J.F., "An Administrative Law Division of the New Zealand Supreme Court – A Proposal for Law Reform" (1969) 7 Alta. L. Rev. 62.

Northey, J.F., "The Administrative Division of the New Zealand Supreme Court – A Postscript" (1977) 17 Alta. L.R. 186.

Habeas Corpus

Cohen, M., "*Habeas Corpus Cum Causa* – The Emergence of the Modern Writ" (1940) 18 Can. Bar Rev. 10 and 172.

Cohen, M., "Some Considerations on the Origins of *Habeas Corpus*" (1938) 16 Can. Bar Rev 92.

Heuston, R.F.V., "*Habeas Corpus Procedure*" (1950) 66 L.Q. Rev. 79.

Manson A., "Extraordinary Remedies – *Habeas Corpus*" (1993) 9 Admin. L.R. (2d) 269.

Sharpe, R.J., *The Law of Habeas Corpus*, (Oxford: Clarendon Press,1976).

Standing

Cromwell, T.A., *Locus Standi: A Commentary on the Law of Standing in Canada* (Toronto: Carswell 1986).

Hay, R.T., "Exactly Who is "Directly Affected"? – A Trilogy on Public Interest Standing before Administrative Tribunals" (1996) 5 R.A.L. 148.

Mercer, P.P., "The *Gouriet Case*: Public Interest Litigation in Britain and Canada" [1979] P.L. 214.

Muldoon, P.R., *Law of Intervention: Status and Practice* (Aurora: Canada Law Book, 1989).

History

de Smith, S.A., "The Prerogative Writs: Historical Origins", published as App. 1 to *Judicial Review of Administrative Action*, 4th ed. by Evans, J.M. (London: Stevens, 1980).

Henderson, E.G., *Foundations of English Administrative Law: Certiorari and Mandamus in the Seventeenth Century* (Cambridge: Harvard University Press, 1963).

Jenks, E., "The Prerogative Writs in English Law" (1923) 32 Yale L.J. 523.

Rubinstein, A., "On the Origins of Judicial Review" (1964) 1 U.B.C. L. Rev. 1.

General References

Dussault, R., *Le Contrôle Judiciaire de l'Administration au Québec* (Quebec Presses de l'Université Laval 1969).

Dussault, R. & Borgeat L., *Traité de droit administratif canadien et québecois* 2d ed., (Quebec Presses de l'Université Laval 1984).

Dussault, R., and Borgeat, L., *Administrative Law: A Treatise* (Toronto: Carswell, 1986), esp. Volume 4.

Evans, J.M., "Judicial Review in Ontario – Some Problems of Pouring Old Wine Into New Bottles" (1977) 55 Can. Bar Rev. 148.

Hogg P.W. & Monahan P.J., *Liability of the Crown,* 3d ed. (Toronto: Carswell, 2000).

Jones, D.P., "Out of Nowhere – Inherent Jurisdiction to Solve Operational Conflicts" (1996) 31 Admin.L.R. (2d) 284.

Report of the Committee of the JUSTICE – All Souls Review of Administrative Law in the United Kingdom (1988), especially c. 6 ("Application for Judicial Review"), and c. 8 ("Standing").

Le Dain, G., "The Supervisory Jurisdiction in Quebec" (1957) 35 Can. Bar Rev. 788.

Lemieux, D., "Supervisory Judicial Control of Federal and Provincial Public Authorities in Quebec" (1979) 17 Osgoode Hall L.J. 133.

Letourneau, G., *The Prerogative Writs in Canadian Criminal Law and Procedure* (Toronto: Butterworths 1976).

Lordon P., *Crown Law* (Toronto: Butterworths, 1991).

Zamir I., *The Declaratory Judgment* (London: Stevens, 1962).

16

Private Law Remedies and The Tort Liability of Public Authorities[1]

---

1 This chapter has been updated by Professor John M. Law of the Faculty of Law at the University of Alberta, Edmonton.

1. Introduction

In addition to statutory appeals[2] and prerogative remedies,[3] redress for illegal governmental actions may sometimes be achieved by using private law actions for damages, injunctions or declarations. Although these private law remedies could historically only be sought by an action, applications for an injunction or a declaration (but not damages) can be included in an application for judicial review, either on their own or in combination with an application for a prerogative remedy.[4]

This chapter provides an overview of the circumstances in which private law remedies may give effective redress to a person aggrieved by governmental action or inaction, as well as some of the limitations inherent in the use of the private law remedies in administrative law.[5]

2. Damages

For centuries, damages have been available against public authorities and officials whose tortious acts or omissions have caused loss or injury to private

---

2 See Chapter 14.

3 See Chapter 15.

4 Part 56.1 of the Alberta Rules of Court provides for a single form of application for the remedies of *certiorari*, prohibition, *mandamus*, *habeas corpus*, *quo warranto*, injunction and declaration (see Appendix 4). Similarly, sections 18, 18.1 and 28 of the *Federal Courts Act*, R.S.C. 1985, c. F.7 (reproduced in Appendix 5), provide for a single form of application when seeking the remedies of *certiorari*, prohibition, *mandamus*, injunction, and declaration against "federal boards, commissions and other tribunals". See the discussion of the procedure in Chapter 15.

5 For a more comprehensive discussion, see: P.W. Hogg and P.J. Monahan, *Liability of the Crown*, 3rd ed. (Toronto: Carswell, 2000) (hereafter "Hogg and Monahan"); R. Sharpe, *Injunctions and Specific Performance,* 2nd ed. (Aurora: Canada Law Book Co., 1996) and Susan Kneebone, *Tort Liability of Public Authorities* (North Ryde, L.B.C. Information Services, 1998).

citizens. As a basic principle, public authorities and officials are personally liable in damages for their injurious misconduct to the same extent as any private citizen or entity would be. Where the governmental action is not lawfully authorized, a public official is liable where the injurious action constitutes one of the nominate torts (such as trespass, nuisance, assault and battery or false imprisonment), defamation[6] or where the action is found to be negligent in relation to a person to whom there is owed a duty of care.[7] In addition, a public officer or authority may be held liable in damages in situations where a private citizen would not. A public officer may be held liable for an abuse of official power under the tort of misfeasance in a public office or for the violation of an individual's constitutional rights or freedoms. In all of these cases, an injured party may seek a remedy by way of damages.[8]

Official liability in damages depends on two necessary pre-conditions: the action complained of must be tortious, and it must also be illegal or *ultra vires*.[9] Hence, a damage action against a public body in tort involves, of necessity, a form of judicial review of the legality of governmental action. Government action which causes loss or injury must be *ultra vires* before it is actionable in tort; *intra vires* action by an official does not generally give rise to tortious liability.[10] However, the relationship between the public law concept of *ultra vires* and the private law concept of tortious liability is not always clear from the cases.[11] In the context of negligence actions against public authorities, the determination of *ultra vires* is often not specifically articulated, probably be-

---

6   J.P.S. McLaren, "The Defamation Action and Municipal Politics" (1980) 29 U.N.L.B. L.J. 123. For a recent defamation action, see *Prud'homme c. Prud'homme*, [2002] 4 S.C.R. 663, 221 D.L.R. (4th) 115 (S.C.C.).

7   The negligent exercise of statutory authority can generally never be authorized, and so implicit within a finding of negligence is a determination that the injurious action was *ultra vires*.

8   This common law right is not restricted unless the injurious public action is permitted by statute. Then the injured party is restricted to the statutory remedy provided in the legislation: *Johannes, Prinz von Thurn und Taxis v. Edmonton (City)*, [1982] 4 W.W.R. 457 (Alta. Q.B.). See also *Marriage v. East Norfolk Rivers Catchment Board* (1949), [1950] 1 K.B. 284 (Eng. C.A.); *Raleigh (Township) v. Williams*, [1893] A.C. 540 (Ontario P.C.); *Canadian National Railway v. Trudeau*, [1962] S.C.R. 398 (S.C.C.); *Leighton v. British Columbia Electric Railway* (1914), 6 W.W.R. 1472 (B.C. C.A.); *North Vancouver (Municipality) v. McKenzie Barge & Marine Ways Ltd.*, [1965] S.C.R. 377 (S.C.C.); *Groat v. Edmonton (City)*, [1928] S.C.R. 522 (S.C.C.); *British Columbia Pea Growers Ltd. v. Portage la Prairie (City)* (1965), [1966] S.C.R. 150 (S.C.C.); *Klimenko v. Winnipeg (City)* (1965), 55 W.W.R. 180 (Man. C.A.). But, compliance with statutory standards does not preclude a finding of civil liability: see *Ryan v. Victoria (City)*, [1999] 1 S.C.R. 201 (S.C.C.).

9   Invalidity, by itself, is necessary but not sufficient to find liability. In *Welbridge Holdings Ltd. v. Greater Winnipeg (Municipality)* (1970), [1971] S.C.R. 957 at 969 (S.C.C.), the Supreme Court of Canada accepted the statement by the distinguished American scholar, K.C. Davis, that invalidity is not the test of fault and it should not be the test of liability (*Administrative Law Treatise*, Vol. 3 (St. Paul, Minn.: West Publishing Co., 1958) at 487.

10 P.W. Hogg, "Government Liability: Assimilating Crown and Subject" (1994) 16 Advocates Quarterly 366 at 374.

11 P.P. Craig, *Administrative Law*, 3rd ed. (London: Sweet & Maxwell, 1994) at 629-32; see also Craig, 5th ed. (London: Sweet & Maxwell, 2003) at 906-08.

cause a decision that the defendant's action was unreasonable necessarily implies that it was *ultra vires*.[12]

The principle that public authorities are liable in damages for their tortious misconduct to the same extent as any private person accords with the Rule of Law.[13] It subjects all levels of public officials to the general law, and it resonates with our belief that every legal system should aspire to remedy every significant wrong: those injured by official wrongdoing should be made whole and official misconduct should be deterred.[14]

Until the statutory reform of the Crown's immunity from tort in the 1950s and 1960s, the primary focus of liability was on particular public officials or employees who were fixed with personal liability when the impugned conduct was held to be tortious. However, the burden of personal liability for official misconduct was limited in a number of ways. First, a public official could advance the defence of statutory authority to an action in tort. If such authority were established, the official would be excused from liability. Secondly, an officer might be able to seek protection from liability under one of a number of common law or statutory immunities. These immunities can be viewed as a legal response to the policy concern that actual or potential liability might impair the proper discharge of official functions. By insulating the official from liability on a qualified (good faith) or an absolute basis, immunities promote the fearless and efficient administration of government. Thirdly, the burden of liability could frequently be shifted, through the principle of vicarious liability, to a public employer of the official, provided it did not constitute "the Crown" with its historical immunity from liability in tort. The public entity, as employer, would then become the primary focus of liability for the tortious misconduct of its employees. Finally, liability could be avoided altogether if the impugned conduct was not tortious, even though it caused injury.[15] In other words, official liability was limited to loss or injury which fell within a recognized heading of tort liability.

This apparently simple scheme of liability has led to significant problems in practice. The scope and character of common law and statutory immunities are often uncertain. Statutory immunity provisions have been haphazardly utilized by the legislature in a variety of statutory settings without any consistency. Different judges at different times have given either limited or liberal effect to these provisions, with the interpretation depending on an unexpressed weighting of the goal of finding liability (so that there can be compensation) with the competing goal of providing immunity (to protect effective decision-making by the government). Similar comments can be made with respect to

---

12   The relationship between the *ultra vires* nature of the action and the tort of negligence is more apparent in cases involving the liability of the government for errors made in the exercise of discretionary authority, where it is clear that the plaintiff must establish that the action was *ultra vires* before a duty of care can arise.

13   A.V. Dicey, *The Law of the Constitution*, 10th ed. (London: MacMillan, 1959) at 193-94; P.W. Hogg, *supra* note 10 at 366-67.

14   P. Shuck, "Suing our Servants: the Court, the Congress and the Liability of Public Officials for Damages" [1980] Sup. Ct. Rev. 281 at 283.

15   "*Damnum sine injuria*".

the common law immunities from liability, which are predicated on imprecise categorizations of government functions and a loose definition of "jurisdiction", making the application of these immunities unpredictable and susceptible to judicial manipulation.

The historic absolute immunity of the Crown from liability in tort has also made a significant contribution to the unsettled nature of the law concerning the liability of public authorities for damages. The existence of such an immunity compelled the courts to define the character and extent of "the Crown" in the context of an ever-widening array of government activities. Although the definition of Crown status still continues to plague the law, the issue of liability has been alleviated somewhat in recent years by the statutory abolition of the Crown's immunity in tort at both the federal and provincial level.

Perhaps the greatest challenge has involved the application of tort law principles of negligence liability to the activities of public bodies and employees. Government action (or inaction) can cause injury in ways that have no counterpart in private activity. Government decision-making is frequently prompted by different considerations from those which motivate private action. Relations between government and private citizens often differ from those of private individuals. We depend on government to protect us both from ourselves and from others. We increasingly expect government to provide a wide range of goods and services essential to our survival or personal status. The uniqueness of government activity is often reflected in the difficult determination of public authority liability.

Where official action or inaction is either identical or bears a strong analogy to private activity, there has been little trouble in applying private law tort principles to determine governmental liability.[16] But where the complaint involves government action which is unique, the courts have had to adapt the principles of tort law so as to recognize the distinctive nature of government and its multifaceted relationship with its citizens. The courts have struggled with the need to strike a balance between the conflicting goals of compensation (on the one hand) and vigorous, effective and efficient governance (on the other hand). In many ways, what has evolved is a "distinct" set of legal principles to govern the legal liability of governmental bodies. The balance of this section on damages will address the basic principles of governmental liability.

(a) Nominate Torts

The nominate torts include actions for trespass, nuisance,[17] assault and battery, false imprisonment, and malicious prosecution.[18]

---

16 The Supreme Court of Canada explicitly recognized this recently in *Cooper v. Hobart* (2001), 206 D.L.R. (4th) 193 (S.C.C.), a negligence action against the British Columbia Registrar of Mortgage Brokers, where the court suggested that broader policy considerations would not operate to negate a duty of care and liability in situations which fell within or were analogous to recognized categories of recovery.

17 While the Supreme Court of Canada created some uncertainty over the liability of governmental authorities in nuisance in *Tock v. St. John's (City) Metropolitan Area Board*, [1989] 2 S.C.R. 1181 (S.C.C.), particularly in relation to the defence of statutory authority, it has

The famous administrative law decision in *Cooper v. Wandsworth Board of Works*[19] is an example where the plaintiff recovered damages for trespass. The Board had demolished the plaintiff's house, purporting to act under the authority given to it in the *Metropolis Management Act 1855*.[20] The Act required a person to give seven days' notice to the Board of his or her intention to build a house; failure to give the required notice made it lawful for the Board to demolish the structure. Mr. Cooper gave no notice. However, the court held that the demolition of the house by the Board was *ultra vires* because the Board had failed to give Mr. Cooper an opportunity to be heard before it acted, even though the legislation did not expressly require this. Thus, the two elements for a successful action in damages were present – the demolition of the house constituted a trespass (an actionable wrong); and the trespass was not lawfully authorized because the Board had acted in an *ultra vires* manner.

A more recent example occurred in Alberta in *Muir v. Alberta*.[21] There the government was held liable for the wrongful detention and wrongful sterilization of the plaintiff (as a young woman) under the province's eugenics legislation, the *Sexual Sterilization Act*.[22] Again, the two necessary elements were present: trespass and a lack of lawful authority.

Although the nominate torts still have a role to play, most actions for damages against governmental agencies or public officials will today probably be brought in negligence, due to the flexible nature of this action's principles.

(b) Negligence

Negligence actions constitute one of the most common forms of suit against public authorities and officials. With its flexible principles, the modern tort of negligence can address a wide range of harmful government activity including novel situations of liability. Plaintiffs complaining of injury by the government have turned to the tort of negligence when they have been unable to fit their loss under another head of tort liability. As a result, the negligence actions have provided a major opportunity for the courts to shape the private

---

now clarified the situation in *Ryan v. Victoria (City)*, [1999] 1 S.C.R. 201 (S.C.C.), by unanimously adopting a formulation of the defence of statutory authorization that would be effective only in limited circumstances, that is, where there is no discretion as to the method of carrying on the activity. For a recent nuisance action against the Crown, see *Sutherland v. Canada (Attorney General)* (2002), 4 B.C.L.R. (4th) 205 (B.C. C.A.), additional reasons at 2003 BCCA 14 (B.C. C.A.), leave to appeal refused (2003), 2003 CarswellBC 1102 (S.C.C.).

18   Despite the limited scope of the tort action, malicious prosecution suits against Crown prosecutors and the Crown have increased over the last decade even though lawyers and judges have been portrayed as cautious in taking advantage of the possibilities under the *Charter of Rights and Freedoms*. See J. Sopinka, "Malicious Prosecution: Invasion of Charter Interests: Remedies: *Nelles v. Ontario*; *R. v. Jednack*; *R. v. Simpson*" (1995) 84 Can. Bar. Rev. 366.

19   (1863), 14 C.B.N.S. 180 (Eng. C.P.).

20   18 & 19 Vict., c. 120.

21   (1996), 132 D.L.R. (4th) 695 (Alta. Q.B.).

22   R.S.A. 1955, c. 311; repealed 1972, c. 87, s. 1. The Government of Alberta admitted liability in respect of the sterilization, but not the detention of the plaintiff, Muir. The Court awarded damages in respect of both heads of liability.

law principles of civil liability to accommodate both novel claims and the unique needs and functions of government.

The negligence liability of public authorities has long been recognized.[23] In some of the early cases, the public character of the defendant did not appear to be of critical importance particularly if the authority's positive acts directly caused physical loss or damage to the plaintiff or the plaintiff's property. However, in other cases,[24] the courts demonstrated a reluctance to hold public authorities to the same standard of civil liability as private persons. Typically, these latter cases concerned allegations of negligence in the exercise of statutory discretion or in the performance of what were considered to be uniquely governmental activities (such as the operation of prison systems, the economic regulation of industry, or military action[25]). Therefore, the law of negligence did not apply uniformly to the wide and ever-expanding field of government activity. Where the government action bore a strong analogy to private activity, the courts have had little trouble in applying established private law principles. The classic example of this would be a government employee driving a government vehicle on government business. The employee would be held to the same standard of care as a private individual in the operation of a motor vehicle. On the other hand, where the claim against government was novel and did not have a strong private analogue, the courts have either adjusted the ordinary principles of negligence liability in applying them to the actions of public authorities, or they have denied the claim on the basis that no duty of care was owed. The classic example in this respect would be loss or injury stemming from the exercise of discretionary authority by a public body or official.

The courts' reluctance to subject certain governmental activities to scrutiny on the basis of the ordinary law of negligence is reflected in the recognition of a number of distinctions designed to restrict the scope of governmental liability in negligence. At one time, a distinction was drawn between a statutory duty and a statutory power.[26] Negligence in the performance of a statutory duty (or the negligent failure to perform a statutory duty) would give rise to liability. On the other hand, negligence in the exercise of a statutory power (or the failure to exercise such a power) would not generally give rise to liability. Another recognized distinction was drawn between misfeasance and nonfeasance in the exercise of a statutory power. A failure to exercise a statutory power ("nonfeasance") would not give rise to liability. However, negligence in the exercise of a statutory power ("misfeasance") would result in liability, but only if the action occasioned fresh or additional damage to the plaintiff or the plaintiff's property (beyond that which would have occurred through the authority's failure to act).

These distinctions, and others like them, represent the judicial belief that it would be inappropriate to hold all government activities to the standards of

---

23 *Mersey Docks & Harbour Board v. Gibbs* (1866), 11 H.L.C. 686 (U.K. H.L.); *Geddis v. Bann Reservoir* (1878), 3 App. Cas. 430 (U.K. H.L.).

24 *Kent v. East Suffolk Rivers Catchment Board* (1940), [1941] A.C. 74 (U.K. H.L.); and *Sheppard v. Glossop (Borough)*, [1921] 3 K.B. 132 (Eng. C.A.).

25 *Anthony v. R.*, [1946] S.C.R. 569 (S.C.C.).

26 *Kent v. East Suffolk Rivers Catchment Board, supra* note 24.

private negligence law. Several reasons can be advanced for this.[27] One concerns the respective roles of the courts and of the executive branch of government. Those who make political decisions should be held accountable in the court of public opinion, not a court of law. Further, it is inappropriate for the courts to second-guess the merits of governmental decision-making – the courts should restrict themselves to evaluating the legality of official decision-making and refrain from judging the merits of political decisions, the difficult balancing of interests or the allocation of scarce resources (which judges may not be well-equipped to evaluate).[28] If all governmental activity and decision-making were amenable to suits in negligence, the floodgates of litigation might be opened, public officers might be intimidated by the possibility of suit and deterred from the forthright discharge of their duties, and public administration would be susceptible to retrial in the courts of law.

Apart from the specific policy concerns, the scope of governmental liability in negligence has also been affected by the limited scope of negligence liability generally. For example, the common law of negligence has only permitted recovery for pure economic loss (as opposed to personal or property damage) in a restricted number of circumstances. Moreover, the common law has not recognized a general duty to take affirmative action to protect persons from harmful actions by themselves or others. These common law restrictions have tended to hamper the imposition of liability on government for errors committed in the course of public regulation. Such regulation is frequently undertaken to protect private citizens from the consequences of the misconduct of others; and a lack of reasonable care in such regulation often results in pure economic loss rather than personal injury or property damage. Nevertheless, the negligence liability of governmental or public authorities has expanded over the last 25 years as courts in England and Canada have recognized more and more instances of government liability for negligence. Based upon a broad and flexible approach to the fundamental duty of care issue, English and Canadian courts have imposed liability on a variety of government actors for negligence in the conduct of uniquely public functions – activities for which there is no strong private analogue. This trend has become more pronounced in Canada than in the United Kingdom as English courts, in recent years, have retreated to more traditional principles when determining liability.

(i) The Starting Point: Anns

The starting point for any discussion of the negligence liability of public authorities is the now discredited decision of the House of Lords in *Anns v. Merton London Borough Council*.[29] The case involved liability for the defective

---

27 See L.N. Klar, *Tort Law*, 2d ed. (Toronto: Carswell, 1996) at 224-25; and Craig, *supra* note 11 at 619-20.

28 Craig describes these types of decisions as "non-justiciable": *ibid.* at 621-23.

29 (1977), [1978] A.C. 728 (U.K. H.L.). The Privy Council in *Rowling* v. *Takaro Properties Ltd.* [1988] A.C. 473 (New Zealand P.C.), and *Yuen Kun Yeu* v. *Hong Kong (Attorney General)* (1987), [1988] A.C. 175 (Hong Kong P.C.) rejected the two stage *Anns* approach as the exclusive test of liability. Subsequently, in *Murphy* v. *Brentwood District Council*, [1990] 2 All E.R. 908 (U.K. H.L.), the House of Lords overruled *Anns*.

foundations of a two-storey block of flats which had been approved by the Council's inspectors even though they did not conform to the approved plans. The key question was whether the Council owed the plaintiff a duty to exercise care in the inspection of the foundations. In the leading judgment, Lord Wilberforce suggested a two-stage approach to the duty issue:[30]

> ... the position has now been reached that in order to establish that a duty of care arises in a particular situation, it is not necessary to bring the facts of that situation within those previous situations in which a duty of care was held to exist. Rather, the question has to be approached in two stages. First, one has to ask whether, as between the alleged wrongdoer and the person who suffered damage, there is a sufficient relationship of proximity or neighbourhood, such that, in the reasonable contemplation of the former, carelessness on his part may be likely to cause damage to the latter – in which case, a *prima facie* duty of care arises. Secondly, if the first question is answered affirmatively, it is necessary to consider whether there are any considerations which ought to negative, or to reduce or limit the scope of the duty or the class of person to whom it is owed or the damages to which a breach of it may arise.

This formulation of the duty issue was of great significance to an expanded concept of governmental liability in negligence. It replaced the classic "categories" approach to the duty issue, which was based on a close analogy between existing and new duty relationships, with a general flexible principle of liability, which is predicated on a concept of proximity defined largely in terms of the foreseeability of harm. This approach to the duty issue permitted an extension of negligence liability to include novel situations involving peculiarly governmental activity, which had no counterparts in the realm of private activity. Further, the two-stage approach to the duty issue recognized that real policy concerns may operate to limit or negate a duty of care based solely upon foreseeability of harm. The second stage of the inquiry stood as an acknowledgement of the belief that some governmental activity cannot be judged on the same basis as private activity. An adjustment of private law principles is required to account for the uniqueness of the government conduct under scrutiny.

As indicated previously, a policy factor that has served to limit or negate the recognition of a duty of care is the fact that many public authorities are clothed with discretionary powers. Traditionally, the courts have refused to hold the exercise of discretionary authority up to scrutiny in negligence actions. In recognition of the courts' historic reluctance to judge the reasonableness of discretionary governmental action Lord Wilberforce in *Anns* drew a distinction

---

30 *Ibid.* at 751-52.

between a public authority's policy area of responsibility and its operational area of action:[31]

> Most, indeed probably all, statutes relating to public authorities or public bodies, contain in them a large area of policy. The courts called this "discretion" meaning that the decision is one for the authority or body to make, and not for the courts. Many statutes also prescribe or at least presuppose the practical execution of policy decisions: a convenient description of this is to say that in addition to the area of policy or discretion, there is an operational area. Although this distinction between the policy and the operational area is convenient, and illuminating, it is probably a distinction of degree; many "operational" powers or duties have in them some element of "discretion". It can safely be said that the more "operational" a power or duty may be, the easier it is to superimpose on it a common law duty of care.

On the basis of this distinction, acts or omissions at the operational level may give rise to a common law duty of care, while decisions taken at the policy level would not (and would therefore be immune from liability in negligence). The term "policy" is used in this distinction to describe certain kinds of discretionary decisions which would not be suitable subjects for judicial re-evaluation. It refers to high-level discretionary decisions dependent on considerations of social, economic or political factors beyond the knowledge or expertise of the courts.[32] In contrast, the term "operational" is used to describe the process of implementation. It refers to a host of lower-level governmental decisions or actions associated with the practical execution of a policy decision. These decisions may involve the exercise of discretion in a sense of making a choice between alternative courses of action. However, these choices are of a more specific or technical nature and are more susceptible to judicial scrutiny through the medium of a negligence suit.

Lord Wilberforce's recognition in *Anns* of the discretionary element in operational activity led him to suggest that the plaintiff would have to establish that the impugned decision fell outside the bounds of a *bona fide* exercise of discretion[33] before liability would arise for negligence at the operational level. This suggests some immunity or exemption from liability at the operational level; and this, in turn, could result in an unwarranted expansion in govern-

---

31   This distinction first appeared in a number of American cases concerning the "discretionary function exception contained in the *Federal Tort Claims Act, 1946*. See *Dalehite v. United States*, 346 U.S. 15 (U.S. Tex., 1953) and *Indian Towing Co. v. United States*, 350 U.S. 61 (1955). As Kneebone points out, *supra* note 5 at 121, the distinction has been "applied as a general test of justiciability".

32   As Craig observes in "Negligence in the Exercise of Statutory Authority" (1978) 94 L.Q.R. 429 at 433:

> A public body should not be liable when the alleged negligence challenges the method of using scarce resources, of balancing thrift and efficiency, or when it results from a risk cautiously taken by that body to achieve a policy pursuant to a discretionary power given by statute.

33   *Anns v. London Borough of Merton, supra* note 29.

mental immunity from liability for negligence. The policy concerns supporting an immunity for discretionary decisions do not apply with equal force to the myriad of technical decisions and choices associated with the practical implementation of a policy decision. To recognize a discretionary immunity at the operational level, based on the *vires* of the official action or inaction, would extend a far greater immunity to public authorities than can be justified. Operational decisions involving an element of discretionary judgment should not be immune from liability for negligence.

While Lord Wilberforce's reference to an *ultra vires* requirement at the operational level complicated the issue of negligence liability, most commentators have agreed that it really has no application to the general run of negligent acts or omissions at this level. As Craig suggests, ". . . a proven lack of care at the operational level involves a finding of *ultra vires*".[34] In other words, in most cases of operational negligence, the issue of *ultra vires* is subsumed in the determination of a lack of reasonable care. A determination that a statutory delegate has acted negligently implicitly involves a finding that it has stepped outside its authority in failing to exercise its powers with reasonable care so as to avoid causing injury to others.[35] In *Anns*, a duty of care was owed to those likely to be affected by a failure to take care in the exercise of the council's statutory authority; that is, to the owners and occupiers of the flats whose health and safety was jeopardized by its approval of the defective foundations.

In the area of its policy decision-making, however, the council must exercise its discretion by giving proper consideration to whether and how it will exercise the statutory power given to it: in *Anns*, whether or not to set up a system of inspection. In doing so, the council had to make its discretionary decisions responsibly having in mind the public interest or purpose the statute contemplates. It could not simply decide not to exercise the power. If a public body, like the council, has the power to act in ways to promote and protect public safety, then it cannot abdicate its responsibilities by deciding not to act out of fear that it may be negligent in the way it discharges those duties. Once the council decided to inspect and established a system of inspection, then the scope of its duty in the operational area was to exercise reasonable care when conducting inspections.[36]

The decision in *Anns* had a profound effect on the negligence liability of public authorities. Many plaintiffs relied on its broad, flexible principles to advance novel claims in negligence against public authorities. Some courts, particularly in Canada, fully embraced and refined the key principles of *Anns* to broaden the scope of governmental liability in negligence. However, other

---

34 Craig, *supra* note 11 at 631.

35 While in general agreement with Craig's analysis, Hogg argues for an exemption from liability for certain operational decisions – those which involve the allocation of scarce or limited resources. Operational decisions of this type should be treated as policy decisions which do not give rise to an actionable duty of care. See Hogg and Monahan, *supra* note 5 at 178-79.

36 Some discretionary decisions at the operational level (such as those relating to the timing, method and manner of inspection) may be protected from liability if they involve a conscious allocation of limited human and technical resources.

courts were concerned about the radical nature of the *Anns* approach to establishing a duty of care and the corresponding increased potential for liability; these courts expressed reservations about the decision in *Anns*, and either rejected it or sought to limit its scope. As a result, a marked divergence of opinion occurred between English and Australian courts on one hand, and Canadian courts on the other.

(ii) Subsequent English and Australian Developments

In 1985, in *Sutherland Shire Council v. Heyman*,[37] the High Court of Australia rejected the two-stage *Anns*-approach to the duty of care issue. Concerned that the *Anns*-approach would lead to an unwarranted expansion in the liability of public authorities for negligence, the members of the court advocated a more traditional and controlled approach to the duty issue in novel situations.[38] Even though the circumstances of the case were remarkably similar to those in *Anns*, the court was of the opinion that the mere foreseeability of harm was not sufficient to establish a *prima facie* duty of care. In order to rely on a common law duty of care, the plaintiff would in addition have to establish that a reasonable relationship of reliance existed between the council and himself. Absent evidence of such reliance, a duty of care would not be imposed on the defendant council to take positive steps to protect the plaintiff from the negligence of the builders.

Clearly, the High Court took the view that proximity was a separate issue from the question of foreseeability of harm. Proximity served as a limiting device on the test of foreseeability in determining whether a duty of care existed. Moreover, foreseeability of harm was seen to be only one element in the establishment of the necessary proximate relationship. While foreseeability may be the key element in the ordinary case of negligence involving the direct infliction of physical loss or damage, it should not be determinative of the duty issue in cases involving pure economic loss, a failure to act, or other "less developed areas of the law of negligence".[39] In situations such as these, the plaintiff will have to establish a close proximate relationship with the defendant, one that "will reflect, among other things, reliance by the plaintiff upon care being taken by the defendant to avoid or prevent injury, loss or damage

---

37   (1985), 60 A.L.R. 1 (Australia H.C.).

38   Illustrative of this is the following observation of Brennan J. with respect to *Anns*, *ibid.* at 43-44:

> Of course, if foreseeability of injury to another were the exhaustive criterion of a *prima facie* duty to act to prevent the occurrence of that injury, it would be essential to introduce some kind of restrictive qualification – perhaps a qualification of the kind stated in the second stage of the general proposition in *Anns*. I am unable to accept that approach. It is preferable, in my view, that the law should develop novel categories of negligence incrementally and by analogy with established categories, rather than by a massive extension of a *prima facie* of care restrained only by indefinable "considerations which ought to negative, or to reduce or to limit the scope of the duty or the class of person to whom it is owed".

39   *Ibid.* at 63 per Deane J.

to the plaintiff or his property in circumstances where the defendant had induced or encouraged such reliance or was or should have been aware of it".[40]

The formulation of the duty issue by the Australian High Court in *Heyman* therefore considerably narrowed the scope of any positive duty to act to prevent harm to others. In the absence of reliance or a similar extremely close proximate relationship, pure non-feasance in the exercise of statutory authority would not give rise to liability in negligence. This result was clearly at odds with *Anns* and the leading Canadian cases.

However, while the High Court rejected the *Anns* formulation of the duty issue, it appeared to accept the policy/operational distinction as a""logical and convenient" approach to the issue of government liability in negligence.[41] In particular, Mason J. added to our understanding of the distinction through the following description:[42]

> The distinction between policy and operational factors is not easy to formulate, but the dividing line between them will be observed if we recognize that a public authority is under no duty of care in relation to decisions which involve or are dictated by financial, social or political factors or constraints. Thus budgetary allocations and the constraints which they entail in terms of allocation of resources cannot be made the subject of a duty of care. But it may be otherwise when the courts are called upon to apply a standard of care to action or inaction that is merely the product of administrative direction, expert or professional opinion, technical standards or general standards of reasonableness.

Only a few years elapsed before the English courts also began to express reservations about *Anns*. Motivated by concerns similar to those expressed by the Australian High Court in *Heyman*, both the House of Lords and the Privy Council cautioned against an expansive interpretation of the approach in *Anns* to the duty issue. For example, in *Peabody Donation Fund v. Sir Lindsay Parkinson & Co.*,[43] Lord Keith cautioned against the acceptance of the *Anns* approach as a test of general liability:[44]

> There has been a tendency in some recent cases to treat these passages as being themselves of a definitive character. This is a temptation which should be resisted. The true question in each case is whether a particular defendant owed to the particular plaintiff a duty of care having the scope which is contended for and whether he was in breach of that duty with consequence loss to the plaintiff. . . . So in determining whether or not a duty of care of a particular scope was incumbent

---

40 *Ibid.*
41 *Ibid.* at 14 per Gibbs C.J.
42 *Ibid.* at 35.
43 [1984] 3 All E.R. 529 (U.K. H.L.).
44 *Ibid.* at 534.

upon the defendant it is material to take into consideration whether it was just and reasonable that it should be so.

The "just and reasonable" requirement reflected a concern about an unwarranted expansion of negligent liability and demonstrated that the duty issue was, above all, a policy question which varied from circumstance to circumstance. Subsequently, similar doubts about *Anns* were expressed by the Privy Council in *Yuen Kun Yeu v. Hong Kong (Attorney General)*[45] and in *Rowling v. Takaro Properties Ltd.*[46] Both cases involved novel claims in negligence against high level government officials. In both decisions, the Privy Council asserted that the existence of a duty of care must be determined by reference to a number of factors apart from foreseeability of harm.[47] At the same time, the House of Lords continued to question the two-stage duty test enunciated in *Anns* in a series of cases involving public authorities or public officials.[48] Again in these cases, the court suggested that the recognition of a duty relationship in novel situations was predicated on a consideration of a variety of policy factors, not just the fact that the harm was foreseeable. In the words of a leading commentator on the law of torts, "[t]he House of Lords and Privy Council . . . have reaffirmed the importance of policy considerations not merely as factors to deny the existence of a *prima facie* duty, but as essential ingredients of the duty relationships themselves".[49]

Any continuing doubt about the viability of the *Anns*-approach were laid to rest by the House of Lords in 1990. In *Murphy v. Brentwood District Council*,[50] the court decided to overrule its previous decision in *Anns* on the grounds that the decision was unsatisfactory and contrary to long-established principles concerning liability for pure economic loss. While the judgments concentrated on issues relating to recovery for pure economic loss rather than the more general question of public tort liability in negligence, it was clear that a more conservative approach to the duty issue was being taken in England. In determining whether a duty of care exists in a particular dispute, the English courts will move cautiously, incrementally and by analogy with existing categories.[51] Where the injury is physical loss or damage which was directly caused by the actions of a public body, there will often be little difficulty in

---

45   (1987), [1988] A.C. 175 (Hong Kong P.C.).

46   [1988] A.C. 473 (New Zealand P.C.).

47   In *Yuen Kun Yeu*, the Privy Council was of the opinion that foreseeability of harm was but one factor in determining the duty issue; in deciding whether the defendant public official, the commissioner of deposit-taking companies, owed the plaintiff depositors a duty of care in the regulation of a failed financial institution, the court looked for factors such as: the purpose of the legislation, the quasi-judicial nature of the defendant's functions, the defendant's lack of control of the day-to-day operations of the company and the absence of a specific relationship of reliance between the plaintiff depositors and the defendant regulator.

48   *Curran v. Northern Ireland Co-ownership Housing Assn.*, [1987] 2 All E.R. 13 (U.K. H.L.); *Hill v. Chief Constable of West Yorkshire*, [1988] 2 All E.R. 238 (U.K. H.L.).

49   L. Klar, *Tort Law* (Toronto: Carswell, 1991) at 124; see also discussion in Klar's 2d ed. (Toronto: Carswell, 1996) at 139*ff.*

50   [1990] 2 All E.R. 908 (U.K. H.L.).

51   The House of Lords approved of the approach taken by the Australian High Court in *Sutherland Shire Council v. Heyman* (1985), 60 A.L.R. 1 (Australia H.C.).

establishing the necessary duty relationship. But where the claim is novel (for example, it involves pure economic loss or arises from a governmental failure to act), the establishment of the necessary duty relationship will be difficult and will depend on a variety of factors. The *Anns*-approach was overruled because the general principle of civil liability, based on the foreseeability of harm, tended towards a broad expansive concept of liability, which in turn obscured many of the policy considerations which have been used historically to limit such liability. The duty issue often involves a variety of policy concerns whose significance has varied from category to category of case. In the opinion of both the Privy Council and the House of Lords, these concerns are fundamental in the determination of the duty issue, and they should not be obscured or devalued by leaving them to a second stage of analysis as in *Anns*. When confronted by novel claims in negligence, the courts should proceed incrementally and by analogy with established categories - a three part test was to be utilized: whether the damage was foreseeable; whether the parties' relationship was proximate and whether it was "just, fair and reasonable" to impose a duty of care.[52]

(iii) Canadian Authorities

Canadian case law on the liability of public authorities for negligence apparently stands in sharp contrast to the position in England and Australia. For twenty or so years, the Supreme Court of Canada[53] and lower courts[54] have whole-heartedly embraced the *Anns* approach to the negligence liability of public authorities. Yet, in two recent judgments concerning the liability of statutory regulations, the Supreme Court of Canada appears to be moving towards the position of the English and Australian courts, which have taken a more restrictive approach towards public authority liability through a cautious, policy oriented approach to the duty question.

---

52 *Capro Industries plc v. Dickman*, [1990] 2 A.C. 605 (U.K. H.L.). The state of English law on the liability of public authorities is well canvassed in the recent article by Bailey and Bowman, "Public Authority and Negligence Revisited" (2000) 59 Cambridge L.J. 85.

53 *Barratt v. North Vancouver (District)* (1980), 14 C.C.L.T. 169 (S.C.C.); *Nielsen v. Kamloops (City)*, [1984] 2 S.C.R. 2 (S.C.C.); *Just v. British Columbia* (1989), 103 N.R. 1 (S.C.C.); *Manolakos v. Gohmann*, [1989] 2 S.C.R. 1259 (S.C.C.), reconsideration refused [1990] 1 W.W.R. lxxii (note) (S.C.C.); *Laurentide Motels Ltd. c. Beauport (Ville)*, [1989] 1 S.C.R. 705 (S.C.C.); *Brown v. British Columbia (Minister of Transportation & Highways)* (1994), 112 D.L.R. (4th) 1 (S.C.C.); *Swinamer v. Nova Scotia (Attorney General)* (1994), 112 D.L.R. (4th) 18 (S.C.C.).

54 See for example, *Brewer Brothers v. Canada (Attorney General)* (1991), 80 D.L.R. (4th) 321 (Fed. C.A.); *Swanson Estate v. R.* (1991), 80 D.L.R. (4th) 741 (Fed. C.A.); *Comeau's Sea Foods Ltd. v. Canada (Minister of Fisheries & Oceans)* (1992), 11 C.C.L.T. (2d) 241 (Fed. T.D.), reversed (1995), 24 C.C.L.T. (2d) 1 (Fed. C.A.), dismissed on other grounds [1997] 1 S.C.R. 12 (S.C.C.), leave to appeal allowed (1995), 198 N.R. 80 (note) (S.C.C.); *Atlantic Leasing Ltd. v. Newfoundland* (1998), 162 D.L.R. (4th) 54 (Nfld. C.A.); *Kuczerpa v. R.* (1993), 152 N.R. 207 (Fed. C.A.), leave to appeal refused (1993), 160 N.R. 319 (note) (S.C.C.); *Hunt v. Westbank Irrigation District*, [1991] 6 W.W.R. 549 (B.C. S.C.), affirmed [1994] 6 W.W.R 107 (B.C. C.A.); *Dorman Timber Ltd. v. British Columbia* (1997), 152 D.L.R. (4th) 271 (B.C. C.A.).

(A) Kamloops

The early leading authority was the decision of the Supreme Court in *Nielsen v. Kamloops (City)*.[55] Like *Anns* and *Heyman*, it arose out of structural damage to a building arising from inadequate foundations. However, unlike these cases, the action in negligence against the municipal authority did not arise out of its failure to inspect the foundations or for its failure to exercise reasonable care in its inspections. Rather, the cause of action was based on the municipality's failure to take any steps to secure compliance with its building bylaws. During the course of construction, city inspectors had determined that the buildings foundations were inadequate. Stop-work orders were issued by the building inspectors, but construction continued. No further steps were taken by the municipality to enforce the orders (either because the building was owned by an alderman, or because the strike of city employees had left the relevant department short-staffed).

Relying on the formulation in *Anns*, Wilson J., writing for the majority of the Supreme Court of Canada, held that the defendant municipality owed a duty of care to the plaintiff (a subsequent owner of the house) in the exercise of its statutory authority, because the damage to the property was a reasonably foreseeable consequence of the defendant's negligence. Further, Wilson J. held that this *prima facie* duty of care was not negated either by statute or by the common law immunity accorded to policy decisions. On the basis of *Anns*, Wilson J. reasoned that, before liability could arise, the plaintiff must establish that the defendant's acts or omissions fell outside the *bona fide* exercise of discretion. In enacting a bylaw to regulate building construction, the defendant municipality had made policy decisions which could not be questioned in subsequent negligence actions. However, the bylaw imposed a duty of an operational nature on the defendant's building inspector to enforce the provisions of the bylaw through the issuance of stop-work orders or by the withholding of an occupancy permit. The court did not view the failure of the city or its inspector to take further action to secure compliance with the bylaw as the product of a conscious policy decision (which would be entitled to immunity). Indeed, Wilson J. held that the city had acted outside the limits of its discretion in failing to give proper (or any) consideration to the question of whether further action should be taken to enforce the bylaw.[56] This was not a case of the city having made a discretionary policy decision which later turned out to be wrong, because the evidence suggested that the city's failure to take further action was prompted by improper considerations, that is, the house under construction was owned by an alderman:[57]

---

55 *Supra* note 53.

56 In this, she appeared to adopt Lord Wilberforce's view in *Anns* that there can be liability for a public authority's unreasonable failure to consider matters of policy. Kneebone, *supra* note 5 at 83 suggests that Lord Wilberforce in *Anns* used the term *bona fide* "in a looser sense to indicate his concern with the proper and rational exercise of statutory powers in accordance with statutory purposes."

57 *Nielsen v. Kamloops (City)*, *supra* note 53 at 24.

In my view, inaction for no reason, or inaction for an improper purpose, cannot be a policy decision taken in the *bona fide* exercise of discretion. Where the question whether the requisite act should be taken has not even been considered by the public authority, or at least has not been considered in good faith, it seems clear that for that very reason, the authority has not acted with reasonable care.

The majority judgment in *Kamloops* presents a number of difficulties. First, Wilson J. appears to confuse the responsibilities of the city's building inspector and the council. Arguably, the building inspector did not fail in his duty to take steps to secure compliance with the building bylaws. He did everything he could. The next course of action involved the commencement of legal proceedings to compel the builder and owner to comply with the city's orders. Any decision to institute legal proceedings appears to have been within the authority of council, not the inspector. In other words, the negligence occurred at the level of council, and not through any failure on the part of the inspector to take reasonable care.

This confusion illustrates the practical difficulties associated with the application of the policy/operational dichotomy. As indicated earlier, the distinction reflects the belief that certain government activities are inappropriate subjects for judicial scrutiny in a negligence action. While the dichotomy exempts certain government activity from review in a negligence suit, it does not define where the line is to be drawn between conduct which should be subject to scrutiny and that which should not. Further, its practical application is complicated by the fact that almost all government activity involves the exercise of some degree of judgment or discretion. In the words of Klar:[58]

> Despite its attractive simplicity, the policy/operational dichotomy has proven to be very difficult for courts to apply. This has produced a mass of inconsistent and seemingly irreconcilable judgments. This is attributable to the fact that one cannot clearly separate the policy or discretionary stages of an activity from its operational or implimentational stages. The two are intermeshed, with most activities containing elements of both in varying degrees. Numerous operational activities occur during the policy stages of governmental activity. Similarly, during the operational end of an activity, matters of policy or discretion will invariably arise. Although there has been general agreement on those factors which incline specific conduct towards either the policy or operational end of the scale, the fact that all activities contain elements of both has caused great difficulties for the courts.

In *Kamloops*, the negligence lay in the council's failure to take steps to enforce the bylaw. Wilson J. saw this as a discretionary decision at the operational level of the City's functions. Liability arose because the council's failure to give proper consideration to the question of further action was outside

---

58 L. Klar, *supra* note 27 at 233.

the limits of a *bona fide* exercise of discretion. However, the decision could also be characterized as a policy activity of the council.[59] If this is the correct characterization, then any immunity for policy activities is great but not absolute. Even at the policy level, liability can arise where the authority has failed to consider the exercise of its powers, or where it has exercised its discretion so unreasonably that it is tantamount to bad faith.[60] Such a characterization would of course complicate the question of whether there is absolute immunity at the policy level. Perhaps to avoid this, Wilson J. characterized the negligence as occurring at the operational level, which does facilitate the imposition of liability. The possibility of manipulating the policy/operational dichotomy has given rise to a concern that ". . . it is a way of stating rather than arriving at a result".[61]

(B) Just

In *Just v. British Columbia*,[62] the appellant's car was struck by a falling boulder while stopped in traffic on a mountain highway. The appellant was severely injured and his daughter was killed. Although the boulder was dislodged by natural forces, an action was brought against the provincial Crown alleging negligence in both its system of rock-face inspection and in the removal of potential hazards. The province had an extensive program of rock-face inspection in place. At trial,[63] McLachlin J. held that the decisions relating to the method and manner of inspection and the elimination of hazards fell within the policy area of the highway department's functions; and, accordingly, were incapable of supporting a duty of care. The British Columbia Court of Appeal agreed with this characterization.[64] However, the Supreme Court of

---

59   In his minority judgment, McIntyre J. characterized the negligence as occurring at the policy level; *supra* note 53 at 48.

60   This analysis may run contrary to an earlier line of authority which held that a public authority will not owe a duty of care in deciding whether it will exercise its power or to what extent it will exercise its powers. In *Sheppard v. Glossop (Borough)*, [1921] 3 K.B. 132 at 150 (Eng. C.A.), Atkin L.J. stated:

> If a local authority having statutory powers decides to exercise those powers, it is under a duty to persons interested to take reasonable care not to cause damage, so far as the avoidance of damage is consistent with the exercise of the statutory powers. But is under no legal duty to act reasonably in deciding whether it shall exercise its statutory powers or not, or in deciding to what extent, over what particular area, or for what particular time, it shall exercise its powers.

This principle was later affirmed by the House of Lords in *Dorset Yacht Co. v. Home Office*, [1970] A.C. 1004 (U.K. H.L.).

61   L. Jaffe, "Suits Against Government and Officers: Sovereign Immunity (Part I) and Damage Actions (Part II)" (1963-64) 77 Harv. L. Rev. 1 at 218.

62   [1989] 2 S.C.R. 1228 (S.C.C.). The decision was one in a group of three public tort law decisions handed down at about the same time. For a more complete discussion of the trilogy see L.N. Klar, "The Supreme Court of Canada: Extending the Tort Liability of Public Authorities" (1990) 28 Alta. L. Rev. 648; and M.K. Woodall, "Private Law Liability of Public Authorities for Negligent Inspection and Regulation" (1992) 37 McGill L.J. 83 at 98-110.

63   (1985), 33 C.C.L.T. 49 (B.C. S.C.), affirmed (1986), [1987] 2 W.W.R. 231 (B.C. C.A.), reversed [1989] 2 S.C.R. 1228 (S.C.C.).

64   (1986), [1987] 2 W.W.R. 231 (B.C. C.A.), reversed [1989] 2 S.C.R. 1228 (S.C.C.).

Canada (per Cory J. for the majority) held that the decisions relating to the means and manner of inspection fell within the operational area of the defendant's functions. This characterization was the product of His Lordship's view that the "policy" label should not be used expansively so as to clothe governmental decision-making with an extensive immunity from liability in tort. In Cory J.'s opinion, only true or pure policy decisions should be excepted from liability – that is, high-level policy decisions based on a consideration of political, social and economic factors. For the most part, these will be "broad formulative decisions, which have been described by one commentator as ". . . threshold decisions, i.e., the initial decision as to whether something will or will not be done".[65] Clearly, such a narrow or limited definition of the scope of the policy immunity would include a decision of a legislative nature.[66] Apart from these true policy decisions, Cory J. was of the view that all other governmental decisions and actions should be subjected to a duty of care on the basis that they would fall within the operational area of the authority's activity. His Lordship described these operational decisions as ". . . manifestations of the implementation of the policy decision"[67] and ". . . the product of administrative discretion, expert or professional opinion, technical standards or general standards of care".[68]

The impact of the Supreme Court's analysis of the policy/operational distinction in *Just* is that a much broader range of governmental activity will be subject to judicial scrutiny and evaluation in a negligence action on the ground that the activity was operational in nature. Indeed, the bulk of governmental activity will be subject to such scrutiny.[69]

---

65 L. Klar, *supra* note 27 at 231.

66 *Welbridge Holdings Ltd. v. Greater Winnipeg (Municipality)* (1970), [1971] S.C.R. 957 (S.C.C.); *Dunlop v. Woollahra Municipal Council*, [1981] 2 W.L.R. 693 (Australia P.C.); *Birch Builders Ltd. v. Esquimalt (Township)*, [1992] 4 W.W.R. 391 (B.C. C.A.), leave to appeal refused [1992] 3 S.C.R. v (S.C.C.).

67 *Supra* note 53 at 20.

68 *Ibid.* at 19-20, quoting from the judgment of Mason J. in *Sutherland Shire Council v. Heyman* (1985), 60 A.L.R. 1 (Australia H.C.).

69 In dissent, Sopinka J. argued against such an unwarranted and unsupported expansion in the scope of negligence liability. *ibid.* at 30, he pointed out:

    In stating that the authority "must specifically consider whether to inspect, and if so, the system must be a reasonable one in all the circumstances", my colleague is exceeding liability beyond what was decided in *Anns v. Merton London Borough Council*, *Barratt v. District of North Vancouver*, and *City of Kamloops v. Neilson*, *supra*. The system would include the time, manner and technique of inspection. On that basis, it is difficult to determine what aspect of a policy decision would be immune from review. All that is left is the decision to inspect. It can hardly be suggested that all the learning that has been expended on the difference between policy and operational was expended to immunize the decision of a public body that something will be done but not the content of what will be done. It seems to me the decision to inspect rather than not inspect hardly needs protection from review. The concern that has resulted in extending an immunity from review in respect of policy decisions is that those entrusted with the exercise of the statutory powers make the decision to expend public revenues. It is not engaged by a decision simply to do something. It is the decision as to what is to be done that will entail the taxation of the public purse.

    Moreover, it is ironic that the second prong of the *Anns* approach, which was designed to

(C) Brown, Swinamer

In two subsequent cases,[70] the Supreme Court of Canada has reaffirmed that the two stage *Anns* analysis, as articulated in *Just*, will govern the negligence liability of public authorities, despite academic criticism[71] and contrary decisions in the United Kingdom and Australia.[72] Each of these cases involved a negligence action against a provincial Crown for its failure to maintain its highways in a safe condition so as to prevent the injuries suffered by the plaintiffs. Even though the respective Highways Departments had a statutory power, but not a duty, to maintain their highways, the Supreme Court held that they owed the plaintiffs, as users of the highways, a legal duty of care to take reasonable steps to maintain them. Therefore, the central issue in each case was whether the actions or decisions complained of were "policy" or "operational" in nature.

In *Brown v. British Columbia (Minister of Transportation & Highways)*,[73] the Court held that the department's decision to operate on the basis of a summer maintenance schedule, with fewer resources, rather than a winter maintenance schedule, was a policy decision to which no liability could attach. It was, in the words of Cory J., ". . . a policy decision involving classic policy considerations of financial resources, personnel and, as well, significant negotiations with government unions. It was truly a governmental decision involving social, political and economic factors."[74] Moreover, he made it clear that policy decisions can occur at any stage of the planning or operational levels of government activity. By this, he wished to expressly repudiate the suggestion made by some that policy decisions are few in number and are threshold decisions which occur at a high level of policy development. While he intended to clarify his remarks in *Just*, in reality, he only added to the

---

limit the scope of public authority liability, has lead to a significant expansion in such liability, through a narrow interpretation of the policy exception contained in the policy/operational dichotomy. In this regard see generally Sgayias, Kinnear, Rennie & Saunders, *The Annotated Crown Liability and Proceedings Act, 1995* (Toronto: Carswell, 1994) at 56-59.

70 *Brown v. British Columbia (Minister of Transportation & Highways)* (1994), 112 D.L.R. (4th) 1 (S.C.C.) and *Swinamer v. Nova Scotia (Attorney General)* (1994), 112 D.L.R. (4th) 18 (S.C.C.). See also *Lewis (Guardian ad litem of) v. British Columbia* (1977), [1998] 5 W.W.R. 732 (S.C.C.). The facts are similar to *Just*, and on the basis of the *Anns* formulation the Supreme Court held the Crown owed a duty to users of the highway not only to take care in the maintenance and repair of the highway but to ensure that care was taken by others undertaking the work. Thus, not only was an independent contractor held liable for its negligent repair of a rock face above the highway, the Crown was also held liable in negligence.

71 See the authorities referred to by Sopinka J., in *Brown, supra* note 53 at 3-4. See also L. Klar, *Tort Law, supra* note 27 at 233-37; L. Klar, "Case Comment: Falling Boulders, Falling Trees and Icy Highways: The Policy/Operational Test Revisited" (1994) 33 Alta. L.R. 167.

72 Indeed, despite the overruling of *Anns* in *Murphy v. Brentwood*, the Supreme Court of Canada in a number of cases, not involving public authorities, has emphatically stated that the two stage *Anns* test is the governing authority in actions involving claims for economic loss. See *Winnipeg Condominium Corp. No. 36 v. Bird Construction Co.*, [1995] 1 S.C.R. 85 (S.C.C.) and *Hercules Management Ltd. v. Ernst & Young*, [1997] 8 W.W.R. 80 (S.C.C.).

73 (1994), 112 D.L.R. (4th) 1 (S.C.C.).

74 *Ibid.* at 16.

confusion concerning where to draw the line between policy decisions and operational activities.

The court then turned to the operational aspect of the defendant's activities to determine whether it was negligent in responding to the icy road conditions which caused the accident. In this regard, the court concluded that the defendant acted reasonably given the unexpected nature of the climatic conditions and the limited resources available to remedy the situation. The plaintiff's suit failed.

The companion case, *Swinamer v. Nova Scotia (Attorney General)*,[75] involved the unexpected collapse of a large, diseased tree on to a provincial highway, injuring the plaintiff in his truck. The highway department was aware of the risk to users of the highway from falling trees and had decided to survey the roads to identify dead and diseased trees which posed such a hazard. These trees were marked and funding to remove them was then made available over a number of years. In response to the plaintiff's argument, that the defendant department was negligent in its inspection and removal of dead and diseased trees, the court concluded no liability would stem from the decision to undertake the survey as it was part of a policy rather than an operational decision. Cory J. described it as "an example of a preliminary step in what would eventually become a policy decision involving the expenditure and allocation of funds."[76] A policy decision to remove dead and diseased trees would involve the reallocation of funds from other highway projects. This was a decision for government to make. The court also concluded that the department was not negligent in the operational aspects of carrying out the policy decision to conduct a survey. Given the need to act quickly and the limited budget available, the department acted reasonably in conducting a visual survey of trees adjacent to the highway to identify the dangers posed by those which were obviously dead and diseased.

In closing, it should also be noted that Sopinka J. cautioned against the use of the policy/ operational dichotomy as the "touchstone of liability" in negligence actions against public authorities.[77] Even though he concurred in the result in both *Brown* and *Swinamer*, he preferred to rest his judgment on the fact that the governing legislation conferred a power, rather than imposing a duty, to maintain the highways. Provided that the defendants exercised their discretion in a *bona fide* manner, their actions were not reviewable by the court in a negligence action.

Brown and *Swinamer* have been criticized for their inconsistency with other cases and for the confusion that they have brought to the application of the policy/operational dichotomy.[78] Apparently, not only are high level, threshold, policy decisions immune from review or evaluation by a court in negligence actions but so are a host of discretionary decisions made at lower levels of government activity associated with the implementation of policy – as one

---

75 (1994), 112 D.L.R. (4th) 18 (S.C.C.).

76 *Ibid.* at 30.

77 Indeed, he suggested that the court reconsider the usefulness of the test at some future time, *Brown, supra* note 73 at 4.

78 For example, see L. Klar, "*Case* Comment", *supra* note 71 at 167.

leading commentator has stated in relation to *Brown*: "[t]hus, not only is the decision to implement a system of road inspection and repair a matter of policy, but so is the decision to operate the system on two schedules."[79]

This seems to be a step back from the position taken in *Just* which appeared to set the stage for an expansion in the scope of government negligence liability.

In recognition of the fact that many governmental decisions are discretionary and involve the allocation of limited resources, Cory J. was of the view that a different standard of care will have to be recognized when judging the "reasonableness" of official activity. Such a standard of care would take into account the limitations and constraints placed on the public authority's actions. As a result, it appears that the courts will sometimes hold public authorities to a lower standard of care in respect of "policy" decisions made at the operational level.

(D) Other cases - Regulatory failure

Despite the lack of clarity surrounding the policy/operational distinction, the Courts continue to rely on the distinction in a variety of negligence actions against government for regulatory failure. Since the recognition by the Supreme Court of Canada of liability for purely economic loss[80] these claims of regulatory failure have involved physical and economic loss. Several decisions are noteworthy.

In *Brewer Brothers v. Canada (Attorney General)*[81] the Federal Court of Appeal held the Canadian Grain Commission liable in negligence for its failure to require a licensed grain elevator operator to post sufficient security to cover its outstanding liabilities. The plaintiff grain producers had suffered loss when the operator failed to fully pay for grain delivered to it. The practical administration of the financial monitoring of operators fell into the operational as opposed to the policy area. In another decision, *Swanson Estate v. R.*[82] the Federal Court of Appeal imposed liability on Transport Canada for its negligent enforcement of aircraft safety standards. As a result of its failure to cancel the license of an airline which had failed to comply with regulatory flight safety standards, a fatal crash had occurred. In its decision, the court recognized the need to immunize some governmental decisions but suggested that this immunity would not be readily available in the negligent administration of regulatory mandates over private activities which resulted in personal injury or death. Such administration was seen largely as a case of government supplying services to its citizens as opposed to "governing".[83]

---

79   *Ibid.* at 175.

80   *Canadian National Railway v. Norsk Pacific Steamship Co.*, [1992] 1 S.C.R. 1021 (S.C.C.), reconsideration refused (July 23, 1992), Doc. 21838 (S.C.C.).

81   (1991), 80 D.L.R. (4th) 321 (Fed. C.A.). See also *Layden v. Canada (Attorney General)* (1991), 8 C.C.L.T. (2d) 41 (Fed. C.A.); *Devloo v. R.* (1991), 8 C.C.L.T. (2d) 93 (Fed. C.A.).

82   (1991), 80 D.L.R. (4th) 741 (Fed. C.A.).

83   It may also be a case of general reliance leading to a sufficient relationship of proximity between the government body and the travelling public. In the case of compelling airlines to comply with safety standards, the government has control over the activity and clearly

Yet another decision, *Comeau's Sea Foods Ltd. v. Canada (Minister of Fisheries & Oceans)*,[84] demonstrates the difficulties associated with the practical application of the policy/operational distinction. The case involved economic loss occasioned by a ministerial decision to revoke the authorization of lobster fishery licences to the plaintiff. Having authorized the licenses, the trial court found the decision to revoke the authorization was not only *ultra vires* but negligent as a breach of a duty of care owed to the plaintiff.[85] The court characterized the decision to authorize the licences as "policy" but held that the formal, routine issuance of the licences was operational in nature. At the Federal Court of Appeal,[86] the majority of the court, for different reasons, allowed the Crown's appeal and held that the Minister was not negligent. Stone J.A. agreed with his colleagues and the trial judge that the decision to revoke the authorization was *ultra vires* but he could not characterize it as either "policy" or "operational". Further, while the parties were in a sufficiently proximate relationship to give rise to a duty of care on the part of the Minister, this *prima facie* duty was negated by the existence of adequate and effective administrative law remedies.[87] Robertson J.A. used the policy/operational distinction in a subtle and somewhat different fashion. A distinction was drawn between the merits of the decision to revoke, characterized as "policy" and the legality of the decision, characterized as "operational" in nature. Thus, the Minister could not be held liable in negligence for the harmful consequences of the decision to revoke - but, he would be liable if he was negligent in determining he had the authority to revoke, that is, negligent in his misconstruction of the statute. As there was no evidence that the Minister misconstrued his authority under the Act, there was no breach of the standard of care.[88] In dissent, Linden J.A., after an extensive review of the authorities, held the Crown liable for the *ultra vires* and negligent revocation of the licence authorization. The revocation decision was not immune from liability on the basis of a policy exemption which was limited to a few decisions which involved policy considerations or peculiarly government activity. On this reasoning, most government activity was susceptible to scrutiny in a negligence action, even if some element of discretion or policy judgment was involved. The Supreme Court upheld unanimously the decision of the Federal Court of Appeal. For the Court,

---

engenders reliance on the part of the travelling public who are unable to adequately address the risk and take steps to protect themselves.

84 (1997), 43 Admin. L.R. (2d) 1 (S.C.C.), leave to appeal allowed (1995), 198 N.R. 80 (note) (S.C.C.).

85 [1992] 3 F.C. 54 (Fed. T.D.), reversed [1995] 2 F.C. 467 (Fed. C.A.), affirmed [1997] 1 S.C.R. 12 (S.C.C.), leave to appeal allowed (1995), 198 N.R. 80 (note) (S.C.C.).

86 [1995] 2 F.C. 467 (Fed. C.A.), affirmed [1997] 1 S.C.R. 12 (S.C.C.), leave to appeal allowed (1995), 198 N.R. 80 (note) (S.C.C.).

87 This reasoning reflects the view that the Minister's decision is nonjusticiable in tort proceedings, and should only be adjudicated upon in judicial review proceedings. The policy against justiciability "is that administrative or public law sanctions are adequate for ensuring "public accountability" without the need for a damages remedy where the tort claim amounts to an indirect challenge to an administrative decision." Kneebone, *supra* note 5 at 132.

88 A determination of *ultra vires* cannot be equated with the finding of negligence or lack of due care.

Major J. ruled that the Minister had not acted *ultra vires* his authority which vested in him continuing discretion until the licences were finally issued. As the Minister acted within his authority, he was not in breach of a duty owed to Comeau to due care in ascertaining his authority under the statute.[89]

(E) A new direction - Cooper, Edwards?

Two recent Supreme Court of Canada cases, involving regulatory failure and economic loss, *Cooper v. Hobart*[90] and *Edwards v. Law Society of Upper Canada*[91] represent a movement away from, or at least a reformulation of, the two stage, general principle, approach of the House of Lords in *Anns*. In *Cooper v. Hobart*, the appellant, one of 3,000 investors who lost money advanced to a registered mortgage broker, brought an action against the provincial Registrar of Mortgage Brokers, for negligence in the regulation of a particular broker. The appellant claimed that the Registrar owed a duty of care to all members of the investing public in its oversight of licenced mortgage brokers - a duty of care which it breached in its failure to cancel or suspend the broker's licence when it became aware of serious violations of the Act. The claim was a novel one entailing potential liability to thousands of persons who sustained losses as a result of the failure of their investments. The Supreme Court of Canada upheld the decision of the British Columbia Court of Appeal that the action must fail as the Registrar did not owe a duty of care to investors. In coming to this decision, the court affirmed that the two stage approach set out in *Anns* was still appropriate in determining negligence actions against public authorities and it clarified what each stage of the analysis entailed. On the basis of the Privy Council decision in *Yuen Kun Yeu v. Hong Kong (Attorney General)*[92] the court held that the first stage, the *prima facie* duty stage, involved more than a determination that the harm suffered was a reasonably foreseeable consequence of the defendant's conduct. There must be something more. Proximity must supplement the reasonable foreseeability test.[93] The latter is not the determinant of the former. In the mind of the Court, proximity means

---

89   Hogg and Monahan, *supra* note 5 at 170, were of the view that the court was incorrect in its analysis of the Minister's actions as "policy" in nature. They suggest that the Minister was acting at the operational level in authorizing the issuance of licences to fishing companies and, accordingly, would have been under a duty of care owed to the plaintiff. In this respect, they refer to *Carpenter Fishing Corp. v. Canada* (1997), 155 D.L.R. (4th) 572 (Fed. C.A.), leave to appeal refused (1998), 230 N.R. 398 (note) (S.C.C.), reconsideration refused (November 19, 1998), Doc. 26484 (S.C.C.), leave to appeal refused (1999), 249 N.R. 200 (note) (S.C.C.) which held that the imposition of a fishing code, as opposed to the granting of specific licences, was a discretionary decision. To the authors, this suggests that the issuance of licences would fall in the operational area.

90   (2001), 206 (D.L.R. (4th) 193 (S.C.C.).

91   (2001), 206 D.L.R. (4th) 211 (S.C.C.).

92   (1987), [1988] A.C. 175 (Hong Kong P.C.).

93   The court seemed to adopt the tripartite formulation of the duty issue, expressed in *Caparo Industries plc v. Dickman, supra* note 52, which involved three criteria: foreseeability of loss, proximity and fairness, justice and reasonableness. Later, in *Stovin v. Wise*, [1996] 3 W.L.R. 388 at 395 (U.K. H.L.) Lord Nicholls, in his dissent, suggested that proximity was not a legal concept or ingredient separate and apart from fairness and reasonableness.

not only a close and direct relationship between the parties, but a relationship of a type which would warrant the imposition of a duty of care. Whether or not a relationship is sufficiently proximate will depend on factors such as "expectations, representations, reliance, and the property and other interests involved"[94] and will often be determined by reference to existing categories of negligence. Above all, proximity is a question of policy and a balancing of interests.

If the first stage is concerned with questions of policy, what purpose is served by the second stage of the *Anns* analysis? In *Yuen Kun Yeu*[95], the Privy Council suggested that the second stage would be rarely used, but the Supreme Court of Canada was of the view that it would arise in novel situations of liability where the courts must consider policy concerns outside the relationship of the parties that may negate the imposition of duties of care. In situations which fell within or were analogous to recognized categories of negligence, the second stage may not arise as the courts may be satisfied that no overriding policy concerns exist. The policy considerations of the second stage are those involving "other legal obligations, the legal system and society more generally"[96] and may include matters such as: the existence of alternate legal remedies, the risk of indeterminate liability, the policy or operational nature of the decision, or in other words, its justiciability, and the existence of statutory or common law immunities. Clearly, in its reformulation of the two stage analysis, the court has given itself and other courts two kicks at the "policy cat".

Applying the restated, two stage *Anns* analysis to the case before it, the court held that the registrar did not owe the plaintiff investors a duty of care. While the plaintiffs may have been able to establish the harm was a reasonably foreseeable consequence of the defendant's negligence, they failed to establish a sufficient relationship of proximity. The case did not fall within, nor was it analogous to other cases where a duty of care had been recognized. The Registrar's duties under the legislation were directed towards the public, not individual investors. Given the multifaceted nature of his responsibilities, it would not be just to impose a duty of care on the Registrar.

Even though it did not have to, the court then moved to the second stage of the *Anns* analysis. Here, it found overriding policy considerations which would have served to negate any *prima facie* duty of care. The decision to suspend a broker's licence was quasi-judicial and policy oriented in nature, requiring a careful balancing of public and private interests. It fell within the policy as opposed to the operational area of government activity and was entitled to deference; that is, it was not justiciable in the context of a tort action. Moreover, the recognition of a duty of care in this case would raise the prospect of indeterminate liability to an unlimited class as the legislation imposed no limit on the number of investors or the amount of money invested. This was not a case of specific reliance by an investor on representations made by the Registrar. Finally, liability would unjustly transfer the burden of loss from

---

94   *Cooper v. Hobart, supra* note 90 at 204.
95   *Supra* note 92.
96   *Cooper v. Hobart, supra* note 90 at 206.

private investors to taxpayers - there was no evidence that the legislation was designed to be an insurance scheme.

The companion case to *Cooper, Edwards v. Law Society of Upper Canada*[97] involved a suit against the Law Society alleging negligence in its regulation of a lawyer's trust account as a result of which the appellants lost money in a gold delivery fraud. They, and others, deposited money with the lawyer in payment for gold, but they were not clients of the lawyer. In essence, they argued that the Society was negligent in its failure to take steps to prevent the improper use of the trust account. The Supreme Court of Canada denied the appeal and upheld the decision of the trial judge[98] and the Court of Appeal[99] dismissing the action for lack of a cause of action.

The court applied the two stage *Anns* approach enunciated in *Cooper*. In terms of the first stage, it concluded that the case did not fall within or was not analogous to any category of case in which liability had been imposed. As a novel situation, the existence of a duty of care depended first, on foreseeability and proximity, and then on the existence of any overriding policy considerations. A review of the legislation lead the court to the conclusion that no *prima facie* duty of care arose. The requirement of proximity was not satisfied in the sense of a direct and close relationship as the appellants were not the clients of the lawyers regulated by the respondents but "participants in a third party business promotion".[100] Also, the discharge of the Law Society's investigative and disciplinary functions involved the exercise of discretionary powers in a careful balancing of public and private interests. Given the multifaceted nature of these functions, it would not be just to impose a duty of care. Finally, the legislation, on which the issue of proximity was grounded, did not support compensation to members of the general public – compensation to clients was provided in the form of professional liability insurance and client compensation funds. Moreover, the legislation immunized the governing body of the society and its officials from liability for loss occasioned by the good faith discharge or purported discharge of their responsibilities.

The Supreme Court did not proceed to the second stage of the analysis although it indicated that any *prima facie* duty of care was negated by unstated overriding policy considerations which did not arise from the relationship of the parties. Some of these, the policy nature of the decision, the existence of a quasi-judicial immunity and the risk of indeterminate liability, had already been touched upon in the first stage. As the court had indicated in *Cooper*, it did not matter at which stage the relevant policy factors were addressed, so long as they were addressed[101] but the heavy emphasis on policy at the *prima*

---

97   *Supra* note 91.

98   (1998), 37 O.R. (3d) 279 (Ont. Gen. Div.), additional reasons at (1998), 38 C.P.C. (4th) 136 (Ont. Gen. Div.), reversed (2000), 48 O.R. (3d) 321 (Ont. C.A.), affirmed (2000), 48 O.R. (3d) 329 (Ont. C.A.), leave to appeal refused (2000), 265 N.R. 400 (note) (S.C.C.), leave to appeal allowed (2000), 266 N.R. 196 (note) (S.C.C.), affirmed [2001] 3 S.C.R. 562 (S.C.C.).

99   (2000), 48 O.R. (3d) 329 (Ont. C.A.), leave to appeal allowed (2000), 266 N.R. 196 (note) (S.C.C.), affirmed [2001] 3 S.C.R. 562 (S.C.C.).

100   *Supra* note 91 at 220.

101   *Cooper, supra* note 90 at 202.

facie duty of care stage does suggest that, over time, the courts will have less and less resort to the second stage of the *Anns* analysis even though the cases before them raise novel situations in terms of duties of care.[102]

(iv) Conclusion on Negligence by Public Authorities

The common law concerning the liability of public authorities has, over the last decade or so, become less settled and more uncertain. While, at one time, it was thought that *Anns* provided a comprehensive, and general approach to the duty issue in public authority negligence cases, courts in Canada, Australia and England have taken different approaches to the issue, even though the basic principles of tort liability are the same and even though the issues surrounding public authority liability are essentially the same. The Canadian courts, at all levels, have continued to apply and refine the *Anns* two stage approach to liability[103] until recently with the result that the negligence liability of public authorities has expanded significantly. However, the reformulation of the *Anns* test by the Supreme Court of Canada in *Cooper* and *Edwards*, with its increased emphasis on policy factors at the *prima facie* duty stage may lead to a restriction on the scope of public authority negligence liability at least in relation to novel claims.

The Australian courts refused to follow *Anns*, early on, and have relied instead on ordinary principles of negligence liability in actions concerning public authorities. In particular, the courts have focussed on issues of proximity in determining the existence of a duty of care in the exercise of statutory functions. In this respect, the liability of public authorities for omissions was severely limited – absence a close and direct relationship of reliance a statutory authority would not be held liable in negligence for failing to act when under no duty to do so. *Anns* was overruled by The House of Lords in England after years of judicial criticism of its general principle. The two stage approach was replaced by a three part test which distinguished between foreseeability and proximity. The latter was used to limit or control the potentially expansive nature of the *Anns* approach in relation to categories of injury such as pure economic loss. A third criteria, whether it is "fair, just and reasonable"" to impose a duty, has been used to limit the liability of public authorities to situations which are analogous to or fall within recognized categories of liability.[104] As a result, the English law has been protective of public authorities particularly in relation to claims involving economic loss, nonfeasance, and novel situations of liability,[105] However, one author has suggested on the basis

---

102 This suggestion is premised on the leading English authorities where the courts have not adopted a two stage approach to the duty issue since the overruling of *Anns* but have indiscriminately addressed a wide range of policy factors in the context of the proximity issue; in particular, see Lord Nicholls' judgement in *Stovin v. Wise, supra* note 93.

103 *Ingles v. Tutkaluk Construction Ltd.* (2000), 183 D.L.R. (4th) 193 (S.C.C.).

104 Kneebone, *supra* note 5 at 87.

105 *X (minors) v. Bedfordshire County Council*, [1995] 3 W.L.R. 152 (U.K. H.L.), County Councils held not to owe a duty of care to children in their exercise of statutory functions under social welfare and education legislation; *Stovin v. Wise, supra* note 93, County Council held not to owe a duty of care to an injured cyclist to remedy a dangerous situation

of two recent cases, that the English courts may be moving away from a restrictive attitude in terms of recognizing duties of care lying on public authorities in the provision of educational services.[106]

The divergent approaches taken by English, Canadian and Australian courts to the issue of public authority liability in negligence present a challenging, complex and somewhat contradictory body of case law whose principles can be said to constitute a loosely defined public law of negligence. These principles have been shaped by a number of fundamental ideas. First, they reflect the idea that government should not be immune from liability because it is government; that public authorities, in the exercise of their statutory functions, should be held, like private individuals in their activities, to a legal duty to take reasonable care so as not to cause foreseeable harm to others. Indeed, the denial of a broad immunity for public authorities has lead to the recognition of liability in situations where private individuals would not be held liable. This is not surprising, as government undertakes activities which are different than those carried on by private individuals. Secondly, these principles reflect the idea that the imposition of a legal duty of care on public authorities must take into account the unique role and position of government in society; that some public authorities act in the public interest which, in turn, may cause harm to private interests in some cases. Some adjustment of the private law principles of negligence liability is required in recognition of the fact that government activity often has no private counterpart and is motivated by social, economic and political factors which are ill suited to judicial evaluation in a negligence action. Thus, in operation, these principles seek to strike a balance between the need to hold public authorities legally responsible for their harmful acts or omissions and the need to ensure that they are not subjected to a scheme of negligence liability which unduly impedes their freedom of action and effectiveness or seeks to replace a "political and technical administration" with "a judicial and legal regime."

The adoption of *Anns* in Canada, and its subsequent refinement by the Supreme Court in *Just*, lead to a significant expansion in the negligence liability of public authorities. In part, this was driven by the *Anns* formulation itself, which is receptive to an expansion of liability. This extension of public authority has manifested itself in a number of ways. First, public authorities have been held to owe a duty of care in novel situations, involving peculiarly governmental activity, such as: the maintenance and repair of highways;[107] the regulation of building construction;[108] the regulation of airline safety;[109] and

---

at a road junction; *Hill v. Chief Constable of West Yorkshire*, [1988] 2 All E.R. 238 (U.K. H.L.), police authorities held not to owe a duty of care in respect of their conduct of a criminal investigation.

106   *Barrett v. Enfield L.B.C.*, [1999] 3 W.L.R. 79 and *Phelps v. Hillingdon L.B.C.*, [2001] 2 A.C. 619 (H.L.). See D. Fairgreve, "Pushing Back the Boundaries of Public Authority Liability: Tort Law Enters the Classroom", [2002] P.L. 288.

107   *Just v. British Columbia*, [1989] 2 S.C.R. 1228 (S.C.C.); *Brown v. British Columbia (Minister of Transportation & Highways)* (1994), 112 D.L.R. (4th) 1 (S.C.C.); *Swinamer v. Nova Scotia (Attorney General)* (1994), 112 D.L.R. (4th) 18 (S.C.C.).

108   *Nielsen v. Kamloops (City)*, [1984] 2 S.C.R. 2 (S.C.C.).

109   *Swanson Estate v. R.* (1991), 80 D.L.R. (4th) 741 (Fed. C.A.).

the administration of prisons.[110] In the past, the courts were often reluctant to recognize a duty of care in these kinds of situations as the lack of a private analogy would not support an incremental expansion in the scope of negligence liability or the activity involved the exercise of discretionary authority with which the courts did not wish to interfere.

Secondly, in several cases, the courts have indicated that public authority liability is not limited to recovery for physical loss or injury, but will also include claims for pure economic loss. Recovery will be permitted where the citizen has relied, to his detriment, on a particular representation or decision of an authority[111] or where the economic loss suffered is the type of loss the statutory regime is designed to guard against.[112] This position is consistent with the general attitude of Canadian courts, in negligence actions for pure economic loss, that claims will be permitted where recovery is manifestly fair and just.[113] In other words, recovery for pure economic loss will be allowed when the principal policy concern of fear for indeterminate and unlimited liability can be addressed through the existence of a close proximate relationship between the defendant's negligence and the plaintiff's loss, and no other policy reasons exist that would negate the duty of care.[114] The attitude of the Canadian courts towards pure economic loss claims represents a marked departure from the traditional exclusionary rule which denied recovery out of a fear of unlimited and indeterminate liability. While this fear may be justified in cases involving private defendants with limited resources, it is often less compelling in an action against government which possesses the resources (or the means to obtain the resources) to meet wide ranging claims for economic loss. Also the imposition of liability may cause government to reform its scheme of regulation to avoid future losses.[115] The receptiveness of Canadian

---

110 *Hill v. British Columbia* (1997), 50 Admin. L.R. (2d) 309 (B.C. C.A.).

111 *Comeau's Sea Foods Ltd. v. Canada (Minister of Fisheries & Oceans)* (1992), 11 C.C.L.T. (2d) 241 (Fed. T.D.), reversed (1995), 24 C.C.L.T. (2d) 1 (Fed. C.A.), dismissed on other grounds [1997] 1 S.C.R. 12 (S.C.C.), leave to appeal allowed (1995), 198 N.R. 80 (note) (S.C.C.); *Windsor Motors Ltd. v. Powell River (Municipality)* (1969), 4 D.L.R. (3d) 155 (B.C. C.A.).

112 *Kamloops, supra* note 108; *Brewer Brothers v. Canada (Attorney General)* (1991), 80 D.L.R. (4th) 321 (Fed. C.A.). See also *Wirth v. Vancouver (City)*, [1990] 6 W.W.R. 225 (B.C. C.A.) where the court denied a claim for economic loss, arising out of operational negligence in the issuance of a building permit on the ground that the rate payers of a municipality should not have to pay for this kind of loss.

113 *Canadian National Railway v. Norsk Pacific Steamship Co.*, [1992] 1 S.C.R. 1021 (S.C.C.), reconsideration refused (July 23, 1992), Doc. 21838 (S.C.C.).

114 L. Klar, *supra* note 27 at 204-08.

115 However, it should be noted that the attitude of the Canadian courts is not shared by their counterparts in England and Australia. In general, these courts have taken a more cautious and restrictive approach to the tort liability of public authorities and, in particular, they have followed the traditional exclusionary rule which precludes recovery for purely economic loss unless a close relationship of proximity (such as a specific reliance relationship) has been established. This is, of course, only true in England since the decision of the House of Lords in *Murphy v. Brentwood District Council*, [1990] 2 All E.R. 908 (U.K. H.L.), overruled *Anns* and reaffirmed the exclusionary rule in negligence actions for economic loss. The *Anns* undifferentiated approach to economic loss recovery had been earlier criticized by the Privy Council in *Yuen Ken Yeu v. Hong Kong (Attorney General), supra* note

law toward economic loss claims should have a significant impact on the scope of the negligence liability of public authorities as government regulation of economic activity is pervasive. However, the recent reformulation of the *Anns* test in *Cooper* and *Edwards* suggests that the impact may be limited in situations involving the failure of statutory regulators to act so as to prevent or minimize economic losses caused by the actions of regulated parties. The existence of a duty of care will be restricted to relationships of sufficient proximity as determined by a consideration of policy factors such as a statutory context, the exercise of discretion, the public interest and the prospect of indeterminate liability.

Thirdly, the scope of public authority liability has been expanded, beyond that normally imposed on private individuals, to include cases of "non-feasance"; that is, liability has been imposed on public authorities for their failure to act or their failure to act with due care when under no statutory duty to act.[116] Historically, out of a concern for individual liberty, the common law has been reluctant to hold private citizens to a general duty of affirmative action. However, these sentiments have increasingly given way in the face of "heightened social obligation and other collectivist tendencies."[117] As a result, affirmative duties to act have been recognized in a number of situations: where the parties are in a commercial relationship from which one party derives an economic benefit,[118] where the relationship between the parties engenders reliance on the part of one party that the other will take precautions for its benefit[119] or where a party's right to control certain persons or a particular activity carries with it the duty to exercise that control reasonably for the protection of others.[120]

In light of these developments, the extension of governmental liability to cases of nonfeasance seems appropriate. Government not only acts in the public interest, it often acts for the specific purpose of regulating private activity so as to prevent persons from harming themselves or others. This, in turn, engenders reliance, on the part of those who the statutory scheme is designed to protect, that government will in fact act with reasonable care to protect them

---

92, and specifically rejected by the Australian High Court in *Sutherland Shire Council v. Heyman* (1985), 60 A.L.R. 1 (Australia H.C.).

116 *Woodall, supra* note 62 , suggests that governmental failures to inspect buildings competently or to inspect and maintain highways are truly cases of "nonfeasance". It should noted that the English courts have generally refused to hold public authorities liable for their failure to act when under no statutory duty to do so. See *X (minors) v. Bedfordshire County Council, supra* note 105, and *Stovin v. Wise, supra* note 93.

117 J.G. Fleming, *The Law of Torts*, 7th ed. (Sydney: The Law Book Company, 1987) at 134.

118 For example, a commercial host has been held in a number of cases to a duty or care to assist of prevent an intoxicated person from injuring himself or others; see *Menow v. Honsberger* (1973), 38 D.L.R. (3d) 105 (S.C.C.); *Stewart v. Pettie* (1995), 121 D.L.R. (4th) 222 (S.C.C.).

119 Fleming, *supra* note 117 at 136-37.

120 For example, a parent is under a duty to exercise reasonable control over his or her children to protect them from harm or to protect others from their injurious activities. Similarly, in *Dorset Yacht Co. v. Home Office*, [1970] A.C. 1004 (U.K. H.L.), the Home Office was held liable for the negligence of its officers in failing to exercise reasonable care to control persons in their custody.

even though it is empowered, but not required by statute, to do so.[121] The existence of a relationship of reasonable reliance should be the basis of any legal duty of care, not whether the statute imposes a statutory duty on the public authority to act or not. Moreover, the concern for individual freedom of action seems out of place in negligence actions against public authorities. An analogy between private individuals and public authorities is often weak, because government is empowered to act, not in its own interest, but for the benefit of individual members of the public, even though its authority is cast in discretionary terms.

The expansion of the negligence liability of public authorities in Canada has not been without its problems. Chief among these is the operation of the policy/operational dichotomy. This simple distinction, designed to exclude from negligence review, non-justiciable, discretionary, policy decisions, has been embraced by the Canadian courts as the touchstone of liability in a variety of negligence actions against public authorities with the result that case law is often confusing and inconsistent. Indeed, one commentator, after a review of the cases, emphatically concludes, "[t]here is no apparent pattern in the judgments or any way to predict whether a court will decide that a specific governmental activity is a matter of policy or operations."[122] The confused and uncertain state of the case law demonstrates that the courts have found it difficult to draw the distinction in individual cases. Part of this difficulty stems from the fact that the dichotomy states the conclusion that policy, and not operational, activities are to be exempted from liability but it does not articulate a test, except in the most vague and ambiguous terms, which defines or describes how the distinction is to be made in practice. However, most of the difficulty stems from the fact that it is often impossible to clearly separate policy activities from operational activities. Policy decisions usually have operational aspects and the operational implementation of policy decisions inevitably involves the exercise of discretion. Thus, it is not surprising that the courts have come to different conclusions in many cases about where the line is to be drawn between policy decisions and operational activities.

At one time, it was thought that the decision of the Supreme Court of Canada in *Just* clarified the situation somewhat. Many interpreted the majority judgment of Cory J. to mean that the policy exemption would be narrowly construed to include only a few threshold decisions made at a high level of authority. The bulk of government activity would therefore fall within the operational area even though it involved some measure of discretionary decision making. The reasonableness of operational decisions and actions would then be determined on the basis of a variable standard of care which took into

---

121   Specific, rather than general reliance may be required for the recognition of a duty of care in situations involving the failure of a public authority to act when under no statutory duty to do so. Lord Hoffman, in *Stovin v. Wise*, *supra* note 93 at 409-18 suggests that general reliance may only be sufficient to impose a duty to act in cases of routine services or powers granted to protect the public from risks which they could not guard themselves against. See also, Kneebone, *supra* note 5 at 118-20 for a categorization of reliance situations which may satisfy the proximity requirement.

122   L. Klar, *supra* note 27 at 235.

account the nature of the defendant and the financial and political constraints it operated under. This interpretation suggested a broad scope for government liability in negligence as, on the basis of foreseeability, a duty of care would be imposed on most government activity. Unfortunately, the judgment of Cory J. may have been misunderstood. In two later cases, *Brown* and *Swinamer*, the courts specifically rejected the notion that the policy exemption applied to only a few, high level threshold decisions. Therefore, it appears that the policy exemption from liability is broader than was thought as it includes decisions prompted by social, economic and political factors or constraints at any level of the governmental decision-making process. As a result, greater uncertainty now attends the practical application of the policy, operational dichotomy.

The efficacy of the policy/operational distinction is further undermined by the fact that English and Australian courts have refused to apply it in negligence actions against public authorities except as one factor in the determination of the duty issue. Rather, they have decided to proceed cautiously in response to novel negligence claims against public authorities. In these situations, the existence of a duty of care will depend on factors other than either the foreseeability of harm suffered or the policy/operational dichotomy – factors such as: whether there is a strong analogy to an existing situation of liability; whether it is "just and reasonable" to impose a duty of care on the public authority;[123] whether there is a relationship of reliance between the parties;[124] whether an adequate form of alternate relief, such as judicial review is available;[125] and whether the statutory powers were conferred for a purpose which would support the imposition of a duty of care.[126] With the reformulation of the *Anns* two stage approach, the Supreme Court of Canada has apparently signalled a move towards the Australian and English approaches to the duty issue. The policy/operational distinction will be a test of justiciability; that is, whether or not the decision is one which the courts ought to assess? As an overriding policy consideration, it will be addressed at the second stage of the analysis which will arise only in novel situations of liability.

The difficulties associated with the policy/operational distinction, the inconsistent and uncertain nature of the case law and the attitudes of the English and Australian courts have lead some courts and commentators to argue that the policy/operational distinction should not be used as the exclusive touchstone of liability.[127] Rather, other approaches to the duty issue should be employed. These would include: the rejection of common law liability in favour of a scheme of statutory liability; the cautious, restrictive approach of the English courts which involves the consideration of a number of factors in the

---

123 *Peabody Donation Fund v. Sir Lindsay Parkinson & Co.*, [1984] 3 All E.R. 529 (U.K. H.L.).

124 *Sutherland Shire Council v. Heyman* (1985), 60 A.L.R. 1 (Australia H.C.); *Murphy v. Brentwood District Council*, [1990] 2 All E.R. 908 (U.K. H.L.).

125 *Rowling v. Takaro Properties Ltd.*, [1988] A.C. 473 (New Zealand P.C.).

126 *Stovin v. Wise*, [1996] 3 W.L.R. 388 (U.K. H.L.). For Canadian authorities, see *Birchard v. Alberta (Securities Commission)*, [1987] 6 W.W.R. 536 (Alta. Q.B.); *Gutek v. Sunshine Village Corp.* (1990), 65 D.L.R. (4th) 406 (Alta. Q.B.).

127 See the comments of Sopinka J. in *Brown*, *supra* note 107 at 4.

determination of the duty issue; and the use of a varying standard of care to account for the fact that different types of government activity may be in issue.[128] While each of these approaches may have some benefits, it is unlikely that any one will bring greater certainty to the law or provide the solution to the problems of public authority tort liability. This is a complex issue which, so far, has not lent itself to simple solutions. Any solution must deal with the diverse activities of a wide range of public actors. This suggests that a multi-faceted approach to the duty issue is perhaps the best. The recognition of a duty of care in particular cases will depend on the circumstances of the case, the public policy factors involved and the balancing of the various interests at stake, as the imposition of negligence liability on public authorities is part of a larger political question concerning the nature and extent of legal controls over government activity. Therefore, it seems appropriate for Canadian courts to turn away from artificial distinctions to a more open, policy based approach. This will at least facilitate an informed debate over the extent to which governments should be held accountable monetarily for the losses or injuries occasioned by their activities.

(c) Misfeasance in a Public Office

The still evolving tort action entitled "misfeasance in a public office" is a form of tort liability unique to government. While its existence was once doubted because it was predicated on a few disparate cases, this is no longer the case as the action has been recognized by courts in the United Kingdom, Australia and Canada,[129] and by leading commentators on administrative law and tort law.[130]

Misfeasance in a public office can only be committed by a public officer or authority in the exercise of either a statutory or prerogative power.[131] The

---

128 For a more detailed discussion of these and other approaches, see L. Klar, *supra* note 27 at 233-46 and L. Klar, *supra* note 71 at 176-77.

129 See the judgment of the Privy Council in *Dunlop v. Woollahra Municipal Council*, [1981] 2 W.L.R. 693 (Australia P.C.), and the judgment of Robertson J.A. in *Comeau's Sea Foods Ltd. v. Canada (Minister of Fisheries & Oceans)* (1995), 24 C.C.L.T. (2d) 1 (Fed. C.A.), affirmed [1997] 1 S.C.R. 12 (S.C.C.), leave to appeal allowed (1995), 198 N.R. 80 (note) (S.C.C.), and the judgments of the House of Lords in *Three Rivers District Council v. Bank of England (No. 3)*, [2000] 3 All E.R. 1 (U.K. H.L.); [2001] 2 All E.R. 513.

130 See for example, Hogg and Monahan, "Liability of the Crown", *supra* note 5 at 144; McBride, "Damages as a Remedy for Unlawful Administrative Action" [1979] Camb. L.J. 323; Craig, "Compensation in Public Law" (1980) 96 L.Q.R. 413; Phegan, "Damages for Improper Exercise of Statutory Authority" (1980) 9 Syd. L. Rev. 93; D.J. Sadler, "Liability For Misfeasance in a Public Office" (1992) 14 Syd. L. Rev. 137; Mullan, *Administrative Law* (Toronto: Irwin Law, 2001) at 506; Kneebone, *supra* note 5 at 167; Leadem, "Tort of Abuse of Public Office" (2002) 15 C.J.A.L.P. 185; Irvine, "Misfeasance in Public Office: Reflections on Some Recent Developments" (2002) 9 C.C.L.T. (3d) 26.

131 As the Courts have defined public office and public officer in expansive terms, this has rarely proved to be a problem. See *Odhavji Estate v. Woodhouse* (2000), 194 D.L.R. (4th) 577 (Ont. C.A.), additional reasons at (2001), 2001 CarswellOnt 476 (Ont. C.A.), leave to appeal allowed (2001), 276 N.R. 199 (note) (S.C.C.), reversed in part 2003 SCC 69 (S.C.C.), on whether police officers under investigation for a fatal shooting were acting as public officers for the purpose of tort of misfeasance. See also *Price v. British Columbia* (2001),

action affords a remedy in damages for loss or injury arising out of a particular type of *ultra vires* action, namely, one which is actuated by malice or more accurately today, by malice or by knowledge that the harmful action was not authorized.

(i) Origins of the Action

Cases concerning an action in damages for the malicious or abusive exercise of statutory authority have been present in the common law for centuries. For example, in 1703, Holt C.J. held that the malicious denial of a person's right to vote was actionable.[132] In this century, courts have held that an action would lie for the malicious denial of a licence[133] or for the malicious confirmation of a compulsory purchase order.[134] In a negative sense, the courts have held that an action will not lie, in the absence of malice or bad faith, for the *ultra vires* disbarment of a lawyer[135] or the *ultra vires* suspension of a street vendor's licence.[136]

These cases appear to support the existence of an action in damages, available in a limited set of circumstances, to remedy malicious misconduct and extreme bad faith on the part of a public official.[137] However, while the cases make it clear that malice or bad faith was a necessary ingredient in any possible action, they also raise questions about the nature and scope of the suggested action. First, some uncertainty surrounds the role to be played by malice in the action. Is the presence of malice or bad faith, by itself, sufficient to establish liability, on the basis that it renders the action *ultra vires* with nothing more required to justify an award in damages? Or, is malice or bad faith just one of the many elements necessary to maintain a successful action in damages against a public authority where loss or injury is suffered as a result of *ultra vires* action? A clear answer is not suggested. Logic supports the view that malice can serve a number of purposes. It can render an act or decision *ultra vires*, and thereby preclude a defence of statutory authority to an action in tort. Alternatively, malice can serve as the basis both for a finding of *ultra vires* and an action in tort. In any event, where a statutory tribunal acts *ultra vires* but in good faith, in the honest purported exercise of its powers, it will not, in general, be held liable for losses suffered as a consequence of its *ultra vires* action, unless those actions otherwise constitute a recognized tort.[138]

[2001] B.C.J. No. 2284, 2001 CarswellBC 2357 (B.C. S.C. [In Chambers]), where the court held that internal management decisions made by the provincial Liquor Distribution Branch were not the exercise of public powers within the ambit of the tort of misfeasance in a public office.

132   *Ashby v. White* (1703), 2 Ld. Raym. 938 (Eng. K.B.).

133   *David v. Cader*, [1963] 1 W.L.R. 834 (Ceylon P.C.).

134   *Smith v. East Elloe Rural (Rural District)*, [1956] A.C. 736 (U.K. H.L.).

135   *Harris v. Law Society (Alberta)*, [1936] S.C.R. 88 (S.C.C.).

136   *Hlookloff v. Vancouver (City)* (1968), 63 W.W.R. 129 (B.C. S.C.)

137   C. Harlow, *Compensation for Government Torts* (London: Sweet & Maxwell, 1982) at 66.

138   *Harris, supra* note 135; and *Hookloff, supra* note 136 are examples of cases where the plaintiff failed as he was unable to establish that the defendant's actions were not only *ultra vires*, but also tortious. A few, isolated cases would suggest that a pure case of *ultra vires* is sufficient, by itself, to give rise to a remedy in damages: see the decision of the Supreme

Secondly, it is unclear what the term "malice" entails. An older line of authority appeared to define the essential element of malice subjectively. To succeed, a plaintiff would have to establish that the defendant's actions were motivated by feelings of spite or ill will towards the plaintiff with an intention to injure or harm him or her. The scope of such an action would be very limited because situations of this type are probably few in number and notoriously difficult to prove.

(ii) Modern Authority

A more modern line of authority appears to take a broader view of what constitutes malice. In the Australian decision of *Farrington v. Thomson*,[139] the court used the term "misfeasance in a public office" to describe an action in damages for the malicious exercise of statutory authority, which it defined in terms of an act which the officer knew to be both an "abuse of office" and harmful to the plaintiff. This definition suggested a broader concept of misfeasance beyond conduct which was motivated by spite or ill will or an intention to injure. The central element of misfeasance, malice, would also include the exercise of powers which the officer knew he or she did not possess. On this basis, the court held that the defendant officers' order closing the plaintiff's licenced premises was actionable.

The celebrated decision of the Supreme Court of Canada in *Roncarelli v. Duplessis*[140] also suggests a broader meaning for the term "malice". Roncarelli owned a restaurant in Montreal which had a liquor licence. He had posted bail for a number of Jehovah Witnesses when members of that sect were arrested by the Government of Quebec for their religious activities. The General Manager of the Liquor Commission passed along this information to the Premier and Attorney General of Quebec. Duplessis ordered the General Manager to revoke Roncarelli's liquor licence. The relevant legislation gave the General Manager the discretionary power to grant or cancel liquor licences. As a result of this action, Roncarelli's business declined and he suffered economic loss.

Roncarelli brought an action in damages for the illegal cancellation of his liquor licence. Duplessis defended the action on the basis that he, as Attorney General, acted in good faith in giving "advice" to the General Manager of the Liquor Commission. The Supreme Court of Canada decided otherwise. By a majority decision, the Court held that the General Manager had not independently exercised his discretion in cancelling the licence, but rather had acted under the direction of the defendant. As Attorney General, Duplessis should have limited himself to giving advice about the legality of the cancellation for the particular purpose envisioned. His action, however, went beyond the scope of his office, and turned the act into a personal one. Liability arose, not merely because his action was *ultra vires*, but because his underlying motivation was

---

Court of Canada in *McGillivray v. Kimber* (1915), 52 S.C.R. 146 (S.C.C.). However, these cases are generally treated as anomalies–isolated cases arising out of a particular statutory scheme or cases where malice is inferred rather than expressly found to exist.

139 [1959] V.R. 286 (Australia S.C.); See also *Tampion v. Anderson*, [1973] V.R. 715.

140 [1959] S.C.R. 121 (S.C.C.).

improper and wrongful. Although the action was discretionary in nature, this necessarily implied good faith in its exercise. In other words, the Premier's action was not only *ultra vires*, it was malicious.[141] Rand J. noted that "[m]alice in the proper sense is simply acting for a reason knowingly foreign to the administration".[142] Thus, "malice" was held to include not only spite or ill will towards the plaintiff, but also to include the intentional exercise of discretionary authority for an improper purpose.

An objective definition of "malice" would afford greater scope for the action of misfeasance in a public office – indeed, a potential action for all *ultra vires* administrative acts would appear to be suggested. After all, the courts, in individual cases, by reference to enabling legislation and the common law, have limited the proper exercise of discretion to actions within certain bounds. Knowledge of these limitations could then be imputed to the public officer or authority so that a malicious exercise of statutory authority arises whenever the discretionary authority is exercised for a purpose which a court later determines to be improper.[143] However, while the potential exists for a broadly defined action in tort based on this view of the malicious or abusive exercise of statutory authority, the courts have been reluctant to acknowledge its existence. Rather, their tendency has been to restrict such a cause of action to a limited set of circumstances: principally, where malice in the sense of spite or ill will towards the plaintiff or an intention to injure has been established,[144] and, on rare occasions, when the officer or public authority acted intentionally with the knowledge they did not possess the powers they purported to exercise.[145] This limited concept of the action rests on a more subjective view of malice either in the sense of acting with spite or ill will towards the plaintiff or acting with the knowledge that the powers exercised were not possessed.[146] This view reflects the intentional nature of the tort action – both malice and knowingly acting outside the scope of authority involve an element of intention.

The limited nature of the action for misfeasance in a public office was later confirmed in several cases.[147] In *Dunlop v. Woollahra Municipal Coun-*

---

141   Rand J., *ibid.* at 141, characterized the actions of Duplessis in the following terms: ". . . [a] gross abuse of legal power expressly intended to punish him for an act wholly irrelevant to the statute. . .".

142   *Ibid.* at 141.

143   This is the view taken by Gould in his article, "Damages as a Remedy in Administrative Law" (1972) 5 N.Z.U.L.R. 105 at 113-14. Sadler, *supra* note 130 at 144-45 disagrees with Gould's analysis, arguing that knowledge of invalidity must be viewed subjectively not objectively: "[t]he officer must with knowledge of the potential for abuse, proceed and abuse his or her jurisdiction." Sadler's view is supported by the authorities.

144   *David v. Cader, supra* note 133; *Hlookloff, supra* note 136; *Farrington v. Thomson, supra* note 139.

145   *Farrington v. Thomson, ibid.*

146   It must be appreciated that some courts have taken the view that knowledge of invalidity is an alternate ground of liability to "malice" in the subjective sense of an intention to injure. *Bourgoin SA v. Ministry of Agriculture, Fisheries & Food* (1984), [1986] Q.B. 716 at 777 (Eng. Q.B.).

147   For an acknowledgement by a Canadian court of the existence of the tort of misfeasance in a public office; see: *Gerrard v. Manitoba* (1992), 98 D.L.R. (4th) 167 (Man. C.A.); *Francoeur v. R.* (1994), 78 F.T.R. 109 (Fed. T.D.), affirmed (1996), 195 N.R. 313 (Fed. C.A.);

cil,[148] an action was brought against the council, as a result of its passage of two invalid resolutions restricting development of the plaintiff's property. The Privy Council dismissed the claim, holding that "in the absence of malice, passing without knowledge of invalidity a resolution which is devoid of legal effect is not conduct that of itself is capable of amounting to such misfeasance".[149] In *Bourgoin SA v. Ministry of Agriculture, Fisheries & Food*,[150] the English Court of Appeal held that the tort of misfeasance in a public office arose when an officer knew that he did not have the power he purported to exercise and further, he knew that the *ultra vires* actions would injure the plaintiff. In other words, the harm suffered must be a foreseeable consequence of the officer's *ultra vires* action. This was the case in *Bourgoin*, as, even though the Minister's illegal decision was designed to benefit English turkey producers, it caused foreseeable harm to their French competitors, or, to put it another way, the harm was a probable consequence of his unlawful activities.

Further support for an action of limited scope is provided by the judgment of the Australian High Court in *Northern Territory of Australia v. Mengel*.[151] The action arose out of restrictions placed on the movement of the plaintiff's cattle herd under a government disease eradication programme. The plaintiffs were unable to move the herds to market as planned, and significant loss was suffered. The High Court held that the plaintiffs were unable to succeed in a claim for misfeasance in a public office as the cause of action had not been made out. After a review of the authorities, the majority of the court concluded that the action for misfeasance in a public office was a form of deliberate tort "in the sense that there is no liability unless either there is an intention to cause harm or the officer concerned knowingly acts in excess of his or her power."[152] Moreover, it was confined to those situations where the harm suffered was a foreseeable consequence of the officer's actions. While the court was satisfied that the officers' orders were unauthorized, this was not sufficient as there was no evidence that they knew that they were acting without authority. In this respect, the court specifically rejected the argument of the plaintiffs that the tort be reformulated to include liability where the officer *ought* to have know that he or she lacked power. Given existence of a tort of negligence, there was no reason to expand the scope of the tort in this way and thus the officer must

---

Chhabra v. R. (1989), 26 F.T.R. 288 (Fed. T.D.). See also *Jones v. Swansea City Council*, [1990] 1 W.L.R. 54, where the court broadly defined the "public functions" of the council to include not only statutory powers but also powers arising under contract; and *Lapointe v. Canada (Minister of Fisheries & Oceans)* (1992), 4 Admin. L.R. (2d) 298 (Fed. T.D.), additional reasons at (1992), 4 Admin. L.R. (2d) 298 at 319 (Fed. T.D.).

148   *Supra* note 129.

149   *Ibid.* at 703.

150   (1984), [1985] 3 All E.R. 585 (Eng. Q.B.).

151   (1995), 129 A.L.R. 1 (Australia H.C.). For academic commentary see, S. Kneebone, "Misfeasance in a Public Office After Mengel's Case: A "Special" Tort No More?" (1996) Tort L.Rev. 111.

152   *Ibid.* at 17. Two members of the court, who concurred in the result but wrote separate reasons, took a broader view of the tort's constituent elements to include "reckless indifference as to the availability of the power to support the impugned conduct and as to the injury which the impugned conduct is calculated to produce." *Ibid.* at 26 per Brennan J.

have actual, rather than, imputed or constructive, knowledge that he or she lacked authority.

(iii) Recent Authority

In recent years, the uncertain tort of misfeasance in a public office has received more judicial attention as plaintiffs, injured as a consequence of government action but unable to establish the existence of either a nominate tort or a duty of care, have sought redress through a more broadly defined tort of misfeasance. As a result, the courts in England, Australia,[153] New Zealand,[154] and Canada have been forced to consider the scope and content of the action, in a number of statutory contexts ranging from bank licensing to land development. What has emerged is a complex tort action of limited scope, designed to deal with the intentional abuse of public office or deliberate official misconduct.

The seminal authority must be considered to be the decision of the House of Lords in *Three Rivers District Council v. Bank of England*.[155] The case presented the House of Lords with an opportunity to review the constituent elements of the tort, particularly the mental elements that set it apart from judicial review for abuse of discretion and the tort of negligence in the exercise of statutory authority. The action arose out of the failure of the Luxembourg Bank which was licensed by the defendant to take deposits in the United Kingdom. Depositors who lost money when the bank failed, due to the fraud of senior officers of the bank, sued officials of the defendant for misfeasance in licensing the bank and in failing to close it down before it failed. In a difficult judgment, the court confirmed the existence of the misfeasance tort but limited its scope to two forms of abuse. The first is the classic form of the action, widely referred to as "targeted malice", that is, the intentional use of statutory authority to injure or harm the plaintiff. There is clearly an *ultra vires* action or decision as the use of statutory authority to harm someone is undoubtedly the use of statutory authority for an improper purpose. The second form expands the scope of the action to include acts undertaken with the actual knowledge they were unlawful and likely, or probably, would cause harm to the plaintiff. This form of the tort does not require malice, in the sense of an intention to injure the plaintiff or acting out of spite for an ulterior purpose. The required mental element associated with this form of the tort would also include subjective recklessness, in the sense of the officer's reckless indifference to the illegality of the impugned conduct and to the possible consequences of that conduct.[156] The Court also rejected the argument that the tort would be

---

153 For a discussion of Australian authorities, see Kneebone, *supra* note 5 at 115.

154 *Garrett v. New Zealand (Attorney General)*, [1997] 2 N.Z.L.R. 332 (New Zealand C.A.).

155 [2001] 2 All E.R. 513.

156 In terms of the recklessness requirement, Lord Steyn observed at *ibid.* at 9: "A policy underlying it is sound: reckless indifference to consequences is as blameworthy as deliberately seeking such consequences". Moreover, in the case of "untargeted malice", the defendant officer need not know the identity of the plaintiff or of the class of plaintiff - it will be sufficient if it is shown that he was reckless about the consequences of his act. See *Akensua v. Secretary of State*, [2003] 1 All E.R. 35 (C.A.).

established where the officer acted with the knowledge that his or her conduct lacked legal authority and as a result caused damage which was foreseeable. The officer would only be responsible for loss or damage he or she knew was likely to occur.

The action described by the House of Lords in *Three Rivers* is an intentional tort of limited scope even though it extends, in its second form, beyond its classic parameters; targeted malice. The requisite mental element for abuse of office presents a plaintiff with a "pretty stern and demanding"[157] onus which will limit the use of the action to situations of deliberate official misconduct. The required mental element will often be difficult to prove.[158] It will not be available to remedy the harmful consequences of an unlawful act or decision stemming from the good faith, honest error of an official. More is required – deliberate misconduct on the part of the public official or authority. This is in keeping with the nature of the action which is designed to deal with the abuse of office, arising out of malice, knowledge of invalidity or reckless indifference, all of which are states of mind which are inconsistent with an honest attempt to perform the functions of that office.

The limited nature of the misfeasance action is reflected in several recent Canadian cases. For the most part, these cases have followed the line of reasoning espoused by the House of Lords in the *Three Rivers* case.[159] These cases concern allegations of targeted malice and knowledge of invalidity. In the first of these, *Uni-Jet Industrial Pipe Ltd. v. Canada (Attorney General)*,[160] the Manitoba Court of Appeal held an R.C.M.P. officer liable for misfeasance in a public office as a result of his improper and premature release of information to the media concerning the execution of a search warrant against the plaintiff. This action was taken for the purpose of advancing the defendant officer's relations with the media. The court found this to be improper and a violation of the officer's duties under both the *Criminal Code* and the *Royal Canadian Mounted Police Act*.[161] Also, the court was satisfied that the defendant officer was aware that his actions would likely cause embarrassment to the plaintiff and harm to its reputation.

Other cases have arisen in a land use context. In *Alberta (Minister of Public Works, Supply & Services) v. Nilsson*,[162] the Court of Appeal upheld a

---

157 Irvine, *supra* note 130 at 30.

158 Leadem, *supra* note 130 and Kneebone, *supra* note 5.

159 In *Alberta (Minister of Public Works, Supply & Services) v. Nilsson*, [1999] 9 W.W.R. 203 (Alta. Q.B.), leave to appeal allowed (1999), [2000] 2 W.W.R. 688 (Alta. C.A.), affirmed (2002), [2003] 2 W.W.R. 215 (Alta. C.A.), additional reasons at (2003), 18 Alta. L.R. (4th) 9 (Alta. C.A.), leave to appeal refused (2003), [2004] 1 W.W.R. 197 (S.C.C.), a case decided before the House of Lords judgment in *Three Rivers,* Marceau J. proposed an integrated analysis of the action which would call into question the two category classification confirmed by the House of Lords in *Three Rivers*. This approach has been questioned by Irvine, *supra* note 130.

160 (2001), 9 C.C.L.T. (3d) 1 (Man. C.A.).

161 *Criminal Code*, R.S.C. 1985, c. C-46 and *Royal Canadian Mounted Police Act*, R.S.C. 1985, c. R-10.

162 (2002), [2003] 2 W.W.R. 215 (Alta. C.A.), additional reasons at (2003), 18 Alta. L.R. (4th) 9 (Alta. C.A.), leave to appeal refused (2003), [2004] 1 W.W.R. 197 (S.C.C.).

trial decision holding the Crown liable for the second form of the tort; the Crown's actions in severely limiting the appellant's use of his land were seen to constitute reckless indifference to the legality of its actions and their probable consequences. The Crown had made the appellant's land part of a Restricted Development Area which precluded development without ministerial permission. The appellant could not develop his land or sell it. The Restricted Development Area had been created under the *Department of the Environment Act*[163] for the ostensible purpose of environmental protection, but the real purpose was to freeze development of land so as to provide for future highway development. The creation of the Restricted Development Area was later held to be *ultra vires* the statutory authority. The trial judge had inferred from the evidence that the Minister and cabinet were subjectively aware of "a serious risk that they were acting illegally"[164] and that they were aware of the risk of harm to the appellant from the freeze on the development or sale of the land. The necessary elements of the tort were, therefore, made out.

In another case, *Powder Mountain Resorts Ltd. v. British Columbia*,[165] the appellant developer brought an action against the Premier and other provincial officials on a number of grounds including misfeasance in a public office where his proposal to build a ski resort failed to gain the necessary provincial approval. The Court of Appeal dismissed the action for misfeasance on the grounds that the appellant had failed to establish an abuse of power in the sense of an illegal act or an excess of power on the part of the defendants. Both the second and the first branch of the tort of misfeasance require an unlawful act as otherwise a citizen could sue for loss or damage incurred as a result of a legal act or decision. Also, the appellant failed to establish "targeted malice"; that the respondents had acted in order to injure the appellant rather than in the province's interest. A final case concerned targeted malice. In *First National Properties Ltd. v. Highlands (District)*,[166] a property developer brought an action against the Mayor, the Council and other municipal officials for misfeasance in public office. As a result of these officials' actions, the developer was frustrated in its efforts to develop a large area of undeveloped land and failed to make the profits it expected. The Court of Appeal, after review of the authorities, affirmed the two forms of the action and held that the respondent had failed to establish that the Mayor and municipal officials had abused their office by using their authority with the motive of injuring the respondent. The Mayor had acted to further a political agenda, on which he had been elected, to preserve natural lands in an undeveloped state – he had not acted to injure the developer. The court also struck a cautionary note suggesting that courts should be careful not to readily equate political beliefs with improper motives in the exercise of public powers.

These cases demonstrate that the tort of misfeasance in public office is well established in Canada. In keeping with the judgment of the House of

---

163   S.A. 1971, c. 24.

164   *Supra* note 162 at 252.

165   (2001), 8 C.C.L.T. (3d) 170 (B.C. C.A.).

166   (2001), 198 D.L.R. (4th) 443, 9 C.C.L.T. (3d) 34 (B.C. C.A.), leave to appeal refused (2001), 285 N.R. 198 (note) (S.C.C.).

Lords in *Three Rivers*, the action can take one of two forms, both of which impose a significant burden on the plaintiff who must establish that the requisite state of mind was present. Overall, the action is one of limited scope designed to address deliberate misconduct, an intentional abuse of statutory authority – in restricted circumstances, it may provide a remedy for losses caused by intentional wrongful or abusive conduct. That apart, it serves as a means of punishing an official wrongdoer and deterring others from similar misconduct.[167] There is no indication that English or Canadian courts appear willing to expand the scope of this action beyond its purpose as a remedy for deliberate misconduct in the exercise of public office – indeed, they seem to be aware of the dangers of overextending the action, particularly in terms of overlap with judicial review and the tort of negligence.

(d) Constitutional Aspects of Damages

The *Canadian Charter of Rights and Freedoms*[168] may lead to a significant expansion in the liability of government and its officials.[169]

The first possible development may be the recognition of another species of "public" tort liability unique to government. This will involve an award of damages for *ultra vires* governmental action which infringes a citizen's constitutional rights and freedoms. Such a remedy is in the embryonic stages of development in Canada, although in the United States a remedy in damages for "constitutional tort" is well established.[170] In the leading American authority, *Bivens v. Six Unknown Named Agents*,[171] damages were awarded to the

---

167 In this respect, it should be noted that the punishment and deterrence value of the action may be undermined by the fact that the Crown may be held vicariously liable for the actions of its servants which constitute misfeasance in a public office. In *Mengel, supra* note 151, the court indicated that such liability could arise where the officer's actions were clothed with *de facto* authority. See also *Racz v. Home Office*, [1994] 1 All E.R. 97 (H.L.). It should also be noted that the tort offers the potential of an award of punitive damages in addition to general damages. See *Longley v. Minister of National Revenue* (1999), 176 D.L.R. (4th) 445 (B.C. S.C.), affirmed (2000), 184 D.L.R. (4th) 590 (B.C. C.A.), leave to appeal refused (2000), 264 N.R. 398 (note) (S.C.C.); *Uni-Jet Industrial Pipe, supra* note 160.

168 Part 1 of Schedule B to *The Canada Act, 1982* (U.K., 1982, c. 11); also reproduced in the *Constitution Act*, S.C. 1982.

169 See: M. Pilkington, "Damages as a Remedy for Infringement of the Canadian Charter of Rights and Freedoms" (1984) 62 Can. Bar Rev. 517; Cooper-Stephenson, "Tort Theory for the Charter Damages Remedy" (1988) 59 Sask. L. Rev. 1; Cooper-Stephenson, *Charter Damages Claims* (Toronto: Carswell, 1990); K.J.W. Sandstrom, "Damage Liability Under the Charter" (1990) 24 U.B.C. L. Rev. 229; Otis, Ghislain, "Personal Liability of Public Officials For Constitutional Wrongdoing" (1996) 24 Man. L.J. 23; Roach, K., *Constitutional Remedies in Canada* (Aurora: Canada Law Book, 1994) (Looseleaf).

170 A great deal has been written on this subject in the United States. For example, see Shuck, *supra* note 14 at 47-51; Lehmen, "*Bivens* and its Progeny: The Scope of a Constitutional Cause of Action for Torts Committed by Government Officials" (1977) 4 Hastings Const. L.Q. 531.

171 403 U.S. 388 (1971). The existence of a damage remedy for breach of a person's constitutional rights has also been recognized in New Zealand. In *Simpson v. Attorney General*, [1994] 3 N.Z.L.R. 667 (New Zealand C.A.), a claim in damages was recognized for an unreasonable search of the plaintiff's home which amounted to a violation of the New Zealand *Bill of Rights 1990*, even though the *Bill of Rights* did not contain a remedies clause

plaintiff for an unreasonable search of his house by federal narcotics agents in contravention of the American *Bill of Rights*.[172]

A damage remedy for "constitutional tort" in Canada arises from the explicit and broad remedial power vested in the courts by section 24 of the *Charter*. This provision enables anyone whose *Charter* rights have been infringed to "apply to a court of competent jurisdiction to obtain such remedy as the court considers appropriate and just in the circumstances". Such a broad and flexible remedial power gives the Canadian courts a virtually unlimited opportunity to fashion the terms of a damage remedy for the infringement of constitutional rights. In developing principles to govern an award of damages under the *Charter*, the courts will be confronted by a broad variety of issues including such matters as: causation, assessment of damages, and the existence and scope of immunities for government and its officials.[173] The few reported cases to date in which damages have been awarded against the government for breaches of the *Charter*[174] reveal little or no discussion of underlying principles.[175]

However, the potential for constitutional tort claims is illustrated by the recent, highly publicized, decision of the Ontario Court of Justice in *Jane Doe v. Metropolitan Toronto (Municipality) Commissioners of Police*.[176] In this case, the plaintiff, a sexual assault victim, was successful in a *Charter* damage claim against the Toronto City Police, arising out of their conduct in the investigation and apprehension of a serial rapist. The claim against the police was novel in that it sought to hold them liable for either their failure to apprehend an unknown offender before he caused injury to the plaintiff or for their failure to warn the plaintiff of the risk of injury so she could take precautions. However, the court found that the acts and omissions of the police not

---

and was not entrenched. See also *R. v. Secretary of State For Transport, ex p. Factortame Ltd.*, [2000] 1 A.C. 5241, damages awarded against English Crown for the deliberate adoption of fishing legislation which was discriminatory, on the grounds of nationality, and therefore a breach of the E.E.C. Treaty.

172   However, it is generally agreed that the promise of *Bivens* in providing a remedy for unconstitutional official action is unfulfilled. For example, see "Government Tort Liability" (1998) 111 Harvard Law Review 2009.

173   See *Prete*, note 181, below.

174   For example, *Collin v. Lussier*, [1983] 1 F.C. 218 (Fed. T.D.), set aside/quashed (1984), [1985] 1 F.C. 124 (Fed. C.A.); *R. v. Crossman* (1984), 9 D.L.R. (4th) 588 (Fed. T.D.); *Blouin v. R.* (1991), 51 F.T.R. 194 (Fed. T.D.); *Rollinson v. R.*, [1991] 3 F.C. 70 (Fed. T.D.). However, there was some discussion of basic principles in *McGillivray v. New Brunswick* (1993), 26 C.R. (4th) 371 (N.B. Q.B.), affirmed (1994), 149 N.B.R. (2d) 311 (N.B. C.A.), leave to appeal refused (1995), 188 N.R. 319 (note) (S.C.C.), a case of a negligent investigation which also allegedly breached plaintiff's s. 7 rights.

175   For a discussion of suggested principles, see Cooper-Stephenson, *Charter Damage Claims, supra* note 169. The Supreme Court has clarified one question concerning liability for the implementation of legislation declared by the courts to be unconstitutional. In *Guimond c. Québec (Procureur général)*, [1996] 3 S.C.R. 347 (S.C.C.), the court held that a claim for damages under s. 24(1) could not be joined with a claim for a declaration of invalidity under s. 52. An official who acted honestly and in good faith in the enforcement of legislation later held to be unconstitutional was entitled to a qualified immunity or a claim of right defence based upon his compliance with obstensibly valid legislation.

176   (1998), 39 O.R. (3d) 487 (Ont. Gen. Div.).

only constituted the breach of a common law duty of care owed to the plaintiff,[177] but also violated her rights under sections 7 and 15 of the *Charter*. The deliberate failure of the police to warn the plaintiff about the real risk of an assault by a serial rapist and their failure to take adequate steps to protect her and other women at risk amounted to a deprivation of her right to security of the person under section 7 of the *Charter*. Moreover, the court concluded that the conduct of the police was contrary to the principles of fundamental justice as they "exercised their discretion in the investigation of this case in a discriminatory and negligent way."[178] The plaintiff's right to "equal benefit and protection of the law", under section 15 of the *Charter*, was also violated by the poor quality of the police investigation and, in particular, by the failure to warn her of the risk of assault. In this respect, the court was of the opinion that the conduct of the investigation "was motivated and informed by the adherence to rape myths as well as sexist stereotypical reasoning about rape, about women and about women who are raped."[179] Thus, the police investigation discriminated against the plaintiff, and other women, on the basis of their gender.

The constitution may also limit or strike down statutory and common law immunities such as those available to judges and other public officers. In *Nelles v. Ontario*,[180] Lamer J. suggested in an *obiter* comment that immunities may be susceptible to constitutional challenge on the ground they limit the broad remedial powers given to the courts by section 24 of the *Charter*. However, this issue has not been directly addressed by the courts in any detail, and therefore any comment on the constitutionality of common law and statutory immunities must be considered to be purely speculative.[181]

(e) Immunities

Statutory and common law immunities are a common feature limiting public tort liability. In the context of a negligence action, these immunities share a similar function with the policy/operational dichotomy discussed in the preceding section. However, it should be recognized that often these im-

---

177 This decision should be contrasted with the decision of the House of Lords in *Hill v. Chief Constable of West Yorkshire*, [1988] 2 All E.R. 238 (U.K. H.L.), a case which also involved a negligence action against the police for their failure to use reasonable care and skill in the apprehension of a serial murderer and rapist. The court dismissed the action on the grounds that the police did not owe the victim a duty of care in the investigation of the crimes. Mere foreseeability of likely harm was not sufficient to establish the requisite relationship of proximity between the victim and the police–more was required such as the victim was one of a small group of persons at a particular risk of harm. However, even if a legal duty of care did exist, it was negated by a number of policy concerns which supported an immunity for the police from negligence liability arising out of the investigation of crime.

178 *Jane Doe v. Metropolitan Toronto, supra* note 176 at 522.

179 *Ibid.* at 521.

180 (1989), 98 N.R. 321 (S.C.C.).

181 See *Prete v. Ontario* (1993), 110 D.L.R. (4th) 94 (Ont. C.A.), leave to appeal refused [1994] S.C.R. x (S.C.C.). The Court held that statutory immunities in Crown proceedings legislation and *Public Authorities Protection Act (Ontario)*, do not apply to relief under s. 24 of the *Charter*. See also *Falloncrest Financial Corp. v. Ontario* (1995), 33 Admin. L.R. (2d) 87 (Ont. Gen. Div.), reversed (1995), 27 O.R. (3d) 1 (Ont. C.A.).

munities are predicated on a characterization of the public authority's function, and represent a cruder approach to the issue of negligence (and other tortious) liability. Unless reconciled with the general two stage approach to public authority liability in negligence, the authorities underlying these immunities can complicate an already complex area of the law.

(i) Crown Immunity

At common law, the Crown was immune from suit in tort.[182] The exact origins of this immunity are unclear but it appears that they lie in the feudal principle that the King, as an overlord, could not be sued in his own court without his consent.[183] In the 19th century, the principle was reaffirmed and strengthened. The English Courts, relying on the medieval maxim "the King can do no wrong", refused to extend the petition of right procedure to suits in tort against the Crown although the procedure had facilitated suits against the Crown in contract.[184] As there was no means of bringing a suit against the Crown in tort, its immunity from liability was considered complete. Moreover, the courts reasoned that, because the King could do no wrong, he could not authorize the commission of a tort by his servants. Accordingly, the Crown was held to be immune from vicarious liability, as an employer, for the torts of its servants. The personal prerogatives of the monarch became the privileges and immunities of the state.[185]

The recognition of the Crown's total immunity from liability in tort did not leave the citizen, injured through governmental action, without a remedy. A citizen could turn to the doctrine of "official liability" to bring an action in tort against a Crown servant or official personally. "Official liability" refers to the personal liability of a Crown servant for torts committed in the discharge of official responsibilities. Liability would be determined on the basis of the ordinary principles of private tort law. In addition, a citizen could bring a suit in tort against a separate government board or agency, where appropriate. As government broadened the range of its activities in the 19th century through instrumentalities such as boards, incorporated government departments and independent agencies, the courts resisted the extension of the Crown's im-

---

182 For consideration of this historic immunity, see *Air India, Re* (1987), 44 D.L.R. (4th) 317 (Ont. H.C.).

183 E.M. Borchard, "Governmental Responsibility in Tort" (1926-27) 36 Yale L.J. 1 at 19.

184 *Tobin v. R.* (1864), 16 C.B.N.S. 310, 143 E.R. 1148 (Eng. C.P.); *Feather v. R.* (1865), 6 B. & S. 257, 122 E.R. 1191 (Eng. Q.B.). For a discussion about the modern law of Crown contracts, see R. Dussault and L. Borgeat, *Administrative Law: A Treatise*, (Toronto: Carswell, 1985), Vol. 1, Pt. 2, c. 3.

185 This development is not surprising, as in its evolution, executive government has been imbued with the personality of the monarch. Historically, the law has not recognized the clear distinction between the personal prerogatives of the monarch and those of the state. The legal personality of the state has as a result been confused with the legal personality of the monarch.

munity to these bodies.[186] Actions in tort could therefore be brought against them. However, this attempt to limit the scope of the Crown's immunity lead to the creation of a confusing body of case law concerning the precise scope of the status of Crown agency and the immunities and privileges that could be claimed by a Crown agent.[187]

In the face of the Crown's immunity from suit, the personal liability of Crown servants served both a symbolic and practical purpose. Symbolically, it represented the concept of equality under the law – the equal subjection of Crown servants and private citizens to the law of the land in the same manner and to the same extent.[188] Crown servants would not be able to claim preferential or differential treatment under any special regime of law. Moreover, the concept of official liability fit well with prevailing notions of morality and responsibility – a governmental official would be held personally accountable for a wrongful exercise of governmental power;[189] and others would be deterred from similar misconduct by the possibility of liability. From a practical perspective, official liability met a real need. Citizens, injured as a consequence of governmental action, had a means of gaining compensation for their loss or damage.

However, the scheme of official liability was not without its difficulties. To begin with, the burden of responsibility for injurious governmental activity was borne by Crown servants in their personal capacities. In some circumstances, the imposition of liability on an individual Crown employee could only be adjudged harsh or unjust.[190] The threat of personal liability encouraged timid and ineffectual government administration in some instances. Further, from a plaintiff's point of view, official liability often provided only a theoretical remedy. Crown servants usually lacked the funds with which to satisfy any judgments obtained against them, leaving the injured citizen with a hollow victory. In other instances, statutory or common law immunities designed to protect the official from liability left the citizen to bear his or her own loss. And, sometimes, the plaintiff was unable to identify the specific Crown servant who caused the loss leaving him or her with no one to sue.

To provide a more efficacious remedy, the Crown began the practice of standing behind its servants in suits arising out of their employment. In other instances, it nominated a defendant to be sued. In both cases, the Crown would conduct the defence in the servant's name and would satisfy any judgment

---

186 A major step in this regard was taken by the House of Lords in *Mersey Docks & Harbour Board v. Gibbs* (1866), 11 H.L.C. 686 (U.K. H.L.). On the basis of this decision, the courts deprived a large number of public corporations of this shield of Crown immunity. As these public corporations were providing commercial services to the public, the courts reasoned that functions of this nature were not "governmental" and therefore not entitled to share in the protection of the Crown's immunities.

187 For example, see Hogg and Monahan, *supra* note 5 at 331-49.

188 Dicey, *supra* note 13.

189 C. Harlow, *supra* note 137 at 19-20.

190 For example, the imposition of liability on a Crown servant for the good faith enforcement of an ostensibly valid statute which was subsequently determined to be unconstitutional. However, the Supreme Court of Canada has recognized a "claim of right" defence in this respect; *Guimond* v. *Quebec*, *supra* note 175.

obtained against him or her on an *ex gratia* basis. Governments at both the federal and provincial level accepted greater responsibility for their own injurious activities and those of their employees.[191] "Petition of Right" statutes permitted actions in tort against the Crown,[192] provided the consent of the Crown was first obtained by fiat. On the other hand, to protect Crown servants from unwarranted personal liability and to foster the forthright administration of government, greater use was also made of statutory immunity provisions.

Despite its obvious shortcomings, this scheme of government liability, with its twin features of Crown immunity and official liability, remained in place for much of this century. However, it came under increasing attack as an anachronistic and inadequate response to the issue of government liability. As a result, statutory reform occurred in most Commonwealth jurisdictions. In the United Kingdom, the Crown's historic immunity from liability in tort was replaced in 1948 by the enactment of the *Crown Proceedings Act*.[193] In 1950, the Canadian Commissioners on Uniformity of Legislation proposed a model Act for a similar purpose.[194] Over the next two decades, all of the Canadian provinces (except Quebec) enacted legislation substantially adopting the model Act.[195] The federal Parliament enacted the *Crown Liability Act* in 1953.[196] As a result, proceedings in tort can now be brought against the federal government and all provincial governments in Canada.

A detailed examination of the legislation governing proceedings against the Crown is beyond the scope of this section.[197] Suffice it to say that the major purpose underlying Crown proceedings legislation was to end the Crown's common law immunity from liability in tort by making it subject to the same

---

191   Since 1938, the federal government had accepted vicarious responsibility for the negligent conduct of its employees.

192   See for example, the *Alberta Petition of Right Act*, R.S.A. 1955, c. 231.

193   10 & 11 Geo. V, c. 44 (1948). This parallelled a similar development in the United States in the *Federal Tort Claims Act, 1946*, 60 Stat. 842.

194   *An Act Respecting Proceedings Against the Crown*, in the Conference of Commissioners on Uniformity of Legislation in Canada, "Proceedings of 1950" at 76.

195   See *Crown Proceeding Act*, R.S.B.C. 1996, c. 89; *Proceedings Against the Crown Act*, R.S.A. 2000, c. P-25; *Proceedings Against the Crown Act*, R.S.S. 1978, c. P-27; *Proceedings Against the Crown Act*, R.S.M. 1987, c. P-140; *Proceedings Against the Crown Act*, R.S.O. 1990, c. P.27; *Proceedings Against the Crown Act*, R.S.N.B. 1973, c. P-18; *Proceedings Against the Crown Act*, R.S.N.S. 1989, c. 360; *Crown Proceedings Act*, R.S.P.E.I. 1988, c. C-32; *Proceedings Against the Crown Act*, R.S.N. 1990, c. P-26. In Quebec, see *Special Procedure Act*, R.S.Q. 1977, c. P-27, s. 1, and the *Code of Civil Procedure*, R.S.Q. 1977, c. C-25, s. 94.

196   Now *Crown Liability and Proceedings Act*, R.S.C. 1985, c. C-50.

197   See Hogg and Monahan, *supra* note 5; Lorden, *Crown Law* (Toronto: Butterworths, 1991); Goldenberg, "Tort Actions Against the Crown in Ontario" (1973) *L.S.U.C. Special Lectures*: *New Developments in the Law of Torts* at 341; Jack, "Suing the Crown and the Application of the Charter" (1986) 7 Advocates' Quarterly 277; Sgayias *et al.*, *supra* note 69; Lester, "Suing the Federal Crown in Tort; Some Practical Points" (2000) 23 The Advocates Quarterly 444.

general principles of tort liability as if it were a private person of full age and capacity.[198] Thus, section 5(1) of the Alberta Act reads as follows:

> 5(1) Except as otherwise provided in this Act and notwithstanding section 14 of the *Interpretation Act*, the Crown is subject to all those liabilities in tort to which, if it were a person of full age and capacity, it would be subject,
>
>> (a) in respect of a tort committed by any of its officers or agents,
>>
>> (b) in respect of any breach of those duties that a person owes to that person's servants or agents by reason of being their employer,
>>
>> (c) in respect of any breach of the duties attaching to the ownership, occupation, possession or control of property, and
>>
>> (d) under any statute or under any regulation or by-law made or passed under the authority of any statute.

Accordingly, the Crown can now be held liable in damages for the tortious acts or omissions of its servants and agents, and for the breach of its duties as an employer, or as the owner, occupier or possessor of property.[199] Suits can either be brought against the Crown directly,[200] or vicariously for the tortious acts of its servants and agents.[201]

The vicarious liability of the Crown will depend on whether the conduct complained of is tortious[202] and whether the tortfeasor is a servant or agent of the Crown.[203]

---

198 Hogg and Monahan, *ibid.* at 113 note that an identical provision was enacted by the federal Parliament and in all provinces, with the exception of British Columbia and Quebec. The Crown retained some immunities from liability in tort; for example, in relation to the performance of judicial functions. See *Nelles v. Ontario*, [1989] 2 S.C.R. 170 (S.C.C.); *Wiche v. Ontario* (2001), 38 Admin. L.R. (3d) 194 (Ont. S.C.J.), affirmed (2003), [2003] O.J. No. 221, 2003 CarswellOnt 291 (Ont. C.A.); *Pispidikis v. Ontario (Justice of the Peace)* (2002), 62 O.R. (3d) 596 (Ont. S.C.J.), additional reasons at (2003), 2003 CarswellOnt 1357 (Ont. S.C.J.), affirmed (2003), 180 O.A.C. 45 (Ont. C.A.).

199 As Hogg and Monahan, *supra* note 5, observe at 11-15, the term "the Crown" is difficult to define in practice. Generally speaking, the term is used to describe the executive branch of government which consist of a myriad of ministries, departments, boards, agencies, commissions, tribunals and corporations. Many of these public authorities are more properly described as "Crown agencies". This status will depend on whether the public body is controlled by a Minister of the Crown or is declared by statute to be a Crown agent. See discussion at 331-40.

200 A novel, direct action against the Crown arose out of the exercise of its prerogative to participate in the NATO bombing campaign of Yugoslavia. The court decided that the policy decision to participate was not justiciable, nor was it subject to a private law duty of care as it concerned a macro policy decision. See *Aleksic v. Canada (Attorney General)* (2002), 215 D.L.R. (4th) 720 (Ont. Div. Ct.).

201 See for example, *Proceedings Against the Crown Act*, R.S.A. 2000, c. P-25, s. 5(1).

202 This determination will be made on the basis of the ordinary principles of tort law. For example, the tort liability of the federal Crown in negligence will be subject to the policy/ operational distinction. See *Brewer Brothers v. Canada (Attorney General)* (1991), 80

The first issue will be determined according to the substantive law of torts subject, of course, to any statutory or common law immunities.[204] In this regard, it must be borne in mind that the personal liability of the Crown servant did

---

D.L.R. (4th) 321 (Fed. C.A.) and *Swanson Estate v. R.* (1991), 80 D.L.R. (4th) 741 (Fed. C.A.).

203   Although an employer is generally not held to be liable for the torts of independent contractors engaged by him, the courts have imposed liability on the Crown for the tortious conduct of its independent contractors arising out of the performance of non-delegable duties imposed on the Crown. For example, in *Lewis (Guardian ad litem of) v. British Columbia* (1997), [1998] 5 W.W.R. 732 (S.C.C.), the Crown was held vicariously liable for the negligence of an independent contractor employed to perform the Crown's duty to maintain provincial highways.

   The vicarious liability of the Crown has arisen in a number of cases involving child abuse committed by independent contractors or employees of the Crown. On the basis of the principles enunciated by the Supreme Court of Canada in *B. (P.A.) v. Curry*, [1999] 2 S.C.R. 534 (S.C.C.) and *T. (G.) v. Griffiths*, [1999] 2 S.C.R. 570 (S.C.C.), the courts have held the Crown liable for sexual and physical abuse committed by teachers, government employees and independent contractors. For example, *B. (D.) v. Canada (Attorney General)*, [2001] 5 W.W.R. 128 (Sask. Q.B.); *L. (H.) v. Canada (Attorney General)*, [2001] 7 W.W.R. 722 (Sask. Q.B.), additional reasons at [2001] 11 W.W.R. 727 (Sask. Q.B.), additional reasons at [2001] 11 W.W.R. 737 (Sask. Q.B.), reversed (2002), [2003] 5 W.W.R. 421 (Sask. C.A.), leave to appeal granted (2003), [2003] S.J. No. 555, 2003 CarswellSask 574 (Sask. C.A.); *A. (C.) v. C. (J.W.)* (1998), 13 Admin. L.R. (3d) 157 (B.C. C.A.); *White v. Canada (Attorney General)* (2002), 4 B.C.L.R. (4th) 161 (B.C. S.C. [In Chambers]), leave to appeal allowed 2002 BCCA 709 (B.C. C.A. [In Chambers]) where the Federal Crown was held vicariously liable for systemic negligence of its officers and employees in failing to take steps to protect sea cadets from sexual misconduct by other employees, affirmed (2003), [2003] B.C.J. No. 442, 2003 CarswellBC 489 (B.C. C.A.).

204   For example, it is generally accepted that the Attorney General and Crown Prosecutors or attorneys, in the performance of their duties are immune from liability in negligence. While some courts talk in terms of an immunity, *Munro v. Canada* (1993), 16 O.R. (3d) 564 (Ont. Div. Ct.); *Al's Steak House & Tavern v. Deloitte & Touche* (1994), 20 O.R. (3d) 673 (Ont. Gen. Div.), affirmed (1997), 102 O.A.C. 144 (Ont. C.A.), *Falloncrest, supra* note 181; others talk in terms of an absence of a duty of care owed by a prosecutor to an accused; *German v. Major* (1985), 20 D.L.R. (4th) 703 (Alta. C.A.). This immunity has been extended by one court to government investigators, in respect of their investigations and recommendations regarding prosecution: *Al's Steak House.* However, other courts have refused to extend the immunity to police officers in respect of the investigation of crime unless there is some association with the activities of the Crown: *Beckstead v. Ottawa (City)* (1997), 155 D.L.R. (4th) 382 (Ont. C.A.).

   Statutory immunity provisions abound in Canadian legislation at both the provincial and federal level. Generally speaking, the courts have limited the effectiveness of these provisions in their application. They have been interpreted to embrace only the good faith acts or omissions of public officers and employees. Thus, absent clear and strong language to the contrary, these provisions will not protect an officer who acts in bad faith, dishonestly, fraudulently or deliberately in excess of his or her jurisdiction. For a recent example of this, see *Boucher v. Milner* (1997), 155 D.L.R. (4th) 106 (N.B. C.A.); *Dorman Timber Ltd. v. British Columbia* (1997), 152 D.L.R. (4th) 271 (B.C. C.A.).

   It should also be noted that the courts are reluctant to narrow the scope of the Crown's vicarious liability in tort by allowing it to take advantage of a statutory immunity provision designed to protect its servants from personal liability. In this regard, see *Hill v. British Columbia* (1997), 148 D.L.R. (4th) 337 (B.C. C.A.), where the court held that the Crown was not entitled to take advantage of a statutory immunity provision which exempted its servant from liability in negligence.

not end with the recognition of the Crown's vicarious liability in tort. Suits can still be brought against servants personally, but care must be taken to sue government officials in their personal rather than their representative capacities.[205]

The second issue–concerning the definition of who is a Crown agent or servant–is often one of great complexity. The term "Crown servant" is usually used to describe natural persons in the employ of the Crown whereas the term, "Crown agent", is used in reference to a variety of public bodies established outside the departments of government but which are subject to extensive control by a Minister of the Crown or are designated by statutes as agents of the Crown.[206] A Crown agent may be able to share in the Crown's privileges and immunities.[207] Servants of Crown agents are generally considered to be servants of the Crown. Therefore, the Crown will be held vicariously liable for torts committed by the servants of the Crown agent in the course of employment.[208] A Crown agent can be held directly liable in tort[209] provided it possesses the capacity to be sued.[210] An incorporated Crown agent possesses the capacity to sue or be sued as an attribute of its legal personality. Can the Crown be held vicariously liable for the tortious actions of its agents? In theory, yes, because the position of a Crown agent is the same as that of a Crown servant.[211] However, this possibility has been precluded by a provision found in the Crown proceedings statutes of all of the provinces which immunizes the Crown from vicarious liability for torts committed by its corporate Crown agents.[212] Finally, it must be noted that the status as Crown or Crown agent does not extend to all public authorities performing governmental functions. For example, mu-

---

205 *Air India*, *supra* note 182. By way of example, Klar, *supra* note 27 at 223-24 refers to the decision of *M. (M.) v. K. (K.)* (1987), 39 C.C.L.T. 81 (B.C. S.C.), reversed (1989), 50 C.C.L.T. 190 (B.C. C.A.), where the court dismissed actions brought against "The Superintendent of Family and Child Service" and "The Ministry of Human Resources" in their representative capacities as opposed to their personal capacities. See also *Cairns v. Farm Credit Corp.* (1991), 7 Admin. L.R. (2d) 203 (Fed. T.D.); *Tottrup v. Alberta (Minister of Environment)* (2000), 21 Admin. L.R. (3d) 58 (Alta. C.A.).

206 On the subject of Crown agency, see *Lucas v. Manitoba (Taxi Cab Board)*, [1985] 2 W.W.R. 681 (Man. C.A.); *Westeel-Rosco Ltd. v. South Saskatchewan Hospital Centre* (1976), [1977] 2 S.C.R. 238 (S.C.C.); *Perehinec v. Northern Pipeline Agency*, [1983] 2 S.C.R. 513 (S.C.C.).

207 Such as the Crown's immunity from statute. See also *Athabasca Chipewyan First Nation v. Canada (Minister of Indian Affairs & Northern Development)* (2001), 30 Admin. L.R. (3d) 87 (Alta. C.A.), where B.C. Hydro, a crown agency, was not allowed to share in B.C. Crown's immunity from suit.

208 *Brière v. Canada Mortgage & Housing Corp.*, [1986] 2 F.C. 484 (Fed. C.A.).

209 *Canada (National Harbours Board) v. Langelier* (1968), [1969] S.C.R. 60 (S.C.C.).

210 On the question of the suable status of public authorities, see *Westlake v. R.*, [1971] 3 O.R. 533, 21 D.L.R. (3d) 129 (Ont. H.C.), affirmed [1972] 2 O.R. 605, 26 D.L.R. (3d) 273 (Ont. C.A.), affirmed [1973] S.C.R. vii (S.C.C.); *MacLean v. Ontario (Liquor Licence Board)* (1975), 9 O.R. (2d) 597 (Ont. Div. Ct.); *Perchinec v. Northern Pipeline Agency*, *supra* note 206; and *B. v. Canada (Department of Manpower & Immigration)* (1975), 60 D.L.R. (3d) 339 (Fed. T.D.). See also Sgayias *et al.*, *supra* note 69 at 159-61.

211 *Gracey v. Canadian Broadcasting Corp.* (1990), [1991] 1 F.C. 739 (Fed. T.D.); *Rasmussen v. Canada (Minister of Fisheries & Oceans)*, [1986] 2 F.C. 500 (Fed. C.A.).

212 For example see s. 3(c) of the Alberta *Proceedings Against the Crown Act* R.S.A. 2000, c. P-25; and Hogg and Monahan, *supra* note 5 at 344.

nicipal corporations are not agents of the Crown. They can be sued either directly or vicariously for the torts of their officials or employees.[213]

In closing, suits against the Crown in Canada, at either the provincial or federal level, raise a number of difficult issues. Apart from questions concerning the suability of the Crown or its agents, the claimant must deal with: the complexities of the substantive law of tort; the obstacles presented by statutory and common law immunities; and the procedural advantages enjoyed by the Crown in litigation, such as special notice and limitation periods.

(ii) Members of Parliament and Provincial Legislatures

All members of the Federal Parliament and the provincial legislatures enjoy many legal privileges and immunities. These immunities emerged from the constitutional struggles between Parliament and the King in England in the 17th century. No member can be held liable in the courts for his tortious actions committed in the House or while on parliamentary business.[214] Disciplinary proceedings can only be taken against the member by Parliament and Parliament retains the power to impose appropriate sanctions against its members for such behaviour.

(iii) Judicial Officers

For centuries, judges have been accorded an immunity from liability in tort. In some instances, this common law immunity has been buttressed by a statutory immunity.[215] This long-standing principle of the common law is predicated on the need to preserve the independence of the judiciary and to protect judges from fear of liability and harassment from those who consider themselves to have been harshly and wrongly judged. However, this immunity does not extend to the tortious conduct of judges acting in their private capacity.[216]

The general principle of immunity is well established on the basis of older English authorities, although the exact perimeters of the immunity are somewhat uncertain. The early authorities revealed that superior and inferior courts were treated differently in terms of the immunity. Superior courts judges enjoyed an extensive if not absolute immunity from suit – so long as these judges acted within their jurisdiction, they could act negligently, maliciously,

---

213   See generally Boghosian and Davison, *The Law of Municipal Liability in Canada* (Toronto: Butterworths, 1999).

214   *R. c. Atlantic Sugar Refineries Co.* (1976), 72 D.L.R. (3d) 95 (Que. C.A.); *Roman Corp. v. Hudson's Bay Oil & Gas Co.*, [1973] S.C.R. 820 (S.C.C.).

215   For example, *Provincial Court Act*, R.S.M. 1987, c. C-275. In Alberta, the *Provincial Court Act,* R.S.A. 2000, c. P-31, s. 9.51 and the *Justice of the Peace Act*, R.S.A. 2000, c. J-4, s. 13 provide provincial court judges and justices of the peace with an immunity equivalent to that of superior court judges– no action can be maintained unless it is proved that the act or omission complained of was done "maliciously" and, "without reasonable and probable cause". Equivalent legislation is to be found in other provinces. See Hogg and Monahan, *supra* note 5 at 199 n.72.

216   D. Gibson, "Developments in Tort Law, 1985-86 Term" (1987) 9 Sup. Ct. L. Rev. 455 at 460.

or corruptly without fear of civil liability.[217] "Jurisdiction" was defined broadly for the purpose of this immunity. However, in theory, a superior court judge could be held liable for tortious actions outside of jurisdiction. There are, however, no reported cases of this occurring, leading Lord Denning to suggest that a superior judge can never be held liable as he or she possesses the jurisdiction to determine his or her jurisdiction or that his or her jurisdiction is so extensive that he or she can never step outside of it.[218] Perhaps, the real answer lies in the fact that jurisdiction was defined liberally by superior court judges in cases involving superior court judges.

Inferior court judges were accorded a lesser measure of immunity. Like superior court judges, inferior court judges were immune from civil liability when acting within their jurisdiction. This immunity, however, was subject to a major exception–inferior court judges would be held liable for malicious acts within jurisdiction.[219] Moreover, the term "jurisdiction" was used in a more technical sense in the case of inferior court judges, thereby restricting the scope of immunity. There is no doubt that superior court judges treated inferior court judges more harshly than themselves. Perhaps this attitude stemmed from the fact that superior court judges had long exercised a judicial review authority over inferior courts on the basis that they were bodies with limited jurisdictions. In any event, inferior court judges were historically held liable for tortious acts outside their jurisdiction[220] and for malicious acts within jurisdiction.

More recently, courts in United Kingdom and Canada have had the opportunity to consider the nature and scope of the common law immunity for judges. In *Sirros v. Moore*,[221] Lord Denning M.R. undertook an extensive review of the older authorities. Judicial immunity was not based on an expansive view of jurisdiction, but on the fact the judge was acting in his judicial capacity. In his opinion, the key to the immunity was whether the judge entertained an honest belief that he or she had jurisdiction:[222]

> So long as he does his work in the honest belief that it is within his jurisdiction, then he is not liable to an action. He may be mistaken in

---

217 The *Marshalsea* (1613), 10 Co. Rep. 68b; *Fray v. Blackburn* (1863), 3 B. & S. 576; see also the judgment of Lord Denning M.R. in *Sirros v. Moore* (1974), [1975] Q.B. 118 (Eng. C.A.).

218 *Sirros v. Moore*, *ibid.* at 135. In support of this absolute immunity, it is usually argued that superior courts, as courts as general jurisdiction, can never act outside of their jurisdiction. In response, Hogg and Monahan, *supra* note 5 at 195, argue that :

> This explanation is far fetched. There are limits to the jurisdiction of even a Superior Court. If a judge of a Superior Court, believing a jury's verdict to be perverse, were to order the imprisonment of a person who had just been acquitted, it would be plain that the judge had acted without jurisdiction. In such a case, the better view . . . is that the judge who acted knowingly without jurisdiction would be liable for the tort of false imprisonment.

In this respect, the authors suggest that reckless indifference to the question of invalidity would not suffice, actual knowledge of invalidity must be proven.

219 *Ibid.* at 134.

220 *Houlden v. Smith* (1850), 14 Q.B. 841.

221 *Supra* note 217.

222 *Ibid.* at 136.

fact. He may be ignorant in law. What he does may be outside his jurisdiction – in fact or in law – but so long as he honestly believes it to be within his jurisdiction, he should not be liable. Once he honestly entertains his belief, nothing else will make him liable.

Only when a judge knowingly acts outside his jurisdiction would liability ensue. Moreover, Lord Denning proposed that his version of the judicial immunity should apply equally to superior and inferior court judges. This would remedy the harsh and unfair treatment of inferior court judges in the past and would recognize the fact that both categories of judges essentially carry out the same function. Lord Denning's statement of the immunity would lessen the historic immunity of the superior court judges and expand the immunity of inferior court judges.[223] It is suggested that superior court judges could be held liable for the malicious exercise of their authority – after all, what could be more malicious than the judge acting in the knowledge that he or she lacks jurisdiction?[224] Also, it expands the immunity of inferior court judges by replacing the technical limitation of jurisdiction with the subjective, honest belief of a judge that he or she had jurisdiction.

Subsequently, the scope of judicial immunity was reviewed by the House of Lords in *McC v. Mullan*.[225] The judgment appears to contradict the key element in Lord Denning's definition of the common law judicial immunity. A magistrate was held liable to a suit for false imprisonment, as he had erred (albeit innocently) in construing his jurisdiction to impose a sentence of detention. Therefore, even though he had acted in good faith, in the honest belief that he had jurisdiction, he was subject to a suit for false imprisonment as he had lost the protective mantle of his jurisdiction. The key factor was that the magistrate had acted outside his jurisdiction.

In the course of his judgment, Lord Bridge made a number of *obiter* comments on the concept of jurisdiction (which he conceived to be central to the immunity) and on the differing treatment of superior and inferior court judges. In the latter respect, he agreed with Lord Denning in *Sirros v. Moore*[226] that inferior court judges should be treated the same as superior court judges in terms of liability for acts within jurisdiction. He then observed that "jurisdiction" was a very malleable concept. In his opinion, not all actions outside of or in excess of jurisdiction would defeat the immunity. Clearly, where the

---

223 Hogg and Monahan, *supra* note 5 at 197 suggest in light of later authority, that Lord Denning was wrong in expanding the scope of judicial immunity. For a New Zealand approach to this issue see *Harvey v. Derrick*, [1995] 1 N.Z.L.R. 314 (C.A.).

224 A contrary view appears to have been taken by the court in the recent case of *Prefontaine v. Gosman*, [2000] 6 W.W.R. 530 (Alta. Q.B.), affirmed [2002] 11 W.W.R. 45 (Alta. C.A.). There, the court, at 545, defined the immunity in broadest terms:

> . . . a judge acting in her or his judicial capacity will not be liable civilly for any actions done in such judicial capacity whether the judge was acting within or outside of her or his jurisdiction, and even if the judge was acting out of hatred, envy or malice, if the judge believed that he or she was acting with jurisdiction and in the course of his or her judicial duties.

225 (1984), [1985] A.C. 528 (U.K. H.L.).

226 *Supra* note 217.

judge had no jurisdiction over the cause at all, the immunity would fail. Also, the immunity would fail when the court committed a gross and obvious irregularity in procedure in the course of the proceeding. But an error of law committed in reaching a determination of guilt would not cause the immunity to fail. On this reasoning, one must conclude that the immunity available to judges is great but is not absolute.

These cases raise questions about the nature and scope of the common law judicial immunity in Canada: Are inferior court judges and superior court judges entitled to the same immunity? Does malice defeat the immunity? What types of excesses of jurisdiction are sufficient to cause the immunity to fail?[227]

The Supreme Court of Canada had an opportunity to consider these questions and the doctrine of judicial immunity in Canada in *Rivard c. Morier*,[228] which involved the scope of a statutory provision purporting to clothe the Quebec Police Commission with the same immunity as that possessed by superior court judges. Unfortunately, the court did not address these issues. It affirmed the absolute immunity of superior court judges. It dismissed the suit as it found that the commissioners' actions fell within the scope of the statutory immunity. The court gave the immunity provision a large and liberal construction; the language, "in the execution of their duty" was seen to be broad enough to include acts outside their jurisdiction. This may bode well for inferior court judges and members of administrative tribunals who seek the shelter of statutory immunity provisions.

More recently, the concept of judicial immunity was considered by the Federal Court of Appeal in *Taylor v. Canada (Attorney General)*.[229] This decision arose out of a complaint to the Canadian Human Rights Commission about a judge's order, in proceedings before him, that a party either remove his religious headgear or leave the courtroom. The Human Rights Commission decided that it could not hear the complaint as judges were immune at common law. After a review of the authorities, the Federal Court of Appeal dismissed the appeal on the grounds that the judge was protected by an immunity which applied to his judicial actions unless he knowingly acted outside his jurisdiction. That was not the case here as the judge was found to have the authority to make the order, even though it was held, in other proceedings, that he had erred in the exercise of his discretion in this respect. In the court's opinion, the broad based immunity afforded to judges was "rooted in the need to protect the public, not on a need to protect judges."[230] It secured for the benefit of the public, an independent and impartial judiciary – given the fundamental importance of an independent judiciary, a judicial immunity was seen to be a constitutional principle which was not inconsistent with the protections af-

---

227 D. Gibson, *supra* note 216 at 455.
228 [1985] 2 S.C.R. 716 (S.C.C.).
229 (2000), 184 D.L.R. (4th) 706 (Fed. C.A.), leave to appeal refused (2000), 263 N.R. 399 (note) (S.C.C.); see also *Taylor v. Canada (Attorney General)* (2003), 223 D.L.R. (4th) 475 (Fed. C.A.), leave to appeal refused (2003), 2003 CarswellNat 2874 (S.C.C.) for subsequent discussion on judicial review of chairperson of Canadian Judicial Council's decision concerning complaint against judge.
230 *Ibid.* at para 29.

forded to citizens by the *Charter*. Therefore, this immunity is constitutional even though it limited the court's power to give a remedy for breach of a constitutional or human rights violation.

(iv) Public Officials Acting Legislatively

A public body engaged in a legislative activity is immune from suit, even though acting negligently. The leading Canadian authority in this regard is the decision of the Supreme Court of Canada in *Welbridge Holdings Ltd. v. Greater Winnipeg (Municipality)*.[231] In that case, the Metropolitan Corporation of Greater Winnipeg had passed a bylaw rezoning certain property to permit a high-rise development. Acting in reliance on the bylaw, Welbridge, the developer, expended large sums of money on the development of the site and partial construction of the building. However, adjacent property owners challenged the validity of the bylaw on the grounds of a lack of notice and the denial of a proper hearing before the municipal council. This challenge was ultimately upheld by the Supreme Court of Canada and it declared the bylaw invalid. The previous zoning bylaw was revived and stop work orders were issued against Welbridge which, as a result, suffered considerable financial loss. It sued the municipality for negligence in the enactment of the bylaw, that is, for failure to follow the correct legal procedures, but was unsuccessful.

Welbridge argued that the council owed it a duty of care to ensure that the proper procedures were followed when enacting the by-law. Furthermore, the case for the existence of a duty of care was even stronger because there was a direct link between the by-law in question and those with an interest in the property. The alleged duty was not merely one owed to the citizens of the municipality in general. Nevertheless, the court held that there was no responsibility in negligence when the statutory body was exercising a legislative power.[232] Nor would the principle in *Hedley Byrne & Co. v. Heller & Partners Ltd.*[233] apply where the action was legislative in nature.[234] Although a municipality may be liable in tort at the operational level or in the exercise of business powers, its legislative activities do not attract tortious liability. As Laskin J. said:[235]

> In exercising such [legislative] authority, a municipality (no less than a provincial Legislature or the Parliament of Canada) may act beyond its powers in the ultimate view of a Court, albeit it acted on the advice of counsel. It would be incredible to say in such circumstances that it

---

231   (1970), [1971] S.C.R. 957 (S.C.C.).

232   *Kwong v. R.* (1978), [1979] 2 W.W.R. 1 (Alta. C.A.), affirmed [1979] 2 S.C.R. 1010 (S.C.C.). See also *Berryland Canning Co. v. R.*, [1974] 1 F.C. 91 (Fed. T.D.).

233   (1963), [1964] A.C. 465 (U.K. H.L.).

234   *Hedley Byrne* was applied in *Windsor Motors Ltd. v. Powell River (Municipality)* (1969), 4 D.L.R. (3d) 155 (B.C. C.A.), where the municipality was held vicariously liable for the administrative action of its licence inspector in giving negligent advice and issuing a licence for a used car business on land whose zoning forbade such a use. The plaintiff had relied on the advice and the inspector's special knowledge and had suffered loss as a result.

235   *Welbridge Holdings*, *supra* note 231 at 969.

owed a duty of care giving rise to liability in damages for its breach. "Invalidity is not the test of fault and it should not be the test of liability": see Davis, *3 Administrative Law Treatise* (1958), at p. 487.

The policy behind the Supreme Court of Canada's decision in *Welbridge* appears to be that the risk of loss from the exercise of legislative powers is a general public one and that no private duty of care can arise in these circumstances.[236] It should be noted that the immunity applies solely to the legislative action itself, not to negligence in actions taken to implement the legislation which may constitute a breach of a duty of care.[237]

(v) Public Officials Acting Quasi-Judicially

In *Welbridge Holdings*, the Supreme Court of Canada drew a distinction between the legislative, judicial and quasi-judicial functions of a public authority and its administrative or business powers. The former would be immune from liability and negligence, while the latter would not. This distinction resurrected an older line of authorities where the focus was on the characterization of the nature of the function performed by the public authority or public officer, rather than on the existence of a private law duty of care.[238] In some instances, the cases represent an attempt by the plaintiff to hold the defendant authority liable in damages for the *ultra vires* exercise of discretionary authority.[239] In other words, the plaintiff sought to hold the defendant liable for a substantive or procedural error in the exercise of a statutory discretion which occasioned loss or damage to the plaintiff. By analogy to the immunity enjoyed by judges, the courts often responded to these claims by holding the defendant immune on the basis of quasi-judicial immunity.[240] The courts reasoned that it would be unduly harsh to hold a statutory decision-maker liable for an honest, good-faith error in the exercise of its powers. In some cases, the courts could have disposed with the claim on the basis that, absent malice, the defendant's actions, while *ultra vires*, were not tortious.[241]

In more recent times, the courts have recognized the immunity in a number of cases.[242] Although in *Welbridge Holdings*, the rezoning function of council seems to have been characterized as a legislative function with a quasi-judicial

---

236 *Kimpton v. Canada (Attorney General)* (2002), 9 B.C.L.R. (4th) 139 (B.C. S.C.), affirmed 2004 BCCA 72 (B.C. C.A.), where an action against the province for negligent drafting of a provincial Building Code was dismissed. See also *A.O. Farms Inc. v. Canada* (2000), 28 Admin. L.R. (3d) 315 (Fed. T.D.).

237 *Welbridge Holdings, supra* note 231 at 970.

238 A. Rubinstein, "Tort Liability of Judicial Officers" (1963-64), 15 U. of T. L.J. 317.

239 See for example, *Harris v. Law Society (Alberta)*, [1936] S.C.R. 88 (S.C.C.).

240 *Everett c. Griffiths*, [1920] 3 K.B. 163 (Eng. K.B.), affirmed [1921] 1 A.C. 631 (U.K. H.L.); *Partridge v. General Council of Medical Education* (1890), 25 Q.B.D. 90 (Eng. Q.B.).

241 *Harris v. Law Society (Alberta), supra* note 239.

242 See for example, *French v. Law Society of Upper Canada* (1975), 9 O.R. (2d) 473 (Ont. C.A.); *Birchard v. Law Society (Alberta)* (1985), 65 A.R. 222 (Alta. C.A.); *Akhtar v. MacGillivray & Co.* (1990), [1991] 2 W.W.R. 489 (Alta. Q.B.); *Stenner v. British Columbia (Securities Commission)* (1996), 141 D.L.R. (4th) 122 (B.C. C.A.), leave to appeal refused (1997), 219 N.R. 160 (note) (S.C.C.).

element or flavour, Laskin J. specifically extended the common law immunity from liability for negligence to include a quasi-judicial function by itself.[243]

The immunity was also recognized in the case of *Bowen v. Edmonton (City)*,[244] where the city authorized a re-plot of land to create smaller building lots in an existing subdivision. The Provincial Planning Advisory Board advised the city that soil stability tests were necessary before a new subdivision could be approved but no tests were made. The plaintiffs purchased one of the lots, after which soil stability tests were done which showed that the land was unstable and unsuitable for building. The city forbid the plaintiffs to build their residence. They could neither build nor sell. However, their action for damages against the city for negligently authorizing the re-plot failed.

Although the court found that the city had been negligent in failing to conduct soil stability tests before authorizing the re-plot, it also found that there was no duty of care owed by the city to the plaintiff in the exercise of its statutory powers, because the city was acting quasi-judicially. The court found a strong analogy between a zoning function in *Welbridge* (considered by the Supreme Court to be a legislative in nature with a quasi-judicial element) and the subdivision function (which the Alberta Court of Appeal also considered to be quasi-judicial in nature).

The correctness of the decision in *Bowen* is now questionable in light of recent developments in the law of governing the liability of a public authority for negligence, such as *Kamloops* and *Just*. The city's failure to conduct soil stability tests when it knew they were required does not appear to arise out of the exercise of a policy discretion. With the knowledge that the land was possibly unstable, the city ought to have had potential purchasers such as the plaintiffs reasonably in mind before authorizing the re-plot. Moreover, if there was an element of discretion involved, the city should have been liable because it exercised its discretion so carelessly or unreasonably as to amount to no real exercise of its discretion at all.[245]

Further doubt is cast on *Bowen* by a decision of the Nova Scotia Court of Appeal in *Nova Scotia (Attorney General) v. Aza Avramovitch Associates Ltd.*[246] In that case, officers of the Provincial Health Department approved the location and design of a sewage system and authorized the installation of a septic tank. The regulations empowered the department to require test holes to be dug to determine soil stability before approving any installation. If the test hole revealed that the soil was unstable, the regulations required the permit to be denied. The officers decided not to require test holes, as they believed (on the basis of previous tests and other information) that the soil was stable. Unfortunately, this decision was in error and test holes would have revealed that the soil was unstable. In the subsequent negligence action, the question was whether the decision not to require the test holes was policy or operational

---

243 *Welbridge Holdings Ltd. v. Greater Winnipeg (Municipality)*, *supra* note 231 at 969.
244 [1977] 6 W.W.R. 344 (Alta. T.D.).
245 This line of reasoning finds support in the judgment of Lord Reid in *Dorset Yacht Co. v. Home Office*, [1970] A.C. 1004 (U.K. H.L.), and the judgment of Lord Wilberforce in *Anns v. Merton London Borough Council* (1977), [1978] A.C. 728 (U.K. H.L.).
246 (1984), 11 D.L.R. (4th) 588 (N.S. C.A.).

in nature. While the court acknowledged that the officers possessed wide discretion and that their decision to approve the construction called for the exercise of independent judgment, it nevertheless imposed liability on the officers for their lack of reasonable care in not requiring the soil to be tested.[247] Cannot the same conclusion be reached about the actions of the city in *Bowen*?

In sum, recent developments in the law of the liability of public authorities for negligence raise significant doubts as to the continuing viability of the quasi-judicial immunity. The immunity represents a dated approach, resting as it does on a now largely discredited distinction between judicial, quasi-judicial and administrative functions.[248] It would appear far better to utilize the policy/operational distinction. This approach is in fact illustrated by two recent Federal Court of Appeal decisions[249] in which the court addressed the issue of liability on the basis of the policy/operational dichotomy, rather than on the basis of any quasi judicial immunity.[250]

(vi) Conclusion on Immunities

To conclude this section on immunities, it appears that recent developments in the law governing the liability of public authorities in negligence have left unaffected only those common law immunities relating to the exercise of purely judicial or legislative functions. The so-called quasi-judicial immunity seems to have been largely subsumed in the policy/operational distinction.[251] Most quasi-judicial functions should fall within the scope of the policy immunity as they involve the making of discretionary decisions which are not appropriate subjects for review in a subsequent negligence action. Of course, that does not mean that the immunity afforded to these types of policy decisions is unlimited. The English Courts in *Dorset Yacht*[252] and *Anns*[253] have suggested that a duty of care may arise even in the policy area where the decision is negligently made by a public authority acting outside the limits of its discretion.

---

247   The case was dismissed on other grounds.

248   This distinction was formerly used to govern the availability of the remedy of *certiorari* and the obligation to adhere to the rules of natural justice. See *Ridge v. Baldwin* (1963), [1964] A.C. 40 (U.K. H.L.) and the discussion in Chapter 8.

249   *Brewer Brothers v. Canada (Attorney General)* (1991), 80 D.L.R. (4th) 321 (Fed. C.A.); and *Swanson Estate v. R.* (1991), 80 D.L.R. (4th) 741 (Fed. C.A.).

250   However, the Ontario Court of Appeal recognized that the discipline process of a law society was protected by a quasi judicial immunity which negated any *prima facie* duty of care in *Edwards v. Law Society of Upper Canada* (2000), 188 D.L.R. (4th) 613 (Ont. C.A.), leave to appeal allowed (2000), 266 N.R. 196 (note) (S.C.C.). This decision was later upheld by the Supreme Court of Canada: (2001), 206 D.L.R. (4th) 211 (S.C.C.).

251   Even though the distinction is often difficult to apply in practice, it is preferable that the law in this area develop on the basis of a consistent set of principles.

252   *Supra* note 245.

253   *Supra* note 245.

3. Injunctions

(a) Introduction

The use of the injunction as a public law remedy is a relatively modern development. From its early origins in the Court of Chancery, it has been employed as an equitable remedy in disputes between private persons to protect proprietary rights.[254] Nevertheless, by the 19th century, it was established as a remedy in public law proceedings. Largely, these matters arose as a result of a suit by the Attorney General to enjoin the commission of a public wrong. In a substantial number of cases, the Attorney General invoked the Crown's *parens patriae* jurisdiction to seek injunctive relief in the public interest to restrain corporations and statutory or public authorities from acting outside their powers.[255] Also, the Attorney General frequently sued, in the public interest, to enjoin the commission of public nuisances. From these roots, the injunction evolved as a public law remedy.

Today, injunctions are used in a variety of public law settings to remedy the *ultra vires* acts or omissions of public authorities. Often this may take the form of a collateral attack against official action where the *vires* of the action is not directly in issue. For example, an injunction may be sought to restrain the enforcement of an *ultra vires* order or regulation which infringes some right of a plaintiff. Or, an injunction may be sought in the form of a direct challenge to official action or inaction, to restrain the *ultra vires* exercise of authority or to compel a performance of a duty. Also, it should be noted that injunctions have been sought in proceedings against private bodies, such as voluntary associations, to challenge acts or decisions with public consequences. As there is some question as to the availability of *certiorari* or prohibition, in such cases, affected parties have resorted to the private law remedies of declaration and injunction.[256]

In constitutional litigation, the courts may grant a "structural injunction"[257] which requires a public body to reorganize itself so as to comply with constitutional requirements. Usually, this entails some ongoing supervision by the courts in the administration of a public agency.

(b) Nature of Injunctions

Injunctions can take a number of forms. They can be cast in either prohibitory or mandatory terms. Mandatory injunctions require the defendant to act

---

254 For example, as a remedy in tort, for breach of contract and for breach of confidence.

255 See R. Sharpe, *supra* note 5 at 3-1, and the cases cited therein.

256 See for example, *Ripley v. Pommier* (1990), 99 N.S.R. (2d) 338 (N.S. T.D.), additional reasons at (1990), 101 N.S.R. (2d) 108 (N.S. T.D.), affirmed (1991), 108 N.S.R. (2d) 38 (N.S. C.A.), leave to appeal refused (1992), 139 N.R. 399 (note) (S.C.C.); *Peerless (Guardian ad litem of) v. B.C. School Sports* (1998), 7 Admin. L.R. (3d) 106 (B.C. C.A.), leave to appeal refused (1998), 233 N.R. 396 (note) (S.C.C.).

257 On the subject of structural injunctions, see generally, Sharpe, *supra* note 5 at 3-72 to 3-84. See also *Marchand v. Simcoe (County) Board of Education* (1986), 29 D.L.R. (4th) 596 (Ont. H.C.), additional reasons at (1986), 12 C.P.C. (2d) 140 (Ont. H.C.), respecting an order requiring funding and facilities sufficient to secure minority language rights.

positively. They can be used to order the defendant to act positively to undo some past wrong to the plaintiff or they can be used to order the defendant to carry out some duty which has not been performed. Because a mandatory injunction requires a positive act on the part of the defendant, it gives rise to special problems[258] and is a less common form of injunction. The most common form of injunction, a prohibitory injunction, is one which forbids or restrains the defendant from doing a specified act such as the execution of an invalid order or decision.

A mandatory injunction bears a strong resemblance to the prerogative remedy of mandamus, because both will lie to compel the performance of a legal duty.[259] At one time, the tendency was to treat these two remedies as mutually exclusive. Mandamus was the remedy to be used when seeking to compel a performance of a legal duty.[260] The primacy of mandamus can be explained on the basis of the narrower standing requirements associated with an injunction–in order to obtain an injunction to enforce a public duty, the plaintiff had to show the infringement of some private right or special interest. Also, uncertainty surrounding the availability of an injunction against the Crown[261] or Crown servants may have stilted its development in the public law area. Likewise, a prohibitory injunction can be similar in effect to the prerogative remedy of prohibition, particularly when a remedy is sought to prohibit illegal proceedings or to restrain the enforcement of an invalid order or decision which threatens to infringe the private rights of an individual. However, the technical nature of these remedies is different because "[a] writ of prohibition issues to the inferior court in the name of the Sovereign and restrains it from pursuing a particular course of action," while "[a]n injunction merely orders a party to the challenged proceedings to refrain from presenting or prosecuting his or her case."[262] Perhaps, for that reason, the order of prohibition, rather than the injunction, has been the preferred remedy when seeking to prohibit proceedings before an inferior tribunal. However, there does not appear to be any principled reason why one remedy is to be preferred over the other.[263]

---

258 See Sharpe, *supra* note 5 at 1-20 to 1-26.

259 The overlap between the two remedies becomes even more pronounced in some jurisdictions, such as Alberta, where a single form of proceedings for judicial review has led to the assimilation of the public law and private law remedies.

260 As Wade and Forsyth state in *Administrative Law*, 7th ed. (Oxford: Clarendon Press, 1994) at 611-12:

> To enforce a duty requires a mandatory inunction, which the court will grant only where the duty is owed to the plaintiff personally, i.e. where he has a legal right to protect. . . . Although there is no reason in principle why a mandatory injunction should not be granted against a public authority, the prerogative remedy of *mandamus* is usually more suitable, particularly since the procedure is quicker and the rules as to standing are less strict. Where the duty is owed to the public generally and not to the plaintiff personally an injunction to enforce performance of a duty will not be granted.

261 See for example, s. 17(1) of the *Proceedings Against the Crown Act*, R.S.A. 2000, c. P-25.

262 Sharpe, *supra* note 5 at 3-43.

263 See the judgment of Bayda J.A. in *Regina (City) v. Police Assn. (Regina)* (1982), 131 D.L.R. (3d) 496 (Sask. C.A.), where he suggested that a more liberal approach to the question should be taken.

Injunctions may also be categorized on the basis of the time at which they are granted. Injunctions may be permanent in nature, in which case they define rights. This type of injunction is granted at the end of the trial as a final remedy.[264] Injunctions may also be interim or interlocutory in nature, granted before the trial or at some stage in the action to preserve the *status quo* until the merits of the action are determined. Interlocutory injunctions can be granted *ex parte*; for example, in cases where either the giving of notice to the defendant or the time taken to give such notice would cause the plaintiff irreparable harm. As no notice is given to the defendant on an *ex parte* application, the courts are cautious in granting such orders, and, usually, the defendant does not have to wait until the end of the trial as he or she is given an opportunity to challenge the interlocutory injunction within a short time of its issuance.

An interim injunction must be regarded as a drastic remedy because it calls upon the court to make an order without the benefit of a full adjudication on the merits of the matter. This is particularly so in the case of public authorities because it entails the possible consequence of interfering with government administration or bringing it to a halt. Aware of this consequence, the courts have been especially cautious when dealing with applications for interim injunctions against public authorities.[265]

In determining an application for an interim injunction, the court is essentially balancing the risk of granting an injunction against the risk of not granting an injunction. Where the balance lies in a particular case will depend on a consideration of a number of factors. In the leading case, *American Cyanamid Co. v. Ethicon Ltd.*,[266] the House of Lords attempted to set out, in a structured fashion, the factors that should be considered in an application for an interim injunction. First, the plaintiff must satisfy the court that ". . . the claim is not frivolous or vexatious; in other words, that there is a serious question to be tried".[267] Previously, the plaintiff was required to establish a strong *prima facie* case. Secondly, the plaintiff must establish that he or she will suffer irreparable harm if the injunction is not granted; *i.e.*, harm which cannot be adequately compensated for through a subsequent award of damages. If no such potential harm is demonstrated, then the injunction should not be granted. Thirdly, the court must ask whether the plaintiff's undertaking in damages will provide adequate compensation if the defendant is ultimately successful at trial. If no

---

264   Although they may include a time limitation; for example, they may be granted for a fixed period of time only, or be in effect only until the fulfilment of certain conditions.

265   Indeed, section 17(1) of the *Proceedings Against the Crown Act*, R.S.A. 2000, c. P-25, prevents the issuance of an injunction against the Crown (as opposed to other statutory delegates), substituting a declaration instead. However, one cannot obtain an interim declaration, because a declaration is a final order. Rule 753.15 permits the court to grant a stay in the course of an application for judicial review, but it is not clear how this relates to the prohibition against injunctions against the Crown. See the discussion below about *Metropolitan Stores (MTS) Ltd. v. Manitoba Food & Commercial Workers, Local 832*, [1987] 1 S.C.R. 110 (S.C.C.), and *RJR-MacDonald Inc. v. Canada (Attorney General)*, [1994] 1 S.C.R. 311 (S.C.C.).

266   [1975] A.C. 396 (U.K. H.L.). See also Ahern, "Interlocutory Injunctions in Administrative Law: What is the Test?" (1991-92) 5 C.J.A.L.P. 1.

267   *American Cyanamid, ibid.* at 407.

potential harm is demonstrated, then the interim injunction should not be granted. Fourthly, if there is doubt as to the adequacy of damages in either case, the court must consider where the balance of convenience lies. This final question involves an assessment of the relative risk of harm to be suffered by either party, and may involve a consideration of the relative strength of each party's case.

While *American Cyanamid* has generally been followed in Canada and England,[268] some doubts have been expressed about its suitability as a governing statement of principle. Courts have pointed to the difficulties created in some cases when the relative strength of the plaintiff's case is ignored after a determination of the threshold issue of a serious issue to be tried.[269] The English Court of Appeal in *Smith v. Inner London Education Authority*[270] concluded that *American Cyanamid* was not applicable in certain cases against public authorities. It discharged an interim injunction that had been granted to the plaintiffs because there was no real prospect of success in a claim for a permanent injunction at trial. Because the remedy sought was one which would interfere with the defendant's exercise of statutory authority, the court was of the opinion that it must assess the merits of the plaintiffs' claim. Moreover, one member of the court indicated that the balance of convenience should be considered from a wider perspective in cases involving public authorities in the performance of their public duties, in order to take into account the interest of the public to whom the duties are owed.

A similar approach has been adopted by the Supreme Court of Canada in a case arising out of a constitutional challenge to legislation. In *Metropolitan Stores (MTS) Ltd. v. Manitoba Food & Commercial Workers, Local 832*,[271] an employer challenged the provisions of the Manitoba *Labour Relations Act*[272] (which provided for the imposition of a first collective agreement) on the ground that the legislation contravened the *Charter of Rights and Freedoms*. During the course of these proceedings, the employer also applied for an order to stay any action on the part of the provincial Labour Relations Board until the constitutional challenge to the legislation could be determined. The stay was refused by the trial judge, but this decision was overturned by the Court of Appeal. On appeal to the Supreme Court of Canada, the court held that the basic principles governing the granting of an interim injunction, as set out in *American Cyanamid*, applied with equal force to the granting of a stay. The first issue involved a preliminary assessment as to the merits of the case. In this respect, the court was of the opinion that the plaintiff need only establish that its case raised a serious question. This seemed to be an appropriate thresh-

---

268 See the cases cited by Sharpe, *supra* note 5 at 2-15 to 2-18.

269 *Kamloops (City) v. Southern Sand & Gravel Co.* (1987), 43 D.L.R. (4th) 369 (B.C. S.C.). In cases involving breaches of contract, the courts have sometimes used the strong *prima facie* case test. See for example *University of Regina Faculty Assn. v. University of Regina*, [1999] 12 W.W.R. 253 (Sask. Q.B.).

270 (1977), [1978] 1 All E.R. 411 (Eng. C.A.).

271 [1987] 1 S.C.R. 110 (S.C.C.).

272 S.M., c. L-10.

old for a case involving a constitutional challenge to legislation.[273] Next, the court considered whether the plaintiff would suffer irreparable harm if the injunction was not granted. Finally, it looked to where the balance of convenience lay between the plaintiff and the defendant. In a constitutional case, this issue was seen to be one of greater complexity than in an ordinary action between private litigants where only their rights and interests were in conflict. Accordingly, the court held that the traditional criteria governing an application for an interim injunction must be broadened to include a consideration of the public interest.[274] The public interest is necessarily implicated when an injunction or stay is granted suspending the operation of legislation until a trial, on the merits, of its constitutional validity. The public is likely to suffer great harm and inconvenience if the legislation, in question, is broad in nature and general in scope. On the other hand, the public interest may suffer little or no harm if the suspended law is a regulation which affects only a limited number of persons. Moreover, the public interest is less likely affected in exemption cases, when a limited and discreet group of persons seek to be exempted from the application of the legislation. The Supreme Court restored the judgment of the trial judge because it was of the opinion that he had correctly considered the public interest in rejecting the application for a stay.[275]

The principles in *Metropolitan Stores* were later reaffirmed by the Supreme Court in *RJR-MacDonald Inc. v. Canada (Attorney General)*,[276] another case involving a constitutional challenge to legislation. Pending the hearing of their appeal the appellants sought a stay of a judgement of the Quebec Court of

---

273 In this respect, the court rejected the position taken by some courts that a more stringent review of the merits must be taken. Such a review may not be possible at this stage as: there is limited evidence on which to decide complex legal and factual issues; it is impractical to conduct a section 1 analysis and a tentative decision on the merits may be given in the absence of complete pleadings. However, there are a number of exceptions to this rule when a more extensive review of the merits must be undertaken: the case is one in which the interim order is, in effect, a final determination or the case is one which involves only a simple question of law. Some courts have refused to grant interim relief where it has the affect of granting the final relief sought. See *Gould v. Canada (Attorney General)* (1984), 13 D.L.R. (4th) 485 (Fed. C.A.), affirmed [1984] 2 S.C.R. 124 (S.C.C.) where the Federal Court of Appeal refused to uphold a mandatory interim injunction allowing a prisoner to vote in an election pending his *Charter* challenge to the *Canada Elections Act* which prohibited prisoners from voting.

274 As Beetz J. stated, *supra* note 271 at 149:
    In short, I conclude that in a case where the authority of a law enforcement agency is constitutionally challenged, no interlocutory injunction or stay should issue to restrain that authority from performing its duties to the public unless, in the balance of convenience, the public interest is taken into consideration and given the weight it should carry.

275 Prior to the decision in *Metropolitan Stores*, the Federal Court Trial Division in *Gariepy v. Canada (Administrator of Federal Court)* (1988), [1989] 1 F.C. 544 (Fed. T.D.), held that, because an application for an interim injunction was directed towards a public authority, an assessment of the balance of convenience must include a consideration of the public interest. See also *Monks v. Canada (Attorney General)* (1992), 58 F.T.R. 196 (Fed. T.D.); *Horii v. R.* (1991), [1992] 1 F.C. 142 (Fed. C.A.); *Bigstone v. Big Eagle* (1992), 52 F.T.R. 109 (Fed. T.D.); *Modern Organics Inc. v. R.* (1991), 45 F.T.R. 134 (Fed. T.D.); *Harper v. Canada (Attorney General)*, [2000] 2 S.C.R. 764 (S.C.C.).

276 [1994] 1 S.C.R. 311 (S.C.C.).

Appeal, upholding the constitutionality of federal legislation, *The Tobacco Products Control Act*,[277] designed to regulate the advertisement of tobacco products. In effect, they wished to be relieved of immediate compliance with the regulations which imposed new packaging requirements.

On the basis of the three stage test, the court dismissed the applicants' application. To begin with, the court agreed with the applicants' contention that the case involved serious constitutional issues. On two occasions, courts had granted leave to appeal and a preliminary assessment of the merits revealed that the case raised several unresolved questions about the application of section 1 of the *Charter*. In this respect, the nature, not the magnitude, of the harm was the key consideration. Accordingly, the court focussed on the tenuous nature of the appellant's claim for damages under the *Charter,* given the uncertain state of the law governing such claims, and not on the magnitude of the loss suffered by the applicants under the legislation. However, at the third stage of the inquiry, the applicants failed to establish that the balance of convenience lay in their favour. In this regard, the public interest was the important consideration and not the maintenance of the *status quo* which was of little or no value in cases which involved the alleged violation of constitutional rights. The court was satisfied that the public interest lay in the government's favour. While the impugned legislation would impose considerable economic hardship on the applicants, it would not impair their long term viability and, in any event, this loss was outweighed by the public's interest in its health. Moreover, the application was a suspension case where the public interest inclined towards compliance with the legislation. And finally, the applicants failed to establish that the implementation of the impugned legislation would result in greater harm to the public interest. In this, the applicants had a difficult onus and the court assumed that there would be irreparable harm to the public interest if the operation of legislation, designed to further the common good through the protection of public health, was suspended.[278] The applicant failed to meet this onus in that they could not demonstrate any harm to the public beyond that of increased prices for the consumers of tobacco products.

In conclusion, while the *American Cyanamid* formulation is well established in Canada, it should not be applied as a mechanistic approach to the question of whether an interim injunction should be granted. Rather, the courts should continue to respond flexibly to the circumstances of each case in the manner suggested by a leading commentator:[279]

> The checklist of factors which the courts have developed – relative strength of case, irreparable harm and balance of convenience – shall not be employed as a series of independent hurdles. They should be seen in the nature of evidence relevant to the central issue of assessing

---

277 S.C. 1988, c. 20.
278 This view was affirmed by the Supreme Court of Canada in *Harper v. Canada (Attorney General), supra* note 275 where it took the view that the public interest in enforcing legislation should be assumed.
279 Sharpe, *supra* note 5 at 2-46.

the relative risk of harm to the parties from granting or withholding interlocutory relief.

The decisions of the Supreme Court of Canada in *Metropolitan Stores* and *RJR-MacDonald* demonstrate that the courts are prepared to do just that.[280]

Finally, it should be noted that injunctions are an equitable remedy and discretionary in nature. Generally speaking, all the reasons why a court may exercise its discretion to refuse one of the prerogative remedies[281] apply to injunctive relief also.

(c) Procedure

In Alberta, an action for a permanent injunction is commenced by issuing a statement of claim,[282] and follows the usual course of trial procedure allowing for interlocutory applications and discovery. This procedure can be lengthy and an application for one of the faster prerogative remedies may be more satisfactory. As part of the parent action, a plaintiff may serve notice of an application for an interim injunction,[283] and the plaintiff can seek his interim injunction *ex parte* where the court is satisfied that no notice is necessary or where notice might entail serious mischief.[284]

Historically, a claim for an injunction could not be joined with an application for one of the prerogative remedies,[285] and there were other procedural difficulties inherent in the different natures of the prerogative and private law remedies.[286] As a result, several jurisdictions have now reformed their proce-

---

280   For example, see *Ontario Federation of Anglers & Hunters v. Ontario (Ministry of Natural Resources)* (1999), 43 O.R. (3d) 760 (Ont. S.C.J.), where the court refused to issue an injunction to suspend the operation of a regulation cancelling the bear hunt on the grounds that applicants failed to show that the public interest was served by an order suspending, on an interim basis, the regulation. See also *International Fund for Animal Welfare Inc. v. Canada* (1998), 6 Admin. L.R. (3d) 76 (Ont. Gen. Div.); *Weatherill v. Canada (Attorney General)* (1998), 6 Admin. L.R. (3d) 137 (Fed. T.D.), where the court refused to grant a stay against the Governor in Council, as the balance of convenience did not favour restraining the Governor in Council from exercising its statutory and prerogative powers. See also *Canada (Attorney General) v. Maritime Harbours Society* (2001), 197 N.S.R. (2d) 322 (N.S. S.C. [In Chambers]), where the court held that public criticism of government was insufficient to constitute irreparable harm.

281   See the discussion on this point in Chapter 15. For example, *University of Regina Faculty Assn. v. University of Regina, supra* note 269 (delay in seeking interim injunction).

282   Alberta *Rules of Court*, R. 6(1).

283   *Ibid.* R. 392(1).

284   *Ibid.* R. 387(1).

285   *O.C.A.W., Local 9-14 v. Polymer Corp.*, [1966] 1 O.R. 774 (Ont. H.C.); *McCarthy v. Calgary Roman Catholic Separate School District No. 1*, [1979] 4 W.W.R. 725 (Alta. T.D.), affirmed (1979), 145 D.L.R. (3d) 765 (Alta. C.A.).

286   For example, they were subject to different time limitations. Also private law remedies can be granted against non-statutory or private authorities, but prerogative remedies cannot: *Howe Sound Co. v. International Union of Mine, Mill & Smelter Workers (Can.), Local 663*, [1962] S.C.R. 318 (S.C.C.). On the other hand, prerogative remedies may be granted against entities which do not have the capacity to be sued, whereas actions for injunctions and declarations require the respondent to have legal personality: *Hollinger Bus Lines Ltd. v. Ontario (Labour Relations Board)*, [1952] O.R. 366 (Ont. C.A.). Query whether the

dures to create an "application for judicial review" which provides for a single form of proceeding for all of the prerogative remedies and the private law remedies of injunctions and declarations.[287]

(d) *Locus Standi*

There is considerable controversy and doubt about the requirements concerning the requisite standing to obtain an injunction to prevent the commission of a public wrong. Whereas a plaintiff in a private law matter must have a direct legal or proprietary interest at stake, a plaintiff in a suit to enforce public rights often has no particular legal or proprietary interest of his or her own at stake. For example, when an individual seeks a mandatory injunction to compel the relevant authorities to enforce the law, the plaintiff may well have suffered no more injury from the lack of enforcement than any other member of the public. Does such a plaintiff have standing to seek the vindication of the public right? Generally speaking, the courts have adopted a cautious approach to the issue of standing to seek an injunction in these circumstances, and have tended to define standing more restrictively here than with some of the other remedies of administrative law.[288] This cautious approach stems from several concerns. First, if standing were broadened too much, the courts fear a flood of unnecessary litigation. Secondly, there are concerns about the appropriateness of using a coercive remedy, supported by criminal sanctions, in situations replete with sensitive political issues.

The restrictive view of standing is classically stated in the judgment of Buckley J. in *Boyce v. Paddington Borough Council*,[289] a case of public nuisance. On the basis of this decision, a private person is said to have standing to seek an injunction to enjoin a public wrong in two situations: first, where the interference with a public right also interferes with a private right of his or her own; and, secondly, where the plaintiff has suffered special damage as a result of interference with the public right (even though no private right has been interfered with).[290] However, some authorities suggest that merely suffering special damages is insufficient: that the plaintiff must suffer an actionable wrong.[291] Certainly where illegal governmental action would result in an

---

requirement for legal personality is required if an "application for judicial review" is used to apply for an injunction or declaration in the public law context?

287 In these jurisdictions injunctions may be sought by a more summary procedure, as one of the remedies associated with judicial review. See for example Alberta *Rules of Court*, Part 56.1, Rules 753.04(1), 753.04(2) (reproduced in Appendix 4).

288 For a detailed examination of the question of standing, consult: Sharpe, *supra* note 5 at 3-24 to 3-40; de Smith, Woolf and Jowell, *Judicial Review of Administrative Action*, 5th ed. (London: Sweet & Maxwell, 1995) at 99-154; de Smith, Woolf and Jowell, *Judicial Review of Administrative Action, First Cumulative Supplement to the Fifth Edition* (London: Sweet & Maxwell, 1998) at 21-27; Craig, *supra* note 11 at 480-515.

289 (1902), [1903] 1 Ch. 109 (Eng. Ch. Div.), reversed [1903] 2 Ch. 556 (Eng. C.A.), reversed (1905), [1906] A.C. 1 (U.K. H.L.).

290 *Halsey v. Esso Petroleum Co.*, [1961] 1 W.L.R. 683 (Q.B.); *Birmingham & Midland Motor Omnibus Co. v. Worcestershire County Council*, [1967] 1 W.L.R. 409 (C.A.).

291 *Stockport District Waterworks Co. v. Manchester Corporation* (1863), 7 L.T. 545; *Pudsey Coal Gas Co. v. Bradford Corporation* (1873), L.R. 15 Eq. 167.

actionable wrong (such as trespass or breach of contract), the plaintiff would have standing to seek an injunction. In any event, the term "special damage" has given rise to a number of varying interpretations and, as a result, there is significant confusion in the law.[292]

Where the harm arising from the unlawful action is suffered by the public generally, then a private individual has no capacity to sue for an injunction to restrain the wrongful action. This is the function of the Attorney General who has standing to restrain illegal governmental action over a broad field. The Attorney General represents the general public to ensure that excesses of statutory authority or breaches of statutory duties are restrained.

The traditional view of standing to obtain an injunction was affirmed by the House of Lords in *Gouriet v. Union of Post Office Workers*.[293] There, a private citizen sought an injunction to restrain the defendant union from breaching the criminal law. The plaintiff sought the injunction on his own behalf because the Attorney General had refused to consent to relator proceedings. The House of Lords held that the plaintiff did not have standing because the defendant's actions did not interfere with any private right of the plaintiff, nor had the plaintiff suffered any special or particular damage. However, the House of Lords subsequently adopted a more liberal view towards standing in *Inland Revenue Commissioners v. National Federation of Self-Employed & Small Businesses Ltd.*[294] It held that an individual does have standing to seek an injunction and a declaration in public law matters if he or she has sufficient interest in the matter.[295] The court's change of attitude was prompted by the more liberal view of standing applicable to the prerogative remedies and the assimilation of these remedies with injunctive and declaratory relief in the new application for judicial review.[296]

In Canada, the rules of standing with respect to injunctions in public law matters have also been liberalized. This has occurred as a result of a series of cases involving actions for declarations arising out of constitutional challenges

---

292 L.A. Stein (ed.), *Locus Standi* (Sydney: Law Book Company, 1979) at 39:
    What is "special damage"? Does it mean merely inconvenience? Or must a loss express-
    ible in money terms be proved? And must that loss be suffered only by the plaintiff, so
    that the worse and more widespread the effects of the injurious conduct the less likely it
    is that anyone else can sue?

293 (1977), [1978] A.C. 435 (U.K. H.L.).

294 (1981), [1982] A.C. 617 (U.K. H.L.). See Craig, *supra* note 11 at 489-98 for a full discussion of the case and its potential effects.

295 The decision in *Gouriet*, *supra* note 293, was distinguished on the dubious ground that it dealt with standing in a private law rather than a public law matter. Having regard to the facts of *Gouriet*, this characterization is curious.

296 The Australian High Court has also apparently broadened the rules of standing for declarations and injunctions in public law matters. See *Australian Conservation Fund Inc. v. The Commonwealth* (1980), 54 A.L.J.R. 176. See also *Reese v. Alberta* (1992), 87 D.L.R. (4th) 1 (Alta. Q.B.), additional reasons at (1992), [1993] 1 W.W.R. 450 (Alta. Q.B.), where D.C. McDonald J. concluded that the effect of the consolidation of all of the remedies of judicial review into a single form of application was to replace the previously disparate rules of standing with a single rule based on the liberal standing principles associated with *certiorari* and prohibition.

to legislation.[297] Because there is a growing tendency to assimilate the rules of standing for injunctions with those of declarations in public law matters, this development will be discussed in the next section dealing with declarations.[298]

(e) Relator Actions

These actions are brought by the Attorney General at the relation of a private individual who agrees to bear the costs and who takes the benefit of the remedy. Usually the relator's counsel conducts the proceedings, although the Attorney General has complete control over the action. The Attorney General's decision whether to take the case is unfettered, and cannot be questioned by the courts.[299]

(f) Availability of Injunctive Relief

As a discretionary, flexible remedy of general application, the injunction has been used in conjunction with a wide variety of public law matters. This makes it very difficult to discuss and define, with precision, the scope of injunctive relief in public law. To do so would require an exhaustive review of the authorities which is beyond the scope of this work and best left to specialized texts on injunctions.[300] However, some idea as to the scope of injunctive relief, as a public law remedy, can be gained through a brief review of the chief purposes to which the remedy has been put in that setting.

At the outset, it should be noted that the development of the injunction, as a public law remedy, has been hampered by a number of factors: first, an apparent overlap between it and the prerogative remedies of *mandamus* and prohibition; secondly, the restricted scope of standing rules, and, thirdly, the uncertain scope of Crown's immunity from injunctive relief. As a result, the injunction has remained on the "periphery of public law"[301] and has never reached its full potential as an all purpose remedy. Nevertheless, the use of injunctions in public law appears to be growing, particularly as a form of interim relief, designed to preserve the *status quo* until the determination of the dispute between the citizen and the public authority. In part, this development can be attributed to the use of injunctions in concert with declaratory relief. Due to its flexible nature, the declaration has become a very popular

---

297 *Friends of Point Pleasant Park v. Canada (Attorney General)* (2000), 188 F.T.R. 280 (Fed. T.D.), where three individuals were found to have sufficient standing to seek an interim injunction restraining the Crown from cutting down trees in the municipal park on the basis that they raised a justiciable issue, had a serious and genuine interest in the matter, and were the most appropriate persons to litigate the issue.

298 Sharpe, *supra* note 5 at 3-32 suggests that because differences exist between injunctive and declaratory forms of relief, the tendency to assimilate the rules of standing for one remedy with those of the others is to be regretted.

299 *London County Council v. Attorney General*, [1902] A.C. 165 (U.K. H.L.); *Attorney General v. Parish*, [1913] 2 Ch. 444 (Eng. C.A.); *A.G. v. Westminster City Council*, [1924] 2 Ch. 416 (C.A.); *Gouriet v. Union of Post Office Workers, supra* note 293.

300 Sharpe, *supra* note 5 at 3-1 to 3-84. See also D.J.M. Brown and J.M. Evans, *Judicial Review of Administrative Action in Canada* (loose leaf), (Toronto: Canvasback Publishing, 1998) at 1-77*ff*.301 Craig, *supra* note 11 at 540.

remedy in administrative law; used to not only declare the rights of the parties, but the *vires* of administrative action. But, the growing use of the injunction can also be attributed to the adoption in many jurisdictions of a single form of proceeding for judicial review. This has not only identified the injunction as a public law remedy but it has apparently lead to a liberalization of its standing rules through the application of a uniform standard.

In private law, injunctions have been used historically to protect private property rights from wrongful infringement by others and to restrain breaches of contract. It was, thus, a natural development for injunctions to be granted against public authorities to prevent the commission or continuance of a tort[302] (such as trespass or nuisance) or a breach of contract.[303] Often, these actions took the form of collateral attack against the legality of administrative action as the conduct complained of arose out of the enforcement of a regulation or an administrative order or decision. The infringement of the plaintiff's rights would only be justified if the official action was determined to be lawful. It follows, therefore, that an injunction will not be granted to restrain the lawful exercise of statutory authority even though it may result in an order or decision which affects or threatens to affect the rights or interests of the plaintiff.[304] Private individuals have also sought injunctions, in a variety of circumstances, to restrain the wrongful or unlawful conduct of public authorities even though that conduct did not constitute an actionable wrong.[305] For example, proceedings have been brought against governmental and municipal authorities to prevent the operation or enforcement of regulations and bylaws, on the grounds that the subordinate legislation was *ultra vires* or the primary legislation was unconstitutional.[306] Similarly, injunctions have been used against these au-

---

302   Wade and Forsyth, *supra* note 260 at 583. See also *Broadbent v. Rotherham Corporation*, [1917] 2 Ch. 31; *Pride of Derby & Derbyshire Angling Assn. Ltd. v. British Celanese Ltd.* (1952), [1953] Ch. 149 (Eng. C.A.); *Canada (National Harbours Board) v. Langelier* (1968), [1969] S.C.R. 60 (S.C.C.).

303   *Saskatoon Square Ltd. v. Canada Mortgage & Housing Corp.*, [1995] 6 W.W.R. 725 (Sask. Q.B.); *Delta (Municipality) v. Nationwide Auctions Inc.*, [1979] 4 W.W.R. 49 (B.C. S.C.).

304   *Carota v. Jamieson* (1978), [1979] 1 F.C. 735 (Fed. T.D.), affirmed (1979), [1980] 1 F.C. 790 (Fed. C.A.); *Roberts v. Calgary (City)* (1966), 57 W.W.R. 666 (Alta. S.C.); *Beck v. Edmonton (City)* (1991), 118 A.R. 107 (Alta. Q.B.). See also *Cummins v. Canada (Minister of Fisheries & Oceans)* (1996), 41 Admin. L.R. (2d) 151 (Fed. T.D.) where the court refused to grant an interim injunction to restrain a ministerial decision on the grounds that the decision was one for the Minister to make in his discretion.

305   Most commentators agree that an injunction can be used in these circumstances, even though the case law on the subject is limited. See Wade and Forsyth, *supra* note 260 at 582; Craig, *supra* note 11 at 451-52.

306   For example, *Smith v. Canada* (1994), 23 Imm. L.R. (2d) 235 (Ont. Gen. Div.); *RJR-MacDonald, supra* note 276; *Club Country Le Grand Ltée c. Nouveau-Brunswick (Commission des licenses & permis d'alcool)* (1990), 109 N.B.R. (2d) 323 (N.B. Q.B.); *Pacific Trollers Assn. v. Canada (Attorney General)* (1983), [1984] 1 F.C. 846 (Fed. T.D.); *Metropolitan Toronto School Board v. Ontario (Minister of Education)* (1985), 53 O.R. (2d) 70 (Ont. Div. Ct.); *Francen v. Winnipeg (City)* (1987), 48 Man. R. (2d) 276 (Man. Q.B.), reversed (1987), 50 Man. R. (2d) 243 (Man. C.A.); *Gulf Trollers Assn. v. Canada (Minister of Fisheries & Oceans)* (1986), 6 F.T.R. 1 (Fed. T.D.); *London Drugs Ltd. v. Red Deer (City)* (1986), 43 Alta. L.R. (2d) 165 (Alta. Q.B.); *Esquimalt Anglers' Assn. v. R.* (1988), 21 F.T.R. 304 (Fed. T.D.); *Aspen Cleaners & Launderers Ltd. v. Toronto (City)* (1988), 32

thorities to restrain the collection or enforcement of illegal taxes.[307] Also, injunctions have been granted against government and educational authorities to prohibit the implementation of unauthorized programs and policies.[308] And finally, injunctions have been issued against statutory authorities to restrain discipline proceedings or decisions.[309]

A number of comments can be made about these cases. First, the standing of the parties to seek injunctive relief, usually as an interim measure to preserve the *status quo*, was not a significant issue even though they did not suffer an actionable wrong or special damage. While, in some instances, the issue of standing may have been subsumed in the larger question of a *prima facie* case, these authorities do suggest that the courts will take a more liberal view of standing when the action or application involves a challenge to the *vires* of official action. In practical terms, this means that a person will have sufficient standing to seek injunctive relief when he or she is directly and detrimentally affected by an administrative decision or action.[310] This is, generally speaking, the standard employed in judicial review proceedings;[311] although an even broader standard may be used in constitutional challenges to the validity of legislative or administrative action.[312] However, it should be borne in mind that, ". . . there is always the possibility that the courts will deny *locus standi* to a person who has not suffered a legal wrong, redressible in an action for damages, or alternatively adopt a very strict view of the meaning of a person aggrieved in proceedings where an injunction is claimed."[313]

Secondly, these cases reveal that an injunction will principally be used to restrain or prevent unauthorized action by governmental and public bodies.

C.P.C. (2d) 87 (Ont. H.C.); *Friends of Point Pleasant Park v. Canada (Attorney General)*, *supra* note 297; *Law Society (British Columbia) v. Canada (Attorney General)* (2001), 98 B.C.L.R. (3d) 282 (B.C. S.C. [In Chambers]), affirmed (2002), 98 B.C.L.R. (3d) 310 (B.C. C.A.), leave to appeal allowed (2002), 292 N.R. 397 (note) (S.C.C.).

307   See for example, *Ontario Jockey Club v. Smith* (1922), 22 O.W.N. 373 (Ont. H.C.); *Dominion Express Co. v. Alliston (Town)* (1909), 14 O.W.R. 196 (Ont. C.P.); *Canadian Oil Fields Co. v. Oil Springs (Village)* (1907), 13 O.L.R. 405 (Ont. C.A.); *Dods v. Minitonas (Municipality)*, [1919] 1 W.W.R. 717 (Man. K.B.).

308   See for example, *MacDonald v. Lambton County Board of Education* (1982), 37 O.R. (2d) 221 (Ont. H.C.); *Algonquin Wildlands League v. Ontario (Minister of Natural Resources)* (1996), 21 C.E.L.R. (N.S.) 102 (Ont. Div. Ct.); *Bradbury v. London Borough of Enfield*, [1967] 1 W.L.R. 1311; *Lavoie c. Québec (Procureur général)* (1994), 66 Q.A.C. 201 (Que. C.A.).

309   See for example, *Duncan v. Canada (Minister of National Defence)* (1989), 52 C.C.C. (3d) 86 (Fed. T.D.) (military discipline); *Kenney v. College of Physicians & Surgeons (New Brunswick)* (1994), 120 D.L.R. (4th) 138 (N.B. C.A.), leave to appeal refused (1995), 168 N.B.R. (2d) 80 (note) (S.C.C.) (physician discipline).

310   Dussault and Bourgeat, *Administrative Law, A Treatise*, 2 ed., Vol. 4 (Toronto: Carswell, 1990) at 418-19.

311   In judicial review proceedings, an interim injunction is often sought with an application for a declaratory order of *ultra vires*. Clearly, the broader standing requirements of the latter remedy have influenced those relating to injunctions.

312   *Thorson v. Canada (Attorney General) (No. 2)* (1974), [1975] 1 S.C.R. 138 (S.C.C.); *Finlay v. Canada (Minister of Finance)*, [1986] 2 S.C.R. 607 (S.C.C.).

313   de Smith, *Judicial Review of Administrative Action*, 3d ed. (London: Stevens & Sons, 1973) at 409.

Usually, an injunction will be sought, as an interim form of relief, to enjoin official action pending a determination of *ultra vires* in either an action or a judicial review application for a declaration. Mandatory injunctions are rare. This reflects not only the traditional reluctance of the courts to grant such relief, but also the concern that the courts should not interfere with the merits of administrative decision making. Moreover, in terms of interim relief, there is a practical concern that the courts may not have an opportunity to adequately assess the merits of the claim at a preliminary stage of the proceedings.[314] Nevertheless, mandatory injunctions have been granted to enforce public law rights.[315] In some cases, the relief may be cast in prohibitory terms, that is, it restrains unauthorized action, but the effect is mandatory as the public authority is commanded to act in a certain fashion.[316] However, overall, the scope of mandatory injunctive relief has been severely limited in administrative law by the prerogative remedy of *mandamus*; this is the preferred remedy to enforce legal duties. Although, there is no principled reason why this should be so except that the standing rules are less strict.

Thirdly, and finally, these cases reveal that injunctions are not commonly used to restrain either the commencement or continuance of *ultra vires* proceedings before quasi judicial statutory tribunals. The remedy of prohibition is used in this respect, although this appears to be more a "matter of habit than principle."[317] Courts[318] and commentators[319] alike have suggested that an injunction should be available as an alternative to prohibition. In individual cases one remedy may be more effective than the other and *vice versa*. For example, injunctions, rather than prohibition, are regularly used to restrain proceedings before domestic tribunals and investigatory proceedings,[320] while prohibition is used in relation to quasi-judicial proceedings, particularly if the tribunal lacks sufficient legal personality to be a defendant in an action at private law.[321]

One major limitation on the scope of injunctive relief concerns parliamentary proceedings. Although the proceedings of the Federal Parliament and the provincial legislatures are completely privileged against injunctive proceedings and any other judicial intervention,[322] the constitutionality of any act may

---

314 *Gould v. Canada (Attorney General)* (1984), 13 D.L.R. (4th) 485 (Fed. C.A.), affirmed [1984] 2 S.C.R. 124 (S.C.C.).

315 Sharpe, *supra* note 5 at 3-41 to 3-43; see also, *R. v. Kensington and Chelsea Royal L.B.C. ex p. Hammell*, [1989] Q.B. 518; *Taylor v. Newham L.B.C.*, [1989] 1 W.L.R. 444; *Amireault c. Epiphanie (Paroisse)* (1980), 13 M.P.L.R. 213 (Que. S.C.).

316 For example, *Warwickshire County Council v. British Railways Bd.*, [1969] 1 W.L.R. 1117.

317 Sharpe, *supra* note 5 at 3-44.

318 *Barnard v. National Dock Labour Board*, [1953] 2 Q.B. 18 at 42 (Eng. C.A.) per Denning L.J.

319 Sharpe, *supra* note 5 at 3-44 to 3-47; de Smith, *supra* note 288 at 727-31.

320 For example, *Turnbull v. Canadian Institute of Actuaries*, [1995] 9 W.W.R. 235 (Man. Q.B.), reversed on other grounds (1995), [1996] 1 W.W.R. 1 (Man. C.A.), leave to appeal refused [1996] 2 W.W.R. lxxx (S.C.C.).

321 See the discussion on this point in Chapter 15.

322 On this subject, see generally: Craig, *supra* note 11 at 542-44; Wade and Forsyth, *supra* note 260 at 587-89; de Smith, *supra* note 288 at 727. For a recent example of a decision on this issue see *Hogan v. Newfoundland (Attorney General)* (1998), 166 Nfld. & P.E.I.R. 161 (Nfld. T.D.), affirmed (1998), 163 D.L.R. (4th) 672 (Nfld. C.A.) where the court refused to

be challenged by the special reference procedure, and in this way the courts are able to pronounce on the lawfulness of any parliamentary action, at least insofar as its constitutional validity is concerned.[323] Moreover, prohibitory injunctions, and the associated remedy of a stay, are available to restrain the enforcement of allegedly unconstitutional laws and practices pending a final determination as to their legality.[324]

The use of injunctions in public law is not confined to actions or applications brought by private individuals seeking to remedy, on a permanent or interim basis, wrongful or unlawful government action. Injunctions have been sought, at the suit of the Attorney General, to enforce public rights or to enjoin the commission of public wrongs.[325] Examples of such actions include proceedings to restrain statutory or public bodies from exceeding their powers,[326] suits to enjoin public nuisances;[327] and actions to enforce statutory proscriptions, especially when they are regulatory in nature and the law has been persistently flouted.[328] Where, however, proceedings are not brought by the Attorney General and a private individual wishes to enjoin the commission of a public nuisance or wrong, difficult problems of standing arise. The plaintiff, in such a case, must establish either that the public wrong also amounted to a violation of his or her private rights or that he or she suffered special damage.[329] Apart from actions brought by the Attorney General, municipalities have been granted injunctions to enforce their bylaws.[330] And, professional bodies have

---

grant an injunction to restrain the Governor General from proclaiming an amendment to the Terms of Union between Newfoundland and Canada. See also *Reference re Canada Assistance Plan (Canada)*, [1991] 2 S.C.R. 525 at 558-59 (S.C.C.).

323 For example, the reference to the Supreme Court of Canada over the constitutionality of the federal government's proposed patriation of the *B.N.A. Act*: *Reference re Amendment to the Constitution of Canada*, [1981] 1 S.C.R. 753 (S.C.C.).

324 For example, *Metropolitan Stores (MTS) Ltd. v. Manitoba Food & Commercial Workers, Local 832*, [1987] 1 S.C.R. 110 (S.C.C.); *RJR-MacDonald Inc. v. Canada (Attorney General)*, [1994] 1 S.C.R. 311 (S.C.C.).

325 These suits have been brought either on the initiative of the Attorney General or on the basis of a relator action.

326 *Attorney General v. Manchester (City)*, [1906] 1 Ch. 643 (Eng. Ch. Div.); *Attorney General v. Fulham Corp.*, [1921] 1 Ch. 440 (Eng. Ch. Div.).

327 For recent examples: *Ontario (Attorney General) v. Dieleman* (1994), 117 D.L.R. (4th) 449 (Ont. Gen. Div.), additional reasons at (1995), 22 O.R. (3d) 785 (Ont. Gen. Div.), additional reasons at (1995), 22 O.R. (3d) 785 at 794 (Ont. Gen. Div.) (injunction to limit and constrain anti-abortion picketing); *British Columbia (Attorney General) v. Couillard* (1984), 11 D.L.R. (4th) 567 (B.C. S.C.) (interlocutory injunction to enjoin widespread street prostitution); generally, see: Sharpe, *supra* note 5 at 3.3 to 3.8.

328 See generally, Sharpe, *supra* note 5 at 3.8 to 3.11. See also *Attorney General v. Harris* (1960), [1961] 1 Q.B. 74 (Eng. C.A.); *Ontario (Attorney General) v. Grabarchuk* (1976), 67 D.L.R. (3d) 31 (Ont. Div. Ct.); *Plantation Indoor Plants Ltd. v. Alberta (Attorney General)* (1982), 133 D.L.R. (3d) 741 (Alta. C.A.), reversed on other grounds [1985] 1 S.C.R. 366 (S.C.C.).

329 *Boyce v. Paddington, supra* note 289. The *Gouriet* case, *supra* note 293, reaffirmed the principle that, absent special damage, a private person has no standing to seek an injunction to restrain a breach of the criminal law.

330 *Toronto (Metropolitan) v. N.B. Theatrical Agencies Inc.* (1984), 4 D.L.R. (4th) 678 (Ont. H.C.); *Capital (Regional District) v. Sooke River Hotel Ltd.* (2001), 9 C.P.C. (5th) 293 (B.C. S.C.) (enforcement of smoking bylaws).

obtained injunctions to restrain persons from violating statutory proscriptions of "unauthorized practice."[331] Finally, it should be noted that some administrative tribunals have sought "free standing injunctions" from the courts.[332] The purpose of this remedy is to aid the tribunal in its processes. If granted, the injunction will enjoin one of the parties before the tribunal from certain conduct until the tribunal makes a ruling with respect to that conduct.

(g) Crown Immunity from Injunctions

Any discussion of injunctive relief against public authorities must address the unique position of the Crown. Historically, on the basis of the common law, and currently, on the basis of statute, the Crown has claimed an immunity from injunctive relief. While the existence of an immunity is not in doubt, its nature and scope remains unclear as the courts, in individual cases, have come to different conclusions on whether, and under what circumstances, Crown agents and servants, including Ministers of the Crown can share in the Crown's immunity.

(i) At Common Law

Today, in Canada, the issue of Crown immunity from injunctive relief is governed by legislation. However, as the legislation, enacted over a period of four decades in the various provincial and federal jurisdictions,[333] has not been seen as a radical departure from the common law position, and as the common law has heavily influenced the interpretation of the legislation, a brief review of the common law position is merited.

At common law, the general rule was that the Crown was immune from injunctive relief.[334] As is the case with most of the Crown's immunities, the

---

331   At one time, the courts took a narrow view of standing in this respect. Professional bodies were denied standing to enjoin unauthorized practice unless the statute specifically provided for injunctive relief. *Chartered Institute of Patent Agents v. Lockwood*, [1894] A.C. 347 (U.K. H.L.). However, recent cases indicate that this position may have changed. *College of Physicians & Surgeons (Manitoba) v. Morgentaler* (1985), 22 D.L.R. (4th) 256 (Man. Q.B.), reversed (1986), 28 D.L.R. (4th) 283 (Man. C.A.); *College of Chiropractors (Nova Scotia) v. Kohoot* (2001), 616 A.P.R. 183 (N.S. S.C. [In Chambers]).

332   *Canada (Human Rights Commission) v. Canada Liberty Net* (1992), 90 D.L.R. (4th) 190 (Fed. T.D.), reversed [1996] 1 F.C. 804 (Fed. C.A.), leave to appeal allowed (October 10, 1996), Doc. 25228 (S.C.C.), reversed [1998] 1 S.C.R. 626 (S.C.C.).

333   Federal legislation concerning proceedings against the Crown did not contain a "no injunction" provision until 1990. As a result, the common law governed the issue of injunctive relief against the Crown, and its servants and agents, until that time.

334   *Grand Council of Crees (Quebec) v. R.* (1981), 124 D.L.R. (3d) 574 (Fed. C.A.), leave to appeal to the Supreme Court of Canada refused at (1982), 41 N.R. 354 (S.C.C.); *R. v. The Lords Commissioners of the Treasury* (1872), 7 Q.B. 387; *Lount Corp. v. Canada (Attorney General)* (1983), [1984] 1 F.C. 332 (Fed. T.D.), affirmed (1985), 19 D.L.R. (3d) 304 (Fed. C.A.); *Centre d'information & d'animation communautaire (C.I.A.C.) c. R.* (1984), 7 Admin. L.R. 157 (Fed. C.A.); *Ominayak v. Norcen Energy Resources Ltd.* (1987), 44 D.L.R. (4th) 355 (Alta. Q.B.). On the subject of injunctive relief against the Crown, see Hogg and Monahan, *supra* note 5 at 2-28; Lorden, *supra* note 197 at 176-78; Strayer, "Injunctions Against Crown Officers" (1964) 42 Can. Bar. Rev. 1; Tokar, "Administrative Law: Injunctive Relief Against the Crown" (1985) 15 Man. L.J. 97; and Sharpe, *supra* note 5 at 3-48

exact origins of this particular immunity are not clear. However, several rationales for the immunity have been advanced in the cases and by academic commentators. For example, Hogg has suggested two reasons for the immunity.[335] One concerns the incongruity of the Queen's courts issuing an order to the Queen. Another way of stating this concern is to say that the courts, as emanations of the Crown, lack the jurisdiction or capacity to command the Crown by a coercive order such as an injunction.[336] Another reason concerns the potential problem of enforcing an injunction issued against the Crown. In other words, can the Crown be held in contempt of its own courts if it fails to comply with the terms of any injunction granted against it? While there is no clear answer to this question, one might note that this rationale is predicated on the unlikely possibility that the Crown might not comply with an injunction issued against it. In *Carlic v. R.*,[337] the Manitoba Court of Appeal granted an injunction against the Crown and the Minister of Manpower and Immigration. Because counsel for the Crown had acknowledged that its immunity was based on a practical concern for enforcement, the court reasoned that an injunction could be granted because the Crown was in fact likely to comply. In the event that the Crown refused to obey the order, the injunction could be enforced against the Minister.[338] This decision of the court to enjoin the Crown is probably bad in law, but its practical assessment of the situation is appealing – enjoining the responsible officials effectively binds the Crown.

Neither of the suggested rationales for the Crown's immunity from injunctive relief is persuasive. An immunity from the ordinary processes of law should not be based on a somewhat dated view of government. There is nothing incongruous about the judicial branch of government asserting some measure of control over the executive branch.[339] Moreover, any enforcement problems

---

to 3-60; Wade, "Injunctive Relief Against the Crown and its Ministers" (1991) 107 L.Q.R. 4; Matthews, "Injunctions, Interim Relief and Proceedings Against Crown Servants" (1988) 8 Oxford Journal of Legal Studies 154.

335 Hogg and Monahan, *ibid.* at 31.

336 This rationale was suggested by the Privy Council in *Jaundoo v. Attorney-General of Guyana*, [1971] A.C. 972 at 984 (Guyana P.C.):

> At the time of the hearing of the motion in the High Court an injunction against the government of Guyana would have been an injunction against the Crown. This, a court in her Majesty's dominions, has no jurisdiction to grant. The reason for this unconstitutional theory is that the court exercises its judicial authority on behalf of the Crown. Accordingly, any orders of the court are themselves made on behalf of the Crown and it is in incongruous that the Crown should give orders to itself.

337 (1967), 62 W.W.R. 229 (Man. C.A.).

338 In *M. v. Home Office*, [1993] 1 A.C. 377 (U.K. H.L.), the House of Lords ruled that a finding of contempt could not be made against the Crown but it could be made against an authorized department or a Minister of the Crown in his official capacity. However, Lord Woolf, at 425, reasoned that it should not be necessary to enforce the finding of contempt by punishment as "the Crown's relationship with the courts does not depend on coercion . . . a finding of contempt should suffice."

339 Strayer, *supra* note 334 at 6. See also Sedley, "The Crown in its Own Courts" in Forsyth and Hare "The Golden Metwand and the Crooked Cord" (Oxford: Clarendon Press, 1998) at 253 for a thorough discussion of this important constitutional principle. In Canada, it has been noted by Lamer C.J. in *MacMillan Bloedel Ltd. v. Simpson*, [1995] 4 S.C.R. 725 at

will be rare as the Crown can be expected to obey the court's orders. In the unlikely event the Crown does not comply, some accommodation will have to be worked out to avoid "a damaging or even irreconcilable constitutional confrontation".[340] And there is the possibility that the injunction can be issued against the Crown servant personally to restrain an *ultra vires* official act which will effectively restrain the Crown.[341]

While the Crown's immunity from injunctive relief was well established, great uncertainty surrounded the question as to whether an injunction may be granted against a Crown servant or agent. The true scope of any Crown immunity rested upon the resolution of this vital question, as the Crown, acts through a diverse range of servants and agents. Unfortunately, the answer to this question lies in a confusing and often contradictory body of case law which reflects a number of approaches to the issue.

In terms of prohibitory injunctions against Crown servants, the strongest line of authority supports the proposition that an injunction will lie against Ministers of the Crown and Crown servants when their actions cannot be sustained in law. As a leading commentator puts it:

> The basic principle which emerges is that an injunction will be granted to restrain a Crown servant from exceeding the lawful limits of his authority or from acting without any authority when his acts constitute a violation of the plaintiff's right.[342]

The leading case in this respect is that of the Privy Council in *Tamaki v. Baker*.[343] It arose out of a dispute over the ownership of certain lands which had been advertised for sale by the defendant, the New Zealand Commissioner for Crown Lands. The plaintiff claimed a possessory title to the lands on the grounds of custom and usage. He sought an injunction to restrain the defendant from advertising and selling the lands. The defendant asserted Crown ownership of the disputed lands on the ground they had been ceded to the Crown. As the defendant's authority was derived from statute, the Privy Council held that it had the jurisdiction to determine whether the defendant had the authority he claimed. It issued an injunction to restrain the defendant from acting in a manner that was, in fact, not authorized by the Act of Parliament:

> Their Lordships hold that an aggrieved person may sue an officer of the Crown to restrain a threatened act purporting to be done in sup-

---

753 (S.C.C.):
>   Governance by rule of law requires a judicial system that can ensure its orders are enforced and its process respected.
> Surely that applies with equal force to the situation where the government is the defendant'"

340   Hogg and Monahan, *supra* note 5 at 38.
341   Sharpe, *supra* note 5 states at 3-52:
>   In fact, it matters little whether the Crown itself may be properly enjoined. The Crown is an abstraction that works through individuals and if those individuals can be controlled through injunctions, the Crown is thereby controlled.

342   *Ibid.*
343   [1901] A.C. 569.

posed pursuance of an Act of Parliament, but really outside their statutory authority.[344]

This principle has been subsequently adopted in a number of Canadian cases.[345]

A similar approach was taken in cases concerning injunctive relief against Crown agents. In *Rattenbury v. British Columbia (Land Settlement Board)*,[346] the Supreme Court of Canada followed *Tamaki*, to hold that an injunction would lie against the Board (an incorporated agency of the provincial Crown) to restrain it from levying an allegedly unconstitutional tax. In response to the Board's argument that it could not be restrained as an agency of the Crown, the court held that ". . . it is common practice, founded on general principle, that the court will interfere to restrain *ultra vires* or illegal acts by a statutory body".[347] Later, the Supreme Court took a similar view in *Canada (National Harbours Board) v. Langelier*,[348] a case arising out of a claim in nuisance against a Crown agent. The respondent owned land adjacent to the St. Lawrence River. He obtained an interim injunction restraining the appellant board and its employees from continuing to fill in land on the banks of the river. The appellant brought a motion to have the injunction vacated on the ground that, as an emanation or instrumentality of the Crown, it was immune from an award of injunctive relief. On the basis of *Tamaki*, Martland J., for the Court, held that just as a Crown servant can be enjoined from acting or threatening to act in an unlawful manner, so could a Crown agent. Therefore, the appellant's contention could not be sustained when a Crown agent steps outside its lawful authority or acts (or threatens to act) in an unlawful manner. Any immunities, attendant upon the status of Crown agent, were limited to the lawful exercise of the agent's statutory authority.[349]

These cases can be viewed as an expression of the principle that a Crown servant or agent can be enjoined in a personal capacity, by an injunction, to restrain unauthorized official action which infringed the rights of the plaintiff. This principle is analogous to that employed in tort actions against Crown servants and officers. While the Crown was immune from liability in tort, its servants or officers could be held personally liable even though at the time they were acting in their official capacity. In both settings, the principle is consistent with the constitutional maxim that the sovereign can neither do wrong nor authorize wrongdoing. An officer who commits a legal wrong

---

344 *Ibid.* at 576.
345 *Carlic, supra* note 337; *Lodge v. Canada (Minister of Employment & Immigration)*, [1979] 1 F.C. 775 (Fed. C.A.); *Filion v. R.*, [1972] F.C. 1202 (Fed. T.D.); *Pacific Salmon Industries Inc. v. R.* (1984), [1985] 1 F.C. 504 (Fed. T.D.); *Miskokomon v. Canada (Minister of the Environment)* (1989), 29 F.T.R. 198 (Fed. T.D.); *Smoling v. Canada (Ministry of Health & Welfare)* (1992), 56 F.T.R. 297 (Fed. T.D.).
346 (1928), [1929] S.C.R. 52 (S.C.C.), leave to appeal refused [1929] W.N. 211.
347 *Ibid.* at 63. See also *Canadian Pacific Railway v. Saskatchewan (Attorney General)* (1950), 1 W.W.R. (N.S.) 193 (Sask. K.B.), reversed (1951), 2 W.W.R. (N.S.) 424 (Sask. C.A.), reversed [1952] 2 S.C.R. 231, (S.C.C.); *Baton Broadcasting Ltd. v. Canadian Broadcasting Corp.*, [1966] 2 O.R. 169 (Ont. H.C.).
348 (1968), [1969] S.C.R. 60 (S.C.C.).
349 *Ibid.* at 72 per Martland J.:It is only when the Board is lawfully executing the powers entrusted to it by the Act that it is deemed to be a Crown agent.

therefore acts in his personal capacity, outside the scope of his authority to act on behalf of the Crown.[350]

The capacity in which a Minister or Crown officer was acting or the capacity in which either was sued appears to have been an important consideration in two other lines of authority. In one, the availability of injunctive relief against a Crown servant seemed to rest on an uncertain distinction drawn between the servant acting in his "official" capacity as opposed to his "personal" or "individual" capacity. An injunction would not be available in the former instance, only the latter. Thus, in one leading authority, *Merricks v. Heathcoat-Amory*,[351] the court dismissed an application for a mandatory injunction as the proceedings were brought against the defendant Minister in his official capacity. Although the judgment is unclear, the Court appeared to construe the Minister's official capacity broadly and literally to include not only the exercise of the Crown's powers and duties, but also those conferred on the Minister directly by statute. In either case, he would be "acting in his capacity as a Minister of the Crown, representing the Crown"[352] and would therefore be entitled to share in the Crown's immunity from injunctive relief. The decision, therefore, suggested that a Crown servant's immunity from injunctive relief was very broad, indeed, and almost synonymous with that of the Crown, in that a Crown servant would rarely, if ever, act in his private capacity in the exercise of statutory powers and duties.[353]

The decision of *Merrick v. Heathcoat-Amory* has been subject to academic and judicial criticism. Wade, for example, has argued that the judgment ignores a principle of "primary constitutional importance": that servants of the Crown, including ministers, in the exercise of powers and duties conferred upon them by statute, have never enjoyed the Crown's immunities.[354] As a result, the Crown's immunities have not been allowed to obstruct the rule of law and the effectiveness of legal remedies against the state. In a similar fashion, Lord Woolf, in *M. v. Home Office* has held that, while the outcome in *Merricks* was probably correct,[355] the reasoning of the court was wrong in that it was inconsistent with prior authority which clearly established that a minister, acting in

---

350 This reasoning was accepted by the House of Lords in *M. v. Home Office*, *supra* note 338 at 410.

351 [1955] Ch. 567 (Eng. Ch. Div.). See also *Harper v. Home Secretary*, [1955] 1 Ch. 238 (C.A.).

352 *Merrick v. Heathcoat-Amory, ibid.* at 576.

353 The House of Lords in *R. v. Secretary of State for Transport* (1989), [1990] 2 A.C. 85 (U.K. H.L.), approved of the reasoning in *Merricks* and held that the Minister was immune from injunctive relief, as a servant of the Crown, in both civil proceedings and judicial review proceedings. Hogg and Monahan, *supra* note 5 at 33, note 49, argue that "it is irrelevant and confusing to pay attention to the question of whether a Crown servant is sued in an "official capacity" or a "personal capacity".

354 Wade, *supra* note 334 at 4-5.

355 *Supra* note 338 at 415. The case involved an attempt to restrain a Minister of the Crown from proceeding with the enactment of an allegedly *ultra vires* regulatory scheme. The courts have consistently refused to grant injunctive relief where it would interfere with the legislative process. See: Sharpe, *supra* note 5 at 3-52; *Bertrand v. Quebec (Procureur général)* (1995), 127 D.L.R. (4th) 408 (Que. S.C.); *Hogan v. Newfoundland (Attorney General)*, *supra* note 322.

his official capacity, could be sued personally and be the subject of an injunction. In light of these criticisms, the decision in *Merrick* now appears to be thoroughly discredited.

Capacity also featured prominently in other lines of authority concerning the issue of injunctive relief against Crown servants and agents. In these cases a distinction has been drawn between a minister or official acting in the capacity of a "servant of the Crown" and acting in the capacity of an "agent of the legislature". Injunctive relief would not be available against a servant of the Crown, but it would be against an agent of the legislature. For example, in *Grand Council of Crees (Quebec) v. R.*,[356] the court refused to grant an injunction against the Minister of the Crown on the ground that he was acting in his capacity as a servant of the Crown, as opposed to his capacity as an agent or delegate of the legislature.[357] This difficult distinction appeared to rest on the basis that a servant of the Crown was exercising powers and duties vested in the Crown, under statute or the prerogative, while an agent of the legislature was exercising authority directly delegated to him by statute. Nevertheless, in spite of its difficulty, this distinction did serve to limit the scope of the Crown's common law immunity from injunctive relief, as most statutory powers and duties were delegated directly to a named officer and not to the Crown.

At this point, it should be noted that one commentator has attempted to explain the "capacity" lines of authority on the ground that they reflect "the basic proposition that the courts will control *ultra vires* acts."[358] Accordingly, if a crown servant or agent is seen to be acting in an *ultra vires* manner, then an injunction can be granted because it is assumed that they are acting in their "personal or individual capacities"; but if the servant or agent is seen to be acting *intra vires*, they cannot be enjoined because they are acting in their "official capacities". The distinction is, thus, a crude attempt to distinguish between those actions which are within a Crown servant's authority and those which are not. It is, in fact, a conclusion, often unstated, as to the *vires* of a servant's or agent's actions. Similarly, as the authority of an "agent (or delegate) of the legislature" is defined by legislation, an official can be enjoined when the limits of the legislation have been exceeded. But, the label "servant of the Crown" suggests the exercise of statutory authority, the limits of which have not been transgressed. Again, there is an unstated conclusion as to the legality of the servant's or agent's actions.

A final line of authority has created great confusion in the law. It stands for the proposition that servants or agents of the Crown are immune from injunctive relief. Typically, these cases contain little or no analysis of either the Crown's or its servant's or agent's immunity from injunctive relief. Rather, these decisions appear to rest on the assumption that, as the Crown is immune,

---

356   *Supra* note 334.

357   This difficult distinction was taken from mandamus cases where it was used to limit the Crown's immunity from that remedy. See *R. v. Lords Commissioners of the Treasury, supra* note 334; *R. v. British Columbia (Minister of Finance)*, [1935] S.C.R. 278 (S.C.C.). Its utility in prohibitory injunction cases has been questioned: see Strayer, *supra* note 334 at 19.

358   Sharpe, *supra* note 5 at 3-54 to 3-55.

so are its servants and agents.[359] However, each of these cases involved an attempt on the part of the plaintiff to interfere with the lawful exercise of ministerial or official discretion. Therefore, they are really about the *vires* of official action and, in this regard, they may not represent a different view from the *Tamaki* line of authority. Rather, they may simply stand for the converse proposition that the courts will not grant injunctive relief when a Minister of the Crown or a government official is acting lawfully, within the scope of his or her discretionary powers.

In summation, the common law concerning the immunity of the Crown and its servants and agents is a mess. It is inconsistent, uncertain, and marred by technical distinctions which have only created greater confusion. The strongest line of authority is that, in appropriate circumstances,[360] injunctive relief is available against a Crown servant or agent when they act (or threaten to act) in an *ultra vires* manner or when they wrongfully interfere with the private rights of others without legal justification. This is consistent with the important constitutional principle that Government should be held to obey the law. Apparently contrary lines of authority can be either rejected, as wrong, or reconciled with this basic proposition.

(ii) Under Legislation

Having canvassed the common law position with respect to injunctive relief against the Crown and its servants and agents, it remains to consider briefly the effect of Crown proceedings legislation. With one exception,[361] legislation in all Canadian jurisdictions, federally, and provincially, contains provisions which purport to immunize the Crown, its officers, servants and agents from injunctive relief.[362]

---

359   *Ontario (Attorney General) v. Toronto Junction Recreation Club* (1904), 8 O.L.R. 440 (Ont. H.C.); *Orpen v. Ontario (Attorney General)* (1924), [1925] 2 D.L.R. 366 (Ont. H.C.), varied (1925), 56 O.L.R. 530 (Ont. C.A.); *Amalgamated Builder's v. McGregor* (1929), 36 O.W.N. 344; *Belleau v. Canada (Minister of Health & Welfare)*, [1948] Ex. C.R. 288 (Can. Ex. Ct.); *Webster Industries Ltd. v. R.* (1982), [1983] 1 F.C. 393 (Fed. T.D.); *Physicians for a Smoke-free Canada v. Canada (Minister of Corporate & Consumer Affairs)* (1987), 14 F.T.R. 292 (Fed. T.D.).

360   "Appropriate circumstances" may involve a consideration of the nature of the government function affected by the grant of injunctive relief against a Crown servant or agent. For example, the courts have refused injunctive relief in cases where interference with the legislative process might result. Also, the term refers to considerations which engage the court's discretionary authority to grant or refuse relief–factors such as: the availability of a declaration as a less obtrusive form of relief; the maintenance of the *status quo*, the availability of another remedy such as damages or a statutory appeal. See *Canada (Attorney General) v. Fishing Vessel Owners' Asson. (British Columbia)*, [1985] 1 F.C. 791 (Fed. C.A.); *Pacific Trollers Assn. v. Canada (Attorney General)* (1983), [1984] 1 F.C. 846 (Fed. T.D.).

361   The Province of Quebec.

362   The following provision, found in the Alberta *Proceedings Against the Crown Act*, R.S.A. 2000, c. P-25, s. 17, is representative of the legislation found in all of the other jurisdictions, as virtually identical language is used to define the immunity:

   (1) When in proceedings against the Crown any relief is sought that might, in proceedings between persons, be granted by way of injunction or specific

The stated purpose behind these provisions is to allow the Crown freedom of action when confronted by a crisis or emergency.[363] The statutory immunity also reflects the rationales which have been historically suggested for the Crown's common law immunity from injunctive relief. Nevertheless, the effect of these provisions is unclear. There is little case law interpreting them, and what little there is suggests that a strong division of opinion exists with respect to their possible affect.

To begin with, the effect of these provisions on the availability of permanent injunctive relief against the Crown, it servants and agents, is unimportant because declaratory relief provides the plaintiff with an effective, final remedy. The Crown and its servants can be expected to obey a declaration. The important question, however, concerns the availability of interim or interlocutory relief against the Crown and its servants or agents. This question would appear to arise in both the context of civil proceedings and applications for judicial review. If the legislation precludes the granting of an interim injunction in either context, then the private citizen has no means of immediate remedy with which to meet wrongful or *ultra vires* government action.[364]

As suggested above, there appears to be little consensus amongst courts or commentators with respect to the standard statutory "no injunction" provision.[365] Nevertheless, there is general agreement that such provisions preclude

---

performance, the court shall not, as against the Crown, grant an injunction or make an order for specific performance but may, in lieu of it, make an order declaratory of the rights of the parties.

(2) The court shall not in any proceedings grant an injunction or make an order against an officer of the Crown if the effect of granting the injunction or making the order would be to give any relief against the Crown that could not have been obtained in proceedings against the Crown but may, in lieu of it, make an order declaratory of the rights of the parties.

For the legislation in other jurisdictions, see *supra* notes 195 and 196.

Federal legislation also contains a provision similar to that found in provincial legislation. See *Crown Liability and Proceedings Act*, R.S.C. 1985, c. C-50. For a judicial interpretation of this provision, see *Kahgee v. Canada* (1992), 56 F.T.R. 253 (Fed. T.D.). For a compilation of the case law concerning s. 22, see Sgayias *et al.*, *The Annotated Crown Liability and Proceedings Act, supra* note 69 at 92-109. Also, it also should be noted that s. 22 does not apply to preclude injunctive relief against Crown agents; s. 35.

363 Barnes, *The Crown Proceedings Act, 1947* (1948) 26 Can. Bar Rev. 387.

364 There is, however, another possibility that a court may grant interim relief, in judicial review proceedings against a public officer, or a statutory board, commission or tribunal, restraining further proceedings on their part, including executive implementation of a decision already taken, until such time as the application has been determined. Interim relief, in aid of judicial review proceedings, is specifically provided for in British Columbia's and Ontario's *Judicial Review Procedure Act*, Alberta's *Rules of Court* and the *Federal Courts Act*. The availability of interim relief, in aid of judicial review proceedings under the *Federal Courts Act*, was considered in *Riabko v. Royal Canadian Mounted Police Commissioner* (1993), 24 Admin. L.R. (2d) 35 (Fed. T.D.) and *Membreno-Garcia v. Canada (Minister of Employment & Immigration)* (1992), 7 Admin. L.R. (2d) 38 (Fed. T.D.). Interestingly, there was no mention of the Crown's immunities in these cases–perhaps the immunity does not apply to judicial review proceedings?

365 For a full discussion of this issue, see Hogg and Monahan, *supra* note 5 at 31-39; and Sharpe, *supra* note 5 at 3-56 to 3-58.

interim injunctive relief against the Crown.[366] However, this immunity apparently does not apply to protect the Crown in constitutional cases.[367]

The situation concerning agents of the Crown is less clear as the case law on the question is mixed. A number of decisions indicate that Crown corporations and agencies are entitled to share in the Crown's immunity from injunctive relief.[368] These cases are difficult to classify, but they appear to reflect the principle that corporate Crown agents are entitled to share in the Crown's immunity, provided they act *intra vires* their statutory authority. On the other hand, a number of courts have taken a more liberal approach to the question of injunctive relief against Crown agents. In these cases, the courts have restrictively interpreted or construed strictly the standard statutory "no injunction" provision against Crown agents in any claim for immunity from injunctive relief. As a result, Crown agencies have been held subject to such relief. For example, in *Canada (Attorney General) v. Saskatchewan Water Corp.*,[369] Bayda C.J. held that a fundamental distinction should be drawn between the Crown, itself, and an agent of the Crown. Only if the agent of the Crown is exercising a function or power of the Crown does an immunity attach. He then concluded that the Saskatchewan Water Corporation was exercising statutory powers conferred directly upon it by statute. These powers were not powers of the Crown in that they were not exercisable by order in council, proclamation, writ or some other form. Therefore, the proceedings were characterized as proceedings against the Crown agent, not "proceedings against the Crown". Thus, they fell outside the scope of the standard "no injunction" provision. It should be noted that this reasoning parallels earlier decisions where the courts have taken the position that the Crown agent, sued in its own right, is not entitled to claim the benefit of any Crown immunities.[370] Typically these cases involved actions in contract or tort against a Crown agent.[371]

---

366   *Saanichton Marina Ltd. v. Claxton*, [1989] 5 W.W.R. 82 (B.C. C.A.); *A.U.P.E. v. Alberta* (1996), 41 Admin. L.R. (2d) 33 (Alta. Q.B.); *Mundle v. R.* (1994), 28 Admin. L.R. (2d) 69 (Fed. T.D.); *A.U.P.E. v. Alberta* (1996), 46 Alta. L.R. (3d) 44, 41 Admin. L.R. (2d) 33 (Alta. Q.B.). The legislation, therefore, continues the Crown's common law immunity from injunctive relief.

367   Hogg and Monahan, *supra* note 5 at 36; *Van Mulligen v. Saskatchewan Housing Corp.* (1982), 23 Sask. R. 66 (Sask. Q.B.).

368   See for example, *Taal v. Saskatchewan (Medical Care Insurance Commission)* (1962), 40 W.W.R. 8 (Sask. Q.B.); *Banner Investments Ltd. v. Saskatchewan Telecommunications* (1977), 78 D.L.R. (3d) 127 (Sask. Q.B.); *Gloucester Properties Ltd. v. R.*, [1980] 6 W.W.R. 30 (B.C. S.C.); (1981), [1982] 1 W.W.R. 569 (B.C. C.A.); *Saskatchewan v. Royal Bank* (1981), [1982] 1 W.W.R. 60 (Sask. Q.B.); *Kohler Drugstore Ltd. v. Ontario Lottery Corp.* (1984), 46 O.R. (2d) 333 (Ont. H.C.), *Alberta Shuffleboards (1986) Ltd. v. Alberta* (1992), 132 A.R. 126 (Alta. Q.B.).

369   (1993), 18 Admin. L.R. (2d) 91 (Sask. C.A.).

370   The distinction between the Crown and agents and servants is a principle of "primary constitutional importance", according to Wade, *supra* note 334 at 4.

371   See *Baton Broadcasting Ltd. v. Canadian Broadcasting Corp.*, [1966] 2 O.R. 169 (Ont. H.C.); *Canada (National Harbours Board) v. Langelier* (1968), [1969] S.C.R. 60 (S.C.C.); *Perehinec v. Northern Pipeline Agency*, [1983] 2 S.C.R. 513 (S.C.C.); *Yeats v. Central Mortgage & Housing Corp.*, [1950] S.C.R. 513 (S.C.C.). See also Hogg and Monahan, *supra* note 5 at 342-48.

The question of Crown servant's entitlement to an immunity from injunctive relief, under the standard provision, has also generated controversy. Two schools of thought are acknowledged to exist. One has suggested that the provision should be interpreted pervasively to preclude injunctive relief against the Crown and its servants in all cases.[372] In other words, Crown servants would be immune from injunctive relief even where they were found to be acting outside their statutory powers. Such an interpretation would effectively overrule the significant exception to the Crown's immunity created by the *Tamaki* line of authority. Nevertheless, this interpretation has been urged on the grounds that the Crown's immunity would be effectively undermined if its servants were subject to injunctive relief on the basis they acted or threatened to act *ultra vires* their authority.[373] The other school of thought has rejected this interpretation on the basis that it is not supported by the legislation.[374] It is argued that a clear statement of legislative intent would be required in order to displace or modify well-established common law. Instead, this school has argued for an interpretation which would treat the standard "no-injunction" provision as a mere codification of the common law. A significant exception to the Crown's general immunity from injunctive relief would therefore continue to exist on the basis of the *Tamaki* line of authority. Crown servants would be immune from injunctive relief, provided they acted *intra vires* their authority; and, conversely, they could be enjoined when they act (or threaten to act) *ultra vires* their authority. In the latter instance, the injunction would be directed against the Crown servant in his or her private capacity. On that basis, it is said that the effect of the remedy would not be to give injunctive relief against the Crown. Adherents of this view derive strong support from the decision of the Ontario Divisional Court in *MacLean v. Ontario (Liquor Licence Board)*.[375] There, the Board, and its employees, had threatened to cancel the liquor licences of premises in which the plaintiffs were employed as entertainers, because their performances were seen to be indecent or immoral. The court upheld an injunction, granted against individual members of the Board and Board inspectors, to restrain them from taking action with respect to certain liquor licences. In response to the argument that the injunction granted by the trial judge ought to be vacated because the court had no authority to grant an injunction against servants of the Crown, the Divisional Court ruled that Crown servants could be enjoined at common law when they acted outside their lawful authority. Moreover, the court was of the opinion that the common law position had not been altered by Crown proceedings legislation. In this case, the Board members and inspectors were found to be acting outside the scope of their authority as set out in the Act and regulations. Their actions were described as "arbitrary and wilful".[376] Therefore, an injunction was granted against the defendants individually to restrain their unauthorized ac-

---

372   Strayer, *supra* note 334.
373   *Ibid.* at 42.
374   See for example, Hogg and Monahan, *supra* note 5 at 32-33; Sharpe, *supra* note 5 at 3-56.4
        to 3.58.
375   (1975), 9 O.R. (2d) 597 (Ont. Div. Ct.).
376   *Ibid.* at 610.

tions. An injunction against the Board, as an agency of the Crown, was not possible because it lacked the capacity to be sued.[377]

The standard "no injunction" provision has also created great difficulty in the United Kingdom.[378] Generally, it has been held that interim relief against the Crown and its servants and agents is precluded by a "no injunction" provision, similar to that found in Canadian legislation.[379] However, in a number of recent cases, the English courts have restrictively interpreted the legislation and have held that the provision only precludes interim injunctive relief against a servant of the Crown in civil proceedings. Thus, such relief would remain available in judicial review proceedings against the Crown.[380] This line of authority would create a significant exception to the immunity of Crown servants from injunctive relief, as most challenges to the legality of administrative action are brought by way of judicial review proceedings. However, these cases were subsequently overturned by the House of Lords in *R. v. Secretary of State for Transport*.[381] In that case, the applicants sought to restrain the enforcement of English legislation which they alleged was in contravention of European Community law. The court held that interim injunctive relief was not available against the Crown or servants of the Crown, acting as such. This was the position at common law and it was continued by the "no injunction" provision found in the *Crown Proceedings Act*, 1947.[382] Further, after an analysis of the reformed procedure for judicial review, the House of Lords concluded that the Act of 198[383] did not confer a new jurisdiction on the courts to grant injunctions against the Crown or its servants in judicial review proceedings. Subsequently, after a reference to the European Court of Justice, the House of Lords granted an interim injunction against the Crown to protect rights arising under Community law.[384] Thus, an anomalous situation was created: while an injunction could not be granted against the Crown and its servants to provide interim protection for rights claimed under domestic law, it was available as a means of interim protection for rights asserted under Community law.

The issue of interim injunctive relief was again considered by the House of Lords in *M. v. Home Office*,[385] a case of significant constitutional importance as it concerned the extent to which the courts could enforce the law against the

---

377   See *supra* note 210.
378   The English authority is particularly germaine as the provision in the United Kingdom legislation served as the model for the standard "no injunction" provision in Canadian legislation.
379   See for example, *Merricks v. Heathcoat-Amory, supra* note 351. See also Adler, "Public and Private Law Remedies Against the Crown and its Servants; a Question of Interim Relief" (1986) 5 C.J.Q. 218.
380   *R. v. Secretary of State For the Home Department, ex p. Herbage ex p.*, [1987] Q.B. 872; *R. v. Licencing Authority Established Under the Medicine Act*, 1968, *ex p. Smith Kline & French Laboratories Ltd. (No. 2)*, [1990] 1 Q.B. 574.
381   (1989), [1990] 2 A.C. 85 (U.K. H.L.).
382   Section 21.
383   *Supreme Court Act*, 1981, s. 31.
384   *R. v. Secretary of State for Transport ex p. Factortame Ltd. (No. 2)*, [1991] 1 A.C. 603.
385   [1993] 1 A.C. 377 (U.K. H.L.).

Crown and its servants through coercive remedies such as injunctions. This case involved an appeal from a finding of contempt against the Home Secretary for his failure or refusal to comply with an interim mandatory injunction issued against him in proceedings for a judicial review of a deportation order.[386] The finding of contempt could only be sustained, therefore, if the courts had the power to issue an injunction against the Crown or its servants. The House of Lords, in a unanimous judgment, held that the courts had the jurisdiction to make such an order in appropriate circumstances.[387] In the course of a lengthy and somewhat technical judgment, Lord Woolf, for the court, clarified several issues with respect to injunctive relief against the Crown and its servants. First, while it was clear at common law, that the Crown was immune from injunctive relief in civil proceedings, it was also clear that this immunity did not extend to officers or servants of the Crown. Servants of the Crown, including ministers, could be sued personally in civil proceedings for civil wrongs committed by them in their official capacities. Injunctions, both permanent and interim, could be granted, where appropriate, in these proceedings. Secondly, this common law immunity was continued, but not expanded, by Crown proceedings legislation. Accordingly, the statutory prohibition of injunctive relief in civil proceedings against the Crown could be evaded by identifying the Crown servant or officer who committed or authorized the commission of the wrong and suing them in their personal capacity.[388]

> In such a suit, an injunction could be awarded against the officer, and the officer would be personally obliged to comply with it even if the affect of such compliance would be the enjoining of action which, if done by the officer, would be done in an official capacity on behalf of the Crown.

Thirdly, the standard "no injunction" provision contained in the English Crown proceedings legislation applied only to civil proceedings against the Crown and its servants. The language of the statute was clear; it did not apply to judicial review proceedings against Ministers or other officers of the Crown. In this regard, applications for a judicial review were governed by the Act of 1981 which conferred on the courts the jurisdiction to grant injunctive relief in public law matters.[389] This conclusion was supported by the history of prerogative proceedings against the Crown which clearly established that, while the Crown was immune from the prerogative remedies of *mandamus* and prohibition, Ministers and servants of the Crown were not. As the injunction was now a public law remedy, like prohibition and *mandamus*, there was

---

386 The Minister had refused to comply with the interim order on the grounds that the deportation order was validly made and that the court had no jurisdiction to grant an injunction against the Crown or an officer of the Crown, acting in the course of his duties.

387 The decision in *Factortame* was distinguished on several bases including that it arose from a misunderstanding of the Crown's common law position with respect to injunctive relief.

388 Cane, "The Constitutional Basis of Judicial Remedies in Public Law" in Leyland & Woods, *Administrative Law Facing the Future: Old Constraints and New Horizons* (London: Blackstone Press, 1997) at 250.

389 *Supreme Court Act, supra* note 383.

no principled reason, in the absence of clear statutory language, to restrict its scope.

With the decision of the House of Lords in *M. v. Home Office*, the English law concerning injunctive relief against the Crown and its servants became much clearer. Even though some difficult distinctions remain,[390] it is evident that the scope of Crown immunity for injunctive relief is narrow – in the normal case, interim injunctive relief will be available against a servant of the Crown to enjoin unlawful or wrongful action. Unfortunately, the same cannot be said about the Canadian law on this subject which remains unclear and contradictory.[391] The case law is marked by either unquestioning obedience to the terms of the legislation or sometimes artful attempts to restrict its scope.[392] The resulting uncertainty has enabled government lawyers to plead what is, essentially, a technical defence to often meritorious claims. The attention of the courts is therefore diverted from the real question: whether, and under what circumstances, allegedly unlawful or wrongful government action should be enjoined, not only to protect private rights or interests, but also the public interest in holding government accountable under the law? It is submitted that the answer to this question lies in the *Tamaki* and *MacLean* line of authority. As there is no evidence that the Crown proceedings legislation was designed to expand the Crown's common law immunity to include servants and agents, they should be treated differently from the Crown. Thus, they can be enjoined by injunctive relief personally in respect of civil wrongs or *ultra vires* acts committed by them in their official capacity. This principle should not significantly impair the functioning of government as the courts can be counted upon to give serious consideration to the public interest in applications for interim injunctive relief.

4. Declarations

(a) Nature of Declarations

A declaration, or declaratory judgment, is a judgment of a court of law which determines the legal position of the parties or the law applicable to them. It is an unusual remedy in that it is not coercive in nature as no consequential relief is granted.[393] As a result, there is no penalty or sanction to be imposed on a defendant for failing to act on the declaration. It can be contrasted with an executory judgment of a court, one in which "the court declares the respec-

---

390   Cane, *supra* note 388 at 252-55.

391   On one hand, this is not surprising given the state of the underlying common law. However, on the other, it is surprising as the courts, in the various jurisdictions, are engaged in the interpretation and application of, essentially, the same legislation in the context of the same structure of government.

392   In a similar vein, Binnie J. of the Supreme Court of Canada, held that the bar to injunctive relief in Manitoba's *Proceedings Against the Crown Act*, R.S.M. 1987, c. P140, s. 14 was overcome by the Court's power to grant a stay under its own legislation. See *M & D Farm Ltd. v. Manitoba Agricultural Credit Corp.*, [1998] 1 S.C.R. 1074 (S.C.C.).

393   Unless, of course, the action for a declaration is joined with a claim for injunctive relief or damages.

tive rights of parties and then proceeds to order the defendant to act in a certain way, for example, to pay damages or to refrain from interfering with the plaintiff's rights."[394] Non-compliance with such a judgment can lead to enforcement proceedings.

The courts' authority to grant declaratory relief, is of recent vintage. Until the mid-point of the 19th century, the authority of the courts to grant declarations *per se* was doubted.[395] Parliamentary attempts at reform[396] were largely nullified by judicial interpretation – declaratory judgments were only available if accompanied by a claim for consequential relief or, if not, only in those situations where the plaintiff was entitled to claim consequential relief. In 1873, with the transfer of Chancery's jurisdiction to all of the divisions of the High Court, the jurisdiction to grant declaratory relief was set out in the following terms:[397]

> No action or proceedings shall be open to objection on the ground that merely a declaratory judgment or order is sought thereby, and the court may make binding declarations of right whether any consequential relief is or could be claimed or not.

With their jurisdiction set in such broad, unlimited terms, and in the absence of any statutory guidelines to guide them in the exercise of this jurisdiction, the courts have enjoyed a wide discretion when granting declaratory relief. Even though they initially responded to their new jurisdiction with caution, the courts have subsequently come to embrace it as a flexible remedy suitable for use in a wide variety of circumstances.[398]

One of the more dramatic innovations in this regard has been the employment of the declaration as a remedy in public law. The leading authority in this regard is generally thought to be the case of *Dyson v. Attorney General.*[399] In that case, the Commissioners of Inland Revenue were authorized to obtain information from owners of land so that they could value land which was newly subject to tax. One of the demands made of land owners was for an annual statement as to the value of the land. This was not authorized by the Act. Dyson sought a declaration that the request was improper and that it was not authorized by the legislation. The Court of Appeal held that the proceedings were proper and granted the declarations sought.

The decision in *Dyson* was important in several respects. First, it settled that an action for a declaration was an appropriate response to illegal government action. The Court of Appeal found that a declaration was "the most

---

394 Zamir & Woolf, *The Declaratory Judgment*, 2d ed. (London: Sweet & Maxwell, 1993) at 10-12.

395 Craig, *supra* note 11 at 530; *ibid.* at 8.

396 *Chancery Act, 1850* followed by the *Chancery Procedures Act, 1852.*

397 R.S.C. Order 25, Rule 5. A similar rule has been adopted in all Canadian jurisdictions.

398 For a description of the wide range of circumstances in which courts are granting declaratory relief, see Zamir, *supra* note 394 and P.W. Young, *Declaratory Orders* (Sydney: Butterworths, 1975). See also *Kourtessis v. Minister of National Revenue*, [1993] 2 S.C.R. 53 at 85-86 (S.C.C.), per LaForest J.

399 (1910), [1911] 1 K.B. 410, [1912] 1 Ch. 158 (Eng. C.A.).

convenient method of enabling the subject to test the justifiability of proceedings on the part of permanent officials purporting to act under statutory provisions".[400] Secondly, an action for a declaration was accepted by the courts as an alternative and permissible means of determining the *vires* of government action. A private citizen did not have to wait for enforcement proceedings to be brought against him for non-compliance in order to raise the illegality of the official action as a defence. And finally, the case established that a declaration was an appropriate form of relief in a situation where the plaintiff had no other cause of action. *Dyson* had no other means available to him to challenge the validity of the government's demand.

Since that time, the declaration has become a popular remedy in public law. Courts and litigants alike have been attracted by its flexible nature and the absence of restrictive technical requirements. Declaratory relief can be granted by a court as an original remedy, a supervisory remedy or both. As an original remedy, a declaration is used to declare the rights of the plaintiff.[401] As a supervisory remedy, it is employed, in a more common fashion, to control the *ultra vires* acts or decisions of the defendant. In some instances, a court, in the exercise of its supervisory functions, can declare the impugned action to be *ultra vires*, and then, in the exercise of its original jurisdiction, can issue a declaration as to the rights of the parties.[402] In keeping with its flexible nature, declaratory relief can be cast in a number of forms.[403] Moreover, the fact that the remedy is not encrusted by technical requirements has led more and more litigants to resort to it as a means of judicial review. In this respect, the absence of coercive affect has not been seen as a problem in that it is expected that government and other public authorities will respect declaratory judgments of the courts.[404]

Declarations are chiefly used as a supervisory remedy in administrative law to challenge the legality of legislative or administrative action.[405] Indeed, a declaration may be the chief form of remedy when the constitutionality[406] or legality of primary or subordinate legislation is at issue.[407] As an alternate form of proceeding to an application for *certiorari* or prohibition, declarations also have commonly been used to challenge the legality of administrative action.

---

400   (1910), [1912] 1 Ch. 158 at 168 (Eng. C.A.) per Fletcher Moulton L.J.

401   See for example, *Glynos v. Canada* (1992), 96 D.L.R. (4th) 95 (Fed. C.A.).

402   Craig, *supra* note 11 at 592.

403   de Smith *et al.*, *supra* note 288 at 735-39.

404   *Lount Corp. v. Canada (Attorney General)*, *supra* note 334 at 365; *M. v. Home Office*, *supra* note 338 at 423.

405   In this respect, see generally, de Smith *et al.*, *supra* note 288 at 735-42. See also *S.E.G.U. v. Saskatchewan* (1997), 155 Sask. R. 161 (Sask. Q.B.), affirmed (1997), [1997] S.J. No. 277, 1997 CarswellSask 245 (Sask. C.A.).

406   See for example, *Irwin Toy Ltd. c. Québec (Procureur général)* (1989), 58 D.L.R. (4th) 577 (S.C.C.); *Gonzalez v. Canada (Employment & Immigration Commission)* (1997), 152 D.L.R. (4th) 703 (Fed. T.D.); *Singh v. Canada (Attorney General)*, [1999] 4 F.C. 583 (Fed. T.D.), affirmed [2000] 3 F.C. 185 (Fed. C.A.), leave to appeal refused (2000), 259 N.R. 400 (note) (S.C.C.).

407   See for example, *Chalmers v. Toronto Stock Exchange* (1989), 40 Admin. L.R. 311 (Ont. C.A.), leave to appeal refused (1990), 105 N.R. 398 (note) (S.C.C.); *Bass v. Pharmaceutical Assn. (British Columbia)* (1965), 54 W.W.R. 437 (B.C. C.A.).

Declaratory relief rather than the prerogative order of *certiorari* has been pursued for a number of reasons, including: the absence of a statutory limitation provision in the case of declarations; the ability to join a claim for declaratory relief with an action for an injunction or damages; the opportunity to conduct interlocutory proceedings such as pre-trial discovery and the availability of declaratory relief against private, non-statutory tribunals.[408] A declaration on its own may not be enough. If the applicant wishes to quash a decision of a tribunal or if he or she wishes to stop a tribunal from proceeding, a declaration will not help them.[409] An order in the nature of *certiorari* or prohibition may have to be sought instead. However, a declaration has the procedural advantage that there is no time limitation within which the action must be brought, unlike *certiorari* and prohibition. An action for a declaration also allows for the discovery of documents, which may bring facts to light not previously within the knowledge of the applicant.

Once the issue of *ultra vires* has been determined by the court, it becomes *res judicata* between the parties to the proceedings. If a tribunal continues to act in an unlawful manner, in the face of a declaration of *ultra vires*, then the applicant may safely refuse to comply with its direction or may seek to restrain the tribunal by other means. Moreover, continued *ultra vires* action by a public authority may result in an action for exemplary damages against it on the grounds of its wilful abuse of statutory authority.[410] Finally, it should be noted that a public authority may resort to a declaration itself. It may seek the assistance of a court when it is in doubt as to the extent of its jurisdiction or the nature of the obligations cast upon it by statute.[411]

(b) Procedures

Under the Alberta *Rules of Court*, there are three ways to apply for a declaration.

First, proceedings may be commenced under Rule 410 by originating notice in certain circumstances.[412] This is a chambers application, which has the advantage of speed but has the disadvantage of no pre-trial discovery. Evidence is led by way of affidavits, although the court may permit oral evidence.[413]

---

408   Some of these distinctions have been eliminated with the assimilation of both remedies into a single form of proceedings in some jurisdictions.

409   *Punton v. Ministry of Pensions & National Insurance (No. 2)* (1963) [1964] 1 W.L.R. 226 (Eng. C.A.); compare *Pyx Granite Co. v. Minister of Housing & Local Government* (1959), [1960] A.C. 260 (U.K. H.L.).

410   *LeBar v. Canada* (1988), [1988] F.C.J. No. 940, 1988 CarswellNat 735 (Fed. C.A.); exemplary damages were awarded against the Crown for the failure of a prison warden to release a prisoner whose sentence was completed, according to the decision of a court in a similar case involving another prisoner.

411   For example, *Toronto (City) v. 1291547 Ontario Inc.* (2000), 49 O.R. (3d) 709 (Ont. S.C.J.).

412   R. 410.

413   R. 407.

Secondly, a declaration can be sought as part of the single "application for judicial review".[414] This procedure has the advantage of permitting an application for a declaration to be joined with an application for any of the prerogative remedies or an injunction.

Thirdly, a regular action may be commenced by way of statement of claim which allows all the usual interlocutory steps leading to trial, but this process can take a long time before a final determination is reached.

(c) Availability

Given the flexible nature of the declaration, there are few limitations on its availability. When proceedings for a declaration are brought by way of action, the statutory body must have sufficient legal personality to be sued in its own right. For example, in *B. v. Canada (Department of Manpower & Immigration)*,[415] the Federal Court held that a declaration is not available against a federal board or tribunal unless its enabling legislation expressly states that it is a suable entity. Therefore, a declaratory judgment is not available against such a delegate, although it may be amenable to *certiorari* or prohibition.[416] It is also generally agreed that a declaration is not available to correct an error of law or fact committed *within* a tribunal's jurisdiction,[417] unless the error is found to be patently unreasonable.[418] In such an event, the only effective remedy would be *certiorari* to quash the decision of the tribunal, either because the tribunal exceeded its jurisdiction or erred in law within its jurisdiction.[419] The reason the court could not grant a declaration as to the applicant's rights in such a situation is that the tribunal has made an ostensibly binding decision which a declaration (unlike *certiorari*) will not set aside. As the fourth edition of de Smith observed, such a declaration would be objected to on the ground ". . . it was not for the court to arrogate to itself an appellate or quasi-original

---

414   See Part 56.1 of the Alberta *Rules of Court*, reproduced in Appendix 4; and the discussion in Chapter 15.

415   (1975), 60 D.L.R. (3d) 339 (Fed. T.D.).

416   With the assimilation of public and private law remedies (with the exception of damages) under a single form of proceeding, an application for judicial review, the issue of suable status may no longer be a problem when a declaration is sought by this procedure. See *Bingo Enterprises Ltd. v. Manitoba (Lotteries & Gaming Board)* (1983), 2 Admin. L.R. 286 (Man. C.A.) where the court held that an action for a declaration could not be sustained against the Board because it lacked suable status–an application for a declaration by way of an originating notice was seen to be an appropriate remedy. See also *Klymchuk v. Cowan* (1964), 47 W.W.R. 467 (Man. Q.B.), where the court granted declaratory relief on the basis that there was no other adequate remedy available, without considering the legal status of the defendant. See *supra* note 210.

417   Craig, *supra* note 11 at 532-33.

418   *Blanchard v. Control Data Canada Ltd.* (1984), 14 D.L.R. (4th) 289 (S.C.C.) because the tribunal's decision, although erroneous, was *intra vires*. See Chapter 11.

419   See Chapter 11 for a discussion of the anomalous use of *certiorari* to quash a decision for an intra-jurisdictional error of law.

jurisdiction and make a new determination inconsistent with a binding (although possibly erroneous) determination of the appointed tribunal."[420]

The original jurisdiction of a court to grant declaratory relief may also be excluded when the authority to deal with a particular question or issue is delegated to a statutory body. The question that arises: has the matter been assigned the exclusive jurisdiction of the delegate?[421] If not, then a court, rather than the delegate, may determine the issue by declaring the rights of the plaintiff. However, the courts are somewhat reluctant to permit a plaintiff to circumvent a prescribed statutory procedure by this means unless, under the circumstances, the declaration is seen to be the more appropriate remedy.[422] A court will not grant a declaration in a matter which is not justiciable. The question of justiciability involves a determination as to whether the dispute is suitable for resolution in the courts. Generally speaking, the courts will be opposed to claims based on moral and political grounds which are beyond the capacity of courts to assess. This limitation was reaffirmed by the Supreme Court of Canada in *Canada (Auditor General) v. Canada (Minister of Energy, Mines & Resources)*.[423] The case arose out of the Auditor General's unsuccessful efforts to gain access to cabinet documents and information in the hands of a Crown corporation. The requests for information were turned down and an application to the Federal Court for a declaration of entitlement to the documents was met by a claim of Crown privilege. The Supreme Court upheld the Federal Court of Appeal's decision to deny the application for a declaration. The Auditor General's claim of entitlement was not one capable of enforcement in the courts. The dispute was not justiciable and further, the Auditor General had an adequate alternate remedy through his report to Parliament.

As a discretionary remedy, a declaration will not be granted where the court is of the opinion that the claim was premature or the dispute is either academic or hypothetical.[424] This principle was reaffirmed by the Supreme

---

420   S.A. de Smith, *Judicial Review of Administrative Action*, 4th ed. (London: Stevens & Sons, 1980) at 520. The learned editors of the 5th ed. of de Smith take a more expansive view of the availability of a declaration in these circumstances: see Chapter 18; *Punton v. Ministry of Pensions & National Insurance (No. 2)*, *supra* note 409.

421   *Pyx Granite Co. v. Ministry of Housing & Local Government*, *supra* note 409.

422   Craig, *supra* note 11 at 533-34 and at 597-99. See also *Terrasses Zarolega Inc. c. Quebec (Olympic Installations Board)*, [1981] 1 S.C.R. 94 (S.C.C.).

423   (1989), 40 Admin. L.R. 1 (S.C.C.). The courts will also not grant a declaration where it would be a futile remedy, that is, where it would serve no useful purpose: *Heller v. Greater Vancouver (Regional District)* (1992), 94 D.L.R. (4th) 718 (B.C. C.A.), leave to appeal refused [1993] 2 S.C.R. viii (S.C.C.). See also *Black v. Canada (Prime Minister)* (2001), 199 D.L.R. (4th) 228 (Ont. C.A.); *Brown v. Alberta* (1999), 177 D.L.R. (4th) 349 (Alta. C.A.).

424   See for example, *Russian Commercial & Industrial Bank v. British Bank for Foreign Trade Ltd.*, [1921] 2 A.C. 438 (U.K. H.L.); *Sonego v. Ontario (Attorney General)* (1996), [1996] O.J. No. 3992, 1996 CarswellOnt 4245 (Ont. Gen. Div.); *Islands Protection Society v. R.* (1979), 98 D.L.R. (3d) 504 at 517, 523 (B.C. S.C.); *Western Canada Wilderness Committee v. Alberta (Provincial Treasurer)* (1993), 108 D.L.R. (4th) 495 (Alta. Q.B.); *Operation Dismantle Inc. v. R.*, [1985] 1 S.C.R. 441 (S.C.C.); *Cheslatta Carrier Nation v. British Columbia*, [2000] 10 W.W.R. 426 (B.C. C.A.), leave to appeal refused (2001), 273 N.R. 397 (note) (S.C.C.), but just because a challenge proceeding does not entail legal conse-

Court of Canada in *Solosky v. Canada*.[425] At issue was the right of a prisoner, in a federal penitentiary to correspond with his solicitor in confidence. His correspondence had been censored for some time pursuant to an order of the Director of the Institution. The Federal Court of Appeal[426] had denied the application for a declaration on the ground that it related to a future event (mail not yet written). While the Supreme Court of Canada dismissed the appeal on other grounds, it upheld the availability of a declaration as a remedy in a case like this. While the declaration sought may affect future rights, this did not mean that the dispute was hypothetical. The court was of the opinion that there was a real dispute, not merely a hypothetical one which might not arise.

Finally, it should be noted that the courts, may, in their discretion, refuse to grant declaratory relief if there exists an adequate, alternate remedy which the applicant ought to pursue.

(d) Crown Liability

The declaration has been viewed as a particularly useful remedy against the Crown. Due to the remedy's non-coercive nature, the problems of enforcement against the Crown or the Crown issuing commands to itself are avoided. As indicated before, the lack of coercive effect is not seen to be a problem as the Crown can be expected to comply with the judgments of the courts. On occasion, this expectation may be misplaced.[427]

A declaration can be obtained against the Crown in one of three ways. First a declaration may be sought by way of an action. Usually this occurs when the plaintiff wishes to join his or her claim for a declaration with a claim for either injunctive relief or damages or both. Prior to the enactment of Crown proceedings legislation, a declaration could be obtained against the Crown on the basis of the petition of right procedure.[428] With the abolition of that form of proceeding, a plaintiff could seek a declaratory judgment through an ordinary action against the Crown. No fiat consenting to the suit would be required.

In addition to the petition of right procedure, a declaration could be sought against the Crown on the basis of a procedure commonly known as the *Dyson* procedure. In *Dyson v. Attorney General*,[429] an action was brought against the Attorney General, seeking a declaration with respect to a request for tax information sent by revenue authorities to millions of citizens. The Attorney General responded by arguing that an action could not be maintained against him – the only permissible form of proceeding was a petition of right, which was subject

---

quences, does not mean that a court will not grant a declaration to protect the applicant from harm, *Morneault v. Canada (Attorney General)* (2000), [2001] 1 F.C. 30 (Fed. C.A.) (public inquiry entailed no legal consequences but hurt applicant's reputation).

425   (1979), [1980] 1 S.C.R. 821 (S.C.C.).

426   (1978), 86 D.L.R. (3d) 316 (Fed. C.A.), affirmed (1979), [1980] 1 S.C.R. 821 (S.C.C.).

427   *Peralta v. Ontario (Minister of Natural Resources)* (1984), 46 C.P.C. 218 (Ont. H.C.), leave to appeal to Ont. Div. Ct. refused (1984), 46 C.P.C. 218 at 229 (Ont. H.C.): government enforcement of fishing quotas declared to be *ultra vires*.

428   *De Keyser's Royal Hotel Ltd. v. R.*, [1919] 2 Ch. 197 (Eng. Ch. Div.), affirmed *Attorney General v. De Keyser's Royal Hotel Ltd.*, [1920] A.C. 508 (U.K. H.L.).

429   *Supra* note 399.

to his fiat. The court disagreed with the argument of the Attorney General and held that an action could be maintained against him.

At one time, the *Dyson* procedure was a great improvement on the petition of right proceeding because no fiat consenting to the action was required.[430] Now, with the abolition of the petition of right procedure, the question arises as to whether the *Dyson* procedure is required any longer. Probably not, unless there is some question about the suable status of the Crown agency or entity.[431]

A declaration can also be sought against the Crown in an application for judicial review.[432] This summary form of proceeding extends to claims for injunctions and declarations in public law matters. The distinction between public law and private law issues is a difficult one to make – and it has been a source of great controversy and unnecessary litigation in the United Kingdom.[433] To avoid that difficulty, the Alberta rules, governing applications for judicial review, have granted the court the discretion to determine whether the summary form of proceeding is appropriate given the circumstances of a particular case.

One of the problems in proceedings against the Crown is the lack of interim injunctive relief against the Crown or its servants. As related previously, courts have attempted to circumvent this immunity in a number of ways.[434] One of the devices utilized, from time to time, is an interim declaration to maintain the *status quo* until the issue can be conclusively determined.[435] The existence of such a remedy is strongly doubted by other authorities.[436]

---

430 Hogg and Monahan, *supra* note 5 at 27.

431 See the discussion in note 210.

432 Alberta *Rules of Court*, R. 753.04. See Chapter 15; *Associated Respiratory Services Inc. v. British Columbia (Purchasing Commission)* (1994), 87 B.C.L.R. (2d) 70 (B.C. C.A.), additional reasons at (1994), 95 B.C.L.R. (2d) 357 (B.C. C.A.), leave to appeal refused (1995), 192 N.R. 78 (note) (S.C.C.). See also *Masters v. Ontario* (1993), 18 Admin. L.R. (2d) 179 (Ont. Div. Ct.), affirmed (1994), 27 Admin. L.R. (2d) 152 (Ont. Div. Ct.), where the court dismissed an application for a declaration on the grounds that the impugned actions of government did not involve the exercise of a statutory power.

433 *O'Reilly v. Mackman*, [1982] 3 All E.R. 1124 (U.K. H.L.).

434 See section 3(g) of this chapter, above.

435 For an example of this, see the judgment of the Saskatchewan Court of Appeal in *Wittal v. Saskatchewan Government Insurance*, [1988] 5 W.W.R. 616 (Sask. C.A.); *Ollinger v. Saskatchewan Crop Insurance Corp.*, [1992] 4 W.W.R. 517 (Sask. Q.B.), reversed [1993] 4 W.W.R. 665 (Sask. C.A.); and *Loomis v. Ontario (Minister of Agriculture & Food)* (1993), 16 O.R. (3d) 188 (Ont. Div. Ct.) where the Divisional Court held that, as a general rule, interim injunctions and declarations could not be granted against the Crown. However, this rule is subject to an exception: an interim declaration can be granted where there is evidence of deliberate flouting of established law by a government authority. It is to be noted that such an exception would not be required if the standard "no injunction" provision was narrowly construed.

436 It is generally accepted that an interim declaration does not exist. See *International General Electric (New York) v. Customs Excise Commissioner*, [1962] 1 Ch. 784 (Eng. C.A.); *Inland Revenue Commissioners v. Rossminster Ltd.* (1979), [1980] A.C. 952 (U.K. H.L.) at 1000 and 1027; *Shaw v. R.* (1982), 140 D.L.R. (3d) 178 (B.C. S.C.). For a contrary view, see, Prentice, "Crown Immunity–A New Look at the Availability of Interim Declaratory Relief Against the Crown" in Legal Education Society of Alberta, Dealing With Government Boards and Agencies (1997). For more recent authorities, see *Te'Mexw Treaty Assn. v. W.L.C. Developments Ltd.* (1998), 163 D.L.R. (4th) 180 (B.C. S.C.); *Bush v. Saskatchewan*

(d) *Locus Standi*

Standing is a complex subject, worthy of separate treatment and consideration.[437] Historically, the rules of standing with respect to the private law remedies of declaration and injunction have been more restrictive than those associated with the public law remedies such as *certiorari*. This reflects the origin of the former remedies; they have existed to vindicate private rights, not public rights. Accordingly, the circumstances in which an individual can seek an injunction or a declaration to redress illegal government action have been narrowly construed. Traditionally, in order to seek injunctive or declaratory relief, an applicant had to establish that the official action complained of interfered with a private right of the applicant or, failing that, that the interference with a public right caused the applicant special damage.[438] However, the applicant for a declaration did not have to establish that the action complained of constituted an independent cause of action, such as a tort or a breach of contract.

This restrictive view of standing did not hinder those who could point to a direct interference with their private legal rights but it did create a real obstacle for those who wished to challenge, in the public interest, the legality of government action. In such a case, the plaintiff had to establish that he or she suffered particular harm, over and above that suffered by the general community, in order to invoke the jurisdiction of the court to grant declaratory or injunctive relief. If the plaintiff was unable to establish particular harm, he or she would have to seek the assistance of the Attorney General in vindicating the public interest. The Attorney General could act on his or her own motion or could lend his or her name or standing to a private person in a relator action. Thus the public interest in controlling illegal government action was effectively left in the hands of the Attorney General.

In recent years, the traditional rules have changed as the English and Canadian courts have taken a more liberal approach to the question of standing. This liberalization can be attributed to a heightened judicial awareness of the interest of citizens in the vindication of public rights. In the United Kingdom, a change in the standing requirements for injunctions and declarations was prompted by earlier liberalization of standing rules for the prerogative remedies. Accordingly, an individual would have sufficient standing to seek declaratory or injunctive relief if he or she were found to have "sufficient interest" in the matter.[439] In Canada, the liberalization of standing requirements for

---

(Minister of Environment & Resource Management) (1994), 119 Sask. R. 180 (Sask. Q.B.); *Ochapowace Indian Band No. 71 v. Canada (Department of Indian Affairs & Northern Development)* (1998), 167 Sask. R. 167 (Sask. Q.B.); *Volansky v. British Columbia (Minister of Transportation)* (2002), 41 Admin. L.R. (3d) 300 (B.C. S.C.), additional reasons at 2002 BCSC 591 (B.C. S.C.).

437 See T. Cromwell, *Locus Standi: A Commentary on the Law of Standing in Canada* (Toronto: Carswell, 1986).

438 *Boyce v. Paddington Borough Council* (1902), [1903] 1 Ch. 109 (Eng. Ch. Div.), reversed [1903] 2 Ch. 556 (Eng. C.A.). reversed (1905), [1906] A.C. 1 (U.K. H.L.).

439 *Inland Revenue Commissioners v. National Federation of Self-Employed & Small Businesses Ltd.* (1981), [1982] A.C. 617 (U.K. H.L.).

injunctions and declarations in public law matters was prompted by the recognition of "public interest" standing in cases involving challenges to the
constitutionality of legislation.

The first of these cases, *Thorson v. Canada (Attorney General) (No. 2)*[440]
involved a constitutional challenge, by a taxpayer, to the federal *Official Lan-
guages Act*.[441] The right of the taxpayer to seek a declaration of invalidity was
upheld even though no private interest of his was violated and he could not
point to any special damage. In its discretion, the court accorded the applicant
public interest standing as the issue was justiciable and as the legislation
similarly affected all members of the public and not just a particular person or
class of persons. Moreover, the court was satisfied that there was no other way
to test the validity of the legislation in court. Similarly, in *MacNeil v. Nova
Scotia (Board of Censors)*,[442] the court recognized the standing of a citizen to
seek a declaration of *ultra vires* with respect to provincial legislation which
authorized the censorship of movies. The applicant was accorded public interest standing as he did not meet the traditional requirements for standing. He
was not a theatre owner, nor could he establish that this regulatory legislation
interfered with his public rights. Finally, in *Borowski v. Canada (Minister of
Justice)*,[443] the Supreme Court held that a private citizen had sufficient standing
to challenge the therapeutic abortion provisions of the *Criminal Code* on the
basis that they were contrary to the *Canadian Bill of Rights*. In these cases, the
Supreme Court of Canada developed a broadly based concept of public interest
standing for use in constitutional challenges to legislation. The recognition of
public interest standing, in a particular case, lay in the discretion of the court.

In granting such status, a court must be satisfied that: there is a serious
issue as to the constitutionality of the legislation; the applicant has a genuine
interest in the validity of the legislation; and there is no other reasonable or
effective way of bringing the issue of validity before the court.[444] Further, the
court appeared to be satisfied that this broadly-based concept of standing would
not tax scarce judicial resources by opening the floodgates of litigation. Any
such concerns could be met through the exercise of judicial discretion and,
further, costs could be awarded against applicants, when necessary, to deter
frivolous and vexatious actions.

As this line of authority was concerned with the public interest in the
constitutionality of legislation and the need, in a federal state, to provide access
to the courts to determine issues of constitutionality, there was some question
as to whether the concept of public interest standing would be recognized in
cases involving non-constitutional challenges to administrative action. This
issue was addressed by the Supreme Court of Canada in *Finlay v. Canada
(Minister of Finance)*.[445] At issue was the legality of payments made by the
federal government to the Province of Manitoba under a cost-sharing agree-

---

440 (1974), [1975] 1 S.C.R. 138 (S.C.C.).
441 Then R.S.C. 1970, c. 0-2.
442 (1975), [1976] 2 S.C.R. 265 (S.C.C.).
443 [1981] 2 S.C.R. 575 (S.C.C.).
444 *Ibid.* at 598.
445 [1986] 2 S.C.R. 607 (S.C.C.).

ment. The applicant, a recipient of provincial social assistance, sought a declaration to the effect that these payments were *ultra vires*. Specifically, he argued that the payments were unauthorized under the federal legislation as the province, in implementing the scheme for which the funds were provided, had failed to comply with the conditions imposed by this legislation. The government, in return, argued that the applicant lacked the standing to seek a declaration of invalidity.

To begin with, the Supreme Court held that the applicant did not meet the traditional standing requirements for declaratory or injunctive relief where public rights or wrongs were in issue. While the applicant was the recipient of social assistance from the province, it could not be said he had a direct, personal interest in the legality of the federal payments to the province – there was no nexus between the illegality of the payments and any harm suffered by the applicant.

Nevertheless, on the basis of public interest standing, the Supreme Court exercised its discretion to recognize the status of the applicant to seek a declaration. The public interest in holding the administration to the limits of its lawful authority was seen to be as great as the public interest in holding the legislature to the limits of its constitutional authority. The same policy considerations which supported the recognition of public interest standing in constitutional matters would also support the recognition of public interest standing in a case such as this involving a challenge to the *vires* of administrative action. The challenge to the legality of the federal government's action raised a justiciable issue – a question of law which could be determined by the courts, even though the Supreme Court acknowledged that the issue of provincial compliance with federal cost-sharing arrangements might sometimes raise issues which are inappropriate for judicial resolution. Further, the applicant raised a serious issue in which he had a genuine interest – as a person in need, in receipt of social assistance, he could not be regarded as a mere busybody. And finally, the court was satisfied that the issue of legality was raised by someone with a direct interest in its resolution – indeed, it could not be said that anyone possessed a more direct interest.

For our purposes, the chief significance of *Finlay* lies in the recognition of a broader, discretionary concept of public interest standing in non-constitutional challenges to administrative action. This broader notion of standing would encapsulate both of the private law remedies: injunctions and declarations.[446] A more liberal standing requirement for these remedies, when sought in a public law context seems both sensible and justifiable, given the fundamentally different task of remedies in public law – not only do they serve to protect private interest from *ultra vires* government action but they also serve to vindicate the public interest in holding government to the legal limits of its powers.[447]

---

446   *Ibid.* at 635.
447   It should be noted that the Supreme Court has indicated that there are some limits on public interest standing. Such standing will be denied where there is a strong possibility that the impugned government action will be subject to attack by a private litigant. See: *Canadian Council of Churches v. R.* (1992), 132 N.R. 241 (S.C.C.); J. Ross, "*Canadian Council of*

(f) Relator Actions

The problem of standing can be solved by the use of the relator action. This is an action for a declaration or an injunction or both brought in the name of the Attorney General at the relation of an individual. It allows a private individual to have standing in a matter of general public interest where standing would otherwise be denied to him or her because no personal legal right of his or hers was affected. The courts cannot inquire into why the Attorney General has lent its name in any given case,[448] nor why it has refused.[449] It is a matter entirely within its discretion. However, where the Attorney General has refused to lend its name in a matter where the applicant cannot demonstrate a personal legal right, the courts have sometimes asserted their discretion to give standing to a private individual because otherwise allegedly illegal governmental action would go unchecked.[450] In such cases, the discretion of the court to refuse standing is sufficient to prevent a proliferation of unworthy actions.

Having lent its name, the Attorney General then leaves the carriage of the proceedings to the relator, who is responsible for costs and for all other aspects of the litigation as if it were a private suit.

5. Conclusion

The purpose of this chapter has been to outline the role played by private law remedies in administrative law. Even though these remedies were at one time accorded secondary status, it is clear that they are now indispensable tools for controlling unlawful governmental action. As a result, a citizen affected by illegal governmental action is afforded more comprehensive and flexible means of redress.

Damages are now available to a greater number of citizens injured through governmental action or inaction, largely because the negligence liability of public authorities (including the Crown) has expanded. In Canada, the courts have accepted the broad and flexible approach of the *Anns* formulation to the duty issue although the reformulation of this approach may be a signal that the courts will be more protective of government. Nevertheless, Canadian courts have extended the reach of negligence liability to governmental activities which have no private analogue. These decisions, in turn, will serve as an analogy for other claims. Under *Anns* the courts have recognized that some government decision-making should be protected from judicial scrutiny in a negligence action due to its non-justiciable nature. Unfortunately, there is an

---

Churches v. The Queen, Public Interest Standing Takes a Back Seat" (1992) 3 Constitutional Forum 100.

448 *London County Council v. Attorney General*, [1902] A.C. 165 (U.K. H.L.).

449 *Attorney General v. Independent Broadcasting Authority*, [1973] Q.B. 629 (Eng. C.A.); *Gouriet v. Union of Post Office Workers* (1977), [1978] A.C. 435 (U.K. H.L.). The House of Lords' latest pronouncement on standing can be found in *Inland Revenue Commissioners v. National Federation of Self-Employed & Small Businesses Ltd.* (1981), [1982] A.C. 617 (U.K. H.L.).

450 *Thorson v. Canada (Attorney General) (No. 2)* (1974), 43 D.L.R. (3d) 1 (S.C.C.).

imprecise distinction between the policy and operational aspects of a public authority's activities. While the distinction is difficult to draw in individual cases, it does permit a remedy for careless government action in an increasing number of situations while respecting the unique role played by government in society. In the end result, the degree to which government should bear responsibility for the harmful consequences of its actions is a question of policy, which will vary from circumstance to circumstance. The law, as a result, must be in a state of some uncertainty.

Government will also be held responsible for intentional and abusive misconduct. The emerging tort of misfeasance in a public office promises to provide an injured citizen with a remedy in damages when a public officer acts with malice or intentionally acts in an *ultra vires* manner. While the scope of this action is far from settled, it should serve to deter deliberate official misconduct. Moreover, a citizen may be able to seek a remedy in damages when government action violates constitutional rights.

The private law remedy of injunction has enabled citizens to respond more effectively to unlawful government action or inaction. A prohibitory injunction is available to restrain a public authority which acts (or threatens to act) in an *ultra vires* manner. A mandatory injunction will lie in a narrow range of circumstances to compel government to act lawfully. While there is an obvious overlap between mandatory and prohibitory forms of injunctive relief (on one hand), and the prerogative remedies of mandamus and prohibition (on the other), the use of injunctions has served to supplement the relief offered by the prerogative remedies. For example, injunctions are available against a wider range of public actors, and also offer a means for interim relief. Unfortunately, neither permanent nor interim injunctions are available against the Crown. This significant limitation on the scope of injunctive relief has resulted in a complex and often confusing body of case law which reflects either a literal application of the legislation or a strong attempt to restrict its scope. As either a matter of principle or policy, the Crown's immunity from injunctive relief is questionable, particularly in relation to agents of the Crown or servants of the Crown when they act, or threaten to act, in a wrongful or unlawful manner.

Finally, the declaration offers an efficient and effective means of remedy against *ultra vires* action by governmental authorities of all kinds, including the Crown. The courts can declare governmental action to be *ultra vires* if the actual or proposed conduct is unauthorized by law, or the courts can make an authoritative and binding decision declaratory of the rights of the parties. The non-coercive nature of the remedy has not proven to be a problem. There are few technical requirements associated with declarations, which are therefore available in a number of situations where the prerogative remedies would not lie. The usefulness of declarations has been increased by the recent recognition of public interest standing in constitutional and non-constitutional challenges to government action, which recognizes the need for a remedy to vindicate the public interest in lawful government action.

6. Selected Bibliography

General

Brown, D.J.M. & Evans, J.M. (The Hon.), *Judicial Review of Administrative Action in Canada*, (looseleaf) (Toronto: Canvasback Publishing, 1998).

Craig, P.P., *Administrative Law*, 5th ed. (Toronto: Carswell, 2003).

Cromwell, T.A., *Locus Standi: A Commentary on the Law of Standing in Canada*, (Toronto: Carswell, 1986).

Dussault, R. and Bourgeat L., *Administrative Law: A Treatise*, 2d ed. (Toronto: Carswell, 1986) translated by M. Rankin.

de Smith, S.A., Woolf, Lord & Jowell J., *Judicial Review of Administrative Action*, 5th ed. (London: Sweet & Maxwell, 1995).

English Law Reform Commission, Report No. 73 on *Remedies in Administrative Law*, 1976, Cmnd. 6407.

Evans, J., "Developments in Administrative Law: The 1986-87 Term" (1988) 10 Sup. Ct. L. Rev. 1.

Jack, D.H., "Suing the Crown and the Applications of the *Charter*" (1986-87) 7 Adv. Q. 277.

Klar, L., *Tort Law*, 3d ed. (Toronto: Carswell, 2003).

Lorden, P., *Crown Law* (Toronto: Butterworths, 1991).

Stein, L.A., (ed.) *Locus Standi* (Sydney: The Law Book Company, 1979).

Damages

Aronson, M. and Whitmore H., *Public Torts and Contracts* (Sydney: The Law Book Company, 1982).

Bailey, S.H. and Bowman, M.J., "Public Authority Negligence Revisited" (2000) 59 Cambridge Law Journal, 85.

Borchard, E.M., "Governmental Responsibility in Tort" (1926-27) 36 Yale L.J. 1.

Bridge, M.G., "Governmental Liability, The Tort of Negligence and The House of Lords' Decision in *Anns v. Merton London Borough Council*" (1978) 24 McGill L.J. 277.

Buckley, R.A., "Liability in Tort for Breach of Statutory Duty" (1984) 100 L.Q. Rev. 204.

Cohen, D., and Smith J. C., "Entitlement and the Body Politic: Rethinking Negligence in Public Law" (1986) 64 Can. Bar Rev. 1

Cohen, D. "Suing the State" (1990) 40 U. of T. L.J. 630.

Cohen, D. "Government Liability for Economic Losses; The Case of Regulatory Failure" (1992) 20 Can. Bus. L.J. 215.

Cooper-Stephenson K.D., "Tort Theory for the Charter Damages Remedy" (1988) 59 Sask. L.Rev. 1.

Cooper-Stephenson K.D., *Charter Damages Claims* (Calgary: Carswell, 1990).

Craig, P.P., "Negligence in the Exercise of Statutory Power" (1978) 94 L.Q. Rev. 428.

Dussault, R., and Carrier, D., "Le contrat administratif en droit canadien et québécois" (1970) 48 Can. Bar Rev. 439.

English Law Commission, Working Paper No. 40, *Remedies in Administrative Law* (1971).

English Law Commission, Report No. 73, on *Remedies in Administrative Law*, 1976, Cmnd. 6407.

Ganz, G., "Compensation for Negligent Administrative Action" [1973] P.L. 85.

Goldenberg, S.L., "Tort Actions Against the Crown in Ontario" (1973) *L.S.U.C. Special Lectures* 341.

Gould, B.C., "Damages as a Remedy in Administrative Law" (1972-73) 5 N.Z.U.L. Rev. 105.

Harlow, C., *Compensation and Government Torts* (London: Sweet & Maxwell, 1982).

Hogg, P.W., *Liability of the Crown*, 2d ed. (Toronto: Carswell, 1989).

Hogg, P.W. & Monahan P., *Liability of The Crown*, 3rd ed. (Toronto: Carswell, Thompson, 2000).

Hogg, P.W., "Government Liability: Assimilating Crown and Subject" (1994) 16 Advocates Q. 366.

Irvine, J., "Misfeasance in Public Office: Reflections on Some Recent Developments" (2002) 9 C.C.L.T. (3d) 26.

Jamieson, D.P., "Proceedings By and Against the Crown in Canada" (1948) 26 Can. Bar Rev. 373.

Kennedy, W.P.M., "Suits by and Against the Crown" (1928) 6 Can. Bar Rev. 387.

Klar, L.N., *Tort Law*, 3d ed. (Toronto: Carswell 2003).

Klar, L.N., "The Supreme Court of Canada: Extending the Tort Liability of Public Authorities" (1990) 28 Alta. L.R. 648.

Klar, L.N., "Falling Boulders, Falling Trees and Icy Highways: The Policy/Operational Test Revisited" (1994) 33 Alta. L.R. 167.

Kneebone, S., *Tort Liability of Public Authorities*, (North Ryde, L.B.C. Information Services, 1998).

Laskin, B., "Crown Companies and Civil Liability" (1944) 22 Can. Bar Rev. 927.

Law, J.M., "Damages in Administrative Law – An Old Remedy with New Potential", prepared for the Administrative Law Seminar jointly sponsored by the Faculty of Law at the University of Alberta and the Legal Education Society of Alberta, March 1984.

Law, J.M., "A Tale of Two Immunities" (1990) 28 Alta. L.R. 468.

Law Reform Commission of British Columbia, *Report on Civil Rights, Part I*, "Legal Position of the Crown", 1972.

Law Reform Commission of Canada, *Legal Status of the Federal Administration*, Working Paper 40, 1985.

Linden, A.M., "Public Law and Private Law: The Frontier from the Perspective of a Tort Teacher" (1976) 17 Cahiers de Droit 865.

McBride, J., "Damages as a Remedy for Unlawful Administrative Action" (1979) 38 C.L.J. 323.

Molot, H.L., "Administrative Bodies, Economic Loss, and Tortious Liability", c. 12 in Fridman, G.H.L., *Studies in Canadian Business Law*, (Toronto: Butterworths, 1971).

Moore, W.H., "Misfeasance and Nonfeasance in the Liability of Public Authorities" (1914) 30 L.Q. Rev. 415.

Mueller, W.H.O., "The Liability of the Ontario Government in Tort" (1967) 25 U.T. Fac. L. Rev. 3.

Perrell, P.M., "Negligence Claims Against Public Authorities" (1994) 16 Advocates Quarterly 48.

Phegan, C.S., "Damages for Improper Exercise of Statutory Powers" (1980) 9 Sydney L. Rev. 93.

Rubinstein, A., "Liability in Tort of Judicial Officers" (1963-64) U.T.L.J. 317.

Slutsky, B., "The Liability of Public Authorities for Negligence: Recent Canadian Developments" (1973) 36 Mod. L. Rev. 656.

Smith, A., "Liability to Suit of an Agent of the Crown" (1950) U.T.L.J. 218.

Street, H., *Governmental Liability: A Comparative Study* (Hamden: Archon, 1975).

Todd S., "The Negligence Liability of Public Authorities" (1986) 102 L.Q.R. 370.

Williams, G., *Crown Proceedings, an Account of Civil Proceedings by and against the Crown as Affected by the Crown* (London: Stevens, 1948).

Injunctions

Adler J., "Public and Private Remedies against the Crown and its Servants: The Question of Interim Relief" (1986) 5 Civ. J. Q. 218.

Harris B.V., "Interim Relief against the Crown" (1981-84) 5 Otago L.R. 92.

Matthews, M.H., "Injunctions, Interim Relief and Proceedings against Crown Servants" [1988] 8 Oxford Journal of Legal Studies 154.

Sharpe, R., *Injunctions and Specific Performance*, 2d ed. (Toronto: Canada Law Book Company; 1996), (looseleaf edition).

Strayer, B., "Injunctions Against Crown Officers" (1964) 42 Can. Bar Rev. 1.

Tokar, J., "Administrative Law: Injunctive Relief against the Crown" (1985) 15 Man. L.J. 97.

Wade, H.W.R., "Injunctive Relief Against the Crown and Ministers" (1991) 107 L.Q.R. 4.

Declarations

Mullan, D.J., "The Declaratory Judgment: Its Place as an Administrative Law Remedy in Nova Scotia" (1975) 2 Dal. L.J. 91.

Warren, D.T., "The Declaratory Judgment: Reviewing Administrative Action" (1966) 44 Can. Bar Rev. 610.

Young, P.W., *Declaratory Orders* (Sydney: Butterworths, 1975).

Zamir, I., *The Declaratory Judgment* (London: Stevens, 1962).

Appendix 1

Alberta
Administrative Procedures Act
R.S.A. 2000, c. A-3

HER MAJESTY, by and with the advice and consent of the Legislative Assembly of Alberta, enacts as follows:

Definitions

1 In this Act,

    (a) "authority" means a person authorized to exercise a statutory power;

    (b) "party" means a person whose rights will be varied or affected by the exercise of a statutory power or by an act or thing done pursuant to that power;

    (c) "statutory power" means an administrative, quasi-judicial or judicial power conferred by statute, other than a power conferred on a court of record of civil or criminal jurisdiction or a power to make regulations, and for greater certainty, but without restricting the generality of the foregoing, includes a power

        (i) to grant, suspend or revoke a charter or letters patent,

        (ii) to grant, renew, refuse, suspend or revoke a permission to do an act or thing which, but for the permission, would be unlawful, whether the permission is called a licence or permit or certificate or is in any other form,

        (iii) to declare or establish a status provided for under a statute for a person and to suspend or revoke that status,

        (iv) to approve or authorize the doing or omission by a person of an act or thing that, but for the approval or authorization, would be unlawful or unauthorized,

        (v) to declare or establish a right or duty of a person under a statute, whether in a dispute with another person or otherwise, or

        (vi) to make an order, decision, direction or finding prohibiting a person from doing an act or thing that, but for the order, decision, direction or finding, it would be lawful for the person to do,

or any combination of those powers. [R.S.A. 1980, c. A-2, s.1]

Application of Act

2 The Lieutenant Governor in Council may, by order,

    (a) designate any authority as an authority to which this Act applies in whole or in part,

    (b) designate the statutory power of the authority in respect of which this Act applies in whole or in part, and

    (c) designate the provisions of this Act which are applicable to the authority in the exercise of that statutory power, and the extent to which they apply,

and this Act only applies to an authority to the extent ordered under this section. [R.S.A. 1980. c. . A-2. s. 2]

Notice to parties

3 When

    (a) an application is made to an authority, or

    (b) an authority on its own initiative proposes

to exercise a statutory power, the authority shall give to all parties adequate notice of the application which it has before it or of the power which it intends to exercise. [R.S.A. 1980, c. . A-2, s. 3]

Evidence and representations

4 Before an authority, in the exercise of a statutory power, refuses the application of or makes a decision or order adversely affecting the rights of a party, the authority

    (a) shall give the party a reasonable opportunity of furnishing relevant evidence to the authority,

    (b) shall inform the party of the facts in its possession or the allegations made to it contrary to the interests of the party in sufficient detail

        (i) to permit the party to understand the facts or allegations, and

        (ii) to afford the party a reasonable opportunity to furnish relevant evidence to contradict or explain the facts or allegations,

and

    (c) shall give the party an adequate opportunity of making representations by way of argument to the authority. [R.S.A 1980, c. A-2, s. 4]

Cross-examination

5 When an authority has informed a party of facts or allegations and that party

(a) is entitled under section 4 to contradict or explain them, but

(b) will not have a fair opportunity of doing so without cross-examination of the person making the statements that constitute the facts or allegations,

the authority shall afford the party an opportunity of cross-examination in the presence of the authority or of a person authorized to hear or take evidence for the authority. [R.S.A. 1980, c. A-2, s. 5]

When certain representations not permitted

6 Where by this Act a party is entitled to make representations to an authority with respect to the exercise of a statutory power, the authority is not by this Act required to afford an opportunity to the party

(a) to make oral representations, or

(b) to be represented by counsel,

if the authority affords the party an opportunity to make representations adequately in writing, but nothing in this Act deprives a party of a right conferred by any other Act to make oral representations or to be represented by counsel. [R.S.A. 1980, c. A-2, s. 6]

Written decisions with reasons

7 When an authority exercises a statutory power so as to adversely affect the rights of a party, the authority shall furnish to each party a written statement of its decision setting out

(a) the findings of fact on which it based its decision, and

(b) the reasons for the decision. [R.S.A. 1980, c. A-2, s. 7]

Requirements of other Acts

8 Nothing in this Act relieves an authority from complying with any procedure to be followed by it under any other Act relating to the exercise of its statutory power. [R.S.A. 1980, c. A-2, s. 8]

Rules of evidence

9 Nothing in this Act

(a) requires that any evidence or allegations of fact made to an authority be made under oath, or

(b) requires any authority to adhere to the rules of evidence applicable to courts of civil or criminal jurisdiction. [R.S.A. 1980, c. A-2, s. 9]

Regulations

10 The Lieutenant Governor in Council may make regulations

(a) to prescribe the length of time that is reasonable for the giving of a notice in accordance with this Act, with respect to authorities generally or with respect to a specified authority;

(b) to prescribe forms of notices for the purposes of this Act;

(c) to carry into effect the purposes of this Act. [R.S.A. 1980, c. A-2, s. 10]

Appendix 2

Ontario
Statutory Powers Procedure Act
R.S.O. 1990, c. S.22

Interpretation

1. (1) In this Act,

"electronic hearing" means a hearing held by conference telephone or some other form of electronic technology allowing persons to hear one another; ("audience électronique")

"hearing" means a hearing in any proceeding; ("audience")

"licence" includes any permit, certificate, approval, registration or similar form of permission required by law; ("autorisation")

"municipality" has the same meaning as in the *Municipal Affairs Act*; ("municipalité")

"oral hearing" means a hearing at which the parties or their counsel or agents attend before the tribunal in person; ("audience orale")

"proceeding" means a proceeding to which this Act applies; ("instance")

"statutory power of decision" means a power or right, conferred by or under a statute, to make a decision deciding or prescribing,

(a) the legal rights, powers, privileges, immunities, duties or liabilities of any person or party, or

(b) the eligibility of any person or party to receive, or to the continuation of, a benefit or licence, whether the person is legally entitled thereto or not; ("compétence légale de décision")

"tribunal" means one or more persons, whether or not incorporated and however described, upon which a statutory power of decision is conferred by or under a statute; ("tribunal")

"written hearing" means a hearing held by means of the exchange of documents, whether in written form or by electronic means. ("audience écrite") R.S.O. 1990, c. S.22, s. 1 (1); 1994, c. 27, s. 56 (1-3); 2002, c. 17, Sched. F, Table.

(2) **Meaning of "person" extended**—A municipality, an unincorporated association of employers, a trade union or council of trade unions who may be a party to a proceeding in the exercise of a statutory power of decision under the statute conferring the power shall be deemed to be a person for the purpose of any provision of this Act or of any rule made under this Act that applies to parties. R.S.O. 1990, c. S.22, s. 1 (2).

2. Liberal construction of Act and rules—This Act, and any rule made by a tribunal under section 25.1, shall be liberally construed to secure the just, most expeditious and cost-effective determination of every proceeding on its merits. 1999, c. 12, Sched. B, s. 16 (1).

3. (1) **Application of Act**—Subject to subsection (2), this Act applies to a proceeding by a tribunal in the exercise of a statutory power of decision conferred by or under an Act of the Legislature, where the tribunal is required by or under such Act or otherwise by law to hold or to afford to the parties to the proceeding an opportunity for a hearing before making a decision. R.S.O. 1990, c. S.22, s. 3 (1); 1994, c. 27, s. 56 (5).

(2) **Where Act does not apply**—This Act does not apply to a proceeding,

(a) before the Assembly or any committee of the Assembly;

(b) in or before,

   (i)   the Court of Appeal,

   (ii) the Ontario Court (General Division),

   (iii) the Ontario Court (Provincial Division),

   (iv) the Unified Family Court,

   (v)   the Small Claims Court, or

   (vi) a justice of the peace;

(c) to which the Rules of Civil Procedure apply;

(d) before an arbitrator to which the *Arbitrations Act* or the *Labour Relations Act* applies;

(e) at a coroner's inquest;

(f) of a commission appointed under the *Public Inquiries Act*;

(g) of one or more persons required to make an investigation and to make a report, with or without recommendations, where the report is for the information or advice of the person to whom it is made and does not in any way legally bind or limit that person in any decision he or she may have power to make; or

(h) of a tribunal empowered to make regulations, rules or by-laws in so far as its power to make regulations, rules or by-laws is concerned. R.S.O. 1990, c. S.22, s. 3 (2); 1994, c. 27, s. 56 (6).

4. (1) **Waiver of procedural requirement**—Any procedural requirement of this Act, or of another Act or a regulation that applies to a proceeding, may be waived with the consent of the parties and the tribunal. 1997, c. 23, s. 13 (1).

(2) **Same, rules**—Any provision of a tribunal's rules made under section 25.1 may be waived in accordance with the rules. 1994, c. 27, s. 56 (7).

4.1 Disposition without hearing—If the parties consent, a proceeding may be disposed of by a decision of the tribunal given without a hearing, unless another Act or a regulation that applies to the proceeding provides otherwise. 1997, c. 23, s. 13 (2).

4.2 (1) **Panels, certain matters**—A procedural or interlocutory matter in a proceeding may be heard and determined by a panel consisting of one or more members of the tribunal, as assigned by the chair of the tribunal. 1994, c. 27, s. 56 (8).

(2) **Assignments**—In assigning members of the tribunal to a panel, the chair shall take into consideration any requirement imposed by another Act or a regulation that applies to the proceeding that the tribunal be representative of specific interests. 1997, c. 23, s. 13 (3).

(3) **Decision of panel**—The decision of a majority of the members of a panel, or their unanimous decision in the case of a two-member panel, is the tribunal's decision. 1994, c. 27, s. 56 (8).

4.2.1 (1) **Panel of one, reduced panel**—**Panel of one**—The chair of a tribunal may decide that a proceeding be heard by a panel of one person

and assign the person to hear the proceeding unless there is a statutory requirement in another Act that the proceeding be heard by a panel of more than one person.

(2) **Reduction in number of panel members**—Where there is a statutory requirement in another Act that a proceeding be heard by a panel of a specified number of persons, the chair of the tribunal may assign to the panel one person or any lesser number of persons than the number specified in the other Act if all parties to the proceeding consent. 1999, c. 12, Sched. B, s. 16 (2).

4.3 Expiry of term—If the term of office of a member of a tribunal who has participated in a hearing expires before a decision is given, the term shall be deemed to continue, but only for the purpose of participating in the decision and for no other purpose. 1997, c. 23, s. 13 (4).

4.4 (1) **Incapacity of member**—If a member of a tribunal who has participated in a hearing becomes unable, for any reason, to complete the hearing or to participate in the decision, the remaining member or members may complete the hearing and give a decision. 1994, c. 27, s. 56 (9).

(2) **Other Acts and regulations**—Subsection (1) does not apply if another Act or a regulation specifically deals with the issue of what takes place in the circumstances described in subsection (1). 1997, c. 23, s. 13 (5).

4.5 (1) **Decision not to process commencement of proceeding**—Subject to subsection (3), upon receiving documents relating to the commencement of a proceeding, a tribunal or its administrative staff may decide not to process the documents relating to the commencement of the proceeding if,

(a) the documents are incomplete;

(b) the documents are received after the time required for commencing the proceeding has elapsed;

(c) the fee required for commencing the proceeding is not paid; or

(d) there is some other technical defect in the commencement of the proceeding.

(2) **Notice**—A tribunal or its administrative staff shall give the party who commences a proceeding notice of its decision under subsection (1) and shall set out in the notice the reasons for the decision and the requirements for resuming the processing of the documents.

(3) **Rules under s. 25.1**—A tribunal or its administrative staff shall not make a decision under subsection (1) unless the tribunal has made rules under section 25.1 respecting the making of such decisions and those rules shall set out,

(a) any of the grounds referred to in subsection (1) upon which the tribunal or its administrative staff may decide not to process the documents relating to the commencement of a proceeding; and

(b) the requirements for the processing of the documents to be resumed.

(4) **Continuance of provisions in other statutes**—Despite section 32, nothing in this section shall prevent a tribunal or its administrative staff from deciding not to process documents relating to the commencement of a proceeding on grounds that differ from those referred to in subsection (1) or without complying with subsection (2) or (3) if the tribunal or its staff does so in accordance with the provisions of an Act that are in force on the day this section comes into force. 1999, c. 12, Sched. B, s. 16 (3).

4.6 (1) **Dismissal of proceeding without hearing**—Subject to subsections (5) and (6), a tribunal may dismiss a proceeding without a hearing if,

(a) the proceeding is frivolous, vexatious or is commenced in bad faith;

(b) the proceeding relates to matters that are outside the jurisdiction of the tribunal; or

(c) some aspect of the statutory requirements for bringing the proceeding has not been met.

(2) **Notice**—Before dismissing a proceeding under this section, a tribunal shall give notice of its intention to dismiss the proceeding to,

(a) all parties to the proceeding if the proceeding is being dismissed for reasons referred to in clause (1) (b); or

(b) the party who commences the proceeding if the proceeding is being dismissed for any other reason.

(3) **Same**—The notice of intention to dismiss a proceeding shall set out the reasons for the dismissal and inform the parties of their right to make written submissions to the tribunal with respect to the dismissal within the time specified in the notice.

(4) **Right to make submissions**—A party who receives a notice under subsection (2) may make written submissions to the tribunal with respect to the dismissal within the time specified in the notice.

(5) **Dismissal**—A tribunal shall not dismiss a proceeding under this section until it has given notice under subsection (2) and considered any submissions made under subsection (4).

(6) **Rules**—A tribunal shall not dismiss a proceeding under this section unless it has made rules under section 25.1 respecting the early dismissal of proceedings and those rules shall include,

(a) any of the grounds referred to in subsection (1) upon which a proceeding may be dismissed;

(b) the right of the parties who are entitled to receive notice under subsection (2) to make submissions with respect to the dismissal; and

(c) the time within which the submissions must be made.

(7) **Continuance of provisions in other statutes**—Despite section 32, nothing in this section shall prevent a tribunal from dismissing a proceeding on grounds other than those referred to in subsection (1) or without complying with subsections (2) to (6) if the tribunal dismisses the proceeding in accordance with the provisions of an Act that are in force on the day this section comes into force. 1999, c. 12, Sched. B, s. 16 (3).

4.7 Classifying proceedings—A tribunal may make rules under section 25.1 classifying the types of proceedings that come before it and setting guidelines as to the procedural steps or processes (such as preliminary motions, pre-hearing conferences, alternative dispute resolution mechanisms, expedited hearings) that apply to each type of proceeding and the circumstances in which other procedures may apply. 1999, c. 12, Sched. B, s. 16 (3).

4.8 (1) **Alternative dispute resolution**—A tribunal may direct the parties to a proceeding to participate in an alternative dispute resolution mechanism for the purposes of resolving the proceeding or an issue arising in the proceeding if,

(a) it has made rules under section 25.1 respecting the use of alternative dispute resolution mechanisms; and

(b) all parties consent to participating in the alternative dispute resolution mechanism.

(2) **Definition**—In this section,— "alternative dispute resolution mechanism" includes mediation, conciliation, negotiation or any other means of facilitating the resolution of issues in dispute.

(3) **Rules**—A rule under section 25.1 respecting the use of alternative dispute resolution mechanisms shall include procedural guidelines to deal with the following:

1. The circumstances in which a settlement achieved by means of an alternative dispute resolution mechanism must be reviewed and approved by the tribunal.

2. Any requirement, statutory or otherwise, that there be an order by the tribunal.

(4) **Mandatory alternative dispute resolution**—A rule under subsection (3) may provide that participation in an alternative dispute resolution mechanism is mandatory or that it is mandatory in certain specified circumstances.

(5) **Person appointed to mediate, etc.**—A rule under subsection (3) may provide that a person appointed to mediate, conciliate, negotiate or help resolve a matter by means of an alternative dispute resolution mechanism be a member of the tribunal or a person independent of the tribunal. However, a member of the tribunal who is so appointed with respect to a matter in a proceeding shall not subsequently hear the matter if it comes before the tribunal unless the parties consent.

(6) **Continuance of provisions in other statutes**—Despite section 32, nothing in this section shall prevent a tribunal from directing parties to a proceeding to participate in an alternative dispute resolution mechanism even though the requirements of subsections (1) to (5) have not been met if the tribunal does so in accordance with the provisions of an Act that are in force on the day this section comes into force. 1999, c. 12, Sched. B, s. 16 (3).

4.9 (1) **Mediators, etc.: not compellable, notes not evidence—Mediators, etc., not compellable**—No person employed as a mediator, conciliator or negotiator or otherwise appointed to facilitate the resolution of a matter before a tribunal by means of an alternative dispute resolution mechanism shall be compelled to give testimony or produce documents in a proceeding before the tribunal or in a civil proceeding with respect to matters that come to his or her knowledge in the course of exercising his or her duties under this or any other Act.

(2) **Evidence in civil proceedings**—No notes or records kept by a mediator, conciliator or negotiator or by any other person appointed to facilitate the resolution of a matter before a tribunal by means of an alternative dispute resolution mechanism under this or any other Act are admissible in a civil proceeding. 1999, c. 12, Sched. B, s. 16 (3).

5. Parties—The parties to a proceeding shall be the persons specified as parties by or under the statute under which the proceeding arises or, if not so specified, persons entitled by law to be parties to the proceeding. R.S.O. 1990, c. S.22, s. 5.

5.1 (1) **Written hearings**—A tribunal whose rules made under section 25.1 deal with written hearings may hold a written hearing in a proceeding. 1997, c. 23, s. 13 (6).

(2) **Exception**—The tribunal shall not hold a written hearing if a party satisfies the tribunal that there is good reason for not doing so.

(2.1)**Same**—Subsection (2) does not apply if the only purpose of the hearing is to deal with procedural matters. 1999, c. 12, Sched. B, s. 16 (4).

(3) **Documents**—In a written hearing, all the parties are entitled to receive every document that the tribunal receives in the proceeding. 1994, c. 27, s. 56 (10).

5.2 (1) **Electronic hearings**—A tribunal whose rules made under section 25.1 deal with electronic hearings may hold an electronic hearing in a proceeding. 1997, c. 23, s. 13 (7).

(2) **Exception**—The tribunal shall not hold an electronic hearing if a party satisfies the tribunal that holding an electronic rather than an oral hearing is likely to cause the party significant prejudice.

(3) **Same**—Subsection (2) does not apply if the only purpose of the hearing is to deal with procedural matters.

(4) **Participants to be able to hear one another**—In an electronic hearing, all the parties and the members of the tribunal participating in the hearing must be able to hear one another and any witnesses throughout the hearing. 1994, c. 27, s. 56 (10).

5.2.1 Different kinds of hearings in one proceeding—A tribunal may, in a proceeding, hold any combination of written, electronic and oral hearings. 1997, c. 23, s. 13 (8).

5.3 (1) **Pre-hearing conferences**—If the tribunal's rules made under section 25.1 deal with pre-hearing conferences, the tribunal may direct the parties to participate in a pre-hearing conference to consider,

(a) the settlement of any or all of the issues;

(b) the simplification of the issues;

(c) facts or evidence that may be agreed upon;

(d) the dates by which any steps in the proceeding are to be taken or begun;

(e) the estimated duration of the hearing; and

(f) any other matter that may assist in the just and most expeditious disposition of the proceeding. 1994, c. 27, s. 56 (11); 1997, c. 23, s. 13 (9).

(1.1) **Other Acts and regulations**—The tribunal's power to direct the parties to participate in a pre-hearing conference is subject to any other Act or regulation that applies to the proceeding. 1997, c. 23, s. 13 (10).

(2) **Who presides**—The chair of the tribunal may designate a member of the tribunal or any other person to preside at the pre-hearing conference.

(3) **Orders**—A member who presides at a pre-hearing conference may make such orders as he or she considers necessary or advisable with respect to the conduct of the proceeding, including adding parties.

(4) **Disqualification**—A member who presides at a pre-hearing conference at which the parties attempt to settle issues shall not preside at the hearing of the proceeding unless the parties consent. 1994, c. 27, s. 56 (11).

(5) **Application of s. 5.2**—Section 5.2 applies to a pre-hearing conference, with necessary modifications. 1997, c. 23, s. 13 (10).

5.4 (1) **Disclosure**—If the tribunal's rules made under section 25.1 deal with disclosure, the tribunal may, at any stage of the proceeding before all hearings are complete, make orders for,

(a) the exchange of documents;

(b) the oral or written examination of a party;

(c) the exchange of witness statements and reports of expert witnesses;

(d) the provision of particulars;

(e) any other form of disclosure. 1994, c. 27, s. 56 (12); 1997, c. 23, s. 13 (11).

(1.1) **Other Acts and regulations**—The tribunal's power to make orders for disclosure is subject to any other Act or regulation that applies to the proceeding. 1997, c. 23, s. 13 (12).

(2) **Exception, privileged information**—Subsection (1) does not authorize the making of an order requiring disclosure of privileged information. 1994, c. 27, s. 56 (12).

6. (1) **Notice of hearing**—The parties to a proceeding shall be given reasonable notice of the hearing by the tribunal. R.S.O. 1990, c. S.22, s. 6 (1).

(2) **Statutory authority**—A notice of a hearing shall include a reference to the statutory authority under which the hearing will be held.

(3) **Oral hearing**—A notice of an oral hearing shall include,

(a) a statement of the time, place and purpose of the hearing; and

(b) a statement that if the party notified does not attend at the hearing, the tribunal may proceed in the party's absence and the party will not be entitled to any further notice in the proceeding. 1994, c. 27, s. 56 (13).

(4) **Written hearing**—A notice of a written hearing shall include,

(a) a statement of the date and purpose of the hearing, and details about the manner in which the hearing will be held;

(b) a statement that the hearing shall not be held as a written hearing if the party satisfies the tribunal that there is good reason for not holding a written hearing (in which case the tribunal is required to hold it as an electronic or oral hearing) and an indication of the procedure to be followed for that purpose;

(c) a statement that if the party notified neither acts under clause (b) nor participates in the hearing in accordance with the notice, the tribunal may proceed without the party's participation and the party will not be entitled to any further notice in the proceeding. 1994, c. 27, s. 56 (13); 1997, c. 23, s. 13 (13); 1999, c. 12, Sched. B, s. 16 (5).

(5) **Electronic hearing**—A notice of an electronic hearing shall include,

(a) a statement of the time and purpose of the hearing, and details about the manner in which the hearing will be held;

(b) a statement that the only purpose of the hearing is to deal with procedural matters, if that is the case;

(c) if clause (b) does not apply, a statement that the party notified may, by satisfying the tribunal that holding the hearing as an electronic hearing is likely to cause the party significant prejudice, require the tribunal to hold the hearing as an oral hearing, and an indication of the procedure to be followed for that purpose; and

(d) a statement that if the party notified neither acts under clause (c), if applicable, nor participates in the hearing in accordance with the notice, the tribunal may proceed without the party's participation and the party will not be entitled to any further notice in the proceeding. 1994, c. 27, s. 56 (13).

7. (1) **Effect of non-attendance at hearing after due notice**—Where notice of an oral hearing has been given to a party to a proceeding in accordance with this Act and the party does not attend at the hearing, the tribunal may proceed in the absence of the party and the party is not entitled to any further notice in the proceeding. R.S.O. 1990, c. S.22, s. 7; 1994, c. 27, s. 56 (14).

(2) **Same, written hearings**—Where notice of a written hearing has been given to a party to a proceeding in accordance with this Act and the party neither acts under clause 6 (4) (b) nor participates in the hearing in accordance with the notice, the tribunal may proceed without the party's participation and the party is not entitled to any further notice in the proceeding.

(3) **Same, electronic hearings**—Where notice of an electronic hearing has been given to a party to a proceeding in accordance with this Act and the party neither acts under clause 6 (5) (c), if applicable, nor participates in the hearing in accordance with the notice, the tribunal may proceed without the party's participation and the party is not entitled to any further notice in the proceeding. 1994, c. 27, s. 56 (15).

8. Where character, etc., of a party is in issue—Where the good character, propriety of conduct or competence of a party is an issue in a proceeding, the party is entitled to be furnished prior to the hearing with reasonable information of any allegations with respect thereto. R.S.O. 1990, c. S.22, s. 8.

9. (1) **Hearings to be public; maintenance of order**—Hearings to be public, exceptions—An oral hearing shall be open to the public except where the tribunal is of the opinion that,

(a) matters involving public security may be disclosed; or

(b) intimate financial or personal matters or other matters may be disclosed at the hearing of such a nature, having regard to the circumstances, that the desirability of avoiding disclosure thereof in the interests of any person affected or in the public interest outweighs the desirability of adhering to the principle that hearings be open to the public,

in which case the tribunal may hold the hearing in the absence of the public. R.S.O. 1990, c. S.22, s. 9 (1); 1994, c. 27, s. 56 (16).

(1.1) **Written hearings**—In a written hearing, members of the public are entitled to reasonable access to the documents submitted, unless the tribunal is of the opinion that clause (1) (a) or (b) applies. 1994, c. 27, s. 56 (17).

(1.2) **Electronic hearings**—An electronic hearing shall be open to the public unless the tribunal is of the opinion that,

(a) it is not practical to hold the hearing in a manner that is open to the public; or

(b) clause (1) (a) or (b) applies. 1997, c. 23, s. 13 (14).

(2) **Maintenance of order at hearings**—A tribunal may make such orders or give such directions at an oral or electronic hearing as it considers necessary for the maintenance of order at the hearing, and, if any person disobeys or fails to comply with any such order or direction, the tribunal or a member thereof may call for the assistance of any peace officer to enforce the order or direction, and every peace officer so called upon shall take such action as is necessary to enforce the order or direction and may use such force as is reasonably required for that purpose. R.S.O. 1990, c. S.22, s. 9 (2); 1994, c. 27, s. 56 (18).

9.1 (1) **Proceedings involving similar questions**—If two or more proceedings before a tribunal involve the same or similar questions of fact, law or policy, the tribunal may,

(a) combine the proceedings or any part of them, with the consent of the parties;

(b) hear the proceedings at the same time, with the consent of the parties;

(c) hear the proceedings one immediately after the other; or

(d) stay one or more of the proceedings until after the determination of another one of them.

(2) **Exception**—Subsection (1) does not apply to proceedings to which the *Consolidated Hearings Act* applies. 1994, c. 27, s. 56 (19).

(3) **Same**—Clauses (1) (a) and (b) do not apply to a proceeding if,

(a) any other Act or regulation that applies to the proceeding requires that it be heard in private;

(b) the tribunal is of the opinion that clause 9 (1) (a) or (b) applies to the proceeding. 1994, c. 27, s. 56 (19); 1997, c. 23, s. 13 (15).

(4) **Conflict, consent requirements**—The consent requirements of clauses (1) (a) and (b) do not apply if another Act or a regulation that applies to the proceedings allows the tribunal to combine them or hear them at the same time without the consent of the parties. 1997, c. 23, s. 13 (16).

(5) **Use of same evidence**—If the parties to the second-named proceeding consent, the tribunal may treat evidence that is admitted in a proceeding as if it were also admitted in another proceeding that is heard at the same time under clause (1) (b). 1994, c. 27, s. 56 (19).

10. **Right to counsel**—A party to a proceeding may be represented by counsel or an agent. 1994, c. 27, s. 56 (20).

10.1 **Examination of witnesses**—A party to a proceeding may, at an oral or electronic hearing,

    (a) call and examine witnesses and present evidence and submissions; and

    (b) conduct cross-examinations of witnesses at the hearing reasonably required for a full and fair disclosure of all matters relevant to the issues in the proceeding. 1994, c. 27, s. 56 (20).

11. (1) **Rights of witnesses to counsel**—A witness at an oral or electronic hearing is entitled to be advised by counsel or an agent as to his or her rights but such counsel or agent may take no other part in the hearing without leave of the tribunal. R.S.O. 1990, c. S.22, s. 11 (1); 1994, c. 27, s. 56 (21).

    (2) **Idem**—Where an oral hearing is closed to the public, the counsel or agent for a witness is not entitled to be present except when that witness is giving evidence. R.S.O. 1990, c. S.22, s. 11 (2); 1994, c. 27, s. 56 (22).

12. (1) **Summonses**—A tribunal may require any person, including a party, by summons,

    (a) to give evidence on oath or affirmation at an oral or electronic hearing; and

    (b) to produce in evidence at an oral or electronic hearing documents and things specified by the tribunal,

relevant to the subject-matter of the proceeding and admissible at a hearing. R.S.O. 1990, c. S.22, s. 12 (1); 1994, c. 27, s. 56 (23).

    (2) **Form and service of summons**—A summons issued under subsection (1) shall be in the prescribed form (in English or French) and,

    (a) where the tribunal consists of one person, shall be signed by him or her;

    (b) where the tribunal consists of more than one person, shall be signed by the chair of the tribunal or in such other manner as documents on behalf of the tribunal may be signed under the statute constituting the tribunal.

    (3) **Same**—The summons shall be served personally on the person summoned.

(3.1) **Fees and allowances**—The person summoned is entitled to receive the same fees or allowances for attending at or otherwise participating in the hearing as are paid to a person summoned to attend before the Ontario Court (General Division). 1994, c. 27, s. 56 (24).

    (4) **Bench warrant**—A judge of the Ontario Court (General Division) may issue a warrant against a person if the judge is satisfied that,

    (a) a summons was served on the person under this section;

    (b) the person has failed to attend or to remain in attendance at the hearing (in the case of an oral hearing) or has failed otherwise to participate in the hearing (in the case of an electronic hearing) in accordance with the summons; and

(c) the person's attendance or participation is material to the ends of justice.

(4.1) **Same**—The warrant shall be in the prescribed form (in English or French), directed to any police officer, and shall require the person to be apprehended anywhere within Ontario, brought before the tribunal forthwith and,

(a) detained in custody as the judge may order until the person's presence as a witness is no longer required; or

(b) in the judge's discretion, released on a recognizance, with or without sureties, conditioned for attendance or participation to give evidence. 1994, c. 27, s. 56 (25).

(5) **Proof of service**—Service of a summons may be proved by affidavit in an application to have a warrant issued under subsection (4).

(6) **Certificate of facts**—Where an application to have a warrant issued is made on behalf of a tribunal, the person constituting the tribunal or, if the tribunal consists of more than one person, the chair of the tribunal may certify to the judge the facts relied on to establish that the attendance or other participation of the person summoned is material to the ends of justice, and the judge may accept the certificate as proof of the facts.

(7) **Same**—Where the application is made by a party to the proceeding, the facts relied on to establish that the attendance or other participation of the person is material to the ends of justice may be proved by the party's affidavit. 1994, c. 27, s. 56 (26).

13. (1) **Contempt proceedings**—Where any person without lawful excuse,

(a) on being duly summoned under section 12 as a witness at a hearing makes default in attending at the hearing; or

(b) being in attendance as a witness at an oral hearing or otherwise participating as a witness at an electronic hearing, refuses to take an oath or to make an affirmation legally required by the tribunal to be taken or made, or to produce any document or thing in his or her power or control legally required by the tribunal to be produced by him or her or to answer any question to which the tribunal may legally require an answer; or

(c) does any other thing that would, if the tribunal had been a court of law having power to commit for contempt, have been contempt of that court,

the tribunal may, of its own motion or on the motion of a party to the proceeding, state a case to the Divisional Court setting out the facts and that court may inquire into the matter and, after hearing any witnesses who may be produced against or on behalf of that person and after hearing any statement that may be offered in defence, punish or take steps for the punishment of that person in like manner as if he or she had been guilty of contempt of the court. R.S.O. 1990, c. S.22, s. 13; 1994, c. 27, s. 56 (27).

(2) **Same**—Subsection (1) also applies to a person who,

(a) having objected under clause 6 (4) (b) to a hearing being held as a written hearing, fails without lawful excuse to participate in the oral or electronic hearing of the matter; or

(b) being a party, fails without lawful excuse to attend a pre-hearing conference when so directed by the tribunal. 1997, c. 23, s. 13 (17).

14. (1) **Protection for witnesses**—A witness at an oral or electronic hearing shall be deemed to have objected to answer any question asked him or her upon the ground that the answer may tend to criminate him or her or may tend to establish his or her liability to civil proceedings at the instance of the Crown, or of any person, and no answer given by a witness at a hearing shall be used or be receivable in evidence against the witness in any trial or other proceeding against him or her thereafter taking place, other than a prosecution for perjury in giving such evidence. R.S.O. 1990, c. S.22, s. 14 (1); 1994, c. 27, s. 56 (28).

(2) Repealed: 1994, c. 27, s. 56 (29).

15. (1) **Evidence—What is admissible in evidence at a hearing**—Subject to subsections (2) and (3), a tribunal may admit as evidence at a hearing, whether or not given or proven under oath or affirmation or admissible as evidence in a court,

(a) any oral testimony; and

(b) any document or other thing,

relevant to the subject-matter of the proceeding and may act on such evidence, but the tribunal may exclude anything unduly repetitious.

(2) **What is inadmissible in evidence at a hearing**—Nothing is admissible in evidence at a hearing,

(a) that would be inadmissible in a court by reason of any privilege under the law of evidence; or

(b) that is inadmissible by the statute under which the proceeding arises or any other statute.

(3) **Conflicts**—Nothing in subsection (1) overrides the provisions of any Act expressly limiting the extent to or purposes for which any oral testimony, documents or things may be admitted or used in evidence in any proceeding.

(4) **Copies**—Where a tribunal is satisfied as to its authenticity, a copy of a document or other thing may be admitted as evidence at a hearing.

(5) **Photocopies**—Where a document has been filed in evidence at a hearing, the tribunal may, or the person producing it or entitled to it may with the leave of the tribunal, cause the document to be photocopied and the tribunal may authorize the photocopy to be filed in evidence in the place of the document filed and release the document filed, or may furnish to the person producing it or the person entitled to it a photocopy of the document filed certified by a member of the tribunal.

(6) **Certified copy admissible in evidence**—A document purporting to be a copy of a document filed in evidence at a hearing, certified to be a copy thereof by a member of the tribunal, is admissible in evidence in proceedings in which the document is admissible as evidence of the document. R.S.O. 1990, c. S.22, s. 15.

15.1 (1) **Use of previously admitted evidence**—The tribunal may treat previously admitted evidence as if it had been admitted in a

proceeding before the tribunal, if the parties to the proceeding consent. 1994, c. 27, s. 56 (30).

(2) **Definition**—In subsection (1),

"previously admitted evidence" means evidence that was admitted, before the hearing of the proceeding referred to in that subsection, in any other proceeding before a court or tribunal, whether in or outside Ontario.

(3) **Additional power**—This power conferred by this section is in addition to the tribunal's power to admit evidence under section 15. 1997, c. 23, s. 13 (18).

15.2 Witness panels—A tribunal may receive evidence from panels of witnesses composed of two or more persons, if the parties have first had an opportunity to make submissions in that regard. 1994, c. 27, s. 56 (31).

16. Notice of facts and opinions—A tribunal may, in making its decision in any proceeding,

(a) take notice of facts that may be judicially noticed; and

(b) take notice of any generally recognized scientific or technical facts, information or opinions within its scientific or specialized knowledge. R.S.O. 1990, c. S.22, s. 16.

16.1 (1) **Interim decisions and orders**—A tribunal may make interim decisions and orders.

(2) **Conditions**—A tribunal may impose conditions on an interim decision or order.

(3) **Reasons**—An interim decision or order need not be accompanied by reasons. 1994, c. 27, s. 56 (32).

16.2 Time frames—A tribunal shall establish guidelines setting out the usual time frame for completing proceedings that come before the tribunal and for completing the procedural steps within those proceedings. 1999, c. 12, Sched. B, s. 16 (6).

17. (1) **Decision; interest**—**Decision**—A tribunal shall give its final decision and order, if any, in any proceeding in writing and

shall give reasons in writing therefor if requested by a party. R.S.O. 1990, c. S.22, s. 17; 1993, c. 27, Sched.

(2) **Interest**—A tribunal that makes an order for the payment of money shall set out in the order the principal sum, and if interest is payable, the rate of interest and the date from which it is to be calculated. 1994, c. 27, s. 56 (33).

17.1 (1) **Costs**—Subject to subsection (2), a tribunal may, in the circumstances set out in a rule made

under section 25.1, order a party to pay all or part of another party's costs in a proceeding.

(2) **Exception**—A tribunal shall not make an order to pay costs under this section unless,

(a) the conduct or course of conduct of a party has been unreasonable, frivolous or vexatious or a party has acted in bad faith; and

(b) the tribunal has made rules under section 25.1 with respect to the ordering of costs which include the circumstances in which costs may be ordered and the amount of the costs or the manner in which the amount of the costs is to be determined.

(3) **Amount of costs**—The amount of the costs ordered under this section shall be determined in accordance with the rules made under section 25.1.

(4) **Continuance of provisions in other statutes**—Despite section 32, nothing in this section shall prevent a tribunal from ordering a party to pay all or part of another party's costs in a proceeding in circumstances other than those set out in, and without complying with, subsections (1) to (3) if the tribunal makes the order in accordance with the provisions of an Act that are in force on the day this section comes into force. 1999, c. 12, Sched. B, s. 16 (7).

18. (1) **Notice of decision**—The tribunal shall send each party who participated in the proceeding, or the party's counsel

or agent, a copy of its final decision or order, including the reasons if any have been given,

(a) by regular lettermail;

(b) by electronic transmission;

(c) by telephone transmission of a facsimile; or

(d) by some other method that allows proof of receipt, if the tribunal's rules made under section 25.1 deal with the matter. 1994, c. 27, s. 56 (34); 1997, c. 23, s. 13 (19).

(2) **Use of mail**—If the copy is sent by regular lettermail, it shall be sent to the most recent addresses known to the tribunal and shall be deemed to be received by the party on the fifth day after the day it is mailed.

(3) **Use of electronic or telephone transmission**—If the copy is sent by electronic transmission or by telephone transmission of a facsimile, it shall be deemed to be received on the day after it was sent, unless that day is a holiday, in which case the copy shall be deemed to be received on the next day that is not a holiday.

(4) **Use of other method**—If the copy is sent by a method referred to in clause (1) (d), the tribunal's rules made under section 25.1 govern its deemed day of receipt.

(5) **Failure to receive copy**—If a party that acts in good faith does not, through absence, accident, illness or other cause beyond the party's control, receive the copy until a later date than the deemed day of receipt, subsection (2), (3) or (4), as the case may be, does not apply. 1994, c. 27, s. 56 (34).

19. (1) **Enforcement of orders**—A certified copy of a tribunal's decision or order in a proceeding may be filed in the Ontario

Court (General Division) by the tribunal or by a party and on filing shall be deemed to be an order of that court and is enforceable as such.

(2) **Notice of filing**—A party who files an order under subsection (1) shall notify the tribunal within 10 days after the filing.

(3) **Order for payment of money**—On receiving a certified copy of a tribunal's order for the payment of money, the sheriff shall enforce the order as if it were an execution issued by the Ontario Court (General Division). 1994, c. 27, s. 56 (35).

20. Record of proceeding—A tribunal shall compile a record of any proceeding in which a hearing has been held which shall include,

(a) any application, complaint, reference or other document, if any, by which the proceeding was commenced;

(b) the notice of any hearing;

(c) any interlocutory orders made by the tribunal;

(d) all documentary evidence filed with the tribunal, subject to any limitation expressly imposed by any other Act on the extent to or the purposes for which any such documents may be used in evidence in any proceeding;

(e) the transcript, if any, of the oral evidence given at the hearing; and

(f) the decision of the tribunal and the reasons therefor, where reasons have been given. R.S.O. 1990, c. S.22, s. 20.

21. Adjournments—A hearing may be adjourned from time to time by a tribunal of its own motion or where it is shown to the satisfaction of the tribunal that the adjournment is required to permit an adequate hearing to be held. R.S.O. 1990, c. S.22, s. 21.

21.1 Correction of errors—A tribunal may at any time correct a typographical error, error of calculation or similar error made in its decision or order. 1994, c. 27, s. 56 (36).

21.2 (1) **Power to review**—A tribunal may, if it considers it advisable and if its rules made under section 25.1 deal

with the matter, review all or part of its own decision or order, and may confirm, vary, suspend or cancel the decision or order. 1997, c. 23, s. 13 (20).

(2) **Time for review**—The review shall take place within a reasonable time after the decision or order is made.

(3) **Conflict**—In the event of a conflict between this section and any other Act, the other Act prevails. 1994, c. 27, s. 56 (36).

22. Administration of oaths—A member of a tribunal has power to administer oaths and affirmations for the purpose of any of its proceedings and the tribunal may require evidence before it to be given under oath or affirmation. R.S.O. 1990, c. S.22, s. 22.

23. (1) **Powers re control of proceedings**—**Abuse of processes**—A tribunal may make such orders or give such directions in proceedings before it as it considers proper to prevent abuse of its processes. R.S.O. 1990, c. S.22, s. 23 (1).

(2) **Limitation on examination**—A tribunal may reasonably limit further examination or cross-examination of a witness where it is satisfied that the examination or cross-examination has been sufficient to disclose fully and fairly all matters relevant to the issues in the proceeding. 1994, c. 27, s. 56 (37).

(3) **Exclusion of agents**—A tribunal may exclude from a hearing anyone, other than a barrister and solicitor qualified to practise in Ontario, appearing as an agent on behalf of a party or as an adviser to a witness if it finds that such person is not competent properly to represent or to advise the party or witness or does not understand and comply at the hearing with the duties and responsibilities of an advocate or adviser. R.S.O. 1990, c. S.22, s. 23 (3).

24. (1) **Notice, etc.**—Where a tribunal is of the opinion that because the parties to any proceeding before it are so numerous or for any other reason, it is impracticable,

(a) to give notice of the hearing; or

(b) to send its decision and the material mentioned in section 18,

to all or any of the parties individually, the tribunal may, instead of doing so, cause reasonable notice of the hearing or of its decision to be given to such parties by public advertisement or otherwise as the tribunal may direct.

(2) **Contents of notice**—A notice of a decision given by a tribunal under clause (1) (b) shall inform the parties of the place where copies of the decision and the reasons therefor, if reasons were given, may be obtained. R.S.O. 1990, c. S.22, s. 24.

25. (1) **Appeal operates as stay, exception**—An appeal from a decision of a tribunal to a court or other appellate body operates as a stay in the matter unless,

(a) another Act or a regulation that applies to the proceeding expressly provides to the contrary; or

(b) the tribunal or the court or other appellate body orders otherwise. 1997, c. 23, s. 13 (21).

(2) **Idem**—An application for judicial review under the *Judicial Review Procedure Act*, or the bringing of proceedings specified in subsection 2 (1) of that Act is not an appeal within the meaning of subsection (1). R.S.O. 1990, c. S.22, s. 25 (2).

25.0.1 Control of process—A tribunal has the power to determine its own procedures and practices and may for that purpose,

(a) make orders with respect to the procedures and practices that apply in any particular proceeding; and

(b) establish rules under section 25.1. 1999, c. 12, Sched. B, s. 16 (8).

25.1 (1) **Rules**—A tribunal may make rules governing the practice and procedure before it.

(2) **Application**—The rules may be of general or particular application.

(3) **Consistency with Acts**—The rules shall be consistent with this Act and with the other Acts to which they relate.

(4) **Public access**—The tribunal shall make the rules available to the public in English and in French.

(5) **Regulations Act**—Rules adopted under this section are not regulations as defined in the *Regulations Act*.

(6) **Additional power**—The power conferred by this section is in addition

to any power to adopt rules that the tribunal may have under another Act. 1994, c. 27, s. 56 (38).

26. Regulations—The Lieutenant Governor in Council may make regulations prescribing forms for the purpose of section 12. 1994, c. 27, s. 56 (41).

27. Rules, etc., available to public—A tribunal shall make any rules or guidelines established under this or any other Act available for examination by the public. 1999, c. 12, Sched. B, s. 16 (9).

28. Substantial compliance—Substantial compliance with requirements respecting the content of forms, notices or documents under this Act or any rule made under this or any other Act is sufficient. 1999, c. 12, Sched. B, s. 16 (9).

29.-31. Repealed: 1994, c. 27, s. 56 (40).

32. Conflict—Unless it is expressly provided in any other Act that its provisions and regulations, rules or by-laws made under it apply despite anything in this Act, the provisions of this Act prevail over the provisions of such other Act and over regulations, rules or by-laws made under such other Act which conflict therewith. R.S.O. 1990, c. S.22, s. 32; 1994, c. 27, s. 56 (42).

33., 34. Repealed: 1994, c. 27, s. 56 (43).

Forms 1, 2 Repealed: 1994, c. 27, s. 56 (44).

Appendix 3

Ontario
Judicial Review Procedure Act
R.S.O. 1990, c. J.1

Definitions

1. In this Act,

"**application for judicial review**" means an application under subsection 2 (1); ("requête en révision judiciaire")

"**court**" means the Ontario Court (General Division); ("Cour")

"**licence**" includes any permit, certificate, approval, registration or similar form of permission required by law; ("autorisation")

"**municipality**" has the same meaning as in the *Municipal Affairs Act*; ("municipalité")

"**party**" includes a municipality, association of employers, a trade union or council of trade unions which may be a party to any of the proceedings mentioned in subsection 2 (1); ("partie")

"**statutory power**" means a power or right conferred by or under a statute,

(a) to make any regulation, rule, by-law or order, or to give any other direction having force as subordinate legislation,

(b) to exercise a statutory power of decision,

(c) to require any person or party to do or to refrain from doing any act or thing that, but for such requirement, such person or party would not be required by law to do or to refrain from doing,

(d) to do any act or thing that would, but for such power or right, be a breach of the legal rights of any person or party; ("compétence légale")

"**statutory power of decision**" means a power or right conferred by or under a statute to make a decision deciding or prescribing,

(a) the legal rights, powers, privileges, immunities, duties or liabilities of any person or party, or

(b) the eligibility of any person or party to receive, or to the continuation of, a benefit or licence, whether the person or party is legally entitled thereto or not,

and includes the powers of an inferior court. ("compétence légale de décision") R.S.O. 1990, c. J.1, s. 1; 2002, c. 17, Sched. F, Table.

Applications for judicial review

2.   (1) On an application by way of originating notice, which may be styled "Notice of Application for Judicial Review", the court may, despite any right of appeal, by order grant any relief that the applicant would be entitled to in any one or more of the following:

1. Proceedings by way of application for an order in the nature of mandamus, prohibition or certiorari.

2. Proceedings by way of an action for a declaration or for an injunction, or both, in relation to the exercise, refusal to exercise or proposed or purported exercise of a statutory power. R.S.O. 1990, c. J.1, s. 2 (1).

Error of law

(2) The power of the court to set aside a decision for error of law on the face of the record on an application for an order in the nature of certiorari is extended so as to apply on an application for judicial review in relation to any decision made in the exercise of any statutory power of decision to the extent it is not limited or precluded by the Act conferring such power of decision. R.S.O. 1990, c. J.1, s. 2 (2).

Lack of evidence

(3) Where the findings of fact of a tribunal made in the exercise of a statutory power of decision are required by any statute or law to be based exclusively on evidence admissible before it and on facts of which it may take notice and there is no such evidence and there are no such facts to support findings of fact made by the tribunal in making a decision in the exercise of such power, the court may set aside the decision on an application for judicial review. R.S.O. 1990, c. J.1, s. 2 (3).

Power to set aside

(4) Where the applicant on an application for judicial review is entitled to a judgment declaring that a decision made in the exercise of a statutory power of decision is unauthorized or otherwise invalid, the court may, in the place of such declaration, set aside the decision. R.S.O. 1990, c. J.1, s. 2 (4).

Power to refuse relief

(5) Where, in any of the proceedings enumerated in subsection (1), the court had before the 17th day of April, 1972 a discretion to refuse to grant relief on any grounds, the court has a like discretion on like grounds to refuse to grant any relief on an application for judicial review. R.S.O. 1990, c. J.1, s. 2 (5).

Where subs. (5) does not apply

(6) Subsection (5) does not apply to the discretion of the court before the 17th day of April, 1972 to refuse to grant relief in any of the proceedings enumerated in subsection (1) on the ground that the relief should have been sought in other proceedings enumerated in subsection (1). R.S.O. 1990, c. J.1, s. 2 (6).

Defects in form, technical irregularities

3. On an application for judicial review in relation to a statutory power of decision, where the sole ground for relief established is a defect in form or a technical irregularity, if the court finds that no substantial wrong or miscarriage of justice has occurred, the court may refuse relief and, where the decision has already been made, may make an order validating the decision, despite such defect, to have effect from such time and on such terms as the court considers proper. R.S.O. 1990, c. J.1, s. 3.

Interim order

4. On an application for judicial review, the court may make such interim order as it considers proper pending the final determination of the application. R.S.O. 1990, c. J.1, s. 4.

Extension of time for bringing application

5. Despite any limitation of time for the bringing of an application for judicial review fixed by or under any Act, the court may extend the time for making the application, either before or after expiration of the time so limited, on such terms as it considers proper, where it is satisfied that there are apparent grounds for relief and that no substantial prejudice or hardship will result to any person affected by reason of the delay. R.S.O. 1990, c. J.1, s. 5.

Application to Divisional Court

6. (1) Subject to subsection (2), an application for judicial review shall be made to the Divisional Court. R.S.O. 1990, c. J.1, s. 6 (1).

Application to judge of Ontario Court (General Division)

(2) An application for judicial review may be made to the Ontario Court (General Division) with leave of a judge thereof, which may be granted

at the hearing of the application, where it is made to appear to the judge that the case is one of urgency and that the delay required for an application to the Divisional Court is likely to involve a failure of justice. R.S.O. 1990, c. J.1, s. 6 (2).

Transfer to Divisional Court

(3) Where a judge refuses leave for an application under subsection (2), he or she may order that the application be transferred to the Divisional Court. R.S.O. 1990, c. J.1, s. 6 (3).

Appeal to Court of Appeal

(4) An appeal lies to the Court of Appeal, with leave of the Court of Appeal, from a final order of the Ontario Court (General Division) disposing of an application for judicial review pursuant to leave granted under subsection (2). R.S.O. 1990, c. J.1, s. 6 (4).

Summary disposition of mandamus, etc.

7. An application for an order in the nature of mandamus, prohibition or certiorari shall be deemed to be an application for judicial review and shall be made, treated and disposed of as if it were an application for judicial review. R.S.O. 1990, c. J.1, s. 7.

Summary disposition of actions

8. Where an action for a declaration or injunction, or both, whether with or without a claim for other relief, is brought and the exercise, refusal to exercise or proposed or purported exercise of a statutory power is an issue in the action, a judge of the Ontario Court (General Division) may on the application of any party to the action, if he or she considers it appropriate, direct that the action be treated and disposed of summarily, in so far as it relates to the exercise, refusal to exercise or proposed or purported exercise of such power, as if it were an application for judicial review and may order that the hearing on such issue be transferred to the Divisional Court or may grant leave for it to be disposed of in accordance with subsection 6 (2). R.S.O. 1990, c. J.1, s. 8.

Sufficiency of application

9. (1) It is sufficient in an application for judicial review if an applicant sets out in the notice the grounds upon which he is seeking relief and the nature of the relief that he seeks without specifying the proceedings enumerated in subsection 2 (1) in which the claim would have been made before the 17th day of April, 1972. R.S.O. 1990, c. J.1, s. 9 (1).

Exerciser of power may be a party

(2) For the purposes of an application for judicial review in relation to

the exercise, refusal to exercise or proposed or purported exercise of a statutory power, the person who is authorized to exercise the power may be a party to the application. R.S.O. 1990, c. J.1, s. 9 (2).

Idem

(3) For the purposes of subsection (2), any two or more persons who, acting together, may exercise a statutory power, whether styled a board or commission or by any other collective title, shall be deemed to be a person under such collective title. R.S.O. 1990, c. J.1, s. 9 (3).

Notice to Attorney General

(4) Notice of an application for judicial review shall be served upon the Attorney General who is entitled as of right to be heard in person or by counsel on the application. R.S.O. 1990, c. J.1, s. 9 (4).

Record to be filed in Ontario Court (General Division)

10. When notice of an application for judicial review of a decision made in the exercise or purported exercise of a statutory power of decision has been served on the person making the decision, such person shall forthwith file in the court for use on the application the record of the proceedings in which the decision was made. R.S.O. 1990, c. J.1, s. 10.

References in other Acts, etc.

11. (1) Subject to subsection (2), where reference is made in any other Act or in any regulation, rule or by-law to any of the proceedings enumerated in subsection 2 (1), such reference shall be read and construed to include a reference to an application for judicial review. R.S.O. 1990, c. J.1, s. 11 (1).

Proceedings under Habeas Corpus Act

(2) Nothing in this Act affects proceedings under the *Habeas Corpus Act* or the issue of a writ of certiorari thereunder or proceedings pursuant thereto, but an application for judicial review may be brought in aid of an application for a writ of *habeas corpus*. R.S.O. 1990, c. J.1, s. 11 (2).

Appendix 4

Alberta Rules Of Court

PART 56

CROWN PRACTICE RULES IN CIVIL MATTERS

General rules to apply

737. Except where provided specially in this the general Rules, including those relating to abridgment or extension of time, apply in all matters under this Part. (Alta. Reg. 390/68 s.737)

Order not writ shall issue

738 (1) An order in the nature of habeas corpus may be granted upon application by notice of motion returnable before the court.

(1.1) An order in the nature of mandamus, prohibition, certiorari, quo warranto or habeas corpus may be granted upon application for judicial review under Part 56.1.

(2) The writs of mandamus, prohibition, certiorari, habeas corpus and quo warranto shall not be issued, but all necessary provisions shall be made in the judgment or order. (Alta. Reg. 390/68; 457/87)

Service of notice of motion

739 (1) The notice of motion shall be served upon every person who appears to be interested or likely to be affected by the proceedings.

(2) The court may require the notice of motion to be served upon any person not previously served.

(3) Where it is sought to quash a judgment, order, warrant or inquiry, and in all applications for an order in the nature of prohibition, notice of motion shall also be served at least seven days before the return date thereof

   (a) upon the Attorney General, and

   (b) upon the person making the order or holding the inquiry.

(4) Any person not served with the notice of motion may show that he is affected by the proceedings and thereupon may take part in the proceedings as though served. (Alta. Reg. 390/68 s.739)

Appeal

740 An appeal lies from the order of the court to the Court of Appeal. (Alta. Reg. 390/68 s.740; 338/83)

Direction by a judge

741 Any direction required to give effect to an order of the Court of Appeal may be made by a judge of the Court of Appeal. Alta. Reg. 338/83)

742 to **753**   Repealed. Alta. Reg. 457/87 s.2)

PART 56.1

JUDICIAL REVIEW IN CIVIL MATTERS

Person

753.01 In this Part, "person" includes a board, commission, tribunal or other body whose decision, act or omission is subject to judicial review, whether comprised of 1 person or 2 or more persons acting together and whether or not styled by a collective title. Alta. Reg. 457/87 s.3)

Application for Judicial Review

753.02 A proceeding under this Part shall be known as an application for judicial review.

Commencement

753.03 An application for judicial review shall be commenced by originating notice. (Alta. Reg. 457/87 s.3)

Granting of relief

753.04   (1) On an application for judicial review, the court may grant any relief that the applicant would be entitled to in proceedings for any one or more of the following remedies:

(1) an order in the nature of mandamus, prohibition, certiorari, quo warranto or habeas corpus;

   (b) a declaration or injunction.

(2) In such application a declaration may be made or an injunction granted where the court considers that it is just and convenient to do so having regard to all the circumstances of the case including

(1) the nature of the matters in respect of which relief may be granted by orders in the nature of mandamus, prohibition, certiorari or quo warranto, and

(2) the nature of the persons from whose decisions, acts or omissions relief may be granted by such orders.

(3) Subrule (1) applies whether the remedy under which the applicant would be entitled to the relief is or is not specifically named in an application.

(4) Before the court may grant relief under subrule (1), it must be satisfied that the grounds for the remedy under which the applicant would be entitled to the relief have been established. (Alta. Reg. 457/87 s.3)

Setting aside

753.05 Subject to Rule 753.11, where the applicant on an application for judicial review is entitled to a declaration that a decision or act is unauthorized or invalid, the court may, instead of making a declaration, set aside the decision or act. (Alta. Reg. 457/87 s.3)

Reconsideration and determination

753.06 (1) On an application for judicial review, the court may direct the person from whose decision, act or omission relief is claimed to reconsider and determine the whole or any part of a matter to which the application for judicial review relates but in respect of a decision the court may only direct a reconsideration and determination if the decision has been set aside.

(2) In acting under subrule (1), the court may give such directions as it considers appropriate.

Technical defect

753.07 On an application for judicial review where the sole ground for relief established is a defect in form or a technical irregularity, if the court finds that no substantial wrong or miscarriage of justice has occurred, the court may refuse relief and, where a decision has been made, may make an order validating the decision, notwithstanding such defect, to have effect from such time and on such terms as the court considers proper. (Alta. Reg. 457/87 s.3)

Originating notice

753.08 (1) An originating notice taken under this Part shall be in Form G modified in such manner as may be necessary having regard to the nature of the application.

(2) Every originating notice taken under this Part shall include a concise statement of the grounds on which relief is claimed in the proceedings and the nature of the relief claimed. Alta. Reg. 457/87 s.3)

Service of application

753.09 (1) The application for judicial review shall be served on

    (a) the person from whose decision, act or omission relief is claimed,

    (b) the Attorney General, and

    (c) every person directly affected by the proceedings.

(2) The court may require the application for judicial review to be served on any person not previously served. Alta. Reg. 457/87 s.3)

Parties

753.10 (1) The court may direct any person to be added or struck out as a party to proceedings for judicial review.

(2) The Attorney General is entitled as of right to be heard in person or by counsel on the application.

(3) Any person not served with the application for judicial review may show that he is affected by the proceedings and thereon may, in the discretion of the court, take part in the proceedings as though served. Alta. Reg. 457/87 s.3)

Limitation period

753.11 (1) Where the relief sought is an order to set aside a decision or act, the application for judicial review shall be filed and served within six months after the decision or act to which it relates.

(2) Rule 548 does not apply to this Rule. Alta. Reg. 457/87 s.3)

Notice for return

753.12 (1) Where the relief claimed on an application for judicial review is an order to set aside a decision or act, the applicant shall cause to be endorsed on the application for judicial review a notice to the following effect, adapted as may be necessary, addressed to the person from whose decision or act relief is claimed:

> "You are required forthwith after service of this notice to return to the clerk of the Court of Queen's Bench at .... (as the case may be) the judgment, order or decision (or as the case may be) to which this notice refers and reasons, if any, together with the process commencing the proceedings, the evidence and all exhibits filed, if any, and all things touching the matter as fully and entirely as they remain in your custody, together with this notice.
>
> Date ....

To A.B., provincial judge at ....
(or as the case may be)

Signed C.D. ....
(Solicitor for the Applicant)".

(2) All things required by this section to be returned to the clerk of the Court of Queen's Bench shall for the purposes of the application constitute part of the record. Alta. Reg. 457/87 s.3)

Return of judgment

753.13 (1) On receiving the application for judicial review endorsed in accordance with Rule 753.12, the person from whose decision or act relief is claimed shall return forthwith to the office mentioned therein the judgment, order or decision, as the case may be, together with the process commencing the proceedings, the evidence and all exhibits filed, if any, and all things touching the matter and the notice served on him with a certificate endorsed thereon in the following form:

"Pursuant to the accompanying notice, I hereby return to the Honourable Court the following papers and documents, that is to say

> (a) the judgment, order or decision, as the case may be, and the reasons therefor;
>
> (b) the process commencing the proceedings;
>
> (c) the evidence taken at the hearing and all exhibits filed;
>
> (d) all other papers or documents touching the matter.

And I hereby certify to this Honourable Court that I have above truly set forth all the papers and documents in my custody and power relating to the matter set forth in the originating notice".

(2) The certificate prescribed in subrule (1) has the same effect as a return to a writ of certiorari.

(3) If the proceedings are not in the possession of the person required to transmit them, he shall, in lieu of the certificate, so state and explain the circumstances.

(4) If the proceedings have not been received by the officer to whom or the clerk of the office to which they are by law required to be transmitted, that officer or clerk shall return a certificate of the fact.

(5) The court may dispense with the return of the evidence or exhibits or part of them.

(6) A copy of this Rule shall appear on or be annexed to the application for judicial review served on the person from whom the return is required. Alta. Reg. 457/87 s.3)

Return of record

753.14 (1) Where relief other than an order to set aside a decision or act is claimed on an application for judicial review and the applicant is of the opinion that the record is necessary to establish the claim, he may apply to the court to require the person from whose decision or act relief is claimed to make the return unless that person consents to file a return.

(2) The court may in its discretion order or refuse to order the return of the record or any part thereof.

(3) Where the court orders the return of the record, Rules 753.12(2) and 753.13 apply except as altered by the order of the court. Alta. Reg. 457/87 s.3)

Stay of decision

753.15 (1) Unless otherwise provided by statute, the court may, if in its opinion it is necessary for the purpose of preserving the position of the applicant, stay the operation of the decision sought to be set aside pending final determination of the application for judicial review.

(2) No order shall be made under subrule (1) if, in the opinion of the court, such an order would be detrimental either to the public interest or to public safety. Alta. Reg. 457/87 s.3)

Continuation of proceedings

753.16 (1) If the relief claimed in a proceeding begun by statement of claim or originating notice under Rule 410 or another procedure ought to be claimed on an application for judicial review, the court, on application or its own motion, may direct that the proceeding be continued as an application for judicial review.

(2) If the relief claimed on an application for judicial review ought to be claimed in a proceeding begun by statement of claim or originating notice under Rule 410 or another procedure, the court, on application or its own motion, may direct that the proceeding be continued under that other procedure.

(3) The court may give such further directions as are necessary to cause the proceedings to conform to the procedure by which they are to be continued. Alta. Reg. 457/87 s.3)

Appeal

753.17 An appeal from an order granted on an application for judicial review lies to the Court of Appeal. Alta. Reg. 457/87 s.3)

Direction respecting order

753.18 Any direction required to give effect to an order of the Court of Appeal may be made by a judge of the Court of Appeal. Alta. Reg. 457/87 s.3)

Application of general rules

753.19 Except where provided specially in this Part, the general Rules, including the originating notice Rules in Part 33 and those relating to abridgment or extension of time, apply to all matters under this Part. Alta. Reg. 457/87 s. 3)

Appendix 5

Federal Courts Act
R.S.C. 1985, c. F-7

18. (1) Subject to section 28, the Federal Court has exclusive original jurisdiction

    (a) to issue an injunction, writ of *certiorari*, writ of prohibition, writ of *mandamus* or writ of *quo warranto*, or grant declaratory relief, against any federal board, commission or other tribunal; and

    (b) to hear and determine any application or other proceeding for relief in the nature of relief contemplated by paragraph (a), including any proceeding brought against the Attorney General of Canada, to obtain relief against a federal board, commission or other tribunal.

  (2) The Federal Court has exclusive original jurisdiction to hear and determine every application for a writ of *habeas corpus ad subjiciendum*, writ of *certiorari*, writ of prohibition or writ of *mandamus* in relation to any member of the Canadian Forces serving outside Canada.

  (3) The remedies provided for in subsections (1) and (2) may be obtained only on an application for judicial review made under section 18.1.

18.1 (1) An application for judicial review may be made by the Attorney General of Canada or by anyone directly affected by the matter in respect of which relief is sought.

  (2) An application for judicial review in respect of a decision or order of a federal board, commission or other tribunal shall be made within 30 days after the time the decision or order was first communicated by the federal board, commission or other tribunal to the office of the Deputy Attorney General of Canada or to the party directly affected by it, or within such further time as a judge of the Federal Court may fix or allow before or after the end of those 30 days.

  (3) On an application for judicial review, the Federal Court may

    (a) order a federal board, commission or other tribunal to do any act or thing it has unlawfully failed or refused to do or has unreasonably delayed in doing; or

(b) declare invalid or unlawful, or quash, set aside or set aside and refer back for determination in accordance with such directions as it considers to be appropriate, prohibit or restrain, a decision, order, act or proceeding of a federal board, commission or other tribunal.

(4) The Federal Court may grant relief under subsection (3) if it is satisfied that the federal board, commission or other tribunal

(a) acted without jurisdiction, acted beyond its jurisdiction or refused to exercise its jurisdiction;

(b) failed to observe a principle of natural justice, procedural fairness or other procedure that it was required by law to observe;

(c) erred in law in making a decision or an order, whether or not the error appears on the face of the record;

(d) based its decision or order on an erroneous finding of fact that it made in a perverse or capricious manner or without regard for the material before it;

(e) acted, or failed to act, by reason of fraud or perjured evidence; or

(f) acted in any other way that was contrary to law.

(5) If the sole ground for relief established on an application for judicial review is a defect in form or a technical irregularity, the Federal Court may

(a) refuse the relief if it finds that no substantial wrong or miscarriage of justice has occurred; and

(b) in the case of a defect in form or a technical irregularity in a decision or order, make an order validating the decision or order, to have effect from such time and on such terms as it considers appropriate.

28. (1) The Federal Court of Appeal has jurisdiction to hear and determine applications for judicial review made in respect of any of the following federal boards, commissions or other tribunals:

(a) the Board of Arbitration established by the *Canada Agricultural Products Act*;

(b) the Review Tribunal established by the *Canada Agricultural Products Act*;

(c) the Canadian Radio-television and Telecommunications Commission established by the *Canadian Radio-television and Telecommunications Commission Act*;

(d) the Pension Appeals Board established by the *Canada Pension Plan*;

(e) the Canadian International Trade Tribunal established by the *Canadian International Trade Tribunal Act*;

(f) the National Energy Board established by the *National Energy Board Act*;

(g) [Repealed 1992, c. 49, s. 128.]

(h) the Canada Industrial Relations Board established by the *Canada Labour Code;*

(i) the Public Service Staff Relations Board established by the *Public Service Staff Relations Act;*

(j) the Copyright Board established by the *Copyright Act;*

(k) the Canadian Transportation Agency established by the *Canadian Transportation Act*;

(l) [Repealed 2002, c. 8, s. 35(2)].

(m) umpires appointed under the *Employment Insurance Act;* and

(n) the Competition Tribunal established by the *Competition Tribunal Act*; and

(o) assessors appointed under the *Canada Deposit Insurance Corporation Act*.

(p) the Canadian Artists and Producers Professional Relations Tribunal established by subsection 10(1) of the *Status of the Artist Act*.

(2) Sections 18 to 18.5, except subsection 18.4(2), apply, with any modifications that the circumstances require, in respect of any matter within the jurisdiction of the Federal Court of Appeal under subsection (1) and, when they apply, a reference to the Federal Court shall be read as a reference to the Federal Court of Appeal.

(3) If the Federal Court of Appeal has jurisdiction to hear and determine any matter, the Federal Court has no jurisdiction to entertain any proceeding in respect of that matter.

Appendix 6

Bill 56 – BC *Administrative Tribunals Act*[1]

Standard of review if tribunal's enabling Act has privative clause

58 (1) If the tribunal's enabling Act contains a privative clause, relative to the courts the tribunal must be considered to be an expert tribunal in relation to all matters over which it has exclusive jurisdiction.

(2) In a judicial review proceeding relating to expert tribunals under subsection (1)

    (a) a finding of fact or law or an exercise of discretion by the tribunal in respect of a matter over which it has exclusive jurisdiction under a privative clause must not be interfered with unless it is patently unreasonable,

    (b) questions about the application of common law rules of natural justice and procedural fairness must be decided having regard to whether, in all of the circumstances, the tribunal acted fairly, and

    (c) for all matters other than those identified in paragraphs (a) and (b), the standard of review to be applied to the tribunal's decision is correctness.

(3) For the purposes of subsection (2) (a), a discretionary decision is patently unreasonable if the discretion

    (a) is exercised arbitrarily or in bad faith,

    (b) is exercised for an improper purpose,

    (c) is based entirely or predominantly on irrelevant factors, or

    (d) fails to take statutory requirements into account

Standard of review if tribunal's enabling Act has no privative clause

59 (1) In a judicial review proceeding, the standard of review to be applied to a decision of the tribunal is correctness for all questions except those respecting the exercise of discretion, findings of fact and the application of the common law rules of natural justice and procedural fairness.

---

1 The BC *Administrative Tribunals Act* received Royal Assent on May 20, 2004.

(2) A court must not set aside a finding of fact by the tribunal unless there is no evidence to support it or if, in light of all the evidence, the finding is otherwise unreasonable.

(3) A court must not set aside a discretionary decision of the tribunal unless it is patently unreasonable.

(4) For the purposes of subsection (3), a discretionary decision is patently unreasonable if the discretion

(a) is exercised arbitrarily or in bad faith,

(b) is exercised for an improper purpose,

(c) is based entirely or predominantly on irrelevant factors, or

(d) fails to take statutory requirements into account.

(5) Questions about the application of common law rules of natural justice and procedural fairness must be decided having regard to whether, in all of the circumstances, the tribunal acted fairly.

INDEX